# Short Story
# Criticism

# Guide to Thomson Gale Literary Criticism Series

| For criticism on | Consult these Gale series |
|---|---|
| Authors now living or who died after December 31, 1999 | *CONTEMPORARY LITERARY CRITICISM (CLC)* |
| Authors who died between 1900 and 1999 | *TWENTIETH-CENTURY LITERARY CRITICISM (TCLC)* |
| Authors who died between 1800 and 1899 | *NINETEENTH-CENTURY LITERATURE CRITICISM (NCLC)* |
| Authors who died between 1400 and 1799 | *LITERATURE CRITICISM FROM 1400 TO 1800 (LC)*<br><br>*SHAKESPEAREAN CRITICISM (SC)* |
| Authors who died before 1400 | *CLASSICAL AND MEDIEVAL LITERATURE CRITICISM (CMLC)* |
| Authors of books for children and young adults | *CHILDREN'S LITERATURE REVIEW (CLR)* |
| Dramatists | *DRAMA CRITICISM (DC)* |
| Poets | *POETRY CRITICISM (PC)* |
| Short story writers | *SHORT STORY CRITICISM (SSC)* |
| Literary topics and movements | *HARLEM RENAISSANCE: A GALE CRITICAL COMPANION (HR)*<br><br>*THE BEAT GENERATION: A GALE CRITICAL COMPANION (BG)*<br><br>*FEMINISM IN LITERATURE: A GALE CRITICAL COMPANION (FL)*<br><br>*GOTHIC LITERATURE: A GALE CRITICAL COMPANION (GL)* |
| Asian American writers of the last two hundred years | *ASIAN AMERICAN LITERATURE (AAL)* |
| Black writers of the past two hundred years | *BLACK LITERATURE CRITICISM (BLC)*<br><br>*BLACK LITERATURE CRITICISM SUPPLEMENT (BLCS)* |
| Hispanic writers of the late nineteenth and twentieth centuries | *HISPANIC LITERATURE CRITICISM (HLC)*<br><br>*HISPANIC LITERATURE CRITICISM SUPPLEMENT (HLCS)* |
| Native North American writers and orators of the eighteenth, nineteenth, and twentieth centuries | *NATIVE NORTH AMERICAN LITERATURE (NNAL)* |
| Major authors from the Renaissance to the present | *WORLD LITERATURE CRITICISM, 1500 TO THE PRESENT (WLC)*<br><br>*WORLD LITERATURE CRITICISM SUPPLEMENT (WLCS)* |

ISSN 0895-9439

Volume 96

# Short Story Criticism

Criticism of the
Works of Short Fiction Writers

**Jelena Krstović**
**Project Editor**

**THOMSON**
™
**GALE**

Detroit • New York • San Francisco • New Haven, Conn. • Waterville, Maine • London

**THOMSON**

**GALE**

Short Story Criticism, Vol. 96

**Project Editor**
Jelena Krstović

**Editorial**
Kathy D. Darrow, Jeffrey W. Hunter, Michelle Lee, Thomas J. Schoenberg, Noah Schusterbauer, Lawrence J. Trudeau, Russel Whitaker

**Data Capture**
Frances Monroe, Gwen Tucker

**Indexing Services**
Factiva®, a Dow Jones and Reuters Company

**Rights and Acquisitions**
Margaret Abendroth, Margaret Chamberlain-Gaston, Edna Hedblad

**Imaging and Multimedia**
Dean Dauphinais, Leitha Etheridge-Sims, Lezlie Light, Mike Logusz, Dan Newell, Christine O'Bryan, Kelly A. Quin, Denay Wilding, Robyn Young

**Composition and Electronic Capture**
Gary Oudersluys

**Manufacturing**
Rhonda Dover

**Associate Product Manager**
Marc Cormier

LIBRARY OF CONGRESS CATALOG CARD NUMBER 88-641014

ISBN-13: 978-0-7876-8893-6
ISBN-10: 0-7876-8893-2
ISSN 0895-9439

Printed in the United States of America
10 9 8 7 6 5 4 3 2 1

# Contents

Preface vii

Acknowledgments xi

Literary Criticism Series Advisory Board xiii

# Preface

*Short Story Criticism* (SSC) presents significant criticism of the world's greatest short-story writers and provides supplementary biographical and bibliographical materials to guide the interested reader to a greater understanding of the authors of short fiction. This series was developed in response to suggestions from librarians serving high school, college, and public library patrons, who had noted a considerable number of requests for critical material on short-story writers. Although major short-story writers are covered in such Thomson Gale series as *Contemporary Literary Criticism* (*CLC*), *Twentieth-Century Literary Criticism* (*TCLC*), *Nineteenth-Century Literature Criticism* (*NCLC*), and *Literature Criticism from 1400 to 1800* (*LC*), librarians perceived the need for a series devoted solely to writers of the short-story genre.

## Scope of the Series

*SSC* is designed to serve as an introduction to major short-story writers of all eras and nationalities. Since these authors have inspired a great deal of relevant critical material, *SSC* is necessarily selective, and the editors have chosen the most important published criticism to aid readers and students in their research.

Approximately three to six authors, works, or topics are included in each volume, and each entry presents a historical survey of the critical response to the work. The length of an entry is intended to reflect the amount of critical attention the author has received from critics writing in English and from foreign critics in translation. Every attempt has been made to identify and include the most significant essays on each author's work. In order to provide these important critical pieces, the editors sometimes reprint essays that have appeared elsewhere in Thomson Gale's Literary Criticism Series. Such duplication, however, never exceeds twenty percent of an *SSC* volume.

## Organization of the Book

An *SSC* entry consists of the following elements:

- The **Author Heading** cites the name under which the author most commonly wrote, followed by birth and death dates. Also located here are any name variations under which an author wrote, including transliterated forms for authors whose native languages use nonroman alphabets. If the author wrote consistently under a pseudonym, the pseudonym will be listed in the author heading and the author's actual name given in parentheses on the first line of the biographical and critical introduction. Uncertain birth or death dates are indicated by question marks. Single-work entries are preceded by the title of the work and its date of publication.

- The **Introduction** contains background information that introduces the reader to the author and the critical debates surrounding his or her work.

- The list of **Principal Works** is ordered chronologically by date of first publication and lists the most important works by the author. The first section comprises short-story collections, novellas, and novella collections. The second section gives information on other major works by the author. For foreign authors, the editors have provided original foreign-language publication information and have selected what are considered the best and most complete English-language editions of their works.

- Reprinted **Criticism** is arranged chronologically in each entry to provide a useful perspective on changes in critical evaluation over time. All short-story, novella, and collection titles by the author featured in the entry are printed in boldface type. The critic's name and the date of composition or publication of the critical work are given at the beginning of each piece of criticism. Unsigned criticism is preceded by the title of the source in which it appeared. Footnotes are reprinted at the end of each essay or excerpt. In the case of excerpted criticism, only those footnotes that pertain to the excerpted texts are included.

- Critical essays are prefaced by brief **Annotations** explicating each piece.

- A complete **Bibliographical Citation** of the original essay or book precedes each piece of criticism. Source citations in the Literary Criticism Series follow University of Chicago Press style, as outlined in *The Chicago Manual of Style,* 15th ed. (Chicago: The University of Chicago Press, 2006).

- An annotated bibliography of **Further Reading** appears at the end of each entry and suggests resources for additional study. In some cases, significant essays for which the editors could not obtain reprint rights are included here. Boxed material following the further reading list provides references to other biographical and critical sources on the author in series published by Thomson Gale.

# Indexes

A **Cumulative Author Index** lists all of the authors that appear in a wide variety of reference sources published by Thomson Gale, including *SSC*. A complete list of these sources is found facing the first page of the Author Index. The index also includes birth and death dates and cross references between pseudonyms and actual names.

A **Cumulative Nationality Index** lists all authors featured in *SSC* by nationality, followed by the number of the *SSC* volume in which their entry appears.

An alphabetical **Title Index** lists all short-story, novella, and collection titles contained in the *SSC* series. Titles of short-story collections, separately published novellas, and novella collections are printed in italics, while titles of individual short stories are printed in roman type with quotation marks. Each title is followed by the author's last name and corresponding volume and page numbers where commentary on the work is located. English-language translations of original foreign-language titles are cross-referenced to the foreign titles so that all references to discussion of a work are combined in one listing.

In response to numerous suggestions from librarians, Thomson Gale also produces an annual paperbound edition of the SSC cumulative title index. This annual cumulation, which alphabetically lists all titles reviewed in the series, is available to all customers. Additional copies of this index are available upon request. Librarians and patrons will welcome this separate index; it saves shelf space, is easy to use, and is recyclable upon receipt of the next edition.

# Citing *Short Story Criticism*

When citing criticism reprinted in the Literary Criticism Series, students should provide complete bibliographic information so that the cited essay can be located in the original print or electronic source. Students who quote directly from reprinted criticism may use any accepted bibliographic format, such as University of Chicago Press style or Modern Language Association (MLA) style. Both the MLA and the University of Chicago formats are acceptable and recognized as being the current standards for citations. It is important, however, to choose one format for all citations; do not mix the two formats within a list of citations.

The examples below follow recommendations for preparing a bibliography set forth in *The Chicago Manual of Style,* 15th ed. (Chicago: The University of Chicago Press, 2006); the first example pertains to material drawn from periodicals, the second to material reprinted from books:

Morrison, Jago. "Narration and Unease in Ian McEwan's Later Fiction." *Critique* 42, no. 3 (spring 2001): 253-68. Reprinted in *Short Story Criticism.* Vol. 57, edited by Jelena Krstovic, 212-20. Detroit: Gale, 2003.

Brossard, Nicole. "Poetic Politics." In *The Politics of Poetic Form: Poetry and Public Policy,* edited by Charles Bernstein, 73-82. New York: Roof Books, 1990. Reprinted in *Short Story Criticism.* Vol. 57, edited by Jelena Krstovic, 3-8. Detroit: Gale, 2003.

The examples below follow recommendations for preparing a works cited list set forth in the *MLA Handbook for Writers of Research Papers,* 6th ed. (New York: The Modern Language Association of America, 2003); the first example pertains to material drawn from periodicals, the second to material reprinted from books:

Morrison, Jago. "Narration and Unease in Ian McEwan's Later Fiction." *Critique* 42.3 (spring 2001): 253-68. Reprinted in *Short Story Criticism.* Ed. Jelena Krstovic. Vol. 57. Detroit: Gale, 2003. 212-20.

Brossard, Nicole. "Poetic Politics." *The Politics of Poetic Form: Poetry and Public Policy.* Ed. Charles Bernstein. New York: Roof Books, 1990. 73-82. Reprinted in *Short Story Criticism.* Ed. Jelena Krstovic. Vol. 57. Detroit: Gale, 2003. 3-8.

## Suggestions are Welcome

Readers who wish to suggest new features, topics, or authors to appear in future volumes, or who have other suggestions or comments are cordially invited to call, write, or fax the Associate Product Manager:

Associate Product Manager, Literary Criticism Series
Thomson Gale
27500 Drake Road
Farmington Hills, MI 48331-3535
1-800-347-4253 (GALE)
Fax: 248-699-8054

# Acknowledgments

The editors wish to thank the copyright holders of the excerpted criticism included in this volume and the permissions managers of many book and magazine publishing companies for assisting us in securing reproduction rights. Following is a list of the copyright holders who have granted us permission to reproduce material in this volume of *SSC*. Every effort has been made to trace copyright, but if omissions have been made, please let us know.

**COPYRIGHTED MATERIAL IN *SSC*, VOLUME 96, WAS REPRODUCED FROM THE FOLLOWING PERIODICALS:**

*Afro-Hispanic Review,* v. 11, 1992. Copyright © The Board of Curators, the U. of Mo. Reproduced by permission.—*Books from Finland,* v. 21, 1987 for "Tove Jansson: The Art of Travelling Light" by Marianne Bargum. Reproduced by permission of the author.—*Chasqui,* v. 20, May, 1991. Reproduced by permission.—*Children's Literature,* v. 19, 1991. Copyright © 1991 The Johns Hopkins University Press. Reproduced by permission.—*Classical and Modern Literature: A Quarterly,* v. 3, winter, 1983. © 1983 CML, Inc. Reproduced by permission.—*Comparative Literature,* v. 46, winter, 1994 for "Hugo's Gilliatt and Leskov's Golovan: Two Folk-Epic Heroes" by Larry R. Andrews. Copyright © 1994 by the University of Oregon. Reproduced by permission of the author.—*Critical Survey,* v. 17, 2005. Republished with permission of Berghahn Books Inc., conveyed through Copyright Clearance Center, Inc.—*Critique: Studies in Contemporary Fiction,* v. 30, winter, 1989. Copyright © 1989 by Helen Dwight Reid Educational Foundation. Reproduced with permission of the Helen Dwight Reid Educational Foundation, published by Heldref Publications, 1319 18th Street, NW, Washington, DC 20036-1802.—*Critique: Studies in Modern Fiction,* v. 28, spring, 1987. Copyright © 1987 by Helen Dwight Reid Educational Foundation. Reproduced with permission of the Helen Dwight Reid Educational Foundation, published by Heldref Publications, 1319 18th Street, NW, Washington, DC 20036-1802.—*Explicator,* v. 59, summer, 2001; v. 62, winter, 2004 Copyright © 2001, © 2004 by Helen Dwight Reid Educational Foundation. Reproduced with permission of the Helen Dwight Reid Educational Foundation, published by Heldref Publications, 1319 18th Street, NW, Washington, DC 20036-1802.—*Journal of Indian Writing in English,* v. 30, January, 2002. Reproduced by permission.—*MELUS,* v. 29, fall/winter, 2004. Copyright *MELUS: The Society for the Study of Multi-Ethnic Literature of the United States,* 2004. Reproduced by permission.—*New Zealand Slavonic Journal,* 1977. Reproduced by permission.—*North Dakota Quarterly,* v. 70, winter, 2003. Copyright 2003 by The University of North Dakota. Reproduced by permission.—*Russian Literature Triquarterly,* v. 8, 1974. Copyright © 1974 by Ardis. Reproduced by permission.—*Scandinavica: An International Journal of Scandinavian Studies,* v. 22, May, 1983. Copyright © 1983 by James McFarlane. Reproduced by permission.—*Slavic and East European Journal,* v. 12, winter, 1968; v. 18, fall, 1974; v. 25, spring, 1981.Copyright © 1968, 1974, 1981 by AATSEEL of the U.S., Inc. All reproduced by permission.—*Studia Slavica,* v. 48, 2003. Copyright © Akademiai Kiado, Budapest 2003. Reproduced by permission.—*Studies in Short Fiction,* v. 14, fall, 1977; winter, 1977. Copyright © 1977 by Studies in Short Fiction. Both reproduced by permission.—*Studies in Short Fiction,* v. 34, winter, 1997. Copyright © 1997 by Newberry College. Reproduced by permission.—*Style,* v. 29, fall, 1995. Copyright © *Style,* 1995. All rights reserved. Reproduced by permission of the publisher.—*Texas Quarterly,* v. 9, autumn, 1966. Copyright © 1966 by The University of Texas. Reproduced by permission.—*Utopian Studies,* v. 8, 1997. Reproduced by permission.—*World Literature Today,* v. 74, spring, 2000. Copyright © 2000 by *World Literature Today.* Reproduced by permission of the publisher.

**COPYRIGHTED MATERIAL IN *SSC*, VOLUME 96, WAS REPRODUCED FROM THE FOLLOWING BOOKS:**

Bertills, Yvonne. From "Intertextualities, Continued: The Connotations of Proper Names in Tove Jansson," in *Children's Literature as Communication: The ChiLPA Project.* Edited by Roger D. Sell. John Benjamins Publishing Company, 2002. Copyright © 2002 John Benjamins B.V. With kind permission by John Benjamins Publishing Company, Amsterdam/Philadelphia. www.benjamins.com—Brians, Paul. From *Modern South Asian Literature in English.* Greenwood Press, 2003. Copyright © 2003 by Paul Brians. All rights reserved. Reproduced by permission of Greenwood Publishing Group, Inc., Westport, CT.—Cavaliero, Glen. From *A Reading of E. M. Forster.* Macmillan Press, 1979. Copyright © Glen Cavaliero 1979. Reproduced with permission of Palgrave Macmillan.—Elkins, Charles. From "E. M. Forster's &lsdquo;The Machine Stops': Liberal-Humanist Hostility to Technology," in *Clockwork Worlds: Mechanized Environments in SF.* Edited by Richard D. Erlich and Thomas P. Dunn. Greenwood Press, 1983. Copyright © 1983 by Richard D. Erlich and Thomas P. Dunn. All rights reserved. Reproduced by permission of Greenwood Publishing Group, Inc., Westport, CT.—

# Thomson Gale Literature Product Advisory Board

The members of the Thomson Gale Literature Product Advisory Board—reference librarians from public and academic library systems—represent a cross-section of our customer base and offer a variety of informed perspectives on both the presentation and content of our literature products. Advisory board members assess and define such quality issues as the relevance, currency, and usefulness of the author coverage, critical content, and literary topics included in our series; evaluate the layout, presentation, and general quality of our printed volumes; provide feedback on the criteria used for selecting authors and topics covered in our series; provide suggestions for potential enhancements to our series; identify any gaps in our coverage of authors or literary topics, recommending authors or topics for inclusion; analyze the appropriateness of our content and presentation for various user audiences, such as high school students, undergraduates, graduate students, librarians, and educators; and offer feedback on any proposed changes/enhancements to our series. We wish to thank the following advisors for their advice throughout the year.

# E. M. Forster
## 1879-1970

(Full name Edward Morgan Forster) English short story writer, novelist, and essayist.

The following entry presents an overview of Forster's life and works. For additional information on his career, see *SSC*, Volume 27.

## INTRODUCTION

One of the best known writers of the Edwardian period, Forster is primarily studied as a novelist, although he wrote numerous short stories, essays, and other nonfiction pieces. His most popular novels include *Howard's End* (1910) and *A Passage to India* (1924)—both works are characteristic of Forster's concerns in the rest of his writing, which often focuses on issues of morality, social structure, and personal relationships. In addition to his novels, Forster also wrote numerous short stories, many of which appeared in periodicals throughout his literary career. His first collection of short fiction is titled *The Celestial Omnibus, and Other Stories* (1911) and includes one of his most-studied stories, "The Story of a Panic." Forster's short fiction mirrors the concerns he expressed in his novels, such as salvation via love, questions about traditional Christian practices, an examination of English culture and morality, and the importance of interpersonal relationships. Although infused with allusions to liberal humanism and paganism, Forster's writing is also admired for its realistic character development. During his lifetime, he established himself as a major literary figure following the publication of *A Passage to India*. While critical studies of this and other books abounded, Forster did not publish another novel during his lifetime, concentrating instead on nonfiction and short stories, distributed primarily to his close friends and associates.

## BIOGRAPHICAL INFORMATION

Born on January 1, 1879, to Edward Morgan Llewellyn and Alice Whichelo Forster, the young Edward Morgan was primarily brought up by his mother and maternal grandmother—his father died when Forster was an infant. A legacy from his father's sister made it possible for Forster to attend King's College, Cambridge University, from which he graduated in 1897. The inheritance also allowed him the means to travel extensively and to support himself financially while continuing to write. At Cambridge Forster became a member of the Cambridge Apostles, a literary and intellectual group that brought him in contact with many contemporary writers, including Alfred Tennyson, Lytton Strachey, and John Maynard Keynes. Although biographers have since identified these years as the time when Forster acknowledged his homosexual orientation, he kept this aspect of his personal life concealed during his lifetime. He spent the years after Cambridge traveling in Europe and later, India. Following his second trip to India, in the early 1920s, Forster published his most famous novel, *A Passage to India*, to much acclaim. After his mother's death in 1945, he accepted a fellowship at King's College, where he lived for many years. He died in 1970 after a stroke.

## MAJOR WORKS OF SHORT FICTION

One of Forster's earliest published works of short fiction was "The Story of a Panic" (1904), and he is known to have regarded this tale as being better than his first two novels. The story of an upper-middle-class man called Eustace who is forced to review his complacent outlook on life during a picnic in the woods, this work reflects many of the themes and literary concerns Forster explored in his later efforts. It, along with other well-known stories such as "The Road from Colonus" and "The Other Side of the Hedge," was included in Forster's first collection of short stories, *The Celestial Omnibus, and Other Stories*. In the years preceding this publication, Forster had issued a series of novels, including *Where Angels Fear to Tread* (1905), *The Longest Journey* (1907), *A Room with a View* (1908), and *Howard's End*. While the novels focused on familiar Forster concerns about the excessive, prejudicial, and narrow-minded character of contemporary English society, his short fiction used allusion and fantasy to focus on similar themes. In particular, "The Road to Colonus," often lauded as one of his best short stories, brings together the narrative and thematic threads of Forster's novels into the fantastical setting he often used in his short narratives. The story focuses on Mr. Lucas, an older Englishman visiting Greece. His companions are typical travelers, expressing their admiration of well-known tourist attractions such as Athens and Delphi in superficial clichés, while remaining completely unaffected by the vitality of Plataniste, a land alive with natural beauty. Mr. Lucas, in contrast, responds to the power of Plataniste, returning to England a changed man. Back in England, he is unable to sustain his connection to the revival he experienced in Plataniste, but before he can return there to rejuvenate himself, Mr. Lucas learns of the destruction of the little inn where he had planned to stay. The story has been studied for its many parallels with Sophocles' *Oedipus at Colonus*, and is significant because of its literary allusions and thematic concerns. The regenerative power of nature and Forster's contempt for the English establishment are recurring motifs in the other stories of the collection, including "Other Kingdom," "The Curate's Friend," and "The Celestial Omnibus."

In 1928 Forster issued his second collection of short stories, titled *The Eternal Moment*. This anthology contained the last fiction Forster composed, except for his unpublished homosexual narratives and his best known novel, *A Passage to India*. During his lifetime, this collection of stories was almost always compared unfavorably to his first anthology as well as his novels, notably *Howard''s End* and *A Passage to India*. The themes Forster explored in *The Eternal Moment,* however, were a continuation of his concerns in the earlier collection, and include such tales as "The Eternal Moment," "The Machine Stops," "The Point of It," and "The Story of the Siren." Although he published nonfiction extensively in the years following, diary entries from these years reveal that he was unable to concentrate much on fiction. Scholars surmise that Forster's homosexuality affected both his writing and his demeanor during these years, and while he shared some of the stories he wrote during this period with close friends, it is almost certain that Forster did not intend them to be published. Nonetheless, a few of them were included in his next anthology, *The Life to Come, and Other Stories*, published posthumously in 1972. Stories in this anthology include "Albergo Empedocle," the title story "The Life to Come," "The Other Boat," "Dr. Woolacott," and "Arthur Snatchfold." Although he addresses the issue of homosexuality directly in some of these stories, Forster's thematic concerns are consistent with those expressed in his other fiction. The power of nature and primitivism is once again contrasted with the superficiality of organized religion and the industrialized West. Forster's last collection, also published after his death, was titled *Arctic Summer, and Other Fiction* (1980) and contains assorted unfinished works, including stories and parts of novels.

## CRITICAL RECEPTION

Forster was a highly regarded novelist among his contemporaries, and while his short fiction was generally praised, it did not garner the critical accolades that his novels did. More positive critical attention has focused

on his short fiction during the latter half of the century and critics have lauded Forster's short stories for their imagery, literary style, and psychological complexity. Many critics have closely examined Forster's use of myth and allusion in his stories, including Judith Scherer Herz and John H. Stape. Herz's essay focuses on Forster's use of the figure of Hermes, the Greek messenger god, proposing that he serves as a point of cohesion in many of Forster's short stories. In his analysis, Leonard G. Heldreth notes the dual nature of the fantastical elements used by Forster in his short fiction—for example, images of fauns and sirens, important as traditional elements of fantasy, are also key because their significance and power is lost on the characters inhabiting the tales, highlighting the chasm between subconscious desire and the established order of society. Other critics who have written about Forster's use of fantasy include Glen Cavaliero, who remarks on the writer's use of Edwardian literary traditions, especially its veneration of childhood and fantasy, in his early short fiction. According to Cavaliero, Edwardian literature was particularly prone to concealing uncomfortable realities under a veneer of charm and illusion, but Forster used illusion in his short stories to celebrate the innocence that childhood and fantasy represented—especially in such stories as "Other Kingdom" and "The Story of a Panic." In addition to focusing on the imagery and style of his writing, critics have also begun studying the contemporary response to Forster's short fiction as compared to his novels, drawing connections between the two that were not perceived by Forster's contemporaries. In a study of *The Celestial Omnibus and Other Stories,* Herz comments that although many of Forster's contemporaries found his stories whimsical and not to the same standard as his novels, there are distinct thematic connections between the stories in this collection and his novels. Several critics have noted that an underlying personal element that is mostly hinted at in his novels is more fully explored in his short fiction, and much modern critical scholarship has focused on a study of Forster's homosexual point of view as it is presented in these stories. Stephen K. Land, who traces these thematic connections between several of Forster's later short stories and novels, contends that despite the attention Forster has received for this aspect of his writing, the element of explicit homosexuality in his work does not adversely affect the literary balance of his writing.

## PRINCIPAL WORKS

### Short Fiction

"The Story of a Panic" 1904
"The Machine Stops" 1909

## Other Major Works

*Includes "The Story of Panic," "The Other Side of the Hedge," "The Celestial Omnibus," "Other Kingdom," "The Curate's Friend," and "The Road from Colonus."

†Includes "The Machine Stops," "The Point of It," "Mr. Andrews," "Co-Ordination," "The Story of the Siren," and "The Eternal Moment."

‡Includes "Albergo Empedocle," "The Other Boat," "The Purple Envelope," "The Helping Hand," "The Rock," "The Life to Come," "Dr. Woolacott," "Arthur Snatchfold," "The Obelisk," "What Does It Matter?: A Morality," "The Classical Annex," "The Torque," "The Other Boat," and "Three Courses and a Dessert."

---

**James S. Malek (essay date winter 1977)**

SOURCE: Malek, James S. "Persona, Shadow, and Society: A Reading of Forster's 'The Other Boat.'" *Studies in Short Fiction* 14, no. 1 (winter 1977): 21-7.

[*In the following essay, Malek offers a reading of Forster's "The Other Boat," characterizing the story as one of the author's most psychologically complex works.*]

Most reviewers of E. M. Forster's *The Life to Come and Other Stories* agree that **"The Other Boat"** is the best story in this collection.[1] It is certainly the most complex psychologically, and perhaps as complex as any Forster short story. The subtle, shifting nuances in the Lionel March-Cocoa Moraes relationship, Lionel's love/hate feelings toward his peers and mother, the juxtaposition of childhood and adult relationships, and the sudden murder/suicide at the end not only provide a degree of psychological character development unusual in the short story, but pose numerous interpretive problems, especially in character motivation. Many of these problems can be solved with the help of Jungian psychology—specifically, by regarding Cocoa as Lionel's "shadow," one which conflicts both with social pressures exerted on Lionel by his mother and peers and with Lionel's "persona," the "mask" he wears as a British army officer and Mrs. March's eldest son. Ultimately, Lionel finds the conflict unresolvable, and destroys both shadow and persona. Such an interpretation can, I believe, provide a coherent reading and illuminate Forster's achievement in **"The Other Boat."**

**"The Other Boat"** is of course a "realistic" narrative with two main characters—Lionel and Cocoa. I am not suggesting that they are literally one, that Cocoa is merely a projection of Lionel's personal unconscious. But Cocoa embodies exactly certain qualities of Lionel's personal unconscious; hence in contacts with Cocoa, Lionel confronts not only another human individual, but his own shadow—"all those uncivilized desires and emotions that are incompatible with social standards and our ideal personality, all that we are ashamed of, all that we do not want to know about ourselves."[2] Similarly, in his relationship with his mother, Lionel reacts less to her as person than to her role as representative of social conventions and expectations—those social pressures with which he has more or less consciously compromised in establishing his persona. Mrs. March appears only in the opening section of the story; in the remainder, she is seen entirely in terms of Lionel's conception of her, which alters because of his contacts with Cocoa. What is important in both of these relationships is Lionel's changing awareness and increasing understanding of self. Because he embodies the repressed qualities of Lionel's shadow which the latter is forced to confront, Cocoa acts as the primary agent in Lionel's development throughout the story.

Of the story's five sections, the first is set on the "other boat" over ten years before the action of the last four, which take place on the Normannia. This brief first section, depicting the childhood friendships of Cocoa and the March children, is remarkable for its foreshadowing of the story's adult relationships and delineation of forces and traits which will determine Lionel's and Cocoa's adult characters. Lionel plays at soldier, and in a manner his mother deems "proper." Of the Marches, it is he who instinctively likes Cocoa and wants him to join their soldiering, but Cocoa refuses because he has "soh many things to arrange, man" (p. 166). Cocoa's persistent concern for planning continues in subsequent years, and is central to his adult relationship with Lionel, manifesting itself in a struggle for supremacy with the latter's persona. For example, we learn later that Cocoa, the "subtle supple boy who belonged to no race and always got what he wanted," had "longed for [Lionel] ever since their first meeting" and now plans "how he would play with [him] forever" (p. 174). And when Cocoa does play with the March children on the "other boat," he will not "play any game properly" (p. 170); superstitious from the beginning, Cocoa is closest to the unseen world in the story. He introduces the March children to the "m'm m'm m'm" by leading them down to the ship's bow—a disorienting world (a Lascar faces the wrong direction while praying) unfamiliar to the Marches, but a comfortable home to Cocoa. Throughout this first section, Cocoa serves as a threat to the orderly, placid, "proper" world Mrs. March wants for her children. And because he is able to see beneath surface appearances, the challenge he offers to British "decency" is potent, especially in Lionel's case. For Lionel is attracted to Cocoa's unconventionality, and must repress that attraction to satisfy his mother.

Hence it is not surprising that Cocoa's greatest enemy in this section is Mrs. March. "With unusual heat," she tells Cocoa that he is "a silly idle useless unmanly little boy" (p. 170). Later, Lionel reports that she "objected that [Cocoa] made things interesting when they weren't" (p. 182). She dislikes him because he is unconventional and because he poses a sexual threat to Lionel, but Cocoa also serves as a scapegoat for her own guilt. While strolling on the saloon deck with Captain Armstrong, she sees Cocoa and "her children playing in the bows without their topis on" (p. 169). Much later, we learn that Baby, the youngest March child, died of influenza a fortnight after their arrival in England, and that Mrs. March attributed his death to sunstroke. Cocoa guesses that Mrs. March blames him, commenting that "she saw me only, running in the sun with my devil's head, and m'm m'm m'm all you follow me till the last one the tiny one dies, and she, she talking to an officer, a handsome one, oh to sleep in his arms as I shall in yours, so she forgets the sun and it strikes the tiny one. I see." Lionel replies: "Yes, you see in a wrong sort of way" (p. 185). But Cocoa sees in exactly the right way. For Mrs. March, temptation turns to guilt, and this guilt resulting from her momentary glimpse of her shadow—the recognition of a desire her ego cannot accept—strengthens her determination to impose strict social conventions on her children. Lionel believes that she is "outside carnality and incapable of pardoning it" (p. 193). She is incapable of pardoning carnality in others because she cannot pardon it in herself; she is "outside carnality" only insofar as she represses it, and she expects Lionel to do the same.

And when Lionel and Cocoa meet ten years later, it appears that Lionel has accepted her values completely.

He is a highly successful British army officer, playing the role of soldier better now than on the other boat. He is, in every sense, respectable and conventional; his status as an officer demands adherence to a strict code of social standards and moral responsibility, but it is a code which he willingly embraces. His peers like him, and he even shares their racial bigotry in public, although "his colour-prejudices were tribal rather than personal, and only worked when an observer was present" (p. 174). He has not been "much bothered by sex" over the years, although "he had occasionally joined a brothel expedition, so as not to seem better than his fellow officers" (p. 192), and is planning to be reunited with Isabel, the girl he hopes to marry, in India.

Cocoa, on the other hand, is far from respectability, and a seemingly unlikely companion for Lionel. He is largely self-educated, dishonest in his business dealings, possesses two passports of questionable legality, and is of course homosexual. If Lionel's primary allegiance is to duty and country, Cocoa's is to himself. For Cocoa, pleasure is the highest good, and he is willing to employ unethical practices to gratify personal desires. Unlike Lionel, whose position imposes a stringent behavioral code, Cocoa belongs to no race and no country; although he is wealthy, he has no "status" and is therefore a free spirit. His behavioral code is wholly personal.

Cocoa and Lionel are also physical opposites. The latter epitomizes the Nordic ideal—handsome, fair haired, blue eyed, virile, masculine, physically "flawless except for a scar down in the groin" (p. 179). Cocoa is gentle and feminine, has a "funny-shaped head" and "blackish-grayish skin" (p. 173), and gives the impression of physical immaturity. One is a lion, the other a monkey.

There is no outward sign that Lionel would be receptive to the idea of an affair with Cocoa. Indeed, his reaction to Cocoa's first advances is to go "straight to the Master at Arms to report an offence against decency" (p. 174). But their meeting as children had "alerted them towards each other as men" (p. 182). He tells himself that he could not possibly have known Cocoa's tastes, but is dimly aware that he might once have known or that his mother knew—"after ten years' forgetfulness, something stirred in that faraway boat of his childhood and he saw his mother" (p. 176). As is frequently the case in Forster's fiction, genius loci plays an important role. Although Lionel would not have touched Cocoa with tongs in England, curiosity gets the upper hand, "resistance weakened" in the Mediterranean, and "in the Red Sea they slept together as a matter of course" (p. 177). Captain March finds himself falling in love for perhaps the first time in his life.

The rest of the story is devoted to an extremely subtle struggle between Cocoa and Lionel's shadow on one hand, and his persona and various reenforcing social pressures on the other. In seeking control of Lionel, Cocoa has planned carefully and nearly succeeds; having wanted Lionel for years, he "met him again as the omens foretold, and marked him down, spent money to catch him and lime him, and here he lay, caught, and did not know it" (p. 174). But Cocoa underestimates the difficulty of his task: "There *they* lay caught, *both* of them, and did not know it, while the ship carried them inexorably towards Bombay" (p. 174; italics mine). What Cocoa underestimates is the strength of the hold various social pressures have on Lionel and Lionel's resistance to accepting his shadow.

That Cocoa comes as close to succeeding as he does is remarkable, given the strength of the opposition. If Cocoa "had foreseen this meeting and had worked towards it through dreams, why should not an anxious parent have foreseen it too? She had valid reasons for anxiety, for things had actually started on that other boat" (p. 181). Cocoa understands Mrs. March and her influence on Lionel better than Lionel does, and is able to diminish her unhealthy control over him for part of the story. For example, he convinces Lionel that his secretary should get back Lionel's letter to his mother, in which he mentions Cocoa, and helps Lionel understand Mrs. March's reaction to Baby's death more accurately. And Cocoa is instrumental in getting Lionel to accept his physicality. Until the present, Lionel "had been ashamed of being built like a brute" because his "preceptors had condemned carnality" and "his mother had ignored its existence in him" (p. 180); rather than repressing it, he now enjoys "carnality," and the recognition and acceptance of this part of his nature is an important step toward wholeness, toward psychological health.

The long post-coital conversation between Lionel and Cocoa in section four first gives Cocoa a sense of imminent victory, but ends in almost certain defeat. He wonders what "trick" he can "'think of this time that will keep [Lionel] from [Mrs. March]'" (p. 182); he plans to separate Lionel from the army and to dispose of Isabel, but his ultimate reliance is on trying to make Lionel see that his best chance for happiness lies with Cocoa. And Lionel nearly sees that—or perhaps he does see it, but is not prepared to admit it. Lionel has "never had anyone to talk to like [Cocoa]" (p. 185), and when he admits that he has "fallen" for him, Cocoa thinks that "'before morning I shall have enslaved him . . . and he will begin doing whatever I put into his mind'" (p. 187). Although Lionel is troubled because he is, in his words, "'fonder of you than I know how to say'" (p. 187), Cocoa closes his eyes with the certain knowledge that "when morning came and practical life had to be re-entered he would have won" (p. 188).

Not surprisingly, the minor event which spells the beginning of the end of their relationship centers around Lionel's excessive concern for propriety. Although Co-

coa assures him that "'the door shut, the door unshut, is nothing, and is the same'" (p. 189), Lionel worries that the unbolted door could have meant a courtmartial and might have "shocked" the steward. He is angered by Cocoa's saying that he knew the door was unbolted but did not tell him, and resents Cocoa's suggestion that he has been Cocoa's "hireling" (in the sense that Cocoa has planned and spent money to "trap" him). And when he announces that he is going on deck, Cocoa knows that the "movement of love" will never be completed—"'When you come back you will not be you. And I may not be I'" (p. 191). Throughout the story, Lionel's movement has been away from role-playing, from undue concern for propriety and conventionality, toward the realization of his full self—in short, toward the acceptance of his shadow. As the persona retreats and the shadow advances, there are signs that the shadow will not only be recognized, but at least partially integrated into the ego. Cocoa has the feeling "that Lionel knew that he was in the net or almost in it, and did not mind" (p. 183). But Lionel *is* troubled by his fondness for Cocoa, and though he is on the verge of loving Cocoa (and hence his own shadow), he cannot quite make the final leap. His persona resents the shadow's apparently complete disregard of propriety in treating the unbolted door so cavalierly; the event shocks Lionel because it brings the threat of the total destruction of the persona's values and way of life. And the suggestion that he has been a "hireling" makes him recoil in anger because it is untimely; the shadow asserts its dominance before Lionel is ready to accept it (or, rather, after the persona is put on guard by the unbolted door incident). The suggestion offers a direct challenge to the persona at its point of greatest strength—"he whose pride and duty it was to be independent and command!" (p. 190). And, finally, Cocoa knows that all will probably be over if Lionel goes on deck because his peers there will reenforce his persona; the moment of acceptance of the shadow is passing and will be lost on deck.

Cocoa is correct, but Lionel has come so close to embracing his shadow that he ends by rejecting his persona as well. Events on deck do strengthen his resistance to Cocoa, but the reenforcement which he finds for social convention is also self-defeating. Alone on deck, he acknowledges to himself that he has repressed sexual desire, and resents the fact that Cocoa has brought it "charging back like a bull"; Cocoa "had woken up so much that might have slept" (p. 193). He must reject Cocoa, he believes, not only for Isabel and the army, but for his mother. He fears her as a kind of demented omnipotence; he sees her as "blind-eyed in the midst of the enormous web she had spun," one who "understood nothing and controlled everything" (p. 193). But she is a good source to turn to in his panic because she reenforces his guilt—"from the great blank country she inhabited came a voice condemning him and all her children for sin, but condemning him most"

(p. 193). He promises her that he will give up Cocoa, but he also draws reenforcement for this resolution from his British peers on board. As he looks at them sleeping on deck, his dilemma is made manifestly clear: "How decent and reliable they looked, the folk to whom he belonged! He had been born one of them, he had his work with them, he meant to marry into their caste. If he forfeited their companionship he would become nobody and nothing" (p. 192). This is of course his persona's strongest argument, one based on fear, and it works—"what really recalled him to sanity was this quiet sleeping company of his peers" (p. 192). What he does not see in his panic is the emptiness and death-like quality of this world; Lionel has discovered depths unknown to these death-in-life sleepers, and to accept their lives again will certainly bring incompleteness or death to him.

After Lionel's panic has passed, Colonel Arbuthnot awakens and tells him that he is going to "raise hell at Bombay" because Cocoa was placed in Lionel's cabin—"if the Company thinks it can treat a British Officer like that it's very much mistaken" (p. 194). Arbuthnot is wrong, of course; Cocoa has given a bribe to get Lionel, not himself, on board. When Arbuthnot invites Lionel to sleep on deck like "the rest of the gang," who have "managed to cordon off this section of the deck, and woe betide anything black that walks this way" (p. 194), Lionel says that he will; but "something snapped and he heard himself shouting, 'Bloody rubbish, leave the kid alone'" (p. 194), and he rushes back to the cabin. Earlier in the story, Lionel had accepted the bigotry of his peers, but cannot now. If gazing on his sleeping peers and thinking of his mother furthered his determination to reject Cocoa, this final contact with his peers undermines the entire code his persona has accepted. If Arbuthnot's position is founded on ignorance, and Lionel knows that it is, might not all the other social conventions which he has accepted rest on similar bases? Moreover, if Lionel cannot accept completely his shadow, neither can he live satisfactorily in his persona's world of self-deception; personal experience has made him too fully human not to object to Arbuthnot.

Lionel returns to the cabin torn between two worlds, both of which are too painful for him to embrace. In a sense, he is trapped between two irreconcilably conflicting self-conceptions, and is not ready to make a choice. But Cocoa forces the issue. When Lionel sees Cocoa in *Lionel's* bunk, he tells him that he has opted to sleep on deck. Lionel's "own remarks pleased him and he decided to go further" (p. 195), telling Cocoa that they will not meet again after disembarkation. He would like to be kind, "but his talk with the Colonel and his communion with the Mater prevented it" (p. 195). However, Cocoa sees that Lionel is merely role-playing, that the insincere words come only from the surface, and challenges him directly by replying "'Kiss

me!'" (p. 195). And when Lionel refuses, Cocoa bites his arm; that bite literally and figuratively penetrates the surface, shattering Lionel's mask. Deeply confused for some time, Lionel ends his psychomachy by reacting instinctively; reason recedes, "the scar in his groin reopened," and "he was back in a desert fighting savages" (p. 195) as he strangles and makes love to Cocoa. He then commits suicide.

M.-L. von Franz says that "if the shadow figure contains valuable, vital forces, they ought to be assimilated into actual experience and not repressed. It is up to the ego to give up its pride and priggishness and to live out something that seems to be dark, but actually may not be. This can require a sacrifice just as heroic as the conquest of passion, but in an opposite sense."[3] It is exactly this kind of sacrifice which Lionel is not able to make. He *has* seen "valuable, vital forces" in his shadow, and he has gained some awareness of his persona's shortcomings. Mrs. March cannot win the struggle with Cocoa, but Lionel's ego will not give up its "pride and priggishness" easily. Lionel can end his dilemma either by accepting his shadow or by refusing to become whole. But choosing the second course necessarily involves self-destruction; he can no longer live with incompleteness and self-deception, but he is not prepared to surrender when the shadow offers its last desperate challenge. Ultimately, Lionel's rejection of Cocoa is also a rejection of a necessary part of his own being. Hence his strangulation of Cocoa is a form of self-murder, and he merely finishes a partially completed suicide when he dives into the sea.

### Notes

1. For example, see Eudora Welty, rev. of *The Life to Come and Other Stories, New York Times Book Review,* 13 May 1973, pp. 27-30, and Karl Miller, "Forster and His Merry Men," *New York Review of Books,* 28 June 1973, pp. 9-11.

   All citations of "The Other Boat" are from *The Life to Come and Other Stories* (New York: Norton, 1972) and will be parenthetically noted in the text by page number.

2. Frieda Fordham, *An Introduction to Jung's Psychology,* 3rd ed. (Harmondsworth: Penguin, 1966), p. 50.

3. "The Process of Individuation," in *Man and His Symbols,* ed. Carl G. Jung (Garden City: Doubleday, 1964), p. 175.

### John H. Stape (essay date fall 1977)

SOURCE: Stape, John H. "Myth, Allusion, and Symbol in E. M. Forster's 'The Other Side of the Hedge.'" *Studies in Short Fiction* 14, no. 4 (fall 1977): 375-78.

*[In the following essay, Stape argues against the negative reception received by Forster's short stories, focus-*

*ing on specific plot elements of the story "The Other Side of the Hedge."*]

The "generally warm reception" accorded Forster's **The Celestial Omnibus** by contemporary reviewers has, as time has passed, become distinctly less warm.[1] Lionel Trilling articulated the view of the stories that now generally obtains: "Forster's short stories, indeed, are on the whole not successful, and their interest lies not so much in themselves as in their connection with the novels."[2] Only a few of the stories have, in fact, received much attention for themselves, and in the many monographs on Forster that treat the stories few of the discussions can be considered more than cursory or obligatory. Some are, in fact, so cursory as to be of little value. If fantasy, as Forster says, "asks us to pay something extra,"[3] then his stories must receive a closer and more penetrating criticism than they have had. Indeed, judgments of their merit depend on closer scrutiny, and their too casual dismissal as "Pan-ridden" fantasies might be less frequent.[4]

One of the stories that has suffered most from critical unwillingness "to pay something extra" is **"The Other Side of the Hedge,"** first published in *The Independent Review* in 1904, a story that one critic speaks of as "a standard anthology piece."[5] H. J. Oliver characterizes it as "the weakest" of Forster's first collection; Norman Kelvin refers to it as "slight," and George H. Thomson sees it as a failure.[6] Although not nearly as successful as some of Forster's other efforts in this genre, the merit of the story might be better judged by a clearer explication of its elements.

The passage from the road to the other side of the hedge has, as some critics have noted, clear allusions to rebirth and to baptism. The passing of the anonymous narrator from one state to the other is assisted by an old man, a vestigial Charon, who is at once more accommodating and less grim than that of Virgil, but who retains one clearly Virgilian characteristic—a certain youthfulness—"his voice was that of a boy of eighteen"—despite his age.[7] In Virgil he is described as: "Old, but a god's old age has left him green and hale."[8] The Virgilian influence on the story is unmistakeable; only two years after its publication the Temple Classics edition of *The Aeneid* was published with an introduction and annotations by Forster. The passage through water may also be a recollection of Aeneas' sprinkling himself with holy water before he enters the regions of Elysium: "He, with lustral dew / Self-sprinkled, seized the entrance, and in haste / High o'er the fronting door the fateful offering placed" (I, 311). And what might be taken as the generalized underworld of antiquity is also specifically Virgilian:

These dues performed, they reach the realms of rest,
Fortunate groves, where happy souls repair.

And lawns of green, the dwellings of the blest.
A purple light, a more abundant air
Invest the meadows. Sun and stars are there,
Known but to them. There rival athletes train
Their practised limbs, and feats of strength compare.
These run and wrestle on the sandy plain,
Those tread the measured dance, and join the song's
   sweet strain.

(I, 312)

The young man sprinting and the girl "singing exquisitely to herself" (pp. 33-34) are echoes of the activities in Virgil's Elysian Fields as are the luminosity and greenness of Forster's underworld. It is further noteworthy that at the conclusion of Aeneas's Descent into Hades (a section of *The Aeneid* that Forster singles out as "wonderful" in his introduction to Taylor's translation),[9] Aeneas departs by way of the ivory gate, the gate of false dreams.

One further detail in the story also has a Virgilian source. In describing the close of day and the preparations for sleep on the other side of the hedge the narrator observes of the inhabitants: "Already they were lying down for the night like cattle—some out on the bare hillside, others in groups under the beeches" (p. 36). The observation echoes Musaeus's reply to the question about Anchises's abode in the underworld: "Fixt home hath no one; by the streamlet's side, / Or in dark groves, or dewy meads we stray, / Where living waters through the pastures glide" (I, 315).

Wilfred Stone's comments on the conclusion of the story betray a failure to recognize yet another classical allusion. Stone remarks that "After an unconvincing spasm of final struggle, the lad accepts this life-in-death as his true and everlasting home, and the story ends with the discovery of the lost brother and the drinking of a can of beer. . . . Fainting (Forester's early heroes usually faint in crises) plus expansion plus music is a fairly normal formula for salvation in Forster. . . . Inside the hedge, the will-less inherit the earth."[10] The "can of some liquid" (p. 37) carried by the man returning to the hills is, in fact, a draught of the River Lethe, the river of forgetfulness. It is thus that the narrator repeats twice "I forgot" as he approaches the man, and precisely what he forgets is the life of his past—the road and what he has mistakenly taken to be "the destiny of our race," an illusory progress. This allusion is made more complex by the narrator's perception of "the magic song of nightingales" (p. 37), and it is clear that Forster has in mind a particular nightingale—that of Keats:

My heart aches, and a drowsy numbness pains
   My sense, as though of hemlock I had drunk,
Or emptied some dull opiate to the drains
      One minute past, and Lethe-wards had
   sunk. . . .

> O, for a draught of vintage! that hath been
>      Cool'd a long age in the deep-delved earth,
> Tasting of Flora and the country green,
>      Dance, and Provençal song, and sunburnt mirth!
> O for a beaker full of the warm South,
>      Full of the true, the blushful Hippocrene,
> With beaded bubbles winking at the brim,
>      And purple-stained mouth;
> That I might drink, and leave the world unseen,
> And with thee fade away into the forest dim.[11]

The allusion to Keats's poem is also made clear by the narrator's saying "my senses were sinking into oblivion" (p. 37). He is, then, not one of Forster's early fainting heroes saved only by will-lessness. Although the passage from a time-bound to a time-less world is clear enough from other references in the story, the watch that no longer works and the youthful old man among them, Forster's allusion to Keats's "Ode to A Nightingale" completes the range of these references. The immortal bird of Keats gives way to the poetic immortalization of a passing moment, and what Forster does by evoking this poem is to confirm the immortalization of the narrator of the story. It seems equally clear that Forster's version of the underworld experience is adapted from classical sources rather than taken over whole, for the doctrine of the transmigration of the soul as classically defined necessarily implies multiple reincarnations. Forster's is a more permanent heaven.

It is interesting to note that in this early story Forster uses symbols later employed to delineate another contrast—that between the Wilcoxes and the Schlegels in *Howards End.* Dust, here associated with the road and its vision of man's destiny, is in the novel attached to the "progressive" Wilcoxes, whereas hay, here associated with the occupations of a rural Arcadia, is in *Howards End* the bane of the unrural "businessmen." The symbols here differentiating one side of the hedge with the other are expanded in the novel while some of Forster's later themes are embryonically presented in this mythological framework. The usual view of this story—that it is an attack on progress—is too simplistically asserted if one takes into account the full range of its references, and its relationship to Forster's more mature fiction, in particular *Howards End.* Forster's vision of utopia in this early story—a place of rural pursuits and of brotherhood, an environment where the arts have a place—later expands into the richer and more complex realities explored in the novels.[12] That **"The Other Side of the Hedge"** may not, in fact, be a story of great merit should not blind critics to what it is, and attentive explication, rather than a summary dismissal, should yield something of interest to students of Forster's fiction.

*Notes*

1. Philip Gardner, "Introduction," *E. M. Forster: The Critical Heritage,* ed. Philip Gardner (London and Boston: Routledge, 1973), p. 14.

2. *E. M. Forster* (1943; rpt. New York: New Directions, 1964), p. 55.

3. *Aspects of the Novel* (New York: Harcourt, Brace, and Company, 1927), p. 159.

4. The phrase "Pan-ridden" is Leonard Woolf's. Cited in J. B. Beer's *The Achievement of E. M. Forster* (London: Chatto, 1968), p. 173.

5. John V. Hagopian, "Eternal Moments in the Short Fiction of E. M. Forster," *College English,* 27 (December 1965), 209.

6. *The Art of E. M. Forster* (Melbourne: Melbourne University Press, 1960), p. 20; *E. M. Forster* (Carbondale, Ill.: Southern Illinois University Press, 1967), p. 33; *The Fiction of E. M. Forster* (Detroit: Wayne State University Press, 1967), p. 61.

7. "The Other Side of the Hedge," *Collected Short Stories* (London: Sidgwick and Jackson, 1948), p. 32. Subsequent references are to this edition.

8. *The Aeneid of Virgil,* trans. E. Fairfax Taylor with an Introduction and Notes by E. M. Forster (London: Dent, 1906), I, 291. Subsequent references are to this edition.

9. "Introduction," *The Aeneid of Virgil,* I, xvi.

10. *The Cave and the Mountain: A Study of E. M. Forster* (Stanford: Stanford University Press, 1966), p. 148.

11. *The Poems of John Keats,* ed. E. de Selincourt (1905; rpt. London: Methuen, 1961), p. 191.

12. See also "The Abinger Pageant" and Forster's pageant play *England's Pleasant Land* in which rural paradises have threatened existences in the world of machinery and progress.

**Judith Scherer Herz (essay date 1979)**

SOURCE: Herz, Judith Scherer. "The Narrator as Hermes: A Study of the Early Short Fiction." In *E. M. Forster: A Human Exploration—Centenary Essays,* edited by G. K. Das and John Beer, pp. 17-27. New York: Macmillan, 1979.

[*In the following essay, Herz explores the significance of the Greek god Hermes in Forster's fiction, noting that he occupies a space between life and death in the author's stories, often evoked to link reality and fantasy in Forster's fictional world.*]

Perhaps we can even identify the god. In a marvellous group in the British Museum he stands beside Alcestis. The S curve of his body accentuated by his slightly raised left foot, he seems, caduceus in hand, to be urging the group forward. Almost contemporary with the Hermes of Praxiteles, he shares the same languid beauty; indeed, he seems even younger. To the left of Alcestis, if, in fact, the draped female figure between the two beautiful boys *is* the wife of Admetus, stands Death, apparently beckoning her forward. His arm, broken at the hand, his head tilted slightly back, he is framed by two full-length wings that are raised only slightly (much less so than the drapery of either Alcestis or Hermes, more a tracery than a relief) from the marble surface of the column base. To the right of Hermes, but badly broken, is another female figure, possibly Persephone. If that identification is correct, she is well located, for the group as it now stands is directly opposite the seated Demeter of Cnidus. The mother, at once dumpy and divine, is alone on her fragmented throne, although the shrine at Cnidus was, we are assured, dedicated to Demeter and Kore, so that originally a standing figure of Persephone was at her side.

In 1903, when Forster visited Cnidus, he took a wry comfort in knowing that while he was wet and muddied where 'the sea ran into the sky', Demeter was 'at that moment, warm and comfortable in that little recess of hers between the Ephesian Room and the Archaic Room, with the electric light fizzling above her, and casting blue shadows over her chin'.[1] He will not, he explains, turn sentimental on the theme of her exile; rather he appropriates her and makes her a living part of his imaginative world: 'Demeter alone among gods has true immortality. The others continue, perchance, their existence, but are forgotten, because the time came when they could not be loved. But to her, all over the world, rise prayers of idolatry from suffering men as well as suffering women, for she has transcended sex.' He granted her immortality and took from her the special comfort of her double sexuality. Perhaps he responded to her Chthonic nature as well, for, especially in her identification with her daughter Persephone, she is a life/death figure, like Hermes, 'conductor of souls'.

There is certainly no disputing the goddess, but is the Ephesian Hermes across the way part of Forster's active repertoire of images? In a diary entry at about the same time as the 'Cnidus' essay, Forster speaks of the Greek sculptures in the British Museum, in particular of 'that wonderful boy with the broken arm—who I suppose is to be called sugary because he's neo-Attic—[who] stands all the afternoon warm in thick yellow sunshine. He simply radiates light: I never saw anything like it. Right across the Assyrian transept he throbs like something under the sea. He couldn't have done it in Greece.'[2] To be sure, the figure on the drum that fits this description is Death rather than Hermes, but the

two were essentially interchangeable in Forster's imagination, as indeed they are mythologically. One need only think of Mann's Tadzio, in gesture very like this 'wonderful boy'. Moreover, the winged figure of death is iconographically close to Eros both as he is traditionally referred to and as Forster imagines him at the moment of his birth in *The Longest Journey*. We have here a nucleus of important associations for Forster—Hermes, the beautiful young friend and guide, particularly a guide to the dead, and young death, also beautiful and ardent ('I have and hope to keep the power of thinking of death as beautiful.' Diary, 1912),[3] both merged in Eros as a figure of love *and* death. The chain of associations here is similar to Mann's in *Death in Venice* and it is interesting that Mann, whom Kerényi called Dr Hermeticus ('Your work and your nature represent a revelation of that God'), observed in a letter to Kerényi thirty years after the story: 'I could not help being pleased to note that the psychopomp is characterized as essentially a child divinity. I thought of Tadzio in *Death in Venice.*'[4]

Indeed Kerényi's analysis of the Hermes figure is particularly resonant for a reading of Forster's mythic imagination. Kerényi speaks, for example, of the close relationship between Eros and Hermes and of 'the eternal relationship of love, thievery and trade.'[5] He sees the figures of Eros and Aphrodite as essentially one and emphasises their wingedness and bisexuality. The Hermetic span, in his analysis, moves 'from the phallic to the psychopompic' and Hermes is seen, 'like every trickster', as one who 'operates outside the fixed bounds of custom and law'. He is a 'hoverer-between-worlds who dwells in a world of his own'.[6]

Hermes, in Forster's fiction, is both a figure with a name, and a point of view, a way of seeing and acting. He is one of a trinity of male mythological figures, and by far the most significant. Pan, his son, was for a time more in fashion, but, as Patricia Merivale has shown, he had become rather trivialised by the first decade of the twentieth century.[7] Although Pan was still important for Forster, particularly as a figure of sexual awakening, a rough country boy, urgent and importunate, he was easily sentimentalised, not resonant enough mythologically as was his father. Even in his most important appearance, in **'The Story of a Panic',** he belongs to a larger pattern shaped by Hermes.

The third figure in this trinity is also a countryman, the hunter Orion, shining in a cold sky, his frosty glories both a promise and a negation. Orion, 'the central star of whose sword is not a star, but a nebula, the golden seed of worlds to be', is older than either Hermes or Pan. He rises in autumn recalling youth and adventure (**'The Point of It'**). For Kuno in **'The Machine Stops',** Orion provides the pattern of man and that image more than anything else is the source of his desire to reach the surface: 'The last thing that I saw ere the stopper closed after us were certain stars, and I felt that a man of my sort lived in the sky.' Orion provides a recurrent image in Forster's fiction, a promise of freedom, a vision of the enlarged male self, the rough woodsman. Any attempt to chart Forster's myth-making must place him, but it is, none the less, 'the mystifying son of Maia, that enticing divinity who calls forth ever renewed attempts at interpretation',[8] that must claim our attention.

Neither a heavenly presence nor an eruptive natural force, he is Hermes *philanthropotatos,* most friendly of gods to man.[9] For Forster he is an essential component of the double-sexed spirit of fantasy: 'She or he. For fantasy, though often female, sometimes resembles a man, and even functions for Hermes, who used to do the smaller behests of the gods—messenger, machine breaker, and conductor of souls to a not-too-terrible hereafter.'[10] It is this 'lightly built' figure who introduces the stories gathered together in *The Eternal Moment.* Again some years later he leads forth *The Collected Tales.* To him Forster dedicated *Pharos and Pharillon* and he concludes that book as well, presiding over the descent into the asphodel, even though Menelaus, who escaped death on his wife's account, remains with the cotton brokers, as he 'leads forth the pageant with solid tread'.[11]

Forster's association of Hermes and fantasy anticipates Kerényi's much later description of the type of experience symbolised by Hermes. It is that 'which expresses itself not scientifically but mythologically . . . [and] is open to the possibility of suprasensual guide and psychopomp, capable of affording impressions grounded in sense experience, which do not contradict the observations and findings of science, and which yet transcend the scientific view of the world. With Hermes as our guide through life, the world is viewed under a special aspect. This aspect is utterly real and remains within the realm of natural experience.'[12] Hermes belongs neither to the realm of life nor death. His true space—and the one most frequently evoked in Forster's stories—is the space between worlds.

Once we recognise this space as the natural setting for the tales, we still have the tasks of showing how the fantasies evoke this space, how the Hermetic presence operates. This hermeneutics of Hermes requires that we recognise the tales as being strong fictions, by no means juvenilia or whimsical exercises in fashionable turn-of-the century Hellenism. They are structures in which language and myth cohere and where the reader plays the role of translator and of expositor of the story's argument. Determining the roles of narrator, characters and reader and thereby identifying the presence of the god will thus be the major concern for the remainder of the essay.

Although the narrators are often dull and uncomprehending, the reader is placed in the privileged position of initiate in a solemn mystery as he distinguishes between false story and true. As a result the controlling narrative point of view in many of these tales is distinct from the teller of the tale. It will be useful to give that point of view the name Hermes (indeed in **'The Celestial Omnibus'** he even appears under his sign) and watch the forms he takes and the tricks he plays. His repertoire of jokes, for example, allows a Tytler or an Inskip to imagine he is telling a story, whereas, in fact, this putative narrator is totally unaware of the story that is really happening. We are witness to a process of transformation that the teller is ignorant of. The stories that Inskip narrates and Bons experiences (he could have been the narrator except for his nasty fall) never happen. But their pupils, who become in the stories the poetry their teachers imagined themselves to have read and understood, enter the realm of Hermes—death in the world, rebirth in the spirit.

Both **'Other Kingdom'** and **'The Story of a Panic'** use the obvious device of a stupid, obtuse narrator who is treacherously involved in the story's events, but who is unwittingly instrumental in the triumphant conclusion. Tytler in his temptation of Gennaro precipitates the leap that frees Eustace and returns him to his vision of Pan, experienced both as epiphany and human touch. Gennaro is both god and boy, the human evidence of the rapt vision. He is the true shaper of the tale, although, as mere actor, corruptible and weak. 'I made the new note crackle in my pocket; and he heard it. He stuck his hand out with a jerk; and the unsuspecting Eustace gripped it in his own.' Even from the Tytler perspective (although we are not to imagine that he intends any pathos in his use of 'unsuspecting'), there is an intimation of the larger meaning of the embrace. Gennaro, of course, sees it all the more sharply because of his own complicity: 'He longed for a friend, and found none for fifteen years. Then he found me, and the first night I—I who have been in the woods and understand things too—betray him to you and send him in to die.' Ironically it is through his apparent treachery that he provides Eustace with his only means of escape and interprets that escape rightly as salvation. 'He has understood and he is saved. . . . Now, instead of dying he will live!' Although lower-born than Hermes and younger, Pan, too, is conductor of the dead, and dwells, as is carefully glossed in **'Other Kingdom'**, 'most places, as name implies'.

Inskip, the perpetrator of such useful pedantry, is, in many ways, a more interesting figure than Tytler and less of a caricature. He is passionless, neutral, totally the embodiment of the practical world that Miss Beaumont absolutely escapes from at the end. It is those two poles, absolutely/practically, that are in many ways the governing polarities of Forster's fiction. The world of fantasy is absolute, reality is 'practically', in the sense both of 'almost' (i.e. tentative, pre-formed, not yet realised) and of 'useful in the ordinary ways of the world'. In the last sentence of **'Other Kingdom'** the contrast and the triumphant escape are given visionary authority: 'She has escaped you absolutely for ever and ever, as long as there are branches to shade men from the sun.' Ford, whose private joke was to keep a diary called 'Practically a Book', is the spokesman for the absolute, the witness to a transformation so total that it escapes the world of sexuality altogether. We may imagine Eustace reenacting eternally the gesture of awakening to his true sexual identity. But Evelyn in her transformation presides over just such a pre-fallen vegetable world that the Marvellian lover might have given to his coy mistress had there been world enough and time.

The narrative tension is thus between pupil and teacher, between Ford and Inskip, and translation, the ostensible activity of the story's opening, functions finally as a metaphor of its achievement. 'Ah, witless fellow! Gods, I say, even gods have dwelt in the woods ere now.' Inskip, the 'demens, the silly ass' tells a story of an odd, impetuous girl, a handsome wedding present, a clever and cynical ward, an indulgent employer; but in the end it is the gods who inhabit the woods whose deed Harcourt owns in perpetuity and it is Ford who sees them and speaks their tongue.

The different narrative strategy of **'The Celestial Omnibus'** is the result of a slight shift in emphasis and is more apparent than real. Inskip and Tytler have been absorbed into the story as Mr Bons while the nameless narrator plays out a story before his nose which he cannot, he will not, see or hear.

The Celestial Omnibus is under Hermes' direction, as the sign-post in the dark alley tells us. The company will not 'be responsible for any negligence or stupidity on the part of Passengers, nor for Hailstorms, Lightning, Loss of Tickets, nor for any Act of God'. The signature is the caduceus, the emblem **'For the Direction'.**

The story records a double journey, the boy's toward enlightenment and vision, Mr Bons's through darkness into death. The primary action is, of course, a literal version of the journey metaphor, and the two conductors are figures for the narrator himself. At the last, the boy (as nameless as his narrator) is caught up on the shield of Achilles and raised aloft, made to stand upright, while Mr Bons, unheeding of the words of Dante whom he has bound in vellum, sees only London and plummets to his death. It is indeed a conclusion of Dantesque tonality. His punishment is to see and not know how to believe, so atrophied has his library-bound imagination become; his fall and mutilation, emblematic of spiritual death.

In mythic terms, this story is probably the most satisfying, the most completely worked out. The shield of

Achilles is the perfect emblem for the boy's exaltation. It is figuratively the entire world, but is bounded, shaped, indeed a shining version of that enclosed space—dell, cave, cabin, womb—that figures in almost every story and novel, and here made to stand for all experience consecrated by the imagination.

The stories move between two worlds. In them Hermes functions as the mythic analogue of the authorial presence, a device that diminishes the necessity for direct intervention, or rather, turns such intervention into a species of masquerade where, in the person of the god, the narrator can manifest truths and reshape reality. The short story, in Forster's hands, becomes genuinely an epiphany. The god himself inhabits there.

But two crucial aspects of the god remain to be examined: his actualisation as the beautiful young boy whom we saw exiled from Ephesus to the British Museum, and his connection for Forster, via his role as psychopomp, with death and memory. In both of these roles he has a ready place in late-nineteenth-century writing. He is Housman's 'merry guide' and related, too, to Pater's Denys L'Auxerrois, although that figure is, perhaps, more Dionysian or Orphic. He leads the *danse macabre* in *Zuleika Dobson,* but for the purposes of this argument, he makes his most interesting appearance in Henry James's 'The Great Good Place', a story with marked affinities with Forster's **'The Point of It'.**

There is no establishing with certainty whether Forster read James's later stories shortly after they were published, nor is it necessary to argue any direct connection or influence. Using James as a touchstone should serve primarily to remind us that Forster was working within an acknowledged aesthetic, even as he shaped it to his own special voice. None the less the resemblances between the two stories are certainly striking, both in their tonality and the shape of the action. In both stories the central character recapitulates a lifetime as the other acts as a guide. In both there is a calculated blurring of the boundary between reality and fantasy. An event occurs that is neither wholly within the soul or within the world. Where does George Dane go? Who is the young man who takes over his life, whose voice, whose face merge with the voice and face of the Good Brother of the dream? 'I just dropped my burden and he received it', Dane tells the brother as a total explanation.[13] To be sure, the central experience of **'The Point of It'** seems more overtly allegorical, but the vision of a lifetime leading to death and back is vouchsafed to Micky in much the same Hermetic fashion as it is to Dane.

Such a reading of **'The Point of It'** is, at first glance, hard to sustain, but an unpublished version presently in The University of Texas Library confirms it in important ways.[14] The story has always troubled its readers, who echo the title with uncertainty, not quite able to complete the sentence. What is it that Micky finally learns? What is his final transformation? However, the story originally ended with four lines that were cancelled before publication:

'Well rowed,' cried Micky to the ferryman. 'Three more and easy.'

The order was obeyed.

'Ship.'

Harold shipped his oars.

These lines, inasmuch as they imply that Harold did not die, remind us that the sunset with which the story closes locates the same moment in time as the story's opening. The friends are now returning at sunset to the shore they set out from earlier in the day, and this realisation transforms the central part of the story, Micky's life and death, from narration to vision.

Described mythologically, the story arrests the flow of time. In a flash all of Micky's life is unfolded before his eyes. Harold, functioning as Hermes, is the stimulus of a vision which allows both for failure and salvation, death and return. Micky sees, simultaneously, the probable course of his life and that action or gesture which could yet transform it. Thus as he is excited by the total commitment to the moment which Harold's rapt straining at the oars signifies, he is able to transcend the mediocrity that will otherwise characterise his life and return in the blazing sunset, having successfully crossed midstream. No time passes at all, or no more than that split second which it takes for the boat, working against the ebb of the tide, to cross the channel. Harold is at the oars. 'The ferryman', these lines call him, but that identification with Charon serves only to emphasise his role as Hermes. There were many precedents for the conflation of the two names, not the least being Housman's epigraph to 'The Merry Guide'. In that subtitle, subsequently cancelled, the phrase 'Hermes guide of souls' appears, but the line from Euripides generally regarded as the source of the quotation refers instead to Charon.[15] That Forster should have merged the two names is no surprise. For whether his name be Hermes or Charon, Harold remains the psychopomp, the spirit of fantasy itself. He is, however, a silent character, whose function as conductor of souls is taken over by the narrator. For it is the narrator who unfolds and interprets the process whereby Micky transforms his life and becomes capable of that absoluteness which is the total antithesis of the Tomlinson life that would otherwise be his. And—this is the point!—this transformation occurs in the realm of fantasy, it does not occur in reality. *No one dies.*

Thus **'The Point of It'** contains two stories; one lasts a moment, the other a lifetime. Even without the cancelled ending, one could maintain such a reading. The

framing sunset remains. Moreover, Micky enters the visionary realm early in the story when on the second page we see him transform the farmhouse on the shore into 'a star and the boat its attendant satellite'. 'Micky had imagination', Forster tells us. In his eyes 'the tide was the rushing ether stream of the universe, the interstellar surge that beats forever.' It is within this frame that the rest of the story unfolds.

Death is, however, not only the beautiful boy all wings and muscle, but retrospect, memory. Twelve years later, in a letter to John Middleton Murry on the death of Katherine Mansfield, Forster wrote: 'Death interests me for more than one reason. It is largely connected for me with the problem of remembering. Sorrow I find indirectly rather than directly painful; it obscures.'[16] In the story, dying is re-living and the pain of death is particularly the pain of the failure of memory. In another portion of the story that was removed before publication, this is made explicit:

Ah time, is it not enough to snatch the present? need you ruin the past as well? here is your highest crime against man, that man forgets. Even as a [*sic*] write memories are fading, sweet moments are ghostly in the gathering grey, places and friends are passing from my brain as they have long since passed from my eyes; until in the final twilight even this dimness will be a memory, and I shall but remember that once I remembered.

One can more easily guess why Forster cancelled this passage than give reasons for his cancelling of the final lines. The tone is, perhaps, too sententious; the 'I' merges with 'a' in a more than typographical error. The contrast in the story is certainly sharper without it: 'The shades were silent. They could not remember.'

But why did Forster choose to blur the outlines of the finished tale and leave the impression at the end that the channel Micky crosses is the spiritual analogue of the real one, but, for all that, not the same? Perhaps the decision to leave the ending ambiguous had more to do with his own unresolved feelings about death than with purely literary concerns. Certainly, as we learn from Furbank's biography, 1910 to 1911 was a particularly dark time for Forster; in many ways his 1637. And while I make no claims that **'The Point of It'** ranks with *Lycidas* as art, the urgent wrestling with death that both story and poem record are comparable. The 'declaration' to Masood which gets him nowhere, the disappointing New Year's Eve that follows, the illness and death of his grandmother, his own illness that might be tubercular (his father had been not quite two years older when he had died), a birthday shadowed with death. Although **'The Point of It'** was not published until November 1911, it had been completed by March.[17] Without the final lines it is a darker story, or, at least, the terms of the triumph are less certain, the point of it more in doubt.

Return is, none the less, part of the Hermes myth and Alcestis on the temple drum will shortly retrace her journey, Hermes still her guide. The story, in similar fashion, holds life and death in equal suspension, its driving urgency, the sense that life must be seized, followed even to the gates of death, as if only in that heroic straining can there be salvation. Harold is, thus, a purer Gerald Dawes, seen more sculpturally, without the crankiness he wore in the novel. And Micky seems, especially from the vantage afforded by the manuscript version, more fit than Rickie to grasp the point of it, to know that he has been in the presence of the god and that, henceforth, his life must be changed.

The god leaves his traces throughout Forster's writing in his many disguises, from Puck the phallic trickster in **'The Obelisk'** to the angry god in **'The Road from Colonus'**. For Forster he seems to be simultaneously a mythic mode, an artifact of unsettling beauty and a psychological reality. As myth, marble and desire, he presides in the tales. He knows more than the mere narrators, although he sometimes speaks with their voices. Mercurial, elusive, he gives the fiction its shape and informs it with his spirit.

Thus the effectiveness of the tales is in large measure due to their mythic coherence. To say that Hermes inhabits there may be fanciful speech but of the sort congenial to Forster's way of imagining. For, finally, Hermes in his triple incarnation—Hermes, Eros, Death—was for Forster, as he was for Whitman, that 'crown and point which all lives have reference to'. Indeed his evocation in the 1876 Preface to *Leaves of Grass* has many echoes for the present occasion:

> I still feel to keep *Passage to India* for last words even to this Centennial dithyramb. Not as, in antiquity, at highest festival of Egypt, the noisome skeleton of Death was also sent on exhibition to the revellers, for zest and shadow to the occasion's joy and light—but as the perfect marble statue of the normal Greeks at Elis, suggesting death in the form of a beautiful and perfect young man, with closed eyes, leaning on an inverted torch—emblem of rest and aspiration after action—of crown and point which all lives and poems should steadily have reference to, namely, the justified and noble termination of our identity, this grade of it, and outlet-preparation to another grade.

## Notes

1. E. M. Forster, 'Cnidus', AH (1936) 175, 176.

2. Quoted, Furbank I, 110. I am greatly indebted to Mr Furbank for suggesting that the Hermes I had been seeking was part of the British Museum group: Death, Alcestis, Hermes. The group is reproduced on the dust-jacket to his second volume.

3. Furbank I, 218.

4. *Mythology and Humanism: The Correspondence of Thomas Mann and Karl Kerényi,* translated by A. Gelley (Ithaca, 1975) pp. 9 and 101.

5. Karl Kerényi, 'The Primordial Child in Primordial Times', in Kerényi and C. G. Jung, *Essays on a Science of Mythology* (New York, 1949) p. 73.

6. Kerényi in Paul Radin, *The Trickster: A Study in American Indian Mythology* (New York, 1956) pp. 185 and 189. See also W. Otto, *The Homeric Gods* (Boston, 1964) p. 117, and N. O. Brown, *Hermes the Thief* (Wisconsin, 1947).

7. Patricia Merivale, *Pan The Goat-God: His Myth in Modern Times* (Harvard, 1969) *passim,* especially pp. 180-91.

8. Letter of Thomas Mann to Kerényi (1945), Gelley, p. 126.

9. See Otto, p. 105. The phrase is used in Aristophanes, *Peace,* 1. 394.

10. E. M. Forster, Introduction to *Collected Tales* (New York, 1947). A slightly different version was used as the headnote of *The Eternal Moment* (1928).

11. PP (1926) 98.

12. Kerényi in Radin, p. 190.

13. Henry James, 'The Great Good Place', *The Complete Tales of Henry James,* ed. Leon Edel (Philadelphia, 1962-4), Vol. XI, p. 25; originally published in *Scribner's Magazine,* January 1900, and reprinted in *The Soft Side* (1900).

14. Permission to quote from the unpublished manuscript granted by the Provost and Scholars of King's College, Cambridge.

15. See T. B. Huber, *The Making of a Shropshire Lad: A Manuscript Variorum* (Seattle, 1966) p. 208.

16. Letter to John Middleton Murry, 4 January 1923. This letter is at The Humanities Research Center at The University of Texas at Austin.

17. Furbank I, 195-6.

## List of Abbreviations

(i) E. M. Forster

Where a work by Forster has not, at the time of writing, appeared in the Abinger edition, a date or some other identifier is attached to the abbreviation to assist ready identification of the text being used. In the case of *Maurice,* however, it is assumed that the pagination of the Abinger text, when it comes, will correspond with that of the first edition.

WAFT: *Where Angels Fear to Tread* (1905) Abinger edition, edited by O. Stallybrass, 1975.

LJ (WC): *The Longest Journey* (1907) World's Classics edition, 1960.

RWV: *A Room with a View* (1908) Abinger edition, 1977.

HE: *Howards End* (1910) Abinger edition, 1973.

AHG: (1922) *Alexandria: A History and a Guide,* Alexandria, 1922.

PP: (1923) *Pharos and Pharillon,* 1923.

PI: *A Passage to India* (1924) Abinger edition, 1978.

AN: *Aspects of the Novel* (1927) Abinger edition, 1974.

GLD: *Goldsworthy Lowes Dickinson* (1934) Abinger edition, 1973.

AH: (1936) *Abinger Harvest,* 1936.

CSS: (1947) *Collected Short Stories,* 1947.

TCD: *Two Cheers for Democracy* (1951) Abinger edition 1972.

HD: (1953) *The Hill of Devi,* 1953.

M: *Maurice,* 1971.

LTC: *The Life to Come and Other Stories,* 1972.

Furbank: P. N. Furbank, *E. M. Forster: A Life* volume I (1879-1914), 1977; volume II (1914-1970), 1978.

(ii) Virginia Woolf

AWD: Virginia Woolf, *A Writer's Diary,* edited by Leonard Woolf, 1953.

Bell: Quentin Bell, *Virginia Woolf, a biography,* two vols, 1972.

Diary: Virginia Woolf, *Diary,* introduced by Quentin Bell, edited by A. O. Bell, 1977-.

Essays: Virginia Woolf, *Collected Essays,* edited by Leonard Woolf, four vols, 1966-7.

Moments: Virginia Woolf, *Moments of Being,* unpublished autobiographical writings, edited by J. Schulkind, 1976.

**Glen Cavaliero (essay date 1979)**

SOURCE: Cavaliero, Glen. "The Early Stories." In *A Reading of E. M. Forster,* pp. 38-58. London: Macmillan, 1979.

[*In the following essay, Cavaliero discusses Forster's use of Edwardian literary tradition, especially its celebration of childhood and fantasy, to sharpen his own literary style in his early short stories.*]

I

The Fitzwilliam Museum at Cambridge used at one time to display a painting called *The Little Faun.*[1] A table is set beneath flowering cherry trees, and a small boy is standing on it, pulling at the branches. Beside him, also on the table, is the little faun: two young women are standing by, and one of them tweaks its tail. The faun parents, dim animal shapes, watch guardedly through leaves. It is a characteristic piece of Edwardian whimsy, full of shimmering pink and white; but a more knowing generation may detect tell-tale undertones. That domestication of the wild, that dainty sexual titillation, the breaking of taboo as the child stands upon the table—all these things add up to a distillation of the evasively erotic that typifies much writing of the period, an example of the Victorian compromise carried over into the field of sex awareness. 'Naughty but nice'—the coyness of Edwardian music-hall coquetry is an attempt to tame the beast, and an instance of that incurable English tendency to dissolve all uncomfortable realities in charm. It was a temptation to which Forster himself was not immune, and his early short stories in particular provide us with examples of his yielding to it. But, more importantly, they show us the way in which he rose above it, and thus sharpened his literary style so that it could undertake more far-reaching explorations in his novels. Instead of rejecting the feeble literary tradition outright, he worked his way through it to a fully mature comprehension of his own.

The tradition is summed up in J. M. Barrie's enormously popular *Peter Pan,* first produced in 1904, the same year that saw the appearance of Forster's **'The Story of a Panic'.** The play combines ambivalence towards the adult world with a celebration of childhood for its own sake. By the time of Forster's early stories the literary cult of childhood was at its height: Kenneth Grahame's *The Golden Age* (1895) is a characteristic example, and in it children live a life that by virtue of its greater spontaneity and naturalness is an implied rebuke to the adult world—the conjoining of Pan with Peter was not surprising when it came. But this tradition was very different from the radical insights of Wordsworth or Blake: it had become a matter of nostalgia, an alternative vision of reality, persuasive on its own terms merely, and more suggestive of escape than transformation. Ultimately it was the expression of a sense of guilt—as Henry James unforgettably demonstrated in 'The Turn of the Screw', the governess's 'adult' fear of corruption being the force that raises the phantoms and thus injures, in one case fatally, the two children. *Peter Pan* and the later *Mary Rose* (1920), Barrie's logical conclusion of the tradition, would seem to suggest that it is better not to grow up at all.

The fact that in *Peter Pan* the life of the fairy Tinker Bell is made dependent on the audience's belief in her, though dramatically effective, also testifies to a sentimentalising subjectivity where the supernatural is concerned: no self-respecting elemental of earlier traditions would have allowed itself to be extinguished by such disobliging schoolboys as might, when asked if they believed in fairies, choose to bellow 'NO!' But the hey-day of imperial wealth and power was essentially materialistic in its spirituality, a point that both Forster and Lawrence in their very different ways were to make repeatedly. The immaterial in whatever form was just that—of no real significance save as an adornment, a 'civilising' extra, something *added* to the real ends of life, which were money and power. Lawrence in his essay on John Galsworthy unforgettably exposes and deflates this attitude, as he analyses the contemporary usage of the word 'passion'.[2] And Forster too, though less by denunciation than by mockery, was to make a similar point. His story **'Other Kingdom'** is a good example of it.

The short stories, indeed, though rightly accounted the least of his fiction, are essential to any understanding of his imaginative world. Written concurrently with the early novels, they provide, as short stories tend to do, clear instances of authorial obsessions; and they thus highlight the novels, which put those obsessions to more objective use. Revealing a tendency towards violence and shock tactics, they are frequently playful, but as cats are playful—with their claws. They are designed to disconcert, and witness to an imaginative impulse that is fundamentally rebellious. But Forster was not by nature an aggressive man: the protest comes out in the shape of farce and fantasy. As Wilfred Stone observes, the stories 'record the first stage of a rebellion against school, church, and the intolerable chaperonage of loving parents and guardians'.[3] Fantasy is used by Forster as 'an unction for disobedience',[4] and by its means he breaks free from the domestic world which was constricting him. And yet even this statement is questionable, for in his hands fantasy returns us to the life which had occasioned it. Forster is not a fantasist of the mythological kind; he does not create new worlds. A feeling for the supernatural was useful to him as a literary device; it was a means of saying something else, never an end in itself. Its appearance in the various short stories he wrote between the early 'Lucy' fragments and *Maurice* illustrates his treatment of so-called 'reality' in these books, and points to the existence of a kind of imaginative overworld to which he regularly returned. It was out of its elements that the novels were to grow.

In *The Longest Journey* he parodies, in the shape of Rickie Elliot's proposed collection 'Pan Pipes', the kind of tales he himself was writing. But at the same time he satirised the readership for which such stories were designed. Agnes's comment on one tale (which, ironically, Forster wrote himself, as **'Other Kingdom'**) helps us to place both it and her. 'Allegory. Man = modern civilization (in bad sense). Girl = getting into touch with nature.' The misunderstanding, the oversimplification, make the point. So does Stephen Wonham's reaction when he reads it. 'In touch with Nature! The girl was a tree!' The distinction is vital; and at the time in which

these stories were being written it was consistently confused. Forster was attempting to liberate himself from a bad literary tradition.

Indeed, the trivialisation of supernatural themes has been a steady and inevitable process coincident with the growth of materialist philosophies since the seventeenth century. One can trace it in the decline of the *Longaevi* of medieval cosmology through the more playful diminutive fairies of Shakespeare and Drayton to those vestigial presences, half-assumed into classical mythology, that we find in Milton. Victorian fantasy provided a further source for the tradition when such an influential writer as George Macdonald made use of German folklore and philosophy. It is significant that in Macdonald's stories the instruments of redemption are quasi-maternal figures: the Great-Great-Grandmother (fourfold maternal) in *The Princess and the Goblin* (1873) comes readily to mind. But no less prominent in Macdonald's fiction are corrective 'aunt' figures, such as the wise woman in *The Lost Princess* (1875), the successors of such better-known disciplinarians as Mrs Be-Done-By-As-You-Did in Charles Kingsley's *The Water Babies* (1863). In Victorian fantasy the woman plays a dominating role; and it is the more significant that Forster, much encumbered with women in his early life, should in his own fantasies turn instead to the young male or brother figure as his deliverer. And the deliverer is frequently light-hearted. The stories are notably lacking in solemnity or, to use a word much in use in the period, 'wonder'.

Nor do they bear much relation to that other aspect of late-nineteenth-century fantasy, the ghost story. The malign aspects of the supernatural evoked by Sheridan Le Fanu or M. R. James are nowhere to be found in Forster's work, though James was in his heyday at the time these tales were being written; nor was Forster himself influenced by the very different, but equally compelling, use of the paranormal to be found in the novels of Henry James and Dickens. The subconscious fears and bogeys on which all these writers play are absent from his work: they are replaced by high spirits, a caustic wit and a rebellious impishness. And this is interesting in view of the fact that much of this macabre writing was done by bookish unmarried men with dominating maternal influences, men such as the three Benson brothers—or, for that matter, Henry James himself. Forster was perhaps more emancipated than has sometimes been allowed.

The figure of Pan appears a good deal in his early writing, as it does in that of many of his contemporaries. Max Beerbohm's 'Maltby and Braxton' makes merry play with the fashion.

> From the time of Nathaniel Hawthorne to the outbreak of the War, current literature did not suffer from any lack of fauns. . . . We had not yet tired of them and

their hoofs and their slanting eyes and their way of coming suddenly out of woods to wean quiet English villages from respectability. We did tire later.[5]

In this respect it is worthwhile to compare Forster's work with that of two writers whom Beerbohm would have had in mind, Arthur Machen and H. H. Munro, better known as Saki. Machen had first made his name with the (then) luridly sensational novella *The Great God Pan* (1894), in which sexual energies are portrayed as obscene and retrogressive. In time he came to dislike the book, which had pandered all too successfully to contemporary tastes in the occult, and in *The Hill of Dreams* (1907) he produced a novel of genuine visionary power which, in its positive stresses, highlights Forster's work. It represents the quintessence of Machen's imaginative world: a solitary boy growing up in a landscape which both fascinates and scares him; the surrounding enclave of adult obtuseness and conventionality; intimations of an ancient civilisation among the ruins of Roman Caerleon; and, most significantly, the dawning of sexuality during sleep on the summit of an ancient earthwork. But the conflict between the physical and imaginative sides of Lucian's nature results in his self-destruction among the arid terraces of London suburbia. The power of Pan is destructive when the human spirit is unable to contain it: the theme of *The Bacchae* is the theme of much literature of this period. The peculiar distinction of Machen's achievement lies in its evocation of an urban landscape that is seen, through the transfiguring vision, as being no less open to spiritual powers and forces than the wild romantic one of Gwent: there is no imaginative departmentalism in his work. Nonetheless he is unable to envisage any reconciliation between the two realities: the prose and the passion will not connect, and in such a later work as *The Secret Glory* (published in 1922 but written fourteen years earlier) the disconnection leads to a breakdown even of the structure of the book itself.

The quest for a transfigured universe, the poetic insight hailed in Machen's literary manifesto *Hieroglyphics* (1902) as being the life of all genuine literature, is to be found in Forster's early work as well. But in Forster the expression of this feeling is tempered by a sharpness of tone that is closer to that of another minor but vitalising writer of the period, Saki. Most of Saki's tales are social satires of varying degrees of frivolity and anger; but one or two are concerned with the operations of the super-natural, usually in the forms of animal malignity. Pan here is the avenger: Saki, a homosexual and, like Forster, brought up by women (in this case a most dire pair of aunts) frequently depicts the female put to rout, whether in jest, as in 'The Boar-Pig', or in deadly earnest, as in 'Shredni Vashtar' or 'The Music on the Hill'. In the latter story the victim of Pan's destructive power is one of those shallow society women who people many of the author's lighter tales; in the former it is yet

another aunt. The hostility of the animal world—also portrayed effectively in Machen's short novel *The Terror* (1917)—is one which Saki appears to endorse, especially in view of the more ribald treatment of such avenging creatures as the cat Tobermory. His intentions, however, seem ambiguous. One notes that his hero-figure Bassington bears the demonic name of Comus; the disruptive Clovis, on the other hand, is surnamed Sangrail. In Saki's world, destruction and dislocation contain elements of deliverance.

II

When compared with the stories of Machen and Saki, those of Forster seem rather tame; but, although more obviously didactic than the other two, he writes with a deeper and more wide-ranging purpose. Five of his stories are tales of Pan, and the production of all but one of them parallels the writing of his early novels. They deal with possession; but, unlike Machen, Forster shows himself to be as interested in its social consequences as he is in the condition of the possessed themselves.

In '**Albergo Empedocle**' the unimaginative but honest Harold (sterling Anglo-Saxon name) falls asleep in a ruined Sicilian temple, and wakes in the knowledge that he has lived before. For him it is the quality of life—'I was a lot greater than I am now'—which is important; but his 'cultured' fiancée[6] interprets this to mean that he has been a king, and she then, sentimentally, tries to fool herself that she likewise has lived before. But Harold will have none of this: the experience is not for romanticising. He alienates her; and the result is his own despair and gradual withdrawal into the past and into noncommunication. He is consigned to an asylum. The story is funny, sad, and alive with intelligence, compassion and wit. The supernatural theme has been made a vehicle for comment on the outlook of the pseudo-culture of the tourist mentality and on the alienating effects of a socially rigid and imaginatively limited way of life. Harold, first of Forster's athletes, is also the first of his victims. The visitation itself is ambiguous, for its destructive nature is really the result of the rest of the party's rejection of it. Tommy, the narrator, who is Harold's friend, remarks at the end that 'the greater has replaced the less, and he is living the life he knew to be greater than the life he lived with us'. This is the expected 'civilised' response. But Tommy goes on to say that 'if things had happened otherwise he might be living that greater life among us, instead of among friends of two thousand years ago'. It is this which is the distinctively Forsterian touch, the tentative optimism, the concern with quality of life rather than with imaginative indulgence.

'**Albergo Empedocle**' foreshadows much that is to be part of the Forsterian universe: the parenthetical, allusive humour; the amiable inanities of the more gently conventional old lady; the sudden sharp comment; the shared observation as between friend and friend. The tale seems almost as much confided as told. Forster always avoids the spectacular: he prefers to use implication. But there is nothing fey about Harold's experience: this is, in one sense, an anti-romantic story. Regrettably, Forster did not think it good enough to publish in *The Celestial Omnibus,* for it is less vulnerable to criticism than some that he did include there.

'**The Story of a Panic'**, however, can have no place among their number: it is one of the surest, most vigorous tales that Forster wrote. Nearly all the ingredients of his early novels are present in this account of the stampeding of a sedate picnic party by the power of Pan. Here are the middle-class conventionalists (Tunbridge Wells, as it were): the spinster sisters whose nephew Eustace is subjected to the visitation of the God; the sentimental aesthete Leyland; the Reverend Mr Sandbach, ancestor of other clerical guardians of the proprieties; and the narrator, Mr Tytler, a Mr Pembroke who talks with the voice of Mr Pooter. The exchanges between him and Leyland anticipate one of the themes of *Howards End.*

> 'All the poetry is going from Nature,' [Leyland] cried, 'her lakes and marshes are drained, her seas banked up, her forests cut down. Everywhere we see the vulgarity of desolation spreading.'
>
> I have had some experience of estates, and answered that cutting was very necessary for the health of the larger trees. Besides, it was unreasonable to expect the proprietor to derive no income from his lands.
>
> (I)

The two sides are played off against each other and both found wanting.

The Italian characters are likewise to be met again later, most significantly the young waiter Gennaro. He is the ideal friend whose death is to be the price for the English boy's release, but who dies, in mordantly Forsterian fashion, still clasping the fee for his treachery. The transition from sharp social comedy to terror is effortlessly managed, partly because Forster's attention at the moment of the picnic party's flight is concentrated on the characters' reactions. They all reveal themselves appropriately; and it is the aesthete who is most frightened. He knows enough to realise what the onset of Pan can mean, but not enough to accept it. It is far harder for him to recover from it than it is for the unimaginative innocents. In this story, the supernatural element is subordinate to the truth which it conveys. The reader is made to think, not jump; but none the less it is (with the exception of *A Passage to India*) the only one of Forster's tales to produce a genuinely frightening effect. This happens when Eustace perceives the goat's hoofmarks in the mud and rolls in them 'as a dog rolls'. The

brevity of this is immensely forceful, an economy of means which Forster was to develop further; we are persuaded that the violence is real. Here is no sentimental post-Meredithian awakening to the joys of nature: Forster's vision at this point is nearer to that of Machen. Gennaro dies while 'Signora Scafetti burst into screams at the sight of the dead body, and, far down the valley towards the sea, there still resounded the shouts and the laughter of the escaping boy.'

Eustace's escape is from—what? Home? 'Ladies'? Too small a bedroom? The tale has a general social relevance, powered by a more personal urge. Its weakness lies in those passages of would-be lyrical evocation when Forster uses the incantatory prose current among his contemporaries: Tytler's account of Eustace's speech is quite out of character.

> He spoke first of night and the stars and planets above his head, of the swarms of fire-flies below him, of the invisible sea below the fire-flies, of the great rocks covered with anemones and shells that were slumbering in the invisible sea. He spoke of the rivers and waterfalls, of the ripening bunches of grapes, of the smoking cone of Vesuvius and the hidden fire-channels that made the smoke, of the myriads of lizards who were lying curled up in the crannies of the sultry earth, of the showers of white rose-leaves that were tangled in his hair. And then he spoke of the rain and the wind by which all things are changed, of the air through which all things live, and of the woods in which all things can be hidden.
>
> (III)

The prose, though musical and skilfully orchestrated, is archaic: these are not the words of Tytler. And they are not really the words of Eustance either. If anyone's, they are the words of Leyland.

But the escaping boy remains to haunt much of Forster's succeeding fiction, like an ultimately friendly demon. (In *Howards End,* however, and *A Passage to India,* Demeter and the Great Mother make their presence felt.) A substitution is effected: Eustace in one sense here *becomes* Gennaro, the 'clumsy, impertinent fisher lad', who is the one person who understands what has happened. And Gennaro is to be reborn as Gino Carella, as Stephen Wonham, as George Emerson, as Alec Scudder; and in each case he is to be bound up with, even to symbolise, a particular place (Monteriano, Wiltshire, Florence, the English woodland) which has significance for the novel's central consciousness, a significance extended into personal terms: 'for Forster, the raising of a single man to mythopoeic stature disguised and sublimated his homosexual passions'.[7] Certainly a sense of *withheld* passion energises the various manifestations of the demon boy; and in the later novels his role tends to be destructive. In *Howards End* he is to be disguised, almost too effectively, as Leonard Bast; and it is he, on one reading, who attacks Miss Quested in the Marabar cave. He can reduce the conventional and repressed, the muddled spiritual materialists, to 'panic and emptiness': Forster anticipates that phrase in this early tale. Here Eustace is liberated by force, and the cost is the destruction of his personality. The later fictions work towards a more positive outcome; and the distinction between compromise and balance is one which will concern Forster repeatedly from now on. Possession is not enough.

The two other Pan stories of the early period show the author's Edwardian side in more complete control. Of these **'The Curate's Friend'** is particularly revealing. The tale is about compromise; but it is itself a compromised production. The curate, whose sight of the faun enables him to bear the loss of his fiancée to another—tiresomely called 'the little friend'—lives on in the knowledge of what underlies reality; but he none the less stays part of that reality.

> And though I try to communicate that joy to others . . . and though I sometimes succeed, yet I can tell no one exactly how it came to me. For if I breathed one word of that, my present life, so agreeable and profitable, would come to an end, my congregation would depart, and so should I, and instead of being an asset to my parish, I might find myself an expense to the nation.

The irony enunciates the author's own situation as well as constituting his particular slant of vision. The closing words indeed, might serve him for an epigraph.

> Therefore in place of the lyrical and rhetorical treatment, so suitable to the subject, so congenial to my profession, I have been forced to use the unworthy medium of a narrative, and to delude you by declaring that this is a short story, suitable for reading in the train.

But this is a dangerous game to play; and this story in particular suffers from an ambiguity of approach. There is something of Harold Skimpole about the curate. He wants to have things both ways. Moreover, the actual presentation of the faun's arrival is arch, and the dialogue when the curate finds 'the little friend' and Emily embracing is pure fustian—or, if it is not, then it is parody such as gives the game away altogether: 'It is idle to chide. What should you know poor clerical creature, of the mystery of love of the eternal man and the eternal woman, of the self-effectuation of a soul?' This sort of thing collides not only with the narrator's tone, but also with the glimpse of 'the great pagan figure of the Faun' towering 'insolently' above them. And the final message of the faun is too slight (though it is telling) for what has gone before: 'To the end of your life you will swear when you are cross and laugh when you are happy.' This is, of course, a Forsterian ideal; but this kind of tale is not the best way of putting it across. It

may contain a homosexual reference (to quote Wilfred Stone, 'The story . . . is a covert love poem, and the spirit of that love is illicit'[8]) but this does not affect its value.

**'Other Kingdom'** is more successful, partly because it is more like a novel in miniature. The comedy is distinctively Edwardian: we are in the familiar world of the Herritons and the Honeychurches. Harcourt Worters is a male surrounded by sycophantic women, and rendered by them pompous and absurd and thus, on Forster's reckoning, dangerous. (When, in a fit of 'playful' jealousy, he pinches his young nephew's leg, he draws blood.) He is a spiritual materialist who seeks to buy and possess what is intangible—in this case Other Kingdom Wood—as a present to his fiancée, Evelyn Beaumont. Evelyn anticipates Helen Schlegel with her protests against the world of 'rights' and 'apologies' and 'Society' and 'position'; she even anticipates, albeit somewhat drastically, Helen's pastoral solution of her dilemma: she turns into a dryad. Mr Worters is a typically Forsterian Apollo, strangely pathetic as he tries to secure what it will never be his to hold. And he is a perfect specimen of the pseudo-aesthete. Speaking of the classics, he says,

> 'They were written before men began to really feel.' He coloured crimson. 'Hence, the chilliness of classical art—its lack of—of a something. Whereas later things—Dante—a Madonna of Raphael—some bars of Mendelssohn—' His voice trailed reverently away. We sat with our eyes on the ground, not liking to look at Miss Beaumont. It is a fairly open secret that she also lacks a something. She has not yet developed her soul.

(II)

It is a story narrated in Forster's most telling, thrifty manner, though a little weighed down by its symbols. The names—Worters, Ford, even Eve Beaumont (how conscious was that?)—are offset by a more persuasive, Lawrentian type of description, as when the narrator observes 'the pleasant, comfortable landscapes, full of cows and carriage horses out at grass, and civil retainers'. But the tale relies too much on puns, as when Evelyn *fords* the stream to the wood (Ford is the name of Mr Worters's nephew, one of those sexually quelled young men who abound piteously in Forster's fiction) while her lover follows her by way of the bridge. And so it is with the 'supernatural' element: it exists to point a moral, and is a product of the fancy rather than of the imagination. Evelyn's disappearance lacks the dramatic power of Eustace's flight: the demon boy here is not in evidence. As in all these early tales, **'The Story of a Panic'** excepted, it is the young girl who goes free. Forster's frustrated compassion may be with the young men, but it is still a question for him of 'Ladies first'.

Ladies are much in evidence in what is in some ways a companion story, **'The Purple Envelope'**. This, like **'Albergo Empedocle'**, was not included in *The Celes-*

*tial Omnibus* collection.[9] It is Forster's one incursion into the macabre, and it forms an interesting gloss on **'Other Kingdom'.** Once again we have a benevolent household despot surrounded by adoring females; but this time the nephew, Howard, is coarse-grained and triumphant.[10] In this tale pseudo-aestheticism is identified with dishonesty—the uncle has defrauded the nephew of his estate; while the outdoor scenes are far more robust and real than the sylvan glades of **'Other Kingdom'.** There is much that is enigmatic about the story—for example, the identity of the middle-aged woman who brings Howard the oval-bored gun; but, since it is the healthy if brutalised reality of Howard's responses which the author seems to be commending, the enigmatic elements only contribute to our sense of the unreality of any attitude other than his. And an enigma is not the same thing as a muddle.

At one point in *A Passage to India* Mrs Moore remarks that 'I like mysteries but I rather dislike muddles.' **'The Story of the Siren'** is an early tale which did not appear until 1920, when it was published by Leonard and Virginia Woolf at the Hogarth Press. It is certainly a mystery; and nowhere until *A Passage to India* was Forster to evoke so hauntingly the human sense of the supernatural. Once again we have a party—this time a boat-load—of tourists, who are confronted with the physical self-assurance and humility of the Italian. The loss beneath the waves of the narrator's notes on the Deist controversy is the appropriate prelude to the fisherman's story of the siren, the sight of whom converts his brother Giuseppe to a weeping wreck as he contemplates the inevitability of mortality. The legend declares that the child born of a pair who have seen the siren under water will save the world by destroying silence and marrying the siren. It is nearly fulfilled by Giuseppe and Maria; but the priest intervenes, and Maria kills herself. The parents' names are those of the parents of the infant Jesus; the clergy act the part of Antichrist. Now the boatman is haunted by an impossible dream; and it is that haunting, our being in the presence of belief, our knowledge of the supernatural at second hand, that lends power to the story. The madness induced by the siren's face lingers on; but 'silence and loneliness cannot last forever'. The dimension of true belief is the antithesis of spiritual materialism, and survives persecution by the priests—and by the tourists, for this story mentions an English lady who has written a book which has turned the village into a showplace, and thus corrupted it. The story of the siren is the story of the loss of vision in the face of materialism and fear. It is an elusive tale, quite free from allegory, but very moving in its evocation of a way of life that is at once idealistic and robustly sane: there is nothing charming or fey about the boatman. There is a strong sense of the erotic, however, and the juxtaposition of the gleaming reality

of his brown body with the notes on the most impersonal of religious controversies is a striking one. The demon boy here becomes a beautiful and suffering man.

III

In all these tales of Pan we are aware less of a desire to entertain than of a need to protest; and the stronger the protest the more truly entertaining is the story. The power of Pan is believed in not, as it were, metaphysically, as another mode of being, but rather as a natural quality of life, to which these stories point through the use of this particular literary convention. That quality is the 'greater life among us', which Tommy wishes for Harold in **'Albergo Empedocle'.** It is not an escape into another dimension, though under present conditions it has to be shown as such. The flight of the lovers to the greenwood in *Maurice* is a further example of this necessity.

In other tales Forster avoids the need to escape by writing fables. There are five of these, and it is notable that they are generally later in date than the Pan stories, and also that only one, **'The Machine Stops',** is set in the future. The others are concerned with an after, or inner, life. **'The Machine Stops'** does indeed stand alone in the body of Forster's work, and is the most impersonal of his tales. Yet it clearly stems from horror and outrage at the transformations in human life which modern technology even then was bringing about. It contains much that was prophetic—the power of television, the reliance on experience at second hand, the architectural uniformity spread across the globe; and yet one can also read it as a critique of more immediate, comfortable suburban conditions by means of futuristic fantasy. The relationship between mother and son, in itself unusual in a story of this kind, gives it a far more intimate character than one might expect, though in this connection it is worth recalling Lionel Trilling's observation that the mothers in Forster's fiction 'have remarkably little impulse towards their sons'.[11] As always with Forster, generalised views are related to the personal life. In this tale too we have an element that is found in all his finest work—anger. Only through anger, controlled and disciplined, does he speak out.

But it is the absence of anger which is notable in the other fables. Two of them, **'Mr Andrews'** and **'Co-ordination',** are notably amiable in tone. Both are slight. In the former, the preference for friendship, rather than for friendship's reward in heaven, makes for one of Forster's softer tales, and the closing sentence almost amounts to self-parody: 'Then they suffered it to break in upon them, and they, and all the experience they had gained, and all the love and wisdom they had generated, passed into [the world soul], and made it better.' The tone here, as in **'Co-ordination'** and **'The Celestial Omnibus',** is comparable with that of Max Beerbohm in such tales as 'The Small Boy and the Barley Sugar' or 'The Dreadful Dragon of Hay Hill'.[12] But the comparison is not in Forster's favour: he is too passionate to handle the sedate or mock-simple with assurance.

'Co-ordination', more truly light-hearted, is more successful, because the fantasy is less controlled, and full of Forster's own brand of mischief (his feeling for little girls is an example of this—Rose and Violet remind one of Minnie Beebe and Irma Herriton). This inconsequential little tale anticipates the portrayal of sublime cosmic muddle in *A Passage to India.* Both it and **'Mr Andrews'** are pictures rather than stories; and George Thomson remarks with justice on 'how completely Forster's imagination deserted him when vision and anti-vision were expressed through the same characters or when the anti-vision was excluded'.[13]

**'The Celestial Omnibus'** is of sterner stuff, despite its playful opening. Mr Bons, like Leyland in **'The Story of a Panic'**, is a pseudo-aesthete, one who confuses books with their substance, the shadow with the reality; when transported to the world of books in its eternal state he cannot endure it, and falls to his death from the celestial omnibus, just as in other Forster stories books fall to the floor or into rivers. But the boy, the innocent eye, can flourish in the archetypal world which destroys the spiritual materialist. The tone of the story at times resembles Belloc's cheerfully sardonic *Bad Child's Book of Beasts* (1896) and is altogether less whimsical than other contemporary celebrations of childhood vision; but the method of the satire is all Forster's own, deft and telling in its dramatisations. Just as in **'The Story of the Siren'** the narrator tells the boatmen that he has seen the siren 'often and often' (he is trying to be ironic), so here Mr Bons boasts of having seven Shelleys in his house. But the omnibus goes 'the whole way' and this is beyond his reach.

It is interesting to compare Forster's fantasy with a contemporary and much longer one which also deals with famous characters in fiction: Walter de la Mare's *Henry Brocken* (1904). This excessively bookish narrative is the kind of elusive dreaming which, if too highbrow for the boy's parents, would just suit Mr Bons. Forster is in fact assessing a literary tradition even while he is using it. (And his hero, significantly, is called The Boy.) A critique of literary historicism, anticipating that in *Aspects of the Novel,* occurs when Mr Bons asserts that the Duchess of Malfi was older than Mrs Gamp. The story may be in a whimsical tradition, but it uses the whimsy to make its points.

More truly original, however, is **'The Other Side of the Hedge'**. This, an early tale, anticipates many of the themes of *The Longest Journey.* Miss Eliza, like Agnes later and memorably, rides a bicycle, and the distinction between those who see life as consisting of being on the move and those who see its essence as lying outside of time foreshadows the contrast between Herbert Pembroke and Stephen Wonham; it is significant that at the end it is a brother whom the narrator discovers. The allegorical element is strong, and the pool clearly represents a baptism. In its restrained, suggestive poetry, its impatient involvement with the world it denounces, **'The Other Side of the Hedge'** is characteristic of Forster's sense of the unseen. As much as the later **'The Machine Stops'**, it constitutes an attack on the historicism of H. G. Wells.

Indeed, **'The Other Side of the Hedge'** represents Forster's version of what may be called the 'great good place' theme, which Henry James had explored in his story of that name. In Forster's use of the term, however, there is not the sense of benevolent security which we find in James: indeed, **'The Machine Stops'** might be read as his rejection of such an ideal. Instead he represents the place as being in the here and now, a dimension parallel, as it were, to our own, and known in that ecstatic communion which gives human life its highest value. This conception is indeed the 'point' of **'The Point of It'**, the story which, according to Forster, displeased his Bloomsbury friends. '"What *is* the point of it?" they queried thinly, nor did I know how to reply.' That 'thinly' places Forster's attitude to the Bloomsbury point of view rather well: the kind of self-regarding cultivation of qualitative response which they embodied was always the object of his satiric scrutiny. Leyland, Bons, what are they but the Bloomsbury ethic translated into suburban terms? But the cult of the ecstatic moment remained of importance to Forster, and was to provide him with a touchstone in the novels, besides being the subject of the richest of his tales, **'The Eternal Moment'**.

In **'The Point of It'**, the ecstatic moment is known by the athlete Harold (that name again—it was also at one time to have been given to Stephen Wonham) as he overtaxes his strength while rowing. This veneration of the athlete is an endearing feature of Forster's early work (it even qualifies his portrayal of the odious Gerald Dawes in *The Longest Journey*) and is one of the things that stops his sense of the 'eternal moment' from being merely pictorial or aesthetic. The subsequent career of Harold's friend Sir Michael, who writes essays like those of A. C. Benson, ('Their good taste, their lucid style, the tempered Christianity of their ethics') is saved from being a morality piece or one-sided sketch by the dialogue overheard on his deathbed, in which the heartless comments of the sons echo the reader's own reactions with discomfiting effect. The final part of the tale, chronicling Sir Michael's posthumous existence in a sandy Hell, the presentation of which looks forward to the visionary world of Samuel Beckett, is easily the most serious and impressive thing that Forster was to write in this vein. Hell is inaction, sloth, the refusal of response: the end of the tale returns us to the moment when Harold died in ecstasy and when Sir Michael dies a second time into, it is implied, eternal life. No wonder the Bloomsburys disliked the story: it has a theological complexity beyond their normal imaginings. Forster here provides one more gloss on the 'great good place' theme. And what *was* the point of it? Again one is directed to values outside of time, an optimism of the moment. Forster's indictment of Sir Michael compares interestingly with what he has to say of Rickie Elliot in *The Longest Journey.*

The timeless moment is to be subject to more enigmatic treatment in one of the most admired stories, **'The Road to Colonus'.** It is a sardonic and ambiguous tale, an old man's version of **'The Story of a Panic'.** But possession here means vision. Forster's account of the Greek shrine anticipates his response to what he was to find in India.

> Little votive offerings to the presiding Power were fastened on to the bark—tiny arms and legs and eyes in tin; grotesque models of the brain or the heart—all tokens of some recovery of strength or wisdom or love. There was no such thing as the solitude of nature, for the sorrows and joys of humanity had pressed even into the bosom of a tree. He spread out his arms and steadied himself against the soft charred wood, and then slowly leant back, till his body was resting on the trunk behind. His eyes closed, and he had the strange feeling of one who is moving, yet at peace—the feeling of the swimmer, who, after long struggling with chopping seas, finds that after all the tide will sweep him to his goal.
>
> (1)

The transition is beautifully done. The soured and weary Mr Lucas abandons himself to his moment of revelation in a manner that symbolises life in death; his subsequent removal from the place where, momentarily, he would end his days is placed with precision in the final episode, where, older but still alive, querulous and senile, he is told how he would have been killed by an earthquake had he stopped. The irony here is double. Not only is Mr Lucas too wrapped up in a letter to his landlord to take notice of his escape, but also the very things of which he is complaining in his letter are, as John Beer has pointed out, clearly subconscious memories of the life and surroundings that would have been his had he remained.[14] As it is, two modes of death are juxtaposed with an economy that is most effective. The point is presented to the reader, not thrust at him; nor is there any Edwardian whimsy in the references to the gods. The tale eschews the merely literary.

The literary is frequently the enemy where Forster is concerned: it is as though he had an inbuilt mistrust of his own methods. Nowhere is this more apparent than in **'The Eternal Moment'**; but in 'Ansell' too, his earliest story of all, we see it no less clearly. Here we find him consigning a trunk-load of books into a mountain stream, and an entire scholar's career is weighed in the balance with the life known and lived by the coachman Ansell, the boyhood friend who is to reappear under his own name at Cambridge in *The Longest Journey* and anonymously as the gardener's boy in *Maurice*. The tale is so free from didacticism as to be almost too elusive; but this is a story the point of which it is *not* to have a point. What it presents is an attitude, an antithesis: the life of time, of careers, of scholarship, of prudence, set against the life of timelessness, the eternal moment extended into a knowledge of simple being. It is a marvellously accomplished tale for a beginner, and one that is singularly free from Edwardian influences. Not least of its jokes is the rescue of *Elizabeth and Her German Garden* from the river, for that book exemplifies much that Forster was to debunk. (The joke is improved when we remember that the story was written before Forster went to work for the authoress at Nassenheide.)

But the richest of all the tales is **'The Eternal Moment'**; it is almost a miniature novel. Miss Raby is that most dangerous figure in Forster's world, the 'mildly unconventional person'. She declines the kind of marriage that Lilia Herriton makes in *Where Angels Fear to Tread,* meanly distrusting the young guide who professes love for her. 'He was too cheap: he gave us more than our money's worth. That, as you know, is an ominous sign in a low-born person' (1). At a stroke Forster strips bare the financial basis for the muddle in spiritual materialism. But Miss Raby is a sentimentalist as well: she cherishes a romantic dream based on her escapade, and turns it into a book which popularises the little resort she now comes back to visit, in company with a middle-aged admirer called, once again, Leyland. If in outlook she resembles Helen Schlegel, in appearance she suggests, with her 'kind angular face', Adela Quested or Margaret Schlegel—those plain women who are, in Forster's world, the most sensitive recorders. Miss Raby, like them, is forced to see the consequences of her own shortsightedness, in this case the vulgarisation of Vorta consequent upon the success of her novel. She has exploited her own failure of moral vision, and the result is a moral landslide, itself symbolised by the physical landslide which destroys Signora Cantu's little farm.

> A landslip, in that valley, never hurried. Under the green coat of turf water would collect, just as an abscess is formed under the skin. There would be a lump on the sloping meadow, then the lump would break and discharge a slowly-moving stream of mud and stones. Then the whole area seemed to be corrupted; on every side the grass cracked and doubled into fantastic creases, the trees grew awry, the barns and cottages

collapsed, all the beauty turned gradually to indistin-
guishable pulp, which slid downwards till it was
washed away by some stream.

(II)

The tangible excellence of the writing induces confidence in what the author is telling us: the portrayal of
the fortunes of Vorta is precise and delicate. Significantly, the landslide also threatens the bell tower, which
is both the symbol of Miss Raby's achievement and the
celebration of her defeat. But Forster's account of that
defeat is more convincing than the celebration of her
victory.

> Her life had been successful, and on the whole happy.
> She was unaccustomed to that mood, which is termed
> depressed, but which certainly gives visions of wider,
> if greyer, horizons. That morning her outlook altered.
> She walked through the village, scarcely noticing the
> mountains by which it was still surrounded, or the un-
> altered radiance of its sun. But she was fully conscious
> of something new: of the indefinable corruption which
> is produced by the passage of a large number of people.

The scene in which Miss Raby confronts Feo and attempts to discuss their past relationship is desolating:
Feo has indeed been corrupted into just that mercenary
servant she had suspected him of being. The conclusion
is masterly in its irony; for we are all but compelled to
endorse the worldly-wise cheap cynicism of Colonel
Leyland, as the two men put their heads together against
the female threat. (But then the world of Goneril and
Regan is always plausible.)

IV

Forster's short stories are in many ways the key to his
novels: certainly they direct our attention to what is singular about them. Although from its inception the English novel had been a vehicle for social and moral
criticism, it did not, until the emergence of D. H.
Lawrence, reflect a sense of personal alienation in its
practitioners. Fielding, Jane Austen, Thackeray, even
Dickens and George Eliot, had recognised and accepted
the underlying social and economic structure: their criticisms (though this is only partly true of Dickens) took
place in the region of personal, individual relationships.
Hardy was perhaps the first novelist really to perceive
the fundamental contradiction between what that society morally required and the means by which it maintained itself in being—which is why *Jude the Obscure*
(1894) has some claim to be regarded as the first modern novel.

Forster's own personal and necessary alienation has already been referred to: it gave him a stance from which,
as a novelist, he could survey the society of which he
was such an uneasy part, and gauge his place in it. In
the stories this process is seen in terms of deliverance,
conversion, salvation—either proffered, accepted or de-

nied. For him there is no fullness of life *within* society,
and the whole relation of the novel to its setting and to
its readers has become uneasy; as Raymond Williams
observes, 'we can see these radical impulses straining
almost dislocating his early novels'.[15] But Forster's art,
the musicality of his deployment of narrative, commentary and symbol, safeguards him from the kind of war-
ring vision which we find in a minor contemporary
such as Machen. He remains part of his society in confining individual experience to a heightened consciousness and moral sense, in this differing radically from
Lawrence. His art may look forward, but his outlook
was derived from that nineteenth-century individualism
so variously embodied in the writings of Matthew Arnold, George Eliot, and Walter Pater. 'The last
Englishman'—in this particular sense Lawrence was
right. But to be last is not necessarily to be left behind.
The novels, even more than the stories, subject their
premises to critical scrutiny. Forster, no less than
Lawrence, was a writer in dialogue with himself, and
thus among the earliest of the moderns.

*Notes*

1. The artist was Charles Sims (1873-1928), a popular painter of landscapes, portraits and allegorical
   subjects.

2. *Selected Literary Criticism,* ed. Beal, [ed. Anthony Beal. London, 1955] p. 118.

3. Wilfred Stone, *The Cave and the Mountain*
   (Oxford, 1965) p. 123.

4. Ibid., p. 124.

5. Max Beerbohm, *Seven Men* (London, 1919).

6. Mildred Peaslake: the name is worthy of Firbank.
   Peaslake is a village not far from Abinger.

7. John Colmer, *E. M. Forster: The Personal Voice*
   (London, 1975) p. 26.

8. Stone, *The Cave and the Mountain,* [Wilfred
   Stone, *The Cave and the Mountain: A Study of E.
   M. Forster,* (Stanford, Calif.), 1966] p. 157.

9. It was not reprinted until 1972, in *The Life to
   Come* (London).

10. Howard was also the name of a family who for-
    merly lived at Rooksnest. Forster was to put it to
    more complimentary use in his fourth novel.

11. Lionel Trilling, *E. M. Forster: A Study* (London,
    1944), p. 42.

12. Reprinted in *A Variety of Things* (London, 1928).

13. George H. Thomson, *The Fiction of E. M. Forster*
    (Detroit, 1967), p. 59.

14. J. B. Beer, *The Achievement of E. M. Forster*
    (London, 1962), p. 45.

15. Raymond Williams, *The English Novel from Dickens to Lawrence* (London, 1970), p. 138.

**Susan Grove Hall (essay date winter 1983)**

SOURCE: Hall, Susan Grove. "Among E. M. Forster's Idylls: 'The Curate's Friend,'" *Classical and Modern Literature: A Quarterly* 3, no. 2 (winter 1983): 99-105.

[*In the following essay, Hall proposes that Forster's model for his short fiction differs from the conclusive completeness of the traditional short story format. Instead, Forster seems to have drawn heavily on the* Idylls *of Theocritus as inspiration for his stories, leading Hall to draw parallels between the two authors' respective use of humor, mythology, and realism.*]

Since their publication over sixty years ago, Forster's collected short stories have been enjoyed by readers but generally dismissed by critics as light-weight and flawed. The stories are oddities because of their mixture of realism and fantasy and their lack of commitment to either mode; thus the tone, purpose, and significance of the narrative often seem uncertain. Even if we agree with George H. Thomson that Forster's fantastic elements evoke the depths of archetypal romance, we find the stories marred by Forster's gestures toward realism, his suggestions of moral and social commentary, or the apparent sentimentality Thomson describes in **"The Curate's Friend"** and elsewhere.[1] Recent critical and biographical expositions of Forster's Edwardian interest in mythology, paganism, and poetic fiction encourage us to value the visionary moments in the stories, but as whole narratives they still appear uneven combinations of realism and fantasy.[2] If **"The Curate's Friend"** is "only an account of a man's arrival at self-knowledge," symbolized in a Pan figure,[3] it seems also a story of selfish hypocrisy, of a private joke against the harmless society Forster has pictured too fondly.

This apparent failure results from a problem of form. Forster did not entirely convert the short story to a unified individual expression, as did Virginia Woolf; neither did he arrange narration and plot toward a climactic revelation which opens and lays bare experience itself, as James and Joyce did. There is "story" in Forster's early short fiction, but it can be inconclusive or misleading: has Evelyn Beaumont "really" changed into a tree, we may wonder at the end of **"Other Kingdom"**; but Evelyn's fate has little to do with the mystical rapture Forster has conveyed as the heart of the story.[4] Similarly, Mr. Lucas's irritation with life after he has escaped salvation and/or death within the tree in Greece leads **"The Road from Colonus"** to questions of moral responsibility in suburban existence which distract us from the Greek encounter with an ultimate real-

ity, beside which the Lucases' lives are irrelevant. A disdain for "story" which Forster expressed in *Aspects of the Novel* seems at fault when narrative sequence is primarily a vehicle which carries us to the visionary moment and then leads us away to an anti-climax which dissipates interest in the characters and their experience.

Forster had a model for his short fiction different from the conclusive or symbolic plot that supports the traditional short story, however; the source which inspired his imagination in writing of a man within a coffin-like tree being sustained by the gods, and of a bride-to-be immortalized in a beautiful tree, provided him with a formal model that was familiar and important to his Edwardian readers.[5] The Idylls of Theocritus supplied Forster and other writers with the mythological religion of Pan and Demeter, the literary precedent for the pastoral vision which dominates Forster's fiction,[6] and also the classical and original form of romance from which, it was thought, fiction had departed into a decadent realism.[7] The nature of the Idyll, as described by Andrew Lang and subsequent scholars, was that of a "little picture" which combined representation of the natural and supernatural, pastoral and artificial, real and mythological, into one harmonious arrangement. Lang showed that the Idylls were characterized by humor, reverent mythic imagination, and realism,[8] the obvious qualities of Forster's stories. Forster knew Theocritus well and conceived of the Idylls as sources for short stories; in *The Longest Journey* they are the source for the writer Rickie's *Pan Pipes*.[9] Moreover, Forster shared the opinion that the Idylls are "little pictures" which blend various modes and redeem the decadent present by juxtaposing its scenes with those of the bucolic life or the mythological past. In *Alexandria,* he praises the vivid, humorous realism of the opening mime between Alexandrian women in Idyll 15 and the "erudite" poetry in its subsequent hymn to Adonis; and he concludes with this judgment on the mixture of form: "Only through literature can the past be recovered and here Theocritus, wielding the double spell of realism and of poetry, has evoked an entire city from the dead and filled its streets with men."[10]

We can better appreciate both the ironic humor and the lyrical high-seriousness of Forster's stories by approaching them as idylls. Like the Idylls of Theocritus, the stories vary dramatic, lyric, and narrative modes to create a visual image, sometimes composed of several vignettes, which is essentially static and is meant to be grasped in its entirety. The unity of the Idyll, Anna Rist explains, does not appear in one developing ethical design with illustrative details, but must be intuited by the reader from an "amalgam of suggestivities" in its allusions and juxtapositions.[11] Our main impressions of such Forster stories as **"The Road from Colonus"** and **"The Story of a Panic"** are thus generally in agreement and reliable, as they respond to the principal images of encounters with mythic presences, around which are grouped the complementary idyllic motifs of pastoral comradeship, rapture and death, and comic ignorance among crass people. When these stories are read as sequential developments of one ethical theme, however, they lead to conclusions that cast into doubt the truth and worth of the central ecstatic experience with its revelation of a mythic reality.

**"The Curate's Friend"** is more in need of interpretation. This tale, in which a curate at a picnic loses his fiancée to a rival but meets a friendly satyr, fails as either realism or romance. Thomson finds it the worst of Forster's stories which provide "no clash of opposites, no depth of symbolism, no irrevocable judgment and, in consequence, no revelation of essential reality."[12] These qualities do emerge in the idyllic character of the story, and Forster has his curate narrator, now a vicar, conclude with an apology for his pretense of narrative form (*CSS* [*Collected Short Stories*], p. 94).

This "little picture" of pastoral joy in a Wiltshire parish arranges around the figure of the Faun the motifs of spiritual and moral responsibility, heterosexual and homosexual loves, and natural and mythical divinities. The narrator begins with a historical portrait of the faun, tracing him from the slopes of Etna in Theocritus' Sicily to the woods, meadows, and streams of rural Wiltshire. He proceeds to give a picture of himself as a young curate, clear-sighted and lively enough to see a faun, conscientious in his parish duties, but "facetious without humor and serious without conviction" (*CSS*, p. 86). With these two sketches Forster draws our attention to the character of the curate in relation to the Faun and the unseen world. The curate's other world, about which he speaks each Sunday "in the tone of one who has been behind the scenes," consists of transcendental Christian polarities of good and evil, spirit and flesh, heaven and hell; the Faun emerges from the other world of pagan mythological religion wherein man and nature exist in timeless harmony.

The scene of the curate's introduction to the superhuman spirit immanent in nature is a picnic on a chalk down, where he has taken his fiancée Emily, her mother, and a young male friend. Forster emphasizes the idyllic setting and atmosphere by having the curate recount his ritual invocation of an unseen ally, which he intends as a facetious heroic challenge to an imaginary foe: "And who will stand on either hand and keep the bridge with me?" (*CSS*, p. 87). His description of the landscape follows, constituting a pastoral song of the humane and playful creature which is the body of England:

> For here is the body of the great chalk spider who straddles over our island—whose legs are the south downs and the north downs and the Chilterns, and the tips of whose toes poke out at Cromer and Dover. He

> is a clean creature, who grows as few trees as he can, and those few in tidy clumps, and he loves to be tickled by quickly flowing streams. He is pimpled all over with earthworks, for from the beginning of time men have fought for the privilege of standing on him, and the oldest of our temples is built upon his back.

> (*CSS,* p. 88)

Forster has transfigured England in this description with the features of Theocritus' Sicily: a smaller island, dominated by a large mountain and its slopes, hospitable to men and their shrines, a place where, as Lang writes of the bucolic Idylls, one is always made aware of the music of water falling from rocky heights.[13] As the creature of earth is roused by the curate's dropping a lit match on the grass and soon appears before the curate in the person of the Faun, Forster confronts his curate with the male character of nature. Pan, rather than Demeter, roams the expanses of England or Sicily, to befriend or assault a pastor or shepherd.

This contrast of the feminine and domestic with masculine insight and freedom arises in the introductory descriptions of Emily, the curate's life, and nature so that a border for the picnic scene is established, pointing up its significance. Emily is associated with the comfort and confinement of a home and the "smug" country the curate preferred when lonely expanses "were still intolerable" to him. Thus the encounter with the Faun is to depict a change in his character; and Forster presents the scene to dramatize the gradual displacement of the curate from the ladies' tea-time to the company of the Faun. The picnic is represented as an Alexandrian idyll that beomes a pastoral one. The humor and realism Forster noted in Theocritus' Idyll 15 pervade his mime of the party fussing over tea, and Forster uses silly, excited chatter just as Theocritus does in his mime of the women's preparations for and journey to the festival of Adonis, where distracted characters also reveal the presence of a summoned god of love, in such lines as "Oh, how tiresome, Gorgo, my muslin veil is torn in two already!" (Lang's translation).[14] Forster has Emily's mother, prattling of the hunger one feels around tea-time, unwittingly point to the sexual appetite the curate betrays in his next remark, that he was horrified when he mistook the Faun for a naked man. The curate's following outburst against village lads bathing outdoors is more than a humorous mistake; bathing, the narrator will later disclose, is the appropriate ritual, rather than tea, for man in communion with nature.

After the curate runs from the Faun and finds himself in the beech copse, Forster's story shifts from mimetic drama to an exchange of dialogue between the curate and the Faun which recalls the herders' debates in the Idylls. The argument proceeds with epithets ("Dear priest," "Poor woodland creature"), lyrical intensity ("Now I begin to make you happy: lie upon your back or run races, or climb trees, or shall I get you blackberries, or harebells, or wives—"), and high rhetoric ("Get thee behind me!"). Whereas descriptions of humming bees and murmuring streams in the singing debates make nature a participant, here it speaks directly, in a response of the hill to the curate's wish to reach and touch the Faun; the hill's answering echoes—"You have reached him," "You have touched him"—bespeak the unity of the curate's suppressed manhood with the animate nature embodied in the Faun (*CSS,* p. 90). The curate's deepest human nature is one with Nature itself, and his buried passion is at once represented and fulfilled by the figure of the Faun. Forster's pastoral idyll at this point suggests not just that imagination can people the lonely expanses of life, but that man at once creates and discovers a sustaining, super-human divinity in uncovering his natural sexual identity. Forster's picture of the satyr draws upon a theory of Greek mythology popularized by John Addington Symonds, that the gods personify ideal human passions; this theory underlies Bertrand Russell's argument for a post-Christian religion in "The Free Man's Worship" (1903).[15] The debate between curate and Faun takes up the serious current concern for the morality of a pagan religion of self-fulfillment, rather than Christian self-denial; and Forster sketches two serene gestures of the Faun in answer to the Christian charges against paganism. First, when the curate has addressed the Faun as the devil, a proper Christian recognition, the Faun is sadly baffled and asks, "What is to tempt?" Without the Christian concepts of human depravity and metaphysical evil, temptation and sin are as impossible as altruism. The Faun's second gesture demonstrates the limits of self-fulfillment which preclude the meaningless hedonism feared by Christians, including Walter Pater, in paganism. Taking up the curate's challenge to make Emily happy, the Faun stands over her and the young male friend and draws them into a mutual passion of love; as Emily proclaims the "self-effectuation" of her soul and demands respect for the "infinities" that now belong to her, she rejects the curate and his values. The depths of her sexual nature which the Faun has aroused introduce her to a separate destiny which will always conflict with the curate's—in the "great solitude" she has found in herself a feminine divinity (*CSS,* p. 91-92). At the conclusion of the debate with the Faun, then, the curate decides on honest self-fulfillment as a priest serving and being served by a god of his own nature.

The remainder of the story is a pastoral song of the harmony within nature and society. Just as the mime in Idyll 15 leads to a hymn to Adonis or the singing debate to a long, finished song, the vicar's story concludes with a paean to the sustaining joy of nature and its satyr-god. Again, Forster emphasizes the music of water in this Sicilian Wiltshire, where "the hour of darkness is really the hour of water, which has been somewhat stifled all day by the great pulsings of the land"; and he

retraces the homosexual suggestions in the motif of outdoor bathing as his narrator praises the bath after sundown for its intimate communion with nature. In the subsequent description of the vicar's parish life, we are to see him not as a hypocrite secretly serving the devil, but as a humane and helpful man who sees beyond the failure of Christian charity and the artificiality of presentation teapots to a true divinity in human life. The idyll finally brings the conflicting themes of femininity and masculinity, self-denial and fulfillment, Christianity and paganism, together in a glimpse of the harmonious community who worship separate and individual godheads. While the story is slight and humorous, Forster arranges its scenes and songs to suggest the depths of his commitment to a mythological religion that justifies male homosexuality. The vicar is a hypocrite if judged by the values of his society and if seen "realistically", but Forster's realistic vignette gives only the superficial aspect of the pastoral life. Around and within it, the reverent and playful visions of man in nature align the ties of this life to its hidden springs. The vicar as a pastoral hero favored by a god does "keep the bridge" between separate realities, and his role as a mediator reflects the purpose Forster outlined for his "fantasies" in his introduction to the collected stories (*CSS,* p. 5).[16]

*Notes*

1. George H. Thomson, *The Fiction of E. M. Forster* (Detroit: Wayne St. U. Pr., 1967), p. 59.

2. See Patricia Merivale, *Pan the Goat-God: His Myth In Modern Times* (Cambridge: Harvard U. Pr., 1969), p. 184-190; and John Colmer, *E. M. Forster: The Personal Voice* (London: Routledge & Kegan, 1975), p. 28-41.

3. W. R. Irwin, "The Survival of Pan," *PMLA* 76 (1961), 166.

4. E. M. Forster, "Other Kingdom," in his *Collected Short Stories* (Harmondsworth, England: Penguin, 1954), p. 59-85. Subsequent references to Forster's short stories in the Penguin edition will be made in the text with the abbreviated title *CSS.*

5. These images appear in Idylls 7 and 18 of Theocritus. See Andrew Lang, trans., *Theocritus, Bion and Moschus* (London: Macmillan, 1889), p. 42, 99. Forster used Lang's translation of Theocritus in his *Alexandria: A History and a Guide.*

6. See Thomson (above, note 1) p. 80-81; and Stephen Spender, "Elegies for England: E. M. Forster," in his *Love-Hate Relations: English and American Sensibilities* (New York: Random, 1974), p. 223, 228-229.

7. For examples, see Gamaliel Bradford, Jr., "The Novel Two Thousand Years Ago," *FortnR,* n.s., 86 (1909), 1054-1065; and R.E. Prothero, "Greek Prose Romances," *Ed. R.* [*Edwardian Review*] 218 (1913), 136.

8. Lang, "Theocritus and His Age," (above, note 5), p. xiv-xxv.

9. *The Longest Journey* (New York: Vintage, 1962), p. 4, 77-78, 304.

10. *Alexandria: A History and a Guide* (Garden City, New York: Anchor Pr., 1961), p. 35, 37-38.

11. Anna Rist, *The Poems of Theocritus* (Chapel Hill: U. of NC Pr., 1978), p. 13.

12. Thomson (above, note 1) p. 59.

13. Lang (above, note 5) p. xx.

14. Ibid., p. 80.

15. Cf. John Addington Symonds, *Studies of the Greek Poets* (New York: Harper & Bros., 1882), p. 80, 381; and Bertrand Russell, "The Free Man's Worship," *Indep. R.* [*Independent Review*] 1 (1903), 417-424; reprinted as "A Free Man's Worship," in *The Basic Writings of Bertrand Russell,* ed. Robert E. Egner and Lester E. Denonn (New York: Simon and Schuster, 1961), p. 70.

16. The writer acknowledges the aid of a grant from the University of Louisville which supplied research material.

### Charles Elkins (essay date 1983)

SOURCE: Elkins, Charles. "E. M. Forster's 'The Machine Stops': Liberal-Humanist Hostility to Technology." In *Clockwork Worlds: Mechanized Environments in SF,* edited by Richard D. Erlich and Thomas P. Dunn, pp. 47-61. Westport, Conn.: Greenwood Press, 1983.

[*In the following essay, Elkins characterizes Forster's short story "The Machine Stops" as remarkable within its historical and intellectual context, going beyond many contemporaries in its dramatization of reactions to technology.*]

> Intellectuals, in particular literary intellectuals, are natural Luddites.
>
> —C. P. Snow

First published in 1909 in the *Oxford and Cambridge Review,* when Edward Morgan Forster was scarcely thirty years old, **"The Machine Stops"** has been cited by critics as one of the first antitechnological dystopias, "and a remarkable story to have been written so early in this century."[1] However, so pervasive has been the development of the antitechnological bias within the dystopian tradition that, except for the artistry of the presentation, contemporary readers might find Forster's story quite *un*remarkable. Familiar with such novels as Aldous Huxley's *Brave New World* (1932), D. F. Jones's

*Colossus* (1966), George Orwell's *Nineteen Eighty-Four* (1949), Kurt Vonnegut's *Player Piano* (1952), and Yevgeny Zamiatin's *We* (ca. 1920), many readers could view Forster's themes as commonplace if not trite.

Consequently, appreciating Forster's masterful achievement demands that the critic undertake several tasks. The first is to place the work in its historical and intellectual context. It is a truism that writers do not create in a vacuum; **"The Machine Stops"** is a strategic answer to a number of sociopsychological questions and tensions out of which it arose. The next task is to show where and how Forster goes beyond his contemporaries to dramatize and thus create attitudes toward technology which are at the heart of liberal reactions to technology; responses that transcend the sociopolitical fears of his contemporaries and go straight to the heart of the liberal's vision of a technological dystopia. The final effort is to critique Forster's work as a viable strategy for dealing with technology. The results of this investigation lead to three related theses: (1) **"The Machine Stops"** can be seen as one outcome of a general turning away by influential intellectuals and critics from science and technology, especially the perceived technological optimism of H. G. Wells; (2) Forster's work goes beyond the usual antitechnological themes by dramatizing the role of science and technology in the demystification of nature—a process intimately connected with the rise of science and capitalism; and (3) as an alienated writer, ill at ease in his own class and age, Forster could not extricate himself from the ideological constraints of his particular situation and, thus, could do little more than sound a warning to those who are overly optimistic about the future and man's relationship with his creations.

As England proceeded through her Industrial Revolution, there were two major negative responses to developing machine technology—the first from the working class, the second from the intellectuals. Up to and through most of the nineteenth century, most machines were created to increase production. From 1811 to 1816 groups of workingmen called Luddites fought against the encroachment of these machines, which they believed caused unemployment and low wages. The Luddites smashed cotton power looms and wool-shearing machines before being suppressed by the government. However, toward the end of the nineteenth century came machines intended more for consumer use and for personal benefit (for example, telephones, movie projectors, gramophones, bicycles, radios, washing machines, refrigerators, vacuum cleaners, and so forth). And it was this aspect of machine production that encouraged some of Forster's contemporaries, such as George Orwell, to observe that they were living in a civilization that was "air-conditioned, chromium-plated, [and] gadget ridden."[2] As one historian of technology writes: ". . . after 1918 the situation worsened. Unemployment and the inability to sell what could be produced become chronic features of the economy—so much so that some came to believe that too much was being produced (in spite of the fact that most people could not get the things they wanted). . . ."³

Yet, for the intellectual the antipathy toward science and technology went much deeper. In the nineteenth century the growth of technology increasingly enhanced science and its world view. This development

> had . . . many destructive consequences for traditional cultural synthesis, particularly in the sphere of religion. . . . This led, in turn, to the split between science and humanistic culture. . . . *Homo faber* . . . has been fragmented. The active component of culture, altering nature and society, has been allocated to science and technology. The meaningful one, the human self-interpretation which alone could make sense of this activity has been ascribed to those devoid of any practical competence.⁴

This split was disastrous; as Martin Green observes: "In England the conjunction of the Industrial and Scientific Revolutions called forth a tradition of cultural criticism which—though perhaps this country's greatest intellectual achievement—was cripplingly on the defensive, setting literary, cultural, personal values in radical opposition to science and to modern life in general."⁵

This antagonism toward science and technology is registered in the works of practically all of the leading writers of the period. Samuel Hynes, in *The Edwardian Turn of Mind,* writes that George Bernard Shaw was disappointed that science "had not lived up to the hopes we formed of it in the 1860's," and that the interest in psychological and psychic research was a reaction against Victorian mechanism and science.⁶ D. H. Lawrence's attack on science and technology was even more virulent than Shaw's. Lawrence was convinced that Western industrial culture debased man; it overemphasized the rational, analytic intelligence at the expense of man's synthetic, intuitive, natural instincts. Lawrence believed that "science, late Christianity and democracy developed more or less together and cooperated in maintaining the standardized culture he wished destroyed."⁷ Science and technology's link with industrialism made them even more hateful, and Lawrence not only raises the issue of rationality versus intuition that concerned Forster, but he also confronts the issue of control, of autonomous technology, with the question: "After all, we are masters of our own inventions. Are we really so feeble and inane that we cannot get rid of the monsters we have brought forth?"⁸

Lawrence had an unlikely defender in the figure of George Orwell. While H. G. Wells scoffed at Lawrence's primitivism and his critique of progress, Orwell assailed Wells's naively optimistic conviction "that science can solve all the ills that humanity is heir to."⁹ Orwell argued that "one must admit that whether Lawrence's view of life is true or whether it is perverted, it is at least an advance on the science worship of H. G. Wells or the shallow Fabian progressiveness of writers like Bernard Shaw."¹⁰ As he clearly dramatized in *Nineteen Eighty-Four,* Orwell understood how science and technology could be perverted to become instruments not of human liberation, but of terror. As it was for Forster, the development of the airplane was for Orwell a symbol for the corruption of science and technology. Orwell observes that "the equation of science and common sense does not really hold good. The aeroplane, which was looked forward to as a civilizing influence but in practice has hardly been used except for dropping bombs, is a symbol of that fact."¹¹

In 1903 a Frenchman, Henri Farmon, flew a heavier-than-air machine over a kilometer course. Forster observed that "It really *is* a new civilization. I have been born at the end of the age of peace and can't expect to feel anything but despair. Science, instead of freeing man . . . is enslaving him to machines."¹²

Furthermore, like Forster, Orwell understood the political implications of technology. Using the airplane again as the symbol of misguided technology, Orwell writes: "The processes involved in making, say, an aeroplane are so complex as to be only possible in a planned, centralized society, with all the repressive apparatus that that implies."¹³ Likewise, Forster says, "Bureaucracy, in a technical age like ours, is inevitable. The advance of science means the growth of bureaucracy and the reign of the expert. And, as a result, society and the State will be the same thing."¹⁴

Like Orwell and Forster, Aldous Huxley also criticized H. G. Wells's technological optimism. And, like **"The Machine Stops,"** Huxley's *Brave New World* began as Huxley's "having a little fun pulling the leg of H. G. Wells."¹⁵ And, just as he reacted against Lawrence's work, Wells called *Brave New World* "defeatist."¹⁶ Just as Lawrence had made an allusion to Mary Shelley's monster, Huxley observed: ". . . technology was made for man, not man for technology, but unfortunately [we have] created a world in which man seems to be made for technology. . . . We do have to start thinking how we can get control again of our inventions. This is a kind of Frankenstein monster problem."¹⁷ Like Lawrence's and Forster's work, *Brave New World* showed man living in fear of direct, primitive experience; nature is mediated by technology. The Savage had no place in technologically sophisticated society. Furthermore, just as in **"The Machine Stops,"** *Brave New World* depicted the devastating effects of technology on the family with the separation of mother from child.

Clearly, then, Forster is in the chorus with his contemporaries and singing the same tune. Still, it is not unimportant to recognize that **"The Machine Stops"** was one of the first works to voice this protest against technology. Twenty-three years before *Brave New World*, Forster wrote **"The Machine Stops"** as "a reaction against one of the earlier heavens of H. G. Wells."[18] It is, as Mark Hillegas observes, a "Wellsian scientific romance set in a Wellsian future," and it foreshadows many of the sociopolitical elements in the later dystopias of Zamiatin, Huxley, and Orwell.[19]

**"The Machine Stops"** depicts an underground, hive-like world, similar to the society in H. G. Wells's *When the Sleeper Wakes*. Individuals live, isolated, in cells; all of their needs are administered to and controlled by the Committee, which, in turn, acts as a liaison to the Machine. The plot involves the conflict between Vashti, a woman completely integrated into her world, and her son Kuno, a rebel against this society. Kuno desires to visit the surface of the Earth, ultimately a crime punishable by death. Through Vashti's eyes and her debates with Kuno, the reader is able to grasp the essential characteristics of this world. People live alone and communicate with each other via visionphones. Everyday life is regulated by the Book of the Machine, containing instructions "against every possible contingency." Individuals do nothing for themselves; they are seldom required to make even the minimal muscular effort to move from place to place or to pick up a fallen object. Muscles have atrophied because in the society of the Machine it is a "demerit" to have them, and infants who show signs of becoming strong adults are killed.[20] All aspects of life are mediated by technology; people do not touch; empirical, direct experience is denigrated; only secondhand and thirdhand ideas are valued. Despite their claim to have transcended the need for religion, people begin to worship the Machine and to treat the Book of the Machine as a sacred text.

In addition to adopting this new religion, people decide that respirators, those devices which make it possible to visit the Earth's surface, are to be abolished since anyone who wishes knowledge of the surface need only listen to a "gramophone" or look at a "cinematophote."[21] Vashti knew that Kuno was ultimately doomed; he could never agree to this new law. As for herself, in the years that followed Vashti was content with the routine of her life: "her life went peacefully forward until the final disaster."[22]

Beginning with insignificant but annoying mechanical malfunctions, the "final disaster" is precipitated by the mysterious but complete failure of the Machine. The uncomprehending population, degenerate and enfeebled by their total dependence on the Machine, cannot save themselves. They are totally annihilated. The narrator sums up the situation: "Man, the flower of all flesh, the noblest of all creatures visible, man who had once made God in his image, and had mirrored his strength in the constellations, beautiful naked man was dying, strangled in the garments he had woven. Century after century had he toiled, and here was his reward."[23] The "garment" is technology.

In passages such as this, one senses the heavy hand of the narrator, yet, for the most part, Forster handles his story with the artistry characteristic of his later work. He skillfully weaves his imagery, for example, into patterns which create a tightly knit whole. Whiteness and colorlessness become the symbols for this entire degenerate world. Vashti's face is "as white as a fungus."[24] The creatures that pull Kuno from the Earth's surface and back into the interior of the planet are described as "long white worm[s]."[25] The narrator observes that the people had physically degenerated "until the body was white pap."[26] Ultimately, the lack of direct, personal contact and the avoidance of firsthand ideas would produce "a generation absolutely colorless."[27]

So impressed is he by his mother's adventure in crossing the roof of the world to visit him, Kuno does not believe Vashti will be interested in his visit to the Earth's surface and his account of the "little . . . low colourless hills" he has seen; still, he tries to explain to her the impression made on his imagination by the living Earth, recalling the turf of the hills as "a skin, under which their muscles rippled."[28] He feels that people of the past must have responded deeply to the hills and loved them. Memory of a color then returns to him; the color of the mist between "his" hill and those in the distance, he says, was "a belt . . . the colour of pearl."[29] Finally, as they die Kuno kisses his mother and, gasping, explains to her the significance of their adventures: although they are dying they have won back some of the sense of life as it was for Aelfrid when he defeated the Danes and as it still is for those who live on the surface of the Earth and dwell in "the cloud that is the colour of a pearl."[30] Here, nature's color and richness stand in stark contrast to the diseased, "white" society of the Machine. Forster's imagery works superbly to underscore the major themes of his narrative. Mark Hillegas sums up Forster's achievement in **"The Machine Stops."**

> Forster . . . gives expression to some of the most important humanist fears about the machine—the fear that the machine will lead to the mechanization of human life and finally to the control of human life; the fear that the machine will dwarf men and take from them their self-respect, pride, and sense of uniqueness; the fear that reliance on the machine will be not only psychologically and spiritually harmful, but in the end physically destructive; and the fear that men may come to make the machine a fake idol which they will worship.[31]

If one had to summarize Forster's fears, one could argue that **"The Machine Stops"** expresses dramatically what has come to be almost an obsession with modern, liberal humanists—the fear that technology is out of control. In a recent book on the subject, Langdon Winner writes: "One symptom of a profound stress that affects modern thought is the prevalence of the idea of autonomous technology—the belief that somehow technology has gotten out of control and follows its own course independent of human direction."[32] Clearly, Forster's story incorporates this attitude. The people in his society have little or no say in the management of their own lives. No one knows how the Machine works. Directives come from the mysterious Committee or are taken from the Book of the Machine. Mechanical breakdowns are reported to the Committee of the Mending Apparatus, but if questions or complaints are "unmechanical," the Committee will not respond. In the end, when the Machine begins to break down, people are helpless; the idea that the Machine *could* break down is incomprehensible. When Vashti tells one of her friends that Kuno has warned her that the Machine is stopping, her friend replies: "The Machine is stopping? . . . What does that mean? The phrase conveys nothing to me."[33] The society's fate is entirely within the control of the Machine, which no one understands or directs.

As Winner suggests, "Autonomous technology is ultimately nothing more or less than the question of human autonomy held up to a different light."[34] From the middle of the nineteenth century to the present, the question of human autonomy has come to the fore as a crucial issue in any discussion of the human situation. The theological questions concerning the nature of God, determinism, and man's free will have not been entirely abandoned. The secularization of the modern world put the concept of human autonomy in some new contexts but did not diminish its force. Charles Darwin's theory of natural selection confronted thinkers with the possibility of environmental determinism. Karl Marx's concept of the modes of production determining the relations of production and, hence, man's consciousness, seemed to subtract from man's ability to determine his own destiny. And Sigmund Freud's theory that individual behavior was directed by unconscious forces over which one had no control dealt a devastating blow to any argument for human autonomy. Not only did forces external to man limit his freedom, but there were processes within his own mind that severely restricted his range of choices and modes of action. Thus, the fear of autonomous technology is one more theme in modern man's sense of his loss of mastery of himself and his world.

It is, however, a major theme in any discussion of man's place in the modern world. As Hannah Arendt argues, "Whatever touches or enters into a sustained relationship with human life immediately assumes the character of a condition of human existence."[35] In discussing work, she makes a distinction between tools and machines:

There never was any doubt about man's being adjusted or needing special adjustment to the tools he used; one might as well adjust him to his hands. The case of machines is entirely different. Unlike the tools of workmanship, which at every given moment in the work process remain the servants of the hand, the machines demand that the laborer serve them, that he adjust the natural rhythm of his body to their mechanical movement.[36]

Yet the fear of autonomous technology goes far beyond the question of technology's involvement in man's work. Since the late nineteenth century, thinkers have associated technology with a succession of changes in which the world is transformed and encapsulated by a growing scientific technology. This technology comprises a huge technical system which seems to function and expand by "a process of self-generation beyond human intervention. Within this system people are "dwarfed by the complex apparatus surrounding them, which they must employ if they are to survive."[37] In addition to these assumptions comes the realization that technology is *not* neutral; instead technologies "provide a positive content to the area of life in which they are applied, enhancing certain ends, denying or even destroying others."[38] People cannot employ technology in any way they wish; for technology to function, individuals must "see to it that the appropriate operating procedures and techniques are followed and that all the material conditions for operations are met . . . of the meanings of autonomous technology . . . this is the most significant."[39] Finally, if Forster's dystopian world seems in the *totality* of its mechanistic organization a little far-fetched, one should note Winner's remarks: ". . . modern technology is a way of organizing the world . . . potentially, *there is no limit to the extent of this organization*. In the end, literally everything within human reach can or will be rebuilt, resynthesized, reconstructed, and incorporated into the system of technical instrumentality."[40]

The consequences of this fear of autonomous technology reverberated in the political realm as well. While some of Forster's contemporaries flirted with socialism of various hues, many were liberals, as was Forster himself. Yet the political conclusion derived from the assumptions of a technological society—namely, the need for a technocracy—is abhorrent to liberalism. From Francis Bacon's *New Atlantis* through the utopian writings of Claude Henri de Rouvroy Saint-Simon and the versions of R. Buckminster Fuller to the science fiction novels of Isaac Asimov and Robert Heinlein runs the argument that authority and power are a product of knowledge and that those who know should rule. The great mass of men must be excluded from positions of power and authority because they lack the specialized knowledge needed to govern a technological society. Technocrats must rule because only they can. Such a conclusion would surely disturb Forster who, while giving only "two cheers for democracy," nevertheless believed that it was the best form of government we could reasonably expect. As Winner puts it, premises of the technocratic position "are totally incompatible with a central notion that justifies the practice of liberal politics: the idea of responsible, responsive, representative government."[41] It should not be surprising, then, that for Forster and his liberal contemporaries the overwhelming success of science and its application as technology was seen with a good deal of ambivalence and anxiety.

However, Forster's concern with technology goes further than that of his contemporaries and relates to his basic humanism. Central to **"The Machine Stops"** is the theme of isolation. Technology intervenes, cutting people off from direct experience with each other and severing man from nature. Throughout his life, one of Forster's chief concerns was exploring obstacles to human communication and solidarity, be they class, as in *Howards End* (1910), or nationality, as in *A Passage to India* (1924). If there is one sentence which could stand as a symbol for everything in which Forster believed, it would be the epigraph beginning *Howards End*—"Only connect. . . ." This is what matters. In **"The Machine Stops"** people are isolated from one another. There are no families; mother love is destroyed; the Machine had decreed that "Parents, duties of, . . . cease at the moment of birth. P.422327483."[42] Because of the Machine it is no longer customary for people to touch one another. Such behavior has "become obsolete."[43] Vashti is outraged when an airline stewardess tries to steady her to keep her from falling. All human intercourse is mediated by technology. Kuno wants to see his mother, not view her through a visionphone. He tries to explain to Vashti that while the Machine is a great thing the ersatz experiences it provides are no true substitute for the real thing; that while he sees *something like* Vashti in the plate, he does not see *her,* not does he hear the real Vashti. In short, he wants her to come to him so that they can experience each other directly.[44] Vashti listens with uncomprehending disbelief.

Even more than isolating people from each other, technology has isolated man from nature; has come between man and nature. Vashti says that she "dislikes the stars." Flying over Earth in an airplane, she finds the stars distracting—"they seemed intolerable."[45] The landscape below the airplane provided "no ideas." As the narrator explains, man "had harnessed Leviathan. All the old literature, with its praise of Nature, and its fear of Nature, rang false as the prattle of a child."[46] Yet for Kuno (and Forster), nature is a living thing; landscapes take the shape of "prostrate" men; mountains are described as "breasts." The Earth is alive; Kuno feels it. The heavens, the stars in particular, are humanized by Kuno. He described one set of stars to Vashti:

"I had an idea that they were like a man."

"I do not understand."

"The four big stars are the man's shoulders and his knees. The three stars in the middle are like the belts that men wore once, and the three stars hanging are like a sword."[47]

Again, Vashti does not understand. For Kuno, nature must be directly experienced and humanized; it excites *his* imagination and *he* responds to it directly. The Machine does not determine his reality; for Kuno, "Man is the measure. . . . Man's feet are the measure for distance, his hands are the measure for ownership, his body is the measure for all that is lovable and desirable and strong."[48] But for the rest of society, nature has lost her charm; mediated by technology, nature ceases to arouse man's imagination. With the development of technology, man ceases to trust his senses and his common sense. Hannah Arendt argues that

> it was not reason but a man-made instrument, the telescope, which actually changed the physical world view; . . . *Homo faber* . . . as he arose from the great revolution of modernity, though he was to acquire an undreamed of ingenuity in devising instruments to measure the infinitely large and the infinitely small, was deprived of those permanent measures that precede and outlast the fabrication process and form an authentic and reliable absolute with respect to the fabricating activity.[49]

According to computer scientist Joseph Weizenbaum:

> This rejection of direct experience was to become one of the principal characteristics of modern science. Gradually, then ever more rapidly and, it is fair to say more compulsively, experiences of reality had to be represented as numbers in order to appear legitimate in the eyes of the common wisdom. Today enormously intricate manipulations of often huge sets of numbers are thought capable of producing new sets of reality. These are validated by composing the newly derived numbers with pointer readings on still more instruments that mediate between man and nature, and which, of course, produce still more numbers.[50]

What has happened, argue Arendt and Weizenbaum—and this lies at the very center of Forster's thinking—is that as a result of his technology man is no longer at home in his world. He no longer trusts his senses because his environment is mediated by technology, by instruments of his own creation. One critic of that symbol of modern technology, the television, writes:

> Natural environments have given way to human environments.

> What we see, hear, touch, taste, smell, feel, and understand about the world has been processed for us. Our experiences of the world can no longer be called direct, or primary. They are secondary, mediated experiences. . . . living within artificial, reconstructed, arbitrary environments that are strictly the products of hu-

man conception, we have no way to be sure that we know what is true and what is not. We have lost context and perspective.[51]

In addition, and related to this loss of a personal, direct contact with the world as a consequence of technology, come the growth of bureaucracy and what might be called the rationalization of everyday life. Like Orwell, Forster believed that "bureaucracy in a technical age like ours, is inevitable."[52] In **"The Machine Stops,"** all regulations are codified in the Book of the Machine; all directions come from and all requests must be addressed to the Committee of the Machine. No one knows who this committee is or how it functions; when it ceases to function, no explanations are given. The world of **"The Machine Stops"** is very similar to some of Franz Kafka's creations. The impersonal but powerful bureaucracy is organized around the model of the Machine.

> The choice of the machine as a paradigm of organization is not accidental. . . . The growth of modern technology and the improvement of machine design . . . demanded . . . the development of appropriate social accommodations to insure their smooth and fruitful functioning. . . . In time, a profound symbiosis has arisen between man and machine in which the orderly operation, the sustained control, and the predictability necessary for the efficient functioning of the machine have inevitably been reflected in an ever greater measure of social order, systemization, and organization—affecting every aspect of human affairs.[53]

It is a world that leaves little room for the poetic, the irrational, and the fantastic.

That world is not congenial to the likes of Forster. Writing about Samuel Butler's *Erewhon* (1872), a Victorian novel satirizing society's dependence on machines, Forster says that he was influenced by Butler's style: "I liked that idea of fantasy, of muddling up the actual and impossible until the reader isn't sure which is which."[54] In **"The Machine Stops,"** Kuno's imagination and fantasies serve only to condemn him. A society controlled by the Machine has no place for the poet. It is a world regulated, systematized and, above all, rational. Its inhabitants scorn any romantic notions of nature and the very mention of religion. Even as they worship the Machine, the people avoid the label "religion" since the Machine protects them against superstition.[55]

In this calculating, rational world, magic has been eliminated. Irritated by any waste of his time, Vashti keeps scolding Kuno to "be quick." She herself is constantly engaged in meaningless activity. It is a world where, as Max Weber observes, "Waste of time is thus the first, and in principle the deadliest of sins."[56] It is a society and culture built upon "the combination of rationalism and empiricism" described by Robert K. Merton, except that the empiricism has been abandoned as useless because everything is mediated by the Machine.[57] It is a culture dominated by the "process of spreading rationality" characterized by economist Joseph Schumpeter: "The capitalist process rationalizes behavior and ideas and by doing so chases from our minds, along with metaphysical belief, mystic and romantic ideas of all sorts . . . capitalistic [organization] is rationalistic and anti-heroic."[58] In short, it is Forster's own world, taken to its logical conclusion. It is a world we recognize.

**"The Machine Stops"** provides its audience with a particular way of seeing the world, and it names that world in such a way as to communicate an attitude toward it. Moreover, that world is as much Edwardian England as it is the remote future. As the philosopher George Herbert Mead tells us in his *The Philosophy of the Present* (1959), we create images of the past and future in order to solve problems in the present.[59] For Forster as well as many of his contemporaries, one of the most pressing problems was how to deal with an emerging industrial technological society whose basic values and social organization appeared to be a clear threat to man's imaginative life and to intimate, personal human relationships. **"The Machine Stops"** does not suggest any solutions to these problems. As they are dying, Kuno tells Vashti that there are humans on the surface of the Earth who have escaped destruction and will rekindle civilization but will not repeat man's enslavement to the Machine. But Kuno is totally unconvincing.

Kuno assumes that man can control his technology and, hence, his destiny. However, at least from the narrative of **"The Machine Stops,"** his position is unearned and unpersuasive. When Vashti says, "Oh, tomorrow—some fool will start the Machine again, tomorrow," the reader can just as easily believe her. Forster has certainly communicated an attitude toward this mechanized world, but since no compelling reasons are given as to *why* and *how* man lost control of his technology, there are no cogent justifications for believing that history will not repeat itself. The narrator explains: ". . . Humanity, in its desire for comfort, had over-reached itself. It had exploited the reaches of nature too far. Quietly and complacently, it was sinking into decadence, and progress had come to mean the progress of the Machine."[60] One is tempted to ask how all this happened. It is perhaps an unfair question. Forster is dramatizing the *effects* of a totally mechanized world rather than its causes and the events that lead up to it. The repulsion one has for this society works to create attitudes toward an overdependence on technology which may assist its readers in rethinking their priorities and restructuring their relationships to technology. In this way **"The Machine Stops"** links with other works by Forster's contemporaries to produce a cultural critique of Edwardian industrial-technological society.

At the same time, while **"The Machine Stops"** satirizes and rejects this mechanized hell, the satire and antipathy is mixed with a sense of resignation and futility.

It is a curious mixture inasmuch as satire's goal is the improvement of man's institutions and the correction of his foibles. Yet **"The Machine Stops"** presents such a discouraging picture of man in general that it is difficult to see wherein lies his hope for the future. Except for Kuno—and we are not certain why he is different—everyone seems to acquiesce in their slavery to the Machine. There is no collective resistance; Vashti and her friends seem lobotomized. They routinely accept the most absurd rituals and ideas. They are sheep; hence their slaughter is inevitable and undistinguished. The reader has little sympathy for them; they had lost most vestiges of their humanity before the story begins. They live in their hives like insects, and it is difficult to feel any emotional involvement in the death of a bee.[61]

Nor can bees control their destiny. Since they are not conscious of nature and her laws, they are her victims. They are totally biologically and environmentally determined. Again the question is raised: Given this view of man, what is the point of the satire? One might answer that Forster is implying that man is not now but could evolve into this insectlike creature, but since there will always be mutants like Kuno, there is hope.

However, the hope is muted. No real alternatives are presented. Forster voices the concerns of liberal humanists who were reacting to events, the future consequences of which seemed to put people such as Forster in even more peripheral situations vis-á-vis their functions in society. What **"The Machine Stops"** fails to communicate is that the relationship between society and technology is a dialectical one. While technology influences social relationships, social relationships also influence the nature and direction of technology. The first theorist to formulate a coherent view of autonomous technology, Karl Marx, understood this.[62] Marx insisted that "technology has to be understood as a social process."[63] And while he clearly was aware that under capitalism, "technology had taken on an independent, malevolent, lifelike existence and stood opposed to man as an alien and even monstrous force,"[64] Marx was *not* a technological determinist.[65] Marx argued that our "mastery over technology has not been really lost. It has simply been removed to a small segment of the social order, the capitalist class."[66]

Marx's answer to the problem of technology is not the whole answer. Forster touched on something quite fundamental. Whatever form of social arrangement one envisions, there is still the question of technology itself, especially its function as a mediator between man and his social and physical world. Moreover, as one thinker has observed, man is not only "separated from his natural conditions by instruments of his own making," but he is rotten with perfection.[67] There seems to be a compulsion in man to take things to their logical conclusion, regardless of the consequences. Science and technology stand as supreme examples of man's imaginative reach, and there is no reason to believe that man will cease in his attempts to extend his reach or perfect his grasp.

*Notes*

1. Rex Warner, "E. M. Forster," in *British Writers and Their Work No. 3,* gen. ed. Bonamy Dobree (Lincoln, NB: University of Nebraska Press, 1964), p. 59. See also Mark Hillegas, *The Future as Nightmare: H. G. Wells and the Anti-utopians* (New York: Oxford University Press, 1967), p. 82.

2. George Orwell, *The Collected Essays, Journalism and Letters of George Orwell,* ed. Sonia Orwell and Ian Angus, 4 vols. (Harmondsworth, England: Penguin, 1970), IV, 70.

3. Samuel Lilley, *Men, Machines and History* (New York: International Publishers, 1965), p. 139.

4. Norman Birnbaum, *The Crisis of Industrial Society* (New York: Oxford University Press, 1969), pp. 131-32.

5. Martin Green, *Science and the Shabby Curate of Poetry: Essays About the Two Cultures* (New York: W. W. Norton, 1965), p. 69.

6. Samuel Hynes, *The Edwardian Turn of Mind* (Princeton, NJ: Princeton University Press, 1968), pp. 132, 142.

7. Mary Freeman, *D. H. Lawrence: A Basic Study of His Ideas* (New York: Grosset and Dunlap, 1955), p. 109.

8. Ibid.

9. Orwell, *Collected Essays,* II, p. 234.

10. Ibid., p. 235. As was often his custom, Orwell overstates his case. Wells, according to such scholars as Mark Hillegas, was not nearly the naive optimist he was taken to be.

11. Ibid, p. 170.

12. Quoted in P. N. Furbank, *E. M. Forster: A Life,* 2 vols. (London: Secker and Warburg, 1977), I, 161-62.

13. Orwell, *Collected Essays,* IV, p. 70.

14. E. M. Forster, *Two Cheers for Democracy* (London: Edward Arnold, 1951), p. 94.

15. Sybille Bedford, *Aldous Huxley: A Biography* (New York: Knopf and Harper and Row, 1974), p. 244, quoting Huxley.

16. Ibid, p. 253.

17. Ibid, pp. 674-75.

18. Furbank, *E. M. Forster,* I, p. 162, quoting Forster. Mark Hillegas argues that Forster was thinking not only of Wells's five scientific romances but of his *Modern Utopia* as well; see Hillegas, *Future as Nightmare,* pp. 85-87.

19. Hillegas, pp. 85, 88, 94-95.

20. E. M. Forster, "The Machine Stops," in *The Eternal Moment and Other Stories* (1928; rpt. New York: Grosset and Dunlap, 1964), section II, p. 43.

21. Ibid., section III, p. 64.

22. Ibid., p. 69.

23. Ibid., p. 83.

24. Ibid., section I, p. 13.

25. Ibid., section II, p. 59.

26. Ibid., section III, p. 83.

27. Ibid., p. 65.

28. Ibid., section II, p. 55.

29. Ibid., p. 56.

30. Ibid., section III, p. 84.

31. Hillegas, *Future as Nightmare,* pp. 89-90.

32. Langdon Winner, *Autonomous Technology: Technics-out-of-Control as a Theme in Political Thought* (Cambridge, MA, and London: MIT Press, 1977), p. 13.

33. Forster, "Machine Stops," section III, p. 71.

34. Winner, *Autonomous Technology,* p. 43.

35. Hannah Arendt, *The Human Condition: A Study of the Central Dilemmas Facing Modern Man* (1958; rpt. Garden City, NY: Doubleday, Anchor, 1959), p. 11.

36. Ibid., pp. 128-29.

37. Winner, *Autonomous Technology,* p. 17.

38. Ibid., p. 29.

39. Ibid., p. 198.

40. Ibid., p. 191 (emphasis mine).

41. Ibid., p. 146.

42. Forster, "Machine Stops," section I, p. 27.

43. Ibid., p. 36.

44. Ibid., p. 16.

45. Ibid., p. 32.

46. Ibid., p. 29.

47. Ibid., p. 17.

48. Ibid., section II, p. 44.

49. Arendt, *Human Condition,* pp. 249, 280-81.

50. Joseph Weizenbaum, *Computer, Power and Human Reason: From Judgment to Calculation* (San Francisco: W. H. Freeman, 1976), p. 25.

51. Jerry Mander, *Four Arguments for the Elimination of Television* (New York: Morrow Quill Paperbacks, 1978), pp. 55, 68.

52. Forster, *Two Cheers,* p. 94.

53. Roderick Seidenberg, *Anatomy of the Future* (Chapel Hill, NC: University of North Carolina Press, 1961), pp. 48-49.

54. Quoted in Hillegas, *Future as Nightmare,* p. 185, n. 13.

55. Forster, "Machine Stops," section III, p. 67.

56. Max Weber, *The Protestant Ethic and the Spirit of Capitalism* (1904-05; trans. Talcott Parsons, New York: Charles Scribner's Sons, 1958), p. 157.

57. Robert K. Merton, "Puritanism, Pietism and Science," in *Social Theory and Social Structures* (Glencoe, IL: Free Press, 1949), p. 333.

58. Joseph Schumpeter, *Capitalism, Socialism and Democracy* (New York: Harper and Row, 1947), p. 127.

59. George Herbert Mead, *The Philosophy of the Present,* ed. Arthur E. Murphy (LaSalle, IL: The Open Court Publishing Co., 1959).

60. Forster, "Machine Stops," section III, p. 69.

61. In *A Passage to India* (1924), Forster examines the Hindu concept of the unity of all living creatures and the sacredness of *all* creation.

62. Winner, *Autonomous Technology,* p. 39.

63. Nathan Rosenberg, "Marx as a Student of Technology," *Monthly Review,* 28 (July-August 1976), 70.

64. Winner, *Autonomous Technology,* p. 36.

65. Rosenberg, "Marx as a Student," pp. 58-61.

66. Winner, *Autonomous Technology,* p. 40.

67. Kenneth Burke, *Language as Symbolic Action: Essays on Life, Literature, and Method* (Berkeley: University of California Press, 1966), pp. 13, 16.

**Leonard G. Heldreth (essay date 1986)**

SOURCE: Heldreth, Leonard G. "Fantasy as Criticism in Forster's Short Fiction." In *The Shape of the Fantas-*

*tic: Selected Essays from the Seventh Annual Conference on the Fantastic in the Arts,* edited by Olena H. Saciuk, pp. 9-19. Westport, Conn.: Greenwood Press, 1986.

[*In the following essay, Heldreth explores Forster's use of fantasy in his short fiction, highlighting his use of the fantastic to stress the conflict between individual desires and social restrictions.*]

The fantasy elements in E. M. Forster's short fiction are traditional ones—a faun, a siren, a metamorphosis from woman to tree, scenes of heaven and hell. The narrator of his short story **"Other Kingdom"** says it is part of his system "to make classical allusions" (*Tales* [*The Collected Tales of E. M. Forster*] 89), and Forster uses a similar system; yet the narrator of **"Other Kingdom"** cannot be trusted, and to see these standard elements as classical drawing-room images is to miss their power. Like most modern fantasy images they are "preoccupied with unconscious desire" which is related to the cultural order (Jackson 63).

In the introduction to his collected stories, Forster states that fantasy "functions for Hermes" as "messenger, machine-breaker, and conductor of souls to a not-too-terrible hereafter" (*Tales* v). This discussion focuses upon these three aspects of fantasy in Forster's short fiction. The first part covers stories in which messengers come to free individuals from lives of social limitations and boredom. The second part examines fantasy as a machine-breaker, a force to oppose society's stifling of any desire that threatens the dominant social machine. The third function of fantasy, to convey people to a mild afterlife, will be examined here as a dominative theme of fantasy in general, the breaking down of boundaries that merges the individual into something greater than or beyond himself. Not discussed are two of Forster's best-known stories, **"The Machine Stops"** and **"The Other Side of the Hedge."** Their symbols and didactic dialogue make clear their messages, and their relationships to the second and third aspects of this discussion need no elaboration.

Through most of his fiction, long or short, fantastic or realistic, Forster stresses the conflict between individual desires and social restrictions, especially those that deny the physical being.[1] The Victorian desire to ignore or gloss over such needs—"the unsaid and the unseen of culture: that which has been silenced, made invisible, covered over and made 'absent'" (Jackson 4)—still dominated Forster's society, and he emphasizes through his fantasies that individuals must develop their physical and emotional sides as well as their intellects, or they will miss much that is valuable in existence. For example, in a minor story, **"The Classical Annex,"** the curator dislikes a nude statue of a Roman athlete or gladiator (*Life* [*The Life to Come*] 147), and when the

statue's unusually large fig leaf falls off, he ties it back on and drives the fig leaf into position with his fist. But the statue comes to life with an "obscene change" in its physique and pops the fig leaf again. This emphasis on physicality and sexuality is decried by the curator as "some obscene breath from the past" (*Life* 149), a conclusion with which Forster (and the curator's son) obviously do not agree. Indeed, physicality can counteract excessive intellectuality and strengthen healthy ties with reality, as the narrator of **"The Rock"** demonstrates when he prays "that my grossness preserve me" (*Life* 64).

Forster often presents the physical and emotional point of view through doubling. In this technique a secondary character appears who represents all that the main character lacks, a character or place acquires "an unconscious *projection* . . . those 'qualities, feelings, wishes, objects, which the subject refuses to recognize or rejects in himself [are] located in another person or thing'" (Laplanche and Pontalis in Jackson 349). In Forster's doubling, a cerebral character, emotionally and physically undeveloped, encounters his opposite.[2] In the short story **"Ansell,"** Edward visits his cousin and renews acquaintance with Ansell, the former gardener and now gamekeeper, with whom as a teenager he had been "intimate" (*Life* 2). Edward has brought a large crate of books with which to write his dissertation, but on the way to the hall the horse rears, and the box of books falls down a ravine where it splits and dumps most of its contents into the river. Ansell asserts that "them books saved us" (*Life* 6), and his remark applies both to the boys' not falling down the ravine and to the saving of their relationship through the loss of the books, for Edward now cannot write the dissertation. Ansell shortly adds, "There's other things but books" (*Life* 6), and by the end of the story Edward acknowledges that he "cannot fend" Ansell off (*Life* 9). This "degeneration" to the physical and nonacademic is exactly what his upper-class cousin had feared, and, as Norman Page points out, the ending is equivocal. Edward's not thinking of the future will not hinder its arrival, and his giving in totally to the physical self is as lopsided as becoming totally intellectual.

"The problem of self to other is mediated through desire . . . usually in transgressive forms" (Jackson 51), and the homoeroticism implied in "Ansell" is stated as explicitly as Forster ever stated such matters in **"The Other Boat,"** an erotic fantasy that, except for doubling, is presented as a realistic story.[3] A blond muscular British officer, Lionel March, meets and shares a cabin on a voyage to Bombay with an Indian whom he had known as a child. In the heat of the Mediterranean, "the setting of so many scenes, in Forster's fiction, of the discarding or disappearance of restraints and the surrendering to the instinctive and the irrational" (Page 58), British propriety surrenders to Indian persistence, and the two sleep together every night. March is worried about discovery while the Indian is little concerned, priding himself on his English conquest. In a disagreement one night, Lionel decides he will sleep on deck in the future, and the Indian bites him on the arm, drawing blood; in the following fight, Lionel strangles his lover and then leaps to his death in the sea. Each of the two men found in the other what was lacking in himself: Lionel's social position and color gave Cocoanut status, and Cocoanut awakens the sexual nature that Lionel had ignored. Social pressures, however, prevented their happiness, and the two halves died together.[4] Despite the story's realistic mode, the two major characters share their secret lives as a fantasy of doubling in the ship's cabin, a fantasy so disgusting to the British that death is the only possible outcome for its discovery.[5]

A similar pattern of doubling occurs in another realistic story, **"Arthur Snatchfold."** At dinner Sir Richard Conway had seen his own gray head, reflected in a mirror, as the brightest object in the room. This perception anticipates his feeling the next morning when, leaning out his bedroom window, he sees in Trevor Donaldson's garden a distinct lack of color; it also anticipates the appearance of his double, the milkman wearing a bright canary shirt. This dramatic entrance, just as Conway was looking for someone exactly like the person who appears, almost breaks the realistic mode. The following morning, to escape the tedium induced by his hosts and their discussions of aluminum, Conway seduces the milkman to a roll in the bracken; only months later does he find out that they had been observed, but that the young man, after being arrested, had refused to identify Conway. The conflict of individual desire with official policy is summed up in the young man's earlier comment, "What can it matter to anyone else if you and I don't mind?" (*Life* 104). This moral is belabored further in another story, a **"Utopian Political Fantasy"** (Colmer 130) with a similar title, **"What Does It Matter? A Morality."** Here the president of a European country admits to having carnal knowledge of his wife, his mistress, and a young soldier. The subsequent social uproar results in no one's really caring what anyone does with anyone else, and the country shuts itself off from the rest of the area and enjoys itself.

At the end of **"Arthur Snatchfold"** is another device common to dreams and to Forster's fantasy: an event that appears unfamiliar at first turns out, on reexamination, to be intimately involved with the self. On first hearing of a young man apprehended for unnatural actions, Conway makes no connection between his own affair and the arrest. But as the details are told, he reinterprets the information and recognizes his affair with the milkman. Then, he abandons his sensual self, the milkman, to prison, concealing the affair and noting only the name, just as he had earlier concealed his desires for men, lived a life of respectability, and sired

two daughters. Such a changing pattern of interpretation, common in dreams and fantasies, forms the basis for the story **"The Rock,"** whose narrator points out, "It was the crisis of his life. But, in a story about his life, it is not the crisis" (*Life* 62). And, again, at the end of **"The Obelisk,"** as the wife realizes she must reinterpret what has happened, she finds that "depth beneath depth seemed to open" (*Life* 129).[6]

Although **"Ansell," "The Other Boat,"** and **"Arthur Snatchfold"** are essentially realistic fiction, such doubling and a reinterpretation of actions and values that at first seem to be obvious are also the major points of **"The Curate's Friend,"** one of Forster's unmistakable fantasies. At the beginning of the story the curate is a conceited youth, facetious and shallow. He takes his fiancée Emily, her mother, and a young friend on an outing for tea where he encounters what he thinks is a naked boy. When he is seized by the boy, he cries out, "Go away!" and then he sees the tail. As often happens with doubles, no one sees the faun but Harry. For years it has spoken only to children, but now it assures the curate it will be with him until his death. When Harry accepts the faun's reality, he orders it to make his fiancée happy, and the faun promptly causes her to fall in love with the young friend. Harry feigns despair at losing Emily, but the faun points out the happiness at the bottom of his heart. Harry finally accepts the joy brought to him by the faun, which functions as the voice of his subconscious and, like most of these doubles, as his suppressed self, his Jungian shadow. Harry prospers, but he acknowledges at the end of the story the dangers of following his true self: "If I breathe one word . . . my present life . . . would come to an end" (*Tales* 124). In a hypocritical and repressive society, the animalistic, pagan self must be hidden, so he presents the account of his faun as fiction. A more serious messenger, one from the dead who brings death as his message, appears in **"Dr. Woolacott,"** a story in which Forster presents an early death for love as preferable to a long but isolated and passionless life. Here also the messenger can be seen as the repressed sensual side of the major character.

Messengers are not the only way fantasy reaches out for the individual. Sometimes the intrusion is more direct: "the supernatural irrupts and shatters the surface of polite society, the infinite invades the finite world of politics and civilized chatter" (Colmer 28). One of Forster's best-known fantasy stories, **"The Celestial Omnibus,"** contrasts the innocence and spontaneous behavior that enable a young boy to see the gods with the polite pomposity and elitist chatter of Mr. Bons, president of the Literary Society, who prides himself on how many copies of Shelley he owns. On his first trip in the omnibus, the boy finds great joy beyond the rainbow, but when he returns, he is caned by his father and called a liar. For verification he takes with him the next evening Mr. Bons, who is at first terrified and then lectures the boy and cows him into timidity. But Mr. Bons has too many books and cannot see the campfires, the Rhine maidens, or Achilles, and when he asks for help from Dante, the poet replies, "Poetry is a spirit; and they that would worship it must worship in spirit and in truth" (*Tales* 73), not with the self-serving hypocrisy that Mr. Bons has exhibited. Yet the ending to the fantasy is a little too pat: Bons falls through the clouds to his death and the boy, crowned with oak leaves, escapes to live in the world of myth and literature.

An older boy, Eustace Robinson, fourteen, also escapes from the dreary routines of civilized English life through supernatural intervention in **"The Story of a Panic,"** but his Italian alter ego, Gennaro, pays for the escape with his life. As Jackson points out, the fantastic "points to or suggests the basis upon which cultural order rests, for it opens up, for a brief moment, on to disorder, on to . . . that which is outside dominant value systems" (Jackson 4). The basis of the cultural order in **"Panic"** is personified by the narrator, Tytler, an Englishman traveling in Ravello with his wife and two daughters. A practical man, he understands that trees have to be managed and that the owner of oak trees might have to cut some down for cash. He likes boys and "was quite disposed to be friendly" to Eustace, but he asserts he would "insist on prompt and cheerful obedience, if I had a son" (*Tales* 4, 7).[7] Like Forster's other narrators,[8] Mr. Tytler exemplifies the social structure of the British Empire, and the tale is presented through his preconceptions.[9] Our interpretation of events "is based on our total understanding of the narrative world, an understanding that not only grows from attention to the overt action reported in the text, but that intimately involves the perspectives unconsciously vivified by the grapholect in which the narrative is presented" (Rabkin 23-24).[10] Tytler reveals his English snobbery in his speeches about Italians and his lecturing Gennaro to "always behave respectfully" to Eustace "for he is a young English gentleman, and you are a poor Italian fisher-boy.' I know that speech sounds terribly snobbish, but in Italian one can say things that one would never dream of saying in English. Besides, it is no good speaking delicately to persons of that class" (*Tales* 24). Although the appearance of Pan throws the narrator into a frenzy of fear, he recovers as does the narrator of **"The Classical Annex":** "Oxford had taught him to admit the supernatural willingly" (*Life* 149). Sandbach's assertion that "the Evil One has been very near us in bodily form" (*Tales* 16) is typical of encounters with the fantastic, for "the other tends to be identified as an otherworldly, evil force: Satan, the devil, the demon" (Jackson 53), and Tytler kneels with the others, although he does not believe Satan is permitted to approach men in visible form (*Tales* 17).

The evening after the panic Gennaro explains that Eustace must be outdoors the first night after the encounter, but no one believes him. Because we see the events through Tytler's eyes, we never understand why Caterina died or why Eustace will die if he remains indoors; nor do we completely understand why Gennaro, sitting on the asphalt path in the garden, falls over dead while Eustace utters "a strange loud cry" when his feet touch the bare earth. "The tale . . . permits no internal explanation of the strangeness—the protagonist cannot understand what is going on—and this confusion spreads outward to affect the reader in similar ways" (Jackson 27). Even though eight years have gone by since the event and Eustace's picture is beginning to get into the illustrated papers, we learn no more.

Such intrusion of the fantastic may begin with an unexpected vision, but the experience may be so overwhelming, as it is with Eustace, that the individual loses touch with his normal life. In **"Albergo Empedocle"** it begins innocuously as Harold falls asleep between two columns, but as he slips back into a previous life, he loses touch with the current world and is finally committed to an institution.

Fantasy thrives on the unsatisfied desire exhibited by the boy in **"Omnibus,"** Eustace, and Harold; and it wanes with satisfaction. So when a society deliberately ignores basic human needs, fantasy has much room for growth, even though the source of frustration may not be obvious. Conway, in **"Arthur Snatchfold,"** "got the feeling that they were all of them looking for something which was not there" (*Life* 100). This void at the center of things is a loss of passion and a neglect of the physical, something the English upper class had relegated to its servants, leaving only empty social routines and business to occupy itself. At another point Conway, a father, gentleman, and successful businessman, says to himself, "We're not stupid or uncultivated. . . . But I'm afraid we don't get much pleasure out of it all" (*Life* 98). In such conditions, as it does for Conway, fantasy becomes rebellious, a "machine-breaker," and "Forster may often have resorted to fantasy . . . because it permitted statements and situations to be presented or hinted at which could hardly otherwise have found their way into print" (Page 32). Such situations occur in **"The Road from Colonus"** and **"The Point of It,"** and in both stories the mere *preservation* of desire and discontent becomes a sufficient goal.

Mr. Lucas, in **"The Road from Colonus,"** could be an older Conway, now traveling with his daughter. He has worked steadily, made money, educated his children, and led a healthy, active life. Forty years before he had become interested in Hellenism, and he now hopes that a visit to Greece will revitalize him. Finding a hollowed tree trunk from which water wells up, he enters the trunk and experiences that traditional function of the uncanny, "to discover, reveal, expose areas normally kept out of sight" and, by doing so, to effect "a disturbing transformation of the familiar into the unfamiliar" (Jackson 65). He drinks from the spring inside the tree, and when he looks up, he feels more than just refreshed; he closes his eyes for a few moments, and when he opens them again, "something unimagined, indefinable, had passed over all things, and made them intelligible and good" (*Tales* 130). As he lunches with his daughter and their friends, "the whole place called with one voice, articulate to him," just as the downs had called to the curate after the faun appeared, and Lucas begins to think that "a supreme event was awaiting him which would transfigure the face of the world" (*Tales* 137). But his family literally drag him away, although the townspeople struggle to keep him there. Lucas then spends the rest of his years in a London flat where he hates the children next door and the sound of running water. Months later, his daughter reads to him from an old newspaper that the house where he wanted to stay in Greece had been completely destroyed on the night that they left by a falling tree.

Wilfred Stone argues that Forster's fantasies "are youthful productions and deal with problems of youth—problems of revolt and belief, of self-justification and self-discovery" (Stone 122) even though he later admits that **"The Eternal Moment"** is "preoccupied with the problems of age" (Stone 138). Self-justification and self-discovery are not solely the concerns of youth, and Mr. Lucas's problem, despite Stone's comment, *is* primarily one of age. Like Sir Richard Conway, he finds something missing in his life; his momentary vision in Greece, however, cannot survive the unimaginative lifestyle imposed by his daughter or the mediocrity of his subsequent life in England.

Critics have also objected to the title of the story, arguing that Mr. Lucas is "a charade of 'tragedy'" (Stone 146) or that the windstorm "is a facile coincidence in order to end the story with an ironic punch" (Martin 59). The point of the title is to accentuate the irony of a civilization that denies old men the right to end their lives as they see fit. Oedipus in his old age was revered in Greece, while Mr. Lucas's simple request is ignored and, for his own good, he is dumped into the cart like so much baggage and carried off. He cannot even choose to die cleanly rather than measure out his life in coffee spoons. Mr. Lucas is not tragic, for he is not permitted the free will that could have resulted in tragic action. Forster presents a picture of a civilization so sunk in mediocrity and hypocrisy, one which has come so far down the road from Colonus, that the tragic vision is no longer possible.

Mr. Lucas's attempt to die in action rather than in bed (*Tales* 128) is also the unspoken objective in a three-part story, **"The Point of It,"** but only Harold achieves this goal. In the first section, Mickey, in his early twenties, supervises Harold, who has been sick and who, like Clesant in **"Dr. Woolacott,"** is urged not to exert himself. The two boys, caught up in animal good spirits, have spent the day on the sand dunes running, bathing, and eating (*Tales* 199). As they row back, Mickey urges Harold to exert himself against the tide, and as he does so, Harold begins to approach a "mystic state . . . he was beginning to be" (*Tales* 198-99). Mickey urges him to stop, saying, "I don't see the point of it," but Harold replies, "Well, you will some day," and dies of a heart attack, half in and half out of the boat.

The second section traces Mickey's subsequent life for the next fifty years until his death. He marries Janet, a person bent on improving other people (*Tales* 204); he fathers three children who produce grandchildren; and at the end of his life he is reconciled to everything. Lying in bed in a coma, he then hears his son berate both him and society for being too mediocre and too tactful (*Tales* 211), and he dies in cold anger.

The third section presents Mickey's experiences in hell, which for him is an illimitable plain of sand in which he is buried up to his mouth. He and the others buried about him, those who have attempted to be agreeable and make the most of their situations, regard their location not as hell but as heaven. Mickey also realizes that his wife is buried in the hills behind him with the tough souls, the crusaders and reformers (*Tales* 218). Only the young are missing and Mickey wonders briefly what the point was of their brief existence (*Tales* 219). A wandering spirit from across the river of the damned reminds the buried souls of their past, and they fight against it. The spirit is desire itself, and Mickey chooses the pain of desire over the monotony of the sand and dies a second time. He finds himself in a boat where someone undistinguishable is rowing, hears the "crack of angelic muscles," and finds himself once again crossing the river and coming toward a farm, "full to the brim with fire" (*Tales* 224). If this fire is the "sunshine" mentioned earlier, then Mickey has reached the "Happy Isles" that he mentions at the beginning of the story. On the other hand, what lies ahead may be the flames of hell. Lawrence Brander sees this story as "corrosive" and as "the only dangerous fantasy Forster wrote" (Brander 215); certainly the story rejects as "soft" and damning the lives led by most people, including critics, and argues that a fiery afterlife rather than a dry one may be the best one can expect. The oarsman is angelic, but the farmhouse brims with fire. Mickey, despite the ambiguity of the approaching flames, now knows that desire and the struggle itself are "the point of it." However much this point may offend critics who want a philosophical rationale and more "mature" concerns in Forster's writing,[11] such a conclusion, that desiring and living life fully is the only point of life, is consistent with much of Forster's other stories and looks forward to some of the tenets of literary existentialism. **"The Point of It"** and **"The Road from Colonus"** both exemplify Forster's belief that dying in a struggle is much preferable to living in mediocre ease, that desire and its accompanying fantasies are one way of opposing a stultifying social structure and one way of preserving the integrity of the individual.

One major aspect of fantasy in the short fiction remains to be discussed, that "which lies behind all fantastic art, to a greater or lesser degree, the arrival at a point of absolute unity of self and other, subject and object, at a zero point of entropy" (Jackson 77). This drive toward unity questions the limitations set up by society and the individual; it "throws back on the dominant culture a constant reminder of something 'other,' thereby 'indicating the vanity of notions of limit and discrimination . . . making that vanity its subject'" (Bessiere in Jackson 70). Freud describes it as "the most fundamental drive in man: a drive toward a state of inorganicism . . . the most radical form of the pleasure principle, a longing for nirvana, where all tensions are reduced" (Jackson 72). Loss of shape or metamorphosis, a characteristic of this tendency, appears in Forster's first published fiction, **"The Story of a Panic,"** when Eustace, walking the paths of the garden at night, seems to take on many shapes—a great dog, an enormous white bat, a mass of cloud which bounced like a ball or took short flights like a bird or glided slowly like a wraith (*Tales* 26).

This urge toward metamorphosis has its fullest development, however, in **"Other Kingdom,"** his updating of Ovid. The conflict is again between the natural or romantic and the civilized or practical, and these opposing forces are personified in Harcourt Worters and his fiancée, Evelyn Beaumont. Harcourt contains the qualities of civilized, materialistic England. He is very good at business and enjoys culture while remaining eminently practical. "Radiating energy and wealth, like a terrestrial sun" (*Tales* 100), he is associated with the golden touch of Midas as well as with the sun god; the legend of Daphne and Apollo is cited, and Ford, Mr. Worters's nephew, warns Miss Beaumont what will happen if Midas touches her and what to do if Apollo approaches her (*Tales* 76).

In contrast, Miss Beaumont, a "crude, unsophisticated person" from Ireland, is said to have not yet developed her soul (*Tales* 103, 90). Associated with druidic mysteries, she hates enclosures (*Tales* 96), and she urges her guests to "throw to the Naiad a pinch of tea," for the reigning wood spirit, disturbed by Christianity, has a nineteen-hundred-year-old headache (*Tales* 189). While her remark allies her with the old religions, Miss Beaumont is also associated metaphorically with trees early in the story when her body and dress quivered "with the suggestion of countless leaves" (*Tales* 80).

She and Harcourt argue about the future of Other Kingdom Copse, a section of woods that Harcourt has purchased and given to her. She wants it left wild and he wants to enclose it with fences and divide it with asphalt paths. He wins, and she goes into a decline, "dressing no longer in green but in brown" (*Tales* 105). After the copse is fenced, a terrific storm appears, and wind blows a branch across the stream and up onto the terrace. Evelyn rushes out and touches it with her hand. She tells Harcourt the wind will never cease as long as she remains in the house (*Tales* 106), but she agrees to cross to the new copse with him and formally take possession of it. She changes the brown dress for the green one, and in the meadow she dances for them: "She danced away, . . . back, back, through the centuries till houses and fences fell and the earth lay wild to the sun" (*Tales* 108-9). Harcourt follows her passionately into the woods but loses her among the trees, and she is never seen again.

Although metamorphosis dissolves the boundaries of shape, the ideal of dissolution is to return to that animism of the young child that removes the distinction between the self and the world, a return that can be achieved only when the human body and society are broken down and differentiation is removed. This goal is achieved at the end of **"Mr. Andrews,"** when the two men abandon heaven as boring and permit the world soul to break their forms and absorb their experiences to make the world soul better (*Tales* 22). A similar pattern is anticipated for society in **"The Song of the Siren"** when the siren will be brought up from the sea to destroy Christian restrictions (*Life* 258).

Despite the realistic aspects of Forster's major novels, Norman Page is right that "fantasy was not a sort of literary acne which Forster outgrew . . . it was a mode to which he chose to return from time to time even after he had achieved success in writing novels in the traditional mode of English realism" (Page 61). He uses fantasy in his short fiction to indicate the superiority of physical desire, striving, and communion over intellectual sterility, smug complacency, and isolation. He was not optimistic about the future of fantasy, saying that she has "become apocalyptic out of deference to the atom . . . or wings her way with even less justification towards the countries of the future" (*Tales* v). But his fantastic muse, dubbed "Hermes Psychopompus," is "lightly built" to "stand in the prow and watch the disintegrating sea, the twisted sky" (*Tales* viii), so he may survive in the modern world, where fantasy's functions of messenger, machine-breaker, and unifier will certainly be needed.

### Notes

1. While the laws and attitudes against homosexuality undoubtedly restricted Forster's satisfaction of *his* physical desires, the drives of the flesh were

officially repressed even for heterosexuals; thus, the need to acknowledge and incorporate the physical was a universal one.

2. In addition to the stories discussed here, doubling of this type occurs in "The Story of a Panic," "The Point of It," "The Story of the Siren," "The Purple Envelope," "Dr. Woolacott," and "The Obelisk."

3. Summers points out the "balance of realism and fantasy that characterizes the entire canon" of Forster's writings (Summers 237). Fantasy and romance dominate the short fiction while realism dominates the novels.

4. Page rightly points out that Forster "found great difficulty in dealing imaginatively with a serious homosexual relationship without seeing it heading for disaster, or in envisaging such a relationship without sensing within it the seeds of tragedy" (Page 42). Seeing such a situation in any other fashion, given Forster's social milieu, would have been too fantastic even for a writer of fantasy.

5. This story has many parallels with another famous short story of doubling and sexuality in a ship's cabin, Conrad's "The Secret Sharer."

6. Forster's interest in alternatives and in alternate interpretations of parallel patterns are evident in his titles: "The Other Side of the Hedge," "Other Kingdom," and "The Other Boat."

7. Wilfred Stone's argument that Tytler and Eustace represent Forster at different stages in his life seems untenable given the character of Tytler (Stone 132).

8. See "The Other Side of the Hedge," "Other Kingdom," "The Classical Annex," and the beginning of "The Curate's Friend."

9. See Rabkin's discussion of the narrator in fantasy literature (Rabkin 10).

10. Rabkin uses *grapholect* to mean the language that marks the narrator as coming from a particular time, place, and social group.

11. See Stone's comment about Forster's outgrowing the "puerility implicit in the form" of fantasy (Stone 161).

### Works Cited

Brander, Laurence. *E. M. Forster: A Critical Study.* Lewisberg, Penna.: Bucknell Univ. Press, 1968.

Colmer, John. *E. M. Forster: The Personal Voice.* London: Routledge & Kegan Paul, 1975.

Forster, E. M. *The Collected Tales of E. M. Forster.* New York: Alfred A. Knopf, 1964.

————. *The Life to Come and Other Short Stories.* Ed. Oliver Stallybrass. New York: Norton, 1972.

Jackson, Rosemary. *Fantasy: The Literature of Subversion.* New York: Methuen, 1981.

McDowell, Frederick P. W. *E. M. Forster.* New York: Twayne, 1969.

Martin, John Sayre. *E. M. Forster: The Endless Journey.* Cambridge: Cambridge Univ. Press, 1976.

Page, Norman. *E. M. Forster's Posthumous Fiction.* ELS Monograph Series No. 10. Victoria, B.C.: University of Victoria, 1977.

Rabkin, Eric S. *The Fantastic in Literature.* Princeton, N.J.: Princeton Univ. Press, 1976.

Stone, Wilfred. *The Cave and the Mountain: A Study of E. M. Forster.* Stanford: Stanford Univ. Press, 1966.

Summers, Claude J. *E. M. Forster.* New York: Ungar, 1983.

### Judith Scherer Herz (essay date 1988)

SOURCE: Herz, Judith Scherer. "The Stories I: Mythic Fictions." In *The Short Narratives of E. M. Forster,* pp. 24-47. London: Macmillan Press, 1988.

[*In the following essay, Herz offers a thematic and stylistic evaluation of Forster's short story collection* The Celestial Omnibus and Other Stories.]

Six months after the publication of *Howards End,* Forster wrote to Edward Garnett about those of his short stories that would soon be published as ***The Celestial Omnibus and Other Stories*** (1911). 'Do you remember some short stories of mine? I have at last entrapped a publisher into taking them. I am very glad, for I think them better than my long books—the only point of criticism on which I have ever disagreed with you!' (12 Nov 1910, L&F, ɪ, 117). And in the September of the following year he made the point even more emphatically in a letter to Jessica Darling: 'Thank you for what you say about my short stories. I would rather people praised them than anything else I wrote' (24 Sept 1911, L&F, ɪ, 125).

As the letter to Garnett suggests, however, Forster's assessment of the stories was by no means the common one among his friends, whose responses were similar to that of the anonymous reviewer for the *Athenaeum* who found them whimsical and facetious. The vogue for the Machen type of fantasy with an underlayer of mysterious horror hardly interested Bloomsbury (or Forster, although that might not have been perceived at the time), but it may have been an inducement to the publisher. In a letter to Edward Marsh, Forster wrote that Sidgwick and Jackson are 'nibbling, but oh so feebly, and I am afraid that only those to which we refer as "of a mythological nature" will be published' (22 Aug 1910, L&F, I, 115). Even so, this type of story was not a fictional form appreciated by his Bloomsbury contemporaries. Indeed Virginia Woolf later referred to this volume in her essay 'The Novels of E. M. Forster' as 'that curious interlude, *The Celestial Omnibus*' (CE, I, 346). Forster, himself, gave a voice to that kind of response when in *The Longest Journey* he allowed Agnes Pembroke, probably the least sympathetic of all his characters, to demand flatly, 'How could . . . anyone make a living by pretending that Greeek gods were alive or that young ladies could vanish into trees?'[1]

But it is also in *The Longest Journey*, the novel closest in spirit to the stories (and the one that Forster repeatedly referred to as his favourite), that he not only answered Agnes, but also defined the critical difference between the social gestures of the novels and the short fiction's parables, visions and prophecies. There Rickie Elliott, justifying his liking for the unsuitable Mr Jackson, provides the essential metaphor for the distinction. Mr Jackson, he explains, 'tries to express all modern life in terms of Greek mythology, because the Greeks looked very straight at things, and Demeter and Aphrodite are thinner veils than the 'survival of the fittest' or 'a marriage has been arranged' and other draperies of modern journalism'.[2] What Forster was able to accomplish in his fiction (but Rickie only partially and that posthumously) was the creation of a narrative mode in which Demeter and Aphrodite share the same fictional space as those 'journalistic' phrases. The two realms coexist in the novels so closely and subtly that one never has the sense that one has left the knowable world for some 'other kingdom'. But in the short stories not only are both present, but one can find oneself on the other side of the hedge at the sudden turning of a sentence.

If some of his readers found this a baffling or unsettling aesthetic, there were others who did know how to respond to it. Forrest Reid, for example, in his first letter to Forster to thank him for his unsolicited kind words about Reid's novel *The Bracknells*, wrote,

> I remember very well reading it [*The Celestial Omnibus*] last summer, lying on my back in a punt under trees, & how the beauty of everything around me melted into & became part of the delicate beauty of your stories. . . . I liked your short stories more than your novels. . . . But in the novels too, & particularly *The Longest Journey*, there is the same spirit if not quite so clearly revealed. That is to say the visible world is not everything, there are deeper and more hidden things touched on, & above all there is a sense of beauty, both of material beauty & spiritual beauty, without which, I confess, no book is of much interest to me.

(Quoted in Fur, I, 211)

Reid was in part responding to the implicit homoerotic quality of many of the stories, a quality present as well in his own writing but in a far less resonant and complex form. For it is the intensely personal re-creation of mythic materials that gives Forster's fiction its reverberative power, suggestive of those 'deeper and more hidden things' that Reid spoke of in his letter. And it is precisely this power that made these stories of such value for Forster that he 'would rather people praised them than anything else [he] wrote'.

Milton wrote of the 'cool element' of prose, knowing '[him]self inferior to [him]self' in that medium, for 'led by the genial power of nature to another task, I have the use as I may account of it, but of my left hand'.[3] Forster, I am suggesting, regarded most of his novels as his 'prose', written but with the left hand. In the letter to Jessica Darling cited earlier, he made a similar point but with a quite different metaphor. 'But I *have* a tall hat (only used for funerals however), which shows that one can get the best of both worlds.' The world that really mattered, however, was less the 'bright and merry' one of *A Room with a View* than the darker, more vexing world of *The Longest Journey* and the stories. Certainly it was that world that he imaginatively inhabited, while the other he looked at and reconstructed—meticulously, comically, ironically—but essentially from the outside, from the vantage of the observer and not from the vital centre.

In the last chapter I suggested that Forster used the essay 'Macolnia Shops' to authenticate his own artistic enterprise, as it provided both a set of images and a way of handling and organizing those images. The essay 'Cnidus' (1904) carries this process even further, for it is not only a record of an experience, but creates the experience it records. And it is an experience, moreover, that is the centrally generating one of all the short stories—the confrontation with a god who is at once human and divine. In several diary entries from this period he describes the Greek gods from such a point of view. In one he talks of the gods in the British Museum, how each time he sees them 'they are more beautiful and more hopeless. It is simple to say they are gods—down to the bulls going to sacrifice on the Parthenon frieze. But I don't believe gods would make one so unhappy. Up to Demeter and Persephone on the pediment they are human and our perpetual rebuke' (13 Mar 1904, KCC). A few months later, in an entry prompted by an exhibition of Siennese painting, he develops the point: 'They puzzle me these Renaissance portraits:

they're much further off than the Demeter of Cnidus who's made of flesh like ourselves, though of nobler texture' (15 July 1904, KCC).

In the essay, Demeter is described as the one who 'alone among gods has true immortality', for 'to her, all over the world, rise prayers of idolatry from suffering men as well as suffering women, for she has transcended sex' (*AH*, p. 172). This is an immortality, however, that is in some sense distinct from divinity; it derives, rather, from her humanity, her connection with human suffering. The goddess who generates such reverence occupies a curious position in the essay, particularly in the creation of the essay, for in a sense she is both presence and absence, the more powerfully there because she is not. For neither in the diary entry in which he first recorded his visit (6 Apr 1903, KCC), nor in the notebook in which he shortly thereafter worked up that description as a first draft of the essay, is she mentioned at all. It is no exaggeration to say that she fills the essay and that the encounter with her is what the essay is about, but it is an encounter that in a literal sense never took place. Forster describes himself in Cnidus, peering at the place where 'the mountain had been scarped and a platform levelled' (*AH*, p. 171), but seeing nothing. For, at that moment while the travellers are wet and muddy before the empty shrine, the goddess is warm and dry in the British Museum, safe in her recess, dusted twice weekly and with a railing and a no-admittance sign before her. Thus the essay is primarily a memoir of an imaginary encounter, no matter how grounded it was in actuality. Demeter is a fiction that both permits and validates a real experience. Indeed she is a double fiction in so far as she goes on to inhabit nearly all his subsequent writing. She appears, for example, as visible icon in *The Longest Journey* in the picture in Stephen's room. She is present, too, at the novel's close and at the close of *Maurice,* and in the mythic sub-structures of the Italian novels and of **'Other Kingdom',** and, most potently of all, as the presiding mother deity of *A Passage to India*—Esmiss Esmoor.

The encounter with Demeter is not the only epiphany of the essay. Pan makes an appearance, too. Suddenly, mysteriously, their group contains twenty-two instead of twenty-one.[4] Who is the stranger? The essayist is unsure, for the real experience as he writes keeps resolving into something else. He is left finally with no souvenirs, no photographs or sketches, only the memory's urge to transform: 'I never cease to dry up its puddles, and brush away its clouds.' 'Even over that extra person', he concludes, 'the brain will not keep steady' (*AH*, p. 174). But that extra person never entirely departs; he comes back almost at once in **'The Story of a Panic'**, and, related to Hermes, he is a presence in nearly all Forster's writing.

Although Demeter occupies an important place in Forster's private pantheon, it is Hermes who will occupy us for the greater part of this chapter, for he provides the best access to many of the short stories. In particular he names an important strategy for making memory the focus of creation, for fashioning what Forster, in his 1929 essay on Proust, called the 'artist's instant', that moment when the artist sets out to be a writer, when 'he must simultaneously recollect and create' (*AH*, p. 98). It is possible that we may even be able to identify the precise image of the god who provided this generating 'instant'. In a marvellous group in the British Museum, a temple drum from the shrine of Diana at Ephesus, Hermes stands beside Alcestis. The S-curve of his body is accentuated by his slightly raised left foot, so that he seems, caduceus in hand, to be urging the group forward. Almost contemporary with the Hermes of Praxiteles, he has the same languid beauty; indeed, he seems even younger. To the left of Alcestis, if, in fact, the draped female figure between the two beautiful boys *is* the wife of Admetus, stands Death, apparently beckoning her forward. His arm broken at the hand, his head tilted slightly back, he is framed by two full-length wings that are raised only slightly from the marble surface of the drum base (much less so than the drapery of the other two figures, more a tracery than a relief). To the right of Hermes, but badly broken, stands another female figure, possibly Persephone. If that identification is correct, she is well located, for the group as it now stands is directly opposite the Demeter of Cnidus (in Forster's day, she was opposite the Choiseul Apollo). Although the mother is now alone on her fragmented throne, her shrine at Cnidus was dedicated to both Demeter and Kore, so that originally a standing figure of Persephone was at her side.

There is certainly no disputing the goddess, but is the Ephesian Hermes across the way part of Forster's active repertoire of images? In the same diary entry in which he spoke of the Parthenon frieze, he described another sculpture: 'that wonderful boy with the broken arm—who I suppose is to be called sugary because he's neo-Attic—[who] stands all the afternoon warm in thick yellow sunshine. He simply radiates light: I never saw anything like it. Right across the Assyrian transept he throbs like something under the sea. He couldn't have done it in Greece.' To be sure, the figure on the drum that fits this description is Death rather than Hermes, but the two were essentially interchangeable in Forster's imagination, as indeed they are mythologically. One need only think of Mann's Tadzio, in gesture very like this 'wonderful boy'. Moreover, the winged figure of Death is iconographically close to Eros both as he is traditionally referred to and as Forster imagines him at the moment of his birth in *The Longest Journey*. We have here a nucleus of important associations for Forster: Hermes, the beautiful young friend and guide, particularly a guide to the dead, and young Death, also beautiful and ardent. A diary entry of 1912 makes the association explicit, 'I have and hope to keep the power of thinking of death as beautiful' (quoted in *Fur*, I, 218). Both are merged in Eros, who thus becomes a figure of love *and* death. The chain of associations here is similar to Mann's in *Death in Venice,* and it is interesting that Mann, whom Kerényi called 'Dr Hermeticus' ('Your work and your nature represent a revelation of that God'), observed in a letter to Kerényi thirty years after the story, 'I could not help being pleased to note that the psychopomp is characterized as essentially a child divinity. I thought of Tadzio in *Death in Venice.*'[5]

Indeed Kerényi's analysis of the Hermes figure is particularly resonant for a reading of Forster's mythic imagination, although Forster's association of Hermes and fantasy anticipates Kerényi's analysis by many years. Kerényi speaks, for example, of the close connection between Eros and Hermes and of 'the eternal relationship of love, thievery and trade'.[6] He sees the figures of Eros and Aphrodite as essentially one and emphasises their wingedness and bisexuality. The Hermetic span, in his analysis, moves 'from the phallic to the psychopompic', and Hermes is seen, 'like every trickster', as one who 'operates outside the fixed bounds of custom and law'. He is a 'hoverer-between-worlds who dwells in a world of his own'.[7]

Hermes, in Forster's fiction, is both a figure with a name, and a point of view, a way of seeing and acting. He is one of a trinity of male mythological figures, and by far the most significant. Pan, his son, was, for a time, more in fashion, but, as Patricia Merivale has shown, he had become a relatively trivialized figure by the first decade of the twentieth century.[8] Although Pan was still important for Forster, particularly as a figure of sexual awakening, he was too easily sentimentalized, not as resonant mythologically as was his father. Even in his most important appearance, in **'The Story of a Panic',** he belongs to a larger pattern shaped by Hermes. Orion, the hunter, completes the trinity. He provides a recurrent image in Forster's fiction, a promise of freedom, a vision of the enlarged male self, the rough woodsman.[9] Both Pan and Orion will figure in this study, but it is 'the mystifying son of Maia, that enticing divinity who calls forth ever renewed attempts at interpretation', that must claim our attention.[10]

Neither a heavenly presence nor an eruptive natural force, he is Hermes *philanthropotatos,* most friendly of gods to man. For Forster he is an essential component of the double-sexed spirit of fantasy: 'She or he. For Fantasy, though often female, sometimes resembles a man, and even functions for Hermes, who used to do the smaller behests of the gods—messenger, machine breaker, and conductor of souls to a not-too-terrible hereafter' (*CT* [*The Collected Tales*], Intro., p. v).[11] It is this 'lightly built' figure who introduces the stories gathered together in *The Eternal Moment* (1928). Again, some years later, he leads forth the **Collected Tales.** To

him Forster dedicated *Pharos and Pharillon,* and he concludes that book as well, as he presides over the descent into the asphodel. Hermes belongs completely neither to the realm of life nor to that of death. His true space—and the one most frequently evoked in Forster's stories—is the space between worlds.

The Hermetic presence is chiefly felt in the shaping of the narrative. He informs the controlling point of view, which is often distinct from the teller of the tale. For the narrators can be dull and uncomprehending, unaware of the story that is really happening on the other side of their narration. For the purposes of this discussion, I shall give that controlling point of view the name 'Hermes' (indeed in **'The Celestial Omnibus'** he even appears under his sign) and watch the forms he takes and the tricks he plays. His repertoire of jokes, for example, allows a Tytler or an Inskip to imagine that he is telling a story, whereas, in fact, the stories they narrate, or the one that Bons experiences (he could have been the narrator except for his nasty fall), do not happen as they imagine. We are witness to a process of transformation of which the teller is ignorant. But their pupils, who become in the stories the poetry their teachers imagined themselves to have read and understood, enter the realm of Hermes—death in the world, rebirth in the spirit.

**'The Story of a Panic'** (1904) uses the obvious device of an obtuse narrator who is treacherously involved in the story's events, but who is unwittingly instrumental in the triumphant conclusion. Tytler, in his temptation of Gennaro, precipitates the leap that frees Eustace and returns him to his vision of Pan, experienced both as epiphany and human touch. Gennaro is both god and boy, the human evidence of the rapt vision. He is the true shaper of the tale, although as mere actor, corruptible and weak. 'I made the new note crackle in my pocket; and he heard it', Tytler explains. 'He stuck his hand out with a jerk; and the unsuspecting Eustace gripped it in his own' (*CT,* p. 33). Even from the Tytler perspective (although we are not to imagine that he intends any pathos in his use of 'unsuspecting'), there is an intimation of the larger meaning of the embrace. Gennaro, of course, sees it all the more sharply because of his own complicity: 'He longed for a friend, and found none for fifteen years. Then he found me, and the first night I—I who have been in the woods and understood things too—betray him to you, and send him in to die' (p. 35). Ironically, it is through his apparent treachery that he provides Eustace with his only means of escape and interprets that escape rightly as salvation: 'He has understood and he is saved. . . . Now, instead of dying he will live!' (p. 38).

Although Gennaro participates in the Pan myth—indeed, completes what was begun in the 'little clearing' on the mountain—he also performs the function of Hermes in his chthonic aspect. For the 'life' he leads Eustace to is, within the givens of the story's world, death, although the story does not, indeed in its narrator's hands cannot, follow him there. Nonetheless, it is through the narrator's language that such an interpretation emerges. When the narrator, by way of ordering his materials, says, for example, 'but the day was nothing to the night' (*CT,* p. 25), he is only interested in establishing a time frame and generating a heightened interest in the events he is recounting. The statement further functions as part of his characterization in so far as it catches something of his exasperation and confusion. But the line also works allusively, enlarging the moment, suggesting that this is no ordinary day and night, but a metaphor for the entire human span.

The allusion is to a passage from Pindar's Eighth Pythian Ode, lines which, as Furbank explains, became a kind of 'charm or maxim' for Forster. He even inscribed them on a piece of paper which he took with him on his 1903 trip to Greece:

Man's life is a day. What is he, what is he not?

Man is the dream of a shadow. But when the god-given brightness comes

A bright light is among men, and an age that is gentle comes to birth.

(Fur, I, 101[12])

Thus the day and night the narrator refers to in fact constitute the sum of Eustace's life. As he will two decades later in **'The Life to Come'** (although there he will invert the structure, moving from night to evening to day to morning), Forster uses the allusion both to frame the experience and to extend its meaning. The double note of poignancy and triumph that one hears in these lines from Pindar is also sounded at the story's conclusion. 'Signora Scafetti burst into screams at the sight of the dead body, but far down the valley towards the sea, there still resounded the shouts and laughter of the escaping boy' (*CT,* p. 38).

In **'The Story of a Panic',** Pan's presence is felt as a sudden eruption; in **'Other Kingdom'** (1909), by contrast, he is a constant presence, for he dwells, as is carefully glossed, 'most places, as name implies' (*CT,* p. 76). Inkskip, the perpetrator of such useful pedantry, is, in many ways, a more interesting figure than Tytler and less a caricature. He is passionless, neutral, the embodiment of the practical world that Evelyn absolutely escapes from at the end. Those two words—'absolute(ly)', 'practical(ly)'—construct the story between them. Indeed they are the governing polarities of all Forster's fiction. The world of fantasy exists 'absolutely'; that of reality only 'practically' in the sense both of 'almost' (i.e. tentative, preformed, unrealized) and of 'useful in the ordinary ways of the

world'. In the last sentence of **'Other Kingdom',** the contrast and the triumphant escape are given visionary authority: 'She has escaped you absolutely, for ever and ever, as long as there are branches to shade men from the sun' (p. 112). It is Ford, whose private joke is to keep a diary called 'Practically a Book', who, in this utterance, becomes the spokesman for the absolute, a witness to a transformation so total that it escapes the world of sexuality altogether. We may imagine Eustace re-enacting eternally the gesture of awakening to his true sexual identity. But Evelyn, in her transformation, presides over just such a pre-fallen vegetable world as the Marvellian lover might have given to his coy mistress had there been world enough and time.

Ford is the primary agent of translation and interpretation, and, like Gennaro in **'The Story of a Panic',** is the human evidence of the god. But he is more Hermes than Pan, for there is little of the earlier story's rough sexual energy in him. He is both a repository of mythological and literary allusions and mischief-maker and messenger. Exempt from the consequences of passion himself (his physicality is almost an abstraction; he believed, in Forster's comic phrasing, that his muscles grew while reading Pindar), he provides the literary contexts (Ovid, Virgil, Pindar, Sophocles) for Evelyn's literal translation and becomes its scholar-interpreter. Indeed that role is his from the start as he records her words in his 'Practically a Book' and thus attests to their truth.

One of these statements becomes, in fact, the pivot on which the entire story turns. It records her description of the classics: 'They are so natural. Just writing down things' (p. 89). Her fiancé, Worters, seems to assent, but he makes a fatal change, for by saying, 'it *only* writes things down' (emphasis added), he ranges himself 'absolutely' with those who would split literature off from life to the trivializing and emptying of both. Evelyn's definition is, of course, the true one. In a non-metaphoric way (she is herself all metaphor, which allows her words and acts to be literal), she affirms Rickie's view of Greek myth as a way of looking straight at things. The conflict between these two definitions frames the story's fiction, as it illustrates in abstract terms what is played out on the level of plot. There the conflict is between the cool, almost soulless desires of a human dryad and the greedy, acquisitive instincts of her guardian-fiancé, who, while he might have a vegetable name (Worters) is altogether incapable of vegetable love. Pan might have made his piping music from the reed that was Syrinx, but Worters discovers to his uncomprehending bewilderment that no such solace is available to him (Evelyn's name is also hardly accidental, as it recalls John Evelyn, whose *Sylva* was written about those woods around Abinger that Forster would later celebrate in his *Abinger Pageant.*)

Although the narrator finds Evelyn's definition silly, 'Just writing down things', he still has some glimmers of sympathy for his subversive charges. He is not completely untouched by those books on which his livelihood depends, aware, for example, of the nature of Ford's 'robust dreams, which take him, not to heaven, but to another earth' (*CT*, p. 84). Yet he is a toady, a tale-bearer; his instinct is to trivialize human relations just as he debases the classical style: 'Oh, my goodness! Oh, all ye goddesses and gods! Here's a mess' (p. 97). For him, translation is merely exchanging one set of words for another, whereas the story he tells, but does not understand, demonstrates that translation is in fact transformation. Thus translation, the activity of the story's opening, functions at the conclusion as a metaphor for its accomplishment. 'Ah, witless fellow!' Inkskip teaches them pedantically to repeat. 'Gods, I say, even gods have dwelt in the woods ere now' (p. 75). Inkskip, this 'witless fellow', thus tells what from his point of view is a story of an odd, impetuous girl, a handsome engagement present, a clever and cynical ward, an indulgent employer. But in the end it is the gods who inhabit the woods whose deed Worters holds in perpetuity, and it is Ford who sees them and speaks their tongue.

The different narrative strategy of '**The Celestial Omnibus**' (1908) is the result of a slight shift in emphasis and is more apparent than real. Inkskip and Tytler have been here absorbed into the narrative as Mr Bons, while the nameless narrator plays out a story before his nose which he cannot, indeed will not, see or hear. The story belongs to the boy (it is told entirely from his point of view), although the narrator allows Mr Bons to imagine that, as a reader of books, he is fit to interpret it. It is, for example, the boy's judgement of Mr Bons, 'In short, he was probably the wisest person alive' (*CT*, p. 50), that we hear, although the words are spoken by the narrator as if they were his own. His angle of vision, however, includes both the boy's innocence and Mr Bons's pretensions; it can place the social setting satirically ('after No. 39 the quality of the houses dropped very suddenly, and 64 had not even a separate servants' entrance'—p. 51), and enter, at the same time, into the spirit of the boy's dreams. By the end it withdraws to the ironic detachment of the newspaper account, but the 'end', the 'Telos'—the last word of the narrator before the neutral, external voice of the newspaper—has already been accomplished. For the true objective or aim (i.e. the 'telos' in its primary definition) had been realized in the boy's exaltation.

The exaltation is figured in an extraordinarily resonant image. The boy is caught up on the shield of Achilles and raised aloft, made to stand upright. The shield, as in Homer, is figuratively the entire world, but it is also bounded, shaped, indeed a shining version of that enclosed space—dell, cave, cabin, womb—that figures in almost every story and novel by Forster, and is here made to stand for the transforming power of the imagination. But Mr Bons, unheeding of the words of Dante, whom he has bound in vellum, sees only London and plummets to his death. It is indeed a conclusion of Dantesque tonality. His punishment is to see and not know how to believe, so atrophied has his library-bound imagination become, his fall and mutilation emblematic of his spiritual death.

The story thus records a double journey, the boy's toward enlightenment and vision, Mr Bons's through darkness into death. It is a journey shaped by Hermes, for, as the signpost in the dark alley tells us, the Celestial Omnibus is under his direction. The company, the sign states, will not 'be responsible for any negligence or stupidity on the part of Passengers, nor for Hailstorms, Lightning, Loss of Tickets, nor for any Act of God'. The signature, '**For the Direction**', has as its emblem the caduceus (p. 53). As the story unfolds, however, Hermes appears under other names—Sir Thomas Browne, Jane Austen, Dante. They accomplish the narrator's role of witness to the transforming power of imagination as they take the role of conductors to that realm.

These stories move between two worlds. In them Hermes functions as the mythic analogue of the authorial presence, a device that diminishes the necessity for direct intervention, or, rather, turns such intervention into a species of masquerade, where, in the person of the god, the narrator can manifest truths and reshape reality. The short story, in Forster's hands, becomes literally an epiphany. The god himself inhabits there.

But there are two further aspects of the god to be examined: his actualization as the beautiful young boy whom we saw exiled from Ephesus to the British Museum; and his connection for Forster, via his role as psychopomp, with death and memory. In both of these roles he has a ready place in late-nineteenth-century writing. He is Housman's 'merry guide', and related, too, to Pater's Denys L'Auxerrois, although that figure is, perhaps, more Dionysian or Orphic. He leads the *danse macabre* in *Zuleika Dobson* (although Forster did not read this until 1912), but, for the purposes of this argument, he makes his most interesting appearance in Henry James's 'The Great Good Place', a story with marked affinities with Forster's '**The Point of It**' (1911).

There is no establishing with certainty whether Forster read James's later stories shortly after they were published, nor is it necessary to argue any direct connection or influence. Using James as a touchstone serves primarily to remind us that Forster was working within an acknowledged aesthetic, even as he shaped it to his own special voice. Yet the resemblances, both of tone and structure, between the two stories are striking. In each the central character recapitulates a lifetime while the other acts as his guide. There is, too, a calculated blurring of the boundary between fantasy and reality. An event occurs that is neither wholly within the soul nor within the world. Where does George Dane go in James's story? Who is the young man who takes over his life, whose voice and face merge with the voice and face of the Good Brother of the dream? 'I just dropped my burden and he received it', Dane tells the Brother as the entire explanation.[13] To be sure, the central experience of **'The Point of It'** seems more overtly allegorical, but the vision of a lifetime leading to death and back to life is vouchsafed to Micky in much the same Hermetic fashion as it is to Dane.

The emphasis in my approach to **'The Point of It',** that there is a return from death to life, depends to some degree on an unpublished version, a typescript that contains cancelled passages of considerable help in constructing a reading of the story.[14] For it is a story that has always troubled its readers, who echo the title uncertainly, unable to complete the title sentence. But it originally ended with four lines that were cancelled before publication:

> 'Well rowed', cried Micky to the ferryman. 'Three more and easy.'
>
> The order was obeyed.
>
> 'Ship.'
>
> Harold shipped his oars.

These lines, inasmuch as they imply that Harold does not die, remind us that the sunset with which the story closes locates the same moment as the story's opening. The friends are now returning at sunset to the shore they set out from earlier in the day, and this realization transforms the central part of the story, Micky's life and death, from event to vision.

From this perspective, the story arrests the flow of time. Harold, functioning as Hermes, is the stimulus of a vision that allows both for failure and salvation, death and return. Micky sees simultaneously the probable course of his life and that action or gesture which could yet transform it. Thus, as he is excited by the total commitment to the moment which Harold's rapt straining at the oars signifies, he is able to transcend the mediocrity that would otherwise characterize his life and return in the blazing sunset, having successfully crossed midstream. No time passes at all, or no more than the split second which it takes for the boat, working against the ebb of the tide, to cross the channel.

Harold is at the oars. 'The Ferryman', the cancelled lines call him, but that identification with Charon serves only to emphasize his role as Hermes, an association that Mann also makes in *Death in Venice,* published in the same year as Forster's story. There were many precedents for the conflation of the two names, not the least being Housman's epigraph to 'The Merry Guide'. There the phrase 'Hermes guide of souls' appears; it was subsequently cancelled, but the line from Euripides generally regarded as the source for the quotation refers instead to Charon.[15] That Forster should have merged the two names is no surprise. For, whether his name be Hermes or Charon, Harold remains the psychopomp, the spirit of fantasy itself. He is, however, a silent character, whose function as guide of souls is taken over by the narrator. For it is the narrator who unfolds and interprets the process whereby Micky transforms his life. But the transformation is more metaphoric than actual: *no one dies.*

Thus **'The Point of It'** contains two stories; one lasts a moment, the other a lifetime. Even without the cancelled ending, one could maintain such a reading. The framing sunset remains. Moreover, Micky had entered the visionary realm quite early when on the second page we see him transform the farmhouse on the shore into 'a star and the boat its attendant satellite'. 'Micky had imagination', Forster tells us. In his eyes, 'the tide was the rushing ether stream of the universe, the interstellar surge that beats for ever' (*CT,* p. 200). It is within this visionary frame that the rest of story unfolds.

Certainly 'the point of it' would have been less in doubt had Forster not cancelled those lines. However, even in its present form, the story hints at that original ending. The chance of salvation that is offered Micky after death, for example, is oddly linked to that opening scene of the holiday outing. Further, the concluding lines seem to erase the intervening years and return the story to its opening moment. Problems arise either way, however. The narrator, after all, says that Harold has died, and gives no hint in his narration that he is continuing his account in a different mode. It is as if Forster had attempted to rewrite Tolstoy's 'The Death of Ivan Ilyich', but from the perspective of the other side of the grave and in a mythic mode that calls into question the actuality of the story's elements. Indeed, one way of looking at the story is to imagine Micky as a reader of Tolstoy's story in that one instant when the boat hung in the tide, and, as a result of that reading, transforming his life.

The power of **'The Point of It'** arises chiefly from the strength of its meditation on death—in particular, its suggestion of the relationship between death and memory. In the story, dying is imagined as reliving, and the pain of death as the pain of the failure of memory. This is made explicit in another portion of the story that was removed before publication:

> Ah time, is it not enough to snatch the present? need you ruin the past as well? here is your highest crime against man, that man forgets. Even as a [*sic*] write

memories are fading, sweet moments are ghostly in the gathering grey, places and friends are passing from my brain as they have long since passed from my eyes; until in the final twilight even this dimness will be a memory, and I shall remember that once I remembered.

One can more easily guess why Forster cancelled this passage than give reasons for the cancelling of the final lines. The tone is, perhaps, too sententious; the 'a' merges with 'I' in a more than typographical error. The contrast in the published story is certainly sharper without it: 'The shades were silent. They could not remember' (p. 222).

Return is, nonetheless, part of the Hermes myth and Alcestis on the temple drum will shortly retrace her journey, Hermes still her guide. The story, in similar fashion, holds life and death in equal suspension, its driving urgency, the sense that life must be seized, followed even to the gates of death, as if only in that heroic striving can there be salvation. Harold is thus a purer Gerald Dawes, seen more sculpturally, without the crankiness he wore in *The Longest Journey*. And Micky seems, especially from the vantage afforded by the manuscript version, more fit than Rickie to grasp the point of it, to know that he has been in the presence of the god and that, henceforth, his life must be changed.

The god leaves his traces throughout Forster's writing in his many disguises from Puck the phallic trickster in **'The Obelisk'** to the angry god in **'The Road from Colonus'**. For Forster he seems to be simultaneously a mythic mode, an artifact of unsettling beauty and a psychological reality. As myth, marble and desire, he presides in the tales. He knows more than the mere narrators, although he sometimes speaks with their voices. Mercurial, elusive, he gives the fiction its shape and informs it with his spirit.

He is certainly there several decades later in **'Dr Woolacott'** (1927), which can be described as a darker and more passionate version of **'The Point of It'**. It is a story that turns midway into myth in Clesant's encounter with Death as the beautiful boy, Death as Hermes. But Death in this story is double-faced. He is not only the 'charming new friend' (*LTC* [*The Life to Come and Other Stories*], p. 89), but also Clesant's wasting-disease, his death in life, the evidence of those social assumptions that deny the boy. (Disease says that the boy 'does not exist. He is an illusion'.) These two versions of death play out a psychomachia over the dying Clesant. Disease, long his intimate ('nor was this colloquy their first'—p. 94) enacts his nature by denying experience, denying touch. The other, indeed a ghostly lover, denies the death in life that disease offers and offers instead life in death. His paradoxical demand is to ask for life—that is, Clesant's life—from the dying Clesant: 'pour life into me', he urges. And so Clesant does—and dies.

The release that brings death is explicitly orgasmic, the partner a boy long dead of his war wounds. The figure that links them is Dr Woolacott. He is an anti-Hermetic figure, however, ironically invoked as 'life's universal lord' (p. 95), while in fact identified with death as disease. He is explicitly the other in the duel with Death as the beautiful boy; nor was this their first combat. For what Dr Woolacott dimly recalls when he sees the dead Clesant at the story's conclusion is a hospital ward and his words 'to a mutilated recruit. "Do let me patch you up, oh but you must just let me patch you up"' (p. 96). His is a negative presence underlined by his absence from the narrative except as a name until this last page. His absence thus becomes the narrative equivalent of his collusion with Death.

Clesant, on the other hand, is all presence. Indeed, for all that the story is set in the apparently real world of an English country house, it seems to take place entirely within him. He is described as 'barricaded . . . in the circle of his thoughts'. The others appear indistinctly, through a fevered vision. 'They flitted out and in, pursuing their affairs like birds, and troubling him only with the external glint of their plumage. He knew nothing about them, although they were his guardians and familiars' (p. 85). So completely is the narrative space interiorized that specifying details of the story's social reality gradually become endowed with symbolic force as they become absorbed into this internal drama. The violin, for example, which he had been forced to put aside, its excitement too dangerous for him according to his doctor, suddenly starts to play at the moment of his first, incomplete encounter with Death. It is a spectral, disembodied music, signifying release, but also incompletion: 'Always breaking off. A beautiful instrument. Yet so unsatisfying' (p. 93). It is a detail that functions on each of the narrative levels: psychomachia, visionary parable, ghost story.

However, the ghost-story conventions are here so subtly attuned to Clesant's internal situation that they take on human dimensions. There is nothing gratuitous in the deployment of the uncanny; it is neither decorative nor atmospheric. It offers, rather, another way of establishing the Hermetic space, the space between worlds. And it endows the fiction with a sensuality and an urgency not present in many of the earlier tales. These qualities may very well have been what prompted T. E. Lawrence's extreme praise of the story: 'It's the most powerful thing I ever read . . . more charged with the real high explosive than anything I've ever met yet'. (quoted in Fur, II, 149). They certainly are confirmed in Forster's reply:

Yes I know Doctor Woolacott is the best thing I've done and also unlike anyone else's work. I am very glad it got you. . . . I want to know, among other things, when you first guessed the oncomer was a spook. Not until the cupboard, or before? The story makes me happy. It gives bodily ecstacy outside time and place. I shall never be able to give it again, but once is something.

(L&F, II, 81)

'Dr Woolacott' is a ghost story, but not Forster's first attempt in the genre. In 1905, while he was working on 'The Purple Envelope', he wrote to Trevelyan about his difficulties with it, worrying that it might not work: 'I somehow think I am too refined to write a ghost story' (1 Jan 1905, L&F, I, 62). The result of that early experiment was nonetheless more interesting than its publication history or the critical comment it has received would suggest, although it contains an odd disjunction between its constituent parts and its frame, and a rationalizing point of view that works against its ghost-story assumptions. 'Dr Woolacott', however, has none of these problems. It is genuinely a ghost story and it is certainly not refined.[16]

In many ways 'Dr Woolacott' sums up Forster's achievement in the Hermetic story. Five years earlier, however, he had used several of the motifs, metaphors and structures of this form in 'The Life to Come' (1912), a story that is on the one hand related, through Hermes, to 'The Celestial Omnibus', 'The Story of a Panic', 'The Point of It' and 'The Curate's Friend', and, on the other, through its language and imagery and its handling of the motif of conversion, to 'Ansell', 'The Story of the Siren' and 'The Road from Colonus'. Although 'The Life to Come' is the text I shall examine most closely for the remainder of this chapter, I want to backtrack briefly and approach it from the point of view of these last three stories, since they are so densely interrelated that tracing one motif or pattern inevitably involves a criss-crossing of nearly the entire corpus.

In both 'Ansell' (1903) and 'The Story of the Siren' (1904), books are cast into the water, although the gesture carries a quite different meaning in each. In the first it is a relatively simple plot device for freeing the scholar-narrator from his false burden and, through the friendship of the gardener, Ansell, teaching him how to laugh. The image is slightly complicated by the surrounding episode, for, had the books not fallen from the cart, gardener and scholar both would have been killed. But the irony is not elaborated; it works suggestively in much the same way as does the irony that arises from the subject of the lost dissertation, the Greek optative, the tense of wish and desire as well as hypothesis, the assertion of 'what might have happened but did not'. As Robert Martin has demonstrated, the movement of tenses in the story goes from the past to the future conditional to the continuous present, a process in which 'the former philologist presents philologically his renunciation of the optative for the indicative, of hypoth-

esis for reality'.[17] However, the final image of the fallen book ends the story somewhat ambiguously, for that book is a Greek lexicon, its pages turned by the wind as if 'an invisible person [were] . . . hurrying from one word to another' (*LTC*, p. 8). The image thus suggests a provisional quality to any reading one might derive from the fiction; indeed, the narrative procedure works against fixing meaning, as the very last words suggest. The narrator may join Ansell in hearty laughter whenever they pass that spot, but, he concludes, 'I have not yet realized what has happened' (p. 9). Yet, if meaning is provisional, it is still open. The dictionary's words are there to be shaped, even if the dissertation and the notes for it have all been swept out to sea.

Pages turned as if by an invisible hand, a book falling through the water, are motifs that occur again in 'The Story of the Siren', written very shortly after 'Ansell'. There, however, they function chiefly as a framing device, although they have, as well, a bearing on the story of Giuseppe. They both generate the occasion for the story, by isolating the two narrators, and serve as a metaphor for the transformation the story describes. As the book descends through the water, it expands into fantastic shapes, like 'a piece of magical india-rubber stretching out to infinity' (*CT,* p. 245). Furthermore, this notebook on the Deist controversy, seen magnified under water, becomes 'bigger than the book of all knowledge', a metamorphosis that lends authority to the story's visionary conclusion: 'Silence and loneliness cannot last for ever. It may be a hundred or a thousand years, but the sea lasts longer and she shall come out of it and sing' (p. 258). The concluding image suggests that, when this transformation occurs, the new book of knowledge will be the scripture for this revelation.

Writing a scripture for a new revelation of love is the main business of 'The Life to Come' (1922), which also uses the motif of the book cast into the water. However, in this story it is a voluntary act with far more drastic consequences. As soon as the missionary sees the flower-covered Bible on the floor of the hut which had been the scene of his passion, he hurls flowers and scripture into the stream, attempting, too late, to retrieve the holy book. But there is no sense here, as there was in 'Ansell', that he is freed by his act. Rather it becomes a commentary on his denial of what has happened. For it is the scripture that is freed, carried away by the stream to become part of the 'darkness and beauty' of the night. One can describe the remainder of the story as an attempt to recover that scripture in a revised prophetic language. Like 'The Story of the Siren' it uses a visionary idiom to speak of salvation.

Salvation, or, more precisely, failed salvation, is the subject of one of the earlier stories that also stands in an interesting relationship to 'The Life to Come'. For both 'The Road from Colonus' (1904) and 'The Life to Come' are about the experience of conversion, and, in the figure of the enclosure formed by a tree, both use a similar setting for the experience. But the earlier story doubles back on itself; its second half resists the visionary experience of the first and refuses any enlargement beyond irony. Forster is certainly in his novel-writing element in the concluding breakfast-room scene, when the bulbs of asphodel, the plant of the gods, arrive in a newspaper detailing the wrath of those same gods (the device is similar to the one he used at the conclusion of **'The Celestial Omnibus'**). He skilfully maintains the breakfast-room chatter at the same time as he activates a mass of those specifying details that yield the ironic so deftly. Even so, it is only in the first half of the story that one feels the pressure of Forster's engagement with his materials. There he accomplishes a mythic enlargement of the moment without diminishing the social actuality. Mrs Forman, Mr Graham, Ethel are all created out of the breakfast-room materials, but in section I they belong to a larger enterprise which pits Mr Lucas against them in his last attempt to contradict that logic of experience which flatly asserts that there are no 'supreme events', that there is only a steady dying. Thus unlike **'Dr Woolacott',** which turned midway into myth, **'The Road from Colonus'** turns away from myth to story. The gods are angry, to be sure, but they do not strike Mr Lucas directly. His death in life (from his daughter's point of view, a providential escape) is punishment enough.

Thus in **'The Road from Colonus'** there is no consequence to the action, no transformation occurs. When divinity suddenly erupts in **'The Life to Come'**, however, the consequences are immense. For there the analogue text is not Sophocles' play, but Euripides' *The Bacchae*, when Paul Pinmay as Pentheus discovers the perils of toying with sacred mysteries. This is admittedly a somewhat portentous way of describing a fiction that is, at least on one level, a holy joke. T. E. Lawrence's reaction, for example, was to laugh.[18] But it is a holy joke in which the comic and serious curiously mingle. Although the love that is God is by no means the same as the sexual act in the missionary's hut, it is closer to it than the desiccated suburban Christianity that the missionaries, themselves all wrapped in their 'decent' clothing, attempt to export to naked savages. Pinmay, who is the emissary of the God that is Love, has critically mistaken his role. Like the Worters, Tytlers and the Inkskips of the earlier stories, he finds the revelations of divinity sudden, inexplicable and overwhelming. He discovers that the words he has so easily preached have a life of their own, a life to come. Thus the story demands—in part facetiously, in greater measure seriously—that religion must be true to its word, that words mean, that the opening lines are no idle pun, no merely linguistic or even cultural misunderstanding.

But how to deal with the story's words, how to hear its tone and negotiate its mythic universe as well as its socially dense detailing—indeed, how to read it—are questions that most of the commentary it has received over the last decade has not solved. Although it is occasionally singled out, along with **'The Other Boat',** as the best of the posthumously published fiction, most readings still seem to work with inadequate assumptions. Norman Page, for example, claims that Forster 'shirks the question' of whether the love experienced by Vithobai and Paul was 'the genuine article or a momentary indulgence in the flesh'.[19] However, from the point of view I am advancing here, such a 'question' cannot arise, for it depends on a world where human relations have a clock measure, in which the social world in its accumulated detail points to the eternal, but keeps its own rhythm and time. In a fiction which records such a world (most of the novels do, although some more than others), Paul and Vithobai could fall into love and out of love, that is test the genuineness of the article. But that is neither Forster's manner nor matter here, where instead of clock measure there is mythic measure, a day made equivalent to the life of man.

The story's end is its beginning. The opening moment, which so soon as it occurs is denied, is steadily reapproched through the time structure, which moves backwards from night to evening to day to morning (the story's four divisions). It is a time scheme that Vithobai acknowledges, but not Paul, who is conscious only of the forward movement of the ten years of official time, for since time, he assumes, cannot run back, perhaps that event will stay buried in the forest darkness. But Vithobai knows better. Offering his gift on the eve of Paul's marriage, he cries out when repulsed, 'First the grapes of my body are pressed. Then I am silenced. Now I am punished. Night, evening and a day. What remains?' (*LTC*, p. 76). What remains, of course, is the morning, the death scene, the dawning of the eternal day of the life to come. It is particularly ironic that Paul, the preacher of such a promise, should find this outburst 'meaningless'. He is, of course, unaware of the true direction in which the events of the story are moving. Each action he takes is intended to cancel out the past, but with every action the past is made part of the present, until finally the event he will not name is named and Paul, now no mere spokesman for the God that is Love, becomes the sacrifice to Him. Several religious motifs mingle strangely here. From one point of view Paul is Pentheus and Vithobai Dionysus, the flirtation is fatal, and the god triumphs in his power. From another, Paul Pinmay is both a type of Christ and Paul his proselytizer. The conclusion is thus a kind of sacred parody in which Paul's final punishment is a grotesquely inverted *imitatio Christi*. You don't play games with the gods is the conclusion that both Euripidean and Christian readings provide.

The role that Forster seems to cast for himself in this story is part *trouvère,* the poet of a religion of love, and part Mosaic scribe, offering a new scripture for this religion. If Frederick Crews's description, some years ago, of Forster as one who had 'a theological preoccupation without a theology to satisfy it'[20] is one we can readily recognize, then what I am suggesting here is that Forster was attempting to go beyond this by imagining a theology that was true to the full range of man's longings and desires. This is not, as Page and others claim, to equate sex with love, but to demand a place for the sexual experience in the most serious love of all. It is not a debasement or trivializing of Christianity that results, rather a complexly layered theological fiction whose language and metaphors are at one with its meaning. This layering begins with the first line and is most elaborately worked out in the first section, 'Night'. There the reader is placed in the position of the exegete, interpreter of the word 'love'. We are given at the start four versions of the same event, four meanings of the same word. The first statement uses the language of myth, its terms reminiscent of Aristophanes' *The Birds,* the source for a scene that recurs in Forster's writing, most notably in the vision of the birth of love in *The Longest Journey*: 'In full unison was love born, flame of the flame, flushing the dark river beneath him.'[21] In the story, however, the the tone is less visionary, the moment of birth qualified by the darkness and vastness of the world into which love is born. The second version goes slightly forward in time but then retraces the first in a comic pantomime of guns, servants, noise, confusion. The third does greatest violence to the episode; both its language ('a mixture of missionary jargon and of slang'—*LTC,* p. 67) and its truth are debased. In what is almost a parody of a speaking voice, Paul tells the official lie, or, more precisely, the official truth, rendered a lie by the crucial omission. The fourth version is the first to record what in fact took place. But by the time it occurs it contains the other three, and even this version is mediated, for it is the event as it is recalled, not as it happened; the event as it now contains both desire and guilt, the experience and the denial of the experience. This recessive effect of going back and back over the same event sets up a pattern that the story will continue, first as Paul attempts to look back at his ever-altering 'sin', and then in the working out of the backward-moving time scheme.

It is in the first section, as well, that the biblical style of simple and compound sentences and paratactic syntax is most conspicuous. In the paragraph that describes the fourth version of the birth of love, for example, 'and' is used twenty-two times, piling up to the climax of the last four sentences, all of which begin with 'and'. In the two centre sections, in which the narrator follows Paul and watches events unfold from a point of view close to his, the style moves in the direction of the complex sentence and ironic tone of the novels, but never completely, and at the end of each section, when Paul and Vithobai meet, a modified parataxis returns. The final section reverts to the syntax of the opening: 'And confusedly, and with many changes . . . and shiftings . . . and reservations . . . and its present consequences' (p. 79). Then, of course, there is that threefold repetition of 'who calls me?' at the close (pp. 78-80).

I do not know if one can decide absolutely if this language succeeds or fails. Taste, notions of decorum, just plain notions, all may skew our response. But it is important that we attempt to determine what Forster was doing and not prejudge the result. To be sure it is a difficult voice to control—Page dismisses it as 'inflated'; Alan Wilde calls it 'poetic by intention, but . . . flat, thin' in its effect[22]—but such comments seem to me to miss the point, for the language here is directly a function of the materials. If the story attacks a Christian orthodoxy that has platonized and disembodied its sacred metaphors, it does so by way of offering a reconsecrated language and theology that are sufficiently inclusive to contain all human experience. It is a notion of inclusiveness best illustrated by the remark in *A Passage to India* that attempts to explain Hamidullah's inability to understand Adela's honesty and sense of justice: 'How indeed is it possible for one human being to be sorry for all the sadness that meets him on the face of the earth, for the pain that is endured not only by men, but by animals and plants, and perhaps by stones.'[23] That same idea had been phrased a few years earlier, in *Alexandria: A History and a Guide,* 'We're all part of God, even the stones.'[24] In **'The Life to Come',** it takes a paradoxical form that is almost Donnean in its physical punning on sacred matters: 'Love's mysteries in souls do grow, / But yet the body is his book'; or, more extravagantly still: 'Full nakedness! All joys are due to thee. / As souls unbodied, bodies unclothed must be.'[25] For neither Forster nor Donne do we have to choose between tenor and vehicle. The story *is* its language; there is no prettying-up process going on, no merely being 'poetic'. And the conclusion offers no gratuitous bit of violence either, but a final spending of all the energies that have built up through the story. From the moment of that ejaculatory sentence, 'and he stabbed the missionary through the heart' (p. 81), there is a strengthening of voice and a quickening of tempo. The earlier figure of the leap of Vithobai from the cart ('his soul uncoiled like a spring'—p. 75) is completed in the final sentence of the plummet from the parapet, half in this life, half in the next.

Thus, both in its imitation of biblical language and in its realization of biblical metaphor, the story objectifies its content in its preaching of a new scripture in a new language. One way of describing the theological matter of this new scripture is as the testing of Christianity from the Indian point of view from which nothing can be excluded. Although it is a testing in which Christianity is found wanting, Indian religions, much on Forster's mind at this time, are not offered as conclusion either. For this story, even more than *A Passage to India,* is religiously syncretic. Its presiding deity is a rather Dionysian Christ and the life to come that both protagonists approach at the story's end is as much Vithobai's 'solid and eternal . . . kingdom of the dead' (p. 82), where he will once again be king, as Paul's Christian Heaven where master and disciple will meet in true spiritual knowledge.

There is an important private dimension to the story as well. Identifying it returns us to Hermes and the starting point of this argument. In a letter to Sassoon, Forster wrote that **'The Life to Come'** embodied 'a great deal of sorrow and passion that I have myself experienced' (L&F, ɪɪ, 45), referring, in particular, to the dismal death by tuberculosis of his Alexandrian friend Mohammed el Adl. In a notebook in the form of a 'letter' to this dead friend Forster wrote, 'I have written a story ['**The Life to Come**'] because of you and have dedicated a book to you.'²⁶ The dedication of which he speaks is to *Pharos and Pharillon*; it reads, 'Hermes Psychopompos', for that is the role he is cast in in that book, as we shall see in Chapter 5. In the story, however, the psychompompic motif is more complexly and ironically embedded in the closing episode. For it is Paul who plays that role for the now-victorious Vithobai, who 'swoop[s] like a falcon from the parapet in pursuit of the terrified shade' (*LTC,* p. 82). A diary entry in 1922 along with Forster's letters to Florence Barger help to explicate the autobiographical aspect of this moment: 'All that is satisfactory [he is discussing the difficulty of holding Mohammed in memory] is **"The Life to Come"** where my indignation found an outlet through my art' (KCC). It is an indignation that was directed against the Pinmays and their missions and institutions, which Forster held responsible for the terrible sequence of events that led up to Mohammed's sickness and death, just as they lead to Vithobai's in the story. The most personal element in the story is thus transmuted into the most public—the death of a beloved yielding a powerful analysis of the ways in which a society can be corrupted and, indeed, made to die.

### Notes

1. *The Longest Journey* (New York: Random House, 1962) p. 165.

2. Ibid., p. 189.

3. John Milton, 'The Reason of Church Government', in *John Milton: The Complete Poems and Major Prose,* ed. M. Hughes (Indianapolis: Bobbs-Merrill, 1957) p. 667.

4. The description evokes Pan, although the incident suggests Hermes in his role as God of travellers.

5. *Mythology and Humanism: The Correspondence of Thomas Mann and Karl Kerényi,* tr. A. Gelley (Ithaca, NY: Cornell University Press, 1975) pp. 9, 101.

6. Kerényi, 'The Primordial Child in Primordial Times', in Karl Kerényi and Carl Jung, *Essays on a Science of Mythology* (New York: Pantheon Books, 1949) p. 73.

7. Kerényi in Paul Radin, *The Trickster: A Study in American Indian Mythology* (New York: Philosophical Library, 1956) pp. 185, 189. See also W. Otto, *The Homeric Gods* (Boston, Mass.: Beacon Press, 1964) p. 117; and N. O. Brown, *Hermes the Thief* (Madison: University of Wisconsin Press, 1947).

8. Patricia Merivale, *Pan the Goat-God: His Myth in Modern Times* (Cambridge, Mass.: Harvard University Press, 1969) pp. 180-91.

9. 'Orion, a ghost, but the sight of him gives physical joy as if a man of the kind I care for was in heaven' (Diary, 11 Jan 1908, KCC). See discussion of 'The Machine Stops' in Chapter 4.

10. Letter of Mann to Kerényi, 1945, in *Mythology and Humanism,* p. 126.

11. A slightly different version was used as the headnote to *The Eternal Moment* (1928).

12. See Fur, ɪ, illustration on back of dust jacket.

13. Henry James, 'The Great Good Place', *The Complete Tales of Henry James,* ed. Leon Edel, xɪ (Philadelphia: Lippincott, 1962-4) p. 25; originally published in *Scribner's Magazine,* Jan 1900, and repr. in *The Soft Side* (1900).

14. The typescript is at the Humanities Research Center at the University of Texas at Austin.

15. See T. B. Huber, *The Making of a Shropshire Lad: A Manuscript Variorum* (Seattle: University of Washington Press, 1966) p. 208.

16. The original title for the story, 'Dummy', makes the generic classification clearer. Letter to J. R. Ackerley, 28 May 1927, Humanities Research Center, University of Texas.

17. Robert K. Martin, 'Forster's Greek: From Optative to Present Indicative', *Kansas Quarterly,* 9 (1977) p. 72.

18. On 30 April 1924 Lawrence wrote, 'Comment? Oh, it's very difficult . . . in my first avid reading of it I ended it, & laughed & laughed' (quoted in L&F, ɪɪ, 56).

19. Norman Page, *E. M. Forster's Posthumous Fiction* (Victoria, BC: University of Victoria Press, 1977) p. 39.

20. Frederick Crews, *The Perils of Humanism* (Princeton, NJ: Princeton University Press, 1962) p. 14.

21. *The Longest Journey,* p. 43. Forster used this passage from 'The Birds' in his biography, *Goldsworthy Lowes Dickinson,* as the setting for Dickinson's first awareness of a world of passion and imagination. See Abinger Edition, (London: Edward Arnold, 1973) p. 18.

22. Alan Wilde, 'Depths and Surfaces: Dimensions of Forsterian Irony', *English Literature in Transition,* 16 (1973) p. 267.

23. *A Passage to India,* Abinger Edition (London: Edward Arnold, 1978) p. 235.

24. *Alexandria: A History and a Guide* (New York: Doubleday, 1961) p. 71.

25. John Donne, 'The Extasie', lines 71-2; Elegie XIX, lines 33-4.

26. Forster wrote in the small, fawn-coloured notebook, 'The Letter-Book to Mohammed el Adl: who died at Mansourah shortly after the 8th of May, 1922', for several years. It was begun on 5 August 1922; the last entry is dated 27 December 1929 (KCC).

*List of Abbreviations*

Page references to the sources listed below appear, where convenient, in the text, identified by the abbreviations given below. Abbreviations relating to published works are omitted where there is repeated reference to the same text. In Chapter 6 references to Montaigne also appear in the text, as explained in note 2 to that chapter.

*AE*: Forster, *Albergo Empedocle and Other Writings,* ed. George Thomson (New York: Liveright, 1971)

*AH*: Forster, *Abinger Harvest* (London: Edward Arnold, 1936)

*AS*: Forster, *Arctic Summer and Other Fiction,* Abinger Edition (London: Edward Arnold, 1980)

*CB*: Forster, *Commonplace Book,* facsimile edition, ed. Philip Gardner (Stanford, Calif.: Stanford University Press, 1985)

*CE*: Virginia Woolf, *Collected Essays,* ed. Leonard Woolf (London: Chatto and Windus, 1966-7)

*CT*: Forster, *Collected Tales* (New York: Alfred A. Knopf, 1975)

*LTC*: Forster, *The Life to Come and Other Stories,* Abinger Edition (London: Edward Arnold, 1972)

*PP*: Forster, *Pharos and Pharillon* (London: Hogarth Press, 1923)

*TC*: Forster, *Two Cheers for Democracy,* Abinger Edition (London: Edward Arnold, 1972)

*Fur*: P. N. Furbank, *E. M. Forster: A Life,* 2 vols (London: Secker and Warburg, 1977, 1978)

*L&F*: Mary Lago and P. N. Furbank (eds), *Selected Letters of E. M. Forster,* 2 vols (Cambridge, Mass.: Harvard University Press, 1983, 1985)

*KCC*: Unpublished materials in the Forster archives, King's College, Cambridge

**Stephen K. Land (essay date 1990)**

SOURCE: Land, Stephen K. "The Later Short Stories." In *Challenge and Conventionality in the Fiction of E. M. Forster,* pp. 219-30. New York: AMS Press, 1990.

[*In the following essay, Land traces thematic connections between several of Forster's later short stories and his novels, contending that, despite the attention it has received, the element of explicit homosexuality in Forster's work does not affect the structure or balance of his writing.*]

Forster wrote **"The Life to Come"** in 1922 during the composition of *A Passage to India*. The connection between the two stories is obvious in their common choice of subject: the relations between "black" man and white, the confrontation between the natural liberalism of the native and the conventional rigidity of the white man's code.

The short story has only two chief figures, the white hero, Paul Pinmay, and the native challenger, Vithobai. The role of the villain, rather as in *A Passage to India,* is taken by a group, in this case the community of missionaries who represent collectively the assumption of white cultural and spiritual superiority. Pinmay begins, rather like Rickie and Cyril, with the belief that "human nature is the same all over the world" (*LTC* [*The Life to Come and Other Stories*]. 95) and that in consequence the social, racial and religious differences among men can all be reconciled through the channels of "love, kindness and personal influence" (*LTC.* 99). In this naively open spirit, rather like Margaret meeting Leonard, or like Cyril inviting Aziz to tea, Pinmay first encounters Vithobai, despite their differences of background, on a level of personal friendship. Like the earlier heroes, however, he soon finds that friendship with the challenger demands more than he had anticipated having to give.

Like Lucy after George's first kiss, or like Margaret after she has witnessed the mutual jealousy of Leonard and Henry, Pinmay recoils from the challenger when he finds his prejudices offended. Like Rickie under the influence of the Pembrokes, he retreats to the closed ranks of his own people and embarks upon a campaign of deliberate repression. "He who had been wont to lay such stress on the Gospel teaching, on love, kindness, and personal influence, he who had preached that the Kingdom of Heaven is intimacy and emotion, now reacted with violence and treated the new converts and even Barnabas [Vithobai] himself with the gloomy severity of the Old Law" (*LTC.* 99).

In this phase of the story, and as a direct result of his contact with the hero, the challenger suffers a form of persecution at the hands of the conventional party. There is nothing so dramatic here as the imprisonment of Aziz or as the assault upon Leonard, although there is a close parallel with the expulsion of Stephen from Cadover. Vithobai is gradually deprived, after his conversion at the hands of Pinmay, of his chiefly splendors, and he loses most of his land to the white colonists who follow in the footsteps of the missionaries. His decline, moreover, is not merely economic, for like Leonard and like Aziz he deteriorates personally in the course of the story from an attractive openness to a condition of embittered suspicion and hostility.

"The Life to Come" brings out a theme which is implicit but less obvious in *Howards End* and *A Passage to India,* namely the corrupting effect of the hero and his way of life upon the challenger. Vithobai has initially, like Stephen and Leonard, a natural freedom of spirit, but he can enjoy this only in his native "primitive" (of the sense of "unspoiled") environment. Contact with the hero and his people turns the challenger, through no real fault of his own, to less innocent ways. Leonard becomes a beggar and a blackmailer, Aziz adopts the prejudices of the nationalist party, and Vithobai becomes first sycophantic and later vindictive. The corruption of the human spirit is linked in "The Life to Come," as it is in a number of the early short stories, with the corruption (or "economic development") of the natural environment. "Civilization," in the ironic sense which allows it to be represented by the expanding conurbation of London in *Howards End* and by the British Raj in *A Passage to India,* is destructive of the natural balance in which the challenger's innocence flourishes. Civilization in this sense can be justified only as providing remedies for problems, but Forster suggests that the problems exist only in the eyes of the civilized or as a result of their own activities. "Can't you grasp," says Pinmay to Vithobai, with magnificent irony, "that under God's permission certain evils attend civilization, but that if men do God's will the remedies for the evils keep pace? Five years ago you had not a single hospital in this valley." When Vithobai protests that neither had they had any disease, Pinmay can only point out that there were the diseases of "vice and superstition" (*LTC.* 104).

Vithobai is presented as initially in close association with his natural environment, much like Stephen in Wiltshire. His hut built over the roots of an aged tree, a tree with significance comparable to that of the trees in **"The Road to Colonus"** and **"The Other Kingdom."** After his conversion, and as a result of it, the forests are cut down and much of the land taken over for mining. As the environment decays, so does Vithobai, becoming lethargic, drab, diminished is status, and eventually terminally ill.

As Vithobai lies dying there is a moment of partial reconciliation between the two men. Pinmay tries to explain his feelings about the episode in the hut and feels the longing to "do something human" for his former friend (*LTC.* 110). Having explained himself, he asks forgiveness. Although Pinmay is a much lesser character than Fielding, and is much more plainly "to blame" for the sad events of his story, there is nonetheless some similarity between this partial reconciliation and that between Cyril and Aziz. The white man in each case explains his actions, while the native still feels that the basis of their original friendship has been betrayed.

The ending of the story, in which Vithobai, himself close to death, kills Pinmay, appears to be a new twist to the plot, since no previous challenger has murdered his hero. The appearance, however, is deceptive and needs closer scrutiny. Vithobai's purpose in killing Pinmay is not only revenge but also spiritual reunion in "the life to come." The murder is an expression not of pure hostility but of corrupted love. A similar element of antagonism, arising from the hero's failure to respond to the love he has evoked from the challenger, can be traced in many of the earlier stories. Stephen, albeit unwittingly, is the cause of Rickie's death, and heroes suffer comparable symbolic deaths at the endings of **"Albergo Empedocle," "The Other Side of the Hedge,"** and **"The Machine Stops."** Hostility between hero and challenger on account of the hero's defection in the middle section of the plot is Forster's norm, and there are no stories in which the two characters survive in unalloyed amity at the end.

"The Life to Come" exhibits the usual three-phase movement; the hero's initial approach to the challenger (here covered retrospectively in the opening paragraph), the middle section of reaction and separation, and the closing movement (in this case heavily ironic) towards reconciliation. The story's title and ending emphasize that, as in some of the early "fantasies," a perfect accord between hero and challenger can be reached only in another world, a point which is repeated in the next story, **"Dr Woolacott."**

"The Life to Come" is the first of the small collection of late short stories with explicitly sexual—and mostly homosexual—themes, stories which Forster preserved but did not publish. Because of the clear similarity between the circumstances within these stories and those within the novels (the similarity in this case, for example, between Pinmay and Vithobai on the one hand and Cyril and Aziz on the other), it becomes tempting to search for latent homosexual elements in corresponding places in the plots of the published works (between Cyril and Aziz in *A Passage to India,* for instance). This activity, harmless enough, will at least yield a list of interesting observations (for instance, the number of "bedroom scenes" between males in the published novels); but it becomes pernicious when, knowing as we now do Forster's own homosexual preferences, we adopt the Freudian view that the published stories, in which the homosexual element may be said to be "repressed," may be somehow lacking in an area in which the explicitly homosexual stories are more complete. The fact remains that Forster's explicitly sexual stories, including *Maurice,* fail to achieve the level and intensity of his published novels and of most of his published short stories.

The element of explicit homosexuality does not change the structure or moral balance of Forster's plots. The homosexuality invariably subsists between the challenger and the hero; and its presence merely contributes to the tension, already built into the earlier plots, between the conflicting demands of natural freedom and conventional social expectations. The "guilt" Pinmay feels at having entered into a sexual relationship with Vithobai may be more severe but is not radically different in purpose from the shame Rickie experiences on discovering that Stephen is his illegitimate half-brother, or Lucy's embarrassment at first being kissed by George. In his fiction Forster employs homosexuality as one among the several areas across which conventional barriers have been erected, along with such others as friendship, heterosexuality and sympathy.

In **"The Life to Come"** the practice of homosexuality is an image of freedom from conventional restraints, restraints which are in this story represented chiefly by evangelical Christianity.[1] In the next story, **"Dr Woolacott,"** written in 1927,[2] these restraints are represented as medical. The hero, Clesant, is ordered by his doctor, Woolacott, to avoid any kind of emotional or physical exertion, including particularly "intimacy" (i.e. sexual relationships). Clesant is not quite content with this regime, since he occasionally wants to do such things as play the violin, which is forbidden him; but in general he accepts Woolacott's directions until he meets an attractive farm laborer who offers him "intimacy." Clesant is on the verge of responding when the recollection of Woolacott causes a reaction.

> Clesant had often been proud of his disease but never, never of his body, it had never occurred to him that he could provoke desire. The sudden revelation shattered

him, he fell from his pedestal, but not alone, there was someone to cling to, broad shoulders, a sunburnt throat, lips that parted as they touched him to murmur—"And to hell with Woolacott."

> Woolacott! He had completely forgotten the doctor's existence. Woolacott! The word crashed between them and exploded with a sober light, and he saw in the light of the years that had passed and would come how ridiculously he was behaving

> (*LTC.* 119).

The hero is now in the usual Forsterian dilemma, caught between the demands of his emotional impulse to connect with the outsider who offers him friendship and, on the other hand, the requirements of the code by which he has lived hitherto.

Cleasant begins to argue with his new friend, and in the course of their discussion two points emerge: first that, from the laborer's point of view, Woolacott is not only not a good doctor but is actually dangerous, and secondly that the laborer, from the point of view of conventional society, is a guilty man. We are given no specifics of either case; we never find out the nature of either Woolacott's incompetence or the laborer's crime. The details do not matter, since the story is an allegory. Woolacott may preserve life in a narrow, materialistic sense, but he does so at a spiritual price which the challenger cannot accept. The challenger himself is by his very nature "guilty" in the eyes of Woolacott, much as Aziz is considered guilty even before trial by the Anglo-Indians.

The situation among Clesant, the laborer, and Woolacott is thus an allegorical representation of that among hero, challenger, and villain in the novels, with the hero caught between the opposing values of the other two. As Clesant reacts against the challenger and resigns himself into the hands of nurses and servants (Woolacott's agents), the laborer at first suffers from fear of persecution and eventually disappears, his very existence being denied by the nurses. His voice continues to plead, however, in Clesant's mind, and as Woolacott himself arrives on the scene Clesant relents and hides the laborer (whose physical reality is now reestablished) in his bed as a symbolic affirmation of their union. Consequently when Woolacott examines the patient he finds him "dead."

Woolacott is "life's universal lord" (*LTC.* 126), the preserver of life, but of life in the negative sense in which Shelley uses the term in *The Triumph of Life* or in the famous stanza 52 of *Adonais.* Woolacott represents a spiritually restricted life, subject to conventional restraints and lived much as Mrs. Herriton, Herbert, and Henry live life. Life in this sense is incompatible with the liberal values of the challenger, and therefore, like Pinmay, Clesant has to die if he is to win freedom.

Whereas **"Dr Woolacott"** presents us with a miniature version of the Forsterian three-phase plot, **"Arthur Snatchfold"** stops short. In this story, written in 1928, the three central character-types are again in evidence—a hero (Conway), a group of repressive villains (the country magistrates, of whom Trevor Donaldson is the most prominent), and the challenger (Snatchfold)—but there is no second meeting between the hero and the friendly milkman. The story ends at the point where, as a result of his (homosexual) encounter with the hero, the challenger is being persecuted by the establishment, being subjected, rather like Aziz, to trial and imprisonment on a charge of sexual misconduct. The hero hears of the trial only later and is not involved in it. He reacts with sadness and sobriety, but with this reaction the story stops; there is evidently no likelihood that Conway will meet Snatchfold again or make any move to alleviate his distress.

The characters belong to types by now familiar. Donaldson and his like have much in common with the Wilcoxes, wealthy, dominating and generally shallow people imposing themselves with little real success upon the traditional framework of English country society. Snatchfold is only thinly drawn, but his working-class background, his geniality, his willingness to defy the law, and the carelessness which results in his eventually being caught and punished, put him clearly in the class of Stephen, Leonard, Scudder, and the unnamed laborer in **"Dr Woolacott."** Conway is an older version of the usual hero, an unattached male, well established as a member of the conventional group, but secretly discontented and seeking for something more in life, something which he finds temporarily in the challenger.

This ironic and pregnant little story emphasizes two particular points, both of which can be traced significantly in most of the longer works. First it shows clearly the hero's responsibility for the sufferings of the relatively innocent challenger. Conway, like Cyril and Margaret, takes the initiative in forming a casual relationship with a social inferior, as a result of which that individual later comes to grief. Second, the way in which Snatchfold, at some cost to himself, conceals Conway's part in the affair and so protects him, shows the true nobility of the character. We are reminded of Gennaro's sacrifice for Eustace, of Leonard's urge to apologize to Margaret (at the cost, it turns out, of his life), and of the natural generosity of Aziz, including his eventual forgiveness of Adela.

The next three surviving stories—**"The Classical Annex," "What Does It Matter?"** and **"The Obelisk"**—all belonging probably to the 1930's, are light-hearted sexual comedies. They share with Forster's more serious work something of the fundamental dualism, the conflict between convention and liberalism, between restraint and license; but they are concerned, like classical and Shakespearian comedy, to burst the bonds of repression with wit and laughter. There is nothing here of the moral tension experienced by the succession of Forsterian heroes, and indeed these stories have no true heroes or heroines. They belong, like **"The Helping Hand,"** in a different, lesser genre from that of the novels and other short stories.

**"The Torque"** (which may have been written as late as 1959) has a hero, Marcian, who stands, a little like Pinmay, between the two worlds of asexual Roman Christianity and primitive pagan vitality. There is here, as in **"The Life to Come"** and at many points elsewhere in Forster's fiction, a good deal of fun at the expense of religious hypocrisy. Institutionalized religion figures here as the body of orthodoxy from which the hero eventually revolts, and its agents, Perpetua and the Bishop, are the story's villains. The challenger is Euric who, as a Goth, is hostile to Roman civilization in general, and who, as a virile homosexual male, is hostile in particular to the social morals of Christian society. The story therefore has the central characters of the usual Forsterian plot, but it remains a slight piece because little is done with them. Marcian clearly dislikes the repressive Christianity of his sister, but he abandons it with neither effort nor difficulty. The story lacks Forster's usual depth of conflict and makes its simple point with a heavy hand.

**"The Other Boat"** is probably the latest of Forster's fictional works, and it is the only piece of non-comic writing of his to have survived from the last forty years of his life. Its composition, however, spanned several decades, the first part, the "childhood" episode, having been drafted around 1913 as a possible opening for a novel, and the remainder written in 1958. It is the most substantial of the posthumously published short stories and shows that Forster had by no means lost his touch thirty-five years after finishing *A Passage to India.*

The hero is Lionel March, a young officer returning by boat to join his regiment and his fiancée in India. The underlying tension, as in *A Passage to India,* is created by the racial prejudices of the Anglo-Indians, exacerbated by the fact that March's association with the native challenger, in this case a half-caste named Moraes, is not only friendly but also homosexual. March meets Moraes at the beginning of the voyage, and when circumstances result in their sharing a cabin they become lovers. After a time March has second thoughts and remorsefully remembers his mother, his fiancée, and his place among his own people. When he tells Moraes of his intention to end the relationship there is a violent lovers' quarrel in which Moraes is killed. March then drowns himself, and the story ends with the disapproval of his mother and English fellow-passengers when the circumstances are discovered.

The characters are broadly true to Forster's established types. March is rather naive, with an open disposition but a limited, conventional upbringing. We learn a lot about his background, not only that he once played as a child with Moraes (on the "other boat") but also that he has fought in a colonial war and killed a "savage," an act of mindless bravery which won him respect and promotion among the whites. Although he slips easily into friendship with Moraes, he soon suffers a reaction of guilt, a guilt associated particularly with his mental image of his mother. Like Rickie, he is the product of a "broken home," his father having set the precedent, which Lionel abhors but almost follows, of deserting his own people and "going native." Much of the depth of the story consists in the interaction of these conflicting background influences—his mother, his career, his childhood friendship, his father's notorious example—as March moves first towards and then away from the challenger.

Moraes turns out to be wealthy, much more affluent than March, and a successful man of the world. This makes him seem at first unusual among challengers, who are generally either downtrodden, like Leonard, or cheerfully unworldly, like Stephen and Arthur Snatchfold. He is nonetheless still treated as inferior by the English on account of his color, and the usual hint of persecution comes in towards the end when Colonel Arbuthnot plans to make official trouble for him in Bombay. In common with other challengers he has a genial, attractive personality, a lively simplicity which made him a pleasant playfellow as a child and which makes him an engaging companion as an adult. He has something of the generosity of Aziz, being anxious to shower his white friend with gifts and to spend money freely for their mutual entertainment.

Like other challengers Moraes has a negative side when seen from a conventional point of view. He is amoral and unscrupulous, showing no shame and convinced that he can bribe his way through any situation. (It is his use of bribes which lays him open to the wrath of Colonel Arbuthnot.) The legality of his business dealings is suspect, and he cheerfully discloses to the shocked March that he possesses two different passports. Even as a child he had an uninhibited openness which appeared as rudeness to illiberal adults, arousing strong antipathy. Mrs. March, on no ground beyond instinctive antipathy, holds him responsible for the death of her youngest child.

The story is a tragic one, and the lines of conflict are even more sharply drawn than in *A Passage to India*, where tragedy is averted. Lionel, although emotionally drawn to Moraes, is building a career upon such deeds as the killing of black men, while Moraes is held responsible by March's mother for the death of his brother. The two men agree that these factors shall not

inhibit their friendship, but March is unable to avoid second thoughts. There is no reconciliation in this story, as there is in most of Forster's fiction. (Even **"The Life to Come"** has in its ending the positive note of possible union in a better world.) When March returns to Moraes after his walk among his own people on deck the outcome is not understanding but mutual destruction. Forster's last story is also his most grim.

*Notes*

1. Forster, rather like Shelley, appears to have admired the spirit of Christianity (he refers, for instance, to the "marvellous chapter" of I Cor.13 in *LTC*. 96), but to have detested its institutions.

2. Dates for Forster's late short stories are taken from Oliver Stallybrass's Introduction to *The Life to Come and Other Stories* originally published in 1972.

*References*

References in the text are to the editions of Forster's novels and stories currently published by Penguin Books. The titles are abbreviated as follows:

*AFT: Where Angels Fear to Tread*

*LJ: The Longest Journey*

*RV: A Room With a View*

*HE: Howards End*

*M: Maurice*

*PI: A Passage to India*

*CSS: Collected Short Stories*

*LTC: The Life to Come and Other Stories*

### Tamera Dorland (essay date fall 1995)

SOURCE: Dorland, Tamera. "'Contrary to the Prevailing Current'? Homoeroticism and the Voice of Maternal Law in Forster's 'The Other Boat.'" *Style* 29, no. 3 (fall 1995): 474-97.

[*In the following essay, Dorland suggests that Forster's "The Other Boat" reveals his ambivalence toward breaking away completely from the Edwardian point of view expressed in his earlier works.*]

In his posthumously published **"The Other Boat"** (1972), E. M. Forster seeks to transform proscribed desire into a "confession of the flesh."[1] Captain Lionel March's "stumbling confession" and "open avowal" of having "'fallen for'" his bunkmate Cocoanut (**"Other Boat"** 186-87) attests to Foucault's rather poetic claim in "A Preface to Transgression" that sexuality exposes "the limit of language, since it traces that line of foam showing just how far speech may advance upon the sands of silence" (*Language* 30). Liminally caught between speech and silence, confession and suppression, the narrative disclosure of Lionel March's "tribal" transgressions against Victorian puritanism and British imperialism adheres, in Foucault's words, to "the authority of a language that had been carefully expurgated so that [sex] was no longer directly named" but was relentlessly "tracked down" (*History* 20). In spite of its post-Victorian context, a rhetoric of indirection and discretion still inscribes the narrative's scenes of illicit homoerotic intercourse between the quintessential British officer and a "wog" (**"Other Boat"** 175). In effect, this discrepancy between literary form and pornographic content constitutes an "open avowal" that belies its own openness.

In his critique of Forster's typescript of *Maurice* in *Christopher and His Kind,* Christopher Isherwood personally notes in 1932 that his "Master's" prudish or "antique locutions bothered him, here and there," while he concedes that "the wonder of the novel was that it had been written when it had been written; the wonder was Forster himself, imprisoned within the jungle of pre-war prejudice, putting these unthinkable thoughts into words" (126). More than four decades after having completed the original draft of *Maurice* in 1913,[2] Forster appears "imprisoned" by continued prejudice and post-war proscriptions against homosexuality. In **"The Other Boat,"** primarily composed during 1957 and 1958, the author still betrays a reluctance to let go of "antique locutions" that essentially expurgate the language but not the contents of the carnal narrative. Fashioned by conventions of euphemism and circumlocution, narrative descriptions of the captain's acts of sodomy and eventual homicide ironically seem to "date" themselves, despite the author's "franker declaration" of his "faith" (Isherwood 126).[3] In the successive scenes of the lovers' illicit intercourse "below deck," the narrator on the one hand counts on concrete referents that obliquely expose yet mock the squeamish enterprise of finding figurative substitutes for depictions of sexual excitement, as in the following image suggesting intercourse: "Pop went a cork and hit the partition wall. Sounds of feminine protest became audible, and they [Lionel and Cocoanut] both laughed" (**"Other Boat"** 178). On the other hand, the narrator purges the erotic plot of concrete reference and clear personal agency by embedding descriptions of physical orgasm and coitus in mystic abstractions. For instance, the narrative reads, presumably from Cocoanut's perspective: "Meanwhile the other one, the deep one, watched. To him the moment of ecstasy was sometimes the moment of vision, and his cry of delight when they closed had wavered into fear" (178). Marked thus by shifts in tone and focalization, Forster's narrative vacillates between identi-

fying the various stages of homosexual intercourse and providing a screen for its pornographic content through a stylistics of evasion. Such subterfuge in turn mirrors the secrecy Lionel himself must vigilantly secure about his deviation from the normative ideal—from being "what any *rising* young officer ought to be" in the context of a threatened British imperialism (**"Other Boat"** 171; my emphasis). This subterfuge above all reflects the officer's wary concealment of his transgression from the British sahibs and memsahibs of the story proper.

The parliamentary resistance to accepting recommendations of *The Wolfenden Report of the Departmental Committee on Homosexual Offenses and Prostitution,* initiated in 1954 and published in 1957,[4] reveals the stylistic subterfuge of **"The Other Boat"** as an element of Forster's necessary concealment of "'a wrong channel for [his] pen'" (Forster, *Life* xii). In his biographical introduction to Forster's *The Life to Come,* Oliver Stallybrass offers an excerpt from Forster's diary, dated 8 April 1922, in which the author confesses that he has "this moment burnt [his] indecent writings" (xii). Whether apocryphal or not, this confession refers to the bulk of his pornographic stories, yet excludes his novel *Maurice,* which nonetheless remained unpublished until 1971, a year after Forster's death. Characterizing these "indecent writings" as clogs to his development as a recognized novelist, Forster refers to them as a channel for personal excitement rather than literary expression (xii).[5] Originally composed for a novel, the early pages of **"The Other Boat"** were drafted about 1913, during approximately the same period, says Norman Page, as Forster's initial completion of *Maurice* and his first incomplete start with *A Passage to India* (54). Clearly, these early pages were not among those burned writings, which, as Forster explains, included only "as many as the fire [would] take" (*Life* xii). Presumably abandoned until 1948, the initial fragment of **"The Other Boat"** was published under the titles **"Entrance to an Unwritten Novel"** in *The Listener* (23 December 1948) and **"Cocoanut & Co.: Entrance to an Abandoned Novel"** in the *New York Times Book Review* (6 February 1949).[6] Providing the groundwork for the first section of the completed **"Other Boat,"** both publications focus on the childhood encounter of Lionel and Cocoanut on the original or "other boat," but neither features their later homoerotic exchange as adults on the second boat. As the "abandoned" novel evolves into its final form as a story, **"The Other Boat"** acquires four additional sections that reconstruct the events precipitating Lionel's lapse from rigid British propriety into interracial and homosexual "abandon." While the novel-fragment provides the origins for the reunion of the British captain and "the wog" as adults, the ensuing four sections developing from this brief childhood interaction confirm retroactively the illicit sexuality that lies at and threatens the very surface of a colonial past played out in the voices of "little boys" who don "paper cocked hats" and die "stiffly" as proud soldiers. More-over, the voice of the abandoned mother, so important in the completed story, can also be heard as she attempts to keep such play within bounds of "what is customary" and proper (166).

With the "passage" of the Aryan officer and homosexual, Captain Lionel March, on board the *S. S. Normannia,*[7] Forster ultimately constructs a narrative that violates and in turn reveals the moral boundaries defined by an absent yet repressive England. Even when concealed from public readership until its posthumous publication in 1972, this five-sectioned story betrays the author's ambivalence toward breaking fully with the Edwardian voice of his published novels. I argue this in spite of James Creech's recent suggestion that Forster "overtly claimed" to try "to speak unprophylactically from, for, or about a homosexual subject position" (54). In *Closet Writing/Gay Reading,* Creech bases his assertion on Forster's contention that he wrote the earlier "indecent" stories of *The Life to Come* "not to express myself but to excite myself" (Creech 55; Forster, *Life* xii). Using the author's testimony against aesthetic intent, Creech speculates: "to state the obvious, what would Forster's stories themselves have resembled if, in the writing itself, he had felt compelled to perform the prophylactic function which, as it turned out, fell to the homophobic intellectual?" (55). While the homosexual subject matter of **"The Other Boat"** signifies a resistance toward performing "the prophylactic function," I submit that Forster's enduring stylistics of indirection and abstraction suggests otherwise. I propose, rather, that it is the mother, "Mater," or imperial memsahib who is posited as an agent of the son's conscience and Law; her ostensibly marginal yet critical position in all five sections of the story signals the figurative presence of a cautionary agency that still inhibits attempts to confess or "speak unprophylactically" in the "homosexual subject position." In effect, with the mother's presence as an indirect arbiter of imperialist and British propriety, Captain March's "open avowal" proves instead a "stumbling confession" that never loses sight of the heterosexual or "homophobic intellectual."

From an orthodox perspective on morality, the fatal resolution to the homoerotic plot of **"The Other Boat"** conforms to contemporaneous proscriptions against homosexuality. By contrast, Forster's *Maurice* unconventionally provides a "happy ending" of bucolic exile for its homosexual lovers. In its well-known "Terminal Note" (1960), dated nearly a half-century after the novel's original completion in 1913 and a decade before its posthumous publication in 1971, the author characterizes this "keynote" of "[h]appiness" as a virtual "crime." Despite societal demands for retribution, the lovers manage to evade punishment by way of a more permissive fiction that allows them "still [to] roam the green-wood" existing beyond the boundaries of the law and

the printed text (*Maurice* 250). The final form of **"The Other Boat"** offers the alternate ending that Forster rejects for *Maurice.* In his retrospective "Note" to that novel, he reflects on the unhappy finale that might have led to earlier publication: "If it ended unhappily, with a lad dangling from a noose or with a suicide pact, all would be well, for there is no pornography or seduction of minors" (250). Addressing the demands of the orthodox reader, Forster's story does conclude unhappily, with the murder of the seductive "wog" and the suicide of the transgressive officer. In spite of the discretion of its language, the story nonetheless works against these demands and violates a condition of publishability because of the pornographic content it implies.

In effect, **"The Other Boat"** bears the long-standing legacy of Victorian vigilance over sexual normalization, namely that of bourgeois heterosexuality. Its focus on Lionel's deviation documents Foucault's claim that homosexuality responded with a "reverse" discourse: "homosexuality began to speak in its own behalf, to demand that its legitimacy or 'naturality' be acknowledged, often in the same vocabulary, using the same categories by which it was medically disqualified" (*History* 101). The narrative confessions of Lionel's sexual transgression thus reflect the indirection, if not ambi-direction, of the post-Freudian writer's attempt to write within yet against a heritage of sexual conduct paradoxically characterized by "an injunction to silence" and an "incitement to speak" the truth of sexuality (*History* 4, 18). The posthumous publication of **"The Other Boat"** (not to mention that of *Maurice* and the remaining stories of buggery in *The Life to Come*) testifies to Forster's own inability to transgress publicly the boundaries of a social conscience or repression signified by an England most notably represented by the maternal figure. Thus, Forster's final censorship of any direct evidence of Lionel March's homosexual activities parallels the author's necessary suppression of these homoerotic texts from his record of conventional literary publications.

While Captain March's disclosure of homosexual transgression tests and exposes the limits of British codes of normative sexuality, it also reveals the extent to which the officer's conscience is held in check by the chaste and chastising mother. The maternal image of Mrs. March hence becomes both sign of and impetus for suppression. But it is through her son's guilt-ridden projection that she ultimately personifies both individual and British social conscience. Allotted a peripheral part in the actual plot, she nonetheless proves to be a potent phantasm of her transgressive son's tormented psyche, an image signifying both repressed desire and repressive prohibition. As the preoedipal and post-oedipal single parent, Mrs. March is still identified only by her marital and maternal names; by virtue of her procreating in the name of the father, she secures a position in the symbolic order that formally locates her on the side of the socio-symbolic community.[8] Absent from the social and family structure because of his own transgression of "tribal" codes of propriety, Lionel's father exists in name only since the patrilineal surname alone survives, the father's Christian name having been expunged from social discourse because of his disgraceful abandonment of this community. On board the *S. S. Normannia*, such community and "tribal" order are chiefly held in check by an *ad hoc* group of British passengers who, reports Lionel in his correspondence with his mother, "make up two Bridge tables every night besides hanging together at other times, and get called the Big Eight, which I suppose must be regarded as a compliment" (171).[9] Referring to the "Big Eight" as a gauge for social propriety and an agency of exclusion, Lionel relates to Cocoanut how his own name has been purged of his father's identity: "He has made our name stink in these parts. As it is I've had to change my name, or rather drop half of it. He called himself Major Corrie March. We were all proud of the 'Corrie' and had reason to be. Try saying 'Corrie March' to the Big Eight here, and watch the effect" (183-84).

Aboard the "other boat," Mrs. March must assume single-handedly the central position as parent and sign of the socio-symbolic community. Confronted with an endangered family order, she alone must preserve a semblance of social harmony and structure and uphold the law of prohibition against so-called "pathological" sexualities. In this narrative context, the name of the mother (or *nom de la mère,* if you will) comes to signify conscience, the Law, or the Phallus.[10] This signification, however, is not based on a direct representation of the mother; rather, it derives from the fatherless son's reconstruction of her as a "phallic mother." Paraphrasing Lacan, Jane Gallop characterizes this conception of the mother as "the silent interlocutor, the second person who never assumes the first person pronoun, . . . the subject presumed to know, the object of transference" (115). In the last four sections of **"The Other Boat,"** Mrs. March, as the phallicized mother, never directly assumes the first-person subject position, in spite of her socio-symbolic position as the central parent. (Only the childhood scene of the first section offers an unmediated presentation of Mrs. March among her children; located at the very beginning of the second section, Lionel's overseas correspondence to the "Mater" instantly signals the disappearance of her physical presence from the narrative.[11]) Textually, she represents the "silent interlocutor" or "second person" that harrows the adult son's conscience, but she does so with a voice projected only in terms of an indirect subjectivity focalized through either the son or the narrator. Invoking the figure of the mother, this narrative of sexual transgression fabricates a dialogic relation between son and mother that reflects the "Idea of Mother and Son" Forster explained in his 1930 entry in *Commonplace Book*:

> She dominates him in youth. Manhood brings him emancipation—perhaps through friendship or a happy marriage. But the mother is waiting. Her vitality depends on character, and asserts itself as the sap drains out of him. She gets her way and reestablishes his childhood, with the difference that his subjection is conscious now and causes him humiliation and pain. Is her tyranny conscious? I think not. Could the same relationship occur between father and daughter? No.
>
> (55)

Ultimately, the mother-son relationship proves to be as tyrannical between son and conscience as between self and culture, because the narrative of Lionel March reconstitutes the biological mother as an internalized voice of conscience. Although unconscious of "her tyranny," the "waiting" mother inhabits and inhibits "the great blank country" (**"Other Boat"** 193) of the son's textual "confession of the flesh" (*History* 19). As disembodied voice and Paternal/Maternal sign of conscience, the marginalized mother of Freudian psychoanalytics symbolically delineates the limits of the discourse of sexual transgression. In this sense, the "confession of flesh" in Forster's text effectively fixes on the indivisible dyad of transgressive son and symbolic mother—of son and an inescapable Maternal Law reinforcing the limits of Victorian England, that censorial and far-reaching "blank country."

As the silent interlocutor, the figure of the mother in **"The Other Boat"** signifies an absolute arbiter of culture through whom the transgressive son condemns or harrows himself. In *Freud and the Crisis of Our Culture,* Lionel Trilling locates this dialogue or "standing quarrel" between the modern self and culture/mother within a broader literary context (58). Crediting "the layman Freud" with the notion that the self is implicated in the culture and "that the surrogates of culture are established in the mind itself," Trilling elaborates: "By what he said or suggested of the depth and subtlety of the influence of the family upon the individual, he made plain how the culture suffuses the remotest parts of the individual mind, being taken in almost literally with the mother's milk" (36-37). Trilling figuratively defines the lactating mother as the nurturing agent of cultural suffusion; he further characterizes the Freudian and post-Freudian self as one who ambivalently resists yet submits to culture as an absolute (or surrogate God) by which the self is constituted and judged (58).[12] Forster's Lionel March, through his own narrative and psychical "standing quarrels," exposes the extent to which the "surrogates of culture" become irrevocably implanted in the "remotest parts of the individual mind," quite literally through the Freudianized trope of the mother.[13]

As a biographical parallel with the mother-son dialectic between Lionel and Mrs. March, Forster perceives his own mother as the source of his repression as a writer.

In a letter dated 10 August 1915, the thirty-six-year-old author equates the presence of his mother (or his infantilized presence within her household) to a form of writer's block:

> I am leading the life of a little girl so long as I am tied to home. It isn't even as if I make mother happy by stopping—she is always wanting me to be 5 years old again, so happiness is obviously impossible for her, and she never realises that the cardinal fact in my life is my writing, and that at present I am not writing.
>
> (1: 229)

In this instance, the maternal figure not only signifies an obstacle to the identity and development of the adult male (the "little girl" possibly suggesting a counterpart to Freud's "little man" in his discussion of the initial stages of female development), but also as an obstacle to those of the author. Biographically, this role links the topos of "the great blank country" with Lionel's repressed sexuality and with Forster's blank pages while living at home, for the mother's presence is targeted as a direct agent of the son's inhibition and self-censorship.

As testimony to Freud's influence, the narrative of **"The Other Boat"** essentially posits Mrs. March as the center of Lionel's continual negotiations between a "long long ago" of colonial and sexual innocence and a fallen present marked by his turn away from those ideal codes of decorum that putatively held such innocence in check. Captain March's "stumbling confession" in effect manifests two conflicting desires. His first desire is to continue with his culture; therefore, he maintains a link with his mother through overseas correspondence and secures social ties with the British caste, the Big Eight, through participation in their nightly bridge games. Conversely, his second desire is to go against the sexual and racial codes of his imperialist caste—that is, it is a desire to "see England recede" not only from the horizon but from his psyche (175). In a figurative sense, the contrary directions of the two boats reflect the officer's contrary responses to being "stabled" with a "dago," a set-up that is "too damn awkward for words" (174). In the story's first section, the original or "other boat" of a nostalgic past travels the Red Sea with its bow directed toward the motherland; in the last four sections, the *S. S. Normannia* journeys through the same waters, but in the opposite direction, with its stern turned on England. With either direction, the imperial motherland remains a geographical and, above all, cultural or moral referent of which the Aryan officer never loses clear sight. The opposing directions of the two boats toward and away from England, although separated by a ten-year gap, parallel Captain March's own ambivalence toward those British precepts of "tribal" decorum he chooses to turn his back on. Whereas his first home-bound passage grounds his cultural conscience in the maternal injunction to "play properly" at

soldiering, the second passage during early adulthood documents the extent to which repressive ties to past lessons are inseverable for the officer/homosexual. Critical to a psychoanalytic consideration of the narrative, the opening section from childhood offers a direct context for the reminiscences Lionel later has of his mother as she censures Cocoanut for his immoral influence on "her doomed offspring" (169). This first section consequently provides the foundation for Lionel's internal conflicts between an awakened or induced (homo)sexuality and an inescapable conscience represented by the embedded voice of his mother.

Since Mr. March had abandoned the family or ship, so to speak, and gone "native somewhere out East" (183), the childhood scene suggests a preoedipal or imaginary stage during which the mother-son relationship appears unchallenged by paternal authority. The authority of the abandoned mother over her children is nonetheless challenged by a prevailing patriarchal or masculine order that strictly observes gender divisions in terms of territorial space:

> A sailor—an Englishman—leapt out of the hatchway with a piece of chalk and drew a little circle round her where she stood. Cocoanut screamed, "He's caught you. He's come."
>
> "You're on dangerous ground, lady," said the sailor respectfully. "Men's quarters. Of course we leave it to your generosity."
>
> Tired with the voyage and the noise of the children, worried by what she had left in India and might find in England, Mrs. March fell into a sort of trance. She stared at the circle stupidly, unable to move out of it, while Cocoanut danced round her and gibbered.
>
> (170)

As sole responsible parent, Mrs. March must serve as both nurturer and head of the household; yet, based on "what is customary," she is barred from following her sons into "Men's quarters" (170). In this first and fleeting staging of Mrs. March, the narrative selectively portrays her restricted role as both mother and father in a society that upholds "the old custom" of distinguishing "ladies" from "gentlemen" by rigidly preserving masculine territory (170). As the only direct presentation of her more human aspects, this scene reveals her fatigue as the abandoned parent, along with her apparently unquestioning surrender to custom. Her relative helplessness against the "independent" though "rapacious" English sailor and the gibbering Cocoanut clearly signals her ineffectual authority over her son's later seduction into "dangerous ground." By contrast with this perspective on the mother, in which her paternal authority is temporarily undermined, the narrative's earlier view exposes a less compassionate and relenting figure. Shifting from distant third-person narrative to free-indirect discourse, the narrator characterizes Mrs. March's familial and moral concerns in terms of a high-browed imperialist racism: "A clergyman's daughter and a soldier's wife, she could not admit that Christianity had ever been oriental. What good thing can come out of the Levant, and is it likely that the apostles ever had a touch of the tar-brush?" (169). This caricature implicitly echoes the discussion by Mahmoud Ali and Aziz of a Mrs. Turton, whose "haughty and venal" supremacism characterizes the "average" Englishwoman in *A Passage to India* (9). Purporting to represent Mrs. March's internal thoughts, which are signaled by a shift to a relatively informal or colloquial tone, the narrator establishes her as a model of moral and racial, if not supremacist, conscience, the basis for Lionel's guilty consciousness of British propriety. But Mrs. March never directly voices a distinct imperialist stance; her imperative to "play properly" and her commitment to doing "what is customary" nevertheless reinforce this severe stereotype of the Englishwoman and diminish her relative leniency towards her children's playing with Cocoanut during the voyage outside the formal boundaries of British territory (169-70).

As the progenitor of "doomed offspring" and agent of family dishonor and shame, Lionel's father remains a covert topic of conversation in the adult sections of **"The Other Boat."** In his place, Lionel has posited his mother as the voice of authority ("Mother said so" [166]) that attempts but fails to shield her vulnerable children from a potentially hostile environment and threatened colonial world. He addresses her as the "Mater" and endows her with an omnipotence projected not through her own minimal actions within the narrative, but through his intensification and recuperation of her controlling image from his own repressive conscience—a conscience founded on the highly emblematic childhood scene of the first section. In line with her initial characterization as a racist, Forster's account of the adult Lionel casts Mrs. March as an Arachne spinning entangling "filaments" as extensive as British imperialism:[14]

> [B]ehind the Army, was another power, whom he could not consider calmly: his mother, blind-eyed in the midst of the enormous web she had spun—filaments drifting everywhere, strands catching. There was no reasoning with her or about her, she understood nothing and controlled everything. She had suffered too much and was too high-minded to be judged like other people, she was outside carnality and incapable of pardoning it. . . . From the great blank country she inhabited came a voice condemning him and all her children for sin, but condemning him most. There was no parleying with her—she was a voice. God had not granted her ears—nor could she see, mercifully: the sight of him stripping would have killed her. He, her first-born, set apart for the redemption of the family name.
>
> (193)

Lionel March renders his own mother as unresponsive and "catching" as the image of a Mother Hag, perhaps resembling Pound's depiction of England as "an old bitch" in "Hugh Selwyn Mauberley." This potent yet misogynist trope links with an earlier brief allusion to an imagined threat of castration occurring when, left alone, Cocoanut covers his nakedness in fear of the hag: "Jealous of what she sees, the hag comes with her scimitar" (191-92).[15] The potential castration or emasculation of male characters in turn parallels the masculinization of female characters. Whereas the narrator reveals that Lionel was "nearly unmanned" by a past battle injury (179) and Cocoanut is proclaimed "unmanly" by an angered Mrs. March (170),[16] a female member of the Big Eight is notably named "Lady Manning" and Mrs. March must assume the absent father's role within the March family, not to mention the role or "voice" of imperialist conscience and racial and moral propriety.

Because of her son's conflicts with his conscience, Mrs. March is both aligned with "the great blank country she inhabited" and reduced to a disembodied "voice" from the past. She thus symbolizes untainted British propriety, purity, and omnipotence, ideals of the Empire (and perhaps a carry-over of the "*divina virago,*" Queen Elizabeth I[17]) that his own sexuality transgresses. Characterizing his mother as having "suffered too much" and as being "too high-minded," Lionel envisions her as a type of *Mater dolorosa* who appears both immune to and therefore unforgiving of "carnality," especially that involving a "wog" or "half-caste." As an obverse image of the father, who, as Lionel euphemistically asserts, "went native" (183), she is imagined by Lionel as witnessing and passing merciless judgment on his acts of sexual transgression. Because of her moralistic stance, he remains conscious of jeopardizing both personal and genealogical redemption, his own chastity previously atoning for his father's "unspeakable" sin. Lionel's homosexual and interracial copulation with the "half-caste" Cocoanut retroactively informs the expression, "He went native." In mocking his lover's hypocritical resistance to acknowledging the possible details of his father's transgression, Cocoanut suggests Lionel's father's defection may have been as illicit as Lionel's own when he asks whether the man went

> "With a girl or with a boy?"
>
> "A boy? Good God! Well, I mean to say, with a girl, naturally—I mean, it was somewhere right away in the depths of Burma."
>
> "Even in Burma there are boys. At least I once heard so. But the Dad went native with a girl. Ver' well. Might not therefore there be offspring?"
>
> "If there were, they'd be half-castes. Pretty depressing prospect. Well, you know what I mean. My family— Dad's, that's to say—can trace itself back nearly two

hundred years, and the Mater's goes back to the War of Roses. It's really pretty awful, Cocoa."

The half-caste smiled as the warrior floundered.

(183)

Lying in bed with the "half-caste" Cocoa, "in the depths" of the boat heading East, Lionel side-steps his lover's claim that "[e]ven in Burma there are boys," ironically denying the implied homosexuality of his "unfortunate parent" (184).[18] In response to the suggestion of miscegenation, however, Lionel disparages but does not dismiss the "depressing prospect" of his father's adulterating the family's pure lineage. The floundering "warrior" banks on genealogical longevity to preserve British imperialist notions of caste and continual progeny. Obliquely aligned with the "hostile" sun whose "mighty power" signifies doom to the unprotected offspring of the "Ruling Race" (169), Cocoanut, as the narrator claims, has "no scruples at perverting Lionel's instincts" nor "at endangering his prospects of paternity" (182). Homosexual intercourse with the "half-caste," rather than "with a girl, naturally," violates normative, biological, or Darwinian codes of sexuality. To the conscientious Lionel, who regards himself as the sole means of redeeming the sullied "family name," it also threatens extinction of acceptable patrilineage, since "[h]is surviving brother was too much a bookworm to be of any use, and the other two [siblings] were girls" (193).[19] His fostering extinction also implicates the self; regaining his sense of self-composure on deck, Lionel favorably surveys the Big Eight sahibs and acknowledges the conditionality of his own social survival: "How decent and reliable they looked, the folk to whom he belonged! He had been born one of them, he had his work with them, he meant to marry into their caste. If he forfeited their companionship he would become nobody and nothing" (192). This thought clearly counters an earlier assertion that his "colour-prejudices were tribal rather than personal, and only worked when an observer was present" (174). Public and private sexual identities ultimately prove inextricable in terms of a family honor and moral stance already jeopardized by the father's fall into the "depths of Burma" (183).

Both son and narrator cast Mrs. March, in contrast to Mr. March, as the Jehovah-like arbiter of the inextricable codes of normative sexuality, morality, and culture required for ensuring caste affiliation and public honor. Presented through the son's guilt-ridden conscience, her disembodied voice denotes both condemnation of and suffering from the past and present falls of father and son. Simultaneously, the adult Lionel venerates his mother's high-mindedness, while denigrating her self-righteous and condemnatory presence in his conscience. Based on a distortion of childhood reminiscence, his veneration and denigration objectify the maternal figure as both ideal mother and ideal Ego.[20]

Aboard the "other boat" of childhood, Mrs. March is featured as a woman who has allowed the colonial restraints of the "Ruling Race" to relax while at sea (167-69); even so, in Lionel's reminiscence, she becomes desexualized and, as his image of sexual restraint and conscience, is internalized as a "Mater" or disembodied Mother.

Significantly, the first section of **"The Other Boat"** serves both as a crucial foreshadowing of "this particular night" depicted in the fourth section and as a foundation for the self-generated strife the adult Lionel undergoes with a mother who is absent, but present in his consciousness (177). Although narrated *in medias res,* with the immediacy of dialogue and free-indirect discourse, this opening scene aboard the "other boat" designates a distant past of "long long ago" (166) "in those far-off days" (169).[21] The "other boat" thereby symbolizes a nostalgia for a childhood located in the colonial past, when "little boys" postured as "soldiers" who "still went to their deaths stiffly" (166); yet it also refers to a biblical or archetypal past when Old Testament male progenitors codified the world. Here, in this first section, the subtext of sexuality and potential fatality underlies the narrative's innocent tone and adumbrates the fatal outcome of the homoerotic relationship between Lionel March and Cocoanut, who in playing soldiers is the "only one who falls down when he's killed" (166). Retreating from this opening battle play among the March children, Cocoanut directs himself toward what he coins the "m'm m'm m'm" that inhabit the bow of the ship. In response to the Marches' curious inquiries about this cryptonym, he inscribes chalk marks on the ship's planks—a cipher that he decodes as the "M'm," which he insists "have no name" (167). Cocoanut's reference to these imaginary "m'm m'm m'm" challenges the inculcated belief of the March children that all God's creations have been securely codified. The young Lionel then holds up Adam and Noah—those male progenitors of a "long long ago" whose biblical accounts illustrate the imperative of naming everything, not to mention organizing the world heterosexually for regeneration:

> "They must have a name," said Lionel, recollecting, "because Adam named all the animals when the Bible was beginning."
>
> "They weren't in the Bible, m'm m'm m'm; they were all the time up in the thin part of the sheep, and when you pop out they pop in, so how could Adam have?"
>
> "Noah's ark is what he's got to now."
>
> Baby said "Noah's ark, Noah's ark, Noah's ark," and they all bounced up and down and roared.

(167)

The "half-caste" Cocoanut's conception of the "m'm m'm m'm" violates this archetypal imperative, for "they" evade the authority of language (or the Divine Word) to systematize the world. As the narrator follows the March children into the ship's bow, "where the m'm m'm m'm were said to be" (168), the intradiegetic but indeterminate narrator shifts from a third-person to a second-person perspective that implicates the reader in the pursuit of these unnameables:

> *Here* opened a glorious country, much the best in the boat. None of the March children had explored *there* before, but Cocoanut, having few domesticities, knew it well. That bell that hung in the very peak—it was the ship's bell and if you rang it the ship would stop. Those big ropes were tied into knots—twelve knots an hour. This paint was wet, but only as far as there. Up that hole was coming a Lascar. But of the m'm m'm he said nothing until asked. Then he explained in offhand tones that if you popped out they popped in, so that you couldn't expect to see them.
>
> (168; my emphasis)

The elusive and cryptonymic "m'm m'm m'm" are disjointedly designated as both "here" and "there," "in" and "out" of the holes of what Cocoanut locates as the "thin part of the sheep," or ship (167). The half-caste's vocalic mispronunciation of "ship" in itself betrays a biblical notion of bestial sodomy, while implying an area of this "other boat" (and perhaps of carnal knowledge) that is shared by Cocoanut and the Lascar, but not by the innocent and vulnerable March children. Consequently, the "new game" of "m'm m'm m'm," once reported to Mrs. March, is promptly checked by her injunction to "Go back and play properly" at soldiering (169).

Suggesting a game of unspeakable impropriety, Cocoanut's sounds take on multiple meanings. The bilabial utterance of "m'm m'm m'm" sounds like a rapid repetition of "mum" if we replace the apostrophe with the more common English schwa and represent this substitution with the grapheme "u." The term "mum" thereby subjects the contraction "m'm" to various denotations: the suppression of speech or the injunction to be silent; the act of masquerading, or masking oneself; or, thirdly, the informal yet chiefly British reference to "Mama." Given this potential multivalence, the unnameable "m'm m'm m'm" conflates the idiomatic expression, "mum's the word," with notions of concealment and mother; hence, as the March children reveal the "new game" to their mother, they phonetically and syntactically link her name with this cryptonym of suppression and deception: "M'm m'm m'm, mummy" (169).[22] This effectively, although innocently, adumbrates Captain Lionel March's vigilant efforts to mask any word of his "offence against decency" aboard the *S. S. Normannia* (174). In addition, Cocoanut's neologism works with the notion of "mummery" ("a pretentious or hypocritical show or ceremony"), which aptly portrays the upstanding officer's conscious attempts to keep up appearances and continue playing at soldiers, so to speak, for Colonel Arbuthnot and the Big Eight sahibs—not to mention for his "mum," with whom he corresponds while at sea.

Lionel's overseas correspondence with his mother functions as primary evidence of his contrition and his need to allude to yet mask his reunion with Cocoanut: "He is on board too," he tells his mother, "but our paths seldom cross" (171). Most notably, this epistle to the "Mater," which opens the story's second section and signals the narrative's transition from the "other boat" to the second boat, constitutes the core of Lionel's "stumbling confession." In projecting his mother as his confessor, as a Jehovah-like "voice condemning him and all her children for sin, but condemning him most," Lionel necessarily locates her "outside carnality" and deprives her of senses, sensations, and sensuality (193). He is mocked by Cocoanut because, by idealizing his mother as "the very soul of purity," Lionel denies the possibility of her sexuality and establishes her as the absolute gauge by which to condemn and restrain his own (185). Lionel later reveals his self-repulsion as he confesses his attempt to imagine his mother engaging in sexual intercourse: "Earlier in the evening, when Cocoa mentioned her, he had tried to imagine her with his father, enjoying the sensations he was beginning to find so pleasant, but the attempt was sacrilegious and he was shocked at himself" (193). That Lionel appears shocked at the vicarious sexual sensations the image of parental intercourse incites falls in line with Freud's discussion of *primal phantasies* commonly generated by neurotics (*Introductory* 371). Syntactically ambiguous, the phrase "enjoying the sensations" may refer to Lionel and to either the mother or the father, any of whom may be enjoying sexual pleasures. But Lionel's sense of profaning his puritanical mother arises from his locating her inside carnality and vicariously identifying with either her or the father as lover. If his identification is with the father as the mother's lover, then the image clearly suggests oedipal and perhaps incestuous implications. But if his identification is with the mother, then it appears equally sacrilegious, yet more "unnatural," and more clearly posits her as the son's object of transference. Lionel envisions his mother, as the cynosure of his fantasy, in his own sexual position. More significantly, he locates himself in the position of his mother, the feminine object of a male lover, as had Cocoanut in the earlier scene.[23] His shock then appears a response not only to the incestuous implications of this imagined scene of parental intercourse, but also to the feminization of his role as homosexual lover.

In his letter to his mother, Lionel addresses her as "Mater"; this term of endearment suggests various dimensions of her role. Polysemously, it signifies the mother, the matriarch, and, ironically, one who breeds. The Latinate *Mater* also signifies the Madonna, whose virginity and procreation secure her as the pure composite sign of maternity and femininity to the Son.[24] Mrs. March's asexuality surfaces as a son's fabrication that Cocoanut derisively discloses. Lionel's or the narrator's image of her as the spider both controlling and condemning her children for sin connects to Freud's discussion in "Femininity" of the aggressivity of the female spider, an image used to deconstruct the binarism of female passivity and male aggressivity and to suggest an alternate figure of the phallic mother (*Standard Edition* 22:115). In *Thinking About Women,* Mary Ellmann extends the Freudian imagery of mother and spider:

> As the stereotyped ideal grows intolerable, reaction against it takes the form of emphasis upon those who misapply it. It is, after all, Freud who described, simultaneously, the duty of the mother to sacrifice herself to the children and her demand that they sacrifice their wishes to her. Properly, she weaves her life about the children, and then in the children's dreams she is a spider (or, for Jung, a serpent or sarcophagus or specter). The more ideal the conception of a human function, the more resentment and suspicion it arouses: we are entirely accustomed, in the consideration of maternity, to this jolting between soul and damnation. We are as familiar with the accusation of consumptive attachment as with the praise of selfless care. In this sense, women are at once the child makers and breakers; no idea is more commonly fixed than that of the filocidal influence of the mother.
>
> (135)

In his own "consideration of maternity" and his "jolting between soul and damnation," propriety and condemnation, Lionel transmutes his mother into an ideal or symbol against which to judge his own guilt for having violated sexual as well as racial norms. Simultaneously, he praises and disparages his mother for a purity that he finds both repressive and critical to his own consciousness of imperialism and a genealogy that "can trace itself back nearly two hundred years" (183).

In the colonial context, Mrs. March, with her imperial "filaments drifting everywhere," represents not only the Empire but its surrogate, the "memsahib," a male construct designed to preserve the genealogical purity and political supremacy of the "Ruling Race."[25] Prior to the memsahib's introduction into India, the British colony was depicted as a "Moloch" primarily populated by males who engaged in interracial as well as homoerotic promiscuity (Hyam 91). This historical image of an exclusively male territory is symbolically portrayed in the scene aboard the "other boat" when Mrs. March enters the area of the boat designated as "Men's quarters" (**"Other Boat"** 170). There, the English sailor draws a circle around her and proscribes her movement into a portion of the boat in which male intercourse can transpire without "the sounds of feminine protest" (178). As Mrs. March agrees to pay for her trespass, Cocoanut, later described as "like a monkey" (173) and ironically as one who is "influential in shipping circles" (171), mockingly supersedes her position within the circle, to which Mrs. March retorts: "You never will play any game properly and you stop the others. You're

a silly idle useless unmanly little boy" (170). Within this narrative context, the "game" most directly refers to Cocoanut's enigmatic game of "m'm m'm m'm." But within a colonial context, it suggests the Indian male's political means of subverting the British imperialist hierarchy through homoerotic bonding. In his article "Forster's Friends," Rustom Bharucha insists upon not only the rebellious yet clandestine role homosexuality played in England against "the authoritarian and paternalistic rule of [the] government," but also the role it served in India as the Indian male's stratagem for "defeating the British at their own game" (109-10):

> In psychoanalytic terms, Indians had begun to "identify with the aggressor." Elaborating on this phenomenon in his brilliant study *The Intimate Enemy,* Ashis Nandy situates the opposition between *purusatva* (the essence of masculinity) with *klibatva* (the essence of hermaphroditism) as the essential conflict in the colonial psychology of Indians. "Femininity-in-masculinity," he claims, "was perceived as the final negation of a man's political identity, a pathology more dangerous than femininity itself."
>
> (110)

Attempting to bring "the feminine instincts of man to the surface" (Bharucha 112), to shake or negate the British officer's solid identity as "entirely the simple soldier man" (**"Other Boat"** 174), Cocoanut nearly enslaves Lionel through tactics of homoerotic bondage. Possessed of "thick fairish hair, blue eyes, glowing cheeks and strong white teeth," "a combination irresistible to the fair sex" (172), Lionel epitomizes the virile Aryan officer and perhaps mirrors Herman Melville's "Handsome Sailor," the "pristine and unadulterate" object of desire, of *Billy Budd, Sailor* (331), which Forster had recently converted into a libretto with Eric Crozier (*Selected Letters* 2:223).[26] The "fair sex" attracted to Lionel ironically proves to be the unfair—that is, the dark—"wog" who engages in foreplay "like a monkey" (173). Initially, Lionel maintains his conventionally masculine role as he "manhandle[s]" and "close[s] on" the physically weaker, effeminate Cocoanut—the act of manhandling referring not only to the lover's manpower but to his object of handling (173). In the penultimate act of sodomy, however, Lionel reverses his role. As visual evidence of Cocoanut's effeminizing the British soldier, Lionel ascends to the boat's deck, unconsciously attired in "effeminate pyjamas" (195). Previously described as "being built like a brute" (180), Lionel, or "Lion of the Night" (189), proves disarmed by the stratagems of the "monkey" (181); the half-caste Cocoanut unmasks (or unmans) the latent sexual identity of the "Nordic warrior" (174) and reveals it to be "[h]alf Ganymede, half Goth" (178)—giving an ironic half-caste distinction to the blue-blooded Aryan. The final evidence of Cocoanut's snake-like seduction and successful exposure of the British officer's "femininity-in-masculinity" comes from Lionel's previous identification with his mother; comparing her pleasures of lovemaking to his own, he progressively breaks with his rigidly-defined masculinity and accepts Cocoanut's feminine gifts as would a prostitute. The appearance of the image of Mrs. March, however, serves as continual self-reproof of his deviation from normative manhood and racial supremacy.

Throughout the course of his seduction, Cocoanut foresees Mrs. March as the primary obstacle to his homoerotic bonding with (or bondage of) Lionel. Historically speaking, this viewpoint represents that of the Indian male who, according to Bharucha on *A Passage to India,* viewed the memsahib as his primary rival for the British colonialist: "The real antagonists of Indian men were not their sahibs but the memsahibs who . . . saw themselves, as Nandy puts it, as 'the sexual competitors of Indian men with whom their men had established an unconscious homoeroticized bonding'" (110). In the fourth section of **"The Other Boat,"** Cocoanut recalls the memsahib March as "[t]hat vengeful onswishing of skirts" that disrupted a "trivial collision" between Cocoanut and Lionel, the collision an adumbration in childhood of their adult homoerotic relationship (182). This metonymic denigration of the maternal figure as swishing skirts echoes Forster's critical assessment of the "barrenness" of the characters in his earlier novel *Howards End* (1910) and his preference for "*Where Angels* [*Fear to Tread*] Gino, in *L. J.* [*The Longest Journey*] Stephen, in *R. with V.* [*A Room with a View*] Lucy, in *P. to I.* [*A Passage to India*] Aziz . . . and Maurice and Alec . . . and Lionel and Cocoa" (*Commonplace* 204; Forster's ellipses). Dated the same year he completed **"The Other Boat,"** Forster's entry in *Commonplace Book* reflects his distaste for the "onswishing of skirts" and provides an insight into his finding no pleasure in his "best novel": "I feel pride in the achievement, but cannot love it, and occasionally the swish of the skirts and the non-sexual embraces irritate. Perhaps too I am more hedonistic than I was, and resent not being caused pleasure personally" (203-04).

In Lionel's own internalized diatribe against the power of his mother, Lionel, or "lion" (the British emblem), envisions the scene of his transgression and ultimately castigates himself for violating filial duty. We are told: "the sight of him stripping would have killed her. He, her first-born, set apart for the redemption of the family name" (193). According to Oliver Stallybrass's footnote to the text, Forster was originally more sexually explicit: he has substituted "stripping" for "topping a dago" (193n). In censoring out direct evidence of homoerotic as well as interracial copulation, Forster in turn has edited or suppressed his initial impulse to offend flippantly both mother and culture (or potential reader). Lionel's disclosure of his "hedonistic" (*Commonplace* 204) sexuality at first seems to represent the primary "offence against decency" (**"Other Boat"**

174). Narratively, he shifts his concern, however, to "the redemption of the family name" that has been sullied by the "unspeakable" fact that his "hundred percent Aryan" father had abandoned both family and caste in order to go "native" "in the depths of Burma" (183-84), an act implying miscegenation or—if Cocoanut is right—homosexuality. Condemning his own libidinal and social lapse, Lionel resolves that he "must keep with his own people" for personal, as well as genealogical and imperial, survival (195). In spite of his resoluteness to submit to cultural norms of sexual conduct, Lionel's "standing quarrel" between erotic desire and "tribal" affiliation can only be extinguished, personally and textually, by the death of both lovers. As Cocoanut is purportedly strangled to death by Lionel, the "scandal" of homicide and suicide, that "sweet act of vengeance," subsequently undergoes its own form of "strangulation" or suppression of details (195-96). Following three elliptically-narrated paragraphs, stylistically mirroring the Big Eight's censorial efforts, the narrative ends with Mrs. March's final act as repressive mother: "she never mentioned his name again" (197). With this statement, the text itself becomes "silent" or as "blank" as the "country she inhabited" (193).

"Confessions of the flesh" in **"The Other Boat"** are not only silenced or mummed by the censorial and decorous memsahib and Big Eight sahibs—and by the childhood game of "m'm m'm m'm," which the adult Lionel enigmatically recalls as the "oddities on the other boat," but ultimately by Forster's own euphemistic rendering of homoerotics. Forster reduces the final sadomasochistic scene leading to Cocoanut's murder to the point of syntactical and emotional abstraction. He says only, "ecstasy hardened into agony" (195). Similarly, he translates Lionel's submission to Cocoanut's sexual advances into compressed abstract nouns: "Resistance weakened under the balmier sky, curiosity increased" (177). Stallybrass remarks that in the story the figurative "a muscle thickened up out of gold" comes closest to corporeal description (173). But through stylistic innuendoes, Forster makes the post-coital "ritual" of smoking a cigarette stand for the entire course of an act of fellatio or sodomy:

> [Smoking] was an established ritual, an assertion deeper than speech that they belonged to each other and in their own way. Lionel assented and lit the thing, pushed it between dusky lips, pulled it out, pulled at it, replaced it, and they smoked it alternately with their faces touching. When it was finished Cocoa refused to extinguish the butt in an ashtray but consigned it through the porthole into the flying waters with incomprehensible words. He thought the words might protect them, though he could not explain how, or what they were.
>
> (178-79)

Indeterminate nouns and pronouns, "the thing" and "it," replace "cigarette"; such referential indirection allows for alternate yet otherwise unspeakable readings of the lovers' "ritual" or "assertion deeper than speech." As Cocoanut pitches the live but finished butt into the "flying waters" with words as "incomprehensible" as "m'm m'm m'm," Lionel, in his post-coital act of suicide and "with the seeds of love on him," later pitches himself into the Red Sea, where his body "quickly attract[s] the sharks" (196).

As the "native crew" then consigns the murdered Cocoanut "to the deep with all possible speed," his corpse floats "contrary to the prevailing current" (196). Here, I read "the prevailing current" as a metaphor for imperialist decorum and British law proscribing homosexual conduct of the sort in which Lionel and Cocoanut engage. Lionel earlier alludes to the legal consequences of homosexuality and describes such illicit behavior as "the worst thing for which Tommies got the maximum" (175), as Oscar Wilde's conviction in 1895 proved. As Elaine Showalter points out, at the *fin-de-siècle* this "pathology" had been made illegal by the Labouchère Amendment to the Criminal Law Amendment Act of 1885 (14). Positing Stevenson's *Dr. Jekyll and Mr. Hyde* as a "fable of *fin-de-siècle* homosexual panic, the discovery and resistance of the homosexual self," Showalter further explains that death (suicide and/or homicide) provided such stories the "only [acceptable] form of narrative closure" (107), for death demonstrated that "it is self-destructive to violate the sexual codes of one's society" (113).[27] Perhaps drawing on this "Gay Gothic" finale, Forster also chooses to end with passionate murder and suicide. Forster's narrator attributes Lionel's guilt to the inexorable "power" of the arachnoid, phallic "Mater," whose socio-symbolic link or "filament" to her son is confirmed by a letter that he has written out of a sense of filial duty. The "red English pillar-box" in which he deposits this letter or masked confession serves as a signpost of the law—of his mother's and/or Britain's inseverable bond and imperialist network even at sea (187). The letter to "Mater" provides textual evidence of the son's self-inflicted need both to confess and translate his sexuality into acceptable discourse; Forster's story, also posthumously disclosed, offers evidence of a similar need. The prevalent mediation of the maternal figure in this closing scene complicates the author's bold claim that his intent was to end narratively on a climactic note of romantic tragedy, "when both crash at the height of their powers" (*Letters to Donald Windham* qtd. in Beauman 369).

In **"The Other Boat,"** Lionel March's repeated invocation of the socio-symbolic mother reflects the son's association of mother with cultural and sexual repression—with imperatives to "keep with his own people" (195) and, as voiced by Colonel Arbuthnot (whose possible namesake published the satirical *Law Is a Bottomless Pit* [1712]), to "come and sleep . . . like the rest of the gang" (194). Lionel establishes a solitary "commun-

ion with the Mater" (195) and promises his absent mother "'Never again'" (193). Submitting to maternal/cultural "imperatives," the son discovers that the mother's repressive voice is ultimately his own, for, as Trilling's Freud asserts, "the surrogates of culture are established in the mind itself" (36). The son's inexorable voicing of Maternal Law can therefore be silenced only by death or the inaudible act of writing—by the "silent, cautious deposition of the word upon the whiteness of a piece of paper, where it can possess neither sound nor interlocutor" (Foucault, *Order* 300).

*Notes*

1. In his discussion of the "repressive hypothesis" in *The History of Sexuality,* Michel Foucault translates the "good Christian" act of confessing "the flesh" into a laconic second-person imperative (19): "Not only will you confess to acts contravening the law, but you will seek to transform your desire, your every desire, into discourse" (21).

2. See June Perry Levine's "The Tame in Pursuit of the Savage: The Posthumous Fiction of E. M. Forster" for an informative analysis of the various manuscripts of *Maurice* (76-79).

3. I borrow this issue of the dated text from Isherwood's own personal account of his "Master," Forster, in *Christopher and His Kind*: "At their meeting in 1932, the Master had praised the Pupil. This time, the Pupil was being asked by the Master, quite humbly, how *Maurice* appeared to a member of the thirties generation. 'Does it date?' Forster was asking. To which Christopher, I am proud to say, replied, 'Why shouldn't it date?'" (126).

4. Using contemporaneous biographies and memoirs and the findings of *The Wolfenden Report,* Antony Grey, in *Quest for Justice: Towards Homosexual Emancipation,* depicts the period between the 1890s and the 1950s as the "silent years," during which transpired "a great deal of homosexual behaviour, most of it discreet and undetected" (19). Because legal proscription did not deter homosexual activity, *The Wolfenden Report* advocated its decriminalization when performed in private by consenting adults: "We do not think that it is proper for the law to concern itself with what a man does in private unless it can be shown to be so contrary to the public good that the law ought to intervene in its function as the guardian of that public good" (*Wolfenden* 43).

5. Norman Page, in *E. M. Forster's Posthumous Fiction,* finds this assertion implausible: "Self-excitation hardly demands so evident an exercise of art, and one has the sense of their being written for an appreciative audience" (54).

6. Representing earlier, stylistically more formal versions of the first section of "The Other Boat," both publications mark the author's first appearance in print since the publication of his novel *A Passage to India* in 1924. In the *New York Times Book Review,* the editor also mentions that the "fragment" was originally broadcast by the BBC "a short time ago." Most interestingly, the editor alludes to a concealed yet nameless novel, presumably *Maurice:* "It is known that there reposes in the British Museum the manuscript of a completed Forster novel, but the impression is general that he will never consent to its publication" (6 February 1949).

7. The *Normannia* is also evident in *Maurice* as the ship on which the gamekeeper, Alec, intends to emigrate to the Argentine (232, 234). In light of Captain March's internal and social struggle with normative ideals, the ship's title also appears an implicit pun on "norm" and "man," if not "mania."

8. See Julia Kristeva's "The Virgin of the Word" in *About Chinese Women* for a further discussion of the participation of the mother in the symbolic Christian order (25-33).

9. The formation of the exclusive Big Eight sahibs parallels that of the "Cambridge group" on board the 1912 voyage that provided the "germ" for Forster's story (Furbank 223). "The Other Boat" clearly adapts biographical elements of this memorable voyage to the East as well as Forster's intimate and lifelong relationship with Syed Ross Masood, the Oxford undergraduate with whom Forster initially posed as Latin tutor. Ostensibly, the character of Captain March borrows from the "fair-haired Byronic-looking" officer who boldly announced his homosexuality to the author while voyaging in 1912 toward his station in India (Furbank 224). While Cocoanut inherits the "volatile" (Furbank 143) and "despotic" (Bharucha 107) features of Masood's personality, he contrasts with the educated Indian with upper-class advantages and physical magnificence. In this light, Cocoanut signifies a hybridized or composite caricature of the perverse seducer and the racial pariah; while his diabolic features perhaps mirror British societal (or Big Eight) conceptions of both the aberrant homosexual and the liminal "wog," such views would clearly oppose the author's own homoerotic attraction to Masood. In turn, "The Other Boat" proves a hybridization of Forster's narrative of homosexuality in *Maurice* and his focus on issues of Anglo-Indian sexuality and Oriental seductiveness in *A Passage to India.*

10. In *About Chinese Women,* Julia Kristeva describes the rationale behind conceiving of a mother with a Phallus: "In a symbolic productive/reproductive economy centered on the Paternal Word (the Phallus, if you like), one can make a woman believe that she *is* (the Phallus, if you like), even if she doesn't have it (the serpent—the penis): Doesn't she have the child? In this way, social harmony is preserved: the structure functions, produces, and reproduces. Without it, the very foundation of this society is endangered" (22).

11. As Judith Scherer Herz observes in *The Short Narratives of E. M. Forster,* Mrs. March only appears as a "'character' in the conventional sense" in the beginning; yet she evolves into a "pure symbol" and, by apparent contrast, a "purely negative creation" (an inferior inversion of Mrs. Moore) in the end.

12. Trilling designates the time of Rousseau as the juncture at which the individual self became most profoundly implicated in the concept of culture or society: "At some point in the history of the West—let us say, for convenience, at the time of Rousseau—men began to think of their fates as being lived out not in relation to God, or to the individual persons who are their neighbors, or to material circumstance, but to the ideas and assumptions and manners of a large social totality" (35).

13. In the biographical *Samuel Beckett,* Deirdre Bair substantiates the profound influence both Freud and Jung had on writers and artists of the earlier twentieth century: "In fact, so many writers and artists of this period were either undergoing analysis or writing their own criticisms of psychoanalytic publications that Ezra Pound, a staunch unbeliever, hooted in derision that he was the only sane writer left in Europe" (177).

Ironically, Forster may have taken his Freud from Trilling. Indeed, Trilling's description of the mother figure may well fit Forster's story because Forster had read Trilling's Freudian study. In a letter to Trilling, dated 1 August 1955, Forster cites *Freud and the Crisis of Our Culture (Selected Letters* 2:259-60); and, in a subsequent letter to William Plomer, dated 12 December 1957, he describes his secondhand access to the literary Freud:

> I had an interesting day's reading yesterday, with the sudden sensation of being in close contact with what I was reading. It doesn't often come to me. What I read is not important, but it radiated ("believe it or not") from Freud. Trilling[']s cluttered-up meditation on him switched me over to Auden's poem ["In Memory of Sigmund Freud"].

*(Selected Letters* 2: 268)

Thus, Forster's reading of Trilling's and Auden's tributes to literary interpretations of Freud precedes his 1957-58 revision of "The Other Boat" by as much as two years. This may account for how and why the internal or "standing quarrel" that Lionel March undergoes with his mother, the omnipresent and absolute sign of culture, narratively illustrates Trilling's perspective on Freud and the "crisis" of culture. Furthermore, in this light, it seems plausible to trace Lionel March's given name, not to mention literary paternity, to Lionel Trilling himself.

14. Etymologically related to "Arachne" and "arachnid," the term "arachnoid" denotes the delicate (cobweblike) membrane enclosing the spinal cord and brain, and significantly located between the *pia mater* (Latin for "tender mother") and the *dura mater* ("hard mother"). This anatomical polarity of tender and hard mother parallels Lionel's construction of Mrs. March as both the unimpeachable caretaker of her fatherless children and the "power," if not backbone, to the imperial "Army."

15. Forster's complete sentence reads: "Jealous of what she sees, the hag comes with her scimitar, and she. . . . Or she lifts up a man when he feels lighter than air" (191-92; Forster's ellipses). The image of the hag lifting up a man connotes the image of the mother as bird, an image perhaps related to Leonardo da Vinci's fantasy of his mother as a vulture endowed with a penis. Freud aligns this androgynous or phallic mother image with the Egyptian maternal goddess "Mut," a symbol of parthenogenetic motherhood ("At a certain time these birds pause in mid-flight, open their vagina and are impregnated by the wind") who was iconographically depicted with breasts as well as an erect penis (*Standard Edition* 11: 88-89, 94). Freud likens da Vinci's fantasy of the "vulture-child"—the paradigm of the fatherless son or bastard child of the "vulture mother"—to the virginal conception of Christ: "The allusion made by the Fathers of the Church to the idea of the Blessed Virgin and her child—an idea cherished by every artist—must have played its part in helping the phantasy to appear valuable and important to him. Indeed in this way he was able to identify himself with the child Christ, the comforter and saviour not of this one woman alone" (90).

16. Mrs. March's invective against Cocoanut's unmanliness biographically recalls Masood's recorded experience with a similar charge when Oxford undergraduates denigrated his "unmanly" use of scents (Furbank 144). This in turn links with Cocoanut's "aromatic smell" (173).

17. See Winfried Schleiner, "*Divina virago*: Queen Elizabeth as an Amazon." Also, Louis Adrian Montrose's "'Shaping Fantasies': Figurations of Gender and Power in Elizabethan Culture," argues that Queen Elizabeth I, as the gynarchic paragon of virginity and power, proves to be Britain's own complex configuration of the sublime and perhaps phallic mother figure (or Mater) of the growing Empire: "Elizabeth's self-mastery and mastery of others were enhanced by an elaboration of her maidenhood into a cult of virginity . . . ; [by] the displacement of her wifely duties from a household to a nation; and [by] the sublimation of her temporal and ecclesiastical authority into a nurturing maternity. She appropriated not only the suppressed cult of the Blessed Virgin but also the Tudor conception of the Ages of Woman. By fashioning herself into a singular combination of Maiden, Matron, and Mother, the Queen transformed the normal domestic life-cycle of an Elizabethan female into what was at once a social paradox and a religious mystery" (79-80).

18. While I have reservations about Forster's most recent biography, Nicola Beauman's account of the immediate Forster family concurs with the implicit depiction of the Marches as homophobic. In several instances, Beauman characterizes Forster's mother, Lily, as not simply one who was dominating or overprotective, but as one who was vigilant against her son inheriting his father's legacy of putative homosexuality: "It may not have been chance alone that took her and Morgan abroad in the very month of the Oscar Wilde trials: might it have been her long repressed feelings about Eddie [her husband] and Ted that prompted her first holiday in France since Paris, 1878?" (69-70); elsewhere, Beauman writes, "Homosexuality was something she would rather not think about, yet she [Lily] must have seen for herself that her son was, like Eddie (about whom she had had her doubts), lacking in some of the characteristics of the active heterosexual" (94-95).

19. Clearly, Lionel's family structure only resembles Forster's in terms of the absent father; the marked absence of Forster's father is, however, related to his premature death from a family disease, as recorded in the author's autobiographical segment of *Marianne Thornton: A Domestic Biography 1797-1887*. In this curious combination of his great-aunt's biography and his early autobiography, published a year before his writing of "The Other Boat," Forster describes his female relatives' over-indulgence of him after his father's death: "They centred round me. I succeeded my father as the favourite nephew. . . . I received the deplorable nickname of The Important One, and when my mother showed signs of despondency she was reminded that she had me to live for" (289). In spite of the presence of three other sib-

lings, Lionel also succeeds his own father and, in a similar sense, carries the moral and genealogical burden of being "The Important One."

20. In *Tales of Love,* Kristeva elaborates: "Phallic power, in the sense of a symbolic power that thwarts the traps of penial performance, would in short begin with an appropriation of archaic maternal power. Man, as he displaces his desires onto the field of knowledge, finally works out the recipes of a Diotima who relieves him of the deadly unleashing of his erotic passion and holds up to him the enthusiastic vision of an immortal, unalterable object. A tracing of the ideal mother, that object of ideal knowledge allows man to build up his ideal Ego. Based on Diotimas as solid as they are overbearing, the ideal Ego of man powerfully withstands the devastating upheavals that are to the contrary induced by sexual, homosexual passions. It is in tearing himself away from homosexual Eros, usually by means of a heterosexual partner who paves the way for desexualizing the male libido, that man achieves a reconciliation with his ideal Ego as well as with the ideal, plain and simple" (75-76).

21. In his fragment to an "abandoned novel," Forster more directly refers to a time when "[w]ar had not yet assumed its colonial aspect" ("Cocoanut" 3); this phrase has been edited from the final version of "The Other Boat."

22. Lionel's "open avowal" of his homoerotic desire for Cocoanut can, in this light, be read as a clever play on the open(-ended) vowel of "m'm m'm m'm" (187). I credit Kathryn Stockton, at the University of Utah, with this insight.

23. In "The Hand That Rocks the Cradle," Coppélia Kahn discusses the son's feminine identification with the mother; borrowing from Adrienne Rich, she describes this potential transference in terms of "'matrophobia'—not the fear of one's mother or of motherhood, but of becoming like one's mother as in the original identification of the child with its mother, and thus losing one's gender identity as a male" ((M)other Tongue 79).

24. Kristeva refers to this condensed if not incestuous configuration of the trinitarian Virgin in "Stabat Mater": "Indeed, *mother* of her son and his *daughter* as well, Mary is also, and besides, his *wife:* she therefore actualizes the threefold metamorphosis of a woman in the tightest parenthood structure" (*Tales of Love* 243).

25. In *Empire and Sexuality,* Ronald Hyam documents this historical phenomenon of the "memsahib": "Few groups of women have been so negatively described as the memsahibs. It has long been said

that the biggest mistake the British made in India was to bring their women out, thus making it impossible to meet Indians as friends. New standards of racial prejudice were, it was said, imposed by hostesses drawing intricate distinctions between shades of colour, as the memsahibs elaborated an imperial social etiquette. . . . The memsahib's function was political: to maintain 'civilised standards,' especially sexual standards, and to contain the temptations of the male. 'Social distance' between ruler and ruled was the policy, especially after the Mutiny, and the memsahibs were its instrument" (118-19).

26. I previously noted that the Aryan Captain March derives from the "Byronic-looking" officer whom Forster encountered during his 1912 voyage. Because of the snake imagery incorporated into the narrative of his seduction by Cocoanut ("The bolt unbolted, the little snake not driven back into its hole" [190]; "the body curved away seductively into darkness" [195]) and the purity initially ascribed to the "half Goth" Lionel ("He had stepped on board at Tilbury entirely the simple soldier man, without an inkling of his fate" [174]), I compare Forster's short story with Melville's in terms of their homoerotic adaptation of man's Fall: "Billy in many respects was little more than a sort of upright barbarian, much such perhaps as Adam presumably might have been ere the urbane Serpent wriggled himself into his company" (Melville 330-31).

According to Mary Lago and P. N. Furbank's biographical introduction to the final phase (1947-70) of his letters, Forster was invited by Benjamin Britten to collaborate on an opera; with Eric Crozier, he produced the libretto for *Billy Budd,* which premiered on 1 December 1951 (2:223, 246n2). Boosey & Hawkes published two versions of the libretto: *Billy Budd: Opera in Four Acts* (1951) and the revised *Billy Budd: Opera in Two Acts* (1961) (*Selected Letters* 2:240n2). These two dates frame the year(s) Forster worked on "The Other Boat" (1957-58).

27. Both June Perry Levine and Judith Scherer Herz describe Lionel's suicide as an "inevitable" resolution to his internal division between caste affiliation and homosexuality or homoerotic desire for Cocoanut. But given that the narrative comes to a halt with the censorial mother, I can view the fatal outcome neither as an easy reconciliation of psychic conflict nor as a triumphant escape into boundless eternity for the two lovers. (The latter, I believe, more aptly reflects Vithobai's final triumph in "The Life to Come.") Calling attention to Lionel's progressive disdain for the bigotry of the Big Eight, Levine does claim that Forster offers

his readers a "cautionary tale for all the world's Lionels who participate in professional and social institutions without distance, without questions, without skepticism, and whose self-knowledge, when it comes, collides against the closed doors of the established order, which they still consider the citadel of self-validation" (86-87). Levine's textual illustrations focus on Lionel's relationship to the Big Eight, which would suggest that this "tale" views them as symbolic if not allegorical representatives of the world's social institutions. But her brief consideration of "The Other Boat" does not include the mother as an agency of social conscience and censorship as well. On the other hand, Herz does associate the mother with Lionel's "fatal split" between "deck" and "cabin." I agree with this direct association, although our readings of the mother as a symbol differ in the end. Examining Mrs. March's "felt presence throughout the story," Herz aligns the mother with the sea, into which Lionel eventually dives to his death. Herz in turn reads the final suicide as a symbolic union (or communion) of son and mother/sea and as an after-life reunion of Lionel and Cocoanut, whose corpse is thrown into the sea and travels with the undertow towards Lionel's (although the narrative only mentions that Lionel's body is quickly consumed by sharks) (54). I am more inclined to agree with her subsequent consideration of Mrs. March as a "purely negative creation" who "consume[s]," or rather censors, the final story of her son (55; see my note 11); but, since I ascribe primary agency to the son and narrator in their construction of the maternal image, I would not venture to place the mother in the position of an implied omniscient narrator who in the end "understands the story better than the others" and who "can reconstitute it from its partial narrations" (54). We are simply told that "she never mentioned [Lionel's] name again," and the narrative enacts this final silencing.

### Works Cited

Bair, Deirdre. *Samuel Beckett*. New York: Harcourt, 1978.

Beauman, Nicola. *E. M. Forster: A Biography*. New York: Knopf, 1994.

Bharucha, Rustom. "Forster's Friends." *Raritan* 4 (1986): 105-22.

Creech, James. *Closet Writing/Gay Reading*. Chicago: U of Chicago P, 1993.

Ellmann, Mary. *Thinking About Women*. New York: Harcourt, 1968.

Forster, E. M. "Cocoanut & Co.: Entrance to an Abandoned Novel." *New York Times Book Review* 6 Feb. 1949: 3, 31.

———. *Commonplace Book*. Ed. Philip Gardner. Stanford: Stanford UP, 1985.

———. "Entrance to an Unwritten Novel." *The Listener* 23 Dec. 1948: 975-76.

———. *The Life to Come*. New York: Norton, 1972.

———. *Marianne Thornton: A Domestic Biography 1797-1887*. New York: Harcourt, 1956.

———. *Maurice*. New York: Norton, 1971.

———. "The Other Boat." *The Life to Come*. New York: Norton, 1972. 166-97.

———. *A Passage to India*. San Diego: Harcourt, 1984.

———. *Selected Letters of E. M. Forster*. Ed. Mary Lago and P. N. Furbank. 2 vols. Cambridge: Harvard UP, 1983.

Foucault, Michel. *The History of Sexuality*. Vol. 1. Trans. Robert Hurley. New York: Vintage, 1990.

———. *The Order of Things*. New York: Pantheon, 1970.

———. "A Preface to Transgression." *Language, Counter-Memory, Practice*. Ed. Donald F. Bouchard. Trans. Donald F. Bouchard and Sherry Simon. Ithaca: Cornell UP, 1977. 29-52.

Freud, Sigmund. *Introductory Lectures on Psychoanalysis*. Ed. and trans. James Strachey. New York: Norton, 1966.

———. *The Standard Edition of the Complete Psychological Works of Sigmund Freud*. 24 vols. Ed. and trans. James Strachey. London: Hogarth, 1953-81.

Furbank, P. N. *E. M. Forster: A Life*. 2 vols. London: Secker & Warburg, 1977.

Gallop, Jane. *The Daughter's Seduction*. Ithaca: Cornell UP, 1982.

Grey, Antony. *Quest for Justice*. London: Sinclair-Stevenson, 1992.

Herz, Judith Scherer. *The Short Narratives of E. M. Forster*. New York: St. Martin's, 1988.

Hyam, Ronald. *Empire and Sexuality*. Manchester: Manchester UP, 1990.

Isherwood, Christopher. *Christopher and His Kind: 1929-1939*. New York: Farrar, 1976.

Kahn, Coppélia. "The Hand That Rocks the Cradle: Recent Gender Theories and Their Implications." *The (M)other Tongue*. Ed. Shirley Nelson Garner, Claire Kahane, and Madelon Sprengnether. Ithaca: Cornell UP, 1985. 72-88.

Kristeva, Julia. *About Chinese Women*. Trans. Anita Barrows. London: Marion Boyars, 1977.

————. *Tales of Love.* Trans. Leon S. Roudiez. New York: Columbia UP, 1987.

Levine, June Perry. "The Tame in Pursuit of the Savage: The Posthumous Fiction of E. M. Forster." *PMLA* 99 (January 1984): 72-88.

Melville, Herman. *Billy Budd, Sailor and Other Stories.* Ed. Harold Beaver. Middlesex, England: Penguin, 1970.

Montrose, Louis Adrian. "'Shaping Fantasies': Figurations of Gender and Power in Elizabethan Culture." *Representations* 1.2 (Spring 1983): 61-94.

Page, Norman. *E. M. Forster's Posthumous Fiction.* Victoria, B.C.: English Literary Studies, 1977.

Pound, Ezra. *Selected Poems.* New York: New Directions, 1957.

Schleiner, Winfried. "*Divina virago*: Queen Elizabeth as an Amazon." *Studies in Philology* 75 (Spring 1978): 163-80.

Showalter, Elaine. *Sexual Anarchy.* New York: Viking, 1990.

Trilling, Lionel. *Freud and the Crisis of Our Culture.* Boston: Beacon, 1955.

*The Wolfenden Report of the Departmental Committee on Homosexual Offenses and Prostitution.* New York: Stein and Day, 1963.

## Marcia Bundy Seabury (essay date winter 1997)

SOURCE: Seabury, Marcia Bundy. "Images of a Networked Society: E. M. Forster's 'The Machine Stops.'" *Studies in Short Fiction* 34, no. 1 (winter 1997): 61-71.

[*In the following essay, Seabury discusses the intersection between religion and technology in modern life, using Forster's "The Machine Stops" as the basis for her discussion.*]

It is a commonplace that we are in the midst of a computer revolution that will change our society perhaps more radically than the Industrial Revolution, and likewise a commonplace that the literary imagination has often gone before us in envisioning not only the shape but the possible significance of such changes. A striking example is E. M. Forster's dystopian story **"The Machine Stops"** (1909), which deserves renewed attention as the computer age accelerates and as the breakup of the Soviet Union may make Orwell's world of totalitarian control and fear, *1984,* seem less imminent than Forster's of satisfied individuals sitting before their networked personal computers.

Forster scholars have frequently either ignored **"The Machine Stops,"** Forster's only portrayal of a future world, or devoted only a couple sentences or paragraphs to it; through the 1970s many judged it a limited creation. Those treating it at greater length have typically focused on how it develops Forster's recurring humanist concerns about connection—of individuals with themselves, senses plus spirit, or individuals with each other and with the natural world—while some recent critics have looked at narrative technique. But some scholars, including those critical of the story, have also seen it as prophetic. And beginning with Mark Hillegas's *The Future as Nightmare* (1967), discussions of the story began to appear in another kind of forum: books and articles on science fiction and dystopian fiction. **"The Machine Stops"** has come to be hailed as influential, the earliest of the twentieth-century dystopias exploring attitudes toward science and technology.[1]

Even the more recent of such commentaries have focused on the story's portrayal of technology in general: for example, people do not have to work and have become soft since the machine works for them. These analyses either predate the widespread use of home computers or do not discuss them. Further, none devotes sustained attention to the religious issues so central to the story. By looking at intersections between religious thinking and computerization in **"The Machine Stops,"** this essay can explore some key questions about the effects of computerization on our lives and values. The citizens in the world of **"The Machine Stops"** live in individual cells, empty except for a chair, a desk, and the controls of a machine. What happens to people's relationship to a power outside themselves, and to their relationships with each other, when their days are increasingly spent in relationship with a networked communication device? I will explore these issues through images and metaphors, assuming as does Robert Frost in his "Education by Metaphor: A Meditative Monologue" that humankind's most profound thinking is metaphorical.

First, Forster portrays an entirely indoor society, a society that looks only at the man-made. This condition began well before the citizens' underground life, as people had increasingly homogenized the earth: "What was the good of going to Pekin when it was just like Shrewsbury?" (10). Then the environment was somehow poisoned, made uninhabitable for all higher life forms, so that people had to move underground—all this written decades before nuclear fission, bomb shelters, and the Swiss's reputed ability to house their entire nation in shelters under their mountains.

Forster is of course not alone in imagining the future city as underground. H. G. Wells's *The Time Machine* (1895) places the workers, the Morlocks, underground, while the Eloi live above. Fritz Lang's movie *Metropolis* (1927), based on the novel by Thea von Harbou, shows an above-ground society of the well-to-do undergirded by workers in a hellish world of overwork and steam. In these cases, however, note that there is a clear division: an at least apparently good life above ground and a hell below. In **"The Machine Stops,"** all inhabit an underground "good life" that is hell.

Moreover, the issue of class, so important in those other works and in Forster's own novels, is nonexistent here. People's cells, their technological appurtenances, will not increase in size or sophistication depending on their birth or accomplishments. Thus our attention is focused not on how this brave new world affects its various classes but on how it affects everyone. As Northrop Frye puts it, today we may have the "growing sense that the whole world is destined to the same social fate with no place to hide" (29). Whether corporation executive or auto mechanic, we all increasingly interact with our technology at work and at home.

In this enclosed world, "night and day, wind and storm, tide and earthquake, impeded man no longer. He had harnessed Leviathan" (**"Machine"** 10). People see not the forces of nature but rather only the machine and the walls of their man-made rooms. Forster's underground citizens can still travel above ground in airships; Forster published his story in the same year as the first airplane flight across the English Channel, foreseeing the age of widespread commercial flights. But the citizens' supposed exposure to the larger world is thus high-speed travel, with windows sealed. Gradually, any travel people do is with the shades pulled, so that they can concentrate better on their own affairs.

Increasingly shut off visually from a world they did not make, Forster's citizens focus their attention on what their own hands have wrought, and look less and less toward an ultimate maker. The mother in the story, Vashti, expresses in a sentence the belief haunting the nineteenth century under the impact of the Industrial Revolution and the ongoing discoveries in the sciences: "I worship nothing. I'm most advanced." As the narrator puts it, ironically, no longer were men "compacted by thinking of a power outside the world" (13). A city underground, then, suggests the danger that modern man become literally and figuratively contained, physically and also spiritually.

A second key image is of course the machine itself. Writing long before the giant ENIAC of 1946, Forster describes a machine that electronically controls the various aspects of daily life in the underground city—dare we call it a computer? One of its aspects is simple mechanization: pushing a button produces results. The machine is also explicitly described as a communications system—a reaction to the then-new possibility of telephones (with a prediction of the videophones most of us still do not have), plus a prevision of "a sort of television," as Furbank describes it (262; cf. Shusterman 52)? But the machine is more. Nominally a Central Committee and a Committee of the Mending Apparatus are in charge, but the narrator and the characters consistently use verbs of agency for the machine. It seems to store and process information and operate automatically, two features distinguishing a computer; it seems to make decisions and evolve on its own.

Such a giant machine has become common fare in science fiction stories and novels of the post-ENIAC decades. Forster prefigures those often night-marish stories in showing the varied dangers, both physical and spiritual, arising from its creation. The well-known archetype underlying his portrayal is the Frankenstein myth, man arrogating to himself the powers of the creator and ultimately being destroyed by his own creation. As with Frankenstein, the creators of Forster's society intend not evil but good, the betterment of human life. But the finite creator does not fully understand what he has created; the created takes on a life of its own; monster becomes master.

Many have followed Forster in considering this theme. In Karel Capek's play *R. U. R.* (1923), containing the first use of the term *robot,* the robots take over from their arrogant, would-be-God creators. Aldous Huxley writes explicitly that "we do have to start thinking how we can get control again of our inventions. This is a kind of Frankenstein monster problem" (qtd. in Bedford 674-75).[2] But Forster's work has the additional dimension that not just particular created beings or inventions but the very environment itself is seen as the monster. He writes that as time passes, "there was not one who understood the monster as a whole." Lest we miss the Frankenstein parallel, in the same paragraph he refers to the Romantic concept of the overreacher that Mary Shelley explored: "Humanity, in its desire for comfort, had overreached itself" (29).

This wording highlights a variation that Forster rings on the Frankenstein motif: Frankenstein rejects his creature, who turns out not to be what he expected, his act in the moment being followed by a nervous breakdown. But with his man-made, mechanical environment, man gets what he wanted. And he does not suddenly abdicate responsibility; he enjoys the results of his inventiveness. As Forster puts it, "quietly and complacently, it [mankind] was sinking into decadence" (30).

A significant part of this slide is the citizens' developing reliance on the machine. Isaac Asimov suggests that "man has always been at the mercy of forces beyond his control—consider economic and sociological forces, whims of climate, and the disasters of war. Machine control is just a different kind of control, and a superior kind since man himself designs it" (Asimov et al. 251). But Forster sees a problematic displacing of the religious impulse that results from this shift. Supposedly having mastered their environment, having banished, as

Vashti says, "all the fear and the superstition" (17), Forster's citizens of the machine inadvertently find themselves once again in an environment where they are not masters of the universe. It is disconcerting, in the new man-made machine world as well as in the old, to feel our lives are controlled by forces beyond ourselves. We look to whatever guide we can find to the world we must inhabit. Thus Forster's citizens turn their backs on one kind of religious belief only to embrace, at first unwittingly, another. Vashti's son Kuno tells her accurately, "You are beginning to worship the machine" (17). Forster's citizens look to "the Book"—the computer manual. The Book of the Machine is grounded in realities beyond people's comprehension and inspires reverence. People get a sense of security from it and actually begin to pray to it (7-8, 33). Indeed, as the society progresses, religion is explicitly reestablished—a religion of the machine.[3]

Forster himself had lost faith, and commented that "Faith . . . is a stiffening process, a sort of mental starch, which ought to be applied as sparingly as possible" ("What I Believe" 67). But in **"The Machine Stops"** he does not leave us with the simple view that any religion is a stiffening agent, and thus that the characters have escaped from one set of beliefs only to embrace another equally constricting. While he objected to religious dogmatism, Forster was deeply interested in the great questions that religions have asked, as witnessed in such works as *A Passage to India*. In **"The Machine Stops,"** he clearly portrays a sense of loss, man's having confined his sights to the man-made and then transferred his worship to the machine. Instead of the music of the spheres, we now hear only a different eternal hum—the hum of the Machine (8). When Kuno's mother tells him to throw himself on the mercy of the machine, he replies, "I prefer the mercy of God!" (25). Forster consistently conveys sympathy with Kuno's yearnings for mystery, for meaning.

Forster's society, then, is man-made and machine-sustained—a world in which, quite literally, people live and move and have their being, (Biblical language Forster adopts 29)[4]. A third aspect of Forster's future world is its networked mode of life. More prescient than Forster's central computer is his portrayal—long before the 1971 invention of microprocessors—of remote terminals, the home computer, a global computer network to which all are connected. Murray Leinster's "A Logic Named Joe" (1946) has been lauded as a groundbreaking work for its vision of home computers (Asimov et al. 10, 279), but Forster's work long preceded it. More recent science-fiction continued to focus on the giant computers (e.g. Arthur C. Clarke's *The City and the Stars* or James Blish's *A Life for the Stars*), being surprisingly slow to foresee or deal with the implications of home computers (cf. Mowshowitz 84-85).

People communicate through the network, learn through the network, entertain themselves through the network. Edward Bellamy, in his utopian novel *Looking Backward* (1888), had envisioned many activities becoming more communal—for example meals cooked at common dining halls—but other activities becoming more private, for example concerts brought electronically into each person's room. Forster shows only the latter part of Bellamy's package: technological progress leading toward increased isolation. Information, basic needs, and public "events" all come to the individual, electronically, instead, the individual going in search of them.[5] What is lost by communication through the machine? Only the "nuances," says Forster ironically; the result is "good enough for all practical purposes" (5).

Networked life consistently interposes a device between people and direct experience.[6] Hillegas sees Forster's citizens as "avoiding direct experience and living only in their imaginations" (86); the point is rather that by avoiding direct experience they have no imaginations, and live only in their sterile circles of responding to what so-and-so said about so-and-so's response to so-and-so (27)—worded by Forster in a delightful parody of academic scholarship that may become still more apt as computer networks allow us to respond ever more quickly to someone else's secondhand thoughts. These circles do spread widely. Paradoxically accompanying the privatization of experience is an enormous increase in the individual's range of contacts. Through her vast network Vashti knows several thousand people (3). The representative citizen, she does not see any dangers from either the dearth of immediate experience or the accompanying information glut.[7]

Forster's portrayal of the networked city compares interestingly with the images for the social shape of "technopolis" that Harvey Cox offered in his 1965 landmark book *The Secular City*: the switchboard and the cloverleaf.[8] Cox wrote, "Technopolitan man sits as at a vast and immensely complicated switchboard. He is *homo symbolicus,* man the communicator, and the metropolis is a massive network of communications" (35). Cox used this image in refuting what he saw as the pervasive negative connotations of urban anonymity; with so many possible connections, modern man enjoys enormous freedom to choose. Cox also described modern urban man as in a highway cloverleaf, an "image of simultaneous mobility in many different directions" (33). Countering what he saw as pervasive criticism of this mobility, he emphasized ways that it frees man.

Cox did not develop any tension between these images. He assumed both would increasingly describe modern urban man. But in at least one sense, they may come to suggest opposite pulls. Cox claimed that "every tendency in modern society points to accelerated mobility" (43); we may instead find the switchboard becoming an increasingly literal image, with people, at least in their daily routines, becoming less mobile physically. The range of connections increases enormously, but physical mobility decreases as both work and entertainment operate through computer and television. Lewis Mumford discussed a similar vision in pre-computer terms: "Instead of his travelling, the world moves before the Megalopolitan, on paper; instead of his venturing forth on the highways of the world, adventure comes to him, on paper . . ." (227). Now, of course, we have the information superhighway.

A further question about Cox's description of the enormous freedom of urban man at the switchboard arises when the switchboard becomes increasingly literal: the extent to which the switchboard demands our attention, leaving us open to the pull of others. Forster's city differs radically in a physical sense from Evgeny Zamyatin's city in *We* (1922): there, individuals live in individual glass cubicles with glass walls, so that everyone can see his neighbors, while in **"The Machine Stops"** the walls are physically opaque. But the electronic lines of Forster's citizens are open, raising related questions about individuality and freedom. When Vashti goes to sleep, the messages keep coming, backing up on her answering machine; even in the moments she is private, the call of the group weighs on her, the pressure of the switchboard constrains her.

Forster's image of the cell of a beehive brings together the several aspects of the man-made, machine-sustained, networked society. He uses the image both literally and figuratively, beginning from his first sentence asking the reader to "imagine, if you can, a small room, hexagonal in shape, like the cell of a bee" (3). We can think of a hive of activity as suggesting order and energy. In ancient Greece, bees were seen as admirable symbols of work, obedience, "industry, creative activity and wealth" (Cirlot 22), and modern utopias have typically been based on the "beehive ideal" (Langer 110). But Susanne Langer goes on to emphasize the essential differences between human societies and hives, and as Lewis Thomas notes, we are generally not flattered today by comparisons between ourselves and swarming insects (6). Two essays written in the 1980s—the first by Thomas P. Dunn and Richard D. Erlich and a second by Arthur O. Lewis—trace the historical shift in use of this image from positive to negative connotations.

Forster draws on several familiar aspects of the hive image, the potentially positive as well as the negative, to critique the society in **"The Machine Stops"**:

  • Hives contain a great many creatures organized into an efficient, stable whole. The whole world here is a hive, made up of tier upon tier of cells—well organized indeed but nightmarish in its tessellated uniformity.

  • Bees seem continually busy, as our laudatory cliché emphasizes. Forster's individuals bustle self-importantly about their activities. Vashti is far from

idle: she has people to get back to on her network, lectures to listen to, a lecture to write, always something to do. She keeps telling Kuno to "be quick." Forster, like Huxley later, in *Brave New World,* shows people becoming consumed by their busy daily round of activities and thus shielded from thought and question about their lives, their values.

  • The individual bee seems subsumed by the group. The individual is not only small but essentially helpless, dwarfed by the system, serving it. Vashti, like almost all other members of her society, lacks the power to think or act as an individual. She talks about the growth of her soul, but all we see her doing is keeping the electronic circuits active while her soul atrophies.

Subsequent twentieth-century dystopias, such as Huxley's *Brave New World* and Zamyatin's *We,* also use the hive metaphor. Forster goes further by providing a striking visual image of a hive, but these other worlds are more hive-like insofar as the bees come and go from their hive (a feature of hives Dunn and Erlich point out in discussion of *We* [49]). In fact, Forster emphasizes the *cell* as much as the hive itself, which further defines his work. Focusing on the cell helps us to see that the differences between a beehive and a computerized, networked society matter as much as the similarities:

  • While we think of bees in a teeming mass, the modern human hive, as discussed above, is increasingly decentralized. Since the interaction is electronic, individuals are increasingly alone in their cells rather than brought together.

  • The bee is physically busy; we in our networked cells are mentally busy while our bodies are passive. Our "buzz" is electronic.

  • Beehives are stratified. People in individual cells with their machines have become homogeneous. The queen bee in such a world is the machine itself.

  • A beehive is an organic structure, with bees following natural instincts and thus fulfilling their nature. When people live in cells that totally exclude the natural world, and suppress many of their natural instincts, the result is not honey, or "sweetness and light." Living the lifestyle they think they love, Vashti and her fellows reap a recurring but unacknowledged irritability.

  • An organic hive endures, subject to the intervention of outside forces; its modern human counterpart can collapse from internal causes. In contrast to a story like Asimov's "The Evitable Conflict," in which a computer keeps the whole world's systems running smoothly, even allowing for human perversity in its calculations, Forster offers a vision that rings true to our daily experience: a computer can break down.

Forster's world of hive/cell, then, can best be described in a series of paradoxes: many people yet isolation; centralized authority, control, power, yet a decentralized lifestyle; busyness yet physical and spiritual stasis; stability yet fragility. However, Forster does not leave us with only a dark vision of a future world; like his more famous dystopian successors, he includes a rebel. El-kins comments that "we are not certain why he [Kuno] is different" (58). That very lack of explanation about Kuno may express Forster's belief in the human spirit: despite conditioning, despite counter pressures, some-thing in the best of us will remain unsatisfied and searching amidst life in an environment created by man, sustained by machine, and lived as part of an electronic network. In this sense Forster's story is more optimistic than *Brave New World,* in which both Bernard and Helmholtz Watson have inborn reasons for thinking dif-ferently from others in their society.

Kuno wants to rediscover what really matters. His con-clusions, like Forster's own, are not explicitly religious. He determines that "man is the measure"—not machine but also not God. But his understanding of man clearly includes nature, history, mystery—the big questions that we may get too busy in front of our personal computers to ask.

### Notes

1. Frederic Crews (1962), Barbara Rosecrance (1982), the 1985 *Twentieth Century Literature* spe-cial issue on Forster, and the collections of essays edited by Herz and Martin (1982, one sentence excepted) and Alan Wilde (1985, one phrase excepted), e.g., offer no discussion of the story. Critics making brief and critical mention of it in-clude Oliver, Wilde, Kelvin, Macauley, and Mar-tin; Thomson's treatment is lengthier but also criti-cal. Other somewhat lengthier treatments include Stone and Colmer; recent discussions focusing more on narrative technique include Lesser, Herz, and Widdicombe. Those citing the work as pro-phetic include Warner, Shusterman, Brander, Mar-tin, Cavaliero, Gillie, and Lesser. Critics discuss-ing it within the context of science fiction or dystopian fiction include Hillegas, Wolfe, Warrick, Dunn and Erlich, Lewis, Elkins, Beauchamp, and Pierce. Given what we have now seen of comput-erization, contemporary critics are far less likely to find Forster's central image "a problem . . . too dominant . . . too vast and inescapable" (Thomson 63), but still in 1987 Lesser comments that "part of the reason we cannot sympathize much with Forster's characters is that they inhabit a world which is defined as strictly other than ours" (179). Is it?

2. Asimov frequently comments about the "Franken-stein complex" in science fiction (e.g., 5-6).

3. Cf. Neil Postman's discussion of "technopoly," "the deification of technology, which means that the culture seeks its authorization in technology, finds its satisfactions in technology, and takes its orders from technology" (70). The "Technopoly story is without a moral center . . . [It says] there is indeed a common culture whose name is Tech-nopoly and whose key symbol is now the com-puter, toward which there must be neither irrever-ence nor blasphemy" (179). Also cf. Roszak's comments about the "Information Age, which makes every computer around us what the relics of the True Cross were in the Age of Faith"; a "cultlike mystique . . . has come to surround the computer"; there is "the real danger that we fall prey to a technological idolatry, allowing an in-vention of our own hands to become the image that dominates our understanding of ourselves and all nature around us" (x, xi, 40).

4. "'The Machine,' they exclaimed, 'feeds us and clothes us and houses us; through it we speak to one another, through it we see one another, in it we have our being'" (29): this passage echoes Acts of the Apostles 17: 28: "For in him we live, and move, and have our being" (King James Version).

5. Cf. Roszak: futurologists have promised that "no-body need ever leave the house, which will be-come school and workplace by virtue of the earth-girdling information networks that serve it"; meanwhile today's university spends "millions to spare its students the exercise of leaving their dorms" (33, 61). It is indeed tempting to indulge in detailed comparisons between Forster's story and aspects of today's computerized lifestyle—especially the Internet, video games (our children in front of a machine learning their "stops and buttons" ["Machine" 21]), a paperless environ-ment to replace the "ages of litter" (7), distance learning, virtual reality, and so on—illustrated by an aerial photo of people at computer work sta-tions. But most of that will be left to the reader's imagination. (By the way, I use as much of the above technology myself as I or my university's budget can afford.)

6. Elkins develops, without focus on computers, the issue of mediated experiences in "The Machine Stops," as technology intervenes "between man and his social and physical world" (see 55-59).

7. A term and concept Postman explores (70); cf. Roszak's discussion of "data glut" (162 ff.). With regard to Vashti's responses, cf. Postman's claim that "those who feel most comfortable in Tech-nopoly . . . believe that information is an un-mixed blessing, which through its continued and uncontrolled production and dissemination offers increased freedom, creativity, and peace of mind . . . the computer redefines humans as 'informa-

tion processors' and nature itself as information to be processed" (71, 111).

8. Note that Cox has modified or changed many of his predictions about the secular city, as he discusses in his 1995 book *Fire from Heaven*.

## Works Cited

Asimov, Isaac. *Robot Visions*. New York: Penguin Roc, 1990.

Asimov, Isaac,, Patricia S. Warrick, and Martin H. Greenberg, eds. *Machines That Think: The Best Science Fiction Stories about Robots and Computers*. New York: Holt, 1984.

Beauchamp, Gorman. "Technology in the Dystopian Novel." *Modern Fiction Studies* 32 (1986): 53-63.

Brander, Laurence. *E. M. Forster: A Critical Study*. Lewisburg, Pennsylvania: Bucknell UP, 1970.

Cirlot, Juan Eduardo. *A Dictionary of Symbols*. Trans. Jack Sage. London: Routledge, 1962.

Colmer, John. *E. M. Forster: The Personal Voice*. London: Routledge, 1975.

Cox, Harvey. *The Secular City: Secularization and Urbanization in Theological Perspective*. New York: Macmillan, 1966.

Dunn, Thomas P., and Richard D. Erlich. "A Vision of Dystopia: Beehives and Mechanization." *The Journal of General Education* 33 (1981): 45-57.

Elkins, Charles. "E. M. Forster's 'The Machine Stops': Liberal-Humanist Hostility to Technology." Erlich and Dunn 47-61.

Erlich, Richard D., and Thomas P. Dunn, ed. *Clockwork Worlds: Mechanized Environments in SF*. Westport Connecticut: Greenwood, 1983.

Forster, E. M. "The Machine Stops." *The Eternal Moment and Other Stories*. New York: Harcourt, 1956. 3-37.

———. "What I Believe." *Two Cheers for Democracy*. 1938. New York: Harcourt, 1951. 67-76.

Frost, Robert. "Education by Poetry: A Meditative Monologue." *Robert Frost: Poetry and Prose*. Ed. Edward Connery Lathem and Lawrance Thompson. New York: Holt, 1972. 329-40.

Frye, Northrop. "Varieties of Literary Utopias." *Utopias and Utopian Thought: A Timely Appraisal*. Ed. Frank E. Manuel. Boston: Beacon, 1965. 25-49.

Furbank, P. N. *E. M. Forster: A Life*. Vol. 1: *The Growth of the Novelist (1879-1914)*. London: Secker & Warburg, 1977.

Gillie, Christopher. *A Preface to Forster*. New York: Longman, 1983.

Herz, Judith Scherer. *The Short Narratives of E. M. Forster*. New York: St. Martin's, 1988.

Hillegas, Mark E. *The Future as Nightmare: H. G. Wells and the Anti-Utopians*. New York: Oxford UP, 1967.

Kelvin, Norman. *E. M. Forster*. Carbondale: Southern Illinois UP, 1967.

Langer, Susanne K. "Man and Animal: The City and the Hive." *Philosophical Sketches*. Baltimore: Johns Hopkins UP, 1962. 108-22.

Lesser, Wendy. *The Life Below the Ground: A Study of the Subterranean in Literature and History*. Boston: Faber, 1987.

Lewis, Arthur O. Introduction. Erlich and Dunn 3-18.

Macaulay, Rose. *The Writings of E. M. Forster*. New York: Harcourt, 1938.

Martin, John Sayre. *E. M. Forster: The Endless Journey*. Cambridge: Cambridge UP, 1976.

McDowell, Frederick P. W. *E. M. Forster*. Boston: Twayne, 1982.

Mowshowitz, Abbe. *Inside Information: Computers in Fiction*. Reading, Massachusetts: Addison-Wesley, 1977.

Mumford, Lewis. *The Story of Utopias*. New York: Viking, 1962.

Oliver, H. J. *The Art of E. M. Forster*. Australia: Melbourne UP, 1960.

Pierce, John J. *Foundations of Science Fiction: A Study in Imagination and Evolution*. Westport, Connecticut: Greenwood, 1987.

Postman, Neil. *Technopoly: The Surrender of Culture to Technology*. New York: Knopf, 1992.

Roszak, Theodore. *The Cult of Information: The Folklore of Computers and the True Art of Thinking*. New York: Pantheon, 1986.

Shusterman, David. *The Quest for Certitude in E. M. Forster's Fiction*. Bloomington: Indiana UP, 1965.

Stone, Wilfred. *The Cave and the Mountain: A Study of E. M. Forster*. Stanford: Stanford UP, 1966.

Thomas, Lewis. "On Societies as Organisms." *The Lives of a Cell: Notes of a Biology Watcher*. New York: Viking, 1974. 11-16.

Thomson, George H. *The Fiction of E. M. Forster*. Detroit: Wayne State UP, 1967.

Warner, Rex. *E. M. Forster*. New York: Longmans, 1950.

Warrick, Patricia S. *The Cybernetic Imagination in Science Fiction.* Cambridge: MIT P, 1980.

Widdicombe, Richard Toby. "Eutopia, Dystopia, Aporia: The Obstruction of Meaning in Fin-de-Siècle Utopian Texts." *Utopian Studies* 1 (1990): 93-102.

Wilde, Alan. *Art and Order: A Study of E. M. Forster.* New York: New York UP, 1964.

Wolfe, Gary K. *The Known and the Unknown: The Iconography of Science Fiction.* Kent, Ohio: Kent State UP, 1979.

## Silvana Caporaletti (essay date 1997)

SOURCE: Caporaletti, Silvana. "Science as Nightmare: 'The Machine Stops' by E. M. Forster." *Utopian Studies* 8, no. 2 (1997): 32-47.

[*In the following essay, Caporaletti characterizes "The Machine Stops" as one of the first contributions to twentieth-century dystopian literature, presaging many of the themes developed by later authors.*]

No matter how exalted its inventiveness, utopian literature, if it is to explicate the cognitive function that is inherent in the genre, can never be pure fantasy: it is inescapably both fictio and mimesis, poised in uneasy balance on the edge between invention and reality.[1] Because of its dual nature, the lie that the utopian text utters is then, in a way, a "true" lie. The imaginative, ideal worlds that it constructs are firmly grounded in concrete reality, being essentially isomorphic projections of those developmental tendencies that, though latent, the authors are able to perceive in the world around them. The relation between utopian literature and reality is therefore particularly problematic. By distorting and exaggerating human situations, the utopian text acts as a criticism of life, and by offering a possible, alternative model of social organization, whether positive or negative, it also acts as an implicit or explicit proposal of a substitutive reorganization. Its message is strictly related to the socio-cultural context which generates it, but seldom remains confined to it. The critical interpretation of human life that it offers and the hope in a timely, positive change that it transmits can speak to very different people in very different times.

The relation of the utopian text to reality can vary, indeed, with time, because human history and science may develop in directions that narrow the gap between imagination and reality, attenuating the fictional aspect of the text and accentuating the mimetic one, in a never ending dialectical process that gives new vigor to the text and updates it, redefining its finality and reinforc-

ing its impact on present reality. This indeed is the case of **"The Machine Stops,"** a rather long short story published by E. M. Forster in 1909. **"The Machine Stops"** is the first example of twentieth century dystopian literature and the prototypical mechanical beehive story that brings together most of the relevant motifs later developed by twentieth century dystopian authors.[2] The significance of this text seems to have increased with time, yet it has received less attention than it deserves by the major scholars of utopian literature and S/F.[3] To analyze it in order to bring out its thematic implications and show how relevant the issues that it debates are still to us, is the main aim of the following discussion.

In **"The Machine Stops"** Forster depicts an imaginary "reality" that bears the disquieting aspect of a world in which fiction has little by little substituted reality until it has replaced it almost completely. In the world of the Machine human beings live isolated in the confined and protective space of small subterranean rooms, refusing all contact with the external world because they prefer the simulation of experience to experience itself. Little more than simulacra themselves, they are fulfilled in a pseudoreality made up of voices, sounds and evanescent images, abstract sensations that can be evoked by pressing a few buttons. Feeble and colorless, unaware of their unnatural condition because completely forgetful of their true human dimension, Forster's creatures move in a hypertechnological world which electronic devices and the advent of virtual reality make today alarmingly possible. The fictional reality that Forster depicts does not appear incredible nor absurd, not only because it is validated by the internal coherence of the narrative, but also because it is the projection of scientific trends which were already at work in his time. Grounded in the fast and exalting progress of science and technology, the strange world of the Machine poses itself as the ultimate development of real scientific premises: notwithstanding its evident diversity, it stems from the same roots as the concrete, familiar world of the reader and is, therefore, hyperbole rather than paradox.

The access to the world of the Machine is direct, unmediated by a narrator: an omniscient impersonal voice, external to the story, authoritatively relates events and situations to the reader. Such a discursive technique tends to distance readers from the narrated matter and to discourage their active participation in it, rather disposing them to accept passively the recounting of long concluded events without questioning their veracity.[4] This technique is usually employed to accentuate the illusion of "truth" that the text produces, because the unique perspective, by excluding the presence of contradictory viewpoints that might destabilize the text, guarantees its internal coherence, while the absence of the mediating mind of a narrator eliminates the doubt of a possible distortion of the observer's perception. The story, that is, seems to reconstruct the events in an objective way and the "reality" of the world that it projects appears to be ontologically founded. Forster's use of this narrative technique is, however, rather anomalous, because he does not seem at all interested in generating an illusion of "true reality" in the reader. The opening words of the story, "Imagine, if you can" (109), are a clear invitation to participate imaginatively in the experience which is to be communicated, and though they do not explicitly exclude its ontological foundation, nevertheless they indirectly stress its imaginative nature. The initial uncertainty is soon resolved by two metanarrative elements that completely strip of reality the world about to be presented. The pseudotemporal definition of the description that follows, "at the moment of my meditation" (109) and the exhortation to the reader to actively intervene in the construction of the fictional world, "think of her as without teeth or hair" (115), imagining, that is, the protagonist, Vashti, toothless or bald at the reader's own liking, resolve any epistemological uncertainty. The explicit identification of the narrative matter as a mere mental matter and the authorial address to the reader subvert the usual function of this narrative technique, and the pact of complicity which is established between the author and the reader is immediate and clear.

At the thematic level, the identification of the fictional world is, in the beginning, somewhat problematic: nothing connects it explicitly with our familiar reality and it appears autonomous and totally alien. Only subsequently some clear references in the text link that world to ours, indeed identify it as ours, but dislocated at an unspecified point in the future. The topos of **"The Machine Stops"** is that of "the future world," but its recognition is delayed by the zero degree of the temporal shift.[5] This topos is, of its nature, a figure of erasure, because the illusion of reality that the text produces depends, in this case, on the assumption of the non-existence of present reality. Future world and present world, that is, are mutually exclusive because the condition for the imaginative existence of the one is the imaginative negation of the other. In order to connect worlds which are synchronically incompatible and allow a direct comparison between them, utopian writers frequently resort to narrative devices such as the time machine, for example, or the unforeseen discovery of a long-lost land, or the "sleeperwakes" motif, all fictional expedients that can bridge the diachronic gap and make plausible the simultaneous existence of two evolutionary stages very distant in time. In **"The Machine Stops,"** though, there are no time travelers, nor waking oversleepers, nor accidentally discovered long-lost lands: Forster simply eliminates the time journey and begins inside the future world without bothering to fill

the temporal gap that separates it from the present. The world-to-come thus cancels the present world, which is absent from the text and is only evoked as a mere conceptual presence in the mind of the reader. Without a character that experiences it, the contrast between the hypothetical and the real worlds remains implicit and the recognition of the relation between fiction and reality can take place only a posteriori, through metaphorical reflection.

The reader is directly introduced into a strange artificial ambience, a wide space of geometrical proportions fragmented into billions of small metallic regular cells, all self-enclosed and bare, but full of buttons, screens and marvelous mechanisms (electronic we would say today) that transform them into complete and autosufficient microcosms.

> There were buttons and switches everywhere—buttons to call for food, for music, for clothing. There was the hot-bath button, by pressure of which a basin of (imitation) marble rose out of the floor, filled to the brim with a warm deodorized liquid. There was the cold bath button. There was the button that produced literature. And there were of course buttons by which she communicated with her friends. The room, though it contained nothing, was in touch with all she cared for in the world.
>
> (112-13)

It is the inside of an apparently perfect centralized machine that extends throughout the whole planet. Human life evolves entirely in this artificial space: every cell is a protective and impenetrable receptacle that contains one individual ensuring him or her an easy existence, free of worries and need. "Human life," though, is scarcely an appropriate expression here, because the creatures that inhabit the world of the Machine hardly conform to our idea of human beings: Vashti is described as "a swaddled lump of flesh . . . with a face as white as a fungus" (109), and they are all very similar to one another. Wrapped in swaddling bands, in their impotent immobility they rather resemble larvae whose existence, entirely consumed inside their cocoons, never reaches the threshold of life. Their time is an equally unnatural dimension, measured by the intensification or the reduction of artificial illumination which signals an arbitrary alternation of night and day.

The unspecified temporal distance that separates that world from ours appears immense. Forster imagines that in the course of several millennia extraordinary scientific and technological discoveries have enabled human beings to conquer the elements and gain absolute control over nature's forces: "Night and day, wind and storm, tide and earthquake, impeded man no longer. They had harnessed Leviathan" (117). Once they became the masters of earth, water and air, intoxicated by their own power, human beings had thought of conquering light and dared the sun, trying to force it constantly above the horizon by artificially speeding up the westward movement of the earth. Frustrated in their Promethean ambition, they had then decided to conquer darkness, and excavated the interior of our planet in order to build there their realm, filling it with artificial light and the continuous, humming voice of the Machine. Darkness was so conquered, reduced into corners: everywhere, as Kuno, the young protagonist, says, "darkness is the exception" (126).

When the story opens, the surface of the earth is only dust and mud, a place of exile and death. It is the "homelessness" disseminated with the bleached whiteness of the bones of the last rebels expelled there by the Machine a long time before. The outside air is believed to be lethal for the pale and weak descendants of those ancient scientists, who have been degraded to a subhuman condition by centuries of an existence entirely spent in the protective and plentiful womb of the Machine, the big mechanical mother upon which they now totally depend. Their sickly passivity seems to be reflected in the weak dynamism of the plot which, though rich on the allegorical and symbolical levels, is almost non-existent at the level of action. Rather insubstantial in itself, the plot is further weakened by the narrative device of the tale within the tale: the only relevant episode before the tragic conclusion is narrated by Kuno to his mother Vashti, thus reaching the reader in the attenuated from of a second degree narration. Kuno tells Vashti that he had got out to the surface through an airing tube, had seen the stars in the sky and recognized his own image in them. Before being pulled back by the flexible tubes of the Mending Apparatus, he had also dimly seen a pearly luminosity, the edge of a bush and a female figure who, coming towards him in answer to his cry for help, fell on the ground with her throat perforated by a metal tentacle.

Kuno has committed no crime, because the surface of the earth is not a forbidden place, but only a place of non-desire. His transgression is behavioral: instead of applying to the Machine, he found the passage by himself and used his own poor muscles to emerge to the surface. His guilt is all in his extravagantly independent conduct, which is regarded as illicit or, as Vashti says, "unmechanical." Kuno is the only anomaly in the uniformity that reigns absolute in the world of the Machine, and from him alone a dialectical conflict could emerge; but he has no opponents and any expectation of diversity in the story is quenched in a disquieting symmetry.[6] His tale crumbles before his mother's scepticism and indignation and the voices of the only two protagonists fade into the silence of a long separation. Nothing more happens until the end when the Machine stops, causing the destruction of the billions of human

beings that depend on it. The cells disgorge then a multitude of agonizing creatures who in their powerless terror pour down the underground passages, acquiring an ephemeral solidity only at the moment of their death. With a slightly exaggerated sentimentality, Forster's story closes on Kuno's tears and on his first and last kiss of his mother while darkness and the void reappropriate to themselves their natural kingdom.

**"The Machine Stops"** basically expresses the same ethical and social preoccupations that inform all the other works of Forster, who repeatedly denounces the dangers of a materialistic ethos and of a general conformism imposed by rigid social conventions, exposing the spiritual barrenness and the emotional impoverishment generated by the repression of diversity, spontaneity and creativity. This short story belongs to the dystopian tradition but is quite different from the negative utopias close to it in time. If we compare it with Wells's *The Time Machine* or Huxley's *Brave New World* or Orwell's *Nineteen Eighty-Four* for example, we realize that, although the dystopian component that informs Forster's world is no less evident and forceful, still it remains exempt from the elements of horrific violence that darken the vision of those authors, and even displays unusually striking positive aspects. Like those writers Forster clearly perceives what Freud defined as the tragic paradox of human civilization, the impossibility of rationally reconciling two incompatible ideals, a stable and well organized society with complete individual freedom. He too is aware that stability and peace cannot exist without careful centralized planning: they inevitably depend, in part at least, on the restriction of individual will. Yet whereas their dream of social justice and equality disintegrates in a common nightmare of political violence and of a forced crystallization of society into distinct and leveled classes, Forster seems to resolve the paradox by placing at the center of his social organization the powerfulness and impersonality of a mechanical engine. With its incessant, perfectly programmed activity, the mechanical heart which sustains that world dissolves the nightmare of the cannibalistic bestiality of Wells's Morlocks or the scientifically induced monstrosity of Huxley's Deltas, Gammas and Epsilons, the horrifying prospect, that is, of a scientifically induced genetic diversification as the solution to the need of diversified social functionalities.[7] It also obviates the nightmare of a physical and mental slavery enforced on the masses by a cruel and tyrannical dominating class, such as we find, for example, in Orwell's *Nineteen Eighty-Four*. The repulsive effect of Forster's dystopian vision is, consequently, of a different nature: in part it depends, paradoxically, on the presence of essentially positive elements which, if considered in themselves, in isolation from the general context, might render the world of the Machine deceptively attractive.

There are no degrading jobs nor heavy nor unpleasant tasks to accomplish in this hypothetical society, because the mechanical apparatus, tentacular and omnipresent, wonderfully differentiated in all its innumerable functions, provides everything for everybody. Being impersonal, moreover, it is perfectly impartial, so that there are no discriminations of any kind. There are neither masters nor servants in this world: all people are equal, all engaged in one and the same pseudointellectual activity, a futile exchange of ideas in the form of short "lectures" which they in turn deliver from the sealed off space of their cells. The general fulfillment of one's needs and wishes has naturally eliminated delinquency, and individual existence appears free from danger, work, illness and pain, even from the fear of death which has assumed the attractive form of voluntary euthanasia. Neither science nor any of the sophisticated mechanisms that characterize Forster's world are conceived or used malevolently against human beings.[8] The only form of violence, the inverted Spartan ritual of examining infants at birth and eliminating "those who promised undue strength," finds a paradoxical justification in the living conditions established by the Machine: "it would have been no true kindness to let an athlete live; he would never have been happy in that state of life to which the Machine had called him" (124). This society does not know the violence of political oppression nor the horror of State torture: the Machine or the Committee that lends it its voice (probably a mechanism itself) does not impose arbitrary laws nor restrictions of any kind. It only requires a general adaptation of human behavior to its preprogrammed and scarcely adaptable mechanical nature, and this one rule is universally accepted as necessary for survival. The mechanical system is also endowed with some margin of tolerance towards diversity; those who, like Kuno, behave in an anomalous way are neither physically eliminated nor mentally reconditioned: in the past they were expelled outside into the "homelessness" of the surface and now are simply not allowed to reproduce themselves.[9] Forster's vision, then, remains exempt from the horror of the forceful enslavement of the many by the stronger few, a topos that recurs in most political dystopias and reaches its climax in *Nineteen Eighty-Four*, where the odd one out, Winston, is even deprived of his freedom to die.[10] If compared with other negative utopias of the first half of our century, the technological solution of Forster offers advantages that cannot be denied. Nevertheless **"The Machine Stops"** poses some very disquieting questions on the ethical and social evolution of a civilization that expects to find in science an answer to its many problems.[11]

This short story has been defined as a "neo-Luddite assault"[12] by those who have interpreted it as an expression of an outdated and reactionary attitude on the part of Forster. Such a view, though, appears simplistic. For-

ster's reaction is not directed against machines but against the Machine as a negative emblem of human exaggeration; his campaign, that is, is against the blindness of an absurd scientific fundamentalism that prefers to ignore the possible consequences of an excess of mechanization and technology and its inevitable effects on man's life.[13] The "meditation" that he offers us with this story is a theoretical bulwark against the facile promulgation, in this century, of a dogmatic scientific exaltation which might demolish our vulnerable humanistic ethos. A liberal and a humanist at heart, Forster does not believe in a scientific panacea; indeed he fears that the progressive mechanization of the human environment, accomplished with the illusion of rendering it more and more adequate to man's needs, might instead in time reduce man to the measure of his artificial environment. In this short story he forcefully expresses this fear by closing the human being and the Machine in a kind of systemic binomial in which, through a strange process of compensatory symbiosis, the one gains what the other loses; in his vision, that is, the evolution of the Machine will inevitably coincide, sooner or later, with the involution of the human race.

In this respect **"The Machine Stops"** seems to have greater affinities with Edward Bulwer-Lytton's *The Coming Race,* the first "modern" utopia,[14] and Samuel Butler's *Erewhon,* which were published respectively in 1970 and 1871, than with contemporary utopian fiction. In *The Coming Race* Bulwer-Lytton raises the doubt that the process of natural evolution, which many interpreted as an unlimited progress of the human species, might not necessarily be positive and even carry with it some dangers and negative implications, to the detriment of spirituality and art. In *Erewhon* Butler puts forward the hypothesis that the extraordinary technological advancement of his age, though in many respects beneficial, might escape man's control and overcome him. Parodying Darwin's theories in "The Book of the Machines," he imagines that, with time, machines might evolve an independent existence of their own and become the dominating race, reducing their creators to the abject situation of "machine-tickling aphids." These are essentially the same doubts and worries as, in a much more serious vein, inspire Forster's dystopian vision.

The rationality of the many generations of scientists who spent their energy in perfecting the Machine and making it more and more powerful and autonomous, triumphed in extending its control over what is, by nature, irrational, until, little by little, mechanical muscles and "electronic" cells replaced almost completely the physical and mental functions of human beings, expropriating them of their human prerogatives. So, at the time of the story, not only have they become so weakened as not to be able to pick up what they drop unless the floor raises it back to them, but they are also incapable of original thought. Music, literature, even poetry are produced exclusively by "electronic" devices. In their blind enthusiasm for scientific discoveries human beings have exceeded the limits allowed to them by nature and provoked the trespassing fo the mechanical into the human; so the Machine, that stupendous and tangible testimony to human intellect, almost perfect in its capacity for autoregulation and autoregeneration, has gradually and inadvertently deprived human existence of all significance, negating it almost completely in the pale and inept beings that are entirely dependent now on its obscure and omnipresent power.

The topos of the creation of monsters or of the monstrous metamorphosis provoked by human beings' disrespect for nature or by their irresponsible tampering with nature's genetic laws is central in **"The Machine Stops."** This topos recurs in S/F with significant variations. In Mary Shelley's *Frankenstein,* for example, the physical monstrosity of the "Thing" is essentially to be seen as the objective correlative of the monstrosity of the scientist's godlike ambition. Similarly, in Wells's *The Island of Doctor Moreau,* the prevailing of the beastly over the human reflects the "bestiality" of the scientist's pretense to creation through genetic manipulation. In other cases, as in Wells's *The Food of the God,* for instance, or Huxley's *Brave New World,* an unnatural mutation is provoked in human creatures, either because of eugenic ideals or a perverse political ideology, aimed at ensuring a stable and functional society. In all these cases, whether the outcome of the experiments does or does not correspond to the scientists' expectations, the creation of monstrosity is the result of a deliberate individual or collective choice. In other cases, as in Wells's *The Time Machine* or in **"The Machine Stops,"** the monstrous metamorphosis is the consequence of a process initiated unwittingly by human beings in a distant past, an unforeseen and irremediable side effect of human error. In these latter cases the vision that the texts project, usually a quasi-terminal phase of an irreversible evolutionary trend, appears particularly dismal and hopeless, because the new creatures either ignore their ancient human past or are incapable of rebellion. There seems not to be, for them, any possibility of redemption: the ferocious, cannibalesque coexistence of the Morlocks and the Eloi shall last as long as there is human life on the planet, and the spiritual monstrosity of the natural clones that inhabit the Machine, more horrific than the physical monstrosity that their bands conceal, will end only with the disappearance of their civilization.

The ancient myth of Zeus, the son who kills his father, the creature that becomes stronger than his creator and destroys him, almost a leit-motif in S/F, is also clearly perceptible in this story. Here, though, the two terms of the relation are complicated by an ironical inversion,

because in its complexity and apparent perfection the Machine, men's creature, is conceptually unattainable to its creators and appears to them eternal, mysterious, noumenal, assuming in their eyes the aspect of a benevolent God. And like a God it is secretly adored. But its superiority is purely mechanical of course: the Machine is a chthonic "divinity" without face or soul, unknown and incomprehensible, that in the end sweeps everything away in its own ruin.

The topos of the "future world" is soon revealed as that of the "death world," not so much because the story ends in a final apocalypse, but mainly because the world of the Machine is a world of death. The recurring image that describes it is the "honeycomb": it is like an immense hive that extends "tier below tier, reaching far into the earth," full of isolated cells containing each "a human being, eating, or sleeping, or producing ideas" (118). The kind of life that unrolls underground is repetitive and static, it is a condition of "life in death," closer to death than to life. The hive resembles a huge metallic mausoleum, cold and impenetrable, whose many walls each reflect an identical image; it is like a sealed labyrinth, threatening and sinister in its infinite circularity. Much more than its extraordinary "electronic" devices, by now dimmed by the daring imagination of the more recent S/F literature, what makes the world of the Machine most alien to the contemporary reader is its absolute homogeneity, the absence in it of any form of diversity. Every small cell is a perfect replica of every other, every place is the same as every other place and every individual is the same as every other individual. Because of a natural process of adaptation to the environment, the geometrical symmetry of the immense structure built by man, that concrete symbol of scientific rationality, now reflects itself in the human beings that inhabit it, imposing a single identity on all of them: "People were exactly alike all over the world" (120). The similarity of all places has deprived travel of meaning and encouraged sedentariness: "Few travelled in these days, for, thanks to the advance of science, the earth was exactly alike all over" (117). The system of space ships that still serves the whole planet is "a relic from the former age," a survival from a barbaric "civilization which had mistaken the functions of the system, and had used it for bringing people to things, instead of for bringing things to people" (117). It is a residual testimony of those "funny old days, when men went for a change of air instead of changing air in their rooms" (115).

With the exception of the few transfers decreed by the Machine "for purposes of propagating the race" (122) or for the occupation of vacant rooms, human existence unfolds entirely inside the cells, and people are so used to physical isolation that any direct contact with others repels them. Kuno's urge for experience and direct human contact is unique: "People at any time repelled her" (143), we are told of Vashti, and the few passengers that travel with her in the same space ship "sat each in his cabin, avoiding one another with an almost physical repulsion and longing to be once more under the surface of the earth" (122). The young hostess that instinctively holds out her hand to support Vashti, is aware that her gesture is "barbaric" and offensive and apologizes "for not having let her fall" (120). To leave one's cell is a painful experience because external reality arouses anguish and horror, and the proximity of others is lived as a violation of one's own privacy. The people of the Machine can tolerate only indirect contact with the outside, through the mediation of the Machine, so individual experience consists almost exclusively of metallic voices and vague faces that appear on bluish videos when they press some buttons. Nor does it matter if those images, inaccurate and blurred, render "only . . . a general idea of people" (111), canceling the "nuances of expression" and "the imponderable bloom, declared by a discredited philosophy to be the actual essence of intercourse" (111), because the impersonality of the Machine has depersonalized human beings and impressed the same likeness on everyone.

Human time is similarly stagnant: past and present paradoxically coincide, because the present is a repetition of the past and the future too is a monotonous recurrence of the past. The words, thoughts, sensations, gestures, even the "ideas" that form the present are nothing but repetition and memory: "let your ideas be second-hand, and if possible tenth-hand" is the authoritative and pressing recommendation of a respected "advanced thinker" (135). Enclosed and regulated by the wider temporality of the Machine, human time is but an empty interval consumed in artificial light, time come to a standstill, immobilized in an eternal replica that makes it revolve continually. Custom and habit are the rule of everybody's existence; novelty is abhorred as it represents disorder and perturbation. Every individual life is nothing more than a re-enactment of antecedent lives, all extinguished in the same uniformity and monotony. Stasis is almost absolute in this world made of acquiescence and passivity. The easy, comfortable, protected life that, generation after generation, the Machine people have spent within the cells of their immense hive, has quenched in them all desire for experience and knowledge, and their utmost aspiration is to consume their lives among the uncorporeal images that monitors and microphones import to their rooms. The surrogate reality that the Machine offers them is both their desire and the fulfillment of their desire.

The veil of metaphor in **"The Machine Stops"** is very thin, even too transparent: the withdrawal from the surface and the descent into subterranean cavities signal the passage of mankind from the light of logos to the obscurity of mythos. Devoured by its own excess, rationality has extinguished itself in obscurantism and superstition. The mechanical all-providing mother conceived by human beings to attain a merely material happiness detains in her womb, in perpetual gestation, human existences that are consumed in a pre-natal state. The flexible tentacle that holds Kuno and takes him back is an obscene umbilical cord that impedes his birth. The swaddling bands that cover the poor degraded bodies (larvae or mummies, the meaning is the same) are a shroud that signals their interior death and impotence. The ethical message of the author is equally clear: if not counterbalanced by a careful preservation of spiritual values, science will not lead to the elevation but to the degradation of mankind, and an uncontrolled technological progress, pursued as a goal in itself, will in the end result in human regression and involution. The Machine era may have eliminated hardship and injustice, but it has dehumanized people, deprived them of emotion, desire, passion, thought, and excised their capacity for love. It is not by chance that Vashti represents the annihilation of the strongest and most lasting form of love, the instinctive bond between a mother and her son.[15] The apparent, general "happiness" is merely a negative condition of non-pain, non-unhappiness; it is, as in Huxley's *Brave New World*, an unnatural condition artificially induced by eliminating individual desire and aspiration. In comparison with the dystopian vision of Huxley, Forster's is indeed more desolate, because in the world of the Machine there is no Savage to claim his own right to unhappiness and sorrow.[16]

The final destruction is received by the reader with a sense of painful relief, not so much because the female figure dimly seen by Kuno seems to attest to the survival of an unknown alternative human race, but because it puts an end to a civilization that barely retains any human trait. Even more than the total absence of values, emotions and creative capacity, what makes the world of the Machine so subtly disquieting is the general acritical acquiescence of its inhabitants, their mental sterility, their refusal of or even their non-desire for knowledge. In this story, that is, Forster subverts the most precious myth of humankind, the myth of Ulysses, dooming the human race forever to the brutality of ignorance.[17]

After the apocalypse Forster's story deliberately leaves open a space in what has not been said and an unresolved question hovers around this silence. Several references in the text to "the ages of litter" (144), when "forests had been destroyed . . . for the purpose of making newspaper-pulp" (121-22), to the triumph of rationality and the death of religion, and some parodic hints to an epoch of general irritability, continuous inconclusive overactivity and lack of originality, clearly indicate the close link between that world and ours. The reader is thus obliged to recognize that this link is metonymic rather than metaphorical and is awakened to the distressing awareness that the world of Kuno and Vashti does not stand for our world but is our world at the end of a process of metamorphosis that develops on a level of temporal contiguity. He must recognize himself as the progenitor of that degraded humankind and is compelled to interrogate himself on the temporal gap that separates that future world from the present.

Nowadays that gap seems to have greatly shortened. Physical weakening is a concrete danger in western societies, where motorized vehicles, automation and remote-controls have considerably reduced the need of movement, and physical exercise is for many a self-imposed practice rather than a natural necessity. Hurriedness as a mental state, irritability, emotional and physical isolation, selfishness, lack of human understanding and a general decline of religious faith, are all features of today's life. Human spaces tend to contract and fill with sophisticated electronic devices. In small flats, rooms or offices the lives of many people, constrained both in space and in time, are not really so different from the existential condition described in Forster's story. In its enthusiasm for scientific research, in its rapid technological and electronic evolution, our epoch begins to appear dangerously similar to Forster's hypothetical world.

Though obsolete in many of its aspects, the mechanical futurism of Forster's world appears threateningly close in others. Fax, e-mail, internet and other forms of telecommunication have rendered physical presence almost superfluous in human interchange, and the book, replaced by electronic sounds and images, might well be on the way to becoming a "survival from the ages of litter" (114). The advent of virtual reality is now opening new vistas which are difficult to fully evaluate. With its bedazzling wonders this new "reality" offers the possibility of individual access, in the very near future, to all kinds of experience, physical, emotional, intellectual. Poor and rich, young and old, able and disabled people alike, they will all be able to live realistic emotions and sensations in the enclosed space of their rooms—artificial experiences, of course, but with full semblance of reality. The prospect of satisfying the most daring desires of every individual is in itself exalting, but once that is achieved would it not be more comfortable and pleasant to enjoy the realization of one's aspirations in the silent tranquillity of individual solitude? May one exclude that, in time, people will come to reject any direct contact with external reality and with others? Instead of pushing human beings towards the world the new electronic technology undertakes to transport the world to them, and in the near future it may not be necessary—or desirable—to move

towards experience, because every small place will encapsulate the universe. A real unreality, a concrete illusion, virtual reality proposes to break down all boundaries between dream and life, but in the unresolvable mental confusion that might ensue between what is lived and what is imagined, between shadow and reality, human desire for life and knowledge might then be extinguished, as in the world of the Machine.

Forster's short-story is not a mere indulging in fantasy, but a serious intellectual engagement: by proposing a perverted and paradoxical version of future reality, his imaginative exaggerations and deformations provide us with an interpretative key that helps us to read our present more correctly. The effect of estrangement that the text produces, that destabilization which we find in all dystopian texts, has, as we said in the beginning, a precise cognitive value. This is true today even more than yesterday, because a century after its publication Forster's story is still very topical, it has indeed acquired an "increment of signification" (Segre, 229-30) that renders it more sinister and disquieting. The ideological message that it conveys is also very topical. It sounds a political warning to our civilization, because in this epoch, so heavily characterized by social instability, conflicts and ferocious cruelties, the safety and protection ensured by a uterine existence, wholly consumed within the sterile "womb" of a superior and all-providing authority, might appear to some perversely ideal.

*Notes*

1. Utopian literature, a definition that covers both categories of "positive utopia" and "negative utopia," tends nowadays to be considered a subgenre of S/F. Hillegas, for example, affirms that utopia (and dystopia, a term he prefers to anti-utopia) is a kind of S/F (8), and Suvin, in distinguishing between S/F stricto sensu and S/F lato sensu, defines the latter as "a literary genre whose necessary and sufficient conditions are the presence and the interaction of estrangement and cognition, and whose main formal device is an imaginative framework alternative to the author's empirical environment" (7-8), that is, as a literary genre that subsumes within itself both utopian and dystopian fiction.

2. "The Machine Stops" is a seminal work. It embodies "two symbols for human helplessness and triviality: the beehive and the machine" (Thomas P. Dunn and Richard D. Erlich, "A Vision of Dystopia," 46) that become almost commonplace in twentieth century dystopian literature. Entries in Clute and Nicholls's *The Encyclopedia of Science Fiction* (1993), Gunn's *The New Encyclopedia of Science Fiction* (1988), Nicholls's *The Science*

*Fiction Encyclopedia* (1979) and Magill's *Survey of Science Fiction Literature* (1979), for example, acknowledge its influence over works as different as David H. Keller's "The Revolt of the Pedestrians" (1928), Laurence Manning's "The City of Sleep" (1933) and "Call of the Mech-Men" (1933), John W. Campbell, Jr.'s, "Twilight" (1934), Paul Fairman's *The Machine* (1935), Eric Frank Russell's "Mechanistra" (1942), Isaac Asimov's *The Caves of Steel* (1954) and *The Naked Sun* (1956), Arthur C. Clarke's *The City and the Stars* (1956), Herbert W. Franke's *The Orchid Cage* (1961) and Robert Silverberg's *The World Inside* (1971), just to give a few examples. Leonard Heldreth (218) correctly regards Forster's short story as the prime source of the theme of the lone individual's rebellion against a totally automated or mechanized society, a theme central to many Science Fiction films, like *Logan's Run,* THX 1138, *A Boy and His Dog* and *Metropolis,* and now a commonplace motif.

3. The several reprints of "The Machine Stops" in the last decades are an indication of its constant success with the reading public, yet this work has received less attention than it deserves by literary critics. Many of the best-known scholarly works on utopian literature, such as Gerber, Walsh, Hillegas, Suvin and Kumar, either ignore it or mention it only in passing. Woodcock discusses it briefly, pointing out the recurrence of some of its motifs in Huxley's *Brave New World* and in Zamiatin's *We.* He affirms that with this short story Forster reacts against something that remains "still outside practical probability" (85), and completely overlooks its metaphorical significance. More interestingly, Berman relates Forster's "novella" to the "Myth of the Cave" section of Plato's *Republic,* stressing their affinity (they are both "myths in that they are imaginative stories dealing with the most universal of human fears and needs . . . expressed in powerful ways" and both "contain elements bearing an affinity to allegory," 179) and emphasizing Forster's "impassioned warnings against the growing nightmare of technological dehumanization" (173). Aldridge devotes some attention to "The Machine Stops," which she defines as "a neo-Luddite assault" (9). Pagetti discusses it more at length, indicating the thematic affinities that link this short story with Forster's *Maurice* and *A Passage to India,* and Lewis defines it "an excellent example of what goes wrong when people place too much reliance on their technological creations" (279). One essay, Elkins, offers a thorough and convincing discussion of the ideological relevance of "The Machine Stops." The author points out that "Forster's antagonism

towards science and technology is registered in the works of practically all the leading writers of the period," but that "his work goes beyond the usual antitechnological themes by dramatizing the role of science and technology in the demystification of nature" (48). Elkins's interesting references to Max Weber, Hannah Arendt, Roderick Seidenberg, George Herbert Mead, Robert K. Merton and Kenneth Burke (among others), prove that the issues so early raised by Forster in "The Machine Stops" remain central to the socio-political debate current in our century.

4. In describing the effects of the impersonal technique on the reader, Jackson observes that the impersonal narrator is "an authoritative, knowing voice . . . It has complete knowledge of completed events, its version of history is not questioned and the tale seems to deny the process of its own telling—it is merely reproducing established 'true' versions of what happened. . . . The effect of such narrative is one of a passive relation to history. The reader, like the protagonist, is merely a receiver of events which enact a preconceived pattern" (33).

5. For a classification of the narrative conventions typical of S/F, see Suvin's *Metamorphoses.* Fortunati discusses the variants of "stereotypy of plot" in utopian novels (41 and ff.).

6. This diffused "sense of resignation and futility" is remarked on by Elkins (58) and implicitly noted by Thomson, who remarks that the central image of Forster's story "remains a problem. It is too dominant in the narrative, too vast and inescapable" (60).

7. Notwithstanding its apparently edenic peacefulness, *Brave New World* is pervaded with subtle, hardly visible violence, no less horrible for being the more concealed. The social stability of the New World is founded on a strictly planned genetic conditioning—on the systematic violation of natural genetic laws, a most hideous form of protracted violence on foetuses, against human beings, that is, at the most vulnerable and helpless phase of their existence—and on the forced administration of drugs to the inferior classes in order to induce general contentment and prevent rebellion.

8. There are no narrative elements in the text which indicate that the Machine persecutes in any way the surface people, whose existence does not pose any danger to the mechanical society and seems to have been almost forgotten. To interpret the death of the girl seen by Kuno as a deliberate murder would not find objective textual support; it

rather appears as an accident caused by the groping movement of the tentacle searching for Kuno.

9. There is no objective evidence in the text that external air is really deadly for the Machine people; the survival of Kuno and the presence of living creatures on the surface seem rather to attest to the contrary. The equivalence between homelessness and death is probably a superstitious tradition.

10. Winston's physical survival in *Nineteen Eighty-Four* is, in my opinion, more hopeless than the suicide of the Savage in *Brave New World.*

11. The optimistic view of technological development as a positive solution to various social problems, a fundamental topos of positive utopia as we find, for example, in Edward Bellamy's *Looking Backward 2000-1887* (1888) or H. G. Well's *A Modern Utopia* (1905)—in reaction to which Forster's dystopian story was written—is quite alive in contemporary thought. As Lodge points out, the "utopian" vision that Claude Lévi-Strauss expresses in *Anthropologie* structurelle is of a world in which technological automatization will restore man to the happy condition of a mythical golden era (235). Also Marshall McLuhan and Herbert Marcuse seem to consider the extraordinary technological and electronical progress of our age full of positive potentialities for the future evolution of human life.

12. The definition is by Aldridge (9). The attitude of Forster towards technological development seems to be ambivalent, a mixture of enthusiasm and diffidence, rather similar to the reaction of the Victorians to the machine that has been convincingly described by Sussman. In particular Forster seems to share the Victorian prejudice "that as mechanization expands the affective life declines . . . that the very qualities which make for the success of the machine, its power, its precision, its unwearied ability to repeat the same action, pose the greatest danger to the psyche" (4).

13. As Beauchamp correctly remarks, "Forster early on grasped the truth that the Machine creates its own politics, its own sociology, its own rationality, its own epistemology, its own axiology and, indeed, its own theology. Modern totalitarism . . . would itself be impossible without a highly complex technological apparatus" (92).

14. In the second half of the XIX century a change occurs in the utopian tradition. Under the influence of evolutionary theories utopia tends to become anticipatory and "possibilistic" in character rather than normative and idealistic. It no longer poses the model of an ideal society, immutable and unattainable in its perfection, but begins to explore the potentialities inherent in human evolution and to anticipate some possible future "scenarios." With few exceptions (like William Morris's *Nowhere,* for example), "modern" utopian fiction does not turn to the past, to a mythical and lost golden age, but projects itself towards a possible future, while questioning the present. Once grounded in history, though, it tends to interpret not only the desires and aspirations of mankind, but also its fears and preoccupations, and the utopian dream inevitably begins to show its dark, nightmarish side. *The Coming Race* by Edward Bulwer-Lytton (1870), the first "modern" utopia written under the influence of Darwin's theories, is also a dystopia.

15. Vashti's affection for her son seems to have no genuine "maternal" quality. Quite content to communicate with him through the Machine, she is unwilling to have any direct contact with him, and the tears with which she reacts to his tale are not of pity and love, but of shame because of her son's offensive conduct. Even at the end, when they are both dying, it is Kuno who wishes to touch and kiss her. Nor is there anything surprising in her behavior, because, as the Book of the Machine, the Bible of the mechanical era, prescribes, "Parents, duties of, . . . cease at the moment of birth" (116).

16. There is Kuno, of course, who learns that "man is the measure" (125), but his acquiescence with Vashti and his solitary exploration have little resemblance with the Savage's forceful rebellion.

17. The reference here is to Ulysses as an embodiment of *libido sciendi,* the personification of a passion for knowledge which, according to Dante, most fully distinguishes man from beast: "Nati non foste a viver come bruti / ma per seguir virtude e conoscenza" (You were not born to live like beasts, but to pursue virtue and knowledge: *Divine Comedy, Inferno,* XXVI) Tennyson and Joyce, though the latter in a parodic vein, both stress this archetypal aspect of the Greek hero.

## References

Aldridge, Alexandra. *The Scientific World View in Dystopia.* Ann Arbour, MI: UMI, 1984.

Beauchamp, Gorman. "Cultural Primitivism as Norm in the Dystopian Novel." *Extrapolation* 19 (December 1977), 88-96.

Berman, Jeffrey. "Forster's Other Cave: The Platonic Structure of 'The Machine Stops.'" *Extrapolation* 17 (May 1976), 172-81.

Clute, John and Nicholls, Peter, eds. *The Encyclopedia of Science Fiction.* NY: St. Martin's P, 1993.

Dunn, Thomas P. and Erlich, Richard D. "A Vision of Dystopia: Beehives and Mechanization," *Journal of General Education* 33 (Spring 1981), 45-58.

Elkins, Charles. "E. M. Forster's 'The Machine Stops': Liberal-Humanist Hostility to Technology." In Erlich and Dunn, 47-61.

Erlich, D. and Dunn, Thomas P., eds. *Clockwork Worlds. Mechanized Environments in SF.* Westport, CT: Greenwood P, 1983.

Forster, E. M. "The Machine Stops." *Collected Short Stories.* Harmondsworth: Penguin, 1972.

Fortunati, Vita. *La letteratura utopica inglese: Morfologia e grammatica di un genere letterario.* Ravenna: Longo Editore, 1979.

Gerber, Richard. *Utopian Fantasy: A Study of English Utopian Fiction since the End of the The Nineteenth Century* London: Routledge and Kegan Paul, 1955.

Gunn, James, ed. *New Encyclopedia of Science Fiction.* Harmondsworth: Penguin, 1988.

Hillegas, Mark R. *The Future as Nightmare: H. G. Wells and the Anti-utopians.* London: Oxford, 1967.

Heldreth, Leonard. "Clockwork Reels, Mechanized Environments in Science Fiction Films." In Erlich and Dunn, 213-33.

Jackson, Rosemary. *Fantasy: The Literature of Subversion.* London: Methuen, 1981.

Kumar, Krishan. *Utopia and Anti-Utopia in Modern Times.* Oxford: Blackwell, 1987.

Lewis, Arthur O. *Of Men and Machines (1963)* cit. in his "Introduction" to Erlich and Dunn, 3-18.

Lodge, David. *The Novelist at the Crossroads.* London: Ark Edition, 1986.

Magill, Frank N. ed. *Survey of Science Fiction Literature.* Englewood Cliffs, NJ: Salem P, 1979.

Nicholls, Peter, general ed. *The Science Fiction Encyclopedia.* Garden City, NY: Doubleday, 1979.

Pagetti, Carlo. "Una utopia negativa di E. M. Forster." *Studi Inglesi* 1 (1974): 203-230.

Segre, Cesare. *Avviamento all'analisi del testo letterario.* Torino: Einaudi, 1985.

Sussman, Herbert L. *Victorians and the Machine. The Literary Response to Technology.* Cambridge, MA: Harvard UP, 1969.

Suvin, Darko. *Metamorphoses of Science Fiction: On the Poetics and History of a Literary Genre.* New Haven: Yale UP, 1979.

Thomson, George H. *The Fiction of E. M. Forster.* Detroit: Wayne State UP, 1967.

Walsh, Chad. *From Utopia to Nightmare.* Westport, CT: Greenwood P, 1962.

Woodcock, George. "Utopias in Negative." *Sewanee Review* 64 (1956): 81-97.

**Thomas March (essay date 2000)**

SOURCE: March, Thomas. "A Viable Alternative: Homosexuality as Fantastic Narrative in E. M. Forster's 'Little Imber.'" In *Literature and Homosexuality,* edited by Michael J. Meyer, pp. 93-109. Amsterdam, The Netherlands: Rodopi, 2000.

[*In the following essay, March examines Forster's "Little Imber" as an optimistic narrative of homosexual fantasy.*]

I.

*Introduction: Homosexuality, Fantasy, and Arcadia*

Considering the abundance of fantastic narrative contexts in E. M. Forster's more widely-read homoerotic short fiction, it comes as no surprise to find that in **"Little Imber,"** an unfinished and widely-ignored short story written in 1961[1], Forster once again narrates homosexual experience from within a fantastic mode. Elizabeth Heine notes **"Little Imber"**'s "fantastic dissolution of the obstacles to fatherhood ordinarily raised by homosexuality" (xxvi), and this dissolution is precisely what the fantastic narrative mode allows Forster's narrator to explore. Indeed, in "'It Must Have Been the Umbrella': Forster's Queer Begetting", Robert Martin writes briefly that "[h]ow to give permanence and continuation in time for the homosexual or anyone who does not biologically reproduce was one of Forster's most abiding concerns, echoed in life in his friendship with the Buckinghams and his godson and finding an ultimate expression in **'Little Imber'**".[2] Martin's is one of the few critical mentions of **"Little Imber"** and is the only one that provides a reading of that text's representation of homosexuality in terms of its relation to Forster's other work and his idealism. What follows is a sustained exploration of the narrativity of hetero- and homosexuality within **"Little Imber"**'s particularly optimistic homosexual fantasy

In "This Other Eden: Arcadia and the Homosexual Imagination," Byrne R. S. Fone outlines the especial appeal of Arcadian myrthology in representations of homosexuality. He writes:

> The homosexual imagination finds a special value and a particular use for this ideal, employing it in three major ways: 1) to suggest a place where it is safe to be

gay: where gay men can be free from the outlaw status society confers upon us, where homosexuality can be revealed and spoken of without reprisal, and where homosexual love can be consummated without concern for the punishment or scorn of the world; 2) to imply the presence of gay love and sensibility in a text that otherwise makes no explicit statement about homosexuality; and 3) to establish a metaphor for certain spiritual values and myths prevalent in homosexual literature and life, namely, that homosexuality is superior to heterosexuality and is a divinely sanctioned means to an understanding of the good and the beautiful. . . . Only in this metaphoric land can certain rituals take place, rituals that celebrate this mythology.[3]

"**Little Imber**" embodies the first and third of Fone's modes. In the fantastic narrative context of *this* Arcadia, the metaphorical legitimization of homosexual desire comes via the emergence of a homosexual procreative ability that replaces a sterile, outmoded heterosexuality. "**Little Imber**" not only creates a mythical space for "safe" homosexual expression but suggests its superiority to heterosexuality. However, it is a specific *type* of heterosexuality that "**Little Imber**" discounts—one that insists upon an exclusive claim to procreative viability. "**Little Imber**" explores a third alternative to these two conceptions of homosexual Arcadia by positing homosexual superiority only provisionally, in the service of a narrative whose ultimate aim is the creation of a world in which *both* sexualities share procreative power and, thus, metaphorical legitimacy.

The importance of the fact that the manuscript of "**Little Imber**" remains unfinished—or not clearly finished—extends beyond any biographical significance that such an apparent lack of closure might indicate.[4] Each ending creates its own implications concerning the feasibility of an Arcadia that transcends the mere fantasies of homosexual acceptance or superiority.

## II.

*THE HETEROSEXUAL PROCREATION NARRATIVE*

"**Little Imber**" takes place in a "lamentable future"[5] where heterosexual procreation teeters on the verge of obsolescence, plagued by the sterility of most of the male population. In a world that places a premium on their procreative potential, the few men who can produce vital sperm are flown to various impregnation camps, where they will bed numerous women during their stay, in the hope of producing offspring and offsetting the terrible sexual imbalance that plagues this society. Clearly, it is this imbalance, and not the procreative revolution that it provokes, that constitutes the lamentability of this future for Forster's narrator, who, in order to create his homosexual Arcadia, must first undermine assumptions of the (exclusive) naturalness of heterosexual procreation that persist even in this fantastic

context. Thus, from the beginning, Forster's narrator limits the fantastic mode's transformative power in order to engage in a more thorough examination of the very prejudices that make the allegorical representation of homosexual acceptability necessary.

The story begins with Warham, an elderly but still potent impregnator, whose arrival is the occasion for the narrator's first observations of the cult of heterosexual procreation that has sprung up as a result of this supposed sexual crisis. Warham's arrival at this particular enclave of fertile women signals the beginning of a critique of the assumption heterosexual procreation's exclusive naturalness to which Warham and the other members of this cult adhere with zealous severity. It is only later, upon Imber's arrival, that Warham becomes one of the progenitors of the "new" pansexuality that this text fantasizes.

In order to combat a literal sterility, heterosexuality in "**Little Imber**" has become figuratively sterile, narratable only in terms of its cult-like regimentation, its roteness. The fantastic premise of this narrative, that homosexual procreation offers a viable and vital alternative to a defunct heterosexuality, requires first a representation of the heterosexual procreation cult as incapable of masking its dysfunction: the inability of the cult's members to consider alternatives that might undermine their claims to naturalness. The sex farm itself is a wry inversion of the nunnery, a secluded space inhabited by women whose devotion does not preclude sexuality but finds its basis *in* sexual activity. Indeed, the matron of this establishment is first described as having "an abbess-like quality" (226) and is referred to throughout as the "Abbess". But her domain is decidedly unlike what one might expect a nunnery to be; her charges are "by no means nuns, and . . . [are] dressed to please" (226). The body has replaced the soul as the locus and foundation of religious practice.

Even so, this new religion is not freely hedonistic; its devotion to the body is a mechanical one, concerned not with the spontaneity of pleasure but with the end result of viable offspring. (As we will see later, the full progression from spontaneous lust to pleasure to procreation remains coded as natural in this text, but only in terms of homosexuality, at least at first). The Abbess, as representative of the institutional forces governing these procedures, rules with the proverbial iron fist. When one girl complains that Warham looks "rather thin" (227), the Abbess chastises her: "Very well, that rules you out" (227). Fascist dogmatism and an unquestioning adherence to protocol have replaced the spontaneity of pleasure in sexual activity. Ironically, a renewed effectiveness in mating does not result from this regimentation. When the Abbess meets Warham, we are told that "[i]t was not their first meeting. Their previous one had been attended by no fruitful consequences, so they ignored it as was the custom" (227). Failure is so widespread within this rigorous machine as to allow the establishment of customary practices for dealing with that failure.

Yet, in a move that foreshadows the era of pansexual tolerance yet to emerge, Forster's narrator mediates the harsh representation of the heterosexual cult by revealing Warham's honorable intentions:

> [H]e was profoundly concerned by the sterility that was nibbling into the human race, and particularly by the shortage of males. Thoughtful, high-minded and intelligent, he was devoting his autumn to counteracting this . . . saddened—though he never said so—by the inadequate results.
>
> (227)

Although we find yet another reference to the inefficiency of this regimentation, its "inadequate results," we are not to dislike Warham for his involvement in this cult. His actions stem from his profound sense of civic—even humane—duty. But like the others, Warham remains unable to see an alternative, a blindness that indicates an acquiescence in that structure's assumption of naturalness, even in the face of its most unnatural attributes. Clearly, a solution to the problem cannot begin here, on these terms, among these people. Some sort of provocation is needed to disturb the cult's self-satisfaction.

### III.

*IMBER'S DISRUPTION*

Warham's conversion begins with the introduction of Imber, a rambunctious youth whom the cult's bureaucrats have dispatched mistakenly to the same enclave that Warham is servicing. His unexpectedness effects a disruption of the order that signifies the further disruption tthat will result from his continued presence. Although his role as stud makes him a part of this order, Imber is completely irreverent in regard to it. He calls the Abbess "old Lady" (227), and in response to the Abbess' query as to why he is there, he responds, not that he is doing his duty—the response one would expect from the dutiful Warham—but simply, "To fuck" (228). Even before she has learned the purpose of his visit, the Abbess refers to Imber's arrival as "Another routine breakdown" (227), simultaneously underscoring the inefficiency of the heterosexual procreative cult and marking the beginning of its obsolescence.

Not only is Imber disruptive and irreverent, but he has an effect on Warham that undermines the latter's belief in his place in this structure. The Abbess, out of deference to Warham, has proposed keeping the two apart during their stay; but, by refusing to grant him the status normally accorded to one in his role as stud, her action attempts to remove Imber's symbolic threat Warham's response to Imber, following Imber's treating him like a doddering old man and before their sexual encounter(s), indicates the moment at which Imber's influence as an *alternative* sexual ideology begins:

> He had been terribly hurt personally—a snake had reared up—he was jealous of youth, he was angry with age, and though he was not impotent he was frightened of being accused of it. . . . All this was a terrible worry, but beyond it was something more urgent: the decay of the human race. If he couldn't arrest it, who would? People like Imber. . . . "He's not a gentleman," he said, speaking aloud. The word was an old-fashioned one, long out of use.
>
> (229)

Warham's anachronistic defensive posture indicates his inability to discredit Imber in terms of the procreational structure of which they are both a part. Indeed, Warham's fear is that Imber will prove *more* valuable than he in this capacity. To counteract this surge of jealousy (or *attraction,* far more frightening!), Warham assures himself with a rehearsal of his own noble reasons for involvement in this practice. In effect, the only criticism that Warham can direct at Imber is that he does not share this lofty morality. The resistance to Imber, then, is a resistance to a cavalier attitude toward this work, and to an unabashed *enjoyment* of one's sexuality, attitudes clearly antithetical to the procedural and devotional tone with which such matters have been treated heretofore. And, even at the moment of these objections, a rejection of Imber on these grounds has already begun to enter obsolescence. The reared snake has entered Warham's consciousness not only as a personal rival, but as an alternative to Warham's sacred rationalizations of his position, and, ultimately, to the heterosexual procreative cult's assumption of naturalness

### IV.

*THE TRANSITION FROM A HETEROSEXUAL TO A HOMOSEXUAL PROCREATION NARRATIVE*

Robert Martin comments that "[i]t is not, of course, the fantasy biology that is of interest here, but rather the agonistic relationships between men that had by now preoccupied Forster for 60 years."[6] Though Martin's identification of **"Little Imber"** as a tale of male-male "agonistic relationships" is certainly worth exploring, the text's "fantasy biology" *is* of interest precisely in terms of what it allows these kinds of relationships to signify. It is this fantastic narrative context that allows an allegorical representation of homosexuality's viability, though the initial narrative function of homosexual sex is to allow the heterosexual procreative narrative to continue. When the very impotence that Warham dreads does come, its only solution is Imber, first as an accomplice in effecting the coherence of the heterosexual procreation narrative, and then as a vehicle in the establishment of its alternative. The act that inaugurates homosexuality's alternative viability actually occurs under the auspices of the heterosexual procreation narrative. It is only later that its results become apparent, indicating the homosexual plot's gradual pulling away from the heterosexual plot, an incremental narrating of its own potentials within this fantastic Arcadian narrative.

Indeed, the first sexual encounter between Warham and Imber is anything but lovely, or even capable of embodying a complete opposition to the heterosexual cult in whose domain it occurs. Just prior to this scene, Warham meditates once again on the significance of Imber's presence at the compound:

> The carelessness of Headquarters in sending two males to one smallcommunity was most reprehensible. How can fertilization prosper unless properly directed? Phrases like this kept coming to him as he changed his raiment in preparation for his promised visit [to impregnate one of the women], but they would not hang together as in the old days. Could Imber be inhibiting him? And just as this idea occurred Imber blundered in. He had been allotted the other half of the Birth House and had lost his way.[7]

Thus, even before the sexual encounter occurs, it is clear that Imber's disruption has entered a new phase, that he represents more than the simple irreverence or potential rivalry that initially so horrified Warham. Warham now finds himself unable to find comfort in the doctrine according to which he has proceeded thus far under an assumption of humane nobility. Such assurances fail to "hang together as in the old days"—the days, in other words, prior to Imber's arrival.

Following this intrusion, Imber and Warham compare and confirm their respective virilities by displaying their erections. The standoff ends in a sexual encounter:

> Their hatred passed into wrestling which presently quietened, and they parted without looking at each other or at the seed that they had both dropped onto the Birth House floor.
>
> (230)

However, the homosexual act has not yet differentiated itself from the heterosexual one by legitimizing lust. The two men refuse to acknowledge what they have done, and cannot face each other or the product of their union. Warham, still the embodiment of the principles of the heterosexual procreation regime, nevertheless finds his commitment to these principles wavering even further following this incident:

> Undisturbed, Warham continued his preparations to visit the women. Or rather, he refused to be disturbed. What had happened was a bestial trifle which he proposed to ignore, and exactly what was to be expected from such a man. . . . He would not admit that he too had been involved and had expended virility at an inappropriate time. This truth, with much else that was disquieting, only dawned on him when he rejoined his hostesses.
>
> (230)

It is not that Warham is *un*disturbed but that he resists the disturbance of his principles that a recognition of the significance of this act would effect. Imber here begins to take on the full force of his signifying power; his oppositional position consists not merely in his irreverence but in his association with the alternative of homosexuality. Thus, his apparent lack of interest in what has just happened seems more likely to be the result not of revulsion but of his being accustomed to such experiences. It is only upon his return to his hostesses that Warham begins to realize the significance of his participation; that is, it is only in the presence of the representatives of the cult and its oppressive regimentation that the potentialities represented by Imber's opposition become most apparent to Warham. He is unable to deny his own participation and must, therefore, acknowledge the significance of his oppositional position, the very awareness of which has only been made possible by his encounter with those whose expectations of his commitment he can no longer share.

However, all of this simply serves to establish homosexuality in an oppositional position, not in itself a startling achievement, and certainly not one that requires such a fantastic narrative context for its assertion. Although the encounter between Imber and Warham will result in the assertion of homosexuality as a viable procreative option, homosexuality's narrative role is still one of subordination to the heterosexual procreation plot. Although Warham has begun to realize the possibilities that Imber represents, if for nothing else than for pleasure, he invokes Imber in the service of his own role in the heterosexual cult: "[H]e realized . . . that he could not consummate any intimate relationship unless Imber said fuck" (232). It is in Warham's requiring Imber's invitation to sex in order to achieve erection, that the homosexual procreation narrative gains viability, even though it is not yet clear that procreation is a possibility that it can claim. As an auxiliary force in the heterosexual narrative, however, homosexuality *is* taking part in procreation, and with its opposition to heterosexuality not established in terms of procreative impediment, the ground is broken for the development of a uniquely homosexual procreation narrative.

V.

The text endeavors to associate a naturalness with homosexual procreation that underscores and continues to define the unnaturalness of the heterosexual regimentation that it has already put in place. With Warham's and Imber's realization that the semen they have expended has taken on a life of its own, the significance of their earlier homosexual act becomes apparent. No longer something either repulsive or, on the other hand, routine, homosexual intercourse is revealed as capable of procreation. It would seem that the homosexual narrative can now be weaned away from its dependence upon the heterosexual procreation narrative in order to establish one of its own. The Birth House remains a birth house, the site not only of a literal birth whose cause is homosexual intercourse, but of the birth of a homosexual procreational viability whose naturalness can now be fully articulated.

The presentation of this fantasy of the naturalness of homosexual experience in **"Little Imber"** is consistent with what Alan Wilde characterizes, in his essay "The Naturalisation of Eden," as the overwhelmingly Priapean tone of Forster's later short fiction. Wilde writes:

> Priapus . . . concentrates desire to a burning point, heedless of what else, outside its narrow limits, is consumed in the flames. The naturalisation of other kingdom—of Eden or Arcadia—produces, then, a world of random, multiple, and fractured incidents. . . . In the landscape of unmediated desire, everything exists, and though it is not true that nothing has value, still value is now a function of a Priapic assent to disconnection and to the unrelated, intermittent, and isolated pleasures it entails.[8]

The homosexual act in **"Little Imber",** however, is far from an "unrelated, intermittent, and isolated pleasure." While the satisfaction of homosexual desire begins in this text with a brutal act, an act of rebellious discontinuity with the sexual ideology already in place, the emergence of homosexual procreative possibility signals the beginning of a new era of pansexual liberation, an "other kingdom" whose inhabitants no longer *think* in terms of the oppositions between heterosexuality and homosexuality—or sterility and fecundity—that are in place at the text's beginning. And this ideological upheaval is just as fantastic as the homosexual procreation that has brought it into being.

In the aftermath of Warham's and Imber's capitulation to passion, the representation of homosexual procreation proceeds according to a strategy of differentiation from the specific deficiencies of the heterosexual procreative paradigm already established. It is already obvious from the method according to which the concep-

tion has occurred that homosexual procreation is more efficient than the regimented heterosexual methods that customarily fail even here among the most virile and fertile of its practitioners. The child is conceived and born in a space of hours, rather than months, and is the fruit of only one spontaneous encounter, rather than dozens of labored attempts at conception. This ease of conception, its almost primordial spontaneity, signals an attempt to establish this homosexual procreation as more natural in opposition to the mechanistic heterosexual method.

When Warham and Imber arrive to witness the death throes of their creation, it is Imber who observes: "Well it's life isn't it and we're instructed to make life if we can. It's what we've been trained for."[9] Life is life, for Imber, and this new life no less naturally so than that which results from heterosexual efforts. Imber blames himself and Warham for the death of their child, who has been left alone while they have been off attempting to procreate in the old way. This attitude represents an attempt by Forster's narrator to establish an opposition between these two methods on the basis of their respect for life; but this is an opposition that will not hold, as the text's (primary) conclusion will indicate. The naturalness of life's new cause, here, is reiterated when Imber and Warham devote themselves to the service of this new, homosexual procreative method:

> Retiring to a pagan grove, the whereabouts of which they concealed, they perfected their technique and produced Romuloids and Remoids in masses. It was impossible to walk in that countryside without finding a foundling, or to leave two together without finding a third. The women were stimulated and began to conceive normally as of old, their sons got raped by the wild boys and buggered their daughters who bore sons, the pleasing confusion increased and the population graph shot up until it hit the jackpot. Males had won."

(235)

The stiflingly mechanical religion of the heterosexual procreative cult is replaced by an ostensibly more natural primal sexuality, whose procreative power far outstrips the method it has replaced. In spite of the troubling reference to rape here, it is clear that the population crisis has been solved with a return to a natural lustfulness and impulsiveness, coded here as natural in its return to a pastoral ideal, that the heterosexual *cult* does not possess.

This ending casts Imber and homosexual procreation as disruptive not of heterosexuality's *validity* but of its failure to acknowledge life-giving alternatives—in short, of its sexual fascism.[10] Homosexual procreation has still functioned as a corollary of the heterosexual procreation narrative, but by serving as the impulse and rationale for heterosexuality's disassociation from the cult.

In the first instance, as we have seen in Warham's need to invoke Imber in order to perform his duty, homosexual impulses serve the propulsion of the heterosexual cult's procreation narrative. When it becomes clear that these methods—both "natural" now—can co-exist, the oppositions already established lose their narrative significance. Heterosexuality itself is no longer sustainable in an oppositional position, indicating that its original oppositional status has been a function not of its *un*-naturalness but of the failure of its cult to accommodate the naturalness of homosexuality's procreative viability. That is, the most artful irony of this story is that the opposition it establishes upon codes of naturalness and efficiency is not one that is sustainable once the narrative of homosexual procreation has been established upon that foundation.

## VI.

### THE "INCOMPLETENESS" OF "LITTLE IMBER"

This "new" method is not adopted universally. But even more important, the text does not end in a definitive manner[11] that establishes a final tone according to which we may interpret the significance of these ultimate arrangements. Is it a problem that, even within a fantastic context, this narrative of homosexuality does not end conclusively? Taking all of these endings as viable parts of the text, it becomes clear that Forster's narrator is attempting to navigate a very difficult passage that will allow the homosexual allegory to retain its potency while also undoing the oppositions that the text has required early on.

In his "Terminal Note" to *Maurice,* Forster discusses similar difficulties in relation to the conclusion of that text's sentimental homosexual narrative.[12] I look to this text not to endow my discussion of **"Little Imber"** with an authority founded in Forster's intention, but in order to identify difficulties that arise in a Forsterian narration of homosexuality. I read the "Terminal Note," then, in much the same way that I read the alternative endings available for **"Little Imber"**—as a *part* of that text. Although the narrator makes his presence known here, which he does not in **"Little Imber"**, the effect of this presence is to underscore the narrator's anxiety concerning the viability of the sentimental narrative that he has ostensibly given us in its completion.

The "Terminal Note" begins with an apology for *Maurice*'s happy ending:

> A happy ending was imperative. I shouldn't have bothered to write otherwise. I was determined that in fiction anyway two men should fall in love and remain in it for the ever and ever that fiction allows, and in this sense Maurice and Alec still roam the greenwood. I dedicated it 'To a Happier Year' and not altogether vainly. Happiness is its keynote-which by the way has

had an unexpected result: it has made the book more difficult to publish. Unless the Wolfenden Report becomes law, it will probably have to remain in manuscript. If it ended unhappily, with a lad dangling from a noose or with a suicide pact, all would be well, for there is no pornography or seduction of minors. But the lovers get away unpunished and consequently recommend crime.[13]

As a sentimental narrative, the homosexual *bildungsroman* is necessarily fantastic, for Forster's narrator. The narrative space is conceived especially for an exploration of "happiness" that the narrator identifies as available *only* in this fictional space—which, of course, it is, whether written of homosexuality or heterosexuality or any variant in between. Forster's *expression* of these historical and political concerns as fundamental in the shaping of this narrative's conclusion indicates a profound anxiety concerning the status of homosexuality as a narrative that is also apparent in his adamance in defending the definitiveness of the book's conclusion:

> The chapter after their reunion, where Maurice ticks off Clive, is *the only possible end* to the book. I did not always think so, nor did others, and I was encouraged to write an epilogue. It took the form of Kitty encountering two woodcutters some years later and gave universal dissatisfaction.
>
> (254, my emphasis)

The only way to narrate the sentimentality of the text is to make it fantastic in the sincerity of its belief in the possibility of enduring love in a distinctly homosexual space, the greenwood, an Arcadian safe haven of the kind Fone describes. The professed necessity of the rejection of Clive indicates the narrator's anxious impulse to effect a clean break from the heterosexual/homosexual oppositional tensions that have driven the narrative throughout and have allowed the articulation of homosexual experience only that it may break free of this defining dialectic in order to roam the greenwood in an imaginary vacuum. But since this is a sentimental narrative, the ingenuousness of the conclusion should need no further modification. The very necessity of an extended defense indicates not only a dissatisfaction with the narrative's conclusion, but, as is clear from the political and social impeti the narrator identifies for the novel's ending, the perceived *necessity* of writing homosexual experience in this way.

The many available conclusions of **"Little Imber"** indicate a similarly anxious dissatisfaction with the writing of homosexuality within the very fantastic narrative mode that has allowed the metaphorical expression of its vitality and legitimacy. Although these do not represent an exhaustion of the material available in the manuscript notes, two of the story's endings are especially interesting in terms of the potential implications they represent for the narration of homosexuality within a fantastic context. In the manuscript notes, Heine gives us the following information regarding a more flippant ending than that which ends the story in the main text:[14]

> The opening of the earlier version of the conclusion shown in the text inserts "male" before "babe" but is otherwise identical through "strain" and fairly close thereafter: *"The women cherished it and it duly repaid them but what it really <wanted>÷esired/ was a mate of its own type, and as soon as it found one things hummed. They retired to a pagan grove to perfect their technique <and until they produced a male daily and twins on Sundays."*
>
> (336, my emphasis)

The withdrawal into a natural landscape in order to establish a homosexual procreative space is the same here, but the reference to the production of "a male daily and twins on Sundays," injects a far more flippant tone than exists in the ending I've already examined. If not a return to the very mechanization of sexuality against which homosexuality in this story has asserted itself, this comment is at the very least a reduction of the significance of the achievement by presenting it in terms more suited to a train schedule. Heine also provides the following information regarding a more foreboding conclusion:

> The last words of the conclusion shown in the text originally read: "the population graph shot up <though no one had the leisure to read it> §harply until <the bell rang> a bell rang/. Hope, energy, enterprise hen/ returned to the world. So unfortunately did warfare."
>
> (336)

The return of warfare here would serve to undermine the unique positivity that homosexuality has achieved in the narrative. The restorative aspect of homosexuality's procreative viability becomes undermined by its ultimate complicity in returning the world to a state in which the very life that has been so lovingly cultivated loses its value.

What is the significance of these contrary endings in terms of the narratability of homosexuality in **"Little Imber"**? Neither the flippancy of the one nor the horror of the other would serve to reinforce the allegory of the dawning of homosexual *procreative* viability whose emergence is the primary purpose of the text's fantastic narration. Just as *Maurice* requires a "happy ending" in order to create the possibility of the "greenwood," a fictional space reserved exclusively for the dream of the durability of homosexual love, **"Little Imber"** requires an ending that will allow its revolutionary sexuality to remain untainted by scorn or disaster. For this reason, the ending that Heine includes in the text of the story itself, rather than in the notes, is perhaps the most narratively appropriate. Ending on a comic or violent note would begin to reestablish a hierarchization of sexuali-

ties that the text otherwise successfully topples, by virtue of a reduction of homosexual procreation to a joke or an accomplice in horror. What the accepted ending accomplishes, however, is the establishment of the co-existence of both procreational alternatives within the same narrative space. The opposition of the two on the basis of *either*'s claim to naturalness has been replaced by an abundance of procreational viabilities, neither of which claims a more "natural" status than the other.

VII.

*CONCLUSION: MISOGYNY?*

If "[m]ales had won" (235), what of the women? It might seem that the advent of homosexual procreation signals a transition for men in their role as studs that undermines the importance of women in the procreative process. No longer required to service the women of the cult, men can now turn to servicing themselves, independently. However, the continued viability of heterosexual procreation ensures that women do not vanish from the procreative picture. A reading of the representation of women in this story in terms of misogyny is further undermined by the fact that women are not represented in a consistently negative manner throughout. By the story's end, they are a vital—and not rigid or disciplinarian or deceitful—part of the resurgent heterosexual procreative population. Negative characterizations of women die with the old heterosexual cult, although before its demise, they are especially blatant. The most negative of these representations occurs in the following passage, in which we learn of Warham's condescending "tolerance" of what he views as the necessary flaws of female character:

> How clever and pleasant the Abbess was! He knew by experience that she was not always straightforward. . . . But he never resented duplicity in women, it was part of their charm—and she certainly felt as he did over the grim curse of sterility, this growing unbalance between the sexes. Everything had been tried—pills, injections, transferences, everything failed, and there was a theory in favour—she told him now about it—that male and female had got tired of each other without knowing it and refused to breed because of boredom.[15]

Warham may make misogynistic observations about the Abbess and about women in general, but these come only *before* his awakening at the hands of Imber. If the women are represented early on in a negative fashion, so too are the men, in Warham's stodginess and inflexibility, as well as in his dogmatic attitude toward sex. Of course, Imber's disregard for the Abbess is a function of his irreverence toward the entire system; however, when Warham makes these remarks, as a fully functioning member of the cult, he is contributing to a narrative opposition between heterosexuality and homosexuality that will eventually undermine the very ideological framework from within which he speaks.

Thus, it is not woman but rigid heterosexuality that is evil, and instead of taking advantage of the fantastic narrative context of the text in order to postulate an exclusively homosexual world, **"Little Imber"** confronts the divisiveness of such a tactic by making it available only in order to reject it. Certainly, with the establishment of the opposition between heterosexuality's cult and the new homosexuality in terms of naturalness, the text could have ended with the complete demise of heterosexual reproduction, in order to reinforce the metaphorical representation of homosexuality's viability that homosexual procreation makes available. Such a move, however, would simply have re-enacted the divisive sexual politics against which homosexuality is postulated in the first place. But **"Little Imber"** refuses these narrative availabilities and seeks instead to interrogate and undermine the notion of sexual "naturalness" in a way that allows both sexualities to remain intact. The text's ending—in any of its endings—suggests the ongoing practice of homosexual procreative methods, thus maintaining the availability of an allegorical reading of the naturalness of non-procreative homosexuality itself.

### Notes

1. Elizabeth Heine, "Editor's Introduction," *Arctic Summer and Other Fiction.* by E. M. Forster. (New York: Holmes & Meier, 1981.), xxvi. Vol. 9 of *The Abinger Edition of E. M. Forster.*

2. Robert K. Martin, "'It Must Have Been the Umbrella': Forster's Queer Begetting," *Queer Forster.* Eds. Robert J. Martin and George Piggford. (Chicago: The University of Chicago Press, 1997), 272.

3. Byrne R. S. Fone, "This Other Eden: Arcadia and the Homosexual Imagination," *Literary Visions of Homosexuality,* ed. Stuart Kellogg (New York: The Haworth Press, 1983), 13. Also published as *Journal of Homosexuality* Vol. 8. Numbers 3/4 (Spring/Summer 1983).

4. "Although Forster seems to have regarded the story as complete, his final decisions are not indicated in the manuscript. Nor is the transition to the most obvious conclusion clear, for two poems intervene, and it is uncertain whether Forster tested the various versions of the ending in the back of the tiny notebook he used for the story before or after he wrote out its main body in the front. But fuller explanations of these manuscript difficulties and editorial choices will be found . . . among the notes" (Heine xxvii-xxviii). For more information on the status of the manuscript, see Heine's notes in this edition, pp. 334-336.

5. E. M. Forster, "Little Imber." *Arctic Summer and Other Fiction.* Ed. Elizabeth Heine. (New York: Holmes & Meier, 1981), 226. Vol. 9 of *The Abinger Edition of E. M. Forster.*

6. Martin, 272.

7. Forster, "Little Imber," 229.

8. Alan Wilde, "The Naturalisation of Eden," *E. M. Forster: A Human Exploration,* ed. G. K. Das and John Beer. (New York: NYU Press, 1979), 206.

9. Forster, "Little Imber," 233.

10. In *Political Inversions: Homosexuality, Fascism, & the Modernist Imaginary* (Stanford: Stanford UP, 1996), Andrew Hewitt explores 20th century theoretical and cultural associations of homosexuality with Fascism. He writes in Chapter 7, "Murder and Melancholy: Homosexual Allegory in the Postwar Novel": "I propose . . . that the prevailing tactic of post-World War II culture has been to enclose fascism as the figure of an unclosable, irrational logic, and that it is through the trope of homosexuality that this enclosure takes place. What is at issue is not simply the alterity of fascism—that its homosexualization ensures from the perspective of a heterosexist critical theory—but the *nonproductive* function of fascism that homosexuality is assumed to replicate. Homosexuality cannot (re-)produce a discourse of truth any more than fascism: yet as the negative representation (or allegory) of this radical negativity, the homosexual trope in fact opens up both itself and fascism to the production of truth and meaning. As an allegory of fascism, homosexuality re-presents an absence, and turns it into a loss. The structure of allegory (which-as we shall see—is itself used to figure the structure of a self-defeating homosexual desire) ascribes to fascism a meaning: meaninglessness." (245-6). "Little Imber" accomplishes the opposite characterization—a non (re-)productive heterosexual fascism is undone by a (re-)productive homosexuality.

11. Heine notes in the text of "Little Imber," just before providing the ending that I have already discussed, that "[t]here is no direct connection to the most conclusive ending" (234). Nevertheless, what I hope to show is that this ending is in many ways preferable to two earlier versions.

12. Martin identifies "Little Imber", interestingly, as the fulfillment of *Maurice's* sexual promise, what I would refer to as this text's fantastic fulfillment of *Maurice's* sentimentality. Martin writes that "[a]lthough cast in a comic and sometimes misogynistic mode, the story is in many ways a continuation not only of the erotic desires of *Maurice*

. . . but also of the other novels and their preoccupation with the intersections of death and desire" (273).

13. E. M. Forster, *Maurice: A Novel*, (New York: W. W. Norton & Company, Inc., 1993), 250.

14. The following is a partial list of Heine's explanation of the editing marks found in these passages:

(1)  . ./ words between oboli inserted by Forster

(2) < . . . words within angle brackets deleted by Forster

(3) < . . . . . / (*a*) words deleted, then reinserted by Forster; or (*b*) words between oboli substituted by Forster for words within angle brackets (xxxiii).

15. Forster, "Little Imber," 231.

*Works Cited*

Fone, Byrne R. S. "This Other Eden: Arcadia and the Homosexual Imagination." In *Literary Visions of Homosexuality,* edited by Stuart Kellogg, 13-34. New York: The Haworth Press, 1983. Also published as *Journal of Homosexuality* Vol. 8. Numbers 3/4. Spring/Summer 1983.

Forster, E. M. "Little Imber." In *Arctic Summer and Other Fiction,* edited by Elizabeth Heine, 226-235. New York: Holmes & Meier, 1981. Vol. 9 of *The Abinger Edition of E. M. Forster.*

———. *Maurice: A Novel.* New York: W. W. Norton & Company, Inc., 1993.

Heine, Elizabeth, ed. "Editor's Introduction." In *Arctic Summer and Other Fiction.* By E. M. Forster,. vii-xxxv. New York: Holmes & Meier, 1981. Vol. 9 of *The Abinger Edition of E. M. Forster.*

Hewitt, Andrew. *Political Inversions: Homosexuality, Fascism, & the Modernist Imaginary.* Stanford: Stanford UP, 1996.

Martin, Robert K. "'It Must Have Been the Umbrella': Forster's Queer Begetting." In *Queer Forster,* edited by Robert J. Martin and George Piggford, 255-273. Chicago: The University of Chicago Press, 1997.

Wilde, Alan. "The Naturalisation of Eden." In *E. M. Forster: A Human Exploration,* edited by G. K. Das and John Beer, 196-207. New York: NYU Press, 1979.

## Paul March-Russell (essay date 2005)

SOURCE: March-Russell, Paul. "'Imagine, if you can': Love, Time, and the Impossibility of Utopia in E. M. Forster's 'The Machine Stops.'" *Critical Survey* 17, no. 1 (2005): 56-71.

[*In the following essay, March-Russell studies Forster's "The Machine Stops" as a key science fiction narrative, calling it a reactive response to the writings of H. G. Wells as well as a precursor to later works by such authors as George Orwell and Aldous Huxley.*]

In 1909, E. M. Forster published his only work of science fiction, the dystopian fable, **"The Machine Stops".**[1] The story portrays a futuristic world-state that exists underground, and in which the inhabitants lead separate lives united only by the Machine, a gigantic technological network that supplies all the citizens' needs. The narrative focuses upon Kuno, who disobeys the Machine and ventures aboveground, and his estranged mother, Vashti. Taking as its cue David Ayers' recent discussion of *A Passage to India* (1924), the following analysis argues that the reconciliation between Vashti and Kuno, once the Machine has stopped, describes a transgressive notion of love that is also related to the need for imagination within an otherwise rationalised existence. In other words, while the social setting of Forster's story is dystopian, the narrative retains a residual utopian element. As Krishan Kumar has argued, utopia and dystopia are inextricably related and in earlier, pre-Victorian texts both elements often co-exist. Kumar writes that 'this balance was destroyed' only once 'utopia appeared a real possibility, an actual prospect'.[2] During the late nineteenth century, the tradition of the satirical utopia, embodied by works such as Sir Thomas More's *Utopia* (1516) or Jonathan Swift's *Gulliver's Travels* (1726), divided into distinct subgenres: utopias such as Edward Bellamy's *Looking Backward* (1888) and dystopias such as H. G. Wells' *The Island of Dr Moreau* (1896). Nonetheless, as Kumar suggests, the reader's competence in reading a dystopian fiction is informed by their awareness of its counterpart, the utopia. In other words, the effectiveness of dystopian fiction depends upon its invocation of utopia as its mirror image. The reciprocity between the two forms can be seen in writers' responses to each other's utopias and dystopias, or in a writer's decision to switch between them (again, most notably, Wells).

Though **"The Machine Stops"** is rarely mentioned by mainstream Forster scholarship, Forster's comment, made nearly forty years after the text's original publication, that the story was written as 'a reaction to one of the earlier heavens of H. G. Wells' (6) has established **"The Machine Stops"** as a key text within science fiction studies. In this context, the story becomes the harbinger of an anti-Wellsian tradition within British literature and a precursor to the dystopian writings of Aldous Huxley, George Orwell and Yevgeny Zamyatin.[3] While reclaiming the story, this response has also narrowed its capacity to be reread by fixing the text into a dialogue with Wells. The dilemma arising from this critical appropriation is highlighted when critics attempt to account for the story's cultural politics. Tom Shippey, for example, plays Forster off against Wells by characterising the latter as innovative and forward-looking and the former as reactionary and nostalgic.[4] This kind of opposition fails to describe the ambiguities that exist both within and between the authors' respective ideological positions. Charles Elkins, similarly, refers to Forster's 'liberal humanism' without sufficient acknowledgement of either term's changing historical significance.[5] In fact, the most arresting feature of Forster's story (the vast communications network that links the otherwise isolated citizens of the world-state) owes little to Wells but instead, as Marcia Bundy Seabury has argued, anticipates contemporary fears surrounding gated communities and the World Wide Web.[6] By rereading Forster's account of utopia as part of a critical engagement with Hegel, as opposed to the alleged dispute with Wells, the story can be repositioned within the evolution of a modernist aesthetic that reaches its apogee in the 1920s.[7]

In his recent study, *English Literature of the 1920s* (1999), David Ayers associates Hegel's notion of 'the Unhappy Consciousness' with the stalled liberalism of *A Passage to India* (1924). For Hegel, the Unhappy Consciousness occurs when one self-consciousness gazes into another, but remains unaware of the union of self and other as its own fundamental nature. In Forster's novel, the misconceived and frustrated desires of Adela and Fielding for some form of reconciliation with, what they perceive to be as, an alien culture exhibit this state of unhappiness. Ayers writes that since Adela and Fielding 'doubt the possibility of the universality of reason, doubt the meaning of their own capacity to engage the other and, while ardently wishing that others will continue to want love, renounce it for themselves'.[8] Nevertheless, whereas Hegel bases his optimism upon a rationality that subsumes internal disagreements, Ayers argues that Forster proposes a model of friendship based upon difference and the acceptance of cultural relativism, which can be found in the camaraderie between Aziz and Mrs Moore. Instead of the pathos of Adela and Fielding, Aziz and Mrs Moore base their friendship upon their irreducible divide from one another. This endless difference and constant negotiation at the heart of their relationship prefigures, Ayers suggests, Jacques Derrida's concept of *aimance* from the *Politics of Friendship* (1997): 'a form of loving which goes beyond the socially determined forms of love and friendship, and beyond the existing cultures and traditions'.[9] If this is the case, then the relationship between Aziz and Mrs Moore gestures towards a utopianism that might transform the present social and imperial order. Nonetheless, by locating Forster as a Twenties writer alongside high modernists such as Wyndham

Lewis and Virginia Woolf, Ayers tends to present *A Passage to India* as an exceptional novel in Forster's *oeuvre*. **'The Machine Stops'**, though, reveals a similar element of utopian love that not only surfaces in *A Passage to India* but which also appears as central in Forster's consideration of personal creativity and artistic imagination.

The citizens of Forster's world-state see themselves as members of a realised utopia: 'How we have advanced, thanks to the Machine!' (121). They define themselves in relation to what they regard as reactionary or inefficient. Forster portrays this kind of binary thinking as the unconscious effect of ideology, while the attendant lack of critical self-awareness is symbolised in the populace's retreat underground. While this metaphor alludes to Plato's parable of 'the Cave', the self-deluding confidence of rationality also refers to Hegel. Vashti's comment that Kuno's behaviour 'is contrary to the spirit of the age' (112) indicates that the state mantra of historical progress is Hegelian in character. Hegel's philosophy of Spirit, summarised in the claim that 'Reason is Spirit when its certainty of being all reality has been raised to truth, and it is conscious of itself as its own world, and of the world as itself',[10] is arguably motivated by a fear of the Other and a need to transcend difference. The subject's search for knowledge is generated both by the very otherness of the object—its resistance to comprehension—and by the realisation that the subject is itself an object within the gaze of the Other. In the most famous passage from Hegel's *Phenomenology,* that of the dialectic between master and slave, this conflict leads inexorably to violence where both participants assert their subjectivity:

> This presentation is a twofold action: action on the part of the other, and action on its own part. In so far as it is the action of the *other,* each seeks the death of the other. But in doing so, the second kind of action, action on its own part, is also involved; for the former involves the staking of its own life. Thus the relation of the two self-conscious individuals is such that they prove themselves and each other through a life-and-death struggle. They must engage in this struggle, for they must raise their certainty of being *for themselves* to truth.[11]

In **'The Machine Stops'** this contest is played-out in terms of the mother-son relationship, home and homelessness, advancement and barbarism. By dramatising this struggle throughout the narrative rather than in the form of a single allegorical battle, Forster foregrounds and questions its rational basis. At its most visceral, the fear of the Other is experienced as a revulsion of physical contact:

> People were almost exactly alike all over the world, but the attendant of the air-ship, perhaps owing to her exceptional duties, had grown a little out of the com-

mon. She had often to address passengers with direct speech, and this had given her a certain roughness and originality of manner. When Vashti swerved away from the sunbeams with a cry, she behaved barbarically— she put out her hand to steady her.

'How dare you!' exclaimed the passenger. 'You forget yourself!'

(120)

The attendant's invasion of Vashti's physical space, in contravention of social custom, confirms her degenerate appearance in Vashti's eyes. Yet, this alleged degeneration has been produced by the attendant's adaptation to her environment: the same pseudo-Darwinist principle that Vashti and her neighbours take to be the basis for their own advancement over their predecessors. Here, then, Forster makes a distinction between history and ideology. Whereas the world-state harnesses social Darwinist precepts of natural selection to its own model of historical progress in order to ensure the perfectibility of its citizens (very much in keeping with the views of Forster's contemporaries such as Wells and Karl Pearson), Forster emphasises that this misuse of evolutionary theory is purely ideological. In acknowledging the more general Darwinist notion of constant change and adaptation, Forster asserts that the rationalisation of evolutionary theory will founder upon its own impossibility. Instead of ensuring perfection, the world-state will itself be subject to historical forces of change and decay. What turns the utopia of **'The Machine Stops'** into a dystopia is its failure to allow for the necessity of change and its abolition of personal and cultural difference. In equating stasis with utopia and uniformity with perfection, the world-state precipitates its own perfectibility. The story's wondrous technology is, nevertheless, insidiously ideological insofar as it appears to suggest that utopia is already now rather than in a continual state of evolution. In that sense, Forster's world-state is prematurely utopian or, in short, dystopian.

Whereas, in *The Secret Agent* (1907), Joseph Conrad satirises his anarchists' eugenic beliefs by emphasising their own degenerate characteristics, Forster undermines the social Darwinism of his world-state by accentuating the relative distinctions between sophistication and barbarism. These distinctions often take place in the context of efficiency and time-management. Forster offers no explanation for the emergence of his world-state—no war or famine or disease—but he does briefly mention the civilisation that preceded it:

> To 'keep pace with the sun', or even to outstrip it, had been the aim of the civilisation preceding this. Racing aeroplanes had been built for the purpose, capable of enormous speed, and steered by the greatest intellects of the epoch. Round the globe they went, round and round, westward, westward, round and round, amidst

humanity's applause. In vain. The globe went eastward quicker still, horrible accidents occurred, and the Committee of the Machine, at that time rising into prominence, declared the pursuit illegal, unmechanical and punishable by Homelessness.

(119)

Whereas the previous society had, however foolishly, pursued the goal of speed with the sun as its creative inspiration, the movement underground and the replacement of the sun with artificial light constitute a management of time and nature, including that of human nature, by their very abolition. Science retreats 'to concentrate herself upon problems that she was certain of solving' whilst 'dawn, midday, twilight, the zodiacal path, touched neither men's lives nor their hearts' (120). The romantic opposition between science and nature, and the gendering of this debate in terms of the domestication of masculine impulses, are given more nuanced expression in the relationship between Vashti and Kuno. For the moment, though, I want to pursue further the interaction between time-management and state ideology in Forster's imagined community.

The quantification of time and the rationalisation of human contact are highlighted early on in the story. Vashti knows 'several thousand people; in certain directions human intercourse had advanced enormously', but she can only give Kuno 'fully five minutes' (109). The cultural orthodoxy of efficiency and advancement—that is to say, of *being seen to be* efficient and advanced—is predicated upon a notion of temporality: of being on time and in command of one's time-keeping. Vashti urges Kuno to 'be quick' and reprimands him: 'how slow you are' (110). Kuno's deliberate 'dawdling' marks him out as a dissident element even before the reader learns of his attempts to escape overground or of his abnormal physicality: 'On atavism the Machine can have no mercy' (128). To refuse to be on time but to enjoy its passing, as Kuno does, is to be automatically considered as degenerate. Only by the effective management of one's time can an individual ensure their true citizen status and, by extension, the organisation of the state. The penalty of Homelessness—of being exposed upon the upper earth—confirms the subject's descent into atavism by forcibly returning them to nature. The notion of Home, therefore, is based not only upon what it opposes (nature, wastage and change) but also by being more temporally advanced than its opponent; of being on time and calibrated to the instant.

The extensive study of the relationship between speed, time and politics by the philosopher, Paul Virilio, offers a useful illustration of this temporal disjuncture between those included within and those excluded from the locus of Home. Virilio's meditation upon the conduct of war and the evolution of the city-state turns upon a consideration of time and speed:

The rudimentary hillock, the elevated observatory, already give the pastoral assembly quicker information on the surroundings, and thus the time to choose between the various military attitudes at their disposal. They avoid the uncalculated spontaneity of primitive struggle (a situation which would immediately be imposed upon them by the aggressor), and thus find themselves confronted with a *new freedom* since they can choose the solution they deem the most advantageous, depending on the size of the enemy group: i.e., either flee with all their goods and flocks, taking advantage of their head start; or face the enemy.[12]

The conversion of the landscape into an armed fortress with ramparts, moats and other defensive strategies is intended to preserve and strengthen that original 'head start' by slowing the antagonist down and giving the protagonists more time in which to act. By extension, the transition of the city-state from armed fortress is motivated by both the effective management of time and the speedy processing of information in order to stay ahead of enemies and competitors alike. The state's acquisition of new freedoms, including, in time, democratic and economic systems, is determined by the advantageous growth of time and speed at the expense of those outside the state or, increasingly, those marginalized from within. Virilio's reminder that civic existence is not an inevitable historical goal, but a product that is both mutable and discriminatory, illuminates Forster's story in a couple of ways. Firstly, it helps to illustrate why time-management is deemed to be essential for the preservation of good citizenship and the running of the state. Vashti's lament for her son's poor time-keeping is tantamount to her pitying his ostracism. Secondly, Virilio indicates that, however advanced the state is in terms of its time-management, it will always be in a condition of crisis because of the paramount need to manage a quality that is, by its very nature, mutable and elusive. St Augustine describes this uncertainty in his consideration of the fleeting moment:

> In fact the only time that can be called present is an instant, if we can conceive of such, that cannot be divided even into the most minute fractions, and a point of time as small as this passes so rapidly from the future to the past that its duration is without length. For if its duration were prolonged, it could be divided into past and future. When it is present it has no duration.[13]

While the calibration of time effectively conceals its elusiveness, the need for political self-preservation is also stimulated by an anxious awareness of time's ineffability. In **'The Machine Stops'** this anxiety takes the form of a revitalised, quasi-religious devotion to the Machine and a superstitious regard towards its Book (or user's manual).

The increasing instability that Virilio sees in the relationship between civic society and time-management underlines an additional impossibility: the realisation of utopia itself. Paul Ricoeur has usefully described the linguistic figure of utopia as 'a place that has no place, a ghost city':

> From this 'no place', an exterior glance is cast on our reality, which suddenly looks strange, nothing more being taken for granted. The field of the possible is now opened beyond that of the actual, a field for alternative ways of living. The question therefore is whether imagination could have any constitutive role without this leap outside.[14]

Ricoeur neatly summarises some of the contradictions associated with the idea of utopia. In literature it is figured as a place, usually a city or an island set in an exotic and remote location, but it also has no material existence. Utopia is therefore a place positioned in-between absence and presence—in that sense, it is spectral—but which also recalls Augustine's description of the instant as something that must exist so as to link past and future but is, at the same time, so fleeting to be without content. The connection between the impossibility of utopia and the inherent uncertainty of time-management can thus be made. Nevertheless, Ricoeur ponders whether imagination could exist without this, in itself imaginative, 'leap outside'. The act of imagination is implicitly tied to the utopian impulse insofar as it hails from a neutral space outside of rational consciousness. Ricoeur equates this hypothetical zone with Kant's notion of the schema as 'a method for giving an image to a concept':

> In the sense that it is the very operation of grasping the similar, by performing the predictive assimilation answering to the initial semantic shock. Suddenly, we are seeing as . . . ; [*sic*] we see old age as the dusk of day, time as a beggar, nature as a temple with living pillars . . . In brief, the work of imagination is to schematize metaphorical attribution. Like the Kantian schema, it gives an image to an emerging meaning.[15]

Kuno's description of Orion's belt as a huntsman bearing a sword (111) exemplifies Ricoeur's analysis of the imaginative process. The poetic image is both 'an emerging meaning', by reordering factual modes of perception in terms of metaphor, and implicitly utopian insofar as it gestures towards a knowledge outside common-sense experience without being either emergent or substantive. The equivocation associated with metaphor communicates the same sense of ambiguity associated with utopian discourse or, as Tom Moylan describes, 'what cannot yet be said within present conceptual language'.[16]

In an essay on anonymity, written in 1925, Forster writes:

> Imagination is our only guide into the world created by words. Whether those words are signed or unsigned becomes, as soon as the imagination redeems us, a matter

of no importance, because we have approximated to
the state in which they were written, and there are no
names down there, no personality as we understand
personality, no marrying or giving in marriage.

Whereas Forster disdains study as only 'a serious form
of gossip', imagination on the part of the reader is a
creative act since it communicates with the unconscious
realm—in Ricoeur's sense, the neutral zone—from
which the text is produced:

> Creation comes from the depths—the mystic will say
> from God. The signature, the name, belongs to the
> surface-personality, and pertains to the world of infor-
> mation, it is a ticket, not the spirit of life. While the au-
> thor wrote he forgot his name; while we read him we
> forget both his name and our own.

Forster is not arguing for uncritical reverence but
against a biographical criticism that omits the unconscious in favour of factual explanations. Artistry is
thereby absorbed into the world of administration even
though 'all literature tends towards a condition of anonymity . . . It is always tugging in that direction and
saying in effect: "I, not my author, exist really" . . . To
forget its Creator is one of the functions of a Creation'.[17]
Forster's valorisation of imagination as necessary to the
artistic process dispels the imposed egotism of the social subject and, by so doing, recognises the irrational-
ity of the unconscious self. Imagination works at the
expense of the ego and in an encounter with the un-
knowable.

In contrast, the citizens of **'The Machine Stops'** have
exchanged imagination for ideas: 'she had no ideas of
her own but had just been told one—that four stars and
three in the middle were like a man: she doubted there
was much in it' (113). The reduction of ideas to empirical data and of their function to social utility is central
to Forster's critique of a planned society. Whereas the
derivation of the word 'idea' from the Greek *idein* (to
see) indicates the role of insight within the work of representation, this critical act has been removed from the
world-state. Instead, ideas do not comment upon the
mind's capacity for imaging the world but mirror the
world as an objective given. Ideas are praised for their
factual accuracy not for their psychological insight as,
for example, in the contact between two speaking subjects. Vashti distances Kuno because the presence of his
subjectivity would be painful for her to accept. She prefers instead the objectification supplied by the Machine:

> It only gave a general idea of people—an idea that was
> good enough for all practical purposes, Vashti thought.
> The imponderable bloom, declared by a discredited
> philosophy to be the actual essence of intercourse, was
> rightly ignored by the Machine, just as the imponder-
> able bloom of the grape was ignored by the manufac-
> turers of artificial fruit.
>
>                                                      (111-2)

The rationalisation of ideas as data complements the
quantification of time and space that underpins existence lived under the Machine. This act of rationalisation is not only shown to be physically corrupting—the
cramped quarters, the paleness of the citizens, the loss
of personal taste and the increasing irritability as time
becomes shorter—but it also undercuts the very notion
of utopia that the state supposedly embodies.

The image of a technocratic, over-rationalised, hyper-
bureaucratic community is most closely associated in
the popular mind with Aldous Huxley's *Brave New
World* (1932). A brief comparison of Forster's short
story with Huxley's novel illuminates the central, dissident element of imagination in Forster's work. Towards
the end of *Brave New World,* Huxley stages a debate
between the Controller, Mustapha Mond, and John Savage on the role of literature as a vehicle for emotional
and spiritual values. The Savage's insistence that '*Othello*'s good, *Othello*'s better than those feelies' is contested by Mond's observation that the loss of high art is
'the price we have to pay for stability'.[18] Without social
unease there is no emotional lexicon with which to understand Shakespeare's tragedies: 'if it were really like
*Othello* nobody could understand it, however new it
might be. And if it were new, it couldn't possibly be
like *Othello*'.[19] The Savage's attempts to persuade Mond
for the necessity of art and religion prove fruitless because the exclusion of Art's irrational and anachronistic
content is *a priori* to the utopia's existence. Consequently, despite the appearance of dialogue, the debate
is predetermined in favour of Mond's position and
against that of the Savage. The effect, though, is that
the narrative gradually expires, symbolised in the pathos of the Savage's suicide, since the novel's premise
has already ruled out the alternative as illusory.

By contrast, Forster does not make a similar opposition
in which the antithesis is projected as merely other. Literature is not banned but produced at the press of a button for the purposes of thought and reflection if not, exactly, for pleasure or edification. Art exists, then, as one
of the appendages of the Machine so as to maintain social order. It is not reified, as in *Brave New World,* as
an unobtainable revolutionary spirit. Though the possibilities of Art are held in check through its subservience
to the Machine, it nonetheless remains a latent, neutral-
ising force that is actively reconstituted through the
workings of the state. Whereas Huxley resigns himself
to the futility of change, his novel's fatalism affirmed
by the Savage's suicide, Forster emphasises that the
state can only identify itself through what it denies.
This ambiguous relationship is stressed in the story's
opening words: 'Imagine, if you can, a small room,
hexagonal in shape like the cell of a bee'. For a story
concerned with arid technology, the direct address to
the reader seems inappropriate: 'yet, at the moment that

my meditation opens, this room is throbbing with melodious sounds' (109). The inscription of an addresser and an addressee counterpoints the lack of contact between Vashti and Kuno, yet the recourse to an oral mode or address can also appear romantic and compensatory. Alternatively, the very inappropriateness of the form (derived, as it is, from the fable) emphasises the discrepancy between speech and text engendered by technology. As Kuno complains to Vashti: 'I see something like you in this plate, but I do not see you. I hear something like you through this telephone, but I do not hear you' (110). Seen in this light, Forster's deliberately awkward language use emphasises not only the intimacy and imagination disallowed by the world-state but also the loss of orality observed by Walter Benjamin within the modern short story:

> We have witnessed the evolution of the 'short story', which has removed itself from oral tradition and no longer permits that slow piling one on top of the other of thin, transparent layers which constitutes the most appropriate picture of the way in which the perfect narrative is revealed through the layers of a variety of re-tellings.

For Benjamin, the ascendancy of the short story over the folk-tale is 'a concomitant symptom of the secular productive forces of history, a concomitant that has quite gradually removed narrative from the realm of living speech'.[20] Equally for Forster, the modern short story's preference for naturalistic as opposed to fantastical settings, and for 'well-made' structures as opposed to the mutability of fable, complements the dry empiricism of the world-state. The equivocal opening phrase, 'imagine, if you can', suggests that the capacity for imagination is already dwindling and that the disappearance of orality in the short story is, in part, symptomatic of this decline. To that extent, **'The Machine Stops'** is not a tale of the future but an allegory of the present where formal inconsistencies describe tensions in contemporary cultural thought.

Underpinning this struggle is Kuno's embodiment of a natural mysticism. As Kuno says, 'we die, but we have recaptured life' (146). Other than his vitality though, which can itself be attributed to one of the malfunctions of the Machine, Kuno has 'no remedy' (131). Following his recapture, Kuno waits for the Machine to decay. Whereas, in the figure of the Savage, Huxley laments the redundancy of Art, Kuno turns his uselessness to his advantage. To understand Kuno's behaviour, though, it is necessary to return to Virilio's notion of the city-state.

As argued earlier, Virilio sees the evolution of the state from armed fortress as a question of speed: of gaining time over the enemy. As was also argued, the regulation of time in the form of data is fundamentally unstable

since the processing of information is itself conditioned by the passing of time. Thomas Docherty writes that 'the problematic temporal nature of subjectivity (and hence of politics) is displaced onto a spatial representation of the problem (in questions of colonial space, relations of hierarchy, strategies of exclusion, or inclusion)'.[21] In other words, the physical omnipresence of the city-state comes to obscure the problems of temporality upon which its foundations are laid. The gaining of time becomes equated with the controlling of appearances: the degree to which the state can conceal itself whilst rendering its opponent visible and vulnerable to attack. In the period nominally known as 'peacetime', when there is no apparent external enemy, this strategy turns inwards and the state identifies itself in relation to internal enemies. For Virilio, contemporary society is characterised not only by an emphasis upon surveillance, but also by an internalisation of its practices that safeguards the social only by calling it into question. Mass disappearances of people under military regimes become 'symptomatic of a more generalized "legal disappearance" of the citizen' in the form, for example, of a government statistic.[22] Nonetheless, since the development of military strategy is towards the mastery of appearances with invisibility as the goal, the guerrilla (or band of lone fighters) assumes a more effective weapon than the all-too visible fortress. This, then, is the present state of political struggle: a contest between a civic society that renders itself transparent for the purposes of social order and individuals who consciously withdraw from that society (for example, computer hackers and the moral panic that subsequently surrounds them).

Kuno's withdrawal can also be read as a deliberate denial of the visibility and constant availability conferred upon the citizens by the Machine. Kuno briefly returns as a kind of spectre:

> He refused to visualize his face upon the blue plate, and speaking out of the darkness with solemnity said:
>
> 'The Machine stops.'
>
> 'What do you say?'
>
> The Machine is stopping, I know it, I know the signs.'
>
> She burst into a peal of laughter. He heard her and was angry, and they spoke no more.
>
> (139)

This spectral effect recurs in the final scene when Vashti and Kuno blindly feel one another and in Kuno's sight of one of the Homeless 'in the twilight' (134). Kuno's invisibility signifies all of those elements, such as love and imagination, which have been rendered Other by the state. Yet, Kuno cannot be taken as the story's authorial presence. Forster balances Kuno's optimism with

Vashti's response that 'some fool will start the Machine again, to-morrow'. Kuno's response that 'humanity has learnt its lesson' is simultaneously shattered by the city breaking 'like a honeycomb' (146). Forster resists both the resignation of dystopian fiction, as in *Brave New World,* and the romanticism characterised by Kuno which, in its optimism, elides with an Hegelian belief in progress: the same principle that, in other words, motivates the world-state. Instead, in its inconclusiveness, the text gestures towards an imaginative return that will not only compensate the present but also radically transform it. The form of this return can be described as the recognition of love.

In his essay, 'What I Believe' (1939), Forster writes that 'The memory of birth and the expectation of death always lurk within the human being, making him separate from his fellows and consequently capable of intercourse with them'. Dialogue, or more specifically friendship, is engendered by a breach between individuals that is itself inculcated by the passing of time and of oneself. Born into 'the fag-end of Victorian liberalism', Forster values free speech and parliamentary democracy but cannot raise more than two cheers: 'there is no occasion to give three. Only Love the Beloved Republic deserves that'.[23] Love is itself 'beloved': it is the condition to which democracy aspires. But, for democracy to claim that it can administer love would be prematurely utopian, which is to say, dystopian. Love remains an ideal for Forster to which we, as individuals, should strive.

In comparison, love in the world-state is merely 'a carnal act' whilst child-rearing is conducted through state nurseries. Love is reduced to procreation with the survival of the species (or, rather, the Machine) being safeguarded by the elimination of undesirables: 'if it could work without us, it would let us die' (131). Vashti's maternal instincts have slowly atrophied and though, at the very end, her feelings of kinship are recaptured in the tunnel, the idea of the tunnel initially scares her: 'she had not seen it since her last child was born' (115). The tunnel is associated with both literal production—of being displayed in human company—and, metaphorically, reproduction: the tunnel as a kind of Fallopian tube. Insofar as the Machine creates a womb-like space for its inhabitants, the story can be read, like Mary Shelley's *Frankenstein* (1818), as a patriarchal attempt to appropriate female powers of human creativity that ends disastrously: the Machine, unlike the female, does not create but merely maintains.

Insofar as love under the Machine is defined in terms of technique, the friendship of Kuno and Vashti can be compared to the Derridean concept of *aimance* introduced in Ayers' discussion of *A Passage to India.* Their

relationship transgresses the isolationism that is imposed by social convention: 'we touch, we talk, not through the Machine' (145). Significantly, Kuno loves Vashti before she loves him. As Derrida writes: 'The argument seems, in fact, simple: it is possible to be loved (passive voice) *without knowing it,* but it is impossible to love (active voice) *without knowing it . . .* . The friend is the person who loves before being the person who is loved'.[24] As Docherty notes, there is a temporal discrepancy between the two participants, since the lover loves '*in advance* of the loved: friendship is an affair of the lover *before* it is an affair of the loved'.[25] It is this divide that underlines the social sphere according to Derrida: 'One can love being loved, but loving will always be more, better and something other than being loved . . . The truth of friendship, if there is one, is found there, in darkness, and with it the truth of the political'.[26]

The breach that Derrida detects dovetails with the separation that Forster observes and which makes possible the intercourse of friendship and imagination. The discrepancy that exists between Kuno loving Vashti, and her slow realisation of that love, offsets the temporal advantage that the state seeks to establish over the Homeless. Whereas the citizens achieve a limited form of subjectivity by their willing inclusion under the Machine, Kuno and Vashti acquire a deeper self-knowledge through their realisation of their dependency upon one another. This understanding, though, is predicated upon the immediacy of death and with it a glimpse of utopia: 'For a moment they saw the nations of the dead, and, before they joined them, scraps of the untainted sky' (146). Instead of being a later turn in Forster's writing, this utopian impulse can be seen as a recurrent theme in stories such as **'The Machine Stops'.** In that regard, Forster's fables form an important phase in his aspiration for literature: 'Not completion. Not rounding off but opening out'.[27]

*Notes*

1. All subsequent references are to E. M. Forster, *Collected Short Stories* (London: Penguin, 1954).

2. Krishan Kumar, *Utopia and Anti-Utopia in Modern Times* (Oxford: Basil Blackwell, 1987), 125.

3. See, for example, Mark R. Hillegas, *The Future as Nightmare: H. G. Wells and the Anti-Utopians* (New York: Oxford University Press, 1967) and, more recently, Nicholas Ruddick, *Ultimate Island: On the Nature of British Science Fiction* (Westport, Connecticut and London: Greenwood Press, 1993), p. 175.

4. Tom Shippey, introduction to *The Oxford Book of Science Fiction Stories* (Oxford: Oxford University Press, 1992), p. x.

5. Charles Elkins, 'E. M. Forster's "The Machine Stops": Liberal-Humanist Hostility to Technology', in *Clockwork Worlds: Mechanized Environments in S.F.,* ed. Richard D. Erlich and Thomas P. Dunn (Westport, Connecticut and London: Greenwood Press, 1983), pp. 47-61.

6. Marcia Bundy Seabury, 'Images of a Networked Society: E. M. Forster's 'The Machine Stops", *Studies in Short Fiction,* 34:1 (1997), 61-71.

7. M. Keith Booker, in *The Dystopian Impulse in Modern Literature: Fiction as Social Criticism* (Westport, Connecticut and London: Greenwood Press, 1994), groups 'The Machine Stops' with 'certain modernist works that seem to be aimed less toward critiques of a given kind of political system' and 'are more concerned with the general philosophical concerns of modernity' (23).

8. David Ayers, *English Literature of the 1920s* (Edinburgh: Edinburgh University Press, 1999), 215.

9. Ayers, 220.

10. G. W. F. Hegel, *Phenomenology of Spirit,* trans. A.V. Miller (Oxford: Clarendon Press, 1977), p. 263.

11. Hegel, 113-4.

12. Paul Virilio, *Popular Defense and Ecological Struggles,* trans. Mark Polizzotti (New York: Semiotext(e), 1990), 15.

13. St Augustine, *Confessions,* trans. R. S. Pine-Coffin (Harmondsworth: Penguin, 1961), 266.

14. Paul Ricoeur, *From Text to Action: Essays in Hermeneutics, II,* trans. Kathleen Blamey and John B. Thompson (London: Athlone, 1991), 320. I am grateful to Stephen Kelly for bringing Ricoeur's work to my attention.

15. Ricoeur, 173.

16. Tom Moylan, *Demand the Impossible: Science Fiction and the Utopian Imagination* (London: Methuen, 1986), 39.

17. Forster, *Two Cheers for Democracy* (Harmondsworth: Penguin, 1965), 90. 93 & 95-6.

18. Aldous Huxley, *Brave New World* (London: Flamingo, 1994), 201.

19. Huxley, 200.

20. Walter Benjamin, 'The Storyteller' (1936), in *Illuminations,* ed. Hannah Arendt, trans. Harry Zohn, 2nd edn (London: Fontana, 1992), 92.

21. Thomas Docherty, *Alterities: Criticism, History, Representation* (Oxford: Clarendon Press, 1996), 181.

22. Docherty, 183.

23. Forster, *Two Cheers,* 84. 65 & 78.

24. Jacques Derrida, *Politics of Friendship,* trans. George Collins (London: Verso, 1997), p. 9.

25. Docherty, *Criticism and Modernity: Aesthetics, Literature and Nations in Europe and Its Academies* (Oxford: Oxford University Press, 1999), 64-5.

26. Derrida, 11 & 16.

27. Forster, *Aspects of the Novel* (Harmondsworth: Pelican, 1962), 170.

---

# FURTHER READING

## Bibliographies

Kirkpatrick, B. J. *A Bibliography of E. M. Forster.* Oxford: Clarendon Press, 1985, 327 p.
    Contains citations for Forster's known contributions to periodicals and newspapers.

McDowell, Frederick P. W. *E. M. Forster: An Annotated Bibliography of Writings about Him.* DeKalb: Northern Illinois University Press, 1976, 924 p.
    Complete listing of all of Forster's works, as well as an annotated bibliography of writings about him.

## Biography

Beauman, Nicola. *Morgan: A Biography of E. M. Forster.* London: Hodder & Stoughton, 1993, 404 p.
    Detailed biography of Forster's life, including chapters focusing on his major works.

## Criticism

Caporaletti, Silvana. "The Thematization of Time in E. M. Forster's 'The Eternal Moment' and Joyce's 'The Dead.'" *Twentieth Century Literature,* 43, no. 4 (winter, 1997): 406-19.
    Comparative analysis of the treatment of time and temporality in two short stories by Forster and James Joyce.

Das, G. K., and John Beer, eds. *E. M. Forster: A Human Exploration—Centenary Essays.* New York: New York University Press, 1979, 314 p.

Compilation of critical essays commemorating the centenary of Forster.

Gardner, Philip, ed. *E. M. Forster: The Critical Heritage*. London: Routledge & Kegan Paul, 1973, 490 p.
   Contains an introduction to Forster's life and works, as well as a collection of material relating to the early stages of his critical reception.

Godfrey, Denis. "The Short Stories." In *E. M. Forster's Other Kingdom*, pp. 9-19. New York: Barnes & Noble, 1968.
   Provides an assessment of Forster's short stories written before 1914, collected in *The Celestial Omnibus* and *The Eternal Moment*.

Meyers, Doris. "Breaking Free: The Closed Universe Theme in E. M. Forster, Owen Barfield, and C. S. Lewis." *Mythlore*, 21, no. 3 (summer, 1996): 7-11.
   Comparative discussion of Forster's, Barfield's, and Lewis's writings in the context of fantasy and language as a means of exploring the unknown universe.

Wilde, Alan, ed. *Critical Essays on E. M. Forster*. Boston: G. K. Hall & Co., 1985, 181 p.
   Deals with the consistency of Forster's work, placing him within the canon of modern British literature, as well as addressing the issue of his homosexuality within the framework of his liberal humanism and morality.

---

**Additional coverage of Forster's life and career is contained in the following sources published by Thomson Gale:** *Authors and Artists for Young Adults*, Vols. 2, 37; *Beacham's Guide to Literature for Young Adults*, Vol. 12; *British Writers*, Vol. 6; *British Writers Retrospective Supplement*, Vol. 2; *Concise Dictionary of British Literary Biography, 1914-1945*; *Contemporary Authors*, Vols. 13-14; *Contemporary Authors New Revision Series*, Vol. 45; *Contemporary Authors—Obituary*, Vols. 25-28R; *Contemporary Authors Permanent Series*, Vol. 1; *Contemporary Literary Criticism*, Vols. 1, 2, 3, 4, 9, 10, 13, 15, 22, 45, 77; *Dictionary of Literary Biography*, Vols. 34, 98, 162, 178, 195; *Dictionary of Literary Biography Documentary Series*, Vol. 10; *DISCovering Authors*; *DISCovering Authors 3.0 DISCovering Authors: British Edition*; *DISCovering Authors: Canadian Edition*; *DISCovering Authors Modules: Most-Studied Authors and Novelists*; *Encyclopedia of World Literature in the 20th Century*, Ed. 3; *Exploring Novels*; *Literary Movements for Students*, Vol. 1; *Literature and Its Times*, Vol. 3; *Literature Resource Center*; *Major 20th-Century Writers*, Vols. 1, 2; *Major 21st-Century Writers* (eBook), Ed. 2005; *Nonfiction Classics for Students*, Vol. 1; *Novels for Students*, Vols. 3, 10, 11; *Reference Guide to English Literature*, Ed. 2; *Reference Guide to Short Fiction*, Ed. 2; *Short Story Criticism*, Vol. 27; *Something about the Author*, Vol. 57; *Supernatural Fiction Writers*, Vol. 1; *Twayne's English Authors*; *Twentieth Century Literary Criticism*, Vol. 125; *World Literature and Its Times*, Ed. 4; **and** *World Literature Criticism*, Vol. 2.

# Tove Jansson
## 1914-2001

(Full name Tove Marika Jansson; also wrote under pseudonym Vera Haij) Finnish short story writer, novelist, children's writer, nonfiction writer, and visual artist.

## INTRODUCTION

Jansson's books have been translated into more than thirty languages and include several collections of stories—some for children, others, later in her career, for adults. She is most widely known for creating the Moomin World in books and stories for children, all of which she also illustrated. The Moomin family, a happy group who lives in their own beautiful valley, must contend with the larger world impinging on their lives. While Moomin works dominated the first half of her career, Jansson's artistic interests developed beyond children's literature. She spent the latter three decades of her life writing for adult audiences, producing five highly regarded collections of stories as well as six novels. Jansson's work has been lauded as profound and original, and she has won several national, regional, and international awards.

## BIOGRAPHICAL INFORMATION

Jansson was born August 9, 1914, in Helsinki, the eldest of three children in a family that was part of the Swedish-speaking minority, a distinct community in Finland. Both parents were artists—her Finnish father a sculptor and her Swedish mother a graphic designer and illustrator. Being raised in a home filled with artistic activity had the effect of creating a sense of inevitability about an artistic career for Jansson, and this, coupled with her father's flair for adventure and her mother's interest in storytelling, contributed to Jansson's early interest in writing illustrated stories. She began writing at an early age even as she was being trained as a visual artist. Her first illustrated story appeared in a children's magazine when she was fifteen, and at nineteen she had published *Sara och Pelle och Neckens bläckfiskar* (1933; *Sara and Pelle and the Water-Sprite's Octopuses*), her first picture book. Jansson studied graphic design and industrial art at Tekniska skolan (The School of Applied Arts) in Stockholm from 1930 to 1933 and then returned to Helsinki, where she studied painting at the Ateneum (Finnish Art Society) until 1937. She then left for Paris to continue her artistic training. During the early part of her career she supported herself by working as an illustrator in various genres. In the early forties Jansson began to develop the characters and concepts that would form the Moomin World stories, her best-known work. It appeared as a series of nine books, published from 1945 to 1970, and was supplemented by four picture books as well as several scripts for theatre, radio, and television. The series became well-known internationally in translation and in the mid-fifties took the form of a cartoon strip, first in London's *Evening News* and then syndicated worldwide. Jansson received the Hans Christian Anderson Medal in 1966, the highest award possible for a writer of children's stories. In 1968, between the eighth and ninth Moomin books, she published an autobiographical novel for adult readers, and in 1970 she ended the Moomin series, after which she wrote solely for an adult audience. In 1971 Jansson published *Lyssnerskan* (1971; *The Listener*), the first of five story collections for adults, and from 1972 to 1989 she wrote five novels, followed by two more story collections, in 1991 and 1998. Jansson received several awards from the Swedish Literary Society in Finland and in 1973 one from the Swedish Academy; in 1978 she was awarded the title of an Honorary Doctor at the Åbo Academy in Finland. She died on June 27, 2001.

## MAJOR WORKS OF SHORT FICTION

The episodic nature of many of Jansson's earlier books as well as the novels written for adult readers reveal her preference for short forms, but of her well-known, nine-part series of Moomin books, only one is a collection of stories, *Det osynliga barnet och andra berättelser* (1962; *Tales from Moominvalley*). The *Tales* are set in the Moomin Valley locale familiar from the earlier books, and some stories such as "The Last Dragon in the World" are accessible to children. However, as the Moomin series progressed, Jansson's thematic interests evolved and the personalities of the characters became more developed, leading some critics to view the stories in this collection as being far too advanced for children. The theme of the transformation of a character's inner nature occurs in several stories: for example, in "The Fillijonk Who Believed in Disasters," a neurotic creature is cured by a storm. In the title story (the Swedish title translates as "The Invisible Child and Other Stories"), a child disappears because she was badly frightened by someone who should have been caring for her, but the love of her family restores her sense of security and she gradually becomes visible and whole again. In 1971 Jansson published her first story collection written solely for adults, *Lyssnerkan (The Listener)*, in which dramatic changes in characters' personalities predominate. The theme of art and artists is apparent in "Black and White," where an artist struggles to fully express himself. Many of the stories deal with obsessive tendencies or difficulty in distinguishing various states of reality, such as "Letters to an Idol," where a reader of romances imagines herself in a relationship with their author, and "A Love Story," which concerns a character's obsessive attraction to a sculptor. Many of the stories reveal the difficulty people have in making contact with each other, such as "Suggestion for an Introduction," "Wolves," and "Lucio's Friends." Other stories, for example "Rain," "The Listener," "The Grey Duchess," and "Children's Party," revolve around problems inherent in the aging process and loneliness.

By the time *Dockskåpet och andra berättelser (The Doll's House and Other Tales)* was published in 1978, Jansson had fully developed her skills as a writer of short fiction for adults. Themes such as change and instability, obsession, conflicts between various perceptions of reality, and the difficulty of achieving authentic contact between people are all present in this work. In addition, in several stories Jansson again deals with creative problems faced by artists. The title story concerns a person who becomes more and more isolated as he attempts to create the perfect doll's house. In "Locomotive" the obsessive narrator carefully studies people he meets so that he can use their 'secret' in his failed attempts at art. "Huvudrollen" is about an actress who, in an attempt to portray a boring character, nearly destroys an uninteresting person she studies for insight into that role. "The Strip Cartoon Artist" addresses the commercial pressures on a successful artist, something with which Jansson was all too familiar after the 1950s; in this story the need for solitude conflicts with the need for human contact, and expedience undermines integrity. Since these stories all have characters who live in their own private, alternative reality, they seem to suggest the need for a world of one's own imagining to complement the circumstances of one's life. In *Resa med lätt* (1987; *Traveling Light*), themes of loneliness and personal difficulties with human contact again appear. For example, "Correspondence" is a collection of letters from a Japanese girl who is anxious to meet a much-admired author, but who finally realizes that she can only know the author through his texts. The thirteen stories of *Brev från Klara* (1991; *Letters from Klara*) also address familiar themes. "The Pictures" concerns the compulsive search for true artistic expression, and in another story a lonely art student writes each of his classmates to tell them he no longer has a relationship with them. In "Journey to Barcelona" a woman travels with her elderly mother to the Mediter-

ranean, and "In August" deals with two aged sisters quarreling about their mother's death. "Emmelina" is an incorporeal nineteen year old who enables death for the elderly and suicide for unhappy youths. Jansson's final collection, *Meddelande: Noveller I urval 1971-1997* (1998; *Message: Selected Stories 1971-1997*), consists of short "messages" from the author, all different from each other, in which eight new stories are collected with previously published material. The title story, "Message," consists of bits taken from Jansson's correspondence and includes such things as reader commentary and merchandising suggestions from entrepreneurs.

## CRITICAL RECEPTION

Jansson's works have brought her great distinction as the creator of a series of books for children as well as high praise for her story collections for adults. Nancy Huse describes Jansson's *Tales from Moomin Valley* as "perhaps the best of Jansson's work and as fine as any children's book" she has encountered. However, Jansson's interests in writing eventually developed beyond what could be presented as stories for children, even before she had finished her Moomin World books, and she began to publish for an adult audience in 1968. Biographer W. Glyn Jones emphasizes that "the theme of the artist's dilemma . . . contributes to a unity in her work as a whole" and forms one of the links between the Moomin books and her later works for adults. Jansson's first story collection for adults, *The Listener,* ably explored such thematic material as the irrational aspects of human nature, obsessive impulses, and the instability of the elderly. Jones describes the stories in *The Doll's House and Other Tales* as those of an "adult writer, firmly in control of her art" and "her most powerful work to date," while Marianne Bargum states that Jansson's *Traveling Light* "strengthens her position as a writer for adults."

---

# PRINCIPAL WORKS

### Short Fiction

*Sara och Pelle och Neckens bläckfiskar* [as Vera Haij; *Sara and Pelle and the Water-Sprite's Octopuses*] (picture book) 1933

*Hur gick det sen? Boken om Mymlan, Mumintrollet och Lilla My* [*The Book about Moomin, Mymble, and Little My*] (picture book) 1952

*Vem ska trösta knyttet?* [*Who Will Comfort Toffle?*] (picture book) 1960

*Det osynliga barnet och andra berättelser* [*Tales from Moominvalley*] (short stories) 1962

*Lyssnerskan* [*The Listener*] 1971

*Dockskåpet och andra berättelser* [*The Doll's House and Other Tales*] 1978

*Resa med lätt* [*Traveling Light*] 1987

*Brev från Klara* [*Letters from Klara*] 1991

*Meddelande: Noveller I urval 1971-1997* [*Message: Selected Stories 1971-1997*] 1998

**Other Major Works**

*Småtrollen och den stora översvämningen* [*The Little Trolls and the Great Flood*] (novel) 1945

*Kometjakten* [*Comet in Moominland*] (novel) 1946; revised as *Mumintrollet på kometjakt* (1956) and *Kometen kommer* (1968)

*Trollkarlens hatt* [*Finn Family Moomintroll*] (novel) 1948

*Muminpappans Bravader: Skrivna av Honom Själv* [*The Exploits of Moominpappa, Described by Himself*] (novel) 1950

*Farlig midsommar* [*Moominsummer Madness*] (novel) 1954

*Trollvinter* [*Moominland Midwinter*] (novel) 1957

*Pappan och havet* [*Moominpappa at Sea*] (novel) 1965

*Bildhuggarens dotter* [*Sculptor's Daughter*] (novel) 1968

*Sent i november* [*Moominvalley in November*] (novel) 1970

*Sommarboken* [*The Summer Book*] (novel) 1972

*Solstaden* [*Sun City*] (novel) 1974

*Den ärliga bendragaren* [*The Honest Imposter*] (novel) 1982

*Stenåkern* [*The Stone Field*] (novel) 1984

*Rent spel* [*Fair Play*] (novel) 1989

*Anteckningar från en ö* [with Tuulikki Pietilä; *Notations from an Island*] (nonfiction) 1996

---

# CRITICISM

**Frederic Fleisher and Boel Fleisher (essay date March 1963)**

SOURCE: Fleisher, Frederic, and Boel Fleisher. "Tove Jansson and the Moomin Family." *American-Scandinavian Review* 51, no. 1 (March 1963): 47-54.

[*In this essay, the Fleishers discuss the first part of Jansson's career, focusing on her writings about the adventures of the Moomin family and her motivations for its creation.*]

When contemporary Scandinavian literature is discussed by non-specialists in other parts of the world a dozen or more names are usually mentioned. But the Scandinavian author whose works have the largest number of foreign readers and followers is apt to be overlooked, is even largely unknown. Still, the adventures of Tove Jansson's Moomin family, their friends and their enemies, have been published in many languages, on several continents and are being read by hundreds of thousands daily.

Someone who is not acquainted with Tove Jansson's works may assume that they are not worthy of the attention of literary connoisseurs. This view could be rooted in the conventional attitude towards children's books and comic strips. Tove Jansson feels that many people are embarrassed to admit that they enjoy reading about a friendly world, where security is never boring and danger is never really dangerous. Tove Jansson believes that some people read detective stories to give vent to certain emotions while others choose children's books as an outlet for a sort of "forbidden kindness."

The problems of launching and establishing the works of a Scandinavian author on the international market are very great. Despite many attempts only very few succeed. Tove Jansson's stories and illustrations caught on quickly, and a number of critics have already called them "classics." At times one wonders whether somewhat older readers are not more moved and fascinated by Tove Jansson's world, but a closer look reveals that the different age groups experience it in different ways. Many adults are charmed by the soft and sensitive illusions, the soapbubble dreams of the individualistic characters who inhabit Moomin Valley, which is untouched by the modern age; when the characters' illusions burst they quickly develop new ones. Children are more fascinated by the Moomin family's adventures, their battle for survival against storms, floods, and other natural disasters, and the sudden appearance of frightening beasts. In Tove Jansson's works kindness always wins out over meanness, which children often accept as rather natural and adults tend to regard as a wish-filled illusion. In Moomin Valley the idealists and optimists are never defeated.

Tove Jansson first introduced the Moomin family in books with drawings. Later, she presented them in comic strips that were syndicated to many parts of the world. The characters' popularity was soon followed by requests to mass create and mass produce them for mass distribution and mass consumption. Tove Jansson did not want her individualistic characters to get out of her hands and she decided to keep them under her control. But through mass culture, the Moomin family have become a symbol of Finland for many young foreigners.

The Moomin stories are set in Moomin Valley, which is located in the Finnish archipelago, where Tove Jansson has spent many months almost every year since her childhood. She was born in Helsinki, in 1914, and she has sketched her development in the following words: "I knew so little in my childhood. All I knew was that I was going to make pictures because that was what father and mother did." In her middle teens, Tove Jansson studied drawing and decorative art at an industrial art school in Stockholm: "After that, I naturally started to work with oils and entered the Atheneum academy of art in Helsinki." Later on Tove Jansson drew cartoons for magazines, illustrated books, and painted.

Tove Jansson is a Swedish Finn who has maintained strong ties with Sweden through her Swedish mother and relatives. Her mother is an artist who, among other things, has designed about two hundred stamps and has also drawn numerous maps of Finland to be used in history books and similar works. Her father was a sculptor. Although she has spent most of her life in Finland, Tove Jansson has lived in Sweden a good deal. Her Swedo-Finnish dialect is noticeable, but not very marked. When she speaks about her "mumintroll," as they are called in Swedish, she says "moomintroll." She feels that the Swedo-Finnish pronunciation "moomin" conveys a round and kind impression. As a result, she is delighted that in English her characters are called "Moomins."

During an afternoon we spent with Tove Jansson in her studio-apartment in Helsinki, she remembered that she gained the initial impulse to the Moomin family in the early 'thirties: "The story may sound like an afterthought, but it is really true. In our house hidden away in the Finnish archipelago we used to write things upon the walls. One summer a lengthy discussion developed along the walls. It all started when my brother, Lars, jotted down a quasi-philosophical statement and I tried to refute it, and our dispute continued daily. Finally, Lars quoted Kant, and the controversy came to an immediate end as this was irrefutable. In annoyance, I drew something that was intended to be extremely ugly, something that resembled a Moomin. So, in a way, Immanuel Kant inspired the first Moomin. Later, I used this character as a mark of identification on cartoons I did for a magazine."

Tove Jansson says that she did not start writing until 1939: "The first thing I wrote was a rather peculiar story for children that was sold in soft drink stands in Stockholm. It was about a flood—I am very fond of natural disasters."

Moomins are small and fat. They have very large noses and stomachs and a fair-sized tail. Their bodies are white and their eyes are blue. They live in Finland and love sun and warmth, and sleep throughout the winter. Moominmamma always carries a large handbag and usually has her apron on. Moominpappa wears a top hat and often carries a cane. Snork Maiden has golden bangs and wears a bracelet around her left ankle. Moomintroll does not carry or wear anything.

Tove Jansson describes some of her major characters as follows. Moominpappa "is the incurable personification of manliness, the boy who never really grows up. It must also be admitted that he has a certain weakness for whiskey, but sometimes I only let him drink some punch. . . . He is sweet and moody." Moominmamma is the most down-to-earth of the characters and is seldom moved by the dreams of the others even though she understands and encourages them. She realizes the importance of allowing the others to have their dreams, and she is always prepared to help them back on their feet when they are disillusioned. Moominmamma is steady and humorous and "has enough motherliness for everyone." (Tove Jansson admits that she has been modeled on her own mother). "It is true that the whole valley has been named after Moomintroll, but he is still the most indefinable of them all. He is strongly attached to his mother and is also rather naive. He is extremely kind and easily feels sorry for others. Sometimes this leads to complications. Moomintroll is very emotional and playful, possibly because he has a good deal of curiosity." Snork Maiden is "the most female of the female." She is superficial and most fond of jewelry, attracted to dashing, somewhat elderly men, and movie stars.

Of all her characters, Tove Jansson says that she is probably most fond of Little My: "She is refreshingly angry and gay at the same time. . . . She enjoys life and is delighted when someone has frightening stories to tell." There are also a number of "hemulens" in the Moomin stories. Hemulens are always "conscientious, loyal and extremely capable. They often use their leisure time to collect things or become policemen. A hemulen has no feeling for nuances, but he or she always has good intentions and is never mean." Hemulens have no sense of humor and Tove Jansson's rather carefree characters often find them a bit boring and irritating. Snufkin is the valley's philosopher in the art of living: "he is wise and gentle, a thinker who wants to be left alone and meditate." With the exception of Moominmamma Tove Jansson claims that her characters are seldom modeled on any one person; they are a composite of several people and at the same time they are none of them.

During the years the looks of the Moomin family have changed considerably. Their bodies have become rounder and "kinder." Their formerly rather small and narrow noses have grown much larger and rounder and they now remind many of hippopotamuses. The stories about the Moomin family have also gone through some changes.

Tove Jansson's first book opened in late August when Moominmamma and Moomintroll entered a large forest in search of a suitable place to build a house for the winter. Moomins cannot stand cold and therefore their winter home must be ready by the end of October, when they crawl into bed with their stomachs filled with pine needles for a long winter sleep. When the story opened Moominpappa had been missing ever since he disappeared with the Hattifatteners, very restless creatures who move in large groups without any goal, who do not hear and continue on their way completely indifferent to what is going on around them. (In her most recent book, *The Invisible Child,* published in the fall of 1962, Tove Jansson revealed the tale of Moominpappa's life among the Hattifatteners). After a number of exciting experiences, Moominmamma and Moomintroll were met by a flood and then they found Moominpappa sitting on the top branches of a tree.

The background of the family was presented in quite another version somewhat later. Moomintroll was without a mother or a father and driven by his loneliness he decided to drown himself, but he found that he swam too well to succeed. By pure accident, Moominmamma and Moominpappa came rowing along at this time and picked him up without realizing that he was their long lost son. When they took him home certain objects reminded him of his childhood and then the Moomin family suddenly discovered that it had been re-united.

In another book, Moominpappa wrote his memoirs, *The Exploits of Moominpappa.* As an infant Moominpappa, wrapped in a newspaper, was discovered on the steps of the home for "found" Moomin children. He remembered that he had been "super-gifted" and unwilling to conform to the rules of the "hemulens" that ran the home. Even as a child Moominpappa was a bit of a Bohemian dreamer, constantly looking for excitement. One night, after everyone else had fallen asleep, he slipped out of the home. On his own, Moominpappa met three individualistic creatures—the fathers of three of Moomintroll's friends. They devoted themselves to a carefree life of adventure. But one stormy night, Moominpappa caught sight of a female Moomin who was frantically holding on to a board that was being mercilessly tossed about by enormous waves. Moominpappa courageously saved her and then his youthful bachelor days came to an end.

Moomintroll met his girl friend, Snork Maiden, under rather dramatic circumstances. One day when he was out with his friend Sniff, who had big plans for success and fortune, Moomintroll heard a lady in distress who was screaming for help by the seashore. Running to her assistance, Moomintroll discovered that a large crab had her tail in his claws. Picking up an enormous rock, Moomintroll crushed the crab. This incident marked the couple's first meeting and the overture to their romance.

During the later 'forties Tove Jansson's books about the Moomin family with illustrations became quite popular and a decade ago the Associated Newspapers in London contacted her and suggested that she should relate the tales of her characters in a comic strip. She remembers that "at first, when it was new to me, it was fun to work with strips. It was a new medium of expression." The Moomin comic strip caught on almost immediately and was printed in many parts of the world and in several languages. Tove Jansson recalls:

> After a while I found myself in a dreadful hunt for subjects, which is the curse of all comic strip authors. I had all the faces of the characters staring at me constantly and everywhere I went. I took them with me to parties and I picked them up as if they were something I was knitting and eventually people got used to it. You become a slave in the hunt for subject matter, which you must constantly vary in order to avoid repetition. For four years I did the drawings and texts entirely on my own. The hunt for subject matter went so far that when my friends came to me with their problems, I started to think: can I use this in my stories? Then I became afraid and realized that I couldn't continue. Later, my brother, Lars, handled the stories for two years and I did only the illustrations. Then when my contract ran out, I turned the strips entirely over to my brother. The transition was made smoother as Lars had two years to get used to the work.

As to why she started to relate the Moomin stories more than twenty years ago, Tove Jansson says: "I suppose I wrote to largely re-live my childhood, to describe the happy memories from childhood's summer veranda. I wrote probably for the sake of my own childishness, but as I was full-grown the result was a mixture of maturity and childishness." When we asked her why she thought her stories appealed to readers she replied: "I suppose it is because they look so crazy and yet they do normal everyday human things."

In the early days of the Moomin stories, Tove Jansson used to tell people that she was primarily an artist, but over the years the stories have gained an increasingly important position in her art. The commercialization of the characters reached its peak about five years ago. Partly as a reaction she wrote *Moominland Midwinter,* which marked a definite turning-point in her work. She says that this was the first book in which she consciously created the characters in one way or another: "It was during a winter, when business life became too much for me and I had to get away from things through writing."

*Moominland Midwinter* differed considerably from Tove Jansson's earlier works and was probably her most mature book. In this story friendly Moomin Valley was transformed into an alien and frightening winter world of loneliness and darkness, which was "not made for Moomins to live in." Moomintroll woke up one day in the middle of winter and was unable to fall asleep again. Moominmamma, Moominpappa, and Snork Maiden were sleeping soundly and there was no way of waking them. Moomintroll was entirely alone in this foreign world.

Not only was Moomintroll's own family asleep, but his friends had left the valley for the winter. In contrast to the open and friendly creatures Moomintroll had met during the summers, he met secretive and reserved creatures during this winter. A winter acquaintance he made told him once that "there are such a lot of things that have no place in summer and autumn and spring. Everything that's a little shy and a little odd. Some kinds of night animals and people that don't fit in with others and that nobody really believes. They keep out of the way all the year. And then when everything's quiet and white and the nights are long and most people are asleep—then they appear."

In many ways, *Moominland Midwinter,* is the most Nordic of Tove Jansson's books; it conveys moods that are very important to the people in Scandinavia: the seemingly endless wait for the sun, warmth and the reawakening of nature.

Tove Jansson found that one of the most dissatisfying aspects of the comic strip was the necessity to "build up a climax within three or four pictures. The readers should be left in constant tension as to what will happen next, new excitement and the tension towards a new climax and so on." In contrast to her comic strips and her earlier books, Tove Jansson let one main theme tie together the different elements of *Moominland Midwinter.* In earlier books, she had related numerous short stories that hung together rather loosely.

Tove Jansson's experiences with comic strips seem to be one of the reasons why she told us that "the text is the main thing for me. Writing is and always has been my most natural medium." She still devotes a good deal of time to painting. Some of her works are on display at the Atheneum, Finland's national gallery of art.

In one of the comic strip stories, Moomintroll once said: "Is it always this difficult to become wealthy and famous? In that case, I think we shouldn't bother and have a good time instead!" When we left Tove Jansson in her studio-apartment in Helsinki, she was leaving the next day for her lonely island in the Finnish archipelago. She said that she wants to live on an isolated island or in an enormous city, where there is freedom and anonymity. She added: "Lots of people go around with a similar dream about islands; there is some sort of intensive symbolism in these dreams." Tove Jansson owns her own island and she seems to regard it as her home, her own refuge, a place for "forbidden kindness."

## W. Glyn Jones (essay date May 1983)

SOURCE: Jones, W. Glyn. "Tove Jansson and the Artist's Problem." *Scandinavica* 22, no. 1 (May 1983): 33-45.

[*In the following essay, Jones examines the issue of public pressure on the writer as well as moral and artistic conflicts as evidenced in Jansson's work.*]

Tove Jansson's mother and father were both serious artists deeply engaged in their work, and so it is scarcely surprising that Tove Jansson's own works from the early Moomin books right through to her latest novel *Den ärliga bedragaren* should reflect a high degree of artistic consciousness. Artistic consciousness in this case does not merely imply the writer's own sense of artistry or the obvious interplay of visual art and the written word in her work. Both are clearly present, but in addition Tove Jansson draws directly on her own experience of an artistic home background, and in particular constantly keeps returning to a consideration of certain aspects of the artist's dilemma as she herself has felt it. She examines the demands made on the artist by his or her public as opposed to the need for isolation and reflection; she discusses the pressures placed on the artist faced with commercialisation; she reveals the moral, ethical dilemma of the artist seeking inspiration, and she indicates that there is sometimes a close approximation between artistic creativity and obsession. Some of these problems emerge at an early stage in the Moomin books, obviously given a degree of urgency by the commercial success of the Moomins. They are then subsequently debated at greater length both in the later Moomin books themselves and more particularly in the works written for adults to which Tove Jansson has turned in recent years.

Tove Jansson has always been reticent in giving information about herself and her personal background. However, in a presentation of herself and her work published in London around 1971 (the pamphlet is without publication date), she has the following to say of her childhood home:

> We lived in a large, dilapidated studio in Helsinki and I pitied other children who had to live in ordinary flats—nothing like the mysterious jumble of turn-tables, sacks with plaster and cases of clay, pieces of wood and iron constructions where one could hide and build in peace. A home without sculptures seemed as naked to me as one without books.

It is, of course, in the autobiographical novel *Bildhuggarens dotter* from 1968 (English translation: *The Sculptor's Daughter,* 1969) that Tove Jansson gives the clearest, though still partly fictitious account of her artistic background. The entire book is concerned with the childhood experiences of a girl growing up in a predominantly artistic milieu, and seeing the world not as yet with an artist's eye but with the eye of a child for whom art and a reverence for art are part and parcel of her daily life. Her behaviour shows clearly how she accepts as perfectly normal and natural the particular way of life which results from her being a member of an artistic family at the same time as she realises that there is something special—'heligt' is the word used on more than one occasion—about artistic creation. Even the very first chapter, 'Guldkalven', reveals the artist's eye, not so much from the general description, precise and visual as this is, as from an apparently chance comment to the effect that:

> Jag gjorde min guldkalv i granbersån därför att den var en hednisk plats och en cirkelformad omgivning är alltid bra för skulptur.

> (2nd ed. p. 10)

> I made my golden calf in the ring of fir trees because it was a heathen place and a circular background is always good for sculpture.*

There is, of course, no indication as to whether this really represents the little girl's awareness. The same intention is fundamental to 'Mörkret', a chapter in which the art rationalisation of her childhood, and the interplay of the child's fantasy world and the adult's presentation of it is one of the characteristic elements in this book. On this occasion, however, it is surely the intention that the reader should accept the child's awareness. The same intention is fundamental to 'Mörket', a chapter in which the art theme is closely related to other ideas commonly found in Tove Jansson's work such as obsession and the ability of the imagination to develop an impetus of its own. Tove and her friend Poju are building a secret passage, and here Tove's artistic background has a purely practical application when she is able to use one of her father's tools (a hammer intended for chiselling marble!) to further the project: 'Pojus hål är mycket mindre men hans pappa har ju så dåliga verktyg att det är en skam' ('Poju's hole is much smaller, but his father has such poor tools that it is a disgrace')* is the somewhat condescending remark of the well-equipped artist's daughter whose dawning artistic sensitivity also appears elsewhere in this story. Tove and Poju hide their secret passage behind a picture which Tove's mother did on sacking when a girl:

> Det är mammas väggbonad som hon målade på säckväv när hon var ung. Den föreställer en kväll. Det är raka stammar som stiger upp ur mossan och bakom stammarna är himlen röd därför att solen går ner. Allting utom himlen har mörknat i obestämt gråbrunt men de smala röda strimmorna lyser som eld. Jag älskar hennes målning. Den går djupt in i väggen, djupare än mitt hål, djupare än Pojus salong, den går oändligt och man kommer aldrig fram för att se var solen går ner men det röda blir bara starkare.

> (ibid. pp. 18-19)

> It is Mamma's tapestry, which she did on sacking when she was young. It represents an evening. There are some straight tree trunks rising above the moss, and behind the trunks the sky is red because the sun is setting. Everything except the sky has darkened to an indeterminate greyish brown, but the narrow red stripes shine like fire. I am very fond of her picture. It goes deep into the wall, deeper than the hole I have made, and deeper than Poju's room; it is never-ending, and you never get far enough to see where the sun is going down, but the red simply becomes deeper.*

The unquestioning acceptance of the artistic background is again quite clear, but the passage implies far more than this, indicating the power of a work of art to fire the imagination of the viewer, and is thus linked to the scene in *Pappan och havet* where Mamma creates a painted garden for herself on the wall of the lighthouse with such powerful artistry and expressive of such longing that she can actually disappear into it. The intensity of artistic experience is linked to the imaginative process, and Tove Jansson's work contains numerous examples, both at Moomintroll level and beyond, of the—sometimes dangerous—power of the imagination.

* * *

*Bildhuggarens dotter* contains many scenes such as these, but it also contains much more. The child's awareness of the role of art in her home and of the difference between art and non-art is clearly observable in several of the chapters, sometimes leading to quite serious consideration of artistic techniques. A temperamental househelp makes a deprecatory remark about the books which Tove's mother reads, and Tove immediately comes to her mother's defence:

> Jag förklarade för Anna att mamma inte hinner läsa andra böcker än dem hon ska rita omslag till för att veta vad boken handlar om och hur hjältinnan ser ut. Somliga bara ritar på som det känns och struntar i författaren. Det får man inte. En illustratör måste tänka på både författaren och läsaren och tillochmed på förlaget ibland.

> (ibid. p. 36)

> I explained to Anna that Mamma can't manage to read any books apart from those she is doing the covers for so that she can know what the book is about and what the heroine looks like. Some just draw what they feel like and don't give a fig for the author. You can't do that. An illustrator has to think of both the author and the reader and sometimes of the publisher as well.*

The role and problems of the book illustrator—amongst whom Tove Jansson can count herself—are obvious in this, and in this same story the child goes further, explaining the different colour considerations which force her mother to paint hair in different colours from what she knows it to be from the text. The artistic imagination, the artist's freedom to create according to an idiosyncratic vision, is clearly the subject of such brief episodes written in defence of the artist's freedom to break down the barrier of realism which the inartistic tend to erect. It is scarcely going too far to argue that passages such as this suggest a philosophy of art, even if it is couched in simple and apparently unsophisticated terms.

Together with this go repeated indications of the reverence with which Tove views art. When the family moves to an island for the summer, the most important problem is to find a place where her father can do his sculpturing. The boathouse is the obvious place, and he takes it over, at which stage this boathouse becomes a sacred place, not to be defiled in any way, and the beach nearby is left deserted by those who have no (artistic) right to be there. The boathouse has become a temple, something sacred where Pappa can create his art, and where he must not be disturbed. He needs his solitude, a craving which the rest of the family understands and respects, in contrast to the uninitiated philistines and outsiders, who come to watch him, disturb him, call him 'the sculptor' and even, to the horror of his daughter, ask how the inspiration is going. Pappa can only resign himself to the situation, whereby he becomes the picture of the frustrated artist, torn between his need for solitude and the demands of his less than artistic public.

*Bildhuggarens dotter* is essential to an understanding of Tove Jansson's work, related, as it is, to the Moomin books and yet more clearly than they pointing to the deeper problems with which the writer of those books was faced. It contains a direct statement of the artist's situation, though there are few explicit signs of the intense awareness of specific problems associated with that situation, which are hinted at in the Moomin books and dealt with at much greater length in the adult work.

The question of the innate tension between the artist's need for solitude and his need to maintain some kind of contact with those around him, to play some kind of positive role in society, is implicit from a very early stage. It is originally reflected in a story entitled 'Vårvisan' through the figure of Snusmumrik, the curious elusive person in the Moomintroll books with whom the Troll himself feels a special affinity. Hitherto Snusmumrik has appeared intermittently in the stories, usually turning up in the spring and leaving again with the approach of winter. He has stood as the type of the independent individualist, a bohemian, a wanderer who knows of no ties, gentle, well-liked, but something of an enigma.

Snusmumrik is first seen in the second of the Moomin stories, the early *Kometjakten* from 1946 (English version: *Comet in Moominland*, 1951), when the Troll and Sniff are sailing down a river on a raft and come across his tent as the only patch of colour in a desolate landscape. He is playing his mouth-organ, obviously enjoying the solitude. The Troll and Sniff are fascinated by this creature who merely calls himself a 'landstrykare'. However, he has the eye of a visual artist and points out the beauties of a landscape which to the unexpected visitors has been seen as anything but beautiful:

> 'Inte är du väl—hm—målare?' frågade mumintrollet lite generad.
>
> 'Kanske en diktare?' undrade Sniff.
>
> 'Jag är allting!' sa Snusmumriken och satte kaffet på elden.
>
> > (1st ed. pp. 47-48)
>
> 'You aren't by any chance—er—a painter?' asked Moomintroll rather shyly.
>
> 'Or perhaps a poet?' suggested Sniff.
>
> 'I am everything!' said Snufkin, putting on the kettle.

This passage, significant as it is, has been removed from the radically revised version published in 1969 under the title of *Kometen kommer*. One assumes that its removal was for stylistic reasons, but this remains nevertheless a very clear early indication of the role assigned to Snusmumrik.

As is the case with most of the figures in the early Moomin books, Snusmumrik is at first only superficially drawn, a type—albeit of an unusual kind of person—showing no sign of development or any of those inner qualities which make a character real. In 'Vårvisan', however, published in 1962 in the collection of short stories *Det osynliga barnet* (English version: *Tales from Moominvalley,* 1963), Snusmumrik becomes a character in his own right. Care has always to be taken in suggesting any degree of identity between Tove Jansson and any of her characters, and indeed she has herself said that Mamma and Tooticki are the only two real portraits. Nevertheless, it is difficult not to see certain personal elements in some of the figures she creates. Snusmumrik is early identified with the artist; here that aspect of him emerges fully, and he is confronted with one of the problems at the centre of Tove Jansson's artistic considerations, the relationship between the artist and his surroundings.

Snusmumrik is first seen wandering in the forest, trying to compose a spring tune, but inspiration is elusive, the tune has a life of its own and will not come until the moment is right. Snusmumrik feels it is lurking somewhere in the solitude he is enjoying, but he cannot quite catch it. At this point he is disturbed by a tiny, insignificant creature, a 'creep', who recognises him as a well-known figure, is drawn to him as an admirer and stares at him, thus disturbing him and finally dispelling his inspiration. Then he speaks to him:

> Får jag värma mig vid din brasa? fortsatte det lilla djuret och strålade med hela sin våta nuna. Tänk, jag kommer at bli Den som en gång fick sitta vid Snusmumrikens lägereld.
>
> > (3rd ed. p. 12)

'May I warm myself by your fire?' the creep continued, its wet little face shining with happiness. 'Just think of it, then I'll be the creep who has sat by Snufkin's campfire.'

Snusmumrik is understandably less than forthcoming, knowing well that his melody has gone. However, his problems are only just beginning, as the 'creep', who is so insignificant as to have no name, asks Snusmumrik to invent one for him, which he reluctantly does. Even then the melody does not return, and instead Snusmumrik is plagued by thoughts of the miserable little creature to whom he has been so dismissive. He goes back to find him and discovers that the creep, now named Titi-oo, no longer has need of him. Freed from the demands of which he has been conscious, he can now settle down to his composing again:

Nånstans under hatten började hans melodi röra på sig, med en del förväntan och två delar vårmelankoli och resten bara hejdlös förtjusning över att vara ensam.

(ibid. p. 19)

Somewhere under his hat the tune began to move, one part expectation, and two parts spring sadness, and for the rest just a colossal delight at being alone.

There can be no doubt about the artist's need for solitude, but it is equally clear that it must be a solitude attained after Snusmumrik has fulfilled what he feels to be the demands made on him by others, not one determined by selfishness and egocentricity. He has to acknowledge his responsibility towards the creep, and once he has become aware of it he can only regain his peace by doing what he knows in his conscience that he must do. As long as there is a justified need for him he cannot find peace until he has done what he feels, even unwillingly, to be his duty.

The importance which Tove Jansson has attached to this particular aspect of the artist's problem is indicated by her returning to virtually the same situation in the last of the Moomin novels, *Sent i november* from 1971 (English version: *Moominvalley in November,* 1971), which starts by showing Snusmumrik going off on his autumn wanderings with the sole object of being alone: 'Snusmumriken steg in i sin skog med hundra mil av tystnad framför sig.' (3rd ed. p.10) ('Snufkin entered his forest, with a hundred miles of silence ahead of him'). The whole of *Sent i november* is concerned with the way in which a small group of characters, each with certain exaggerated characteristics, is forced to adapt to each other's personalities. Each of them undergoes a transformation, a modification of the claims of exaggerated individuality. Snusmumrik is no exception to this process, though he is as unwilling to accommodate himself to his surroundings here as he was in **'Vårvisan'**. As in the earlier short story, Snusmumrik is on the point of composing a melody, and the surroundings in which

he is seen are described in strikingly poetical language. Nevertheless, the melody eludes him: 'Hann förstod att de fem takterna fanns kvar i dalen och att han inte skulle kunna hitta dem förrän han gick tilbaka.' (ibid. p.24) ('He knew that the five bars must be somewhere in Moominvalley and that he wouldn't find them until he went back again') It is this realisation that forces him to go back to Moomin Valley where he is obliged to fit into a society of living beings. And it is only by doing so that he can find his true artistic inspiration: there are plenty of melodies in the air which he could have taken, but they are 'sommarvisor för vemsomhelst', ie not the real products of inspiration, for which he himself is looking. The distinction between art and non-art is again indicated here, and it is clearly related to the question of personal integrity, a problem which becomes of great importance as Tove Jansson's work develops.

On arriving in Moomin Valley Snusmumrik remains true to his nature and does not live in the house with the others, choosing instead to remain isolated in his own tent. However, he cannot entirely avoid the others in the group, who disturb him and even force themselves on him, and he finally allows the hemulen, the noisiest of them all, to stay in his tent for the night. Before this, at the beginning of Chapter 10, it is expressly stated that the five bars he is seeking have not come any nearer, but only one chapter later, when he gets up early to have at least a little time to himself before the noisy hemulen wakes up, the five bars have got closer. As the story progresses it is Snusmumrik who almost without realising it begins to have a greater and greater influence on the other members of the party, changing some of their negative characteristics into positive ones, and even inspiring the otherwise very uninspired fillifjonka. In doing so, however, he moves away from the esoteric, egocentric aspect of his own art and is forced to create art for others, on their level. Only then, when all the transformations have taken place and the guests have dispersed does his melody come:

I det första dagsljuset gick Snusmumriken för att hämta sina fem takter, de fanns på havsstranden. Han steg över vallen av tång och drivved och stod på sanden och väntade. De kom genast och var ännu vackrare och enklare än han hade hoppats att de skulle vara.

Snusmumriken gick tillbaka til bron medan visan om regn kom närmare och närmare, han krängde ryggsäcken över axlarna och gick rakt in i skogen.

(ibid. p. 157)

At first light Snufkin went to the beach to fetch his five bars of music. He climbed over the banks of seaweed and driftwood and stood on the sand waiting. They came immediately and they were more beautiful and even simpler than he had hoped they would be.

Snufkin went back to the bridge as the song about the rain got nearer and nearer, he slung his rucksack over his shoulders and walked straight into the forest.

The situation is almost exactly parallel to that in **'Vårvisan'**.

A further examination of the need for the right conditions in which to create—though this time not concerned with general ethical demands made on the artist—is found in **'Svart-vitt'**, a story included in *Lyssnerskan* (**'The Listener'**) from 1973, and thus closely related in time to *Sent i november*. In this story the problems of artistic conception are interwoven with those of human relationships. The title refers not only to the illustrations which the principal character, an artist who, like many of Tove Jansson's characters, is unnamed, is trying to create, but to the contrast between the house which his wife has designed, cold, light and impersonal, with nowhere where he can be himself, and the one to which he retires to work: old, dark and dilapidated, but one in which a human being can live and fulfil himself. When faced with the task of illustrating a volume of horror stories, the artist finds he cannot achieve the right balance between black and white in his work, and his wife suggests that he should go and work in the old villa instead. This he does; he *can* live in that house, and he *can* produce the black element in his drawings, the black which seems also to represent the more sombre sides of his own nature, the side which it is necessary to express in order to express his full self.

Along with this goes a consideration of what artistic creation is, the problem of what an artist seeks to achieve:

> Det är det outtalade som intresserar mig, tänkte han. Jag har tecknat för tydligt, man ska inte förklara allting, så är det . . . Jag ser mina bilder som ett stycke verklighet eller overklighet skuret på måfå ur ett långt och ohjälpligt skeende, mörkret jag tecknar fortsätter hur långt som helst . . . Stella, jag illustrerar inte längre. Jag gör mina egna bilder och de följer ingen text.
>
> (Delfin ed. 1973, p. 49)

> It's what isn't directly expressed that interests me, he thought. I have been too precise in my drawings; you mustn't explain everything, that's what it is . . . I see my pictures as a piece of reality or unreality carved at random out of a long inevitable series of events; the darkness I draw extends as far as you want it to . . . Stella, I'm not illustrating any longer. I'm making my own pictures, and they don't follow any text.*

The text contains obvious echoes of the sunset picture, where the sunset, like the darkness here, went as far back as the viewer wished, and likewise the artist's freedom vis-à-vis the texts to be illustrated, similarly touched on in *Bildhuggarens dotter*, is a matter of concern. It is possible to discern some development, for whereas the infant Tove in *Bildhuggarens dotter* insists on the artist's need to understand the text, here the unnamed artist knows his text but feels his freedom to go

beyond it. Previously freedom has only consisted in the colour of hair. This passage from **'Svart-vitt'** indicates the fundamental difference between the uninspired book illustrator and the true artist who can produce real art, but who must do so in the right circumstances. This artist's personality and creative dynamism can only find their expression when he is removed from the impersonality by which he has so far been surrounded, an impersonality which is capable of killing his art. This particular text is followed by the significant sentence: 'Någon kommer at ge dem en förklaring' (Someone will find an interpretation for them)*, surely with the implication that his drawings have now gone far beyond mere slavish illustrations and have become art in their own right open to more than one interpretation.

This is one of the relatively few passages where Tove Jansson directly, even if through the medium of her characters, actually discusses artistic creation as such. She does, in *Bildhuggarens dotter*, talk admiringly of John Bauer, to whose technique her own forest scenes may appear to be indebted, and she returns in fairly general terms to artistic intention in the story **'Konst i naturen'** from *Dockskåpet* (*The Doll's House*), 1978, in which the custodian of an open air exhibition himself experiences the suggestive power of the sculptures in his charge:

> De växte upp ur gräsmattan, väldiga mörka monument i slät obegriplig oformlighet eller sönderhuggna taggigheter, utmanande och oroande.
>
> (1st ed. p. 141)

> They grew up from the lawn, vast dark monuments, smooth and shapeless and incomprehensible or fragmented and spiny, challenging and disturbing.*

He is confronted by a young couple who have bought an abstract painting on the meaning of which they cannot agree, and he tries to convince them that they should keep it wrapped up and interpret it according to the way in which they experience it individually:

> Det är det hemlighetsfulla som är viktigt, på något sätt mycket viktigt.
>
> (ibid. p. 147)

> It is what is mysterious that is important, somehow very important.*

His words clearly echo the thoughts of the artist in **'Svart-vitt'**, even if the kind of art he is discussing is a completely different one.

The twofold tension between on the one hand the need for solitude and the outside pressures to which an artist is subject, and on the other the need for clarity as opposed to the need for some mysterious depth resulting from independent artistic inspiration, lies behind the story **'Serietecknaren'** (**'The Strip Cartoon Artist'**) from *Dockskåpet.* It is a problem with which Tove Jansson herself was obviously confronted and which she felt to an increasing extent during the seven-year period from 1953 when she was producing the Moomin cartoon series for the London Evening Standard. She is, of course, a black and white artist as well as a writer, and the combination of the popularity of the Moomintrolls in the Moomin stories and the obligation to produce a cartoon strip every day exposed her to pressures which were new to her. There was the need for some kind of inspiration upon which to base the cartoons, together with the longing for a breathing space in which to gain some measure of mental peace. If she has ever written a story in which her own subjective experiences shine through, it must be this. Certainly, an article in *Hufvud-stadsbladet* on 9 April 1971 talks of Tove Jansson as having been driven almost to despair by the demands of the series, while in an interview in the *American-Scandinavian Review* in the Spring of 1963 she herself says:

> At first, when it was new to me, it was fun to work with strips. It was a new medium of expression . . . After a while I found myself in a dreadful hunt for subjects, which is the curse of all comic strip writers. I had all the faces of the characters staring at me constantly and everywhere I went.
>
> (p. 53)

The situation in the story, with its obvious overtones, is basically simple. Allington, presumably an American, has done a highly successful cartoon strip called Blubby for twenty years. He has given up and is replaced by a young man, Stein, who significantly is given a seven year contract. Stein has no sense of being a great artist, but he is asked directly whether he is one of those who feel they are prevented from producing true art because they are engaged on this particular kind of task—a question which cannot have been entirely unknown to Tove Jansson while she was working on the Evening Standard. In answer to Stein's question as to why Allington gave up, he simply receives the answer that he got tired. One of the objectives in the remainder of this short story is now plainly to find out what has happened to Allington, and to discover why he gave up. As the new Blubby artist Stein now begins to receive hosts of letters from admirers, mostly children, and he is faced with the moral choice of what to do about these letters. His colleague, Carter, has no problem, simply refusing to answer any letters at all, while Stein has certain misgivings about allowing his to be answered by another member of the newspaper staff and signed with Allington's stamp. The problem is obviously a real one, and it is increased when Stein is actually visited by one boy who has written to 'Allington' persistently, and who is now suspicious when Stein cannot remember him. However, through this boy Stein manages to trace Allington, whom he visits. Allington, too, has replied to his corre-

spondents in one way or another; he is a man of integrity who has sought to do a good job, and who has suffered from the strain. He has moreover experienced the burden of the search for inspiration which is part and parcel of this particular kind of artistic production: and he discovers that he has to draw on the people he meets:

> Man börjar leta motiv. Bland folk man känner, bland sina vänner. Ens eget är tömt och då tar man ut allt vad de har och använder det och kramar ur det och vad de än talar om för en så tänker man bara, kan det användas.
>
> (1st ed. p. 124)

> You start looking for themes. Among people you know, among your friends. Your own store is exhausted, and then you take out everything they have and make use of it and squeeze it out, and whatever they talk to you about you just wonder whether it can be used.*

It is clear that creation of this kind has become an obsession in which Allington's own integrity as a human being has been brought into question. He has been put into the position where he cannot have a relaxed and casual relationship with other people because he is constantly on the look-out for some way of exploiting them in his search for new stories.

This same problem is found elsewhere in *Dockskåpet,* principally in **'Huvudrollen',** the story of the actress Maria Mickelsen who is given an uninteresting role but discovers that the very drabness of the person she is to play is beyond her. She finally has to overcome her problem by inviting her cousin Frida, whose insipid, colourless nature is exactly what is necessary for the part, to stay with her for a time at her house in the country. The irony of the story is that the cousin is filled with gratitude for the invitation and enjoys to the full the days she spends with Maria, while Maria is secretly merely exploiting her, drawing on her personality for her own ends.

There is a vampire-like quality about Maria. The same quality is seen again in **'Lokomotiv',** though this story is only indirectly linked to the artistic problem. The narrator is *not* an artist, though he is convinced that his creations of the idea of the locomotive are products of great artistic quality. In order to find his inspiration he deliberately sets about exploring the character of the people whom he meets in an effort to discover their innermost secret. When he finally persuades himself that they have given themselves away, in what he calls 'the moment of the locomotive', he feels he is able to draw on their personalities and find inspiration for his own drawings. In point of fact, of course, the man is a hopeless psychological case, in no way an artist, but in the present context the interesting feature is that his problem, of deriving inspiration from anyone and everyone he meets, is exactly parallel to that experienced by real artists of different kinds, and thus becomes a travestied version of the artist's situation in Tove Jansson's work.

In her latest novel, *Den ärliga bedragaren* (*The Honest Cheat*), 1982, Tove Jansson returns to the theme of the artist, centring herself on Anna Aemelin and her artistic and human integrity. At the beginning of the novel Anna is something of a recluse and something of a legend in the village on the outskirts of which she lives. She exists exclusively for her art, in which rabbits are somehow an essential feature, and she inhabits the house known locally as Kaninhuset, outside the village proper and with very little real contact with the inhabitants. The rabbits in her watercolours are always expected of her, but even at this early stage there are signs that she is not personally committed to them, and when she reads the reviews of her latest work she always gives up on reaching their references to her rabbits. What the reviewers say about the rest of her work is far more important to her:

> Aemelin förvånar oss än en gång genom sin anspråkslösa, närmast kärleksfulla behandling av den miniatyrvärld som endast är hennes: skogsmarken. Varje detalj, minutiöst utformad, är för oss andra ett igenkännande och samtidig en överraskning, hon lär oss att se, att verkligen betrakta . . . Men Aemelins akvareller är ständigt förnyade. I ett både naivt och mycket skickligt grodperspektiv har hon fångat skogens idé, dess stillhet och dunkel, det är en orörd urtidsskog vi har framför oss.
>
> (45)

> Aemelin surprises us yet again with her unassuming, almost tender recreation of the miniature world which is hers and hers alone: the floor of the forest. Every detail, fashioned with infinite care, is something we both recognise and at the same time are surprised by. She teaches us to see, to observe in the proper sense of the term . . . But Aemelin's watercolours show a constant renewal. In what is at one and the same time a naive and yet highly sophisticated worm's-eye view she has captured the idea of the forest, its silence, its darkness. We are presented with a primeval forest untouched by mankind.*

Although Anna is aware of a quality in her watercolours which is not always appreciated by those who are only concerned with her rabbits, she is tied to her 'blommiga kaniner' simply because people expect them of her. In the course of the novel she undergoes a development which is of a psychological rather than an artistic kind, a trauma forced upon her by the self-assured, ruthless 'ärliga bedragaren' Katri Kling. Her peace and her isolation are disturbed. Anna emerges unscathed but changed, and after a period during which she can no longer see her woodland, she begins to produce a new, adult art without her 'blommiga kaniner'.

Katri Kling's role belongs to the category of human relationships in Tove Jansson's work, and her direct significance for Anna's artistry is limited. However, the two subjects cannot be entirely separated. The immediate artistic problems are related to those in 'Serietecknaren'. There is, for instance, a renewed consideration of the question of the artist vis-à-vis the commercial pressures to which he or she is subjected. Anna produces her rabbits very largely because it is expected of her and because business firms are earning money from them as they do from Blubby. One of Katri's aims is to break down the relationship between Anna and those exploiting her, and Anna is disinclined to let her do this, though she does give in.

Then there is the question of Anna's relationship to her correspondents. Like Stein in **'Serietecknaren',** and like Tove Jansson in real life, she is inundated by letters from youthful admirers, and it is her principle to answer them all individually. In the problems caused by this Tove Jansson is returning to her consideration of the uneasy balance between seclusion and the need to have some kind of relationship with her public, which can be traced right back to Snusmumrik's attempts to find his Spring melody.

Anna is seen answering letters from children:

> Hon hade ordnat deras brev i tre högar, högen a var från de mycket små som skänkte henne sin beundran i bilder, mest teckningar av kaniner, og fanns det text hade mammorna skrivit den. Högen b innehöll önskningar som det ofta var bråttom med, isynnerhet ifråga om födelsedagar. Nummer c kallade Anna Dem det är Synd om och här behövdes stor omsorg och eftertanke.
>
> (99)

> She had arranged their letters in three piles. Pile a was from the very little ones who were expressing their admiration in pictures, mostly drawings of rabbits, and if there was a text to them, it had been written by the mums. Pile b contained wishes which were often urgent, especially concerning birthdays. The ones in c Anna called The Ones I feel Sorry for, and they required a great deal of thought and consideration.*

In her confusion Anna asks Katri what she advises her to do:

> Att låta bli att svara, sa Katri.
>
> Det kann jag inte.
>
> Men ni har ju ingen överenskommelse med dem.
>
> Hur menar ni, överenskommelse . . .
>
> Jag menar ett löfte. Ni har ju skrivit til varje barn bara en enda gång, inte sant. Och ni har ingenting lovat.
>
> Nåja, som det nu blir . . .
>
> Ni har alltså skrivit till somliga barn flera gånger?
>
> Vad ska man göra! de skriver och skriver och tror man är vän med dem . . .
>
> (100)

> 'Don't reply,' said Katri.
>
> 'I can't do that.'

'But you've no agreement with them.'

'What do you mean, agreement . . .'

'I mean a promise. You've written just once to each child, haven't you. And you haven't promised anything.'

'Well, that depends . . .'

'So you've written more than once to some children?'

'What can I do? They write and write and think I'm a friend of theirs . . .'*

The conflict is solved, or at least removed, when Anna agrees to let Katri answer her letters for her, not least in such a way that the children will realise that there is no question of a continuous correspondence of any kind. But this is at the cost of Anna's sense of personal integrity. The problem implicit in **'Vårvisan'** is still present, and although it is treated in greater depth, the dilemma persists.

There is, obviously, no solution to it, real as it is. It is probably to be seen as part of the dynamic process which produces art, and as such can be incorporated into Tove Jansson's general view of art, its potential, its categories, the demands it makes on the artist.

Art and the artistic problem in its various guises is a regularly recurring theme in Tove Jansson's work, sometimes openly treated, as in *Bildhuggarens dotter,* sometimes disguised in the scenario of the Moomin books, sometimes seen in the form of adult fiction in the later works. It would probably not be correct to call Tove Jansson an artist's artist, or an artist's writer, but the theme of the artist's dilemma is of such fundamental importance that her work in its entirety cannot be appreciated unless her preoccupation with the problems of the artist is taken very seriously indeed. This is one of the themes contributing to a unity in her work as a whole, and one which is inextricably linked to the gradual transition from the Moomintroll books, with their increasingly adult element, to the later works written exclusively for adults.

### Notes

(Translated passages: All English translations marked with an asterisk are my own. All others are taken from the standard English translations of Tove Jansson's work as published in Puffin Books.)

## W. Glyn Jones (essay date 1984)

SOURCE: Jones, W. Glyn. "Background, Ideas, and Influences." In *Tove Jansson,* pp. 1-13. Boston: Twayne Publishers, 1984.

[*In the following essay, Jones outlines influences on Jansson's work as it has evolved from children's stories into adult literature.*]

The twentieth century has seen the emergence in Scandinavia of two children's writers, Tove Jansson and Astrid Lindgren, whose names have become household words throughout the world. They have both at an early stage created their own fantasy worlds, different as they are, centered in the one instance on the Moomin family and in the other on Pippi Longstocking, the first quiet, gentle, romantic at times, the other boisterous and full of fun. Both writers have, after creating their own fantasy worlds, felt the necessity to explore other fields. Astrid Lindgren has kept, broadly speaking, within the field of children's stories, though they reflect a vast register of mood and genre, whereas Tove Jansson has moved further and further away from the children's story into the realm of adult literature—which nevertheless has themes and motifs in common with her earlier work. Meanwhile, within the earlier creations, parallels have been sought and drawn between these two outstanding authors. Writing in the Danish newspaper *Information* in 1966, Ulla-Stina Nilsson argued that "Moomintroll becomes a dream figure in just the same way as Pippi Longstocking, whose great popularity without doubt can be ascribed to the fact that she is a girl doing just what she wants to do—and what we probably want to do but do not dare"[1].

This article was written on the occasion of Tove Jansson's being awarded the Hans Christian Andersen Medal, "the greatest distinction which can be made to a children's author." It was only one of the many awards and prizes she won. Her books have been translated into twenty-five languages, and she receives some fifteen hundred letters a year from enthusiastic devotees all over the world. The story goes that after publishing her picture book **Who Shall Comfort Toffle?,** Tove Jansson received a letter from an English child who wrote that he would send four pence a week to her to help comfort Toffle, and then he changed the sum to six pence. A slightly different version of this story is found in Ebba Elfving's article in *Hufvudstadsbladet* of 9 July 1976, in which the child in question is an American boy who at first promises five cents a year and then alters his offer to a once and for all payment of twenty-five cents!

The secret of Tove Jansson's remarkable popularity is not hard to learn. Her Moomin family represents what has been called a "liberal humanism," a slightly confused, tolerant, semi-Bohemian attitude to life that has been compared to the philosophy of Henry Miller or Jacques Tati, an opposition to the conformism that seems irrevocably to follow in the wake of commercialism and technical progress[2]. The Moomin world is a fantasy world, an escapist paradise even, but one that attracts children and adults alike because of the security it ultimately offers, even if that security is subject to outside threats and dangers. As early as spring 1963, Frederic and Boel Fleischer viewed Tove Jansson's world in this way in an article in the *American Scandinavian Review*:

> . . . Tove Jansson's stories and illustrations caught on quickly, and a number of critics have already called them "Classics." At times one wonders whether somewhat older readers are not more moved and fascinated by the soft and sensitive illusions, the soap-bubble dreams of the individualistic characters who inhabit Moomin Valley, which is untouched by the modern age; when the characters' illusions burst they quickly develop new ones. Children are more fascinated by the Moomin family's adventures, their battle for survival against storms, floods, and other natural disasters, and the sudden appearance of frightening beasts. In Tove Jansson's works kindness always wins out over meanness, which children often accept as rather natural and adults tend to regard as wish-fulfilled illusion. In Moomin Valley the idealists and optimists are never defeated.[3]

Any philosophy to be found in the Moomin books seems to have been fortuitous, and Tove Jansson denies seeking to educate her readers: "I make no conscious effort to educate. I do not try to put over any particular view, least of all any 'philosophy.' I try to describe what fascinates and frightens me, what I see and remember, and I let it all take place around a family whose main characteristics are perhaps a kindly confusion, acceptance of the world around it and the very unusual way in which its members get on with each other"[4]. In this same discussion with Bo Carpelan, Tove Jansson touches on the accusation that she is an escapist. In answer to the suggestion that Moomin Valley is a paradise for escapists, she replies:

> To be honest, isn't escapism an integral part of writing for children? At least it is with me. Let's put it this way: if I don't write to amuse or educate little children, I must presumably be writing for my own childish qualities. Either those I have lost or those I can't fit into an adult society, a rather discreet kind of escapism.[5]

The theme is taken up again in an unpublished manuscript:

> Escapism, why not? . . . I know that it is supposed to be dreadfully negative. I suppose I am an escapist. I have enclosed a family in a valley paradise, surrounded them with lofty mountains on all sides and only given them a narrow outlet to the sea—which of course is itself an escapist symbol. Perhaps the excuse is that I am writing children's books—for surely children have the right to escape.

However, she adds that her books are written less for children than for herself, a significant comment, which may well be an indication of the forces that have led her away from children's books and turned her into a highly individual adult author[6].

No author is born in a cultural or historical or national vacuum, and for some, a knowledge of the influences—cultural and social—brought to bear on them through-

out their lives is important, even necessary, if their work is to be properly understood. Tove Jansson, however, is one of those who have the quality of timelessness; for her the Finnish national and cultural background certainly makes its impact, but it is of secondary importance in understanding her writing. The countless thousands of children the world over who read the Moomin books scarcely wonder about cultural backgrounds: they find themes of a timeless nature and with a universal appeal, and the character types must surely be recognizable whatever the background of the reader.

As for the significance of Tove Jansson's own life and background, interviews with her and articles about her, her childhood, or her life on the island to which she repairs in the summer all show clearly that there is a direct connection between what she writes in her books and what she has experienced. She has also admitted that people have often seen aspects of themselves in her characters, though she maintains that only two of the figures in the Moomin books are actual portraits: Moominmamma is based on her own mother and Tooticky on the artist Tuulikki Pietilä. Apart from this, Tove Jansson is reticent about relating her life to her work, and published articles and interviews tend to be imprecise when it comes to details of her nonliterary life.

Suffice it, then, to say that Tove Jansson belongs to the Swedish-speaking minority in Finland. She was born of a Swedish mother and a Finland-Swedish father and brought up against the solidly middle-class background that the Swedish-speaking Finns of Helsinki represented; her own artistically minded parents, however, were less inclined to conform to the norms laid down by the respectable middle classes than were many other Finland Swedes. The obvious contrast between the narrow respectability of certain members of this class and the more relaxed attitude of her own immediate surroundings is doubtlessly responsible for some of the contrasts portrayed in her books between, for instance, the fillyjonks and hemulens on the one hand and the Moomin family on the other.

Modest as her background might have been, the home *was* middle class, and this is reflected in all Tove Jansson's work. Like many Finland-Swedes—indeed like many Finns in general—the family did move out of town and spend the summer months in the country or—in their case—on an island in the archipelago, where they occupied a cabin. The similarity has been pointed out between the Finland-Swedish ritual of closing down the summer residence for the winter and reopening and refurbishing it the following spring, and the way in which the Moomins close down *their* house to hibernate:

> Life in summer residences in Finland was a very Finland-Swedish phenomenon. It was a way of life for

fairly well-to-do and well-established people, and right up to the first world war it was the Swedish speakers who dominated the establishment.

And I (with my roots in that class) recognised Tove Jansson's playful portrayal of the middle class pattern which is so effortlessly merged with a Bohemian way of life. A traditional way of living, and yet with its unconventional features.[7]

Even the architecture of some of these Finnish summer residences, with their towers and romantic roofs, is reminiscent of the Moomin house—though that is supposed to have been inspired by an old-fashioned stove. The mixture of the petit bourgeois and the Bohemian is also pointed out by Lennart Utterström, who emphasizes that the Moomin family—and *mutatis mutandi* Tove Jansson's own family?—seldom consciously breaks with accepted concepts and conventions[8].

There are in Tove Jansson's work occasional glimpses of rather bedraggled and woebegone creatures, but in general the surroundings reflect a certain standard of life, and her illustrations all represent sizable houses. The same holds true of the adult books: there are very few glimpses of the working classes in them, and whether the action takes place in Tove Jansson's native Helsinki or, occasionally, abroad, the solid middle classes usually assert themselves. There is no sign of social conflict and only here and there, of what could be called social awareness.

There is, however, a constantly recurring motif of security that is threatened from outside. It is not possible to explain this fully, though various reasons for the sense of lurking danger might be pointed out. While Tove was still a very small child, Finland underwent a bloody civil war between the Reds—the communists—and the Whites—the conservative forces—and it may well be that this left traces. Or perhaps the sense of belonging to a minority of 11 percent in a country where the majority was becoming increasingly influential played a part. Or perhaps it can be ascribed to the general sense of insecurity caused by events abroad as well as at home.

Tove Jansson herself makes no direct allusion to any of this in her work, and she has vehemently denied any political parallels, such as those that have been suggested in the conflict between the red spiders and the white hattifatteners in the short story, **"The Secret of the Hattifatteners."** She does, however, accept that the general situation in which she has been brought up has left its mark on her work:

Why not? It is a Finland-Swedish family I have described. And there may be traces of the isolation which is inevitably present in any minority. But it is done absolutely without pathos. They are content with each other, with their surroundings and the place in which

they live. But of course they must have recognisable Finland-Swedish characteristics—that isn't intended to be either a good or a bad thing. It's simply how it is.[9]

Tove Jansson's family was "different" in Finland because on the one hand it was Swedish speaking—though this would scarcely be felt in the Swedish-speaking enclave—and on the other because it was a family of artists which maintained a strong artistic tradition with all this meant for the family's life-style. Her mother, the daughter of a Swedish clergyman, was Signe Hammersten Jansson, known by the pseudonym of Ham; she was first and foremost a highly gifted caricaturist, but she was also responsible for the design of many of Finland's banknotes and about two hundred Finnish stamps as well as a large number of book covers, illustrations, and maps. She was, according to all accounts, a practical woman who managed to combine her artistic activities with caring for her husband and three children as well as running a home and a cabin[10]. She used to tell stories to her children, and Tove Jansson acknowledges her debt to her for this and for the feeling of comfort and security she experienced as her mother sat near the stove in the dark studio.

Her father was the sculptor Viktor Jansson, known to his friends as Faffan. His artistic creations, some of which are seen on the dust cover of the autobiographical *The Sculptor's Daughter,* set their stamp on the home. Tove Jansson says that she has powerful visual memories of her childhood home:

I saw that studio much later, when other artists had been living in it and stamped it with their personalities. I saw how tiny it was, and how changed. But that did not spoil my original picture of the studio, big and mysterious with a fire in the stove, the shadows and the sculptures. Since then I have felt that any home without sculptures is empty.[11]

According to the author herself, both her parents were active in the Finnish Civil War in 1918, and her father in particular was of a very patriotic disposition. (One remembers Moominpappa, who on one occasion declares himself to be a staunch royalist.) Tove was the eldest of three children (her first brother, Per Olov, was born in 1920 and the second, Lars, in 1926), and she has emphasized that her childhood was a happy one despite uncertain financial circumstances. The members of the family were devoted to one another, but Tove felt herself particularly close to her mother. She has already been acknowledged as the model for Moominmamma, and the question will inevitably arise as to whether Viktor Jansson was the model for Moominpappa. The answer seems to be rather that certain of his characteristics have been borrowed, though Moominpappa falls short of being a re-creation of the author's father.

One aspect of Tove Jansson's work that strikes the reader is her love of islands and her fascination with storms. It seems that her father was at least in part responsible for this.

> In the summer [my parents] rented a fisherman's cottage on an island in the eastern part of the Finnish archipelago; it was wild and beautiful and uninhabited. Every time there was a storm Father would take us out in the boat—he loved storms. We sailed to islets which were even wilder and more isolated, and spent the night under the sail during thunderstorms which were far more violent and dangerous than they are now; the waterspouts were higher, and when you got lost in the mushroom woods the autumn darkness was blacker.
>
> We used to save shipwrecked smugglers. Father could waken us in the middle of the night to put out forest fires miles away from our island, and when the water began to rise he was delighted and said: I fear the worst.
>
> But it was Mother who then lit the lamp in the evening.[12]

There is hardly a word in the account that cannot be directly related to the Moomin books and *The Sculptor's Daughter,* a demonstration beyond doubt of the close relationship between Tove Jansson's own experience and the poeticized reality of the Moomin world.

Tove Jansson has continued the family tradition of retiring to an island, and she comments on this in an unpublished manuscript, in which she uses Moominpappa's island as her point of departure:

> That lonely island in the sea? Well, it was perhaps created less because I didn't like people than because I did like the sea. And if I am now moving out to an even smaller island out in the Finnish archipelago, it is because I have grown even fonder of the sea.

Tove Jansson's cottage "reminds one of an old-fashioned fisherman's cottage or pilot's house, a perfectly ordinary house with four windows, rag rugs, a rocking chair and so on. Even an ornate iron stove which it was difficult to find now that everything is black or white and artistically designed. In this cottage Tove works, writes, illustrates, paints"[13]. In another article, the same writer points out that Tove Jansson has done all the planning work on the island, which explains the obvious technical knowledge she exhibits in *Moominpappa at Sea,* with its glimpses of Pappa in his workshop and building breakwaters on his island.

Tove Jansson at an early age revealed her artistic propensities, and at the age of fifteen, after nine years at school, she went to study art in Stockholm, Helsinki, and Paris. She recalls that her father would not allow her to become a sculptor—but it is apparent that painting was the art form to which she was most attracted from the start.

> My father was a sculptor, but he would never let us touch clay. He said it was enough with one sculptor, I think he tried to protect us. Well, then, I started as a

painter and illustrator, and as a young woman I did a lot of illustrations for periodicals and newspapers. I designed book covers, anything at all; no one would buy my paintings, so I managed on illustrations. Later, I only illustrated my own books, but recently I have had some really interesting other jobs. I did them for Bonniers' Swedish versions of *Alice in Wonderland* and *The Hunting of the Snark,* and it was great fun, though very difficult.[14]

The principles guiding her in her illustrations are indicated by her in an article in *Mediernas värld.*

> To illustrate a children's book gives me a feeling of being an intruder in alien territory. I only draw in order to make things clearer, to emphasise or to tone down. The illustrations are nothing but a note in the margin, an attempt to be "considerate." What is too frightening can be modified by a picture, what is not plain can be given a clear outline, a happy moment can be captured and prolonged.[15]

In view of the intimate relationship between illustration and text in the Moomin books (there are no illustrations to Tove Jansson's adult work with the sole exception of a late edition of *The Summer Book*), it is interesting to note the indication in the first of the above quotations that it is difficult to illustrate the work of others. Tove Jansson herself feels a natural affinity between her illustrations and her text, and she realizes that illustrating her own text means the elimination of possible differences of interpretation between writer and illustrator.

The artists to whom she says she owes the greatest debt are the Impressionists, but she also mentions John Bauer[16] (to whom she devotes some discussion in *The Sculptor's Daughter*), Arosenius[17], and Elsa Beskow[18]. A later interest has been old engravings, "those very intricate ones with masses of detail and mysterious landscapes and volcanoes in eruption."[19] It may well be that these engravings have had their influence on some of her later illustrations, such as those in *Moominpappa at Sea.*

Tove Jansson has often been asked how she originally thought of the Moomintrolls. The inspiration for their shape at least appears to have come almost by chance.

> The story may sound like an afterthought, but it is really true. In our house hidden away in the Finnish archipelago we used to write things upon the walls. One summer a lengthy discussion developed along the walls. It all started when my brother, Per Olov, jotted down a quasi-philosophical statement and I tried to refute it, and our dispute continued daily. Finally, Per Olov quoted Kant, and the controversy came to an immediate end as this was irrefutable. In annoyance, I drew something that was intended to be extremely ugly, something that resembled a Moomin. So, in a way, Immanuel Kant inspired the first Moomin.[20]

Although it had been her original intention to concentrate exclusively on painting, in 1938 she turned to writing. Her first book, *The Little Trolls and the Great*

*Flood*—"a rather peculiar story for children that was sold in soft drink stands in Stockholm"[21]—was then published in Helsinki in 1945 and subsequently in Stockholm; from then onward the children's books took shape. In the mid-1940s, she began experimenting with strip cartoons in the Swedish-language paper *Ny Tid,* but it was not until 1954 that she made an international name for herself in this field with the Moomintroll cartoons which appeared in the *London Evening News* and were then syndicated all over the world in forty countries[22]. She continued this series for many years, gradually working on it with her brother Lars (Lasse) and finally leaving it entirely to him. She comments on this period of her life:

> At first, when it was new to me, it was fun to work with strips. It was a new medium of expression. . . . After a while I found myself in a dreadful hunt for subjects, which is the curse of all comic strip writers. I had all the faces of the characters staring at me constantly and everywhere I went.[23]

This experience had its literary expression in the short story for adults, **"The Strip Cartoon Artist,"** from *The Doll's House.*

According to an article in *Hufvudstadsbladet,* 9 April 1971, Tove Jansson was driven almost to despair over the demands made on her by her strip cartoon work. In the 1950s she had met the artist Tuulikki Pietilä, who "taught her to take a more relaxed attitude to life and take things as they came. And Tove gave Moomintroll difficulties instead of adventures"[24]. It was this same Tuulikki Pietilä who served as the model for Tooticki in *Moominland Midwinter* and **"The Invisible Child,"** the mentor who induces Moomintroll to accept the new reality with which he is surrounded.

The Moomintroll series continued until 1970, when the last of the novels, *Moominvalley in November,* appeared. Since then Moomin books have been sporadic and of a rather different nature—colored picture books with short texts. If, as appears to be the case, Tove Jansson has left the Moomins as her major work, it seems she is still tempted to take short, unassuming, and undemanding trips back into the fantasy world she created, a sign, perhaps, that although she has had to break new ground, the attraction of the children's books still remains. Again, she has commented on this:

> My first books were very naive and ordinary stories intended for very little children, but I feel that since then there has been a clear line . . . in my work, in the course of which my books have become less and less childish. I finally reached the point when I simply couldn't write for children any more. I think this is quite a natural change; perhaps I wasn't sufficiently childish myself any longer.[25]

And she goes on to say that her move from the Moomin books was regretted by many people, but that it was necessary.

I am convinced that if a writer sits down with the sole intention of writing a children's book, the result will be poor. Whatever you do, you must do it because you *want* to do it, because of a *need* to express yourself in this way, and if you do it for any other reason the result will be pretty meagre.[26]

The question of literary influences inevitably arises, and the answer might at first seem surprising. Tove Jansson has herself listed some of them in a brief presentation of herself that she wrote in 1960:

> As a little girl I was very fond of Arosenius' *The Cat's Journey,* and then came Elsa Beskow and Topelius[27]. The books which made the greatest impression on me as a young teenager were Kipling's *Jungle Book,* Conrad's *Typhoon,* Poe's *Tales of Mystery and Imagination,* Burroughs' first Tarzan book, Curwood's *Nomads of the North,* Lagerlöf's[28] *Herr Arnes penningar* (Sir Arne's Money), Čapek's *Krakatit,* Hugo's *Les travailleurs de la mer,* London's *The Sea Wolf,* Hardy's *Far from the Madding Crowd* and Karlfeldt's[29] *Vildmarksdikter* (Poems of the heath).

In her interview with Bo Carpelan, she produces much the same list, though she expands it slightly in a way that throws a good deal of light on her own approach to literature:

> If everything goes wrong one day I can still take out some of the romantic and naive fairy tales by Topelius. Unless I choose science fiction or horror stories. They calm me down. Take Ray Bradbury, for instance: he works with such small means, but he makes events *credible.* And so he has a calming effect.[30]

She then adds that from the age of thirteen she avidly read everything that came her way:

> Ham—my mother—used to get the books for which she designed covers, and I read everything she brought home. If it was a book she thought unsuitable for me—and she seldom thought that—all she needed to do was say: this is a very worthwhile historical novel, you should read it—and it remained unread. When I was forced out to have some fresh air I sat down behind a dustbin on the farm and went on reading. And at nights with an electric torch under the bedclothes.[31]

In a letter, Tove Jansson has added Collodi's *Pinocchio* and Jules Verne's *Captain Grant's Children* to these sources of inspiration, seeing the influence of *Pinocchio* in Tulippa's blue hair in *Comet in Moominland* and of the Jules Verne novel in the idea of the marooned Pappa sending his plea for help in a bottle[32]. On the other hand, she rejects what might look like an obvious influence, A. A. Milne's *Winnie the Pooh,* acknowledging certain similarities but stating that she did not read Milne until after she had started her own Moomin books.

Over the years Tove Jansson has become one of the most widely read of all Scandinavian authors. At the same time, she has had many exhibitions of her visual art and has been awarded a large number of prizes and medals, mainly for her books for children. Her fame as the creator of the Moomintrolls has spread still further, thanks to a number of television plays and series based on the Moomin family. She has also written a number of television plays for adults: "a little strange, with a touch of the horrific, to frighten the viewers"[33]. She has written a number of radio plays of a similar nature.

Despite, or perhaps because of, the success of the series, the Moomin books have made great demands on her time and her imagination. Her increasing preoccupation with human psychology (often the abnormal or overdimensioned aspects of human personality, which was apparent in some of the later Moomin books and occasionally in the very early ones) meant that these books, originally conceived for children, became more and more disguised adult literature. Consequently, over the past ten years or so, Tove Jansson has experimented with various forms of adult literature—the semiautobiographical novel, the short story, the novel—and with works for radio and television. As she has become more at home in the adult genre, she has shown an increasing intensity, until her latest volume of short stories, **The Doll's House,** stands as a new climax to her work. Everything seems to indicate that she has now found a medium in which she can express herself more freely than she could in the Moomin books. With hindsight it is apparent that her work as a whole shows a clear line of development: the children's books gradually take on a new character and merge into adult literature. This development is the theme of the present study.

*Notes*

Page references are given in the text. Those enclosed in parentheses refer to the English translations, Puffin editions. Those in brackets refer to the original Swedish editions, and in these cases, the translations are my own.

1. Ulla-Stina Nilsson, "Mumindalen, vort genoplevede barndomsland," *Information,* 24 May 1966, p. 8.

2. Ibid.

3. Frederic and Boel Fleischer, "Tove Jansson and the Moominfamily," *American Scandinavian Review,* Spring 1963, p. 47.

4. Bo Carpelan, Interview, in *Min väg till barnboken,* ed. Bo Strömstedt (Stockholm, 1971), p. 102.

5. Ibid., pp. 97-98.

6. A similar comment is found in Tove Jansson's interview with Fleischer "Tove Jansson," p. 52.

7. Harriet Clayhill, "Drömmen om Muminhuset," *Allt i Hemmet,* no. 2 (1976), p. 29.

8. Lennart Utterström, "Möte med Mumin," *Hufvudstadsbladet,* 30 September 1973, p. 3.

9. W. Glyn Jones, "Tove Jansson. My Books and Characters," *Books from Finland* 11, no. 3 (1978): 93.

10. *Look at Finland,* no. 3 (1979), p. 47.

11. Private MS.

12. Private MS.

13. Ebba Elfving, "Muminmammans värld," *Damernas värld,* 20-28 June 1965, p. 19.

14. Jones, "Tove Jansson," p. 96.

15. "Trygghet och skräck i barnboken," *Mediernas värld,* Sveriges Radio, Stockholm 1977, p. 104.

16. John Bauer, Swedish artist (1882-1918).

17. Ivar Arosenius, Swedish artist and writer (1878-1909).

18. Elsa Beskow, Swedish children's writer (1874-1953).

19. Jones, "Tove Jansson," p. 97.

20. Fleischer, "Tove Jansson," p. 49.

21. Ibid.

22. "Moomintrolls in many ways," *Books from Finland,* no. 3 (1980), p. 128.

23. Fleischer, "Tove Jansson," p. 53.

24. At this point, the books seem to change from what might be called children's tales to novels proper, with the development of character and the consideration of problems that rightly belong to that genre.

25. Jones, "Tove Jansson," p. 91.

26. Ibid., p. 95.

27. Zachris Topelius, Finland-Swedish author (1818-98).

28. Selma Lagerlöf, Swedish author (1858-1931).

29. Erik Axel Karlfeldt, Swedish poet (1864-1931).

30. Carpelan, Interview, in *Min väg till barnboken,* ed. Strömstedt, p. 100.

31. Ibid.

32. Letter, 15 June 1981.

33. Jones, "Tove Jansson," p. 95.

*Selected Bibliography*

PRIMARY SOURCES

*1. TOVE JANSSON'S WORKS IN SWEDISH*

Note: All first editions published by Schildt, except *Småtrollen och den stora översvämningen* which was published by Söderström.

*Småtrollen och den stora översvämningen.* Helsinki 1945.

*Kometjakten.* Helsinki 1946.

*Trollkarlens hatt.* Helsinki 1948. Edition quoted: Helsinki 1968.

*Muminpappans Bravader.* Helsinki 1950.

*Farlig Midsommar.* Helsinki 1954. Edition quoted: Helsinki 1969.

*Trollvinter.* Helsinki 1957. Edition quoted: Helsinki 1970.

*Det osynliga barnet.* Helsinki 1962. Edition quoted: Stockholm 1974.

*Pappan och havet.* Helsinki 1965.

*Kometen kommer.* Helsinki 1968.

*Sent i november.* Helsinki 1971. Edition quoted: Stockholm 1974.

*Bildhuggarens dotter.* Helsinki 1968. Edition quoted: Helsinki 1969.

*Lyssnerskan.* Helsinki 1971. Edition quoted: Stockholm 1973.

*Sommarboken.* Helsinki 1972.

*Solstaden.* Helsinki 1974.

*Dockskåpet.* Helsinki 1978.

2. *Tove Jansson in English*

Note: All first editions of the novels in translation were published by Ernest Benn. Permission to quote from the English editions of Tove Jansson's Moomin books has been given by the copyright holders, Messrs. Ernest Benn Ltd.

*Finn Family Moomintroll.* Translated by Elizabeth Portch. London 1951. Edition quoted: Puffin Books, 1980.

*Comet in Moominland.* Translated by Elizabeth Portch. London 1951. Edition quoted: Puffin Books, 1980.

*The Exploits of Moominpappa.* Translated by Thomas Warburton. London 1952. Edition quoted: Puffin Books, 1980.

*Moominsummer Madness.* Translated by Thomas Warburton. London 1955. Edition quoted: Puffin Books, 1979.

*Moominland Midwinter.* Translated by Thomas Warburton. London 1958. Edition quoted: Puffin Books, 1980.

*Tales from Moomin Valley.* Translated by Thomas Warburton. London 1963. Edition quoted: Puffin Books, 1980.

*Moominpappa at Sea.* Translated by Kingsley Hart. London 1965. Edition quoted: Puffin Books, 1980.

*Moominvalley in November.* Translated by Kingsley Hart. London 1971. Edition quoted: Puffin Books, 1977.

*The Sculptor's Daughter.* Translated by Kingsley Hart. London 1969.

*The Summer Book.* Translated by Thomas Neal. London 1972.

"The Monkey." Translated by W. Glyn Jones, *Books from Finland* 14, no. 2 (1981): 62-63.

"Locomotive." Translated by W. Glyn Jones, *Books from Finland* 14, no. 2 (1981): 64-71.

SECONDARY SOURCES

1. *Bibliography*

Tarkka, Pekka. *Suomalaisia nykykirjailijoita.* Helsinki: Tammi, 1980, pp. 65-67. Two-page article in book of similar brief descriptions of major modern Finnish writers. Contains main biographical details and list of TJ's work.

2. *Books*

Hageman, Sonja. *Mummitrollbøkene.* Oslo: Aschehoug, 1967. Discussion of TJ's principal characters and a chronological description of Moomin books up to *Moominpappa at Sea.* A little on TJ's style.

Jones, W. Glyn. *Tove Jansson: Pappan och havet.* Studies in Swedish Literature no. 11. Hull: Department of Scandinavian Studies, University of Hull, 1979. An analysis of *Moominpappa at Sea,* dealing with main themes and aspects of the narrative. Also contains section on TJ and select bibliography.

Jutikkala, Eino, and Perinen, Kauho. *A History of Finland.* Espoo: Wellin & Göös, 1979. A good, fairly long history of Finland, useful for the historical background.

Klinge, Matti. *A Brief History of Finland.* Helsinki: Otava, 1981. A very short review of Finnish history by a leading historian.

Strömstedt, Bo. *Min väg till barnboken.* Stockholm: Bonniers, 1971. A book on various authors' approach to children's writing, containing a stimulating interview with TJ by Bo Carpelan.

3. *Articles*

Fleischer, Frederic and Boel. "Tove Jansson and the Moominfamily," *American-Scandinavian Review,* Spring 1963, pp. 47-54. Brief description of Moomin books, including interview with TJ.

Jones, W. Glyn. "Studies in Obsession. The New Art of Tove Jansson." *Books from Finland* 14, no. 2 (1981): 60-62. Brief introduction to TJ's work, touching on some of the themes developed in the present study.

———. "Tove Jansson and the Artist's Problem," *Scandinavica* 22, no. 1 (May 1983). A discussion of the themes of art and the artist as seen in TJ's work.

———. "Tove Jansson. My Books and Characters." *Books from Finland* 14, no. 3 (1978): 91-97. Lengthy interview with TJ, in which she reviews her approach to writing, her feelings about children's books, the theme of loneliness in her work, her approach to adult writing and her work as an artist.

Ranheim, Kirsten. "Utviklingen i Tove Janssons muminforfatterskap," *Norsk litterær årbok*, 1977. A thorough study of stylistic and thematic development of TJ's Moomin books.

*4. Dissertation*

Omland, Kirsten. "Tryggheten og skrekken. Utviklingen i Tove Janssons Muminforfatterskap." University of Oslo, 1975. A detailed study of TJ's work, mainly the Moomin books, based on the view that the central feature is the contrast between a sense of fear and a sense of security.

## W. Glyn Jones (essay date 1984)

SOURCE: Jones, W. Glyn. "*The Doll's House.*" In *Tove Jansson*, pp. 149-62. Boston: Twayne Publishers, 1984.

[*In the following essay, Jones discusses the thematic content of the stories in* The Doll's House, *describing it as Jansson's "most powerful work to date."*]

*The Doll's House* stands in stark contrast to the books immediately preceding it and is far more closely related to *The Listener* in mood and content than to any of Tove Jansson's other work. It probes the darker recesses of the mind and aims at producing fear in its reader. It is without doubt Tove Jansson's most powerful work to date and is characterized by a new intensity and a new depth of understanding.

**"The Monkey,"** the first story in the book, is the shortest and most optimistic, although even here the optimism is slightly tinged with melancholy. An ageing artist gets up one morning and as usual reads his newspaper, which he is "helped" to do by his pet monkey, who jumps through it. The review of his latest work is negative, though the critics treat him condescendingly rather than harshly; he is himself aware that he is in decline. He carries out a number of aimless tasks, then sleeps for a time, and then takes the monkey out with him to have lunch with some of his fellow artists. Their comments are bitingly sarcastic, and the mood affects the monkey—which has already been infected by the sculptor's own restlessness. They leave, and the monkey finally makes off up a tree; the sculptor

does nothing to stop it, only remarking that it may be cold, but at least the monkey can climb, a final comment intended to indicate that the monkey in a way serves as an inspiration to him to have another try.

Although the artist thus derives something positive from the monkey, the idea of limited contact between two living beings is taken to its farthest limit in the portrayal of the relationship between the man and the animal: they are used to each other and the sculptor knows the monkey's habits, but a closer contact between the human being and the monkey with the "expressionless" eyes is impossible. Yet the monkey is susceptible to atmosphere, sensing the sculptor's own mood in the morning, reacting to the teasing of the children on the way to the café and even more violently to the teasing of the critics. It is an outsider. So, in his way, is the ageing artist, as he gradually feels his diminishing artistic ability. Here, then, is a special instance of the artistic problem, a brief and unsentimental look at the artist who is losing his grip.

This is followed by the title story, **"The Doll's House,"** in which the central character, Alexander, is a carpenter and decorator. He is described as a man with a highly developed sense of taste and an unfailing sense of aesthetic values. He shares a flat with a friend, Erik, and when they both come to retiring age, the harmony that existed between them is put to the test. While Alexander succumbs to his creative bent and starts fashioning a doll's house, Erik, far more earthbound, sees to the food. The kitchen has to be divided between them, and Alexander finally is overcome by the obsession of building the house—which in the course of the story becomes the House. He is a perfectionist, bordering on the fanatical, and he cuts himself off more and more. When the telephone rings, it is now described as being like a sound from another world. Alexander has created his own world, and there he is content to live.

Meanwhile, this spoils the contact between Alexander and Erik, who is less at home in this world. He lacks the artistic gifts of his friend, and when he finally does take a hand in things, it is only with limited success. He is forced out to an ever-increasing extent, and this process is accentuated with the arrival of an electrician, Boy, who helps Alexander and becomes as obsessed with the whole idea as he is. Erik resorts to the television, and his estrangement from his closest friend is underlined by the fact that the hatch between his kitchen and Alexander's workshop is closed while Alexander and Boy are working in there, with the result that Erik can hear the drone of their voices but not distinguish the words.

It becomes obvious that some change is coming over Erik, that a crisis of some kind is approaching. It comes when Boy finishes the tower on the house and shows it to Erik, referring to it as "our house." Erik rejects the implication that it is "theirs" and virtually goes amok, attacking Boy with a metal drill and injuring his face; he threatens to destroy either the house or Boy. He is obviously on the borderline of insanity in his despair at being estranged from his lifelong friend, but a simple, everyday movement—that of taking off his spectacles— brings him to his senses. Alexander returns and understands the implication when Erik says he has saved "our home," and he retrieves the situation by remarking that there never was such a house as Erik's and his.

The story centers on the artistic problem again, though this time it is represented by a skilled craftsman rather than an artist proper. He is at all events a man who is seized by a project and cannot leave it alone. Alexander even gets up in the night to go to his House, and he eats his breakfast in his workshop. His obsessive preoccupation with his project creates a barrier between him and Erik and is itself the result of the need to adapt to the change in life-style resulting from retirement. As in *Sun City,* the innate characteristics of a person emerge more clearly in old age. Alexander even fails at one time to perceive the borderline between reality and fantasy, and he comes close to infecting Erik with his ideas: Erik takes a look at the house's kitchen, typically, of course, for the man who spends his time preparing food in real life, and notices that there is a wood fire in it:

> "Of course. It looks nice."
>
> "Good Lord," said Erik. "I can't imagine a wood fire. It's no use. Not when you're used to a modern kitchen."
>
> "You'll get used to it," said Alexander.

A tragicomedy, this story is nevertheless compelling and thought-provoking. The drama develops consistently and constantly until the climax is reached a couple of pages from the end. At one point, it looks as if the outcome will be tragic, but this is prevented by an ordinary action which reasserts everyday reality and breaks through the charged atmosphere that has gradually built up.

The borderline between the real and the unreal is even less clear in the next story, **"Time Concept,"** a whimsical tale of an elderly grandmother with no sense of time who pesters her grandson by giving him a cup of tea in the middle of the night or trying to get him to go to bed at six in the morning. However, this timeless world of hers is skillfully combined with a different time pattern when she and the grandson travel over the North Pole to Anchorage, to the accompaniment of the time changes that take place on such a journey. When they arrive, there is a red glow in the sky, and Lennart, the grandson, remarks that the sun is rising:

> "No, dear, it's setting," replied the grandmother. "That's what's so interesting. Here we come out of a long arc-

tic night, and when we get here the day has already turned into evening."

> [36]

And she is right. Her complete lack of a sense of time has here won over the grandson with his acute sense of it. The implication may well be that it does not matter in any case.

Time concepts and misconceptions are scattered throughout this story, including the ideas of having enough time or of being short of time. In contrast to the grandmother with her indifference to time comes the rush and bustle in the airport in Anchorage, where everyone is hurrying as though every second counted. The grandson's own sense of time no longer works after his watch symbolically stops on the way—after which there is a surprising change from a first-person to a third-person narrative.

For her part, the grandmother has, in Lennart's own words, created a world within herself, a world in which she is happy and can thrive, and when he seeks to disillusion her, she is upset. At the very end, when Lennart has rushed about trying to find postcards and discover departure times in an empty part of the airport—a scene with distinct Kafkaesque overtones—he finds the grandmother together with her childhood friend, John, a doctor who is said to be able to help people suffering from illusions and lapses. Lennart overhears his grandmother telling John that time has no significance for her—she finds days and nights equally beautiful. She is happy in her world, however it has been fashioned, and John's final words to her as they proceed to their plane are, "We have plenty of time" [39].

After this delightful story, there is a radical change of mood in **"Locomotive,"** undoubtedly the most powerful and intense story in the volume. The narrator, who like many of Tove Jansson's characters is not named, is a loner, a man living entirely in a world of make-believe, obsessed with what he calls the "idea" of the locomotive. He is a draughtsman who in his spare time makes colored drawings of locomotives; in his eyes, however, they are not just drawings, but an attempt to express the innermost being of the locomotive. He cuts himself off from the world around him, but in his sporadic enforced contacts with other people, his aim is always to make them betray themselves by talking and talking until they give away their most profound secrets. This he calls "the moment of the locomotive." From these "moments" he derives a—false—sense of power.

As a child, he has walked to school through the railway station each day, making up stories of trains or shipwrecks in which it is always he who has the power of life and death over others—he is the "imperator," he says. Even now, he sometimes goes to the station, and on one such visit, he meets a woman in the station restaurant. They start talking. She is in the station because she likes watching trains—and the narrator immediately interprets this innocent remark as a sign that she is also interested in the "idea" of the locomotive. He meets her again weeks later, and a "friendship" develops between them. He appoints her as his daily help, and she gradually begins to take him over in the same way as he has taken over other people in his imagination.

He becomes disenchanted when he discovers that the character with which he has endowed her in his imagination has nothing to do with reality: she is not interested in any abstract ideas but is an ordinary woman who, as she herself has said, likes watching trains. However, a relationship of some kind is struck up between them; she gains more and more power in his home, and while she is obviously trying to see to his needs and fuss over him, he feels she is devouring him. When she finally sees one of his color illustrations, her exclamation is as forthright as that of the child in Andersen's story of the emperor's new clothes: "But they are standing still." Frustrated, disillusioned, and weary, he decides "to let her die." The final section of the story tells how she persuades him to go for a weekend in Rovaniemi, and how he plans to dispose of her. It is not clear whether he does actually murder her, but in view of the number of plans he lists for getting rid of her, it can safely be assumed that the one he apparently carries out also merely takes place in the mind. He lacks the strength of purpose to kill her in reality, and the plan to dispose of her is really only another in the long series of imaginary events in which he has been the master of life and death.

In this complex story, Tove Jansson is working on two or three different levels. There is the straightforward portrayal of the narrator living in a world of his own, a world created by a neurotic, perhaps even psychotic, personality. He is interested only in machines, because of their "supreme indifference" to other people, and he is afraid of the demands people might make on him. He dislikes physical contact with people, even avoids such expressions as "to lend a hand" because they imply physical contact, and so when the Woman (whose name, Anna, he can scarcely bring himself to use) stands and holds his hand as a train comes in, she is damning herself in his eyes—though a warm *frisson* goes through him at the same time. When she puts her arms around him, the heat of her body fills him with disgust. His only contact with other people is to try to discover their secret beings, and there is a demonic urge in him to take them over and derive strength from them. However, ironically, this is precisely what he feels that the Woman is doing to him—though as it is all experienced through his eyes, we have only his rather unreliable word for it, and there is no other concrete evidence to

suggest that her approaches to him are anything but those of a woman feeling growing affection for a man with whom she is seeking contact. He speaks to her, compulsively, until he has betrayed everything about himself, and the story is full of expressions indicating the extent to which he feels he has surrendered himself to her. He even dreams of her: ". . . she came closer, hopping like a black bird over the rails, she was hot and smelled of sweat and held her arms outstretched to take hold of me, and at the same time I knew that she already had me, she had the whole of me packed into her stomach, undigested and with no possibility of release" [61]. In committing these strikingly Freudian images to paper, the narrator is, of course, also betraying himself on a different level—to the reader. His jottings are often disjointed, and although for the sake of "objectivity," he tries to tell his story in the third person, he resorts to the first person as he becomes more and more emotional about what he has to tell. And as he becomes increasingly obsessed with the idea that the woman in some way has devoured him, the crisis he is undergoing is underlined by more and more frequent references to how tired he is; he often has to stop his account, sometimes in mid-sentence, and return to it later.

Very little is learned of the woman, as everything is seen through the narrator's eyes. She is the only person he has ever been interested in, but the personality he ascribes to her is one he imagines and is therefore a projection of himself. The general impression of her is that she is a very ordinary, even colorless person who is probably genuinely fond of the narrator—or at least uses him as a relief from her own loneliness.

While **"Locomotive"** examines a sick mind, **"A Tale from Hilo, Hawaii"** turns to the mind of an innocent abroad, a young hippie from America who comes to a small town in Hawaii with the preconceived notions of the ignorant foreigner. Hilo is no paradise: it is a seedy little place, with a lot of rubbish on the shore, and when Frans decides to tidy it up, he merely makes it worse than ever. He stays on, a well-intentioned but unrealistic hanger-on, properly speaking unwanted, but in a way liked by the local population. The narrator points out that unfortunately he took a liking to him—and implies that he was never paid for the board and lodging he gave him.

In contrast to **"Locomotive,"** this is a light and humorous story in which the only sense of tragedy is that of the encroachment of modern civilization on a somewhat backward outlying area of Hawaii. However, it has serious overtones, underlined perhaps by the inability of Frans and the grandmother to communicate, as the grandmother, with her ninety-seven years, does not speak English, thus affording the narrator the opportunity of covering up for her and embarking on a series of lies to placate the young tourist. On a different level, the inability to communicate spreads to the clash of cultures, as the young hippie fails to understand the Hawaiian culture in which he finds himself. He is misunderstood and misunderstanding, and much as people like him, he is an object of gentle fun. By the end of the story, he has been accepted, but only as part of a kind of game.

**"A Memory from the New Country"** is a more everyday tale, drawing on the experiences of three Finnish sisters who have emigrated to the United States. The eldest of them, Johanna, has responsibility for the other two, and of these the younger, Siiri, soon shows signs of irresponsibility. She marries a good-for-nothing Italian, a small-time thief who proceeds to exploit the sisters' meager financial resources. In a final confrontation with the Italian brother-in-law, Johanna threatens him with the police if he does not go away. He leaves, and the three sisters settle down to a normal, uneventful life in their new country.

This is an uncomplicated, though scarcely lightweight story, in which more than one private world is glimpsed. The obvious one is Siiri's marriage to her Italian, a dream that could not possibly come true, an infatuation if not an obsession. However, in a way, this is counterbalanced by Johanna's own private world, as she is trying in America to maintain the Finnish quality of their lives, to create a little bit of Finland in America. Perhaps there is even a hint that a make-believe world, in this case the Finland Society of which Johanna is a member, is necessary in order to survive in alien surroundings. The third of Tove Jansson's essential themes also glimpsed is the inability of the three sisters to communicate with each other. Johanna understands the situation, but she is unable to penetrate Siiri's silence, while Maila, the middle sister, is torn between the two and is in her turn less than open with Johanna. It is an almost archetypal situation, with the eldest sister feeling her responsibility and the younger ones resenting, to varying degrees, the authority that is naturally hers.

Following her custom of varying the weight and seriousness of the stories within one volume, Tove Jansson now proceeds to a longer and more intense story, **"The Strip Cartoon Artist."** It would be wrong to talk of an autobiographical story, but there must be a considerable element of personal experience in it in view of Tove Jansson's own activities in this very field. Despite the American setting and the fictitious action, it is obvious that some of the atmosphere surrounding the strip cartoonist must result from an intimate knowledge of the scene.

Allington, the creator of the world-famous "Blubby' has given up his job, and his paper is desperately trying to find a successor who can continue the series without interruption. A young artist called Stein takes over the task and moves into Allington's spot in the newspaper offices. He tries to discover why Allington has given up, what has become of him, and both his and the reader's curiosity is aroused by the evasive answers he is given. In the end he discovers where Allington lives and goes to visit him. Allington talks at length about the pressures on the artist and the intellectual monotony of the job. As the conversation continues, it becomes apparent that he has suffered a nervous breakdown as a result of his work and the strain it has put on him. In the abrupt but effective ending to the story, he offers to do a few drawings for Stein if he ever needs inspiration.

Possible personal experience apart, this story puts the dilemma of the commercial artist into perspective. He has to create, whether the inspiration is there or not, and what he creates has to be good. There is no time to relax, and it is significant that on glancing in a mirror toward the end of the story, Stein notices that he is looking tired. He, like Allington before him, is living in a world apart, but it is a world created through outside pressures rather than one resulting from some twist in his own personality. Stein is a stable young man at the beginning of the story and indeed also at the end of it, but he has now seen the ravages that stress of this kind can bring about in another human being who was equally normal.

Problems of the artist are also present in **"White Lady,"** in which three ladies of around sixty are out enjoying themselves. The general problem of ageing—as opposed to old age—is implicit in this glimpse of the three in a restaurant on an island outside Helsinki, enjoying the feeling of relaxation and looking back on their youth. Yet they have little contact with the young people they meet there, although they do try to talk to them. Ellinor, the writer, specializes in novels for young people, but she now begins to realize how little she really knows them and how little she has in common with them.

Not unlike the novel *Sun City*, **"White Lady"** portrays ageing people unable to come to terms with the age they have attained and wanting to keep in touch with younger people, but unable to do so. As in the novel, certain facets of their personalities become slightly exaggerated as they age: Regina's sentimentality, and Ellinor's love of metaphors. At the end, the shadow of death passes as the boat approaches to take them back to Helsinki, and May (like Mrs. Rubinstein in the coach in *Sun City*) refers to it as Charon's barge. They have all spent an evening in an artificial world, dreaming of a world that is past—if it ever existed—and in Charon's barge, they are being ferried back to reality.

**"Art in Nature,"** which comes next, also takes place on an island. Again it is a world on its own, a world this time in which art dominates. The only person left in this open-air exhibition at night is a watchman, who lives his own life among the paintings and sculptures. He prefers the sculptures. One evening he is going his rounds and comes across a middle-aged couple having their own little barbecue, and after the inevitable reprimands, he starts talking to them about a parcel they have with them. It is an abstract painting they have bought, and they cannot agree as to what it represents. The watchman suggests that they should wrap it up artistically and hang it unopened on the wall instead of disagreeing: "That's the strange thing about art. Everyone sees in it what he can, and that's the intention" [145]. He avoids having to comment on the subject of the painting by saying that it is too dark to see it, after which he returns to his own unadorned room.

One of the shortest stories in the book, this merely hints at some of the main themes—the artist's problem in communicating with the public, the object of abstract art, and the necessity for the viewer to participate actively in understanding it. Indirectly, the question of communication between human beings is suggested, and the watchman is a clear example of someone living apart from the world of reality. However, none of the motifs is dealt with at length, and the story aims to set the mind in action rather than to provide any kind of answer to the questions it raises.

"Leading Role" continues the study of the artist's problems, in particular the need for some kind of inspiration. In "The Strip Cartoon Artist," Allington has spoken at length on the need he has felt to exploit every chance acquaintance in the quest for material: "Your own resources are dried up, and so you take everything they have and use it and exploit it, and whatever they say to you, you are wondering whether you can use it" [124]. In "Leading Role," the artist is an actress who needs to study and mentally devour an uninteresting and unsuspecting cousin in order to perfect the part she is to play. There is in Maria something of the same demonic need to absorb and live on other people's personalities as there is about Allington and the narrator in "Locomotive."

For the first time, Maria is offered the leading role in a play, but to begin with, she finds the character uninteresting. When it is pointed out to her that it is in fact very difficult to play the part of such a colorless character, she decides that her cousin Frida resembles the part so much that her best way of mastering it is to invite Frida to spend a week with her in her lonely, dismal summer house. The story is concerned with the interplay between these two characters, with Maria watching Frida's every movement and deliberately creating embarrassing silences in order to study her insecure cousin and note both her gestures and the way in which her voice dies away. When Frida finds that she can be useful about the house, her insecurity vanishes, and in order to bring it back, Maria sends for her own housekeeper to take over the work. Little does the cousin realize that on going to her room, Maria is noting her every gesture and trying to rehearse her movements in front of a mirror. The supreme irony comes when Frida fails to understand how Maria can be so considerate of her—a remark that obviously has its parallel in the play under rehearsal, where Ellen, the colorless principal figure, also fails to realize that she is being cruelly treated.

There is little sign of real contact between the two women, but toward the end Maria is overcome with what she sees as Frida's natural goodness, and although there is not sufficient warmth about her completely to efface the impression of a cold, calculating actress, a modicum of sympathy begins to emerge, and Maria decides at least to play the part of a good hostess.

Frida is a type not entirely unknown in Tove Jansson's work, the little, unattractive, and neglected person whom life is obviously passing by. The contrast between her and the calculating Maria is underlined by the scene in which the reader on the one hand sees everything through Maria's eyes and on the other realizes that Maria is consciously studying her. Sympathy is aroused for Frida for the very reason that she *is* experienced through Maria's eyes, and the use to which she is being put is very clear indeed.

"Leading Role" is an examination of artistic integrity and artistic self-sufficiency. How far can an artist create without consciously drawing on others for inspiration? The narrator in "Locomotive" can only with reservations be called an artist, but the signs are that Allington is one on his way and that Maria is at least a capable actress. Yet none of them is able to support his or her art without a deliberate and conscious exploitation of other, unsuspecting people. In different ways and to different extents, all three of these figures have a vampire-like quality, drawing their life strength from other living beings, who might then go on to praise them for their originality. One of the problems for the artist appears to be the necessity of exploiting human beings in order to communicate with—human beings.

In "Flower Child," there is no exploitation of people, but the question of human contact looms large, coupled with the problem of ageing and the changes it brings about within a person or a group of people. Flora Johansson is a svelte young thing who lives a gay life as a young girl, surrounding herself with friends of like mind. She marries an American and goes to live in the United States where she continues her spoiled and carefree life. Time passes and Flora is prevented from going to Finland by the war. Her parents die, and so does her husband. In the end she goes back to Helsinki and rejoins her former friends. All have looked forward to the reunion, but all have aged and changed, and the close contact that formerly existed is no longer to be found. After the first elation, things settle down. Memories can no longer provide the stuff for more than superficial conversation: "The close-knit circle around an all too small table presupposed an intimate contact which no longer existed" [166]. And moreover, that contact cannot be re-established.

Flora's life in Helsinki is now a lonely one. Her friends have other interests and duties—jobs, grandchildren, worries about their health—but she has nothing to live for except her own memories. And that is precisely what she does. She creates her own world of memories, imagining that she has guests, entertaining them, dismissing them when she has had enough. And she plies them with champagne, which she buys in great quantities and needs in order to keep a clear view of what is going on around her. Time begins to have little significance for her, almost as little as for the grandmother in **"Time Concept,"** and she sleeps when she feels the need, at any time of the day: "And Flora went to sleep on her fur, and the day passed into twilight, and she woke up and drank just a little champagne, just a single glass so that she could see and experience everything the clearer" [169]. Like many of the other stories in this collection, this has an open ending, and these final words indicate the hopeless and unchanging situation in which Flora now finds herself.

**"Flower Child"** is the story of a "light" woman, a woman who seeks superficial enjoyment in a world of her own and is finally faced with a reality with which she cannot cope. She has never understood her husband's business, and even the luxury in which she has lived as the wife of a rich businessman has been a false world, as he has been heading for bankruptcy. She has been fêted and spoilt, has scarcely grown up, while her friends have developed in a different direction. What once united them now divides them, and the contact that was there before is there no longer. It is a tragic story of loneliness and a hunger for contact growing with the years.

The last of the stories, **"The Great Journey,"** takes up the theme of the imaginary journey found in **"Locomotive,"** though the story itself is very different. It tells of a triangle. Rosa is torn between her friend, Elena, and her mother. Both want to travel with her, but Rosa is tied to her mother and cannot go away with Elena, with whom a very close relationship is indicated. The mother, who has dominated Rosa, has always been promised a trip abroad, but has never managed to go on one, and now she travels in her imagination to places with exotic names such as Gafsa and Bahia. Rosa is like Frida in **"Leading Role,"** a gentle person with a constant bad conscience even if she has done nothing to merit it. Elena tries to persuade her to break the bond that ties her so closely to her mother, but finally changes to persuad-

ing her to take the mother to the Canary Islands. What effect this will have on their relationship is left unclear. The dream world motif and the idea of the limits to understanding, this time among three people, are clearly discernible.

Taken as a whole, **The Doll's House** is a natural continuation of Tove Jansson's earlier work, a book in which she continues to examine the themes on which she has already laid so much emphasis. In all these stories, there is some character living in a dream world or a world not perceived by anyone else, a "doll's house." The extent to which they are divorced from reality varies considerably; in some cases, it is merely a constituent part of a totality, but in others it emerges, takes on a life of its own, and leads either to neurosis or psychosis or demonic fascination. There is even enough to suggest the need in people for some kind of "life dream"— perhaps related to Ibsen's "life lie"—as the basis on which to live their lives. It emerges at least as a book about people's need for some kind of dream with which to supplement the reality of a humdrum or demanding everyday life.

## Selected Bibliography

Page references are given in the text. Those enclosed in parentheses refer to the English translations, Puffin editions. Those in brackets refer to the original Swedish editions, and in these cases, the translations are my own.

### Primary Sources

*1. Tove Jansson's Works in Swedish*

Note: All first editions published by Schildt, except *Småtrollen och den stora översvämningen* which was published by Söderström.

*Småtrollen och den stora översvämningen.* Helsinki 1945.

*Kometjakten.* Helsinki 1946.

*Trollkarlens hatt.* Helsinki 1948. Edition quoted: Helsinki 1968.

*Muminpappans Bravader.* Helsinki 1950.

*Farlig Midsommar.* Helsinki 1954. Edition quoted: Helsinki 1969.

*Trollvinter.* Helsinki 1957. Edition quoted: Helsinki 1970.

*Det osynliga barnet.* Helsinki 1962. Edition quoted: Stockholm 1974.

*Pappan och havet.* Helsinki 1965.

*Kometen kommer.* Helsinki 1968.

*Sent i november.* Helsinki 1971. Edition quoted: Stockholm 1974.

*Bildhuggarens dotter.* Helsinki 1968. Edition quoted: Helsinki 1969.

*Lyssnerskan.* Helsinki 1971. Edition quoted: Stockholm 1973.

*Sommarboken.* Helsinki 1972.

*Solstaden.* Helsinki 1974.

*Dockskåpet.* Helsinki 1978.

2. TOVE JANSSON IN ENGLISH

Note: All first editions of the novels in translation were published by Ernest Benn. Permission to quote from the English editions of Tove Jansson's Moomin books has been given by the copyright holders, Messrs. Ernest Benn Ltd.

*Finn Family Moomintroll.* Translated by Elizabeth Portch. London 1951. Edition quoted: Puffin Books, 1980.

*Comet in Moominland.* Translated by Elizabeth Portch. London 1951. Edition quoted: Puffin Books, 1980.

*The Exploits of Moominpappa.* Translated by Thomas Warburton. London 1952. Edition quoted: Puffin Books, 1980.

*Moominsummer Madness.* Translated by Thomas Warburton. London 1955. Edition quoted: Puffin Books, 1979.

*Moominland Midwinter.* Translated by Thomas Warburton. London 1958. Edition quoted: Puffin Books, 1980.

*Tales from Moomin Valley.* Translated by Thomas Warburton. London 1963. Edition quoted: Puffin Books, 1980.

*Moominpappa at Sea.* Translated by Kingsley Hart. London 1965. Edition quoted: Puffin Books, 1980.

*Moominvalley in November.* Translated by Kingsley Hart. London 1971. Edition quoted: Puffin Books, 1977.

*The Sculptor's Daughter.* Translated by Kingsley Hart. London 1969.

*The Summer Book.* Translated by Thomas Neal. London 1972.

"The Monkey." Translated by W. Glyn Jones, *Books from Finland* 14, no. 2 (1981): 62-63.

"Locomotive." Translated by W. Glyn Jones, *Books from Finland* 14, no. 2 (1981): 64-71.

## Marianne Bargum (essay date 1987)

SOURCE: Bargum, Marianne. "Tove Jansson: The Art of Travelling Light." *Books from Finland* 21, no. 3 (1987): 137-47.

[*In the following excerpt, an introduction to the translation of a short story from* Traveling Light, *Bargum discusses themes of power struggles among adult family members, obsession, and emotional baggage that impedes people as they navigate their lives.*]

Tove Jansson's latest collection of short stories, **Resa med lätt Bagage** (**Travelling Light**)—her third—strengthens her position as a writer for adults, with her own intensely personal style and choice of subject.

At the same time new editions of her Moomin books for children are published continually, and the books go on attracting new readers throughout the world. Tove Jansson says she receives over 2000 letters a year, and she answers them all individually by hand.

Her fame as a children's writer and strip cartoonist is thus something Tove Jansson has to deal with every day of her life, even though the last Moomin book, *Sent i november (November in Moomin Valley)* appeared as long ago as 1970. Fame is something the characters in some of her recent work also have to deal with: the writer Anna Aemelin in the novel *Den ärliga bedragaren* ('The Honest Deceiver', 1982), who is well known for the flowery rabbits she draws. Or the strip cartoonist in the short story **'Serietecknaren'** (**'The cartoonist'**) from *Dockskåpet* (*The Doll's House,* 1978), who packs in his job and goes missing.

There is, nevertheless, a significant difference between the children's books and this more recent work: whereas, in the Moomin books, Tove Jansson attempted to create a family which could live together and who loved each other but left each other in peace and allowed each other their freedom, the main characters in the later stories are not able to live together. It is a question, rather, of a power struggle, of loneliness as a necessity and as a torment.

Kati, a strong-minded woman in *Den ärliga bedragaren,* ruthlessly exploits the weaker Anna Aemelin in order to serve the brother she loves. And the main character in the story **'Lokomotiv'** (**'Locomotive,'**) from *Dockskåpet,* published in *Books from Finland* 2/1981) is a very lonely man, totally obsessed with the idea of the locomotive, who exploits the confidence of the people he meets—they provide him with the warmth and intensity he does not possess, but they must not come too close.

This man illustrates one of Tove Jansson's favourite themes: obsession. In a recent interview for a Japanese issue of *Books from Finland,* she comments on this interest: 'Obsession with an idea, a fixation on one thing, fascinates me. Sometimes it's a question of excess with can become destructive, sometimes a mania which is not escapist or self-reflecting, but an honest attempt to achieve something fruitful right to the extreme limit and beyond, something that takes form, which is larger than oneself. I can't help becoming bewitched by those who try break out of their given limits.'

**Resa med lätt Bagage** is a collection of stories where travelling is the central theme: the characters may wander far, but essentially it is a question of travelling within oneself, with one's mental baggage which sometimes proves heavy to carry. Can one leave old and useless things behind and start anew, travelling light?

## Nancy Lyman Huse (essay date 1987)

SOURCE: Huse, Nancy Lyman. "Equal to Life: Tove Jansson's Moomintrolls." In *Webs and Wardrobes: Humanist and Religious World Views in Children's Literature,* edited by Joseph O'Beirne Milner and Lucy Floyd Morcock Milner, pp. 135-46. Lanham, Md.: University Press of America, 1987.

[*In the following essay, Huse argues that Jansson's Moominland stories and books celebrate human autonomy and combine elements of mythic quest fantasy with those of realistic tales of a rational world.*]

In describing Tove Jansson's Moomintroll fantasies, Eleanor Cameron states that these 1966 Andersen Award books present one of the most unusual worlds in the realm of fantasy. Jansson's characters "are all beings created wholly out of her own imagination."[1] The rounded, funny moomintrolls were originally cartoon characters developed by Jansson. They seem different from the animated toy characters of other comic, episodic fantasies, from the mythic creatures and talking beasts of spiritual or visionary fantasy, and even from such "domestic" beings as *The Borrowers* (sometimes used as a comparison for Jansson's work). Their land, Moominland, is not the kind of symbolic, coherent kingdom found in mythic fantasy, where the triumph of good over evil calls upon supra-human powers; nor does it challenge its creatures to the full use of human potential or lead them to ultimate maturation. Contrary to what we have come to expect in serious, interpretive literature, Jansson does not posit her world at conflict with the powers of the Dark, to use Susan Cooper's term, or engage in a maturation process to reach a balance between self and others, as in the stories of Wilbur the pig and Arrietty the Borrower. Nor does she set out to mock human vanity or simply spin child-toy adventures, as many fantasies which are neither spiritual quests nor humanistic searches do. Jansson's work does not fit into an easily defined position at either end of or even, perhaps, along the continuum between the ordered, mythic worlds of spiritual quest-fantasy and the progressive, rational worlds of humanistic tales.

She bases her characters in family relationships, perceived in much the same way modern psychology perceives them, but places them in a mythic world rich in strange and wonderful beings at whose center is the Moomin family. Moominland's coherence seems to rest in the theme of personal development and friendship,

especially, but not exclusively, as experienced by the young Moomintroll, in the cycle of the seasons passed in a secure but stimulating menage. This fictive creation differs from tales of supra-human powers, even though Moominland is as magical as any fantasy world one can visit. Moominland is not a world which reflects a higher one, nor is it a country which demonstrates the foibles of our own. Instead, in her universally significant fantasy world Jansson celebrates the reality a child encounters with its alternating terror and joy. Her unique, comforting yet strikingly modern world view emerges somewhat randomly in the early Moomin books and with a powerful consistency in the later ones. Jansson's success in depicting a world view which is neither traditionally humanistic nor religious rests in her presentation of character, particularly the Moomin parents, and their relationships to each other and the natural world they inhabit. Two autobiographies clarify the significance of Jansson's own experience in shaping that world view and introduce questions about the relationship of her illustration and her writing.

When I began using the Moomintroll books in my children's literature classes a few years ago, this "originality" intrigued me. Jansson resisted description under the critical framework I was trying to establish with my students. Her galaxy of comic characters first caused me to focus on "originality" rather than on "convention" in describing Jansson. Moominland is inhabited by creatures of varied ages and attitudes: Snufkin, the freedom-loving wanderer; Sniff, the babyish, kangarooish companion of Moomintroll; Moomintroll himself, who looks like a comic rhinoceros with a nice long tail but feels and thinks like a young person of sensitivity and imagination; Moominmamma and Moominpappa, his indispensable parents and fellow adventurers; the Fillyjonk, a reed-like spinster who usually likes to clean her house; and, generated over more than three decades, a host of woodies, creeps, hemuelens and other newly-coined but soon familiar folk.

I was also impressed by the perceptive statement about the value and wonder of life which was evident even in the early, episodic, almost haphazard tales, *Comet in Moominland* and *Finn Family Moomintroll*.[2] World view really becomes the significant dimension in discussing Jansson's originality, for in later works such as **Tales from Moominvalley**, *Moominland Midwinter, Moominpappa at Sea* and *Moominvalley in November* she seems to be consciously developing an overarching thematic structure. The stories depend on continual movement between the core of physical security best represented by Moominmamma's commodious handbag, and the metaphysical risk involved in experiencing and even becoming one with cosmic phenomena like the sea, the seasons, and the sky. "Self-definition in a benevolent universe" is a possible epigrammatic description of Jansson's theme, but this fails to include the loving tension between individual and community essential to her version of self-definition, as well as the cataclysmic proportions of the floods, the storms, the alternately barren or lush topography, and the dark pools and hidden glades which the creatures love and fear.

Central to Jansson's vivified world view are the Moomin parents, particularly Moominmamma. Moominmamma is the core of security in Moominland. She is the pivotal character whose meaning and presence makes Jansson's work both distinctly personal and universal, and who enables this artist to construct narratives which neither hold up external standards of perfection nor suggest that human (troll) nature is in need of improvement. With her strong, loving mother figure, Jansson seems to defy our usual expectations that serious literature is in some way heroic, in some way about our need to improve. In Moominland, it is true, creatures do change—especially in the later books. But the difference between Jansson and many other writers is that in her books there is no imperative for this change, either with the other characters in a tale or with the reader. The creature has a place and will be loved regardless of inner or outer change or the lack of it. Moominmamma does not view others as flawed. As nearly as I have seen it done, Jansson captures in art the notion of "mother" as it exists for the very young child. Recalling her childhood impression of growing up in a "tremendously rich and generous and problem-free home,"[3] the writer comments that she was unaware of the economic difficulties of her artist parents, as well as of other problems they faced. "Anything was possible, everything was exciting . . . My mother, especially, had an unusual capacity for mixing stern morality with an almost exhilarating tolerance, a quality I have never met with in anyone else."[4] In Jansson's fantasy world, Moominmamma does provide essential values and norms, but she will not exclude those who do not meet them. She is friend or mamma to the fussy fillyjonk, the obnoxious mymble (a round, contented, free type) and the introverted hermit-fisherman of *Moominpappa at Sea.* Existence gives one an intrinsic right to Moominmamma's love.

One of Jansson's best stories, **"The Invisible Child,"** collected in *Tales From Moominvalley* and, fortunately, anthologized in Arbuthnot, is a clear example of the troll mamma's central role in the books.[5] Ninny, introduced to the Moomintroll household by their fuzzy-haired friend Too-ticky, is the "invisible child" who has faded away from sight because she had been "frightened the wrong way by a lady who had taken care of her without really liking her,"[6] the icily ironical kind" who ridiculed instead of scolded. At first, the Moomins can see only the silver bell and ribbon the child wears around her neck. Mamma declines the suggestion to

take Ninny to a doctor, and tucks her in just as she tucks in Moomintroll, leaving "the apple, the glass of juice and the three striped pieces of candy everyone in the house was given at bedtime" (p. 113). Luckily, a recipe left by Granny has a few lines for a medicine "if people start getting misty and difficult to see." Even before she starts to take the medicine, however, Ninny's paws—"very small, with anxiously bunched toes"— appear (p. 114). Though Ninny's paws fade each time she is frightened by bumbling family members, Moominmamma's strong affirmation of *the way she is* causes more and more of her to appear. Wearing a new pink dress and hair ribbon made from Mamma's shawl, Ninny soon lacks only a face and a sense of humor. The medicine doesn't seem to have any more power, so Moominmamma decides that "many people had managed all right before without a head, and besides, perhaps Ninny wasn't very good-looking" (p. 122).

When Ninny, terrified of the sea, notices Pappa threatening (teasingly) to push Mamma off the dock, the invisible child hisses, screams, bites Pappa's tail, and appears at last in full face—snub-nosed, red-headed. Startled Moominpappa falls into the water himself, and Ninny shouts with laughter—now the most uninhibited child in the family. Security has given Ninny the power to act on her emotions.

Numerous examples of Moominmamma's unconditional, intuitive love and its role as the basis for action and the central value of the books appear even in the early stories. In *Comet in Moominland,* when Moomintroll rushes off into danger to rescue a pet, his mother waits quietly and alone outside of the cave which shelters the other creatures, until her son returns. In *Finn Family Moomintroll,* she alone knows her child when he has been physically transformed by the goblin's hat. She is seen at the beginning of *Moominsummer Madness* carving a bark boat for Moomintroll—the first of the season, which always goes to him. Although interrupted by an enormous flood and a summer of foreign adventure (including a hilarious interlude in the theater), she remembers, without being asked, to complete her gift by carving a dinghy for the tiny boat. She thus seals the experience of the summer within the safe and pleasant rituals of home and the now tranquil sea. When she wakes from hibernation in *Moominland Midwinter* (moomintrolls hibernate with their stomachs full of pine needles) she joins with her child in enjoying the early spring even though his winter hospitality has emptied the pantry of jam and pressed the silver tray into service as a sled. "Mother, I love you terribly," Moomintroll tells her,[7] this is his realization after a winter awake, during which he has learned, "One has to discover everything for oneself. And get over it all alone" (p. 143). In the last Moomin books, Jansson depicts Moominmamma, too, as someone who needs time to herself; yet she remains an expert at getting the family off on picnics when danger threatens.

As a literary creation, Moominmamma has as yet few peers, for as Too-Ticky remarks, very few stories are written about those who welcome heroes home. Beyond her loving tolerance and acceptance, Moominmamma exemplifies the ability to let people alone. She thus provides both absolute freedom and absolute security, essential to wholeness but not a way of shaping a *bildungsroman.*

Jansson's autobiography, *Sculptor's Daughter,* offers us much direct evidence of the experiences which forged such a unique world view. The incidents she chooses to relate from her childhood clearly demonstrate how dependent the Moomintroll books are on her own experience and on her memories of her parents. For example, she narrates a mood-piece in which, "doing just what she wanted to do," she burns old rolls of film left from her mother's work as an illustrator, simply to enjoy the sight and smell of the burning. In *Moominland Midwinter,* this odd activity is the choice of Moominmamma in her encounter with early spring. Other physical descriptions based on her childhood memories, such as the experience of *enjoyable* ocean storms and tidal disturbances which reveal lunar landscapes, and fascination with candles deemed "interesting" because they might burn nearby walls—all examples of the secure child venturing out into the unfamiliar with confidence and exhilaration—are incorporated into the fantasies as very natural aspects of Moomin life.

Two episodes in *Sculptor's Daughter* give charming testimony to the origins of Moominmamma. The child-narrator describes the bohemian parties given by her colorful father, all dependent for success on being "improvised" at the last minute. "Mummy has everything ready"—a well-stocked pantry so one can "improvise something."[8] The ideal life must include openness, freedom, spontaneity; yet the enjoyment of these things depends on the core of safety, the design and framework within which one acts. The notion of "making a whole" of things, of being equal to the task of arranging the reality one encounters as flux, and of seeking out danger in order to make yet more beautiful designs, is intrinsic to the Moomin tales. This same secure bravado and potential artistry is apparent in an early memory Jansson has of building a golden calf (taken, alas, to be a lamb by her grandmother) for the purpose of "clamoring for God's attention." Such spirit as that of the five-year-old would-be-idolator-sculptor, and of the Moomins themselves, is explained by the islands of complete security and safety in Jansson's memoir. The most notable for its relationship to her mother, and to Moominmamma, occurs when Tove and her mother are snowed in alone for several days. Her mother tells her they have gone

into hibernation: "Nobody can get in any longer and no one can get out!" (p. 165). The child's delight in their underground life is complete; she laughs, shouts I LOVE YOU and throws cushions, rejoicing alone with her wonderful mother in front of the fire. The image of utter safety, repeated in various ways in the autobiography, is extended beyond the hibernation the Moomins engage in, to the light on the verandah of the blue house, a power so great that it draws all creatures to it.

The narration of *Sculptor's Daughter,* by a child whose age may be five or six, spells out the premises of life as Jansson deals with it in Moominvalley. Maturing, moving from childhood to adulthood, is not the issue. Security and the courage to live are focal. Self-affirmation, rooted in a secure love relationship and eagerness for experience, is not a goal but a reality in the stories; in some sense, the tales are metaphoric shouts of joy and love. In demonstrating the child's exhilaration, Jansson seems to be one of those writers who, according to Arthur N. Applebee, shows the implications of a familiar paradigm rather than challenges beliefs.[9] Jansson's work constitutes a series of images of a familiar paradigm rather than a conflict-centered drama. Travel and discovery are frequent in the tales, but occur as a result of the undemanding love at the center of each book; adventure is a response intrinsic to reality as much as mother's love is inherent in reality. Going forth into the unknown is a natural function, like breathing and eating. To a large extent, travel and adventure constitute the "Pappa" side of life, but they are narrated in reference to the "Mamma" source of security.

The light on the verandah has its deepest meaning when it burns for a returning voyager. The core of safety must center in a whirlpool, a raging storm, a comet's path, or its value as a refuge and haven is lost. From time to time, Moominpappa (and Moomintroll) must venture out, away from the verandah, to explore the world. For Moominpappa, this is a way of fueling his art, the writing of memoirs and the keeping of diaries. While the journey-quest device seems a more conventional element than the intuitive, accepting home-image, the *Adventure* (Moominpappa's boat) also has its origins directly in the writer's childhood. Her father, the sculptor Viktor Jansson, "gave the necessary background of excitement."[10] The autobiography reflects the wildness of his parties and music, the antics of his numerous pets, the nerve-wracking but hallowed time of casting a mold in the studio, and his Viking love for the challenge of a storm at sea. It was his choice to spend each summer with the family on an island in a fisherman's cottage, creating the sources and settings for some of Jansson's adult books as well as the Moomin tales.

While the *Sculptor's Daughter* offers a rather clear explanation of Jansson's central thematic impulse, it is

*The Summer Book* which explains the intimate relationship Jansson enjoys with nature which is essential to the Moomin books. *The Summer Book* is the story of a young child and an old woman passing their summers on an island in the Gulf of Finland.[11] This work, drawn from Jansson's adult experience as well as from her childhood, recreates the strength and beauty of lives so much a part of the sea that the child is certain she has conjured up an especially fierce storm by her prayers on a too-quiet day. She needs to know the limitations of her own powers in relation to the wild, churning sea, yet her confidence in these powers must be preserved. Thus, her grandmother takes credit and blame for the terrible storm. Belief in the mind's power to interact with natural forces occurs repeatedly in the Moomin books, but without recourse to supernatural powers. It is Moominpappa's boisterous confidence which supplies the energy for the episodic adventures from which the family sometimes needs the rescue of a Moominmamma picnic.

Encounters with the natural world within and without the Happy Valley, where the round blue Moominhouse and its verandah shelter the extended family of creatures who happen along, fit neither a good-versus-evil pattern nor a nature-versus-culture one. The sea, the most pervasive and decisive force and image in the books, is the object of Moominpappa's scientific scrutiny until his child tells him that the sea "seems to do just what it likes . . . There's just no rhyme or reason in it."[12] The sea is a living thing, "a weak character you can't rely on," unpredictable as a person and just as worthy of love, respect, and tolerance. Pappa declares, "It's an enemy worth fighting, anyway," as the little trolls shout over the breakers, equal to the task of braving the ocean and making friends with it. Like other of their friends such as the ski-enthusiast hemuelen (another funny rhino-type with an elongated snout suggesting the inherent qualities of the bureaucrat who loves to arrange other people's lives), the sea is a fearsome but wonderful mix to be accepted as it is. The trolls and their companions are part of the mysterious tides, storms, and sunshine; the essence of life is experience, the unfolding experience of a child who knows the incredible terror of separation, yet knows even more fully the comfort and safety of a parent's presence.

In *The Summer Book,* a seafaring neighbor elicits the comment: "A person can find anything if he takes the time, that is, if he can afford to look. And while he's looking, he's free, and he finds things he never expected" (p. 67). Almost a summary of Jansson's work in the Moomin books, the comment especially describes her father's zest for life and Moominpappa's intrepid curiosity. With its assumption that "looking" is essential to a fully realized life, the statement calls attention to the essentially visual nature of the Moomin books. As the daughter of two artists and a painter herself, Jansson has created a fantasy world in which sensory observation and stretching the limits of experience are vital, and occur as a natural part of living. Not only the themes of her books, but her illustrations of them, exhibit the cozy security in the midst of chaotic adventure Jansson offers as a child's eye view of the world.

The illustrations are full of the sweet absurdities and intense enjoyment characteristic of the Moomins. A well-educated artist, Jansson has extended her intuitive, spatial powers into her verbal constructs. This is a significant factor in her use of emotion as the real "inner logic" of her fantasies—emotion not subject to critical evaluation, but simply presented as "being" rather than "becoming." Hers is not a linear artistry; while the early books use more loosely bound episodes and the later ones more emphasis on "states of mind" (really "states of feeling"), the pictures remain constant and show that each Moomin book is about the loving embrace of unfolding reality. Jansson says that her works are centered in love—"I love my characters and I love my readers"—and that she writes for the "ones easily frightened."[13]

Clearly, Jansson's own artistic sensitivity, rooted in her childhood with her loving, daring parents, has made her aware of the terrors of separation, of not belonging, of being in actual physical danger. Her childhood in Finland was upset by World War I, a fact which has caused Scandinavian critics to assert that her works are about security in catastrophe.[14] She has even been compared with Harry Martinson (Swedish winner of the Nobel prize for literature in 1974) because of her tenderness and cosmic anxiety.[15] Just as the "Mamma" core of the Moomin books sets them apart from such domestic adventure tales as those of Laura Ingalls Wilder (where the father figure is far more important to the narrative than the mother), the "Pappa" quest for danger enlarges the scope of the works and validates the security theme. The presence of fear, Jansson believes, is as strong a principle in childhood as the presence of love.[16] Thus, her books have fear as their "negative" side. The crushing waves, the burning comet, the desolate island, the enormous flood, are met in love.

Significant examples of this duality occur throughout the books; the clearest may be the "Groke," a creature who seems to represent the Nordic cold. Her name is the Swedish word for "growl," and she is the closest to a "pure evil" the Moomin books have. Wherever the Groke sits, she turns the ground to a frozen grave. Yet, Moominmamma says the Groke is lonely; it is her doom never to be liked by anyone. Moomintroll, disliking her as everyone does, nonetheless leaves a lamp burning for her at night when the family is living on an island in *Moominpappa at Sea.* He realizes that the lamp is her one comfort, even though if she comes too close to the light she will put it out forever. Characteristically, Jansson does not explain why Moomintroll is not afraid of the Groke, beyond establishing the general principle that nothing in the world need be shunned. While such plot incidents suggest a joyful response even to the most awesome natural phenomena, the illustrations do so even more effectively. The books are replete with them; the creatures tumble up and down the pages. Strategically placed full-page drawings throughout the series are deliberately used to allay the terror the printed word may cause the child reader.[17] Jansson's definition of herself as an artist by profession, her essentially non-linear story-telling, and her dependence on illustration to mitigate the fear aroused by verbal constructs all demonstrate the existential nature of her work.

The difficulty of discussing a graphic artist in a print medium may be one reason why literary critics outside of Scandinavia have not found Jansson a rich subject for analysis; readers unfamiliar with her work need to look at it as much as they need to listen to it in the act of reading the stories or reviews of them. Discussion of a few full-page illustrations which mitigate fear through reassuring design will, I hope, make more vivid the abandon I am suggesting as the mood of the Moomin books. Unfortunately, readers of the English and American editions miss the use of color to create an "undersea" effect in the original illustrations.

In *Comet in Moominland,* one of the earliest, most catastrophic and least domestic of the books, the illustrations are especially effective in their mitigating role. At the end of the book, the creatures huddle in a cave waiting for the descent of a huge, flaming comet, pictured as a frightening spectacle (p. 187). Yet the illustrated page before this, and the one after it, show respectively the waiting animals round-eyed with fear while nonetheless safely huddled together; and Moominmamma, handbag and all, giving a solid hug to the most frightened creatures. *Finn Family Moomintroll,* also filled with the terrors of the unpredictable, has a marvelous plate showing the way the Moomin drawing room looks when it is accidentally (via the hobgoblin's hat, a device like the magic pebble which trips up Sylvester in William Steig's classic) turned into a florid jungle. Creatures swing on jungle creepers from the hurricane lamp to the drapery rods; they look afraid, but the picture is funny. In *Tales From Moominvalley,* perhaps the best of Jansson's work and as fine as any children's book I have read, a fillyjonk knows that something terrible is going to happen before a wild ocean storm shatters the knick-knacks, furniture and window-glass she spends her time fussing with. The picture (p. 57) shows her standing in the midst of her possessions as they are crashing about. Significantly, she is unharmed by the storm, and in fact freed by it to

sit on the beach and know real safety there. While the picture itself could be terrifying were it not for the funny-looking fillyjonk, the illustrated storm becomes concrete and better known, more fully experienced by the reader, and thus less frightening.

In the last of the books to date, *Moominvalley in November,* an excellent tale in which an assortment of creatures travel to Moomin Valley to visit the trolls, only to find that they have gone off in the *Adventure,* the pictures convey the sense of separateness the creatures bring with them and retain despite their becoming used to one another, family-like, during their stay. One plate (p. 154), used as the cover design for the paperback edition, shows them—each representative of various stages from infancy (Toft) to old age (Grandpa Grumble), and various modes of life (settled spinster, itinerant musician, bureaucrat)—assembled on the verandah. Each is markedly different from the others in appearance; all are shown in the relaxed complacency of daily family life. This picture follows a more frenzied domestic scene in which the fillyjonk leads an assault known as spring cleaning before she leaves, recovered from the scare which brought her to visit Moominmamma in the first place. The fears each of the six had responded to in making their journey to the valley have been dealt with through the simple actions of keeping the household going. Only Toft, the baby-creature, waits on the dock as Moominmamma and her family return; the others, grown-ups, have gone home—unchanged from their essential selves. Knowing they have been loved and loving, they are equal to life.

The self-affirmation and individualism which constitute Jansson's world view, with her exuberance for life and thus for human nature, cannot be dismissed as a light-hearted, truth-dodging representation of existence. Viewed as a whole, and with contemplation of the illustrations in relation to the text, the Moomin books give a needed sense of the beauty of life to the modern child. Neither the all-encompassing framework of spiritual fantasy (a type often categorized as the "highest," most valuable kind)[18] nor the witty self-criticism of the rational humanist offers the kind of celebration of new life which must ground a human being in a world which eludes totalized mythic explanations and can often seem too disappointing under the satirist's pen. Jansson's consistent joy does not omit terror, but—and in this respect she does what other serious writers do—enables the reader/viewer to include the terrifying among the familiar, through the process of discovery and experimentation typical of childhood.

The child-protagonist, Moomintroll, need not change. Like the sea, his life is one of flux, of unpredictability, variation and surprise. In the early books, he is more apt to be on an external odyssey, in the later (beginning with his acquaintance with winter in *Moominland Midwinter*) on an inner journey. Nonetheless, each book shows him loving and being loved, and acting in response to the natural world. As an individual, Moomintroll is exceptionally sensitive and dreamy—a presumed self-portrait of Jansson herself. Just as her funny, fussy fillyjonks and stubborn, dull hemuelens are adults who are loved as they are, and who are free to change or not to change as they determine for themselves, so Jansson's cast of child-characters demonstrates the principle of being-loved-as-one-is. Even more than Moomintroll, the other child characters tend to be artfully unchanging.

Little My, a tiny mymble or self-absorbed, uninhibited, life-celebrating creature, is the adopted sister of Moomintroll who says what only a "brat" can say. She is the one who goes sledding in Moominmamma's tea-cosy, tells more fibs even than a Whomper (who tells so many he has to go to bed at sundown in *Tales from Moominvalley*), and who asks Ninny if she wants a biff on the nose when the poor thing is still the terrified invisible child. Little My is indestructible, and glories in her own being; no one tells her, or expects her, to grow up. Toft, another baby-creature, is one of the "easily frightened," who are in danger from too much fearing, too much separation from the core of safety. He knows he belongs in Moomin Valley, knows he will be a welcome sight as the Moomins return at the end of the last tale. Though they needed to be away and alone, there is no doubt about his place with them. In fact, he has chosen to grow a little bit, to alter his idyllic conception of the Moomins to include the notion that, like him, they are all at times sad or angry; however, had he remained as unaware of others as he had been at the start of the book, his embrace from Moominmamma would have been as warm.

Speaking of her own creatures in the tone of tolerance and affirmation her mother character projects, Jansson says, "What would happen to this world of ours if a *misabel* [gloomy creature who finds a home in the theater exactly suited to her tragic sense] suddenly acted like a *mymble*?"[19]

Although Tove Jansson has received little more than generalized praise or quick dismissal from critics outside of Scandinavia who include her because she is an Andersen medalist but rarely discuss her in detail, she is the object of a good deal of scholarship in Sweden. Moreover, she is enormously popular there, even with the dominant sociological critics, who seem to forgive her uncritical tales because she offers something "necessary" to childhood.[20] Various comparisons to fantasists such as John Bunyan and Lewis Carroll have been suggested; a French critic, Isabelle Jan, states that Jansson resembles realistic writers such as Laura Ingalls Wilder

and Louisa May Alcott more than she does fantasists.[21] Jan's comment is especially interesting, for she dramatizes the fact that our usual notion of "fantasy" assumes a significant encounter with the supernatural, or with some failing inherent in human nature or reality itself. Jansson's celebration of storms, modeled on her father but enabled by her mother, shows that certain artists evade our categories at the same time that they enlarge and clarify them. An original mythology; a dazzling image of autonomy: Jansson offers both.

*Notes*

1. Eleanor Cameron. *The Green and the Burning Tree.* New York: Little, Brown, 1969, p. 12.

2. Moomin books have appeared in twenty-two languages, beginning in 1946. Jansson's English publisher is Ernest Benn. In the United States, most of her books have been brought out by Henry Z. Walck, Inc. In the 1970's, her books have been available in Avon paperbacks. I have used these except where indicated below. Titles and dates of U.S. publications are as follows: *Comet in Momminland,* 1959; *Finn Family Moomintroll,* 1951; *Exploits of Moominpappa,* 1966; *Moominsummer Madness,* 1961; *Tales From Moominvalley,* 1963; *Moominland Midwinter,* 1962; *Moominpappa at Sea,* 1968; and *Moominvalley in November,* 1972. At least two other titles, and comic books about the Moomins, have appeared in England but not in America.

3. Jansson, quoted in Eva von Zweigbergk, *Barnboken i Sverige 1750-1950.* Stockholm: Raben and Sjogren, 1965, p. 468.

4. *Ibid.*

5. Tove Jansson. *Tales from Moominvalley,* Trans. Thomas Warburton. New York: Henry Z. Walck, Inc., 1963.

6. *Tales,* p. 109. Subsequent references in the text are to this edition.

7. Tove Jansson. *Moominland Midwinter,* Trans. Thomas Warburton. New York: Henry Z. Walck, 1962, p. 159. Subsequent references are to this edition.

8. Tove Jansson. *Sculptor's Daughter,* Trans. Kingsley Hart. New York: Avon Books, 1976, p. 40. Subsequent references are to this edition.

9. Arthur N. Applebee. *The Child's Concept of Story.* Chicago: University of Chicago Press, 1978, p. 24.

10. Jansson, quoted in Anne Commire, ed., *Something about the Author,* v. 3. New York: Gale, 1972, p. 90.

11. Tove Jansson. *The Summer Book,* Trans. Thomas Teal. New York: Random House, 1974. Subsequent references are to this edition.

12. Tove Jansson. *Moominpappa at Sea,* Trans. Kingsley Hart. New York: Avon, 1977, p. 158.

13. Tove Jansson. quoted in Stromstedt, p. 97.

14. von Zweigbergk, p. 469.

15. Birgitta Goteman, in *Tove Jansson pa Svenska,* ed. Birgit Antonsson. Stockholm: Uppsala, 1976, p. 72.

16. Jansson, in Stromstedt, p. 101.

17. *Ibid.*

18. Ruth Nodelman Lynn. *Fantasy for Children.* New York: Browker, 1979.

19. Jansson, quoted in von Zweigbergk, p. 470.

20. Lars Backstrom, in Antonsson, p. 71.

21. Isabelle Jan. *On Children's Literature.* London: Allen Lane, 1973, p. 120.

*Bibliography*

*Chapters in which the books are discussed are indicated at the end of each citation.

Jansson, Tove. *Comet In Moominland.* New York: Henry Z. Walck, 1959. Chapter 13.

———. *Exploits of Moominpappa.* New York: Henry Z. Walck, 1966. Chapter 13.

———. *Finn Family Moomintroll.* New York: Henry Z. Walck, 1951. Chapter 13.

———. *Moominland Midwinter.* Trans. by Thomas Warburton. New York: Henry Z. Walck, 1962. Chapter 13.

———. *Moominpappa at Sea.* Trans. by Kingsley Hart. New York: Avon, 1977. Chapter 13.

———. *Moominsummer Madness.* New York: Henry Z. Walck, 1961. Chapter 13.

———. *Moominvalley in November.* New York: Avon, 1972. Chapter 13.

———. *Tales from Moominvalley.* Trans. by Thomas Warburton. New York: Henry Z. Walck, 1963. Chapter 13.

**Nancy Huse (essay date 1991)**

SOURCE: Huse, Nancy. "Tove Jansson and Her Readers: No One Excluded." *Children's Literature* 19 (1991): 149-61.

[*In the following essay, Huse discusses Jansson's awareness of children's responses to her work.*]

Tove Jansson has not written a Moomintroll novel since 1970, when *Moominvalley in November* left the Moomins somewhere at sea, with only the youngest member of their extended household, Toft, awaiting their return. Those who know the Moomins are alive, however, include the large number of Jansson readers whose twelve cartons of letters, drawings, and artifacts (such as a pebble found by a four-year-old in Sweden, a purse for Moominmamma's handbag from a Japanese woman, a condensed thesis from a British psychologist) are stored in the Åbo Akademi library in Åbo (Turku), Finland. While many writers receive such mail, few engage in extensive correspondence with their readers, and fewer still seem to depend on such correspondence as a way of keeping intact a hard-won psychological stance intrinsic to ongoing work as an artist. For three decades, Jansson answered personally the approximately two thousand letters she received each year. An examination of this reader-writer interaction provides insight into Jansson's particular history. It also suggests some of the implications of the adult-child connection in literature, when the adult draws from her socialization as a daughter to create art and the child perceives the adult woman's ambivalence about the act of writing truthfully. Furthermore, it underscores the importance of children's responses in the literary system.

The daughter of two visual artists, the sculptor Viktor Jansson and the illustrator-engraver Signe Hamer Jansson, and a member of Finland's Swedish-speaking minority, Tove Jansson was educated as a painter. But the stories she constructed around her Moomin cartoons marked a transition to verbal art and to a life that continued her family's aesthetic tradition while delineating a new channel for it. Despite the difficulty of producing new fiction based on her adult identity, Jansson maintains her ties to her birth family and to her child readers via continuing contact with the Moomin family, thereby demonstrating the complex female perspective discussed by Nancy Chodorow (*The Reproduction of Mothering*) and Carol Gilligan (*In a Different Voice*).

Gilligan's work in developmental psychology indicates that women mature into "the vision that everyone will be responded to and included, that no one will be left alone or hurt" (63). According to Gilligan, women are socialized to preserve relationships, achieving integrity by caring for others while defining their own needs. Jansson, in a letter to a librarian, simply says, "One can't very well leave the letter of a child unanswered." Unlike Michel Tournier, however, who writes gleefully of his exchanges and visits with children but seems to view his young readers as clearly separate from his own identity (183), Jansson's immersion in her correspondence and visits with children seems directly related to her understanding of her moral selfhood. This is evident in some of her replies, such as the thoughtful and lengthy letter she writes to an American girl who wonders if the bombing of Hiroshima could in any way be justified by the creator of the Happy Valley. Persistently in such letters Jansson rejects an end-justifying-means ethic, yet she credits her correspondents with forcing her to confront questions she has avoided.

Such a perspective involves balancing rights and responsibilities, aggression and tenderness; it differs from twentieth-century images of maturity as independence and separateness, and of art as a unique product of isolation or alienation. Jansson acts the way a writing mother is said to do, alternating between "'resentment and tenderness, negation of the child and reaching out for the child'" (Adrienne Rich in Suleiman, 366).

The first Moomin book, *Smaatrollen och den Stora Oversvamningen* (*The Small Troll and the Big Flood*), appeared in 1942, when Jansson was twenty-eight. From the episodic adventure structure of the first few novels (there are nine novels and a collection of stories in the series), the books evolved into complex psychological fantasy, with accompanying shifts in illustration style from romantic to surreal (Hollander). A story collection, published in Swedish as **Det Osynliga Barnet** (**The Invisible Child,** 1963) and in English as **Tales from Moominvalley,** was followed by two additional novels, *Moominpappa at Sea* (1965) and *Moominvalley in November* (1971), exploring adult-child relationships and the aging process. In 1966, Jansson received the Hans Christian Andersen medal. Over the next decade, she gradually separated her writing from her drawing, seeing fiction as a means of exploring adult themes and pictures as a way of providing children with humor and support. Continuing her children's literature involvement only with Moomin picture books, the writer has since produced a number of stories, novels, and autobiographical works for a sophisticated adult audience.

Across the manuscript of her first short story for adults, **"The Listener"** (1971), Jansson scrawled "*Inte for barn!*" (not for children); her theme in this and later fiction is the power of language, a "mind-game called Words That Kill—." Despite her wish to keep children at a distance from such themes, to avoid projecting her own needs onto them over a long process of accepting and articulating a lesbian identity (interview), many child readers have traced themes of alienation, doubt, artistic isolation, and maturation in the Moomin series books which precede Jansson's conscious attempt to write only for adults. The children's letters, and Jansson's replies to them, suggest how Jansson's creative process depends on the links to her own childhood that the Moomins represent. The correspondence also shows that—despite notions of children's radical difference from adults which lead such critics as Glyn Jones to assert that the later Moomin novels are not children's

books at all, and that children "do not interpret"—young readers' responses are in fact rich strategies for explicating and extending the Moomin books as literary texts.

By some criteria Jansson's inability to prevent children from "reading" her own deepest concerns could signal the writer's lack of control of her craft. For example, Michael Egan has used the term "Double Address" to identify a convention of children's literature whereby writers explore their unconscious while seeming not to (46). Yet to call Jansson an unskilled writer would be preposterous. A better explanation for the responses her work evokes from children lies in the novels themselves, where adults and children have richly connected lives. Children who write comments like "Why don't you write a book of Moomin poems" or "on the laws of nature according to a whomper" or who show keen sensitivity in observing that "the books are getting sadder and sadder" with advice such as "You like *November* best. I'll read it again if you'll read *Midwinter* (my favorite) again" demonstrate first-rate ability to interpret. Contrary to some developmental theory (Piaget's, for example), such child-readers can enter into the viewpoints of others, and they provide a valuable, often whimsical ("Do snorks have pockets?") commentary unavailable in reviews or formal criticism of the books. Their mode of interpretation centers on producing new versions of the books they read. Many write creatively in the persona of Snufkin or Sniff, addressing their letters not to Jansson but to Moominmamma; and new characters (such as "Smicker"), new forms (such as "Snufkin's log book"), or new plot ideas (such as "Snufkin as Heraclitus") abound. This process makes the children "collaborator(s) in the polysemic life of the text" (Corti 44), disseminating Jansson's characters and ideas within the literary system, somewhat like directors who both replicate and alter Shakespeare's texts. Perhaps because of a general devaluing of metaphor and playful language, children's discourse seems unrelated to interpretation or criticism. Yet in an era when many critics have deliberately engaged in playful elaborations of texts, it may be possible to recognize children's abilities as interpreters.

Though Jansson's lesbian orientation has remained hidden from them, child readers have recognized and empathized with her shifting existential beliefs, the yearning of the artist for solitude and of the person for affection, and the questioning of the nature of reality and illusion. Frequently children exchanged letters with Jansson over a period of years because her combined sense of responsibility and pleasure in the correspondence prolonged it. "I can't resist the little devils" is one bemused description of her letter-writing; she also describes herself as "cornered" by these readers (interview). Thus, she articulates in the letters to children her dual wish for relationality and solitude. To Japanese children who ask her what she would do if she learned of her imminent death, she writes, "I would walk along the sea with one I love best and not betray" (that is, not cause pain). To a reader who loves Jansson's poet-philosopher Snufkin, she comments ruefully, "He is free to come and go as he wishes and be silent without a bad conscience." More than once, Jansson has defended writers who, like Astrid Lindgren, send printed messages to children who write to them. But the children who address her as "Dear Moominmamma" may have correctly interpreted the centrality of that character's pre-oedipal, steady presence in the author's own personality—despite her admiration for the freer Snufkin.

An example of the creative tension in the correspondence is Jansson's habit of pasting an insightful letter on her studio wall or carrying one (as Moominmamma would) in her handbag, hoping to sustain inspiration and even to stimulate the allegedly impossible and undesirable return to writing Moomin books (interview). One such letter, from a boy in Sweden, detailed the way **"The Invisible Child"** (in *Tales from Moominvalley*) had brought peace to a classroom full of emotionally disturbed children on one especially desperate afternoon. The teacher (mother of the boy, Dan) had been unable to reach the children that day. But the account of how an unloved child becomes a rambunctious Moomin daughter, able to push Moominpappa into the sea without herself disappearing from fright, fulfilled a therapeutic function which the boy described eloquently. The children grew calm, intent on Ninny's gradual recovery from abuse. Jansson's reply to Dan explained how the famous story originated in her own family, with the adoption of a troubled child. This deeply personal and functional tale is one of Jansson's earliest attempts to probe her own subconscious and to experiment with language, and the letter shows how fully children understand it.

The children represented in the collection are, of course, often similar to Dan—and to Moomintroll himself—in being sensitive dreamers and already fluent writers. Yet letters from a range of ages and personalities indicate that various kinds of children make valid interpretations of even the later Moomin books. Many letters show the comic zest with which young readers enter into the wordplay and illogic of the early books; they send their own drawings of Moomins, hemulens, fillyjonks, and hattifatteners, characters which even in the first books embody odd moods and personality structures found in adults who live alone, become bureaucrats, or are caught in self-destructive moods of long duration. These children frequently move from playing with verbal and pictorial elements to a mode of interpretation in which they comment on how their own fears and delights have

been reflected and made comprehensible in new ways through the stories. Child readers explicate such passages as the one in which Moomintroll is enchanted by the goblin's hat and recognized only by his mother, or they note that they were "achingly sorry for the hemulen, when no one would play with him." When readers say which character represents them, Little My, Sniff, Snufkin, and Toffle are cited nearly as often as the protagonist, Moomintroll, thus underscoring the multidimensional affective structure of the tales and their complex cumulative meanings. Child readers, not yet bound by the convention of identifying with a single main character, readily enter and describe Jansson's mythic world, where all child and adult creatures are welcome and necessary.

Some children then move from what James Britton would call the expressive and poetic modes to that which is more discursive and rational, the transactional. To one English child who wrote, "I enjoy the Moomins so much, because they are so unreal in form, and so real in person," Jansson replied, "I couldn't have got a finer compliment from a child." Nor, one might suspect, from an adult; the comment recognizes the psychological aspects of the fantasies. Noting the unique elements of the books, an American girl wrote, "They are wonderful, because they are different from any stories I've ever read"—a perceptive remark, since Jansson has been difficult for Anglo-American critics to describe and she herself stresses the personal (and Scandinavian) nature of the tales. Most such analytic comments appear in letters that individuals have chosen to write rather than in the school-generated packets Jansson despises and fears (because of her compulsion to answer even these letters).

More interesting, and probably more disturbing to Jansson's wish to be free of the demands childhood makes of her female moral self, is the outpouring of advice from young readers who recognize the doubt and anguish in *Moominpappa at Sea* and *Moominvalley in November*—books they name as favorites. Readers as young as nine, begging for a new Moomin book to follow the *November* text's focus on aging, suggest ways Jansson can write herself out of a corner, picking up with integrity the unwoven threads in her Moomin tapestry. Some of these letters, no doubt, have spent time on the studio wall or in Jansson's handbag as a help in her struggle and determination to retain creativity. Certain children (including Dan, the teacher's son) write to Jansson well into adulthood, further obscuring boundaries between "child" and "adult." A Norwegian boy, Einar, sent Jansson poems over a span of fifteen years. Another child, Tom, continued his habit of sending postcards signed "Sniff" from all over the world, writing of his adult search for love and work. Another, Richard, sent Jansson a copy of his novel, an achievement hardly surprising to a reader of the letters and stories he had written her in his boyhood. Simon Short, a frequent letter writer in boyhood, took a university degree in philosophy and as a young adult wrote again to discuss the existential themes of the books which fascinated him still.

A persistent theme of the child readers has been their wanting, like Holden Caulfield, to be with their favorite writer in actuality. In more than one instance, Japanese children have shown a particularly future-oriented response that Jansson thinks distinguishes them from more present-oriented American children. Some Japanese children have saved their money until they could make a pilgrimage to Helsinki to meet Jansson. Others have written to say that they want to come to Finland to live. One teenager realized that her childhood reading of the Moomin books had been a significant part of her development: "I found your books. I met your world. Always they make me a human." Another youth wrote to Jansson throughout his orphaned adolescence, receiving encouragement from her to become a teacher and find a place in Japanese society despite his yearning to be the writer's adopted son. While other writers or celebrities might have ignored the stream of letters from these young people, Jansson must follow up on the relationships her writing initiates, even though she says the role of "guru" is exhausting and debilitating (interview).

Unerringly sensitive to the needs of the individual child, the author explains her obsession—when amused rather than disgusted by it—with such comments as "They *tell* me things. They tell me about their cat. . . ." Fluent in English, Jansson has some mastery of German, French, and Finnish in addition to her first language. She gets help in reading messages in Russian, Polish, and Japanese. Nearly half the letters are in English, and she frequently replies in English. The children who "tell" her things range from the articulate and wealthy Pablo writing in German from Barcelona, at first at his mother's urging, to the Puerto Rican child in the East Bronx who copied out a long passage from *The Exploits of Moominpappa* on his own volition. The child's teacher sent a note explaining that the boy had never before done sustained reading or writing and needed the writer's encouragement. The children less needy than these, such as the American girl who sent her picture in a Moomin costume, or the schoolchildren who demand to know how Jansson gets ideas for books, receive witty replies. But the author explains at some length to Pablo, for instance, why he must first learn the thoughts of others in order to be truly original. Jansson writes that the Moomin texts are "memories of a happy childhood mixed with the comments of an adult," a distinction which helps her to view her newer work as "adult," linked not to her childhood directly but to experiences

she has had as an adult woman artist whose almost cruel voice in her recent fiction represents a world she is determined to claim as her own.

The lengthy correspondence with individual children shows that Jansson is working through her sense of artistic vocation even as she takes care of the child she is writing to. Touched especially by the Japanese girl who signed herself "One of Your Children," Jansson seems willing to share with such young readers her most personal concerns—concerns she had hoped would be inaccessible to child readers of her Moomin books but which actually inspire letters to the author. For such readers, Jansson will allude to the "dry dust" of her mind; the potential for stories in her dreams and travel; her fears that the Moomin pictures will not be suitably recognized as art; her frequent regret that she created the Moomin comic strip in her youth and thus assured herself of "no peace ever since" to be an artist. In these letters, it is clear that the writer is willing to be mother, teacher, and mentor because these roles meet the artist's need for community. At the same time, the children's perspicuity has apparently made final Jansson's determination not to write anything but letters (and picture books) for child readers. Believing that children should not be burdened with adult concerns but given reassurance and cheerfulness by those who care for them, Jansson seems nevertheless to have accepted into her private circle those children who divine her secrets—and made up her mind to avoid future invitations to the young into her rich and hidden life. Thus, her canon—with its shift to an adult audience made explicit by a transition from fantasy to autobiography to surrealism—can be understood in developmental terms, especially in female developmental terms. Those letters to children who demand attention because they know Jansson's pain and sensitivity to others constitute an act of integration similar, as mentioned above, to the propitiation of crying children by mothers who are writers and whose continuing creativity is bound up in the continuing life of their children, even though this means interruption and diffusion of their thoughts.

Jansson's attachment to her own mother (who died at age eighty-eight) and wry affection for children are integral to both the Moomin books and the letters. Instead of separating from the all-good mother as Moomintroll does in his adolescence, the writer-daughter refuses to forget or abandon either the mother or the children who claim her attention through their letters and their insight into her books. In her autobiography, *Sculptor's Daughter* (1969), Jansson discusses an immediate source for the Moomin characters in "Snow," a chapter describing a few days sequestered with her mother in winter. For part of that time, she remembers, "Mummy didn't draw. We were bears with pine needles in our stomachs. . . . Only Mummy and I were left" (165).

Jansson's extensive, even obsessive letter-writing has taken away time and energy from other things. Yet the messages to and from Moomin readers sustain her creative powers as much as the process limits her. Unless she answers the letters, she can't work; yet the letter-writing keeps her from other writing (interview). It is apparent that Jansson's letters from and to child readers have neither simply encouraged her to write nor kept her from doing so; instead, they have caused her to write in certain ways, and her body of work has taken shape from the intensity of her involvement with children and her commitment to them as well as from her desire to be solitary and free of the demands of those who, in her judgment, need protection she cannot give.

One of Jansson's reasons for moving consciously into the writing of books directed toward adults was her fear that in her struggle to attain a clear sense of sexual identity, she would manipulate child readers. Aware of the artist's dependence on the unconscious, and fearing the psychoanalytic readings of such critics as Jacqueline Rose (*The Case of Peter Pan*), Tove Jansson has been wary of comparisons of her work to that of Andersen and Carroll, though in recent adult work, such as the 1982 *Den Erliga Bedraggeran* (*The Honest Deceiver*), she has been open about her lesbian partnership with Tuulikki Pietela, characterized as the helpful and spontaneous Too-Ticky in *Moominland Midwinter* (1957). Because Jansson's search for female artistic identity takes place in the context of her famous family (Viktor Jansson's sculptures dot Helsinki; Signe Hamer Jansson designed Finland's postage stamps) her personal life is always in markedly public view, thus heightening the sense of responsibility she feels and demonstrates toward her child audience.

Jansson turned to other art forms because, while continuing to keep the Moomins alive in pictures for children and for herself, she dared no longer allow the Moomin family to play out for children the terms of her psychosexual development. As she tells one reader, "it isn't a question of deciding. It comes to you or it doesn't. I am open for everything. But sometimes doors close and there is nothing to do about it" (1973 letter). Regardless of whether Jansson's later work endures—and such texts as *Sculptor's Daughter* (1969) and some stories in **The Doll's House** (1978) certainly have a resonance of their own—her Moomin novels and tales deserve more textual and historical criticism than they have received in English. Her integration of picture and narrative invites comparison with Sendak and Potter; her Moomin odyssey ought also to be addressed in the context of fantasy criticism. Above all, critics need to address the ways in which Jansson—like Anna Wulf, Doris Lessing's protagonist in *The Golden Notebook*—has discovered and dealt with the emotional difficulty of creating for oneself, for others, and for those others

one must protect. These concerns make Jansson one of a relatively limited company of serious artists totally aware of a child audience.

Theories of projective poetics and reader response criticism come closest to explaining the relationship she has had with her child readers and its effect on her work. Georges Poulet, for example, emphasizes that in reading we are thinking the thoughts of another, experiencing the consciousness of another as if it were our own (44). Readers who write about the books they read, according to Wolfgang Iser, help to make conscious those aspects of the work which would otherwise remain in the subconscious (157). That readers and writers engage in "an intimate interaction . . . in and through which each defines for the other what s/he is about" is a familiar premise within much feminist criticism (Kolodny 244). In such a relationship, writers and readers create the works as well as each other's understanding of them. Such theories seem fully validated by this writer's continued involvement with her readers. The frequent and damaging assumptions that children cannot interpret, or that they are entirely victimized or controlled by the adults who produce children's books, are certainly called into deep question by the letters Jansson receives and answers.

Adults represented in the Åbo collection explicate some of the same themes as child readers do. But they make few demands on Jansson, supplying encouragement rather than requests or implicit pleas for attention. The adult readers typically write analytically, expressing their views by references to their other reading and learning rather than by sending story ideas or asking for the comfort they see as promised by the stories.

Although none of the letters has launched a return voyage for the Moomins, through them Jansson has engaged with readers in the quest for integration that remains primary to her. Aside from the therapeutic benefits of the correspondence, it has had the function of ordering her roles and values, allowing her to maintain an ethic of care while asserting an ethic of rights in her artistic and personal life. Like the hemulen who loved silence (**Tales**) but ultimately was unable to keep children out of the amusement park to which he had retired, Jansson has needed to live with the Moomins in the correspondence and in numerous exhibits and picture books concurrent with her adult books. In some ways, the correspondence may serve as pre-writing for these adult books, a moving in the letters through the stage of "innocence" to the "experience" of the surreal stories about art.

The child who told Jansson, "I hope you keep writing all your life," recognizing the terror of failed imagination in *Moominpappa at Sea* (1965), is one of several who have given Jansson their own hope. The connections between Jansson and her readers, a paradox of community and individuation, play out the dilemmas of the female writer which enable, even necessitate, the writer's growth and change. Jansson's examples—children's writer turned adult author who still enters tangibly into the lives of children who understand her books—may not be followed by many other writers. Yet her wish to respect childhood as a period relatively free of adult pressures, her contradictory creation of fantasies which portray the full emotional range of human life, and, above all, her sense of responsibility for the effect of those fictions upon children suggest provocatively that the child readers of such authors may have a share in constructing not only their "own" literature but "adult" literature, too. **Tales from Moominvalley,** possibly Jansson's masterpiece, was produced at the height of the correspondence and generated some of the most insightful letters at Åbo, and perhaps "the voyage out" represented by the Moomin books which followed. For me, the protectiveness of Jansson toward her child readers is a reenactment of the stories she wrote for them, in which no one is excluded or hurt—not even a hemulen or a fillyjonk.

## Notes

1. Solveig Widen, librarian at Åbo Akademi, helped to make the Jansson correspondence available for my visit. Petra Wrede, Marita Rajalin, and Tove Hollander of the Åbo Akademi community provided a helpful context for interpreting the materials.

2. I am indebted to Petra Wrede for this information about Jansson's recent novel, *Den Erliga Bedraggeran (The Honest Deceiver).*

## Works Cited

Britton, James. *Language and Learning.* London: Penguin, 1970.

Chodorow, Nancy. *The Reproduction of Mothering: Psychoanalysis and the Sociology of Gender.* Berkeley: University of California Press, 1978.

Corti, Maria. *An Introduction to Literary Semiotics.* Trans. Margherita Bogat and Allen Mendelbaum. Bloomington: University of Indiana Press, 1978.

Egan, Michael. "The Neverland of Id: Barrie, *Peter Pan,* and Freud." *Children's Literature,* 10 (1982): 37-55.

Garner, Shirley Nelson, Claire Kahane, and Madelon Sprengnether, ed. *The (M)other Tongue: Essays in Feminist Psychoanalytic Interpretation.* Ithaca: Cornell University Press, 1985.

Gilligan, Carol. *In a Different Voice.* Cambridge: Harvard University Press, 1982.

Hollander, Tove. Interview with author in Åbo, 1983.

Huse, Nancy. "Tove Jansson's Moomintrolls: Equal to Life." *Proceedings of the Children's Literature Association* (1981): 44-49. Reprinted in *Webs and Wardrobes: Humanist and Religious World Views in Children's Literature,* ed. Joseph O. Milner and Lucy Floyd Morcock Milner. Lanham, New York: University Press of America, 1987. 136-46.

Iser, Wolfgang. *The Act of Reading: A Theory of Aesthetic Response.* Baltimore: The Johns Hopkins University Press, 1978.

Jansson, Tove. Interview with author in Helsinki, 1983.

———. *Comet in Moominland.* London 1951.

———. *Finn Family Moomintroll.* London 1951.

———. *The Exploits of Moominpappa.* London 1952.

———. *Moominsummer Madness.* London 1955.

———. *Moominland Midwinter.* London 1958.

———. *Tales from Moominvalley.* London 1963.

———. *Moominpappa at Sea.* London 1965.

———. *Sculptor's Daughter.* London 1969.

———. *Moominvalley in November.* London 1971.

———. *The Doll's House.* Helsinki 1978.

———. "The Monkey." Trans. W. Glyn Jones. *Books from Finland* 14 (1981): 62-63.

———. "Locomotive." Trans. W. Glyn Jones. *Books from Finland* 14 (1981): 64-71.

———. *Den Erliga Bedraggeran.* Helsinki 1982.

———. "The Listener." Trans. Nils J. Anderson in correspondence with author, 1984.

Jones, W. Glyn. "Studies in Obsession: The New Art of Tove Jansson." *Books from Finland* 14 (1981): 60-71.

———. *Tove Jansson.* Twayne World Authors Series. Boston: G. K. Hall, 1985.

Kolodny, Annette. "A Map for Rereading; or, Gender in the Interpretation of Literary Texts." In Garner et al., 241-59.

Poulet, Georges. "Criticism and the Experience of Interiority." In *Reader Response Criticism,* ed. Jane P. Tompkins. Baltimore: The Johns Hopkins University Press, 1980, 41-49.

Rose, Jacqueline. *The Case of Peter Pan or The Impossibility of Children's Fiction.* London: Macmillan, 1984.

Suleiman, Susan Rubin. "Writing and Motherhood." In Garner et al., 352-77.

Tournier, Michael. "Writer Devoured by Children." *Children's Literature,* 13 (1985): 180-87.

Wrede, Petra. Conversation with author, 1983.

**Yvonne Bertills (essay date 2002)**

SOURCE: Bertills, Yvonne. "Intertextualities, Continued: The Connotations of Proper Names in Tove Jansson." In *Children's Literature as Communication: The ChiLPA Project,* edited by Roger D. Sell, pp. 71-83. Amsterdam: John Benjamins Publishing, 2002.

[*In the following essay, Bertills discusses the challenge of preserving the specific connotations of Swedish names when they are translated into English in Jansson's Moominworld stories.*]

1. Intertextualities at the Micro-Level

[Kaisu Rättyä has shown] how one postmodernist children's writer has drawn on the resources of intertextuality by alluding to whole texts. Some of these then serve as subtexts sustained throughout his own text, so entering into a kind of dialogue with it. What now remains to be emphasized is that intertextuality concerns not just whole texts, but units which are much smaller. Every new use of every expression, word, and even morpheme in a language happens in intertextual relationship with every use of it in other contexts earlier and elsewhere. In theory, the here-and-now occurrence of any linguistic item recapitulates and modifies all its previous occurrences, and bears a differential relation to the occurrences of every other expression in the same language culture as well.

In practice, this is not something of which language users can ever be entirely conscious. The amount of language use that any individual is exposed to is in any case only an infinitessimally small part of all the language use there has ever been. And from that tiny cross-section, we develop a kind of linguistic *savoir-faire* that is for the most part highly automated. Yet even so, every once in a while we do think about these things. If we ourselves are trying to say or write something to which we attach particular importance, or which has to be suitable for a particular kind of setting or situation, then we sometimes begin to wonder whether this word doesn't "go better" with that word than some other word does, or whether such and such a phrase somehow doesn't "sound" as well as it might do. In terms of grammar and broad-brushstroke semantics, these dilemmas may seem irrelevant. Yet often we decide without

the slightest hesitation that some particular expression would be simply unsatisfactory through having "the wrong connotations".

Connotations are also something we can fairly consciously respond to in the language use of other people. Our admiration of a poem, for instance, may well be expressed in terms of what the phrases, words and morphemes, in combination with each other, seem to "hint" or "suggest". By this we do not mean something as specific and substantial as the Kivian subtext underlying Parkkinen's Suvi Kinos novels, but something which, without being any the less fore-present, and without having any the less significant a dialogic relationship with the text in hand, is nevertheless at the micro-level, so to speak. From our own point of view as readers, it is for ever slipping away into subliminality.

Presumably, literary writers try to handle this dimension of intertextuality with sensitivity and skill. At the very least, they will not want to turn off their readers by *mis*handling it. But some writers, whom we tend to think of as playful and linguistically creative, use it in a more positive spirit, as a resource which can be adapted and expanded to their own ends, sometimes even rather conspicuously. This is what T. S. Eliot noticed in certain Elizabethan dramatists, for instance, whom he praised for their "perpetual slight alteration of language, words perpetually juxtaposed in new and sudden combinations, meanings perpetually *eingeschachtelt* into meanings" ([1920] 1951, p.209). As for children's writers, their position is specially interesting here, since on the one hand they cannot expect a child reader to have the previous exposure to intertextuality that an adult has, while on the other hand they may well feel that they want to develop their young readers' sensibility— and perhaps to throw in some intertextual pleasures for co-reading adults as well.

One children's writer who certainly seems to have these aims is Tove Jansson, probably the most famous Finland-Swedish author of all, and best known for her Moomintroll books: the nine novels (1945-1970) and the four picturebooks (1952-1980). In addition to having been the object of biographical scholarship, Jansson has also come in for a fair amount of literary-critical commentary (e.g. Westin, 1988; Jones, 1984; Aejmelaus, 1994). But more can still be said, I would suggest, about her actual handling of language. Here I shall be paying particular attention to some of the names she gives her characters, and in order to highlight their intertextual workings I shall approach them from the standpoint of a translator. The intertextualities I shall consider are specific to the Swedish language, sometimes still more restrictedly to the Swedish language as used in Finland. My question is, then: What happens when an attempt is made to translate these Finland-

Swedish intertextualities into the intertextualities of English as used in English-speaking cultures?

## 2. WHAT'S IN A NAME?

In part, the answer has to do with vocabulary, and with differences between the vocabularies of the different languages. In point of fact, there are at least four ways of transferring proper names from one language into another, all of which can be variously combined (Hermans, 1988, pp.13-14). A name can be *copied,* i.e. transferred in exactly the same form as that of the source language; it can be *transcribed,* i.e. transliterated or adapted on the levels of spelling and phonology; it can be *substituted,* i.e. replaced by an expression which bears no real relation to the original; or, when the name has some connection with the standard lexicon, it can be *translated,* i.e. rendered by an expression which seeks to be semantically "equivalent". But as my scare-quotes hint, in the target language a real equivalent may be difficult to find, or to concoct.

Then there are issues of pragmatics. The way a proper name operates in a fictional work and its translations depends on the relationship between the texts and their various kinds of readers. Even when a name is untranslated and read within the source culture, it may well make a different impact on an adult reader than on a child reader, for instance. When somehow or other transferred to another language and read within a correspondingly different culture, its range of effect is likely to be still more complicated. Crucial here is what readers themselves are able to bring to their understanding of it—what range of linguistic and other knowledge, what preconceptions, associations, values, and so on. Two of the pragmatic variables most likely to make a difference are precisely readers' age and cultural background. As Hunt (1991, p.87) points out, children are *developing* readers; their approach to life and text stems from a different set of cultural standards than that of adult readers.

So however much translators may aim to render a name by some "natural" parallel, the effect they achieve may at times be quite new, sometimes bearing little or no relation to the effect created by the original, and perhaps prompting readers to have thoughts and feelings which the original author would have found surprising—pleasantly or otherwise. Beyond a certain point, translators, whether they like it or not, probably have to accept that their own role calls for great sensitivity, good judgement, and creativity.

This immediately opens the door to controversy, since a critic is likely to find some of their solutions less appropriate than others. According to Riitta Oittinen (1993), translators' strongest obligation is towards their own readers. Although, as much as possible, they will want to convey the same feelings and associations as the source text, in Oittinen's view exact equivalence is a secondary aim, and the most important thing is to arrive at a mode of expression in the target language which really works. My own view, by contrast, is that, especially as regards proper names, if the translation's reader is to get anything like the same impression as the source text's reader, then the ideal of semantic equivalence should not be abandoned too easily, and if a name also involves some special phonetic features, an attempt should be made to recapture these as well. As for cases where semantic equivalence and formal equivalence cannot be achieved simultaneously, much will depend on the function of the name in a larger context. It is important that the translation's reader gets the same notion of the character as the source text's reader. But it is also important that in both the source and target text the proper name should have the same function.

According to the language philosopher J. R. Searle (1958, p.172), "proper names [in fiction] function not as descriptions, but as pegs on which to hang descriptions." Searle seems to think that proper names are not descriptions, and that it is the context which describes a character. This is of course partly true, especially with conventional names such as "John" or "Alice". But even some conventional names may arouse certain expectations, and with names which are both unusual and semantically loaded a description will already be suggested by the mere name itself. In Jansson, there are even some characters whose name tells us almost all there is to know about them. In such cases, it seems to me, the ideal of translation equivalence is especially important.

The distinction between conventional and semantically loaded names has been discussed by Hermans (1988). The reason why ordinary surnames, and christian names such as John and Alice, are not very strongly loaded is partly that they will not be motivated by the personal characterstics of the people who bear them, and partly that they often do not consist of elements which already belong to, or are reminiscent of, the standard language. Loaded names, by contrast, are names which recall other words and thereby suggest meanings, some of which may be somehow appropriate to their bearer. Such names, says Hermans, can "range from faintly suggestive to overtly expressive names and nicknames" (Hermans, 1988, p.13).

When Jansson introduces characters by name and then goes on to give a fuller picture of their appearance, behaviour and personality in her illustrations and in the continuing narrative, the appropriateness of their name to the total impression she gives of them is not always straightforward. In Jansson, names do tend to draw attention to themselves and are not simply neutral. Admittedly, some of her names are less surprising than others, so that if the characters to whom they are attached come across as fascinating and exciting this will be largely thanks to what they are reported as saying, doing or thinking in the rest of the text. But many other names certainly are suggestive, and usually rather amusingly so, and in ways that turn out to be truly appropriate to their bearers. Some names, again, though no less playful and suggestive, are rather more thought-provoking, in that their appropriateness to their bearers is not obvious, and readers may well find themselves asking, "How on earth did a character like this end up with a name like that?" Sometimes, too, it may be difficult to decide whether the name really conveys any "meaning" at all. For all one knows, it may actually be quite opaque.

But much depends on who "one" is, for we inevitably come back to the pragmatic variables. The distinctions between the obvious and more problematic kinds of appropriateness will not be equally apparent to every kind of reader, and for this reason represent an even greater challenge to any translator.

### 3. TRANSPARENCY

Some of Jansson's names, then, are not particularly humorous, and do not convey particularly strong connotations at all. Instead, they are appropriate in a rather transparent and neutral way. This is where a reader's main impressions of the characters concerned will depend on Jansson's illustrations, and on the text's descriptions of what they say and do and think.

One such name is *Trollkarlen.* This is a standard Swedish noun, which would normally be rendered into English as *The Wizard/Sorcerer/Magician,* and with no necessary suggestion of anything frightening or sinister. Jansson's English translator, however, calls this character *The Hobgoblin,* which suggests something like "evil troll", "mischievous imp", "ugly evil spirit". In the Swedish original, the character does gain a rather disturbing aura, but mainly because of the way he is introduced. To quote the translation:

> "Good", said Snufkin. "It's strange story, and I got it from the Magpie. Well, at the end of the world there lies a mountain so high it makes you dizzy even to think about it. It is as black as soot, as smooth as silk, terribly steep, and where there should be a bottom, there are only clouds. But high up on the peak stands the Hobgoblin's House, and it looks like this." And Snufkin drew a house in the sand.
>
> "Hasn't it got any windows?" asked Sniff.
>
> "No", said Snufkin, "and it hasn't got a door either, because the Hobgoblin always goes home by air riding on a black panther. He goes out every night and col-

lects rubies in his hat. [. . .] The Hobgoblin can change himself into anything he likes, [. . .] and then he can crawl under the ground and even down onto the sea bed where buried treasure lies."

(Jansson, [1958] 1990, pp. 91-92)

From this passage it is clear that the character in the novel cannot be ascribed the same traits as an "ordinary" wizard, and by choosing *hobgoblin* rather than *wizard* the translator has simply translated on the basis of the descriptions in the source text. That a hobgoblin should be dressed in black, disappear as suddenly as he appears, and ride on a big black panther may seem almost natural. What is lost, however, is any immediate sense that this is a person who can perform magic tricks—a wizard's main attribute. The translator has used a name which is *more* atmospherically loaded that Jansson's original, and one which leaves out her more transparent term's main implication.

### 4. PLAYFULLY APPROPRIATE SUGGESTIVENESS

Then there are the names which are more strongly and humorously loaded, and which turn out to be appropriate to their bearers. Here there are a fair number of nonsense words or nonce words, in which the element which has the "funny" ring to it will tend to be the name's most prominent feature, and carry a very strong connotative meaning.

One example is connected with the Finland-Swedish verb *rådda,* which means something like "to make a mess, to be in a mess, to be mentally confused". A mess or a state of mental confusion, similarly, is describable by the noun-adjective pair *rådd-råddig.* In the Moomin books there is a character named *Rådd-djuret,* which literally means "the mess/confusion animal", but which the English tranlator translates as *The Muddler,* perhaps somewhat lessening the hint of *mental* chaos.

The name *Filifjonkan,* by contrast, which belongs to certain female characters, does not have any meaning in standard Swedish usage in either Sweden or Finland. It is Jansson's coinage. Yet a reader who knows Swedish fairly well is likely to associate it with a number of words which sound rather like *-fjonka,* and which seem to share among themselves one particular type of meaning: *fjompa* and *fjompig,* plus *fjolla* and *fjollig.* Both of these noun-adjective pairs are used mainly in reference to women, and mean roughly *silliness/foolishness* and *silly/foolish.* The English translation of *Filifjonkan* is *Fillyjonk,* which transcribes the name at the level of spelling, and which almost manages to achieve a degree of semantic appropriateness as well. The standard English word *filly* means a female foal, and in upper-class male slang could once upon a time refer to a lively young girl. But *lively* is not really the same thing as *silly/foolish,* so that readers of the translation will be jumping to different conclusions than readers of the original. The translator has been less concerned to replicate the name's "meaning" than its form.

Another amusing yet appropriate name is *Hatifnattarna,* a group name whose second element is derived from the verb *fnatta,* which means something like "to flutter madly around". The name strongly suggests something about the behaviour of its bearers, and especially about their style of movement, a suggestion which is further developed by passages of description. What do these white creatures do?—*"de små vandrarna som ständigt färdas över jorden utan att stanna nånstans, drivna av längtan och oro"* (1946, p.44). (Translation: they "are for ever wandering restlessly from place to place in their aimless quest for nobody knows what" (1951, pp.52-3)). Such creatures *"har ingen ro i sig. Jämt på resa nånstans. Bara far och far och säger aldrig ett ord"* ([1950] 1961, p.53). (Translation: have "[n]o peace, no rest. Always travelling. Travel and travel without a word." ([1952] 1969, p.50)). The proper name and the descriptive passages do not exactly cover the same meaning, since the descriptions add the idea that the reason why these beings flutter madly around is that they *lack the patience* to stay still in any one place. But clearly, this is not exactly a contradiction, and thanks to the link with standard Swedish, the connotations of a particular kind of physical movement are especially strong. As for *hati-,* the name's first element, there is an obvious suggestion of *hatt,* the Swedish word for "hat", and Jansson's illustrations, together with some further descriptive passages, clearly narrow this down to *hatt* in the standard Swedish sense of "the top part of a mushroom". The characters carrying the name resemble small snowball-like mushrooms, and are also referred to as such; they seem to grow in groups of white blobs on a neatly mown lawn (1955, p.86). The English translation, however, is a transcription of their name as *Hattifatteners,* which connotes something completely different. Its most prominent suggestion is roughly "people or beings who make something or somebody fat", which bears no meaningful relation to any peculiarity of the characters it describes. English idiom does not have such an obvious connection between the idea of a hat and the idea of a mushroom, and the characters' style of movement is not suggested at all. There are merely the ongoing text's descriptive passages to say that these characters travel all the time because they are restless. Here again, then, the translator has saved the form of the name, but at the sacrifice of connotation. Another possibility would have been to use the English verb *flutter.* Not only that, but something could surely have been done with *fungus.* In terms of both form and content, **Fungiflutterers* would have been a creative compromise.

To take one last example of this typically Janssonesque kind, there is the name *Hemulen.* It so happens that *hemul* does actually exist as a Swedish noun, but is extremely limited in meaning, and largely confined to legal language, particularly to the expression *det finns hemul för [detta],* meaning "there is good authority/ warrant for [this]". There is also the very rare adjective *ohemul,* meaning "unwarranted, unjustified, improper, incorrect". For a reader who is aware of this, Jansson's invented name would have a clear appropriateness, in that the group of characters to whom it applies are very orderly and law-abiding. Such a reader would also appreciate the humour of Jansson's using the negating prefix *o-* to make the adjective *ohemul* as if it was a coinage deriving from the name of the characters (rather than the other way round), and would also enjoy the adjective *överhemul* (= "super-correct"), which probably really is a coinage ([1958] 1990, pp.64, 96, 112). As for the English translation, *Hemulen* is simply copied, preceded by the definite adjective: *the Hemulen.* And the adjectives become *un-Hemulenish* and *super-Hemulenish.* This is as true as possible to the form, obviously, but the hints of meaning are quite lost. The translator may or may not have considered the possibility of **the Warranted,* **un-Warranted,* and **super-Warranted,* but these solutions would perhaps have lost too much of the original's sound effects, and for Anglophone readers an unconventional and totally opaque name such as *Hemulen* is in any case not without its charm. As a peg on which to hang meanings as they gradually emerge from the story, it has its own memorability.

### 5. Appropriateness versus Playfulness

Then there are the names which are playfully suggestive, but in ways which do not obviously fit their bearer. One of the strangest examples is *Snusmumriken.* In form, this name is the same as an existing Swedish compound, derived from the noun *snus,* meaning "snuff", and the noun *mumrik,* meaning something like "old codger". *Snusmumrik* and *mumrik* can both mean just "old codger", except that *snusmumrik* means roughly "an old codger who uses snuff", or more generally just "an old bore". Since snuff-taking is a practice not universally admired, and since *snus* is also phonetically close to the Swedish words for "dirt" and "dirty" (*snusk, snuskig*), the old man conjured up by *snusmumrik* may even be rather disgusting. Leaving aside this unpleasant connotation for the moment, the name is at least in certain other respects fairly well motivated. The character who bears it is not a boring or nasty old man, but he is certainly something of a vagabond, and is also older—and wiser—than any other character, and actually rather a hermit. His greatest pleasure is to sit by himself, and he does not talk without due cause. His distinctive attributes include his old green suit, his old green hat, his pipe, and his mouth-organ: "He was quite happy wearing the old suit he had had since he was born (nobody knows where and when that happened), and the only possession he didn't give away was his mouth-organ" ([1958] 1990, p.21). These details, backed up by Jansson's own book illustrations, probably give most readers a strong enough hold on the character, and, to return to pragmatics, his name's perjorative connotations may actually not register with many readers, including even many adults, since in standard Swedish *smusmumriken* is now virtually obsolete. Yet if the unpleasant associations do come across, then since this character is actually a very pleasant person, the proper name becomes rather confusing, in a playful way which the English translator does nothing to capture. *Snusmumriken*'s English name is *Snufkin*. Here the noun *snus* is translated to "snuff", and *mumrik* becomes the particle *-kin,* which is very common in English children's stories, but which does not convey suggestions of age, let alone derogatory ones. On the contrary, *-kin* usually suggests diminutive size and immature years, and in a way that is unreservedly pleasant, and even rather quaint and sentimental. Another difference is that the translation does not try to convey Jansson's variation between *Snusmumriken* and just plain *Mumrik,* which serves as a kind of nickname ([1948] 1992, pp.62, 96). In the English translation, the character is always called *Snufkin,* which because of the diminutive particle almost sounds like a nickname already.

Another example would be the name *Snorkfröken,* translated into English as *Snork Maiden.* The link to the lexicon is quite obvious to the source text reader, because *fröken* really is the Swedish word for "Miss" (as in *Miss Marple*) or "maiden", and *snork* immediately associates to the Swedish adjective *snorkig,* meaning something like "snooty". Yet although very clearly invoked, the association with snootiness is not really appropriate for this particular character, and in the Moomin books as a whole the meaning of *snork* is merely something like "pertaining to the Snorks". In the English translation, the first part of the character's Swedish name, "Snork", is simply copied, so that the English word *Snork* means the same as Jansson's Swedish one: "pertaining to the Snorks". What the translation again fails to convey is anything corresponding to Jansson's play with a dictionary meaning in the standard language. Given the playful inappropriateness of her nod towards *snorkig,* it would be unfair to say that the English translation is simply inadequate. Yet playfulness is, after all, a bonus, and can even be taken here as Jansson's wink to the reader behind the character's back. The effect is something like: "'Snorkig' by name but not by nature". If the English translator had gone in for *Snoot Maiden* or even *Snob Maiden,* something of this might still have come across.

Then there is the name *Snorken,* also copied into English as "the Snork". On the level of form, *Snorken* is obviously derived from *snorkig,* but as with *Snorkfröken,* the name is not really appropriate for the character. Taken together, *Snorken* and *Snorkfröken,* merely hint at the characters' kinship (as do also the names *My* and *Mymlan*). The specific characteristics of the Snorks are explained to Moomintroll by Snufkin: "They must be the same family as you I should think, because they look the same, except that they aren't often white. They can be any colour in the world (like an Easter egg), and they change colour when they get upset" (1951, p.78). But no such features could have been predicted from a knowledge of the name's etymology. As a name, *Snorken* is a kind of little joke, which in the English translation is quite lost, but which *The Snoot* might have captured.

## 6. MISTRANSLATIONS

Even out of context, many of Jansson's proper names amuse and tease. Used in a passage of continuous narrative, and especially when the related adjectives are drawn in, the effects are even more richly humorous. Take this, for instance:

> Maka på dig, sa hemulen. Det har regnat in i min säng. Värst för dig själv, sa snorken och vände sig på andra sidan. Därför tänkte jag sova i din grop, förklarade hemulen. Var inte snorkig nu. Men snorken bara morrade lite och sov vidare. Då fylldes hemulens hjärta av hämndlust och han grävde en kanal i sanden mellan sin egen sovgrop och snorkens. Det där var ohemult, sa snorken och satte sig upp i sin våta filt.
>
> (Jansson, [1948] 1992, p. 94)

Here the Hemulen complains that it has rained into his bed, and asks the Snork to move over and let him sleep in his (the Snork's) own hole in the sand. He accompanies this request or command with the exhortation, "Var inte snorkig nu" (= "Don't be *snorkig* [standoffish-snooty/Snorkish] now".) When the Snork just growls and goes on sleeping, the Hemulen gets revenge by digging a trench between his own, waterlogged hole in the sand and the Snork's dry hole. "That was *ohemult* [= unwarranted/un-Hemulenish]", the Snork said, and sat up in his wet blanket.

As already noted, the English translator has decided that any such puns on *snorkig* and *ohemult* are less worth having than the proper names' actual forms. And even though *the Snob* or *the Snoot* would have been close in both sound and sense to *Snorken,* the English translator's *the Snork* can at least be defended on grounds of greater phonetic fidelity. What certainly is much harder to defend, I feel, is the pursuit of phonetic fidelity when translating, not the proper nouns themselves, but the related adjectives. The translator's rendering of the passage just quoted is as follows:

"Look!" said the Hemulen, "it has rained in my bed." "Bad luck", said the Snork, and turned over on his other side. "So I think I shall sleep in your hole", announced the Hemulen. "No snoring now!" But the Snork only grunted a little and slept on. Then the Hemulen's heart was filled with a desire for revenge, and he dug a trench between his own sand-hole and the Snork's. "That was most un-Hemulenish!" said the Snork, sitting up in his wet blanket.

(Jansson, [1958] 1990, p. 96)

In sound, *"No snoring now!"* is marginally closer to *"Var inte snorkig nu!"* than *"Don't be snooty now!"* would have been. But it has nothing at all to do with the meaning of what Jansson has written, and the phonetic quasi-fidelity can hardly justify the semantic infidelity. To point out that the Swedish verb for "to snore" is *snarka,* and to suggest that Jansson *might have* invented a nonce-adjective *\*snarkig* (*\*snore-y/snore-ish*) does not help matters.

Yet the English translator's sacrifice of meaning for sound is not a matter of sustained principle. There are cases where both sense and sound go by the board. The names *Tofslan* and *Vifslan,* for instance, are translated as *Thingumy* and *Bob.* The phonetic discrepancies are obvious enough, but the semantics are more complicated. *Tofslan* suggests *tofs,* which means "tuft", while *Vifslan* suggests *vifta,* the verb meaning "to wave", connotations which Jansson's illustrations and ongoing descriptions of these characters support. As so often, the English translation makes no attempt to catch the semantic loadedness. Similarly, the translator does not catch the fact that, in the Swedish original, these two characters' distinctive mode of speech is reminiscent of their actual names: to various words they tend to add on the syllable *-sla-*. But even more serious here is that the English renderings are gender-specific. It would be unusual for a girl to have the nickname *Thingumy,* and *Bob,* unlike *Bobbie,* can only refer to a boy. In Swedish, names ending in *-a/-an* more often belong to girls, though they are sometimes also boys' names. In point of fact, biographical research on Jansson has revealed that *Tofslan* and *Vifslan* allude to Jansson herself and to one of her female friends, though this is something which many readers will not know. The issue here is that in Jansson's text as a whole the sex of Tofslan and Vifslan is left open. This significantly affects a reader's overall impression of the story she is telling.

## 7. CHILD/ADULT, NATIVE/NON-NATIVE

Names like *Snusmumriken* and *Hemulen* will be semantically loaded for a reader with a well developed command of Swedish. For a Swedish-speaking child, they will be opaque. *Snufkin* will be semantically loaded for both younger and older native speakers of English. But the younger ones may get more out of the *-kin* than the

*Snuf-*, and neither grouping will get the same things as some adult Swedish-speaking readers from *Snusmumriken.* And for both adult and child readers who know no Swedish, *the Hemulen* will be as opaque as *Hemulen* to a Swedish-speaking child.

Given the double nature of the problem—the differences between the vocabularies of the different languages, and the influence of these pragmatic variables—, one might well ask whether it is even remotely possible for several different groupings of readers to receive more or less one and the same impression from even a single Jansson name. Are there, or are there not, cases in which Swedish-speaking child-readers and Swedish-speaking adult readers of the original text, and English-speaking child-readers and English-speaking adult readers of the English translation, are at all likely to end up with roughly the same idea?

Well, sometimes Swedish and English are fairly close to each other. So a translator, even by simply copying a name, may be able to achieve an effect very similar to that of the original. One example is the name *Sniff.* In both English and Swedish, *sniff* onomatopoeically imitates the noise made by somebody sniffing. In Swedish it does not, as in English, occur as an ordinary word. But it does recall words whose meaning is fairly closely related: *snuva,* meaning "head cold", and *snyfta,* meaning "to sob/to simper". In the first Moomin book, the character concerned here is actually referred to as "the little creep". The name *Sniff* is used from the second book onwards, and it harmonizes fairly well with his sobbing and lamenting. Somewhat piteous, timid, and childish, Sniff complains about his own smallness, and uses it as his excuse when he is too bored to do something, or when things go wrong (Jones, 1984, pp.22, 39-40). The name could also allude more directly to his physical appearance, and particularly to his nose, which Jansson's illustrations make very prominent. In this case, then, the associations conveyed by the name are closely connected to the character's actual behaviour and physique, and the translation and the original can be said to be in agreement. What is more, a reader of any age is likely to get more or less the same impression from both.

Another example is the name *Mårran.* This suggests the Swedish noun-verb pair *morr* and *morra,* meaning "growl/snarl" and "to growl/to snarl", in which the *m*-can be sounded, and the *-rr-* trilled, in ways which are felt to be onomatopoeic—in reference to, say, the noise made by a large and angrily suspicious dog. In Jansson's stories, the character carrying this name does not actually growl at the other characters, but is always thought to be the source of a distant howling they sometimes hear. In trying to suggest the nature of this strange creature to the Hemulen, Bob bares his teeth, draws himself up to his full height, and gives an intense stare. But even before this display, the Hemulen has already started to tremble, just because of the creature's name, the awesomeness of which would be similarly quite apparent to a Swedish-speaking reader of any age. Here the English translator also goes in for onomatopoeia, not through a phonetic copying of the Swedish word, however, but through a coinage which is onomatopoeic in English: *the Groke*. As well as suggesting an unnerving sound, this relates to other words by which such sounds can be described: *groan, growl, croak, crow*. Here, then, we can perhaps credit the translator with a fairly reasonable equivalent, which will again be well understood by both children and adults.

The only problem is that *Mårran* has that *-an* suffix, which often, though not always, indicates feminine gender. *The Groke*, by contrast, will perhaps come across as male, or as a simply neutral sort of monster. As so often, it all depends on who "one" is. Jansson herself is obviously aware that her various names will strike different categories of readers in different ways. It is clearly part of her intention that one and the same book should be, paradoxically, at least two books at once. The plurality of her implied reader, which can also be seen in the ambiguity of the names, accounts for her popularity with both children and adults. But inevitably, there are things quite beyond an author's own control. Some real readers, in what they bring to a text, will simply be very different from any aspect of its implied reader, and one such differently constituted real reader may also be the person entrusted with the job of translating it into some other language. In turn, the translator creates the implied reader anew, inevitably a somewhat different one from the author's own implied reader, and the translation's real readers will resemble this new implied reader to a greater or lesser extent, depending on their own age and other circumstances. And although all human beings are capable of acts of imaginative empathy, so that they can indeed communicate with people who are unlike themselves, they can nevertheless not exceed the limits of their own understanding. Readers can read Jansson, and can read translations of her, and can thereby greatly enjoy themselves. But the number of readers who receive one and the same impression of even her proper names will probably be limited. Unless, of course, scholars and critics are able to intervene in the role of mediatior.

### References

Aejmelaeus, S. (1994). *Kun lyhdyt syttyvät. Tove Jansson ja muumimaailma.* [With a summary in English: *When the Lanterns Are Lit—Tove Jansson and Moominworld*]. *Suomen Nuorisokirjallisuuden Instituutin Jalkaisuja* 18.

Baldick, C. ([1990] 1996). *The concise Oxford dictionary of literary terms.* Oxford: Oxford University Press.

Bassnett, S. ([1980] 1994). *Translation studies.* London: Routledge.

Connolly, P. T. (1995). *Winnie-the-Pooh and the House at Pooh Corner. Recovering Arcadia.* New York: Twayne.

Docherty, T. (1983). *Reading (absent) character: Towards a Characterization in Fiction.* Oxford: Clarendon Press.

Eliot, T. S. ([1920] 1951). Philip Massinger. In T. S. Eliot, *Selected Essays* (pp.205-20). London: Faber.

Hermans, T. (1988). "On translating proper names, with reference to De Witte and Max Havelaar." In M. Wintle and P. Vincent (Eds.), *Modern Dutch Studies: Essays in Honour of Peter King* (pp.11-24). London: Athlone.

Hunt, P. (1991). *Criticism, Theory, and Children's Literature.* Oxford: Blackwell.

Hunt, Peter. 1992. "Winnie-the-Pooh and domestic fantasy." In D. Butts (Ed.), *Stories and Society. Children's Literature in Its Social Context* (pp.112-125). Basingstoke: Macmillan.

Jansson, T. (1946). *Kometjakten.* Esbo: Schildt.

———. (1951). *Comet in Moominland* (trans. E. Portch). London: Benn.

———. ([1958] 1990). *Finn Family Moomintroll* (trans.E. Portch). Harmondsworth: Penguin.

———. (1955). *Moominsummer Madness* (trans. T. Warburton). London, Benn.

———. ([1950] 1961). *Muminpappans bravader skrivna av honom själv.* Helsingfors: Schildt.

———. ([1952] 1969). *The Exploits of Moominpappa* (trans. T. Warburton). Harmondsworth: Penguin.

———. ([1948] 1992). *Trollkarlens hatt.* Esbo: Schildt.

Jones, W. G. (1984). *Vägen från Mumindalen* (trans. T. Warburton). Hangö: Schildt. [Original title: *Tove Jansson: Moominvalley and beyond,* 1984]

Klingberg, G. (1978). Teori, arbetsbregrepp och terminologi i barnlitteraturforskningen. (Studies published by the Swedish institute for Children's Books, 9). In G. Klingberg (Ed.), *Children's Books in Translation* (pp.33-43). Stockholm: Almqvist & Wiksell.

Klingberg, G. (1986). *Children's Literature in the Hands of the Translators.* Lund: CWK: Gleerup.

Koskinen, A. (1984). Kulttuurikonteksti käännösongelmana: Günther Grassin Kampela suomalaisissa vesissä. *Sananjalka 26* (Suomen Kielen Seuran Vuosikirja) (pp.61-79). Turku: Suomen Kielen Seura.

Newmark, P. (1988). *A Textbook of Translation.* London: Prentice Hall.

Nida, E. A. and Taber, C. R. (1969). *The Theory and Practice of Translation.* Leiden: E. J. Brill.

Nikolajeva, M. (1996). *Children's Literature Comes of Age: Towards a New Aesthetic.* New York: Garland.

Nikula, K. (1994). Översättning av namn: Bo Carpelans *Urwind. LSP and Theory of Translation: 14th VAKKI Symposium* (pp.210-224). Vaasa, Vaasan yliopisto.

Oittinen, R. (1993). *I Am Me—I Am Other: On the Dialogics of Translating for Children.* Vammala: Vammalan kirjapaino.

Schogt, H. (1988). *Linguistics, Literary Analysis, and Literary Translation.* Toronto: University of Toronto Press.

Searle, J. R. (1958). "Proper Names." *Mind,* 67, 166-173.

Stephens, J. (1992). *Language and Ideology in Children's Fiction.* London: Longman.

# FURTHER READING

### Criticism

Jansson, Tove, and W. Glyn Jones. "Tove Jansson: My Books and Characters." *Books from Finland* 12, no. 3 (1978): 91-7.
  Interview in which Jansson talks about her literary output, including the Moomin books, adult stories, artwork, and dramatic productions.

Jones, W. Glyn. "Studies in Obsession: The New Art of Tove Jansson." *Books from Finland* 14, no. 2 (1981): 60-2.
  Focuses on thematic development in Jansson's writing.

Spenader, Jennifer. "Modality Realization as Contrast in Discourse." *Journal of Semantics* 21, no. 2 (May 2004):113-31.
  Uses examples from Jansson's Moomin books to illustrate a discussion of the use of a phonetic marker indicating "truth value" in speech.

**Additional coverage of Jansson's life and career is contained in the following sources published by Thomson Gale:** *Children's Literature Review,* **Vol. 2;** *Contemporary Authors,* **Vol. 17-20R;** *Contemporary Authors New Revision Series,* **Vols. 38, 118;** *Contemporary Authors-Obituary,* **Vol. 196;** *Contemporary World Writers,* **Ed. 2;** *Dictionary of Literary Biography,* **Vol. 257;** *Encyclopedia of World Literature in the 20th Century,* **Ed. 3;** *Literature Resource Center*; *Major Authors and Illustrators for Children and Young Adults,* **Eds. 1, 2;** *Reference Guide to Short Fiction,* **Ed 2; and** *Something about the Author,* **Vols. 3, 41.**

# Jhumpa Lahiri
## 1967-

(Full name Nilanjana Sudeshna Lahiri) English-born American short-story writer and novelist.

## INTRODUCTION

Lahiri is critically acclaimed for her short stories, many of them focusing on the problems faced by immigrant Indians living in the United States. She does not limit herself solely to these bicultural issues, however, as she explores general themes of the human condition including miscommunication, alienation, love, and self-realization. Her Indian characters maintain links to their original culture as they engage with their new one in the United States, and it is this tension, mixed with the strain of interpersonal relationships, that pervades Lahiri's stories. Her first book, *The Interpreter of Maladies* (1999), received high praise from several reviewers and won Lahiri the Pulitzer Prize in fiction in 2000—the first time that prize had been awarded individually to a South Asian. Additionally, the title story from this volume won an O. Henry Award in 1999 and was included in *The Best American Short Stories* for that year. *The Interpreter of Maladies* also met remarkable popular success, becoming a bestseller; it has been translated into twenty-nine languages. Lahiri's second book, a novel titled *The Namesake* (2003), develops many themes she has also explored in her short stories.

## BIOGRAPHICAL INFORMATION

Lahiri was born to Bengali parents in London, England, where she lived for her first two years. She grew up in South Kingstown, Rhode Island, where she began writing fiction at age seven, and where she received the nickname Jhumpa from one of her teachers in elementary school. While a child, she made lengthy visits to Calcutta every two years with her parents. Lahiri became a U.S. citizen at eighteen and later graduated from Barnard College with a Bachelor's degree in English literature. After being rejected for admission by numerous graduate schools, she was accepted by Boston University and earned Master's degrees in English, creative writing, and comparative studies in literature and the arts, as well as a Ph.D. in Renaissance studies. She has taught creative writing at Boston University and the Rhode Island School of Design. Lahiri married in 2001 in Calcutta and now resides in New York with her husband and two children.

## MAJOR WORKS OF SHORT FICTION

*The Interpreter of Maladies* consists of nine stories, eight of which were previously published (over a several-year period) in earlier versions in assorted publications including the *New Yorker,* the *Harvard Review, Salamander,* and *Story Quarterly.* Lahiri got the idea for the title story after meeting an old acquaintance who was working as an interpreter for a doctor—who served many patients who could only speak Russian. Lahiri now views the title as somewhat reflective of her own task as an author. Three of the stories in the collection are set in India: "The Interpreter of Maladies," "A Real Durwan," and "The Treatment of Bibi Haldar"; the balance are set in the United States. The only story appearing for the first time in this collection, "The Third and Final Continent," is based on the experiences of Lahiri's Bengali father as he made his way from Calcutta to London and then to Boston, adjusting to each culture along the way.

## CRITICAL RECEPTION

Lahiri's work has been well received by critics, with the *New Yorker* in 1999 designating her as one of the twenty best writers under the age of forty. While many reviewers focus on aspects of her work specific to immigrants, others emphasize that the problems examined by Lahiri are not specific to people from one culture; indeed, Ronny Noor contends that what makes the stories so valuable is that they "transcend the confined borders of immigrant experience to embrace larger human issues." Noor notes that while several of Lahiri's stories involve secrets kept from spouses or show her characters lacking in understanding, at other times compassion takes center stage. Basudeb Chakrabarti and Angana Chakrabarti discuss the short story "A Temporary Matter," focusing on its self-obsessed characters laboring under modern existential maladies. Jennifer Bess points out that Lahiri's characters wrestle with the problem of managing the universal and the unique simultaneously, as they seek to find "the union between understanding the human experience and finding satisfaction in their individual lives." Several critics have attempted to categorize Lahiri or place her in context with other expatriate writers. Paul Brians notes that Lahiri is considered a post-Salman Rushdie author who rejects magic realism and other experiments in fiction. Instead, Brians writes, Lahiri's stories "belong to the long tradition of delicate character sketches, avoiding sensational effects and overly clever endings." In her analysis of "When Mr. Pirzada Came to Dine," Judith Caesar states that Lahiri's short stories do not fit neatly into such standard subcategories of contemporary fiction as postcolonial literature, Indo-Anglican literature, or Asian-American literature; rather, she writes American fiction, but American fiction that is informed by the sensibility of one who is not American. In his critique, Simon Lewis contends that "The Interpreter of Maladies" is a reworking of *A Passage to India,* E. M. Forster's classic 1924 novel. Lewis emphasizes that the key update in Lahiri's work is the perspective that misunderstanding stems from cultural rather than racial differences. Lahiri's literary techniques are also examined by Gita Rajan, who analyzes the ethics of "When Mr. Pirzada Came to Dine" and notes Lahiri's skillful use of the reportage form to engage the reader's interest. Noelle Brada-Williams regards *The Interpreter of Maladies* as a much more ambitious work than is generally recognized—a delicately balanced short story cycle that draws parallels between certain stories, with recurring patterns and motifs—connected by a single theme, the need for care, presented by Lahiri through dichotomous examples of carefulness and carelessness.

# PRINCIPAL WORKS

## Short Fiction

*The Interpreter of Maladies* (short stories) 1999

## Other Major Works

*The Namesake* (novel) 2003

# CRITICISM

## Ronny Noor (review date spring 2000)

SOURCE: Noor, Ronny. Review of *Interpreter of Maladies. World Literature Today* 74, no. 2 (spring 2000): 365-66.

[*In the following review, Noor praises* The Interpreter of Maladies *not only for exploring the experiences of immigrants, but also for considering larger human issues.*]

Born in England of Indian parents and raised in America, Jhumpa Lahiri has evidently benefited from all three cultures. Their aroma drifts from the pages of her first collection of short fiction, titled *Interpreter of Maladies,* where she has woven their idiosyncrasies into well-crafted stories with a keen eye for observation and an admirable gift for details. Eight of the nine stories have been previously published, in slightly different form, in various literary and nonliterary journals across the nation. They not only study the experiences of immigrants but also deal with perennial universal issues.

The title story, **"Interpreter of Maladies,"** is about a young couple named Mr. and Mrs. Das, by birth American, who go to India with their three children to visit the land of their ancestors. While viewing monastic dwellings on the hills of Udayagiri, Mrs. Das confides in the car driver, a translator for a doctor, that her husband has not sired their eight-year-old boy. He is the product of an encounter with a guest in the house. This is the secret, the malady if you will, which she hides from her husband, just the way Dev hides his extramarital affair from his wife in **"Sexy."** Shoba is not so lucky in **"A Temporary Matter."** She thinks that her husband did not see the stillborn baby she had delivered while he was away at a conference. But when Shukumar tells her that he returned early from the conference to hold his son in his arms before the boy was cremated, the secret is out, adding more pain to their already miserable marriage.

Lahiri's stories are not just about this malady of secrets between spouses, but also concern broader social issues. In **"A Real Durwan"** the residents of a Calcutta tenement unjustly cast out an old sweeper because of a theft in the building while she was away in town. They show no sympathy for the innocent victim despite her pleading. Such lack of understanding forces Bibi to lead a desolate life in **"The Treatment of Bibi Haldar,"** and pushes a professor's wife into an embarrassing car accident in **"Mrs. Sen's."** Compassion, on the other hand, goes a long way toward resolving differences in **"This Blessed House," "When Mr. Pirzada Came to Dine,"** and **"The Third and Final Continent."** The last story, hitherto unpublished, is a first-person narrative of a man who has journeyed from India to America via England in search of a livelihood. He marries a traditional Indian woman who seems to be steeped in her native customs, which he, as a modern man, finds hard to accept. But when they visit his former landlady, an ancient who once found happiness in his sympathy, the old woman thinks his wife is "a perfect lady," a compliment that makes the couple smile at each other, lessening the distance between them. Thus, with sympathy, understanding, and a smile, one can narrow the gap not only between spouses but also between continents. E. M. Forster expressed it best with his "only connect" precept.

The value of these stories—although some of them are loosely constructed—lies in the fact they transcend the confined borders of immigrant experience to embrace larger human issues, age-old issues that are, in the words of Ralph Waldo Emerson, "cast into the mould of these new times" redefining America. So it is not surprising that the title story of Jhumpa Lahiri's laudable collection has been selected for both *The Best American Short Stories* and the year 1999's O. Henry Award.

**Simon Lewis (essay date summer 2001)**

SOURCE: Lewis, Simon. "Lahiri's *Interpreter of Maladies.*" *Explicator* 59, no. 4 (summer 2001): 219-21.

[*In the following essay, Lewis analyzes the short story "The Interpreter of Maladies" as an update to E. M. Forster's novel* A Passage to India.]

Jhumpa Lahiri's short story **"Interpreter of Maladies,"** from her 1999 Pulitzer Prize-winning collection of the same name, is likely to become a classic of literature anthologies not just because of its great narrative and verbal craft, but also because it updates E. M. Forster's 1924 novel *A Passage to India.* The plots of both texts hinge on a misconceived tourist excursion—to the Marabar Caves in *A Passage to India,* to the monastic cells at Udayagiri and Khandagiri in **"Interpreter of Maladies"**—during which a male Indian guide and a female visitor misinterpret each other's verbal and nonverbal signals. In both cases the male guide's perceptions of the foreign visitor are at odds with those of the woman who, apparently prompted by her extraordinary and unfamiliar surroundings, tries to come to terms with pre-existing emotional dilemmas.

As one might expect in a postcolonial rewrite, Lahiri narrates her story from the point of view of the Indian host, the interpreter of maladies-cum-tourist guide Mr. Kapasi. What makes Lahiri's reworking of Forster so intriguing, however, is that the gulf of misunderstanding between Mr. Kapasi and the visiting Mrs. Das results from cultural rather than racial difference. Lahiri thus moves beyond Eurocentric or Oriental images of India to those of a contemporary postcolonial nation more concerned with dialogue with its own diaspora than with its former colonizers. The story may repeat the Forsterian theme of mutual human incomprehension, but the world of **"Interpreter of Maladies"** is an exclusively Indian one, in which Indians define notions of self and other, in which Indians move freely among countries and cultures, and in which India itself is an object of scrutiny by Indian eyes.

Although Mr. Kapasi and Mrs. Das are both Indian, the difference between them is just as gaping as that between Forster's Dr. Aziz and Adela Quested. With both Forster and Lahiri the question of misunderstanding is supposed to go even deeper than race and culture, representing something fundamental to the human condition. After fleeing from the first of the Marabar Caves, for instance, Forster's Mrs. Moore—so intuitively sympathetic to India and Indians up to this point—becomes exasperated with the emotional turmoil around her and formulates the thought that despite "centuries of carnal embracement, [. . .] man is no nearer to understanding man" (Forster 147-48). Likewise, in the novel's famous closing, the connection between Fielding and Aziz is denied by their material circumstances: the rocks between which they rode "didn't want it, they said in their hundred voices, 'No, not yet,' and the sky said, 'No, not there'" (Forster 316, original punctuation). In **"Interpreter of Maladies"** the material symbol of Kapasi's and Mrs. Das's non-connection, the "slip of paper with Mr. Kapasi's address on it" (69) flutters away unnoticed by anyone but Mr. Kapasi, who is left with a mental impression only of the Das family instead of the personal correspondence with Mrs. Das that he had anticipated.

Kapasi's final disappointment comes after he realizes how self-absorbed Mrs. Das is. After listening to her confession that her younger son Bobby had been fathered by an unnamed "Punjabi friend," Kapasi realizes that this confession is not the shared intimacy he had been hoping for, but that Mrs. Das had told him the story more or less to purge herself of it. When he fails to offer either absolution or a cure and instead quite reasonably asks, "'Is it really pain you feel, Mrs. Das, or is it guilt?'" (66), her withering glare "crushed him; he knew at that moment that he was not even important enough to be properly insulted" (66).

This moment has its analogue in *A Passage to India* when Adela's naive question to Aziz as to whether he has more than one wife irritates Aziz so much that he has to leave her and smoke a cigarette in order to regain his composure as host. Forster goes to some length to stress that there is absolutely no erotic charge in their encounter—the narrative records that Aziz "had never liked Miss Quested as much as Mrs. Moore" and that his mind was preoccupied with organizational details of the recent breakfast (162). Nonetheless, out of that encounter (or non-encounter) and Adela's subsequent hysterical experience come the accusation of rape and the raising of stereotypical issues of transracial desire that are so central to colonial fiction.

In **"Interpreter of Maladies,"** by contrast, Kapasi's desire for Mrs. Das, though never physically expressed, is more frankly acknowledged. Right from the opening paragraph Lahiri shows Kapasi as intensely aware of Mrs. Das's physical presence: of "her shaved, largely bare legs" (43) and her clothes. Her "close-fitting blouse styled like a man's undershirt" and "decorated at chest level with a calico appliqué in the shape of a strawberry" (46) persistently draws his attention, and toward the end of the story he fantasizes about "complimenting her strawberry shirt, which he found irresistibly becoming" (60).

However whereas Kapasi, unlike Aziz, clearly finds his tourist-guest sexually attractive, his desire for her does not fit the stock transracial model of colonial fiction. Instead, part of her appeal seems to be his sense of Mrs. Das's similarity to him; she and her family all "looked Indian" even though they "dressed as foreigners did" (43-44). Because it is almost impossible to ascribe exoticness or foreignness either to the Dases or to Mr. Kapasi, Lahiri's story here as elsewhere thoroughly confounds the Manichean sense of self and other that underlies the tension that Forster creates between the unmarried white woman visitor and her married Indian host. Each is partly familiar to the other, but neither is wholly representative of "Indianness."

Mr. Kapasi, for instance, in his crucial role as interpreter, refers easily to the television show *Dallas* (a reference the Das daughter does not recognize because it is so dated), and his English is more British than Indian or American. Indeed, unlike Aziz, whose idiosyncratically Indian English is the source of some humor in *A Passage to India,* Lahiri has Mr. Kapasi comment on the idiosyncrasies of Mrs. Das's American usage. At the height of his fantasy about Mrs. Das, for instance, Kapasi is rather perplexed by her casual use of "Neat" in response to his explanation of the significance of a bronze statue of Surya (59). His hope that her noncommittal comment will allow him to continue his relationship with her, acting as an "interpreter between nations" (59) rather than of maladies, is finally quashed no less emphatically than Forster quashes the hope of Indian-British connection in *A Passage to India.*

Ultimately, although Lahiri's story reiterates Forster's elegant pessimism concerning human relations, it denies that the malady that comes between people has its origin in race or geographical location. To be sure, there is a Forsterian theme—that although Mr. Kapasi might be able to interpret both his own maladies (of thwarted ambitions, thwarted desire) and those of others, no one can bridge the communicative gaps that inevitably separate human beings. Yet in rendering this world in exclusively Indian terms, Lahiri's story tacitly exposes the outdated racialism of Forster's novel.

### Works Cited

Forster, E. M. *A Passage to India.* Harmondsworth: Penguin, 1980.

Lahiri, Jhumpa. *Interpreter of Maladies.* Boston: Houghton, 1999.

## Basudeb Chakrabarti and Angana Chakrabarti (essay date January 2002)

SOURCE: Chakrabarti, Basudeb, and Angana Chakrabarti. "Context: A Comparative Study of Jhumpa Lahiri's 'A Temporary Matter,' and Shubodh Ghosh's *Jatugriha." Journal of Indian Writing in English* 30, no. 2 (January 2002): 23-9.

[*In the following essay, the Chakrabartis contrast the literary approaches taken by Lahiri and Shubodh Ghosh, who writes about life in Bengal during the period between 1950 and 1960.*]

The comment on the literature written in different regional languages in India during the last 50 years, made by Salman Rudhdie is indeed unfortunate. In the introduction of a jointly edited book, Salman Rushidie comments:

> The prose writing—both fiction and nonfiction created in this period (1947-1997) by Indian writers writing in English—is proving to be a stronger and more important body of work than of what has been produced in the 16 'official' languages of India, the so-called 'vernacular languages' during the same time, indeed, this new, and still burgeoning 'Indo-Anglian' Literature represents perhaps the most valuable contribution India has made to the world of book[1].

One may or may not contest what Rushdie thinks of the role and the importance of Indian writings in English in the 'world of books'. But his comparison of Indian writings in English with Indian literature written in different regional languages—Indian literature which according to him is of minimal importance to the world of books shows his callow competence and infantile analysis of what has been written in Indian vernacular languages during the last fifty years. Indeed a comment like this is unfortunate.

Many Indian languages have rich traditions. Hindi speaking states in India have produced a variety of literature. Marathi literature has contributed a lot to the world of books, particularly literature dealing with Dalit community:

> . . . One the other hand, in an Indian laguage like Marathi an entire school of Dalit writers of the lowest of the low classes has arisen during the last two decades, they have broadened the scope of Marathi literature, both in themes and style. The Dalit experience is one of the most tragic in the world, showing what man has made of Man, and since this experience is expressed in the Dalit's own words, Marathi literature has gained a new vocabulary and idiom, a new register and idiolect[2].

The modern Bengali literature after the Indian Independence has inherited a very strong line of tradition. The Bengali language itself is rich with lexical varieties pertaining to different registers. References to Samaresh Basu, Naren Mitra, Bimal Kar, Subodh Ghosh, Shyamal Gangopadhyay, Sunil Ganguly, Manoj Basu, Jibananda Das, Sukanta Bhattacharya and lots of others are evidences of the literary richness transmuted through the Bengali language after the Indian freedom. Great writer in Bangladesh like Sayed Walliallah, Humayun Ahmed, Aal Mamud, Akhtarujjamam Ilias, Samsur Rahaman and others have made experiments not only with forms of novel but also with themes. Only reference to either Samaresh Basu's 'Ganga' or 'B. T. Roder Dhare' or Chilakothar Sipai' of Akhtarujjaman is sufficient in evaluating the richness of literature written in Bengali language. Had Samaresh Basu been translated into English and the translated version of his novel been sent to the Noble Prize committee, who knows Samaresh Basu would not have been the Nobel Prize winner. Salman Rushdie's comment on the richness of Indian literature written in regional languages is unjust and so insulting.

An attempt to assess the merits of Indian literature written in regional languages in objective and proper perspective does not mean any indifference to big volume of literary writings in English in India during the last fifty years. Salman Rushdie, Nirod C. Chaudhuri, Jayanta Mahapatra, A. K. Ramanujan, Mulk Raj Anand, Anita Desai, Amitav Ghosh, Arundhati Ray, Jhumpa Lahiri and others have been already awarded many national as well as international prizes. Some of these writers of Indian diaspora have contributed much to the world literature. Indian English has developed already a particular variety of standard British English. Indian literature written in regional languages needs not to be undermined or ignored for the appreciation of Indian Writings in English.

Shubodh Ghosh and Jhumpa Lahiri are writers residing in two different parts of the globe, yet they are both in one way or another interpreters of the maladies of their contemporary societies. Shubodh Ghosh's milieu is the 1950-1960 society of Bengal, Jhumpa experiments with Bengal, Boston and other places of today. She is herself an immigrant and therefore feels the importance of family and how it ties man to his homeland. In the words of Lahiri herself: "I went to Calcutta neither as a tourist nor as a outsider and yet I also know that as different as Calcutta is from Rhode Island, I belong there is some fundamental way, in the ways I didn't seem to belong in the United States.'" Hence this sense of belonging to a particular place and culture and yet at the same time being an outsider to another creates a tension in individuals which happens to be a distinguishing feature of Lahiri's characters. Reminiscences of Bengal throng Jhumpa's **"A Temporary Matter."** As Shoba remarks: "I remember during power failures at my grandmother's house, we all had to say something" and again: "It's like India . . . sometimes the current disapears for

hours at a stretch. I once had to attend an entire rice ceremony in the dark. The baby just cried and cried. It must have been so hot." (**Interpreter of Maladies**, *p. 12*)

But this kind of cultural tension is not the raw material for Shubodh Ghosh's *Jatugriha*. In this remarkable short story, Madhuri and Shatadal are born and brought up in West Bengal and speak the Bengali language. And so the malady which he describes in one of his own society. The local moves locally from Rajpur to Ghatshila but never changes internationally. And so Shubodh Ghosh's society is much smaller than Jhumpa's cross cultural society.

But such cultural difference cannot erase the basic points of similarities in interpreting a social malady. For both Lahiri and Ghosh deal with broken marriages and the reader tries to search the cause for it. Is it the 20th century material mindedness which destroys the basic human feelings and sentiments? Or is it the basic existential temperament of looking at life? In Jhumpa's story Shoba gives birth to a still-born baby and this creates in them a mental vacuum which is difficult to be filled up and which partly seems to be made up by their reminiscences in the darkness of load shedding "a temporary matter". Shubodh Ghosh's Madhuri and Shatadal are a childless couple who decides to separate and take the help of law. They meet after 5 years at a railway station. Shatadal was travelling to Calcutta and Madhuri to Rajgir. The rift in the relationship between Jhumpa's and Shubodh Ghosh's couples is certainly a malady of the Existential modern society.

Modern Existentialism takes us back to the philosophical thinking of Soren Kierkegaard (1813-1855), Martin Heideggar (b-1889) and Jean-Paul Sartre (b-1905). All these philosophical thinkers accept the priority of the actual being of the individual i.e. the particular human being. They deny the importance of 'essence' which focuses only on human nature, i.e., humanity. One can conceive of 'essence' only by reason or intellect whereas existence can only be grasped by one's own immediate experience. Existentialists are in one way or another individualists, particularists, empiricists, voluntarists and subjectivists. They are more concerned with their own individual freedom in social, cultural, political matters. In one way or other these thinkers emphasize anti-intellectualism and anti-objectivism.

Shubodh Ghosh's Madhuri and Shatadal and Lahiri's Shoba and Shukumar are individualists who accord primacy to the particular human being. The still born child therefore becomes merely a kind of a lame excuse to severe all marital relationship in **"A Temporary Matter."** The death of the child instantly rubs away all sacred emotional ties which marriage confirms:

> The more Shoba stayed out, the more She began putting in extra hours at work and taking on additional

projects, the more he wanted to stay in, not even leaving to get the mail, or to buy fruit or wine at the stores by the trolley stop.

*(Interpreter of Maladies,* p. 2)

Both Shoba and Shukumar try to fill in the void, created in them by the death of their child, by different assignments. As Jhumpa once more remarks:

Instead he thought of how he and Shoba had become experts at avoiding each other in their three-bedroom house, spending as much time on separate floors as possible.

*(Interpreter of Maladies,* p. 4)

This reminds one of Sartre's subjective and passive conditions of man. For, Sartre formulating his 'existential phychoanalysis' has remarked that individuals feel it proper to live only their specific lives. In Sartre's own words, 'existence comes before essence' and we must being from the subjective'.

This excessive subjectivity becomes the crux of Shoba's way of life. It is only her existence and her particular self with which she seems to have been preoccupied. Jhumpa delineates how Shoba is easily able to put off all her familial responsibilities and duties. A certain aloof and detached temperament overcomes her:

. . . She wasn't this way before. She used to put her coat on a hanger, her sneakers in the closet, and she paid bills as soon as they came. But how she treated the house as if it were a hotel.

*(Interpreter of Maladies,* p. 6)

A similar avoidance of responsibilities happens to be a marked feature of Shukumar's way of life:

Shukumar had dissembled it all before bringing Shoba back from the hospital, scraping off the rabbits and ducks with a spatula. . . . In January, when he stopped working at his carrel in the library, he set up his desk there deliberately, party because the room soothed him, and partly because it was a place Shoba avoided.

*(Interpreter of Maladies,* p. 8)

Shobodh Ghosh's Jatugriha also reveals the dullness in marital relationship between Madhuri and Shatadal. When Shatadal is about to leave on a tour to Bhubaneshwar for certain archeological research project, Madhuri never for a single moment comes to bid adieu. On the contrary, she was busy reading her own books without any concern for her husband. Similarly, when Madhuri gets ready for an outing one summer evening, Shatadal hardly pays any heed to her wishes. He remains untouched by his wife's desires and engages himself with an architectural sketch of the foundation of a temple.

Actually Shoba and Shukumar in **"A Temporary Matter"** on Madhuri and Shatadal in *Jatugriha* are strong individualists who believe in complete freedom in social and familial matters. In both these couples there is nothing outside the preoccupation with their own selves. A still-born baby or a childless marriage is enough to draw them apart from one another. They lead a life which is passive and void. This excessive preoccupation with Being takes them to a state of Nothingness. For Nothingness is an integral part of Being. As Sartre has concluded:

the permanent possibility of non-being outside us and within, conditions our questions about being.[4]

And this is not the subjectivity. This is non-being which is a new component of the real.

So it is undeniable that both Lahiri and Shubodh Ghosh deal with the existential problems of modern men although in different cultural contexts. But apart from this commonality of theme, the approaches of Lahiri and Ghosh are poles apart.

Shubodh Ghosh's prose has certain poetry and rhythm which imparts a particular stature to his writing. Ghosh becomes almost a delineator of minute details. Each of these details becomes a distinguishing feature of the estranged relationship of Madhuri and Shatadal. Shatadal now wears his watch with a black leather band, something he refused to wear as a mark of respect for Madhuri's choice. The floral prints of the pillow-cover suggest that shatadal's newly married school teacher wife has selected it for him unlike Madhuri who usually opted for the plain white cover. Madhuri also notices that Shatadal has reduced a lot and concludes that probably his present wife takes little care of him. Shatadal also finds a change in Madhuri's hair style and sari. She now wears a crepe-sari instead of the Dhakai or the Bengal Handloom variety. These changes in their physical appearances seem to match those in their mental makeup. Each realizes that they are far away from their earlier selves.

Shoba and Shukumar's mental void and a rupture in their relationships have been delineated by Jhumpa Lahiri in concrete and too prosaic a manner. One is not struck by the sweetness of rhythm which spreads over Shubodh Ghosh's *Jatugriha*. Lahiri is more a dispassionate chronicler of the lives of Shoba and Shukumar in a modern society:

It was nearly lunch time when Shukumar would finally pull himself out of bed and head down stairs to the coffeepot, pouring out the extra bit Shoba left for him, along with an empty mug on the counter top.

*(Interpreter of Maladies* p. 5)

Lahiri further adds:

These days Shoba was always gone by the time Shukumar woke up. He would open his eyes and see the long black hairs she shed on her pillow and think of her, dressed, sipping her third cup of the coffee already, in her office down town, where she searched for typographical errors in text books. . . .

*(Interpreter of Maladies* p. 4)

It is the matter of fact tone of her language which strikes any reader of **"A Temporary Matter."** The writer is merely a detached observer of the daily events in the lives of her characters. But Shubodh Ghosh appears to be more involved in the mental conflicts and turmoils of Madhuri and Shatadal.

Thus just as in *Jatugriha,* the brief meeting of Madhuri and Shatadal at Rajpur railway station becomes a means of retrospecting their past lives, so also the power failure at Boston, though a temporary matter enables the couples, Shoba and Shukumar to reminisce their earlier lives. In this respect, the power cuts in Lahiri's story and the meeting of Madhuri and Shatadal at Rajpur become symbols of a tattered relationship and acquire symbolic overnotes.

*Notes*

1. Quoted, M. K. Naik, "Towards the New Millennium: Indian English Literature Today", in *The Journal of Indian Writting in English,* Vol. 29, No. 1, p. 15, Jan 2001.

2. Ibid., p.2.

3. Jha, Parmanand, "Home and Abroad: Jhumpa Lahiri's Interpreter of Maladies", *The Indian Journal of English Studies,* Vol. XXXVIII, 2000-2001, p. 107.

4. Danto, Arthur C., Sartre, Glasgow: 1975, p. 66.

**Judith Caesar (essay date winter 2003)**

SOURCE: Caesar, Judith. "Beyond Cultural Identity in Jhumpa Lahiri's 'When Mr. Pirzada Came to Dine.'" *North Dakota Quarterly* 70, no. 1 (winter 2003): 82-91.

[*In the following essay, Caesar analyzes the short story "When Mr. Pirzada Came to Dine," describing how Lahiri uses certain key images and emblems to build meaning.*]

Jhumpa Lahiri's Pulitzer Prize-winning short story collection, *The Interpreter of Maladies* is informed by at least three types of contemporary fiction while remaining just outside all of these categories. It is not postcolonial literature, or even what Salman Rushdie termed "Indo-Anglian literature" (50), because most of the stories take place in the United States, not in post-colonial India, and they concern the psychic development, or the failure to develop, of cosmopolitan and multicultural characters, not Indians struggling to understand the

meaning of their personal and national past. It is unlike most previous Asian-American literature in that few of the characters are American-born Asians trying to understand their ancestral culture and make it part of their American identities, as Amy Tan's and Maxine Hong Kingston's characters do, nor, for the most part, do the stories focus on the rigidity of the ancestral culture and the protagonist's attempts to rebel and redefine herself in opposition to those strictures, as some of Bharati Mukherjee's stories do. However, the stories are not simply American fiction, although they are written to an American audience and often concern American problems. What makes Lahiri's work unique is that the American problems that it identifies are ones that most Americans wouldn't be able to see unless they had examined America through eyes that have seen and minds that have understood other places. Moreover the stories expand the definition not only of what it can mean to be bicultural, but of post-colonial, Asian American, and American literatures. This transcendence of the boundaries of what have been rather insulated subcategories of contemporary fiction is particularly evident in the second story of the collection, **"When Mr. Pirzada Came to Dine."**

The story takes place in 1971, in a small American college town in New England where ten-year-old Lilia lives with her Indian-born parents and tries to learn how to live in multiple worlds. Lilia's home is a version of the best her parents remember of India—the food, the customs, the warm family life—without the sexism or the meddlesome extended family that plague the protagonists of so much Indo-Anglian fiction. And yet her parents apparently feel isolated and lonely, for every year they go through the father's university faculty directory looking for Indian names and inviting these people home. Mr. Pirzada, a visiting scholar from what is then East Pakistan, thus becomes a temporary part of this family world, having dinner and spending the evening with the family almost every night, bringing Lilia more candy than she knows what to do with, and calling her "the lady of the house." And he also shares another world with Lilia's parents, the world of what is going on outside the United States, on the subcontinent, where East and West Pakistan are fighting a particularly cruel and bloody war, where refugees from East Pakistan are flooding into India, and where India and Pakistan are then going to war. Mr. Pirzada can get no word from his family back in East Pakistan—his wife and seven daughters. He doesn't know if they have been forced to flee the country, or even if they are still alive. He lives in that world, the world where his family lives, and every night as they watch the war on television, Lilia's family lives in that world too. But Lilia lives much of her life in a world where neither of these other worlds exists, an American world of Halloween and history lessons about the American Revolutionary War and unhyphenated American friends whose parents don't watch the news or think much about the world outside their own neighborhood.

The plot of the story is slim because the meaning of the story resides in its images and emblems, not in its story line. Lilia comes to like Mr. Pirzada very much—indeed, he becomes like a favorite uncle, although in this case, he is a favorite uncle that is soon to disappear from her life forever. She becomes increasingly concerned about Mr. Pirzada's family back in Dacca, about little girls just like herself who might be homeless—or dead. And so she performs a magic ritual. Every night, she eats a piece of Mr. Pirzada's candy and says a prayer for the safety of his family, being careful not to brush her teeth afterward for fear that this will brush away the prayer as well. She hasn't been taught any prayers, so this ritual is her own invention. The plot comes to its climax on Halloween when Lilia goes off into the American world of make believe scariness to trick-or-treat with her friend Dora, and India declares war on Pakistan. When Lilia comes home,

> I opened the door, expecting the three of them to be standing in the foyer, waiting to receive me and to grieve for our ruined pumpkin, but there was no one. In the living room Mr. Pirzada, my father, and mother were sitting side by side on the sofa. The television was turned off, and Mr. Pirzada had his head in his hands.
>
> (Lahiri 40)

But in fact, there has been no tragedy, at least not for Mr. Pirzada. Lilia continues with her candy-coated prayers, adding the Halloween haul to her store, Mr. Pirzada goes back to what is now Bangladesh, and the semester ends with Lilia's family going off to see friends over the Christmas break. Months later, the family gets a thank-you letter from Mr. Pirzada, telling them that his family is safe, that they had fled to a family estate in the countryside when the fighting began, and that they are now happily reunited. He thanks them profusely for their kindness, understanding, and generosity, and they never hear from him again. Lilia, unsure about what to do now with her carefully saved hoard of candy, finally throws it away.

The meaning of the story, however, comes not from the linear plot, but from the images and emblems of the meaningful moments in which Lilia's separate worlds touch in ways that only she can notice and sometimes only the reader can understand. The story is not a film depicting an unrolling of events, but a collage of snapshots which explores the meaning of being an American and a person outside America at the same time, of the multiple mental and physical places coexisting at the same instant. Sometimes these snapshots are simple and fairly obvious, as when Lilia notes that Mr. Pirzada keeps a second watch set on Dacca time so he will al-

ways know what time it is at home, and she realizes that it is that time in which he truly lives. It is almost as if a shadow Mr. Pirzada is trapped there in New England, while the true Mr. Pirzada goes about his life in East Pakistan.

This image, which occurs early in the story, creates a context for the more complex encounters with other worlds later when Lilia's American world runs smack against her Indian world without even realizing that it is there. Only Lilia sees the collision, which she is too young to comprehend fully and so presents without comment. She and her friend Dora are sent to the library to do a book report about the American Revolutionary War. While in the library, Lilia sees a book about Pakistan, and remembering what her parents have told her about Mr. Pirzada's not being an Indian "any more" but a Pakistani, she is curious about this country which, her parents tell her, make Mr. Pirzada different from them in ways that she can't see. However, as she is leafing through the book, her teacher returns and reprimands her for wasting time.

> She glanced at the cover, then at me.
>
> "Is this book part of your report, Lilia?"
>
> "No, Mrs. Kenyon."
>
> "Then I see no reason to consult it," she said, replacing it in the slim gap on the shelf. "Do you?"
>
> (33)

Mrs. Kenyon apparently can't understand why a child whose parents are Indian might want to read about the subcontinent rather than America, probably because she cannot imagine a history other than the American history she was taught and is now teaching. The War of Independence is the war that took place in America two hundred years earlier, not the war then going on between East and West Pakistan. Presumably, Mrs. Kenyon doesn't mean to be unkind or to stifle Lilia's intellectual curiosity. To her, the world outside America simply doesn't exist, and Lilia is just playing when she is supposed to be working. The world in which Lilia lives every night when she watches the news with her parents is invisible to the people like Mrs. Kenyon who inhabit her school day world. In fact, Lahiri's description of the American television news coverage of the Indian-Pakistani War is a fictive device rather than verisimilitude. From what I remember of the American news in 1971, it was devoted almost exclusively to that other cruel and bloody war, the war in Vietnam. The war on the subcontinent had even less of an American reality in "real" life than it does in Lahiri's story—which makes the fictive insights of the story even more "true." To live in America, Lilia has to learn to negotiate her way through worlds that are invisible to the very adults who should be guiding her. At ten, she is on her own in deciphering the meaning of her encounters and learning how to respond appropriately to differing assumptions about the world.

Even her parents can't give her much formal guidance in the American world because they don't seem to live in America but in their own private India, an American India which they have recreated in their own image as a place of safety, plenty, and tolerance. Lilia's father is distressed that Lilia doesn't know about the partition of India, apparently unaware that American schools teach very little modern world history. Lilia's mother can only define America in terms of its contrast to India. In her America, there are "no rationing, no curfews, no riots" (26), and she finds her American coworkers at the bank curious in their customs and eating habits. Of course, in the real America of 1971, as opposed to the private American India in which the family lives, there were indeed riots and violence, as Black ghettoes burned, police beat anti-war protesters, and students took over buildings on American college campuses. The family is oblivious of all this.

But their American India is a place where a non-Muslim family (since they are non-religious, the family's religious background is unclear) can invite a Muslim like Mr. Pirzada without a second thought because in their world religious differences no longer matter. Religion is no longer identity to them; what matters is that they share a culture with him that they do not with their American neighbors and colleagues. When I taught the story to Indian and Arab students at the American University of Sharjah in the United Arab Emirates, however, the family's religion was very important to these students, and some students suggested that the fact that the family went away to spend Christmas with friends must mean that the family was Christian. It seems to me that Lahiri deliberately left the family's religious affiliation vague in order to emphasize the idea that without any formal religious instruction (and my Hindu, Christian, and Muslim students were equally scandalized that Lilia hadn't been taught any prayers) Lilia has found within herself the sort of disinterested compassion for others central to the spirit of many religions. Presumably she has learned some of this compassion from the example of her parents. Many of my students were astonished that a non-Muslim family would treat a Muslim with such hospitality and thought that Lilia's parents were incredibly kindhearted and tolerant people. In the world outside Lilia's family, religion still matters a great deal, but inside, the family's beautifully hybrid utopia is nurturing a child who is spiritually alive without being formally religious.

In the American world of the story, this private world stops at their doorstep, and it is in the real America that Lilia must live, an America that is not quite as safe as her parents imagine and in which Lilia faces difficulties

that they do not know about. And yet these very difficulties may have the effect of giving Lilia a maturity and depth that children raised monoculturally do not have. Like monoculture in farming, social monoculture seems to be depleting, but nevertheless its practitioners adhere to it because it is what they know. Thus, the worlds outside the family want to label Lilia. To Mrs. Kenyon, Lilia is too "American" to need to know anything about any history other than America's, but when Lilia goes trick-or-treating, several neighbors jokingly remark that they have never seen an Indian witch before. Why isn't she an American to other Americans? My students wanted to know. After all, she was born and raised in the United States, she speaks American English, she goes to American schools, and she has never even been to India. Probably for the rest of her life, Lilia would be an American to some Americans but an Indian to others, no matter how she chose to define herself. If religion isn't necessarily an identity in the American world, nationality and ethnicity are. Yet Lilia does not seem distressed by these thoughtless labels, perhaps because she is in the process of forging for herself an identity that transcends the identities the outside worlds seek to project onto her. She is not monocultural, and she moves through these curious worlds with the self-possession of Alice in Wonderland.

When Lilia's separate and mutually invisible worlds bump into each other, the result is not conflict but understanding, not between the people of those worlds, who remain ignorant of one another, but within the reader and often within Lilia herself. When Lilia and Dora go trick-or-treating, Mr. Pirzada offers to go with them to make sure that they are safe, although the only danger he can imagine is that they might get lost.

> "Why did that man want to come with us?" Dora asked.
>
> "His daughters are missing." As soon as I said it, I wished I had not. I felt that my saying it made it true, that Mr. Pirzada's daughters really were missing, and that he would never see them again.
>
> "You mean they were kidnapped?" Dora continued. "From a park or something?"
>
> "I don't mean they were missing. I meant he misses them. They live in a different country, and he hasn't seen them for awhile, that's all."
>
> (39)

This image, more complex than the others, is a miniature portrait of the mutual incomprehension of the inhabitants of the worlds through which Lilia moves. Living exclusively in an American world, Dora can't imagine a world in which children could be war refugees, in which the infrastructure has been so destroyed that desperate parents can't find out if their children are safe, or in which the organized violence of war targets the innocent and vulnerable. It is difficult for her to understand why a family friend would offer to go trick-or-treating with other people's children, as Mr. Pirzada does in Lilia's family world. However, she can imagine a world of random violence in which children can be kidnapped from parks because it is the America she lives in. In both these American and outside worlds, "missing" has a different but equally sinister meaning, a meaning which Lilia can only try to negate by transforming it into the innocuous "misses," restoring it to the safety of the world of her home. And yet both these ideas, that Mr. Pirzada is concerned about Lilia because his children are missing, and that he showers attention and candy on Lilia because he misses his own little girls, are amazingly mature insights for a ten-year-old to whom adults would more usually seem to be inscrutable authorities without motives or vulnerabilities. In fact, she has a kind of compassion rare even in adults: the ability to feel concern and sympathy for someone who is facing problems she has never faced herself. (She later says that she never "knew what it meant to miss someone . . . just as he had missed his wife and daughters for so many months" (42) until she realized that she would never see Mr. Pirzada again.) In addition, Lilia wishes to protect Mr. Pirzada's family by not putting into words the idea that they are in real danger, even though her white lie isolates her from her playmate. It seems that the very process of negotiating such conflicting worlds on her own has sensitized her and made her more thoughtful and perceptive than a child raised in one culture only. Far from being the "ABCD" (American-born confused Desi) of the Indian stereotype, Lilia has an understanding of herself and her relationships to others that goes far beyond labels. Because of this knowledge, she has an opportunity to become a more complete person than the people around her who know one world only.

In the story's conclusion, the three worlds touch again in moments that are the most ambiguous in the story. First, Mr. Pirzada writes the family a thank-you letter. Earlier in the story, Mr. Pirzada had made fun of the American verbal tic of thanking everyone for everything. "'What is this 'Thank you'? The lady at the bank thanks me, the cashier in the shop thanks me, the librarian thanks me when I return an overdue book'" (29). And yet when he returns home, he realizes what an extraordinary thing Lilia's parents have done in treating a stranger of another religion as a member of their family—although actually their generosity of spirit goes beyond that, since family members are bound together by mutual obligations and self-interest as well as love, whereas Lilia's parents have acted without any expectation of repayment or even of a continued relationship. Significantly, Lilia's parents always address him by his title, never by his first name, nor do they expect Lilia to call him "uncle." The relationship remains slightly formal, and always respectful of his separateness from them. In the letter, he adds "that although he now un-

derstands the meaning of the words 'Thank you,' they were still not adequate to express his gratitude" (42). He, it seems, has been changed and deepened by his experience of another world, in this case, the hybrid world of Lilia's family.

And as for Lilia herself, why does she throw the candy away in the end? The ending is open to several interpretations, not necessarily any more mutually exclusive than her many worlds. One can say that Lilia can throw the candy away because it is no longer needed, not as a means of ensuring the safety of Mr. Pirzada's family or even as memento of Mr. Pirzada himself because, as Lilia seems to understand and accept, he is now back where he belongs and will not be a part of her world except as a memory. She also may throw the candy away because she is "sweet" enough already. She has become a compassionate person who can imagine herself in other people's conditions and want desperately to help them. The candy has been a vehicle of the compassion that Lilia can only express in secret, and now that ability to feel compassion is a part of who she is. Whether she is Indian or American or Indian-American or Hindu or Christian doesn't matter; she has become a generous-spirited person who resists labels. She has learned to become this not because her parents have consciously taught how to do this or guided her through her worlds, but in part because her awareness of the simultaneous existence of these different systems of thinking has expanded her knowledge of what it means to be human. Lilia's growth as she passes through her mutually invisible worlds has not just been intellectual but also spiritual as she learns to respect humanity and to feel concern for people whom her various worlds would label as different from her.

And yet this reading, taken alone, belies the sense of loss at the end of the story. Lilia has become a compassionate person, but her compassion is both secret and a source of pain. She misses Mr. Pirzada. In throwing the candy away, she is also trying to throw away feelings that now have no object. The story is about spiritual growth, but it does not minimize the degree to which the process is also painful and sometimes lonely.

This slightly melancholy tone and Lilia's essential aloneness in facing her various worlds put the story in the tradition of much of American short-story writing, from Hawthorne's spiritually isolated Puritans to Sherwood Anderson's small town grotesques and the haunted and inarticulate protagonists of Raymond Carver. This is part of why the story, and indeed all of Lahiri's work, resonates with American readers. This motif of loneliness is part of what makes the collection feel familiar to American readers. The collection seems to be both within the American literary tradition and outside it, just as the characters (like Lilia) are both Americans and outsiders in America.

One of the most obvious reasons that the stories interest American readers (according to *The Chronicle of Higher Education,* Lahiri's collection is the most popular book on American college campuses) is the way in which it reveals monocultural Americans' limitations. The American characters—not just Mrs. Kenyon, Dora, Dora's parents, and the neighbors in **"When Mr. Pirzada Came to Dine,"** but the non-bicultural Americans in the entire collection—are all well-meaning enough, but annoyingly and embarrassingly ignorant of the world outside the United States and of how they look to the educated foreign-born. Lahiri makes her American readers realize their own provinciality, but she does so without satire; indeed, she depicts the narrowness without comment, either authorial or through the consciousness of the characters.

But the story and the collection have an impact that goes far beyond this in the ways in which they expand the themes and motifs of mainstream American literature, minority American literature, and post-colonial literature. This story, and the collection as a whole, is a new kind of hybrid composed of literary trends that are often at odds with one another.

Much of the classic American literary fiction of the 19th and 20th centuries (from *Huckleberry Finn* to *Catcher in the Rye* and *The Member of the Wedding* and *Housekeeping*) focuses on an individual, often a child or adolescent, trying to develop a system of moral values without the help of either trustworthy conventional morals or outside guidance—no one can tell these children how they should act. The characters are both lonely and alone. Lilia too is alone—but her parents do provide trustworthy models. Moreover, unlike Lahiri, other American authors, fearful of didacticism, frequently do not go beyond the adolescent sensibility to show the character's development of meaningful adult values. For the best American writers, this is tragic; the tragedy is that the past is gone forever without having taught Americans what they needed to know about themselves. This past is often a dangerously mythic Eden, a falsely remembered childhood to which the characters need to return because something went wrong in the process of becoming an adult, either personally (*You Can't Go Home Again*) or nationally (*Beloved*). For less gifted American writers, the protagonist as a lonely outsider with a skeptical adolescent's attitude toward authority has become a stock character, a tradition that may have been romanticized too much and examined too little. Lahiri's fiction, with her characters who are not just alienated but literal aliens, who face unpredictable problems and mature as they confront these problems, or whose immaturity is never romanticized, makes us see beyond this self-indulgent formula.

Growth is also central to the other stories in ***The Interpreter of Maladies.*** Unlike the experiences depicted in much of traditional American fiction, it is the contact with what is different that causes Lahiri's characters to mature—including the differences in personality and values between her married couples who imagine their spouses to be like themselves and find, sometimes too late to save the marriage, that marriage entails an accommodation of differentness (**"A Temporary Matter," "This Blessed House"**). Nor is this experience limited to her Indian-American characters. In other stories in the collection, such as **"Sexy"** and **"Mrs. Sen,"** American characters can learn about themselves and create a richer system of values as a result of encountering the other, foreign customs and ways of thinking of the Indian characters—sometimes without even fully realizing what they have come to understand or the opportunity they have missed. And yet the reader does understand how they have grown or what they have missed.

However, Lahiri does not oversimplify the difficulty of living in several worlds at once. In Lahiri's world, as in life, becoming bicultural is not the inevitable result of encountering values and assumptions different from one's own. Confronted with the existence of another culture, many people prefer to become homocultural, associating only with people from their own cultures (as many expatriates do), or schizocultural, adopting the manners of whatever culture they find themselves in without considering the values those manners imply. Being bicultural requires both intelligence and a capacity for empathy, but the result can be intellectual and emotional maturity. The conditions are right for such growth, if the characters have the capacity to make use of this opportunity.

*The Interpreter of Maladies* is unlike much of Asian American fiction. Instead of showing the problems of growing up with the knowledge of two different sets of values and of being perceived as foreign by one's countrymen, as so many minority American writers do, Lahiri depicts being bicultural as a blessing—a mixed blessing, assuredly, but a blessing. Moreover, when her Indian-American characters travel to India, as in the title story **"The Interpreter of Maladies,"** they do not discover a new cultural identity, for such things are not picked up in passing, like curios; instead, the readers sometimes discover the characters' (and perhaps their own) insensitivity and shallowness. This knowledge can be a starting point.

In contrast to American literatures, post-colonial literature (*Things Fall Apart, The God of Small Things*) has tended to depict characters struggling against stifling or hypocritical traditions at the same time that they must contend with an entirely different set of imposed false values that come from the West—too many people are telling them how they should act rather than too few. Moreover, for the post-colonial world, the tragedy is not that the past is lost forever, but that no one can escape the past (consider Mahfouz's *Cairo Trilogy,* for instance, where each generation repeats the mistakes of the previous one). *The Interpreter of Maladies* goes beyond post-colonial fiction just as it goes beyond traditional mainstream American fiction and hyphenated American fiction. In Lahiri's world, the past is not a revenge tragedy that will never play itself out. Mr. Pirzada can go back home, to his own life and his own past, and Lilia can throw away the past like stale candy because she has already absorbed and digested what it has to give her. Lahiri has done the same with a series of literary formulas.

### Works Cited

Lahiri, Jhumpa. "When Mr. Pirzada Came to Dine." *The Interpreter of Maladies.* Boston: Houghton Mifflin, 1999.

Rushdie, Salman. "Damme, This Is the Oriental Scene for You!" *The New Yorker* 23-30 June 1997: 50-59.

"What They're Reading on College Campuses." *The Chronicle of Higher Education* 2 Feb. 2001: A9.

## Paul Brians (essay date 2003)

SOURCE: Brians, Paul. "Jhumpa Lahiri: *Interpreter of Maladies* (2000)." In *Modern South Asian Literature in English,* pp. 195-204. Westport, Conn.: Greenwood Press, 2003.

[*In the following essay, Brians discusses the stories that comprise* The Interpreter of Maladies *and explains that their theme is not so much the problems of immigrants as it is miscommunication between couples.*]

In recent times the literary world has become used to brilliant new writers emerging from South Asia. But when a book by a previously little-known woman author won the prestigious Pulitzer Prize for best American work of fiction in 2000, it was sensational news, partly because Jhumpa Lahiri's *Interpreter of Maladies* was a collection of short stories in an age when the novel is dominant. Two of the stories had appeared previously in the premier American outlet for short fiction, *The New Yorker,* and six others in less widely read periodicals; but to most reviewers and readers her brilliant writing came as a complete surprise. The book earned other major honors as well, including the PEN/ Hemingway Award and an award from the American Academy of Arts and Letters.

Lahiri was born in London in 1967 to Bengali immigrant parents from Calcutta. Her father is a librarian at the University of Rhode Island, and her mother a teacher who earned an MA in Bengali literature. The family had moved to the little town of South Kingston, Rhode Island, when she was three, so she has spent most of her life as an American and became a U.S. citizen at age eighteen, although from childhood on she has made many long visits to India. Some Indian critics have criticized Lahiri as an "outsider," but considerable praise for her work has also appeared in the South Asian press. So strong has the interest in her writing been in India that translations have been commissioned into Bengali, Hindi, and Marathi.

She studied English literature at Barnard College in New York City, and then at Boston University earned three master's degrees (in English, creative writing, and comparative literature and the arts), capping her academic career with a Ph.D. in Renaissance studies. Such a course of study would normally be a prelude to a career of teaching about literature, but Lahiri realized that her true love was creating literature. Indeed, she had been writing fiction steadily since the age of seven; her most influential educational experience was a two-year fellowship in writing at the Fine Arts Work Center in Provincetown, Massachusetts; and her only academic appointments have been in creative writing, at Boston University and the Rhode Island School of Design. In January 2001 Lahiri married Alberto Vourvoulias-Bush, deputy editor of *Time Latin America,* in a traditional Bengali ceremony in Calcutta. They now reside in New York City. She published a novel, *The Namesake,* to general acclaim in 2003, too late for inclusion here.

Lahiri has been hailed as an outstanding member of a post-Rushdie generation of Indian writers who have turned their backs on magical realism and other experiments to write well-crafted traditional realist fiction. Her stories belong to the long tradition of delicate character sketches, avoiding sensational effects and overly clever endings. Although her work has often been described as focusing on the problems of immigrants—and it is true that such characters dominate her writing—her real subject is miscommunication. The relationships in her stories are a series of missed connections.

The first story in the collection, **"A Temporary Matter"** (originally published Apr. 20, 1998, in *The New Yorker* as **"A Temporary Prayer: What Happens When the Lights Go Out"**), is a fine example. A husband and wife who have drifted apart in the wake of the death of their child seem to find intimacy during a series of planned power outages, but the conclusion reveals that the wife is experiencing their relationship very differently from her husband.

Women sometimes criticize men for being so emotionally insensitive as to be unaware that their wives are drifting away until the eve of their departure. It is true that Shukumar, the husband, has not made much of an effort to penetrate his wife Shoba's grief. Like many married male students, he is supported by his wife's work, and it was his academic conference that prevented him from being with her when the stillbirth occurred.

But this is no anti-male tract. He hadn't wanted to go to the conference: she had insisted. He clearly cares for her and worries about her. Since she has become depressed, he has taken over the cooking, and enjoys it. Earlier in their marriage, she was the organized, disciplined one while he drifted. Now he keeps the household running. Shoba is a very private person, and at the very least may be said to send mixed signals to her husband. Lahiri doesn't seek to assess blame, merely to portray the way in which a marriage stricken by the death of a child may collapse as grief drives the couple apart.

As the narrator explains, power outages (called "load sheddings") are commonplace in India. It perhaps strains credibility that an American power company would shut off electricity for five nights running to repair local line damage, but if the reader accepts this premise, it is easy to be moved by the intimacy that blooms in the dark as the two begin to tell each other their secrets. These exchanges are full of subtle details, like the fact that he notes her fading beauty just before he tells her how he first realized they would marry.

From Shoba's perspective she is delicately, even affectionately, disentangling herself from Shukumar, but we experience the process from his point of view, which is very different. When he is stunned by her final declaration, he flings out the most hurtful secret he can think of: he had held and seen the infant. It is not clear whether Shoba had also seen him before falling asleep, although that seems likely. It may be that her husband's absence during this crisis marked him irrevocably in her mind as an outsider (her mother certainly seems to regard the incident that way).

Although he means to assert himself and perhaps hurt her by describing the dead child, his confession seems to bring them together in sorrow in a way that does not suggest their marriage can be saved, but that they now understand each other better. Maturity and sensitivity cannot necessarily heal all wounds. As another couple walks arm in arm past their window, they sit together for the last time, weeping. Like the power outage, both their intimacy and the marriage are "temporary matters." The distinguished Indian director Mira Nair (*Monsoon Wedding*) announced a plan to make this story into a film for PBS, but it is not clear whether that project is still under development.

**"When Mr. Pirzada Came to Dine"** (first published in 1999 in *The Louisville Review*) is set in 1971, at the height of the crisis that resulted in the secession of Bangladesh from Pakistan, with support from India. The British and American news was full of stories of starving refugees from the brutal assaults of the Pakistani forces ordered by General Yahyah Khan on the Bengalis in Pakistan's Eastern Wing. Although Lilia, the narrator of this story, is a little older than Lahiri herself would have been at the time, she may well have experienced the news in the same distanced, confused way.

The first sentence of the story underlines the irony of Mr. Pirzada coming to feast on Indian food at the home of fellow Bengalis and handing out sweets while agonizing over the dangers his wife and seven daughters are facing at home. He can express his parental affection only for this substitute child. Lilia is old enough to understand something of what is going on, but to her Mr. Pirzada is principally a source of candy. For the adults, his visits are a mirror of the growing alliance between Bengali Indians and Pakistanis in their homeland. In another ironic contrast, Lilia is studying the American Revolution in a typically celebratory way while she witnesses the all too vivid tragedy of another nation being born on the news that is not being studied at school—indeed, her teacher rebukes her for reading about Pakistan.

At first, this is another story of misunderstandings and miscommunications, as Lilia reveals her ignorance of the matters that most concern Mr. Pirzada and her parents. But it is also a very subtle coming of age story, in which her growing understanding of the tragedy in South Asia finally makes her reluctant to eat their guest's sweets. She is no longer the innocent, pampered object of affection, but an aware participant in the ongoing history of her parents' homeland.

The book's title story, **"Interpreter of Maladies"** (first published 1998 in *Agni Review*), resembles in plot the episode in Narayan's *Guide* in which a tour guide is drawn to the Westernized wife of an Indian traveler; but the encounter here is much more ambiguous, and the outcome far more unexpected. Lahiri has said that the phrase "interpreter of maladies" came to her when she encountered a man who made a living translating Russian for immigrants trying to explain their ailments to a non-Russian-speaking doctor.

She tried for years to work it into a story, and finally succeeded by transplanting the interpreter to India and giving the phrase a metaphorical twist. Mrs. Das chooses Mr. Kapasi to hear her confession because she thinks of him as a professional listener-to-troubles; but he is startled to find himself in this unwelcome role because he has been dreaming instead of himself as her potential lover. Like **"A Temporary Matter,"** this is a story of two people crossing at an angle through each other's lives, neither satisfied with the response of the other.

The fact that Mr. and Mrs. Das were born and raised in America, where women are used to a good deal of independence and privacy, makes her affair more credible than if she had been a native-born resident of India. But this story is not ultimately about South Asians living abroad or in exile. Lahiri skillfully builds the tension as we gradually realize how much Mr. Kapasi desires Mrs. Das, and how much he has let his fantasies carry him away in dreams of a romantic future. Shocked at her heartless confession, he somewhat hypocritically rebukes her, considering that he has just been dreaming of seducing her himself. Yet he is clearly also aware of her suffering, realizing that she has "fallen out of love with life."

The final scene is typical of Lahiri's subtle ambiguity: Mr. Kapasi, who has lost his own child, watches the unloving mother brushing her rescued son's hair while the slip of paper that once promised him so much flutters away in the wind. No one is simple in this story, which is a mark of Lahiri's mastery.

**"A Real Durwan"** is the first story in this volume entirely about Indians living in India. A *durwan* is someone who watches over a building, a caretaker who guards the entrance against intruders and keeps track of the residents' comings and goings. Some Indian readers have criticized this story as distorting Indian reality. Lahiri tells amusingly of having been sternly rebuked by an Indian for suggesting that Calcutta apartment buildings ever lack sinks, when in her own grandparents' building where she had just been before writing the story in 1992, there were only plastic buckets on each landing.

The story is not really about the inadequacies of Calcutta plumbing, but more about the casual cruelty the poor can be subjected to in any culture. Even more important, it is a character sketch of the destitute old woman called "Boori Ma," reportedly based on a old woman who lived in the house of Lahiri's uncle and aunt in Calcutta. Although she is welcome at first, the kindliness of the apartment dwellers in her building evaporates when their new sink is stolen, and they blame her for not being "a real durwan," even though she has suffered a theft of her own far more disastrous, considering her poverty. Boori Ma is not portrayed as a particularly sympathetic victim; it is never quite clear whether she is lying about having come from a wealthy *zamindar* (landowning) family. Clearly she greatly resents her fall in the world to the point that she cannot qualify even as a durwan. Lacking wealth and power, she also lacks the humility and submissiveness that might appeal to well-off people in a poor woman, and that is her downfall.

**"Sexy"** (originally published in *The New Yorker*, Dec. 28, 1999) is another story of three different perspectives: that of Miranda, a twenty-two-year-old woman

having an affair with a married Indian man; that of the wife of such a man (via her cousin Laxmi); and that of an innocent young boy (Laxmi's son). Like most of Lahiri's stories, the presentation is complex and subtle. We learn little of Miranda's inner thoughts; in fact, we may suspect that she avoids thinking clearly about the implications of the affair she has fallen into. Lahiri introduces the topic of infidelity by telling us first how badly Laxmi's cousin and son have been hurt by the husband's affair. The narrative implies that this story leads Miranda to think about her own affair with Dev, but that she resists thinking about it as harmful. She is still enjoying the bliss of a budding relationship. She is young enough to find it difficult to identify with a married woman's problems; she belongs to the generation from which mistresses are commonly chosen.

Her name suggests wonderment at the discovery of the new, which is associated with Shakespeare's Miranda in *The Tempest,* but Dev seeks to make her a naturalized Indian by associating her name with "Mira." She is charmed by her older lover's romantic gestures, so unlike the clumsiness of previous younger boyfriends. This is her first true love affair. In contrast, for Dev she is simply "the first woman I've known with legs this long," which implies he's had the opportunity to study the anatomy of a substantial number of women. His whispered message in the mapparium that gives the story its title thrills her, but it also clearly demonstrates the limits of his interest in her: she's sexy.

The story of their continuing affair is counterpointed against the unfolding disaster of the cousin's marriage. Gradually Dev seems to take her more for granted, make fewer romantic gestures, especially after his wife has returned to town. This behavior makes the reader wonder whether he has just been seeking some diversion in his wife's absence rather than seeking a substitute for her.

But more threatening is the fact that Dev says his wife looks like the famously beautiful Bollywood actress Madhuri Dixit (b. 1967), famous in part, incidentally, for her long legs. The story does not explicitly articulate the worry and jealousy Miranda feels, but her quest for a picture of the actress in the Indian grocery store reveals that she cannot take it for granted Dev will ultimately choose her over his wife. The fact that she can't even correctly spell the name of this wildly popular Indian star underlines the fact that she's only playing on the fringes of a world she knows little of.

The fact that Miranda's only other association with Indian people involves the fearsome goddess Kali may be meant to suggest potential vengefulness: Kali is a fierce warrior, slayer of demons, bedecked with the heads and limbs of her victims. Another threatening image is the "too spicy" Hot Mix, which implies that she may not have what it takes to hang on to Dev.

Thus far Miranda has been able to cling to her attachment to Dev successfully, despite the discouraging stories she is hearing from Laxmi. But her encounter with Rohin finally causes her to face the harm she is doing by continuing her affair. A simpler story would simply present Rohin as a brokenhearted damaged child, but Lahiri does something considerably more complex. When the boy says to Miranda "you're sexy," he draws a clear connection between his father's behavior and Dev's that is powerful precisely because is so young and naïve that he doesn't even realize she will feel stung by his words. He has arrived at his childish definition of "sexy" by deducing its meaning based on his father's case: "sexy means loving someone you don't know." Without meaning to, he has revealed to Miranda what she should have known all along: Dev doesn't love her, he just finds her sexy.

Lahiri again avoids the obvious by choosing not to end the story with a tumultuous confrontation between the two lovers or with Miranda experiencing a dramatic change of heart. Even now, she yearns for Dev and would like to prolong the affair. This is much truer to most people's lived experience than a sudden and dramatic conversion. It is not so easy to disentangle oneself from a love affair, even when the basis of that love affair is purely sexual. It is too easy to speak dismissively of "mere" sex; Miranda shows us how powerful it can be, and she is not even shown as repentant. But the driving force of the relationship, the belief that she was something truly special for Dev, has been drained away. Yes, Miranda is sexy, but so is Dev's wife, and the mistress of Rohin's father—and in the end that's not enough to sustain the relationship. She's left with her memories—and with the emptiness of the sky over Boston.

**"Mrs. Sen's"** (first published 1999 in *Salamander*) is the story of an unhappy immigrant. Mrs. Sen is not just constitutionally timid; she is terribly homesick. The United States is famously a country dominated by individualists, people eager to break out of the shackles of identity forged in small hometowns and create new identities in the anonymity of the big city. Sons and daughters who remain at home after they have turned adult are frowned on as failures. In countries like India, the successful family tends to be regarded as one that stays together, in which everyone knows what everyone else is up to, and in which the rewards of individualism are sacrificed for the rewards of *belonging*. Mrs. Sen yearns for a culture in which she would be cared for simply because of who she is.

She isn't comfortable in a country where it's routine for a mother to hire someone to care for her child while she works, even though that pattern provides her with a job she seems genuinely to enjoy. She's depressed to be living in a place where the neighbors call you up only to complain about the noise you're making. She lacks the drive for independence that would motivate her to master the art of driving, content to have her husband pick up the fresh fish she so longs for. Unfortunately, he does not feel the same. He's just the sort of immigrant that has built America: eager to move on, impatient with tradition, bent on change.

What Lahiri accomplishes in this story is to show us that Mrs. Sen's point of view has a good deal to be said for it. Good seafood and the intimacy of family connections are worth having; and it is not clear that the independence Eliot gets by becoming a latchkey child at the age of eleven is superior. But the story is not trying to establish that one pattern is good, the other bad. It simply portrays two characters crossing paths, headed in opposite directions, Eliot becoming more typically American, and Mrs. Sen more typically Indian.

We never learn whether Eliot's mother is a divorcee, a widow, or simply a single mother. A father doesn't feature in his world. Lahiri is particularly good at portraying the point of view of children. Much of what Mrs. Sen says goes over Eliot's head. He has no way of understanding a great deal about India, including the fact that the bald man at a spinning wheel on the stamps Mrs. Sen receives is Mahatma Gandhi, who vigorously promoted the production of homemade cloth to help Indians break free of the dominance of imported English goods. It would be unrealistic to expect him to have arrived at any deep insights about this intercultural encounter, but we can guess that some day he will look back on this experience with deeper understanding and an appreciation for another way of life.

**"This Blessed House"** (first published in *Epoch,* 1999) is another story of a mismatched couple drifting past each other, but with a comic undertone. We can tell they are not on the same wavelength when Sanjeev reads how Mahler expressed his love for his wife in what must be the fourth movement of his Symphony no. 5 and Twinkle's response is to flush the toilet and pronounce the music boring.

Twinkle is delighted by the array of Christian artifacts she finds in the couple's new home, not because she is particularly religious, but because they amuse her. When her husband repeatedly insists "but we are not Christian," she dismissively waves aside his objections. Lahiri does not draw the parallel, but it is difficult not to be reminded of Westerners who collect Hindu images, buy lunch boxes with images of Kali or Ganesh on them because they find them exotic and entertaining, with no sense of the religious sentiments attached to them by believers.

There is nothing uniquely Indian about this story. True, their marriage was an arranged one, but they had a Western-style courtship as well, in which they might have been expected to learn to know each other better. Yet it is commonplace for couples everywhere to discover after marriage that they have married strangers with tastes and habits that are distinctly not shared. But Sanjeev's conservatism never has a chance against her exuberance.

It would be a mistake to regard Twinkle, despite her frivolous nickname, as merely childish. She is writing a thesis on an obscure Irish poet for a graduate degree at Stanford, likes depressing German films, has sophisticated taste in music, and is capable of inventing a tasty fish dish, although she's a sloppy housekeeper. Her witticism about the "virgin on the half shell" is a clever reference to the traditional image—borrowed from pagan images of Venus rising from the sea—of Mary standing on a scallop shell. "Oysters on the half shell" is a traditional way of serving this seafood raw, and Lahiri probably got the idea for this joke from a Kurt Vonnegut-inspired novel called *Venus on the Half-Shell.*

Her friends appreciate her sense of play and find her charming; it is Sanjeev who is the odd man out in this setting. He is not sure he loves her and not sure she loves him; but by the end of the story it is clear that she is the one whose tastes will prevail in their home. She dances off barefoot at the end of the story while he lumbers reluctantly along under the weight of the silver statue of Christ that delights her, doomed to live under its gaze for the rest of his days—or at least for the rest of their marriage.

**"The Treatment of Bibi Halder"** (originally published in *Story Quarterly* 30, in 1994) resembles **"A Real Durwan"** in being the story of an unfortunate woman treated badly by those around her. It should not be assumed that Lahiri means to imply that Indians are particularly heartless: consider how family supportiveness is emphasized in **"Mrs. Sen's."** But not every family is a loving one, and Bibi's parents' treatment of their epileptic daughter is particularly heartless in ways that can be found in any culture.

Many societies have believed that a woman who lacks a man may fall ill as a result. Shakespeare's generation spoke of "green-sickness" as the malady afflicting young women ripe for marriage, which could be cured by a fulfilling wedding night and ensuing love life. Sigmund Freud argued that unsatisfied suppressed yearnings for sex caused the neuroses of many of his women patients, with little more evidence than the Elizabethans had.

This early story lacks the subtlety and complexity of Lahiri's best work. She seems to share the amusement of the neighbors at the afflicted girl's fantasies of marriage, the unflattering matrimonial ad her father places for her is played for laughs, and her eventual "cure" is almost a joke.

The volume's moving concluding story, **"The Third and Final Continent,"** is more typical of Lahiri at her best and indeed one of her most admired works. Traces of the story of Lahiri's parents appear in this tale. Mukesh, like the author's father, is an immigrant to England from Calcutta who moves on to the United States where he becomes a librarian at a prominent New England university (North America being, of course, the "final continent").

In this story two distant relationships develop warmth: The narrator's growing affection for the senile and irritable Mrs. Croft and his growing affection for his wife. If the latter illustrates an Indian tradition in which the partners in an arranged marriage are expected to gradually fall in love after the wedding rather than before, his relationship with Mrs. Croft reflects much more universal patterns. She does try to assert American supremacy by forcing him to celebrate the American landing on the moon, but she seems otherwise welcoming of her South Asian border. Her prejudices are not racial or nationalistic, but academic: she rents only to "boys" from the prestigious schools of Harvard or the Massachusetts Institute of Technology ("Tech"). Mukesh, with his training at the famous London School of Economics (LSE), fits in nicely.

Their relationship cannot be called an intimate one: she reigns haughtily from her centenarian perch of superiority without the slightest comprehension of her tenant, not even grasping he is married. The antiquated prudery with which she forbids her aged daughter from visiting with Mukesh in his room is comic. Even her pride in asserting that an American flag stands on the moon is rendered somewhat amusing by Sanjeev's awareness that the flag has in fact toppled over.

Yet he grows to care for this irascible old woman, and when his wife arrives to join him, he feels he must present her to his former landlady. She pronounces Mala, who had had difficulty attracting suitors in India because of her dark skin, "a perfect lady." His days with Mrs. Croft become a family legend, and her appreciation of his wife seems to be echoed in Sanjeev's growing affection for her. After so many stories of couples drifting apart, it is comforting to see that the volume, which appeared as the author was planning her own wedding, concludes with a marriage that—after a very unpromising beginning—ends in mutual love and affection.

*Selected Bibliography*

Aguilar, Arun. "One on One with Jhumpa Lahiri." *PIF* 28 (1 Sept. 1999). <http://www.pifmagazine.com/vol28/i_agui.shtml>.

A particularly interesting interview with Lahiri.

Bushi, R. "Death in the Hills: False Reality and Realisation in 'Interpreter of Maladies.'" (2001). <http://members.lycos.co.uk/thaz/RedGhost/lahiri.htm>.

An interesting essay on the title story in *Interpreter of Maladies.*

Choubey, Asha. "Food Metaphor in Jhumpa Lahiri's 'Interpreter of Maladies.'" *Postcolonial Web: The Literature & Culture of the Indian Subcontinent (South Asia).* <http://www.scholars.nus.edu.sg/landow/post/india/literature/choubey1.html>.

Discusses food in her stories.

Flynn, Sean. "Women We Love: Jhumpa Lahiri." *Esquire* (Oct. 2000): 172-73.

Clearly captivated by Lahiri's beauty, Flynn also has some interesting comments about her writing.

Houghton Mifflin. "A Reader's Guide: *Interpreter of Maladies* by Jhumpa Lahiri." <http://www.houghtonmifflinbooks.com/readers_guides/interpreter_maladies.shtml>.

Study questions, background information, and a brief interview.

Kakutani, Michiko. *The Interpreter of Maladies.* Boston: Houghton Mifflin, 1999.

————. "Liking America, but Longing for India." *New York Times* 6 Aug. 1999: 48.

A follow-up article, more interesting than the *New York Times Book Review*'s original review on July 11, 1999—which is, however, available on the Web at <http://www.nytimes.com/pages/books/review/index.html> for "Interpreter of Maladies."

Lahiri, Jhumpa. "Translato ergo sum." *Himal* (October 2000). <http://www.himalmag.com/oct2000/voices.html>.

Excerpt from an article that originally appeared in *Feed Magazine* as "Jhumpa on Jhumpa." A response to Indian critics and others who find Lahiri's stories inauthentic because she is was born and lives abroad.

————. *The Namesake.* Boston: Houghton Mifflin, 2003.

Lahiri's first novel.

Patel, Vibhuti. "The Maladies of Belonging." *Newsweek* 20 Sept. 1999: 80.

A good, readily accessible review.

SAWNET (South Asian Women's NETwork). "Jhumpa Lahiri." <http://www.umiacs.umd.edu/users/sawweb/sawnet/books/jhumpa_lahiri.html>.

Brief article with links.

*Voices from the Gaps: Women Writers of Color.* "Jhumpa Lahiri." <http://voices.cla.umn.edu/authors/jhumpalahiri.html>.

Useful overview and bibliography.

## Jennifer Bess (essay date winter 2004)

SOURCE: Bess, Jennifer. "Lahiri's *Interpreter of Maladies.*" *Explicator* 62, no. 2 (winter 2004): 125-28.

[*In the following essay, Bess focuses on irony in Lahiri's stories, noting how the most fleeting of relationships may result in the greatest self-understanding.*]

A plate of peanut butter crackers and a Jesus trivet become, in Jhumpa Lahiri's **Interpreter of Maladies,** icons of alienation and loneliness. In the Pulitzer Prize winning collection of short stories, everyday items and events expose the liminal situation unique to the first- and second-generation immigrant characters, but also embody the author's timely lament over the failure of global living to bridge the gaps between cultures and between individuals (cf. Dubey 23: Lewis 219). In fact, although firmly grounded in the concrete and in the present, Lahiri's collection weaves together universal themes of alienation, connection, and loss as her characters embark on unique quests to find the union between understanding the human experience and finding satisfaction in their individual lives. Moving between values of collectivist and individualist cultures, they are perfectly suited to navigate the relationship between the universal and the unique, but they find that the homogenizing forces of globalization, the chaos of mechanized living, and the silence of loneliness threaten cultural identity instead of fostering a sense of community and that they threaten individual identity instead of nurturing self-knowledge. It is, ironically, only in the most transient of relationships that the sought-after union between understanding humanity and understanding self is found, creating in the collection a dialectic between the failure to understand the human condition and the hope of embracing its richness.

In **"Mrs. Sen's,"** the title character attempts to become a global citizen by maintaining her Indian identity at the same time she adapts to American culture. Newly arrived from Calcutta with her husband, she struggles to maintain the traditional role of the wife to Mr. Sen through her careful attention in preparing Indian cuisine. Although she laments the fact that *bhetki* is not available, she finds that fresh halibut will suffice. Collected from a seaside fishmonger, the fish is prepared with a special blade from India. This blade, Mrs. Sen explains to the young boy she baby-sits, recalls to her the community of women she has left behind: "'Whenever there is a wedding in the family [. . .] my mother sends out word in the evening for all the neighborhood women to bring blades just like this one, and then they sit in an enormous circle on the roof of our building, laughing and gossiping'" (Lahiri 115). In India the women's "chatter" extends into the night, filling the silence with meaningful companionship and common purpose (115). In the United States, however, Mrs. Sen is assaulted sometimes by a cacophony of voices and street noises and other times by an unbearable "silence" that keeps her awake at night (115). Longing for her home, where anyone who raised her voice to "'express grief or joy of any kind'" would find the "'whole neighborhood'" at her doorstep, Mrs. Sen has lost her sense of belonging, her sense of shared human experience (116). Likewise, she loses her own uniqueness as she must make a traditional meal without green bananas, an essential ingredient, thereby failing to fulfill the role she finds most satisfying. Finally, when the chaos of the city street causes her to get into an accident, she becomes a victim of the noisy flow of machinery with which she cannot merge. If the commonality she found in communal cooking fostered her identification with others and her own sense of purpose, then the despair with which she abandons her cutting blade in favor of peanut butter and crackers after the accident exposes the fact that she has lost the only identity she has ever known—nurturer, homemaker, wife of Mr. Sen. In her effort to adapt, Mrs. Sen has lost herself to the silence of loneliness and the noise of modern life.

If Mrs. Sen, a recent immigrant, loses both her sense of community and her sense of identity to the forces of the global market that called her husband to work at an American university, Sanjeev and Twinkle of **"This Blessed House"** suffer a similar fate as they are overwhelmed after settling into a lovely suburban home, which they find hides "a sizeable collection of Christian paraphernalia" in its corners and closets (137). Whereas Twinkle delights in uncovering and displaying trinkets, including a Jesus trivet and a paint-by-number portrait of the three wise men, Sanjeev feels only irritation and repeatedly reminds his bride that they are not Christian, but Hindu. To him the objects lack "a sense of sacredness," a spiritual value and meaning, but to her, they bring joy (138). Like the din of the traffic in **"Mrs. Sen's,"** the trinkets in **"This Blessed House"** expose the relationship between the characters and the modern, global world they inhabit: While Sanjeev pursues happiness in the form of the American Dream through his job, his pretty bride, and his home, Twinkle pursues her own whims, finding happiness in the search for trinkets. In a sense, they are both seeking meaningless tokens and avoiding the complexities of communication with each other, thereby distancing themselves from their humanity. By the end of the story, when Twinkle descends the stairway carrying a huge silver bust of Christ (a scene that fills Sanjeev with hatred), an object which emanates "dignity, solemnity, beauty" yields in him the

same silence, the same lack of meaning and intimacy, that haunts Mrs. Sen (157). Although Sanjeev knows Twinkle will display the bust proudly on their mantle, he says nothing. Her joy remains unknown to him and his animosity is unknown to her. The invasion of the Christian tokens into the Hindu household has created a personal and spiritual vacuum; the clutter—in this case the visual cacophony compared to the aural assault Mrs. Sen experiences on the roadway—overcomes any opportunity for a meaningful exchange of religious or cultural experience and any opportunity for two people to understand each other or themselves.

Although the married characters in the collection tend to suffer silently and separately, the most transient of relationships are the ones that offer a hope of fostering individual and universal understanding, an understanding of what it is to be unique and of what it is to be part of the human collective. The silence suffered by Mrs. Sen, Sanjeev, and Twinkle is finally shattered in **"The Third and Final Continent,"** in which a single word, "splendid," punctuates the story like a refrain. Significantly, the first-person narrator is unnamed. Although the use of the first person emphasizes his individuality, his namelessness simultaneously celebrates his universality, thus creating a glimpse of a unity that the other characters have not experienced. In this final story in the collection, the narrator seeks temporary housing with a centenarian, Mrs. Croft, when he first moves to America. She welcomes him into her boarding house in her own idiosyncratic way, insisting that he say "splendid" after she tells him of the recent moon-landing (179). This brief conversation becomes a nightly routine for them, one which he first finds awkward. But after time passes, the seemingly trivial exchange becomes the foundation of something more intimate than the feelings revealed between the two married couples. Through their brief exchange, the narrator pleases Mrs. Croft and, in doing so, satisfies himself. He discovers that if he was unable to care properly for his own mother when she went insane, he can care for his landlady in this exchange and in handing her his weekly rent money. In "these simple gestures," the unnamed narrator finds his humanity and confirms hers (189). As a result, he evolves from the groom who could not console his weeping bride on their wedding night to a husband who prepares thoughtfully for her arrival to America. Thirty years later, the narrator has described what Mrs. Sen, Sanjeev, and Twinkle cannot: "As ordinary as it all appears," he says, referring to his own life, "there are times when it is beyond the imagination" (198). He mourned, he loved, and he raised a child; he has, in other words, lived a life that is rich with the universal feelings that bind men and women together across continents and across time. But at the same time that his life has been "ordinary," universally human, it has also been unique, unimaginable, for he has lived on three continents, he has been profoundly touched by Mrs. Croft, and he has loved a woman named Mala. The universal and the individual have converged.

## Works Cited

Dubey, Ashutosh. "Immigrant Experience in Jhumpa Lahiri's *Interpreter of Maladies*." *The Journal of Indian Writing in English* 30.2 (2002): 22-26.

Lahiri, Jhumpa. *Interpreter of Maladies*. Boston: Houghton Mifflin, 1999.

Lewis, Simon. "Lahiri's 'Interpreter of Maladies.'" *Explicator* 59.4 (2001): 219.

## Noelle Brada-Williams (essay date fall/winter 2004)

SOURCE: Brada-Williams, Noelle. "Reading Jhumpa Lahiri's *Interpreter of Maladies* as a Short Story Cycle." *MELUS* 29, nos. 3 & 4 (fall/winter 2004): 451-64.

[*In the following essay, Brada-Williams contends that* The Interpreter of Maladies *is more than a random collection of short stories, as evidenced by its careful structural balance and recurring motifs.*]

It may at first seem strange to describe Jhumpa Lahiri's *Interpreter of Maladies* as a short story cycle rather than simply as a collection of separate and independent stories. After all, from Sherwood Anderson's *Winesburg, Ohio* to Sandra Cisneros' *House on Mango Street*, readers of the modern short story cycle are often cued to the unity of a collection by a single location and/or a small ensemble of recurring characters that serve to unite the various components into a whole, while Lahiri's Pulitzer Prize-winning work features diverse and unrelated characters, a variety of narrative styles, and no common locale. Indeed, the text even transcends national boundaries, being set in both India and the United States. However, a deeper look reveals the intricate use of pattern and motif to bind the stories together, including the recurring themes of the barriers to and opportunities for human communication; community, including marital, extra-marital, and parent-child relationships; and the dichotomy of care and neglect.

The short story cycle is a notoriously difficult genre to define. Forrest L. Ingram points out this difficulty by describing the cycle's method of making meaning:

> Like the moving parts of a mobile, the interconnected parts of some short story cycles seem to shift their positions with relation to the other parts, as the cycle moves forward in its typical pattern of recurrent development. Shifting internal relationships, of course, continually alter the originally perceived pattern of the whole cycle. A cycle's form is elusive.
>
> (13)

Susan Garland Mann asserts that the essential characteristic of the short story cycle is the "simultaneous self-sufficiency and interdependence" of the stories which make up the whole (17). Mann comments on Ingram's conception of the tension which short story cycles create between the individuality of its components and the unity of the whole by noting that the "tension is revealed in the way people read cycles" (18).

An analogous tension can be found in the way people read ethnic literature. The unique vision of an individual artist and the unique representation he or she provides of a community are often challenged by readers from both within and outside the community being represented as various readers lobby for the value of one representation over another. Such claims on writers include the demand for more sanitized, more stereotype-affirming, or simply more diverse, representations.[1] Examples range from controversies over the use of dialect in early twentieth-century African American literature to the depictions of sexuality and gender roles in virtually all ethnic American literatures up to the present time, including, most recently, Lois-Ann Yamanaka's depiction of a Filipino American sexual predator in *Blu's Hanging*. Although most rational readers are aware of the diversity and individuality of any given ethnic group (especially the vast population Lahiri engages of South Asia and its diaspora), the logic of representation implies, especially with regards to groups under-represented within a national literature, that a work depicting a part of a community "represents" the whole.

We see the logic of representation at work in the naïve[2] reader who naturally bases his or her understanding of a particular demographic unit on the few representations he or she has come across, as well as the experienced literature professor who attempts to create a syllabus that is "representative" of diverse populations through what can be read in a single term. Readers both new to ethnic literature and those who are experts in the field thus face the common dilemma of obscuring part and whole due to the inevitably finite nature of both available representations and one's own reading. Not only does this problem of obscuring part and whole work to the advantage of the short story cycle as a genre but the genre can, as we see in *Interpreter of Maladies*, work towards solving the problem of representing an entire community within the necessarily limited confines of a single work by balancing a variety of representations rather than offering the single representation provided by the novel or the individual short story.

The popularity and critical success of Lahiri's *Interpreter of Maladies* in both the United States and India could in part be due to the delicate balancing of representations she provides through the cycle as a whole. For example, the cheating husbands of **"Sexy"** are balanced by the depiction of the unfaithful Mrs. Das of **"Interpreter of Maladies."** The relative ease with which Lilia of **"When Mr. Pirzada Came to Dine"** participates in an American childhood is contrasted with the separation and stigmatization that the Dixit children experience in the story **"Sexy."** Mrs. Sen's severe homesickness and separation from US culture is contrasted with the adaptability of Lilia's mother and Mala in **"The Third and Final Continent."** The balancing of the generally negative depiction of an Indian community in **"A Real Durwan"** with the generally positive portrayal in **"The Treatment of Bibi Haldar"** is yet another example not only of the resulting balanced representations that the genre affords Lahiri but is itself one of many ways through which Lahiri constructs a conversation among her pieces.

The first and last stories in the cycle most clearly evoke a balancing dialogue through a careful mirroring of their basic plots. **"The Third and Final Continent"** both reflects and reverses the plot of the first story, **"A Temporary Matter."** While the first story of the cycle relates the tale of the death of a son and the possible destruction of a marriage, the concluding story provides a tale of the survival and resilience of both the parents' marriage and their son. The plot of the final story emphasizes the "ordinary" heroism of the narrator and his wife through the trials of migrating across continents and coming to care for a stranger by contrasting the pair to the narrator's fragile mother and their life in the United States to the short stay of the astronauts on the moon. They are also connected to the elderly Mrs. Croft and her near-miraculous ability to survive; she seems to have traveled as far in time as the main characters have in space. By placing Shoba and Shukumar's story in her readers' minds first, Lahiri is able to inform readers of the final story of the ways Mala and her husband could have failed as a couple and as parents, thus emphasizing their experiences as achievements rather than mere norms. The placement of these two stories at the beginning and end of the collection also helps to signal readers of the cyclical nature of the collection.[3]

Susan Mann notes that titles are key "generic signals" and that "collections that are not cycles have traditionally been named after a single story to which the phrase 'and other stories' is appended. . . . Generally placed first or last in the volume, the title story represents what the author feels is the best work or, in some cases, the best-known work" (14). Mann cites Faulkner's insistence on having "and Other Stories" removed from *Go Down, Moses* as support for the absence of the phrase as a conscious signaling device, as can be seen in Lahiri's text. Other critics have described the title of Lahiri's cycle as descriptive of her talents and her subject matter in all of the stories, rather than just a naming of the third story in the collection.

Scholars have noted many common themes among the stories, often focusing on the sense of displacement attached to the immigrant experience. In their analysis of **"A Temporary Matter,"** Basudeb and Angana Chakrabarti make several claims regarding common themes in Lahiri's stories, for example, that "this sense of belonging to a particular place and culture and yet at the same time being an outsider to another creates a tension in individuals which happens to be a distinguishing feature of Lahiri's characters" and that Lahiri deals "with broken marriages" (24-25). Ashutosh Dubey looks at the immigrant experience in three of the nine stories and notes that three more stories dealing with second generation Indian immigrants focus on the "themes of emotional struggles of love, relationships, communication against the backdrop of immigrant experience" (25). In "Food Metaphor in Jhumpa Lahiri's *Interpreter of Maladies*," Asha Choubey traces her theme through five of the nine stories, analyzing their representation of Indian food and the use of food as metaphors for home and the connection between people. She also asserts that Lahiri's "protagonists—all Indians—settled abroad are afflicted with a 'sense of exile'" (par. 4). A sense of exile and the potential for—and frequent denial of—human communication can be found in all of Lahiri's short stories and indeed are the defining, structuring elements of her short story cycle.[4] Yet despite their insights, many of the critics cited above ignore the two stories set wholly in India and without any American characters, **"A Real Durwan"** and **"The Treatment of Bibi Haldar."** Choubey's statement also ignores the non-Indian protagonists of Miranda (**"Sexy"**) and Eliot (**"Mrs. Sen's"**). Common themes are important to defining a story cycle; but to distinguish between a collection containing stories merely characteristic of a writer's dominant interests and a true short story cycle, a single theme tying every story together is needed.

Many critics have suggested marriage as the unifying theme for the collection, and marriage is indeed a key element of most of the stories. Even **"A Real Durwan"** has the subplot of Mr. and Mrs. Dalal's bickering and reconciliation. Mrs. Sen's marriage to Mr. Sen may not be the main focus of her story, but it does create an important backdrop for her homesickness and several of her more pertinent observations to Eliot. The one story that breaks with the theme of marriage or marital problems is **"When Mr. Pirzada Came to Dine."** Although it depicts a married couple and their friend Mr. Pirzada, who is himself a married man, the relationships at the focus of the text are those between Lilia and Mr. Pirzada and the trio that Mr. Pirzada and Lilia's parents temporarily create during East Pakistan's war of independence. As Lilia notes, "Most of all I remember the three of them operating during that time as if they were a single person, sharing a single meal, a single body, a single silence, and a single fear" (41). Ironically they achieve this unity as their nations enter into the war that will eventually allow East Pakistan to become the independent nation of Bangladesh. Not only human connection but human communication is yet another important theme for the cycle which runs through this story as Mr. Pirzada learns to interpret the American "thank you" just as Miranda in **"Sexy"** gradually comes to interpret the title of her story.

What has not been sufficiently noticed is that carefully executed rituals mark the relationships in *Interpreter of Maladies.* For instance, **"When Mr. Pirzada Came to Dine"**: Lilia takes care to save up the candy Mr. Pirzada gives her, treating it like an offering in her prayers for Mr. Pirzada's family. Each evening at dinner Mr. Pirzada carefully winds and sets out the pocket watch he keeps set to the time of his homeland, which is one of the things Lilia notices after she begins "to study him *with extra care*" (30, emphasis mine). These details evoke the most important theme running throughout the cycle: all nine stories are woven together with the frequent representations of extreme care and neglect. Repetitions of this dichotomy occur in a variety of communities including whole neighborhoods, marital and extramarital relationships, and relationships between children and adults. Sometimes carelessness as a trait in *Interpreter of Maladies* defines a period of significant tension or even mourning as Lilia's parents shift from carefully prepared meals to simple boiled eggs and rice as the crisis in East Pakistan deepens. At other moments in the collection, a lack of care signifies fundamental differences between peoples or is represented as a permanent flaw, a human failing central to an individual character or even a whole community. The needs for "care" are linked to love, duty or responsibility, and homesickness. Images of neglect range from a dress that has slipped off its hanger to a car accident. Such images serve as augurs of the characters' emotional states and processes.

**"A Temporary Matter"** opens with a description of a woman arriving home: Shoba "let the strap of her leather satchel . . . slip from her shoulders, and left it in the hallway" (1). We are then told that she looks "like the type of woman she'd once claimed she would never resemble," namely, one who came home in gym clothes and with her makeup either rubbed off or smeared (1). Readers quickly come to realize that a dramatic change has come over the woman once marked not only by her physical beauty but her careful and meticulous manner in all things. We learn these details indirectly through a third-person narration that is filtered through Shoba's husband's point of view, the husband who will later put her things away but who is himself marked by personal neglect. He has not yet brushed his teeth by the evening of the day on which the story begins and has taken to lying in bed and avoiding work on his dissertation or even leaving his home.

Lahiri uses a variety of such small details to evoke not only the vast change that has come over the couple since the stillbirth of their son, but to reveal the great neglect in which their own relationship as a couple has fallen since that tragedy. One small image of neglect and decay is particularly resonant with the state of their marriage: When Shukumar, the husband, picks up a potted ivy in order to use it as a makeshift candle holder while the electricity will be turned off, he finds that "Even though the plant was inches from the tap, the soil was so dry that he had to water it first before the candles would stand straight" (10). Thus, Lahiri subtly evokes the couple's common state of shock and lack of interest in their shared environment as both have failed to water a plant even when doing so would have taken almost no effort at all. Taken together, the sheer number of these small failures to provide care helps to define the depths of Shoba and Shukumar's common yet isolated experience of grief for their lost child as well as their waning care and love for each other.

**"Interpreter of Maladies"** similarly focuses on a young couple with severe marital problems, but their carelessness is most often evoked in their treatment of their three children. **"Interpreter of Maladies"** is a third-person narrative filtered through the point of view of Mr. Kapasi, the family's driver while sight-seeing in India. The story opens with the parents bickering over who will take their daughter to the restroom. Mr. Kapasi will later think that the family is "all like siblings . . . it was hard to believe [Mr. and Mrs. Das] were regularly responsible for anything other than themselves" (49). The first paragraph of the story notes that the mother "did not hold the little girl's hand as they walked to the restroom" (43). As in **"A Temporary Matter,"** small signs of negligence add up to reveal deeper emotional difficulties and detachments. This otherwise unremarkable scene acts as foreshadowing for what may be called the twin climaxes of the story: the attack on one of the boys by monkeys and the revelation of his illegitimate birth. Notably it is the popcorn that his mother has carelessly dropped that draws the monkeys to her son as well as the fact that he is left unsupervised that leads to the attack.

Mr. and Mrs. Das's lack of carefulness in raising their children extends to their carelessness in maintaining their marriage vows, at least on Mrs. Das's part. Although their driver, Mr. Kapasi, recognizes similarities between the Das's marriage and his own, he himself functions as a stark contrast to Mr. and Mrs. Das's lack of care. Not unlike Mr. Pirzada, Mr. Kapasi is characterized by his carefully tailored clothing and meticulous manners. Simon Lewis has read this story as a rewriting and updating of the trip to the Marabar Caves in E. M. Forster's *A Passage to India,* this time from the perspective of an Indian national, Mr. Kapasi in the role formerly held by Dr. Aziz (219). Lewis's argument can be supported by Mr. Kapasi's dream "of serving as an interpreter between nations" (Lahiri 59) which he fantasizes fulfilling through a future correspondence with Mrs. Das. The way in which Mr. Kapasi gives Mrs. Das his contact information is illustrative of their essential differences as characters: she hands "him a scrap of paper which she had hastily ripped from a page of her film magazine" upon which he writes "his address in clear, careful letters" (55). She then tosses "it into the jumble of her bag" (56). The clear differences in these two characters in their relationship to care or lack of care, specifically in relation to responsibility, makes their final disconnect inevitable. While they both can be seen longing for communication with others, Mrs. Das is a woman with a life of relative comfort and case who yearns to be freed of the responsibilities of marriage and children, and Mr. Karpasi is a man who has given up his dreams to support his family and who only yearns for some recognition and interest in his life. By the time his address falls out of Mrs. Das's bag and is borne off by the wind, Mr. Kapasi has already let go of his fantasy of communicating across continents and between individuals.

In **"Mrs. Sen's"** the title character takes excellent care of the eleven-year old Eliot, the filter of the third-person narrative, for most of the story. One period when she acts differently is when she learns of her grandfather's death. As in **"A Temporary Matter,"** images of carelessness and the cessation of past routines are used to evoke characters in mourning. Mrs. Sen's care-giving activities include not only feeding Eliot as well as his mother when she arrives to pick him up but in preparing elaborate meals for her and Mr. Sen's evening meal. During her hour-long daily ritual of chopping up ingredients, Mrs. Sen has Eliot stay on the couch, far from her chopping blade: "She would have roped off the area if she could. Once, though, she broke her own rule; in need of additional supplies . . . she asked Eliot to fetch something from the kitchen . . . 'Careful, oh dear, be careful,' she cautioned as he approached" (115). This same daily ritual or routine connects Mrs. Sen with India. Describing the scene before a wedding when the neighborhood women would gather to prepare food with blades such as hers, she states, "It is impossible to fall asleep those nights, listening to their chatter. [. . .] Here in this place where Mr. Sen has brought me, I cannot sometimes sleep in so much silence" (115). She also asks Eliot, "if I began to scream right now at the top of my lungs, would someone come?" (116). Drawing on his own experience, Eliot can only answer, "Maybe. . . . They might call you, . . . But they might complain that you were making too much noise" (116-17).

Mrs. Sen is homesick for the kind of community she had in India, a community defined by a responsibility to participate in the lives of others rather than a responsi-

bility not to interfere or be in any way intrusive in the lives of others. Mrs. Sen's statement when she is contemplating the fearful task of driving is ironically applicable to both the other drivers and herself: "'Everyone, this people, too much in their world'" (121). The American model of polite behavior depicted in Lahiri's work is to be wholly in one's own world and to maintain the smells, sounds, and emotions of that world so that they do not encroach upon another individual's life. Mrs. Sen's notion of community is the opposite. Yet her ability to become distracted while driving marks her as someone lost in her own world and oblivious to the needs and safety of other drivers.[5] While Eliot's mom views the other cars as mere scenery, as inanimate objects, and is able to negotiate the road to the beach with ease, Mrs. Sen is hyper-conscious of the existence of other beings on the street but unable to perform in such a way as not to intrude in the lives of other drivers. This otherwise careful person becomes an extremely careless driver, and an accident results. Although the accident causes very little physical damage to Eliot or Mrs. Sen, it puts an end even to the limited form of community that the two had come to share with each other.

Lahiri represents examples of Indian community in two stories that are set off from the other seven stories not only by being set wholly in India and with all Indian nationals as characters but in their distinctive narrative style. **"A Real Durwan"** and **"The Treatment of Bibi Haldar"** continue to focus on a central dichotomy of care*less*ness and care*ful*ness. Both stories shift from Lahiri's usual practice of using a filtered third-person or first-person narrative. While elsewhere this technique provides a detailed look into the interior life of most of Lahiri's characters, the lives and unspoken thoughts of Boori Ma and Bibi Haldar are left unknown to the reader. Each story resembles a legend as it depicts characters who manage to suffer through and survive extreme adversity. The lack of representation of their individual thoughts, memories, and motivations also lends the title characters a mythic or allegorical quality. In these two stories the community surrounding the character referred to in the title is as much the focus of the tale as any single character.

Boori Ma is a refugee who, although a woman, performs the duties of **"A Real Durwan"** or doorman in a Calcutta apartment building. We are told that she "maintained a vigil no less punctilious than if she were the gatekeeper of a house on Lower Circular Road, or Jodhpur Park, or any other fancy neighborhood" (73). When we first meet her, she is inspecting her tattered bedding for insects. A sympathetic resident of the building asks, "Do you think it's beyond us to provide you with clean quilts?" (75). As this statement reveals, the neighbor's good intentions are mixed with her sensitivity to her own limited social status. The same day will bring a change in the neighbor's status and will propel the entire building into a fury of building renovations aimed at increasing each resident's relative status in the world. Boori Ma, who had previously swept the stairs twice a day and kept suspicious characters away from the building, is pushed out of her routine and even her post by the renovation efforts. The residents seem to forget to be hospitable in the rush to be genteel. Boori Ma begins wandering the neighborhood and spending her life savings on snacks. Eventually the keys and savings that she had so carefully saved despite partition, dislocation, and the loss of her family, are stolen from her. In the meantime, the sink that began the renovation craze is stolen and Boori Ma is blamed for carelessness and literally thrown out onto the street. In the focus on and care for material status and the material repair of the building that physically defines the community, the apartment community has failed to care for its members, including Boori Ma who for years had been the primary *caretaker* of the building.

**"The Treatment of Bibi Haldar"** provides a depiction of community in opposition to that described in **"A Real Durwan."** Lahiri's technique in this story is similar to Faulkner's method in "A Rose For Emily," even down to the use of a first person plural narrator, a communal "we." Lahiri acknowledges her debt to Faulkner in an interview with *Pif Magazine,* where she states it "was an experiment for" herself to replicate the nonspecific collective narrative voice of Faulkner's tale. She describes the narrator of her story as "a group of women [with] no particular identity." The first person plural inevitably emphasizes the role of the community in the story. In contrast to the neighbors in **"A Real Durwan,"** the community represented in **"The Treatment of Bibi Haldar"** take their responsibility to a fellow community member very seriously.

In **"The Treatment of Bibi Haldar,"** set in an unnamed small town outside Calcutta, the narrative "we" take turns feeding, clothing, teaching, chaperoning, and generally looking out for Bibi. The care given to Bibi, first by her father and then by an army of "family, friends, priests, palmists, spinsters, gem therapists, prophets, and fools"—as well as other "concerned members of our town," at least in treating her epilepsy-like illness, is so great that it is burdensome (158). But after she loses her father and is left in the neglectful care of her only remaining family, her cousin Haldar and his wife, she begins to yearn for marriage. As much as they do for her, the neighbors admit "she was not our responsibility, and in our private moments we were thankful for it" (167). Incensed by her family's ill treatment of Bibi, the neighbors boycott the cousin's cosmetics shop and succeed in driving him out of business and out of town. The neighbors "At every opportunity [. . .] reminded her that we surrounded her, that she could come to us if she ever needed advice or aid of any kind" (171). But

they leave her to herself at night and eventually Bibi is found to be pregnant. This pregnancy leads to an amazing transformation in which she is almost miraculously healed and becomes a capable, self-supporting businesswoman who now takes great care not only of her business but, as newly trained by the community of women around her, of her son as well. Bibi's desire for marriage and seemingly magical cure by motherhood balances and contrasts the depiction of Mrs. Das, who is seeking a remedy for the responsibility of marriage and motherhood. The mystery of Bibi's pregnancy is never solved. Although several possibilities are suggested, it is ultimately unclear not only who the father of her child is but even whether the birth arose out of an unreported crime or through Bibi's own choice and willing consent. Lahiri leaves it up to the reader to decide.

We see Lahiri's characteristic refusal of definite closure in many other stories as well, including **"This Blessed House"** which is similar to **"The Treatment of Bibi Haldar"** in that both stories offer a more nuanced depiction of the collection's general valuing of carefulness. Bibi flourishes only once she is *without* the continual care of others and yet is herself given the responsibility for caring for another. The carefulness of Sanjeev in **"This Blessed House"** seems more related to his own worries about what other people think and the rituals he had established as a bachelor than anything positive for his marriage. His wife Twinkle's carelessness is ultimately connected with creativity and *joie de vivre* as much as it is with selfishness. While everpractical Sanjeev can recognize, via the opinions of his friends, his wife's objective value, he seems unable to appreciate it. The silver bust of Jesus that they find in the attic becomes symbolic of Twinkle herself:

> He hated its immensity, and its flawless, polished surface, and its undeniable value. He hated that it was in his house, and that he owned it. Unlike the other things they'd found, this contained dignity, solemnity, beauty even. But to his surprise these qualities made him hate it all the more. Most of all he hated it because he knew that Twinkle loved it.
>
> (157)

The story closes with Sanjeev carrying the silver bust to the living room where Twinkle has asked it to be placed on the mantel, against Sanjeev's wishes. Our last image is of Sanjeev in a balancing act, being "careful not to let the feather hat slip" from the statue and following his wife. Readers can interpret this as one of Sanjeev's last acts to please his wife or, in stark contrast, as indicative of an eventual balancing of their character differences and Sanjeev's following of Twinkle into a more spontaneous and playful approach to life.

We are given the freedom to create our own closure, and in many cases our own judgments as to the outcomes suggested by Lahiri's narratives. But with this freedom comes our responsibility to read *with care.* Reading the text as a short story cycle and not just a collection reveals Lahiri's careful balancing of a range of representations and her intricate use of pattern and motif. By reading the stories as a cycle, readers not only receive the additional layers of meaning produced by the dialogue between stories but a more diverse and nuanced interpretation of members of the South Asian diaspora.

## Notes

1. Such controversies over representation are not new. In 1926, W. E. B. Du Bois, in "Criteria of Negro Art," described what artists face more eloquently than I can here.

2. I use the term "naïve" to describe a variety of readers, including students who may be new to reading ethnic literature as well as individuals of any age or level of education who may be ignorant of the communities depicted in ethnic literature. This lack of knowledge, willful or not, may stem from the varied regional demographics of the US or from the still segregated nature of American society.

3. The truly cyclical nature of the structure of this collection, in addition to the fact that *Interpreter of Maladies* is much closer to a selection of short stories than a novel on the spectrum that Ingram defines, leads me to use the term "short story cycle" rather than Dunn and Morris's "composite novel." For more discussion specifically on ethnic short-story cycles, see Nagel and Davis. I am grateful to Dr. Cheng Lok Chua for suggesting these sources as well as for the advice and encouragement I received on this essay from both Drs. Chua and Amritjit Singh.

4. Mann notes that "Because cycles consist of discrete, self-sufficient stories, they are especially well suited to handle certain subjects, including the sense of isolation or fragmentation or indeterminacy that many twentieth-century characters experience" (11). Ingram's study of Kafka's *Hunger Artist* cycle focuses on the barriers in communication depicted. Lahiri has said that "characters [that she is] drawn to all face some barrier of communication" and she links this to growing up in two countries ("Maladies of Belonging").

5. Dubey asserts that her "stubborn refusal to learn [to drive] can be seen as a subconscious . . . resistance to the dictated terms of this new world" (24).

## Works Cited

Chakrabarti, Basudeb and Angana Chakrabarti. "Context: A Comparative Study of Jhumpa Lahiri's 'A Tem-

porary Matter' and Shubodh Ghosh's 'Jatugriha.'" *The Journal of Indian Writing in English* 30.1 (2002): 23-29.

Choubey, Asha. "Food Metaphor in Jhumpa Lahiri's *Interpreter of Maladies.*" *The Literature & Culture of the Indian Subcontinent (South Asia) in the Postcolonial Web.* 2001. 3 May, 2003. <http://www.scholars.nus.edu.sg/landow/post/india/literature/choubey>.

Davis, Rocío G. *Transcultural Reinventions: Asian American and Asian Canadian Short-story Cycles.* Toronto: Tsar Publications, 2001.

Dubey, Ashutosh. "Immigrant Experience in Jhumpa Lahiri's *Interpreter of Maladies.*" *The Journal of Indian Writing in English* 30.2 (2002): 22-26.

Du Bois, W. E. B. "Criteria of Negro Art." *Call & Response: The Riverside Anthology of the African American Literary Tradition.* Ed. Patricia Liggins Hill. New York: Houghton Mifflin, 1998. 850-55.

Dunn, Maggie and Ann Morris. *The Composite Novel: The Short Story Cycle in Transition.* Studies in Literary Themes and Genres 6. New York: Twayne, 1995.

Ingram, Forrest L. *Representative Short Story Cycles of the Twentieth Century: Studies in a Literary Genre.* The Hague: Mouton, 1971.

Lahiri, Jhumpa. *Interpreter of Maladies.* New York: Houghton Mifflin, 1999.

——. Interview with Arun Aguiar. *Pif Magazine* 28 (2000). 3 May 2003. <http://www.pifmagazine.com/vol28/i_agui.shtml>.

——. "Maladies of Belonging." Interview by Vibhuti Patel. *Newsweek International* 20 Sept. 1990: 80.

Lewis, Simon. "Lahiri's 'Interpreter of Maladies.'" *The Explicator* 59.4 (2001): 219. Infotrac. 16 April 2003. <http://web5.infotrac.galegroup.com>.

Mann, Susan Garland. *The Short Story Cycle: A Genre Companion and Reference Guide.* New York: Greenwood, 1989.

Nagel, James. *The Contemporary American Short-Story Cycle: The Ethnic Resonance of the Genre.* Baton Rouge: Louisiana State UP, 2001.

## Jhumpa Lahiri and Paul Mandelbaum (interview date 2005)

SOURCE: Lahiri, Jhumpa, and Paul Mandelbaum. "Jhumpa Lahiri Discusses 'The Third and Final Continent,' Setting, Cornflakes, and the 'Perfect Lady.'" In *12 Short Stories and Their Making,* edited by Paul Mandelbaum, pp. 234-42. New York: Persea Books, 2005.

*[In the following interview, Mandelbaum encourages Lahiri to discuss how both real-life experiences and imagined ones emerge in her writings.]*

*[Mandelbaum]: Your fiction often explores the tension between the place where it's unfolding and some other place—the place left behind, say, or a place the character tries to imagine.*

[Lahiri]: There were two physical landscapes in my upbringing. I lived exclusively in the United States, but because my parents remain so closely tied to India and their family, I could never think of myself as being part of just one place.

And I think that still continues to interest me as a writer. Even the more subtle shift of someone growing up in a small town and moving to a city, or growing up in a certain way and then finding him or herself in a new environment, yields a lot for me dramatically.

*In "The Third and Final Continent" you have your narrator buy his guide to North America in London and not in India. On the plane to Boston, he reads: "Don't expect an English cup of tea," a nice irony given that his own cultural adjustments will undoubtedly be larger. Do you recall anything about making that choice?*

I actually found this book in a closet in our house somewhere. It was my father's book and he had obviously bought it in London. He wouldn't have needed it in India. When he lived in India, he was only going to England, and it was from England that he came here. I based my character on that same path that my father took.

I've never written anything as close to real life as that story. It wasn't my life I was writing about, but still, I was basing quite a bit of it on events that happened.

*Did you interview your father for background information when you were writing it, or by that point had you internalized the family stories?*

I had always heard this story, this anecdote about my father coming over in 1969 and renting a house in Cambridge that belonged to the one-hundred-three-year-old woman, and how she would want to speak to him every evening about the men who had just been to the moon—all of that my father would relate from time to time. I think it struck me when I was growing up because my father is not a big storyteller.

When I was up at the Fine Arts Work Center in Provincetown, on a writing fellowship for seven months, I invited my father to come and spend a week there. He did, and one evening I invited a few fellow writers over for dinner. One of them happened to ask my father:

why did you come to America, talk about that. And so he eventually wound up telling this story again, and for some reason, I saw it not just as a part of my father's past but as a possible story that I could write.

*The simultaneity with the moon landing gives the material an amazing shapeliness.*

I never thought about it as a parallel or significant in any way. Even when I started writing, it was so much a part of my family lore that it's one of those things you feel so close to, you can't see it. It was only after I had spent quite a bit of time wrestling with the making of the story that it occurred to me that it was such a fascinating confluence of events—one very personal and one so very, very public that changed the world and how human beings think of themselves in relation to the rest of the universe. It was very gratifying to discover. But it was only in the course of the writing. I worked on this story I would say for six or seven months in total.

*His plane touches down in Boston as news of the moon landing is announced. I assume there's a certain amount of poetic license you're taking there; it's just too wonderful to have actually been the case.*

I think I got that detail from reading accounts of the moon landing and how it was announced on airplanes and things like that. But I think that my father had already been here for a while, and then the moon landing happened. He had maybe been here for a month, but I don't know. At this point it's all sort of mixed up, and it's very hard for me to tease out what was real and what wasn't.

*How did you immerse your imagination in the world of the late sixties? Did you look up archived editions of the Boston newspapers?*

I did. I got some issues of the *Globe*—the day of the moon landing, and a few follow-up articles on it. And I read one or two books about that particular mission.

*You provide a few crisp details about the row house in London, and nothing gets across the chaotic, transitory living space of bachelors quite like dirty dishes soaking in a bathtub.*

That was a detail from my parents' early married life in London. The chronology of the story is off. My parents were already married, and I was already born, when this story took place. The timing is delayed. I did that because first of all I wasn't interested in writing any sort of family history. I wanted it to be fiction. And also I felt that the arrival of this man's wife would contribute to his situation. My mother told me, on various occasions, about one of the places they lived in in London, where they didn't have access to a sink and they had to do their dishes in the bathroom. They lived in various shared lodgings and shared a kitchen. And it was either that there was no sink or the sink was far too small. My parents, even back then, entertained a lot of people on a regular basis. So I think there was need for ample sink space.

*Your narrator's next stop is the YMCA, and you evoke its unpleasantness with just a couple of very choice sensory details, most importantly the street sounds. Do you recall how you arrived at that? Trying to sleep with your fingers in your ears—that's an elegantly simple yet unendurable situation.*

I imagined it would be loud because I know where it is in Cambridge, on Massachusetts Avenue, which is a very busy central avenue. I had never been inside the YMCA until very recently; I actually did a reading there, which bizarrely brought this whole experience full circle. My father never stayed in the YMCA, but he would go there to read the newspapers and pass the time in the evenings. I asked a friend who had lived in Cambridge for many years about the YMCA. I think he had been there and knew people who stayed there, so he gave me some details.

Regarding the matter of the fingers in the ears, when I first started writing that story, I was up in Provincetown, which is probably the most quiet place on earth. I was there in the wintertime and would hear the sea and the wind and that was about it. But after my fellowship ended, I moved to Manhattan and I was working on this story, in an apartment on Fourteenth Street on the East Side. It was an incredibly noisy apartment facing the street. So I just worked that detail in—what it's like to live in a really noisy place.

*Sometimes the mere fact that the narrator is observing a certain detail implies its novelty to him—the wood-shingled house and chain-link fence of Mrs. Croft's house, for instance.*

There are certainly no wood-shingled houses in Calcutta to speak of. Nor are there very many in north London. I imagined that the narrator would observe the exterior of the house carefully before entering. I wanted it to be a specific image of Cambridge and its architecture.

*As a traveler, he's particularly aware of things that a resident might not be.*

I think that's true for anyone who feels new to a place. Your powers of observation are sharpened, heightened. And especially so in a situation where you're contemplating taking up residence there. Basic questions would go through one's mind: Is it safe? Is it solid? So the details, I imagine, would be important.

*These powers of observation coincide nicely with your task as a writer: to see things through fresh eyes. Maybe every writer should try a travel story as an exercise.*

That's how I see everything in the world. It's hard for me *not* to notice those things.

*What do you attribute that to?*

I think I'm just hard-wired that way. It's how I relate to the physical world. I am a very visual person and I just tend to notice things. But I don't think I'm unique. I think most writers and painters would say the same thing.

*Are you a big walker? Josip Novakovich supposes in the* Fiction Writer's Workshop *that writers had a much more intimate relationship with their cities before driving became so predominant.*

I've never owned a car in my life. My parents had a car when I was growing up, obviously, so I rode in cars. But when I went to college in New York City I didn't have a car. I moved to Boston after college—I lived there for eight years—and never had a car. I had a car for those seven months when I was living on Cape Cod, but I rarely used it, except when I had to leave the Cape for some reason. And now I'm back in New York and we still don't have a car, so I do walk a lot, just out of necessity, I suppose.

*Do you keep any kind of notebook with details observed either in your daily life or your travels?*

I keep a journal. I record this and that, but don't really think of it as material for writing. It's just more of a writing exercise, a sort of daily warm-up for me.

*In this story and others, you really tap into food being a huge source of comfort and discomfort.*

Yes, absolutely.

*When Mala pre-pours the narrator's cornflakes for him, that's a rich gesture: It's touching and gently funny too, and revealing of her character. She doesn't question his choice, she continues to dutifully prepare his breakfast, even a breakfast whose very essence is convenience and lack of preparation.*

She's a new wife, and she wants to please and be helpful and do the wifely thing. That would mean doing things so that her husband wouldn't have to. I imagine her as a very traditionally raised woman with a strong sense of duty toward her husband. So that would include what she does with the cornflakes.

*Mrs. Croft must have grown up in a world without cornflakes herself, and would probably find it a less than proper breakfast. What does Mrs. Croft's kitchen—its contents and the soup regimen—convey about her character and situation?*

She's sort of eating to survive, in the same way that the narrator is—eating to live, and not the other way around. She's too old and too frail to do anything more elaborate. She can't even open up the cans. I think that for the narrator it would be a very startling thing to find a woman of her age living alone. It is simply unheard of in India, and I think in many other parts of the world as well, but certainly in India. The thought of an elderly person on his or her own would be quite disturbing and upsetting, but also kind of fascinating for the narrator to see. And she does manage, even though she's limited in what she can do.

*It's interesting that you mentioned the narrator's in a sort of similar position. He's not yet a householder, and she isn't much of one any longer. And they're both at this crossroads where they're passing one another, and that's something they have in common, two people who at first blush might seem more different than similar.*

Right.

*There's that nice detail about the table legs in Mrs. Croft's living room, being concealed, as are Mrs. Croft's—the story specifically compares the two on page 216—implying a modesty that is old-fashioned in 1960s Cambridge, but ironically more fitting I'd guess with 1960s Calcutta.*

Probably. The Victorian influence in Calcutta is quite strong, and the cultural changes that were in the air during the sixties in the United States had not hit Calcutta.

*Miniskirts among them, which seems to scandalize Mrs. Croft. Certainly regarding the propriety between the sexes, Mrs. Croft seems as though she'd be much more at home in Calcutta.*

Yes. *(Laughs.)* Probably.

*I wanted to talk about the piano bench. When we meet up with Mrs. Croft, it's at the bottom of the stairs, so right after she lets him in, she sits back down, and that's where she's to be found, most of the time.*

Right, that's her spot. That was a detail I took from my father's account. The real Mrs. Croft was a piano teacher, and the bench was central to the way he told the story: that she would be sitting there on the bench and would ask him to sit down beside her.

*There's a poignance to its being away from the piano—it's clear she no longer plays it.*

She's sort of disconnected from her former life. At the end of the story, the bench is back at the piano, because then Mala sits on it.

*She does, which also feels like a significant choice.*

It seems like that was the place the narrator associates himself and Mrs. Croft being together and now it's he and Mala who are a couple, a true couple. So I suppose that's why her sitting there would be significant.

*I also read into it some kind of connection between Mala and Mrs. Croft, because it's shortly afterward that Mrs. Croft deems her "a perfect lady." It makes a kind of quirky sense, given Mrs. Croft's Victorian propriety, that she'd be especially appreciative of Mala's virtues.*

Yes, that's another detail that's taken from the real life account. Apparently the real Mrs. Croft pronounced my mother a perfect lady.

*It's amazing that such a key element actually occurred. You know how you can read certain works of fiction and they feel constrained by a kind of over-autobiographical feeling and the sense that they're not fully imagined? But that's certainly not the case with this story.*

I think the difference is that I am at such a remove. It's one thing to write autobiographically about things that you've experienced. That's when the lack of imagination comes into play because you rely on what you know—but I knew nothing of this story apart from a two- or three-minute anecdote with scattered details about a piano bench, and cornflakes, and the "perfect lady." The rest of it was a completely alien world to me. I was two years old in 1969. I have no memory of the moon landing, I have no idea what it's like to immigrate, I have no idea what it's like to be a man. I have no idea what it was like for my father. I've never experienced anything remotely similar. The closest I've ever come is going to a foreign country for a week or two and struggling along in a foreign language, with a foreign currency. So even though all of these details were given to me in terms of family history, I had to work extra hard to make them ring true, and to make them seem credible. I was writing about both a time and an experience that I had no consciousness of.

*And you've done more than just make them credible. When Mrs. Croft pronounces Mala a perfect lady, it feels like so much has led to that moment. Their coupleness is being formally recognized in America, and in his mind.*

Yes. Because I managed to manipulate the details and the chronology of events, I think that the pronouncement is more significant in the world of the story than perhaps it was in real life. In real life, my parents may have just chuckled over that. I was also in that living room at the time. My parents took me on the visit to the real Mrs. Croft. I was two; god knows what I was doing. It was very funny and interesting to write a scene in which I knew I had been present but I erased myself completely.

*I wanted to talk about that small scene on pages 226-27 where the narrator is witnessing the woman in the sari with the baby stroller and there's another woman with a pet dog. There's a sort of mini-drama that's being played out before the narrator, and a small culture clash. I'm guessing that pet dogs are not nearly so popular in 1960s Calcutta?*

Not as much, no. I vaguely remember, when I lived in Boston, observing an Indian woman once walking down Mass Avenue; I think I was walking behind her. But you know it could have been a weird image in a dream that lingered. I don't know about the bit with the dog, either. I think I just invented it, but I can't be sure.

*The pet seems to convey a sense of American privilege and triviality, as well as a slight menace.*

I think of it as the narrator does: The woman is somehow vulnerable, because of her clothing and appearance, which are superficial traits standing for something deeper. Seeing it happen to an Indian woman who isn't his wife allows that realization to penetrate a bit more.

*How have some of your readers in India responded to your work?*

Oh, very different opinions. *(Laughs.)* Hatred and admiration and everything in between—it's sort of like here.

*Hatred? Why?*

I don't know. Why not? I mean it's just a matter of personal opinion. There are people who can't stand my writing and don't think I deserve to be published, and then there are other people who are very kind and say nice things. I think for some reason, because my book got more attention than certainly most people, including myself, thought it would, people react very strongly to it, both good and bad.

*What has your father had to say about* **"The Third and Final Continent"***?*

As I mentioned earlier, my father is generally a man of few words. When he read the story, his reply was, "My whole life is there."

## Gita Rajan (essay date 2006)

SOURCE: Rajan, Gita. "Poignant Pleasures: Feminist Ethics as Aesthetics in Jhumpa Lahiri and Anita Rao Badami." In *Literary Gestures: The Aesthetic in Asian American Writing,* edited by Rocío G. Davis and Sue-Im Lee, pp. 104-20. Philadelphia, Penn.: Temple University Press, 2006.

*[In the following essay, Rajan compares the ethical components of "When Mr. Pirzada Came to Dine" with those of another work featuring a child protagonist—the novel* A Hero's Walk, *written by Anita Rao Badami.]*

In the last few years, some South Asian writers in the United States have moved away from recounting thinly veiled, sociopolitical accounts of immigrant experiences to fashion aesthetically rich narratives that create a different kind frisson and reading pleasure. This difference, evident in select contemporary South Asian fiction in North America, is based upon an aesthetic of affect, i.e., evoking levels of poignant pleasure through conventional literary tropes and formal devices, as for example, through a child's narrative perspective, which blends together innocence with a sense of helplessness in order to generate pathos. In contrast, the narrative fulcrum in the works of Bharati Mukherjee, Sara Suleri, and Ved Mehta, for example—works that spanned the period from the 1970s to the late 1980s—was situated in the complex identity politics of diasporic, marginalized subjects on the cultural landscapes of Western, majority populations. In other words, these authors relied upon the reader's ability to blend together the American immigrant-dream metaphor with relics of images of the Raj days from which South Asians fled real or imagined oppressions, and decode plots that either reiterated the model minority success story or opted for the victim rhetoric of racial marginalization. Mukherjee's *Jasmine* or Bapsi Sidhwa's *American Brat* come to mind as representing these two modalities, which incorporated cliché́d norms from traditional narratives in an attempt to assimilate their characters into a multicultural America as the nation of newer immigrants.[1] Mukherjee, Sidhwa, and others crafted novels that evoked sympathy for their characters by focusing upon sociocultural inequities and injustices, with the objective of conveying a political message that was amplified in an environment of uncomfortable race relations in the nation. Such fiction serves as an example of a kind of realism, similar to that of nineteenth-century European writers whose ideology lay just under the surface of their literature, however, that is not our focus now.

By comparison, the recent works of Asian American authors such as Chitra Divakaruni, Jhumpa Lahiri, Mohsin Hamid, and Kirin Desai, for example portray subjects and situations that become memorable by invoking other kinds of aesthetic responses, something akin to brief or fleeting but pleasurable instances of shared cultural reminiscences or poignant memories of loss as they grapple with new realities. An important difference visible in the new set of South Asian American authors writing at the turn of this century, is a shift in focus that brings into play a distinctive affect through ethics. The formal devices they use create a space between readers and texts to locate one's aesthetic responses in the dynamic gap, where one encounters crises in the narratives and formulates a reaction that is based upon assessing the risk factor in not acting ethically. While the fiction of earlier writers foregrounded historical and political injustices, this new kind of fiction creates a frisson of awareness about ethical questions. Such an ethical component seems to be the simultaneous result of a younger generation of writers entering the arena (who perceive themselves as rooted within the nation space and not as diasporic or exilic actors) and a contemporary trend in fiction that responds to our globalized milieu[2] of an explosive, uncontrolled capitalism, and all its cultural accoutrements. This difference, as practiced by writers at the turn of the 20th century, more than simply marking a generational attitude, is also discernable in the morality-ethics divide. At the risk of generalizing,[3] moral codes articulated in a public sphere rely on external, institutional mandates of good and evil, reflect upon the actor, and usually result in or from institutional initiatives (like church or state-based morés of charity). In contrast, ethical conventions are grounded in internal, intuitive notions of right and wrong, and reflect upon the actor's individual actions in the community as enacted by shouldering civic responsibilities. In other words, in our globalized, multiethnic, multicultural environment, ethics is based upon mediated and negotiated actions of one's accountability to others in society and through civic notions of *doing the right thing,* while morality suggests a set of fixed principles or actions that apply to monocultures. In praxis, the contingency of aesthetic evaluation when measured as actions in the public sphere require a moving away from the universality of standards of conduct to locality or positionality of the subject in society and in the text.[4] This form of fiction which incorporates a strand of ethics as a device to deliver pleasure is an interesting experiment in the realist tradition, and is the focus of this essay.

Speaking of ethics and this newly fashioned aesthetic in South Asian American literature in the same breath puts the problematic relationship between these two categories in a different light.[5] While older debates about aesthetics and ethics ranged from the autonomous and transcendent nature of art to the abstract and universal responsibilities of art in society, contemporary scholars broaden the scope of these arguments by incorporating the specificity of cultural productions via grounded subject positions of gender and race. Such comprehensive or inclusive theorizing not only avoids the blind spot of European (and Enlightenment) models that barred non-Western points of view from entering the debate, but also sidesteps the inherent crisis produced by the postcolonial moment that resisted a hierarchized aesthetic based upon devaluing non-Western cultural productions. Almost running parallel with this recent change in the shaping of literatures, which reflects a move from the postcolonial phase to something loosely called globalization, there is a concomitant inclination of scholars to redeploy Emmanuel Levinas's theories of the Other for debating aesthetics and ethics. The passage often quoted for this purposes is Levinas's comment, "I am defined as a subjectivity, as a singular person, as an 'I' precisely because I am exposed to the other. It is my inescapable

and incontrovertible answerability to the other that makes me an individual 'I' to the extent that I agree to depose or dethrone myself—to abdicate my position of centrality—in favor of the vulnerable other."[6] Dorota Glowacka and Stephen Boos modify this view in their Introduction to *Between Ethics And Aesthetics: Crossing the Boundaries* to write, "for Levinas, Western representational paradigms are the project of an egological, imperial subject, while aesthetics, traditionally understood as producing a likeness of the Other, colludes in the appropriation of Otherness by the same. Levinas himself has never attempted to redefine aesthetics within the parameters of the Other, yet his critique has precipitated various searches for the possibility of an 'other' aesthetics, capable of accommodating radical alterity without reducing it to the measure of the same.'"[7]

While granting the appeal and perhaps even appropriateness of positioning Levinas as the main figure in reanimating the question of ethics inside aesthetics, some feminist scholars have taken Levinas to task for ignoring the woman question. Vicki Bell, for example, systematically challenges Levinas' statement that "indeed politics obliges one to engage in the non-ethical, so that the ethical cannot be understood as a basis of feminist politics,"[8] by responding that "ethics figures neither as a source of politics nor as a political weapon but as a check on freedom, an inspiration that prompts a continual questioning of one's own positionality, including the conditions of possibility of one's ethical sensibilities."[9] Sadly, Bell's assessment of Levinas remains bounded inside feminist critiques instead of being engaged in the wider arena of discourses on ethics. From an aesthetic angle, Marjorie Stone in a recent essay, "Between Ethics and Anguish," critiques Levinas's glaring omission or subjugation of female/feminine/gendered subjectivities vis-à-vis the Other.[10] Beyond the simplistic tendency of placing woman in the Other category, Stone's argument shows how the deeply personal moment in female subjectivity is part of an ethical crisis; yet another point of view that has not figured much in scholarly discussions of Levinas thus far. While I allude to Bell's position in rereading Levinas through a feminist lens to widen the circle of critical engagements of narrative discourses, in this essay, I will use Stone's logic to examine two South Asian texts.[11] Stone's "question [of] the relative neglect of the aesthetic in the developing work in feminist ethics and call for a more concerted analysis of the relations between feminist ethics and feminist aesthetics, between the 'real' and the representational"[12] resonates with my own scrutiny of unutterable trauma and the call to ethics in specific works of Jhumpa Lahiri and Anita Rau Badami. Consequently, I borrow some ideas from Stone's framework to explore a feminist granting of subjectivity and to read the ethical realism at work in Anita Rau Badami's *A Hero's Walk* (2001) and Jhumpa Lahiri's **"Mr. Pirzada Comes to Dine"** [*sic*] from her collection, ***The***

*Interpreter of Maladies* (1999).[13] In each of the works the protagonist is a young girl who impels readers to witness the anguish of making the right choice.

### THE LOGIC OF ASSOCIATIONS: VALIDATING COMPARISONS

It is necessary to explain why I thread together Badami's novel *A Hero's Walk* with Lahiri's short story, **"Mr. Pirzada Comes to Dine"**. To grasp the ethical import of new trends in literatures, Badami's novel about a young Asian Canadian girl's journey to India needs to be placed alongside Lahiri's short story about the experiences of a young Asian American girl in New England, and read as analogous texts. The point of comparison begins with the narrative perspective of a young girl in each case, who feels the West is her abode, and who is genuinely mystified by the idea of home that the other characters have. The reader's aesthetic responses to the two works are guided by the confident but naïve vision that the young girls have of themselves in society. Both authors deploy their own brand of ethical realism to assert their protagonists' childlike but firm sense of belonging. Upon reflection, this shows that Badami and Lahiri have crafted an identity for their heroes inside majority cultures without engaging in identity politics of minority race relations as the earlier set of authors from 1970s-80s had done. This is a crucial factor in understanding the shift from a morality undergirded by ideological motives to one that invokes an ethical response, i.e., these narratives do not solicit moral responses based upon rewriting history to correct a past injustice or racial, colonial oppressions. Instead, they create spaces through formal devices that allow readers to enter the narrative and glimpse a viable course of actions in terms of accountability to others. In fact, Lahiri and Badami deliberately use the childlike perspectives to show gaps between the actions of the older people in the works and what the readers perceive as the ethical choice in moments of crisis. Finally, reading the two works with and against each other challenges our orientation of centers and peripheries and changes our understanding of the cartography of global flows in an age of mobile cosmopolitanism—whether it is the United States or Canada—the condition of globality makes us reevaluate our paradigms of travel, migration, community and belonging, and the concomitant obligation to treat with courtesy and respect those whom we encounter. That is to say, it is not the deterritorialization of subjects that comes with *dislocation* that is fascinating in this comparison, but rather it is the unmooring of our notion of *national literatures* that comes with globalization, and our ways of reading new literatures.

But, there is also a critical difference. Lahiri's child protagonist intimates her ethical stance by glimpsing the world through television news to understand (albeit in a limited sense), the horrors of war, i.e., there is an aesthetic distance to her distress that is dramatized in Lahiri's use of the reportage genre. Badami's child protagonist hesitantly propels those around her to act ethically when she is viscerally imbricated in the unutterable trauma of loss through instances of interior monologue, i.e., the weight of non-ethical choices is more immediate as the consequences are borne by the young narrator. By looking through the prism of mirrored and distorted similarities of American and Canadian experiences of citizens of Asian origins, I posit an aesthetics that embodies the potential to articulate an ethics of/in local-global interactions. As a point of interest, there are examples of other Asian American narratives that have used child narrators,[14] such as Lan Cao's Mai Ngyen in *Monkey Bridge,* Christina Chiu's Eric Tsui in *Troublemaker and Other Stories,* and Lois Ann Yamanaka's Ivah in *Blue's Hanging.*[15] But the difference in Lahiri's and Badami's works are recognizable through their historical connections to the United States and Canada, respectively. The Vietnamese, Chinese, and Japanese-Hawaiian authors reflect their colonial relationship to the United States and consequently touch upon oppression and marginalization, and even though seen through a child's eyes, these issues are structured along majority/minority and class/race/sexuality lines, and are confined to national boundaries. In contrast, Lahiri and Badami work from a global level, but also paradoxically from within same race familial bonds. Lahiri's protagonist Lilia, the Indian American, is unable to see the Bangladeshi, Mr. Pirzada, through the lens of geographic proximity as a neighbor or another South Asian. Similarly, Badami's Nandana, the Indian Canadian is incapable of identifying with her own maternal grandparents within the essentialized domestic space of "India." That is to say, Lahiri and Badami inflect the details of time and space—the coordinates of realism—to shade the estrangement and the process of reengagement of the two girls within their own circles of class and culture so as to enable ethical choices, even as their actions require a global context, so that social justice is articulated in vocabularies of responsibility to community and accountability to one's fellow human beings.

### BADAMI'S *A HERO'S WALK*

Do certain experiences of human anguish become so intense that a threshold is crossed when it is no longer a matter of pleasure or beauty or their absence because the very possibility of artistic expression and aesthetic response is annihilated? The substitution of anguish for aesthetics . . . is meant to shadow forth this possibility, as well as to pose the question of how such anguish affects the first (and some might say) the primary term in the coupling of ethics and aesthetics, a binary that may take the form of a dialectical opposition as well as a continuum or space of mediation? Does it become unethical even to attempt to represent what seems unspeakable? And, does such unspeakable anguish also limit our ability to make ethical judgments in the realm of the 'real' as opposed to the representational?[16]

Anita Rau Badami's story focuses upon the travails of her protagonist, seven-year-old, biracial Nandana, whose parents die in a car crash in Vancouver, to explore how she narrowly escapes becoming a ward of the state because her maternal grandfather in India is discovered to be her legal guardian. Contrary to so many diaspora stories, Badami focuses upon the dislocation and traumatic experiences of a self-proclaimed "Canadian" child in India, so that the significance of home and family are not simply reversed but radically altered. Further, the most difficult aspects of nostalgia and loss are uttered in clear, childlike tones with a beguiling banality, making understatement the artistic or aesthetic device to shed light on the girl's unspeakable trauma. The abject horror of this child's plight and the utter cruelty to which she is subjected allows readers to see the gaps in ethical action and the lapses in responsible behavior of the adults in the novel. Thus, at a formal level, Badami uses the representational power of art and the pathos of the real and deploys interior monologue as a device to create a verisimilitude to keep within the tradition of realism. This strategy further enhances the dramatic irony of Nandana's situation. It is this masterful combination of aesthetics and ethics that systematically evokes poignant pleasure in the narrative.

The novel begins with Nandana not knowing that her parents have been killed, and her inability to understand why the older people in the story will not allow her to go home, "her father had often said it was only a hop, a skip, and a jump away. She knew her address—her parents had made her repeat it nearly every day—250 Melfa Lane, Vancouver, BC, Canada, North America, The World. Her father had always added the last two, and it had made her mother laugh and say, 'Don't confuse the child, Alan'" (16). Because she doesn't know, she tries to go back *spatially to the time* when "home" was accessible and constantly attempts to escape the people who want to protect her from the trauma. A few pages later this impulse is repeated, when she runs away from Kiran's place: "She was nervous about being alone on the road, but she knew it was only a hop, a skip, and a jump away" (28). Even when she is physically transported to India to her grandparents' house, she believes "home" was just a "hop, a skip, and a jump away" (164). The father's hyperbolic humor in positioning home as always being a "hop, skip, and jump" and located in the "world" gives Nandana a concrete sense of belonging, which in turn, creates a narrative disjuncture for the reader to glimpse the aesthetic *representational* factor of belonging that is balanced against the ethical *real* fact of not being in the right place. That is to say, the gap structured on a humorous ploy adults use teasingly, but one that Nandana believes to be legitimate,

allows readers to enter the narrative and recognize the pathos of her situation and wonder what actions the adults in her life will take to correct it. This gap is heightened when Nandana, who does not fully comprehend the fact that her parents have been killed, attempts to contact her parents as spoken in interior monologue:

> Earlier today, she had tried calling home when Aunty Kiran had gone for her bath. She got the answering machine. "Mummy, Daddy, please come and take me home," she said to the machine. Then she added, in case they had forgotten where she was sleeping over, "I am at Anjali's house. It's the white one with the maple tree, behind Safeway"
>
> . . . . .
>
> Nobody called her back or came to get her. She was beginning to think that Aunty Kiran had decided to keep her here for ever and ever. Hadn't she often said as much to her mother? "Maya, your daughter's such a cutie pie, I think I shall keep her." And her mother would laugh, "Ah, not so cute all the time, believe me. She can be a little pest." Then, she would stroke Nandana's cheek and say, "I wouldn't give her away for a zillion dollars."
>
> She wondered if her mother had changed her mind.
>
> (18)

Recognizable signposts of diaspora narratives—the differences in cultures, in national geographies, and social and psychic environments, and the longing for home as both imagined and real—operate at an aesthetic remove, or a radical angle in Badami's novel. For Nandana, home is the private space of family, of memories, of laughter and happiness with her mother and father, and she feels consistently destabilized, be it by Kiran, who lives on the next street "behind Safeway" or her grandmother, who lives across the seas in India. Badami aestheticizes the incomprehensibility of the situation for a child by layering Nandana's grief with bewilderment, thus nudging us toward empathy by intensifying our sense of pathos:

> On her last visit Nandana had crawled into her mother's closet. The clothes had smelled sweet: the white silky blouse that she wore when she had a meeting; special black pants and the regular brown ones; the sleeveless yellow cotton shirt that her father had said made her mother look like a sun drop. She sat silent as a mouse inside the closet, hoping that Aunty Kiran would leave without her. She spotted a spider creeping across the floor, towards the door and the light outside. Stupid spider, she thought and crushed it under her shoe. Dead, she told it. You are dead. Then she waited for Aunty Kiran to call her name.
>
> (117)

Here nostalgia, memory, life experiences, and trauma are all packed into Nandana's very being. It is the child's severe sense of confusion, misplaced rage, and a quiet desperation that readers glimpse. Her senseless

brutality in killing the spider hints at her partial awareness of death as an intrusive fact in her life, but she is
not able to deal with all the accompanying emotions.
Badami begins by slowly constructing Nandana's helplessness and gradually escalates it to hysterical proportions through interior monologue, "I want to go home
. . . homehomehome" (90) signaling the rising panic in
the child's body as she loses control of her world, imagining "her father would be wondering where Nandana
had gone. For *sure*" (90, original italics). The authorial
emphasis on *sure* ironically anchors Nandana in a safe
place and simultaneously reveals the threat to that safety
when it is taken away. Her hopelessness becomes real
when Kiran takes her back to her house to collect some
things for another overnight stay, "she ran inside eagerly. She thought that the house had a lonesome smell"
(91), which indicates to the reader that Nandana herself
is beginning to sense "home" as a place of loss.

But, Badami does not indulge in the stereotyping of minority subjects as victims by allowing the narrative to
be a litany of loss-filled events; instead, she introduces
an ethical sensor, and rescues Nandana through the actions of her grandmother. It is now worthwhile to explore the potential for feminist ethics (and feminist
aesthetics) in Badami's novel. In an attempt to explain
the practical meaning of feminist ethics, I borrow the
arguments that Robin Fiore and Hilde Linderman Nelson make in *Recognition, Responsibility, and Rights*
(2000), where they write, "Responsibility, as feminists
deploy the concept, is not exhausted by traditional
philosophical issues of freewill and the possibility of
moral judgments, of holding people accountable. For
feminists, it involves human practices of responsiveness
to particular contexts, of being accountable, that is taking as well as assigning responsibility."[17] The grandmother takes center stage in the child's shattered world,
the person who embraces Nandana by enmeshing her in
the familiarity of household routine, so that the child
begins to build a sense of normalcy through the very
monotony of performing habitual tasks. The grandmother serves as a stark contrast to the grandfather,
who refused to speak to his daughter when she married
a Canadian. And Nandana tells the reader through interior monologue that he is the "stranger," the "Old Man"
who made "her mother cry," while she remembers her
grandmother as the "kind Mamma lady" (154). In feminist vocabulary, the grandmother works through an *ethic
of care* allowing Badami to experiment with new structures of power, where the grandmother emerges as the
ethical actor in contrast to her daughter, Maya. Living
in Vancouver and inhabiting the modern West, Nandana's mother Maya, for all her enlightened outlook, is
only able to put in place patriarchal and juridical structures for safeguarding Nandana by *naming* her father in
her will. He "saw this trusteeship as an attempt by Maya

to force herself back into his life. But he signed the
documents nevertheless" (86). Though resentful, he
does accept this patriarchal authority.

The father, the "Old Man" resents the fact that he had
to lose face when Maya broke her promise to marry an
Indian man, saying "he would never avoid doing his
duty, even though Maya had no compunctions about ignoring hers" (116). The power of this sentiment lies in
the fact that the "Old Man" remains aloof from Nandana in Vancouver (inept at handling grief, perhaps),
and stoically fulfills his duty but fails in his ethical obligation to give solace to his granddaughter. It is the
grandmother, interestingly, from a small town in South
India, who from within traditional, matrilineal, familial
networks "pointed out, it was his duty" (116), and wel-
comed the distraught child into their midst. It is she
who metaphorically takes Nandana's hand and walks
the "hero's walk." The grandmother explains the meaning of "a hero's walk" to her dance students, urging
them to "walk with dignity. Walk with courage, and humility. Lift your head high" (136). Badami's message,
one could posit, is articulated in a feminist aesthetic so
as to give voice both to the granddaughter and grandmother; one silenced by grief and the other by tradition,
to portray a life that can be lived ethically. As Misha
Strauss says, "in trying to understand one's own role in
a particular situation or deliberating over a course of
actions, members of a person's community can help a
person reflect upon who she is and who she wants to
be. Members of one's community do important emotional work . . . that both contributes to the construction of one's self understanding and provides opportunities for transformation of one's self-
understanding. . . . It names the management of
others' emotions—soothes tempers, boosting confidence, fueling pride, preventing frictions and mending
egos."[18] In the end, Nandana and her grandmother form
family and community bonds that sustain them together,
as they walk the "the hero's walk."

LAHIRI'S "WHEN MR. PIRZADA CAME TO
DINE"

**"When Mr. Pirzada Came to Dine"** spotlights ethical
issues in large-scale global contexts about wars and
violence, and addresses the potential of a complex connectivity between global citizens and local subjects. Lahiri choreographs the reader's memories and embedded
images of war to dramatize the difference between acting out of an abstract sense of moral convention and
acting with pragmatic, ethical responsibility. The former
requires little personal involvement or sacrifice, while
the latter is based upon actual, transformative action,
however small those gestures might be. Lilia is the
young narrator who carries this message. The story is
about Mr. Pirzada, a figure in crisis from war-torn Bangladesh, who benefits from the benevolence of strangers

in a small, college town in New England, and who ultimately belies popular (xenophobic) expectations by going back home. Pirzada's situation, i.e., quasi refugee status, calls attention to a particular kind of discourse that is in circulation in different spaces of public culture in the United States about people's responsibility in a transnational arena in moments of global crisis. Lahiri's aesthetic device is the formalistic deployment of the reportage genre even as it negotiates the fiction-documentary divide. The duo—Lilia and Pirzada—enable discussions about the reader's preconceptions of unstable, third world countries where violence erupts as a result of national and ethnic conflicts (reiterated, for example, by media reports of Bosnia or Croatia, and more recently, of Afghanistan, or Iraq, Israel, and Palestine). The premise of such discourses is that these nations are not capable of managing their affairs, and thus need the developed West to intervene. The scope and nature of this intervention is precisely what shows the difference between ethics and morality in a global arena. By excavating memories from random spaces of public culture and United States's responses to war and disempowerment in distant countries, the story hints at the reader's own potential to act ethically by using the child as exemplum.

A comment Zygmunt Bauman made in *Liquid Modernity* (2000) is useful in understanding the sentimental responses to crises that are rooted in popular culture.[19] He notes how the United States has come to nurture *a culture of giving* over the last half a century:

> It was exactly that "emancipation"—from want, "low standards of life", paucity of needs, doing what the community has done rather than "being able" to do whatever one may still wish in the future—that loomed vaguely in Harry Truman's 1947 declaration of war on "underdevelopment." . . . Most obviously, "development" develops the dependency of men and women on things and events they can neither produce, control, see, nor understand. Other humans' deeds send long waves which, when they reach our doorstep, look strikingly like floods and other natural disasters; like them they come from nowhere, unannounced, and like them, they make a mockery of foresight, cunning, and prudence.[20]

The reportage genre is Lahiri's formal device to wrench Mr. Pirzada's national identity from Pakistan and assigns him a Bangladeshi citizenship. By using news reports and TV coverage Lahiri knits the story together and explains the intricacies of a civil war between East and West Pakistan that created Bangladesh. In choosing this reportage mode, which lends itself to her brand of realism, she catalogues the violence of war with concise, historical, and geographical precision. Lilia, the child protagonist, begins the story with: "In the autumn of 1971 a man used to come to our house, bearing confections in his pocket and hopes of ascertaining the life and death of his family" (23), and ends by saying, "Mr.

Pirzada flew back to his three-story home in Dacca, to discover what was left of it," while she and her family "went to Philadelphia to spend Christmas with friends of my parents" (41).

Lilia's guileless voice makes readers vigilant about Pirzada's precarious powerlessness and her family's unselfish response and commonsense understanding of generosity. However, the child's vision is telescoped by the author's ironical gaze that points to the inevitable limit of liberal generosity. Lilia's casual documentation of her family's willingness to help a stranger motors the story, and shows how Pirzada accepts their benevolence (comes to dinner) and its limit (returns to Dacca). It also reveals how Lilia's parents have assimilated into a form of public culture in the United States and, as members of the general public, have unconsciously internalized Truman's dictum of "emancipation" from "want" (Bauman). But once that obligation is fulfilled, the interruption is glossed over and their lives go on, as seen in their Christmas jaunt. In contrast, Pirzada is permanently marked by their kindness, as Lilia reveals in the end saying he "thanked us for our hospitality [upon returning to Dacca], adding that although he now understood the meaning of the words 'thank you' they still were not adequate to express his gratitude" (42).

By not making Pirzada a permanent liability, Lahiri reveals the other face of liberal generosity, i.e., the moral obligation and the necessarily temporary nature of transnational aid in today's tense geopolitical reality. Lilia's comment of Pirzada's "gratitude" points to public sentiments about social obligations, which in turn, enables readers to access sedimented memories about expected responses to human suffering while ensconced in the safety of their own homes. Lilia helps excavate such submerged memories by relaying the events as a composite report of the horrors of war overlaid upon the normalcy of everyday life:

> That year Pakistan was engaged in civil war. In March, Dacca had been invaded, torched, and shelled by the Pakistani army. Teachers were dragged onto streets and shot, women dragged into barracks and raped. By the end of the summer, three hundred thousand people were said to have died. In Dacca Mr. Pirzada had a three-story home, a lectureship in botany at the university, a wife of twenty years, and seven daughters between the ages of six and sixteen whose names all began with the letter A.
>
> (23)

By juxtaposing scenes of rape and genocide in the violent splitting of Pakistan with the placidity of hearth and home, and the familiarity of a modern university life with the strangeness of other's cultural practices, Lahiri allows readers to go back to the hazy *topoi* of news reports they, too, might have witnessed over the years. The scene brings back memories of other wars fought elsewhere, gradually creating a fundamental similarity about peoples' lives in war-torn zones. By skillfully using the reportage form, Lahiri couples distance and immediacy, war and peace, and a chaotic sameness out there with the stable sanctuary in here so as to suture together the representational aspect of aesthetics with the real issues of ethics. The next scene emphasizes this fact, when Lilia recounts, "That night, like every other night, we did not eat at the dining table, because it did not provide an unobstructed view of the television set. Instead we huddled around the coffee table, without conversing, our plates perched on the edges of our knees. From the kitchen my mother brought forth the succession of dishes: lentils with fried onions, green beans with coconut, fish cooked with raisins in a yogurt sauce" (30). Lahiri may be speaking of a war that birthed Bangladesh in 1971 while eating exotic Indian food, but today, the scene could very well trigger images of atrocities in other war-torn parts of the globe, as we too watch the evening news and eat dinner. These images of war, haphazardly stored and evoked from public memory sites become Lahiri's pretext for asking questions about one's ethical conduct in global contexts.

The latent sense of distance, safety (and privilege) that readers have stored in the vast and irregular spaces of public culture in the United States often gets mediated through communal acts of generosity. Giving money to feed the hungry and tending to refugees are familiar responses to war, which allows readers to engage their moral obligation, albeit impersonally. Lahiri's story suggests that the impulse behind such impersonal, institutionalized gestures of goodwill needs to be examined, and Lilia serves as her heuristic device. Lahiri manipulates public memory to probe this question by appealing to two sets of readers. On the first level there is the general reader, who merely recalls war scenes and formulates obligatory responses of generosity, and on the second level there is the more astute reader, who recognizes the subtle message about flaws in liberal humanism (and its corollary, liberal guilt). Lilia aligns herself with the first set of readers by saying "my father and Mr. Pirzada deplored the policies of a general named Yahyah Khan. They discussed intrigues I did not know, a catastrophe I could not comprehend. 'See, children your age, what they do to survive,' my father said as he served me another piece of fish" (31). Obligation here arises simply out of one's sense of safety in the face of the other's danger. Images of distant wars mapped outside the borders of the United States underscore one's security while also requiring one to engage in appropriate action. Lahiri adroitly builds upon such an unclear or unsure sentiment of moral obligation by having Lilia admit that her understanding of war came from learning about the American Revolution in school, a war that had both rational purpose and moral underpinnings.

Interestingly, Lilia's comment about her mother is meant to appeal to the second set of readers who know, and now are reminded again of fault lines in liberal generosity. The mother says, "'We live here now, she was born here.' She [mother] seemed genuinely proud of the fact, as if it were a reflection of my character. In her estimation, I knew, I was assured of a safe life, an easy life, a fine education, every opportunity" (26). The mother fits the outmoded, melting pot paradigm of immigrants, and reveals dichotomous moral impulses of gratitude and guilt based upon gifts received and sacrifices made in her life in the United States. She manifests such confused motives by cooking elaborate meals for Pirzada's daily dinner visits. Guilt, an unpredictable emotion, makes the cost of liberal humanism high indeed. Readers catch a brief glimpse of the fraying edges of her conflicting emotions when Lilia recalls that during the actual days of the war between East and West Pakistan, "my mother refused to serve anything other than boiled eggs with rice for dinner" (40). The mother's scaled-down dinner preparation points to this "procedural" sense of obligation. And, by switching to a quasi omniscient, news-anchor voice, the narrative gestures toward the fact that, in reality, liberal humanism is founded on the *unspeakable* immunity of first worldism. Her generosity is based upon parochial nationalism rather than a real willingness to help, and is seen in Lilia's remark that is informed by a nascent understanding of local-global connectivity:

> What they heard that evening . . . was that India and Pakistan were drawing closer and closer to war. Troops from both sides lined the border, and Dacca was insisting nothing short of independence. The war was to be waged on East Pakistani soil. The United States was siding with West Pakistan, the Soviet Union with India and what was soon to be Bangladesh.

(40)

The matter-of-fact reporting of the bloody exchange glosses over the fact that super powers tend to divide parts of the globe with self-serving political and economic motives, while using euphemisms to formulate policies. Lilia's factual tone gives the reader an opportunity to reflect upon *ethical responsibilities* to Pirzada, given that the United States is ideologically at odds with a Soviet-backed Bangladesh. Lahiri tries now to point to the sequel nature of international accountability, i.e., figuring out which nations the United States needs to help, and for how long its citizens feel responsible for those in war-ravaged nations. This implication of liberal generosity is underscored, particularly as the media seems invested in routinely and graphically proliferating reports of overwhelming global chaos aided by its unrelenting coverage of sensationalized violence.

That is to say, when images and information about war and ethnic cleansing in Croatia, for example, get sequentially superimposed upon images from Afghanistan, it becomes increasingly difficult to imagine the world out there, and to prioritize which nation and for how long disempowered people merit generosity. Political alliances, which add to the confusion of one's willingness to help, further problematize such a blurring of nations and peoples in need, especially in a world gone mad with violence. Using Lilia as the narrator and the reportage genre as her vehicle, Lahiri's story draws attention to the media's technique of creating a repository of indiscriminately blurred images in the public sphere, such that differences between moral obligation and ethical responsibility become distorted. Lahiri uses the form, i.e., the reportage genre, to challenge the *meaning of truth,* and alerts readers to their own roles as global citizens. Lilia's parents feel they owe Pirzada some charity and kindness, but Lilia connects with him at a visceral level in a not-yet-articulated effort of ethical, global community building.[21] Bauman expresses this sense of obligation in another way when he writes, "that to live is to live *with others* (other human beings; other beings *like us*)—is obvious to the point of banality. What is less obvious and not at all banal, is the fact that what we call 'the others' we live with . . . is what we *know* of them. Each of us 'construes' his or her own assortment of 'others' out of the sedimented, selected and processed memory of past encounters, communications, exchanges, joint ventures, and battles."[22] When horrendous images of war-torn places promote immediate but uncritical responses from people, how does one decipher the nature, meaning, and significance of ethical responsibility? If one agrees that the media obliterates national, ethnic, and religious barriers in order to sensationalize information and grab viewer attention (playing the ratings game), where does one turn for getting and assessing the *truth of the events in order to enact social justice*?

The ethical fulcrum of Lahiri's story rests on awakening readers to their own actions in this messy world. She points to the difference between an older generation of liberal humanists like Lilia's parents who feel morally obliged to be kind, and a younger generation of Lilias who are still working out a complex, ethical connectivity between peoples of this globe. Lahiri marks Lilia's place in a new generation of global citizens, citizens forging connections through genuine, radical kinship bonds. The story ushers in a cautious note of optimism through Lilia, a child who is not yet socialized or internalized that ideology of liberal generosity. When she hears Pirzada and his family are finally safe, Lilia recalls:

> To celebrate the good news my mother prepared a special dinner that evening, and when we sat down to eat at the coffee table, we toasted our water glasses, but I did not feel like celebrating. Though I had not seen him for months, it was only then that I felt Mr. Pirzada's absence. It was only then, raising my water glass in his name, that I knew what it was to miss someone

who was so many miles and hours away, just as he had missed his wife and daughters for so many months.

(42)

As a child who has not yet internalized the codes of adult gestures of civility, she embodies Lahiri's powerful note about the interdependency of human lives in a disproportionately globalized society. Lilia's sorrow, nay her empathy, is her bond of solidarity with Pirzada, one that reaches across transnational spaces.

Throughout the story, Lilia sees Pirzada as a friend, for example, by accepting his little gifts of candy, initiating him in the foreign act of carving a Halloween pumpkin, and praying each night that his "family was safe and sound" (32). But her parents see him merely as an object to be used as repayment for their good fortune in the United States, and thus feel a need to feed him curries. Lilia's sentiments and actions hint at the possibility of a nascent understanding of ethical, reciprocal community building. In today's world, alliances are temporary, fickle, and often politically motivated and/or market driven, hence ethical action cannot be based upon absolute commitments but upon small and consistent efforts of valuing and nurturing connections, even fleeting ones, between people. Lilia symbolizes such a connectivity that will make asking for and giving help not a matter of generosity, but one of solidarity. In this story, the Bangladesh war is a ploy for readers to reflect on the volatility in developing nations, the willingness of developed nations to help maintain peace, albeit a fragile peace, and the necessary actions each one of us takes as global citizens in this negotiation. Lilia tries, but doesn't fully succeed in revealing the full potential of global citizens to forge an equitable society that can affirm individual freedom and communal existence on a slippery balance between self-interest and responsible group interest.[23] Lahiri takes up the challenge of articulating an *ethical discourse* when claiming she is *telling us a story.*

## CONCLUSION

A child's voice, whether spoken in interior monologue as in Badami's case or articulated lucidly as in Lahiri's work, becomes a mode of experimentation on numerous registers. As a vehicle for deploying a version of feminist ethics, both authors move away from rigid, universalized moral codes, and suggest instead intimate gestures of friendship and solidarity that help build community. As seen, these bonds are not hierarchized via relations, but enabled through empathetic moments of doing the right thing. At a formal level, as expressions of feminist aesthetics, both authors use a child's voice to bring to the fore a contemporary issue of the ethics of care, taken up by feminists such as Alison Jaggar, Seyela Benhabib, and Marion M. Young in a larger debate that spans the spectrum of the rights and responsibilities of global citizens. Both authors attempt to awaken readers to their own responses and actions when faced with dilemmas that are becoming more and more part of our lived, globalized reality.[24]

### Notes

1. As Sue-Im Lee points out accurately in the Introduction, the problem of representing Asian American life using identity politics, ethnography, and immigration history as transparent criteria both for literary production and critical reception has been the norm. Most notably, the controversy (albeit misogynist) between the editors of *Aiiieeeee!* and Maxine Hong Kingston is a case in point. Using Elaine Kim's *Asian American Literature* (1982) to mark the point of departure, Lee writes, "the artistic and political modality with which Asian American literature entered the U.S. academia demonstrates, in a meta-critical sense, what Raymond Williams identified as the dual condition of 'representation': there 'is a possible degree of overlap between representative and representation in their political and artistic senses.'" That is, Asian American literary criticism served as more than a second level "representation" of the artistic endeavors of literary production. It fundamentally functioned as a discursive "representative" of Asian American subject positions. The case of the listed South Asian authors is more complicated. For one, their experiences reflect the post-1965 Immigration Reform period, so they are further removed from the brutal exclusionary and racist treatment experienced of the early Chinese and Japanese Americans. For another, because of their facility with the English language (thanks to the British), they perform a neat substitutive maneuver by using post-colonial resistance sensibilities and diasporic angst sentiments to assimilate into a multicultural/Asian America. All this notwithstanding, the novels of these authors beg for a political, sociohistorical reading.

2. I have argued this facet of contemporary South Asian writing elsewhere, too, most recently in "Ethical Responsibility in Inter-subjective Space" forthcoming in *Cross Wires: Asian American Imaginations in National, Transnational, and Global Contexts,* eds. Shirley Geok-Lin Lim, et.al., Temple University Press. The principal argument for using ethics is also articulated in different ways by Peter Singer in *The Ethics of Globalization* (New Haven, CT: Yale University Press, 2002) and Amy Chua in *World on Fire: How Exporting Free Market Democracy Breeds Ethnic Hatred and Global Instability* (New York: Doubleday, 2001).

3. I thank the editors for bringing Emory Elliott's *Aesthetics in a Multicultural Age* to my attention.

While many of the essays in his anthology engage in multidisciplinary and multicultural challenges to a Western, classical understanding of aesthetics, my examples are slightly different because I braid ethics with feminist criticism, and create another trajectory for analysis beyond identity politics in explaining the value and pleasures of the text.

4. This line of reasoning mirrors Lee's point in the "Introduction," wherein critical discourses assume "ethnic" can only lead to a sociological or anthropological "aesthetic."

5. Richard Cohen, *Face to Face with Levinas* (Albany, NY: State University of New York Press, 1986): 27.

6. Glowacka Dorota and Stephen Boos, eds. *Between Ethics and Aesthetics: Crossing the Boundaries* (New York: State University of New York, 2001): 3.

7. Passage quoted by Vicky Bell in "Ethics and Feminism" in *Between Ethics and Aesthetics,* eds. Dorota and Boos (Albany, NY: State University of New York Press 2002): 159.

8. Ibid., 159.

9. Marjorie Stone, "Between Ethics and Anguish: Feminist Ethics, Feminist Aesthetics, and Representations of Infanticide" in *Between Ethics and Aesthetics,* eds. Dorota and Boos.

10. Stone situates her argument about feminist ethics in comparing slave infanticide in a little-known poem by Elizabeth Barrett Browning, "The Runaway Slave at Pilgrim's Point" and Toni Morrison's *Beloved.* I find her argument applicable to my South Asian authors because of her careful explanation and coupling of feminist aesthetics and ethics.

11. Stone, "Between Ethics and Anguish": 132.

12. Anita Rau Badami, *A Hero's Walk* (Chapel Hill, NC: Algonquin Books, 2001) and Jhumpa Lahiri, *The Interpreter of Maladies* (New York: Houghton Mifflin, 1999). Direct quotations from these books will be cited parenthetically within the text.

13. See, for example, Alicia Otano's *Speaking the Past: Child Perspective in the Asian American Bildungsroman* (Hamburg: LIT Verlag, 2004).

14. Lan Cao, *Monkey Bridge* (New York: Penguin, 1998); Christina Chiu, *Troublemaker and Other Saints* (New York: G. P. Putnam, 2001); and Lois Ann Yamanaka, *Blu's Hanging* (New York: Avon Books, 1997).

15. Stone, "Between Ethics and Anguish": 136-7.

16. Robin Fiori, et al., eds. *Recognition, Responsibility, and Rights* (Lanham, MD: Rowman & Littlefield, 2003): ix.

17. Misha Strauss, "The Role of Recognition in the Formation of Self-Understanding" in *Recognition, Responsibility, and Rights,* eds. Robin Fiori, et al. (Lanham, MD: Rowman & Littlefield, 2003): 47-8.

18. Zygmunt Bauman, *Liquid Modernity* (Cambridge, UK: Polity Press, 2000). Bauman in discussing the "forms of togetherness" writes, "I propose that the passage from the convention-ruled to the moral condition is not marked by the sudden numbness of the once voluble demand, nor by the dropping of conditions which once circumscribed responsibility, but by the appearance (or reappearance) of what the ethical legislation declares off-limits in the world of morality—namely of the emotional relationship to the Other. I also propose that the kind of emotion which colors the relationship is secondary, regarding the very emotionality of encounter which is primary—and decisive" (62).

19. Ibid., 30-1.

20. Michael Smith writes in *The Moral Problem* (Malden, MA: Blackwell, 1994) that moral problems become apparent when the impossibility of reconciling the objectivity of morality, the action-guided character of judgment, and the foundational subject or the Humean principle of motivation come together. My focus is on the distinction between absolute standards of morality and the fluidity of ethical impulses in the messiness of everyday reality.

21. Bauman: 146, original italics.

22. Bauman makes the distinction between uncritical liberalism and responsible community action in "On Communitarianism and Human Freedom: Or How to Square the Circle," *Theory, Culture and Society,* 13.2 (1996): 79-90.

23. Acknowledgment: I thank Gurudev and Rohin Rajan for their guidance, Orin Grossman for his support, and am grateful to Sue Im Lee and Rocío Davis for their vigilance in making me revise for precision and clarity. I also thank the anonymous readers from Temple University Press for their helpful suggestions.

---

## FURTHER READING

### Criticism

Dubey, Ashutosh. "Immigrant Experience in Jhumpa Lahiri's *Interpreter of Maladies*." *Journal of Indian Writing in English* 30, no. 2 (July 2002): 22-6.

Examines how the cultural perspective of Lahiri's characters influences their attempts to cope with problems.

Jha, Parmanand. "Home and Abroad: Jhumpa Lahiri's *Interpreter of Maladies*." *Indian Journal of English Studies* 38 (2000-01): 106-17.

A comparative analysis of Lahiri's *The Interpreter of Maladies* with works by several other short story writers.

# Nikolai Semenovich Leskov
## 1831-1895

(Also transliterated as Nikolaj Leskov and Nikolay Leskov; wrote under the pseudonyms M. Stebnickij and M. Stebnitsky) Russian short-story writer, novelist, journalist, essayist, and critic.

For further information on Leskov's life and career, see *SSC*, Volume 34.

## INTRODUCTION

Plagued by adversaries and political censors throughout his lifetime, Leskov was considered a writer of secondary importance in his own era. Never mastering the form of the long realist novel, which at the time was considered the only serious literary form, Leskov instead produced an abundance of short fiction, which he published primarily in conservative journals and newspapers. Regarded as one of the most "Russian" of Russian writers, Leskov often featured members of the peasant class in his stories, situating them in tales involving themes of corruption, heroism, prejudice, the search for spiritual truth, tyranny, hypocrisy, religious and political dogmatism, and self-righteousness. These characters, scholars point out, reveal the author's fine ear for language, speaking in dialect and using folk expressions that mimic oral speech rather than more "literary" language. Central to Leskov's body of work is the issue of Christian morality and in particular the role of the Russian Orthodox Church—the state religion until 1917. Though Leskov wrote a vast number of tales in his almost thirty-five-year career, many of his works remained untranslated and thus unavailable to English-speaking readers until the early 1920s, when an English edition of his short stories was released. By the mid-twentieth century Leskov began to receive greater critical attention; he became increasingly well-known among non-Russian readers during the late 1970s and 1980s when the first book-length study of his life and works was published in English and when Russian leader Mikhail Gorbachev instituted the policy of *glasnost* ("openness") in 1985.

## BIOGRAPHICAL INFORMATION

Born on February 4, 1831, in the Russian village of Gorokhovo, Leskov grew up in the small city of Orel, southwest of Moscow. Although he was a member of the gentry, through his extended family he came in contact with virtually every social class in Russia. When Leskov was young, his family moved to a farm near Orel. During these years Leskov was introduced to the Russian countryside, where he came into contact with the common folk of Russia, many of whose types—the hero, the villain, the swindler, the fool, the righteous man—would surface later in his writings. Under the instruction of a tutor until the age of eight, in 1841 Leskov entered the gymnasium, Russia's academic high school. Five years later he dropped out, at the age of fifteen, then worked briefly for the Orel criminal court system. In 1849 he was transferred to a governmental post in Kiev, and while in the employ of the army recruitment office there he married Olga Vasil'evna Smirnova, the daughter of a prosperous merchant. The couple had a brief and unhappy marriage, and by 1862 it ended. In 1857 Leskov began working for his uncle, who managed estates near Kiev. For the next three years Leskov traveled throughout European Russia as the firm's chief Russian agent. These treks through the most remote parts of the Russian countryside gave Leskov the opportunity to study the habits, customs, speech, and mannerisms of country people. As part of his job Leskov sent his uncle letters detailing his progress; according to scholars, these dispatches evidenced an emerging talent for writing.

By 1861, at the age of thirty, Leskov had moved to St. Petersburg, where he began writing articles and columns. From the outset, however, Leskov was an outsider among other writers. He was neither an academic nor a member of the intelligentsia—unusual for a member of the literary world. Calling himself a reformer, Leskov communicated with radical writers, but early in his career he faced a boycott by many in the liberal press. Leskov had written an editorial calling for an investigation into an 1862 fire in St. Petersburg, which was rumored to have been started by radical students. Though it appears that Leskov's intent was simply to see justice served, liberals called him a betrayer and accused him of attacking their cause. For the next several years only the most conservative of publishers would accept Leskov's works.

Leskov produced his first short story in 1862. The following year he began writing novels as a way to legitimize himself as a writer. His first two attempts, both attacks on the radical community, incited so much opposition that for the next two decades the liberal press refused to publish any of his works. From that point on Leskov never published another novel, but turned to shorter forms instead. In 1875 he embarked on a three-month tour of western Europe. Experiencing turmoil in his personal life—his relationship with his common-law wife, Katerina Bubnova, was failing, and he was suffering from financial trouble due to difficulties finding publishers—Leskov found himself for the first time interacting with Western churchgoers. In Europe he was exposed to many Catholic and Protestant works that were either prohibited or simply not available in Russia, and he also completed a thorough reading of the Gospels. Ultimately rejecting many of his former Russian Orthodox beliefs, Leskov began focusing instead on what critics have called "spiritual Christianity," a nondenominational version of Christianity in which the foundation is one's personal faith and relationship with Jesus Christ.

Leskov continued producing short fiction during the last two decades of his life. He completed several collections of tales, including his Christmas stories, fictional works written specifically for the expanded Christmas editions of newspapers. These stories, popular in the 1870s and the 1880s, feature supernatural events combined with moral lessons. Satire became Leskov's major genre during this period and he became known for the carefully constructed narratives in his short stories. Modern critics have pointed out that Leskov began using the literary technique of "skaz," in which a narrator, using an informal, conversational style, retells a story that he himself has heard previously from someone else. In this way Leskov could distance himself from the controversial religious or moral meaning of his stories and avoid arousing the suspicion of political and religious censors. This new way of writing, however, caught the attention of authorities, and in 1883 Leskov lost his position with the Ministry of National Education. Becoming increasingly isolated and suffering from poor health and depression, he became even more despondent when a volume of his collected works was burned by censors. Critics have noted that toward the end of Leskov's life his stories became increasingly bitter and his satire more sharp. He died on February 21, 1895.

## MAJOR WORKS OF SHORT FICTION

From the outset, Leskov considered himself a reformer and an objective observer, and he spent a large part of his career responding to the social, moral, political, and religious issues of his native Russia. When he began writing in 1861, there existed a vast divide between Russia's rural, peasant class—the bulk of its population—and its cultural elite. Much of Leskov's work during the 1860s and early 1870s responds to this situation, and many of his short fictions are set in the rural provinces. According to several critics, Leskov typically situated his fiction in provincial settings in order to make his writing accessible to the general public, who would feel an emotional connection with these familiar backdrops. Featuring the Russian peasantry, who had preserved the rich oral folklore and the old customs and traditions, the tales also reveal the author's sharp ear for dialect, folk expressions, jargon, and proverbs. In 1865 Leskov published one of his best known and most popular stories. Stylistically and thematically unlike any other Leskov narrative, the erotic "Ledi Makbet Mtsenskogo uezda" ("Lady Macbeth of the Mtsensk District") is the author's version of English dramatist William Shakespeare's tragedy. It is also Leskov's attempt to create a distinctly Russian tragedy, one that features a provincial character who would be recognized as embodying as much drama and complexity as one of Shakespeare's tragic figures. In the story, the lustful Katerina L'vovna Izmailova is married to a middle-aged merchant who has in his employ a handsome steward, Sergei. After Katerina and the steward become lovers, their secret liaison is discovered by Katerina's father-in-law, who threatens to expose the affair. Portrayed as a demonic woman roused by passion to murder anyone standing in her way, Katerina first kills her father-in-law, then her husband, and then her nephew. When the lovers are exiled to Siberia as punishment, Katerina feels neither guilt nor remorse. After she finds out that her lover has rejected her for another female prisoner, she drowns both herself and her rival.

Leskov turned again to the moral state of his homeland in *Smekh i gore* (1871; *Laughter and Grief*), about the persecution he felt was rampant in Russia. This work contains a series of tales that depict Russian life as distasteful, full of betrayals, robberies, violence, and meddling by secret police. In one of his best-known stories, "Ocharovannyi strannik" (1873; "The Enchanted Wanderer"), Leskov examined the subject of Russian national identity. The hero of the story, Severianovich Fliagin, who is born a serf, kills a monk by accident. This flawed hero, who plods through life, but loves his country deeply, is seen as representative of the entire Russian people. With this story, as well as with the later "Skaz o tul'skom kosom Levshe i o stal'noi blokhe" (1881; "The Tale of the Crosseyed Lefthander from Tula and the Steel Flea"), Leskov gained a reputation as a defender of the Russian people and their heritage.

Leskov's short fiction after 1875 reveals the author's new spirituality. Written after his trip to Europe, many of these stories criticize what the author regarded as the hypocrisy of Russian politics and religion, pointing out the massive discrepancy between what political and Orthodox church leaders preached and how they lived. According to critics, Leskov was convinced that Russian society was in a state of moral decay, and from this point until his death his major concern was evading the censors so that his works could reach the Russian masses. To that end he used the literary device of "skaz," in which an unreliable narrator provides the "frame" for the story in order to sidetrack readers and keep them from recognizing the subversive voice of the author. Leskov became a master at dodging censors, using complicated titles filled with literary metaphors and indulging his love of wordplay. For example, he attacked the beliefs of the Orthodox Church in "Na kraiu sveta" (1876; "On the Edge of the World"). The tale revolves around a Siberian provincial bishop who hopes to convert the primitive people in his parish to Christianity. However, it is the pagan native and not the bishop who demonstrates true Christian behavior. In "Belyi orel" ("The White Eagle"), published in the Christmas edition of the *New Times* in 1880, Leskov veiled his criticism of political corruption in a simple ghost story. The incident, retold by the narrator, occurred some years prior. According to the narrator, the main character, Galaktion Ilyich, was sent on a mission to investigate the possible abuse of power by government officials. While conducting his investigation, Ilyich is accused of being involved in the sudden death of a man named Ivan Petrovich. Ilyich is then haunted by Petrovich's "ghost"—really Petrovich himself, who has faked his own death. With every other individual "in" on the scheme, Ilyich becomes the victim of a conspiracy by officials to sidetrack him from his job and discredit him as a witness.

Between 1886 and 1891 Leskov published nine tales, among them "Prekrasnaia Aza" (1888; "Beautiful Aza") and "Gora" (1890; "The Mountain"), which are adaptations of the religious narratives found in the *Prolog*. The popular *Prolog* tales were first written in Greek and later translated into Russian and enlarged to include the writings of the Church fathers. Leskov's re-workings emphasize an ecumenical spirit, celebrating the victory of the individual Christian follower over the institution of the Church. In "Beautiful Aza," for instance, a prostitute is eventually baptized by angels. In "The Mountain," a simple goldsmith possesses such a powerful faith that he is able, literally, to move mountains. Leskov's final story contains a masked attack on the inner workings of the Tsar's secret police, the Third Section—a subject no other nineteenth-century Russian writer would touch. Written between 1891 and 1894, "Zaiachii remiz" ("The Rabbit Carriage," "The March Hare," or "The Rabbit Warren") is a satire set in a small Ukrainian town. Bungling police official Onoprii Opanasovich carries out rules and orders blindly and unquestioningly. When it turns out that he has gone after the wrong man, he suffers a complete mental collapse and lands in an insane asylum. Considered too dangerous to print during the author's lifetime, the story was first published more than twenty years after Leskov's death.

## CRITICAL RECEPTION

Prior to the October Revolution of 1917, only a few scattered analyses of Leskov's work existed. During the Soviet regime, Leskov's works were excluded from the official school curriculum because of their "subversive" and "heretical" content. His writings, however, were too popular among general readers to be entirely dismissed by Soviet censors, so they instead passed his stories through a "filter," diluting passages describing his new spirituality and his antinihilism. The idea that Leskov was a key figure in Russian literature emerged slowly in the twentieth century. An English edition of some of his stories appeared in 1922, and beginning in the 1940s several other collections began to be released. Research on Leskov spread for the first time to countries other than his native Russia, and critics in the United States began discussing Leskov's treatment of such topics as religion, folklore, and Russian nationalism. In addition, Leskov's literary technique became a subject widely discussed by scholars. Some critics faulted his complex literary style, calling it excessive and obscure. Later critics noted that Leskov enjoyed confusing his readers and to that end would resist using the literal meaning of a word, instead experimenting with its full array of meanings. In fact, according to K. A. Lantz, Leskov was so accomplished at bewildering his audience that he was able to publish "On the Edge of the World" in a highly conservative paper that was sympathetic to the Orthodox Church. Irmhild Christina Sperrle points out that Leskov's fondness and talent for thinking up complex titles for his tales also attracted the notice of literary colleagues. Further reversing the tendency among earlier critics to simplify Leskov's works, scholar Norman W. Ingham suggests that Leskov's use of the narrative "frame" should quickly alert readers to the existence of a secret, or concealed, meaning behind the surface layer of the narrative.

Another major trend in Leskov criticism involves the tracing of Leskov's move from a "defender of Orthodoxy" to someone with leanings toward personal religion. Exploring the issue of gender identity, Faith Wigzell has studied Leskov's view of Russia as "Matushka Rus" (Mother Russia). Maintaining that during the nineteenth century the maternal image was of primary importance in Russian culture, Wigzell finds that Leskov celebrated this notion but did not embody maternal characteristics in his female characters, only in the males. Male characters, according to Wigzell, therefore constitute the main positive examples of "Russianness" in Leskov's fiction. Other critical discussions focus on the role of sentimentality in Leskov's fiction, the relation between Leskov and nineteenth-century Russian realist writers, the extent of his knowledge of Orthodox theology, and on his portrayal of the many personalities and ethnicities that comprised the Russian Empire.

# PRINCIPAL WORKS

## Short Fiction

*Tri rasskaza* 1863

"Ledi Makbet Mtsenskogo uzeda" ["Lady Macbeth of Mtsensk"] 1865

*Povesti, ocherki i rasskazy M. Stebnitskogo* [*Tales, Sketches, and Stories of M. Stebnitsky*] [as M. Stebnitsky] 1867

*Smekh i gore* ["Laughter and Grief"] 1871

"Ocharovannyi strannik" ["The Enchanted Wanderer"] 1874

"Na kraiu sveta (Iz vospominanii arkhiereia)" ["On the Edge of the World"] 1876

"Belyi orel" ["The White Eagle"] 1880

"Skaz o tul'skom kosom Levshe i o stal'noi blokhe (Tsekhovaia legenda)" ["The Tale of the Crosseyed Lefthander from Tula and the Steel Flea (A Workshop Legend)"] 1881; published in journal *Rus'*; republished as "Skaz o tul'skom Levshe i o stal'noi blokhe" 1882

*Zametki neizvestnogo* ["Notes of the Unknown"] 1884

*Sviatochnye rasskazy* ["Stories of the Christmas Season"] 1886

"Prekrasnaia Aza" ["Beautiful Aza"] 1888

"Gora" ["The Mountain"] 1890

*The Sentry and Other Stories by N. S. Leskov* 1922

"Zaiachii remiz" ["The Rabbit Warren," "The Rabbit Carriage," or "The March Hare"] 1922

*The Tales of N. S. Leskov, I: The Musk-Ox and Other Tales* 1944

*The Enchanted Pilgrim and Other Stories* 1946

*The Amazon and Other Stories* 1949

*Selected Tales* 1961

*Satirical Stories of Nikolai Leskov* 1969

*Five Tales* 1984

*The Sealed Angel and Other Stories* 1984

*Vale of Tears; and, On Quakeresses* 1991

*On the Edge of the World* 1992

## Other Major Works

*Nekuda* [*No Way Out* or *Nowhere to Go*] (novel) 1865

*Na nozhakh* [*At Daggers Drawn*] (novel) 1871

*Soboriane. Stargorodskaia khronika v 5-ti ch.* [*Cathedral Folk*] (chronicle) 1872

*Sobranie sochinenii* (short stories, novels, essays, criticism) vols. 1-10 1889-90; vols. 11-12, 1893 and 1896

*Polnoe sobranie sochinenii.* 30 vols. (short stories, novels, essays, criticism) 1996-

# CRITICISM

## Richard Bridgman (essay date autumn 1966)

SOURCE: Bridgman, Richard. "Leskov under the Bushel of Translation." *Texas Quarterly* 9, no. 3 (autumn 1966): 80-8.

[*In the following essay, Bridgman laments the fact that translations of Leskov's work are few and fairly inadequate, but argues that Leskov's "splendid" talent is nevertheless unmistakable in the texts available to English readers.*]

The Jacobean dramatists most often rise in the mind as one reads Leskov's stories. Like Ben Jonson, he possesses an uncanny range of technical knowledge about crafts and professions, which is complemented by a sharp ear for levels of speech. And like John Webster, Leskov encloses his people in a world clouded with savagery. Events close in upon men without warning, to torment and kill at their pleasure. The characters know this and, by doing their share of murdering, introduce themselves into the inexplicable scheme. This dangerous universe is ringed by terrors created in their own minds, for Leskov's people are unusually subject to hallucinations, visions, and marvels. This much is Websterian, the soup of poisoned paintings, amputated hands, and lycanthropic dukes. Leskov's characters respond to this surreal world as Webster's characters do to theirs. The same energy that animates it and projects delusions forth so invests the characters that they never snivel, never cower, but participate demonically in the world as is, and die dazzlingly. These are courageous, stoic characters, egoistic, demanding, dangerous. But they are not insensitive. This is a point worth making, since today we are not accustomed to the joining of power and sensitivity. They seem to us separate endowments. Leskov reminds us how far we have fallen from a conception of the full man.

Leskov's characters are flesh, bone, and often visible blood. One often thinks of them first as animals because of their brutal, candid activity, and Leskov encourages this metaphorically. But these are abundantly imaginative animals, whose minds teem with concretized images that leap out, blend with the feral scene, and surround them with a peculiar force and beauty. Moreover, these creatures are directly aware of powers controlling them, and worship them unabashedly. Their awe is not servile however, and rarely clots into inert theological forms. Vitality persists and forces religion to adapt to it—whereupon we come full circle, back to the animal energies animating, or put otherwise, making man.

Short of the radical step of learning the Russian language though, it sometimes seems that we shall never know how great a writer Nikolai Semenovich Leskov was. The universal plaint of his translators is that Leskov's style is a hurdle too high, and they have tripped, although capable of brilliant rhetorical turns. The trouble is that his style is essentially colloquial. Some intercultural significance may be made of the fact that Leskov was born in 1831, four years before our own colloquial master, Samuel Clemens. Leskov's translators go on to say that their failures are the more bitter since he is a writer of the first rank, and the most Russian of Russians. Gorki thought him a "magician of the word," and Tolstoi censured him for the winning fault of exuberance. "There were too many good things in his stories."

Painful as it is to be regaled with descriptions of a writer's narrative skill and verbal pyrotechnics and then be told they are hidden from view, still perhaps a strong enough light will burn the bushel. As a priest and his barbaric driver wait out a blizzard in a snow hollow roofed with reindeer skins, Leskov evokes a Siberian snore—"As if a large swarm of bees was humming and knocking gently on the sides of a dry, resonant beehive." The atmosphere of "human sweat, smoke, damp rottenness, dried fish, fish fat, and dirt" generates the following acerbly comic interchange, whose vivacity is a second heartening instance of Leskov's penetrating the barrier of intractable language.

> "Don't snore," I said.
>
> "Why, Bachka? Why shouldn't I snore?"
>
> "You snore horribly, you don't let me sleep."
>
> "You ought to snore too."
>
> "I don't know how to snore."
>
> "And I know how to, Bachka," and he instantly started droning at full speed.

Other metaphors shine forth. Reindeer skins resemble soapsuds. Gay laughter sounds "as if someone was tickling the water nymph of the lake." A Tarter resembles "a fresh and hardy vegetable." A Roman candle goes off "like a fiery bird with a burning tail." And a gypsy's grace is lauded: "I have seen actresses dance at a theatre, but pah, they were like an officer's horse on parade that fidgets for nothing, without any fantasy—there's no fire and no life about it. When this queen stepped out, she seemed to be sailing on a calm sea and yet you could hear her bones crack and her marrow run from bone to bone."

Few people know that Leskov is that exhilirating to read. Not much of his work is available, and what is is indifferently translated. But for the moment the first job is to get Leskov out in the open, to demonstrate that he is a splendid writer. Then we can quibble our way pleasantly toward fidelity.

The portrait of Leskov most frequently reproduced shows a doughty man, seated, arms firmly folded in front of him and supported on the arch of a cane. He is bearded and wears a kind of engineer's cap fixed squarely on his head. Leskov was the son of a civil servant. Like Pushkin and Tolstoi he had peasant nurses, but more important he early came into the aura of an Aunt Polly, whose Quaker beliefs sufficiently permeated him so that near the end of his life he approached sympathetically—but did not go ga-ga over—Tolstoi's radical Christianity. His uncle by marriage, an Englishman named Scott, managed some extensive estates near Kiev, and for ten years he employed his nephew as a business agent. Leskov's letters to Scott—so the story goes—were impressive enough for friends to encourage him to enter journalism.

Leskov's career now took a queer turn. Arriving at St. Petersburg as a committed journalist, he immediately reduced his market with an improvident article. St. Petersburg had been seriously burned in 1862 and the radicals were blamed for it. Leskov, by nature a partisan of objectivity, called for an official investigation to test the validity of these rumors to which, ironically, he seems not to have subscribed. The liberal press thinking they saw an act of betrayal at once denied Leskov publication in a sizable portion of the national press. Since he had intimately observed the condition of the serfs Leskov too desired reform, but he felt the liberals were too often fowl, squawking, pecking, hissing, and quacking in the barnyard while progress toward a genuinely humane and cultured Russia went a-begging in the wilderness. This position, consolidated by the personal attacks upon him, led him to write novels critical of the progressives, the titles of which suggest the Russian political climate: in 1864, *The Impasse* (sometimes translated as *No Way Out*), and in 1870, *At Daggers Drawn*. Being virtually ostracized did not shake Leskov artistically. His great stories are marked by stability, good humor, and under the circumstances, a notable lack of vindictiveness. He does not seem to have been obsessed by his persecution and won a wide reading public in spite of the boycott.

This same poise kept him in later life from falling into the excesses of Tolstoian piety. Although Leskov admired the glowing faith of Russian mystics, he readily satirized the clergy. "On the Edge of the World" (1876) concludes, "Gentlemen, reverence at least the holy modesty of the Orthodox Church, and understand that she has truly maintained the spirit of Christ, if she suffers all that God wills her to suffer. Truly, her humility is worthy of praise; and we must wonder at her vitality and bless God for it." Yet, before this reconciliation is reached, Leskov has led us through a bitterly hilarious account of a young priest on the Siberian frontier learning not to push conversion too strongly among the natives. If their genial pragmatism leads them to yield occasionally to the baptizing efforts of a vodka-peddling missionary, they still view Christ as a kind but essentially weak deity. The priest's driver, for example, admires Christ chiefly because he made a blind man see by spitting in his eyes, an appeal whose literalness naturally troubles the young, idealistic priest. Not long after, though, he awakens in his sledge with his eyelashes frozen shut. With no analogical fuss from Leskov, the driver spits in the priest's eyes and rubs them until they unfreeze.

Such ironic counterpoint is often perceptible in Leskov's work. In **"The Enchanted Wanderer"** (1874), the leading character is purchased at one point as a nurse for a little girl, who suffers from "the English illness," which according to normal nationalistic slurs would be venereal in origin but which here is apparently rickets. As a result, her legs are "round as wheels." Later the Wanderer is captured by Tartars, who slit the soles of his feet and pack chopped horsehairs into the wounds. The prickling forces the Wanderer to walk on his ankles until his legs too become "round as wheels." (The treatment enrages the Wanderer: "You damned Asiatics, what have you made of me? Better to have killed me outright, you vipers!" To which the Tartars reply soothingly, "Never mind, Ivan, never mind. Why make a fuss about nothing?")

Before the story of the young priest in Siberia ends, another savage has gobbled up the Holy Elements of the mass, drunk the consecrated oil, and stolen the ritualistic box in which they are carried. The acquisition of this sort of ruefully comic experience often makes Leskov's priests into sane men who know how to act with vigorous good sense. When the Wanderer turns lay brother, his religious fervor leads to fits of hallucination. Under the illusion that it is a suicide seeking his prayers—which he cannot in good conscience provide—he kills the convent cow. So the Father Prior locks him in a potato cellar. There he falls into incessant prophesying, whereupon the Father's next response is to transfer him to a building stripped of all furniture save the icon "Blessed Silence." When, after a winter in the exclusive company of a silent Christ, the Wanderer has not improved, the Father finally decides to send him "off somewhere to have a good run. Perhaps he has merely grown stale in one place."

This, the tolerant view, is the one most often taken by the ecclesiastical leaders in Leskov's world, but the stupid, the venal, and the petty appear too. In **"The March Hare"** (sometimes known as **"The Hare Park"** and published twenty-two years after Leskov's death in 1895) a priest learns during confession that a boy has stolen watermelons from his garden (Russian Missouri again) and hales the boy up and down the room by the hair. The boy's indignant father in turn berates the priest as a beast and usurer (he is), and as reparation wins

from him a pound of foreign soap, a turkey cock and two turkey hens, a heifer, a young pig, and "a lovely piece of cloth that will make you a very excellent coat" (Russian Washington, D.C.).

Leskov's priesthood stands on the solid base of the simple lay believers. A caveat: these are spiritually simple men whose faith and vision have gradually clarified in the dark cellar of existence. Otherwise, they are demonstrably complex human beings, not in the slightest degree allegorical. The conclusion of the Wanderer's story can be misleading. "He had told us all his story with the unreserved frankness of his simple soul, and his prophecies are concealed in the hands of Him who has kept his decrees from the wise and has revealed them to babes and sucklings." The career of this babe and suckling leavens the simplistic sentiment. It begins when he tumbles a man under the wheels of a coach for which he rides postillion. The dead man comes to haunt the Wanderer, and the two confront one another forthrightly. "What do you want with me? Go away!" "You took my life without leaving me the time to repent my sins." "Things will happen."

This same matter-of-factness reappears when the Wanderer flogs a Tartar to death in an endurance match. In retrospect he comments, "His stubbornness and ambition caused him to depart stupidly from this world. You see, I am not to blame, it was his own fault." The Wanderer is no sadistic scoundrel. We are not appalled by his attitudes so much as we are slowly drawn to accept their inevitability in a pain-ridden and irrational world. Leskov's men are forceful, proud, and active and in a violent existence swirling with nightmarish visions they retain a stoic elan that is compellingly attractive. The Wanderer meets the abandoned mistress of a prince for whom he works. Wolf-eyed and big in stomach, she begs him to plunge a knife into her heart. "I shuddered all over and told her to pray. I couldn't kill her with the knife; I pushed her off the bank into the river." This Wanderer, the one whose way with a wild horse was to jump on his back, "seize him with my left hand by the ear and turn him aside with all my might, whilst I hit him with my right between the ears and ground my teeth most frightfully," *this* Wanderer earns the right to be simple, so fantastically and savagely complex is his enchanted world. His struggles in the weird web of life finally win him direct religious vision.

Leskov introduces us to another variety of spiritual response in **"The Musk Ox"** (1862). Vasilii Petrovich, the clumsy title figure whose arrival is presaged by "a series of heavy movements . . . behind the fence, following which [he] dropped into the little garden like a load of earth" is Leskov's most relentlessly pessimistic character. This tortured, earth-bound idealist plays out the misery of his life against an idyllic backdrop of forest monasteries, between which pilgrims travel slowly in country carts, the air fragrant with lilacs, golden carp and trout leaping in the thin vapours over the surface of wooded lakes, and "jackdaws pottering about in the greenery of the trees."

In the midst of this lyric serenity stands a gruff icono-clast and radical Christian. Accused of impractical ide-alism, the Musk Ox responds irritably, "What will you have me do? My heart cannot stand this civilization, this nobilization, this scoundrelization!" He suffers nei-ther fools nor brutes easily, and as a consequence loses a tutor's job for assaulting a young aristocrat who had trapped and teased a maid on a ladder. And he is pro-foundly upset when he witnesses a governmental roundup of vagrant Jewish children for military service. "I can't follow all your la-di-das," he cries. "Your heads are full of stuff about the sheep being safe and the wolves being in good fettle too; only it can't be done. It never happens that way." His peculiar blend of spiritual pith and ferocious sympathy is caught in this small ex-change: "Your mother is alive and well, I hope," asks the narrator. "Died in a poorhouse." "What, all alone?" "Well, who do people die with?"

The Musk Ox makes a series of unsuccessful withdraw-als from society: to live among the Old Believers—"The truth is they are a lot of hair-splitters"; to a forest hermitage, from which he is soon expelled for holding free-thought seminars with pilgrims; and finally to a family of wealthy ex-serfs. Mooning and snarling at his hosts in the extremity of his spiritual malaise, he is sent to their lumber camp. There the Musk Ox makes his last retreat—to a stifling dark woodland nook where he hangs himself with his belt. The margins of his copy of Plato are filled with self-accusation: "A clown to the people, a curse unto thyself, a killer of ideas." Though Leskov's·men are possessed with God in queer ways, and sometimes seem to win a salvation of sorts, they are quite as likely to end as disastrously as the Musk Ox, with his "bloodshot dilated eyes [staring] at the moon with the expression which is left in the eyes of a bull who has been struck several times on the head with a bludgeon, and then straightaway has had his throat slit."

Writing of peasants, Leskov never seems, like Turg-eniev, to be a god descended temporarily among the commoners. He is sympathetic and shares their attitudes easily. He revels in odd details drawn from country life, so that here and there in his stories we learn that an "astronomer" is a horse that habitually jerks its head up; that the best way to assess the maturity of a pig is to pierce his back fat with an awl; and that if you put a burbot (not a turbot) in a wooden trough, tease it until its liver swells in rage, and then kill it, you are assured of a delicious soup. His eye for detail has a structural counterpart, for he customarily organizes his material in small units of narrative. His chapters are rarely more

that three to five pages long, for he conceives his action in a series of discrete blocks linked by symbolic recur-rence. He is fond of using a narrator; sometimes a brace of them with the first introducing the second who then tells the main story, even as the Conradian narrator in-troduces Marlow.

In **"The March Hare,"** for example, a narrator takes us to an asylum where one of its inmates, O., proceeds to describe how he became a rabid conservative. Although the tone is persistently ironic and the climax high farce, Leskov still generates sympathy for this poor devil of a subdistrict police officer, whose title alone must remind us of Orwell as a young sub-sub in Burma and Melville's sub-sub librarian, and all the attendant iro-nies generated by debased bureaucratic titles.

O.'s route to obsession passes through the Church. Serv-ing as a bishop's choirboy, he is instructed by a marti-net who respects Facts and the kind of authority they breed. O. must memorize that the Virgin was born in the summer of 5486, and that seventy thousand saints were born in January, but only a hundred and thirty in June. Stuffed with such tripe, O. is sent home to be-come a police official. His distorted zeal sets him after those "underminers of foundations," the Socialists. He meticulously traps a governess into writing out and signing two apparently radical remarks ("The deceitful-ness of riches chokes the Word"), which naturally turn out to be quotations from the New Testament. Tricked, cuckolded, and maddened to a frenzy by a real subver-sive in his employ, O. is sent off at last to the asylum where he spends his days knitting socks and his nights sitting on heron eggs in the swamps in order (so he believes) to hatch the fire bird. But as he remarks plain-tively to the narrator: "The fire bird cannot be hatched out, if they all want to eat heron's eggs."

This badgered victim of an authoritarian education owns just one more of the many obsessions Leskov explores. If O. is shallow and mad, the Musk Ox introspective and self-destroying, and the Wanderer robust and per-egrine, each displays a personality bent by the brilliant and mysteriously relentless pressures of life. As a rule, Leskov commiserates with those in the grip of sav-agery, but in at least one instance the savagery itself dominates his interest. In his major work, **"Lady Mac-beth of Mtsensk"** (1865), we read a chilling story of the utmost emotional power and technical skill, totally lacking in pity. It moves from the classic opening of a bored merchant's wife thrown in the company of her handsome lackey, through a history of adultery, murder, and punishment—all without the faintest nod to guilt or remorse. Yet Leskov creates respect for the single-minded intensity of his characters, who, like trapped foxes, gnaw themselves free, indifferent to the mutila-tion they must inflict upon themselves.

The first of many low-keyed symbolic events in **"Lady Macbeth"** occurs when the husband is called away because a dam has burst and damaged his property. The central unifying gesture of the whole story is a symbolic cognate to this—the pressure of Katerina's breast, first felt when Sergei exuberantly squeezes her to him. Shortly he has made her his mistress, whereupon a large grey cat, strokable but—properly for an embodiment of passion—not seizable, lies between her breasts. After the lovers have murdered her father-in-law, this same cat assumes the dead man's face to comment, "I have come from the churchyard on purpose to see how you and Sergei Filipych are warming your husband's bed." Following this sardonic apparition, Katerina's husband arrives to be dispatched with a blow from a candlestick, supplemented by strangulation. "For five quiet minutes" Katerina lies atop her husband's chest as her lover strangles him—listening to his heart slow, and stop.

This bizarre murder is a ghastly counterpart to their sexual passion, which is also consummated in eerie silence. When Sergei first takes Katerina, "a silence fell upon the room, which was broken only by the soft regular ticking of a watch." (It is her husband's.) They spend a passionate night later under an apple tree when "the air was still" and "It was difficult to breathe, and one felt an inclination to laziness, indulgence, and dark desires." A fresh murder takes place in an equally oppressive atmosphere, heightened by whispers, coughs, heavy breathing, hoarseness, candles being snuffed, shutters closed. Then Katerina "with one rapid movement covered the childish face of the victim with a large down pillow and threw herself on it with her firm elastic bosom."

Drunken passersby witness and interrupt the last moments of this murder with "deafening blows" upon the shutters. After this equivalent to the Shakespearian porter scene (which is omitted in Shostakovich's opera based upon this story), the lovers are sentenced to exile in Siberia. "When they handed her child to her [Katerina] only said: 'What do I want with him!' turned to the wall, and fell with her bosom on the hard pallet." During the long journey east, Sergei trifles with other female convicts. Once convinced of his infidelity, Katerina throws her chief rival overboard as the prisoners cross the Volga, then leaps into the water herself. Having this long sustained his remarkable metaphor of the breast's suffocating passion, Leskov concludes: "Katerina Lvovna rose from another wave almost to the waist above the water, and threw herself on Sonetka like a strong pike on a soft-finned minnow, and neither appeared again."

**"Lady Macbeth"**'s ending in a fish simile reminds us that Leskov's fiction swarms with imagery drawn from natural life. Human activity is characteristically punctuated by animal commentary—is, in fact, virtually ab-sorbed in it. When Sergei and Katerina embrace under an apple tree, Leskov rises to a bravura paragraph, flavorsome, mixed, curious:

> A golden night! Stillness, light, aroma and beneficent vivifying warmth. On the other side of the garden, in the distance beyond the ravine, someone struck up a loud song; near the fence in a thicket of bird-cherries a nightingale poured forth its shrill song; in a cage on a high pole a sleepy quail jumped about; the fat horse breathed heavily behind the stable wall; and on the other side of the garden fence a pack of gay dogs ran noiselessly across the common and disappeared in the strange, formless, black shade of the old half-ruined salt warehouse.

Similarly, when the couple make love in a wretched corridor of a way station, a chorus of sounds surrounds them: a guard spitting idly at his boot tip, crickets chirping competitively, convicts snoring, a mouse gnawing a feather under the stove.

Leskov's grotesque juxtapositions of levels of natural life make the delusions his characters often suffer seem part and parcel of a weird whole. Sometimes the illusions are symbolic dreams like Katerina's cat of passion. Sometimes madness brings on the fantasies. One stage of O.'s progress out of hysterical delirium is marked by this vision: "Something dancing before my eyes, something very mysterious, some curiously tiny creatures, the size of pea-pods, just like the dwarfs children sometimes see in dreams, and these dwarfs seemed to be fighting with one another and waving steel spears about which flashed so brilliantly they almost blinded me."

At other times, Leskov's characters face bewildering physical illusions. At the very moment that a drunken priest lies down above a window under which there is a gateway, "a cartload of hay had driven into it, and he, in his fuzzled, sleepy state, imagined that it had driven into his inside." The priest refuses to budge until the cart is driven out again where he can see it. Such roughhouse fancy is matched by lyrical beauty. Caught in a snowstorm and abandoned by his driver, the young priest sees this:

> A gigantic winged figure floated towards me, clad from head to heels in a chiton of silver brocade, which sparkled all over; on its head it had a headdress that seemed to be seven feet high and glittered as if it were covered all over with diamonds, or, more precisely, as if it were a whole diamond mitre. . . . It was like a richly ornamented Indian idol, and to complete this resemblance with an idol and its fantastic appearance, from under the feet of my wonderful visitor sparks of silver dust spurted out on all sides, and he seemed to float upon them as on a light cloud.

Even though this particular vision turns out to be no more than the priest's frost-covered driver returning to rescue him, it is wonderful enough. The drive in his snow miter is no less a representative of salvation than a bishop in his golden one. Leskov's natural world repeatedly produces such scenes that reveal wonders truly beyond madness, and these constitute the last regality of Leskov's imagination. It leaps the boundaries of a perceived world to testify to the awesome splendor of man immersed in his own fantasies. Even as the lower animals envelop his characters' lives, so do these wonders that need not rise from madness or derangement:

> An ancient man came up to me, he mumbled incoherently; he was covered with wax and smelt of honey; yellow bees wriggled in his eyebrows.

What else shall we make of this forest creature than that he is Leskov's measure of life? And note: like the plain cup of water and honey-drenched cucumber that this old man provides as refreshment, Leskov's conceptions have a mysterious adequacy, even in English.

## Thomas L. Aman (essay date winter 1968)

SOURCE: Aman, Thomas L. "Leskov's First Series of Sketches." *Slavic and East European Journal* 12, no. 4 (winter 1968): 424-34.

[*In the following essay, Aman offers an analysis of two of Leskov's earliest short stories—"Razbojnik" (1862) and "V tarantase" (1862)—noting that the two tales contain many of the subjects, character traits, narrative techniques, and verbal wordplay that would typify Leskov's entire career.*]

It is generally considered that Leskov is one of the masters of the short story in Russian literature. But this undisputed fact might be a closely guarded secret, for all the critical acclaim Leskov has received in English. Professor Edgerton has performed a titan's task in sorting through the maze of biographical material on the writer,[1] and Thomas Eekman has contributed to our overall understanding of Leskov's best known novel, *Soborjane*.[2] But Leskov's short stories have received very little attention indeed. Except for V. S. Pritchett's sparse comments,[3] it may almost be said that Hugh McLean has single-handedly contributed to whatever critical literature there is on Leskov's short works.[4]

The story of Leskov's extensive journeys over the wide expanse of Russia is well known. His keen powers of observation coupled with a lively imagination served him in good stead when he eventually determined to make his living by the pen. During his thirty-five years as a writer, Leskov created a prodigious body of literature encompassing an incredible variety of genres, topics, and characters. He was fairly brimming over with ideas, and his work at times gives the impression of having been written down helter-skelter, so much was

he in a rush to get it to the printer's office in order to launch himself into a new project. This is, in most cases, an illusion, however, for what is in force is a technique both carefully contrived and controlled—a technique producing that apparent haphazardness which is the hallmark of Leskov's talent and which is so like life itself.

Occasionally Leskov's hand could not keep pace with Leskov's imagination. At times he planned entire series of stories in advance only to see these plans disappear as he got caught up by a different idea. His Lady Plodomasova, for example, was to be but the first character in a proposed trilogy.[5] In 1864 in a letter to Straxov Leskov mentions a projected series of eleven stories to follow **"The Lady Macbeth of Our District."**[6] Neither of these plans was ever realized. At other times he was more successful in bringing his projects to fruition, as witness his "Rasskazy kstati" and "Rasskazy neizvestnogo." But whether such projected series actually saw publication or remained mere plans, Leskov was attracted to the form.

Leskov's first effort of the pen, which is the first in a series of articles on the distilling industry in the Penza district, is dated 28 April 1860. Two years later, in March, Leskov published his first purely artistic work under the heading **"Pogasšee delo."**[7] This was followed in a month by the sketch **"Razbojnik"**[8] and shortly thereafter by its continuation, **"V tarantase."**[9] The latter two stories were subsequently republished in the collection, *Tri rasskaza* (Peterburg, 1863).

Had Leskov's later works suffered the same fate that these first stories did, he would be utterly unknown to the Russian reading public today. Following the 1863 edition, **"V tarantase"** was never again published. **"Razbojnik"** had to wait 82 years from the time of its republication in 1863 before it again saw the light of day.[10] Then, as in the more recent edition of Leskov's *Collected Works* of 1956, it was presented without the follow-up sketch, **"V tarantase."** It is unfortunate that this should have happened, for the sketches form two parts of one comprehensive whole. It is also surprising, because **"V tarantase"** is, as A. Narkevič points out, at least as good a story as **"Razbojnik."**[11] One even gets the impression that the decision to publish one sketch without the other was purely arbitrary. Although the two stories are far from Leskov's best offerings, I do not believe that they should be so lightly dismissed as they are in Edgerton's statement: "neither of these two sketches is particularly good as a story."[12]

The two stories under discussion deal with a group of travellers on their way to the fair in Makar'eva. The time is fixed as "fair" time; no further definition is given except that it is hot and dry, therefore summer. The travellers' journey takes them through the Penza district, and the settings of the sketches are the open road and various wayhouses along the route. Leskov, the narrator and one of the travellers, is a non-participating observer.

The origin of the stories is unknown, but it is most probable that Leskov heard the anecdotes while journeying over the vast areas of Russia and then transformed them artistically into the state in which they appeared in 1862.[13] It is quite possible that Leskov originally planned a whole series of anecdotes which would have been narrated during the travellers' journey. In any case, the idea was one that certainly appealed to the author. The ancient mode of travel, with the attendant interesting conversations, must have attracted Leskov, for at the end of **"V tarantase"** he comments with a certain amount of nostalgia: "Perhaps, in time, people won't travel in this fashion in Russia, and then, probably, such conversations will disappear and completely different ones will take place."

Almost twenty-five years later Leskov was to reiterate his remarks. In **"Žemčužnoe ožerel'e"** a group of friends sit around tea discussing literature and pondering over why inventiveness seems to have weakened in recent times.[14] Leskov, the narrator, recalls the deceased Pisemskij's ideas on the subject. There is a direct connection, he claims, between lack of inventiveness and the railroad system. With the railroads one can travel a great deal but travel is rapid and in no way offensive. Earlier one had to take his chances on all sorts of travelling conditions and many types of travelling companions. However, this served the keen observer with a wealth of impressions. And because it is a variety of impressions that activates the imagination, the railroads have proved harmful to literature.

The travellers, then, are riding in an old-fashioned springless Russian carriage. "There were five of us sitting there," Leskov informs us, and then proceeds to name them for the reader's future reference: "I, a merchant from Nižnij Lomov, a steward [*prikazčik*] from a certain Astraxan' commercial establishment, two young salesclerks attached to this same steward, and a trading peasant from the village Golovinščina."[15] The peasant rides on top of the *tarantas* with the coachman; the remaining five have assembled themselves in the carriage itself. "According to habit we all soon became acquainted with one another and were drawn together as only Russians are able to draw close while travelling. Our conversations did not cease for a minute. . . ." (1-2.)

The convention is a timeworn and useful one; an author gathers together a group of people, one of these narrates a story he knows or has heard, and the others become his listeners. Such a gathering takes place occasionally in a cozy room before a fireplace, sometimes in a train station, or on board ship, in short, anywhere where two or more people congregate. The assumption is, of course, that in any group of people there will be at least one who has an interesting story to tell. With Leskov the story is usually interrupted at various junctures by the listeners' comments, interjections, and questions. These serve as a kind of punctuation marks in the story and remind the reader both of the listeners' continued presence and of the fact that the narrator of the events is not the author of the story. With Leskov the narrator is usually a participant in the action he relates.

In **"Razbojnik,"** the final statement quoted above not unexpectedly leads the reader to believe that a tale will be told during the journey itself. Actually, this is true; but the travelling tale is postponed till the second part of the story, **"V tarantase."**

Leskov's opening of **"Razbojnik"** is exceptionally felicitous. "We were driving toward Makar'eva, to the fair" (p. 1). A host of ideas must have been conjured up by this simple sentence for the contemporary Russian reader. Fair time, with all its attendant bustle and excitement, always offered a good subject or background for an interesting tale. In those days driving a long distance was at best a hazardous affair. If one did not have difficulty obtaining horses, perhaps the carriage would break down—not to mention the ever-present danger of being terrorized by assorted brigands and robbers. This last foreboding is strengthened by the title itself.

The sketch is divided into three parts: in the first Leskov briefly describes his travelling companions, the second comprises a series of conversations held in the tiny village where the travellers stop for the night, and the third part is dominated by the *skaz* tale of the young peasant from this village. The first two parts offer, as it were, a background and introduction to the third and most important segment. The narrator and his audience are presented to the reader and the scene is set. The entire party is sitting around the table with the exception of the narrator himself, a young local peasant, who remains standing before his audience. The listeners have already been somewhat prepared for the story; the conversation up to now has dealt with recent robberies in the neighborhood and their investigation by the local authorities. The travellers have repeatedly been warned not to drive on the same evening after dark, but rather to wait until dawn.

Fear on the part of the peasants, that same worry over one's skin which Leskov earlier noticed in **"Pogassee delo,"**[16] has conspired to help the robbers in their evil deeds. The peasants drive their passengers from one point to another and could very well shout out warnings when spying these robbers. But, as the peasant reasons, to whom would he yell out when returning along the same route, this time alone? By now the villain would have had time to round up his comrades and would be waiting to ambush the hapless coachman. Eventually the travellers reconsider and put off the continuation of their journey to the morrow.

"But did you ever see one?" The question concerning robbers is put to the young peasant (p. 7). The query serves the purpose of eliciting the subsequently related story in the form of an answer. The narrator begins: "'Bout six years ago, or probably even more, I got so scared that, good God!" Leskov inserts the remark, "We began to listen."

Not too far from where the travellers are resting is situated a village where a peasant wanted to sell his horse. The narrator, as it turned out, was in need of one. Early one morning, therefore, he slipped into his boot some forty rubles, a considerable sum in those days, and set off through the forest. Considering the possibility of being waylaid, he decided to cut a club with which to defend himself if the need should arise. Shortly thereafter he descried through the trees a soldier sitting by the pathway. Apprehensive, yet determined, the narrator continued on his way. When he drew level with the bedraggled soldier the latter suddenly asked him for a crust of bread. Receiving the reply that the peasant had none, the soldier then requested a *groš*. Wishing to help the poor man, yet fearful of showing all his wealth at once, the peasant again answered that he had none. With a cry that he would call his followers, the soldier then bent over and reached into his boot, as if to draw a knife. With no further thought, the narrator immediately took advantage of the opportunity thus afforded him, and gave the soldier a whack with all his strength. The man fell on the spot and "lay there, just like a frog" (p. 8).

A glance at the athletic build of the narrator is enough to assure the listeners that the soldier was either killed or very seriously hurt. The peasant, then, would kill out of fear for his own skin. In answer to the question, "But did you finish him off?" he says, "The Lord only knows. There's a sin on my soul if something happened. Only I didn't want to. . . ." (p. 9.) This, then, plus the fact that he confessed his crime to the priest, absolves him, as it were, from any more responsibility in the matter. The oldsters in the village merely caution him to be quiet about the affair, thus insuring immunity for the village from the authorities. As in the earlier **"Pogaššee delo,"** silence before the law is shown as a primary instinct of the peasant and his community.

The peasant's narrative has produced a very strong impression on one of the listeners, however, the author himself. As the travellers clamber up into the hayloft for a night's rest, he falls into a fitful sleep in which a dream keeps haunting him. In this dream the narrator sees the wounded soldier crawling off toward the woods

with "eyes bulging out, blue lips, tongue clenched between teeth, and blood welling from nose and eyes" (p. 10). From this point the imagination of the author carries him further and further: "There was also a small, cypress cross from Kiev, and in a bit of rag a pinch of his native earth. He'd surely carried that little piece of ground from afar, from his native land, where his old mother and father are awaiting their son on leave, and perhaps even a young wife is also waiting for him, or is she running after the Cossacks, or is she *already* at the midwife's. Keep waiting, friends, keep waiting." (p. 10.)

There are so many changes in tone and in emphasis in this final paragraph that it is difficult to keep track of them. The first part offers a description of the soldier which is ghastly. The greenish-hued face, blue lips, bloody eyes and nose, bulging eyes, and tongue clenched between teeth are all terms denoting physical corruption specifically utilized to induce terror in the face of death. The little knife with hand-made handle and the tiny cypress cross from Kiev are personal details, say something about the man himself, and evoke sympathy on the part of the reader. Death can be very impersonal, but personal detail increases the pain and fear many times.

The pinch of earth which the soldier has carried about with him for, perhaps, many years is an inserted bit of information which approaches the sentimental. The added touch that this is from his native land where his old parents are awaiting the soldier's return makes the sentimentality extreme, almost unbearable. Pathos is injected in this manner, but a pathos that is almost alien to the story in which it has been introduced. It is almost unfair that the parents have been included at this juncture, for we have already heard the peasant's story, feel sorry for the most probably innocent victim of his fear, and now it is as if the author were asking us to share the pain of the parents also. It is an irony of fate that we simultaneously know both of the soldier's death and of the old parents' expectancy.

It is at this point that Leskov puts in the master's touch. In a manner somewhat reminiscent of Gogol', Leskov succeeds in transforming a hypothetical idea into a living reality. "Perhaps," he writes, "even a young wife is also waiting for him. . . ." By the end of the sentence, however, it has already become ". . . or is she *already* at the midwife's." From the idea that a young woman is, perhaps, waiting for the soldier, comes the fully formed unfaithful wife who, it turned out, was unable to wait and succumbed to the charms of some passing Cossack. By this stroke, Leskov has managed to veil the tragic old parents in a mist and has once again forced the emphasis to return to the tragedy of the soldier, where it properly belongs. Perhaps even a certain relief is felt at realizing that the unhappy soldier will never be subjected to the pain of learning of his wife's infidelity.

If we bear in mind that **"Razbojnik"** is but Leskov's second artistic effort, then the dream sequence becomes even more significant for the sophistication of its representation. Leskov had attempted description of a dream in his earlier work, **"Pogassee delo."**[17] Here, however, the priest's dream appears, if not crude, at least somewhat obvious. The changing of tempo and progression of ideas in the dream with all their implications to the narrator of **"Razbojnik,"** on the other hand, are executed with the best combination of starkness of description and economy of means.

Less than two weeks after the publication of **"Razbojnik"** Leskov's **"V tarantase"** appeared. There can be no doubt that the sketch is a continuation of the one preceding it. The same characters are present; they are still journeying to the fair in their huge, lumbering *tarantas*. The peasant who had told the story of his encounter with the poor soldier is now driving the company and even points out the spot where the confrontation had occurred. The time of the segment is the morning following the evening on which the travellers had prudently decided to postpone their trip.

If one were to judge literature by inventiveness alone (it is, after all, this inventiveness which Leskov has in mind when recalling Pisemskij's words above), then **"V tarantase"** would indeed claim a high place in belles-lettres. The setting of the story and the characters, in fact, even the technique involved, are ordinary enough. But the two anecdotes which constitute the major portion of the sketch are among the most original that Leskov ever described. And it is these anecdotes that are at the basis of both the story's literary purpose and its success.

In this sketch, as in **"Razbojnik"** before it, Leskov does not lead directly into the anecdote portion, but rather spends some time in preparation for it. The travellers have risen and seated themselves in the carriage where they continue to doze for a short while. Soon, however, they are fully awake, and the inevitable conversations begin. Much of this introductory section is monopolized by talk of drinking and by the merchant Gvozdikov's idle chatter. The company halts at a wayside inn, thus offering Leskov the opportunity to describe contemporary conditions in such an establishment. Travelling is enormously facilitated by the aid of a few drinks, for when the passengers resume their journey, the atmosphere becomes much gayer and a lively conversation ensues. As in so many of Leskov's tales a question provokes the central anecdote.

No doubt under the impression of the previous evening's tale about the suspected robber, the peasant riding on top queries, "Whyever would there be this stealing among our people?" The merchant has his predictable answer, "There's stealing among all people." It is Gvozdikov's remark which gives rise to the slight but amusing digression to follow. "But, no," he declares, "there's no stealing amongst the Germans." And, in fact, he adds that the Swedes do not have any robbers either—cheaters aplenty, but no robbers. Anfalov, the steward, with shrewd logic then inquires as to who makes Swedish locks. With sudden dawning, Gvozdikov reluctantly admits that there must be stealing amongst Swedes.

A short silence ensues, after which the peasant inquires about the English. The merchant assures all that the English are constantly employed in trading. Anfalov, or Yellow-eyes, as Gvozdikov calls him, seconds this, mentioning that they have "been destined" for this "from on high." In response to objections from the group, he relates the following story in a tongue that is, if archaic, extremely lively.

In olden times, he recounts, shortly after Christ's ascension, and when the ancient faith flowered throughout the land, a wanderer made his way about the world, preaching a godly life to the people. This wanderer at one time found himself in a country peopled by many nations and situated in the place where Rome now stands. His preaching eventually angered the cruel tsar of these people and the latter commanded that he leave his domain. When the preacher refused to depart, the evil tsar ordered his execution. The arrows shot at the holy man bounced off, however, and when the tsar's warriors returned to report, the various nationalities gathered round the preacher and discussed among themselves how best to free him. The English were the first to come up with a plan and, approaching the bound man, asked him, "Would you like us to go to the tsar and trade you away from him?" The holy man gave vent to his disappointment that his words had gone unheeded. The diverse peoples had failed to attain harmony among themselves. "You were not able to stand up for me as a community," the preacher answered them, "go, therefore, and trade your whole lives through." In similar fashion, he enjoins the French to "make war" and the Russians to "steal your whole lives through."

Thus, says Anfalov, were the different nationalities sent forth according to their calling. The tsar's warriors returned and drove a pike into the holy man's heart, but before the latter died he prophesied that from each drop of his blood would spring forth a man who would go about the people teaching love and harmony.

The tale produces a strong impression on the company, and for a time silence reigns. It is broken, however, by the merchant, who thoughtfully exclaims, "Something's not right." He admits the truth of the English trading all their lives but is skeptical about the remainder of what Anfalov has related. As proof he points to the French employed at a cast-iron works, asking, "What kind of war could be going on there?" The driver backs up the merchant by testifying to the proficiency of the French at stealing.

It is this same driver who now proceeds to tell an alternate version of why some people steal while others make war. Once, he claims, he was driving someone to the station from which this company had yesterday arrived. He had gone some five versts or so when he spied a man walking alongside the road. The peasant offered him a lift and after a short pause the pedestrian accepted and crawled into the wagon. The inevitable conversations immediately began. The wanderer let drop that he had been in Jerusalem and moved on to a discussion of why men were plagued by lechery, drunkenness, stealing, and other sins.

There was a holy man, he said, to whom God had entrusted the commandments written in His own hand on stone tablets. Everything was transcribed there as it should be: thou shalt not steal, thou shalt not kill, etc. This holy man carried the tablets down to his people from the heights of a great mountain. But, descending the mountain, the man froze in his tracks when he caught sight of his people. They had not had the patience to wait for him but had given themselves over to the devil. He was met by music, dancing, revelry, and all sorts of evil. So much did this upset the saint that he dropped the tablets which clattered down, breaking into pieces as they fell. The people, realizing their waywardness, scrambled to gather up the shattered pieces. But in no way could they put them back together again. The holy man continued his descent, surrounded by a heavenly light. So frightened became those holding the tablet fragments that they ran off in all directions, still clutching them in their hands. To those who remained, however, the saint brought a second set of commandments, and these lived out their lives in righteousness. But those who ran off were destined to lives of sin and hardship. The people carrying fragments which said "steal," "kill," etc., spent their days in stealing and killing. Those to whom fell the pieces on which was written "thou shalt not" became wanderers, outcasts without home or family.

Thus ends the coachman's tale of "why there would be stealing among our people." The merchant probably expresses the opinion of the majority when he states, "Now, that's more likely closer to the truth."

There is a remarkable unity in these two stories that could not have been achieved without careful planning. Each story is made up of two basic components, embellished with a certain amount of extraneous detail. In

"**Razbojnik**" the various conversations about robberies in the village district make up the first component. These robberies are "real" events, of course, but somehow vague, impersonal, in a way, almost hypothetical. The second component in the story is the actual encounter with the soldier which the peasant relates. This is something which no longer merely forebodes; it touches the reader first because it *happened,* and secondly because it happened to someone with whom the reader has become acquainted.

The two basic elements in "**V tarantase**" are the two anecdotes themselves. Each of them has the purpose of explaining the events described the evening before. Here again, the first turns out to be the "hypothetical" case, for the explanation is rejected by the company as untrue. The second story is perfectly acceptable to all and thus becomes the established fact. The company continues its journey fully assured that it has discovered the logical reason for the happenings previously described as well as all other events of both the past and the future. Whether Leskov meant to produce such an impression by purposeful implication or whether such implication was inherent in his understanding of the peasant mentality, it seems to me that there is also present here the suggestion of the peasants' attitude of blind and utter subordination to the wiles of fate. In any case, it is significant that it is the same person, namely the young village peasant, who gives voice to the "real" segments in each of the two stories.

Quite apparent in these early stories of Leskov is the writer's essential objectivity. For example, nowhere does he make a definite pronouncement on whether the soldier in "**Razbojnik**" actually intended to rob the peasant. And the peasant's narrative holds just the right note of unconcern. After all, he felt justified in protecting himself and if he killed the soldier, well, he "hadn't wanted to." In "**V tarantase**" it is Leskov's intention to present, not his own, but the people's version of why men sin. His description of the travellers' rejection or acceptance of an explanation and their reasons for such is like a transcript of the participants' remarks. There is absolutely no intrusion by the author.

Present in these stories are the seeds of numerous themes, motifs, and characters which Leskov would later develop more fully. There is, for example, mention of a village priest in "**Razbojnik**," a character for which Leskov would become well known in a few more years. Anfalov, it turns out, is an Old Believer, as is the wanderer who had told the peasant the story of the commandments. The Old Believers will, of course, become an object of extreme interest for Leskov and, eventually, the subject of one of his greatest stories. One may also discern in "**V tarantase**" the rudimentary idea of the *pravednik,* a character existing in almost all of Leskov's works.[18] Akin to the objectivity remarked above, there is a certain casualness, almost nonchalance, in the face of death in the story **"Razbojnik."** But this near callousness in describing death[19] will become tempered with humor as Leskov's literary development progresses. But it is noteworthy that he published very few works in which death of some sort does not figure. One other facet of Leskov's art which is slightly exhibited here is his fondness for animal imagery. When the peasant recalls how he struck down the soldier with his club, he remarks that "he lay there, just like a frog." Not only is the term one which would readily have occurred to the peasant's mind: it is also a most appropriate one for describing the felled soldier's utter helplessness.

Two other elements in the stories bear noticing for the light they shed on Leskov's future artistic development. His descriptions of the peasants' lives, traditions, and superstitions, of the village, the wayside inn, and the open road: all are but miniatures of what was to come later. These were facets of Russian society which Leskov knew well, and he never ceased to draw on his experiences when creating a new work.

Finally, a word about Leskov's language. It may be said without exaggeration that this is the only feature of Leskov's talent which has received anywhere near the recognition due it.[20] In the two stories under discussion many recognizable traits are already observable. Gvozdikov's verbal play in **"V tarantase"** is on a somewhat lower plane than that of Leskov's future characters, but gives an idea of things to come. The speech of the young peasant is full of dialect words and ungrammatical forms. The story told by Anfalov is monopolized by all sorts of archaic words drawn from the Old Church Slavic vocabulary. The important thing to note here is that from the very outset Leskov was attempting to individualize the speech patterns of each of his characters. He himself was occasionally wont to boast of his ability in this respect: "A writer's organization of voices consists in the ability to control the voice and language of his hero and not run off from alto to bass. In my work I tried to develop this ability and attained it, it seems, to the extent that my priests speak like priests, my nihilists like nihilists and my peasants like peasants."[21]

### Notes

1. William B. Edgerton, *Nikolai Leskov: The Intellectual Development of a Literary Nonconformist* (dissertation, Columbia Univ., 1954).

2. Thomas Eekman, "The Genesis of Leskov's *Soborjane*," *California Slavic Studies,* II (1963), 121-140.

3. V. S. Pritchett, "Leskov," *Oxford Slavonic Papers,* X (1962), 18-24.

4. See, e.g., Hugh McLean, "On the Style of a Leskovian *Skaz,*" *Harvard Slavic Studies,* II (1954), 297-322, and "The Priest and the Sorcerer: Leskov's First Short Story," to be published in a Chicago *Festschrift* dedicated to G. V. Bobrinskoy. Also worth mentioning here is A. Ansberg, "Frame Story and First Person Story in N. S. Leskov," *Scando-Slavica,* III (1957), 49-73.

5. Валентина Гебелъ, «Н. С. Лесков в творческой лабораторий» (М., 1945), 130.

6. Letter of 7 December 1864 to Straxov, Н. С. Лесков, «Собрание сочинений» (11 тт.; М., 1956-1958), X, 253.

7. М. Стебницкий, "Погасщее дело," «Век,» No. 12 (25 март 1862).

8. М. Стебницкий, "разбойник," «Северная пчела,» No. 108 (23 апрель 1862).

9. М. Стебницкий, "В тарантасе," «Северная пчела,» No. 119 (4 май 1862).

10. Н. С. Лесков, «Изоранные сочинения,» ред. б. Другов и а. Лесков (М., 1945), 3-7.

11. а. НаркевИч, "Лесков и его комментаторы," «Вопросы литературы,» 1959, No. 12, стр. 195.

12. Edgerton, 166.

13. Professor Edgerton has suggested to me the probability that the two anecdotes in the second of these stories represent undiscovered folklore elements and that these early sketches in general were influenced by as yet unidentified sources. No one, however, has had the opportunity thus far to fully explore these theories.

14. Н. С. Лесков, "Жемчужное ожерелье," «Собр. соч.,» VII, 432.

15. Н. С. Лесков, "разбойник," «Собр. соч.,» I, 1. All further quotations in the text are taken from this edition.

16. М. Стебницкий, «Сборник мелких беллетристических произведений» (СПб., 1873), II, 110, reprinted here under the title "Zasuxa."

17. Ibid., 122.

18. This was mentioned by Edgerton, 166.

19. Cf., e.g., the description of Axilla's brother's death in *Soborjane* (*Sobr. soč.,* IV, 70), and that of the old monk in "Očarovannyj strannik" (*Sobr. soč.,* IV, 398-399). This is, however, only apparent callousness. After all, as Leskov takes great pains to show, these are not his descriptions but rather those of his characters.

20. I list here but a few of the many articles dealing with Leskov's use of language: А. С. Орлов, "Язык Лескова: Материл к статье," «Язык

русских писателей» (М.: Ан СССр, 1948), 144-175; Н. С. Антощин, "о языке Н. С. Лескова," «Наукові записки» (Ужгородський Державний Унів.), XXXVII (1959), 70-97; Валентина Гебель, "о языке Н. С. Лескова," «Литературная учеба,» 1938, No. 5, стр. 39-62.

21. Н. И. фаресов, «Против течений» (СПб., 1904), 273-274.

## Katherine Tiernan O'Connor (essay date 1974)

SOURCE: O'Connor, Katherine Tiernan. "The Specter of Political Corruption: Leskov's 'White Eagle.'" *Russian Literature Triquarterly* 8 (1974): 393-406.

[*In the following essay, O'Connor contends that in "The White Eagle" Leskov used an extremely naive and credulous narrator—Galaktion Ilyich—as a vehicle for exposing the deceit and depravity of governmental bureaucracies.*]

Leskov's **"The White Eagle"** [**"Belyi orel"**], subtitled a "fantastic story," describes a real political intrigue that is "fantastic" by virtue of its extreme subtlety and artistic, albeit perverse, inventiveness. The exact nature of this intrigue is only apparent, however, after a painstaking examination of the various clues contained within the fabric or subtext of what appears to be a traditional ghost story. The surface plot is as follows: Galaktion Ilyich, an official from Petersburg, is sent to the provinces to head a preliminary investigation into the reported misconduct of a particular governor. Once there, he becomes implicated in the sudden death of one of the local officials whom he is accused of having given the evil eye. Preposterous as it may seem, Galaktion's psychological insecurity makes him vulnerable to such a charge and thus he departs from the provinces under compromising circumstances. Our realization that Galaktion's story, which is told in his own words, has a deeper significance than he himself realizes comes gradually. Our curiosity is naturally aroused by the strange coincidences and suggestive details that he fails either to observe or to explore. We are forced, therefore, to take a closer look at the surface narrative and in doing so we achieve a deeper understanding of what happened to Galaktion and why.

The first clue to Galaktion's naiveté as a narrator is provided by the story's first narrator, a curious, skeptical fellow with an almost Jamesian turn of mind, who familiarizes us with the circumstances under which he heard Galaktion's story and who then provides us with a brief but highly revealing character sketch of Galaktion himself. He heard Galaktion tell his story "two or three years ago" when he participated in a story-telling circle that was influenced by the modish spiritualism

[*dukhovidstvo*] of the 70s. Members of the circle exchanged stories concerning their personal experiences with the spirit-world, while agreeing mutually to avoid such touchy subjects as religion or politics. Galaktion fails to grasp the political and ethical implications of his own "ghost story" and hence he is unaware that he actually violated this rule of conduct. The first narrator no doubt realizes this and relishes the irony. When describing his own attitudes toward spiritualism the first narrator is clearly more of a skeptic than a believer. He notes that in stories of the so-called supernatural it is often customary to cover oneself by beginning with the following quotation from "Hamlet" which affirms the existence of the supernatural: "There are more things in heaven and earth than are dreamt of in your philosophy." He, however, chooses the following quotation from Theocritus for his epigraph: "The dog dreams of bread, and the fisherman of fish." In contrast to the "Hamlet" quotation this one maintains that there is a rational explanation for dreams and visions; the dreams that a man has are related to his personality and character. When we consider the "Hamlet" quotation with the aid of hindsight, we note that it bears a subtle and ironic relation to Galaktion's subsequent narrative. Hamlet addresses the above words to Horatio just after he has spoken with his father's ghost (I, v.). Since Horatio, who is commonsensical and skeptical to the extreme, resists believing in the ghost, Hamlet chides him for his narrow rationalism and asserts that there are many phenomena that it fails to explain. Galaktion, in contrast to Horatio, turns out to be too credulous and believes too readily in the ghost that appears to him. Had he been more skeptical he might have seen that there was a rational explanation for the so-called supernatural phenomena that he was witnessing. Whereas Hamlet takes issue with Horatio's skepticism, the first narrator takes issue with Galaktion's credulity. The comparison between the ghost in "Hamlet" and the "ghost" in **"The White Eagle"** yields yet another example of what might be called a reverse parallel between the two texts. In "Hamlet" the ghost that appears is the ghost of Hamlet's murdered father who was the innocent victim of his brother's political and personal ambitions. In Leskov's story, however, the "ghost" himself turns out to be part of an elaborate political intrigue. He claims to be the innocent victim of Galaktion, but when the evidence is in, it appears that the reverse is true.

The character sketch that the first narrator provides of Galaktion before turning over center stage to him is brief but intriguing. After entering the Civil Service Galaktion advanced in the ranks due to the patronage of Count Viktor Nikitych Panin whose private secretary he eventually became. His intellectual or administrative abilities remain in doubt, however, for it is generally assumed that Count Panin relies on him for his more idiosyncratic assets, namely his extraordinarily demoralizing and almost corpse-like appearance. He functions as a receptionist who interviews people coming to see the count. They are understandably so unnerved and intimidated by Galaktion that their subsequent impression of Panin is, by way of contrast, extremely favorable. As we can see, a precedent has been set in Galaktion's past for exploiting him on the basis of his physical unattractiveness. Also, Count Panin emerges as his primary exploiter, a role which we suggest he continues to play throughout the story, although in more subtle and devious ways.

The story that Galaktion relates concerns a series of events that began some twenty-five years ago in the mid-fifties. It was at this time that rumors began to reach the capital about the cruel and tyrannical abuse of power practised by P-v, a certain provincial governor who is also reputed to be an artist and an aesthete.[1] Although rumors about the governor's misconduct continued to reach the authorities in Petersburg, nothing was done for a long while for, as Galaktion reports, the governor and the Marshal of the Nobility, who was in league with him, are on good terms with the tsar himself. Finally, the situation becomes too serious to be ignored and Count Panin, then the Minister of Justice, decides to send one of *his own* men, namely Galaktion, to investigate. Before Galaktion leaves, Panin asks him the name of the last decoration that he received. When he learns that it was the Vladimir, Second Class, he tells Galaktion that he will receive the White Eagle after accomplishing the mission.[2] The way in which this information is communicated is curiously detailed. Galaktion recalls that Panin's "well-known heavy bronze paper-weight, the 'slain bird'" was lying on his desk. Panin first removes his notebook from underneath this paper-weight, and then "with all the five fingers of his right hand [he] takes a thick giant-pencil of black ebony and, making no effort to conceal what he is doing, writes down [Galaktion's] name and opposite it the 'White Eagle'." Thus, the image of the "slain bird" on Panin's paper-weight accompanies the first reference to the White Eagle, the decoration that Panin lets Galaktion assume he will receive. The real significance of such an association will be seen only later.

Upon Galaktion's arrival in the town, the governor and the local officials predictably attempt to curry his favor and to seek out weaknesses in him that they can use to their own advantage. He is, however, impervious to all their lures, including the beautiful young women who make him shameful offers. When told by one of his subordinates that he has been questioned as to his superior's particular preferences, Galaktion directs him to say that what he [Galaktion] likes most is health, and what he is most fond of is people who are "hale and hearty, happy and gay." This seems, on the surface, to be the most innocent of admissions, and hence it is curious that Galaktion at this juncture breaks off his narrative to ask his audience whether he was guilty of any

great indiscretion when he admitted to such a preference. Galaktion's insecurity on this point suggests to the reader that, sub-consciously at least, he realizes how compromising what he said was in view of subsequent events.

Our curiosity is further aroused when we learn that a sudden change was then made in Galaktion's office staff. He is informed by a member of the administrative staff that Ornatsky, the local official assigned to him, can no longer appear for duty since he is off on one of his frequent drinking bouts. When Galaktion expresses a willingness to wait until he is "well" again, the clerk insists that this is impossible since it will take *Ivan Petrovich's* mother a long time to cure him. He goes on to say that this same *Ivan Petrovich* is the very one who has been appointed to take Ornatsky's place. The fact that a man who is yet unknown to him should be mentioned twice by name in such a short space of time strikes Galaktion as odd, and he says as much to the clerk. The latter responds by saying that he is an assistant in the registrar's office whom everyone notices because he is so handsome. Considering the fact that Galaktion has previously described Ornatsky as "elderly, dry and melancholy," it is indeed provocative that he should suddenly be replaced on a rather flimsy excuse by someone who is handsome and robust, particularly since Galaktion has just "confessed" his weakness for such people. When he asks the clerk the surname of his new assistant, the clerk becomes somewhat embarrassed and can't remember his last name. This is rather surprising,—indeed suspicious—considering the fact that he has just testified to Ivan Petrovich's general popularity in the town. He does, however, recover from his brief lapse of memory and announces that his name is Aquilalbov [Lat: "white eagle"], but that everyone calls him "the white eagle" on account of his beauty. Galaktion does note the strange coincidence in the fact that his new assistant has the same name as the decoration he expects to receive. He fails to grasp the irony (and therefore to see the trap) that is implicit in this coincidence.

Ivan Petrovich Aquilalbov is, we suggest, an obvious set-up, the pivotal character in an elaborate scheme that has been designed to discredit Galaktion and his investigation. The fact that the clerk fails to remember his name suggests that "Aquilalbov" is not his real name but rather a "stage-name" with which he's been provided for his role in the plot. We assume that the governor had found out that the White Eagle was the decoration that was promised Galaktion by Count Panin. Once he had conceived a scheme to discredit Galaktion it suited his artistically perverse and theatrical tastes that the agent-provocateur of his plot should bear the name "White Eagle." Galaktion expects to get the White

Eagle, and indeed he shall, but hardly in the form he imagined. Disgrace will come in place of honor, but under the same name.

Despite the suspicious circumstances under which Aquilalbov becomes Galaktion's assistant, he makes a most favorable first impression on Galaktion. Not surprisingly, considering his function as "office spook" in Count Panin's office, Galaktion seems to fear that he'll make an onerous impression on the handsome newcomer, and hence he tries to put him at ease. The White Eagle responds simply and straightforwardly, however, and Galaktion is clearly quite taken with him. When asked to demonstrate his handwriting skills, Ivan Petrovich writes a sentence that is suspiciously in line with what Galaktion admires. This seems also to indicate that he's been carefully prepared for his new assignment: "Life is given to us for joy," he pens. Rather than being suspicious of this remark Galaktion seems delighted. He considers it fortunate that a man who is so much "to his taste" has been placed in his office. Later on, however, when alone, Galaktion confesses that he found it curious that Ivan Petrovich managed to look so good and live so well on such a modest salary. Although his curiosity is more than justified under the circumstances, he doesn't carry it very far. We, however, can assume that Ivan Petrovich is pampered and well-dressed because he is the "darling" of the governor's entourage of corrupt officials. His official salary may be small, but his position has many "fringe benefits." After Galaktion had admitted to admiring men like Ivan Petrovich who are everything he is not, the Governor saw his chance to entrap the Petersburg investigator. He picked Ivan Petrovich to start his scheme in motion because he realized Galaktion would be vulnerable to his beautiful appearance and robust health. The exact nature of the plot to entrap Galaktion is still unknown, however; the governor himself, who subsequently arrives in Galaktion's office, gives him and us a perverse, artistically veiled preview of what is about to happen.

The governor arrives ostensibly to invite Galaktion to a party. The striking thing about his visit, however, is that he talks endlessly about Ivan Petrovich, in glowing terms, and then describes elaborately the various roles that Ivan Petrovich will play in the "tableaux vivants" [*zhivye kartiny*] that will be performed at the party. A close examination of the description of these *tableaux vivants* reveals to the reader, but not to Galaktion, their function in the story: the content of the tableaux provides a veiled allusion to the real role Ivan Petrovich is playing in the Governor's plot to discredit the investigator from Petersburg. The subject of the first tableau, based on Samuel I:29, is Saul's visit to the Witch of Endor. Saul, played by Ivan Petrovich, appears before the witch in disguise, dressed like other men, but recognizable nonetheless as a king. This is oddly reminiscent of Ivan Petrovich's appearance to Galaktion; he was os-

tensibly an ordinary official, but Galaktion couldn't fail to notice his resemblance to a Greek god. The second tableau will feature Ivan Petrovich as Samuel's ghost. When we learn that Galaktion is visited by Ivan Petrovich's ghost we recall his role in this tableau and are suspicious of the ghost's reality: is this really Ivan Petrovich's ghost or is it Ivan Petrovich playing the role of his own ghost? The final tableau has Ivan Petrovich playing the Witch of Endor, for he is, as the governor tells Galaktion, particularly adept at playing old women. The governor stresses how frightening the witch will be; when Galaktion gazes upon her, "[he] will see a face that knows what wise men never dreamed of." [*Vy uvidete litso, kotoroe znaet to, chto snilos' mudretsam*]. This allusion to the "Hamlet" quotation [*Est' veshchi, kotorye ne snilis' mudretsam*] suggests that the horror of the witch's face defies reason. The governor adds that Galaktion will see "how horrible it is to talk with one who has come out of the grave." With hindsight Galaktion views these words as prophetic, for he tells his audience that "within three days he himself was to experience such a torment," that is, when he is visited by what he assumes to be the ghost of Ivan Petrovich. Although the *tableaux vivants* are never performed, they allude to real-life "tableaux" that do take place, disguised however as spontaneous events. Everything that befalls Galaktion in this strange, corrupt town is in effect part of a "tableau" directed by the Governor with Ivan Petrovich as his leading man and Galaktion Ilyich as his dupe. The governor is indeed an artist, as Galaktion reported, but he is as criminally perverse as he is artistic. He delights in giving Galaktion a "preview of coming attractions," knowing that Galaktion will miss the point and fail to recognize the clues for what they are.

Before passing on to the rest of the text we should note the further allusion to "Hamlet" that is implicit in this entire chapter. In both works a dramatic production is used to unmask a political intrigue. The totally contrasting ways in which this device is employed in both texts suggests, however, that the parallel is once again a reverse one. In "Hamlet" the hero, trying to avenge his father's death, has "The Death of Gonzago" performed before his uncle and mother in the hope that its resemblance to their own crimes will so unnerve them that their guilt will become plainly evident. Contrastingly, in **"The White Eagle"** the chief conspirator (the Governor) uses drama to reveal his own plot, perversely amused that his victim will fail to understand the performance. In "Hamlet," then, the innocent party resorts to drama to unmask the guilty, whereas in **"The White Eagle"** the criminal resorts to drama to dupe the innocent.

On the day before the Governor's party the local archpriest visits Galaktion and warns him that Ivan Petrovich's recent transfer into his office was done with some plan in mind. He suggests that Ivan Petrovich's extraordinary "luck" in lotteries and raffles is due to the great popularity he enjoys with the Governor. Galaktion does not seem to heed his warnings, however, for he views him as a gossip with never a good word for anyone.

On the day of the Governor's party the intrigue against Galaktion really gets under way. Ivan Petrovich is very attentive to him, and they converse in more personal tones than previously. Galaktion jokes with him about how he should get married, whereupon he coyly replies that he would rather "remain a virgin." Following this, Galaktion invites him to Petersburg, but he refuses, saying that everyone is fond of him where he is and that his mother and Tanya (the orphan girl whom they have adopted) would "not be suited for Petersburg." Galaktion is touched by his love for his family, and he embraces him before he departs. Considering that Ivan Petrovich will shortly accuse Galaktion of having given him the evil eye, his obvious attentiveness to him during their last conversation strikes one as especially calculated and sinister. Winning Galaktion's affection and gaining his confidence is clearly part of Ivan Petrovich's "game plan" for then Galaktion will be more intimidated by the charges leveled against him. The accusations of a seeming friend always generate more guilt and anxiety than those of any enemy.

Ivan Petrovich first "appears" to Galaktion shortly after their conversation. Galaktion has dined alone, and he is trying to take a nap when he is suddenly disturbed by what he considers to be a most curious dream: Ivan Petrovich enters rather abruptly and pushes aside the chairs in the middle of the room with his foot. He accuses Galaktion of having given him the evil eye, and promises that he will seek revenge. If Ivan Petrovich is appearing in the flesh but masquerading as a ghost (which we suspect), we conclude that he manages to delude Galaktion into believing that it is a dream. Galaktion's credulity is partially explained by the fact that Ivan Petrovich's "dream" personality is so unlike his "real-life" personality of only a few hours before. How could the strangely hostile man who disturbed his sleep possibly be the same man who was chatting so amiably with him moments before? It must be a bad dream. Galaktion composes himself after his "nightmare" and goes off to the Governor's party. There an even more ominous surprise awaits him, for he learns that Ivan Petrovich died shortly before and that Ivan's mother accuses Galaktion of having given her son the evil eye. Despite his depression over this news Galaktion remains at the party only to fall victim to further insinuations. Now the all-encompassing nature of the conspiracy against him becomes fully evident. Everything that occurs at the party seems strangely unspontaneous and calculated solely to strengthen Galaktion's guilt feelings. Firstly, the guests communicate their hostility to Galaktion by whispering ominously in his hearing that "he gave [him] the evil eye." Then, Ivan Petro-

vich himself passes among the guests, but no one seems to see this "apparition" except poor Galaktion. Finally, the Governor whispers in his ear, "It's Ivan Petrovich spoiling things for you: he's avenging himself on you." If Galaktion were in a more rational state of mind, the Governor's precise awareness of what is in fact going on within him might have struck him as suspicious, and he might also have realized the obvious malevolence in such a remark. At this point, however, he is so convinced of the existence of Ivan's "ghost," seemingly visible only to him, and so guilt-ridden as a result, that the governor's words probably strike him as clairvoyant rather than incriminating and hence all the more disturbing.

After Galaktion leaves the party, the ubiquitous Ivan Petrovich accompanies him home in his sleigh and then sits on the edge of his bed as he's about to go to sleep. This forces Galaktion to ask his manservant Egor to sleep in the same room with him. Nothing, however, seems to faze Ivan Petrovich, for he doesn't seem to mind Egor's presence. Egor ostensibly doesn't *see* Ivan Petrovich, or acts as if he doesn't. If Ivan Petrovich is present in the flesh in Galaktion's room, we have to assume that Egor acquiesces in the plot against his master. The text supports this assumption in the form of some seemingly extraneous information provided earlier. Following the visit of the arch-priest, Galaktion relates hearing a buzzing sound coming from Egor's room. He goes to investigate and finds Egor making "holders" *[podstavochki]* out of cigar-box wood. It seems that Ivan Petrovich had observed that Egor was bored in the evenings and thus taught him to occupy himself in this way. A friendly association between Ivan Petrovich and Egor had already been established, in other words, and it is not inconceivable that Egor was first charmed by Ivan Petrovich and then maybe even bribed as well into playing along with all his "pranks."

On the day following Ivan Petrovich's totally improbable "death" Galaktion decides to visit the house of the "deceased" to "have a look at him" and "pay his respects." When describing the impression that Ivan Petrovich's "body" made on him, Galaktion curiously resorts to the following pun on Aquilalbov's last name: "the white eagle lay there as if he'd been winged." The pun calls to mind Panin's famous paper-weight, the "slain bird" and Galaktion's elaborate description of it on the day the Count wrote down the order Galaktion would receive, the White Eagle, Galaktion's subsequent fate and, more specifically, the role that "slain birds" play in such a fate, are ironically foreshadowed in this opening scene. In place of the White Eagle promised him for services rendered, Galaktion finds the "dead" Aquilalbov whom he is accused of slaying. The foreshadowing of Galaktion's fate in the scene in Count Panin's office suggests that the Count himself is the agent of Galaktion's disgrace. Panin's initial exploitation of

Galaktion on the basis of his unprepossessing appearance previews, moreover, the later similar kind of exploitation that he experiences at the hands of the Governor and Ivan Petrovich. Panin is never directly implicated in the conspiracy, although we recall that the Governor's choice of the name Aquilalbov for his prime agent provocateur suggested that he was in communication with Petersburg, and that earlier complaints against the Governor had come to naught because of the influence he had with the Tsar himself. Finally, Panin, knowing Galaktion's vulnerability on the subject of his ugliness, chose namely him to investigate the Governor. There are a sufficient number of hints at Panin's involvement in the plot against Galaktion to imply that the political corruption that victimizes the poor, notoriously ugly civil servant extends from the provincial administration right up to the highest echelons of the Petersburg bureaucracy.

Predictably, Galaktion is rebuffed by Ivan Petrovich's mother at the wake when she refuses to speak with him. Tanya, however, treats him with great civility and even affection. Since the conspiracy which we have outlined would logically implicate both the mother and Tanya, how are we to interpret the latter's seeming kindness to Galaktion and hence her apparent uninvolvement in the plot against him? We suggest she is playing the role of the seemingly innocent party who poses as the victim's friend. By being nice to Galaktion Tanya most subtly aggravates his growing despair and guilt. After all, Galaktion is upset and guilt-ridden about his alleged responsibility for Ivan Petrovich's death largely because the deceased had always treated him with compassion and affection in spite of his ugliness. The interview between Tanya and Galaktion concludes sentimentally when Tanya gives him a keepsake picture of Ivan Petrovich to show him that she bears him no ill will. This gift is itself double-edged; a picture of the "deceased" will aid in keeping his memory alive to Galaktion long after he has left town. Even back in Petersburg Galaktion will continue to be vulnerable to seeing Ivan Petrovich everywhere.

Just before Galaktion's departure the arch-priest pays him a final visit. Once again he casts suspicions on the moral rectitude of the town officials and in so doing he, like Tanya, seems to stand outside the conspiracy. He doesn't deny the existence of the evil eye, but he doubts whether men are as vulnerable to it as animals. He claims, on the contrary that Ivan Petrovich was poisoned because he knew too much and they (i.e., the Governor and his cronies) feared that he could confide in Galaktion. Galaktion is disturbed by this allegation, but he doesn't heed it any more than he did the arch-priest's earlier accusations. We should resist the temptation of viewing the arch-priest as the concerned bystander who tries unsuccessfully to warn Galaktion about the danger surrounding him. His name will reap-

pear later in Galaktion's narrative in a more negative context which suggests his seeming concern is also not without ulterior motive.

Galaktion's return to Petersburg coincides with the annual awarding of decorations at New Year's. He acknowledges feeling little or no anxiety on this score since he assumes, perhaps naively, that he will receive the White Eagle. On the night the awards are to be announced, Ivan Petrovich visits Galaktion once again and proceeds to thumb his nose at him most rudely. The significance of this gesture is revealed shortly when we learn that Galaktion's name does not appear on the list of those who have received decorations. The fact that Ivan's "ghost" knows what will happen is a clear indication of the complicity that exists between the Count (bestower of decorations) and the Governor's set. When Galaktion learns in the morning that his name didn't appear, he rushes to his sister's to find out what happened. His brother-in-law informs him that his name had originally been on the list but that at the last minute the Count himself had crossed it off. The Count promiseth and the Count taketh away—an ironic reversal, to say the least, and one that seems sinister and manipulative. The Count wrote down the order Galaktion would receive in his presence, most alluringly, but he coldly and manipulatively crossed his name off the list behind the unsuspecting Galaktion's back. Galaktion's brother-in-law reports what we have guessed already, that the rumors which implicated Galaktion in the mysterious "death" of a provincial official prevented him from receiving the decoration. The Count had been inundated with letters from the province that compromised Galaktion; the letter singled out for individual attention came from none other than the arch-priest, whose incriminating allegations were the strongest. It now appears that the arch-priest, like everyone else in the town, was playing a part. He posed as a confidant in Galaktion's presence but participated in the plot behind his back. We see proof of the arch-priest's complicity in the obvious fact that any plot calling for a sham death, a sham wake, and a sham funeral would logically involve the foreknowledge of the local priest. The priest's participation enlarges the scope of the plot (both the government and the clergy are involved) lending it an all-encompassing quality that is sinister and awesome.

We are not surprised that Ivan Petrovich's visits to Galaktion stopped at this time. Galaktion's reputation has been compromised and the investigation he headed has presumably been shelved, at least for the time being. Ivan Petrovich's visits are no longer necessary.

Three years after the events described Ivan Petrovich makes his final and most "tangible" *[osiazatel'nyi]* appearance—this epithet alone robs him of any ghostly incorporeity. It is again New Year's, the time when awards and decorations are announced. Galaktion arrives home from a party given by his sister and finds the White Eagle decoration lying on his desk. His sister had given it to him three years ago when it was assumed that he would receive the award, and he had locked it up ever since. He is surprised to see it lying on the desk, but he himself suggests a logical explanation. He might have taken it out himself, possibly reminisced about the past and then forgotten to put it back. It is extremely likely psychologically that he would take it out at the time of year when the awards were given, subconsciously hoping that he would finally receive the long-awaited decoration. On the bedside table he finds an envelope with his name written in Ivan Petrovich's familiar handwriting. Inside is a copy of the order that bestows on him the White Eagle. When asked who brought the envelope, Galaktion's manservant (who is not the same Egor who had been befriended by Ivan Petrovich and even possibly corrupted by him) unhesitatingly points to the picture of Ivan Petrovich that is hanging on the bedroom wall—the same picture that Tanya had given Galaktion at the wake. Such a disinterested observer's testimony to the reality of Ivan Petrovich confirms our suspicions that he was never a ghost, that, indeed, he never "died" at all.

The elaborate, sinister and ingenious *tableau vivant* (with special emphasis on the "vivant," we might add) has at last been brought to an end, an astounding success, as the director himself predicted: the original investigation into corruption headed by Galaktion has been compromised; the Governor and his entourage are free to continue enjoying the fruits of depravity and corruption. Why not applaud their own efforts by finishing the whole play with a mocking, highly ironic anti-climax: let the "white eagle" (i.e., Aquilalbov, whose real name remains unknown) notify Galaktion that he has at last received the White Eagle. Keeping in mind the Governor's covert connections with Petersburg, we assume he was informed when Galaktion would receive the decoration. Perhaps the Governor himself provided the stimulus for awarding Galaktion the decoration. He initially prevented Galaktion from receiving it for services rendered to the authorities, but he gives the go-ahead three years later as an award for services unwittingly rendered to the criminals. Obviously, the White Eagle is now more of a mockery than an honor; Galaktion has really been awarded the symbol of his own disgrace.

**"The White Eagle"** depicts a reality of evil unimpeded that is far more fantastic and uncanny than the sham supernatural that masks it. Galaktion Ilyich is so credulous and biased as a narrator that he finds it easier to believe in so-called supernatural phenomena than to examine and probe reality. Had he been less vulnerable psychologically, less insecure, he might have done so, and as a result the story would have been told quite differently. Galaktion might then have resembled the skeptical first narrator who warned us to question and explain psychologically what Galaktion merely accepted at face value. By employing such a naive narrator, however, Leskov is able to highlight the uncanniness of the evil that pervades the reality of political and bureaucratic life. A conspiracy that implicates an entire provincial administration, including the clergy, and that continues to flourish undaunted by higher authorities is indeed a frightening phenomenon. The personality and character of the conspirators themselves are no less awesome. The Governor is as imaginative as he is perverse, Count Panin as superficially gracious as he is inwardly cruel, and Ivan Petrovich, the great actor, the beautiful mask that hides a rotting soul, as charismatic as he is sinister. The Devil himself must be applauding offstage.

*Notes*

1. We learn from the notes to the story found in the 1958 edition of Leskov's collected works (*Sobranie sochinenii*, T.7, Moskva, 1958) that the character P-v was patterned after a real historical personage, Aleksandr Alekseevich Panchulidzev, who served as the governor of Penza province from 1831 to 1859. Leskov lived in this province in the late fifties, and it was then that he heard about his notorious exploits.

2. There was a prescribed sequence observable in the awarding of decorations. The White Eagle is the decoration that is next in importance following the Vladimir, Second Class.

**Stephen S. Lottridge (essay date fall 1974)**

SOURCE: Lottridge, Stephen S. "Nikolaj Leskov's Moral Vision in the *Prolog* Tales." *Slavic and East European Journal* 18, no. 3 (fall 1974): 252-58.

[*In the following essay, Lottridge examines the nine stories included in Leskov's* Prolog, *published between 1886 and 1891, as his reworkings of a Russian compendium of centuries-old religious tales and moral lessons.*]

Nikolaj Leskov's concern with Christian morality was central to his writing during most of his literary career. While modern criticism has shown a greater interest in his skill as a storyteller and literary craftsman than in his religious ideas, it was for his presentation of positive figures that he was most appreciated during his lifetime. Such figures occur not only in his well-known tales about righteous men (*pravedniki*), on whose moral strength human society depends,[1] but in scores of his short stories, tales, and longer works from the mid 1870's through the end of his life.

The formative history of Leskov's Christian ideal is long and complicated.[2] In his earliest works one can find characters and attitudes that suggest important elements of his later moral vision, and as early as 1875 he began to publish works that contained all the essential elements of his mature Christian view. Nevertheless, he attained the vision of true Christianity that he eventually embodied in his later works only with great difficulty. In December 1891, in a letter to the critic M. A. Protopopov, Leskov wrote:

> Your criticism (in general pleasant to me) lacks historical perspective (*istoričnost'*). Speaking of an author "not finished, but closed within himself," you forgot his time and the fact that he is a child of his time. It was simply a matter of my having to free myself from the fetters that encumber a Russian child of the landowning class from his infancy. In writing about myself I would have called the article not "A Sick Talent," but "Difficult Growth." The tendencies of the landowning class, ecclesiastical piety, narrow nationalism and statism, glorification of the native land—I grew up in the midst of all that, and often it all seemed repulsive to me, but still I could not see "where the truth lay." . . . Katkov had a great deal of influence on me, but it was while *Zaxudalyj rod* was being printed that he himself first said to Voskobojnikov: "We are mistaken; this man is not ours!" . . . He was right, but I did not know *whose* man I was. "A thorough reading of the Gospels" made it clear to me, and I at once returned to the free feelings and inclinations of my childhood.[3]

This "thorough reading of the Gospels" took place during Leskov's trip to Western Europe in 1875, when he spoke with Western churchmen and read a great deal, not only the Bible but also other religious writings, especially Protestant.[4] Leskov conceived the idea of writing about "a Russian heretic—an intelligent and well-read 'spiritual Christian,' who has passed through all doubts for the sake of his search for Christian truth and has found it only in his own soul."[5] Spiritual Christianity as a religious ideal was to be the path that Leskov followed for the rest of his career. Even so, his journey down this path was uncertain, and he felt a strong need for support and verification of his Christian vision. He found this support in great part in the figure and writings of L. N. Tolstoj. Leskov described Tolstoj's importance for him most fully in the letter he wrote to Tolstoj on 4 January 1893.

> You know the good you have done me: from the earliest years of my life I was attracted to questions of faith and began to write about religious people when it was considered improper and impossible . . . , but I kept getting mixed up and being satisfied with the fact that I was "sweeping the rubbish out of the temple," but I didn't know with what to enter into the temple. . . . I *myself* was approaching what I saw in you, but in myself I kept being afraid that it was a mistake because although the very same thing that I recognized in you shone in my own consciousness, still everything in me was in chaos—murky and unclear, and I didn't rely on myself. But when I heard your elucidations, logical and strong, I understood everything as if having "recalled" it, and my own light became unnecessary to me and I began to live in the light which I saw coming from you and which was more pleasant to me because it is incomparably stronger and brighter than that in which I was rummaging with my own strength.

> (XI, 519)

From this statement, reiterated at other times, it is clear that Tolstoj acted as a catalyst for Leskov, focusing and strengthening views that Leskov had held for some time.[6] The vision to which Tolstoj's teachings gave particular support was that of an active, spiritual, nondenominational Christianity, depending entirely on individual conscience and personal faith. While Leskov had written several stories embodying such a vision which antedate Tolstoj's religious writings, Tolstoj's example and eventually his personal encouragement gave Leskov an additional impetus to express his moral vision in fiction.

Leskov's most concentrated attempt to embody his ideal of Christian morality in literary form is a series of nine tales written between 1886 and 1891.[7] These tales, which will be referred to here as the *Prolog* tales, are, in the order of their publication, **"The Woodcutter," "Fedor and Abram," "Pamfalon the Clown," "Conscience-Stricken Daniel," "Beautiful Aza," "Father Gerasim's Lion," "The Brigand of Askalon," "The Mountain,"** and **"Innocent Prudencij."**[8] They are based on narratives found in the Russian *Prolog,* a compendium of religious writings and didactic narratives that had enjoyed considerable popularity in Russia as a source of entertainment as well as instruction for several centuries.[9] Leskov specifically connected his use of the *Prolog* as a literary source with Tolstoj's example. In fact, the first of the *Prolog* tales, **"The Woodcutter,"** is contained in an article defending Tolstoj's use of old religious narratives as a literary source (XI, 100-12). The explicit connection with Tolstoj points up the importance of the *Prolog* tales to any study of Leskov's Christian vision, while the use of early Christian didactic narratives represented Leskov's attempt to return to an earlier vision of Christianity in order to present a positive vision of universal Christian good rather than a negative view of contemporary evil. Finally, the *Prolog* tales are particularly illuminating because they are reworkings of known narratives; by comparing them with Leskov's sources, we can see what was taken over and what was changed. These changes reveal the essential elements of Leskov's positive Christian vision.

The original *Prolog* narratives are short tales or anecdotes that illustrate a particular Christian virtue, such as humility or chastity, or a generally Christian life-style, such as service to one's fellowman. The three main Christian principles which they illustrate are charitable self-sacrifice, active and humble participation in human society, and the infectiousness of good.[10] The heroes of these narratives are for the most part figures of great spiritual strength. Some lead humble lives in a state of material poverty and spiritual purity. Others perform heroic acts of self-sacrifice. Nearly all are nominally Christians, but most feel unworthy and take no pride in their membership in the Church. All the central figures in the *Prolog* narratives are faced with religious dilemmas or challenges which they solve or overcome through the strength of their faith. For the most part Leskov retains these dilemmas in his reworkings and develops a vision of Christian virtue in their resolution. In so doing, however, he alters the emphasis in many of the narratives.

The most important of these changes is in the attitude expressed toward the official Church. The *Prolog* narratives are marked by a strong pro-Church bias, which in Leskov's hands is eliminated and often deliberately attacked. In the source for **"Fedor and Abram,"** Fedor, a Christian, borrows money from Abram, a Jew, pledging on his faith in Christ that he will return it. When Fedor is unable to return the money and must borrow more, Abram blasphemes by doubting Christ's divinity. The money is eventually returned to Abram with a message from Jesus to blaspheme no more. As a result of this miracle Abram and his whole household accept baptism. In Leskov's version the miracle instead of converting Abram to Christianity confirms each man in his own faith and in his respect for the faith of the other. The two men, friends from boyhood despite the persecution this relationship has caused each of them, use their money to establish an interfaith orphanage in which children can learn to live together in harmony and understanding. Leskov's version is much more ecumenical in spirit;[11] true Christianity for him is not a matter of formal affiliation.[12]

In other *Prolog* narratives the entire Church is persecuted and must perform a miraculous feat to emerge triumphant. In the source for **"The Mountain"** the heathen ruler of Alexandria, a "cruel torturer of Christians" and "lawless barbarian," demands that the Christian patriarch and his followers literally move a mountain with their prayers on pain of dire punishment if they fail. By dint of faith, especially the faith of a certain Zenon, they succeed in moving the mountain, and the heathen are converted. In Leskov's version there are several important changes. The ruler of Alexandria makes his demand on the Christians because pressing political and economic reasons force him to look for a scapegoat, not simply because, as a pagan, he hates Christians.[13] The Christians in turn, especially the leaders, are shown to be as venal, cowardly, and self-serving as the pagans.

Genuine spiritual strength is displayed by Zenon, who though a schismatic is alone among the Christians in his calm faith in God. The miraculous moving of the mountain causes the pagans to seek baptism, but Zenon's real triumph lies in the effect of his example on the courtesan Nefora: moved by the purity of Zenon's faith and his capacity for self-sacrifice, she abandons her sinful life, distributes her wealth, and becomes, with Zenon, an active Christian.[14] Leskov's emphasis is on the spiritual triumph of the individual Christian rather than on the triumph of the Church militant.[15]

An important tenet of Leskov's Christian vision, the need to participate actively and humbly in human society, is illustrated in **"Pamfalon the Clown."** In the *Prolog* version a rich and powerful man wins God's favor by giving away his wealth and living thirty years in the desert as an anchorite. As a reward he is sent to Damascus to meet another who is pleasing to God. The man he meets is a clown who cannot leave his frivolous calling because he has given his wealth away to help a woman burdened by debts. Yet it is through this act of self-sacrifice that he has achieved grace. The anchorite is moved by the clown's story, but he returns to his pillar in the desert. In Leskov's version, which is basically the same except for the satirical view of the Damascus Christians who refuse the anchorite charity and shelter, the clown's tale influences the anchorite to go to a village in the desert, live among the people there, and serve them as a shepherd. The lesson he learns from the clown is that humble service to others is more pleasing to God than the moral purity of the hermit. Thus, while accepting the *Prolog*'s emphasis on charitable self-sacrifice, humble service, and the infectiousness of the Christian life, Leskov shifts from a militantly partisan bias in favor of the official Church toward an ecumenical spirit and an emphasis on a personal Christianity that can stand in opposition to the official Church as well as to non-Christians.

Soviet and Western critics have variously described the relation between the *Prolog* tales and the rest of Leskov's writings. Some have viewed the *Prolog* tales as a departure from Leskov's more characteristic work, a departure resulting from his temporary attraction to Tolstoj's Christian teachings.[16] Others have stressed the divergence from Tolstoj's ideas in the attitude expressed in many of the *Prolog* tales, connecting the *Prolog* tales with the body of Leskov's satiric writings in the 1880's and 1890's, especially with his anticlerical satires.[17] It is true that Leskov satirizes the clergy in some of the *Prolog* tales. But he satirizes hypocrisy and false piety in lay Christians and non-Christians as well. His concern was with hypocrisy wherever it is found.

Leskov's "difficult growth" did not end with the final elucidation of his vision of positive Christian morality in the *Prolog* tales. In a letter to Tolstoj on 8 April

1894, less than a year before his death, Leskov again takes up the question of the usefulness of positive and negative treatments of morality in literature. In this letter Leskov invokes anew the image of one who "sweeps the rubbish out of the temple" (cf. the 4 Jan. 1893 letter quoted above). While in the earlier letter Leskov speaks of the importance of Tolstoj's example for his entry "into the temple," i.e., for his positive presentation of the Christian ideal, here Leskov asserts his inability to present positive figures and a positive vision directly and asks for Tolstoj's support of his more recent satiric works: "I cannot 'present the one who is living in the holy of holies,' and I think that I ought not to take that up. . . . In a word, I want to remain *one who sweeps out the rubbish,* and not an interpreter of the Talmud."[18] He had been an "interpreter of the Talmud" in his re-workings of the *Prolog* tales, but by the early 1890's the restrictions of this kind of literary undertaking had begun to chafe. In his last major works, dealing with contemporary Russian life, Leskov presents his positive vision not explicitly but implicitly, through satire of contemporary hypocrisy and immorality. Thus the *Prolog* tales did not mark the final stage in Leskov's literary development. But as the last group of tales in which the central focus is the direct embodiment of his Christian ideal, they may be seen as the literary culmination of his positive moral vision.

*Notes*

1. The first story in this group, "Odnodum," was published in 1879, though several earlier works qualified for inclusion in the series about righteous men. "Odnodum" was originally preceded by a Foreword with the epigraph, "Without three righteous men no city can stand" (*Bez trex pravednyx nest' gradu stojanija*), from which the name of the series is taken.

2. The fullest available discussion of the development of Leskov's moral ideas as expressed in his writings is contained in William B. Edgerton, "Nikolai Leskov: The Intellectual Development of a Literary Non-Conformist" (Diss. Columbia Univ. 1954).

3. N. S. Leskov, *Sobranie sočinenij* (11 vols.; M.: GIXL, 1956-58) XI, 508-09.

4. For a discussion of the significance of this trip for Leskov, see William B. Edgerton, "Leskov's Trip Abroad in 1875," *Indiana Slavic Studies,* 4 (1967), 88-99.

5. Letter to P. K. Ščebal'skij of 10 August 1875 (X, 412).

6. For an analysis of Tolstoj's importance for Leskov, see William B. Edgerton, "Leskov and Tolstoy: Two Literary Heretics," *American Slavic and East European Review,* 12 (1953), 524-34.

7. Several other stories from the period of the *Prolog* tales embody a vision strongly akin to Tolstoj's; for example, "Pugalo" (1885), "Figura" (1889), "Čas voli božiej" (1890), the last of which was based on a subject proposed by Tolstoj. The *Prolog* tales, however, provide the clearest example of Leskov's attempt to present directly and explicitly his vision of Christian morality.

8. The full titles in the original (with year of publication): "Povest' o bogougodnom drovokole" (1886), "Skazanie o Fëdore xristianine i o druge ego Abrame židovine" (1886), "Skomorox Pamfalon" (1887), "Legenda o sovestnom Danile" (1888), "Prekrasnaja Aza" (1888), "Lev starca Gerasima" (1888), "Askalonskij zlodej" (1889), "Gora" (1890), and "Nevinnyj Prudencij" (1891).

9. The *Prolog* was originally a translation of a Greek collection of hagiographic writings. After its translation into Slavic, probably in the 12th or 13th century, the *Prolog* grew to include writings by the Church fathers and also edifying narratives drawn mainly from collections of such works, of which several existed in Slavic. These edifying narratives were primarily responsible for the popularity of the *Prolog,* and it was from them that Leskov took the subjects for the *Prolog* Tales. Leskov did not state which edition of the *Prolog* he used as a source. He insisted, however, that it was the ancient, unexpurgated version, containing much of the poetic and legendary material which was for the most part edited out in the 18th and early 19th centuries. The copy of the *Prolog* used for this study is that published in 1895-96 in two volumes in St. Petersburg by the Sinodal'skaja tipografija. Although this edition is a late one, published even after Leskov's death, it contains the "full" versions of the sources for Leskov's tales, as these versions are to be found in the earliest printed *Prolog*s from the 16th and 17th centuries. The *Prolog* of 1895-96 is held by the Slavonic Room of the New York Public Library. Sixteenth- and 17th-century copies of the *Prolog,* which are listed in A. S. Zernova, *Knigi kirillovskoj pečati izdannye v Moskve v XVI-XVII vekax* (M.: Biblioteka SSSR im. Lenina, 1958), are held in microfilm by the Rockefeller Library of Brown University. For a fuller discussion of various editions of the Prolog and their genesis, see my "Nikolaj Leskov and the Russian *Prolog* as a Literary Source," *Russian Literature,* 3 (1973), 16-39.

10. The only important exception is the source for "Nevinnyj Prudencij," in which lust is overcome by fasting.

11. Throughout his life Leskov was seriously concerned with relations between Jews and Chris-

tians. His attitude was not consistent, but eventually it called, both directly and indirectly, for tolerance and understanding between the two faiths. For a fuller discussion see Hugh McLean, "Theodore the Christian Looks at Abraham the Jew: Leskov and the Jews," *California Slavic Studies,* 7 (1973), 65-98.

12. Leskov's vision is not restricted to relations between Christians and Jews. In "Na kraju sveta" the same idea is presented through the relations between a Christian missionary and a pagan Siberian sled driver, who is more Christian in spirit than are the Siberian tribesmen who have been converted to Christianity.

13. Leskov introduces these reasons not only to modify the religious bias of the *Prolog* but also to meet contemporary demands for social and psychological motivation in literature, rather than purely partisan religious motivation.

14. In fact, in Leskov's tale the mountain is moved not by the prayers of the faithful but by natural causes: a great cloudburst loosens part of the mountain and it slides into the Nile. This shifts the focus of the tale to the more human miracle of Nefora's change of heart.

15. The distrust of organized religion which is in evidence in "The Mountain" may also be seen in several other of the *Prolog* tales: "Pamfalon the Clown," "The Brigand of Askalon," and "Conscience-Stricken Daniel." This distrust was one that Leskov shared with Tolstoj and one which Tolstoj's example encouraged in Leskov. However, even in the *Prolog* tales there is no blanket condemnation of the clergy, and in this regard Leskov was more moderate than Tolstoj.

16. For example, Vsevolod Setschkareff, *N. S. Leskov, Sein Leben und Sein Werk* (Wiesbaden: Otto Harrassowitz, 1959), 126.

17. M. S. Gorjačkina, *Satira Leskova* (M.: AN SSSR, 1963), page 94, argues that the period 1870-90 was marked by a fundamental anticlerical theme in Leskov's works and mentions such works as "Polunoščniki," "Zajačij remiz," "Putešestvie s nigilistom," "Zametki neizvestnogo," and "Meloči arxierejskoj žizni." See also B. M. Drugov, *N. S. Leskov: Očerk tvočestva,* 2nd ed. (M.: GIXL, 1961).

18. L. N. Tolstoj, *Perepiska s russkimi pisateljami,* ed. S. Rozanova (M.: GIXL, 1962), 587-89. Leskov evidently had in mind such recent satiric works as "Zagon," "Zajačij remiz," "Zimnij den'," and "Polunoščniki."

## William Hugh Hopkins (essay date 1977)

Hopkins, William Hugh. "Lermontovian Elements in Leskov's Story 'Deception.'" *New Zealand Slavonic Journal,* no. 1 (1977): 23-34.

[*In the following essay, Hopkins contends that in "Deception" Leskov used many of the motifs, literary devices, and character traits found in Russian writer Mikhail Lermontov's* A Hero of Our Time *(1840). According to Hopkins, Leskov paralleled the structure and content of this well-known work in order to expose and condemn Russian society's latent ethnic prejudice and moral relativism.*]

In Nikolay Leskov's short story **"Deception"** (**"Obman"**)[1] a retired army officer tells a group of fellow train-travellers, who are engaged in a conversation tinged with anti-Semitic overtones, why he is not so much anti-Semitic as anti-Rumanian.[2] In an extended anecdote which constitutes the body of the story within the story, the old gentleman recounts how he, as a debonair young officer stationed in Rumania, was deceived and cheated by the local people. Apparently he expected to receive everything gratis, especially attention from Rumanian ladies, jocularly called *kukony.* In an initial incident with one *kukona,* which foreshadows a more complicated incident with a second, the officer twice lets the *kukona* get away, not realizing that the crone with whom he negotiates is really the object of his affection in disguise.

Later he is again deceived by mistaking appearance for reality. At the farm where his regiment is quartered, the young officer becomes increasingly resentful of the landowner Kholuyan for a number of reasons and contrives to cuckold him. Although he seems to succeed, it turns out that all the Rumanians on the farm were participating in a grand charade. Kholuyan had sequestered his real wife away from the Russian soldiers, and "Madame Kholuyan" was just a local bar girl. Not even Kholuyan himself revealed his true identity. In short through many humorous twists the officer is deceived on every count, and his antics earn him a reprimand from his superiors. He never forgives the Rumanians their "perfidy". **"Deception"** can be described as a humorous, ironic demonstration of the absurdity of anti-Rumanianism and by analogy as a denunciation of anti-Semitism and of all prejudice.[3]

In the story Leskov subtly and unobtrusively employs a number of literary motifs long familiar to the Russian reading public and reminiscent of those used in Mikhail Lermontov's *A Hero of Our Time* (1840). Many devices and allusions in **"Deception,"** as well as its compositional techniques, relate it to that work. Some are parodied, but Leskov does not use these materials in such a way that his story emerges simply as a parody of *A Hero of Our Time*. Rather, he uses familiar, recognizably Lermontovian elements to create his own effects. These new effects then combine to constitute a specifically Leskovian whole. Identification of this relationship provides an expanded range of thematic and philosophical implications for both works.

**"Deception"** was not the first story in which Leskov employed Lermontovian motifs. Links between Lermontov's *Bela* and Leskov's **"The Enchanted Wanderer"** (**"Ocharovannyy strannik,"** 1873) have been observed by I. Z. Serman. In the early 1870s in the works of Turgenev and Tolstoy, among others, there was a revival of many themes and motifs which had been popular in Russian Romantic literature of the 1820s and 1830s. Leskov also revived themes and images from that period in **"The Enchanted Wanderer."** Serman thinks Leskov's artistic echoing (*pereklikaniye*) of Lermontov, Turgenev and Tolstoy, evident in that story, is not accidental. He contends that Leskov felt entitled to rework themes already touched upon by his predecessors and contemporaries.[4]

Lermontov himself frequently drew material from other literary sources. It might be argued that many of the "Lermontovian" elements in **"Deception"** were drawn from various sources, not necessarily from *A Hero of Our Time*. However, Leskov does not permit the attentive reader to miss their point of origin. Early in his conversation the retired officer-narrator describes the idea of free love for the military in his day as being "just as in Lermontov's novels".[5] This is the only such overt allusion to Lermontov's work in the story, but the remark is crucial. Having noticed this allusion, the reader becomes aware of more connections and parallels to Lermontov's work.[6] For example, just the combination of the motifs of travel and the South, which are introduced early in **"Deception,"** would perhaps have suggested something Romantic, Lermontovian, to a nineteenth-century Russian reader. These motifs are present in *A Hero of Our Time* and are similar to the combination Lermontov uses in *Bela*.

The five stories in Lermontov's work are arranged in a chronologically complex fashion. The first two are narrated by an itinerant officer of literary proclivities. In the frame of *Bela* the officer's travel account provides him an opportunity to recount a story told him by Maxim Maximych, an old junior captain, whose story within the story is essentially a first-person narrative. In *Maxim Maximych* the travelling "author"-narrator again encounters the junior captain and the pair meets Pechorin. The "author"-narrator eventually publishes Pechorin's journal, composed of three tales: *Taman'*, a story based on Pechorin's almost fatal encounter with smugglers in a small Black Sea port town; *Princess Mary*, a society tale set in a Caucasian spa and dealing

with a duel arising from the rivalry between Pechorin and Grushnitsky for a young lady's affection, and *Fatalist*, which treats the validity of the idea of predestination.

In **"Deception"** we find a roughly analogous situation. In the frame an unnamed narrator describes the appearance and actions of the retired army officer, who brings to mind Lermontov's character Maxim Maximych. At first this narrator seems well-disposed toward the venerable-looking old man, but his remarks soon begin to create a rather ambiguous impression. The story proper is essentially the retired officer's first-person narrative occasionally punctuated by the interpolated remarks of the original unnamed narrator. Such remarks remind the reader of the old man's inconsiderate and self-centred behaviour described in the frame, making it difficult to sympathise with his past trouble, and he becomes increasingly aware of the discrepancy between the actual events and the old officer's interpretation of them. In providing this data Leskov allows the reader to conclude that the old officer is devious, hypocritical and ludicrous. By association one begins to re-evaluate Maxim Maximych, the junior captain's world view, and the values implicit in the society in which he lived.

Maxim Maximych is perhaps one of the best-known and best-loved Russian literary creations. Since *A Hero of Our Time* was first published both the reading public and the critics have interpreted the character in highly positive terms. A perceptive modern American critic, corroborating the opinion of nineteenth-century Russian critics, calls Maxim Maximych "the incarnation of the truly Russian characteristics of simplicity and Christian humility." He adds that "even for the modern reader he remains a character notable and attractive for his naturalness and rough tenderness." Furthermore, he says there exists "a pathos about this being, who without being aware of his particular virtues is gentle, earnest, and compassionate."[7]

Maxim Maximych is described in physical terms as being about fifty, swarthy, prematurely gray, of firm gait, and of vigorous appearance. The physical description of the retired army officer in **"Deception"** is reminiscent of this. The narrator describes the retired officer as being of athletic build, muscular, white-haired, with strong features and a swarthy face. Moreover, the retired officer is described as "the most remarkable person among the passengers," and as a "positive character" and a "staunchly practical man." The narrator adds that "such men are not to be sneezed at in our time or in any other." All his qualities seem good. However, when the reader becomes better acquainted with the character, such apparently respectful observations about him by the first narrator assume an ironic quality.

If one re-examines the venerable Maxim Maximych against the thematic considerations which obviously interested Leskov in **"Deception,"** it quickly becomes apparent that Maxim Maximych is hardly the epitome of virtue he is so commonly thought to be. Instead, in at least some aspects of his character, he manifests pernicious attitudes which had apparently long been accepted, tolerated, or ignored in Russian society. Upon closer scrutiny this popularly accepted repository of simple Russian virtues can be seen to be a bigot with a warped sense of ethics.

Maxim Maximych's attitude toward the indigenous Caucasian tribes is hostile. He considers them dirty and foolish and characterizes them as "terrible rascals" and "dreadful rogues" who are yet clever enough to be capable of any sort of deviousness. His ambiguous compliments are in truth insults born of prejudice. He damns by faint praise. He is so poorly disposed toward one particular tribe in the vicinity that he considers the manifest blood-thirstiness of certain other tribes to be a positive virtue by comparison. In spite of such sentiments, Maxim Maximych nevertheless enters into "alliances" with these people. He attends a feast at the home of Bela's father, although he is suspicious of his host and the other guests. Discretion is unquestionably the better part of his prejudiced valour. At another point he invites a native, Kazbich, to tea, remarking that although he is a robber, he is still a *kunak* (ally).

When Maxim Maximych comments on Pechorin's plot to abduct Bela, he admits that it was "rotten," but soon he accedes to Pechorin's interpretation of the ethics involved. Finally, the idea seems to be that Bela, only a savage, should in spite of everything have considered herself fortunate to have been abducted. For all his affection for the girl, Maxim Maximych never forgets the fact that she is not a baptized Christian.[8] When Kazbich steals the girl back from Pechorin, Maxim Maximych remarks:

> I'm sorry, but these Circassians are a well-known thieving bunch: whatever's lying around they can't help but swipe; whether they need it or not, they will steal . . . but I guess you can't really hold it against them! And anyhow he's fancied her for a long time.[9]

The ethical justification for both Pechorin's and Kazbich's actions is tenuous. Even Maxim Maximych must perceive this in his limited way. He attempts to exonerate both men, not a particularly noble thing, but even his defense of Kazbich's action only serves to reveal further his prejudice and the inconsistency and relativity of his moral standards. The abduction of Bela by Kazbich was evidence of his savage, thieving nature; Pechorin's abduction of the girl was somehow different.

Maxim Maximych has fixed opinions about non-Asiatic nationalities as well. For example, he is willing rather indiscriminately to characterize Englishmen as always having been inveterate drunkards. Traditional interpretations of the Lermontovian character aside, it is possible that Leskov consciously or unconsciously perceived in Maxim Maximych not the epitome of Russian virtue, but the manifestation of a salient contemporary Russian vice. In addition to Maxim Maximych's bigotry, or perhaps because of it, he frequently distorts ethical considerations. His is in large measure a philosophy of ethnocentric apologetics.

When Maxim Maximych is viewed from such an angle, both the Lermontovian prototype and his literary descendants can be better understood. To see only the good aspects of the figure can lead to certain problems of interpretation of related characters. For example, Leskov had used a character related to Maxim Maximych in a story of 1878 entitled **"The Rakushansky Melamed. A Story on Bivouac."**[10] It has been observed that a character in the story, Major Pleskunov, is "a descendant of Lermontov's Maxim Maximych," "old-fashioned," and "true-blue."[11] Identifying such a connection, while failing to perceive Maxim Maximych's bigotry, almost necessarily leaves a critic confronted with a number of "ambiguities" in the story *vis-à-vis* the theme of anti-Semitism.[12] However, the two characters are more closely related in their negative than in their positive qualities. Keeping in mind as well that Leskov is well known for his use of satire and irony, the comment which **"The Rakushansky Melamed"** has to make about anti-Semitism is not at all ambiguous, but clearly opposed to prejudice.

As has been pointed out, *A Hero of Our Time* has three principal narrators—the "author"-narrator, Maxim Maximych and Pechorin. In **"Deception"** the retired officer also suggests Pechorin, as a young man in the tale which he relates about himself. It is true that the retired officer and the young officer are in fact one individual. However, the frame-story technique, the years which have intervened since the episode occurred and its retelling, the differences between the narrator as a young man and as an old man, and the vastly different physical settings between the frame story and the tale, metaphorically bifurcate the character.

Pechorin's character has always held a strange fascination for Russian readers. It is this figure, rather than Maxim Maximych, who has been thought to be lacking in ethical values. It seems plausible that Leskov was also drawing to some degree on the predictably negative reader attitude toward Pechorin and suggesting Pechorin in the retired officer when seen as a young man in order to help create the final effect of **"Deception."**

The retired officer begins his anti-Rumanian diatribe by stating that man reveals his true nature in love perhaps more than in cards. Even savages, he condescendingly observes, do not live without love. These motifs (cards, "savages," and love) are all encountered in *A Hero of Our Time*. As he continues his anecdote, he reveals a nostalgia for the good old days and their traditional values. He implies that people were more moral in his day, and that there were fewer of the current vices, such as common-law marriage. However, he is quick to grant moral dispensations to the military for infidelity and discreet free love. The permitted remissive behaviour of the military is met in both works, and in both there are apologists for such behaviour.

It is precisely in connection with the idea of free love for the military that the narrator alludes to Lermontov's works. The motifs of free love and infidelity play important thematic roles in *Bela* and *Princess Mary*. In these stories Pechorin ignores the ethical implications of his involvement in certain morally questionable exploits. He is unprincipled in his treatment of Bela, Mary, and Vera. He has devised for himself a pseudo-philosophy of self-justification and rationalization that is blatantly hypocritical. Apparently, the society in which he functions, for the most part, tacitly accepts such a code. Pechorin abducts a Chechen woman and it is he who should assume the major moral responsibility for her death. However, he is not really considered culpable; there are no significant consequences for him. He kills a man in a duel and as punishment he is banished to a remote post. In each situation the perfunctory moral response of the society fosters the egocentric moral relativism of the individual.

The notions of hypocrisy and moral poverty are also developed in **"Deception."** The depiction of Pechorin is essentially a psychological study and no humour is developed in Lermontov's novel. In Leskov's story the retired officer both in the frame and as a young man in the tale manifests the same hypocritical disposition towards ethics that can be identified in Maxim Maximych and Pechorin, i.e., ethnocentric apologetics and egocentric moral relativism. While relativism and forms of self-centredness are characteristic of both, a distinction is useful here, because the characters manifest what are perhaps the same qualities in different contexts. Leskov's treatment of the bifurcated character in his story is humorous, the ethics of the situation notwithstanding. The young officer's warped philosophy backfires on him, but this happens in a situation so trivial that it evokes only amusement.

The first episode with a *kukona* in **"Deception"** has no exact narrative parallel in *A Hero of Our Time;* however, it does introduce motifs of intrigue and infidelity that are to be used again later in the story. In the events that take place on the Kholuyan farm, the Lermontovian motifs of intrigue (as in *Bela* and *Taman'*) and infidelity (as in *Princess Mary*) are developed and treated facetiously, since it is the "hero," and not the heroine, who is finally deceived.

As Leskov's narrator reminisces about the suspicions he had that he was somehow about to be deceived, the tone of his anecdote, i.e., the mood of his story itself, for a time becomes quite similar to the tone of *Taman'*. In *Taman'* a tone of ominousness and apprehension is created through a description of Pechorin's reaction to his surroundings and the local inhabitants, many of whom speak broken Russian. In the first episode of the retired officer's anecdote in **"Deception"** the protagonist finds the unpleasant Rumanian climate, a Jewish pander's behaviour, and the Rumanian *kukona* and her "crone" to be mystifying and threatening.

As the scene shifts to the Kholuyan farm the narrator encounters the regimental versifier. The enigmatic, non-sensical statements of this character can be interpreted as having been designed to perplex the narrator further, to heighten the suspense, and to create a mock-Lermontovian aura of mystery (c f. the undine and her songs in *Taman'*). Even the Lermontovian theme of predestination, or at least presentiment, is introduced:

> Well, anyway, believe if you want, if not, don't believe in a premonition . . . Sure, nowadays skepticism is popular, but I believe in premonitions, because in this rough life of mine I've had plenty of proof; but in my soul when we were going up to that farm-stead I got so sad, so miserable, that it seemed just like I was going to my own execution.[13]

Though highly abbreviated in **"Deception,"** thematically this passage reminds one of Pechorin's frequent reflections about cosmic questions, especially as expressed in *Fatalist* and to a somewhat lesser degree in *Princess Mary* and *Taman'*.

Lermontov's use of the word *nechisto* to describe the atmosphere in *Taman'* introduces the motifs of physical dirt and occult happenings.[14] The description of Kholuyan's farm contains the same motifs. The narrator observes:

> The first impression it made on me was a most disgusting one.

> And there were already some kind of real, open pits like graves. Hell knows when and by what devils and for whom they were dug, but they were really deep. Maybe they used to get clay out of them, or maybe, as some said, there was supposed to be this medicinal mud here, and apparently even the old Romans used to smear themselves with it. But in general the place was really gloomy and really strange.[15]

In *Taman'* Pechorin experiences ominous presentiments, not only because of the physical circumstances and the general ambiance, but also because of the presence of the blind boy. He remarks:

> I admit, I have a strong prejudice against all blind people, one-eyed ones, the deaf, the mute, legless people, armless people, hunchbacks and such. I have

noticed that there is always some kind of strange relationship between a person's exterior and his soul: as if with the loss of a limb the soul loses some part of its feeling . . . Anyway, what could I do? I'm often given to prejudice . . .[16]

The motif of the menace of physical abnormality is a device Lermontov uses to create suggestions of the occult and the grotesque, yet on the thematic level Pechorin's disposition toward physical abnormality is essentially only another manifestation of prejudice. It is apparent that Lermontov uses suggestions of the occult and the grotesque as a literary device to create fear or at least suspense. Pechorin's prejudice, even though used as a literary device to create a certain atmosphere, ultimately derives from fear of that which is different, misunderstood, unknown. Pechorin's manifestation of prejudice just like that of Maxim Maximych is born of those same elements which foster all prejudice.

The boy's nocturnal behaviour, Pechorin's particular prejudice, and the generally ominous atmosphere all make him suspect nefarious activities in *Taman'*. In a similar way the narrator in **"Deception"** does not like the general atmosphere of the Kholuyan farm, and he is particularly repelled by the abundance of some unpleasant flowers, the number of herons, and the pits and hills. For example, he says:

> Here and there you could see little thickets, but just like little graveyards . . .
>
> There weren't any flowers or even cornflowers, but only some kind of stalks that looked like they were sprinkled with fuzz which stuck out here and there, and on them were heavy, yellow pitchers on the order of lilies, but really foul: if you'd go to smell it, your nose would swell up right away. And what else surprised us was how many herons there were . . . I can't stand a place where that buzzard of the Pharoah breeds: it has something about it that reminds you of all the plagues of Egypt . . . It was just like they were planning to do something secret there, undercover. Most probably, I guess, they were counterfeiting our Russian money.[17]

In **"Deception,"** Rumania and its exotic *kukony* replace the Lermontovian Transcaucasia and its storybook princesses. The narrator is particularly vexed at being expected to pay for food and lodging. He considers this irregular and concludes the Rumanians are avaricious. In his retrospective opinion this particular act of Rumanian treachery was exceeded only by Kholuyan's use of the *kukona* to bring him to grief. This *kukona* (at once suggestive of the undine in *Taman'* and of *Bela*) is a flat, stock character, the exotic fairy-tale princess developed only insofar as it is necessary to the action of the story.

It appears that the narrator is going to encounter a rival for the *kukona's* affection with the introduction of the Russian officer Foblaz. In the preface to his tale the retired officer remarked that he would be telling a little anecdote about the privileged Rumanian class and their manners and morals. It becomes clear with the appearance of the love intrigue that this whole anecdote can be viewed as a pastiche of the society tale. *Princess Mary* represents an example of this genre in *A Hero of Our Time*. Since it was a well-known genre even in Lermontov's time, its conventions were familiar to the reading public.[18] A reader acquainted with the genre could anticipate, for example, that Pechorin and Grushnitsky would eventually fight a duel because of rivalry and romantic intrigue. Much of the humour in **"Deception"** arises from the fact that Leskov frustrates such reader anticipation. Foblaz's rival is literally a *chicken*. There *is* no duel. Instead Foblaz commits suicide, morally devastated because a travelling Pole has managed to distract the *kukona* from her chicken—albeit for money. The Russians, led by the hero, decide to avenge Foblaz. After contriving to dupe "Kholuyan" out of some money the officer is able to purchase the lady's attentions. As a consequence of having executed his clever but misguided plot to deceive Kholuyan, and for then having revealed the lady's indiscretion to her "husband," the narrator is deprived of his military rank. The authorities punish him not so much for what he really did as for the fact that they do not think a gentleman should reveal such a thing about a lady. The distorted ethical standards of conventional society are revealed in this episode.

Although the situation in **"Deception"** is humorous, an analogy is apparent here to the warped standards of society so frequently manifested in *A Hero of Our Time*. Although the narrator has shown himself to be devious and unprincipled and although it is evident that he has brought everything upon himself, he is chagrined to think that the real Kholuyan did not want someone like him to be in contact with his family. In a similar, though less ludicrous way, Pechorin also fails to perceive the essential meaning of his experiences. For example, at the conclusion of *Taman'*, it has not occurred to him that he himself was ultimately responsible for his entanglement with the "honest" smugglers and his brush with death.

After the retired officer has completed his story, in a few brief lines narrated principally by the original unnamed narrator, the reader is brought back from Rumania to the train-compartment setting of the frame story. Offering no value judgments, the original narrator again makes innocuous observations which remind the reader that the retired officer is still occupying three times his share of space and is still eating and drinking without offering anyone anything.

The retired officer proposes a morally inconsistent toast "to the Yids" and to the "ruin of the Rumanians." Since it is Christmas Eve another unnamed passenger suggests that instead they wish "good to all and evil to no one." Everyone accedes to this idea, and the vituperative philosophy which the old officer has attempted to generate is dispelled by the perfunctory "Christian" palliative. If anyone has seen through the old officer's self-serving hypocrisy, no one has challenged or reproached him for it. The pious platitude wipes the slate of everyone's conscience clean. The final image of the story is that of the old officer merrily drinking to the good of all. It is clear from the original narrator's abrupt termination of the discourse without further comment that he alone has understood that the warped philosophy at work in this microcosm has only been temporarily suspended by the magnanimous toast, not rectified.

Enough themes converge in **"Deception"** to justify its reading as an indictment of the society's lack of ethical values and its toleration of ethnocentric apologetics and egocentric moral relativism. More than that, for the modern reader the structural and thematic links between **"Deception"** and *A Hero of Our Time* make the two works almost objective correlatives of each other. It is not to our purpose to debate authorial intent. However, a close study of **"Deception"** reveals that Leskov seemingly employs Lermontovian characters and motifs almost hallowed in Russian literary tradition and gives them a new slant. Thereby the thematic and philosophical range of his work extends beyond the story itself. Reshuffled Lermontovian motifs, themes and compositional effects become almost a symbol for the moral and ethical impasse at which Russian society had arrived.

An analysis of Leskov's story likewise provides new thematic perspectives from which to view *A Hero of Our Time*. He does not parody it as a literary work *per se*, rather his story exposes in bold relief the moral bankruptcy of these modes of behaviour, attitudes and values reflected in Lermontov's novel. Leskov thereby debunks some of the comfortable myths that society perpetuates to salve its conscience, and he reveals the ludicrousness of such self-deceiving hypocrisy. Still, there is no shrill denunciation of prejudice or bigotry. The artistic restraint noticeable in his statement is analogous to the moderation implicit in Leskov's reasoned personal approach to the necessity of re-assessing and rectifying the basic philosophical assumptions of Russian society.

### Notes

1. The story originally appeared in *Rossiya,* nos. 10-15 (1883) and was entitled *Kartiny proshlogo: vetrenniki.* It was retitled *Obman* in Leskov's collection *Svyatochnye rasskazy* (St. Petersburg, 1886), and the new title has remained. See Hugh McLean, 'Theodore the Christian Looks at Abraham the Hebrew: Leskov and the Jews', *California Slavic Studies,* 7 (Berkeley, 1973), n. 48, p. 91.

*Obman* was not printed in the most recent Soviet edition: N. S. Leskov, *Sobraniye sochineniy v odinnadtsati tomakh,* Moscow, 1956-58.

2. Leskov wrote a number of stories which include Jewish characters. These stories as well as some of Leskov's non-artistic literary endeavours which concern the Jews are enumerated, described and interpreted by McLean in 'Theodore the Christian . . . ,' *California Slavic Studies,* pp. 65-98.

The article examines certain aspects of Leskov's life and experiences with Jews as well as the author's literary creation apparently in order to determine exactly how Leskov was disposed towards the Jews. In the main the critic finds the author's literary creation indicative of Leskov's personal ambivalence toward them; however, he vindicates Leskov the person from charges of anti-Semitism.

3. There seems to be no critical discussion whatsoever of *Deception* in either pre-revolutionary Russian or Soviet publications. Only Edgerton in his Introduction to *Deception* in Nikolai Leskov, *Satirical Stories of Nikolai Leskov,* trans. and ed. by William B. Edgerton (New York, 1969), pp. 105-06, had offered any critical comment about the story until McLean discussed it in 'Theodore the Christian . . . ,' *California Slavic Studies,* pp. 90-91.

The latter's interpretation is unconvincing due to incursions of the intentional and the affective fallacies. For example, he remarks:

> The presumed moral of 'Deception,' therefore, is that we should set aside not only anti-Semitism, but prejudice itself. . . .

> Yet one wonders whether it is this message of tolerance and good will that Leskov's readers would have derived from 'Deception,' particularly on the emotional level. . . .

> In any case, in the context of pogrom-wracked Russia of the early 1880s such a playful treatment . . . of the subject of ethnic prejudice and especially anti-Semitism seems inappropriate not only artistically, but even morally.

4. Serman links *Ocharovannyy strannik* to Turgenev's *Konets Chertopkhanova* (1872) and to L. N. Tolstoy's *Kavkazsky plennik* (1872), both of which likewise include themes found in *Bela.* See Serman's notes in N. S. Leskov, *Sobraniye sochineniy,* vol. IV, pp. 551-53. The following studies make reference to Serman's notes and discuss the links between the aforementioned stories: Hugh McLean, 'Leskov and the Russian Superman', *Midway,* Spring 1968, pp. 105-23; Vsevolod Setschkareff, *N. S. Leskov: Sein Leben und sein Werk* (Wiesbaden, 1959), p. 90; and I. V. Stolyarova,

'Povest' N. S. Leskova *Ocharovannyy strannik'*, Omsky pedagogichesky institut im. Gor'kogo, *Uchennye zapiski*, Vypusk 21, Trudy Kafedry russkoy i zarubezhnoy literatury (Omsk, 1963), pp. 64-102.

5. The Russian text reads: "Etogo grekha, kak i v romanakh Lermontova, vidno bylo deystvitel'no ochen' mnogo . . ." N. S. Leskov, 'Obman', *Polnoye sobraniye sochineniy*, izd. 3 (St. Petersburg, 1903), XVIII, p. 96.

6. Although the retired officer makes reference to Lermontov's *novels*, we can safely assume that he does not have in mind *Vadim* (1834) or *Knyaginya Ligovskaya* (1838), but only *A Hero of Our Time*. The two former works are unfinished and never enjoyed anything like the popularity of the latter work, which must be known to almost every literate Russian.

7. John Mersereau, *Mikhail Lermontov* (Carbondale, Illinois, 1962), pp. 87; 89.

8. Although he handles it very differently, Leskov also treated the theme of the Christian Russians' attitude toward non-baptized Asiatics in his story *Na krayu sveta* (1876).

9. M. Yu. Lermontov, *Geroy nashego vremeni, Sobraniye sochineniy v chetyrekh tomakh* (Moscow & Leningrad, 1962), vol. IV, p. 321.

10. Leskov, op. cit., XIV, pp. 130-65. (See n. 5.)

11. McLean, op. cit., p. 79.

12. While extended discussion of Leskov's attitude toward the Jews is beyond the scope of this study, it is worth noting that Leskov's treatment of a certain Jewish character in *The Rakushansky Melamed* (his *artistic, literary* treatment) has been one of the reasons for his suspected anti-Semitism.

In McLean's opinion Pleskunov's disdain for the melamed's pietistic religiosity reveals a contradiction in his ostensible defense of the Jews. Unfortunately, this contradictory attitude is extended to Leskov himself. Another "ambiguity" of attitude is resolved in Leskov's favour, for in the story the Russian who outwits the ultra-deceitful Jew is portrayed not as his moral superior but as his immoral equal.

13. Leskov, op. cit., p. 109.

14. Mersereau, op. cit., p. 110.

15. Leskov, op. cit., p. 109.

16. Lermontov, op. cit., p. 342.

17. Leskov, op. cit., p. 110.

18. Mersereau, op. cit., pp. 113-16.

## James Y. Muckle (essay date 1978)

Muckle, James Y. "The Religious and Moral Content of Leskov's Later Works." In *Nikolai Leskov and the "Spirit of Protestantism,"* pp. 127-47. Birmingham, U. K.: University of Birmingham, 1978.

[*In the following excerpt, Muckle focuses on the short stories Leskov wrote from the mid-1880s until his death, suggesting that Leskov's changed his views on a variety of moral and religious issues during this period.*]

In the works of the last ten or eleven years of Leskov's life there is a subtle change in style and spirit. None of the beliefs he cherished up to this time are renounced, but there is a slight, though distinct change in emphasis. The change begins to be discernible in the works conceived in the early to middle 1880s, and it follows and could partly be a consequence of certain upheavals in Leskov's personal and professional life which began in the late 1870s.

His family and personal life was uneasy. The aftereffects of certain events were still making themselves felt in the eighties: he had parted from his mistress, Katerina Bubnova, in 1877. His wife Olga, from whom he had separated many years previously, went mad in 1878 and entered an institution, where Leskov visited her regularly, conscious of his own share of the responsibility for her collapse. His apartment was run by a succession of housekeepers; one of them, Ketti Kukk, had a daughter whom Leskov adopted and looked after from the time he dismissed her mother in 1885 until his death. His son by the relationship with Bubnova, Andrei, had a violent dispute with him in 1885 and left to stay with relations in Kiev—relations whom Leskov had now ceased to visit, sensing perhaps that they no longer had anything in common. Leskov's mother died in 1886. Though he had many friends and acquaintances, his last years seem to have been lonely. He had drifted away from most of his family, and became somewhat isolated from other people. He suffered dismissal from government service in 1883, the banning of Volume VI of his collected works in 1889 and frequent other trouble with censorship. Hallucinations, depression and poor health in general were the consequences of these difficulties, but at least the publication of his collected works ensured an end to financial worries. Until his death in 1895 he was, however, known to officialdom as a rebel and a heretic[1].

The change in the tone of Leskov's stories at this period is not easy to define. Despite the difficulties he was experiencing, there is no strain of bitterness in them. They continue to be witty and persuasive, and are often optimistic in their view of human nature. There is, however, a sharpness in the satire more intense than before. The serious intent of most of the stories is even more obvious than in the earlier works, and a good proportion of them set out to be unashamedly didactic. Several of them are based on the ancient *Prologue* or are set in mythical lands. Despite the appearance of many selfless and saintly characters, there is intensified pessimism in the treatment of the masses: people in general, 'they', are often ignorant, unfeeling, superstitious, credulous, undiscerning or cruel. The character of the later works can be summed up generally by saying that they are extremely serious in intent, occasionally austere in style, they represent a firm moral and religious outlook, they are more critical on the whole of people and groups than the earlier works. The hand that holds the pen is more self-assured than ever before in Leskov's career. Charity and sympathy there still is, but there is less evidence now of an easy-going frame of mind.

Themes dealt with by Leskov include some very important ones: the nature of Christian love, mercy and forgiveness, the age-old puzzle of appearance and reality, what is meant by truth, the place of the artist in society, self-sacrifice, duty, freedom and man's ability to restrict his own freedom. Sexual and spiritual love, life and death, politics and religion, faith and works all figure in some or other of these stories. Fear, obscurantism, belief in miracles and superstition are depicted and discussed. The standpoint from which all these problems are seen is that of the Bible-reading Christian. The most significant sources outside himself to which Leskov went in search of confirmation of his beliefs were the Protestant movements and preachers investigated hitherto (though overt reference to them is much less frequent in this period), Fathers of the Church, ancient ecclesiastical literature and Lev Nikolaevich Tolstoy.

These sources could be summed up in one: the Bible. Leskov quoted directly and referred indirectly to both Old Testament and New. He quotes the prophets, the Acts of the Apostles, Paul's hymn to love and most often of all the teachings of Christ. Like Origen, a father of the early church whom Leskov keenly admired, he used Christ's sayings as the yardstick by which everything else—the rest of the Bible, preachers he knew, religious literature and contemporary moralists—was measured[2]. This is not a change in his outlook of earlier years, but an intensification of an earlier tendency.

Two of the virtues praised by Leskov in these later stories were love and mercy, with their synonyms self-sacrifice and forgiveness. Examples can be multiplied: the girl who impoverishes herself to pay another's debts, **"Prekrasnaya Aza,"** (VIII [all parenthethical volume numbers refer to *Sobranie Sochinenii*, vols. I-II, Moscow, 1956-58]), (**"Beautiful Aza"**), the man who takes in orphans, **"Gora,"** (VIII), (**"The Mountain"**) and another example in **"Pugalo,"** (VIII), (**"The Bogeyman"**). The 'fool' in **"Durachok"** (Marks, vol. 33. [all paren-

thetical references to "Marks," coincide with *Polnoe Sobranie Sochinenii*, I-XXXVI, 3rd ed. St. Petersburg, 1902-03]) takes a beating for another and offers to be tortured in place of someone else; the analogy of Christ is present here. At the simplest level, Christian love is exemplified by the man who does a mundane job without complaint (**"Luchshii bogomolets,"** (XI), (**"The Better Worshipper"**)), and it is seen to extend even to animals (**"Lev startsa Gerasimova,"** (Marks, vol. 30), (**"Father Gerasim's Lion"**)). **"Chas voli Bozhiei,"** (IX), (**"God's Good Time"**), is a discussion of the question 'Who is my neighbour?'

The converting power of the quality of mercy is described by Leskov in a number of stories. In **"Bramadata and Radovan"** (Marks, vol. 30) it is the forgiveness of Radovan's son and the mercy he shows to Bramadata when he has him in his power which persuades him to renounce cruelty and give it no further place in his kingdom. The eponymous hero of **"Figura"** (VIII) forgives a drunken Cossack soldier for assaulting him; this leads to Figura's dismissal from the service; Christianity and the service of the Empire cannot be reconciled! Forgiveness for Beautiful Aza was conditional, as far as the Church was concerned, on certain rites being observed, but Leskov tells his readers that in similar circumstances Christ wrote a woman's sins 'with his finger in the sand and left the wind to blow them away'. This is a happy thought, but not an exact paraphrase of John 8, vv. 7-9, where it is possible that it was the sins of the woman's accusers that were written in the sand[3].

Readiness to stand firm in defence of the truth is a recurrent theme in several stories. Bryanchaninov and Chikhachev in **"Inzhenery-bessrebreniki,"** (VIII), (**"The Disinterested Engineeers"**), believe that warlike activity is incompatible with Christian convictions, but being unable to stand up for this truth they flee. The very nature of truth is the main theme of **"Chelovek na chasakh,"** (VIII), (**"The Sentry"**), in which a bishop shows he is only too ready to compromise in the interests of preserving good relations between Church, army and Tsar. He is skilful in manipulating arguments to show that no conflict of duty and truth has been involved.

The illusory nature of popularly accepted 'truths' is a theme of a number of Leskov's stories, and he often seems to suggest that truth is an elusive quality which must be sought below the surface of events. Selivan, the central character of **"The Bogeyman"**, is a victim of other people's ignorance, superstition and silly talk: his Christian charity is interpreted as evil and sinister. People in a number of stories fail to understand the real truth about the unselfish actions of righteous characters: good people are rewarded by nicknames like 'little fool' or 'muttonhead', or they are ostracised because their behaviour is not conventional, as in **"Zimnii den',"** (IX), (**"A Winter's Day"**). In **"Chortovy kukly,"** (VIII), (**"The Devil's Marionettes"**), an artist becomes a 'marionette' and loses his freedom to depict the truth by accepting the patronage of a prince.

The impossibility of a human being arriving at a full appreciation of moral and religious truth is expressed by Leskov in **"Skazanie o Fedore-khristianine i o druge ego Avrame-zhidovine,"** (Marks, vol. 30), (**"The Tale of Fedor the Christian and Avram the Jew"**). The heroes discuss the nature of truth. 'God created men so that they understand things differently', says Avram. Fedor replies: 'What the Jews don't understand is that Jesus wanted only to do good to all men and was killed by those who couldn't see it'. Avram answers: 'It is not only Jews who do not understand him, but many Christians who . . . don't carry out his teachings.' They conclude that 'in both religions it is possible to be master of oneself, if only one understands the faith correctly, and does not harbour cunning thoughts . . .' This is a reasonably coherent statement of philosophy: truth is understanding and may be perceived in different ways, so toleration is the only possible attitude between Christians and Jews. Love is more important than truth because failure to show love obscures the truth, and good deeds and sound attitudes of mind are possible to members of different faiths.

These three themes of love, truth and mercy are linked in the closing lines of the story **"Malan'ya—golova baran'ya"** (Marks, vol. 33), (**"Malanya Muttonhead"**). This tale has a strange atmosphere: it is a cross between legend, folktale and parable, and introduces the subject of death. Malanya does a good deed and is rewarded by the granting of a wish: 'that Death shall not cross her threshold'. In a hundred years no-one in the village dies—Malanya petrified the figure of Death when it appeared. Since many of the villagers now long to die, she releases Death; he goes about his business, but she herself survives. She is so old that she has forgotten her name. Others say it is *Lyubov'*, love. Love is not on the list of names which Death has come to claim, not, that is, until 'truth and mercy meet and the wolf lies down with the lamb'.

Love, truth and mercy are three key ideas in the stories of this period in Leskov's life, and the linking of them in **"Malanya Muttonhead"** is not fortuitous. It arises out of Leskov's understanding of his reading of two of the fathers of the early Church: Origen and Isaac the Syrian. Origen lived in the second and third centuries of the Christian era, and his ideas are well enough known in both East and West. One feature of Origen's doctrine which must have appealed to Leskov was his keen awareness of the ethical implications of the Gospel. Leskov refers more often to another father of the Church, Isaak Sirin, Isaac the Syrian. Among Orthodox

Christians today and in nineteenth century Russia Isaac's writings were well known[4]. In the West there has been doubt as to whether Isaac was one, two or several different people. Some of the confusion has been cleared up by S. Brock in a recent article[5], in which Isaac the Syrian is identified as Isaac, bishop of Nineveh.

Leskov found a great deal in Isaac to admire. In a letter to Tolstoy of 3 October 1894[6] he reflected that there was much in Isaac which was akin to Tolstoy: Isaac's criticism of the impropriety of selfish prayer, for example, and his sense for justice (meaning fairness rather than a temporal system of law-giving), non-resistance to evil, and mercy. Earlier references to Isaac link love, truth and mercy very clearly. Isaac sought truth and mercy, wrote Leskov to Suvorin (XI, 371). In the article 'Tolstoy and Dostoevsky as Heresiarchs' Leskov paraphrases Isaac in his polemic with Leont'ev. Leont'ev had advanced the notion that fear rather than love is the first healthy step in a man's relationship with God, and had claimed the authority of Isaac for this. On the contrary, replied Leskov, Isaac maintains that 'The mercy of God towards men, revealed in the Gospel will remain for ever his changeless characteristic'. It is interesting and important to note that Leskov first and foremost uses Scripture in this article to attack Leont'ev's position. Isaac (and Origen too) are called in as the second line of attack to back up what Leskov regarded as the Scriptural position.

Everything that Leskov says about Isaac and his faith is quite true, but Brock's account of Isaac's views shows that it is only half the story. Reading Isaac's message, the reader enters into a world of Orthodox spirituality which is quite strange to anyone brought up in the Protestant tradition. Isaac's religion is, as Leskov says, rooted in the love of God, but it is also ecstatic, enthusiastic, fervid, exultant—almost irrational. Isaac writes of 'spiritual drunkenness' and 'tears of joy'. This monograph is primarily concerned with Leskov's intellectual problems in facing religious issues, but it must not be forgotten that he never criticised or mocked the ecstatic side of religion—indeed, the point has been made and will be made again later that his emotions were engaged in his religion just as his intellect was. The enthusiastic response of ordinary people to religion was so much part of Leskov's background that it only occasionally occurred to him to comment upon it.

The consciences of many Christians in Russia were troubled by the requirement on certain occasions to swear oaths. Reluctance to swear is based on Matthew 5, vv. 33-7, which reports the words of Christ: 'Swear not at all . . . Let your communication be Yea, yea; Nay, nay'. Leskov attacks the swearing of oaths, and it was undoubtedly his reading of the Gospel coupled with his moral sense and rationalist way of thinking which led him to do so. Christ's words look like an instruction regarding plain speaking and a criticism of irreverent embellishments to one's utterances rather than a refusal to allow promises to be made which might limit the speaker's freedom[7]. Verse 36, 'Neither shalt thou swear by thy head . . .' may even be a joke.

One occasion when the ordinary man was called upon to swear an oath was when serving as a juryman. In an article of 1882, 'Snedayushchee slovo', Leskov raises this question of conscience. He argues that the swearing of oaths is forbidden by Christ, and that jurymen, knowing this, are omitting to swear or swallowing (*snedat'*, to eat) the words as the oath is administered. Good faith is involved, and the matter should not be forgotten about, he insists. Leskov's article is consistent and justified, according to the letter of the Gospel, but it is rather exaggerated, and not particularly well argued. Does he really need to be indignant because a juryman or a witness promises to act in good faith by swearing 'by Almighty God'?

The swearing of oaths has a much more sinister side, however. A soldier on enlistment swears an oath of allegiance to the Crown. This means in effect that he transfers the control of his conscience to his superior officer. The soldier Postnikov, aptly named with the double pun on *post*, 'fast' and 'post', is placed in a situation in the story **"The Sentry"** in which he has to choose between loyalty to the Emperor and the need to rescue a drowning fellow man. He is punished for opting for the latter: what would happen if soldiers did as they thought and not as they had sworn to do? An important issue is raised here, one which has been argued fiercely in our own time: can a man escape responsibility for his sins of omission or commission by saying he obeyed orders? The conventional answer is 'No', but in practice few men have the mental and spiritual resources to check every decision made on their behalf.

In more than one story Leskov portrays the clergy stifling the qualms of the sensitive. Figura finds his oath of allegiance at variance with his faith, and is asked why he did not go to a priest to resolve his difficulties. In other words, why does he not find another person to take the responsibility for a serious moral decision off his shoulders? This is exactly what Svin'in does in Chapter XVII of **"The Sentry"**; and doubts about the rightness of what has happened are set to rest by a bishop.

The story which puts the case against oaths most clearly and convincingly is **"Tomlenie dukha,"** (Marks, vol.16), (**"Spiritual Torment"**). Some boys have sworn an oath not to tell their father that the Provincial Governor's son stole apples from an orchard, and a peasant lad is flogged for the crime. Their tutor, nicknamed 'Koza', remonstrates with them and their parents and is dismissed for his pains. To the boys he says, 'You relinquished your freedom and became prisoners of your oath . . . You were not free to speak the truth and an innocent boy was flogged in consequence'. We have here a cogent objection to oath-taking. It restricts the freedom of the person who has sworn, and he may therefore fail to do good or speak the truth, even when to do so would prevent wrong from happening. The situation depicted in the story illustrates the moral precept very clearly and appropriately, and at the same time simply. The story probably also reveals that the swearing of oaths was a very much more usual feature of everyday life in Russia than it has ever become in the West. What English boy would swear such an oath as here or regard himself as bound by it? **"The Sentry"** portrays the moral dilemma of men bound by their oath, and the two stories together comprise a good case against oath-taking. **"The Sentry"** exploits an intricate situation and propounds no easy answer; **"Spiritual Torment"** presents a very straightforward moral issue, clear enough to be suitable for children. 'Koza' has a strongly developed religious outlook. Leskov subtly hints at his Christ-like nature. When asked by the children what family he has, he replies, *'Nu, kto svoi . . . eto zhe s kem odno i to zhe lyubish'*, clearly reminiscent of Christ's 'Whosoever shall do the will of God, the same is my brother, and my sister, and mother' (Mark 3, vv. 35).

Marriage, sexual love and their place in the life of a Christian are discussed in several of the works of the last ten years of Leskov's life. Leskov is fond of contrasting selfish physical love with Christian concern for all mankind, or as theologians would say, *eros* with *agape*. *Eros* for Leskov is an emotion sometimes amounting to a passion. *Agape* is manifested by a decision of the will, or it is an attitude of mind liberated by the subject's genuine desire to serve the God he believes in, and is not an emotion. The contrast is expressed and the conflict resolved in **"The Mountain,"** a reworking of an Egyptian legend. The story concerns the moving of a mountain by faith: it does indeed move to the extent that a large piece of it falls into the Nile. However, Leskov's story is really about the moving of a spiritual mountain: the passionate and selfish beauty Nefora perceives that her understanding of 'love' is false and wishes to be united with the man she desires, Zenon, by becoming a 'slave of his lord'. The legend is a confrontation between Zenon and Nefora, and between these two ideas of what love is. Zenon marries her only when she expresses her allegiance to the Christian God in unequivocal terms. This is the 'moving of the mountain'.

The story **"Nevinnyi Prudentsii"** (Marks, vol. 30), (**"Innocent Prudentius"**), concerns another love affair between a Christian and a non-Christian. The ideal of Christian marriage is presented as 'a union of those who harness themselves beneath one yoke by reason of the identity of their ideas and their agreement about the meaning of life'. The innocent Prudentius who is finally rejected by the Christian girl whom he woos, concludes eventually that 'the spirit and not the flesh must be regarded as the master of life'. There is an element of realism in another of his conclusions: that it is better to recognise one's inadequacy than to make excuses, to 'make aprons out of leaves'.

"Innocent Prudentius" is the most uncompromisingly puritanical story on the subject of sexual love. Puritanism was not a feature of Leskov's attitude in his own life in earlier years: the failure of his marriage, the youthful wild oat sowing in Kiev, the relationship with Bubnova are well-known, and it is possible that another sexual relationship with one of his housekeepers took place in later life. In fact, he was no puritan, and was certainly no prude: prudery is made fun of in "A Winter's Day." It is the ideal which is being presented in "Innocent Prudentius," an ideal which Leskov probably did not expect all to attain and which he certainly did not attain himself.

There is a most interesting treatment of sexual love in "Po povodu Kreitserovoi sonaty," (IX), ("Concerning the 'Kreutzer Sonata'"), a story commenting on the more famous one by Tolstoy. Leskov's sketch was written in 1890, but not published in his lifetime; Tolstoy's *Kreutzer Sonata* was not published in Russia either, but was well-known in manuscript. In the sketch a woman approaches Leskov for advice; she is deceiving her husband by sleeping with another man, and deceiving society by enjoying the reputation of a good wife and mother. She does not love the other man, who is shameless and despicable; she longs to be free of the relationship. Should she confess all to her husband, who is kind and upright, but lacks 'heart' or 'poetry'? Leskov's advice is to continue the deception and let matters rest. He believes she will drift apart from her lover and return to her husband; lives will be wrecked unnecessarily if she confesses, and it would be better for her to go on enduring the sense of guilt and to live for the sake of others.

On this evidence Leskov is something less than a stern moralist. His decision involves weighing up two evils and deciding what to do about a 'hard case'. His attitude shows charity and a certain intelligent worldliness. It certainly lacks puritanical distaste for sexual immorality and shows concern for the well-being of a group of people.

The question of violence and war arises in these stories. The moral position adopted by Leskov is ambiguous. There are two characters in "The Disinterested Engineers" who leave the army because they believe that war is incompatible with Christianity. Prince Radovan

in "Bramadata and Radovan" does not love war, and does not resist his enemy Bramadata. Before being executed he instructs his son not to avenge his death, as 'enmity is not overcome by enmity but by mercy'. A splendid sentiment, though Dolgozhiv, the son, is not able to carry his point with Bramadata without holding a sword to his throat and keeping him in terror for his life for a while. The threat of violence is acceptable, it would seem, even if violence itself is not. It is as if Leskov could not avoid the conclusion that in this imperfect world behaviour can rarely be irreproachable. The pessimistic conclusion to the story "God's Good Time," in which the king makes the moral discovery that he should love his neighbours and his enemies, but fears to do it because it does not appear to be practical politics, suggests the same conclusion. The doctrine of non-resistance to evil as preached by Tolstoy was not entirely attractive to Leskov, at least not in 1886. In the article 'O rozhne' ('On Goads'), published in that year, he defends Tolstoy's principle of non-resistance to evil, tracing it back to Plato and Marcus Aurelius, but in practice he finds many hard cases, which he thinks Tolstoy should take into consideration: the American Civil War which freed the slaves, for example; or the case known to him of two little girls, strangled in a park in Kiev, while an adult witness stood by, unwilling to intervene and 'resist evil'.

It is scarcely possible to discuss Leskov's contribution to the debate on oath-taking, sexual morality and resistance to evil without referring to Tolstoy's views, since he was the figure dominating this debate in the last twenty years of the nineteenth century. There are other features of Tolstoy's doctrines which Leskov discusses: 'Judge not, that ye be not judged' and 'Sell that thou hast and give to the poor'. Wealth for Leskov presented no great moral problem. For a start, he himself did not have very much. According to Vera Mikulich, he wished Tolstoy would live up to his own teachings and give his wealth away. She asked him why he did not do likewise. 'I haven't any wealth to give away', was his answer, but he did not reply when she suggested he should give away what little he had[8]. In the stories wealth is seen as a useful means of doing good; morality resides in the correct use of riches, not in disposing of them as if to avoid contamination.

On the question of judgement, there is one story which puts the Tolstoyan view (and we know that Leskov shared this view from the correspondence with Zhirkevich which took place only a month or two before Leskov's death). This is "Pod Rozhdestvo obideli"[9], ("A Wrong Done at Christmas"). It is of particular interest because the central incident in it was used by Tolstoy and re-used by Leskov himself as one of the moral tales put out by such publishing concerns as the *Intermediary* for very cheap sale among ordinary folk[10]. The story is that a respected member of society is called for jury service, but he refuses when called upon to try a thief. His reason is that, when a boy, he was caught red-handed in the act of thieving, forgiven and given a home by his intended victim. Tolstoy's version of the story, called *Vorov syn, (The Thief's Son),* (and published with acknowledgement to Leskov)[11] concentrates on the simple issue that judging people is contrary to Christ's teaching. Leskov's fuller version of the story is more subtle and consequently more persuasive. The question for Leskov is whether to punish or whether to forgive: the commandment not to judge is seen as a corollary of the Christian instruction to forgive. Leskov does not place at the forefront the need for a Christian to refuse to have anything to do with the administration of justice by society, but the need for him to show mercy if faced with the decision to punish or not to punish a wrong-doer.

It is inevitable that differences should be found between Leskov's and Tolstoy's approaches to a number of moral, religious and social problems. These have been examined and established by other writers[12]. For example, Leskov, a towndweller for the last 35 years of his life at least, did not put the peasant on a pedestal, and found qualities to admire in men of all social classes. His attitude to the position of women and their education differed from Tolstoy's, and he did not mistrust scientific advance; indeed, as earlier chapters [of *Nikolai Leskov and the 'Spirit of Protestantism'*] have shown, he was extremely interested in attempts to reconcile science and Christian belief. Whatever the differences, Leskov never criticised Tolstoy publicly, though he was contemptuous both of Tolstoy's detractors and his fawning admirers, as the stories **"A Winter's Day"** and **"Polunoshchniki," ("Night Owls"),** show. In **"Night Owls,"** as H. McLean has demonstrated[13], Leskov puts forward a stirring defence of Tolstoyan views, so skilfully and ironically presented, that the opponents of Tolstoy could not object. There is no doubt that Leskov was deeply indebted to Tolstoy for confirmation of his views and for fertilizing many of his ideas. Moreover, this is relevant to the theme of Protestantism in Leskov's work, if only for one reason, and that is the place of the New Testament in setting both men thinking and in establishing their position. Scripture is called to witness again and again; interpreted not with the 'biblical pietism' of the Pashkovites, but with the intelligence and some of the rigour of such as Farrar and Naville and all of the forthright assurance of the words attributed (perhaps wrongly) to Luther: 'Here I stand. I can do no other.'

Leskov's rejection of ecclesiastical ritual has already been discussed in this chapter with reference to **"Beautiful Aza."** Another important tenet of Protestant belief is sturdily upheld by Leskov in **"The Better Worshipper:"** the right of an individual to work out his own salvation without the intermediacy of a priest. The ar-

ticle is a defence of Tolstoy, who had been attacked for advancing the same view in his stories, especially **"Three Elders."** Leskov uses a skilful, perhaps even cunning, argument. He does not attack Orthodox doctrine, but tries to show that the view people find shocking in Tolstoy's stories is in fact traditional, and he achieves this by examining a story from the *Prologue,* which was held in great esteem by the Orthodox faithful. In the story, which he calls 'Tale of a Worthy Woodcutter', a bishop recognises that a simple woodcutter is as good a Christian or better than himself and approaches him with humility. Leskov comments that the same message today is regarded as dangerous. The article illustrates Leskov's profound admiration for Tolstoy, his growing interest in the *Prologue* as a source of useful material for didactic tales, and one of his favourite lines of argument: to prove that viewpoints which appear unorthodox are in fact scriptural, traditional or even in essence more truly Orthodox than the opinions of their detractors.

Leskov's treatment of the *Prologue* originals is an interesting topic in itself, which has been dealt with in a recent dissertation by S. S. Lottridge: 'N. S. Leskov's Prolog tales' (Columbia University, 1970). The *Prologue* was a translation of a Greek hagiographical collection known as the *Synaxarion.* The title 'Prologue' was a scribe's error: he imagined the first word in the manuscript to be the title. It enjoyed great popularity in Russia, and a series of printed versions was issued, the first in 1641 and the last, apparently, in 1896. Leskov was a collector of the various editions. Lottridge's conclusions include one or two of importance to us here. He states that Leskov transformed medieval moral tales into modern psychological narratives, by developing the characters and exploring their motivation. The *Prologue* always takes the side of the Christian Church, but Leskov's religion was 'personal and spiritual', and he often shows true Christianity opposed by Christians seeking position. Lottridge also detects in Leskov's *Prologue* tales an 'anti-official rebellious spiritual independence', and writes of Leskov's 'strong concern with art as a moral force'. These conclusions are certainly just. Moreover, the use of the *Prologue* as material for stories expressing his own views was a piece of Leskovian cunning. It lent a superficial impression of orthodoxy with which to confuse or embarrass the censor, and readers not closely acquainted with the originals might imagine Leskov's reworkings to present views shared by the Church.

So far we have examined Leskov's views on a series of moral and religious questions without asking what evidence there is of his attitude towards the Russian Orthodox Church in the last two decades of the nineteenth century. We have seen that he greatly admired Isaac and Origen; he also had a little to say about more recent Slav saints. The most important of these was Nil Sorskii (1433-1508) who was a great favourite of the nineteenth-century liberal intelligentsia. Leskov intended in 1878 to write an article on Nil, whose good sense and practical ideas he thought 'unlike all others', and in 1894 he wrote to Tolstoy with approval of Nil's down-to-earth ideas (XI, 589). To read Nil, he said, would be good for people who were tempted to run away from reality in their search for a 'refuge of faith'. A number of incidents in the later stories show that Leskov was still capable of rapture before the beauty of Orthodox liturgy and its musical settings. **"Grabezh,"** (VIII), (**"Robbery"**), contains an entertaining account of a singing contest for deacons, and the narrator betrays his fondness for Orthodox music. Chapter XI of **"Tainstvennye predvestiya"** (Marks, vol. 20), (**"Mysterious Omens"**), shows that Leskov could still convey the magic of Orthodox music, and both of these stories were written at a time when he had clearly ceased to accept the Church's claim to be a unique repository of religious truth. It may well be that the last straw in Leskov's relations with the Orthodox Church was the banning of Volume VI of his collected works in 1889, which he saw as an insult directed against him personally by 'pot-bellied priests'. The banning certainly had a serious effect on his physical health and mental well-being.

The religious content of the later works would be incomplete without examination of the subject of death. It is clear from much that Leskov wrote in his stories and letters that he found it difficult to come to terms with death: he was afraid of dying and he sought assurance that he would survive beyond the grave. There is a notable passage in his early novel *The Outsiders* in which the hero Dolinskii reflects upon the death of his beloved Dora; he is angry that a human being can 'rot' and frustrated before the undeniable fact of death. In stories like **"Father Gerasim's Lion"** and **"Malanya Muttonhead"** Leskov tries to answer his own questions. Mastery over death for some of these characters means having conquered fear. Father Gerasim's indifference to death is complete: he says, 'I act according to God's commandments and will not become a slave to fear'. In **"Dama i Fefela,"** (IX), (**"The Lady and the Gawk"**), life is regarded as 'a training course on earth' whereby people prepare themselves for death. Prasha, the 'gawk' of the title, loses her fear of death in the company of a nun whose conversation is thoughtful and spiritual. The moral of **"Malanya"** is that death has no dominion over love (*agape*, not *eros*).

Certain of Leskov's letters reveal what he himself believed about death. In his published works he showed the intellectual's unwillingness to commit himself, but in a letter to Tolstoy of 1893 (XI, 519-20) he admits to his fear of death and says that he would read Plato and some of Tolstoy's writings for reassurance. In a letter to Chertkov of 1891 (XI, 577) he wrote, 'I think and believe that "I shall not entirely die", but some spiritual remnant will leave my body and continue "an eternal life", but as for what form that will take—it is impossible to form any concept here, and God knows when it will become clear'. In a letter to Tolstoy of the same year[14] he wrote that he found I Corinthians, vv. 12-15 'Very curious and very comforting'. ('If any man's work shall be burned, he shall suffer loss: but he himself shall be saved; yet so as by fire'.) Leskov makes great play with the word 'himself', *sam*. 'No', he writes, 'this "himself" is so well conceived that he cannot be obliterated, "he shall suffer loss, but he *himself* shall be saved."' Leskov underlined the word 'himself', *sam*, three times.

Three years before his death, in 1892, Leskov produced a story **"Yudol'"**, (**"Vale of Tears"**), and an article 'O kvakereyakh', (**"On Quaker Women"**), which contain interesting though ambiguous information about the Protestant influence on his personal development. These works (both in IX) repay close examination, and 'Quakers' figure in both of them. Quaker relief work in Russia, following the poor harvest of 1891 and consequent famine, attracted public attention and admiration, and it has been suggested that this reminded Leskov of long-forgotten events from his youth and encouraged him to write about them. **"Vale of Tears"** is described as a 'rhapsody'. It does not lack unity, despite a certain episodic quality. It portrays a famine fifty years previously in the village where Leskov lived as a small boy, and the closing chapters tell how two women, Leskov's 'Aunt Polly' and an English Quaker Hildegard Vasil'evna work among the people when an epidemic breaks out among the already starving peasants. The public reacted with interest to Leskov's story, but said surely Leskov must be talking about Radstockists— there were no Quakers in Russia in those days. Leskov replied with his article 'On Quaker Women', proving that Quakers had been known in Russia for very much longer than he had suggested in the story.

On the historical point, Leskov is quite right; nevertheless he makes many statements in both **"Vale of Tears"** and "On Quaker Women" which are factually doubtful, but which open a number of very interesting questions, not least about his own intellectual and religious development, and about the way he used memoir material in composing works of art. In "On Quaker Women" he makes the significant assertion that his own upbringing was somewhat influenced by a 'spirit of English religion', and that his family circle had close links with Protestantism. The reason for this was that one of his aunts had married Alexander Scott, a Russified 'anglichanin', and the Scotts' family life was so exemplary as to be held up as a model to all the rest. The Scotts' household was well-known in Moscow because the family kept open house for British girls, including both Methodists and Quakers, who had come to Russia seeking posts as children's nurses and governesses.

At many points in his works, Leskov mentions Alexander Scott, his father James, and his various brothers, and he nearly always calls him an Englishman, though when any of the family go 'home', they go to Scotland. In *Trivia from Archiepiscopal Life* Leskov implies that Alexander Scott was an Anglican, by stating that he was connected with the English chapel in Moscow. Since Scott was a Scotsman, he is much more likely to have been a Presbyterian, and the 'spirit of English religion' which influenced the Leskovs was really the spirit of Scottish religion—a different thing. Examination of the baptismal, marriage and burial registers of the English chapel in Moscow, and certain other related documents[15], shows that Alexander Scott's father, stepmother, a brother, a nephew and two nieces were married, baptised or buried at the chapel. Alexander's signature does not happen to appear as witness to any of the marriages, not even the second marriage of his father in 1831, but that fact certainly does not disprove Leskov's statement that Alexander was an adherent of the English chapel. The fact that the Scotts went to the Anglican chapel in Moscow is not conclusive, as expatriates tend to link up with the native-language-speaking church whatever its denomination. If Scott was an Anglican, then he should more accurately be termed a Scottish Episcopalian—the spirit of this religion, I venture to suggest, is different again. Obviously, there is room here for further investigation, though whether the material exists to clear the matter up is very doubtful indeed: after all, any given Scotsman might belong to any denomination extant in his native country. From what Leskov says about Scott, it is impossible to arrive at any conclusion. Leskov was impressed by his uncle's religion and learnt to respect his faith and his piety, which was Protestant if he was a Presbyterian and at least partly Protestant if he was an Anglican.

The real trouble is that Leskov's accounts of incidents from his own life were very unreliable. He adapted his own past to suit the tale he had to tell, as is only too obvious from **"Vale of Tears."** The central character, 'Aunt Polly', is fictional—but deceived Leskov's biographers for years. He is said to have based her on two of his mother's sisters[16]. As for her English Quaker companion, who at the time of the story had just arrived from England, Hildegard or Gil'degarda Vasil'evna seems a most unlikely name for an English Quaker woman, even if her father was called Basil and the patronymic was made up in honour of the country of her adoption. (Quaker custom is to use Christian name and surname.) There are other, more serious oddities in the story. Though Leskov's knowledge of the history of Quakers in Russia is excellent, there are two points of Quaker practice on which he slips up. He

writes that Hildegard 'most certainly never baptised Aunt Polly into her faith'—without adding that the very idea is ridiculous, since Quakers do not practise baptism. This is not what Leskov appears to mean, however; he merely wishes to emphasise that Aunt Polly never became a Quaker. Then there is the hymn-singing incident translated below. There are several quite serious objections to this, which are discussed later, but an obvious minor one is that hymns are not used in Quaker worship. Quakers might well join with other Christians on other occasions in the singing of hymns, but the scene described below, with its 'concertina' is more reminiscent of other religious traditions.

In view of the importance attached by Leskov to the episode, it is quoted here at length.

> What I had taken to be a travelling medicine-case was a concertina, a primitive one such as we knew in those days, but the sounds it made were full and harmonious, and my aunt and Hildegard softly sang a hymn, to the accompaniment of this instrument.
>
> They sang a *cantique* on the text "Him that cometh to me I will in no wise cast out" (John 6, v. 37), and the words of the hymn sung in the starlight (in a Russian translation) were these:
>
> *Takov kak est',—vo imya krovi*
> *Za nas prolitoi na kreste,*
> > *Za veroi, zren'em i proshcheniem,*
> > *Khristos, ya prikhozhu k tebe.*
>
> I was impressed by the peaceful harmony of these noble sounds which filled our house so unexpectedly, and the simple sense of the comforting words captivated my understanding. I sensed an unusually complete feeling of joy, that every man, *now*, "just as he is", may enter a state of mind in which the stultifying significance of time and space no longer exists. And it seemed to me as if they had approached Him, "for faith, understanding and forgiveness" and He also was coming forth to meet them, and was offering them that which makes his yoke easy and his burden light.
>
> Oh, what a moment that was! I buried myself face downwards in the back of a soft arm-chair and for the first time in my life wept tears of a happiness which until then had been unknown to me, and this brought me to such a pitch of rapture that the room seemed to be full of a beautiful gentle light, and it was as if this light came straight from the stars, through the window where two elderly ladies were singing, and straight to my heart, and at the same time, we all—the starving peasants too and the whole world—were floating off somewhere to meet the Absolute.
>
> Oh, would not all the tribulations of earthly life be worth just one more such moment of rapture when the soul parts from the body!
>
> That evening, which I recall now, when my head is covered with the snow of the winter of life, seems to have had a meaning for the whole of my life.

The episode raises a number of very interesting questions. Was the hymn *sung* 'in a Russian translation' or does Leskov mean that he is quoting it in Russian? If sung in Russian, how would the infant Leskov have known it was a translation; if not sung in Russian how could he have understood it? (He knew no English and his French was very poor until many years after the presumed date of the incident.) If not sung in Russian, the use of the word *cantique* suggests French, but Hildegard's native language was English (and another part of the story illustrates that her knowledge of Russian was grotesque!)

This *cantique* is in fact a misquotation of a well-known Russian translation of the first verse of Charlotte Elliot's popular English hymn: 'Just as I am, without one plea, / But that Thy blood was shed for me, / And that Thou bidd'st me come to Thee, / O Lamb of God, I come!' The third word of the Russian should be *esm'*, and Leskov has given the third line of the *second* verse in mistake for the correct third line, 'Vo imya Bozh'ikh prizyvanii'. Elliot wrote the hymn in 1834 and first published it two years later; it has been translated into dozens of languages and is included in almost every imaginable anthology of English hymns. It could therefore just possibly have been sung in Russian in 1840, but I can find no evidence of a translation into Russian before 1865, when Lady Radstock requested the Religious Tract Society of London to print a very much more sophisticated version on a single sheet. (They did in fact do so.)[17] The version here misquoted by Leskov became very popular during Lord Radstock's time in Russia in the 1870s[18].

The theology of the hymn, however, is scarcely Quaker. Elliot was an Anglican, and she wrote the hymn 'to express the great certainties of her salvation . . . the formulae of her faith'[19]. It is an intensely personal expression of faith, speaking of confidence in the forgiveness of God, and belief in the saving power of the blood of Christ, and the need for the individual to approach his God as a matter of personal decision. Nothing could be more Protestant. It is scarcely surprising that it became so popular. It is doubtful, however, whether many Quakers would think that the words 'vo imya krovi, . . . prolitoi na kreste . . . ya prikhozhu k tebe' expressed a particularly Quaker theology. It is not impossible that Leskov heard a Quaker sing it, but much more likely that he heard it sung by Radstockists or the like in Russia[20], or perhaps by Protestants in the West when he went abroad in 1875.

There is another important aspect of the story which implies that it was not Quaker doctrine Leskov was describing. We must remind ourselves that Aunt Polly was not presented as a member of the Society of Friends. Quakers believe that 'the only valid test of a Christian is whether he lives in the spirit of Christlike love'[21]. Hildegard and Aunt Polly are certainly Christians measured by this yardstick. But it is the approach to religious belief which is not Quakerish in **"Vale of Tears."**

The Quaker approach to faith is from human experience, 'the stillness at the centre of our being'. Aunt Polly does not become a Christian because it is 'from this deep place that her insights into the real meaning of life arise'[22]. Aunt Polly's conversion is rather a classic of evangelical Protestant Christianity: she becomes convinced of her own sinfulness, she resorts to religious ritual observances and finds they are not right *(ne to)*, she tries 'spiritual reading', but again this is *ne to*, and finally she reads the Bible, which contains the answer. To judge by the words of the hymn, this answer is that Christ died for her on the cross and she can approach Him, 'come unto Him', and be refreshed. This knowledge inspires her to believe in the possibility of being reconciled with God, and in the need to work selflessly for others, to love her neighbours and her enemies. The first stages of this progression to understanding and faith—conviction of sin, saving power of Holy Scripture, belief that Christ died to save her personally—could not be any closer to the doctrines of such as Radstock, or so many other Protestants of much greater sophistication. Leskov's critics, who were sceptical about Hildegard the Quakeress, were in a way quite right: Leskov was not writing about Quaker belief in this story. He was writing about Protestantism of a different tradition.

There is a great deal of circumstantial evidence, then, that the incident described did not happen at the time, in the place, in the circumstances or in the way portrayed in **"Vale of Tears."** No single piece of the evidence is conclusive, but the total of it suggests that many of the details must be wrong. But now we come to the author's moving evaluation of the effects the incident had upon him. It 'had a meaning for the whole of his life', and he longs for another moment of such rapture. He recounts in an evocative way a 'mystical experience' by Knowles's definition of the words[23]. Even if we were sure that the hymn-singing incident did not take place, it seems wrong to doubt the genuineness of these sentiments. They must be sincere—but Leskov must be making use of another incident from his own life. Undoubtedly he was moved at some time by the words of Charlotte Elliot. Certainly he admired the good works of the Quakers. But the 'rhapsody' **"Vale of Tears"** expresses clearly that he had been impressed by the Protestant-evangelical approach to religion and believed it to be a valid one.

*Notes*

1. Numerous letters from Leskov at this period were signed humorously 'Eresiarkh Nikolai', 'Lzhesmirennyi eresiarkh N.', 'Smirennyi starets N.'. See V. Mikulich, *Vstrechi s pisatelyami* [Leningrad], 1929, and Klochkova in *Ezhegodnik rukopisnogo otdela Pushkinskogo doma na 1971 g.*, [Leningrad], 1973, 3-105.

2. Benjamin Drewery, *Origen and the Doctrine of Grace,* London, 1960, 203.

3. W. Barclay, in *The Gospel of John,* Edinburgh, (c. 1950), II, 4, attributes this interpretation to an early Armenian translation of the New Testament.

4. At least one Church Slavonic and three Russian editions of Isaac's works were issued in Leskov's lifetime.

5. S. Brock, 'St Isaac of Nineveh and Syriac Spirituality', *Sobornost,* series 7, Winter 1975, No. 2, 79-89.

6. Letter No. 48, in *Pis'ma Tolstogo i k Tolstomu,* ed. S. P. Shesterikov, [Moscow-Leningrad], 1928.

7. Leskov's (and Tolstoy's) interpretation of this saying of Christ is not the obvious understanding of it. It is doubtful even whether the actual text will bear Leskov's interpretation. The moral point—that to swear an oath limits the freedom of action of the oath-taker is one thing, but what Christ said ('Let your communication be Yea, yea; Nay, nay') applies, most likely, to the dealings, say, in a market place, where the prophets and saints are constantly called (perhaps dishonestly) to witness the truth of the speaker's assertions.

8. Mikulich, *Vstrechi s pisatelyami,* 193.

9. In the anthology *Dobroe delo. Sbornik povestei i rasskazov,* [Moscow], 1894, 171-82.

10. See p. 52 and Thais S. Lindstrom, 'From Chapbooks to Classics; the story of the Intermediary', *American Slavic and East European Review,* XVI, 1967, No. 2, 190-201.

11. L. N. Tolstoi, 'Vorov syn', [Moscow], 1911. This item is listed in the Bibliography under Leskov's individual works.

12. Particularly N. K. Gudzii, 'Tolstoi i Leskov', *Iskusstvo,* 1928, No. 1-2, 95-128; W. B. Edgerton, 'Leskov and Tolstoy—two literary heretics', *American Slavic and East European Review,* XII, 1953, 524-34. Of some interest is L. Afonin, 'N. S. Leskov—chitatel' L'va Tolstogo', *Pod''em,* Voronezh, 1960, No. 6, 124-7.

13. Hugh McLean, 'Leskov and Ioann of Kronštadt: on the Origins of *Polunoščniki*', *American Slavic and East European Review,* XII, 1953, No. 1, 93-108.

14. *Pis'ma Tolstogo i k Tolstomu,* 119-20.

15. These papers are held in the Guildhall Library, London.

16. W. B. Edgerton, 'Nikolai Leskov: the intellectual development of a literary nonconformist', Dissertation, Columbia University, 1954, Chapter II. Andrei Leskov, in his biography, *Zhizn' Nikolaya Leskova,* [Moscow], 1954, 33, 342, makes it clear that Polly is 'apocryphal' or 'semi-apocryphal'.

17. A copy of the translated hymn is in the British Library: Charlotte Elliot, *Perevod angliiskogo gimna,* London, 1866. Lady Radstock's request is reported in the Minute Book of the RTS Committee, 31 Oct 1865, now held by the United Society for Christian Literature at Luke house, Guildford, Surrey.

18. Two cuttings, Pashkov papers, III/17, refer: one from *Rossiya,* No. 12, 4 May 1880; the other is unidentified.

19. Quoted by J. Telford, in *The New Methodist Hymn-Book Illustrated,* London, 1934, 187-9.

20. Andrei Leskov, on p. 341 of his biography, describes occasions when such hymns were sung; they relate to 1878-9. 'Just as I am' is not mentioned, but circumstantial evidence linking *Vale of Tears* with the Radstockist circle includes a reference to 'an English concertina'!

21. G. H. Gorman, *Introducing Quakers,* London, 1969, 18.

22. Gorman, *op. cit.,* 14.

23. There is a certain similarity between Leskov's description and the ecstasy experienced by Alesha in Part 3, Book 7, Chapter 4 of *Brothers Karamazov,* 'Cana of Galilee'.

## K. A. Lantz (essay date spring 1981)

SOURCE: Lantz, K. A. "Leskov's 'At the Edge of the World': The Search for an Image of Christ." *Slavic and East European Journal* 25, no. 1 (spring 1981): 34-43.

[*In the essay below, Lantz proposes that in "At the Edge of the World" Leskov succeeded in crafting a formidable, highly subversive attack on the Russian Orthodox Church.*]

The year 1875 was a turning point in Leskov's literary career. The writer, who had earned a reputation as "the scourge of the nihilists," became after this date increasingly notorious as the gadfly of the conservatives who had once claimed him as their own. Toward the end of 1874 an embittered Leskov had broken with Mixail Katkov whose *Russkij vestnik* had published some of his best (and some of his worst) writings. Leskov cast an increasingly baleful eye on the growing conservatism of the society around him and was dismayed to learn of several scandals which strengthened his conviction of that society's moral decay. In the first months of 1875, for example, a former close associate, the conservative novelist and courtier Boleslav Markevič, was exposed in a sordid affair of bribery. Leskov observed that "the fall of this arrogant fop from his five-foot height has tapped such moral dregs of social passions that one wonders if there are not already some sort of Visigoths camped outside the Šlusselburg Gate of your putrid Rome."[1] Leskov had regarded the Orthodox Church as a positive force whose moral authority might serve as a bulwark against the encroaching barbarians, but even his faith in the Church began to erode. On a three-and-a-half month trip to Europe in the summer of 1875 Leskov rested from the ordeals of the previous year (his second marriage was breaking up; he had severe financial problems and many difficulties in finding publishers for his writings), took stock of his literary career, and made a thorough reassessment of his religious views. He read widely in religious literature—largely the writings of Protestant theologians—unavailable or prohibited in Russia.[2] One result of these readings was that he became, in his own words, a "turn-coat" (10:411) who renounced many of his former beliefs in the meaning and function of the Orthodox Church.

The first work of fiction Leskov published after returning from Europe was **"At the Edge of the World"** (**"Na kraju sveta"**)[3]. Apart from its undoubted artistic merits, the story is of interest as a statement of the essence of Leskov's new religious beliefs. This new faith, of course, was scarcely in accord with official Orthodoxy. The fact that Leskov could publish what amounts to a strong attack on some of the fundamental tenets of the Orthodox Church in the arch-conservative *Graždanin,* a newspaper closely identified with official Orthodoxy, is a tribute to his "slyly genial manner" (11:372) of narration in which his real and quite subversive intentions are cleverly concealed behind an innocuous facade.[4] Indeed, at first glance the story seems a solid contribution to the brand of chauvinistic religion often espoused by Prince Meščerskij's *Graždanin.* Leskov must have chortled when he learned that the leading exponent of official Orthodoxy, Konstantin Pobedonoscev, admired the work so much he sent a copy to the heir apparent, the future Alexander III, with a warm recommendation.[5]

The basic plot of the story seems quite straightforward: the bishop of a remote Siberian diocese sets out to bring the light of the Church's teachings to the primitive Yakut nomads in his spiritual charge, only to find that he is in greater need of enlightenment than they are.[6] The story, told by the bishop himself as an episode from his younger days, is "framed" in Leskov's favored manner, and the frame itself unobtrusively introduces the major theme. The bishop and his guests are discussing the Russian Church's missionary work; one visitor argues that the Orthodox missionaries have little success because their notions of Christ and Christianity are too narrow. The bishop disagrees: the Russians simply have their own unique concept of Christ. To prove his point he shows his guests a collection of reproductions of Christ as portrayed by western artists. The bishop criticizes each of these in turn: in some, Christ appears indifferent, squeamish, or scornful when confronting sinners; in others He seems either pitiable or too idealized to be convincing. At last the bishop points to his own icon, "a typical Russian portrayal" (5:454), utterly simple and even rustic (*mužikovat*) in comparison with the more sophisticated western images. The face on the icon is expressive, yet without passion. In this simplicity and homeliness, the bishop argues, the unknown artist has caught the real essence of the Russian image of Christ.

Such a beginning must have struck a responsive chord in the editors and readers of *Graždanin* and thus drew their attention away from the highly sensitive issues raised later. In fact the opening, with its narrowly nationalistic view of religion, is only the bait to lure the complacent Russian chauvinist into Leskov's trap. Leskov then goes on to convey his new religious views in two ways: first, he undermines the credibility of the existing state Church, and second, he proposes a reasonable and attractive alternative.

As the bishop sets forth to "defend" the Russian conception of Christianity, Leskov is in fact launching a devastating attack on the public image of Orthodoxy, advancing under a heavy screen of incense smoke to point out the intellectual and moral failings of the clergy, the Church's stress on empty ritual at the expense of genuine religious spirit, its fundamental indifference to the material and spiritual welfare of its members. The bishop tells of his first experiences in his Siberian diocese where he was shocked to find that the majority of the clergy were barely literate, addicted to drink, and utterly cynical about their vocation. He recounts some of the absurdities that result when the ill-educated clergy uncomprehendingly stumble through the complexities of the liturgy. One illiterate deacon tries to bluff his way through the service by memory but each time he repeats the words "in heaven" he continues mechanically with: "hallowed by Thy name, Thy kingdom come . . . ," and is unstoppable until he has finished reciting the Lord's Prayer. In another case an arch-priest who has overindulged at a christening banquet convinces himself that a cart-load of hay has been driven into him and is only cured of his malady by a local sorceress. The bishop does what he can to improve the external aspect of the Church by curtailing excessive formalism and by trying to educate the clergy and raise their moral standards in order to stop them from being an object of derision. The effect of the bishop's anecdotes is to suggest that ritual is dead; it has long ceased to have any meaning for those who perform it since they neither understand it not take it seriously. Neither is it in keeping with the primitive simplicity of the image of Christ in the icon.

Leskov then moves to a much more hazardous area: he shifts his attack to the dogmas of the Church. The bishop tells how, in his eagerness to make contact with his potential converts, he began studying the Yakut language. He soon realizes that its meager vocabulary, "nothing more than the language of animal life, not of intellectual life," is simply incapable of expressing even elementary theological concepts:

> How could you explain to them the meanings of the words: "Be as crafty as the serpent and as gentle as the dove," when they have never seen a serpent or a dove and cannot even imagine what they look like? It is impossible to find words for them to express "martyr," "baptist," "forerunner," and if you translated "Holy Virgin" into their language—Sočmo Abja—it turns out not to be our Virgin Mary but some sort of Shamanist female deity, a goddess in fact. It is even more difficult to speak of the merits of the Holy Blood or of any other mysteries of our faith. And there is no point even thinking of constructing any theological system for them or of mentioning a child born of a Virgin, without a husband: either they would understand nothing, and that would be best, or else they would probably laugh right in your face.

> (5: 468)

This is a compelling argument against the complexity of Christian theology. If Christianity is universal, Leskov implies, then it must be accessible to all. Accordingly, concepts that cannot be expressed in the simple and basic terms of the Yakut language should be dispensed with. The theology and dogmas of the established church are thus criticized as a barrier to the spread of Christianity.

Leskov goes on to deal with the sacraments of the Church—specifically Baptism. The bishop finds the missionary work in the diocese is flagging: there are few converts, and those who agree to be baptized—often under coercion or after being plied with vodka—have little understanding of their new faith and freely blend Shamanist or Lamaist concepts with it. The few successful missionaries in the area are only concerned with adding new names to their lists of converts and care little for what happens to their flock after baptism. The bishop seeks advice from a Siberian veteran, Father Kiriak, only to find that Kiriak stubbornly refuses to have anything to do with baptizing natives. While Father Kiriak never entirely denies the worth of the sacrament of Baptism, he cites a number of sources—the New Testament, the Church fathers—to argue that it is a meaningless rite unless accompanied by a genuine acceptance and understanding of Christ's teachings.

The bishop eventually learns that baptism has had no positive effect on the local nomads and it has undermined their traditionally high moral standards. The bap-

tized man is a lost man, a native tells him: both the shaman and the lama beat him and steal his reindeer. To make matters worse, no one trusts the convert since the natives regard baptism as little more than a license to commit crime. For example, a baptized tribesman will steal, since he knows that the priest will forgive him his sin. The native argues that the priest should forgive only those who have sinned against him personally.

Some final blows are struck at the sacraments at the end of the story. Father Kiriak has been abandoned in a blizzard by his native, Christian guide while on an expedition, and the bishop finds him on his deathbed. Wishing to administer the last rites, the bishop learns that the native guide has eaten the Holy Elements Father Kiriak was carrying: the guide knew that a priest would forgive him. The bishop hears Father Kiriak's confession, while a native sorceress simultaneously conducts her ceremonies over the dying priest. The implication is that there is little difference between the two rites.

Once Leskov has knocked down, or at least dealt some telling blows to the structure of organized religion, he proceeds with the second stage of his program: to establish a practicable and simple alternative to current organized religion. To do this he first uses the credible and appealing figure of Father Kiriak. Father Kiriak emerges as a man of strong—if somewhat less than orthodox—faith. His ideas on religion have developed from many years of practical experience; and for Leskov wisdom bought by experience was the only wisdom that mattered. Furthermore, Kiriak is a simple, slightly eccentric figure and can express views that might seem heretical coming from the bishop's mouth.

Kiriak's strongest religious experiences have been direct and personal and have had nothing to do with the formalities of life within the Church. He tells of two incidents from his childhood which he rather naively interprets as miracles. Once he prayed to be spared from a beating and, after "something moved in [his] heart like a warm little dove" (5:464), he was spared. A second time he prayed to be exempted from a difficult examination in school, and again his prayer was answered. The point of these anecdotes is not in Kiriak's "miraculous" deliverance but in his own experience at the time. On both occasions, he claims, he felt a genuine personal contact with the Deity: "It is not enough that He has the whole universe to enfold and yet, seeing the childish grief of a small boy under a bench in a bath house, He crept up, bringing a breath of coolness to his soul, and came to dwell in his little bosom" (5:465). Like Dostoevskij's Zosima, a figure with whom he has much in common,[7] Kiriak is filled with joy and wonder at the mystery he has experienced. The "bosom" (*pazuška*) is central to his religion. "It is there," he tells the bishop, "it is all there; only through the heart will you call it forth, not through reason. Reason cannot construct it, it destroys. Reason gives birth to doubt, My Lord; faith gives peace, gives joy" (5:471-72).

Kiriak will not baptize the natives nor will he even preach to them. The Church, he says, should limit itself to teaching, to practical charity, and to setting a good example: "Let him who is wise and skillful show them goodness through his life; then they will understand Christ" (5:481). Kiriak has deep faith in this image of Christ as an ideal of goodness. He preaches one simple rule, applicable in all situations and readily understood by the local tribesmen: whatever one does, one must ask oneself if it can be done for the glory of Christ. Unlike the bishop, Kiriak never speaks of a specifically Russian understanding of Christ, opposed in its simplicity and homeliness to the "pompous Byzantism" (5:465) of the Greeks; the center of his religiosity is clearly the personal experience of the Deity and as such it is hardly limited by nationality.

The heart of the story completes Leskov's attempt to evoke a simple and persuasive image of Christ by having his bishop experience it directly himself. Despite Kiriak's arguments against further missionary work and despite the abuses he has seen himself, the bishop has not yet been convinced that his urge to proselytize is misguided. He decides to inspect a distant corner of his mission field, hoping to find new ways of winning converts. He and Kiriak set off in two sledges, each with a native guide. One of the guides is unbaptized, and Kiriak insists that the bishop travel with him. The bishop questions this guide about Christianity and learns that he knows of Christ as a good man and a miracle worker: "He spat on a blind man's eyes, Father, and the blind man saw; he fed the people with bread and little fishes" (5:487). Although the guide admires this image of Christ, he refuses to be baptized. The bishop tries to preach to him, but the native's concept of Christianity does not go beyond these few miracles. The bishop despairs that the guide is beyond salvation:

> Nothing could be done for him, either with Massillon or Bourdaloue or Eckhartshausen. There he is, poking his long staff into the snow and swinging it about; his face, like a well worn lump of soap, expresses nothing. There is not the slightest spark of the soul's fire in his peepholes (it would be shameful to call them eyes). The very sounds of the words that issue from his larynx seem somehow dead: in grief or joy there is always the same intonation—dull and passionless. He articulates half his words somewhere in his gullet, and compresses the other half with his teeth. How is he to seek for abstract truths with these means, and what use are they to him? They are a burden to him: he must die out with his whole race as the Aztecs died and as the Red Indians are dying . . . A terrible law!
>
> (5: 489)

The party is suddenly overtaken by a violent blizzard. This is the most crucial point of the story: the bishop is brought from despair that his guide will never understand Christianity to an awareness that it is the same guide who in fact is a living manifestation of the image of Christ. This reversal is accomplished gradually and subtly through a series of Biblical allusions in which the guide's actions deliberately parallel Christ's miracles. The bishop awakens during the blizzard unable to see because his eyelids have frozen shut; the guide spits on his eyes, rubs them, and restores his sight. The two cover themselves with snow and huddle together to wait out the storm. The guide presses close and breathes in the bishop's face to warm him. The bishop is repelled by the guide's stench, compounded of "stinking reindeer skins, the pungent odor of human sweat, soot, damp mould, dried fish, fish fat, and dirt" (5:491), worse, he thinks, than the stench of the corpse of Lazarus after four days in the tomb. Their refuge itself seems like a coffin, a snowy grave where the bishop is certain he will end his days. But the guide's concern for him helps him survive and enables him to crawl from the icy tomb when the blizzard ends. And finally it is the guide who saves the bishop's life by finding food for him, a miracle that impresses the bishop as much as Christ's feeding of the multitudes.

The two have become separated from Father Kiriak, who has the food supplies, and have lost their way. The dogs are exhausted, and when the guide finally sets off alone over the snow, the bishop is certain that the unreliable heathen has deserted him. He resigns himself to a slow and painful death, envying Kiriak who, it would seem, has a more trustworthy Christian guide to look after him. After several days alone in the snow the bishop, scarcely knowing whether he is alive or dead, sees something that seems to be flying across the snow toward him. Hunger and exhaustion combine with the eerie half-light of the short Siberian day to play tricks with the bishop's vision. He sees "a gigantic winged figure clad from head to heels in a *chiton* of silver brocade that sparkled all over; on its head was an enormous headdress that seemed almost seven feet high and glittered as if covered all over with diamonds, or more precisely, as if it were a whole diamond miter" (5:505-6). As the figure draws closer the bishop realizes that it is not an angel but his guide, covered with snow and with his frozen hair piled high on his head. (The guide, unwilling to steal, had left his hat as a pledge in the deserted yurt where he had taken food). The bishop realizes that this pagan, who has risked his life to save him, "being moved, of course, not only by the *natural* feeling of compassion for me, but also having 'religio,' prizing the *reunification* with that master 'who looks from above'" (5:509) is in no need of his ministrations. The bishop had once lamented the poverty of the guide's language and intellect; now he realizes that this pagan has 'religio,' that he acts in accordance with the image of Christ and that his actions derive not from his intellect but from his heart. Just as Father Kiriak had experienced the Deity, so the bishop feels something move in his own heart and he prays: "I believe that Thou has revealed Thyself to him as much as he requires it, and he knows Thee as everything knows Thee" (5:510).

The effect of the story derives in large part from the neat but subtle irony of its ending. The bishop's change of heart is all the more convincing since he is portrayed from the outset not as a bigoted fanatic but as an enlightened and sensible man who quickly gains the reader's sympathy. The reversal at the end of the story is therefore all the more likely to prove convincing. The story is also effective because Leskov manages to create an appealing positive character in his native guide, a completely unsentimentalized figure reeking of fish and sweat, laconic, unemotional, yet very human. Finally, the setting of the story adds to its impact. Leskov wants to reveal the essence of religion and so takes his characters into the barren Siberian landscape, the world's edge, where the distractions and complications of civilization are removed, and matters are very quickly reduced to the essential ones of life and death. In such a setting, where nature is stripped to its very minimum, Leskov is quickly able to strip away the redundancies of religion and expose its essence as well.

What is left when Leskov peels away the dead outer layers from the living heart of the matter? One must be careful to distinguish between the overt and cheerfully positive conclusion, designed to disarm the censor and the editors of *Graždanin,* from the covert, subversive impact of the story as a whole. The bishop ends his story on an optimistic note, assuring his listeners that "the Church is indestructible like the apostolic edifice" (5:517). The clergy's roles as set out in the story include teaching, providing a good example of an ethical life, and, less important, administering the sacraments. Yet the significance of the sacraments has been minimized, and in some cases they have been shown to be definitely harmful. The bishop has made some progress in raising the moral and intellectual level of his clergy, yet he ends with a diatribe against the bureaucracy within the Church and its subservience to the state, facts which he claims prohibit any serious effort to spread enlightenment and improve morals. Leskov takes pains to underline the bishop's change of heart over his own function within the Church. At the beginning of the story he arrives in his new diocese full of zeal and thankful that "it had fallen [his] lot to do more than cut the hair of ordinants and settle the quarrels of drunken psalm-readers" (5:456). But after his experiences in the mission field he realizes that all he can do within the structure of the Church is "quietly cut the hair of ordinants and reconcile deacons with laymen" (5:513). Little evidence is offered to suggest the Church is indestruc-

tible. Indeed, not one of the positive figures in the story—Kiriak, the guide, the bishop—works wholly and effectively toward the expressed aims of the Church.

Even the idea with which the story began—that the Russians have their distinct, national concept of Christianity—runs counter to the remainder of the work.[8] Kiriak, to be sure, exemplifies this homely religion, but he is very much an exceptional figure, considered an eccentric and even a heretic by his colleagues. While the simple and straightforward tradition of Christianity may have once been widespread in Russia, there is nothing in the story to indicate that it is prevalent or even common any more. In fact the figure that best exemplifies this basic Christianity is neither Russian nor Orthodox nor even nominally Christian but an anonymous and unbaptized Yakut guide. By clearly identifying this pagan with the miracles of Christ, Leskov suggests that the guide acts in accordance with the image of Christ and that this image is present in every man. Leskov of course does not exclude Russians from an understanding of Christ—Father Kiriak and the bishop himself surely have it—but he does affirm that they have no monopoly on genuine Christianity.

The religious spirit suggested by the story has more in common with Protestantism than with Orthodoxy, but in fact Leskov is little concerned with labels or churches of any sort. The organized church, whatever its denomination, may play a useful role by teaching, by providing an example of ethical behavior, and even by administering the sacraments. But the implication is that the image of Christ is far more essential to the religious life than is the church. Leskov seeks to demonstrate that living religion is a matter of an individual's purely personal consciousness of his link with the Deity, a consciousness that expresses itself in decency and practical charity rather than in dogma and ritual. Father Kiriak experiences this as a small boy in a bath house; the bishop as an adult in the frozen desert of Yakutia. Neither experience is confined within the framework of any church. Leskov suggests that the image of Christ is more likely to be found *"za pazuškoi,"*—in the bosom of good people such as the anonymous "heathen" guide—than amid the Byzantine splendors and incense of Orthodoxy. The guide's language may be impoverished and his intellectual horizons narrow, but his religious sense needs neither translation nor deep understanding, since it is a matter of emotions and actions that are universal. The spirit of the story is not one of religious chauvinism as might first appear, but of genuine ecumenicity.

### Notes

1. N. S. Leskov, *Sobranie sočinenij v odinnadcati tomax,* (M.: GIXL, 1955-58), 10:381. All further citations from Leskov are from this edition and are indicated in the text by volume and page number.

2. See William Edgerton, "Leskov's Trip Abroad in 1875," *Indiana Slavic Studies,* 4 (1967); 88-99, and James Y. Muckle, *Nikolai Leskov and the "Spirit of Protestantism"* (Birmingham: Dept of Russian Language and Literature, University of Birmingham, 1978).

3. Published as a Christmas story in *Graždanin,* no. 52 (1875), nos. 1-4, 6 (1876).

4. William Edgerton, in his introduction" to *Satirical Stories of Nikolai Leskov* (New York: Pegasus, 1969), 13-14, first noted the "heretical implications" of the story. He also comments on Leskov's satirical technique of concealing criticisms behind praise.

5. "Permit me to offer you as well the little book 'At the Edge of the World,' the work of Mr. Leskov— the same one who wrote the story you already know, *The Cathedral Folk.* This little book is well written and I think that you will like it when you have the leisure to read it." *Pis'ma Pobedonosceva k Aleksandru III,* I (Moscow: Novaja Moskva, 1925), 44. 14 May 1876.

6. Leskov based his story on incidents from the life of Bishop Nil of Jaroslavl' who spent many years as a missionary in Siberia. Although most of Leskov's information seems to have come to him second hand via the Bishop's friend, V. A. Kokorev, Leskov probably read Nil's *Putevye zapiski* (Jaroslavl', 1869). Like Leskov's bishop, Nil is fond of studding his writings with Biblical and Latin quotations. Nil, too, was shocked by the low intellectual and moral level of the clergy in isolated villages. Although Nil saw his task primarily as proselytizing, he was dismayed by the poverty and general barrenness of the lives of the native tribes and was concerned not only to baptize but to bring them the benefits of civilization: ". . . It is long past time for our nomads to begin their exodus, as from some Egypt, from the darkness that lies over them and to follow in the steps of other peoples, notably Orthodox Russia, toward moral, intellectual and material development" (331).

7. E. M. Pul'xritudova, in "Dostoevskij i Leskov (K istorii tvorčeskix vzaimootnošenij)," *Dostoevskij i russkie pisateli: tradicii, novatorstvo, masterstvo* (M.: Sovestkij pisatel', 1971), 87-138, argues that the chapter "The Russian Monk," with its *skaz* technique and episodic structure, was influenced by Leskov's writings in general, although she does not specifically mention "At the Edge of the World." The fact that the story appeared in *Graždanin,* which Dostoevskij had edited until 1874 and to which he still contributed, suggests he must surely have read it at the very time he

was planning his last novel. The episodes Father Kiriak recalls from his youth are strongly suggestive, both in content and in tone, of Zosima's biography. Both Kiriak's language, with its combination of diminutives, homely colloquialisms and solemn ecclesiastical vocabulary, as well as his sense of the miraculous present in everyday life, surely influenced Dostoevskij in creating his elder. Kiriak makes an analogy that baptism is like a ticket to salvation, but a man who appears at a banquet without a ticket would surely not be turned away. This recalls Ivan Karamazov's "respectful return" of his entrance ticket. The episode of the bishop and his reeking guide pressing close together to keep one another alive recalls Ivan Karamazov's legend of John the Merciful who revived a stinking beggar by breathing directly into his mouth (Book 5, Chapter 4). Apart from its possible influence on Dostoevskij, the story may well have had some effect on Tolstoj's "Master and Man," as Hugh McLean suggests in *Nikolai Leskov: The Man and His Art* (Cambridge: Harvard Univ. Press, 1977), 303.

8. Leskov seems to be taking issue here with Dostoevskij's messianism and religious chauvinism. Dostoevskij wrote in 1873: "Doesn't Orthodoxy contain everything, everything that [our people] are seeking? Isn't there in Orthodoxy alone both the truth and the salvation of the Russian people and, in the coming centuries, the salvation of mankind as a whole? Hasn't Orthodoxy alone preserved the Divine image of Christ in all its purity? And, perhaps, the most significant preordained destiny of the Russian people, within the destinies of mankind as a whole, consists simply in preserving this divine image of Christ in all its purity and, when the time arrives, in revealing this image to a world that has lost its way." *Dnevnik pisatelja za 1873 god* (Paris: YMCA Press, n.d.). As shown above, Leskov initially seems to support the Russians' exclusive claim to possession of the "Divine image of Christ", but the story itself suggests something quite different. In the same article Dostoevskij notes ". . . and our priest, indeed, is no functionary! Isn't he the preacher of the sole great truth capable of reviving the whole world?" (259). Leskov's priests in fact are functionaries who, if capable of preaching, are prevented from doing so by church bureaucracy and state interference. Dostoevskij and Leskov had a complex and often stormy relationship. Further details can be found in K. P. Bogaevskaja, "N. S. Leskov o Dostoevskom (1880-e gody)," *Literaturnoe nasledstvo, 86: F. M. Dostoevskij. Novye materialy i issledovanija (Moscow: Nauka, 1973), 606-20;* I. P. Vidučtskaja, "Dostoevskij i Leskov," *Russkaja literatura,* 4 (1975), 127-37; V. V. Vinogradov,

"Dostoevskij i Leskov (70-e gody XIX veka),"
*Russkaja literatura,* 1 (1961), 63-84 and 2 (1961),
65-94.

## Norman W. Ingham (essay date 1986)

SOURCE: Ingham, Norman W. "The Case of the Unreliable Narrator: Leskov's 'White Eagle.'" In *Studies in Russian Literature in Honor of Vsevolod Setchkarev,* edited by Julian W. Connolly and Sonia I. Ketchian, pp. 153-65. Columbus, Ohio: Slavica Publishers, Inc., 1986.

[*In the following essay, Ingham explores Leskov's story "The White Eagle" as an expertly veiled critique of the corruption of government officials. Ingham is a Professor Emeritus of the Universtiy of Chicago.*]

In the more than a century since its publication, how many people must have read Nikolai Leskov's **"Belyi orel"** (**"The White Eagle"**; 1880) and not even noticed that it is a puzzle story, let alone solved the puzzle for themselves? Leskov was a master at concealing his true message and evading the censorship.[1] But in this instance—as with **"Levsha"** (**"The Lefthanded Smith"**)—he may have done his work too well. His contemporaries seem to have been fooled by the smoke-screen of supernaturalism he threw up, and critics to our day have continued to view **"The White Eagle"** as an entertaining but rather inconsequential spook tale written for the Christmas trade.[2] In truth it is a cleverly disguised satirical story of political corruption and conspiracy. It is also a remarkable exercise in narrative technique, the trick to which is the use of an unreliable narrator.[3] Galaktion Il'ich, who relates to a circle of acquaintances his experiences of twenty-five years ago, has never come to understand what really happened to him. Yet the author, in a *tour de force* of mystery narration, salts Galaktion Il'ich's own account with enough clues so that we readers can uncover the truth.[4]

There are in fact two untrustworthy narrators in **"The White Eagle."** The speaker in the introductory frame (who should be distinguished from the implied author) is the first teller who misleads us while also dropping clues. But he, unlike Galaktion Il'ich, seems to do it knowingly, and his irony puts him outside Wayne Booth's definition of the unreliable narrator. The very manner in which Leskov used the frame device serves notice that we ought to be on the lookout for ulterior purposes. In the opening frame the main narrator raises provocative questions about the story that is to follow, and then—he never returns to give answers. Leskov deliberately leaves the frame of the story unclosed, thereby challenging the reader to draw his own conclusions. He allows **"The White Eagle"** to trail off suggestively with Galaktion Il'ich's words to his audience, "That is something I do not understand."[5]

What appears to be a casual, bantering introduction of the story by the first teller in chapter one is, on closer look, a masterpiece of mystification in which significant clues are embedded. The narrator makes a pretense of saying that he believes in the supernatural, humorously invoking Hamlet as his authority ("There are more things in heaven and earth . . ."). We may be lulled by this into a false sense of security and suppose that we are merely asked to relax, suspend disbelief, and enjoy "A Fantastic Story" (the deliberately misleading subtitle of Leskov's tale). But then the narrator equivocates about the supernatural. He makes light of the contemporary fad of spiritualism and hints that some of the stories told by members of his circle may be made up and that discrepancies could be due to the teller's lack of art. He also insinuates that "supernatural" experiences can have a subjective, i.e., psychological basis. (The story's epigraph already had to do with subjectivity: "Of meat the dog dreams, and of fish, the fisherman.") Contradicting himself in one sentence, the narrator mentions again the things philosophers never dreamt of, but adds that what is interesting is, "which things appear to whom and how" ("kak kakie veshchi komu predstavlyayutsya"). "And indeed," he goes on, "the subjectivity here is worthy of great attention." Then he gives the reader a final nudge: "And you can no longer tell what is lie and what is truth, but at the same time it is interesting to pursue this. . . ."

The questions which Leskov has his narrator raise and never answer are red herrings. They are subtly designed to make us think but deceptive concerning what we are to think about. The real question Leskov wants us to ponder—and he cannot say so openly—is not whether the supernatural exists, whether the story is invented, or even how the experiences of Galaktion Il'ich might be explained by his psychological make-up. The question is: What actually happened to Galaktion Il'ich?

Unobtrusively brought into the chatter of the opening chapter are clues to the real theme. At the social gatherings where fantastic stories were told, it was not permitted, says the narrator, to hold conversations about "the powers and rulers of this world," or to "take great names in vain," or even to talk about "conserving and saving Russia." "There were, of course, occasional infractions of the rules, but even these were done with great caution." He mingles the forbidden subjects with references to the only accepted topic, insubstantial ghosts from the other world that have a way of coming down into our world and interfering in the lives of living people. Here Leskov has planted hints that the ghost in the story is all too concrete, and that the real subject is not the supernatural but the malfeasance of government officials. It is the author who has to proceed "s bol'shoyu ostorozhkoi" (with great caution) when leaving the bounds of permissible subjects; and that is the reason for the elaborate deception he practices. In this light, the host's good-natured threat of a penalty (*shtraf*) for infractions of the rules takes on ironic meaning; and a whispered remark in private conversation, "Pas si haut!" (Not so loud!) might as well be a reminder to the author himself.

Galaktion Il'ich is the "martyr of the day" whose turn has come to tell a supernatural experience from his past. The first speaker offers a brief sketch of this strange man before yielding the floor to him. Known behind his back as "khudorodnyi vel'mozha," Galaktion Il'ich is indeed a thin, rather high-placed person of humble origin, just as the punning nickname suggests. His father was a mere servant in an aristocratic house but experienced a spectacular rise, became a man of substance, and received a decoration (order). Count Viktor Nikitich Panin took a special interest in him, for mysterious qualities known only to the count. Leskov, through his narrator, seems to be hinting that Panin was the patron behind Galaktion Il'ich's father from the beginning and that the latter performed a shady service of some magnitude in order to be so rewarded. Later the count took on the son at an early age as his assistant.[6]

"Vechnaya pamyat'" (the prayer "Eternal Memory") sung over the grave of the servant father continued to hang over the son, remarks the first speaker. And apart from his humble background, Galaktion Il'ich has another thing to be sensitive about—the "fatal countenance" he possesses, which shocks and cowers people and is the ostensible reason why Count Panin employs him as receptionist in the office. He looks like both a "country lackey" and a "living corpse" (graphically described by the narrator). Afflicted with this appalling exterior and poor health, he is deprived of ordinary human joys and any success in society, though in his secret heart he is a sentimental dreamer who loves life.

Such is the doleful but sensitive and vulnerable narrator who tells the circle a story of the odd supernatural experiences he had many years ago when he was sent by Count Panin (then Minister of Justice) to look into allegations of corruption by a certain governor and his officials. While in the provincial capital, Galaktion Il'ich, according to his account, came under suspicion of having somehow caused the sudden death of a young local man named Ivan Petrovich; and afterward the man's impudent ghost returned to haunt him in an animated and rather comical manner.

Let me violate the etiquette of mystery writing by revealing the solution to the puzzle at once. The truth which Leskov so cleverly disguised is that Galaktion Il'ich was the victim of an elaborate plot by the governor and townspeople—a conspiracy that had the purpose of distracting him from his investigation of corruption and discrediting him personally so that his report could be suppressed. Ivan Petrovich only pretended to

die. Being a consummate actor, he played the roles of his own corpse, perhaps his mother, and certainly the ghost who so effectively kept the hapless Galaktion Il'ich occupied.

But is it plausible that so many people, including (it would seem) the whole town and Count Panin himself, would engage in so ambitious a conspiracy? Yes, it is, when we consider what was at stake. The corrupt governor and the marshal of nobility were highly regarded ("na luchshem schete") by the tsar himself, the formidable Nicholas I. Obviously, they and their fellow malefactors had to be protected by high officials in Petersburg; and no doubt they possessed enough power on their own to force cooperation by the local people. The central government had found it convenient to ignore mere rumors of the governor's extensive wrongdoing; but when a formal, written complaint was received in Petersburg detailing the crimes, at least a semblance of official action had to be taken. Galaktion Il'ich remarks that by rights there should have been a formal investigation (*reviziya*), but that first Count Panin wanted to ascertain the facts for himself by sending his "own man" ("chelovek," the same word used for calling the father a "servant").

What Galaktion Il'ich takes to be a way of most reliably finding out the truth of the charges is actually a device for hushing it up. Superficially, Count Panin's instructions to him seem dictated by a need for secrecy and discretion. He tells Galaktion Il'ich to pretend he is inspecting only one department, and to return to Petersburg when he is recalled by the count.[7] But these orders would be preposterous if a serious investigation were intended. Nobody is going to be fooled by the "cover" given to Galaktion Il'ich, and indeed he quickly learns that the whole town knows what his mission is. It also makes no sense to terminate the inquiry abruptly upon an order from Petersburg, regardless of what progress has been made. The instructions can only be meant to limit the scope of Galaktion Il'ich's investigation and cut it short. Count Panin merely wants to say that he looked into the charges himself through his own trustworthy agent.

It remains to find a way to distract the emissary from his work while he is there and squelch his report. Count Panin leaves this part to the governor and his people, who exert their considerable ingenuity. Evidently, Panin communicates to the governor some information about Galaktion Il'ich, as otherwise the conspirators would not know enough to capitalize on the White Eagle motif—the name for the decoration which the count has promised him upon completion of the assignment. One further measure taken by Panin is to send along two young assistants not of Galaktion Il'ich's choosing. We do not need to suppose they play a conscious role in the plan, even though they are called "lovkie" (clever, adroit)—the same word that is applied to the governor. They are selected because they are inclined to the social life ("svetskogo napravleniya") and can be easily led astray by the townspeople.

On site, Galaktion Il'ich does not succumb to the same temptations—the lures he knows perfectly well local society is dangling in order to "catch" and "embroil" him. He turns down the governor's offer of a better apartment and limits his social engagements. He resists the astonishing "plans" (as he euphemistically put it) that ladies come to him with, while his two associates have "successes" in that department (he requires only that there be no scandal). Apart from his determination to remain impartial in the investigation, he feels unsuited to the enticements.

The people, persevering, use his assistants to ferret out Galaktion Il'ich's weakness. He incautiously relays the message that he likes "health": "ya bol'she vsego lyublyu lyudei bodrykh, schastlivykh i veselykh" (more than anything else I like lively, happy, jovial people). For once Galaktion Il'ich breaks the thread of his story to ask his listeners a question: whether he was guilty of an indiscretion. They politely say "no," but of course the answer is a resounding "yes!" Knowing that the townspeople were trying to entrap him, he voluntarily provided exactly the angle they needed.[8]

Since Galaktion Il'ich turned down the women (some of whom surely were "lively, happy, and jovial"!), the plotters send him a man who meets the requirements ideally.[9] They replace Galaktion Il'ich's receptionist (a lugubrious creature like himself, in the same kind of job he holds in Count Panin's office) with "the most handsome man" from the registrar's office, "Ivan Petrovich himself." Tall, proportionately built, blond, and the flower of health—he also has just the right manners and joyous attitude toward life. He answers a greeting with the military, "Zdraviya zhelayu" (literally: I wish you health). Asked for a sample of his handwriting, he boldly pens, "Zhizn' na radost' nam dana" (Life is given to us for joy). Galaktion Il'ich quickly concludes he is "wholly a man according to my taste."

Our first clue that Ivan Petrovich is not entirely on the up and up is his supposed surname, Akvilyal'bov, an improbable blend of Latin and Russian that is all the more unexpected in a family of priestly origin. It has been made up from the Latin *aquila alba* (white eagle), and the giveaway is that the adminstrative clerk has trouble remembering the name, even though Ivan Petrovich's family is said to be very well known in town. Galaktion Il'ich immediately notices the coincidence of the name but does not seem to suspect it has been invented for his benefit. (The leitmotif of the White Eagle, which might appear to be a coincidence of fate, is in fact carefully nurtured by the plotters in order to con-

fuse Galaktion Il'ich.) Another point that should arouse his suspicions and ours is that Ivan Petrovich is said to be "na schetu u nachal'stva" (well regarded by his superiors)—which echoes the phrase about the governor and marshal being well thought of by the tsar and hints that Ivan Petrovich is the governor's man.

The new strategy immediately begins to work. Normally splenetic Galaktion Il'ich lets his official files and documents lie unstudied while he pleasantly daydreams about the happy life which healthy and lucky Ivan Petrovich must lead. With perfect timing, the governor arrives and breezily invites him to a soirée at which none other than Ivan Petrovich will star in a series of tableaux vivants. The governor fairly bubbles over with praises for the young "White Eagle's" talents and charitable activities, which have made him "a universal favorite in the town." He dwells upon the variety of roles Ivan Petrovich will enact in swift sequence, including the majestic King Saul, the ghost of Samuel, and the witch of Endor (he is especially good at portraying old women). What the governor really does here is anticipate the parts Ivan Petrovich will play, not on the stage, but in the life of Galaktion Il'ich.

Ivan Petrovich spends the morning of the fateful day with Galaktion Il'ich and leaves him only three hours before the party. The latter's parting remark, "Neterpelivo zhdu vas videt' v raznykh vidakh" (I look forward to seeing you in various parts), and Ivan Petrovich's pregnant one-word response, "Nadoem" (I'll bore you), are ironically prophetic of the actual performance to come. So implausible is the announced scenario that we would never be taken in by it if we had not been made to expect the fantastic. We are asked to believe that robust, happy Ivan Petrovich goes home, lies down, and promptly dies—for no discernible reason other than that *perhaps* Galaktion Il'ich accidentally jinxed him. We are also to believe that, despite the sudden death of the most popular man in town and the star of the evening's entertainment, the governor puts on his party anyway and (what is completely impossible) keeps the sad news from the guests.

As things turn out, Ivan Petrovich is a very lively presence at the soirée after all. Supposedly a ghost seen only by the distraught Galaktion Il'ich, he darts about the rooms and among the guests, taunting and distracting the poor man. Granted, we might be willing to accept on this occasion that he is a genuine spook (the supernatural explanation) or that he exists only in Galaktion Il'ich's fevered brain (the psychological)—if it were not for the evidence elsewhere that the apparition is played by a real man. All the governor's guests are well-coached actors in the farce; they go about their socializing and pretend not to notice Ivan Petrovich's presence. On cue some of them repeat in a whisper the word that has upset Galaktion Il'ich: "sglazil" (he gave him the evil eye), said by Ivan Petrovich's mother (as quoted by the governor) in blaming Galaktion Il'ich for her son's death.

"Vy menya sglazili" (You gave me the evil eye) was also said by the rambunctious ghost himself in an earlier "dream" visit to Galaktion Il'ich's bedroom, before it became known that Ivan Petrovich had "died." The manner of this first haunting during Galaktion Il'ich's nap betrays how corporeal the spirit actually is. He "noisily kicked aside the chairs that were standing in the center of the room."[10] Galaktion Il'ich was amazed "how clearly Ivan Petrovich appeared in my dream!" For the perceptive reader there is no mystery about how the real Ivan Petrovich gets into the room now and later to perform his spectral act. We are told that he has taken an interest in the welfare of his victim's valet, Egor. Obviously, he buys his cooperation. That same night the pesky ghost is back sitting on Galaktion Il'ich's bed and reproaching him: "You really did give me the evil eye." Not even ordering the servant to sleep in the same room keeps Ivan Petrovich away (naturally).

When Galaktion Il'ich goes the next evening to pay his respects, it is, of course, the actor Ivan Petrovich he views laid out on the table, playing dead (he mastered staying perfectly motionless in tableaux vivants).[11] What is not entirely clear is whether Ivan Petrovich also plays the role of the mother. It was emphasized that he impersonates old women especially well; and Ivan Petrovich's mother (depicted as a fortune-teller and healer who believes in the evil eye) bears a suspicious resemblance to the witch of Endor. The governor also claimed that Ivan Petrovich can make costume changes very quickly. Even so, it looks as though the corpse would have to become instantaneously the mother in the adjoining room—too much of a trick even for him (unless Galaktion Il'ich waits briefly in a third room or hallway—something which he does not make clear). The governor reported earlier that the mother was so upset she might come looking for Galaktion Il'ich and accuse him of responsibility for her son's death. Were Ivan Petrovich acting her role, we would expect him to stage a melodramatic scene. Instead, the mother excuses herself and quickly leaves the room. Perhaps Galaktion Il'ich's request to see her takes the conspirators somewhat by surprise and the woman drafted for the role (the real mother?) is unprepared.

It falls to Tanya, the fifteen-year-old foster daughter, to converse with Galaktion Il'ich. Her behavior and remarks are calculated to confirm how noble Ivan Petrovich was and how devoted she was to him. While refusing money from Galaktion Il'ich, she pretends to prove her good will by presenting him with a photograph of the deceased, a picture she says Ivan Petrovich himself placed in her French grammar at the page where he ended their lesson the previous day. This is a revealing claim. Apart from the fact that one's own portrait would be an odd choice for bookmark, the reported version of how Ivan Petrovich died seems to leave no time in the day when he could have given Tanya a French lesson.[12] Here is a flaw in the conspirators' story that should rejoice any reader of detective tales. The hidden purpose in bestowing the photograph is that the plotters want their dupe to be constantly reminded of Ivan Petrovich.

Galaktion Il'ich remains in the town eight more days, tormented by his grief over the young man's death and by a vague sense of guilt. Now, can he really believe that he jinxed Ivan Petrovich and caused his death? It is not clear just how superstitious he is; possibly he could be persuaded that his own ill fortune might rub off on Ivan Petrovich.[13] But the conspirators are too smart to offer a jinx as the only explanation. From the first moment, the governor brushes aside the evil-eye rumor as provincial superstition. Having carefully planted the suggestion, he distances himself from it, deferring to the Petersburg official's presumed sophistication. By that same gesture the author makes a concession to his readers.

An attractive alternative explanation is proposed to Galaktion Il'ich by the local archpriest, who gossips that people poisoned Ivan Petrovich to prevent him from revealing damaging information.[14] The idea cleverly builds on a remark Galaktion Il'ich himself made to the governor when informed that the dead man's mother blamed him for the death ("What, was he poisoned at my place or something?"); and this suggests that the archpriest may be in on the plot.[15] Whether he is or not, his allegation furthers the conspirators' cause exceptionally well. It holds out to Galaktion Il'ich (and, for Leskov's purposes, the reader) the possibility of a rational explanation for the abrupt demise of Ivan Petrovich; and at the same time it slyly reinforces Galaktion Il'ich's feeling of guilt. If he did not destroy Ivan Petrovich with a jinx, perhaps he did so by dragging him into his investigation. In either case, the paragon of youthful health and happiness died because of him.

Reflection ought to tell Galaktion Il'ich that there are difficulties with the poisoning rumor. He has reason to know that Ivan Petrovich was deliberately chosen to work in his office; and the archpriest earlier told him the switch of assistants was made with an ulterior purpose. As far as we are aware, the young man was discreet and showed no inclination to volunteer local secrets. What reason is there to think that he would become a dangerous informer? More plausible, perhaps, would be a variant explanation that they planted an innocent victim in the office and then killed him in order to frame Galaktion Il'ich. But if so, why do they not accuse him of murder? Ultimately the poisoning theory may turn on the question of opportunity. When and where could he have been poisoned by outsiders in such a way as to cause sudden death?

Galaktion Il'ich is too upset and too occupied with the ghost and other incidents to reason out what can have happened. And before he is able to recover, an unexpected order arrives from Count Panin that he return to the capital at once. (Eight days should be sufficient time for a message from the conspirators to reach Petersburg and instructions to be returned.) The hidden reason for his recall, of course, is that he has served his purpose and must be rushed away while his investigation is in disarray. Clearly, the strategy has worked very well, for we hear no more about Galaktion Il'ich's work or the report he should be expected to file in Petersburg. He has been distracted from his inquiries, and nothing seems to come of them—which was exactly the intention.[16]

Back in the capital, he finds himself under a cloud, supposedly because of his rumored involvement in Ivan Petrovich's death.[17] Count Panin strikes Galaktion Il'ich's name off the New Year's honors list, and the faithful servant does not receive his Order of the White Eagle. Instead, he is insulted by the vulgar ghost of "White Eagle" Ivan Petrovich in his Petersburg flat. What, we may wonder, can be the conspirators' purpose in keeping up the charade there? Evidently, they need to continue discrediting Galaktion Il'ich (even in his own eyes) and thereby divert attention from the governor's crimes long enough to "take the heat off." Three years later, on another New Year's, Ivan Petrovich's ghost puts in a final appearance—and delivers the decoration. Again he gatecrashes a party, this one thrown by Galaktion Il'ich's sister;[18] but the difference is that these people are not in on the conspiracy, and therefore the specter has to keep out of sight. Nevertheless, they become aware of his distinctly physical presence. When he slams the door on exiting, they rush to see whether someone has stolen the guests' coats.

Returning home from the party, Galaktion Il'ich learns from his valet that the man in Ivan Petrovich's photograph has paid a visit. The servant is new and not the Egor in whom Ivan Petrovich took an interest (as Galaktion Il'ich mentions). This unimpeachable witness recognizes the supposed ghost as a real human being—the very man in the picture.[19] A final clue to Ivan Petrovich's true nature and connections is the fact that he has delivered the order for conferral of the White Eagle—a duty, we learned earlier, that is normally performed by official couriers.

After the decent interval of three years, Galaktion Il'ich has fully earned his decoration, although he never will suspect exactly how.

### Notes

1. Hugh McLean talks about the clever tricks of "crafty old fox" Leskov, in his "On the Style of a Leskovian *skaz*," in *Harvard Slavic Studies*, 2 (1954), 297. William B. Edgerton, in *Satirical Stories of Nikolai Leskov* (New York: Pegasus, 1969), 14, discusses Leskov's use of limited narrators—a device with which "Leskov accomplishes two things: he throws dust in the eyes of the censor, and he gives his reader the pleasure of perceiving Leskov's irony for himself."

2. For the major critics, see Vsevolod Setschkareff [Setchkarev], *N. S. Leskov: Sein Leben und sein Werk* (Wiesbaden: Otto Harrassowitz, 1959), 110; and Hugh McLean, *Nikolai Leskov: The Man and His Art* (Cambridge, Mass.: Harvard University Press, 1977), 376-78. Leonid Grossman (*N. S. Leskov: Zhizn'—tvorchestvo—poetika* [Moscow: Ogiz, 1945], 192) took the somewhat eccentric view that "The White Eagle" is a psychological study of an insane civil servant and as such fits into a long line of Leskovian stories.

3. An unreliable narrator, in Wayne Booth's definition, is one who does not speak or act for the norms of the work (i.e., the norms of the "implied author"). See Wayne C. Booth, *The Rhetoric of Fiction* (Chicago: University of Chicago Press, 1961), 158-59. Booth does not apply the term to narrators who are deliberately ironic ("difficult irony is not sufficient to make a narrator unreliable"). Thus the first narrator of "The White Eagle" is not unreliable (assuming that he knows the truth of the matter), only cunning.

4. My thanks to "generations" of students who have listened patiently to my interpretation of "Belyi orel" and contributed their insights.

5. The text of "Belyi orel (fantasticheskii rasskaz)" is cited from N. S. Leskov, *Sobranie sochinenii*, 7 (Moscow: Khud. lit., 1958), 5-25. I make some use of the English translation by David Magarshack in Nikolai Leskov, *Selected Tales* (New York: Farrar, Straus & Giroux, 1961), 275-300. Magarshack associated "The White Eagle" with "spooky ghost stories" (p. xviii).

6. A partial resemblance of Galaktion Il'ich to Count Panin, and the unaccountable rise of father and son to positions of favor suggest that possibly Galaktion Il'ich is the count's illegitimate son and that the service performed by the "father" was to marry the pregnant girl who afterward bore Galaktion Il'ich. It may be an indicative fact that all mention of his mother is omitted.

7. Panin also stresses that he pretend to concentrate on office routine and court procedures; and Galaktion Il'ich does seem to spend his time over paperwork. Yet most of the crimes alleged against the governor are of a kind that is unlikely to be exposed by review of official records and procedures.

8. The supposed supernatural events do fit Galaktion Il'ich's psychological profile—not because that is the way spirits from beyond the grave work; not because he imagines or invents experiences suited to him; but because the conspirators cleverly exploit his weaknesses.

9. Several motifs suggest a feminine side to Ivan Petrovich, beginning with his "delicate pink complexion with a wide flush" (as though rouged), his dark eyelashes, and the deep red sash with flamboyant bow that he wears across his shoulder. However we look at the matter, it is certain that Galaktion Il'ich takes a more than usual interest in this young clerk whom he describes as "nastoyashchii krasavets" (a truly handsome man). In chapter 8 he "jokingly" tells Ivan Petrovich he ought to get married, and almost in the same breath that he should come to Petersburg. This reads rather like a parody of a marriage proposal. Ivan Petrovich replies that he prefers to "remain an 'old maid'" (*ostat'sya "v devushkakh"*), and that he wants to stay with his mother and Tanya. Galaktion Il'ich uses this as a transparent excuse for a hug: "I even embraced him for that love for his mother and the little orphan." After Ivan Petrovich's supposed demise, the older man tells Tanya, "ya polyubil ego"—an ambiguous expression meaning, "I came to like (or love) him." In the last chapter we learn that Galaktion Il'ich has Ivan Petrovich's photograph on view in his bedroom three years later ("in memory of dear little Tanya"!).

10. The liveliness of the ghost fits Galaktion Il'ich's love of gypsies and their animated dancing and singing. Ivan Petrovich was said to play the guitar; and his ghost "serenades" Galaktion Il'ich. There is abundant mockery here, yet Galaktion Il'ich comes almost to like the spook and trades quips with him.

11. Significantly, Galaktion Il'ich mentions only that Ivan Petrovich was buried the next day, without saying whether he was present. His attendance would require a disappearing act from Ivan Petrovich, in view of the Russian custom of carrying the open casket to the grave.

12. The curious thing is that Ivan Petrovich hardly knows French himself and claims to be "self-taught." Later his ghost puzzles Galaktion Il'ich by singing in a comical mixture of broken French and Russian ("Do svidans, do svidans,—zhe ale o kontradans"). The French language motif runs pretty much throughout the story, beginning with the overheard "Pas si haut!" Its relevance seems to be that French speech is a mark of the upper classes in which Galaktion Il'ich holds a tenuous claim to membership. What he does not quite understand (last words of the story) is the ghost's mockery in using mangled French.

13. Galaktion Il'ich seems to be devastated by the total reversal in Ivan Petrovich's fortunes. The healthy, active, lucky (he won lotteries), joyous young man is suddenly dead, motionless, unfortunate, and discontent (judging by his ill-natured and abusive ghost). The only thing unchanged is that everyone loves and respects him. Their universal condemnation of Galaktion Il'ich, however unfounded from a rational point of view, must weigh heavily on him.

14. Vsevolod Setcharev (110) suggested that the poisoning theory may be correct. Indeed, if Ivan Petrovich is really dead, then poison may offer the best chance for a rational explanation.

15. The archpriest's role remains ambiguous. Certainly by the end of the story he has been pressured into helping the conspirators, because he joins others in writing denunciations of Galaktion Il'ich to Petersburg.

16. If we did not accept the conspiracy theory, how would we explain the extraordinary fact that not a word is said at the end of the story about the outcome of the criminal investigation that started it all? And how would we justify the awarding of a decoration to Galaktion Il'ich after he involved himself in a scandal and apparently did not complete his mission?

17. Surely his superiors do not believe in the evil eye; and if Galaktion Il'ich is accused of criminal wrongdoing, why do they not order an inquiry? No doubt even vague and unsupported rumors of a scandal are enough to discredit him for a time. There are sufficient clues in the text (see especially note 9 above) to indicate that the rumors concern a homoerotic attraction to Ivan Petrovich.

18. Or is she a cousin (*dvoyurodnaya sestra*)? Earlier he referred to her as his "rodstvennitsa" (relative, kinswoman), which would be an odd thing to call one's own sister. She is married to the director of Galaktion Il'ich's office, but she and her husband seem to have been kept in the dark about the conspiracy.

19. Galaktion Il'ich remarks that the spirit was the most "palpable" on his last visit. Earlier clues to his tangible reality (in addition to those already pointed out) are that Galaktion Il'ich heard his feet crunching in the snow before Ivan Petrovich passed under a window, and that Ivan Petrovich woke him on New Year's Day by poking him in the side.

**Michael Prokurat (essay date 1992)**

SOURCE: Prokurat, Michael. "Translator's Preface." In *On the Edge of the World*, by Nikolai Leskov, translated by Michael Prokurat, pp. 7-21. Crestwood, N.Y.: St. Vladimir's Seminary Press, 1992.

*[In the following excerpt from his introduction to Leskov's story "On the Edge of the World," Prokurat offers a brief overview of Leskov's beginnings as a writer, his literary technique, and his attitude toward religion.]*

Nikolai S. Leskov (1831-1895) wrote and rewrote **"On the Edge of the World"** until it took its present, final shape in late 1875 and 1876. Neither the novel nor the author won critical acclaim, although a wide readership liked both. In fact, Leskov's reputation was acknowledged only rarely during his lifetime; but it grew in Russia (and in Germany) after his death, due to a new edition of his works in 1902-3, a few positive critical books, and some new literary disciples. **"On the Edge of the World"** (hereafter **"On the Edge"**) was somewhat dangerous. It criticized the church using the church's own theology, and challenged views of government and religion which were widespread in Europe.

Leskov was not a member of the aristocracy nor of the intelligentsia, both supposed requirements for literati in Russia. He dropped out of school early in life, without even completing the gymnasium, and later became a traveling government employee and a businessman. When he began writing professionally at age thirty he considered himself a journalist—but quickly transformed these same journalistic skills into tools for the art of the short story, much as Tolstoy transformed his skills as a diarist. Thus, Leskov wrote no juvenilia but emerged as a mature, developed writer. Still, he never mastered the "great form" of his time, the long novel; and it was probably a combination of these factors which deprived him of the recognition from his contemporaries he deserved. After he established his professional reputation, Leskov often felt cheated out of his rightful glory and continually battled feelings of inadequacy.

The characteristics which marred Leskov's artistic reputation during his lifetime—no formal education, ex-itinerant employee, writer of the shorter forms, etc.—were the very features of his artistic genius. They gave him his identity, his self-image as the man of experience, the man well-traveled on the byroads of the most unfamiliar of the Russian provinces. Resultingly, Leskov chose the travelogue, as in this novel, to be one of his favorite genres. In the travelogue or travel diary, as in other of his journalistic modes, the contents were usually half fact and half fiction, though this remained indiscernible to the reader. Hugh McLean, the international dean of Leskov studies, has described this type of writing as "ambiguous fictionality: dancing continually on the very border separating reality from art."

Leskov's out-of-the-way peregrinations and his peculiarly acute ear for language enabled him to portray characters in dialect, just as revolutionary a concept in Russia as in America for his contemporary, Mark Twain. Both Leskov and Twain enjoy many other similarities: beginnings in itinerant work and then in journalism, devotion to narration or basic storytelling, mastery of style, thematic utilization of travel, extensive use of the tongue in cheek manner, personal interest in religion, usage of spoken—as opposed to literary—language, etc. Unlike Twain, Leskov created characters in dialect solely through "mannered" language and "the pitching of the voice," not with the added tools of defective spelling and mispronunciation which Twain so successfully employed. Leskov did this primarily through the selection of vocabulary. Leskov's stylized vocabulary alone fostered the individualization of speech, giving the impression of words spoken, of oralization. McLean tells us, "In matters of Russian vocabulary he was perhaps the greatest connoisseur of all the foremost Russian writers, the one most at home in unfrequented byways of regional and class dialects, the most inventive linguistic innovator."

Leskov's linguistic innovation (a nightmare for translators) was seldom appreciated by his conservative literary colleagues. First of all, from time to time he used what experts term "macaronics" and "blend-words," or what might more familiarly be called "nonexistent words" (*slovechki*) or "unwords." He sparked a continuing debate in Russia on the legitimacy of his invention and on his sense of proportion. (As an illustration of the literary difficulty at issue, it is notable that writers like Lewis Carroll or Gerard Manley Hopkins were not known in nineteenth-century Russia.) Second, Leskov employed folk etymologies to "redefine" words and give them peculiar new definitions, a type of neologism. Although his use of this device in **"On the Edge"** is limited, one may consult the Book of Genesis which is replete with Hebrew folk etymologies[1] for more examples of the phenomenon. This too did not endear him to literary purists—but it makes him fun to read!

After the completion of *Cathedral Folk* (1872), a masterful portrayal of Russian parish clergy, Leskov was considered the leading writer on, and defender of, Orthodoxy. Authorship of **"On the Edge"** reinforced this view. The type of "defender of Orthodoxy" that Leskov was for the first part of his literary career should be examined, since the nuances are appreciable. Leskov was champion of the parish priest, a priest as he imagined his paternal grandfather to be, kind to his flock and steadfast before the arbitrary decisions of civil and ecclesiastical authorities. If champion of the parish clergy, he was equally the declared foe of the bishops and church-state officialdom. His dislike of the hierarchy, the Holy Synod, and the Ober-Procurator remained relatively undisguised. However, his knowledge of theology, theological literature, and liturgy was formidable. Many of the materials he selected from church tradition to publish were recommended readings by parish clergy to their flocks, and occasionally were even republished by the church. Some of this publication activity occurred late in his career. Thus, the title won early in his career, "defender of Orthodoxy," is to be qualified and understood with some reservations.

In a brief analysis of Leskov's attitude toward Christianity, it should be pointed out that during this period in his life Roman Catholicism and Protestantism do not seem to have fared any better, or worse, than Orthodoxy. Shortly after writing **"On the Edge"** on a trip to Paris—the most significant feature of which was a long, cordial stay and dialogue with Russian Jesuits there—Leskov expressed sympathy with Jesuit ideas and ministry. Still, he did not shy away from roundly criticizing certain Roman doctrinal positions he considered recent and innovative, as well as the tendency of the Roman Church to provide sure answers where there are none, to paraphrase his complaint.

His attitude toward Radstockism . . . and Protestantism bears similar marks of praise and scepticism. One might have expected more sympathy from Leskov toward Lord Radstock (comparable in spirit to Billy Graham) in Russia. The evangelical Englishman did not speak against any denomination, but characterized organized religion as dominated by a formalism that eclipsed the essence and true spirit of the Christian faith—notes that Leskov himself would play. However, in 1876 he published a treatise which became a book the next year, *A High-Society Schism: Lord Radstock, His Doctrine and Preaching.* In this Leskov asked whether Radstock had not erred in his personal judgment by claiming too much authority for his own rationale and faith. Edmund Heier comments:

> Leskov's criticism touches the very essence of Radstockism, and with it also the entire Protestant doctrine of justification by faith. He argues against the concept of salvation by faith and redemption through the atoning death of Jesus Christ. Against any passage which Lord Radstock cites from the Bible in defence of his teaching, others may be selected which express the very opposite.[2]

As the scholar W. B. Edgerton and others have observed, Leskov took to task anyone who dogmatically claimed "he [had] found the one correct path to the truth." He was capable of positively appreciating any belief that promoted practical Christianity, "true Christianity"—but denominational exclusivity expressed by any religious group brought his wrath. This might explain his dual attitude, praise and condemnation, toward every Christian church body. It was not entirely a doctrinal or ecclesiastical position, but possibly a reflection of his own search for religious truth.

By the 1870s and to the end of his life, Leskov both exhibited a knowledge of the tenets of Protestantism and evolved into a Tolstoyan of sorts, although he was never officially excommunicated as was his idol, Tolstoy. Given his "transvaluation of faith," one goal of scholarship has been to plot the course of this evolutionary journey in his life and writings. Sorting out the dynamics of that process is far beyond the scope of this preface, but whereas Leskov began as a "defender of Orthodoxy" and that he ended up as a modified Tolstoyan are beyond dispute. Briefly put, depending on how one views Leskov's development, **"On the Edge"** may be attributed to his "Orthodox period," his "Protestant leanings," or to his "abandonment of Orthodoxy." Unfortunately, this type of analysis—as logical and necessary as it is—runs the risk of overlooking what might be the most important aspect of Leskov's legitimate understanding of Orthodox Christianity.

The point glossed over is that Leskov used traditional (or Traditional in the Orthodox Christian sense), ancient ecclesiastical authorities to express views on what should be done by Christians, and to oppose Christianity improperly practiced in Russia. When this was subterfuge to avoid censorship or diminution of his social position is extremely difficult to discern, since the positions taken were not merely contentious, but were by and large expert argumentations, correct according to Holy Tradition. When Leskov through the mouth of the archbishop opposed modern novelty in religious painting, he appealed to the traditional canon of classical iconography. When through the words of Kiriak he criticized baptism without preparation and catechesis, he quoted Saint Cyril of Jerusalem on the sacrament of baptism. When again, through Kiriak, he critiqued the minimalistic morality of Christian urban society, he cited Tertullian. When he gave a final and sole example of real missionary activity among natives, he deferred to the martyrdom of a good soul. (In Holy Tradition the martyr, or witness, of the faith is the true missionary.) Examples could be multiplied, such as the bishop's native driver's consistent moral behavior, his "orthopraxy" of the Gospel. The Scriptural, Patristic (Church Fathers), and hagiographical (lives of saints) authorities Leskov referenced—applied in context—are familiar and appealing to Orthodox theologians, past and present. (Leskov attained a respectable level of expertise in these areas, so much so that he wrote articles on Patristic commentaries on Scripture and on hagiography.) Whether Leskov would have considered himself postured for or against the Russian church or the Church universal during this period is hard to determine with certainty; but assuredly his critique had a great sensitivity to Holy Tradition, even if the man himself was not "Orthodox-minded" at the time of writing.

The only proponent of religious belief Leskov did not take to task was Leo Tolstoy, although Leskov appears to have had a more traditional personal faith than Tolstoy. Tolstoy's doctrine, or rather the moralistic positivism of an educated sectarian (complete with an uncritical approach to the gospels as literature!), was ripe for cross-examination. Nonetheless, late in life Leskov acceded to Tolstoy's position and claimed it as a better articulation of his own. In summarizing Leskov's religious questionings, perhaps it is appropriate to remember an observation of the philosopher Nicholas Berdyaev: Late nineteenth-century Russian literature exhibited a strong religious and moral character, along with its political and social natures; and this was an indicator of Russian spiritual life, regardless of the express personal beliefs of the epoch's authors.

Leskov's sense of irony and command of genres were such that he would be comfortable expressing a birthday congratulation in the form of a newspaper obituary, leaving the general readership of the paper to wonder whether the birthday greeting was "dark humor" or a murder wish. If ironies and table-turnings punctuated his writing, they might have originated in the conundrums that accentuated his changing personal views. It is extremely rare, if not unprecedented, that a social critic of Leskov's caliber could alternately court the political Left, the ultra-Right, and the Left again; could write pieces disparaging to Jews, then write paid, pro-Jewish tracts, then write disparaging ones again, and finally be sympathetic; could manage to offend both the proponents and opponents of a religious movement with the same article (Pashkovists/Radstockists); could make saints of anti-establishment revolutionaries and ridicule a man recognized as a saint in his own time (John of Kronstadt); could be identified as a defender of Orthodoxy and as an anti-church Tolstoyan; and so on. Surely, all of this did not proceed simply from an evolved psychological predisposition or a mercenary's compromise of integrity, though perhaps some of it did. I suspect that an artistic genius unsure of his personal worth severely tested society time and time again over the years—and most often found it wanting. What was and is valuable in his critical assessments probably provoked his contemporaries because of its accuracy. Besides, no one accused Leskov of being a likeable person. His relationships were seldom lukewarm, and friendships were always fleeting.

Many of the attitudes Leskov expressed through his characters were very unpopular at the time, but now may be viewed, to a certain degree, as prophetic. His affirmation of missionizing natives without supplanting their indigenous languages and cultures, long a professed ideal of Orthodox Christianity, has met with acceptance in recent decades in Roman Catholic and Protestant churches. The work of the Russian Church with the Alaskan natives, begun before Leskov's birth and concluded during his lifetime, stands as a living monument to this ideal today.[3] In particular his stand on tra-ditional iconography as superior to western art for purposes of worship and on the value of Christian education preceding baptism have both been vindicated, albeit recently, within the seminaries of the Orthodox Church. Nevertheless, Leskov is a man of his time; and he expresses typical nineteenth-century, Russian prejudices—usually with cleverness and irony. He is content to disparage groups such as Roman Catholics and borderland native tribes, and to ventilate Russian chauvanistic views towards things non-Russian. These expressions are not characteristic of present-day Russian society or the Russian Orthodox Church, for the most part.

The author is an experienced, master crafter of stories who encourages the reader to embrace the characters in this short novel. The narrative is powerful; and given the fact that the book's narrator is based on a historical personage, the appeal is heightened. The combination of an interesting story and superb storywriting makes for a riveting and fascinating reading experience. Most people come away from **"On the Edge"** with a vivid, lasting memory of particular characters and scenes. Of special note, the snowstorm description in the later chapters is widely recognized as one of the greatest in Russian literature.

### The Historical Identity of the Bishop

The question of the identity of the story's narrator is an interesting one, since there were a number of eighteenth- and nineteenth-century missionary bishops whose experiences were similar to those Leskov described. Fortunately, Leskov himself belatedly cleared up the mystery. Archbishop Nil or Nilus (Isakovich) of Irkutsk (1799-1874), and subsequently of Yaroslavl', was one of the more likely candidates. He was author of the analysis, *Buddhism: An Examination of Its Relationship to Its Followers Dwelling in Siberia* (1858, in Russian) and *Travel Notes* (1874), two items which correspond with elements in **"On the Edge"**; but during the bishop's lifetime Leskov never divulged his secret. Whether out of respect for the man's modesty or privacy, out of regard for the mystique of the historical novel, out of Leskov's deference to his personal ideological agenda, or for some other reason, the question was left unanswered for several years. After Nil's death Leskov indicated the man's connection with the story in the preface to the 1877 essay "Episcopal Justice":

> I no longer see the need to hide the fact that the hierarch from whose memoirs this story was made up was none other than the recently departed Archbishop of Yaroslavl', His Eminence Nil, who himself told the incidents which formerly happened to him, presently under consideration, to one living and thriving in Petersburg, the honorable and trustworthy person, V. A. Kokorev.
>
> V.A.Kokorev reported this to me.

Leskov's relationship with the financier-banker V. A. Kokorev (1817-1889) is recorded in the biography, *The Life of Nikolai Leskov,* written by his son, Andrei Leskov. Thus, we may certainly identify the inspiration for the main character of the following pages with Archbishop Nil (Isakovich). [For a description of nineteenth-century Russian missionary work in English, similar in many respects to the above, see Paul Garrett, *St. Innocent: Apostle to America.* Crestwood, NY: SVS Press, 1979.]

### THE SOCIAL AND RELIGIOUS CONTEXT

Most western readers assume that the tsarist government in Russia always supported Orthodox Christianity to the exclusion of other faiths during the time of the Empire. The historical record does not entirely confirm this supposition; and the reader should accept as factual the incidents related herein in regard to government interference in support of Buddhism. The winds of government, and we may include here the opinions of the intelligensia as well, blew in many directions in tsarist Russia.

During the eighteenth and nineteenth centuries the spread of Christianity among the peoples of eastern Siberia met with obstacles not only from the side of the old pagan religion under the auspices of shamanism, but also from lamas who competed there with the Russian Orthodox missionaries. The lamas cultivated Buddhism among these peoples in its Tibetan-Mongolian form, so-called lamaism. They easily adapted to prevailing social conditions, included in their pantheon the local gods, and enlarged their cult with the local rites. By the first half of the eighteenth century they obtained from the tsarist government recognition of independent Siberian lamaism, which was advancing as the chief agent of tsarism in Buryat-Mongolia. This accounted for the sympathy shown lamaism by the central, as well as the provincial, governments. In *Buddhism* Nil put forward the entire confrontation with Siberian lamaism:

> Almost no one decided to accept baptism from paganism, afraid of going against the lamas. Besides this, before they were baptized they didn't have any peace. They [the lamas] chased them, they burdened them with all measures . . . The children grew up idol-worshippers, having Christian parents. Fathers and mothers, formerly Christians, had their faith and betrayed it for paganism in order not to fall into the clutches of the lamas.

> (p. 254)

Correspondingly, Nil made reference in *Travel Notes* to the situation wherein the Christianization of the indigenous population of Siberia was aided by the Russian imperial military command. He quoted from an ukaz or edict of the Holy Synod to Bishop Benjamin of Irkutsk, dated August 27, 1805:

His royal, imperial majesty is pleased to make this announcement to the Diocese of Irkutsk and to the Protopresbyter and preacher Gregory Sleptsov of the Nativity of the Mother of God Church in Irkutsk regarding the protection of the military chapel. It was given to you by the royal command for the dissemination of the Faith among the foreign peoples, and in particular, the Chukots. Jurisdiction of the chapel is not to be military—since military arms could disturb the tranquility of the savage peoples and the uneducated—but it is to be civilian.

Sleptsov explained that he was thankful for such help for ten years, 1805-1815, "not less than 1,000 heterodox were converted to Christianity" (pp. 349, 353). Thus, either of these political contexts, government support of Christian missions or government support of Buddhist missions, could occur; and occasionally they existed side-by-side.

Tragically, the lamas often employed violence against the populations, preventing their conversion to Christianity; and unprincipled Christians baptized to command the obedience of their new "godchildren." A "dual-faith" or "two beliefs" sprang up—a mixture of the various religions which were foisted on the natives all at the same time. The term "dual-faith" is a familiar one to the Russian reader, since it was used to describe the popular mixture of Christianity and paganism in ancient Rus' after the conversion of Vladimir. During Nil's tenure as bishop Buddhism, Christianity, and shamanism were mixed together to varying degrees. Such was the religious context we find in the historical period of the present novel.

In order to understand the native peoples which appear throughout the novel, the following brief summaries are offered. Yakut is the Turkic language of the northernmost Turkic people, which people, language, and religion are all known as Yakut. Living in northeastern Siberia in the Lena River basin, they herd horses and cattle, hunt, fish, produce crafts, and trade. Subjugated by Russia in the first half of the seventeenth century, many adopted Christianity by the end of the next century. Nominally Russian Orthodox, some preserved their own shamanism modifying it with Christianity, for example attributing traits of God, Mary, and angels to shaman spirits—as above, a "dual-faith." In 1979 the Yakut numbered approximately 328,000.

Tungus (or Tunguz) refers to the Tungusic languages of the Tungus peoples, including the Evenki and Eveny among others. Again, the term designates the people, their language, and their religion. This Mongoloid hunting tribe is possibly related to the Manchu, and through small groups dominated the area bordered by the Arctic Ocean on the north, Lake Baikal on the south, the Sea of Okhotsk on the east, and the Yenisei River on the west. Tribal mythology, including myths of creation, heroic deeds, the bear ceremony, etc., is reproduced in their religious ceremony. . . . Today many of these nomadic groups still exist, numbering about 56,000 individuals in 1979.

The Zyryans (or Zyrians) are known also as Komi, and constitute one of two parts of the Permyak branch of the Finno-Ugric populations of central Russia. In the ninth century the Permians divided into Komi and Udmurts. The Komi still live between the upper Western Dvina River, Kama, and Pechora, a large region west of the northern Urals toward Arkhangel'sk. In 1979 the Komi numbered over 325,000.

Historically, the Komi came into contact with Christianity as early as the twelfth century since they were trading partners with Novgorod. Their conversion is associated with Saint Stephen of Perm (c. 1345-1396), who was a Russian born among the Zyryans. In 1370 after spending thirteen years as a monk at Rostov, Stephen traveled to this people situated east of the Volga. He believed, in concert with Orthodox Tradition, that the people should worship in their own language, so he created an alphabet for them from the line design in their embroidery and carving. Following this, he translated the Bible and the liturgy of the Church from Greek into Zyryan. He also is known to have founded schools and seminaries to train native clergy. For information on the non-Christian religion of the Zyryans see the articles "Finnic Religions" and "Finno-Ugric Religions" in *The Encyclopedia of Religion* edited by Mircea Eliade.

### The Genre

The genre, or type of literature, represented by **"On the Edge"** is the Leskovian *skaz,* meaning a tale within a tale. The general term *skaz* is a bit more complicated than this brief description, of course, but it may be approximated here.[4] This type of literature has a formal frame, begun by a first narrator, and then an internal unit or kernel which is told by a storyteller—a story ostensibly told orally by a second narrator. The last part of the frame, or the end of the novel, is completed by the first narrator, however short a conclusion. One way in which this novel departs from the *skaz* more broadly defined is that the story is not told by an unlettered person having the appeal of local color, but on the contrary, by an educated, cultivated churchman of high rank. Another more traditional *skaz* by Leskov is **"The Night Owls" ("Polunoshchniki")**. As examples of literature with similar genre characteristics, the story within a story, one might call to mind the Book of Job[5] or *The Canterbury Tales.* Each of these contains a first narrator's frame within which the principal story, or stories, is secondarily told.

Certain characteristics of the Leskovian *skaz* provide us with insights into the author's technique. First, the frame is always shorter and more formal, using polished language and a more sophisticated vocabulary, than the "oral" story which it frames. The single episode surrounded by a frame has very much the tone and color of a story told orally. It has been made to "sound like" a storyteller's tale by the choice of vocabulary, colloquialisms, narrative technique, etc. Though the internal kernel of the *skaz* approximates a tale told orally, it is in fact literary, or a literary device, and not oral speech—which may be ascertained by reading the text aloud. (If only casual speech were as lively and varied as that of Leskov's characters!)

Second, Leskov used the *skaz* genre "politically" to distance himself, somewhat, from controversial ideas he wanted to express. The Russian imperial and ecclesiastical censors frequently were unable to discover Leskov's own "subversive" opinions, since they were voiced by characters seemingly twice-removed from the author. In the present work, for example, the consistent and poignant critique of practices of the nineteenth-century Russian church are greatly softened in the perception of the reader when spoken by a monk who was willing to die for his faith or by an old archbishop whose Orthodoxy and allegiance were not in question. If that critique stood alone, without the sympathetic reading ensured by the set-up of the genre, it might have proved overbearing, an unacceptable affront, and as a result would not have been printed. Curiously, Leskov was aware of the fact that his readers more often took away entertaining memories and an appreciation of character portrayals from his writings—in spite of camouflaged deeper meanings and hidden agendas— than they did his latest social commentary.

### The Translation

Finally, a few words are in order regarding this translation. My aim was to be as faithful as possible to the original Russian, using modern idiomatic American English, while avoiding a paraphrastic translation style. Particular dialects, without a doubt, could not be reproduced; but proper and improper grammar, earthiness and hominess, and a propensity for slang could. One criterion used in translating was whether the words were believable speech in a particular character's mouth, respecting the strength of Leskov's personifications and their consistent word coloration. As an added check I attempted to maintain the approximate number of words and variation in vocabulary which occur in the Russian, so that the length of narrative and dialogue corresponds closely to the original.

In the many places Leskov has placed incorrect or awkward speech in the mouths of his characters, I have put forward incorrect or awkward English equivalents. Also, where Leskov has lured the reader by using a new pronoun without any apparent antecedent, creating anticipation or tension, I have done the same. The technique involved is a simple and effective one, but sometimes leaves the reader with the impression he has missed something. He has, but by the author's design; and usually the contrived question is answered momentarily.

In an early draft of this translation I attempted to preserve all of Leskov's method and style of punctuation—which seems to contribute favorably to the illusion of "orality" or oral speech. Everyone who read the draft agreed that the punctuation proved too cumbersome for the modern reader, especially since the conventions of style of nineteenth-century Russia are so different from our own. Nevertheless, wherever practical I did try to maintain the author's propensity for sentences punctuated by dashes and suspension points (dots or ellipsis points). In the frequent cases where suspension points are found in the Russian text it is not always clear what Leskov had in mind: a pause in speech, an interruption, a break in thought, an unrecorded piece of obvious dialogue, or simply a trailing off of the conversation. Although Leskov's usage of suspension points goes beyond the definitions of the manuals of style for proper English—or Russian, for that matter—it seemed prudent to maintain his own system with its flexibility and ambiguities, since he clearly intended it as a feature of his art. . . .

**"On the Edge of the World"** has been read in the Russian emigré community, the now-defunct Soviet Union, and Germany, and is seen cited from time to time in secular and theological literature. An earlier English language translation—available in Chamot's *The Sentry* from 1922—is literally accurate, for the most part, but difficult to obtain and, by now, dated. Some years ago Mr. Andrew Rayburn shared his personal translation of the novel with me and I was immediately captivated. I am indebted to both Chamot and Rayburn for the work they have done and for their appreciation of Leskov and his inimitable characters. Important to the present work are the Russian text and the invaluable notes provided by L. B. Domanovsky in the Soviet edition of Leskov's collected works [V. G. Bazanov, et al., eds., *N. S. Leskov: Sobranie Sochinenii*, Tom 5 (Moskva: Gosudarstvennoe Izdatel'stvo Xudozhestvennoi Literatury, 1957)] which are the basis of a number of entries in the Notes and of Archbishop Nil's writings, to which I did not have direct access. . . .

*Notes*

A Note on Non-Christian Religions.

Although precise information regarding the nature religions or the forms of paganism of these different native peoples cannot be given here, some characteristics of nature religion in general might be helpful for those unfamiliar with the phenomenon. First of all, the world view of non-urban pagan societies was dependent largely on nature. In them it was common to find the elemental forces of nature—wind, water, earth, thunder, frost, sun, moon, etc.—personified, or even deified, and interacting with human society or particular human beings. Similarly, animals were frequently found with voice and rationality in folk tales, imparting the wisdom of their ways to humankind. Since all these forces were thought to control crop growth, vital to agricultural peoples, and fecundity and availability of game, vital to herdsmen and hunters, knowing and respecting them appeared necessary for human survival. Sacrifice fit mechanically into the perceived cause and effect of those forces in daily life. The calendar, which marks such things as the times of rainfall, fertility of crops and animals, and the movement of herds, was associated with astrology, and took on the same central significance of sustaining life.

On the human side of the equation, two social institutions complemented nature religion. The first was the tribal, gens religion, sometimes called the cult of the ancestors. The second was the development of a priestly class of society. In the first social institution one finds such phenomena as the cult of the clan and the cult of the dead. Both emphasize kinship associations and the importance of tribal and familial membership. Through this institution one learned the value of the group for survival, the respect of persons, the knowledge of tradition—a living, communal experience—and so forth.

The second institution provided human society with applied knowledge as well as the religious functions of priestcraft. Members of this caste might be called shaman, druid, sorcerer, wizard, magician, etc. All knowledge was doubtless considered esoteric by everyone involved, so that understanding the calendar, treating people medically, and advising people on the properties of herbs were placed on the same level as forecasting the future, casting spells, and training villains: all had religious connotations. The shaman was given the status of a gnostic, one who knew or one who was a "keeper of secrets." He was to remember and repeat the archaic spells. Sometimes he also performed a religious role in tribal leadership.

Unlike missionaries in the West who were often given to minimizing or disparaging the paganism of native groups, the Eastern Church since the time of Clement of Alexandria (second century) has taken a different tack. Thus, these religions—including the nature religions—were not to be off-handedly condemned or even disregarded. They were to be considered a necessary preparation for the proclamation of the Gospel to the peoples. This approach produced both positive and negative results. The most significant positive consequence was that indigenous cultures were not destroyed by assimilation; but they were gradually transformed into bearers of the Christian tradition, insofar as Christianity over time could show itself to be legitimately superior to the "old ways." The obvious negative consequence was that the "old ways" might well continue unabated for centuries, with idolatry and superstition consuming human resources and retarding cultural development.

1. E.g., "No longer shall your name be Abram ('exalted ancestor'), but your name shall be Abraham (here, understood as 'ancestor of a multitude')." In point of fact the name Abraham is a dialectical variant of Abram.

2. Edmund Heier, *Religious Schism in the Russian Aristocracy 1860-1900: Radstockism and Pashkovism* (The Hague: Martinus Nijhoff, 1970), p. 69.

3. During the thirty years after Russia's sale of Alaska to the United States in 1867, the Russian Church spent more money on the education of Alaskan natives than did the U.S. Government. The U.S. government dealt with the natives by suppressing their languages and cultures, separating children from their families, and reeducating them, policies directly opposed to those of the Russian Church. Not only the U.S. government deserves stricture. It should be pointed out that prior to this period the Russian missionaries in Alaska expended considerable energy in protecting the native population from Russian adventurers who had exploited these peoples in other ways.

4. The technical definition of the Leskovian *skaz* is, "stylistically individualized inner narrative placed in the mouth of a fictional character and designed to produce the illusion of oral speech." Hugh McLean, "On the Style of a Leskovian *Skaz*," *Harvard Slavic Studies,* II (Cambridge, MA, 1954), p. 299.

5. That is to say, the original ending of Job is, according to most scholars, the final speech of God. Thus, the structure of Job is a) the first frame section, the discussion in the heavenly council, b) the internal oral units, the dialogues of Job and his friends, and c) the second frame section, the theophanic answer of God. Under this reconstruction the ending, wherein Job receives everything back, and the discourse of Elihu, which clearly anticipates God's theophanic answer, are considered as secondary accretions to the original.

### Larry R. Andrews (essay date winter 1994)

SOURCE: Andrews, Larry R. "Hugo's Gilliatt and Leskov's Golovan: Two Folk-Epic Heroes." *Comparative Literature* 46, no. 1 (winter 1994): 65-83.

[*In the essay below, Andrews outlines similarities and differences between the folk hero of Leskov's* Deathless Golovan *and that of Victor Hugo's* Toilers of the Sea, *exploring whether Leskov was influenced by Hugo's novel.*]

Midway through his literary career Nikolaj Leskov set out to create a series of positive heroes for nineteenth-century Russia. Among his most impressive "righteous men" (*pravedniki*) is the "immortal" Golovan, protagonist of the 1880 novella *Nesmertel'nyj Golovan: iz rasskazov o trex pravednikax (Deathless Golovan: from Tales of Three Righteous Men)*. At the end of the sixth chapter Leskov's narrator, a transparently autobiographical representation of Leskov himself, introduces an impromptu digression that enthusiastically compares Golovan to Victor Hugo's Gilliatt, protagonist of his 1866 novel *Les travailleurs de la mer*:

> When I avidly went through the pages of Victor Hugo's novel *Toilers of the Sea* and encountered Gilliatt with his severity toward himself and indulgence toward others (outlined with such genius), having attained the height of perfect selflessness, I was struck not only by the grandeur of this cast of mind and the power of his portrayal, but also by the identity [*toždestvom*] of the Guernsey hero with the living person I knew by the name of Golovan. One spirit lived in them, and their similar hearts both beat with a selfless impulse. Nor did they differ much in their fate: a sort of mystery grew thick about them their whole life just because they were too pure and clear, and there fell to the lot of one as well as the other not one bit of personal happiness.
>
> (*Sobr. Soč* 6: 372; my translation here and subsequently)

This paragraph is striking because of its abrupt interruption of the story; it seems a spontaneous and happy recognition. Chapter 7 opens immediately thereafter with a further juxtaposition of the two characters' unorthodox positions vis-à-vis organized religion. A comparative study of the two characters, starting from Leskov's own remarks and including not only their striking similarities but also their equally striking differences, suggests that the two are folk-epic heroes with a peculiar twist: they have certain personal quirks or eccentricities and they are situated inappropriately in a problematic and unheroic social environment, a world that no longer seems to produce or support heroes. The comparison also suggests that Leskov's conception of his character and its literary vehicle is the more original, if less powerful, of the two. Further, speculation about influence suggests that, much as Leskov apparently admired Hugo's work, his conception of Golovan and the literary form that embodies him was more probably rooted in his own reminiscences and native traditions.

In the text of the story Leskov's comparisons of the two characters are unusually direct; he makes few other literary allusions (e.g., a quotation from an old Russian tale and a mention that Golovan had memorized Pope's

*Essay on Man*[1]). Leskov's comparison is also entirely positive—he mentions no differences between the two characters and speaks of them with unqualified praise. Leskov also speaks as if comparing indiscriminately a literary character (Hugo's) to someone in real life, supporting his claim to be writing a biographical sketch ("I want to try to put down on paper what I have known and heard about him [Golovan] so that in this way his memory, so worthy of notice, will endure in the world" (*Sobr. Soč* [Leskov, *Sobranie sočinenij,* 1956-58] 6:352).

The context of the comparison with Gilliatt in Chapter 6 is Golovan's most legendary exploit in the eyes of the villagers, an exploit which epitomized Golovan's selflessness: during the plague he had cut off a piece of his own flesh and cast it into the river, supposedly as a propitiatory sacrifice to save the people. (We find out later that he had simply cut off a plague sore to save himself, though he had, in fact, tended plague victims at great risk.) The comparison with Gilliatt (cited earlier) crowns this story and heightens the image of heroism it conveys.

The context of the comparison in Chapter 7 is Golovan's "free-thinking"—his tolerant, deistic quasi-Protestantism that partly reflects Leskov's own beliefs at the time. And again the viewpoint is that of the common people, who are baffled by Golovan's friendship with the Jew Juška and the "crazy" freethinker, Anton the astronomer: "Golovan, like Gilliatt, appeared 'doubtful in faith'" (6:373). The quotation marks, the use of *sumnitelen* instead of *somnitelen,* and the verb "appeared" suggest the people's view, not that of the reliable author-narrator. Two pages later, to crown the peasants' doubts about Golovan's orthodoxy, Leskov mentions the uncertainty of his parish membership, an uncertainty created when Golovan's hut slid part way down a hill and apparently crossed the parish boundary. Here the comparison with Gilliatt is very precise; when questioned insistently about his parish affiliation (about which he seemed quite indifferent), Golovan would say:

> "I'm of the parish of the Almighty Creator"—but there was no such church in all Orel.
>
> Gilliatt, in reply to the question of where his parish was, just raised his finger and, pointing to the sky, said:
>
> "Up there," but the essence of both these replies was one and the same.
>
> (6: 375)[2]

Golovan does, however, visit the priest for "confession" when he is dissatisfied with himself, and the priest affirms that "his conscience is whiter than snow" (6:375). The comparisons with Gilliatt help round out the end of the first half of the story, the general and anecdotal characterization of Golovan, before Leskov focuses on the religious pilgrimage to the unveiling of a new relic.

What essential similarities between the two heroes does Leskov emphasize in these passages? The most important is their altruism. Both men set high standards for themselves—Golovan's good deeds and sexual continence and Gilliatt's heroic conduct—but have compassion for others' weaknesses. Leskov cites many examples of Golovan's "perfect selflessness" (*soveršennogo samootverženija*): purchasing his family out of serfdom, succoring the plague victims, turning the other cheek to the insults of his rival Fotej, renouncing carnal love with Pavla, sharing "bread from his own hunk indiscriminately with everyone who asked" (6:373), and finally drowning in a cesspool while trying to save someone's life or property in a fire. Hugo's Gilliatt serves the community as a sailor, saves the lives of Landoys and of his eventual rival Caudray, rescues Lethierry's boat engine and money with heroic physical and mental labors, and then renounces his love for Déruchette, the prize his efforts have won, when he discovers that she loves another. He goes so far as to arrange Déruchette's quick marriage, provide a ring and the trousseau intended for his own bride, and then efface himself in suicide. The moral purity of both characters lends them "sublimity" or "grandeur" (*veličiem*)—an aesthetic appeal—as positive ethical and epic heroes. They are prototypes of the possibility of human greatness among the common people.

Precisely because both characters are "too pure and clear" compared to the society around them and are quiet, even taciturn men, their lives seem mysterious, even miraculous—their second point in common. The common people in both novels tend to exaggerate the heroes' virtues and distort their motives with superstitious assumptions. Thus in both cases the authors show not only the substance of a folk hero but also his accrued legend in the perceptions of others. Throughout his story Leskov often focuses more on these perceptions of Golovan than on Golovan himself, suggesting that he is equally interested in characterizing the mentality of the folk surrounding his hero. Hugo's early characterization of Gilliatt stresses the mystery of his foreign background, his isolation from the native Guernseyites, his taciturnity and dreaminess, and his reputation as an uncannily expert sailor. His practical knowledge of sailing, gardening, and the weather earns him the distrust of the Guernseyites, who regard him as a sorcerer, a *marcou*. When Gilliatt returns triumphant from the rescue, Lethierry suggests that the common people might with justice look on him as demonic for his incredible feat: "Mais comment as-tu fait? Tout le diantre était contre toi, le vent et la marée, la marée et le vent. C'est vrai que tu es sorcier. Ceux qui disent ça ne sont déjà pas si bêtes" (3: 201-02). Although, or perhaps because, the people in both stories find these heroes somewhat alien beings, they consult them for advice and willingly grant them mythical status as heroes.

Their third similarity is their inability to achieve "one bit of personal happiness," expressed in their unfulfilled loves. Golovan is forcibly separated from his youthful love, Pavla, when their master sends him to the army and marries her off to Fotej. Later he takes her into his household when she has been abandoned and left destitute by her husband. Although the villagers refer to her as "Golovan's sin" (*Golovanovym grexom*), he has maintained a chaste relationship with her because she is still married. Hugo's Gilliatt endures a tacit, four-year love for Déruchette and undertakes his grand rescue in order to win her as a bride. At the end, however, she has fallen in love with the clergyman Caudray, and he learns of this love in the most painful way at the most ironic moment. The loss of his love directly motivates his suicide.

Finally, although Leskov sees both characters as examples of Christian altruism, he points out that neither possesses conventional faith or adherence to an established church. Leskov was moving in this Tolstoyan direction perhaps sooner than Tolstoy himself. His righteous men can express their uprightness outside the bounds of organized religion, partly *because* they are independent of it. Golovan's ethical values transcend church attitudes about parish boundaries, the sectarians, and the sacraments. Gilliatt, too, in pointing to the sky as his parish, expresses both his Revolutionary background and Hugo's skepticism toward the church. Gilliatt transcends the narrow views of both Anglican and Catholic residents of the island. His parish is cosmic creation itself, and most of his drama occurs in the vast context of the sea, sky, and animal life. The portrayal of both Golovan and Gilliatt emphasizes less their doubts than their positive faith in life and in a power greater than themselves.

Besides these similarities to which Leskov explicitly calls attention, the two heroes share other qualities as well. Both are common workmen of the lower middle class—Golovan the dairyman and Gilliatt the fisherman and gardener—in a rural setting close to nature.[3] Both authors here and in other works (the left-handed gunsmith from Tula and Jean Valjean come to mind) show enormous respect for work and for practical know-how and good sense. Leskov emphasizes Golovan's practical skills in expanding his herd of cows and giving good advice to others about cures and dowsing. Hugo catalogs in expansive detail Gilliatt's knowledge of gardening, the weather, and the sea, his carpentry and smithing skills, and his amazing resourcefulness in saving the wrecked Durande. Furthermore, both men are physically healthy and strong, except for Golovan's game leg. Both act with heroic courage in a physical struggle with the elements—Golovan with the plague and the Orel fire and Gilliatt with the sea, the storm, and the gi-

ant octopus. Both demonstrate what Leskov describes as the sudden emergence of folk heroes in times of crisis:

> In such sorrowful times of general disaster the folk puts forth from its midst heroes of great spirit, fearless and selfless people. In ordinary times they are invisible and often stand out in no way from the crowd; but when a "pimple" [*pupyrušek*—a colorful colloquialism for a plague sore] has a go at people, the folk puts forth a chosen one, and he works wonders that make him a mythical, legendary, "deathless" figure.
>
> (6: 364)

In addition to these folk-heroic qualities, both characters also possess similar personal quirks. Both men are extremely neat and tidy in their personal habits. Both combine with their skills and practical shrewdness a certain innocence and simplicity. Both seem abnormally shy around women and are, in fact, virgins. Both are viewed as odd and set apart from normal society, and their physical dwellings are set apart spatially and looked on as peculiar (Golovan's) or haunted (Gilliatt's).

The literary vehicles that dramatize the two heroes are also similar in some ways. Both stories are narrated at a historical distance from the events. Leskov constantly refers to "those days" of what must have been the 1830s and 1840s and tries to recapture what life was like in old Orel. Hugo writes of the Guernsey of 40 years earlier (1820s), contrasting it with present-day (1860s) conditions. This historical distance in both cases enhances the "legendary" quality of the heroes and may imply, especially in Hugo's case, that present times are no longer capable of producing such heroes. As a corollary, both works also have local color as part of their design. Leskov's eye always wanders from his protagonist to the general customs and conditions of life, the *byt*, surrounding him. He pauses lovingly over minor characters and describes at length a religious festival whose connection to his hero primarily as a contrast. Hugo wrote a long prologue on the channel islands that he eventually decided to publish separately. And with his customary amplification, he frequently pauses in the novel itself to describe weather and sea conditions around Guernsey, the state of trade, local superstitions, local flora, and technical details of labor. Both works thus have a digressive narrative style, and in both, local color—important and interesting in its own right—also establishes a base in the people and their way of life for the emergence of a folk hero and the popular legends surrounding him.

In both works, too, the narrators strike an autobiographical stance, creating in *Golovan* what McLean calls an "ambiguous fictionality" (95). The narrator's point of departure in *Golovan* is an early childhood memory of Golovan's rescuing him from a mad dog. Leskov's home town of Orel furnishes the setting, his grandmother and uncle appear as characters who can tell him about Golovan, and the narrator refers directly to later events in Leskov's life as if it were his own. The author-narrator also freely offers opinions and generalizations on his material ("Great personal disaster is a bad teacher of charity," 6:364). Notably, Leskov does not use his *skaz* technique, with its colorful and unreliable narrator, here or in most of the *pravedniki* stories. Hugo also obviously speaks out of his experience and love of the island that gave him refuge during his years of political exile and to which he dedicated his novel. As narrator he refers to himself as a resident and to his earlier writings, and, in typical Hugolian fashion, never resists an opportunity to expatiate at large on a subject. Both narrators are also great lovers of language, including archaisms, colloquialisms, and trade jargon. This metadiscourse, this authorial presence dominating both works, is characterized abundantly by ironic distance. The educated narrators ultimately speak of uneducated commoners from the outside, with a mixture of admiration for their colorfulness, strength, and virtue and tongue-in-cheek irony regarding their superstitiousness and ignorance. Both authors find models of moral excellence in their folk heroes and models of stupidity and rascality (Leskov's Fotej) or hypocrisy and evil (Hugo's Clubin) in secondary characters. Both authors satirize institutionalized religion.

Less obviously, both works mix epic and novelistic genres in attempting to portray the possibility of heroism in an unheroic age. Marjorie Ferry, in her excellent dissertation applying narrative theory of Georg Lukàcs to Leskov's *pravedniki* tales, shows convincingly that **Deathless Golovan** and ten other tales experimentally combine the epic conception of a moral hero with a novelistic conception of a problematic, amoral world. The resulting hybrid "is designed to provide concrete evidence of the existence of a wholeness behind the chaos of Russian life" (Ferry 148; the tension between the two is explored further by Luigi Volta). His personal eccentricities make Golovan more of an individual than the traditional epic hero, though his positive qualities still make him rather static as a result of Leskov's quasi-hagiographic approach. At the same time Leskov redeems the work's didacticism from utopianism by showing that the protagonist's moral wholeness is "already active in the midst of a more novelistically interpreted society"; the protagonist realistically demonstrates a "successful existence in and occasional opposition to a seemingly meaningless world" (Ferry 148).[4] Gilliatt, too, represents an individuated folk hero who is contrasted, in his straightforward simplicity, with the problematic nineteenth-century world of criminality, class stratification, and disillusionment, as well as to such metaphysical problems as the ambiguity of destruction and creation in the forces of nature. In calling attention to the latter theme, Victor Brombert acknowledges that the novel has an epic intention and tone and that Gilliatt has the traits of the mythical hero engaged in a quest. But he further suggests that this "pattern of myth points to spiritual rather than strictly epic values," thus justifying the work's description as a "visionary novel" (150-52).

This account of the similarities of character and genre must, however, be heavily qualified. The same four qualities that Leskov singles out for resemblance of character also reveal significant differences. Although Leskov praises Gilliatt's "severity toward himself and indulgence toward others," altruism is not so clearly Gilliatt's key virtue as it is Golovan's. In addition to his service to others, Gilliatt is also competitive, as in the boat race. Above all, his main heroic feat, the rescue of the Durande, is motivated more by the desire to obtain Lethierry's niece as his wife than by the wish to help his neighbor. Golovan's parallel deeds, helping victims of the plague and the fire—communal, not personal, disasters—show no signs of self-interest. In Hugo the great deed dominates the plot, emphasizing Gilliatt's individual power, whereas in Leskov the great deeds receive the same emphasis as smaller, more down-to-earth examples of charity. We see in Golovan none of Gilliatt's defiant posture before the elements, and Golovan is presented more often in an active social role: for example, because of his honesty and fairness he is chosen to distribute food at communal tables and to record property sales. Gilliatt's selflessness and generosity are shown largely at the end, where his humble arrangement of the marriage (an arrangement which, incidentally, employs deceit) is so exaggerated a reversal that it stretches credulity and perhaps expresses the despair and resignation that leads to his death. Golovan's selfless behavior is constantly shown in more believable and practical acts of kindness throughout the work. Then, too, although both characters experience ironic reversals, Gilliatt's bitter sense of the futility of his herculean labors turns him against life—his self-effacement becomes self-erasure.[5] Golovan's sense of irony is constant, as seen in his "eyes, intelligent and good, but as if a bit mocking" (6:353), and it supports his amused tolerance of others and his positive attitude towards life. He is quite content to live in full awareness of the discrepancy between his apparently sinful relationship to Pavla and his real, chaste one. Golovan's ethical strength is intended to evoke an ur-Christian, eschatological standard of behavior; his simple advice to peasants seeking his help is to "pray and then act as you would if you were about to die" (6:358). Golovan's *caritas* is so clearly more exemplary than Gilliatt's general tolerance and ultimate resignation that one wonders if Leskov did not misread Hugo on this issue of altruism.

The mysterious and legendary quality of the two heroes also admits significant differences. Golovan is not the brooding dreamer Gilliatt is, and he keeps silent about his relationship with Pavla for the sake of her privacy, silent about cutting the plague sore from his leg out of a respect for folk belief: "Golovan . . . was so little burdened by the mystical cloud with which popular rumor surrounded him that he did not, it seems, make any effort at all to destroy anything that had taken shape around him. He knew that it would be in vain" (6:372). The people, too, seem more tolerant of his mysterious oddness than do the Guernseyites of Gilliatt's. His reputation as a savior of the people is positive, unlike Gilliatt's negative reputation as a sorcerer. Orel society is more open than Guernsey society to all kinds of sectarians and eccentrics; the Russian villagers give great freedom to Anton the astronomer by labeling him mad, and they worry little about Golovan's lack of religious affiliation.

More important are the differences in the two characters' supposed lack of "personal happiness." Both heroes, in fact, lead useful, stable, and generally contented lives. But Gilliatt undergoes a trial that crushes his hopes for love and his purpose for living. Golovan remains stable and optimistic; although he cannot marry Pavla and abstains from sex with her, he does live long and contentedly with her. An early description emphasizes his cheerfulness—the "calm and happy smile" perpetually on his lips and in his eyes (6:353). Leskov's comment about both heroes' not having found any happiness must therefore be qualified. Leskov himself provides the distinction at the end of his story. When the narrator remarks that Golovan and Pavla "deprived themselves of all their own happiness" on account of a good-for-nothing, his grandmother defines two kinds of happiness:

> "But happiness is to be understood in this way: there is righteous happiness [*sčast'e pravednoe*] and there is sinful happiness [*sčast'e grešnoe*]. The righteous kind will never transgress against anyone, but the sinful kind will step over everything. And they [Golovan and Pavla] preferred the first to the second."
>
> (6: 397)

In renouncing Déruchette, whose uncle would force her to marry him, and in renouncing life, Gilliatt does not seem to earn the same degree of "righteous happiness." Leskov's simple comparison of the two heroes thus conceals a difference. Gilliatt's suicide over the loss of his love reveals the absence of any of Golovan's higher sources of sustaining happiness in life.

This difference is underlined by the differences in the two heroes' religious attitudes, in the broader sense. Although both transcend conventional religion and both show an intimate relationship with nature's life force, Golovan's reverence for the Creator and for creation is more consistent and his attunement to life more convincing. He is known for having unusually high-quality livestock and dairy products, for feeding people, and for divining water for wells. And as perceived by the folk mind, he fuses pagan and Christian values: his sacrifice of part of his leg to the river of life ends the plague, restores fertility, and "pays" for the community. His flexibility and resilience also reveal an Eastern patience with time and the elements. Gilliatt, in contrast, despite his gardening, fishing, life-saving, and extraordinary kinship with the sea and sky, becomes a brooding obsessive who must endure and outwit nature and kill its menacing monster for the sake of an unrequited love. On the one hand Hugo portrays Gilliatt as a dreamer immersed in the infinite mystery and power of the elements, and on the other he makes Gilliatt a "gladiator" striving to conquer these elements with his dauntless human will and ingenuity. Both traits belong to European romanticism—one thinks of Faust yearning to follow the sun in Part 1 yet building dikes to control the sea in Part 2. By introducing a conventional love motive into Gilliatt's character, Hugo unbalances him. It is then difficult to see his sea-suicide as a positive return to transcendent nature. When Golovan loses his love when she is married off to another, he does not lose faith in life but becomes a good cook in the army, calmly buys his freedom, and frees and supports his relatives. When he is reunited with his love but remains frustratingly celibate, their relationship is integrated happily into a larger life of productivity and community. In terms of world-view, his consistent quality of acceptance, shown even in the smile the narrator remembers so clearly at the very moment Golovan snatched the mad dog and flung it into a cellar, is more convincing and interesting, if less emotionally powerful as fiction, than Gilliatt's mixed extremes of reverence, resistance, and resignation.

In addition to character differences, differences in style and genre also modify the similarities Leskov so emphasized in the two characters. Despite numerous stylistic parallels, Hugo's blend of the epic and the problematic (in Lukàcsian terms) in the relationship of the hero to his world is more dramatic and less unified than Leskov's. Gilliatt's sublime conquest of nature in the rescue resembles the traditional epic hero's feats of valor more than do any of Golovan's actions. In fact, however, the daily, practical "righteousness" of a person such as Golovan, as Leskov implies at the end of the story and in an 1881 article ("O gerojax i pravednikax"), is much more difficult to achieve than the traditional heroic deed (Muckle 51). Although Gilliatt seems more the epic hero, his personality is at the same time invaded more by the "problematic," through the love story and suicide, than is Golovan's. Because Golovan's heroism is embedded in daily life, the two modes—epic and novelistic—are more seamlessly interwoven.

Hugo's *Les travailleurs de la mer* is also a full-scale romantic novel with leisurely descriptions of a number of characters and a complicated, carefully structured plot. It draws on traditions of the gothic and exotic tale, the adventure novel, romantic love stories, and the fairy-tale quest (the rescuer of Lethierry's engine and "treasure" is promised marriage to his niece, the "princess"). It draws on all the resources of romantic style—protracted suspense, extravagant diction, high dramatic contrasts, clear moral conflicts, grotesque and exotic detail, coincidence, eavesdropping, emotional descriptions, clear internal characterization, and intense situational irony. Only secondarily is it a realistic novel about *travailleurs*. *Nesmertel'nyj Golovan*, in contrast, claims to be a biographical sketch, looks like a realistic, anecdotal *povest'*, and draws on traditions of moral fable, folk legend, and saints' lives. Its very linguistic texture, including the voice of the narrator, is permeated by oral folk traditions in a way Hugo's is not. Despite the work's far smaller size, its plot is less focused than Hugo's. The chronology is loose, the tone is casual and understated, and the lengthy treatment of the religious procession bears only indirectly on the protagonist. Some of Golovan's most interesting and heroic actions have already occurred when the story opens, and all information except the incident with the mad dog comes to the narrator at second hand. Leskov treats characters from the outside and refrains from artificially heightening the deeds of his hero. The surprise revelation of "Golovan's sin" at the end is but modestly climactic. Leskov introduces a Western love element only to submerge it and deprive it of traditional sentimental and romantic significance.[6] Despite the narrator's open admiration of Golovan, Leskov does a great deal to emphasize Golovan's realistic, concrete individuality by giving him eccentricities (his smile, his "gentlemanly" sash, his odd house, his single garment, his sisters' "spittle" yarn) and by avoiding romantic methods of portraying his hero.

Yet a hero Golovan is, emerging from the common background much as a folk hero or saint, and as basically unchanging and static as they are in their respective genres. He seems more static, despite the greater realism of Leskov's style, than Gilliatt, who is deeply affected by seeing his name in the snow in the opening incident and then conducts a near-silent courtship of Déruchette from a distance. If Golovan's consistency and quirky ordinariness are more convincing, Gilliatt's emotional intensity and sustained physical prowess are more gripping in the course of the plot. At the same time Leskov's treatment of an epic hero in an unheroic world is more original because he shuns the romantic clichés Hugo was still using in 1866 and because the contrast between his hero's heroic nature and the surrounding *byt* is less sharply drawn. Golovan is extraordinary in his very ordinariness; Gilliatt is extraordinary chiefly because of his one superhuman exploit.

This account of the differences between the two heroes and their literary frames suggests that Leskov's comments on Gilliatt in the story need not be taken as precise analysis or definitive appraisal. Leskov is acknowledging his admiration for Hugo, but he is also "doubling" his own character with another similar one and thus extending the number of *pravedniki* in this series of tales. At this time of transition in Leskov's life he was deliberately searching for examples of virtue to prove to himself (and to Pisemskij, with whom he debated the issue[7]) that the modern world was not doomed to moral disintegration. The literary example of a Gilliatt may have struck his imagination as a confirmation across national boundaries of the *pravedniki* he was discovering among the Russian people.

But did Hugo's character actually influence the composition of *Nesmertel'nyj Golovan* in a significant way? Leskov was a wide and voracious reader, copying passages from numerous Western authors into his notebooks (Gebel' 56) and referring to them in letters. But references to Hugo are sparse. Leskov seldom dealt with foreign writers in his journalistic articles, although in an 1869 article refuting complaints about the poverty of Russian literature, he does say that the French can boast only of Hugo (*O lit.* [Leskov, *O Literature i isskustve*, 1984] 33). In an essay on Turgenev ("Čudesa i znamenija," 1878) he quotes in passing a wolf analogy from Hugo (*O lit.* 64), and in an 1891 letter advising the young artist Z. P. Axočinskaja to become better educated by studying great works of art, he says, "Make a first conquest over yourself: Read all of Puškin, then Shakespeare, and then Vict[or] Hugo" (*Sobr. soč.* 11: 481) In *Ostrovitjane* (*The Islanders,* 1866) the narrator reports that a priest told him that he had never seen "a condemned man in such state of mind as Victor Hugo clumsily depicts in his *Dernier jour d'un condamné*" (title cited in French: *Sobr. soč.* 3:165-66) He alludes to Hugo in "Skaz o tul'skom kosom Levše i o stal'noj bloxe" in an insignificant reference to Quasimodo from *Notre Dame de Paris,* and one wonders if traces of Bishop Myriel from *Les Misérables* persist in the priest Tuberozov in *Soborjane* and in some of Leskov's good bishops, as they do somewhat in Dostoevskij's Zosima. But in general Leskov's creative thinking was not dominated by Western literature. He always asserted that experience of Russian life and knowledge of people were the most important things for a writer. He was not a typical aristocratic intellectual, thinking largely in terms of European literary tradition.

Most Russian, Soviet, and Western scholars are silent about Leskov's knowledge of Hugo (e.g., Drugov, Troitskij, Volynskij/Flekser, McLean, Edgerton, Macher) and have amply shown the plausible Russian literary and autobiographical sources for Leskov's *pravedniki*.[8] M. P. Alekseev emphasizes the great attention Hugo drew from translators and critics in the 1860s and 1870s but says nothing of Leskov (884-90). Vladimir Kostršica offhandedly mentions that **Deathless Golovan** "comments on . . . an episode from Victor Hugo's *Travailleurs de la mer*" (74), but he does not specify which episode; perhaps he is thinking simply of Leskov's explicit reference to Gilliatt's reply about his parish. Leonid Grossman quotes at length from Leskov's paragraph comparing the two heroes but does not explore the possible influence or compare the two characters in detail (199). Piero Cazzola mentions, without development, the comparison about parishes (745). Vladimir Semenov quotes and reaffirms Leskov's comparisons of Golovan with Gilliatt but without development or differentiation (129-30). Pierre Kovalewsky cites the possible influence of Hugo's novel but says that the subjects are so different that there could be no serious influence (210-11).

In the story itself, of course, Leskov as narrator says that he avidly read Hugo's novel. Did he read it in French? Andrej Leskov says that Leskov received very low scores in French in the gymnasium and that only his mother spoke French in the family (73-74). Leskov was apparently less comfortable in French than other major Russian writers were, and though he attended French theatre during his second sojourn in Paris in 1875, he visited primarily Russians.[9] He did not meet Hugo then, as, for example, Turgenev did in the 1870s. McLean speculates that "although he knew French literature reasonably well, he had probably read most of it in Russian translation. He could, however, and sometimes did, read French books" (28). He could have read *Les travailleurs de la mer* in Russian translation, either in its installments in *Otečestvennye zapiski* in 1866 (Nos. 6-8, 15-17) or in one of its book editions published in the same year. But he doubtless read the novel in French because in November 1872 he published a simplified version for young people of Hugo's novel, *Truženiki morja,* ostensibly his own translation, under his pseudonym M. Stebnickij.[10] Thus Leskov read *Les travailleurs de la mer* between 1866 and 1872, three to nine years before his second trip to France and eight to fourteen years before the composition of **Nesmertel'nyj Golovan.** (Semenov is thus a bit loose when he says that "At the time of composition of his **Golovan** Leskov became acquainted with V. Hugo's novel," 129.) The very fact that Leskov published a children's version of Hugo's novel, doubtless for its captivating adventure narrative and for its exemplary hero, supports the idea that the work had a great impact on him.

An examination of that translation produces two further revelations. The first is in Leskov's foreword (or, as he calls it, "In Place of a Foreword"), where he answers potential parental objections that the book is unsuitable for children. He argues:

> aside from an acquaintance with the customs of a little-known maritime population—an acquaintance that furnishes fresh and very interesting reading—the young reader can draw from it images of lofty spirit and worthy imitation of character, images whose outline is met far from often in children's novellas in that artistic form in which they appear in Victor Hugo.
>
> (M. Stebnickij, n.p.)

He is alluding here, of course, to the exemplary moral character of the protagonist Gilliatt, especially as captured imaginatively by Hugo in stirring scenes. This justification of the didactic suitability of his translation confirms Leskov's high opinion of Hugo's hero.

The second revelation comes out of the changes Leskov makes in rendering Hugo's original. Not unexpectedly, Leskov deletes many details and most of Hugo's expansive digressions on such topics as sorcerers, sailors' jargon, English aristocratic titles, French protestants, octopus lore, and the relations of the natural elements of wind and sea. These would tend to impede the plot movement for young readers. He also deletes passages that might be construed as objectionable on political, religious, or moral grounds (e.g., Norman jokes against royalty, a reference to the Tsar's repression of Poland, details about Lethierry's atheism, and descriptions of Déruchette's beauty and of naked girls bathing). But what is most relevant to this study is the way Leskov changes Hugo's ending. First, he completely veils Gilliatt's suicide by drowning in the cliff chair Gild-Holm-Ur. He deletes the details of Gilliatt's calculated progress to the rock and the painful, step-by-step rise of the tide until it covers his head, coinciding with the steady retreat of the boat bearing away the young lovers Déruchette and Caudray. He also eliminates the description of the complex expression on Gilliatt's face. The reader surely still gathers that Gilliatt is going to drown—the seat is mentioned by name and Gilliatt's rescue of Caudray from the seat earlier is still fresh. But the result of Leskov's change is that the suicide is minimized instead of being protractedly emphasized as in the original. Perhaps Leskov found such a scene too painful for his youthful readers, or he felt that this suicide ill-suited the noble character of Gilliatt. Leskov certainly sympathized with suicides, as in *Očarovannyj strannik,* but he preferred heroes attached to life, like his *pravedniki.* Surely, too, he had no desire to transmit without qualification what he considered the stale plot formula referred to earlier—"he fell in love and shot himself." If so, his changed ending is a critique or correction of Hugo, and Golovan could be considered a further response to Hugo's final treatment of his hero.

More important, besides deleting the description of Gilliatt's death, Leskov *inserts* several generalizations about Gilliatt's virtue that leave no doubt that Gilliatt evoked his highest admiration. These final didactic comments begin when he has Déruchette recognize Gilliatt on the rock (she does not recognize him in the original): "'Look, there's a person [*čelovek*, i.e., human being] there on the rock: it's he!' And it actually was *he*, it was Gilliatt, a *human being* in the full and great meaning of this word" (Stebnicki 440; Leskov's emphasis).[11] Here Leskov emphasizes Gilliatt's fulfillment of the highest conception of human potential.

After a brief literal translation of the boat's passing, Leskov concludes the novel with a fade-out that distances us as it generalizes about Gilliatt:

> Gilliatt remained on his spot as a model of sublime love, which stood higher than love for his own happiness.
>
> Let him thus remain on this rock and in the imagination of the reader as a model of noble energy [*obrazcom blagorodnoj ènergii*], goodness [*dobroty*], and submission to the holy will of Providence, which everyone who wishes to be a worthy human being should foster in himself.
>
> (440-41)

Leskov praises Gilliatt's self-sacrificing love—his altruism—just as he does eight years later in Golovan. He also singles out Gilliatt's tireless work ("noble energy") in the service of practical love and his essential kindness and goodness, again key qualities in Golovan himself. The final note, about Gilliatt's "submission" (*pokornosti*) to Providence, blurs Gilliatt's suicide, which in Hugo's work may be interpreted as either resignation or revolt and thus resembles only Golovan's resignation to his love's inaccessibility even in her proximity (an act of resignation not dramatized in the story). Leskov thus provides a generalized, didactic ending in place of Hugo's original concrete ending. It is a choice that reflects both Leskov's perception of his young audience and his enthusiasm for Gilliatt's moral qualities.

Still, it is a fair distance from noting Leskov's great admiration for Hugo's novel to ascribing significant influence to it in the conception and composition of ***Deathless Golovan.*** Despite the similarities between the two heroes, the differences between them, along with what we know of Leskov's Russian sources, suggest that Leskov was directly and almost entirely influenced by native experience and tradition in creating his character Golovan. After all, Golovan was a historical person known to Leskov's family. Further, Leskov seemed to want to distance himself deliberately from Western genre traditions in fiction, as he had earlier in the *skaz* and the novel-chronicles. In *Nesmertel'nyj Golovan* he counters the romantic style, the obligatory love interest,

the tight plotting, and the individualistic hero of Western novels such as Hugo's with an anomalous, hybrid Russian genre[12] and a hero intimately related to his community and intended didactically to represent a general moral ideal and a specific virtue in the Russian people. In concluding this comparison of the two heroes of these novels, we might very well find the differences between them more interesting and instructive than the resemblances with which Leskov was so taken.[13]

*Notes*

1. Although "having approved" of Pope's work, Golovan may have learned it partly because it was given to him by his patron, General Ermolov, and partly because he liked "lofty thoughts" in general; his memorization of it is presented as a bit eccentric—he knew Pope "not in the way people usually know an author, *by having read through his works*" (*Sobr. Soč.* 6: 375, Leskov's emphasis).

2. The original passage in Hugo comes in the scene in which Gilliatt has just rescued Caudray from the sea:

   "De quelle paroisse êtes-vous?"

   Gilliatt leva la main droite, montra le ciel, et dit:

   "De celle-ci."

   (Hugo 1: 204)

3. Hugh McLean (358-59) and Danilo Cavaion (47-48) both appropriately emphasize the petit-bourgeois economic independence and self-reliance of Leskov's *pravedniki;* Hugo's Gilliatt fits this description as well.

4. In a parallel fashion, O. E. Majorova also calls attention to two narrative levels in the story, the mythic and the social-psychological, as well as the mingling of two narrative points of view, those of the peasants and of the educated narrator (174).

5. Cf. Victor Brombert: "Gilliatt's ultimate sacrifice . . . cannot be attributed solely to selflessness and higher love . . . Gilliatt's withdrawal from life is not a simple matter of generosity; it is a refusal of the violence of passion, perceived as a threat and a fundamental evil . . . Gilliatt turns his back on the allurements of life" (159-60).

6. McLean alludes to Leskov's heavy guilt about sex in describing "puritan" desexualization as one of the three chief traits of the *pravedniki* (360). He finds Golovan's case especially remarkable because Leskov makes Golovan's relations with the women living with him the object of climactic interest, whereas the courage shown in the epidemic and fire seems more promising literary material for development (361). Walter Benjamin, however, finds the asexuality or bisexuality of Lesk-

ov's "maternal males" not something "privative" but the "pinnacle of creation" and "a bridge to a higher world" (97-98). If Leskov skirts the problematics of sex and Hugo touches on them (in Gilliatt's fantasies and subsequent pain), it is partly a question of genre, of Leskov's rejection of Western fictional treatments of love, about which he often complained. In his 1882 book review, "Žitie kak literaturnyj istočnik," for example, he scornfully characterizes some of Tolstoy's critics as "sorry that such a great artist is concerned with ascetics and not with ladies and cavaliers . . . It is incomprehensible and annoying to these people that it is possible to love something in another way than the endless variations on the theme: 'He fell in love and got married' or 'He fell in love and shot himself'" (*O Lit.* 39). See also A. I. Faresov's account of an interview with Leskov near the end of his life in which he said that the French, with their addiction to the trite love themes cited above, cannot hope to understand characters in Russian novels (241-43).

7. In his "Foreword" to the first edition of *Odnodum* Leskov tells amusingly how his talks with the "dying" Pisemskij were the genesis of his search for "righteous men" and the series of stories about them (*Sobr. soč.* 6: 641-43).

8. The key study here is Majorova's detailed comparison of *Golovan* with a number of saints' lives and the epic song of Egorij. See also A. A. Gorelov, *N. S. Leskov* (245-48), and A. A. Kretova. N. C. Mixajlova discusses Leskov's imitation of folk legend about the bogatyrs and finds that the juxtaposition of folkloristic and realistic elements works well (51). D. Straukaite and V. Gebel' (81) also point to folk sources. Andrej Leskov speaks of the influence of the *One Hundred Four Sacred Stories* (67)—mentioned in the story itself—and of several childhood incidents (43, 52-53). McLean points to hagiographic models for the *pravedniki* (350) as well as personal models in Leskov's uncle Scott and in his early acquaintances Markovich, Benni, and the Kiev intellectuals (34, 54, 70). Leskov himself called attention to the saints' lives as rich sources for positive heroes in literature, including references to Tolstoy and Flaubert, in his 1882 "žitie kak literaturnyj istočnik" (*O lit.* 38-40).

9. Particularly two Russian Jesuits, as McLean (28) and William B. Edgerton (89) make clear. In fact, this trip may have influenced the development of his *pravedniki* because he was thoroughly rereading the gospels and was engaged in serious religious reconsiderations. This process would outweigh by far any influence of French literature at this time. Leonid Grossman also notes Leskov's weakness in French during his first stay in Paris in 1862-63, when he studied the Russian colony there (82, 92-93).

10. I am deeply indebted to Ljudmila Ivanovna Koval'čuk, head of the Information and Bibliography Group at Volgograd State University Library, for obtaining a microfilm of this rare book for me to use during my exchange visit in Volgograd.

11. Compare the original:

    "Vois donc. Il semblerait qu'il y a un homme dans le rocher."

    Cette apparition passa.

    Le *Cashmere* laissa la pointe . . .

    (Hugo 3: 270)

12. Earl Sampson notes the difficulty of genre classification for *Nesmertel'nyj Golovan* and Leskov's other stories and cites a number of Leskov's own invented genre terms (317-18).

13. I am indebted to the Research Council of Kent State University for a summer research grant that made the completion of this article possible. I am also indebted to Prof. Hugh McLean for pointing out in private correspondence several of Leskov's references to Hugo.

## Works Cited

Alekseev, M. P. "Viktor Gjugo i ego russkie znakomstva: vstreči; pis'ma; vospominanija." *Literaturnoe nasledstvo* 31-32. Moscow, 1937. 777-932.

Benjamin, Walter. "The Story-Teller: Reflections on the Works of Nicolai Leskov." Trans. Harry Zohn. *Chicago Review* 16 (1963): 80-101.

Brombert, Victor. *Victor Hugo and the Visionary Novel.* Cambridge, Mass.: Harvard University Press, 1984.

Cavaion, Danilo. "Per una tipologia dei 'Giusti' di Leskov." Cavaion and Cazzola 35-49.

Cavaion, Danilo and Piero Cazzola, eds. *Leskoviana.* Bologna: Editrice CLUEB, 1982.

Cazzola, Piero. "I 'Giusti' di Leskov." *Convivium* (Bologna) 36 (1968): 732-51.

Drugov, Boris. *N. S. Leskov: očerk tvorčestva.* Moscow: Xudožestvennaja literatura, 1961.

Edgerton, William B. "Leskov's Trip Abroad in 1875." *Indiana Slavic Studies* 4. Bloomington: Indiana University Press; The Hague: Mouton, 1967. 88-99.

———. *Nikolai Leskov: The Intellectual Development of a Literary Nonconformist.* Diss. Columbia University, 1954.

Faresov, A. I. *Protiv tečenij: N. S. Leskov. Ego žizn', sočinenija, polemika i vospominanija o nem.* St. Petersburg: M. Merkuševa, 1904.

Ferry, Marjorie Ann. *N. S. Leskov's Tales About the Three Righteous Men: A Study in the Positive Type.* Diss. Yale University, 1977.

Gebel', Valentina. *N. S. Leskov v tvorčeskoj laboratorii.* Moscow: Sovetskij pisatel', 1945.

Gorelov, A. A. *N. S. Leskov i narodnaja kul'tura.* Leningrad: Nauka, 1988.

———. "'Pravedniki' i 'pravedničeskij' cikl v tvorčeskoj èvoljucii N. S. Leskova." *Leskov i russkaja literatura.* Ed. K. N. Lomunov and V. Ju. Troickij. Moscow: Nauka, 1988. 39-61.

Grossman, Leonid. *N. S. Leskov: žizn'—tvorčestvo—poètika.* Moscow: Xudožestvennaja literatura, 1945.

Hugo, Victor. *Les travailleurs de la mer.* 5th ed. 3 vols. Paris: Librairie Internationale, 1866.

Kostršica, Vladimir. "O žanrovom svoeobrazii prozy N. S. Leskova." *Filologičeskie nauki* 2 (1974):70-75.

Kovalewsky, Pierre. *N. S. Leskov: peintre méconnu de la vie nationale russe.* Paris: Presses universitaires de France, 1925.

Kretova, A. A. "Fol'klornye tradicii v povestjax N. S. Leskova 'Očarovannyj strannik' i 'Nesmertel'nyj Golovan.'" *Fol'klornye tradicii v russkoj i sovetskoj literature: Mežvuzovskij sbornik naučnyx trudov.* Ed. B. P. Kirdan et al. Moscow: Moskovskij gos. ped. inst. im. V. I. Lenina, 1987. 88-100.

Leskov, Andrej. *N. S. Leskov. Po ego ličnym, semejnym i nesemejnym zapisjam i pamjatijam.* Moscow: Xudožestvennaja literatura, 1954.

Leskov, N. S. *O literature i iskusstve.* Ed. I. V. Stoljarova. Leningrad: Leningrad University Press, 1984.

———. *Sobranie sočinenij v odinnadcati tomax.* Moscow: Xudožestvennaja literatura, 1956-58.

Lužanovskij, A. V. "Dokumental'nost' povestvovanija—žanrovyj priznak rasskazov N. S. Leskova." *Russkaja literatura* 4 (1980): 144-50.

Macher, Brigitte. *Nikolai Leskovs Verhältnis zur Orthodoxie.* Diss. Marburg University, 1952.

Majorova, O. E. "Rasskaz N. S. Leskova 'Nesmertel'nyj Golovan' i žitijnye tradicii." *Russkaja literatura* 3 (1987): 170-79.

McLean, Hugh. *Nikolai Leskov: The Man and His Art.* Cambridge, Mass.: Harvard University Press, 1977.

Mixajlova, N. G. "Tvorčestvo Leskova v svjazi s nekotorymi obrazami narodnogo èposa." *Vestnik moskovskogo universyteta: filologija* 3 (1966): 49-57.

Muckle, James Y. *Nikolai Leskov and the "Spirit of Protestantism."* Birmingham: Dept. of Russian Language and Literature, University of Birmingham, 1978.

Sampson, Earl. "The Madman and the Monk: Two Types of Narrative Construction in Leskov." *Mnemozina: Studia litteraria russica in honorem Vsevolod Setchkarev.* Ed. Joachim T. Baer and Norman W. Ingham. Munich: Wilhelm Fink, 1974. 317-24.

Semenov, Vladimir. *Nikolaj Leskov: vremja i knigi.* Moscow: Sovremennik, 1981.

Setschkareff, Vsevolod. *N. S. Leskov: Sein Leben und sein Werk.* Wiesbaden: Harrassowitz, 1959.

Stebnicki, M. [N. S. Leskov]. *Truženiki Morja. Roman Viktora Gjugo prisposoblennyj dlja detej.* St. Petersburg and Moscow: Izdanie knigoprodavca—tipografa M. O. Vol'fa, 1872.

Stoljarova, I. V. *V poiskax ideala (tvorčestvo N. S. Leskova).* Leningrad: Leningrad University Press, 1978.

Straukaite, D. "Antiklerikal'nye motivy v skazax N. S. Leskova i narodnaja satiričeskaja skazka." *Lietuvos TSR aukstyjy mokykly mokslo darbai, literatura* 6 (1963): 125-40.

Troickij, V. Ju. *Leskov-xudožnik.* Moscow: Nauka, 1974.

Volta, Luigi. "Aspetti tipologici e comparatistici della scrittura di N. S. Leskov." *Cavaion and Cazzola* 337-49.

Volynskij, A. L. [A. L. Flekser]. *N. S. Leskov: kritičeskij očerk.* 1898. St. Petersburg: Èpoxa, 1923.

Xaližev, V. and O. Majorova. "Leskovskaja koncepcija pravedničestva." *V mire Leskova: sbornik statej.* Ed. Viktor Bogdanov. Moscow: Sovetskij pisatel', 1983. 196-232.

## Knut Andreas Grimstad (essay date 1999)

SOURCE: Grimstad, Knut Andreas. "Micro-Harmony in Russian Realism: Leskov's Language of Feeling." In *Dialogue and Rhetoric: Communication Strategies in Russian Text and Theory,* edited by Ingunn Lunde, pp. 55-71. Bergen, Norway: University of Bergen, 1999.

[*In the following essay, Grimstad discusses the shift toward sentimentality and emphasis on feelings and emotionality exhibited in the works of late nineteenth-century Russian realist writers, focusing in particular on Leskov's* Cathedral Folk.]

Запел и я себе от восторга и умиленно заплакал.
В этих целебных слезах я облегчил мои
досаждения и понял, сколь глупа была скорбь

моя, и долго после дивился, как дивно врачует
природа недуги души человеческой!

By the second half of the nineteenth century, many
Russian writers sought to answer the so-called "accursed questions," hoping to revitalize their Orthodox
belief in the direction of a less dogmatic, more "natural" Christianity. Thus joining the Russian tradition of
(heterodox) lay theology, they would represent religious
problems in fictional literature in such a manner that
conceptions of faith were creatively transposed into "realist" literature. Theological principles such as regeneration, resurrection, and a New Life were openly developed in stories and novels that no longer wished to
represent merely the love between human beings, but a
transcendent aspect of this love, aspiring to overcome
death. Although in this process, the (pre-)romantic, sentimentalist shift from "head to heart" played a substantial role, Russian realist prose instigated its own version
of *Empfindsamkeit* which was nurtured, stylistically and
rhetorically, by the edificatory writings of the *Philokalia*. Intended for lay people living in the world as well
as for monks, this "neo-Hesychast" anthology of early
Christian and medieval texts combined the ascetic and
mystical with the corporate and social aspect of monastic life. In particular, it laid emphasis on the idea of the
*heart* as the embodiment of the *whole* person, compris-
ing both intellect, will and emotions; the practice of the
continual "prayer of the heart," which was offered spontaneously by the whole of one's being; and the need for
obedience to a *starets* or elder, for whom the spiritual
ward (*dukhovnyi syn*) could reveal each of his thoughts.[1]
It is precisely the Hesychast tradition which informs
Nikolai Leskov's texts of the 1870s: the values of emotionality, or the spontaneity of feelings, shape the representation of contemporary Russian characters, whose
spiritual power to observe and understand life in its
simple, everyday manifestations is often idealized as a
specifically Russian trait (cf. *dukhovnost'*). In this light,
the objective of my essay will be to explore the view of
man as constructed in Leskov's "national romantic" fiction, as well as the attitudes that underlie his rendering
of cultural encounters within the Empire.

I propose to focus on one salient feature of his texts,
the critical opinion of which include everything from
praise to pity: that is, the sentimental mode of writing.[2]
Here Victor Terras' description of Leskov's narrative
prose as "funny, entertaining, moving, and wholesomely
sentimental"[3] is actually quite useful, as it points to the
competitive relationship between bathos and pathos,
which is typical of the writer's humorous hero worship.[4] However, to my mind, the degree of sentimentality (*sentimental'-nost'*) as such, of indulging excessively in or appealing directly to emotions, seems less
important than the rhetorical implications of the sentimental dimension in his fictional universe as a whole.
Before embarking upon our analysis of one of Leskov's

best-known works, the chronicle-novel *Cathedral Folk
(Soboriane,* 1872), it will be useful to point to the significance of the primary locale for most texts produced
in this decade: the Russian provinces.

In order to appear "real," and to take on the function of
a memory site (*locus*), this non-urban setting must be
recognized as distinctly Russian and provincial through
well-established, easily remembered, descriptive features. The idea is to use certain *topoi,* which implement
a mode of narration that is capable of evoking a social
response, of creating an illusion that may be perceived
by more than one reader. Rhetorically speaking, the
sentimental dimension in Leskov's representation of life
in the *uezdy* is thus geared towards the creation of an
accessible fiction, capable of inspiring the reader's affa-
bility and sympathetic disposition. Further, it informs
the narrator's role in the storytelling process, which intensifies the emotional charge of the events narrated,
and which he or she can do, not by modifying the manner or content of the narrative itself, but by leaning on
the reader to effect a more intense receptivity. In brief,
the fictional world of the Russian provinces is designed
to *affect* the reader's moral sensibility, and yet it should
provide an image of a truthful, unmanipulative representation of reality. We might speak of the sentimental
dimension in Leskov's "realism" as a kind of fictionalizing impact-making.[5] Interestingly, this impact works
not only in relation to the memorableness, or "sociabil-
ity" of the text as fiction, but also to the tendency of
groups or persons to live in communities and develop
social links, as represented in the fictional text.

While Leskov's Russian heroes of the 1870s are disposed to associate together with their fellows in terms
of class, religion, or nationality, they are also constantly
forming new and unexpected alliances. In this sense,
sociality is a controlling influence on his way of writing, which is committed to the resources of a *language
of feeling* in order to represent necessary social bonds.[6]
Far from being a facile indulgence, this mode of expression can be said to reflect the difficulty which a
multicultural Empire has in imagining the nature of social relations. Hence the importance of Hesychast ideals, the notions of heartfelt sincerity and emotional response to deep and tender feeling (*umilenie*) that are so
characteristic of the manner in which the fictive characters think, act and express themselves. In other words,
Leskov's aim, in moving the reader's heart through the
use of provincial characters, appears to be to convey a
sense of the moral beauty that affects the way human
beings relate to each other, and how they perceive these
relations. As we shall see, the *idealization of responsiveness to emotion* in Leskov's texts seems to reflect,
on the one hand, the romantic, affirmative notion that
the simple people of the provinces share a "natural"
Christian faith in the divine scheme; on the other, the
case for emotional spontaneity implies the more critical

view that non-urbanized man too has moved from a state of primeval innocence, virtue, happiness and freedom, to an enlightened and over-civilized society that is morally depraved. In this way, the realization of various "sentimentalist" figurations in the text contributes to an affective verisimilitude,[7] the tensions of which ultimately guide our modern interpretation of Leskov's fiction in terms of anthropology.

### THE IMPERFECTIONS OF THE SOCIETAL IDYLL

A book of both seriousness and laughter, *Cathedral Folk* depicts the arduous life-battle of the Archpriest Savelii Tuberozov, who hopes to bring about a reform of the Russian Orthodox Church from within. As indicated by the opening pages, the narrator concentrates on the vicissitudes in the everyday lives of a clerical trinity, the members of which are simple, ingenuous, caring, sharing a sense of affinity with surrounding nature, myths and traditions; they lead their habitual lives in a sleepy, little town in "Little Russia" (Ukraine), far away from the urban capitals of Moscow and St Petersburg. The initial appeal to the reader's imaginative powers (*voobrazhenie*), the use of the folk-colloquial phrase *zhit'e-byt'e,* in the meaning of the daily grind or the quotidian, as well as the highlighting of the Archpriest's advanced age, strikes a nostalgic accent which serves as a preparation for the narrative cohesion of the *khronika* as a whole. By the same token, the quaint, slightly obsolete-sounding names of the two priests and the deacon, Tuberozov, Benefaktov and Akhilla Desnitsyn, evoke the fragrance of lilies (Latin *tuberosa*), charity (*bene factus*) and loyal service (Church Slavonic *desnitsa,* "right hand"), alluding both to low clergy tradition[8] and to the world of the Scriptures. As a memory site, the "ideal Russian town" of Stargorod ("Old-Town") takes on symbolic value as a microcosm pointing to the glory of medieval *Rus',* whilst the *topos* of the Cathedral, the *sobor,* signals the centrality of religious unity. In brief, the chronicler-narrator has established a associative field of traditionalism, ecclesiasticality and provinciality.

Typically, the ageing Tuberozov is presented to the reader as an attractive man whose head is "extremely handsome" (отлично красива) and whose eyes have both a "capacity for lighting up with the presence of intellect" (способность освещаться присутствием разума) and for yielding "the flash of joyous rapture, clouds of grief, and tears of emotion" (блеск радостного восториа, и туманы скорби, и слезы умиления, 6).[9] The Archpriest and his fellow townsfolk aspire to social justice, truth and progress, though in their day-to-day interaction, so the narrator tells us, they are striving "to vary their life by those scenes of slight enmity and misunderstanding, which beneficially aroused the natures of men lulled by the inactivity of provincial existence" (разнообразить жизнь сценами

легкой вражды и недоразумений, благодетельно будящими человеческие натуры, усыпляемые бездействием уездной жизни, 11). Amounting to little more than various ways of diverting themselves through "quarreling in order to become reconciled" (ссорились для того, чтобы мириться, 129), such reciprocity permeates the representation of Tuberozov's parish, where "night, in this quiet little town, gathers all to their nests and hearths at an early hour . . . From the far-off forest wafts a beneficent freshness" (ночь в тихом городке рано собирает всех в гнезда свои и на пепелища свои . . . Из далеких лесов доносится благотворная свежесть, 23). Characteristic of the Stargorod style of life depicted in the novel are the numerous references to rural "quietness" and "fresh" existence, which point to a fundamental *idyllizing vision* manifested in the different tonalities and different levels of narration. To the extent that the modern reader recognizes life in the cathedral town as specifically Russian and provincial, we may infer that our response results from the fictionalizing impact of the sentimental dimension. If we "believe" in the religious sensibility of the rendered characters and their stories, this is also an effect of the narrator's *re-presentation* of Tuberozov's own emotionalized idyllization:

> . . . запел и я себе от восторга и умиленно заплакал. В этих целебных слезах я облегчил мои досаждения и понял, сколь глупа была скорбь моя, и долго после дивился, как дивно врачует природа недуги души человеческой!

(36)[10]

Covering more than 35 years of his life, Tuberozov's diary, the *Demikotonovaia kniga,* is animated by sensitivity throughout. The text is informed by a distinct preoccupation with harmony, tender emotions, a moving love of man, and enlightened generosity. It is significant that although these properties fit well within the scheme of the sentimentalized idyll,[11] they come nowhere near an all-permeating, definite poetic genre, but should be seen as recurring traces of such a genre, or, better still, as transformations or hybrid forms of the idyll in contrast to the idyll *sensu stricto.* The idyll proper serves as a reservoir, out of which the idyllization can feed, as it is constructed, on different narrative levels, from topics originating from a traditional grammar of forms, imagery and stylistics. In this manner, idyllization in Leskov's novel becomes something variable and unstable.[12] In fact, it is highly ambiguous. For example, as a hero opposing both the ecclesiastical and secular authorities, the Archpriest is also a courageous preacher, who repeatedly breaks away from the enclosed world of his environment, an action which is mirrored by his pupil, the deacon Akhilla, who sets off for the big city only to return to the bosom of the family where he resumes his parochial living. Given that the sentimental dimension is instrumental, above all, in the representation of the alienated individual, the tendency of idyllize the Russian provinces does not work without its contradictions. As a world-image turned aesthetic object, *the idyllic* here coincides with Ernst Robert Curtius' definition of the idyll as *extended topos,* an intellectual theme suited to various kinds of development and adaptation.[13] The same may be said of the representation of Russian provincial life in *Cathedral Folk,* where both feelings and ideas are treated within an idyllic macro-image of human society.

In his work on the idyllic as a way of organizing fictional reality, Virgil Nemoianu establishes the *societal model* as a compact, non-utopian microcosm, which is to a great extent isolated from the wide world outside.[14] Likewise, the world of Stargorod presents a secure and protected society in close contact with nature, though not subordinated to it or identified with it, the townsfolk simply following its rhythm on a human level. Since fertility, growth and slow obsolescence are part of the pattern of life, the idyllic universe is, as Nemoianu points out, sceptical of rush, violence, abnormal and oversized actions, seeking to keep the whole together by moving slowly. However, the interference between the microcosm and the world is always troublesome. Similarly, the representation of the fictive characters in Leskov appears to be governed by a co-presence of different, separate laws—sacred and secular, irrationalist and rationalist—so that certain "oversized" actions, emotions and moral states are *not* excluded: on the contrary, ecstasy and despair, heroism and sainthood, interfere with the desired regularity and predictability. In this sense, the societal idyll in *Cathedral Folk* is "a stylized version of part of an existing society. It functions in different texts besides literary ones—in sociology, philosophy, politics, and other areas—and is thus immediately recognized by members of a society."[15] Just as the representation of Russian provincial life (*byt*) is generally marked by a heterogeneity of "texts" and styles, so the tendency towards idyllization itself consists in imperfection. Within the novel's idyllizing vision, the non-idyllic elements trigger a creative dynamism that works on the level of semantic suspension.

One example of such idyllic imperfection, as manifested in the combination of different texts, styles, and *topoi,* features Tuberozov's factotum, the deacon Akhilla. As indicated by the incongruous interior of his dwelling, Akhilla represents a multiplicity of mythic values from both the Orthodox and folkloric registers of culture; he is a "Cossack in a cassock,"[16] both fierce and feeble, internalizing, as it were, the tension between the idyll and the non-idyll. The essential variability within the idyllic microcosm is more clearly illustrated in a bathing scene, which, imbued with false mystery and mock-epic stature, opens with a description of the somnolent morning mood: "Over everything lay the shadows of twilight, and nowhere, either inside the houses, nor on the squares and in the streets, were any signs of awakening perceptible" (на всем еще лежат тени полусвета, и нигде, ни внутри домов, ни на площадях и улицах, не заметно никаких признаков пробуждения, 84). It is important that the gathering of Stargorod bathers who meet daily at the riverside, represent all social strata of the town. Collectively, they form a sentimental-romantic complex consisting of easily recognizable folk types from Russian literary and oral tradition.[17] Typical of "the simplicity of life in Stargorod" (простота старогородской жизни, 89), the uncomplicated action of this "landscape and genre picture" (пейзаж и жанр) is developed, in a similar vein, around one picturesque event: the assisting of the elderly Prefect in his matutinal bath! The innocent naturalness of the characters being complete, Mother Felisata, the only woman in the group, is at ease among the naked men; "to her, there existed no difference of sex" (различие пола для нее не существовало, 90). The weather is fine, time stands almost still, and, as the simple-hearted eccentric (*chudak*) Pizonskii puts it:

> . . . без новостей мы вот сидим как в раю; сами мы наги, а видим красу: видим йес, вдилмгоры, видим храмы, воды, зелень; вон там выводки утиные под бережком попискивают; вон рыбья мелкота целою стаей играет. Сила господня!
>
> (91)[18]

Although the idyllized description of nature is further amplified by elements of Christian rhetoric, or vice versa, the emotional words of the latter-day Holy Fool seem to carry an omen. Behind the peaceful atmosphere of what the narrator refers to as a "northern," "mysterious saga" looms the wide world outside full of people incapable of appreciating such perfect harmony; if an intruder should arrive, "everything will seem wrong to him, and he will go and pick things to pieces . . ." (все это ему покажется не так, и пойдет он разбирать . . . 91). When the Stargorodians go on to discuss the God-given privileges of living and dying in provincial tranquillity, Akhilla turns out to be extremely provoked ("remember that I'm an ecclesiastical person!"; ты помни, что я духовная особа! 92) by the young, "nihilist," seminarian-cum-schoolteacher Varnavka, who has refused to return a skeleton, so the deacon can arrange an Orthodox funeral for it. Soon, he ends up boldly accusing one of his fellow-bathers, the District Doctor, of agnosticism, declaring that he himself is prepared to take necessary measures to curb this widespread tendency—especially, since Father Savelii "doesn't know how to manage" it (он не умеет, 93). After a series of provocations, he grabs the frightened doctor and hurls himself with him into the water. Pathos and bathos co-act; in the mildly ironical words of the narrator: "Thus did Deacon Akhilla begin the eradication of the pernicious free-thinking which had established itself in Stargorod" (Так диякон Ахилла начал искоренение водворившегося в Старгороде пагубного вольномыслия, 93).

This is but one of several humorous examples of how the cathedral folk fight "in order to become reconciled": within the imperfections of the societal idyll, they mostly remain friends. But although Akhilla's larger-than-life spontaneity may be amusing on the whole, the depiction of his readiness to combat "heterodox" influences strikes a more sober note when related to the competition between different world-views and value judgements—Russian/non-Russian, Orthodox/non-Orthodox, Christian/atheist, and so on. As signalled by the deacon's reference to his spiritual father (*dukhovnyi otets*) in the bathing scene, the clash of ideologies on the level of plot shows how idyllic meaning is constantly being disturbed on the level of the text. Pertaining to both the stylistic and the rhetorical registers, the representation of an imperfect idyll in the world of *both* cathedral men highlights antagonistic ways of understanding culture, which challenge any one reading of the novel in terms of meaning. At the same time, however, a counteractive strategy is implied, where meaning is advanced through boundary crossing and transgression.

ORTHODOXY AS MICRO-HARMONY

Let us consider Tuberozov's life-long struggle against the many ills that he perceives as threatening to the very foundations of Russian culture and society.[19] Confronted by a multicultural Empire, where the virulent ideological forces of his time collide, the societal idyll holds the provincial whole together. However, due to the imperfections of the societal model, it remains vulnerable and fragile, whilst chaos becomes a viable alternative. Eagerly awaiting a future renewal of the faith of his *own* people, Tuberozov describes repeatedly in his diary how he must deal with *other* individuals who upset the Stargorod harmony: the "nihilist" activities of Varnavka; the two scheming ladies, who are corrupted by "un-Russian" ideas; and, notably, Ishmael Termosesov, a mercenary high government official, who has arrived from St Petersburg. As for Tuberozov's apocalyptic interpretation of events, idyllization seems to point towards a fictional "as if,"[20] an attempt to bridge the gap between the given and the unfathomable. The fact that the "foreign" Russian from the capital brings about the Archpriest's downfall, leaves the latter's project of renewal unresolved in the conflict between old and new; in a semantic limbo between closedness and openness, stability and change. Chaos may now be said to enter into the novel's fictional world so that mutability might exist, implying an opposition between reality and perfection, but also the possibility of other worlds. Within the novel's idyllizing vision, the language of feeling appears to be impelled by a hunger for these other worlds.

When approached through the lens of literary anthropology, the representation of idyllic imperfection in *Cathedral Folk* could be seen in terms of a *micro-harmony*. This is a "bracketed-off" world which is achieved, above all, by way of a comprehensive mythopoetic backward glance on the part of the fictive character. Instead of reconstructing the catastrophe, the battling protagonist, behind whose back the world seems about to collapse, revives congruous elements of the *status quo ante*. Rhetorically speaking, Tuberozov resorts to *simulacra*.[21] In trying to tackle the multi-layered incongruousness of his time, he often evokes images which for him (and the reader) represent mythic Russianness: national pride, religious unity, moral ideals, and so on. As we shall see, this idyllic re-presentation of cultural used-to-be's—the calling back into presence what is absent—resembles a mnemonic exercise, a way of remembering (the past) that produces an act of boundary-crossing, a doubling mechanism, where what has been overstepped (the present) is constantly kept in view. For the Archpriest and his friends, the images of the Old Russian cultural heritage only acquire meaning in the face of chaos and the threat of forgetting. Hence the need for retrospective nostalgia. So too for the narrator: the establishing of a micro-harmony by way of "remembering" Orthodox ideas and rituals, functions well in the portrayal of the relationship between Tuberozov and his tenderhearted, all-sacrificing spouse (*popad'ia*), Natal'ia Nikolaevna:

> Протопопица сама никогда не ужинала. она обыкновенно только сидела перед мужем, пока он закусывал, и оказывала ему небольШие услуги, то что-нибудь подавая, то принимая и убирая. Потом они оба вставали, молились пред образом и непосредственно за тем оба начинали крестить один другого . . . Получив взаимные благословения, супруги напутствоваги друг друга и взаимным поцелуем, причем отец протопоп целовал свою низенькую жену в лоб, а она его в сердце; затем они расставались: протопоп уходил в свою гостиную и вскоре ложился.
>
> (27-28)[22]

This is one of many idyllized descriptions where the narrative atmosphere is permeated by unpretentious love and companionship. Sexuality is toned down—now child-like and playful, now serene, almost "angelic"—which, in turn, makes the ritualistic tenderness between husband and wife all the more conspicuous. In Tuberozov's own sentimental-romantic depiction, the focus is on *kisses*:

> . . . подхожу к ней спящей и спящую ее целую, и если чем огорчен, то в сем отрадном поцелуе почерпаю снова бодрость и силу и тогда засыпая покойно. . . . чувствовал плохую женку мою в душе моей, и поелику душа моя лобзала ее, я не вздумал ни однажды подойти к ней и поцеловать ее.
>
> (39-40)[23]

—and on *tears*:

> В тихой грусти, двое бездетные, сели мы за чай,
> но был то не чай, а слезы наши растворялись нам
> в питие, и незаметно для себя мы оба заплакали,
> и оборучь пали мы ниц пред образом Спаса . . .
> [Я] пал пред ней на колени и, поклонясь ей до
> земли, зарыдал тем рыданием, которому нет на
> свете описания. Да и вправду, поведайте мне вре-
> мена и народы, где, кроме святой Руси нашей,
> родятся такие женйдны, как сия добродетель?

(38, 39)[24]

The ingenuousness of the couple's married life points to a simplicity (*prostota*) that reveals an Orthodox sub-text, or way of perceiving the world, which is linked to "the attitude of the ordinary man towards God, in his prayer and his moral life" (Fedotov),[25] to the natural-ness, as it were, of life itself (*samaia zhizn'*). However, just as the social innocence of Akhilla and the bathers is challenged by "foreign," "un-provincial" elements, so too the everyday bliss of Tuberozov. Simplicity is coun-tered by complexity. Therefore, the Archpriest is con-tinually creating micro-harmony through idyllization.

For instance, degraded and frustrated by the duty im-posed on him by his church superiors to combat sectari-anism, he pursues fortitude through various forms of af-firmation.[26] Eager to reinforce his opposition to the proselytizing policy of the official Church, as well as his struggle against the morally corrupt elements of the Empire ("the Schismatics live up to their errors, while we neglect our right path; and that, I think, is the most important"; раскольники блюдут свое заблуждение, а мы своим правым путем небрежем; а сие, мню, яко важнейшее, 32), he rejoices in the news of his wife's pregnancy. Typically, the Archpriest seeks tem-porary relief from overwhelming negativity by donning the mask of positive domesticity: "This morning. *March 18, 1836,* my wife Natal'ia Nikolaevna, hinted to me that she felt herself heavy with child. May the Lord grant us that joy!" (Сегодня утром. *18- о     ce о 1836    od ,* попаппя наталья Николаевна, Намекнула мне, что она чувствует себя неп-орожнею. Подай господи нам сию радость! 33). Sadly, the expectancy turns out to be "the fruit of her kind imagination" (плод ее доброй фантазии, 38). At one point, his wife discreetly suggests they adopt any bastard child from her husband's supposed frivolous past ("Isn't there an orphan somewhere?"; то нет ли где какого сиротки? 39), her will to sacrifice herself being so overwhelming to Tuberozov that he falls on his knees and bows down in front of her, sobbing and giving praise to her, to the virtuous women of Russia, and to the Lord, who has bestowed such a happiness upon him. As the ideas of piety and moral rectitude are explained in terms of tears and kisses, that is, of simple and sincere emotions, the micro-harmony often takes on the form of an *Orthodox idyll.*

Here the interrelated images of children and parent-hood, orphans and childlessness, so frequent in the speech of the novel's narrator and characters, are firmly established within an Orthodox anthropology. For all Orthodox Russians, the ultimate task in life is to create in themselves the likeness of God the Father in imita-tion of the archetype of Christ the Son. This kind of Christian self-realization is carried out many times over in the portrayal of the interaction between the novel's provincial characters: the father-son theme is introduced by Tuberozov in his idyllization of Pizonskii, "the nour-isher of orphans" (сирых питатель, 37), who adopts the baby boy of a half-witted girl and whose simplicity of faith becomes a major source of homiletic inspira-tion; incidentally, the Archpriest's mild, but constant, patronization of his "simple-minded Natasha" (простодушная Наташа моя, 51) reflects in many ways a traditional spiritual father-daughter relationship. The *topos* of the father-figure (*starets*), however, is most effectively developed in the depiction of his spon-taneous love for Akhilla: "I love him terribly—without myself knowing why"; "May God forgive and bless him, for the fascinating simplicity of his heart . . . I feel that I have come to love that kindly man with a truly paternal weakness"; (я его смертельно люблю—сам за что не ведая; Бог прости и благослови его за его пленительную сердца простоту . . . Чувст-вую, я со всею отеческою слабостию полюбил сего доброго человека, 65, 69). After the death of his wife, the two men decide to live together, their profound companionship being modelled "sentimentally" on the Hesychast idea of monastic eldership (*starchestvo*), as described in the popular *Philokalia* compilation. Tu-berozov aspires to provide Akhilla with personal guid-ance and to let him hear the judgement of the Holy Fa-thers. More importantly, the representation of the *chudak*, the Archpriest's wife and the deacon as epito-mes of compassion and emotional simplicity, comple-ments Tuberozov's "reading" of his own life as an *imi-tatio Christi*, that is, an imitation of the ultimate father-son relationship.[27]

Throughout the Archpriest's endeavour to understand his place as a priest in Stargorodian society, idyllization serves as a way of world-making in order to postpone the inevitable "sense of an ending."[28] Therefore, consid-ering that he has a wife, but is deprived of a family—and tends to seek other forms of sociality in, for ex-ample, his fellow countryman Akhilla and various officials of foreign origin—it is striking that in the cosy company of Natal'ia Nikolaevna his being *out of place* is actually confirmed. When she, at one point, dozes off—her husband's enthused speech on Russia's pre-dicament being far beyond her—Tuberozov seems to realize that a marginalized outsider, like himself, will always struggle alone: "every one who sees a little fur-ther than his brother will be lone among his own people" (всяк, кто подальше брата видит, будет одинок промеж своих, 203). Within the novel's senti-mentalized rendering of Orthodox domesticity, the themes of childlessness, orphan- and parenthood are linked here to that of a more *universal* alienation, which, in marked contrast to the Russian Orthodox ideal of unity in multiplicity (*sobornost'*), represents rather *un*-Orthodox forms of being.[29] In this way, the struggle of the Archpriest, who as fictive character is placed in an in-between-sphere of two views on culture, one affirmative and closed, one negative and open, becomes another example of how idyllic imperfection is revealed in the text.

Typically, the narrator employs the rhetorical strategy of "loyally" rendering Tuberozov's idyllizing mind: having recognized the distance between himself and his beloved spouse, the Archpriest is immersed in the micro-harmony of the ordinary and the prosaic, now Christian in a more general sense: "And the old man rose softly from the bed, in order not to disturb the repose of his sleeping wife, made the sign of the cross over her, and having filled his pipe, went outside and seated himself on the porch" (И старик тихо под-нялся с кровати, чтобы не нарушить покоя спящей жены, перекрестил ее и, набив свою трубку, вы-шел с нею на двор и присел на крылечке, 203). Here the crossing of boundaries in the text between unity and separation, openness and closedness, implies that idyllic meaning is suspended. The thoughts and actions of the Russian parish priest emerge in an ambiguous light, which, in turn, motivates a number of different readings of the way Russian provincial life is represented in the novel as a whole.

### The Multiple Facets of the Idyllic

In accordance with our understanding of "sentiment" as the capacity for responding to emotion and impression, as well as a thought, opinion or attitude, the sentimental mode of writing in Leskov's fiction of the 1870s fulfils several functions. First, it makes his prose affable and accessible by creating an impact. The use of material which is easily recognized as Russian, provincial, and "of the Empire," facilitates the reader's emotional response to the text, so that he or she can fictionalize the characters and their interrelationships represented within it. Second, the "straddling of feeling and idea"[30] reflects the co-presence in Leskov's text of two sets of perspectives upon man and culture, two prevalent ideological spheres, which are inspired by Romanticism and the Enlightenment respectively. On the one hand, we have an idealistic understanding of culture that is informed by unity and integrity, roots and tradition, affinity and a given identity—on the other, one which is shaped by change and disruption, complexity, disorder, openness and unpredictability. The friction between the emotional-romantic (particularism) and the "realistic"-enlightened (universalism) is manifested on the level of competing

stylistic attitudes, edifying ones and critical ones, which are the hallmark of Leskov's "language of feeling." To be sure, we are not interested in dualities and binarisms as such, but in the space between, the middle ground, where styles, texts and values commingle and establish relations, in "the playful mixing together of such heterogeneous elements."[31] In this sense, the sentimental dimension, or the creative play on the emotions, in *Cathedral Folk* becomes important as a rhetorical force.

The idyllic is structured according to its own rules using the societal model almost as if it were an epithet or a metaphor. As a hybrid form, the societal idyll in the novel can be seen as a macro-image constituted by the combination of several *topoi* and motifs, with different intellectual themes and fragments of world views. As I have shown, the sentimental idyllization of the Russian provinces often therefore takes the form of an Orthodox micro-harmony, whose existence is delicately dependent on the interplay of different textual elements (or codes) in the semiotic space of the text. In this way, the semantic tension within the "imperfect" idyllizing vision itself contributes towards the novel's affective verisimilitude, or, to use another of Michael Bell's terms, its *sentiment of reality*.[32]

Finally, bearing in mind the fictive characters' striving to deal with chaotic reality, the constant failure of the text to establish the quiet repetitive predictability of an idyllic framework points to the changeability of provincial life itself. Here the constant crossing of *cultural* boundaries would seem to indicate that the semantic potential of sentimental idyllization, or micro-harmony, has many facets: it counteracts various aspects of the foreign or the strange (*chuzhoe*) within the complexity of the contemporary Empire. However, as may be witnessed on the different levels of narration, the urge for sameness is always doubled by the urge for otherness, so that any one-sided idea of Russianness and of a Russian national character is contradicted. In this sense, Leskov's "national romantic" novel offers an intriguing example of how Orthodox conceptions of faith, man and culture, have been transposed ambivalently into Russian Realism.

### *Notes*

1. Timothy Ware, 1997, *The Orthodox Church,* London, p. 117ff.

2. I. V. Stoliarova, 1978, *V poiskakh ideala: tvorchestvo N. S. Leskova,* Leningrad, p. 86, writes about "the warmth of feeling" and "the emotional surplus" of the fictive heroes, linking the manifestation of emotions, especially of romantic feelings, to the Russian national character, while Hugh McLean, 1977, *Nikolai Leskov: The Man and His Art,* Cambridge, Mass., p. 120, 144, states that certain works "veer perilously close to sentimen-

tality" or are "sentimental and lacking in psychological validity."

3. Victor Terras, 1991, *A History of Russian Literature,* New Haven, p. 363.

4. D. S. Mirsky, 1949, *A History of Russian Literature,* London, p. 316.

5. Cf. Wolfgang Iser, 1989, "Toward a Literary Anthropology," *Prospecting: From Reader Response to Literary Anthropology,* Baltimore, pp. 262-284.

6. John Mullan, 1989, *Sentiment and Sociality: The Language of Feeling in the Eighteenth Century,* Oxford, p. 2ff.

7. I here use Michael Bell's term, which denotes "the unstable tensions within any literalistically conceived fiction that has a manifest moral design upon its reader." See Michael Bell, 1983, *The Sentiment of Reality: Truth of Feeling in the European Novel,* London, p. 3.

8. Lennart Kjellberg, 1964, *Den klassiska romanens Ryssland,* Gothenburg, p. 152.

9. My translation of Leskov's text is in some places rather loosely based on *The Cathedral Folk,* transl. I. F. Hapgood, Westport, Conn., 1924. Page numbers refer to the Russian original, N. S. Leskov, 1956-1958, *Sobranie sochinenii v odinnadtsati tomakh,* vol. 4, Moscow.

10. "I too began to sing, and in my rapture, fell to weeping with emotion. In those healing tears, I alleviated my vexations, and realized how stupid was my grief, and for a long time thereafter I was lost in amazement at the wonderful way in which Nature heals the ills of the human soul!"

11. Cf. Gitta Hammarberg, 1991, *From the Idyll to the Novel: Karamzin's Sentimentalist Prose,* Cambridge, p. 50.

12. Wolfgang Preisendanz, 1986, "Reduktionsformen des Idyllischen im Roman des neunzehnten Jahrhunderts (Flaubert, Fontane)," *Idylle und Modernisierung in der europäischen Literatur des 19. Jahrhunderts,* eds. H. U. Seeber & P. G. Klussmann, Bonn, pp. 81-92, pp. 81-82, has shown how the idyll in nineteenth-century narrative literature is a plotless text capable of appearing only as a partial aspect of represented reality, establishing a "semantic field" in the reality model of the text, which stands in opposition to other "semantic fields."

13. Ernst Robert Curtius, 1948, *Europäische Literatur und Lateinisches Mittelalter,* Bern, p. 77.

14. Virgil Nemoianu, 1977, *Micro-Harmony: The Growth and Uses of the Idyllic Model in Literature,* Bern, p. 18ff.

15. Virgil Nemoianu, 1989, *A Theory of the Secondary: Literature, Progress, and Reaction,* Baltimore, p. 128.

16. McLean, 1977, p. 192.

17. Faith Wigzell, 1988, "Leskov's *Soboryane*: A Tale of Good and Evil in the Russian Provinces," *Modern Language Review* 83 (4), pp. 901-910.

18. ". . . here we sit without novelties, as though we were in paradise; we are naked ourselves, and we behold beauty: we see the forest, we see the mountains, we see the temples, the water, the green; yonder are the broods of ducklings cheeping near the shore; yonder are the little fishes playing in a regular school. 'Tis the power of the Lord."

19. In this connection, considerable attention has been given to the points of similarity between the life of the Archpriest in *Cathedral Folk* and the seventeenth-century *vita* (*zhitie*) of the Archpriest Avvakum, the Schismatic leader who also fought against the ecclesiastical authorities.

20. Wolfgang Iser, 1993, *The Fictive and the Imaginary: Charting Literary Anthropology,* Baltimore, p. 12ff.

21. See Renate Lachmann, 1997, *Memory and Literature: Intertextuality in Russian Modernism,* Minneapolis, pp. 8-9.

22. "The Archpriest's wife herself never supped. As a rule, she merely sat opposite her husband while he had a bite, and rendered him small services, now handing him something, again receiving and removing a dish. Then they both rose, prayed in front of the holy picture, and immediately afterwards began to make the sign of the cross over each other . . . Having received this mutual blessing, the husband and wife took leave with a mutual kiss, the Father Archpriest kissing his diminutive wife on the brow, and she kissing him on the heart. Then they parted: the Archpriest went to his parlour, and soon into bed."

23. ". . . I go up to her as she sleeps and kiss her in her slumber, and if I am pained at anything, in that consoling kiss, I drink fresh courage and strength, and then I go calmly to sleep. . . . I felt my naughty little wife in my soul, and so long as my soul kissed her, it never once occurred to me to go to her and kiss her."

24. "In quiet grief, we two childless people sat down to drink tea—but it was not the tea, but our tears that became our drink, and without noticing it ourselves, we both began to weep, and hand in hand fell down upon our knees before the Holy Image of the Saviour . . . I fell on my knees in front of her, and bowing to the ground before her,

I began to sob; it was a sobbing which no one on this earth can describe. Really and truly, show me a time or a nation outside of our Holy Russia where women are born such as this image of virtue!"

25. George P. Fedotov, 1946, *The Russian Religious Mind,* Cambridge, Mass., vol. 1, p. 213.

26. In this respect, the diary entries can be said to illustrate Tuberozov's *narrative thinking.*

27. For an analysis of Tuberozov as an *imitator Christi,* and of Akhilla who echoes the transformational aspect of the Archpriest's life, see my article "The Rhetoric of an Archpriest: Nikolai Leskov and the Orthodox Heritage," *Cultural Discontinuity and Reconstruction: The Byzanto-Slav Heritage and the Creation of a Russian National Literature in the Nineteenth Century,* eds. J. Børtnes & I. Lunde, Oslo, 1997, pp. 217-236.

28. Frank Kermode, 1967, *The Sense of an Ending: Studies in the Theory of Fiction,* Oxford, pp. 3-35.

29. I. A. Esaulov, 1995, *Kategoriia sobornosti v russkoi literature,* Petrozavodsk, p. 61ff.

30. Bell, 1983, p. 121.

31. Lachmann, 1997, p. 33.

32. Bell, 1983.

## Knut Andreas Grimstad (essay date 2000)

SOURCE: Grimstad, Knut Andreas. "Styles and Stories in the Fiction of Nikolai Leskov." In *Severnyi sbornik: Proceedings of the NorFA Network in Russian Literature 1995-2000,* edited by Peter Alberg Jensen and Ingunn Lunde, pp. 158-70. Stockholm: Almqvist & Wiksell International, 2000.

[*In the following essay, Grimstad considers Leskov's use of a multitude of different styles in his fiction and examines how this technique affected his ideas concerning the making and unmaking of Russian myths.*]

While the literary prose of Nikolai Leskov is usually praised for its storytelling and stylistic qualities, its "verbal wizardry" still raises some problematic issues. The nineteenth-century idea of an exuberant prose writer who "could not keep his talent within bounds," whose stories consist of "too many good things" (Tolstoy),[1] has been largely accepted by modern scholars. Many of his longer prose works are considered to be brilliantly narrated, but weakly composed; generically composite, they come across as either "too leisurely, too uneventful, too placid"[2] or "diffuse," "flabby, disorganized and incoherent."[3] If we look at Leskov's formal *bricolage*

from the point of view of his blatantly complex language, current criticism is similarly influenced by the view that a disunity of style[4] opposes the unobtrusive stylistic standard that is assumed to be characteristic of mainstream nineteenth-century Russian Realism. Typically, the writer is rated charming, but secondary—that is, outstanding within the Russian tradition, but not canonical in the Bloomian sense; or, to cite Victor Terras: a "genius" of linguistic originality, whose language is "unfortunately, untranslatable." Due to his "mannerist" form, which foregrounds "fortuitous detail of language," Leskov's prose takes on an "ephemeral quality, so that people can no longer read him."[5]

When the copiousness of Leskov's language does not comfortably fit within the framework of what is considered the "classic" Russian literature,[6] this is because, in my view, the multitude of social and cultural voices in his texts have been difficult to deal with productively, or in a fashion that anticipates the needs of the contemporary reader. In taking up this challenge, I propose to focus on some structuring mechanisms in Leskov's texts on the level of stylistic multiplicity. Accumulation, inventories of stylistic qualities, listed according to some pre-determined scheme, concern me very little, partly because such extensive analyses are available elsewhere,[7] and partly because my ambition is to provide a more "synthetic" account. Concentrating on the relationship between styles and the telling of stories, I am more eager to consider different (con)textual relations within Leskov's fiction, between styles, rhetoric, and culture.

### MINGLING, CONFLICT AND SYNCRETISM

Although a verbal-ideological centre for Leskov's fictional texts does exist, the lack of a unitary language or style should be viewed as a higher order of style, a *style of styles.*[8] The diverse languages of everyday life are orchestrated into a heterogeneous whole, whilst the author, as the creator of this whole, cannot be found at any one of the text's language levels. The author is, as Bakhtin insists with regard to the novel, "to be found at the center of organization where all levels intersect."[9] Viewed in this light, the multiplicity of styles, or the *stylistic mingling,* in Leskov's narrative prose is better taken as part of a fundamental heterogeneity—as a textual *modus operandi* pertaining to various levels of design and designation.

As indicated by Hugh McLean, the concentration of "coloured" language in the speech of the Leskovian hero-narrator brings together voices from different eras, cultures and milieus, thereby informing the text with a larger resonance.[10] To my mind, the *linking of stylistic diversity to cultural difference* seems even more valuable when considered within the bounds of "a rhetorical theory of the text."[11] In Leskov's fiction, the blending of stylistic levels—oral, written, secular, religious, provincial, urban, church, non-church, archaic, contemporary—can be said to compete with a *decorum*-oriented system, thus suspending the border between the rhetorical spheres of the official and the unofficial, on the one hand, and the native and the foreign on the other. In turn, this boundary crossing allows two contexts, or utterances, to enter into conflictual contact, so that a permanent semantic difference is released which is likely to disturb any reading based on a single meaning. Conceived of as a motley representation of people and places in the Russian Empire, Leskov's fiction, then, may be said to "resonate" with a multiplicity of meanings caused by rhetorical transgression.[12]

In so far as *decorum* as a stylistic criterion locates itself finally in the beholder and not in the speech or text (no textual pattern *per se* is decorous or not), it may be described as a kind of intuitive judgement dependent on patterns of inherited, "tacit" knowledge. Such a judgement is not only a rhetorical criterion; it becomes a general test of basic acculturation. For example, in order to establish the "decorum" of a particular situation, say, somewhere in the Russian provinces, the fictive character of a priest or deacon (and the "beholding" reader) has to learn to find his or her footing in that culture. This cognitive process will always involve the assimilation of cultural traits belonging to other subgroups.[13] In thus understanding rhetoric as a cultural model, a way of both possessing and processing culture,[14] our main interest in Leskov's representation of Russia is motivated by the productive potential of multicultural communication.

In talking about styles we are talking about choice or, more precisely, the rhetorical choice between the various shades of meaning that cluster around a given subject.[15] While most of Leskov's texts are permeated by the "rhetorical choice" of the Russian Orthodox heritage, the stylistic mingling reflects a collision of different value judgements, world-views, or ways of understanding culture, as well as the possibility of competition and exchange between them. A fictive character may resort to Russian Orthodox literature, wishing to consolidate his idea of a great national tradition, yet may be just as prone to exploit non-Russian, non-Orthodox journals from abroad. By the same token, another character may express his wish to emulate the moral attitudes of his devout co-religionists, whilst he advocates "athetist" ideas acquired from foreign friends. In both cases, the hybridization of styles[16] points to the phenomenon of *syncretism,* which not only presupposes a confrontation of antithetical stylistic attitudes, but also requires further textual instances of how these conflictual attitudes are intertwined with the cultural models with which they correspond. As Renate Lachmann explains, "in the intertextual text, syncretism brings about the synchronization, as well as the contamination, of

both heterogenous styles and the semantic and cultural experience accumulated within them."[17] Stylistic mingling, then, appears to indicate an intertextual common ground where colliding views on humankind and culture are exchanged and mutually interfere.

Let me try to demonstrate how Leskov's representation of people and society in Imperial Russia is structured by means of a basic syncretism, so that two opposite semantic potentials interact and are developed simultaneously: *mythopoeia,* that is, the creation of Russian myths, and *mythic decomposition,* the deflation of Russianness and ideas of national superiority. Through examples taken from the novel *Cathedral Folk* (1872), I will illustrate how various myth-making movements contribute to the design, or constitution, of the texts of the two central characters as well as that of the primary narrator. One question I will address is how syncretism, with all its cultural and ideological implications, acts on different levels of storytelling; another will be why the author, a syncretic thinker, who oversteps generic as well as textual limits in his intertextual practices, has a predilection for this type of verbal expression. It seems useful to begin with the diary of the novel's main hero, the Archpriest Savelii Tuberozov, which constitutes a "matrix" for the Leskovian stylistic material, as it were, in distilled form.

### Meaning in-between Styles/Texts

Presented by the narrator as a written life account, "whispered" forth by the diarist to himself (станем тихо и почтительно слушать тихий шепот его старческих уст, 29),[18] the *Demikotonovaia kniga* combines the intimate and anecdotal.[19] Judging from the frequent use of hortatives and apostrophes (Оле и вам, ближние мои, братья мои [. . .]! 34; о слепец [. . .] о глупец! скажу тебе 57; О, ляше правителю, будете вы теперь сию проделку свою помнить! 57; and so on), the Archpriest is imagining a reader. As creating subject, he displays a rather self-conscious literary mind with a bent towards the confessional mode of writing. He attempts, in various ways, to come to terms with the "exasperated enmity and hatred towards faith" (ожесточенная вражда и ненависть к вере, 83), which he takes to be clear indicators of the steadily eroding fabric of Russian society, of its internal strife, corruption and lack of unity. For our own purposes, we observe that the second entry, where Tuberozov recounts how he is reprimanded as a young, newly ordained priest by his bishop for alluding in his sermons to real life, points to his preoccupation with style and various means of expression: дабы в проповедях прямого отношения к жизни делать опасался, особливо же насчет чиновников, ибо от них-де чем дальше, тем и освященнее (30). The quoting of these admonitory words reflects a certain homiletic standard by which the Archpriest measures his pastoral work. As we shall see, the problem of religious "naturalness" and the urge to communicate the ideals of Russian culture's pervasive spirituality (*dukhovnost'*) lie at the core of a whole sequence of confrontations he describes between those who *genuinely* cherish their faith and those who pay lip-service, "who officially defend it" (кои официально за нее заступаются, 83).

In this process, Tuberozov tends to confront the corruption of moral and religious ideals in Imperial Russia with an idea of genuine Russianness, the stress being on religious sensibility, on the values of simplicity, sincerity and sensitivity (*prostota, iskrennost', chuvstvitel'nost'*). For instance, his all-sacrificing wife (*popad'ia*) and the town's simpleton and latter day Holy Fool (*iurodivyi*), are both portrayed as bearers of the Russian Orthodox tradition, of what he terms the *staraia skazka* (literally, "the old fairytale").[20] Both characters emerge as innocent personifications of an imaginary, "tender-hearted *Rus'*," (мягкосердечная Русь, 36) of bygone days, but also as natural evidence of "our being constantly transfigured" (всегдашнего себя преображения, 36), that is, of the spiritual importance of ordinary, everyday life (*byt*). When Tuberozov is reprimanded a second time by his superiors for having "improvised" (импровизация, 43) a sermon scandalously dedicated to a "live person" (живое лицо, 43), he refuses to be a preacher working under duress: he cannot express himself through "rhetorical exercises" (риторические упражнения, 43) and insists on creating "living speech" (живая речь, 43). As can be seen in an apostrophe to contemporary writers and thinkers, the rhetoric of his narrative continues to be informed by a yearning for "real life" (Аах, сколь у нас везде всего живого боятся! 43) and a wish to stress the relevance of the quotidian. . . .

As his anti-dogmatic crusade against the official Church unfolds, a stylistic juxtaposition is developed in the text between a positive and a negative sphere, and—its rhetorical corollary—between the genuine and the artificial. . . .

In paraphrasing the prophet Isaiah and the Psalms, the Archpriest achieves a parallel between his own plight as a struggling archpriest and the heroic mission of two biblical figures.[21] It is here important that Moses is not only a majestic leader and law-maker, who guides his wandering people towards the Promised Land, but also the person who communicates most intimately with God.[22] Similarly, the sacred songs of King David are an expression of faith in national salvation within a larger divine scheme, as well as one of personal joy and sorrow. In alluding to the two heroes of the Bible, whilst, at the same time, exhorting Russian writers of literary fiction to avoid "empty-worded lectures" and to pay heed to "the actual life which people live," the Archpriest brings together the "official" scriptural text with

his own "unofficial" text in such a way that the real-life relevance of both is highlighted. As a consequence, he emerges as an advocate of genuineness and sincerity, as a bearer of that great old Russian tradition, which he is prone to ascribe to his wife and to the town simpleton.

However, the dual "pre-text" of a prophet well-known for his condemnation of religious hypocrisy and moral corruption, on the one hand, and of a king who repeatedly succumbs to wordly temptations, on the other, challenges the intended intertextuality. Especially so, since the allusion to Moses as a model mediator is also dubious: the fact that Moses' wish to be shown the divine glory of God's face is never fulfilled, indicates a rather insufficient communication.[23] Considering that the Archpriest aspires throughout his life to preach a "natural" faith to his countrymen (христианство еще на Руси не проповедано, 59), but resigns himself only too often to trivia and spiritual indifference, the significance of the parallel as "intertext" lies primarily in the production of semantic difference. As a fictive figure, Tuberozov fluctuates here between two stylistic spheres—one affirmative, that of the biblical universe; the other critical, that of provincial "reality"—in such a way that several world-views are embraced simultaneously, Russian as well as non-Russian. This ambiguous composition of mythic naturalness is reinforced with the arrival of the new Deacon, Akhilla Desnitsyn, who appeals immediately to the Archpriest and his ideal of "a very heartfelt sincerity" (весьма добрая искренность, 68).

Racing around like a Kirghiz horseman, the "Cossack-like Deacon" (какаковатый дъякон, 65) steals, fights, and lashes out; he bestows unwarranted blessings on the parishoners, teaches the children absurdist verse to be performed before the town mayor, sings in a Polish Catholic choir and, to top it all, acts in a scandalous amateur play. Although he ends up condoning the behaviour of his factotum, Tuberozov finds it difficult to accept fully such uncontrolled levity (легкомысленность, 71). An interesting tension now emerges in the text, as the mythopoetic line is blurred, between the natural responsiveness to feelings—which Tuberozov attributes to the Deacon (Сколъ детски близок этот Ахилла к природе, и сколъ все его в ней занимает! 75)—and the emotional, yet highly mundane, "propensities" that underlie the outrageous actions of "his Achilles" (живые наклонности моего любезного Ахиллеса, 69). Given that the Archpriest is constantly subjected to ridicule and degradation, the craziness of the Deacon reflects back on him, upsetting the more ambitious side of his aspirations—both his personal ones, as a husband, friend and Christian fellow being striving for self-improvement, and his social ones, as a "useless Russian priest," struggling for the religious reform of both his own parish and Imperial Russia as a whole.

The ambiguousness of the Deacon in the context of mythmaking is modified with the homecoming of the young seminarian Varnava Prepotenskii. Through a series of anecdotes, Tuberozov describes how the "nihilist" cynically corrupts schoolchildren with foreign ideas, conspires with other scheming "free-thinkers" in the town, socializes disgracefully with Polish officials, and even condemns the Empire's expansion in Poland. Severe disapproval and outrage underlie the Archpriest's account of how the "enlightener" (просветителъ, 74) boils the bones of a drowned man "in the interests of enlightenment" (в интересах просвещения, 82). Just as the Deacon is described as a trusted friend in terms of idealized old "Russian" virtues, so the seminarian is represented in the image of the traditional demonized arch-enemy (научителъ пакостей; супостат; ехидный враг, 73-74). Whilst making local discord the driving force behind the mythopoetic movements in his storytelling, Tuberozov typically interprets people and events "antithetically", by opposing the emotional with the rational, the familiar with the foreign.

But the depiction of Varnava's "un-Russian" provocations takes on additional meaning when viewed in the light of the many diary references to the Marshal of the Nobility as "this Voltairian of mine" (волътерянин-то мой, 76). In the heat of the battle, Tuberozov demands from his collaborator (человек земли, а не наемщик, и пожалеет ee, 75) that the seminarian be reprimanded. Then, as his problems are greeted with sympathy but little action, his tone becomes more ironical (Сей Туганов, некогда чтителъ Волътера, заговорид со мною с грустъю и в наидруженнейшем тоне, 79-80). Then he seems to recognize insincerity and indifference in the Marshal's speech: Какая сухменностъ в этих словах, но я уже не воздражал [. . .]. Что уж делатъ! Боже! помози ты хотя *се ееи*, а то взаправду не доспетъ бы нам до табунного скитания, пожирания корней и конского ржания (80). His attitude towards "Voltairian" thinking and to other forms of foreign influence is, of course, far from unequivocal.

Further evidence of Tuberozov's ambivalence towards reason and rationality emerges from his appetite for illegal books, which he, interestingly, has to borrow from his enemies, from Polish and German government officials. One example of such *unofficial* literature are the memoirs of the eighteenth-century Russian woman intellectual, Princess Dashkova (с мнениями Дашковой во многом я согласен, 64). More importantly, his clandestine reading also includes the "non-conformist" writer Laurence Sterne. . . .

In quoting the life and opinions of two foreign, non-Orthodox novelists (Sterne, Cervantes) to back up his "conclusion" with regard to the state of affairs in present-day Russia, Tuberozov blends together a variety of stylistic levels. Thus, the register of Russian apocalypticism ("nihilism is at an end [. . .] Shandyism is commencing"; "Rus' has entered upon the phase") *and* the references to the "witty Reverend Sterne" are linked to the Russian priest's conviction about the moral frivolousness of his own people. Rhetorically, we might say that he resorts to the style and ideas of the enlightened English writer with the purpose of identifying the ills of the Empire, as well as of describing his own predicament within it. In spite of the prediction that one non-Russian evil ("nihilism") will be followed by another (Shandyism)—and that these elements hamper the revival of Russian moral rectitude—Tuberozov's understanding of the nation's future originates, intertextually, *in-between* a multitude of opposing ways of understanding culture and the world: sincere-artificial, emotional-rational, foreign-Russian, official-unofficial, Orthodox-non-Orthodox, and so on. Consequently, whilst the Archpriest's interpretation complies with the usual antithetical pattern, his favourite myth of Russia's unique place in history, and, ultimately, his idea of himself as a defender of unique "Russian" values, is no longer unshakeable but punctured and tends towards decomposition.

In the subsequent entries, Tuberozov gives his version of how the *bogatyr'* Akhilla takes upon himself the task of combatting the "madness" (безумие, 75) of the seminarian Varnava. The latter has now made the bones into a skeleton and hung it up in his window, directly "opposite the sanctuary of the Church of St Nicetas" (против алтаря Никитской церкви, 82). This is particularly distressing to his mother, "the widow of Nain"(вдова наинская), as Tuberozov brands her. . . .

With this "productive" anecdote ("and a new story began"), the myth-making movements of the diary text become more complicated. The Archpriest's appeal to the Deacon's faculty for rational argument ("bring to reason"), juxtaposed with the "learnedness" of the widow's son, punctures the positive myth of Russian religious sensibility. With his half-crazy "resolution," Akhilla may appear to be an expression of Russianness, and the boisterous, frivolous Varnava the embodiment of foreignness, "an empty, but harmful man" (пустой, но вредный человек, 81), but actually *both* men are involved in the same trivial *pustiak,* The Battle of the Bones, thus falling into the category of "incessantly laughing" people. In Tuberozov's account of this local scandal, the collaborator and the antagonist exemplify jointly the "new success of buffoonery" (шутовства новое преуспеяние, 80), which contradicts his idea of a "natural" and heartfelt Russian sincerity.

On the level of stylistic mingling, the ambiguousness of the Deacon and the seminarian points to the tension between two "psychic tendencies"[24] in Russian cultural mythology, the creative potential of which underlies the diary text as a whole: religious maximalism and "secular" scepticism. While the maximalist streak in Tuberozov's text is best sensed in the dominant myth of eschatology, or in "the sense of an ending,"[25] the scepticism comes to the fore in the voice of social conscience, or of conscientious opposition to the Empire' *status quo*. Again, the Archpriest fluctuates between two stylistic tendencies, or world-views, so that his self-structuring is permanently wedged in a no man's land between cultures and ideologies. In turn, this multi-levelled conflict indicates a semantic openness which is already present in the early entries, where his two homiletic ideals are expressed—genuineness of feeling and the relevance of the quotidian. . . .

Tuberozov's readiness to improvise "some underhand way" makes him refer to the down-to-earth wisdom of a venerated Russian Orthodox monastery elder (*starets*) on the one hand,[26] and to the pragmatism of Polish Catholic priests on the other. More importantly, as he follows the example of the "enlightened" founder of the Jesuits, in order to avoid official censorship, the semantic and cultural experiences accumulated within the heterogenous stylistic levels—all of which represent different voices co-present within Imperial Russia—are interchanged and contaminate one another. We might say that the confrontation of cultures in Tuberozov's diary is brought about syncretically by the interplay between the novel's multiple structuring mechanisms. In turn, in this crossing between the official and the unofficial, myths are made and unmade, while any onesided idea of national superiority is counteracted. The activation in the priest's text of an outside, non-Russian cultural reservoir contributes to the establishing of a transformed, albeit non-permanent, "neo-Russian" culture, which comes into being especially "when one cannot proceed by the direct road."

As regards the primary narrative, "the great Stargorod drama" (великая старогородская драма, 23) is brought to a climax with the incorporation into the text of the Archpriest's fiery sermon,[27] the controversy surrounding which leads to his downfall, his lengthy sequestration, the loss of his wife, and, finally, his own death. It is significant that the chronicler's text too may be viewed in relation to mythopoeia and mythic decomposition, more precisely, as the *re-presentation* of Tuberozov's tendency to mythologize. Like the medieval annalists, he seems to be guided by a divine and incomphrensible salvational scheme, which informs his "historical" tales and therefore pays little heed to the explicatory burden of evidence. Towards the end of his life, the Archpriest has the Deacon move in with him: Ахилла служил в церкви и домовничал, а Туберозов сидел дома, читал Джона Буниана, думал и молился [. . .]. Он действительно все соби лс и жил усиленной и сосредоточенною жизнью самоповерящгего себя духа (274). Although the two

are typically described in Orthodox eldership terms as spiritual father and son, the Archpriest's turning to the spiritual allegories of John Bunyan[28] signals another passing beyond the bounds of the Russian Orthodox tradition. Like Tuberozov, this Protestant lay clergyman zealously attempted to solve the personal problems of his troubled congregation, whilst being repeatedly confined by high officials for his subversive preaching. On the level of the text, the constant transgression in terms of rhetoric and styles reaches another high point when the Deacon leaves domesticity in the cathedral town for the Synod in St Petersburg as part of the bishop's entourage. Inserted into the main narrative like the diary, his letters to Tuberozov are оригиналъные и странные, не менее чем весъ складъ его мышления и жизни (274).

Akhilla's communications are full of contradictory elements. On the one hand, he admits to melancholy and homesickness, recognizing his own "lack of education" (необразованность) as well as his superior's provincial ignorance (вы этого, по своей провинциалъности, не поймете, 275). On the other, he recounts how he is "sincerely reconciled" (искренно примирился, 276) with Varnava, who has become the editor of a St Petersburg newspaper. It is interesting that the Deacon sympathizes with his former enemy, partly because the latter is "cruelly unhappy" (жестоко несчастливый), partly because he has been apparently transformed into a different, more devout man (готов бы даже за бога в газете заступитъся, 276). As soon as Akhilla is reunited with Tuberozov back in Stargorod, he continues his stylistic mingling in the form of a storytelling frenzy. . . . Then, with a sensitivity to style and rhetoric similar to that of the main hero, the chronicler describes how the Archpriest at first listens to the Deacon's anecdotes "with tender emotions" (с умилением), only to lose his patience, appalled at his excess of language: "Why have you learned to insert such empty words?" (Зачем ты таиъе пустые слова научился вставлятъ? 278). In responding spontaneously to the Deacon's "mixed, vast and incoherent" speech, Tuberozov must relate to the "un-Russian" artificiality of a person to whom he is attached (cf. the similar diary description of Varnava as an insincere person, "empty, but harmful"), but also to Akhilla's confession that he has become an atheist. . . .

According to the chronicler, the Archpriest is extremely provoked by the results of the "enlightenment" the Deacon has received in St Petersburg (петербургская просвещенностъ, 279). Whereas Akhilla dismisses both the English Protestant writer and the Russian Orthodox ideal of simplicity, Tuberozov is actually defending both of these—before the person whom he has earlier identified negatively with the former, and positively with the latter. Here the syncretism of Akhilla's speech upsets the mythopoetic function of the overarching rhetorical principle in Tuberozov's "maximalist" text—the juxtaposition of antitheses—in such a way that the line between the traditional binaries old/new, Russian/non-Russian, true/false, remains ambiguous. The Archpriest then attempts, gradually, to "de-urbanize" the Deacon by means of instruction. . . . In describing how the two men, arms linked, walk out of the house and into the wintry night, the primary narrator thus contributes to the mythopoetic process, or rather to a *reaffirmation* of Orthodox faith: pointing to the cross on the provincial cathedral, where both men have served so long at the altar, Tuberozov commands Akhilla to repent his sins and then joins his soul mate. Проповедник и кающийся молилисъ вместе (282).

COMPLEXITY IN SIMPLICITY: A "RUSSIAN"
EMPIRE?

The aim of this essay has been to suggest a way into Leskov's verbal originality in order to achieve a fuller experience of his prose. As we have seen, the mingling of styles may be explained in terms of an intertextual confrontation engendered by the novel's myth-making movements. Here the stories of Tuberozov, Akhilla and the chronicler may be said to be "styled" by way of syncretism, or by the semantic and cultural experience that accumulates within the heterogeneous styles. In fact, the Archpriest and the Deacon emerge as examples of hybrid consciousness; their "confrontational" speech contributes to new meanings in-between styles and texts in the novel as a whole.

By seeking out the stylistics of confrontation in this way, we discover that the making and un-making of myths in *Cathedral Folk* imply two kinds of meaning potential that are alternately developed: concretion and accumulation, dispersion and fragmentation.[29] Ideas of Russian grandeur and superiority are inflated and deflated, Russianness is never only Russian. In turn, the text's potential for repeatedly transgressing rhetorical boundaries motivates a number of different readings of people and society in Imperial Russia that suspend "monologized" or official truth. As the splitting of singular meaning is an essential trait on all levels of the story-telling, the effect of the myth-making activity is that Russian culture never comes to rest; because the syncretic text refuses to reproduce any culture, culture as such cannot congeal or acquire definite contours. Indeed, several of Leskov's texts of the 1870s may be construed as an aesthetic expression of complexity in simplicity, a rendering of motley provinciality in a manner which is anything but unreadable.[30]

*Notes*

1. D. S. Mirsky, 1949, *A History of Russian Literature,* London, p. 316.

2. Mirsky, 1949, p. 317.

3. Victor Terras, 1991, *A History of Russian Literature,* New Haven, Conn., p. 362.

4. L. P. Grossman 1945, *N. S. Leskov: Zhizn—tvorchestvo—poetika,* Moscow, p. 159, holds that Leskov's disregard of "the unity of style and the wholeness of artistic writing," as well as "the mixed character and the heterogeneity of material (*pestrota i raznokachestvennost' materiala*) [. . .] infringes upon the artistic manner."

5. Terras, 1991, p. 364.

6. Malcom V. Jones and Robin Feuer Miller suggest that Leskov would be counted among the "classics" only by readers with a very "intimate knowledge of the tradition." See "Editors' Preface," *The Cambridge Companion to the Classic Russian Novel,* eds. M. V. Jones & R. Feuer Miller, Cambridge, 1998, p. xiii.

7. Cf. Wolfgang Girke, 1969, *Studien zur Sprache N. S. Leskovs,* (Slavistische Beiträge 39), Munich; and Robert Hodel, 1994, *Betrachtungen zum* skaz *bei N. S. Leskov und Dragoslav Mihailović,* (Slavica Helvetica 44), Bern.

8. Gary Saul Morson & Caryl Emerson, 1990, *Mikhail Bakhtin: Creation of a Prosaics,* Stanford, p. 17.

9. Mikhail Bakhtin, 1990, "From the Prehistory of Novelistic Discourse," *The Dialogic Imagination: Four Essays,* ed M. Holquist, trans. C. Emerson & M. Holquist, Austin, Tex., pp. 48-49.

10. Hugh McLean, 1967, "Russia: The Love-Hate Pendulum and *The Sealed Angel,*" *To Honor Roman Jakobson: Essays on the Occasion of his Seventieth Birthday,* The Hague, vol. 2, pp. 1328-1339; p. 1338, 1333-1334. Hugh McLean, 1977, *Nikolai Leskov: The Man and his Art,* Cambridge, Mass., pp. 195-196.

11. Cf. Josef Kopperschmidt, 1990, "Einleitende Anmerkungen zum heutigen Interesse an Rhetorik," *Rhetorik,* vol.1: *Rhetorik als Texttheorie,* ed. J. Kopperschmidt, Darmstadt, pp. 1-31.

12. Here my line of inquiry differs from that of Irmhild Christina Weinberg, who argues that Leskov's focus on exceptional situations and characters is the organic expression of his worldview: "to find the theory, the one word, that explains it all. For Leskov, the meaning of life is in finding the appropriate word for this very moment, and for this we have to know a lot of words to choose from." (Irmhild Christina Weinberg, 1996, *The Organic Worldview of Nikolai Leskov,* doctoral thesis, Columbia University, p. 339.)

13. I have borrowed the phrase "find one's footing" from Clifford Geertz, who locates the centre of anthropology in something resembling classical

*decorum.* "Although one starts any effort at thick description, beyond the obvious and superficial, from a state of general bewilderment as to what the devil is going on—trying to find one's feet—one does not start (or ought not) intellectually empty-handed." (Clifford Geertz, 1993, *The Interpretation of Culture: Selected Essays,* New York, p. 27.)

14. See Renate Lachmann, 1977, "Rhetorik und kultureller Kontext," *Rhetorik: kritische Positionen zum Stand der Forschung,* Munich, pp. 167-186; p. 167ff.; 1978, "Rhetorik und Kulturmodell," *Slavistische Studien zum* VIII. *Internationalen Slavistenkongress,* eds. J. Holthusen et al., Cologne, pp. 264-288; p. 279ff.

15. Graham Hough, 1969, *Style and Stylistics,* London, p. 10ff.

16. Stylistic mingling understood as conflict can be linked to Bakhtin's concept of "hybrid construction," which may contain mixed within it a stylistic plurality, as well as a number of axiological belief systems. See Bakhtin, 1990, p. 304ff.

17. Renate Lachmann, 1997, *Memory and Literature: Intertextuality in Russian Modernism,* trans. R. Sellars & A. Wall, Minneapolis, p. 123.

18. Quotations are taken from N. S. Leskov, 1956-1958, *Sobranie sochinenii v odinnadtsati tomakh,* Moscow, vol. 4. Unless otherwise indicated, italics are mine.

19. Actually a religious calendar bound in a heavy cotton fabric which was in use in Russia in the *early* nineteenth century, Tuberozov's diary (*Demikotonovaia kniga,* from the French "demicoton") connotes with the quaintness and old-fashionedness of its author.

20. As Faith Wigzell, 1985, "The *staraya skazka* of Leskov's *Soboryane*: Archpriests Tuberozov and Avvakum," *The Slavonic and East European Review* 63 (3), pp. 321-366; p. 321, points out, the term *staraia skazka* defies adequate translation. I prefer her "old fairytale" (Faith Wigzell, 1998, "The Cathedral Folk: Soboriane," *Reference Guide to Russian Literature,* ed. N. Cornwell, London & Chicago, pp. 501-502) to Isabel F. Hapgood's rendering "old tradition," where the tones of enchantment inherent in the Russian word *skazka* is lost (Nicolai Lyeskov (Leskov), 1924, *The Cathedral Folk,* trans. I. F. Hapgood, Westport, Conn.).

21. Is. 11, 15-16, Ps. 104, 33, Is. 2, 5.

22. Ex. 33, 9-11 ("and the Lord spoke with Moses face to face, as a man speaks to his friend"; И говорил Господъ с Моисеем лицем к лицу, как бы говорил кто с другом своим).

23. Ex. 33, 23. I am indebted to Ingunn Lunde for drawing my attention to this point.

24. David M. Bethea, 1998, "Literature," *The Cambridge Companion to Modern Russian Culture,* ed. N. Rzhevsky, Cambridge, pp. 161-204; p. 162ff.

25. Frank Kermode, 1967, *The Sense of an Ending: Studies in the Theory of Fiction,* Oxford, pp. 3-35.

26. As to the practical slant of Kirill Belozerskii's edificatory writings, he is described as "a man, not only sensible, but also sufficiently educated and with a good command of his native language" (Metropolitan Makarii (Bulgakov), 1995, *Istoriia russkoi tserkvi,* Moscow, vol. 3, p. 290).

27. For an analysis of Tuberozov's sermon, see my "The Rhetoric of an Archpriest: Nikolai Leskov and the Orthodox Heritage," MA dissertation, University of London, 1994; also, in *Cultural Discontinuity and Reconstruction: The Byzanto-Slav Heritage and the Creation of a Russian National Literature in the Nineteenth Century,* eds. J. Børtnes & I. Lunde, Oslo, 1997, pp. 217-236.

28. With his Puritan allegory *The Pilgrim's Progress* (1677), Bunyan offended the establishment as well as alarmed his co-religionists by his bold disregard for sectarian protocol. More importantly, the edifying author conceives of Christians as spiritual wanderers, which is close to how Tuberozov sees himself in his own life.

29. Both aspects of meaning-production are implied in Bakhtin's concept of dialogicity.

30. Multivectorial structuring generates cultural ambivalence, in a similar fashion, in *Zapechatlennyi angel, Ocharovannyi strannik, Na kraiu sveta* and *Detskie gody.*

## Faith Wigzell (essay date 2001)

SOURCE: Wigzell, Faith. "Nikolai Leskov, Gender, and Russianness." In *Gender and Sexuality in Russian Civilisation,* edited by Peter I. Barta, pp. 105-20. London: Routledge, 2001.

[*In the essay below, Wigzell examines "the gender bias underlying Leskov's artistic recharacterisations," asserting that the author "defeminizes and, more particularly, dematernalizes his symbols of traditional Russia."*]

Gor'kii's dictum that Leskov was the most Russian of writers ("samobytneishii pisatel' russkii" (Gor'kii 1948-55, 24, 237)) has dominated subsequent critical assessment. While this essay conforms in so far as it discusses Leskovian characters who embody traditional Russian archetypes or ethnic stereotypes (national characterology), it takes as its focus the gender bias underlying Leskov's artistic recharacterisations. From lyrical appeals to his country (Rus'/rodina) to his colourful characters stylized à la russe, I shall argue that Leskov defeminizes and, more particularly, dematernalizes his symbols of traditional Russia. The aim is not to speculate on Leskov's biography, psychology or attitudes to women, but rather to uncover the writer's personal artistic slant on Russian national identity. I am, therefore, neither following the line pursued by Inès Muller de Morogues who examines female portraiture in terms of Leskov's response to the woman question, nor the psychologized approach of Hugh McLean (Muller de Morogues 1991; McLean 1977).

The works that lend themselves best to this type of discussion are those of the 1860s and 1870s where Leskov was responding to contemporary debate about Russian national identity and the Russian way forward. They are all set in the provinces, which was perceived by the Slavophile-inclined, here including Leskov, as the locus of real Russianness; **"The Life of a Peasant Martyress"** (**"Zhitie odnoi baby"**), 1863, **"The Enchanted Pilgrim"** (or **"Wanderer"**) (**"Ocharovannyi strannik"**), 1873, together with three of the remaining parts of the unfinished chronicle of Russian provincial life, the novel *Cathedral Folk* (*Soboriane*), 1872, **"Kotin the He-Cow and Platonida"** (**"Kotin doilets i Platonida"**), 1867, and **"Olden Times in the Village of Plodomasovo"** (**"Starye gody v sele Plodomasove"**), 1869.[1] Some reference will also be made to the well-known story **"Lady Macbeth of Mtsensk"** (**"Ledi Makbet Mtsenskogo uezda"**), 1864.

For a writer to comment on the nature and future of Russia was not of course new. In particular, Leskov shares much with the Gogol' of *Dead Souls,* both in his (albeit more modest) apostrophes to Rus' and in the use of ethnic stereotypes as a basis for character portraits. By contrast with Gogol, however, Leskov's considerable knowledge of ordinary Russians, acquired in childhood and subsequently, as well as of their oral poetic heritage enabled him to broaden his sources for national characterology, thereby largely escaping the conventional negative connotations of ethnic stereotypes (the Russians as, for example, strong, ignorant and fond of drink) which dominate in *Dead Souls* (Møller 1997, 72)). It should have also permitted him to escape the negative gender stereotypes of women so often found in Gogol's work (women as gossip-mongers, obsessed with trivia and so on), but here, as will be argued, Leskov ignored or reworked traditional images.[2] In any case, the debate about the qualities inherent in Russians which made them distinct and might determine their future had moved a long way since the early 1840s.

By the 1860s the question of how to bridge the cultural divide between the secularized culture of the élite and rural Russia's old pre-Petrine world view had become so pressing that few members of the intelligentsia, writers included, could ignore it (Hosking 1997, 263-85; 210-12). To solve the problem meant first defining Russia's essence and then advocating a path for the future. Not least was what to do with the majority of the population, the peasants. On the one hand they seemed irredemiably backward, on the other had preserved ancient customs and a rich national folklore, gems of which were being discovered and published in exactly this period: texts of the folk epic *byliny* with their heroic *bogatyri* (Rybnikov 1861-7) in particular, but Afanas'ev's folk tales and work on mythology (Afanas'ev 1855-7; 1865-9), P. V. Kireevskii's collection of songs (Kireevskii 1860-8) and Barsov's of folk-poetic laments (Barsov 1872) also spring to mind. Much of Leskov's work of this period was a response and artistic contribution to that debate, drawing on folk and religious material. Although he shared the Slavophile interest in the country's indigenous cultural roots, he felt his superior experience of rural Russia and its largely peasant population gave him a more balanced view than many. As Gor'kii remarked: "he loved Rus' in her entirety exactly as she was, with all the absurdities (*neleposti*) of her age-old way of life . . . but he loved it all without shutting his eyes to anything . . ." (Gor'kii, 24, 233). He was contemptuous of those whose ignorance of the "narod" led them to absurd idealisations (witness his ironical quotation from a Maikov poem at the end of **"The Life of a Peasant Martyress"** (1, 385; also 1, xxviii[3])), but equally disliked the semi-fictional ethnographic writings of populist writers with their exaggeratedly gloomy portrayals of peasant life (McLean 1977, 115-6). Leskov's use of folk images and national characterology allowed him to make ironic and sometimes bitter comment on contemporary Russia, while at the same time bringing forward what he saw as the positive heritage and potential of his country. However balanced his assessment of his country, Leskov's own gender bias nonetheless ensured a biassed selection and treatment of the images of Russianness.

His approach is evident even in his treatment of the varied terms for country that reflected the painful cultural divide: "Rus'" and "rodina" versus "Rossiia" and "otechestvo". Conceptually, "Rossiia" and "otechestvo" form a pair, connected to Russia as empire, with "otechestvo" implying concepts of noble duty or military and civil service in a cosmopolitan secular state. The two pairs of terms are gendered; obviously the term "otechestvo" is connected with the word for "father", but, over and above this, the concepts of state service and duty are essentially masculine ones, and so too is the Latinate term "Rossiia", despite its feminine gender (Gachev 1991, 150). The grammatical gender of the capital Petersburg (masculine), from where the tsar, the father of his people ruled (Dal' 1984, 1, 258), further assisted the view of the Russian autocracy and empire as male. Those interested in defining the essence of Russia, Leskov included, preferred the other pair, "Rus'" and "rodina", which are more than simply grammatically feminine. The word "rodina" is cognate with words like "roditel'" (parent) and "urozhai" (harvest). Through the associations with abundance, feeding and reproduction it is connected to the cult of Damp Mother Earth ("Mat' syra-zemlia"), the symbol of nurturing and care, enshrined in many traditional rituals and beliefs. In pre-Christian belief and the peasant world view the earth was seen as the womb of all civilisation, constantly renewing itself and providing succour to its children (Hubbs 1988, xiii-xvi; Barker 1986). "Your home ("rodimaia storona") is your mother—foreign parts are your mother-in-law" reads one of Dal''s proverbs (Dal' 1984, 255). Such concepts were also accepted by the intelligentsia: "I know why it is you weep, mother mine", declares Nekrasov in his poem ("Rodina"). "Rus'" like "rodina" is not simply feminine but, more specifically, possesses strong maternal overtones, often being popularly termed Mother Russia ("Matushka Rus'"). It had ceased to be a geographical term, denoting instead the qualities seen as essentially Russian, the language, tradition and religion located in a land seen as home ("rodina")—hence it was both the embodiment of Russianness and the epitome of the peasant world view. Key qualities were the supposedly female attributes of the submissive and humble, and, above all, of caring and nurturing (see Aizlewood 1996,).[4]

In the work of the 1860s and 1870s under consideration here, Leskov not surprisingly ignores the terms "otechestvo"/"Rossiia", since his concern is the Russia of tradition and how to move the country into the modern world without destroying its essence. By contrast, the terms "Rus'/rodina" appear frequently, albeit often placed in the mouth of a narrator. Thus in the early story, **"The Life of a Peasant Martyress"**, the narrator, a local now resident in Petersburg, concludes a disquisition on the appalling rural habit of child beating, prevalent among the gentry as well as the peasants, as follows:

> O, my Rus', my native Rus' ("Rus' rodimaia"). How much longer will you dawdle in your dirt and squalor? Is it not time to wake, and take hold of yourself? Is it not time to unclench the fist, and turn to the mind? Revive, my own, much praisèd land! Enough of playing the fool, enough of wiping away the tears with fist and cudgel . . .

> (1, 285)[5]

Although Leskov (here clearly perceptible behind the narrator) addresses Rus' in the familiar "ty", lyrically declaring his love for his country, he characterises Rus' as an uncaring mother, who responds to tears with brutality. Violence has overwhelmed caring maternal instincts.

Other instances of Leskov's use of the term "Rus'" reinforce the impression that he underplays the powerful maternal image of Rus'. A few years later, writing about the journey across Lake Ladoga in 1872, which is reflected in **"The Enchanted Pilgrim"**, Leskov expressed both admiration and despair about his "rodina" and its extraordinary people: "Whither are you going, whither are you sailing, oh holy motherland, on your rickety boat with its drunken sailors. How can you digest this combination of peas and cabbage, piety and drunkenness, spiritualist ravings and airy-fairy atheism, ignorance and conceit . . . Oh be strong, my homeland! Be strong for you are crucial" (quoted in Gorelov 1988, 219). Here again Leskov affirms his love of Russia, but this time leaves out all reference to her feminine nature. The focus is instead on the country's incongruous contrasts and appalling problems, and rests partly on ethnic stereotypes (piety, drunkenness, ignorance, love of philosophizing) which are not gendered here. Though this invocation does not form part of **"The Enchanted Wanderer"** itself, the sense of Russia as a land of self-destructive contrasts (including piety versus drunkenness) underlies the story, in which positive features of Russianness are set against the negative in the person of the flawed hero. In this case the image of "Rus'"/"rodina" is not anti-maternal, but neither is it feminized. Only in the third example of an invocation to Russia, which comes in the novel *Cathedral Folk* is there any clear positive presentation of Rus' as feminine. On observing the kindness of the eccentric Pizonskii, who is bringing up an orphan on his own, the main character, Archpriest Savelii Tuberozov, exclaims: "Oh my soft-hearted Russia, how beauteous thou art!" (4, 36). It is no coincidence that this epitome of maternal qualities is a man, a point elaborated later. It may be concluded that, although Leskov is clearly deeply attached to his country as "Rus'"/"rodina", his view minimized the feminine aspects of the conventional concept. As will be seen, defeminizing or rather dematernalising is a feature of Leskov's literary Russianness as a whole.

It does not follow from the suggestion that "Rus'"/"rodina" is essentially feminine and "Rossiia"/"otechestvo" masculine that the former does not incorporate the masculine as well. Traditionally "Matushka Rus'" was seen as married to "Batiushka" (diminutive of father) tsar. Russians were seen as her children. While female positive images tended to replicate the supposed feminine qualities of Rus' (caring, long-suffering, passive and humble), male images were both contrasting and more varied, reflected in the religious and martial aspects of the old saying "Holy, Orthodox, heroic Rus', sacred Russian motherland" ("Rus' sviataia, pravoslavnaia, bogatyrskaia, mat' sviatorusskaia zemlia") (Dal' 1984, 1, 258; Platonov 1993, 6). Although no evidence exists to suggest that Leskov drew directly on the proverb in his depiction of his Russianized characters, this conception of "Rus'" with its tri-

partite division into maternal, religious and heroic qualities makes an excellent yardstick by which to evaluate
Leskov's Russianness, and the respective roles played
by male and female images in it.

The evaluation of Leskov's own selection of archetypes
requires an understanding of the context of gender representation in Russian oral and literary tradition, the
relevant aspects of which I shall, therefore, briefly out-
line. Surprisingly, the situation is more complex than
might be assumed from the patriarchal structure of traditional Russian society. In folklore gender plays an important role, both in the "ownership" of a given genre
and in the creation of typical images. Only the lament
is performed solely by women, but in other genres
women dominate. For example, the ballad, a narrative
song focussing on family conflict, is frequently centred
on female characters and women's problems (such as
their powerlessness in the context of marriage in the patriarchal household). Though the sympathy between
singer and subject matter is not overt, the ballad often
expresses a female point of view and was generally
sung by women (Balashov 1963, 14). It reflects national
characterology in its emphasis on violence in the face
of injustice, as well the figures of the victim heroine,
the bold young man ("dobryi molodets") or the wicked
mother-in-law. Apart from the ballad, a large body of
lyric folk songs, mostly concerning love and marriage,
are the property of women. More often than not they
portray the sadness of a woman who is a victim of circumstances (married to a man she does not love, mourning a lost love and so on).

By contrast, the most obviously male genre in terms of
subject matter and hero is the bylina. Perhaps not surprisingly, these epic songs (and the related genre of the
historical song) were primarily sung by men. All the
main heroes, the bogatyrs, are male, larger-than-life figures who defend Rus' by single-handedly overcoming
hideous monsters, dragons or huge armies. Interestingly, whereas in the bylina and the folk historical song
the ability to down buckets of "green wine" is a male
attribute given positive value in the figure of the
bogatyr, the ethnic stereotype of the Russians as prone
to drink possesses negative connotations. Overall, the
bylina heroes, in particular the best known, Il'ia
Muromets, came to be regarded as the epitome of Russianness in its masculine variant, brave and active
("heroic Rus'").

Nonetheless, this "male" genre features not one, but
two positive female figures. The first of these is the
"polenitsa" (or "polianitsa"), a warrior maiden whose
strength may rival or exceed that of the bogatyr with
whom she fights (e.g. "Dobrynia and Nastas'ia"). It
should, however, be noted that the "polenitsa" is always
either tamed by marriage or killed by her husband for
challenging his superiority (e.g. "Dunai"), and, further-

more, never fights to defend Rus'. The second is the
hero's mother. In the bylina, just as in some folk historical songs, mothers play a significant role as caring
figures who warn their sons not to take foolhardy action
(e.g. "Dobrynia i zmei"), or pick up the pieces after
their advice has been ignored, as in the bylina about
Vasilii Buslaev and some variants of the song about the
death of Mikhail Skopin-Shuiskii. But if the archetypal
wise and caring mother has a raw deal in the bylina, fathers almost never appear.[6]

While positive mythologised images of women (even if
often long-suffering and fatalistic) do exist in Russian
folklore, they are rarities in Russian Orthodoxy. Just as
Christianity is a male-dominated religion, though many
of its most fervent ordinary supporters have always
been women, hagiography, which mythologizes the
deeds of saintly men and holds them up for emulation,
is a genre composed by men, often monks, who mainly
promoted misogynistic ideals. Female saints exist in
Russia, as elsewhere, but they are few and far between
and generally little venerated. The only female Christian figures to be universally venerated in Russia were
those that incorporated age-old beliefs into their cult:
Mary and St Paraskeva-Piatnitsa. In Russia more icons
are devoted to Mary than to any other single figure, her
cult emphasizing less her virginity than her role as the
mother of God (Barker 1986, 87-123), most likely because of a confusion with the pre-Christian cult of
Mother Earth.[7] Paraskeva-Piatnitsa similarly was linked
with a pre-Christian female deity, Mokosh, who specifically protected women. The loving, giving mother is
the supreme female image in Russian folk belief and
folklore, just as the maternal facets of Rus' predominate. Overall the maternal figure is of major importance
in traditional Russian culture (folk and written), certainly more so than the wise maiden of folk tales, or the
unhappy victim of lyric song or ballad, trapped in a
loveless marriage.

Outside hagiography women fare no better. The historical literature of early and Muscovite Rus' focusses on
dominant figures who were overwhelmingly men. Only
when women became widows, like Princess Ol'ga in
the *Tale of Bygone Years* (*Povest' vremennykh let*),
could they hold any real power. Not until the seventeenth century do literary portraits of strong women
emerge in the descriptions of the lives of Uliian'ia Lazarevskaia, Boiarynia Morozova—supporter of the Old
Belief—and Anastas'ia Markovna, the wife of the Archpriest Avvakum. Emphasizing the qualities of loyalty,
steadfastness and infinite forbearance, these works
present women as wives or mothers, to some extent,
therefore, paralleling folk archetypes.

Female images of Russianness were thus available to
Leskov. Despite this, the most distinctive of his epito-
mes of Russianness are male: the narrator hero of **"The**

Enchanted Pilgrim", Ivan Sever'ianovich Fliagin, the priests Tuberozov, Zakhariia Benefaktov and deacon Akhilla Desnitsyn in *Cathedral Folk* as well as the lesser character of Konstantin Pizonskii (*Cathedral Folk* and "Kotin the He-Cow and Platonida"). By contrast, the positive female characters, especially those in the Stargorod cycle and in **"The Enchanted Pilgrim",** are secondary, more passive or conventional. Tuberozov's wife, Natal'ia Nikolaevna, is a much less colourful character than her husband, while Platonida is neither as colourful nor as developed a character as Pizonskii, with whom she shares the story. In **"The Enchanted Pilgrim",** the only striking and stylized female image is that of Grusha, who is not Russian but a gypsy (albeit a striking archetype of the passionate and tempestuous Romany). The sole dominant female character is Marfa Plodomasova (the old landowner from Tuberozov's diary and "Olden Times in the Village of Plodomasovo"). Only the early stories, **"The Life of a Peasant Martyress"** and **"Lady Macbeth of Mstensk",** focus on heroines stylized à la russe. However, these characters and the nature of their Russianness must be understood in the context of Leskov's aims, which were less to create Russian archetypes than to make a polemical point.

The reasons for Leskov's choice of source material for Nast'ia Prokudina and Katerina Izmailova lie in his literary aims which at this very early stage of his writing career were more restricted than they became in the Stargorod cycle and **"The Enchanted Pilgrim".** **"The Life of a Peasant Martyress"** was intended, like **"The Robber"** (1862), **"The Musk-Ox"** (1863) and **"The Mocker"** (1863), as a contribution to the peasant question. The story revolves around the tragic life and love of Nast'ia Prokudina, whose refusal to compromise her essential goodness and moral idealism (she has been forced into marriage to a near idiot as part of a business deal) leads to her destruction by the barbaric peasant environment in which she lives. Using his excellent first-hand knowledge, Leskov demonstrates the moral bankruptcy of the peasantry (McLean 1977, 115; Gorelov 1988, 146). The choice of a victim heroine with the archetypal Russian qualities of purity of soul and steadfastness was a natural one in the circumstances. To lend his character a typicality and enhance the tragedy of her fate, Leskov employed folk sources. The ending in which Nast'ia freezes to death in a forest inverts that of the well-known folk tale, "Jack Frost" ("Morozko"), about a victim heroine who, because of her goodness, escapes death in the forest in winter—real life, Leskov implies, is no fairy tale. Equally natural was the use of folk song as a means of lending a poetic colouring to Nast'ia's plight, and especially to the account of her love affair with an unhappily married man. Nast'ia is first drawn to Stepan because he sings superbly, just like Turgenev's "Singers" in *A Sportsman's Sketches*; she, too, possesses a remarkable voice, and the songs they sing, both separately and together, are carefully chosen to reflect their feelings and situation. Nast'ia is stylized after the manner of the sad female figure of many folk songs, as a way of heightening the pathos of her fate and pointing out the contrast between her feelings and the brutal realism of her surroundings. In this way Leskov disputed the radicals' argument that serfdom was the cause of all peasant ills, suggesting instead that the peasants themselves were too often brutalized by life, causing harm to each other. The parallels render her a symbolic Russianized victim heroine in the service of a polemical argument, rather than an archetypal symbol of Russianness in general.

With Katerina Izmailova Leskov was responding not to political debate about peasant life but to a literary one about the relevance of Shakespearean archetypes in Russian settings (was tragedy possible in the Russia provinces?) as well as Leskov's own comment on the, as he saw it, over-idealised merchant heroine of Ostrovskii's play, *The Thunderstorm* ("Groza") (Guminskii 1983, 243-44; Wigzell 1989, 170-1). However, the desire to create his own versions of Russian archetypes as a function of a growing interest in the question "whither Russia" was already developing. In late 1864, just after completing **"Lady Macbeth",** the writer declared his intention (subsequently unrealised) of making the story part of a cycle about typical Russian female characters (10, 253). The important word here is "typical". At this stage Leskov wanted to create recognisable provincial types, but not yet in characters who would embody the virtues (and failings) of Rus', thereby contributing to a general debate. Like Nast'ia, Katerina represents the victim heroine, but in the variant found in the folk ballad as opposed to magic tale or folk lyric. This heroine is driven by passion to the sort of action of which Nast'ia is incapable, murdering whoever stands between her and her lover, Sergei. The story contains numerous parallels both of plot and treatment with ballads (for details, see Wigzell 1989). As Lantz points out, the story supports the view of Leskov's alter ego in his novel *No Way Out* (1864) that the Russians possess a "direct and uncompromising nature . . . which would give their drama a unique flavour" (Lantz 1979, 44), a quality well expressed in the dramatic plot of the folk ballad. By underscoring the typicality of Katerina in this way, Leskov makes his point.

What becomes clear is that Leskov moved away from female characters as he began to focus on the problems of Russia. The victim heroine could not embody the positive values of old Russia, and in the Stargorod cycle features only once in the person of Platonida, who is given a much lighter Russian stylization than either Nast'ia or Katerina. Furthermore, when it came to depicting a happily married woman in Natal'ia Nikolaevna Tuberozova of *Cathedral Folk*, Leskov had no obvious folk source. Consequently Tuberozov's wife is paragon of wifely virtue according to conventional social norms, certainly also representing Leskov's own ideal spouse (caring, supportive, submissive, quiet, deferring to her husband's intellect and judgement), but Leskov also wanted to make her representative of the best in *traditional* Russian womanhood (Muller de Morogues 1991, 429-32). To this end he modelled Natal'ia Nikolaevna on the wife of Archpriest Avvakum, the most famous opponent of Church reform in the seventeenth century. Both are adjuncts to their husband, only once stepping forward to encourage him when his resolve falters (see Wigzell 1985, 332-4). Described by Deacon Akhilla as a "force", Natal'ia Nikolaevna is a softer, gentler person than her counterpart. Her "force" lies in her meekness and devotion to her husband. For his part, he derives moral and emotional strength from her presence by his side. Whereas there is some suggestion that Tuberozov might have done more to realise his potential and put his ideas into action, there is no such implied criticism of Natal'ia Nikolaevna. Like many, he clearly did not envisage women playing a more active role in the defence of Russianness and the development of his country.

When creating his trinity of clerical heroes in *Cathedral Folk,* Leskov, not surprisingly, shifted from women's to men's folklore. The bylina was an obvious choice, especially since public enthusiasm for it was at a height. Long believed defunct, it had been discovered flourishing in Olonets province. Interest culminated in Vereshchagin's famous portrait of Il'ia Muromets and in performances in Moscow in 1871 by singers brought from their villages (Gorelov 1988, 193). The second most important character in *Cathedral Folk,* the deacon Akhilla Desnitsyn, as well as the hero of **"The Enchanted Pilgrim"**, Fliagin, both draw on the male image of the epic hero. Termed bogatyrs partly because of their enormous size and strength (Leskov 1956-8,4, 86, 298, 304, 386-7), both imbibe huge quantities of vodka, get involved in tests of physical strength (Akhilla in a fight with a German wrestler at a fair, Fliagin with a Tatar), and love their country (even though they do not serve it well). Both are also connected with horses; Fliagin becomes a "koneser", a connoisseur of horseflesh, Akhilla gallops the countryside like a Cossack (4, 67) and furnishes his spartan home in Cossack style (4,10-11) (on Fliagin see Gorelov 1988, 197-204, Mikhailova 1966, Cherednikova 1971; on Akhilla, see Wigzell 1988a, 905-6)). Of course, despite their good qualities, neither has the sense of purpose of the epic bylina hero: Leskov's view of the past was a nostalgic one, but he realised that the epic qualities so admirable in the bogatyr were too often inappropriate or absurd in a latter-day hero. In evaluating aspects of his latter-day epic heroes' behaviour, he therefore drew on the ethnic stereotype of the Russians with its frequently negative connotations. Firstly, he shows how misplaced their strength often is, and, secondly, depicts their attachment to vodka, especially binge drinking, as a failing. None-

theless, their strength, spontaneity, basic decency and love of country make them both sympathetic figures in traditional epic vein and essential components of the nostalgic picture of old Russian life purveyed in *Cathedral Folk* on the one hand and the evocation of Rus' through the hero of **"The Enchanted Pilgrim"** on the other.

Important as the connection with the bylina is for one of Leskov's trinity of clerical heroes, it was not sufficient for the characterisation of the religious aspect of holy, Orthodox, heroic Rus'. Leskov chooses to present Father Savelii Tuberozov as a latter-day Avvakum, the conservative revolutionary who strove to reform Church life and then to protect Orthodoxy, as he conceived of it, from the attacks of the reforming Nikonites (Wigzell 1985, 321-5). Tuberozov's relative ineffectiveness in the modern world (as well as his occasional childishness) make him a more endearing but much weaker figure than the indomitable Avvakum. The counterpoint underlines Leskov's pessimism about the survival of old Russian virtues in a modern world, and rather suggests that, much as he admired the quintessentially Russian male qualities, he doubted how useful they were in the service of Russia.

Designed as a contrast to Tuberozov, the meek, kind Father Zakhariia Benefaktov of *Cathedral Folk* represents a different facet of Orthodox tradition. His humility and gentleness make him the embodiment of Russian kenoticism, like those Russian saints who espoused love and non-resistance to evil. One may observe that meekness and humility are close to the qualities dispayed by Nast'ia Prokudina, but in this instance do not derive from folklore. There the suffering of women stems from their powerlessness in a given situation, these qualities thus forming a strategy for survival rather than a positive stance held up for emulation. One should note that the emphasis on the religious significance of humility and forbearance is to a great extent a nineteenth-century educated construct, just as the ideal of kenoticism has achieved its prominence only with Tolstoi, but its late provenance as part of a mythologised Russian tradition is of course just as valid in Leskov's artistic stylizations. The writer, as ever the pragmatist, could not admire uncritically, and he shows that Father Zakhariia's qualities are totally ineffectual in a Russia beset by atheism and alien Western influences; he is loved but not listened to.

If in *Cathedral Folk,* Leskov drew on the kenotic saint, the religious revolutionary and the heroic bogatyr' for this trinity of heroes, in **"The Enchanted Pilgrim"** he combined heroic and religious archetypes together in one character (male). Having largely given up hope that the reform of Russian life and moral leadership could come through the Orthodox Church, Leskov now focussed on a hero, epitomising the Russian "narod" with its moral strengths and failings, whose pilgrimage through life represents the people's own blundering path. With his propensity for violence and weakness for strong drink, Leskov seems to have found difficulty in finding appropriate models from lives of saints for his all too fallible hero, and hence restricted the hagiographical colouring to separate motifs and episodes, notably the dedication of the infant Pilgrim to God by his mother, his prophetic dreams, and his ultimate career as a monk, albeit of an unconventional kind. As a substitute Leskov turned to the late seventeenth-century literary work, depicting another fallible hero's journey through life, *The Tale of Misery-Ill Fortune* (*Povest' o Gore-Zlochastii*). In this lay morality tale, the foolish young man ("molodets"), ignoring his parents' advice, sets off on his own path in life. After constantly succumbing to the temptations afforded by strong drink, gambling, false friends and his own arrogance, he is hounded by the folk-poetic figure of Misery (Gore) and forced to take refuge in a monastery. Like the "molodets", Fliagin is prone to bouts of drinking and degradation followed by periods where he seems to be doing or making good. He, too, is finally forced to choose the monastery as the only way out (Wigzell 1997). Not least of the parallels is thematic; the "molodets" disobeys his parents and seventeenth-century behavioural precepts, while Fliagin, one of the children of Rus', not only ignores his real mother's dedication of him to God, but fails to pay sufficient respect to his motherland. In captivity among the Tatars Fliagin dreams longingly of the monastery domes in his own "baptised land", the beginning of inner change (4, 434). In the concluding pages of the story, the literally and metaphorically sobered Pilgrim hearkens to his mother's wishes, and places himself at the service of his Orthodox motherland (see Wigzell 1997, 760). Thus **"The Enchanted Pilgrim"** brings together the qualities of Russia, expressed in "holy, Orthodox, heroic Rus', sacred Russian motherland", although it should be noted that the maternal aspects of the saying are restricted to the end of the story, which leaves the reader with no real confidence that the hero can effectively defend his "rodina", doubts Leskov also shared.

Thus the active male Russianized heroes of the Stargorod cycle and **"The Enchanted Pilgrim"** are flawed by failings which reflect ethnic stereotypes of the Russians, but, thanks to their stylization through links with folk and religious literature, remain appealing figures. By contrast, the active Russianized heroine in these works is restricted to a single figure, that of Marfa Plodomasova. In general she represents a version of a historical image, the woman who gains power through widowhood. In early Russian literature this type is best represented by Uliian'ia Lazarevskaia, who dedicates herself to good works in the name of God after the death of her husband, while evidently continuing to care for her children (her biography was composed by

her son). Ever modest and self-abnegating, she uses power simply as a means of disposing of the family income in charitable activities. A more self-willed image is that of Boiarynia Morozova, who, against the wishes of her husband, dedicates herself to the cause of the Old Belief and so becomes a religious martyr. Neither provides a direct model for Marfa Plodomasova. Nor was the image of strong-minded widow relevant for the portrait of the younger Marfa, who, abducted at the age of fifteen by a dissolute neighbour and forced into marriage, refuses to repudiate her brutal husband when she has the chance because of her belief in the sanctity of marriage. Her decision to stand by him results in him reforming his ways. Although the principled Marfa is presented as a historical type, such as no longer exists (this part of the story is set in 1748), it seems likely that here Leskov drew on the contemporary literary archetype of the young heroine, who is morally stronger than the man she loves. He reverted to the historical image when depicting Marfa as a widow, autocratic but morally upright, courageous in the face of torture from bandits who invade her house. For the depiction of Marfa as a mother, on the other hand, he had the choice of numerous models, including that of Uliian'ia and the bylina mother, but Leskov presents her as severely lacking in caring and nurturing qualities. Her moral principles and the patriarchal precepts of the sixteenth-century guide to household management and good behaviour, the *Domostroi*, regulate her relations with her son. When she discovers that the twenty-year-old has made a serf girl pregnant, she orders a humiliating flogging. Although Marfa Plodomasova emerges as a pillar of virtue and a pious Christian, she is also a tyrant who has adopted the mores of male patriarchal society. As a mother she is the opposite of the loving, nurturing figure of folk and Orthodox tradition. That she was based on Leskov's grandmother and, more importantly, his mother (see McLean 1977, 15-23) goes some way to explaining the treatment of maternal images, not only in the person of Marfa but also elsewhere in these works.

While Natal'ia Nikolaevna is an ideal wife in Leskov's terms, she has no children. The decision not to make Tuberozov's wife a mother was certainly deliberate, since Tuberozov was to be seen as an ineffectual latter-day Avvakum who would leave no descendants of any kind. But it is clear that the playing-down of women as mothers goes further. Just as Leskov minimised the traditional maternal aspects of the concept of Rus', so the hugely important female maternal image finds practically no resonance in these stories. Katerina Izmailova's and Nast'ia Prokudina's efforts to become mothers end in tragedy with Katerina's rejection of her child and the death of Nast'ia's at two days old. Important male characters do not have mothers, while the Enchanted Pilgrim's mother dies when he was tiny, leaving no emotional or moral legacy other than her promise to dedicate him to God. By contrast, in the bylina the bogatyr has a mother (but no father), while the "molodets" of the *Tale of Misery-Ill Fortune* has both.

The only other mothers are all minor figures, none of whom is given a folk poetic colouring. In *Cathedral Folk* Zakharii Benefaktov's wife is mother to a whole tribe of children, but she is little more than a cipher, a reproach to Tuberozov's own childless wife. Leskov is so little concerned with her that he does not even bother to give her a name. In one of the episodes in **"The Enchanted Pilgrim"** Fliagin becomes nursemaid to a child whose mother has run off with an officer. He eventually allows the distressed mother to reclaim her child, but the episode is more important for its demonstration of Fliagin's essential humanity than of any point about the mother. What the episode does show is that Fliagin, the epitome of Russianness, carries within him the caring maternal impulse, though his child-care methods would make him the nanny from hell for a contemporary parent (he buries the child in sand up to her waist to keep her from running off).

Predictably, in the Stargorod cycle where the various facets of Russian tradition are largely kept separate, maternal benevolence is epitomised in one individual. The sole positive maternal image is a man, Konstantin (Kotin) Pizonskii. Brought up as a girl, Pizonskii is a ridiculous figure redeemed by his adoption of orphans (two girls in **"Kotin the He-Cow and Platonida"** and a boy in *Cathedral Folk*). His humility, acceptance of poverty and readiness to accept the scorn of others place him in direct line of descent from both the holy fool ("iurodivyi") and the "kaleki perekhozhie", the wandering beggar pilgrims of pre-Revolutionary Russia (who also appear in the bylina). Leskov underlines the resemblance in **"Kotin the He-Cow"** by calling him "nishchii, kaleka i urod" ("a beggar, cripple and freak") (1: 229), which in English translation lack the religious resonances of the Russian counterparts, where traditionally a connection is often, if not necessarily, made between physical deformity and true spirituality. Kotin is an odd and eccentric figure rather than a physical cripple. In his case the contrast is between his eccentricities in general and his inner moral values. As Kenneth Lantz noted, "the absurdity of Pizonsky's behaviour is one of his positive virtues" (Lantz 1979, 51). Although holy fools and "kaleki perekhozhie" could be men or women, Leskov's are male. The integration of a maternal image with theirs is not one found in folk or religious tradition. As already mentioned, Pizonskii's symbolic link with Rus' is made overt in the novel, indicating Leskov's admiration for traditional maternal values, but his unwillingness to embody them in a woman.

It may be concluded that for all Leskov's attachment to the Rus'/rodina pair of terms, his own personal psychological make-up dictated adjustments to the conven-

tional gendered perceptions of "Rus'"/"rodina" as a combination of the strongly maternal, and the male heroic (both secular and religious). Of the archetypal heroic and religious images used by the writer only the holy fool and the "kaleka perekhozhii" could be of either sex, but in Leskov they are male. The maternal image, so powerful and universal in folk belief and folklore as well as in the cult of Mother Earth and of the Mother of God is either neglected or inverted. At the same time, the maternal aspects of Mother Russia are played down, while actual female characters are either not seen in a maternal role or as mothers lack caring nurturing qualities. Indeed, the best "mothers" are men.

Overall, men furnish the great majority of positive embodiments of Russianness in the works examined. Whatever blemishes they possess or lapses they commit (such as a weakness for drink, ignorance or physical aggressiveness), their innate decency remains as a potential for good or for change. Furthermore, very often the particular stereotypical failings Leskov highlights are those which can have positive value in folklore (notably drinking, uncontrolled behaviour and even violence and ignorance). By contrast, few of these supposedly typical Russian failings are given to the women characters, to some extent because many ethnic stereotypes of Russians relate more to men than to women. Exceptions appear of two types, either those which render a character more negative than positive, such as Katerina Izmailova with her unbridled passions (but she is, after all, a type not an epitome of Russianness), or Marfa Plodomasova whose tyrannical behaviour is a means of presenting her as an inadequate mother. Similarly, as has been seen, for his positive female characters Leskov made limited use of models existing in oral tradition and early Russian literature. When it came to the depiction of Natal'ia Nikolaevna Tuberozova, a happily married woman, Leskov downplayed the strength and determination of her model, Archpriest Avakum's wife, to a point where Natal'ia Nikolaevna's "force" lies solely in her meekness and wifely devotion, for which he also drew on non-traditional cultural archetypes. Natal'ia Nikolaevna contributes neither to the heroic nor maternal dimension of Rus', and to the religious only passively. Marfa Plodomasova is an old woman and her principled attitudes are presented as anachronistic. In keeping with the patriarchal attitudes of his day, Leskov saw leadership largely in the hands of men. "Rus'" and "rodina" may be grammatically feminine, but for Leskov they seem to have been predominantly masculine.

### Notes

1. I therefore exclude characters such as the hero of "The Musk-ox" ("Ovtsebyk"), 1863, or "The Battle-Axe" ("Voitel'nitsa"), 1866, because Leskov makes little use of folk or traditional literary images in the creation of the main characters.

2. The situation with Gogol's female characters is similarly more complicated than it appears. The strongly negative tone of his portraits stem from the irreconciliable conflict between his own ideal of woman as the epitome of moral virtue and poetic inspiration, to which he had subscribed in his youthful essay "On Woman" (1831), and his own observations. Disillusion pushed him into the use of popular stereotypes.

3. References to Leskov's works are to the collected works, 1956-8, and are cited by volume and page number.

4. Writers and thinkers throughout the century, while seeing Russia as feminine, tended to emphasize the humble and submissive more than the maternal. Towards the end of the century, other female stereotypes, such as Blok's Russia as gypsy, began to play a role. There was a shift to the use of the term "Rossiia" by, for example, the philosopher Berdiaev, presumably because of the very specific connotations of "Rus'", though Berdiaev nonetheless chooses to refer to the Eternal Feminine as "bab'e", reflecting the peasant term for woman "baba" (Aizlewood 1996).

5. All translations are my own.

6. An obvious exception is "Il'ia Muromets i syn".

7. The Russian agrarian cycle was marked by festivals whose rites were intended to increase fertility and productivity of land, animals or people, sometimes overtly by reference to a mother figure or Mat' syra-zemlia.

### List of Sources

Afanas'ev, A. N., 1855-63. *Narodnye russkie skazki* (Moscow: A. Semen)

———, 1865-9. *Poeticheskie vozzreniia slavian na prirodu* (Moscow: K. Soldatenkov)

Aizlewood, Robin, 1996. "Berdiaev and Chaadaev, Russia and feminine passivity", paper presented at the Conference on Gender and Sexuality in Russian Civilisation at the University of Surrey.

Balashov, D. M., 1963. *Russkie narodnye ballady* (Moscow-Leningrad: Sovetskii pisatel').

Barker, Adèle Marie, 1986. *The Mother Syndrome in the Russian Folk Imagination* (Columbus, Ohio: Slavica).

Barsov, E. V., 1872. *Prichitaniia severnogo kraia,* 2 pts (Moscow: Obshchestvo liubitelei rossiiskoi slovesnosti).

Cherednikova, M. P., 1971. "O siuzhetnykh motirovkakh v povesti N. S. Leskova 'Ocharovannyi strannik'", *Russkaia literatura,* 3, 113-27.

Dal', V. I., 1984. *Poslovitsy russkogo naroda,* 2 vols (Moscow: Khudozhestvennaia literatura).

Gachev, Georgii, 1991. *Russkaia duma: portrety russkikh myslitelei* (Moscow: Novosti).

Gorelov, A. A., 1988. *N. S. Leskov i narodnaia kul'tura* (Leningrad: Nauka).

Gor'kii, M., 1948-55. *Sobranie sochinenii,* 30 vols (Moscow: Khudozhestvennaia literatura).

Guminskii, V., 1983. "Organicheskoe vzaimodeistvie (Ot *Ledi Makbet* k *Soborianam*)", *V mire Leskova. Sbornik statei,* ed. V. Bogdanov (Moscow: Sovetskii pisatel').

Hosking, Geoffrey, 1997. *Russia. People and Empire 1552-1917* (London: Harper Collins)

Hubbs, Joanna, 1988. *Mother Russia: The Feminine Myth in Russian Culture* (Bloomington and Indianapolis: Indiana University Press).

Kireevskii, P. V., 1860-8. *Pesni, sobrannye P. V. Kireevskim* (Moscow: Obshchestvo liubitelei drevnei pis'mennosti).

Lantz, K. A., 1979. *Nikolay Leskov* (Boston: Twayne).

Leskov, N. S., 1956-8. *Sobranie sochinenii N. S. Leskova,* ed. P. Gromov and B. Eikhenbaum, 11 vols (Moscow: Khudozhestvennaia literatura).

McLean, Hugh, 1977. *Nikolai Leskov: The Man and His Art* (Cambridge, Mass./London: Harvard U. P.).

Mikhailova, N. G., 1966. "Tvorchestvo N. S. Leskova v sviazi s nekotorymi obrazami narodnogo eposa", *Vestnik Moskovskogo universiteta. Seriia Filologiia,* no. 3, 49-57.

Møller, Peter Ulf, 1997. "Counter images of Russianness: On the role of national characterology in Gogol's *Dead Souls*", *Celebrating Creativity: Essays in Honour of Jostein Børtnes,* ed. Knut Andreas Grimstad and Ingunn Lunde (Bergen: University of Bergen), 70-81.

Muller de Morogues, Inès, 1991. *"Le probleme feminin" et les portraits des femmes dans l'oeuvre de Nikolaj Leskov* (Slavica Helvetica 38) (Berne/Berlin/Frankfurt/New York/Paris: Peter Lang).

Platonov, O., 1993. "Russkaia tsivilizatsiia: dorogi tsivilizatsii", *Russkii vestnik,* 18-20 (101-03), 1-8.

Rybnikov, P. N., 1989-91. *Pesni, sobrannye P. N. Rybnikovym,* 3 vols, (Petrozavodsk: Karelia) reprinted from the 2nd edition ed. A. E. Gruzinskii Moscow, 1909-10.

Stoliarova, I. V., 1978. *V poiskakh ideala (Tvorchestvo N. S. Leskova* (Leningrad: Izdatel'stvo Leningradskogo universiteta).

Wigzell, F., 1985. "The *staraya skazka* of Leskov's *Soboryane*: Archpriest Tuberozov and Avvakum", *Slavonic and East European Review,* 63, 321-35.

————, 1988a. "Leskov's *Soboryane*: a tale of good and evil in the Russian provinces", *Modern Language Review,* 83, 901-10.

————, 1989. "Folk stylization in *Ledi Makbet Mtsenskogo uezda*", *Slavonic and East European Review,* 67, 1989, 169-82.

————, 1997. "Bludnye synov'ia ili bluzhdaiushchie dushi: 'Povest' o Gore-Zlochastii' i 'Ocharovannyi strannik' Leskova", *Trudy otdela drevnerusskoi literatury,* 50, 754-62.

## Irmhild Christina Sperrle (essay date 2002)

SOURCE: Sperrle, Irmhild Christina. "'The Rabbit Carriage' or the Madness of a Perfect World." In *The Organic Worldview of Nikolai Leskov,* pp. 150-98. Evanston, Ill.: Northwestern University Press, 2002.

[*In the following excerpt, Sperrle offers a detailed analysis of Leskov's last story, "Zaiachii remiz" ("The Rabbit Carriage"), discussing the story's title, narrative structure, language, imagery, and symbolism.*]

> Anybody can be misled, but one has to be crazy to persist in one's delusion.[1]

### A "LIVELY" TITLE

Following the rabbit's tracks they reached the bear.[2]

One of the most enigmatic features of Leskov's last story **"Zaiachii remiz"**[3] (1894; 10:501-91) is its title. Leskov had used it earlier for an unpublished 1891 work that seems not to have survived[4] and it is uncertain now whether this was an early version of the one known presently as **"Zaiachii remiz"** (finished only in 1894). Most scholars agree that there were two different works with the same title, a supposition supported by Leskov's own description of his 1891 story as a conte à clef based on some "reminiscences"—a subject that bears little resemblance to the later work. Yet, it is also possible that Leskov drastically reworked his earlier piece after several publishers had rejected it for censorship reasons and "because the people mentioned in these memoirs were still alive."[5] In 1892, Leskov wrote to the philosopher Vladimir Solov'ev, whom he had asked to take a look at an early version of the manuscript:

> About **"Zaiachii remiz"** I think exactly as you do and therefore I asked that it should be returned to me so that I can *rework* [*perestroit'*] it,—from all the same material but in a different manner and according to a different plan, both of which occurred to me only after you had already left. I didn't offer this story to a single Petersburg editor and won't do so until I have completely redone it, toward fall. The story should come out livelier, funnier, and with more venom. Then I will offer it, but it won't do in its present form.[6]

Since we are only concerned with the title, the pros and cons of this debate—the question whether Leskov borrowed the title from the earlier piece or whether the second work is a radical overhaul of the first—is beside the point. But already in 1891 when Leskov offered his work to Prince Tsertelev, the founder and editor of *Russian Review* (*Russkoe obozrenie*), he commented specifically on the title's cryptic quality: "I entitled the manuscript differently from what it was. It was called 'Invasion of the Barbarians,' and now it will be called **'Zaiachii remiz.'** The new title is gentler and *more incomprehensible,* and at the same time, it is sonorous and seductive which is good for the cover of a journal" (11:507).

Leskov was never at a loss for a title. He often proposed several to his publishers, kept lists of choice titles in his notebooks,[7] and obviously enjoyed experimenting with titles, as is seen in his surviving manuscripts, which frequently reveal series of crossed-out variants. As he wrote in 1882, "What I love in a title is that it should be *lively* and that it should suggest through itself the content of a lively story." He proudly mentioned that his fellow writers (*bratiia*) often came to him with requests "to name the child" (11:266).

With such a talent at his disposal, why would Leskov choose a title for his last work that is "more incomprehensible"? The Russian word *remiz* is a borrowing from French and in its most common meaning defines a penalty in a card game or an insufficient take from the deck of cards. The choice of "rabbitlike" (*zaiachii*)[8] as a qualifying adjective for this activity is truly beyond easy grasp. A highly specialized and more obscure meaning for *remiz* comes from the hunting domain: "a place where wild animals live and breed."[9] This meaning, which makes sense when combined with the attributive "rabbit," was favored by foreign translators. In his 1949 translation, Magarshack used the title **"The March Hare,"** which was adopted by several English-speaking scholars.[10] In his study of Leskov from 1977, McLean offered the new title **"The Rabbit Warren."** Setchkarev translated it into German as "Die Hasenremise" which, due to the identical French loan word, is ingeniously close to the Russian and duplicates the original simplicity and sonorous quality. Among other meanings, the German *Remise* denotes "an enclosed wild animal preserve" (*Wildgatter*). Scholars, however, have refrained from commenting in detail on the connection between the title and the content of the work. In her book on Leskov's rhetorical strategies and work habits, which devotes a whole chapter to his fascination with titles, Gebel counts this choice among the cases where Leskov was "far from taking into account the connection between the content of a given story and its title" and concludes that "in [this] case the title remains unintelligible in relation to the text of the story."[11] The fact that it existed separately from any story, being included in a long list of contrived titles which were kept "in reserve" in one of his late notebooks,[12] and that it freely migrated from one work to the next seemingly supports Gebel's argument.

Leskov, no doubt, was very fond of the title. In 1894, when he proposed his new (or reworked) piece to Stasiulevich, the editor of *The Messenger of Europe* (*Vestnik Evropy*), he once again rejected an alternate choice: "Game With a Dummy" ("Igra s bolvanom") in favor of **"Zaiachii remiz."** He writes: "The manuscript was ready, but all this time I couldn't make peace with the title which seems to me at times too harsh, at others as somehow too incomprehensible [*maloponiatnym*]. However, let it be for a while the one which I have put down now, namely, **'Zaiachii remiz'**. . . ." (11:606).

The title's elusiveness results from the semantic richness encompassed by the original French words *remis* and *remise*, which express concepts ranging from an "undecided game" to "delivery, coach-house, shed, replacement, reduction, remittance, postponement," among others. From these semantic fields further derivations entered the German and Russian languages in the form of foreign borrowings. **"Zaiachii remiz"** is a story about the origin and development of a case of dementia that Leskov attributes to the hero's inability to understand semantic connotations and his fixation on literalness. This gets him into a mess. I therefore propose that Leskov overcame his hesitations about the title's incomprehensibility and stuck to it precisely because it satisfied his criteria for titles most fully: it perfectly conveyed the story's content and essence. Obviously, he made peace with the idea that his readers may not grasp all the different layers of this title. The most common use of *remiz* in Russian is in the derivative verb form *obremizit'sia:* "to get into difficulties, into a mess." In his rejection letter, Stasiulevich was quick to pun on this meaning when he mentioned that with the publication of this piece "he himself could end up in a great mess" (*mozhno ochen' samomu obremizit'sia;* 9:643). So, what about the adjective "rabbitlike"? The hero of the story gets himself into a mess because of strange fantasies that have taken hold of him; in other words, the mess is in his head. Already at the very beginning of his writing career in his novel *No Way Out* (*Nekuda;* 1864) Leskov had made use of the rabbit image to describe the muddledness that characterizes a "blind follower of new ideas":

> The marquise could not reason calmly and logically; she could not, so to speak, *reason reasonably*. She had, as the Poles would say, "a rabbit in her head," and this rabbit jumped about in her skull so aimlessly [*besputno*], that it was completely impossible to catch it. It was even impossible to see its hind legs or its little drawn-in bob-tail. The restless jumping about of this hurrying little animal was only felt because from under its legs came flashing out: "crowns of the social lad-

der" and other clever words which were mixed up into the most stupid phrases.

(2: 321)[13]

As will be shown later, a state of great mental confusion also distinguishes the main character of **"Zaiachii remiz."** Thus, if *Zaiachii remiz,* "a place where wild rabbits live and breed," is understood in this abstract sense, McLean's **"The Rabbit Warren"** or his more recent **"The Rabbit Refuge"**[14] seem appropriate translations of the title which convey very well the story's essence.

I would, however, like to suggest still another possible translation for this title, which plays on still another meaning of the French word *remise,* a meaning Leskov knew. In French, the word *remise* as a masculine noun also denotes a hired or livery carriage (this is a shortened version of the phrase "une voiture de remise," in which *remise* is feminine).[15] To qualify this meaning with the attribute "rabbitlike" creates a paradoxical combination. Usually one hires a cab to get to a specific destination. But if the carriage behaves like a rabbit, it will run along an unpredictable course and most certainly will not end up where one wants to go. Such a title aptly reflects one of the central episodes of the story where the main protagonist, a village police chief, is in hot pursuit of a suspected subversive, a much feared "socialist." The chase is carried out in a carriage driven by the hero's newly hired coachman. But the police chief is not going where he thinks he is, realizing much too late that the person he is pursuing is actually his very own driver. And in good rabbit fashion the hunted party gets away.

Support for translating the title as **"The Rabbit Carriage"** comes first from Leskov's own statement. In the continuation of the letter to Stasiulevich quoted earlier, he explains the title thus: "'**Zaiachii remiz,**' that is, the madness [*iurodstvo*] into which 'rabbits sit down, for whom the rock served as a refuge'" (11:606). One can hardly call this an elucidation of an already obscure title! For the time being, let us concentrate on two words of this statement: "to sit down into" and "madness." Leskov uses the verb "to sit down into" (*v kotoroe sadiatsia*) to describe the rabbits' activity which is appropriate for a carriage. Moreover, such a rabbitlike carriage is made synonymous with *iurodstvo,* the Russian type of holy foolishness which in extreme cases displays distinct traits of madness. Well, to sit down into a carriage of the aforementioned description would drive anybody insane, which is exactly what happened in the aforementioned episode in the text. Perceiving too late that his driver has turned the tables on him and transformed him, the alleged hunter, into the hunted animal who is stuck as in a trap, our overzealous police officer becomes stark-raving mad and ends up in a lunatic asylum. There, he turns into a classic *iurodivii,* a self-proclaimed holy fool and prophet, and in his final feat tries to make the world understand his message of salvation. The second part of Leskov's enigmatic statement—the "rabbits, for whom the rock served as refuge"—contains, in my view, the philosophical meaning of the story. It can be understood only within the context of the text, and I will return to it later.

The meaning of the French word *remise* as a hired carriage is not in current Russian use, nor was it in Leskov's time. This makes this interpretation of the title completely unintelligible, something Leskov was aware of when he chose it. But we have evidence that the word was known to Leskov himself. In an unpublished letter to his stepdaughter Vera Bubnova, who is preparing for a trip to Paris, he shares some of his own experiences in Paris with her and offers practical advice. Among other tips he tells her: "For carriages *don't* take a fiacre,[16] but what is called there 'voiture de rémise[']' [*sic*], that is, a coach *with a railing* on its roof where they'll put your luggage. . . ."[17] Leskov must have known these *voitures de remise* quite well since he proceeds in great detail to tell her how and when to pay and even how much such transportation would cost. I therefore believe that Leskov, who loved to trick readers with lexical richness and ambiguities, was playing on this meaning of *remiz* in addition to those mentioned earlier. My personal preference for translating **"Zaiachii remiz"** as **"The Rabbit Carriage"** is not because I necessarily think that this translation is superior or more plausible—in essence, the variants all come down to one thing, namely, a metaphor for madness—but because it is more accessible to a reader who is uninitiated in Leskovian imagery. Moreover, the carriage plays a central role as the "vehicle" that moves the story forward and in the final chase provides the climax that sends the hero over the edge.

Notwithstanding Leskov's great efforts, his last masterpiece was not published until 1917, more than twenty years after his death.[18] This neglect, however, can hardly be blamed on the obscure title. Nor could it be attributed to a direct rejection by the censors, since in all likelihood no censor ever saw the work. The culprit was so-called self-censorship, since the various editors to whom Leskov proposed the work got cold feet and were put off by the boldness of Leskov's subject matter. Once scorned for his alleged "conservatism," toward the end of his life, Leskov was considered too liberal, so that even the most progressive journals of the time rejected several of his last works.

Leskov finished **"The Rabbit Carriage"** at the end of 1894 and offered it first to Gol'tsev, the main editor of *Russian Thought* (*Russkaia mysl'*) under the title "Game with a Dummy" (*Igra s bolvanom*). Used to dodging the censors in the last decades of his life, Leskov cautioned Gol'tsev that the story contained "delicate mate-

rial" but, as he added, "everything ticklish is very carefully disguised and deliberately made obscure. The coloration is Ukrainian and insane" (11:599). He felt that it would pass the censor more easily than **"A Winter's Day"** (**"Zimnii den'"**), his attack on the Tolstoyans, which had just been published in *Russian Thought*. The editors did not share Leskov's optimism, however, and rejected the story. One of them, V. M. Lavrov, wrote Leskov on December 13, 1894:

> I and V. A. [Gol'tsev] read your manuscript and decided that at the present time it is definitely impossible to print it. Precisely because of those questions which you touch upon the censors will get raving mad at us, as well as at you. This is very sad, but we hope that you do not blame us for what has to be charged totally to the present order of things. We are returning the manuscript, although reluctantly.
>
> (9: 643)

Leskov was not deterred and proposed the story to *The European Messenger,* this time under its final title **"The Rabbit Carriage"** (**"Zaiachii remiz"**). He writes to Stasiulevich: "The piece is written in a whimsical manner, like the narratives of Hoffmann or Sterne with digressions and ricochets. The scene is transferred to the Ukraine [. . .] and with the Ukrainian humor things will seem to go more smoothly and more innocently" (11:606). Unfortunately for Leskov, Stasiulevich was also afraid to accept the work for publication. Although he experienced "great pleasure" on reading the manuscript, he felt that "he could not risk sharing this pleasure with others" (9:643). Less than two weeks before his death, in another letter to Stasiulevich, Leskov resigned himself to "retiring the work":

> There is a saying: "Drunk or not, if others say you are drunk, you'd better go to bed." That is what I will do. I don't consider "the funny story" all that dangerous, but *I will put it to bed.* . . . This has already become a habit with me: *Cathedral Folk* slept in the drawer for three years. "The Survey of the Prolog" [now known as "Legendary Characters"]—five years. Let this one sleep as well. I believe you when you say that there are reasons to be afraid [. . .]. Let's wait. It's possible that the weather will grow milder.
>
> (11: 607)

The "delicate matter" concerned a subject, which—as McLean pointed out—was not touched on by any other Russian writer of the nineteenth century, namely, the inner workings of the Third Section, the czar's secret or political police, and the pursuit of "subversive elements."[19] For Leskov it was not an altogether new theme. In a more lighthearted way, he had ridiculed the gendarmes earlier in **"A Journey With a Nihilist"** (**"Puteshestvie s nigilistom,"** 1882; 8:125-31) and **"Laughter and Grief"** (**"Smekh i gore,"** 1871; 3:382-570). In the latter, one of the characters is even introduced as a "sky-blue being" (*goluboe sushchestvo*)

(3:421) and receives the nickname: the "sky-blue cupid," a reference to the sky-blue uniforms of the members of the Third Section. But the irony of Leskov's earlier period had darkened with the same speed with which Russian society grew more conservative. The satirical stories of his later years no longer spared their targets. As he told Faresov,

> My last works about Russian society are very cruel. **"The Cattle Pen," "A Winter's Day," "The Lady and the Wench."** . . . The public doesn't like these pieces for their cynicism and their directness. Well, I don't want to please the public. Let it choke on my stories as long as it reads them. I know how to please it, but I no longer want to. I want to flog and torture it. The novel becomes an indictment of life.[20]

It is therefore not surprising that another story from 1893 that touches on the subject of the political police as well and depicts the easy and "graceful" removal of undesirable elements among the intelligentsia—a story aptly called **"Administrative Grace"** (**"Administrativnaia gratsiia"**; 9:388-396), "slept in the drawer" even longer, until 1934. Although in **"The Rabbit Carriage"** Leskov set the action in a small Ukrainian village of no consequence and chose as the main protagonist a bungling village policeman who is unsuccessfully trying to catch "underminers of foundations," the madness and the Ukrainian coloration did not sufficiently cover up the underlying targets.

**"The Rabbit Carriage"** carries the subtitle: "Observations, Experiences, and Adventures of Onoprii Peregud from the Clan of the Pereguds," and not only relates the complete life story of the main protagonist, Onoprii Opanasovich Peregud, from birth to death but also includes much background information, such as the founding of the clan and its ancestral village by one of Onoprii's ancestors. One of the two narrators is the hero himself, who as a patient in a lunatic asylum tells his story to the visiting author. The author as the frame narrator, in his turn, at times intercepts, edits, takes over the narrative, and, after Onoprii's death, adds an epilogue to the story.

From the "madman's" perspective the reader learns about Onoprii's family history, his childhood, his half-baked education in the bishop's entourage, and how by chance he becomes a police chief in his native village, Peregud. In this position he at first is very successful, despite his total lack of preparation for the job, until he gets "infected" with the idea of ridding society of "shakers of foundations." From that point on it goes downhill for the hero. Desperately trying to be distinguished for the apprehension of subversive elements, he gets himself into the most ridiculous situations. He denounces a Tolstoyan governess for seditious statements that turn out to be biblical quotations and neglects his time-honored task of catching horse-thieves, with the result

that his own horses get stolen. The latter misfortune lands him in court, where he cuts a sorry figure. His final mix-up is the arrest of a secret agent who is on the track of the real revolutionary, Onoprii's coachman. The recognition that his own driver is the insurgent he is desperately trying to catch and the fact that he himself has unwittingly been the distributor of the seditious leaflets which were hidden under his very own seat finally drives him mad, and he ends up in the lunatic asylum.

Inspired by the very Tolstoyan he had earlier tried to denounce, he devotes himself to useful activity and becomes the asylum's "official sock knitter," work that earns him the respect of the other inmates. At this stage in his life he becomes acquainted with the author and recounts his story in retrospect. From the author's own comments and observations during his visits to the madhouse, we also learn of the hero's predeath spiritual awakening, as well as of the final feat that precipitates his death.

To reduce the content of **"The Rabbit Carriage"** to Onoprii's "antinihilistic" police activities, which begin only after chapter 15 of a thirty-chapter story, means that the first half of the work is being ignored or relegated to the category of "extraneous material." Such a division into two parts usually happens when this work is discussed. Critics often concentrate only on the second part—considered the major part of the story—and besides some general isolated social criticism, see in the first part little relevance to the work as a whole. As McLean puts it,

> [I]f the story is classified as a satire on policemanship, then its whole first half must be viewed as a digression. This digression, dealing with Onopry's early life, consists of a series of disconnected and seemingly harmless anecdotes, [. . .]. On the level of pure narrative development, none of this background geography proves essential to the reader's understanding.[21]

He comes to the conclusion that "[i]n relating episodes from the basic phases in his life, each of them unconnected in any rational way with the one before, Onopry is unconsciously making the same point Leskov had made twenty years earlier in **'Laughter and Grief'**: that human lives, especially in Russia, are existentially absurd."[22] Like Grossman before him and Lantz after him, McLean then puts **"The Rabbit Carriage"** into the category of stories in which a "mad *raisonneur* [. . .] from the vantage point of the lunatic asylum, lays bare the madness of the outside world," and, following Grossman, discusses possible influences on Leskov by the younger generation, such as Chekhov's story "Ward Number Six" ("Palata No. 6," 1892) and Garshin's "Red Flower" ("Krasnyi tsvetok," 1883).[23]

Look Who's Talking

To turn Onoprii into a "mad *raisonneur*," however, ignores the attitude of the frame narrator who, considering the first-person narrative and the autobiographical information, purports to be Leskov himself. In Leskov's *skaz*-like stories, the frame that motivates and encloses the inner *skaz* narrative is not a mere convention but contains authorial correctives that are crucial for understanding how the inner narrative is to be "read." These "spectacles necessary to correct the distortion"[24] become even more indispensable in such stories in which there is a wide discrepancy between views expressed in the inner narrative and those of the author. In **"The Rabbit Carriage,"** the frame narrator (implied author)—functioning once more as a "chronicler"-type narrator—arranges his material in such a way as to stress the hero's "madness" and, as the story unfolds, distances himself more and more from the protagonist's view of the world, thus discrediting the latter's qualifications as *raisonneur*. By the end of the story, which temporally coincides with the fictional time—the "actual" time when the protagonist presents his "observations concerning the outside world"—the author makes the laconic comment: "Now, he had become a real madman whose words not every person would be inclined to believe" (9:589).

In the author's mind there seems to be no doubt that his protagonist is mad, despite the fact that this derangement is barely noticeable, and he reinforces his impression by hints throughout the story. He begins **"The Rabbit Carriage"** with an autobiographical fact, stating that "due to a sad incident, over quite a long period of time" he was in the habit of visiting "a hospital for people suffering from nervous disorders, which in the common everyday language is called 'a madhouse.'"[25] As if to make sure that his readers should not mistake the place for anything but a lunatic asylum, he adds after the word "madhouse" the comment: "which, as a matter of fact, is exactly what it is [*chem ona i est' na samom dele*]" (9:501). He then defines what *he* thinks constitutes insanity: "With the exclusion of a small number of people who are there for examination, all patients of this institution are considered 'insane' and 'not responsible,' that is, they do not answer either for their words or for their acts." He then makes sure that one would not be tempted to count Onoprii among those who are there "merely for examination." On the contrary, as he expressed it, his hero belonged to the category of sick people "who were interesting for the fact that in them the insanity was barely noticeable, while nevertheless they were without doubt insane" (9:501). As if in support of his view, a line from a romantic song, "And maybe my dreams are insane," which the hero applies to himself repeatedly, runs through the text like a leitmotif. Thus, at the very beginning of his autobiography Onoprii tells the author: "I would have lived

until the end of my days [*do veka*] were it not for that song 'And maybe my dreams are insane!'" (9:510)

In this manner, Leskov arranges around Onoprii's type of "insanity" a specific cluster of ideas, such as irresponsibility in *words* as well as in acts; a madness that is barely noticeable; and certain dreams, using for dreams the Russian word *mechty,* which denotes daydreams or desires one desperately wants to have fulfilled in one's life. All these notions appear in the Russian concept of holy foolishness (*iurodstvo*). Thus, one of the most flagrant hallmarks of the Russian holy fool (*iurodivyi*) is his exceedingly irresponsible behavior "in words and acts," which for him is a way to realize the (probably) "insane dream" of total union with God. Specialists who have studied the phenomenon often equate it with various forms of madness, and, in fact, several *iurodivye* lived in mental institutions. This, however, did not deter the simple people. Far from considering *iurodstvo* a deranged mental state, they highly revered it as a form of inspiredness, as a state of being in the possession of real knowledge.[26] Furthermore, as we have seen earlier, when explaining the title, Leskov equated the idea of **"The Rabbit Carriage"** with *iurodstvo*.

I suggest, therefore, reading the story as an exploration of Onoprii's "insanity" instead of concentrating on him as a *raisonneur*. For if we accept his (crazy) view of the world as "social criticism" instead of as a severely distorted view of reality, we fall into the same trap as the Russian common people (as well as certain sections of the intelligentsia) who ran to their holy fools for advice and took their insane babble for the ultimate truth.[27]

**"The Rabbit Carriage"** is a typical Leskovian *skaz* consisting of a frame and an embedded narrative—a quasi-oral tale by a second highly individualized narrator. Despite its acceptance as a critical term, *skaz* has not really been defined satisfactorily. There is a great divergence of opinions of what exactly constitutes a *skaz,* of whether it denotes a style or a genre. Unfortunately, the search for a unified definition has been impeded by polemical considerations. The formalist critics who first paid attention to this phenomenon almost exclusively stressed its formal aspects and defined *skaz* as a narrative that linguistically creates the illusion of oral speech. As concerned the nineteenth century, Leskov was considered the main proponent and uncontested master of this technique.[28] In an excellent article that discusses the particular devices Leskov used to achieve linguistic "oralization," McLean comes up with a good working definition for *skaz,* which he adapted from the various formalist sources: *skaz* "means a stylistically individualized inner narrative placed in the mouth of a fictional character and designed to produce the illusion of oral speech."[29] McLean rightfully avoids the hot water of "style versus genre" debate and calls *skaz* a technique or narrative mode. Rice, who admirably tried to sort out the issue, distinguished *skaz* style from *skaz* as genre but advanced a rather narrow definition of the latter. Since he feels that authorial comments destroy the illusion of orality, he discounts all frame stories, as well as all narratives with first-person self-description, and considers "pure *skaz*" a tale told in a highly idiosyncratic language by a third-person narrator, a definition, as he admitted, that comes close to a story in dialect.[30] Ironically, Leskov, who developed and perfected *skaz* in the nineteenth century and whose influence on twentieth-century proponents of *skaz,* such as Remizov, Zamiatin, and Zoshchenko, is uncontested, would have produced very few "pure *skaz*" examples. Rice only mentions Leskov's **"The Left-hander"** as belonging in this category, omitting the fact that it was first published with a footnote that resembled a frame, in which the author explains the origin of the tale, as well as the background of the narrator. Applying his theory of polyphony to *skaz,* Bakhtin enlarged the notion and offered a fresh angle beyond stylistic considerations but marred his insights considerably by desperately trying to apply his definition to Dostoevsky. Depending on how *skaz* is defined, some examples may be found in Dostoevsky, but given his lack of language differentiation—a fact even Bakhtin admits[31]—it may not have been the wisest strategy to test a theory of *skaz* on this writer; unless, of course, one disparages the importance of orality, one course of argument Bakhtin chose. He states that "to see in *skaz* only oral speech is to miss the main point."[32] Criticizing the formalists for their exclusive stylistic interests, and using Turgenev as an example of why oral speech is an insufficient criterion for *skaz,*[33] Bakhtin sees in *skaz* an orientation "toward another person's discourse."[34] In his view, Leskov belongs to the category of "writer-monologists"[35] and is an unsatisfactory example of *skaz* writer, since he "resorted to a narrator largely for the sake of a socially foreign discourse and socially foreign worldview, and only secondarily for the sake of oral *skaz*."[36] Whereas in the second claim (Leskov's "secondary" interest in orality—it was very primary indeed!) Bakhtin betrays total ignorance of Leskov's intention, in the first he does not explain satisfactorily why a "socially foreign discourse" is an objectified discourse, and what distinguishes it from an orientation "toward another person's discourse," which supposedly is "double-voiced." Bakhtin's stress of the dialogic element in *skaz*—when applied somewhat differently from what he had in mind—proves very useful for a definition of *skaz,* at least as it appears in Leskov.[37] At the same time, however, given the etymological derivation of *skaz* from the root "to tell, to relate," the illusion of orality must be retained as primary. *Skaz,* then, could be defined as an oral narrative that is distinguished from an oral monologue by incorporating dialogic elements. This "dialogue" could take place between the narrator and the reader, the narrator and an imagined listener or listeners, or the narrator and a "present" listener or listeners. The more differentiated the narrator's speech is from the accepted standard—the literary language of the implied author—the greater the implied dialogue between norm and deviation. Since speech reflects worldview, such a dialogue should of course be understood not only stylistically but, more important, philosophically and psychologically. As Leskov said about the writer's task, "Man lives by words, and we must know at which moments of psychological life which of us will use which words."[38] In Leskov there is a strong trend toward the third type of dialogue, a "physical" re-creation of an oral performance. The more typical Leskovian *skaz* will have an elaborate frame which sets the stage, introduces the narrator, and creates a motivation for the narrative that is to follow. This motivation, however, is not of the conventional type, as in Turgenev, for example ("The guests assembled after dinner. . . ."), but derives from a topical issue, or a problem that is "apropos" (*kstati*), in answer to which the *skaz* narrator presents *his* particular point of view. The frame also provides possible clues as to the author's stance in relation to the point of view presented. A very Leskovian element, moreover, is the move away from an embedded *skaz* monologue toward an embedded *skaz* dialogue. Whereas a monologue is determined only by "Shandyanism," the erratic nature of a particular consciousness,[39] a "real" versus an "imagined" dialogue will have the added element of several erratic minds belonging to the various listeners. This adds a "foreign" element to the narrative, an element outside the narrator's control: the presence of listeners will deform a tale as it is being told. An oral narrative, thus, is close to epic poetry, which includes performance—physical gestures as well as rhetorical devices, that is, techniques of improvisation. Leskov seemed to have been particularly interested in the element of distortion, in the fact that *any* speech event is conditioned by its circumstances, its motivation, its particular setup, its participants. Thus, in his *skaz* stories, he re-creates the atmosphere of a fictional oral performance. His "listeners" will interrupt, ask for clarification, make comments, and thus redirect the story. The narrator is only one—although the main—participant of this event. Often, the initial motive for the story changes. In **"The Enchanted Wanderer,"** for example, the character who is to become the *skaz* narrator enters a discussion on suicide and, prompted by his listeners, ends up telling "the story of his life." Such redirections are common in Leskov and account for the prevalence of "loose ends," digressions, and the move away from a tight story.[40] There is, therefore, no sharp division between frame and embedded narrative; the "frame"—the audience or the author—spills into the *skaz.* And as if to stress the discrepancy in dialogue between intention and result, between what is meant to be told and what is told, as well as between what is told and what is "heard," that is, *what the listeners make of it,* Leskov often emphasizes this distortive element by adding additional "unreliable" or untrustworthy situations. Thus, in **"Choice Grain"** (**"Otbornoe zerno,"** 1884), a character recounts a conversation of a *skaz* narrator, which he unwittingly overheard during a train ride while *half asleep.* (What prevented Leskov, the author, from having his character listen to a story by his traveling companions while fully awake?) Or, in **"Night Owls"** (**"Polunoshchniki,"** 1891), the narrator listens through the wall of a hotel room (undependable situation—Did he hear right?) to the story of a woman with "faulty" moral standards. Again, overhearing a conversation in a hotel lobby would have been as equally well or "badly" motivated.[41] Leskov may also deliberately confuse the reader by concocting a whole array of narrators. In **"Antuka"** (**"Antuka,"** 1888), a narrator tells a story about somebody having told him a story about somebody else or some event. Anybody having played the child's game "Telephone," which consists in whispering a message from one person to the next, has experienced surprise at the final distorted outcome. In **"The Co-Functionaries"** (**"Sovmestiteli,"** 1884), the frame narrator promises to retell a story "in almost the same words in which he heard them" (*pochti temi zhe slovami, kak slyshal;* 7:399). Literary convention has enough examples of implied authors claiming to tell a story in "exactly the same words in which he heard them." There was no need for Leskov's disclaimer, were it not for his deliberated attention to the fact that *any* speech event is an example of *polu-byl',* a distortion of the "true" version.

As if "physical" distortion is not enough—the attention paid to the unreliability of circumstances or to the listeners' receptiveness—Leskov often creates a great discrepancy between the psychological, moral, or social makeup of the *skaz* narrator and his audience, and/or the implied author. He seems, in fact, to have a fascination with unreliable narrators, the presence of which often causes what Likhachev called a "'faulty' ethical evaluation" of his stories.[42] The roster of questionable *skaz* narrators includes people with dubious morals, such as the procuress in **"The Amazon"** (**"Voitel'nitsa,"** 1866), the shameless hypocritical female companion in **"Night Owls"** (**"Polunoshchniki,"** 1891), or the "high official" (*sanovnik*) in **"Administrative Grace"** who gleefully reports the "painless" removal of a liberal professor from the university. In these stories the purpose of the story may be less *what* is told than *who* tells it. As Edgerton, who calls these narrators "negated" narrators, says about one such satire, "[It is] told in approving terms by a character who turns out to be himself a target of Leskov's attack."[43]

Such a combination of untrustworthy situations and narrators creates—to use Likhachev's term—"multistoried narrations."[44] It forces a dialogue among various world-views, positions, and individual experiences without necessarily offering a solution. Just like the fictional audience, which is presented with a highly individualized point of view—that may not necessarily be the right solution to the problem stated in the beginning—the reader, somewhat guided by hints in the frame, has to peel off the various distortive layers and try to discover the "final" meaning of the story. The "dialogue" is unfinalized, open-ended. No wonder, then, that Leskov's reader is often surprised by what he comes up with. Grossman is not alone when he expresses the frequently encountered bewilderment on reading a story by Leskov: "Often Leskov's reader is genuinely puzzled as to whose side the satirist is on, whom he is condemning and for whom he is fighting."[45] Leskov himself acknowledged his tendency to confuse the reader morally and reports that it has been attributed to "a certain *ingrown craftiness in* [*his*] *nature.*"[46] However, despite the fact that this may not always be obvious, Leskov's work is intensely moral. Thus, Likhachev considers the Leskovian trait of "moral confusion" a thorough disguise for a moralizing stance, and he calls it "the device of literary intrigue": "In contradistinction to the direct moralizing 'up front' [*v lob*] in Tolstoy, Leskov very often transforms the moral into an element of literary intrigue, and this makes him one of the most original writers in world literature."[47] For Likhachev, the deliberate removal of the author, who turns into merely a stenographer and records conversations, forces "the reader to judge on his own as concerns the character and the moral makeup of those talking and as to the events and life situations which unveil themselves gradually before the reader's eyes in the course of these conversations."[48] Of course, what Likhachev calls "stenographer" has been called "chronicler" here; given Leskov's attitude toward source material, his narrator would not "simply record conversations" but would vary them. The moralizing element is to be sought in the narrator's interference, in how he arranges, presents, and possibly distorts such material.

In **"The Rabbit Carriage,"** there is a deliberate and plainly stated confusion between frame and embedded *skaz* narration. In an apology to the reader, the author outright admits that for the sake of greater accessibility he has "tampered" with the material presented:

> I ask you not to condemn me for the fact that his and my words will be mixed together here. I allowed this to happen so that not everything would be as drawn out as Onoprii Peregud told it in his elaborate fashion during his walks. A lot of what he considered important, in fact, seemed unimportant to me and was cut out [. . .] or retold much more briefly in my own words, but the whole essence of the events was preserved, except that repetitions and other devices of this dreaming madman's [*mechtatel'nii man'iak*] wordiness were eliminated. . . .

> (9: 503)

The second, imbedded narrator, then, is the "dreaming madman" Onoprii, who takes over completely after chapter 4 and, with the exception of a few interferences, continues until almost the end.

Given Leskov's interest in unreliable narrators, one should not be surprised to find a madman as the story's main spokesman. The issue of Leskov's unreliable narrators usually comes up in discussions of his satires or "problematic" stories, in which the reader is challenged to unravel the moral confusion resulting from the discrepancy between the *skaz* narrative and the author's point of view. However, such cases are merely extreme examples of Leskov's notion of *skaz* narration, as discussed earlier. In a letter to Buslaev, in which he lays out his views on the novelistic genre, Leskov agreed with what he called "the old decision" concerning the preference of one genre over another, namely, that "the best form for any writer is the one which best corresponds to his skills" (*s kakoiu on luchshe upravliaetsia*). For himself he chose the "memoir form embedded in a fictitious artistic work" (10:452), which essentially is nothing other than what has previously been called *rasskaz-polu-byl'*—"a half-true story."

Memoirs, or reminiscences in some form or other, play a major part in Leskov's writing. As we have seen in the previous chapter [of *The Organic Worldview of Nikolai Leskov*], they provide the source material for his work. Besides works that are based entirely on memoirs, found notebooks, and life stories, we find in Leskov a very prominent use of the anecdote, of retold isolated events in his own or somebody else's life. Even the *skaz,* one of Leskov's most favored narrative techniques and one in which he is the uncontested nineteenth-century master, falls into this category. The *skaz* may be considered a fictionalized oral memoir ("Let me tell you what happened . . . !"). In contrast to a "written-down" memoir, it reproduces features of orality such as speech habits, intonation, and pitch of voice, which characterize the narrator. The *skaz* narrator tends to be a specific social type, but Leskov often transcends that category by choosing a somewhat outstanding or curious specimen of the given milieu. Character in Leskov is determined by social circumstances, as well as by personal traits. Thus, the narrator in **"The Left-Hander"** (**"Levsha"**), for example, is not merely an ordinary gunsmith but also left-handed and squint-eyed. His professional feat in the story is made all the more extraordinary by his individual "handicaps." Likewise, the narrators' voices reflect their social background (jargon, dialects, specific vocabulary) but also personal idiosyncrasies, what McLean called "tag words," "certain 'favorite' phrases and expressions which they constantly repeat in all possible appropriate and inappropriate situations."[49] The oral traits, then, merely underscore the highly individualistic nature of the story. It is the story of *one* particular person, who is firmly set within a social environment, and is told in an individual and idiosyncratic voice. Leskov may choose *any* kind of narrator, "reliable" or "unreliable," as long as the story he or she tells is good. As he once wrote, "I fully agree with those who think that 'all kinds [of writings] are good, except the boring kind'—I like lively issues and characteristic, serious, and instructive reminiscences . . . what is interesting, cheerful, seasoned in taste, and makes sense is also good."[50] Sorting out the story is the reader's work. Thus Leskov preserves an epic, open-ended quality, which for Benjamin distinguishes a narrative told by a real storyteller from a novelistic work.[51]

Shying away from using an "objective" author, Leskov then makes sure that the chosen *skaz* narrator's milieu, stature, class, background, even his mentality and moral makeup, are known to the reader—usually from the very beginning. He wants his reader to know that what he presents is a very individual perspective on an issue, while he himself remains hidden behind his narrators. He merely "chronicles," that is, records and edits, but usually refrains from direct judgment. But that does not prevent him from passing indirect judgment through well-placed comments or through highlighting the flaws or vices of the narrator, in the *way* he presents the material. Thus, the unreliable or "negated" narrator, if not prevented from talking, will eventually reveal his or her real nature. Sooner or later it will be apparent that the vision presented is that of a distorting mirror. The pitfall in reading Leskov's stories is that the *skaz* narrator is often not fully deciphered, and Leskov, the author-chronicler, is identified with the point of view presented. This is even more true in cases where the *skaz* narrator is essentially a "sympathetic" character, albeit of limited mind, who easily wins the reader's compassion. Even in such an endearing story as **"The Left Hander,"** for example, the point of view is that of an ignorant gunsmith from the provinces and not that of Leskov. This narratological pitfall is represented as well in **"The Rabbit Carriage,"** where the *skaz* narrator elicits our sympathy as we move into the story.

Through his particular use of *skaz* narrators, Leskov exemplifies and stresses the deceptiveness and distortion inherent in any individual perspective, which is all the more true if it pertains to an uneducated person. Thus, distortion, as Leskov uses it, is close to the formalists' notion of estrangement—*ostranenie*—a device that makes familiar aspects of reality appear "unfamiliar" by employing an unusual angle.[52] But unlike the formalists, for whom estrangement was a formal device, a way to "refresh" the text and thereby renew and intensify the perception of reality, in other words, an end in itself, for Leskov it is highly moral. The use of distortion must have a positive motive. It must reveal, open up, and enlarge an aspect of reality and is not justified when it debases the object in question.[53] For example, Leskov does not make fun of people who have "a strange way of talking or behaving," his humor is not ethnic humor, nor does he choose human deficiencies or ridiculous or humiliating situations as comical targets. What makes Leskov's stories highly enjoyable is that his humor may be biting, but is hardly ever nasty.[54] The reader often ends up admiring—while laughing at—the verbal ingenuity of Leskov's characters, even in cases of morally suspect characters.[55] Distortion, then, is a way of stressing differences without necessarily establishing a hierarchy of superiority. For this same reason Leskov may use the voice of the uneducated to teach the educated, or vice versa. One should be wary, though, not to interpret Leskov's frequent use of "uneducated" narrators as an expression of a hidden sympathy for populism on his part, or of any animus against intellectuals. Leskov can and cannot be found on either side. In an unpublished article he attacked what he considered a naive view of the common people advocated by populists:

> I am not a populist [*narodnik*] . . . in the sense that I like everything, even what is bad in the Russian better than what is good in the foreign. I also don't think that learned people should go back once more to learn from the uneducated, but nevertheless I think that one should listen closely to the voice of the people and take the opinions of the people into consideration.[56]

Leskov is not interested in the division of "uneducated" versus "educated," or *narod* versus intelligentsia. He is looking for people who recognize the limits of their perspective and preserve an open and undogmatic mind. They represent for him people of a certain spirit, of what he calls "a spirit that is alive" (*zhivoi dukh*), and he finds them among the common people as well as among the more enlightened bishops and members of the intelligentsia. They are, however, not necessarily Leskov's narrators. They might just as well be found in the "audience" or as a character or characters within the embedded narrative.

### "Digested" versus "Undigested" Knowledge

The theme of limited individual vision is introduced in the epigraph to **"The Rabbit Carriage"** and sets the stage. Leskov chose a passage from the Ukrainian philosopher Hryhory (Grigorii in Russian) Skovoroda (1722-94); a choice that is rather unusual, since, in general, Leskov tended not to pick philosophical epigraphs. It is a slightly shortened paragraph from a piece called "A Dialog or Conversation about the Ancient World" ("Dialog, ili Razglagol o drevnem mire") in which five people discuss the image of man and the world in relation to God. This dialogue was first published in a volume of Skovoroda's work that appeared in 1894 on the occasion of the centennial of the philosopher's death.[57] Two pages of Leskov's last notebook are filled with quotations from Skovoroda that were probably copied from an article on this philosopher from the same year.[58]

All but one quotation from Skovoroda reappear in **"The Rabbit Carriage"** in different parts (five in all, excluding the long epigraph). This creates a strong philosophical undercurrent to the work, which is further reinforced by the fourfold mention of Skovoroda's name throughout the story.

The epigraph touches upon several issues in Skovoroda's philosophy, which are in turn taken up and illustrated in Leskov's work. It reads:

> If you wish, stand on a flat piece of ground and order a hundred mirrors be placed all around you. You will then see that your unique bodily image [*bolvan*] has assumed a hundred different shapes, and as soon as you take away the mirrors, all those copies will disappear. However, our bodily image is itself but a shadow of the true Man. That creature, like an ape, represents through its visible activity the invisible and eternal force and divine substance of that Man of whom all our images are like shadows reflected in a mirror.
>
> (9: 501)

In this passage from Skovoroda's dialog, Longinus, one of the interlocutors, explains the effect of a hall of mirrors to Afanasii, who has never seen one. With the help of this metaphor—a variation of another favorite Skovorodian image, namely, the tree and its ever-changing shadow—he illustrates the relationship of the "two worlds," the Divine, or the ideal, and the real. The ideal is unchangeable but intimately connected to and reflected in the multiplicity of reality.[59] The central image in this passage is the *bolvan,* which in modern Russian designates a blockhead in its literal meaning (that which gives shape to a hat) and in its figurative meaning (a fool or dummy). Skovoroda used a third, now obsolete meaning: "idol" or "image." Man is a *bolvan,* that is, only a crude copy of the Divine, the real Man in the passage. In **"The Rabbit Carriage,"** Leskov takes up and varies all three meanings of *bolvan.*

The epigraph also shows metaphorically people's relationship to the world, as well as to the Divine, the ideal. We are surrounded by the world—the hundred mirrors—and each part of this world—each individual mirror—will see and reflect a different part of us. A singular vision will produce a very limited picture. Only if all the visions are placed together can one get the correct picture. But even this would yield only the external appearance—our *bolvan.* The same is true of our vision of the Divine: we are only one of the mirrors reflecting the Divine, therefore, we cannot perceive its full nature. In their activities, people "ape" the Divine, thus becoming "the blockhead" of the Divine—"giving shape" to the Divine in its earthly manifestations. Our willingness to reveal our real human nature, to open our eyes and act as a mirror, creates the precondition for the Divine to be reflected through our activities. Imagery connected with seeing and blindness becomes central in Leskov's **"The Rabbit Carriage."**

This metaphor aptly expresses Leskov's suspicion of any single perspective or any theory that is hailed as the true situation, when the "reflection" is taken for the "true image." People have a tendency to create their own notion of the Divine—create the hat that fits the blockhead, when it really should be the other way around—we should shape our blockhead to fit the divine "hat."[60] We are not to create the Divine but to *reflect* it. This view once more stresses Leskov's own position of putting deeds over theory, which he tirelessly expressed throughout his works. Thus, already in an 1882 letter he writes: "It is insane and impudent to 'make comments about God' [*kommentirovat' Boga*], but it is totally reasonable and noble to educate one's own spirit to submit to the fates which cannot be negated 'since they themselves negate you.'"[61] Themes that are touched on in this passage all reappear in **"The Rabbit Carriage,"** namely, theorizing about God versus the assimilation of a certain spirit through education; "negation of the fates"—that is, the attempt to control one's life and to overcome death—versus being eliminated by what you are trying to control. Thus, Onoprii finds death as he tries to overcome death.

The difficulty presented by Leskov's prose is his tendency to create a multifaceted picture, which one may call kaleidoscopic or which was earlier called "cubist." He achieves this strange picture through his highly individualized point of view, by presenting *one* view but in such a way that he achieves what Bakhtin called heteroglossia. To use Skovoroda's metaphor: It is as if we are standing in the middle of a room of mirrors and we look at one mirror, which reflects not only us but the reflections of other reflections that come from other mirrors. Moreover, some of these mirrors may be distorting mirrors. But these are all reflections of one thing: *us*. For example, the chronicler-narrator, who pretends to be located outside this setup, merely describes what he sees when looking at certain reflections or reflections of reflections—the uncommented reiterations of other people's opinions would fall into this category. His freedom consists in which mirrors he will single out for his account. This process keeps his own involvement to a minimum, and he betrays his own position less by narrative comments than by the juxtaposition and sequence of descriptions—the chosen arrangement.

Commentators have tended to simplify Leskov and have ignored the numerous "internal reflections," thereby distorting the whole text. This simplification has arisen out of sheer necessity, since in Leskov it is difficult to talk about one issue without first establishing its relation to other issues, which leads to an endless chain of explanations and particular definitions. For example, the earlier quotation from Leskov's letter could superficially be interpreted as a call to submit to fate, an interpretation that has often been given to Leskov's work which renders him a fatalistic conservative. Leskov's

extremely optimistic worldview is forward-looking, however, and assigns personal freedom a central place. This optimism and passion for individual freedom are not evident unless one clarifies first what he meant by "spirit," "education of one's spirit," "submission to fate," "fate," "negation of the fates," and "being negated by fate." Unfortunately, most of these terms can be understood only after distilling their specific "Leskovian" meaning, which necessitates a familiarity with a substantial part of Leskov's work and thought.

His way of thinking—which is not "horizontal" (linear-logical) but "spatial" in that it creates endless internal linkages—also finds expression in his style. Leskov's style has often been called "excessive," and some critics find that at times it gets out of hand and loses its relation to the text. His play with words, however, is just one way of creating overlapping semantic fields. Each word, first, through its original meaning, and second, through its "distorted" (that is, individual and contextual) meanings, creates endless connotations that evoke other passages and other words elsewhere in the text. Often the full meaning of the pun is not understood unless all related references are put together—unless all the mirror images are assembled into one three-dimensional picture.

In Leskov the mind is viewed with a certain wariness, since by its essence it tends toward concretization and finality. He does not, however, *reject* it but, quite the contrary, stresses the importance of its "education." For Leskov education must have the purpose of training the mind to remain open to new stimuli. In this process it should concretize, that is, a person should and must form opinions and have convictions, but these must subsequently be open to modification. The anti-intellectual bent that is occasionally felt in Leskov's work is more precisely a critique of those "who think they know," a category that includes anybody with a rigid worldview, from hermits or so-called wise men, to simple people believing in superstition, to those believing in deterministic and materialistic theories. Knowing, in Leskov, is an open-ended activity. Thus, in his work those who have arrived at solutions are suspect; they have to twist and turn to justify what does not fit their theory, which Leskov is quick to point out. It is not surprising, then, that Leskov found a certain affinity with Skovoroda, whose anti-intellectual bent is expressed in the following saying which, via Leskov's notebook, found its way into **"The Rabbit Carriage"**: "Wise people see with their eyes and cackle with their mouths, show off like monkeys, change like the moon, are restless like Satan, greedy like the dropsy, steady like the sea and as affectionate as a crocodile. And besides they are people, people!"[62] Leskov ukrainianized and shortened this quotation and put it, together with two other sayings by Skovoroda, into the mouth of the bishop. It appears in a passage in which Onoprii relates his experiences in the town where he was taken by the bishop for his education. The bishop was earlier presented in the story as an intelligent, good-natured, well-read, and immensely practical and rather undogmatic person who untiringly fights superstition in all forms. In the passage in question, Onoprii tells how the bishop berated the steward for his superstitious beliefs by showing him the real reasons for his cow's strange behavior. Onoprii then continues by giving a characterization of the bishop, whom he called "more far-sighted than all superstitions:"

> But that couldn't be otherwise because this was a man of great gifts and of such immense learning that he even agreed with Skovoroda in his opinions and answered all suggestions about any improvements in his diocese with the words: "You may turn as you wish, but what is really necessary is to pave the way amidst the piled-up burial mounds of rebellious unbelief and the sordid swamps of slavish superstition," and this, if you remember, is a saying of a certain eternally remembered Grigorii Varsova Skovoroda. And he saw all of this so clearly that he laughed at those who went to foreign lands and returned again with the same type of mind, and "look with their eyes, and cackle with their mouths and show off like monkeys and change like the moon and are restless like Satan. He who is blind in his own house will not see anything either when he goes on a visit."
>
> (9: 526)[63]

In this combined form Skovoroda's original message—in Leskovian fashion—is somewhat distorted and enlarged, since it no longer applies to "wise men" (*mudretsy*) but to superstition, unbelief, and mental blindness, that is, certain fixed ways of thinking which are rigidly based on one's own established view of cause and effect and which do not change despite shifts in physical surroundings. In other words, if one's views do not reflect the change of circumstances, the mirror is blind, since each mirror and each different position reflects a *different* shape.

Although relatively little of Skovoroda's work had been published in the nineteenth century and he had not really begun to be appreciated by the urban Westernized intelligentsia in Russia before the turn of the twentieth century, among the simple people in Ukraine he was indeed an "eternally remembered" figure. In the 1860s, the Russian folklorist and historian Kostomarov noted that "every literate Ukrainian knew of him, as did many of the illiterate folk," and evidence shows that his sayings, songs, and parables had influenced the folklore and popular culture of Ukraine.[64] It is very probable, then, that the bishop and even Onoprii himself knew bits of Skovoroda's thought. But the future readers of **"The Rabbit Carriage"**—the Russian intelligentsia of the two capitals—might scarcely have known the name of the Ukrainian philosopher. What, then, is Leskov's purpose in repeatedly bringing up the name of Skovoroda?

Textual evidence suggests that the philosophy of Skovoroda provides a foil to Onoprii's own rules of life, since in several places throughout the book, Leskov contrasts Onoprii with people who quote Skovoroda. The first instance is the foregoing passage, which is followed by an elaboration of the theme of education and traveling. In this section a dichotomy is set up between traveling and ignorance versus staying at home and still having knowledge. Although Onoprii is not mentioned personally, he must be implicitly put into the first category. He is the only one in the story who leaves home blind—he has to be educated—but returns the same way, having acquired nothing, as the reader is told repeatedly in no uncertain terms. The other side is exemplified by the bishop, who traveled on an official visit in the beginning of the story but essentially prefers to stay at home and educate himself. This we learn from Onoprii, who follows his reiteration of the bishop's statement (which is really Skovoroda's)[65] on the foolish habit of traveling while returning unenlightened, with the comment that the bishop, by contrast, "remained at home in his monastery but understood and knew everything" (9: 526).

The compressed Skovorodian sayings—which constitute the first reference to the philosopher, excluding the epigraph—introduce the theme of erudition in general. Again Onoprii and the bishop are contrasted. After giving an elaborate account of the bishop's knowledge, Onoprii admits his own inability to be taught anything. Thus, he lists all the reading the bishop had done:

> and Plato and Cicero and Tacitus and Plautus and Seneca and Terence, and many others, and good gracious, what else didn't he know and read, and probably even wanted to teach me a lot, but couldn't because of the compatibility of everything [*po vsego sovmestimosti*]. By God, you may not believe this, but, by God, it is the real truth—he couldn't!
>
> (9: 526)

Onoprii blames the failure of being taught anything on some kind of "compatibility." This is a good example of a typical Leskovian *slovechko*—a little word that seems to make little sense but is crucial in understanding the passage. Without it the reader will not know what prevented Onoprii from learning. This term is not explained anywhere in the text, nor does it reappear again. But it must have been a favorite expression of Leskov's, since Faresov mentioned it in a recorded conversation with the writer and stressed it by putting it between quotation marks. In this conversation, which according to Faresov was one of many on the theme in question, the related term *sovmestitels'tvo* was used in the sense of "simultaneous service to two gods." In this case, the argument touched on the idea of being an artist and a bureaucrat at the same time. Leskov strongly opposed this position and considered that such a "'*sovmestitel'stvo*' was always harmful to any thought."[66] Somewhat later in the conversation, he uses the same term that appeared in **"The Rabbit Carriage"** only in its negated form, namely, *po nesovmestimosti,* to denote that same incompatibility of literary—that is, creative—activity and government service.[67] For Leskov, there is a deep-seated organic incompatibility between "serving," that is, blindly following strict rules, and "creating," that is—as has been pointed out previously—"distorting," or applying rules in a liberal, "heretical" manner; an incompatibility of a follower's and an artist's mentality. **"The Rabbit Carriage"** was to be the third part of a trilogy, of which the first part was *No Way Out* (*Nekuda,* 1864) and the second Leskov's unfinished novel *Falcon Flight* (*Sokolii perelet,* 1883).[68] All three deal with the them of follower in some manifestation: focusing on the nihilist movement, *No Way Out* depicts people who slavishly follow someone else's ideas; *Falcon Flight,* which was to portray former nihilists who had turned into faithful government agents (11:656), was to concentrate on those who blindly submit to political power; **"The Rabbit Carriage,"** as we will see, while touching on both types, also transcends the theme in the figure of Onoprii, who becomes a follower, more precisely, a slave, of his own idealistic creations.

**"The Rabbit Carriage"** shows how people who have an unswerving follower's mentality will be determined by this nature in all they do in life. They may "travel," that is, physically change their perspective, but not profit from it, since their dogmatic mind is not swayed by changing external circumstances. Nor are they moved to change their views when offered additional knowledge. They do not learn.

Onoprii is a typical specimen of this mentality. All the bishop's efforts to teach him therefore come to naught. Although Onoprii tried to combine both ways of thinking and be on both sides of the road—the literal meaning of *sovmestimost'* as "placing things together" would probably be a better translation of the term—he cannot "grasp" anything, that is, vary and adapt any received information. Instead, true to his follower's mentality, he excels in memorizing and becomes a favorite altar boy, since he knows to perfection at what point during the liturgy who has to bow how many times and where the prayer carpet has to be moved to (9:531-32). But, as is stressed repeatedly, he did not acquire real learning. Thus, when he leaves the bishop's entourage to take up the position as police chief in his native village, the bishop asks him whether he understood the advice given him by his former teacher. Onoprii answers: "No, [. . .] Your Grace. I haven't understood anything, for, to tell you the truth, having been taught with the other choirboys according to the easy method, I haven't learned anything at all" (9:534).

In the previous pages the reader has been told what this "easy method" was like. The boys' teacher was Vekovechkin, a demoted priest who was hired by the bishop to teach the choirboys. He is the ultimate "wolf in sheep's clothing,"[69] an extremely clever opportunist, who knows how to bend any rule to his advantage and how to get ahead in any game. As a relativist with no fixed rules at all, he embodies the flip side of the dogmatic follower. Even after Onoprii leaves the town and returns to his native village, he returns to call on Vekovechkin whenever he needs advice. Onoprii admits that, as regards learnedness, things were rather bad in the choir and "one couldn't expect any better, since [the boys] were supposed to acquire all knowledge in the shortest possible time and only from one person," from the same Vekovechkin, who was called "inspector" (9:527). They were told the most ridiculous facts, culled from special notebooks made up by their teacher. Examples of Vekovechkin's self-produced, "incestuous" knowledge, which the boys had to memorize, include such pearls as: "In September there are 1,100 saints, in October 2,543, in November as many as 6,500, and in December even more—14,400; in January there are even more than that, namely 70,400, whereas in February the figure falls to just 1,072, and in March there is a further drop to 535, and in June there are only 130 . . ." (9:528). Onoprii then makes the following comment: "Many people are amazed at where and how Karamzin dug up and copied all his material from; and God knows, whether what he tells us is true or not; but in the case of our inspector Vekovechkin it was firmly established that . . ." (9:528), upon which follows another list of ridiculous data concerning the life of Christ and the Mother of God with exact dates and times when the Annunciation, the birth, and so on were to have taken place. Secular history was taught in an "even more shortened version," which resulted in such conclusions as the one on the French Revolution, namely, "since that time the significance of France [was] demolished" (9:530).

When talking about Onoprii's education, Leskov stresses several times that all knowledge came from "one teacher only" and all from "his notebooks," which emphasizes once again the dangers of one perspective, especially when seen against the background of the bishop's varied reading.[70] Another important factor in Vekovechkin's system was the precept "not to doubt but to believe the witnesses" (9:527-528), that is, an original development of thought was not encouraged, which Onoprii stressed once more on another occasion: "We weren't asked for any answers because there was no time to learn the lessons" (9:530).

Learning according to the "easy way," then, is the uncritical acceptance of knowledge which comes from one "teacher" only, without consultation of and verification by other sources, and without proper "digestion" of knowledge. In other words, the adoption of a ready-made truth essentially creates a follower. Upon leaving the bishop, when Onoprii complains that he did not learn anything with the "easy way," Vekovechkin makes the following, rather true comment:

> What are you complaining about, you idiot! You are not the only one educated in this way, but that doesn't mean anything: This is how it has to be, for there is nothing that can be learned the easy way, but, nevertheless, many who got enlightened in this manner function all right in life. You were educated in the easy way, so go and make your judgments according to the easy way.
>
> (9: 534)

Vekovechkin, in fact, rightfully observed that many people want to learn "the easy way"; they want to be done with learning and merely become followers of what they have accepted once and for all.

In discussions of this story, Onoprii's misadventures are frequently blamed on his education. This may be true, but only up to a certain extent. We are told that Onoprii had further opportunities to learn, since the bishop took a liking to him and tried to teach him "a lot," Latin and the appreciation of poetry, among other things. He did not succeed, however, due to Onoprii's inability to have his mind work in two ways, in the creative distorting and in the strict and monist way. The real reason for Onoprii's failure must then be looked for in his nature, which may be incongruous with real learning. And it may not be surprising that certain factors in Onoprii's character are again contrasted to two more ideas by Skovoroda, which crop up in two crucial places in **"The Rabbit Carriage."**

### THE CLAN OF THE PEREGUDS

In the short introduction that precedes chapter 1 of **"The Rabbit Carriage,"** the author rather explicitly and at the same time enigmatically relates what Onoprii's nature was like. Moreover, as a foreshadowing the reader is told that whatever happened to the protagonist up to his finale in the madhouse is a direct consequence of this nature. The statement is made in a peculiar language, an unblended mixture of the author's own words with inserted quotations from Onoprii, whose speech is in itself a concoction of Ukrainian, Church Slavonic, and mangled Russian expressions:

> In his convictions he was "in part ambitious and in part a conservative," and in his life he "loved a nauseous quiet" [*tishnotu*] and that "nobody should dare to show another person a facial expression that resembles an ugly mug." And given these, his special gifts, Onoprii Opanasovich Peregud "in a most astonishing fashion extolled himself by means of 'The Rules for the Manifestation of Truth'" and then "most cruelly diminished and annihilated himself" [*umen'chtozhil*]. This event

was astonishing and sad, but Peregud did not complain about that, for all of this "resulted from his special surprised nature." (9: 502)

In this paragraph the author presents a very compressed synopsis of several stages in the hero's life. It is loaded with references that will be picked up later in the story and may become either clearer at that point or, in good Leskovian fashion, even more obscure by the acquisition of additional meanings and connotations which were not originally associated with them. Moreover, Leskov's ingenious neologisms, his beloved "little words" (*slovechki*), create a subtext that is not readily comprehensible. For example, the kind of quiet that Onoprii loved is conveyed by the Russian neologism "*tishnota*," which is a combination of *tishina* (quiet) and *toshnota* (nausea). The second connotation of this mangled word seems to make little sense at first, but we shall return to it later. Leskov does not explain; he does not supply ready-made meanings. Thus, the reader may never fully know what was meant by Onoprii's "surprised nature" (*udivlennaia priroda*) (nor, incidentally, whether it was Onoprii's own expression about himself or whether somebody else coined it—it is put in quotation marks, thus a "reflection" from some source or other). One can only guess. We are surprised by what we do not understand and by what we are not prepared for. Both elements, the inability to digest knowledge that is contrary to expectation and the inability to cope with unexpected events, indeed, are part of Onoprii's nature.

Luckily for the reader, after this loaded and confusing passage the author jumps in and explains in his own words—in Leskovian fashion, that is, once more enigmatically—what Onoprii's nature was like: "And his nature was such that already in his childhood he chased himself around a barrel stubbornly trying to catch and overtake himself. It is quite natural that a person with such a disposition can't be calm in the end, and it went so far that after many trials Peregud managed to become an inhabitant of the madhouse. . . ." (9:502-3). Thus, the author takes seemingly innocent childhood play to be an expression of a "disposition" which runs through Onoprii's life and finally makes him fit for the lunatic asylum.

Onoprii calls himself part conservative and part ambitious. Although the two notions seem unrelated and sound strange in this combination, they have a common semantic field, namely, temporal direction. And seen from that aspect they are total opposites: conservatism denotes an exclusive focus on the past or on the inside; it is a move toward containment, stagnation, fear of change and foreign influence. It could be represented by the mythological symbol of the snake biting its tail, or Onoprii's attempt to catch himself in the effort to create a closed, self-sufficient circle of himself with nothing alien in between. The second notion, ambition, denotes an aggressive forward movement toward the future, a relentless and somewhat "blind" striving toward a definite aim of one's own devising—one's desire, or *mechta*. Ambition, we are told on several occasions, brings on Onoprii's ruin. Onoprii first talks about ambition when an overwhelming yearning overtakes him to seek distinction and glory in the elimination of state enemies. But his aspirations eventually take on megalomaniac proportions: during his stay in the madhouse he dreams of overcoming death—which is nothing other than the attempt to "overtake oneself,"[71] to overcome the ultimate boundary of one's individual human life.

Although these two essentially opposite movements exist in human life in moderate and somewhat compromised forms and usually are concentrated toward two very different ends, political conservatism and personal ambition, for example, in Onoprii's case they more and more coincide, and the two coveted goals become each other's flip side. He strives first politically and then spiritually toward the establishment of a utopian society that is completely conservative, devoid of foreign or distorting elements. Such a society is, by definition, dead for its negation of change, that is, life. At the same time, Onoprii attempts to overcome death. In other words, he is at one and the same time trying to embrace and eliminate death. The physical realization of such paradoxical ambitions cannot but drive him mad.

The subtitle tells us that **"The Rabbit Carriage"** relates the "Observations, Experiences, and Adventures of Onoprii Peregud from the Clan of the Pereguds." This subtitle explicitly makes Onoprii part of his "clan." In fact, a careful analysis of his background reveals that his nature reflects the nature of his clan as it was laid down by its founder. This would explain why Leskov bothered to "digress" to such an extent by giving Onoprii's family history.

The village of Peregud was created literally "out of nothing"—in other words, ex nihilo—by Onoprii's ancestor, Opanas Opanasovich Peregud, a Cossack elder and a knight. As Onoprii tells the author, "In the beginning there was nothing here" (9:504). The founder, Opanas Opanasovich, was a "true fighter for 'the Orthodox faith'" who would not tolerate any 'unbelievers.'" With the help of his chosen priest he inculcated in his growing clan the superiority of Russian Orthodoxy over any other faith in the world. Consequently, his first concern was to keep his people apart from so-called unbelievers—"Lithuanians and Poles, and even more so from Lutherans and Jews" (9:504). Order was maintained with the help of the Russian and a native type of whip—"between which those who experienced them found little difference"—as well as through the priest's relentless efforts to instill fear of

eternal damnation into the potentially disobedient ones. Through fear of punishment. Old Peregud then was able to settle his Cossacks and enserf them to himself. This was all the more remarkable given, first, the intrinsic rebellious nature of the Cossacks, and second, the time in history, which, as we are told, predates the moment when the Ukrainian peasants, not to speak of Cossacks, were enserfed to their masters.[72]

When the Cossacks plan to petition the empress, Catherine the Great, and complain about their treatment, Old Peregud, having gotten wind of the conspiracy, deals with them using a "whip of native fashion." To put an end to possible recurrences, he decides to "take steps for the future," reasoning that "it is always free people who put temptations of any kind into the head of unfree people, therefore [he] had to see to it that those who were not free should never get close to those who are free" (9:506). To this end, he drove out the Jew who helped the conspirators, since he considered that "all Jews are equally enemies of the Christian people" (9:506).

Old Peregud's "dream" was to create a perfectly organized village under his exclusive control and closed off from any "foreign" interference that might disturb the existing order. The trouble spots for such a society were identified early on as foreignness and freethinking, both of which induce unwanted change. The society's incestuous quality—by which I mean to express a hermetic situation that perpetuates itself by drawing on itself alone, as opposed to a movement that is initiated by outside stimuli, which transform the stagnant status and "renew life"—is reinforced by the order that every male offspring was to be given the first name Opanas, or at least the patronymic Opanasovich (son of Opanas), "in honor of the ancestor." Old Peregud loved his people so much that he would spare neither pains nor money to make life comfortable. His society was to be paradise where everything was fine and easy if you did not ask any questions or doubt the authority of the founder.

This Eden began to fall apart after the death of Opanas Opanasovich, when people started to doubt the veracity of the commandments he whispered into the ear of his priest before he passed away. His testament, as conveyed by the priest, was the following:

> Father, tell all the people at my funeral that I forbid them and any of my heirs and descendants for all eternity to permit any Jew or Catholic to settle among us in our village of Peregud, and that there should never be any Catholic Church or Jewish school; and that in our village there should be always only our one and true Christian faith. Moreover, all should go to confession to you, the priest of Peregud, and should reveal to you what they are thinking. And whosoever will not fulfill this sacred wish of mine and conceals something from you, may "his fate be the fate of Judas who sits

next to the most important devil in hell holding the
money bag in his lap and burning in brimstone."

(9: 508)

Old Peregud ordered that his rules should be observed
for eternity and that there should never be any change
in the village of Peregud. And for quite some time this
is what happened. However, freethinkers soon begin to
appear, and unlike what one would expect, they did not
attack Old Peregud's rules as such but doubted the verbal transmission of them by the priest. Unlike God's
commandments, Old Peregud's were not "written in
stone."

> For a long time all the people believed what he [the
> priest] said, but then some kind of freethinkers began
> to appear who began to say that Father Prokop did not
> always speak the whole truth and that sometimes
> even—the Lord forgive him!—"he fantasizes" in quite
> a shameless way; which, as they argued, gives rise to
> doubts whether the old Peregud really put a curse on
> the village, or maybe it was Father Prokop himself—
> the Lord have mercy on him—who thought it all up in
> order that he should be the only one to intercede to
> God for all the village.

(9: 508)

And this "heresy"—as Onoprii calls it in his account—
took hold of the people and dispelled the "fear of deliverance" and nobody was afraid any longer of "Judas'
fate" (9:508-9).

In this description of Old Peregud's society Leskov
gives a satirical account of several aspects of the institutional Catholic church, and in particular the strict
dogmatic application it received in Western Catholicism. Thus, Opanas Opanasovich, a stout Orthodox believer, borrowed prominent features from a belief he
greatly detested and feared. By circumscribing his territory as Orthodox and keeping out "foreignness," he has
in fact become "foreign" (Western). This paradoxical
feat will be repeated by his offspring, the hero of **"The
Rabbit Carriage."** Old Peregud creates his village "out
of nothing." The doctrine of creation ex nihilo was established in the Nicene Creed as a reaction to Platonic
and Gnostic cosmogonies. To distinguish this act from
human creation, the creed stressed that only God is capable of creating ex nihilo.[73] Old Peregud, therefore,
puts himself in the place of God, rules like a god, and
after "his disappearance" installs a sole intercessor who
alone is ordained to speak on his behalf. Unlike the
Eastern Orthodox Church, which retained a synodical
structure, Catholicism in the West proclaimed the primacy of Peter among the apostles. Since Peter was the
first bishop of Rome, this step led to the doctrine of the
primacy of the pope, who thus established for himself a
direct line as Christ's spokesman on earth. The oral
transmission of Old Peregud's commands echoes the
strong dogmatic nature and the claims of direct apos-

tolic succession made by the institutional Catholic
Church. Another strong "Catholic" feature is the threat
of eternal damnation. Eastern Orthodoxy, with its stress
on God's love instead of God's retribution, has never
gone as far as the Catholic Church with its highly developed system of penance, atonement, and indul-
gences,[74] nor was the East as adamant in its persecution
of heresy.

As Onoprii rightfully remarks, "heresy"—doubts concerning the truthfulness of spoken words—preceded the
loss of paradise, the crumbling apart of Old Peregud's
village. Through similarity in themes, a parallel is established between this process and the biblical story. In
Genesis, the tempting serpent instills doubt as to the veracity of God's rules into Eve as well and thus expels
the fear of punishment (Gen. 3:4). Other biblical motifs
connected with the loss of paradise are brought up in a
little, seemingly unimportant anecdote that explores the
effects of acquiring forbidden, that is, "foreign," knowledge. The center of the village was taken up by a pond
for bathing, and since nobody had anything to hide, everybody bathed stark naked. A sense of shame was absent in Peregud. One of the squires, however, a certain
Dmitrii Afanasevich, screened off his section of the
pool with sheets and created a private swimming pool.
He is introduced as the second of the two most remarkable squires in the village (the first is the narrator
Onoprii). What distinguishes him is his education in a
Moscow boarding school and the fact that he speaks
French with his wife and his mistresses. While his father carried the full "honorable" name of Opanas Opanasovich, Dmitrii, as can be seen, Russified his ancestor's name from the Ukrainian Opanasovich into
Afanasevich.[75] This step already signals a small "revolution." Although Russians were not openly called undesirable elements in Old Peregud's world, this was only
because they were more powerful. Old Peregud very
diplomatically tried not to arouse their attention and
merely prayed silently "that God's power would smash
them to bits" (9:504). Obviously, Dmitrii is set up as
the foil for Onoprii.[76] He has been infected by foreign
knowledge, a type of knowledge considered evil in Old
Peregud's paradise. As in the Bible, the savoring of forbidden knowledge (the search for good versus evil) creates a sense of shame and signals the end of paradise,
here symbolized by Dmitrii's private bathing area.

The "Catholic" leaning, instilled in Onoprii through the
social order of his ancestral village, is reinforced later
on by the "Jesuitical" instruction with its emphasis on
catecheses, to which he is subjected in the town. Many
of the patterns and techniques are familiar to him, as he
had already assimilated them at home. Thus, Old Peregud's manner of establishing the village finds an echo
in the way Vekovechkin looks at the notion of learning.
Both want to create followers for their established truth.
They both cherish incestuousness (exclusion of

foreignness), a static quality (an absence of doubts which would bring about change), and creation "without source," that is, supposedly out of nothing (i.e., a refusal to give credit to what was before; a clean separation with the past). Another similarity is the idea of one teacher/founder who lays down the rules and tolerates no deviation. Old Peregud's notion of an easy life where punishment is reserved for disobedience resonates in Vekovechkin's notion of learning by rote, in his easy, abbreviated method which brooks no questions and is enforced by a frequent use of the rod.

"Education" in Old Peregud's and Vekovechkin's world is understood as a complete acceptance of rules or facts with no deviations—there is no notion of assimilation or growth. The idea of "digesting knowledge," which fosters doubts but also encourages innovations, is spurned in favor of literal repetition of received information. In the example of Old Peregud's verbally transmitted testimony, in **"The Rabbit Carriage"** Leskov establishes a direct link between the questioning of received information, that is, the acquisition of real knowledge, and heresy. Moreover, as we are told, heresy dispelled fear of punishment in the inhabitants of Peregud. Since according to the basic Christian tenet, belief in Christ dispels fear, in Leskov's theology, belief in Christ must therefore be associated with heresy—which indeed it was, as has been shown in the previous chapter [of *The Organic Worldview of Nicolai Leskov*]. Real knowledge is therefore not compatible with the idea of one specific truth, a notion which closes the mind to doubt and stops the true learning process.

The Pereguds were taught by their founder to cherish a happy but static quality in their society, a state of "paradise." For Onoprii, as we have been told, this became part of his nature. He loved quiet. But as the potentially subversive element of Old Peregud's society is merely hidden and waiting for a moment to burst into the open, so does Onoprii's quiet contain a dose of nausea— *toshnota*. In Vekovechkin's and Old Peregud's world, "digestion" of new information is forcefully stopped or prevented altogether by keeping the children busy— "there was no time to learn the lesson." At some point this condition will lead to a violent explosion if no other release is created.

Leskov combines the three semantic fields of quiet, indigestion and/or stomach troubles, and imminent doom in several places in the text. Through this combination of images he expresses the organic idea that any hermetically closed-off matter—a state of stasis—"goes foul in the inside" and will create a violent rupture and force a release, if it is not allowed to be digested, decomposed, that is, be renewed in some way. This danger is merely ignored or beaten down forcefully in Old Peregud's world. The simultaneous state of outward calm and inner unrest is maintained until the death of

the prime authority, when—literally—"the bottom of the whole scheme drops out." The breakdown of the society Old Peregud so carefully preserved is symbolically foreshadowed by the details of his death. Having arranged all to his liking and about "to make peace with the Lord," the old man senses his approaching death by the fact that one day "he got sick in his stomach, and moreover so badly, that his bowels almost dropped out of him" (9:506). This image of the spilling out of undigested material is metaphorical for his society, in which after his death emerge "heresy," strife, quarrels among the squires, and an influx of foreigners.

Other references to stomach ailments in this context— ominous quiet and imminent doom—appear in the much later courtroom scene, when Onoprii describes the circumstances that led to the theft of his horses. Despite the judge's repeated admonitions not to digress, Onoprii insists on mentioning in elaborate and poetic terms the quiet of the night. Again warned to restrict his account to necessary evidence, Onoprii replies that this is just what he is doing and goes on to tell how he "prepared to go to sleep at night when he suddenly felt somehow not well at all, as if [he] were poisoned . . ." (9:565). Again, quiet and indigestion precede the disruption of order.

At another point in the text, indigestion gets linked to "vain dreams." Onoprii tells the author: "But pay attention to that dream of mine! For while there are dreams which are of no significance whatsoever, arising out of a full stomach, there are dreams that are quite important which come from the angels. And those are the remarkable ones!" (9:549). Onoprii had just been recounting one of his dreams in which he was looking for an enemy who turned out to be right under his bed. It obviously is one of the significant types of dreams, since it foretells the outcome of Onoprii's chase. Onoprii completely ignores the warning signal, however, and instead pursues his "mad dream"—his desire to catch "the shakers of foundations"—which, incidentally, was the result of a quiet and contented life, "a full stomach": "Before I used to live a quiet sort of existence, eat, drink, go to the bath house and give myself a steaming and go galloping after a horse thief [. . .] and never gave a thought to dangers that threatened my own life" (9:549). Onoprii's "quiet life" continued after his education, which greatly reinforced his Peregudian nature. As the police chief in his native village, he enjoys great success in catching horse thieves and other bandits. His technique is essentially "Peregudian." On leaving his teacher Vekovechkin, he receives a little book, "Rules for the Revelation of the Truth," which he promptly and thoroughly learns by heart. He becomes a master of these rules and all the fine points of their application. The rules are quite simple. To any criminal he apprehends, he recites the most terrifying accounts of God's punishment after death and continues to do so for however long it takes to break resistance, and thus he is able to make even the most hardened robber scream out in pain and confess. When the author voices objections that the criminals might also not have believed in the veracity of the impending punishment, Onoprii exclaims, "Why shouldn't they have believed me? Isn't it printed in the book?" (9:537) Obviously in Onoprii's mind the printed word has irrefutable validity and tolerates no doubts. By contrast, heresy, earlier connected to the spoken word, could raise doubts as to the veracity of its source. This distinction will become important in his life as a "prophet" later on.

All the information on Onoprii's life up to this point is generally labeled digressive background material. But as can be seen, Leskov uses these extensive "digressions" to prepare and establish early on in the story certain clusters of ideas, which will reappear and create new combinations and associations among themselves. To summarize Old Peregud's world or his "true nature" (9:505), one would have to include stagnation and its maintenance by force and threat of punishment; reliance on one source (the founder who creates out of nothing); one truth; one belief; fear and exclusion of foreign matter and freethinking; clean divisions of good and evil; unfreedom and fixed rules for the followers; knowledge as repetition of received information; and an unmediated and literal transfer of communication. In short, it signals a mentality which cherishes clean divisions of "ours" and "theirs," fears deviation, and believes in the possibility of creating a self-contained and self-sufficient system.

Such a world breaks down with death and organic renewal, which immediately interrupts unmediated communication. The person who put himself up as final authority cannot be consulted any longer. At the same time, the idea of "spokesman" for the truth becomes suspect: The word is no longer a pure representation of its source and can be doubted, since it has passed through "another person's mouth and mind." Doubt creates heresy, plurality of opinions, and interpretations (i.e., "fantasy"), dissension and distortion, and loss of absolute authority. On the positive side, however, doubt creates freedom and generates knowledge, which is the acquisition and productive use of something new or foreign.

Onoprii is first aware of death when his firmly established notions begin to collapse all at once. His boasting about his successes in establishing order by a skillful application of his "rules" prompts a prescient comment by the author. He feels that Onoprii's special ability also gave rise to a great danger,

> since, on the one hand, it not only had encouraged in him the hope that soon he would be able to govern and control everybody according to these rules forever, but also, on the other hand, he was overtaken by an evil fate inasmuch as after the elimination of all horse-thieves, he fell into temptation and there arose an unquenchable thirst in his soul for glory and ambition.
>
> (9: 538)

Vekovechkin soon tells him that real glory is not to be gained through the seizure of home-grown criminals who will always exist in a society, but only through the elimination of a new type of villain who has cropped up, the "socialists, or which is the same thing, underminers of foundations, for it is they who shake the thrones of kings!" (9:542). These new enemies come from the outside. Vekovechkin stresses the foreignness of these subversive elements by first using the mangled Russian word *sitsilisty* for socialists, thus placing their origin somewhere far away in Sicily, and then by giving a totally outlandish physical description of them. Men of this species have long hair and wear "hats from the country of Greece," and the women have short cropped hair and wear dark glasses (9:542).

Whereas Old Peregud had to deal only with a limited and closed society, a village—which he placed under a curse lest it should ever develop into a town—and succeeded by force or diplomacy in keeping all foreign elements out of his territory, the village had changed by Onoprii's time. Although nominally still a village, it had in fact become a town with "foreign influxes"—shakers of foundations, or heretics. Faced with a situation for which he was not prepared, Onoprii first completely abandons his "Rules for the Revelation of the Truth," since they could not help him with the "foreign" situation. For the first time he realizes that his rules do not cover all possible circumstances in life: "What kind of action I was to undertake, of this there was no mention in my 'Rules for the Revelation of the Truth'! Just think! No book could embrace all the manifold situations in life!" (9:540).

Again, he looks for a "printed truth," a book that would explain any possible situation in life. His own mind is not trained to deal with unexpected situations by applying and adapting previously received knowledge. Thus, he gets rid of one rigid truth only to quickly adopt another: Vekovechkin's physical description of the "underminers of foundations," which he applies as literally as any other truth he believed in before. While looking for the men in Greek hats and the women with short hair and spectacles, he gets into the most ridiculous situations and arrests the wrong people while missing the real villain, who does not fit the description.

As police chief, whose job it is to maintain order in society, Onoprii feels himself to be a part of this society's foundation. While he was fearless earlier in his handling of common criminals, now, for the first time in his life, when faced with this new situation, he experiences fear. This is not a simple fear for his life, but an existential fear, the fear that his authority is being "undermined," eliminated. He becomes obsessed with the idea of ridding society of these "underminers of foundations and shakers of thrones," since for him authority is not to be challenged.

Onoprii has learned from his ancestor that a perfect society can be created through fear and exclusion of the outside. Now he finds out that an outside, foreign enemy has already penetrated, but he is unable to identify it. When asked by his live-in maid what the "hats of the Greek country" look like,[77] he cannot really describe them, which, paradoxically, does not stop him from looking for them (9:545). This is the beginning of his muddle-headedness, which does not leave him up to his very death and crops up whenever he is made to deal with complex situations. He is now combining (*sovmestit'*—putting together) two incompatible notions: a rigid adherence to accepted norms, that is, his conservative or follower's mentality, with a search for a new truth, namely, his ambitious or creative nature. The act of combining these two ways of thinking, according to Leskov, was "always harmful to any thought." In other words, it marks the beginning of his madness.

### The Chicken and the Egg

Leskov called **"The Rabbit Carriage"** "a funny story" and considered it not "all that dangerous" (9:607). It is certainly very funny, notwithstanding the dark truth behind it. As for the dangerous aspect, I would suggest that Leskov did not intend to write a satire on policemanship and the workings of the secret police. Those are very strong elements in the story, but they alone do not reveal or explain the numerous and strong subtexts, nor do they help in making sense of all the digressions. Rather than an attack on a police state, **"The Rabbit Carriage"** should be seen as a confrontation of two worlds and two mentalities. One of these is exemplified by the Peregudian world and its attempt to create and maintain a utopia. This mentality tries to sustain a simultaneous coexistence of two opposite movements which eventually will lead to madness—although this madness "is barely noticeable": a strong linear forward movement—ambition, and nonmovement—their fixed "dream." In whatever they do and regardless of the situation in which they find themselves, such people will act in accordance with their firmly established set of rules and their fixed idea of utopia.

The opposing mentality, which is less obvious, appears in **"The Rabbit Carriage"** only in digressions. It corresponds to the worldview of somewhat minor figures, such as the bishop and the marshal of the nobility, and is associated with the Ukrainian philosopher Skovoroda, whom both of these figures cite in the text. Incidentally, it is also shared by the frame narrator, who is possibly

the author. This mentality feels an affinity with an organic and evolutionary movement that progresses through a chain of partial replacement and renewal. Its goal (the future) is not concrete, it cannot be known, and there are no specific rules as to how it can be attained.

The differences between the two worlds are most evident in matters concerning death. The Peregudian fears death while he thinks in an ambitious manner, that is, while his efforts are directed toward his goal, since death would interfere with its attainment. But once he convinces himself that he has found his truth, that he has reached his ideal of imaginary utopia, death is embraced, since he has nothing to look forward to. The second mentality accepts death at any point as part of a necessary renewal process and meets it calmly.

Both views of death are illustrated in **"The Rabbit Carriage."** The organic notion of death is associated with the bishop and once again with the philosophy of Skovoroda. On one occasion, Onoprii talks about the bishop's death:

> [H]e already had departed to his fathers, or to say it more simply, "he had kicked the bucket." Yes, indeed, a man of great piety though he was, yet he died too— and I forgot to tell you, that he died without fear and from his last words it was apparent that he considered himself "a personified idea," this being the will of God, Who "Himself breathes the spirit into us, feeds us, lays out our life for us, mends us, and takes us apart again." He comprehended it all and it is, therefore, all the more astonishing that he should not have bequeathed the same spirit to anyone. . . .
>
> (9: 541)

The internal quotation in this passage, which describes God's control of our life, is a slightly truncated saying of Skovoroda, which is found once again in Leskov's notebook.[78] An even closer, organic connection between death and renewal is made somewhat later with another quotation from the Ukrainian philosopher. It is put into the mouth of the marshal of the nobility, who rescued Onoprii after he had gone mad on being abandoned by his coachman and nursed him back to life. The marshal tells Onoprii: "Your philosopher Skovoroda has a fascinating saying, namely, 'the chick is conceived in the egg only at the moment when the egg is beginning to spoil.' . . ." (9:585). The full quotation of Skovoroda's maxim, as recorded in Leskov's notebook, includes the additional comment: "And thus it goes on for all eternity."[79]

In Skovoroda's view the relationship between death and life is not antagonistic. The rebirth process happens *because* there is a degeneration process, that is, new life is conditioned by the decay of the old. This worldview does not operate with imagery of elimination or separation of good and bad, inside and outside, but with imagery of integration and transformation. Death and life have a common base—the egg in Skovoroda's metaphor, which contains both decay and rebirth. Distortion, which is the demise of the accepted, is then a precedent for new creation, a variant of the earlier pattern of respect and disrespect of authority, which was also connected to development and growth.

In the Peregudian mind, on the other hand, death and life are separated into "them" and "us." Believers in this worldview fear and wish to eliminate those elements or people that are different and are situated at the outside and whose penetration into the static world would initiate a process of change. Death becomes frightening because it is the elimination of the self; it is a process, in which the outside—unknown and hostile—takes over and attacks the secure world inside. This image appears in the elaborate account of Old Peregud's death. The old man not only feels that "his bowels are about to drop out," but he is also plagued by terrifying dreams of meeting the most horrible spirits and devils which "exist on the outside" and are ready to drag him into hell:

> [H]e remembered about "the hour of God's will" and began to imagine in his mind: "What would happen when his Cossack soul little by little and finally altogether would jump out of his body? Oh, it won't escape coming up against those horrible and most terrifying aerial spirits, or to put it more simply, the devils and demons which fly around everywhere and which have been painted on the walls at the exit of the Cave monastery! [. . .]" He was very brave, but, you know, once the thought of such a dreadful encounter enters the head of a man and one who is ill at that, things begin to look bad indeed! To be sure, Peregud tried to drink himself into oblivion and to fall asleep more soundly, but the whole host of those aerial devils chased after him and began to enter his dreams. Peregud saw how they [. . .] were about to seize him by his forelock and drag him down to hell, while others came up from behind with fiery rods. . . .
>
> (9: 506-7)

All his life Old Peregud has successfully been able to shut out all disturbing elements. It seems appropriate, then, that in his last hours, when he is called upon to go beyond the boundary of life, he should meet the imaginary devils he has created in his mind and positioned "on the outside of his periphery."

Another image connected with the death of Old Peregud is the "ugly face" with which he passed away (9:507). For this expression Leskov used the rather strong substandard word—*rozha*. The somewhat startling effect of this word is reinforced by its rather frequent recurrence in the text. It appears first in the beginning of the story, when the reader is told that one of Onoprii's "special gifts" is his abhorrence of an ugly

face, that is, he did not like that anybody should assume "a facial expression of an ugly mug—*poza rozhi*." Its reappearance in the description of Old Peregud's death—when *rozha* is used the next time—would mean that part of Onoprii's "special gift" is his rejection of death. The combination of an ugly facial expression and death resonates all through **"The Rabbit Carriage"** and gets reinforced by the additional connotations of spiritual death and mental blindness. This happens when the bishop dissuades Onoprii's parents from sending their son to become a border guard:

> What kind of pleasure is it to turn your son into a catcher of people! Just read what is written about them in the Book of Enoch: "These guardians of hell who stand like vipers. Their eyes are like extinguished candles and their teeth are bared." Is that the kind of glory you want for your son? No, this won't do. And to prove to you that my sympathy is not in vain I'll repeat again: I like the countenance of his mug [*poza rozhi*] and I propose to take your son with me as an addition to my choir. What better do you want?
>
> (9: 522)

The description of the guardians of hell in this passage is borrowed from the apocryphal Book of Enoch.[80] The bishop applies this description to border guards—to those who protect a territory from foreign intruders, thereby establishing a correlation between border guards and "guardians of a dead society." In his mind, then, if a society is intent on keeping out foreign elements, it will turn into hell, hell being "what comes after life," that is, it will be devoid of life. Moreover, the physical description of the guardians—the extinguished eyes and bared teeth—is that of a skeleton. If a society has turned lifeless, their guards will be the same.

Considering the previous mentions of the ugly facial expression, the bishop's use of the term "ugly mug" for Onoprii means that he already sees a certain spiritual deadness in Onoprii. But he is not afraid of Onoprii's "countenance," since what may signify death to others, in his worldview signals a possibility of renewal. He takes Onoprii for his choir and later employs him in the liturgy, an occupation in which he excels thanks to his memorization skills. In the bishop's mind, a "dead" countenance may be perfect for a vocation that is based on a literal and unalterable repetition of ritual movements, and he predicts a church career for Onoprii. His plans are crossed with the death of Onoprii's father and his mother's wish to have her son return to the village to take up the position of police chief.

In this new position Onoprii does very well as long as he concerns himself only with "internal" enemies, with "bad apples," such as horse thieves and robbers. These elements merely disrupt the existing order but essentially do not try to change it. They can be controlled with force and fear. But as soon as he begins to worry about the "real underminers of foundations"—"the foreigners" who challenge the established authority—his appearance begins to change: "And I began to think about this [how to find these elements] and wore myself out to such a degree, that my face changed and became that of a border guard, and my eyes looked like theirs, like extinguished candles and my teeth were bared . . . fie, how disgusting!" (9:546). Thus, the police chief Onoprii turns into a "border guard"; instead of worrying about criminal "domestic" elements, he concerns himself with "foreign" elements. As Onoprii continues tracking down these subversive forces, he becomes completely confused, since he does not really know what he is looking for.

Having hitherto lived according to fixed rules and their correct application—which had solved all of his problems—Onoprii is now at a loss. His direction has changed. Before he was merely a "conservative," but now he is attempting to create a new society without "any disturbing elements," a utopian society. The only trouble is that he does not know what the new society will look like. In need of a concrete goal, he simply makes one up—he becomes "creative." He tries to explain to his coachman what is ahead:

> And I began to make things up and told him how one has to live in the future, and that we have to stop living in the old way and instead have to do things differently.
>
> And he asks: "How?"
>
> And I tell him: "That's how it will be: You see, now we are driving with two horses and a shaft, but one has to drive with three horses and a shaft-bow and bells. . . ."
>
> (9: 562)

Since Onoprii's imagination is limited, his listener does not really get the point of this new society. So Onoprii engages in evasions and tells him that when the time comes he will "understand" and "see" why this has to be like that. As a result of this conversation, his "naive" native coachman leaves him disgusted by this incomprehensible talk, and Onoprii replaces him with a dashing new fellow he picked up in town, in other words, a foreigner!

He is blind to the disaster he has created by this step, a result of his ambition. Notwithstanding all his constant talk about uncovering subversive elements, he, in fact, invites the "real revolutionary" to come to the village and reside with him. Subversive leaflets appear everywhere, and he does not know where they come from or how to stop them. And he wonders whether "[he himself] is catching someone or whether someone is catching [him]. And [his] spirit became dejected and his eyes became extinguished and his teeth were bared. . . ." (9:570). The invitation of the foreigner into his carriage thus begins the process of decay, and Onoprii begins to

disintegrate physically and mentally. His mental blindness prevents him from realizing that he is the origin of it all, that the man he is looking for is his own man.

What has only been an instinct felt in rare moments through dreams and glimpses of enlightenment—namely, that the hunter and the hunted can be the same—becomes reality in the climactic scene of the carriage chase. He is finally made to realize that one and the same act can have two diametrically opposed interpretations—two mirrors looking at one thing from opposite sides. His mind is trained only to recognize neat and clear divisions: good, bad, right, wrong. Consequently, it works only with literalness and concreteness. Any distortion, any different interpretation, throws him off the track. Coming face-to-face with the paradox that the source of creation and elimination is one and the same—the chick and the spoiled egg—he goes mad. This happens when he is abandoned by his revolutionary coachman in a strange forest during a downpour. The first thing that comes to his mind is to destroy the damning evidence, the subversive leaflets he found under his own seat. As he tells it later, "You see, I wanted to put every last one into some ditch or into a swamp and to bury or stomp them in there, so that they would disappear and wouldn't be remembered" (9:578). He still thinks that any subversive material can be stamped out, eliminated. But instead, he himself falls into a ravine—since he *could not see* where he was going. As for the leaflets, instead of being destroyed, a torrent sweeps them up and carries them off. He finds himself in a compromising situation, since his act had the opposite result from his intent, and the ensuing investigation had to establish whether "[he] wanted to cover up the traces of that most pernicious of propagandists and sweep his evidence into a ravine, or on the contrary, whether [he] was his accomplice and was trying to spread these accursed leaflets all over the world by floating them down the raging torrents" (9:581). To get him out of this incriminating situation, the marshal of the nobility, who had found him wandering about in the forest hallucinating and had taken him home, decides to have him declared mad and committed. This may be the best place for him, since, as we were told in the beginning, the madhouse is for those who are irresponsible in word and deed. A person with a follower's mentality has a tendency to dodge responsibility for unintended and undesirable outcomes of his acts, since he cannot cope with varied interpretations. He thus merely ignores them.

Commentators on the story tend to believe Onoprii when he says that during his convalescent period in the marshal's home "all [his] ideas underwent a radical change" (9:584). Although Onoprii seems to change for the better, this change has to be seen as conditional. He indeed undergoes a rebirth, but *in the same spirit*. Obviously, his mental blindness has not been cured. The next morning, after experiencing "this radical change," he goes to the mirror and becomes frightened upon looking at himself: his face is all wrinkled and "[his] eyes are extinguished and [his] teeth are bared" (9:584). Leskov hints that to judge from his external appearance, Onoprii has not really changed at all and at heart he remains a "guardian of hell."

### THE HATCHING OF THE EGG

> If anything ail a man, so that he does not perform his functions, if he have a pain in his bowels even . . . he forthwith sets about reforming—the world.[81]

To throw light on the nature of Onoprii's "change," one first has to analyze the world that brought about this alleged change. He awakens in the marshal's home after his nighttime bout with the leaflets, and his first reaction is that he has died and entered paradise. However, he reasons that it cannot be the Christian paradise, since there "all sit and sing 'Holy, holy, holy'; instead it must be some Ovidian pagan paradise, because there was no singing, but nauseous quiet" (9:579). With this terse comment we see Leskov setting up the dichotomy of Christian versus pagan and putting Onoprii into the pagan category, since Onoprii's mind is essentially superstitious. It works according to fixed rules. And lo and behold, the type of quiet Onoprii finds is his beloved *tishnota*—quiet with a dose of nausea. And in case we have missed the hint, it is repeated once more. During the examination in the asylum, when asked to explain what brought on his change, he answers that he himself did not notice how it happened, but maybe he "began to love nauseous quiet [*tishnota*] because he was influenced by good people" (9:587).

Among the good people who influenced him were first and foremost a certain Julia Semenovna, the same suspicious Tolstoyan he earlier denounced as an "underminer of foundations." She believes in a form of social Christian utopia without any division of rich and poor. As her own contribution toward this goal, she dedicates herself to charitable work and knits crude woolen peasant socks for those who have none. Again Onoprii "copies" what he thinks is "good," and knitting, as we will see, becomes Onoprii's own vocation in the madhouse. Already in the very introduction to the story the frame narrator makes the following comment about Onoprii:

> The director of the institution, all the personnel, and all of the sick called him "the sock manufacturer" since he was knitting socks continuously and at all times, unless he was eating and sleeping, and gave them to the poor. He was not at all offended at the nickname "sock manufacturer" but on the contrary was flattered by it and considered this activity *his vocation*.
>
> (9: 502)

Knitting socks becomes a prominent theme in the last part of **"The Rabbit Carriage."** The idea behind it is that it keeps people busy and prevents them from doing worse things, so-called *betises*. It preserves a state of *tishnota* and keeps the inner disturbance at bay. As Onoprii says at one point, "Quickly, give me my knitting! . . . Or else I am going to get into a state!" The Tolstoyan Julia who dedicates her life to charitable work is usually seen as a positive figure.[82] But one has to tread carefully in the Leskovian minefield. On one occasion she discusses knitting with the marshal and mentions her grandmother who knitted to keep herself from picking her nose[83] and adds the comment: "This is probably true for all people . . ." (9:583). The marshal, who, as we may remember, quotes Skovoroda and is the foil to the Peregudian world, adds the following comment: "Your grandmother provides a wonderful example for a lesson which all those many enthusiasts, who poke their hands where they shouldn't, should be forced to obey" (9:583-84); and in the case of Julia Semenovna, he tells her: "At least you are probably not inflicting any evil on another person" (9:584). Knitting socks, or charity, is then seen as the best occupation for those who believe in a utopian society, because it prevents them from doing worse, that is, using violence to bring about this supposedly blissful state.

The theme of implementing a utopian state appears symbolically in the last part of **"The Rabbit Carriage"** in the image of hatching out the firebird. The first who engages in this activity is "King Bryndokhlyst" (his name being a combination of idleness and whipping), a madman whom Onoprii meets on entering the asylum (9:585). He has established himself King of the Madhouse and demands slavish devotion from his fellow inmates by beating the rebellious into submission (9:502)—in other words, he is another Peregudian, and his dream echoes Old Peregud's paradise. His only unsolvable problem is not foreign elements (the madhouse is already hermetically sealed off from the outside) but his inability to control the weather in his kingdom. Since he walks around barefooted, he suffers from cold feet. This is where Onoprii comes in: he is promptly turned into a royal vassal, a *leib-viazal'shchik*—a neologism which in one word ingeniously combines the idea of vassalship and of knitting.

Onoprii, first having imitated Julia Semenovna's knitting activity, now becomes infected with Bryndokhlyst's wish to hatch the firebird. He tells the author that at night he flies off into the swamp—and not, as the author suspected, "in thought" but, as Onoprii insists, "with his whole being"—to sit among the hummocks and to hatch herons' eggs from which firebirds were sure to emerge. To the author's inquiry whether this is not a frightening thing to do, Onoprii answers, "No, there are many familiar faces, and all are trying to hatch firebirds but for the time being the firebirds are not appearing because there is too much pride in us" (9:588). We then learn that Julia Semenovna is among those sitting and, in fact, has been sitting "on the very first mound and already for a very long time." Charity as a way of righting the wrongs of the world is an old solution.

But not surprisingly, the marshal is *not* to be found there. As Onoprii explains, "He believes in civilization—and imagine, he tried to convince me that one has to live by one's reason. He is against socks and says that it looks as if 'ever since I stopped imitating one type of folly [*betizy*], I had fallen victim to others.'" Onoprii then relates an example the marshal gave him of a German who got confused since a life situation could not be explained by the grammar he had learned. When Onoprii asks the marshal what grammar has to do with him, the marshal answers: "I am telling you that so that you should realize that if something is done successfully by one person, that does not mean that it should be repeated by everybody ad nauseam. Remember [. . .] at least your Skovoroda: One has to go forward and drag along one's own 'bodily image' [*bolvan*]" (9:588-589). The author emphatically endorses the marshal's philosophy of life: "I said that this seemed to be quite true!" In other words, the author supports the marshal's theory that each person in fact should establish "their own grammar"—or as Skovoroda would put it—drag along their own "bodily image" instead of imitating others.

Onoprii seems to agree as well, repeating the word "truth" twice, and then puts forth *his* own grammar of life: "I walk on the carpet" (*ia khozhu po kovru*). This turns into the homophonic "I walk while I lie" (i.e., distort the truth [*ia khozhu poka vru*]), which he promptly conjugates all the way through—"you walk while you lie, he walks while he lies, we walk while we lie, they walk while they lie. . . ." (9:589). After this effort, he complains that his whole mind has gotten confused, and assuming a "gloomy facial expression" (*ugriumaia poza rozhi*), he leaves. This is the last the reader sees of Onoprii. From that point on the author takes over and recounts the last events in the protagonist's life in an epilogue.

This heavily loaded paragraph combines in one big fireworks many of the images encountered before and explains many of the clues that have been scattered throughout the story. There obviously are two camps: Onoprii, Julia Semenovna, and King Bryndokhlyst on one side, and the marshal, Skovoroda, the bishop, and the author on the other. What the first three have in common is their desire to hatch the firebird, a Russian fairy-tale creature associated with a paradisiacal state. In Russian mythology its image also occasionally overlaps with the mythical phoenix, which burns itself and rises again from its ashes.[84] The activity to hatch the firebird takes place *not* in thought only but *in reality*, or, to be more specific, in what constitutes Onoprii's reality. All three believe in creating a world in which

there is general well-being and no disturbing elements; they believe they can bring about their particular kind of utopia. Bryndokhlyst creates his kingdom in the madhouse by forcefully subjugating all inmates. It is totally isolated from the outside, and the only trouble spot—the control of the cold weather—is climinated with Onoprii's socks. Like Old Peregud, Bryndokhlyst believes in conservative totalitarian structures. Julia Semenovna—who incidentally is another of the characters portrayed as having a "countenance of a mug," although of endearing dimensions (*poza rozhitsy;* 9:554)—attempts to realize her Christian utopia by replacing force with charity and the dedication of one's life to others.

Onoprii first tried the "conservative" brand of utopia during his career as police chief but failed, since he could not close off "his kingdom" from the outside. Always ready to submit to a strong authority and its unshakable rules, he is content to live in the madhouse, since there he has achieved total approval from the ruling authority (King Bryndokhlyst)—something he was denied as police chief. He reproves the author for calling the place a madhouse: "Why do you call it a 'madhouse'! That's enough, Sir! Life is very good here: I knit socks and think what I want, and give away my socks as gifts—and everyone likes me for this. Every man, Sir, likes my gifts! Yes, Sir, they love it and say 'Thank you!'" (9:588). However, he immediately modifies the comment and adds that, like everywhere, even in the madhouse there are ungrateful people, a remark which prompts him to mention other negative features, until at the end of the passage he finally contradicts what he had started out with and calls the place "an abyss of madness." This may be an illustration of his "grammar": he believes that he is walking along a carpet, that is, living a protected, cushioned life, and through his socks provides a cushioned life for others. He immediately realized, however, that he was lying since not everybody was happy and content. The asylum is a place where you can think what you want, where you create your own reality, but as soon as you interact—give away socks—the result may not be what you expect. Just as a string of words may mean two different things, which is illustrated by the homophony—*ia khozhu po kovru* versus *ia khozhu, poka vru*—Onoprii's act of generosity is not understood by all in the same way. It does not solve all the problems as he thought and does not even get him the reward he had hoped for—gratefulness. Thus, as soon as you start walking—moving toward the outside, toward the other—you in fact begin to lie, that is, you have to modify what you said or thought before.

The recognition that the madhouse is in fact a madhouse and that the conservative brand is not doing the trick prompts Onoprii during his last days to come up with a new "dream," his new version of utopia. In this effort he confirms once more his ambitious character. Struck by the goodness of Julia Semenovna, he adopts a religious rhetoric and dreams of "satisfying 'the desire of every living thing'" (*sovershit' "zhivotnoe blagovolenie"*; 9:589).[85] One cannot help but see the two possible interpretations of this term. *Zhivotnoe blagovolenie* is borrowed from Psalm 145 (in the Russian Orthodox Bible, Psalm 144), David's psalm of praise, which describes God's goodness and power. The term itself characterizes God's boundless love toward people. However, in Church Slavonic, *zhivot* means "stomach" as well as "life," which would give a second meaning to the term, namely, "well-wishing in the stomach." After what has been said about stomach troubles which permeate **"The Rabbit Carriage,"** this connotation could be taken to mean that Onoprii wants to offer *his* recipe to remove the nauseous feeling from his type of quiet, to halt the organic process of decay and rebirth.

Indeed, we learn in the author's epilogue that "during his last days on earth, Peregud experienced the great happiness of believing in the possibility of a better life in this deadly vale of tears" (9:589). He wanted to discover how to "begin the renewal of the extinguished mind" and decided that "one would have to invent how to print thoughts," reasoning that printing on paper was useless, since it is powerless against suppression (9:590). Such an invention is in accordance with Onoprii's mind. As we have seen earlier, in Onoprii's world, written words represent infallible truth and cannot be contested. As his own work as police chief shows, however, written material can be suppressed. Now, he reasons that the truth—or what he thinks is the truth—has to be *imprinted* on the mind to prevent any tampering. Thus, his idea of "renewing the mind" is to stop making it think; that is, he wants to find a way to stop the distortion process in the mind that makes people doubt received information and create heresies, that makes old information decay and allows for new knowledge.

Among the truths he wants to convey is his idea that "animals should no longer be killed" and that people should "stop eating those that feed them." He did not arrive at these rules by himself, but they represent a literal repetition of some lines he had managed to remember from his reading of Ovid's *Metamorphosis* under the bishop's guidance. He also desires that "all should recognize and hear not only that but also many other things, and that they should understand the horror of what they are doing and what they ought to do" (9:590). Onoprii's truth should not be seen as mere vegetarianism. He is attacking a worldview that allows people to eat those who feed them, in other words, that is based on renewal and replacement, in which the authorities who nourished you will become obsolete and are "recycled." He rejects a world in which the yolk that feeds the chick has to spoil and be eaten by the offspring.

In Onoprii's world, what is acclaimed as ultimate truth cannot be superseded. In order to spread his message throughout the world, he decides to print it directly in the sky for all to see, an endeavor which becomes his last feat. He considers this to be very simple, since all he has to do is to find out from "whence the light shines and what makes darkness grow so dense" (9:590). He seems to have found the solution to this secret during a particularly violent storm when he grabs two letters he has cut out previously—the two letters that signify "good" and "word"[86]—and jumps onto the window sill to stick them to the glass "so that they should be reflected throughout the whole world" (9:591). This attempt, which the author calls his feat "to overcome death" (9:591), in fact causes his death, since he falls down from the window sill. As for his letters, they were illuminated by "the terrible glory" and indeed "something was reflected on the wall, but what it was nobody understood."

Onoprii repeats what he has condemned earlier but what is nevertheless close to his nature, namely, teaching people by the "easy abbreviated method." He believes that his distilled truth would make people understand the whole truth. Moreover, he wants his abbreviated truth to be indelibly printed on everybody's mind and never be altered. In the last apocalyptic scene during the thunderstorm, when "terror ruled everywhere" (9:590), Onoprii in fact assumes the position of God and sends his "word" which is "good" into the world. Unfortunately, he had not quite figured out "whence shines the light" and could not control the various reflections, the various mirrors in the heads of people who just do not understand things the same way. His "writing on the wall" was of no consequence, since nobody could make out what it was.

In 1889 Leskov wrote to a writer friend: "Life is not what it is, *but how it appears in our imagination.* Your imagination is terrible and torturous, but life *is not for happiness' sake, not for happiness' sake, not for happiness' sake.*"[87] Onoprii's imagination is terrible and torturous as well, since he, too, is looking for happiness. As the frame narrator of **"The Rabbit Carriage"** puts it, he dies filled with "the good-hearted desire to satisfy the desire of every living thing'" (9:589). Putting himself in the place of God, Onoprii wanted to be the agent of transformation of the world. He wanted "to make the whole world happy but the force of things only allowed him to knit socks for his comrades of unfreedom" (9:589).

As we were told, the firebirds do not hatch because of pride. There are many who sit on eggs, and every single one believes that he or she is the one who will hatch out the miraculous transformation that the world is waiting for. But this is only one of the reasons. In his most lucid moment, when he realizes that his mind is totally gone, Onoprii offers another reason: "The firebird will not be conceived when all want to eat the herons' eggs themselves" (9:589). Those sitting on the eggs do not permit the foreign agent to enter the egg and allow the "spoiling" process, which is necessary for the birth of the offspring. Instead of fertilizing their eggs—their ideas—by bringing them in contact with the outside, they protect them and keep them to themselves. They are stopping the natural process of decay and rebirth and thus become Kronos devouring his children.

Leskov presents two ways of transformation in his story: one is advocated by the members of the Peregudian camp who themselves want to have the leading hand in bringing about a utopian state. They want to hatch a firebird from an ordinary heron's egg, in other words, create a perfect society born from their limited imagination. Moreover, they become so enamored of their "egg" that they prevent its distortion by "the force of things." The surrounding world that rejects their ideas is hostile and foreign—a swamp—and they are content to sit in isolation on their ideas. Their mental state borders on madness, although this is "barely visible."

The other side "believes in civilization" and in an organic and alternating process of birth and death. Civilization is a slow evolutionary movement based on the advancement of knowledge: a constant process of refutation and variation of theories. This process depends on people who establish theories which can then be altered and adapted. For this reason, the bishops, marshals, and Leskovs need their sources of authority, their Platos, Skovorodas, and Tolstoys, which, however, they feel completely at liberty to adapt to their own needs and distort if necessary. This "organic" side grows through an alternation of theorizing and critical refutation; its agents are "creators" (theoreticians) and "partial demolishers" (critics).[88] The latter are those who "carry away the dung," who eat "their nourishers," their fathers, when they have lost their usefulness.

Transformation in this system happens more indirectly. "Spoiling" can be encouraged by advancing heretical ideas that undermine the established truth. But this process does not follow an infallible chain of cause and effect: The beginning can be induced, but the effect cannot be controlled. Not every egg that is fertilized will hatch. Therefore, the process of inducing change is dangerous, since it can have two opposite outcomes: it can "spoil" something for good and destroy it or it can "spoil" something and produce something better. Those who do not understand the process—who do not live by their reason, that is, those who think they can impose their rules and control the outcome—should rather knit socks than meddle in the order of things.

For Leskov, people with fixed minds are dangerous to themselves and to society, since they force reality to correspond to their rules of transformation. Although he does not advocate "knitting"—renouncing one's place in the world and dedicating one's life to charitable work—it is the best solution to keep such people from doing worse things—so-called *betises*.

The two camps take the form of prophet and followers. The prophet, an advancer of new ideas and a critic of the old order, belongs to the organic camp, since his ideas are usually heretical; the follower, by contrast, is merely an implementer of these ideas who uncritically, "blindly," accepts and attempts to carry them out in life. The marshal touches upon this in **"The Rabbit Carriage":** the followers merely imitate what works for others.

The divide between the two mentalities may explain why Leskov could love Tolstoy and detest the Tolstoyans. He could recognize the pain of doubt in Tolstoy, which was lacking in his followers who were content to adopt the "abbreviated method." In fact, in his later years Leskov often pointed out the similarity between the Tolstoy followers and the men of the sixties. Both want to create their own utopia and both want to get to their goal not by a slow evolutionary process but by demolishing "for good" the old structure. They do not want to fertilize the egg but merely replace it with their own. Unfortunately, theirs is a hard-boiled egg and will never hatch. But between the two, the Tolstoy followers are less dangerous, since they "content themselves with knitting socks." During a conversation about his "anti-nihilistic" novel *No Way Out*, Leskov stated:

> For the second time in my life I see before me the same lightweight people who get carried away by theories, but on whom you cannot rely. In this, the teachers—in the past Herzen and Chernishevskii, and now Tolstoy—are not to blame. We inherited the lightweight people to whom our teachers had merely given the direction. But if you want to codify your life with big names, then even Lev Nikolaevich gets all mixed up in the details. The Tolstoyans are somewhat cleaner than the nihilists, but the character is the same: the same phrase and the same impossibility of relying on it.[89]

Onoprii belongs to the followers. His mind is closed, since he associates any movement, any distortion, with something sinister, something evil. As he expressed it in his grammar, "I walk while I lie." The fact that the walking and distortion process can be productive and, on the contrary, bring forth a clearer truth, does not enter his head. His world is stagnation and striving for stagnation.

### A Word Is a Word

**"The Rabbit Carriage"** can be read as a philosophical essay, an illustration of what is the true Word, the Logos that God sent into the world and "which was not understood" (John 1:10). In the exuberant digressive material, Leskov presents the reader with several versions of how people try to interpret this word, the true meaning of life. As he did in most of his work, he illustrates in **"The Rabbit Carriage"** how people adopt certain ideas and instead of testing them—fighting with them and adapting them to new situations—proclaim them as a way to salvation. To Faresov he once explained that **"The Rabbit Carriage"** was to show that "ideas should be fought with ideas, and that cruder measures can have sometimes the most unexpected results."[90] People's attempts to recreate a tangible paradise or utopia will lead to the "confusion of the brain," as well as to the chaos that the madman will leave behind him. Onoprii absolves himself completely of the responsibility of the disorder he has created by "leaving," by first entering a madhouse, then by death, thus forcing others to clean up the mess.

People who create utopias go against nature. They impose their rules—allegedly infallible laws of cause and effect, which form a linear structure—on nature, which follows the cyclical movement of death and rebirth and which is furthermore highly unpredictable.[91] Leskov's enigmatic statement about the story's title could be seen as a metaphoric formulation regarding the paradox of forcing nature into a fixed mold: "***'Zaiachii remiz,'*** that is, the madness [*iurodstvo*] into which 'rabbits sit down, for whom the rock served as a refuge'" (11:606). The second part of this statement refers to line 18 of Psalm 104 (in the Russian Orthodox Bible, Psalm 103), which deals with security and salvation. It includes a paradox in itself since rabbits cannot find refuge behind rocks. They are unaware of their large ears, which stick out when they are listening for the enemy and thus give them away. As is well known, the rabbit's salvation lies in its unpredictable way of running. To hide behind a rock—to look for salvation in stagnation—is against the rabbit's nature.[92] Likewise, we are foolish to believe that we can hire a carriage along life's course. We cannot bridle our thoughts and map out the course of life and pretend that we are in control when, in fact, life will take its own course, which is most often contrary to our conceptions.

Leskov wants people to give up their fixed plans and ideas and instead "live by their reason," that is, with an open mind. The Word, the Logos, must be constantly subjected to interpretation. For Leskov, the meaning of life is to let oneself be part of the general renewal process not by enforcing one's rules but by contributing one's effort toward interpreting and revealing the good. Thus, the Word should not be assigned fixed borders, which will result only in a dead interpretation. A Word that is alive does not have any fixed meaning and will already include its opposite within itself—birth and decay. Onoprii's misadventures are caused by his literal application of words. His mind does not work with se-

mantic fields, which can include opposites—for example, he does not recognize that what in his mind signals death could mean rebirth to someone else.

Leskov embodies his theology in his style. His stories do not easily yield to interpretation, since he does not give "a ready message." He lets every reader make his or her own conclusion. Leskov's characters are distinguished by their words, since language reflects our view of the Word, our notion of the Divine, what we cherish in life. Leskov equally resists using words in their literal meaning, since in his view there is no such thing as a "literal meaning." He wants to show the reader the whole range of meanings that are encapsulated in one word, a desire which explains his fascination with puns, word experimentation, and distorted words.

Leskov uses a great number of techniques to incarnate the "living word" into his work. One device that has been mentioned before is characterization through language. For example, Onoprii's language reflects the "muddleheaded" nature of his character: he speaks in an undigested mess of Ukrainian, Church Slavonic, and mangled—or half-digested—Russian and foreign expressions. He has not assimilated any of the three backgrounds into a uniform individual style for himself. Occasionally, however, his own creativity takes over and he comes up with little pearls—transformations, in the "Skovorodian" sense—words in which the spoiling of the old is still visible but gives rise to the new.

Leskov's "little words"—*slovechki*—are not mere decorations or attractive fireworks but contain in a nutshell the essence of a character or the theme of the story. Leskov rarely creates new words—neologisms in the twentieth-century, futurist sense. He does not trash the old and replace it with the new. On the contrary, his words reveal a transformation process in action.

But this is not a fairy-tale transformation, in which a firebird rises out of the ashes or from heron eggs, as the characters in **"The Rabbit Carriage"** expect; in other words, in which the result is of a completely different nature from the material of creation. Leskov subscribes to the Skovorodian chicken—egg transformation, in which the new contains the old in a transformed, enriched way. For example, in *tishnota* there is a common semantic field—the Skovorodian egg, so to speak—which is stagnation. But one half of the word, *tishina*, expresses a calm quiet, whereas the other, *toshnota*, the troubled quiet of a swamp—nausea. The two opposites are not antagonistic but come together and create a new idea, which describes those who live in an illusionary quiet by ignoring the "dung."

The funny combination of the borrowed French word *poza*—a pose, with *rozha*—the substandard word for "face," is another example of this transformation process. In the story, this expression is applied to those who have a fixed mind and who fear the underminers of accepted norms. Such a mind rejects distortion, whether it comes from the inside—the homebred type, that which does not meet the standard established, which is symbolized by the substandard part of the expression—or whether it comes from the outside—the "foreigner," a fact that is symbolized by the French part of the word. Both elements are semantically represented in the wordplay. Another example is Onoprii's designation as *leib-viazalshchik,* which denotes his unfree status as a vassal and his vocation of sock knitter. On an abstract level this expression could be seen as an embodiment of Leskov's idea that charity as vocation means the loss of creative freedom (vassalship). Dmitrii Afanas'evich's *beduar* (9:550) combines a woman's bedroom—*boudoir*—with the sorrow—*beda*—that is perpetrated there, since it is kept in readiness by its owner for the exclusive seduction of unsuspecting girls hired for the job of nanny.

In an earlier novel Leskov gives some hints of the philosophy underlying his word creations. One of the characters complains:

"Again a new word. Before it was *komonnichat'* and now it is *marfunstvovat'*."[93]

"Each word is good, my dear, if it expresses what you want to express with it. The Academy of Sciences doesn't know all the words that are necessary."

Or in another exchange:

"He roughed me up and cheeked me."

"What kind of word is 'cheeked'?"

"How should one express it then?"

"He was cheeky."

"Why use two words instead of one? And by the way, you understood it after all, which means that the word is good."[94]

Leskov's notion of a "good" word is, therefore, not whether it is sanctioned by those who create the canon—the Academy of Sciences, but whether it is necessary, whether it expresses one's ideas most fully, and, most important, whether it is understood.

Leskov's notion of the real Word, the Logos, is by analogy, then, a truth which may not be accepted by those in the business of defining it, for example, the church. Leskov's idea of truth is embodied in those who think heretically, that is, those who subscribe in a general way to the accepted norm (Christian ethics in terms of theology; "Academy of Sciences" in terms of linguistics), but who feel free to interpret this authority in their own—slightly distorted—way. But people should remain heretics, and not become sectarians, that is, create their own separate authority. For Leskov each person expresses his or her own reality, creates his or her own words, his or her idea of God, and, as Skovoroda said, we have to drag around our own bodily image—live with the reality we have created. And we should not impose this reality on others, nor should people imitate what seems to work for some. In Leskov's world, real happiness is not to make others happy—give gifts—although that has a certain conditional value, too, since it is preferable to the use of force in bringing people over to our side. For Leskov, real goodness appears in those rare moments when our composite reality—our created word—is understood by somebody else not abbreviated but in its totality.

*Notes*

1. Leskov made a marginal notation with a violet pencil next to this entry in his copy of N. Makarov, *Entsiklopediia uma ili slovar' izbrannykh myslei avtorov vsekh narodov i vsekh vekov* (St. Petersburg, 1878), 92. See Leskov's Memorial Library, OGLMT, Fond 2.128.

2. Epigraph of an unpublished unfinished manuscript; see N. S. Leskov, "Gidry (Sovremennaia raznovidnost'). Iz zametok cheloveka bez napravleniia [Roman.]," RGALI, Fond 275.1.6.

3. I will use the Russian title until I justify my translation of it.

4. This 1891 work, which is also known under a previous title ("Invasion of the Barbarians" ["Nashestvie varvarov"]), is supposedly not extant except for a typewritten copy of one page that was prepared by Leskov's son, Andrei Leskov, supposedly based on a manuscript scrap found after Leskov's death. See RGALI, Fond 275.1.99. It is also possible, however, that a previously unpublished work with the title "Neotsennye uslugi" is related to this 1891 work, since they share common characters. (Compare Leskov's "Neotsennye uslugi," the text of which is published in O. E. Maiorova, "N. S. Leskov: Neotsennye uslugi [Otryvki iz vospominanii]," *Znamia* no. 1 [1992]: 155-79, with the description Leskov gives of his "Invasion of the Barbarians," in a 1891 letter to V. A. Gol'tsev, the editor of *Russian Thought* [*Russkaia mysl'*] [11:485].)

5. See N. Klestov's comment to Leskov's 1891 letter to V. A. Gol'tsev mentioned above (N. Klestov, "Pis'ma N. S. Leskova [Iz arkhiva V. A. Gol'tseva]," *Golos minuvshago,* nos. 7-8 [1916]: 406, note 3).

6. From an unpublished letter, a copy of which in Andrei Leskov's handwriting is deposited in IRLI, Fond 612.204. The original is kept in the library of Saratov University.

7. See, for example, "Zapisnaia knizhka s zapisiami ustarevshikh slov, frazeologicheskikh oborot i poslovits [1894]," RGALI, Fond 275.1.110, p. 2, and "Zapisnaia knizhka s vypiskami iz knig S. M. Georgievskogo i dr. [1890]," RGALI, Fond 275.1.108a.

8. Of course, *zaiats* really means "hare" and not "rabbit," but as McLean pointed out, "hare" has a distinct British flavor. Americans tend to use "rabbit" for the wild and domestic variant of this animal. See Hugh McLean, *Nikolai Leskov: The Man and His Art* (Cambridge: Harvard University Press, 1977), 744.

9. This meaning appears in Ushakov's four-volume dictionary of the Russian language (D. N. Ushakov, *Tolkovyi slovar' russkogo iazyka*, 4 vols. [Moscow: Gosudarstvennoe izdatel'stvo inostrannykh i natsional'nykh slovarei, 1935-40], 3:1336) as an obsolete hunting term. Such a meaning was obviously not very current in the nineteenth century, since it is not mentioned in Dal''s comprehensive dictionary of the Russian language. I have been, furthermore, unable to locate this meaning in any other nineteenth-century dictionary.

10. Nikolai S. Leskov, *The Amazon and Other Stories*, trans. and intro. David Magarshack (London: Allen and Unwin, 1949).

11. Valentina Gebel', *N. S. Leskov: v tvorcheskoi laboratorii* (Moscow: Sovetskii pisatel', 1945), 104-5.

12. "Zapisnaia knizhka s zapisiami ustarevshikh slov," p. 2. Leskov never used many of these titles.

13. I am grateful to I. V. Stoliarova for reminding me of this passage.

14. Hugh McLean suggested this variant in private correspondence to me.

15. Marguerite-Marie Dubois, *Modern French-English Dictionary* (Paris: Librairie Larousse, 1969), 614.

16. Leskov used *fiakr,* the Russified equivalent of the French *fiacre.*

17. Leskov to Vera M. Bubnova, 22 August 1882; IRLI, Fond 220.32, sheet no. 3.

18. *Niva,* nos. 34-37 (16 September 1917): 518-45.

19. McLean remarked that if the "forbidden topic" was touched on at all by other writers, such as Dostoevskii, Tolstoi, and Chekhov, it dealt with "the related subject of prison and exile, though mostly from the perspective of common rather than political criminals." McLean, *Nikolai Leskov: The Man and His Art,* 622.

20. Anatolii Faresov, *Protiv techenii: N. S. Leskov; ego zhizn', sochineniia, polemika i vospominaniia o nem* (St. Petersburg: Merkushev, 1904), 382.

21. McLean, *Nikolai Leskov: The Man and His Art,* 631.

22. Ibid., 632.

23. Ibid., 634; Leonid Grossman, *N. S. Leskov: Zhizn'—tvorchestvo—poetika* (Moscow: Gozlitizdat, 1945), 249-50; K. A. Lantz, *Nikolay Leskov* (Boston: Twayne, 1979), 145.

24. Hugh McLean, "On the Style of a Leskovian *Skaz,*" *Harvard Slavic Studies,* vol. 2 (Cambridge: Harvard University Press, 1954), 298.

25. Leskov is referring to the initially regular visits he used to make to his wife, Olga Vasil'evna Smirnova, who in 1878 was committed to the Hospital of St. Nikolas in St. Petersburg. When she no longer recognized him due to her progressive illness and given his own failing health, he finally stopped seeing her.

26. On the Russian holy fool, see Ewa M. Thompson, *Understanding Russia: The Holy Fool in Russian Culture* (Lanham, Md.: University Press of America, 1987).

27. Leskov makes fun of this custom in several of his stories. See, for example, "A Little Mistake" ("Malen'kaia oshibka," 1883; 7:252-59) and "The Cattle Pen" ("Zagon," 1893; 9:356-87).

28. *Skaz* or *skaz*-related issues are treated in the following articles by formalist critics: Boris M. Eikhenbaum, "Illiuziia skaza," in *Skvoz' literaturu: Sbornik statei* (Leningrad: Academia, 1924 [written 1918], 152-56); "V poiskakh zhanra," in *Literatura: Teoriia—kritika—polemika* (Leningrad: Priboi, 1927 [written 1924], 291-95); "Leskov i sovremennaia proza," in *Literatura: Teoriia—kritika—polemika* (Leningrad: Priboi, 1927 [written 1925], 210-25); and "Leskov i literaturnoe narodnichestvo," in *Moi vremennik. Slovesnost'. Nauka. Kritika. Smes'* (Leningrad: Izdatel'stvo pisatelei v Leningrade, 1929, 105-8); and V. V. Vinogradov, "Problema skaza v stilistike," in *Poetika: Sbornik statei,* vol. 1 (Leningrad: Academia, 1926 [written 1925], 24-40).

29. McLean, "On the Style of a Leskovian *Skaz,*" 299.

30. Michael P. Rice, "On 'skaz,'" *Russian Literature Triquarterly* 12 (spring 1975): 420.

31. Mikhail M. Bakhtin, *Problems of Dostoevsky's Poetics,* ed. and trans. Caryl Emerson (Minneapolis: University of Minnesota Press, 1984), 182.

32. Ibid., 192.

33. To my knowledge, no theoretician of *skaz* has ever claimed that Turgenev wrote in the *skaz* mode. On the contrary, Eikhenbaum ("Illiuziia

skaza") and Vinogradov ("Problema skaza v stilistike") use Turgenev as an example of what *skaz* is not. Bakhtin is simply setting up a straw man.

34. Bakhtin, *Problems of Dostoevsky's Poetics,* 192.

35. Ibid., 182.

36. Ibid., 192.

37. Despite his insistence to the contrary, the dialogic element may have been "secondary" to orality but was definitely raised already by the formalists in their stress on the "otherness" of the *skaz* narrator as well as in the "otherness" of his language.

38. Faresov, *Protiv techenii,* 274.

39. Of course, the "Shandyan" monologue can have dialogic elements—in Bakhtin's understanding as a dialogue with an imaginary listener or listeners. But it is ultimately "monologized" by one consciousness.

40. Writing about Leskov's "The Enchanted Wanderer," the literary critic N. Mikhailovskii complains that the story has no center and compares its structure to a "string of beads: "And each individual pearl can be very easily removed and exchanged for another, and moreover one can still string however many pearls one wants onto that same string" (Nikolai Mikhailovskii, "Literatura i zhizn'," *Russkoe bogatstvo,* no. 6 [June 1897]: 105).

41. William Edgerton, ed. and trans., *Satirical Stories of Nikolai Leskov* (New York: Pegasus, 1969), 343.

42. Likhachev, "'Lozhnaia' eticheskaia otsenka u N. S. Leskova," in *Literatura—real'nost'—literatura,* 2d. ed. (Leningrad: Sovetskii pisatel', 1984), 131-37.

43. Edgerton, *Satirical Stories of Nikolai Leskov,* 343.

44. Likhachev, "'Lozhnaia' eticheskaia otsenka u N. S. Leskova," 132.

45. Grossman, *N. S. Leskov: Zhizn'—tvorchestvo—poetika,* 236.

46. *Nov',* no. 7 (1 February 1886): 352.

47. Likhachev, "'Lozhnaia' eticheskaia otsenka u N. S. Leskova," 137.

48. D. S. Likhachev, "Osobennosti poetiki proizvedenii N. S. Leskova," in *Literatura—real'nost'—literatura,* 2d. ed. (Leningrad: Sovetskii pisatel', 1984), 141-42.

49. McLean, "On the Style of a Leskovian Skaz," 320.

50. Quoted in Grossman, *N. S. Leskov: Zhizn'—tvorchestvo—poetika,* 259.

51. See Walter Benjamin, "Der Erzähler," *Illuminationen: Ausgewählte Schriften* (Frankfurt am Main: Suhrkamp Verlag, 1961), 409-36. In comparing the novelist to the storyteller, Benjamin advances a position that arrives at opposite ends of Bakhtin. For him, the epic is open-ended, whereas the novel is closed.

52. See Viktor Shklovskii, "Iskusstvo, kak priem," in his *O teorii prozy* (Ann Arbor, Mich.: Ardis, 1985), 7-23.

53. Shklovskii's "classical" example of estrangement, the passage in Tolstoi's *War and Peace* that depicts Natasha's impression of the opera, is really not "revealing" reality but debasing it: opera is shown to be a ridiculous deception. Instead of enlarging the notion of "opera," the distortive element transmits Tolstoi's own contempt for "highbrow" culture (Shklovskii, *O teorii prozy,* 16).

54. The distinction between "bitting" and "nasty" humor is their respective targets. Of course, Leskov could be pretty "nasty" when he wanted to. But that kind of humor was usually directed toward "unveiling" a person with great public esteem, such as Ioann of Kronstadt, for example, whom he detested. Unlike Dostoevskii, Leskov does not make fun of intrinsically pitiful characters (e.g., blubbering drunkards). Leskov obviously was proud of this fact. He wrote in a 1888 letter to Suvorin: "When publishing 'Laughter and Grief' Katkov told Shchebal'skii: 'Where in [Saltykov-]Shchedrin is there such genuine and *kind* satire!'" (11:385)

55. A good example of this is the narrator of the "The Amazon" ("Voitel'nitsa," 1866; 1:144-221), a procuress, who is objectionable for what she does but becomes endearing through the artless simplicity with which she looks at the world and which becomes her downfall. This trait is shown exclusively through her highly idiosyncratic language. Of course, "deformed" language is not always positive. In "Night Owls" ("Polunoshchniki" 1891; 9:117-217) it is used to reveal a highly debased reality (the device of "estrangement"—in language, in this case—is used precisely to expose morally debased behavior, instead of to impose moral judgment, as was the case in the Tolstoi example quoted earlier). On the function of language in "Night Owls," see McLean, "On the Style of a Leskovian *Skaz.*"

56. "Oshibki i pogreshnosti v suzhdeniiakh o gr. L. Tolstom (Neskol'ko prostykh zamechanii protiv dvukh filosofov)," [1886], RGALI, Fond 275.1.71, sheet no. 7, handwritten.

57. Grigorii Skovoroda [Hryhorii Skovoroda], *Sochineniia Grigoriia Savvicha Skovorody: iubileinoe izdanie (1794-1894)*, ed. D. I. Bagalei. Sbornik Khar'kovskago Istoriko-filologicheskago obshchestva [Khar'kov Historical-Philosophical Society Collection], vol. 7 (Khar'kov: Tip. Gubernskogo pravleniia, 1894). Although Leskov was aware of the edition, it is not certain whether he saw or read the book.

58. "Zapisnaia knizhka s vypiskami russkikh i inostrannykh avtorov [1893-94]," IRLI, 612.106, pp. 11, 11v. The article on Skovoroda was by F. A. Zelenogorskii, "Filosofiia Grigoriia Savvicha Skovorody, ukrainskogo filosofa XVIII stoletiia," *Voprosy filosofii i psikhologii*, no. 23 (May 1894: 197-234). By means of textological comparisons, Levandovskii established that Leskov's quotations of Skovoroda's work were taken from excerpts quoted in the aforementioned article. See L. I. Levandovskii, "K tvorcheskoi istorii povesti N. S. Leskova 'Zaiachii remiz,'" *Russkaia literatura*, no. 4 (1971): 125. On Skovoroda and Leskov see also O. V. Ankudinova, "Leskov i Skovoroda: K voprosu ob ideinom smysle povesti Leskova 'Zaiachii remiz,'" *Voprosy russkoi literatury* 1, no. 21 (1973): 71-77.

59. This image should not be confused with Plato's "cave" metaphor in Book 7 of *The Republic* (Plato, *The Republic,* trans. B. Jowett [New York: Vintage, 1991], 253ff.) and the way he viewed the relationship between the real and the ideal. For Skovoroda, the real and the ideal are not separate. Reality "touches" the Divine; there is a point of contiguity as there is between the shadow and the base of the tree: "After all, the farthest part of the shadow is on the ground, but its beginning and base is one with the apple tree" (Grigorii Skovoroda, *Sochineniia v dvukh tomakh,* vol. 1 [Moscow: Mysl', 1973], 299). For Skovoroda, the "two worlds" are paradoxically related: they are separate, yet joined, like the two natures in Christ. On Skovoroda, the tree imagery, and its correspondence to the christological paradigm, see D. Chizhevskii [Tschizhewskij], *Skovoroda: Dichter, Denker, Mystiker,* Harvard Series in Ukranian Studies 18 (Munich: Wilhelm Fink Verlag, 1974), 82-95.

60. There is a great prevalence of hat imagery in the story. The "suspicious" people supposedly wear "hats of the Greek country," wide-rimmed felt hats, which, on the one hand, make their wearers suspect, since they cover up the face. On the other hand, given the anti-idealistic slant of the story and the undercurrent of the *bolvan* imagery, these "Greek hats" could also be interpreted to mean that these people, who are socialists (i.e.,

"idealists") create a god who is philosophically rooted in Greek idealist philosophy.

61. Leskov to E. N. Akhmatova, 2 August 1882, *V mire Leskova: Sbornik statei,* ed. Viktor Bogdanov (Moscow: Sovetsekii pisatel', 1983), 325.

62. "Zapisnaia knizhka s vypiskami russkikh i inostrannykh avtorov," p. 11v.

63. This long quotation contains three separate sayings by Skovoroda, which Leskov put together and shortened slightly. Ibid.

64. Cited by Joseph T. Fuhrmann, "The First Russian Philosopher's Search for the Kingdom of God," in *Essays on Russian Intellectual History,* ed. Leon Borden Blair (Austin and London: University of Texas Press, 1971), 63-64.

65. This would be another example of reflections of reflections without evaluation, this time as used by a *skaz* narrator. The reader would have to establish first whether the bishop cited Skovoroda correctly or whether he distorted his thought, whether he approved or disapproved of the original thought, and what Onoprii's relationship is to (a) Skovoroda, (b) the bishop, and (c) the quotation, and ultimately what the quotation has to do with the text as a whole. Of course, one could also simply label it as a digression and dismiss it.

66. Faresov, *Protiv techenii,* 292.

67. Ibid., 294. As in everything, however, he is not making a categorical statement, saying that a literary person in service can in certain circumstances become a Saltykov-Shchedrin, but that is usually not the case. For a more lighthearted treatment of the problems, difficulties, and dangers of "co-functionism" (*sovmestitel'stvo*), see Leskov's story "The Co-functionaries: A Bucolic Tale on a Historical Canvas" ("Sovmestiteli: bukolicheskaia povest' na istoricheskoi kanve," 1884; 7:399-431).

68. I. A. Shliapkin, "K biografii N. S. Leskova," *Russkaia starina* 26, no. 12 (December 1895): 209.

69. This image is played on when Onoprii relates how and why Vekovechkin changed his name from the "sheepish" Ovechkin (from the Russian *ovets* for "sheep") by adding a *vek*—a century—to it, giving this character an eternal quality (9:527). This word pun is also recorded in one of Leskov's notebooks ("Zapisnaia knizhka s zapisiami ustarevshikh slov").

70. One should not, however, consider the bishop an "ideally" educated person. The Latin, that is, Catholic influence in Ukrainian seminary education is reflected in his reading, which, besides Plato, includes only Roman authors. Moreover,

the practical bent in his thinking is very obvious and would explain—and in fact this is exactly how it is explained in the story—his hiring of Vekovechkin as "teacher."

71. For "overtake" in the foregoing quotation, Leskov uses in place of the standard Russian verb *operedit'* the neologism *vyperedit'*, which through the prefix *vy-* connotes a movement toward the outside. The word therefore carries the additional meaning of "going beyond and out," which is exemplified in Onoprii's desire to go beyond the limits of human nature.

72. Unlike the Russian peasants, who were conclusively enserfed under Boris Godunov at the beginning of the seventeenth century, the Ukrainian peasants were free until Catherine the Great's reign in the second half of the eighteenth century. Ukraine initially escaped the Russian serf laws because it was only incorporated into the Russian Empire at the middle of the seventeenth century. Onoprii's ancestor somewhat forestalled Catherine's politics.

73. Jaroslav Pelikan, *The Spirit of Eastern Christendom (600-1700)* (Chicago and London: University of Chicago Press, 1974), 222-23.

74. Ernst Benz, *Geist und Leben der Ostkirche* (Munich: Wilhelm Fink Verlag, 1971), 44, 47-48.

75. In his account of life in the village, Onoprii goes back and forth, calling this squire sometimes Dmitrii Afanasevich and at other times with the Ukrainian version, Dmitro Opanasovich (9:550).

76. Dmitrii's "education" is by no means exemplary. He represents the other side of Onoprii's rigidity. Instead of slavishly holding onto the past, this squire totally rejects it (spurns his background, speaks French) and has learned to use the present for his self-serving and egotistical purposes. He thus merely replaced Old Peregud's rules by his own self-styled ones. The Moscow school where he studied is called *Galushka,* meaning "dumpling." His education is like dough, without backbone or moral grounding.

77. During this conversation, his maid makes the sharp comment that as a woman she has nothing to fear, since certainly these men will take off their hats when they meet her. If the idea of equating the Greek hats with Greek idealist philosophy is valid, this comment would mean that when it comes to sex, idealist notions are quickly put aside.

78. "Zapisnaia knizhka s vypiskami russkikh i inostrannykh avtorov," p. 11v.

79. Ibid.

80. Leskov's preoccupation with the apocryphal Book of Enoch is seen in one of his last notebooks, which contains several quotations from it, including the one used in "The Rabbit Carriage" (see "Zapisnaia knizhka s vypiskami russkikh i inostrannykh avtorov," p. 5). The book in question is not the Ethiopian apocryphal "Book of Enoch" but the Slavonic "Book of the Secrets of Enoch," which describes Enoch's visit to the seven heavens. It survived only in a Slavonic version. The corresponding passage in the text reads: "I saw the key-holders and guards of the gates of hell standing, like great serpents, and their faces like extinguished lamps, and their eyes of fire, their sharp teeth, . . ." (Rutherford H. Platt Jr., ed., *The Lost Books of the Bible and the Forgotten Books of Eden* [New York and Scarborough, Canada: New American Library, 1974], 96). Once again, Leskov varied and adapted the quotation to fit his needs. Here, he stressed their blindness, which (according to the English translation) is not in the original text.

81. Henry David Thoreau, *Walden and Other Writings,* ed. Brooks Atkinson (New York: Modern Library, 1937), 69.

82. In Leskov criticism Julia Semenovna is usually called a Tolstoyan. She does indeed show strong Tolstoyan influences—but does not reject the city as a center of real learning. The "underminers of foundations" are usually identified as nihilists and the story is said to continue "Leskov's beloved theme of antinihilist attacks." This warrants closer scrutiny. When analyzing the messages on the leaflets, one will find that the subversive message advocates a strongly colored Christian socialism or even anarchism. It would be closer to an aggressive form of Tolstoyanism. In his later years Leskov found that practiced Tolstoyanism and nihilism are in fact two sides of the same coin, and on numerous occasions he called Tolstoi's or Tolstoi's son's activity *iurodstvo* (see, e.g., 11:317, and Leskov to O. M. Men'shikov, 27 June 1893 and 18 February 1894, IRLI, Fond 22574 CLVIIIb.61). The similarity among the three movements—nihilism, Tolstoyanism, and *iurodstvo*—consists in their strong conviction of a found truth and its attempted realization, thus in a follower's mentality.

83. "Picking one's nose" in the Leskovian jargon denotes those who refuse to educate themselves and instead pull all their knowledge out of their nose. See, for example, Leskov to Ol'ga Krokhina, 13 March 1892, IRLI, Fond 220.42.

84. A. Afanas'ev, *Poeticheskiia vozzreniia slavian na prirodu,* vol. 1 (Moscow: Indrik, 1994), 512-14.

85. The translation is taken from the King James Bible (Psalm 145). In the modern Russian and German Bibles this line has a somewhat different meaning. It reads: "You [God] satisfy every living being according to Your goodwill," thus the focus is on what God is willing to give, and not on what we want. A slight cultural difference, perhaps.

86. In Old Slavonic the letters "g" and "d" were called "word" (*glagol*) and "good" (*dobro*).

87. Leskov to E. N. Akhmatova, 14 January 1889, *V mire Leskova*, 331.

88. Despite the fact that Leskov suffered almost all his life from unjust criticism, he greatly believed in the critic's task as such; he himself worked in the capacity of critic and energetically engaged with his critics.

89. Faresov, *Protiv techenii*, 316.

90. Ibid., 382.

91. The notion of unexpectedness, which disrupts a belief system that is based on cause and effect, is a major theme in the story, as it is in general in Leskov's work. The belief in causal relationships is repeatedly associated with superstition and with women (in Onoprii's mind!), which may explain why Onoprii wears a woman's kerchief on his head.

92. It is not certain whether Leskov was aware of the line's mistranslation in the Russian Bible, which creates the paradox and makes it meaningless in the context of the psalm, or if he picked it by instinct. The original Hebrew for what is translated as "rabbits" in the Russian Bible is *shaphan*, which is a species of rock-badger and which includes the primary root for hiding. Others identified it as the *daman*, a small hoofed animal from Syria that does indeed hide in rocks. (The English King James translation of this line is: "The high hills are a refuge for the wild goats; and the rocks for the conies.") The mistranslation has been pointed out by McLean, *Nikolai Leskov: The Man and His Art*, 744.

93. "*Komonnichat'*" is derived from Old Slavonic *komon'*, which meant "horse" (Russian *kon'*) and is used in the novel in the meaning "to show one's character, to kick." *Marfunstvovat'* denotes the quality of being Martha (in Russian *Marfa*), as compared to Mary (Luke 10:38-42).

94. The first quote is from Leskov's novel *Oboidennye* (in *Sobranie sochinenii v dvenadtsati tomakh*, 12 vols. [Moscow, 1989], 3:158). The second passage is quoted in Grossman, *N. S. Leskov: Zhizn'—tvorchestvo—poetica*, 284-85. I have been unable to locate it in Leskov's work.

## Oleg V. Nikitin (essay date 2003)

SOURCE: Nikitin, Oleg V. "Leskov's 'Notes of the Unknown' ('Zametki neizvestnogo')." *Studia Slavica* 48, no. 4 (2003): 413-41.

[*In the essay below, Nikitin studies the narrative content and linguistic style of "Notes of the Unknown," exploring in particular Leskov's use of historic Russian religious, national, and legal texts, as well as Old Slavonic terms.*]

A strange feeling took possession of me when I read Leskov for the first time. An astonishing world from the past opened before me. It was not dead, neither was it crowned with laurels, but it was lively and spontaneous, a bit ironic but cheerful, sometimes severely denouncing and at the same time most human. First of all it was the author's apt and vivid language that struck me as most interesting, where different semantic elements and archaisms lived together used with an original flavour and subtly charged with a new shade of meaning. It was also remarkable to see Leskov's ability to give a truthful representation of geniune Russian reality which at the time was more or less forbidden and was, indeed, skilfully avoided by his contemporaries. And besides, there was Leskov's all-forgiving identification with everything—nature, people, history. This comes from his philosophy and the depth of the suffering of his soul, a soul that was firmly loyal to the motherland and fully committed to serving her most resolutely. Leskov considered this service his mission.

During all his life Nikolaj Leskov would take steps which have never been treated adequately and for which he has been blamed and stigmatized again and again. It is a paradox but a fact now that Leskov's literary works were excluded from the school curriculum after the October Revolution. In higher educational establishments his activities and creative works were studied in selected passages (and so they are even today). For a long time his fiction (to say nothing about his religious and political writings or about his literary criticism) was unaccessible for the common reader. It was only his anti-clerical stories, small domestic sketches and some novels which were discussed, but the critical response was limited due to the moralizing ethos of the time defined by the concept of socialist realism. The critics and advocates of socialist realism were too blind to see Leskov's superb craftsmanship and the disguised implications of his work. When the term socialist realism is used it should be remembered that Russian realism is a very capacious and complicated notion as compared to what it was stated to be in the Soviet theory of literature with its strictly confined boundaries and its submission to the exigencies of the revolutionary movement. There can hardly be any similar definition of realism, for instance, that would apply to the 19th and the 20th centuries. It can even be claimed that the 18th century in Russia was the age of progressive aesthetic and literary norms which are responsible for the kind of realism that appears in the masterpieces of Radiščev and Puškin, Žukovskij and Karamzin. The Russian cultural tradition appeared as a natural source of inspiration for writers. To the abyss of the coming *agitculture* they opposed the only value—man. The humanistic—and, in this sense, realistic—character of classical Russian literature consisted in a humane Weltanschauung which respected the dignity of man, and, in consequence, the principle of the independent, involuntary development of a human being. That was an ideology of добромолюбие (goodness) and wisdom which was eradicated later.

The fact that Leskov swam against the current of the time can be said to have determined the complexity of his vision as well as his creative attitude. On the whole, the entire inner world of his fiction is obviously permeated with an ideal or, better to say, disposition—духовносмъ (spirituality). That is not only a reflection of a system of constant and firm moral values, of a commitment to a definite conception of art as a form of enlightenment but also of the quality of a soul, wistful and searching, tormented and plagued by contradictions. It is a prevalence of spiritual and intellectual interests over material being. It is the lot of few. Not to be crushed by gossip and threats, falsifications and mockery—such was the reward prepared for him. His adversaries never even pretended to forgive Leskov his spiritual truth and pure intentions, on the contrary, they tried to crush him by hook or by crook. Leskov, however, bore no grudge against them. His life and works are evidence of that.

The Russian dictionaries of the Soviet period define the notion духовносмъ as 'obsolete' (!)—as though available but incompatible with the modern mentality and mode of life. Actually, it is not a slogan (that would not be typical of Leskov at all), духовносмъ offers no promises of any kind, neither does it open up false perspectives. Духовносмъ might be to some extent conservative, but it is not hostile to progress. It does not belong to any political party. On the contrary, it pleads for the protection of the best traditions and ideals of the past from inexpert or ruthless usage and interpretation by adherents of 'new' convictions. It should be remembered that the Latin *conservativus* means 'standing guard over smb., safe-guarding, protective'. 'Safeguarding' has often boiled down to a complicity with inertness and stagnation. That is why Leskov was invariably shown to have been a writer of secondary importance, an effort to which the *Okhranka* (Secret Political Police in tsarist Russia) contributed, too. Leskov, however, was a guardian in the primary sense of the word—a guardian of the most important traditional values and ideals, i.e. the humanism and the spontaneity of the Russian character. That is why he resisted every attempt to level its originality, to blunt the intensity of the Russian spirit. In that we can see an actual necessity of our own time: the obligation to uphold the noble ideals of the ancient times, to adjust them to modern social processes and to look for ways in which they can be passed on to the future. That is where the great vitality of Leskov's power lies. His restitution has already come. Leskov for us is one of the modern authors occupying in the civil society of today.

The following note which Leskov jotted down in the album of G. P. Danilevsky seems to reflect his innermost pains; his words will help us to see him in a brighter, more appropriate light:

> In my literary time there was not a writer slandered more than I; nevertheless not in the least have I ever been sorry about that. I've always tried to accept the sufferings which have been falling to my lot through all the malice and libels for my good and have been very thankful for them: they've taught me to put up with them, and God help everybody in that.
>
> Nikolaj Leskov (Stebnitsky). 14th May, 1872. SPb.[1]

A lot has been said about the persuasiveness of Leskov's language, but the specific attributes of his style have never been properly defined, although the clarification of his reasons for the use of specific discourses might disclose much of the nature of his artistic world. It seems to be especially rewarding to try to detect the sources he drew upon while he elaborated his linguistic medium.

His essays and articles often touch upon questions of church life and as a matter of fact they frequently read as investigations of artistic problems. It was natural for the author to base them on documentary materials. For instance, Синодалъные персоны. Период боръбы за дреоблаиание (1820-1840 гг.) ['Representatives of the Synod. The period of struggle for predominance'], Иродова Рабома. русские кармины ВОсмзейском крае ['Tyrant's Work. Russian pictures in the East See region'], Церковные инмриганы. Исморические кармины ['Church intrigants. Historic pictures'], Поповская чехарда и приходская прихомъ. Церковно-исморические нравы и кармины ['Priest's re-shuffle and parish whims. Morals and pictures from the history of the Church'] and some other works written by Leskov and published in the journal *Istoričeskij vestnik* in the 1880s. Some of the aforementioned essays were later included by the author in the larger and prominent short stories and novels, others were organized into cycles like *Zametki neizvestnogo.*

Leskov had testified to their authenticity: in the article Поповская чехарда . . . he says:

> I would like to offer the readers an interesting story (here and further on emphasized phrases are spaced by us—*O. N.*) I have borrowed from the original inquiry

made in the Moscow department of the Holy Synod about priest Kirill about whom forty two persons from the parish of Spas in Nalivki "croaked".[2]

And in the introduction to the **"Notes of the Unknown"** the narrator describes an ancient manuscript which he has found introducing it to the readers in detail, besides declaring its authenticity. Then the author characterizes it substantially, and eventually he adds:

> засим я предлагаю в подлиннике заметки неиз-вестного летописца в том иорядке и под теми же самыми частными заглавиями, под какими они записаны в полууничтоженнои рукописи

(лесков 1973, IV: 257).

(Hereafter I present the original notes of the unknown annalist in that order and with those and the same sepa-rate titles under which they appear in the half-destroyed manuscript.)

This is an interesting peculiarity of Leskov's not only in this instance but in general terms as well. In another article, Бладословенный брак. Харакмерный про-пуск в исмориуеской лимерамуре раскола ["Blessed marriage. A distinctive omission in the annals of the history of the Schism"] the writer again refers to a rare manuscript book entitled О бракосочемании ["On matrimony"], quotes the complete text and gives a minute description of it.[3]

One more important piece of information is offered by Leskov: as he begins his story the author points out to a familiar second-hand bookseller from the Sukharev tower from whom he claims he has bought a manu-script (Лесков 1973, IV: 257). It is known that since the middle of the 19th century Sukharev Square had been the venue of the famous book and art market. That was a centre of antiquities in Moscow (later on, at the time of Stalin, the tower was demolished). We may as-sume that Leskov the bibliographer knew that place and went there often enough to buy books.

Thus, fact and true-to-life fiction seem to merge. Those two references to reality are complemented by the writer in an inobtrusive, a most sophisticated way by a hint to an "artless presentation of events which in its own time seems to have interested an apparently very respectable, seriously disposed social circle" («безыскусственное изображение событий, интересовавших в свое время какой-то, по-видимому весьма достопочтен-ный, оригиналъный и серъезно настроенный об-щественный кружок») (Лесков 1973, IV: 257).[4]

This circle was a mixed group of people including the secretary (from Искусный омвемчик), the assessor's wife with her small son Ignaty (Излищняя мамерин-ская недсносмъ), "the spiritual student" («Чужеземные обычаи толъко с разумением при-

менятъ можно»), etc. But the main characters of the cycle are, among others, a bishop, priests, a consistory man and the principal of the church seminary.

Leskov's acquaintances occasionally tried to exercise some pressure on him disapproving of his sharply criti-cal views on the problems of church life. They wanted to soothe his anti-clerical leanings. Colonel Pashkov wrote to Leskov on the 22nd of September 1884:

> I find it unbearably regrettable to see that you, whose heart responded formerly to everything true and good, now sneer at . . . what was taught by the apostles . . .

(Другов 1957: 88).

The Slavophile I. S. Aksakov also approached Leskov with similar letters. But he had his own notions in this context: he fought for the moral purity of the custodians of religious traditions and despite the pressure of his friends or the censors' prohibition he never wavered in his position. (The cycle of short stories **"Notes of the Unknown"** was first published in *Gazeta A. Gattsuka* in 1884, No. 2, 5, 9-14. Then publication was stopped by censorship, and it was only in 1917-1918 that the last three stories appeared in *The Niva*. In Leskov's view people who are ordained should be inspired, i.e. inwardly ennobled and filled with elevated feelings and aspirations. These are people of Faith. Under the *klobuk* (headgear of Orthodox monk) and black robe with a smooth radiant cross Leskov saw not only a God's min-ister but first of all a man. Observing a deep abyss be-tween the words of God's preachers and their deeds which hardly conformed to the established rules of mor-als the writer could not keep silent. It should be empha-sized that the anti-clerical writings of Leskov should not be seen as an indication of a departure from God or Faith or religious feelings. They reflect no rejection on Leskov's part of God's commandments. They should be seen instead as true sketches of the life of the clergy, their domestic life and relationships. Some arguments of V. O. Klučevskij reflect the same view, e.g. his ironic question: "Do the clergy believe in God? They do not understand that question because they officiate God", or his statement: "In the West the Church has no God, in Russia God has no Church" (Ключевский 1990: 384).[5]

It has been established that it was scrupulous and pro-tracted work in the archives that helped Leskov to real-ize the profound sense of the mentality of the past. That also considerably supplemented the knowledge derived from life. And, indeed, **"Notes of the Unknown"** con-tains much documentary information. Even some traits of the characters of this cycle were taken from the in-quest deeds of the Synod. That is why what is pre-sented in his narrative should be interpreted more than a fruit of Leskov's fantasy. It is the result of persistent research as well as the observation of the actual proto-types of his fiction. Leskov can actually be considered to have been a scholar, an explorer of the Russian antiquities and an investigator of the spirit of the past. Our suppositions are confirmed by looking through the files of the former Record Office of the Synod. A substantial part of them now is concentrated in the Russian State Record Office of Ancient Acts in Moscow. I was fortunate enough to be able to read some manuscripts kept in File No. 1183 'Moscow Synodal Office' and analyze them.

In a manuscript entitled "The case of the shock which hieromonk of Novospassky Monastery, Arseny, had during divine service in Peter-and-Paul's Parish Church" there is the report of the following incident:

> . . . during the service of the hieromonk Arseny was overcome by a shock, he, however, had finished the liturgy; by the time he finished he had lost his tongue, the left arm and leg were paralyzed; soon after that a vomiting followed with eruption of holy donations at the altar; the ejected remained in a washbasin; after the exposure he had been taken to the church ward . . .[6]

At the end of this personal file a resolution was placed: a prohibition of divine service in churches of the Moscow eparchy. Later we shall see how Leskov used these sad and ironic facts in his domestic sketches.

From the other document under the heading "About the presentation of a book for recording the evil deeds to the permanent inhabitants of the abolished George's Monastery" it is clear that a certain Grigory Nikolayev was lazy and negligent in performing his duty and showed no proper industry, and Zakhar Efimov abandoned himself to hard drinking and even violence. With reference to that, the applicant writes, your most humble servant asks the Office of the Holy Synod to give us a book for putting down in it every case of their improper conduct[7].

Here is another interesting and important document which helps us to find the sources of Leskov's prose. It testifies, in our opinion, to a curious accident, or as the writer might have said, to an extraordinary occurrence of a very unpleasant nature. Under the title "About the expulsion of the novice Vasily Shiriayev from Voskresensky Monastery for improper conduct" it is told that "the lay brother Vasily Shiriayev was seen in a drunken state all during the Easter week . . .".[8]

Does not all that is cited above look like artistic discourse? Could not those picturesque passages connected with some actual events and facts be related to Leskov's **"Notes of the Unknown"**? At least we catch a likeness between them and the narrative. For instance, in his conduct and action "the regent of the bishop's choir", who was much of an Adonis (*«красик»—a dandy* in Leskov's view.—*O. N.)*

was so completely confused by the love stories of ladies who arrived for vespers, that . . . [he] wandered away from the choir or started winking at important females who were about to leave the church . . . (так в переплете любовных историй от приезжавших ко всенощной дам запутался, что . . . [он] с хор утекал или с направлявшимися к выходу женскими особами глазами перемигивался . . .)

(Лесков 1973, IV: 287),

and Grigory Nikolayev who "was negligent and showed no proper industry in performing his duties". Who could know what was meant by such an impersonal definition? Only Leskov's creative imagination could see so clearly this cloaca maxima which was engraved on the worn and burnt pages of the invaluable manuscripts.

An old hierodeacon, who during the Lent was crazy about billiard, drank so truly that he became tipsy of empty wine-glasses (Лесков 1973, IV: 284-285), reminds the reader of the very cuctos morum who "all the Easter week was seen in a drunken state".

Lastly, Father Ioann from the story **"Как нехорошо осуждамъ слабосми"** [**"It Is Wrong to Blame Foibles"**] being intoxicated permitted himself an "indecent thing": "having uttered an exclamation fell asleep, and did not wake up for a long time" («сделав возглас, заснул и не скоро лровудпдся») (десков 1973, IV: 259), and hieromonk Arseny who had a "shock" during divine service. In both of the examples veiled irony is implied.

After some possible parallels have been pointed out, a comparison of Leskov's style and approach to the description of every day events with some of the possible sources of his narrative style has been carried out. Our investigation suggests that the style of the business documents of national history, especially those of investigatory evidence connected with church life, is in a certain correlation with the text of Leskov's narrative. That interaction becomes particularly pronounced in the use of the words which have characteristic and determined meanings and may have served as formative models for him like буйсмво (tumult), разоблачение (unmasking), извем (false denunciation), справщик (corrector), дознание (inquiry), обыскная книга (a church book for registration of matrimonies), обыск (a note on marriage in a church book), консисморский приказный (consistorial bailiff). All these words had been used actively in the Old Russian legal system and in manuscripts in their primary meanings with different semantic and stylistic shades. For instance, the lexeme извътъ had nine ways of interpretation: 1. Pretext; excuse. 2. Cause. 3. Fraud, illegal actions. 4. Accusation; slander, calumny. 5. Proof, confirmation, evidence. 6. Denunciation. 7. Report, dispatch. 8. Advice. 9. Justification; apology, forgiveness (Словарь русск. яз. 1979:

116-118). Leskov accumulated them into a specific cover with a new meaning invented by him—'doubt'. On the one hand, it was a peculiar trait of his protagonist, the secretary of the consistory, who, after having been decorated with an order he had coveted, understood that

> after the departure of the foreign predicant (here preacher—*O. N.*) many of the simple folks who before in their lapsed life had never read the Gospel, appeared with the New Testament . . . Though,—the narrator proceeds,—in each of them were printed particulars as to the place and date of the publication, the secretary conceived an anxious doubt that those books were made at some printing-house in London, and the Russian imprint was put in by fraud, in order to reduce the incomes (?!—*O. N.*) of the orthodoxial department in Russia ('по отъезде иностранного предиканта у многих простого звания дюдей, кои в прежде прошедшей жизни никогда Еангедия не читади, появидися в руках книжки Нового Завета . . . ихотя под кажою из оных было подпечатано обозначение выхода их из духовной типографии, но секретарь возымел беспокойное сомнение, что те книги произведены в типографии в Лондне, а выход российский им обозначен обманно, собственно для подрыва доходов (?!—*O. N.*) православного ведомства в России')
>
> (Лесков 1973, IV: 303-304).

On the other hand, the writer ridicules the pathological inclination of some protectors of orthodoxy who give in to the temptation of engaging in an absurd and feigned search of enemies of the national religion. Leskov's irony expressed in a veiled form takes another turn when the narrator gives a parody of the inquiry trial. It is held according to the secretary's извем. Being an expert in the Gospel he asks the chief справщик (corrector) from the gubernia printing-house, a German by birth, . . . to give him an explanation that would lead to conclusive evidence («призвал к себе из губернской типографии главного справщика, происхождением немца, . . . и предложил: не можете ли дать на сей предмет сведущего разъяснительного заключения») (Лесков 1973, IV: 304).

Because he had no doubt that an English publishing company, however hard they strived to falsify a legitimate Russian edition published with established blessings, would never be able to do so

> английское общество сколько бы ни стремилось всеми силами к тому обману, чтобы подделаться к законному русскому изданию, с установленного благословения изданному, никак того достичь не в состоянии.
>
> —а почему?
>
> —Потому, что там с такими грубыми несовершенствами верстки и тиснения и на столь дурной бумаге уже более двухсот лет не печатают
>
> (Лесков 1973, IV: 304)

And why? (asked the secretary—*O. N.*)

Because there with page-reading and editing so imperfect, and on paper of such poor quality nothing has been printed in the last two hundred years).

A fine and subtle hint of the title of this short story, **"Смесненная ограниченносмь англицкого искуссмва"** [**"The Constraining Limitation of English Art"**], gave Leskov the possibility to show the absurdity of the official Church and the pseudo-patriotism of the Russian zealots. It was his manner to invent affected titles, overloaded and intricate. The titles reveal the psychological attitude of Leskov to the specific tradition in question. He created his own system which distinguishes the notions 'book language' and 'local patois', 'living' and 'literary speech'. As a rule, the titles of his works are complicated and full of metaphors. This helped him to protect the original text from censorship covering the content behind the same neutral phrases which were hard to discern. In this episode the Old Russian word извѣтъ could have also been interpreted in a new sense because of the polysemanticism of its root: извѣтъ—вѣсть—вѣкъ—извѣчный, i.e. a primordial, old (difficult) problem. And in our view, the writer meant to make a step toward solving it by means of humour and irony, defending русскосмь (Russianness) and fighting against its mystificators.

The sarcasm with which he describes God's servants might suggest that Leskov's soul was entirely torn by the contradictions of reality. His characters are, to some extent, reflections of his own spiritual conflicts and awareness of social injustice. But his prose does not give the impression of despair concerning man's moral potential or lack of belief in the future. On the contrary, the writer was nourished on quite different stuff. Once he wrote to S. N. Shubinsky: "You should not at all be in time with 'the monde', but keep yourself to whatever is better than what it now approves of and encourages . . ." (Русские писатели 1955: 223). Leskov deeply felt the coming tragedy of nihilism. It was not only a trend in the environment of разночинец.[9] It was the beginning of a tyranny under which everyone would be left to the mercy of fate. That was an absolute negation and rejection of all human and social standards, principles, values established before. In this situation he was looking for bright ideals, and he found them in the rural provinces of Russia. Leskov listened to its spirit and movement with great attention. There he saw natural people and felt at ease. Leskov studied them through their customs and habits, through their language. Explaining the specific manner of the pronunciation and behaviour of people in the countryside Leskov retorted to the opponents of the 'artificiality' of his language:

> That very common, vulgar and artificial language in which many pages of my works are written is no invention of mine, it was collected while eavesdropping

on the speech of a мудсик, of a half-wit, of a крас-
нобай [phrase-monger—*O. N.*], of a юродивый
[God's fool—*O. N.*] and of свямоши [hypocrites—*O. N.*]

(Русские писатели 1955: 221).

When travelling about in the remotest places in Russia
Leskov met uncommon characters having exceptional
fates and strong tempers. Such is Ivan Severyanovich
Flyagin the Очарованный смранник, depicted in a
tale of the same name, who is a «типический, просто-
душный, добрый русский богатырь, напомина-
ющий дедушку Илью Муромца» (Лесков 1973, III:
4-5) ('a typical, open-hearted, kind Russian бодамырь
[Hercules.—*O. N.*] reminding us of grandpa Ilya
Muromets'). All Russia is compressed into his story.
The Archpriest Savely Tuberozov (Соборяне), whose
life is part of Russian hagiography, has gracelessly sunk
into oblivion. In these characters Leskov saw the poen-
tial of a mighty spiritual force able to resist the general
chaos of nihilism.[10] The writer visited a lot of monasteries where he could listen to unusual stories and read the
messages of unusual, desperate souls from the past.
Leskov found a way to reflect in a natural though elaborate form the innocent spontaneity of whatever he came
across. For an example here is the entire text of a manuscript which deserved Leskov's attention:

Честнѣйшіӣ отецъ казначей Епифаній!

Извѣстно вамъ, что уже у насъ на Крестно(м) ос-
тровѣ открылся питѣйный домъ, то во
о(т)вращеніе противны(х) слѣдствій, по хр[и]с-
тіанской любви проши, а по должности моей и
приказываю, сохраните пожалийте какъ себя, так
и други(х) братій в порядочно(м) воздержаніи, в
незазорно(м) поведеніи, и в добродѣте(л)номъ сос-
тояніи, что бидетъ Б[о]жу пріятно, о(т) ближни(х)
заслужите себѣ почтеніе, а мнѣ во утѣшеніе и
спокойствіе диха, ва(м) сіе поручено, и поричаю
наблюда(т) сей порядокъ благосостоянія о чемъ
на васъ надѣюсь и не симнюсь. Знаете, в
потивно(м) случае какая мнѣ о(т)рада, я
приниждён, но биди соо(т)ввтствова(т) моей
доджности. Извѣстны вы, что Б[о]жею милостію,
и монарши(м) благоволеніемъ доволнw пожало-
ваны, со временемъ почивствуете сами свою
ползи. Сіе мое приказаніе, или паче усердіе, об-
явите и про(т)чей братіи. В про(т)чемъ желая
вамъ всѣхъ благъ, пребываю

Вашъ доброжелателный Архимандритъ Макарій.
Маія 28 1780 года. онѣга.[11]

That manner of speaking and style was very close to
Leskov's as he pointed out himself:

My priests speak ecclesiastically, my nihilists—in a ni-
hilistic way, my мужсики—in a manly manner, the
parvenus of them and the скоморохи [buffoons—*O.
N.*]—freakishly, etc.

(Русские писатели 1955: 221).

Without any commentary the document will give an
idea to the reader of the style and manners of the time
so that he can compare it with the text of Leskov's
**"Notes of the Unknown."** The comparison will hope-
fully lead us to a new interpretation and a better understanding of the contents. The manuscript seems to be
rich in the varieties of microstyles and syntactic constructions belonging to the church tradition, distributed
in an appointed succession and with consistency which
must have had an important meaning to Leskov. In the
broad sense the writer drew upon the best traditions of
classical Russian style so highly estimated in former
times. Thus he could convey the inner world of his
characters in a special language where "ornate sound of
the words", he thought, was inadmissible. Here he followed the traditions of the literary language elaborated
by M. V. Lomonosov and N. M. Karamzin, A. F.
Vel'tman and the Russian Romantics, but he preserved,
at the same time, his own individual voice, coherence
of ideas and the linguistic character of his own vivid
and clear style.

In this narrative Leskov, who was an outstanding ex-
perimenter, used striking Old Slavonic collocations and
citations from the Holy Writ. That was an expressive
recreation of the language used by the clergy, and it
was a most ingenious device to achieve the ironic over-
tone of **"Notes of the Unknown."** In the context of his
own time we can call his style even avant-garde because specifically Russian elements are presented alongside with Slavonicisms like « . . . нимало сумн-
яся . . . » (Лесков 1973, IV: 272) (not in the least
doubting), « . . . егоже любяше» (Лесков 1973, IV:
277) (whom he had been loved by), «доумертвия . . .
» (Лесков 1973, IV: 277) (up to death), « . . . в пре-
выспренние . . . » (Лесков 1973, IV: 279) (to the
heavens), «нози» (Лесков 1973, IV: 280) (feet), «но-
воначатие» (Лесков 1973, IV: 259) (innovation), «ми-
оносицы» (Лесков 1973, IV: 304) (here the meaning
is not directly connected with myrrh, the referentiality
of the word is altered and it means: female admirers of
the chief of some sect), «войтвенники» (Лесков 1973,
IV: 326) (put by the author instead of воины—soldiers),
«борзяся» (Лесков 1973, IV: 330) (hastily), and others. And what is more, the writer borrows phrases from
the Bible, which he uses in a slightly altered form to
show the false learning of the ecclesiastics. The quotations in Leskov serve not for argument or evidence.
They have the role of artistic analogies in relation to
events and the characters' inner reality. Such a style
gave the writer the possibility to disclose something of
the secret deeds of God's servants. When explaining an
episode which happened to Father Grigory, who was
undecided as regards the difference between the Roman
Catholic and the Protestant concepts of the sacrament
of the holy penance (Лесков 1973, IV: 270), the narrator put his own thoughts into the Archbishop's words
who "cleared up" the Father's problem in this way:

они (взъляды—*О. N.*) весьма противуположны, но я их не осуждаю, а даже скажу: обои не худы. Но мы, как правосдавные, должны своего не порицать и держаться—тем более, что у нас исповедь на всякий случай и особое применение в гражданском управлении имеет, которого нам лучше не касаться

(Лесков 1973, IV: 270)[12]

(These [views—*O. N.*] are very contradictory but I don't condemn them and even say: neither of them is wrong. But we, as orthodoxials, should not dispute ours and should actually keep to it—especially because our creed has an application to every situation and a particular application in civil life, which should rather not be touched upon).

The passage suggests that the author considers it an obligation for the priest to denounce political offence if he gets to know about it through a confession. It is not too much to say that Leskov, the avant-garde artist, applied Slavonicisms in a function not exploited before. It was not even their phonetic cover (the though decorative phonetic design of the word as a special stylistic method was originally adopted by the writer) he was interested in. Leskov used archaic expressions not for their lack of pleophony and abstruseness of meaning, for specific initial combinations or availability of compound sounds, etc. What mattered for him was the possibility to convey implicating intonations by means of Old Slavonic and express satirical laughter filled with the mixed feeling of sorrow and joy thanks to its spiritual rhythm.

We can find confusion of language units close in form in the prose of Pustozersk, i.e. in Жимие промопопа Аввакума and in his челобимные (petitions) to Tsar Alexey Mikhaylovich, and in 'literary' works (messages) by his coprisoners, инок (anchorite) Epiphany, priest Lazar', deacon Feodor. In these writings we can often see the Holy Scripture as interpreted by the authors correlated with what they want to say, which is similar to Leskov's way of giving parallels to the convulsions of modern life, as for example: « . . . свет его может просветиться пред человеки . . . » (Лесков 1973, IV: 309) (let his light so shine before men)—a free borrowing from the Gospel of Matthew, or « . . . что ми хощете дати?» (Лесков 1973, IV: 312) (what would you give me)—the question of Judas about the reward for his betrayal; or one more example: « . . . мня ся біти яко первым по фараоне . . . » (Лесков 1973, IV: 313) (I imagine myself to be as though the first after Pharaoh)—in Leskov's narrative it is said in honour of Father Pavel who considers himself to be the first after Pharaoh, and who, being very much displeased with refreshments prepared for him on a day of fast, finds an excellent remedy:

a glass of undiluted punch rum with chemists' drops of English mint-*kholodianka* . . . , and, as a token of what it often compels, to alleviate pains . . .

(Лесков 1973, IV: 315).[13]

According to the biblical legend Joseph, who had been sold by his brothers into Egyptian slavery, became the first in Egypt after Pharaoh. A similar method of the interpretation of the Holy Writ was artistically used by Avvakum: he read contemporary events by the light of the holy rites. This elevates the occurrence described to the rank of a holy mystery (Пустозерская проза 1989: 33). In it his life-story and the end of the history of the world gets entangled:

Ты, Господи, изведый мя из чрева матере моея, и от небытия и бытие мя устроил i аще меня задушат, причти мя с митрополитом филиппом Московским . . .

(Пустозерская проза 1989: 45).

Epifany in *Жи ие* says somewhat similarly:

Господи Иисусе Христе, Сыне Божий! Помилуй мя, грешнаго, по благодати спаси мя, а не по долгу, ими ж веси судшбами

(Пустозерская проза 1989: 199).

Like in the case of Avvakum, where the change of the personal tone and the stylization of language lead to exposing the pathos of the preacher, Leskov uses archaic church elements in the oral colloquial speech of the characters in his **"Notes"** as well. In both works we see symbolic parallels corresponding to different parameters of view: жимие-narrative, saturation of the texts with church Slavonic terms, creative intuition to show events which happened during the life of each author, and eventually their religious moral stance is conveyed in the ancient book style in its primordial state. All that gives us the possibility to formulate the following conclusion: the permanent use of the literary aesthetic tradition and language heritage enables Leskov to create his own stylistic system. He was an avant-garde artist searching new ways of using words in their original and nonartificial hypostases. Just as Avvakum himself embodied a novel literary and language intention, Leskov tried to appropriate what he found there and accommodate it to the fresh conditions thereby developing his own standards. Our task is to understand this 'unintelligible' system of material linguistic integument and the means of its interior aesthetic organization.

When studying the problem, however, the danger of mixing up the two notions, style in its diachronic conception and the "normative" comprehension of it, might arise. The historic approach presupposes some system and we may easily be bogged down in multilingual and multicultural problems. Normative style is more or less a static category representing a whole complex of questions. It is a totality of indications characterizing an art or literary piece of a definite period and a tendency in attitude to the substantial idea and the artistic form. Here style has found its position on the basis of timelessness. We have a propensity for source study. It might appear an absolute necessity for anyone to develop analysis in such a key because Leskov compiled his work from original sources, and to elucidate his historic method has always born more substantial fruit than concentrating research exclusively on the text. It is also important to remember that "various styles of speech within limits of one and the same written language . . . can go back to different historic traditions" (Винокур 1959: 232).[14] For instance, it is known that in Russian literary speech of the beginning of the 19th century some Slavonicisms like млеко, бред, выя, вран, etc., which had their primordial Russian synonyms-duplicates, were in active use. In that particular period this trait characterized literary language on the whole in contrast to secular, epistolary or domestic language in its written form. Closer to the '30s the use of Old Slavonic was not any longer an attribute of the artistic mode of speech, it was rather a characteristic of the language of poetry as contra-distinguished from that of prose. Thus it would be an error to consider every language feature in Leskov's narrative as evidence for his use of the real language situation of his time. Here we should keep a linguistic distance and take into consideration essentially different conditions for the language in diverse spheres. That is why the writer's Slavonic world should be explained in the context of the literary aesthetic traditions of his time as well as of his own views expressed in letters, articles, etc. Seen in this way the abundance of Church Slavonic lexemes and syntactic constructions can be said to make no impression of a surcharge of the text as a result of primitive stylization. His comprehension of the notion of stylization is entirely different from some of the definitions we can find in modern dictionaries, e.g. "1. Stylization—imitation of outward [i.e. superficial—*O. N.*] forms, typical illustrations of a certain style. < . . . 2. Literary work being as to the form an imitation of some style" (Лексические трудности 1994: 455). Stylization for him was not mere imitation, it was not even connected seriously to it (in this period of his creative activities). Leskov's inward requirement 'to stylize' comes out of his own artistic struggle against any unreasonable treatment of language ligatures on the one hand, and out of his speculations on artistic taste on the other. It is evident that Slavonicisms have a special part to play in the structure of his texts. Their emotional mood, musical pitch and grammatical harmony create a fascinating atmosphere of skilful puns and whimsical imagination. They are very carefully attributed to the oral characteristics of his protagonists and do not upset the balance of composition. Look at their inner phonation: епимимейка (Лесков 1973, IV: 269) (penance)—here used with the diminutive hypocoristic suffix instead of епимимья; примязание (Лесков 1973, IV: 257) (in the meaning of grabbing); дражае (Лесков 1973, IV: 284) (dearly, here in the sense 'having more

importance'); снемлюмся (Лесков 1973, IV: 299) (are gathering); оспособлямшь хозяев (Лесков 1973, IV: 298) (to help the hosts); . . . воздреваема духом благочесмивой ревносми . . . (Лесков 1973, IV: 299) (warming by the spirit of pious zeal)—describing the anger of a bishop; быв же через немалое время увещеваем . . . (Лесков 1973, IV: 309) (having been admonished during a long period of time); благочинный градских церквей . . . (Лесков 1973, IV: 305) (rural dean of the urban churches); . . . [бытш] в напрасно посмыжающем конфузе (Лесков 1973, IV: 300) ([to be] in unfoundedly shameful embarrassment); . . . помещик . . . возмнил себя уже видящим небо омверсмо и смал проповедо-вамш . . . (Лесков 1973, IV: 298) (the landowner got too high an opinion of himself just seeing the Heaven open and began to preach); . . . омец же Иван . . . благословил его, а помом . . . лег паки (Лесков 1973, IV: 260) (Father Ivan blessed him, and then lay down again). Obviously, the use of archaic models of official business style filled with Slavonicisms and lexemes of religious meaning let us come to the conclusion that there is an appreciable connection between Leskov's language and some of the language features of the 17th century but Leskov's medium is more stylized. Leskov relied on a tradition which emerged in a later period, in the 1700s, when Old Slavonic words which used to have mostly ecclesiastic and cult semantics before were subjected to a redefinition of their language status, sometimes their field of dissemination was narrowed down (or changed in a way) and they preserved their primary sense only in obsolete stylized church speech. Leskov was also right when he noticed the most peculiar feature of written business style in the 18th century: the collation of church speech with phraseological locutions with figurative meaning.[15] This made wordy modifiers metaphoric and inimitable in artistic beauty.

This statement is corroborated by our analysis of changes in Leskov's attitude to the literary language. He began with imitative genres, and the main form of stylization was 'mimicking of style' (of course, we have his fiction and not his essays or journalism in mind). That was not, however, simple imitation or assimilation to the concrete manner of writing but its intentional and spiritually realized reproduction. Moreover, Leskov came to literature with a definite view of Russian existence. In his first story, **"Овцебык" ("The Musk-Ox")** [1862], the principal traits of his artistic stance was already outlined: recollection, aptly combined with fantasy, was based on exposing the biography of a hero by short and impressive episodes (ЛЭС 1987: 216); short stories inserted into the main body of the text; a heightened sensitivity to folk speech and its richness in unexpected turns; trustworthy sketches of the clergy.[16]

"Жимие одной бабы" ("**The Life of a Woman**") [1863] anticipates the characteristic components of his further literary activities—the subtitle «Из гостомелшских воспоминаний» ("**From the Gostomel reminiscences**") suggests that Leskov's interest in giving a biographic turn to his narrative has deepened, and the folk *skaz* (tale) in his fiction obtains a dominant position for the first time.

In the second part of the '60s and '70s, Leskov's writing is notable for the broad range of expression. In this period the following language and style features of his literary works can be distinguished: a significant presence of elements of language naturalism, an active search for style-forming elements and modes of organizing the genre system, heightened sensibility to the minute description of the representatives of national types, and last but not least, a graphically pronounced social orientation of turns of speech *(Соборяне, Запечамленный ангел, Очарованный смранник)*. Historic truth is subordinated to artistic truth in Leskov's literary works of this time just as in A. F. Vel'tman. The fantastic and real were the two principles forming the subject-matter of his fiction during the period. This perhaps indicated a shift from what is called conventional historicity, i.e. Leskov moved away from the important problems of modern life, which are screened by reveries and romantic dreams, to conscious historicism in which the tale as a source blends with a critical insight into the spiritual contradictions of the present.[17]

Later Leskov himself defined the method he used in the last period of his career. "I wrote in small chapters",—he said. L. P. Grossman (Гроссман 1945: 265) comments on Leskov's statement as follows:

> Leskov mastered this gift to cut up a story and enhance the interest of the reader by a skilful distribution of parts to perfection. He created his independent type of short story in sections: the general figure of his stories, which emerges in a series of quickly succeeding short chapters resumed nearly in every page, gives that lucid coherence to the whole which is assimilated by the reader with no strain or tiredness
>
> (Гроссман 1945: 265).

"**Notes of the Unknown,**" indeed, consists of short but richly condensed chapters (all in all twenty two). Each of them has its own plot, each is certainly vivid, satiric and easily retained in memory. Every chapter has its own title, sometimes playful or ironic. Here are some of them: "**Искусный омвемчик**" ["**The Clever Respondent**"], "**О вреде ом чмения свемских книг, бываемом для мнодих**" ["**On the Harm of Reading Secular Books Which Affected a Great Many**"], "**Излишняя мамеринская нежносмь**" ["**Superfluous Motherly Tenderness**"], "**Счасливому осмроумию и непозволимелвная волвносмь прощаемся**" ["**The Lucky wWit Is Forgiven for Inadmissible Familiar-**

ity"], "**О безумии одного князя**" ["**About the Madness of a Prince**"], "**Османовление расмущего языка**" ["**The Stoppage of the Growing Tongue**"], etc. It was one of Leskov's artistic habits to specify the title of the story by a subtitle either in brackets or without them, as for instance, "**О слабосми чувсмв и Онапряженносми оных. (Двоякий приклад ом познаний и наблюдения)**" ["**Of the Weakness of Feelings and the Intensity of Theirs. (The Double Assiduity of Epistemology and Observation)**"] or "**О Пемухе и его демях. Геральический казус**" ["**About Petukh and His Children. A Heraldic Casus**"]. A similar device to specify the main idea was applied by Leskov in his articles and essays, as we have already noticed. He thought that the title should be lively, sonorous, alluring and easy to memorize. Following this principle he created out-of-the-way, enigmatic and inviting titles.

The last story of the cycle is most remarkable in this respect. Let us first examine the title and its complex meaning—"**A Heraldic Casus**". It emphasizes the mystery of the contents and creates a considerable metaphorical aura. This is the result of an unusual concept of the word, of its interior structure. In it the unit of the language appears not in the function of a conditional sign for expressing an idea but like an artistic image (Буслаев 1861: 1). We shall try to penetrate into the substance of this figurativeness. Thus, 'heraldic' can be traced back to the lexeme 'heraldry'. The 'Dictionary' of foreign words (Полный словарь 1894: 266) gives the following definition: it derives from Middle Latin *heraldus* which can be traced back to herald. Heraldry is the science of insignia. The name comes from the fact that in the Middle Ages at the time of a tournament the armorial bearings of a new knight appeared, and the herald was supposed to explain the meaning of the arms depicted on the shield of the new contestant. But this interpretation does not contain the sense we are looking for, the very mysterious implication which Leskov managed to give the word. To reveal its concealed significance we shall follow the writer's mode of treating language: having 'turned' the word to one side we shall now turn it to the other. 'Herald' springs from Old German *hariwalt*—'steward of force'. It had three different meanings:

1. A public or town crier (in Russia—длашамай) in ancient times whose duty was to announce wars; 2. a person who proclaimed the names of knights in a tournament; 3. an official who announced important events to the public, e.g. coronations (Полный словарь 1894: 270). For the understanding of Leskov's intention the third meaning is of special interest. To get closer to it we have to remember that the word дерольдия, which is obsolete today, was still widely used in the 19th century. This lexeme with some accurate definition would contain the main theme of the short story. Герольдия

in Russia was a government institution which was responsible for the scrutiny of the rights of the nobles and for working out the insignia for various places and people. To confirm our hypothesis we shall address the short story **"About Petukh and His Children"**.

In it Leskov made use (with good effect) of events which were connected with the public marriage of an officer, son of a land-owning woman and a serf maid as well as the juridically illegitimate entry of their marriage. Showing the pictures of pre-reform Russia the writer touches lightly upon the very intricate and complicated theme of Russian cryptogamia (here the word is used in the meaning of clandestine marriage). Leskov's story seems true to us because he explains some details of the unusual case by references to one of the legal documents. In the second part ('A simple means') he inserts a footnote with some interesting information which proves that the story is true to historical fact. He mentions in a casual way the forty second paragraph of 'Instruction to Rural Deans', which was published in 1857, and quotes a few words from it:

> . . . in it the necessity is discussed to exercise "prudence in declaring couples husband and wife who were not married here" (где говорится об «осторожности в ноказывании супругами таких лиц, кои здесш не венчаны»),

and in witness of their marriage cannot produce evidence.

> Apparently,—infers the narrator,—there must have been some reason that made this warning necessary (Очевидно, что предостережение это было чем-нибудш вызвано)
>
>                                  (Лесков 1973, IV: 331).

As it becomes obvious by the passage quoted above, by inobtrusive signs and remarks the author tries to bring the reader closer to his true-to-life narrative style and tries to convince him of the authenticity of his words. As far as we can know on the ground of the written evidence, Leskov was elaborating this problem at the time of publishing the cycle and somewhat later in the articles Благословенный брак . . .[18] and Бракоразводное забвение. Причина разводов брачных . . .[19] ["The divorce unconsciousness. A motive of divorce proceedings . . ."]. In particular, the writer cites a curious passage from a rare book which has an indirect relationship to **"The Notes of the Unknown."** That is how Leskov describes an episode of Russian cryptogamia [spacing out and sequence of words made by the writer are presented here without any changes—O. N.]: ". . . in the accomplishment of marriage the church, i.e. 'the gathering of believers' . . . , does not participate neither does any 'executor of *treb*' [occasional religious rites: christening, marriage, funeral, etc.—O. N.]. All the chanters

and benedictors only 'coattend', as witnesses, but 'the performer [of rites—O. N.] is absent'[20]. This elliptical device artistically confirms 'A heraldic casus' in which Leskov, with grotesque metaphorical allusions, represents the fictive marriage (misalliance) of Petukh and Pelageya describing the essence of the matter as a criminal farce. What is more surprising, the writer finds quite a marvelous solution to settle the problem. It was really 'A Simple Means'—such is the title Leskov gave to the final part of this short narrative. The consistory bailiff comes to Luka's rescue who is so much in despair that he has no idea of what to do, saying that

> отчаяние естш смертный грех, а на святой Руси нет невозможности
>
>                                  (Лесков 1973, IV: 332)

(despair is a mortal sin, but in holy Russia nothing is impossible).

What is his 'remedy'? It is not a forgery or a criminal act ("There is a mind not only in big heads but in small ones" = «Ум-то не в одних болшших головах, а и в малых» Лесков 1973, IV: 333). So, Luka Aleksandrovich gets the book from the archives and finds the name 'peasant Petukh' in it written in a different ink in a scraped space. As soon as no one remembers who has done it, an investigation is undertaken. During it all testify that Pelageya married Luka, and Petukh was simply standing by. That proves to be a cogent argument, and the true matrimony is confirmed. ". . . but the bailiff did not do any forgery, he only added in the book the very thing that he had wiped out in it. That was his 'simple means'" («а приказный никакой фалшши не сделал, а только подписал в книге то самое, что в ней и вычистил. То было его "простое средство"» Лесков 1973, IV: 333),—the narrator concludes finishing the story. This final section differs from all the rest. It manifests Leskov's greatness as an artist in the commanding humour, lenient irony and fully particularized (as to characteristics and description) form. This part is satiated with a special colouring supplied by the metaphorical devices and the amazing variety of verbalized emotions. In it we find a most unusual combination of circumstances skilfully brought together by Leskov and joined with various style and language constructions: the tradition of 18th-century business correspondence acquires completely new shades of meaning, the lexis of the inquiry deeds is put to very convincing use, vivid Slavonicisms are combined with picturesque phraseological locutions. Even the very plot seems as if it was borrowed from an ancient forensic manuscript with its typical colophon, and the miscarriage of justice is looked upon as a heraldic *casus*.

The second word of the subtitle has relatively richer semantic colouring. *Casus* means 'case'—this is the well-known definition today. In the earlier period it also had the meaning 'an awkward circumstance' or 'a remarkable case' (Полный словарь 1894: 438). Modern sources add to the aforementioned definitions useful and pertinent semantic explications, i.e. 1. Case, usually difficult, intricate or uncommon, ridiculous; 2. *jur.* A case, an accidental action, having external signs of transgression but deprived of the element of a guilt therefore non-punishable (СИС 1990: 211).

All these possible interpretations of 'heraldic case' are important to take into account as they prompt us the idea that the very word in Leskov's fiction appears in the role of a literary image. It possesses not a single information ground but contains various groups of conditional indications and connotations which Leskov wants to mobilize.

Somewhat later, in 1886, Leskov would reflect on the problem of cases presenting highly convincing proofs based on his own experience in the article Гералъцеский муман. (Эамемки о родовых проэваниях). Alongside with some interesting facts he gives in it an analysis of names and surnames which seem foreign in origin, in term of their genealogy, however, they are primordially Russian[21]. At this point the literary historian, E. P. Karnovich's Родовые проэвания и мимулы в России и слияние русских с иноэемтами (С&ЛБ886) ['Patrimonial nicknames and titles in Russia and the blending of the Russian with the foreign'] should be mentioned; Leskov appreciated his knowledge of life and artistic gifts very highly.

Critics have pointed out the most characteristic peculiarities of Leskov's fiction: his ability to create a language which can convey the inner processes and the speech habits of his protagonists as well as the astonishing vividness of his description of domestic scenes. How is this manifested in the **"Notes of the Unknown,"** and what shades of textual meaning does his language display? We would like to return once more to the short story **"About Petukh and His Children"**. The narrator's speech is imperceptibly inserted into the dialogue so that what was said before could be explained:

> Petukh was a бсмягольный (having no family) *muzhik* in the master's poultry-yard dirty and half-witted, with a red nose, jabbering away in a squeaky voice, and was forty or so (Был жеПетух бстяголъный мужик на господском гтитьем дворе—нетистый и полоумный, с красным носом, и говор гмел дроботливый с выкриком ио-петушьему, а лет уже сорока и поболее)
>
> (Лесков 1973, IV: 324).

Here the author employs specific words to create a true-to-life domestic atmosphere. The words have their own shades of meaning peculiar to the nature of the person implied, e.g. бесмягольный instead of бессемейный. In Old Russian мягло was used basically in

two meanings: labour conscription or a family executing their duties at the time of serfdom. Interesting notes on it are given in the 'Dictionary' (Дал 1994: 900-901):

> . . . мягловой крестьянинъ, который тянетъ полное тягло, за лвѣ луши; . . . обычно крестьянинъ остается мяглымъ отъ женитьбы своей до 60 лѣтъ, затѣмъ либо онъ идетъ в полутяглые, и на четверть тягла, или смѣщается вовсе. . . . Тягло ср. мужб с женою или семья, въ крестьянствѣ, доколь мужикъ, по лѣтамъ своимъ и по здоровью, числится тяглымъ.

Leskov can very well be supposed to have known the numerous proverbs which were connected with this notion and which had wide currency in the social environment described by the writer in his cycle.

In the sentence quoted above Leskov uses дробомливый говор instead of more common words like quick, fast, pattering. And the sentence is immediately followed by the description of the conversation of the priest and his wife which is presented in another manner closer to *skaz:*

> Попдья ничего не внимала, а сказала такой сказ, что если поп ее заранее осведомит, когда бригадиршин сые съедет в город, а Полньку с мужиком свенчают, то она никакого мешанья не сделает, но если он от нее это скроет, то ее любопытство мучить станет, и тогда она за себя не поручится, что от нетерпения вред сделает
>
> (Лесков 1973, IV: 324)[22]

(The priest's wife didn't listen to him but said such a tale that if the priest informed her in advance when the brigadier's wife's son was going to go up to town, and Polen'ka and the *muzhik* were going to be married, then she would not make any мещнья (trouble), but if he hid that from her then she would be tormented by curiosity, and then she could not vouch for herself and might, out of impatience, do some harm).

After this verbose skaz Leskov inserts a single statement: «поп уступил» (Лссков 1973, IV: 324) (the priest gave in). Nothing superfluous is added by the narrator. His syntactic phrases are efficiently constructed and thought out. This fluent passage gives the reader the impression that he can actually arrest the flow of the narrative and try to realize what is behind the narrator's words. That compositional device is called retardation. In connection with Leskov's *skaz* A. S. Orlov was the first to notice that particular narratological element. He claims that "the skaz of Leskov can be characterized by its excitement being supported by the curiosity of the listener to be able to hear how every person speaks in accordance with his typical nature" (Орлв 1948: 146). The priest uses a different language: there are no diffuse phrases, his voice sounds mild, and it is briefly interrupted by the narrator's elucidation:

Ну, ладно,—говорит,—я тебе лучше все скажу, только уж ты знай, да никому здесь не сказывай

(Лесков 1973, IV: 324)

(All right then,—he says,—I would better tell you everything, but remember you must not tell anyone here).

Soon enough the speech of the officers is defined: it is shaped in the imperative mood without any additions and explanations; *skazovost'* here is not an expressive stylistic device to be applied. The traits of the people of this social stratum require another artistic method in another linguistic medium:

—Сейас нам отчеретп! Ибо з аем, что в храме насильный брак совершается, и мы не допустим и сейчас двери вон выбьем . . .

(Лесков 1973, IV: 326)

—(Open now [the door]! Because we know that in the church a forcible matrimony is happening, but we won't let it go on, we'll rather knock out the doors in no time . . .).

Their speech is an expression of their intentions. This approach to representing character is most subtle. As we have already suggested, each estate in Leskov's fiction has its own unique language and style. By the means of speech constituting his characters Leskov creates a comic atmosphere. Manipulating elements of comedy, irony and satire the writer defines the characteristic features of the heroes' interior speech and inner world.[23] Though retardation is a stylistic device widely spread in longer literary pieces, there it has a different function; it appears, for instance, in lyrical digressions, in descriptions of nature or interiors, in insertion of external personages and separate short stories, etc., Leskov's mode of using it in the **"Notes of the Unknown"** differs, to some extent, from his usual treatment of the device. As we have mentioned, the author tried to slow down the speed and delay the events by using various ways of expressing the vocal characteristics of his protagonists. It is attained through a sharp change of textual key and alteration of the tone of narration. There is also one more detail which brings **"Notes"** close to folklore. It is the sequential construction of the narrative and the threefold reduplication of the typical episodes, which builds up tension. We find the latter used four times. Thirst is used in Излняя мамеринская нежносмь in this way: there is a mildly ironic and humorous depiction of Ignaty's fright which arises out of lying near бабка-голландка (Grandma Dutch) who keeps chuckling at him and making smacking noises with her lips up to the very morning (Лесков 1973, IV: 266). Here we see a two-way junction: the reinforcement of the inner tension of the hero (confirmed by him saying that he was looking forward to falling asleep with all his might) which takes place as if in a dream, and the skaz of two kinds when what happened in the past correlates to reality. We call this device an imagi-

nary reduplication because the progress is infringed but the delay of the action is the result of the transmission of the thoughts and the voices of the characters through the sensibility of the narrator. In that particular episode skaz is one of the ways of showing reduplication where the situation of spontaneous improvisation conveys the disposition of the story-teller. We cannot fully affirm that this device is merely borrowed from national folklore. It is rather an element of sentimental prose which itself was affected by the oral folklore of the time. But the less it directly conforms to that dominant tradition or the literary norm the more original and interesting it is as to its form and metaphoricity. The problem is psychological rather than linguistic: it indicates what lies behind the narrator's apperception. Some parallel examples of retardation might be useful to analyze.

In the story **"Об иносмранном предиканме"** retardation appears in a different form: in the dialogue between Father Georgy and владыка (member of the higher orders of the clergy). They discuss the question of the prohibition of preaching to the foreign предиканм (here 'preacher'). First of all the incident is described which arouses the interest in the reader as to why Georgy has refused to forbid the preacher to preach in the house of the предводимельща (the wife of a marshal of the nobility), Elena Ivanovna, who is called Elena Prekrasnaja for her 'delicate face' («за свое изящное лице») (Лесков 1973, IV: 299).

Првая моя пичина,—говорит,—та, что моего запрещения могут не послушаться, и я тогда буду через то только в напрасно постыждающем конфузе

(Лесков 1973, IV: 300)

(My first reason is,—he says,—that they might disobey my prohibition, in which case I put myself in a disreputable *konfuz'* in vain).

That idea does not seem convincing enough to the bishop—«Эо не чо иное как гордость ума» (Лесков 1973, IV: 300) ('This is nothing else but the pride of the mind'). The second argument is as follows:

. . . что предиканта того «развратителем» назвать будет несправедливо, ибо он хотя и иностранец, но человек весьма хороших правил христианской жизни . . .

(Лесков 1973, IV: 300)

(. . . it would be unfair to call that *predicant* "a seducer" because though he is a foreigner, but a person of high Christian principles . . .).

This reason does not seem to the bishop conclusive either who now begins to show his displeasure. To Georgy's third motive the bishop listens with testy impatience: ". . . it is not customary to the spirit of the orthodoxial belief to fear timidly any dissenting opinions, but on the contrary, it is characterized by laudable веромерпимсмво (toleration) and free expression and speech, just like the apostles advise: «Все слшать, а хорощего дериаться» (Лесков 1973, IV: 300) (To listen to everything but hold to *the good*) [italicized by the author—*O. N.*]

The convincing argument for the bishop was that the governor himself was sitting behind the screen listening to the predicant.

> Усліхав это последнее,—продолжает повествователь,—владыка остановился и сказал:—Так для чего же вы мне об этом последнем с самого начала не сказали?
>
> (Лесков 1973, IV: 301)
>
> (Having heard this,—the narrator continued,—the bishop stopped and asked:—Why didn't you tell me about this last thing at the very beginning?).

In this episode retardation comes after the second reduplication, and the dialogue serves the function of setting the story in motion. To some extent, the passage quoted above is connected with folklore motives (the name of the lady ironically corresponds to a similar character of a well-known Russian tale). Leskov used the same device in the story **"About Petukh and His Children"**.

This brings us to an analysis of the syntactic system of the writer which is based (particularly in the last story) on N. G. Kurganov's Latinate syntax together with a sham (бтафория) of the beginning of the 19th century (Орлов 1948: 164-165). Actually, here we come across constructions which are not customary in Russian, i.e. adverbial participles and verbs which change their positions and are placed by the author at the absolute end of the phrase, as for instance:

> The priest's wife his grief умищила (Лесков 1973, IV: 325) (calmed down); the Brigadier's wife took a deep breath and crossed herself, but that was because of a great confusion instead of a wedding ceremony, heaven knows what пемо бяху (had been sung), the deacon did not say . . .
>
> (Лесков 1973, IV: 330),
>
> or And you did not disgrace (пе опали) for that either me or anyone else through the rage of yours, but, by your usual mercy all of us покрыв (shielding), deliberated calmly and decorously . . .
>
> (Лесков 1973, IV: 329), etc.

The examples quoted above are not exceptional. If we examine them we understand the function of the transformations. Leskov seems to have intensified the real semantic and temporal sense of the endings of locutions by means of the utilization of verbal inversion. Thus, the full implication of the events is moved to the verbal forms which speeds up action and precipitates the evolution of the plot. It is in the verbs where the author

perceives the substantial kernel of the passage. In conformity to the positional structure of the sentence Leskov uses the method of substitution. The writer's narrative style requires this in order to determine words and constructions which can freely occupy any syntactical position. This device amplifies the ways of the semantic expansion of the vocabulary because the shift of syntactical position does not always conform to valid aspects of syntax. We can see some elements of the method of transposition here as well where the transfer of words or collocations from one syntactic position to the other creates a different tone and defines the relations between the form of the word and its function in the sentence. As we can see, Leskov's method is experimental and uncommon. We have already touched upon this problem in the discussion of the gamut of the language colours in his prose.

Leskov's special interest in heraldry has already been pointed out. In **"Notes of the Unknown"** the names of the representatives of the clergy are selected very carefully. They can be read as labels which anticipate the roles these protagonist will play in the narrative. Some of them function as mirror reflections of certain tempers and moral characteristics. Of course, behind the form of the bearer of a proper name stands the narrator's ulterior device. Leskov liked one of the statements of Theocritus which he used as an epigraph at the beginning of the article Геральдический муман . . . : "Everyone gets his name at a blessed hour"[24]. Leskov himself followed this dictum in his creative writings. Thus, for instance, Father Ioann (the name is a translation of the Hebrew 'God's grace') «прежде во всю жизнь свою не пил» (Лесков 1973, IV: 259) (he had not drunk all his life before); Father Pavel (from Latin *paulus*— 'small') «был роста высокого, осторожного понимания и в разйоворах нередко шутлив» (Лесков 1973, IV: 261) (was of large stature, of keen comprehension, and in speech often enough jocular); Father Grigory (in Old Greek γρηγορРω—'be awake, cheerful, vigilant') «в слженье хорош и весьма способен, но камоликовам, и то было в нем заимствованное . . . » (Лесков 1973, IV: 268) (in service is good and very capable, but камоликовам (is like a Catholic), and that was borrowed in him . . .); hieromonk Theodosy (the name is compound from the two Old Greek words: θεός—'God' and δόςις—'a gift', 'a donation', i.e. granted to God) «нарицаяся друг, но не верный, и втайне зложелатель . . . » (Лесков 1973, IV: 288) (called a friend, but not faithful, and secretly malevolent . . .); another Father Pavel, who imagined himself "to be as though the first after Pharaoh (мня ся быти яко первым по фараоне), endeavored to sit [in the дрожки] outstreched in a place for two . . ." (Лесков 1973, IV: 313); lastly, junior deacon (причмник) Porphiry (compare to Old Greek πορφύρεος—'purple, crimson; dark-red, violet; generally dark'; the name also has the root meaning 'purple clothes or a mantle') who was named 'the dull-born' (глупороженный) and 'rough' (комованый), was tall and of a very submissive disposition (нрав) (Лесков 1973, IV: 313).

It might be surprising to see that Leskov practically never mentions the surnames of his characters, especially if they belong to the church. Surnames were not used in clerical circles. Besides, it could have been rather a stiff and artificial device. Their real temper and deeds are of the greatest importance for Leskov who in hardly visible traits created picturesque satirical portraits of the local clergy.

Leskov's interest in the meaning of names and in their genealogy is obviously deeply rooted. In the 1870s he elaborated his own system of categorizing the surnames of the Russian priesthood. He established six categories: surnames which go back to the names of holidays (for instance, Rozhdestvensky), to the names of figures in antiquity like Platonov, or to words for virtues of character, etc. (Гроссман 1945: 272). Leskov's names are artistic images which have a life of their own and a complex aura of connotations. Somewhat later, in the 1900-1910s, the philosopher Father P. A. Florensky also expounded his view of names. He thought it was a grave mistake to "declare all the literary names,—*and the name as it is* [italicized by P. A. Florensky—*O. N.*],—arbitrary and accidental . . . Names are the main kernels of the very images . . ." (Флоренский 1993: 25). As well as Leskov, he considered names artistic images forming complex spiritual organisms and characterizing the persons who carry them. According to P. A. Florensky's concept, they possess various moods of their being (бымие): ecclesiastic, humiliated, diminutive (Флоренский 1993: 40, 94-96). The hypostasis of every name determines its significance and should be analyzed as part of the cultural process.[25] It may be interesting to compare the theological tradition with Leskov's own concept of names. His gift as a creative writer, his idealism and severe critical views helped him find an artistic form to convey his experiences as well as the findings of his research. In point of fact he formulated the very group of notions which later on were to become the basis of a modern branch of science—onomastics—the art of giving names (that is calque translation from the corresponding Old Greek word). Leskov's feelings and thoughts combined to find the concrete object of his writing—the representatives of the clergy. It was not only a coincidence but one of his stylistic devices permanently present in his literary works. This combination of satirical literary expressions and intellectual penetration to the depth of a problem seems to be the articulation of two features of his individuality: his intransigence as a social being confronting moral perversion and his profound intellect in search for truth. The very term 'onomastics' covers not only the art of giving names, but also scholarly proficiency in studying them. The latter now belongs to linguistics,

Leskov, however, was the master of both approaches, and what is more, that ability of his appears in two forms: in scholarly conjectures and hypotheses which he managed to translate into the terms of the imaginative world of his art as a writer. Leskov's creative work, his world-view and his understanding of aesthetic problems merged all together in his fiction moulding his style and extending his penetration into national history and culture.

Leskov's work as a writer is most unique in the wide range of the questions he treats and the variety of ways he describes them. His narrative style is constituted of a great diversity of stylistic figures and dialects. The playful language abounds in parodistic elements given in a cover of archaic Slavonic expressions in combination with quotations from the Holy Writ which results in paronomastic effects. On the other hand, there are a lot of professional patterns and words of folk terminological lexis. Sometimes they are simply misrepresented in their meaning and structure. In another case, as though explaining the real sense of the word Leskov binds it in the consciousness of a speaker with a different lexeme. This device—attraction paronymique—is widely applied in **"Notes of the Unknown."** It is used to express the difference in the cultural status of his characters (Орлов 1948: 167). Somewhere he changes the sense, and a wrong letter used by him, as if by mistake, has its own shade of meaning and colour indication. Thus, for instance, in the collocation посморонние вольнодомки (Лесков 1973, IV: 262) the letter o is substituted for u because those people were not 'free thinkers' (the correct root of the second word is дум), but people who stayed at home (па дому). In the sentence «Иеродиакон немолодых лет, но могумной (of mighty flesh) нлоти . . . имел страсть к биллиардной игре . . .» (Лесков 1973, IV: 284) the word могучий (might) is re-vised and changed into могумная which now absorbs the nuance of suggesting a self-indulgent, unrestrained character who never hesitates to take liberties. Father Preferants (whose nickname is associated with a card game preference) has a son богослов (theologian) who would better be called бог ослов (the God of donkeys) (Лесков 1973, IV: 291). In this example folk etymology is combined with the process of redistribution of the stem. As a result, quite an opposite meaning is suggested by the evocation of a curse commonly used in the 19th century in theological seminaries, an ironic nick-name for a foolish person, the same as 'ass' in English. After that statement the narrator defines the word by the following reference: « . . . [сын] по пороку беспамятства никак не мог научиться служению . . .» (Лесков 1973, IV: 291) ". . . [the son] because of a defect of unconsciousness could hardly be taught to preach . . .". This feature illustrates the significance of and the reason for the use of this rather uncommon idiomatic expression.

In the short story **"Удивимельный случай всеоби-
щего недоумения"** [**"A Wonderful Case of General
Perplexity"**] Leskov uses the word combination маде-
муазель попадья (as a reference to a priest's wife)
putting it in inverted commas. It is organized on the
principle of placing together incompatible (because of
their dissonant meanings) notions or of correlating
words having contradictory meanings in a collocation.
Similarly, for instance, to the French oxymoron *une
sage folie* (a wise folly) (see: Марузо 1960: 186); or
the Russian phrase: звонкая мищина (a ringing
silence), etc.

This *alliance des mots* conveys a delicate sense of irony
and humour, especially as those are words of different
origins: *mademoiselle* (Fr.) + попадья (Rus.). When
describing 'the spiritual inclination' to the unfrocked
archimandrite the narrator says that

> в чнсие лпсем, оставшихся поспе смерти
> расстриги, было одно от женщины настоящего
> высокого звания русских фамилий, которая даже
> называть его прежнего сана не умела и заместо
> того, чтобы писать «архимандрит», выражалась:
> «парфемандрит», что ей было более склонно к
> французскому штилю

> (Лесков 1973, IV: 310)

(in the number of letters remaining after the death of
the unfrocked monk was one from a lady of one of the
really high rank Russian families, who did not even
know how to name his former order, and instead of
"archimandrite" she wrote: "parfemandrite", which she
found more familiar since it was closer to her French
style).

In the passage quoted above Leskov's neologism consists of the prefixoid парфе- which could be brought
into correlation with the French adjective *parfait*
(perfect, absolute). That is an instance based on an expression etymologically unclear for the national language environment. Here it is partly paraphrased just
like револьвер at the turn of the 20th century when
many borrowings were in active use. It was understood
owing to its artificial rebuilding as ребродер[26].

Original puns are close in nature to folk etymology.
They used to be organized as metaphoric idioms and
constituted a phrase which had a double sense. Here are
some characteristic examples of Leskov's individual
thinking-in-words: неодолимая пассия (Лесков 1973,
IV: 319) (irresistible passion), опымные резоны
(Лесков 1973, IV: 320) (serious reasons); "And
Polen'ka . . . became idleless, and having, as one can
see, from her mother innate French кокемерия
(coquetry) . . ." (Лесков 1973, IV: 320); "If he [Father
Grigory—*O. N.*] на духу (with courage) for the better
perspicuity exhorted in French, then this moved the audience so intensely that they гисмерически
(hysterically) sobbed violently . . ." (Лесков 1973, IV:

320). The phrases quoted above can be interpreted in
two ways: they provoke laughter because of a contradiction between their meaning and the actual situation
of the characters, on the one hand, and because of the
reference in them to the protagonists' civilized temper
and bent for French manners and mentality, on the other.
This idea has an interesting justification. The Russian
каламбур (pun) has a concrete event for its origin,
which, we may assume, was used by Leskov as a sub-
textual device.

It was known that in 18th-century French aristocratic
memoirs the term *calambour* was explained in terms of
the following genealogy: in a gathering of high society
it was decided that everybody was to make up some
verses for fun. There was a dull-witted abbot who had
no idea about poetry. When his turn came, after some
vain attempts, in a sweat at last he invented the following lines:

> *Pleurons tous dans ce jour*
>     *A bois de calambour . . .*

This rot made the whole *monde* laugh to excess, and
the *casus* was not forgotten for a very long time. Leskov
may be supposed to have wanted to make use of the
episode. We can say that puns (here on the preciosity of
French style and manners) were very popular in Russia
in the 18th-19th centuries.[27]

We can also quote some specifically Russian puns and
language pigments from Leskov's narrative, e.g.
больщая иресмращка (Лесков 1973, IV: 331) (a
great fear), примязание (Лесков 1973, IV: 257)
(grubbing), сивуха (Лесков 1973, IV: 322) (in the
context the horse is meant, but generally the word is associated with raw vodka), усилок (Лесков 1973, IV:
326) (strong man), в живоме (Лесков 1973, IV: 329)
(during his life time), [deacon] положил . . . всему
макое краегранение (Лесков 1973, IV: 328) (began
fabricating a story); «Священник . . . в разговоре
голландский джин, отбивавший во вкусе своем
мозжухой, даже критиковал . . . » (Лесков 1973,
IV: 308) (During the conversation the priest . . . even
criticized the Dutch gin which savoured of моз-
жуха . . . (here the italicized word is associated with
juniper having the specific suffix -ух- (compare to крас-
нуха—ten rouble banknote, etc.). These phrases have
undoubtedly a vivid appeal to the senses. They all look
unusual (as to their structure and meaning), they do not,
however, break the rules of the genre. The analysis of
similar instances would require an approach which is
not exclusively linguistic.

We have tried to correlate the elements of Leskov's language with his peculiar stylistic system, with the facts
of his biography and with the traditions of the history
of literature. Looking for the sources of his fiction we
have also tried to clarify the theoretic positions which
could be useful for textological and source studies.

Thus, in the **"Notes of the Unknown"** different stylistic devices are combined. Creating picturesque portraits of the people of many professions and estates gives Leskov ample scope to charge his style and language with vivid features of various manners of speech and enunciation. Leskov's later style becomes a very complicated system, thoughtfully organized and elaborated to a nicety. His linguistic expressiveness, sophisticated use of words, his kind and keen irony, his ability to bring the narrator's speech closer to the tale tradition as well as the polysemanticism of the plot of each story based on original archive material lead to a conclusion of the following character: stylization in Leskov's later creative activities develops into an artistic principle which enables the writer to convey the complex vision he aspired to articulate.[28]

### Notes

1. GPB. F. 236, No. 174, p. 56. Cited from: (Лесков 1991: 37). [Here as hereafter all translations into English are my own.—*O. N.*].

2. Historическій вѣстник 11 (1883) 2: 265. Though A. N. Leskov did not find a real manuscript with original *Notes* (see: Звезда 1935, 7: 226), I assume that linguistic and source studies will lead us to us some possible parallels.

3. Историескій вѣстник 20 (1885) 6: 506-509.

4. Ibid. P.257. Later on Leskov said that he wanted to write Записки рассмриги ["Notes of the unfrocked"]; the hero of the story would be a young, sensitive and modest gentleman who becomes a priest in order to do what is possible (we keep here the authors spacing out of the words—*O. N.*) *ad majorem Dei gloriam,* and discovers that there is nothing to do for God's glory. But this could hardly be published in our Fatherland,—inferred the writer. (See the epilogue by A. N. Leskov to one of the first publications of some stories from *Notes of the Unknown* in the journal Звезда 1935. 7: 226).

5. When writing this narrative Leskov's personal position was rather difficult. Besides the fact of having to stop publishing the *Notes,* there is one more detail. In that period E. M. Theoktistov (whom the writer called "a pig from Theatre Square") was the Head of the Central Department of State Seal. The Minister for Education D. A. Tolstoy who "disliked people who took their own stand", as Leskov said, was also ill disposed to him.

6. RGADA. F. 1183. L. 1, part 37, No. 129, p. 1.

7. Ibid. No. 134, p. 1.

8. Ibid. No. 176, p. 6.

9. Разночипец—intellectual not belonging to the gentry in 19th-century Russia.

10. Йигилизм in its origin is borrowed from Latin *nihil*—'nothing'. N. O. Lossky gives a substantial analysis of the problem of Russian nihilism and its functions in literature. In his view the word "nihilism", not in an old theological but in the social sense, was used for the first time by N. I. Naдeždin in 1829. At that period it meant new tendencies in literature and philosophy. N. O. Lossky considered nihilism "the seamy side of the good qualities of the Russian people". See: Лосский 1991: 338-350.

11. RGADA. F. 1195. L. 4, No. 445, p. 84 r. s. This manuscript is written in the traditional type of Russian handwriting of the 18th century—скоропись (tachygraphy). It is to some extent more developed as compared to the beginning of the century, and is closer to the modern manner of writing. It is characterized by a variety of letter scripts, an abundance of signs carried above the line and the absence of an elaborated system of punctuation. Figures representing the date of the composition of the document in the second part of the 1700s are not substituted for letters as a rule. In "()" we put letters written in the original above the line; in "<>"—the letters omitted but implied by the author, "[]" are used for the letters carried out under the title. Orthography and punctuation are given without any corrections in the original form.

12. Compare the statement by N. O. Lossky: "Reducing the Church to the stage of servitors of the state, the government converts ecclesiastics into social servants" (Лосский 1991: 248).

13. The very remedy was called by the spiritual males *ес и ис е о и о from ес и и.*

14. In his other article G. O. Vinokur posits an interesting thesis which can be usefully adapted to historical analysis. He claims that "in application to the tasks of the reproduction of an old *glossa* the means of language of the following four types can be distinguished: firstly, the means of generally historic and folk colouring; secondly, the means with bookish colouring imitating Church Slavonic speech; thirdly, the means of narrow chronological colouring; in the fourth place, the means in expressiveness of which the dialectally estranging momentum suppresses the historical momentum proper" (Винокур 1991: 424).

15. Compare also Leskov's following combinations to the business style of the 18th century: he uses the 18th century grammatical concord with prepositions thus ascribing to them the meaning they used to have then and brings them into correlation with one of their sensitive units to polysemantic Slavonicisms (we put them in the bold type):

« . . . по принесении же белья эконом оное весьма смотрел в достоинстве проверял . . . » (Лесков 1973, IV: 278) (when the linen was brought the house-(exchequer-) keeper carefully looked through it and in virtue checked it up); « . . . [граф] в Петербург возвратясь, в мануфактур-совет, для испрошения медали . . . » (Лесков 1973, IV: 308) ([the count] came back to Petersburg, to the manufactory council, for asking a medal); « . . . случился к той поре на селе некий опытный брат, приезжий из недальней обители за нуждою монастырскою. . . . [он] сказал: "Брате, брате! Чего доспел еси?"» (Лесков 1973, IV: 311) (it came about at that time in the village that a certain experienced brother, a visitor from a cloister not far off, for monastery need. . . . [he] said: "Brother, brother! What have you made up?").

16. It can be mentioned here that one of Leskov's sisters, Natalija (1836-1920), was the nun Gennadija. See: Гроссман 1945: 26.

17. Compare, for instance, A. F. Vel'tman's Сердце и думка ('Heart and haze') to Leskov's Очароьанный сранник ('Encharmed wanderer').

18. See: Историескій вѣстникъ 20 (1885) 499 515.

19. See: Историескій вѣстникъ 22 (1885) 509 524.

20. Cited from: Историескій вѣстникъ 20 (1885) 503.

21. See: Историескій вѣстникъ 24 (1886) 598 613.

22. The usage of the rusificated French borrowing брииагирща is extremely significant. By probing into its genealogy the real contextual time can be revealed. The Russian бригадир springs from бригада (brigade) which has been known in Russia from the very outset of the 18th century. Since that time бригадир has been used as a military term. It was 'a brigade commander', an officer of the fifth class in the tsarist army of the 18th century, in between the colonel and the major-general, and in the navy it was the rank corresponding to the captain-commodore. Consequently, бригадирща (in the dictionaries it is defined as 'obsolete')—the wife of a brigadier—as a character's prototype could not exist beyond the first third of the 19th century. That is why we suppose that the real contextual time of this short story was the period between 1800 and the 1840s. See: Даль 1994: 313; Черных 1993: III; Макаров и Матвеева 1993: 47; ССРЛЯ 1991: 759. In the broad sense, Leskov gave a free rein to his imagination when describing pictures of pre-reform Russia. Apart from the aforementioned phenom-

enon, we think that there are some other striking illustrations of our conjecture, i.e. the problem of Russian *cryptogamia* described in this sketch, and the presence of tableaux vivants of the patriarchal mode of life in the Russian provinces in that period.

23. L. P. Grossman observed that "[Leskov] liked the inner world of his heroes by recreating their enunciation: one had a speech dull and unintelligible—his character is reserved and sullen; another spoke with such canning word ligatures (илвимия слов), that one is likely to get astounded by his speech,—but had a light and captivating temper" (Гроссман 1945: 270). See also the article Опекоморых особеппосмях языка «Замемок неизвесмпого» (Азбукин 1963: 59-63).

24. Историческій вѣстникъ 24 (1886) 598.

25. Compare the following definition made by bishop Antony (Florensov): "Name is an omen of the moral education of a person, of a Christian, a testimonial of his individuality and inclination to one or another kind of activity". See: андроник (Трубачев) 1981: 76.

26. See the publication of 'Terminological Glossary on Linguistics (1935-1937)' from the Archives of the Academy of Sciences of the USSR (now RAN) in: Поливанов 1991: 392-393.

27. Some scholars have supposed that the term can be traced back to an anecdote about priest Kalember or about the German count Kalember whose command of French was poor. See: Поливанов 1991: 463; ЭРЯ 1982: 24. P. Ja. Černych quotes a passage from "The Letters of the Russian Traveller" by N. M. Karamzin where the word "calanbur" was used, and considered that already from the beginning of the 19th century this expression was in use. In Russian dictionaries it is mentioned from 1804. See: Черных 1993: 370. As we know, anecdote is one of Leskov's vivid devices, which was artistically employed by him for language disguise.

28. I would like to thank Prof. Dr. V. Yu. Troitsky for his helpful comments while I was preparing this article and express special thanks to Prof. Dr. T. V. Androsova whose generous assistance and moral support I had ready at hand while working on it. I would also like to thank Mr. D. A. Dogadin for his technical recommendations and gestures of generosity during the time I was writing this article.

### Literature

Азбукин В. И. О некоторых особенностях языка «Заметок неизвестного»: Ученые записки Томского гос. ун-та. 1963. No. 45. 59-63.

Андроник (Трубачев), иеродиакон. Епископ Антоний (Флоренсов)—духовник священника Павла Флоренского: Журнал Московской Патриархии. 1981. No. 9. 71-77.

Буслаев Ф. И. Эпческая поэзия: Буслаев Ф. И. Исторические очерки русской народной словесности и искусства. 1. С.-Петербург 1861.

Даль В. И. Толовый словарь Живого великорусскойо языка, 1-4. Москва 1994.

Друеов Б. М. Н. С. Лесков. Очерк творчества. Москва 1957.

Випокур R. О. Об изучении языка литературных произведений: Винокур R. О. Изранные работы по русскому языку. Москва 1959.

Випокур Г. О. О языке художественной литературы. Москва 1991.

Гроссмап Л. П. Н. С. Лесков. Жизнь—Творчество—Поэтика. Ленинград 1945.

Ключевский В. О. Собрание сочинении. В 9 т. ix. Материалы разных лет. Москва 1990.

Лексиуеские трудности русского языка: Словаръ-справочник. Москва 1994.

Лесков Н. С. Рукопсное наследие. Каталог. Ленинград 1991.

лесков Н. С. Собрание сочинений в шести томах. III, IV. Москва 1973.

Лосский. О. Характер русского народа: Лосский Н. О. Условия абсолютного дочра. Москва 1991. 338-350.

Макаров В. И., Мамвеева Н. Р. От ромул до наших дней: Словарь лексических трудностей художественной литературы. Москва 1993.

Марузо Ж. Словарь Лингвистических терминов. Москва 1960.

ЛЭс = литературный энцклопедический словарь. Москва 1987.

орлов а. С. язык Лескова. (Материалы к статее): орлов а. С. язык русских писателей. Москва-Ленинград 1948.

Ноливанов Е. Д. Толковый терминологический сйоварь по лингвистике (1935-1937). В кн.: Лоливанов Е. Д. Избранные труды по восточному и русскому языкознанию. Москва 1991. 318-506.

Нолный словарь иностранных слов, вошедших в употребление в русском языке с означением их корней. Сост. Бурдон и Михельсон. С.-Петербрг 1894.

Лустозерская лнроза: Сборник. Сост. М. Б. Ллюханова. Москва 1989.

Русские лисатели о литературном труде, 3. Денинград 1955.

СИС = Словарь иностранных слов. Москва 1990.

ДРС = Словарь русского языка XI-XVII вв. Вып. 6. Москва 1979.

ССРЛЯ = Словарь современного русского литературного языка: В 20-и томах. Т. 1. Москва 1991.

Флоренский П. А. Имена: Малое собрание сочинений. Вып. 1 (Архив священника Павла Флоренского). купина 1993.

Черных П. Я. Историко-этимологический словарь современного русского языка: В 2-х томах. Т. 1. Москва 1993.

ЭСРЯ = Этимологический словарь русского языка. Под ред. Н. М. шанского, ii/8. Москва 1982.

*Abbreviations*

Ed.: Edition

F.: Fund

GPB: Госудрственная публичная библиотека им. М. Е. Салтыкова-Щедрина (St. Petersburg). (now: Россчиская националъная библиотека).

L.: List (= описъ)

RAN: Российская академия наук.

RGADA: Российский государственный архив древних актов.

R. s.: Reverse side

---

# FURTHER READING

### Criticism

Edgerton, William B. Introduction to *Satirical Stories of Nikolai Leskov,* translated and edited by William B. Edgerton, pp. 9-16. New York: Pegasus, 1969.

General discussion of the progression of Leskov's career and writing style.

———. "Leskov and Gogol." In *American Contributions to the Ninth International Congress of Slavists, Vol. II: Literature, Poetics, History,* edited by Paul Debreczeny, pp. 135-47. Columbus, Oh.: Slavica Publishers, Inc., 1983.

Explores the vast influence that Edgerton claims fellow nineteenth-century Russian writer Nikolai Vasilevich Gogol had on Leskov's literary style.

Keenan, William. "Leskov's Left-Handed Craftsman and Zamyatin's Flea: Irony into Allegory." *Forum for Modern Language Studies* 16, no. 1 (January 1980): 66-78.

Examines dramatist Yevgeny Zamyatin's attempts to adapt Leskov's "Levsha" for the stage.

McLean, Hugh. *Nikolai Leskov: The Man and His Art.* Cambridge: Harvard University Press, 1977, 780 p.

First English-language book-length study of Leskov's life and major works.

Muckle, James. "Scholars, Critics, and Nikolay Leskov." *Journal of Russian Studies,* no. 36 (1978): 35-42.

Reviews a variety of books on Leskov and discusses assessments of his work by critics, both Russian and otherwise.

Nagibin, Yuri. "Nikolai Leskov," translated by Laura Beraha. In *N. Leskov: "The Enchanted Wanderer" and Other Stories,* by Nikolai Leskov, translated by George H. Hanna, edited by Julius Katzer, pp. 7-24. Moscow, U.S.S.R.: Raduga Publishers, 1983.

Brief account of the author's life and career. This work was originally published in Russian in 1982.

Wachtel, Andrew B. "The Adventures of a Leskov Story in Soviet Russia, or the Socialist Realist Opera That Wasn't." In *Epic Revisionism: Russian History and Literature as Stalinist Propaganda,* edited by Kevin M. F. Platt and David Brandenberger, pp. 117-34. Madison: University of Wisconsin Press, 2006.

Examines how in the 1930s, Soviet composer Dmitrii Shostakovich attempted to "rehabilitate" Leskov's place in literature, offering an operatic reinterpretation of "Lady Macbeth of the Mtsensk District" in order to give the story a place within the Socialist Realism canon.

Wigzell, Faith. "Folk Stylization in Leskov's 'Ledi Makbet Mtsenskogo uezda.'" *Slavonic and East European Review* 67, no. 2 (April 1989): 169-82.

Discusses Leskov's choice of folk settings in his works.

**Additional coverage of Leskov's life and career is contained in the following sources published by Thomson Gale:** *Dictionary of Literary Biography,* **Vol. 238;** *Literature Resource Center; Nineteenth-Century Literature Criticism,* **Vol. 25; and** *Short Story Criticism,* **Vol. 34.**

# "The Smallest Woman in the World"

## Clarice Lispector

The following entry presents criticism of Lispector's short story "The Smallest Woman in the World." For discussion of Lispector's complete career, see *SSC,* Volume 34.

## INTRODUCTION

Lispector is best known for her short fiction, including several anthologies for children and adults. One of her most reviewed stories is "The Smallest Woman in the World," included in her collection *Laços de família* (1960; *Family Ties*). The story is considered unique because of its strong and successful female protagonist, as well as because of its focus on race relations and subsequent stereotypes.

## BIOGRAPHICAL INFORMATION

Lispector was born in a Ukrainian village in 1925, as her Russian émigré parents were enroute to Brazil with their young family. She spent her early childhood in Recife before the family relocated to Rio de Janeiro, where she finished her secondary education in 1937. During her course of studies at a Rio law school, Lispector was a news agency editor and interviewer before finding work on a newspaper, where she encountered several writers who would prove influential to her literary career. After graduating law school in 1944, Lispector accompanied her husband on his diplomatic postings to Europe and England. Her first story collection, *Alguns contos, (Some Stories)* was published in 1952, the year in which the Lispectors came to the United States. In 1959 she separated from her husband and returned to Rio with her children. In 1960 Lispector published *Family Ties,* followed by her third story collection, *A legião estrangeira (The Foreign Legion),* in 1964. She began to publish her stories for children in 1967, the same year that she was also badly burned in an apartment fire. Lispector died of cancer in 1977.

## PLOT AND MAJOR CHARACTERS

The stories in *Family Ties* emphasize the familial bonds that control Lispector's female protagonists. However, Little Flower's experience in "Smallest Woman" is an exception to the book's pattern. The story opens as the French explorer Pretre encounters a tribe of pygmies in the jungle of central Africa, including an eighteen-inch-tall pregnant woman. Pretre gathers data for his report, which includes his careful observations about the woman. At the precise moment in this process when Pretre decides to call the woman Little Flower, she scratches her naked genitals and he looks away in embarrassment. His findings are published in several newspapers accompanied by a life-sized color photo of Little Flower; the central part of Lispector's story consists of the omniscient narrator's report of several readers' responses to what they see in the newspaper. As these characters project their ideas or personal experiences onto Little Flower's image and story, they reveal things about their own lives: a young girl perceives that females are continually in the possession of others; a young bride and her mother express their condescension toward Little Flower's race and culture; a family's love is revealed as a "malign and cruel necessity" by a mother who does not see the truth of her own observations; and an old woman refuses to admit any connection between herself and the female in the photo. In the final part of the story, the narrator relates Little Flower's thoughts, although she just smiles in response to Pretre's observations. She enjoys herself and her situation completely, partly because she has not yet been "devoured," even though she is completely vulnerable as a small, pregnant woman whose tribe is fair game for all its jungle neighbors. The narrator reveals that Pretre would be disturbed to know that the pygmy woman loves him, but also loves, in exactly the same way, his boots, his ring, and his pale skin. The reader understands Little Flower's personal autonomy when the narrator comments that she is at peace, living in her very own tree.

## THEMES

"The Smallest Woman in the World" traces the perception of and responses to the protagonist, Little Flower, by Pretre and the readers of his newspaper report. The story exemplifies the sometimes corrosive effects of love while it also comments on the possibilities for female power. As Pretre, and through him his readers, encounters Little Flower, he objectifies her and attempts to possess her. Pretre is taken aback by her; in order to regain control, he responds by first naming the pygmy woman and then beginning to record his observations of her. Pretre and his readers seem to relish her vulnerability, and her "civilized" observers reduce her still further by referring to her as monkey, dog, and animal. Much of the story consists of individuals' responses to Pretre's newspaper report presented in a context of the readers' family relationships. Frequently they seem to focus on maternal love: a mother who has failed in marriage rebukes her bride-to-be daughter for identifying with the animal image of the pigmy; another mother is horrified that her child would like Little Flower for a toy or pet and comments on the damaging power of love, which she herself sees as a savage force. As a family views the newspaper photo together, the narrator tells us that each of them wants to own Little Flower. Pretre's response to Little Flower illustrates the futility of such hopes because in the end, he is unable to classify her smiling response to him. Among the story's many defeated women, only Little Flower retains her natural autonomy. Diminutive and pregnant, she enjoys herself and her situation completely, and thus she is unique among the women of *Family Ties* in maintaining her female power and the integrity of her identity.

## CRITICAL RECEPTION

Critics generally regard the "The Smallest Woman in the World" as a positive example of the possibility for female power. Lispector uses animal symbolism in several stories in *Family Ties* to show the "dilemma of women trapped in conventional roles," as A. M. Wheeler contends, arguing that unlike the collection's other protagonists, Little Flower is portrayed as a woman who is not a powerless object, but rather a subject in possession of herself. However, partly because of Little Flower's cultural situation, Kamala Platt describes "Smallest Woman" as a tale with racist implications, accusing Lispector of ignoring the multiracial nature of Brazilian culture. Ingrid Muller views "Smallest Woman" as a key to understanding the entire story collection because Little Flower's personal integrity shows that she is untroubled by anything like the mind/body split that is a common experience in Western civilization. While Earl Fitz has written (see Further Reading) that feminist issues are not an "easily defined feature" of Lispector's work, many critics have commented on Lispector's stories in a feminist context. In fact, Judith Rosenberg asserts that the tendency to identify Lispector with such major Western philosophers as Albert Camus and Jean-Paul Sartre has often constricted her to a male-dominated critical position. Rosenberg's feminist reading contends that the sexual politics of "Smallest Woman" reveal "a female fantasy of autonomy . . . [that] competes with the male fantasies of domination." Barbara Mathie shows how "patriarchal discourses" predominate in *Family Ties* and recognizes Little Flower

as a woman who has "succeeded in preserving her identity" in a threatening world because she does not participate in those discourses. Marta Peixoto notes the "predominantly bleak view of feminine possibilities in *Family Ties*" but regards "Smallest Woman" as an exception to that pattern because Little Flower's experience becomes the "wry symbol of an effective female power." Fitz has written that "the stories of *Family Ties* rank among the very best produced by a Latin American author in the mid-twentieth century," and Lispector's "The Smallest Woman in the World" continues to be ranked as one of the strongest stories in this distinguished collection.

## PRINCIPAL WORKS

### Short Fiction

*Alguns contos* [*Some Stories*] 1952
*\*Laços de família* [*Family Ties*] 1960
*A legião estrangeira* [*The Foreign Legion*] 1964
*A mulher que matou os peixes* [*The Woman Who Killed the Fish*] (children's story) 1968
*Felicidade clandestina* 1971
*A imitação da rosa* 1973
*A via crucis do corpo* 1974
*Onde estivestes de noite* 1974
*A bela e a fera* 1979

### Other Major Works

*Perto do coração selvagem* (novel) 1944
*O lustre* (novel) 1946
*A cidade sitiada* (novel) 1949
*A maçã no escuro* [*The Apple in the Dark*] (novel) 1961
*A paixão Segundo G. H.* [*The Passion According to G. H.*] (novel) 1964
*Uma aprendizagem ou o livro dos prazeres* (novel) 1969
*Água viva* [*White Water*] (novel) 1973
*A hora da estrela* (novel) 1977
*Um sopo de vida: pulsações* (novel) 1978

*Includes "The Smallest Woman in the World."

## CRITICISM

### A. M. Wheeler (essay date spring 1987)

SOURCE: Wheeler, A. M. "Animal Imagery as Reflection of Gender Roles in Clarice Lispector's *Family Ties*." *Critique* 28, no. 3 (spring 1987): 125-34.

[*In the following essay, Wheeler argues that Lispector uses animal imagery to present her ideas about gender roles and authenticity, and that she shows how the protagonist in "The Smallest Woman in the World" achieves personal autonomy.*]

Although the Brazilian writer Clarice Lispector's link with the existentialist thought of Jean-Paul Sartre has long been recognized, the similarity of her female characters to the female roles defined by Sartre's companion Simone de Beauvoir has only recently begun to be acknowledged.[1] Beauvoir writes in *The Second Sex*:

> Humanity is male and men define woman not in herself but as relative to him; she is not regarded as an autonomous being. . . . She is defined and differentiated with reference to man and not he with her; she is the incidental, the inessential, as opposed to the essential. He is the Subject, he is the absolute—she is the other.[2]

Indeed, the stories in Lispector's **Family Ties** primarily relate the struggle of women to realize themselves as subjects and to escape their role as objects. Few of them successfully make this break, but, because their failure usually involves a return to the traditional roles of wife and mother, their defeat has often been interpreted as victory.[3] The dilemma faced by Lispector's women and, indeed, her men is more clearly reflected in her portrayal of animals.[4] Through her use of animals in her stories, she shows the essence of her vision of male and female gender roles, unobscured by preconceived social roles, and the difficulty of breaking through these roles to achieve authentic being.

The dilemma of the woman trapped in conventional roles is portrayed most clearly in **"The Chicken."** In the opening of the story, the chicken is perceived by the family solely as an object: "Even when they had chosen the chicken, feeling the intimacy of her body with indifference, they could not tell if she were plump or thin."[5] This chicken's value is based solely on her physical character, as the value of women has often been in the past, but, even as they judge her body, the family members take little real notice of her. They see her as an individual entity only when she begins to behave in an unaccustomed manner, fleeing from slaughter to freedom on the roofs. Through the flight, she asserts her own being apart from the role the family has defined for her:

> And she seemed so free. Stupid, timid and free. Not victorious as a cock would be in flight. What was it in the chicken's entrails that made her a being? The chicken is, in fact, a being.
>
> (50)

Just as Lispector's female characters are often condemned for their attempts to escape their conventional roles, the chicken in her flight for freedom seems not heroic but ridiculous. In spite of her absurdity, though, in flight the chicken is a Subject. In freeing herself from the family, she saves herself from being literally devoured to serve their needs.

The family does not recognize her autonomy, however, and pursues her; finally she can only save herself by reverting to a purely biological role. She lays an egg, and for this feminine act, volitionless though it is, the family applauds her as they did not applaud her uncharacteristic escapade on the roof. The chicken herself, however, once again becomes merely an object: "she was nothing, she was simply a chicken—a fact that did not suggest any particular feeling" (51). After this renunciation, she becomes the queen of the household, reflecting again woman's traditional role as both ruler and prisoner of the house. In her apparent triumph, nonetheless, she is haunted by the memory of her brief escape, when "she had stood out against the sky on the roof edge ready to cry out" (52). By returning to her biological role, she has bought herself a measure of physical safety at the cost of her existence as a being.[6] Unfortunately, this safety is only temporary: she ultimately becomes the family's dinner, as they had originally intended. Although her role in the house may have seemed more appropriate to her role as a chicken, her only real salvation lay on the roofs.

In this story, placed early in the collection, the chicken is the sole focus. However, the two stories that end the collection show an animal in direct relation to a human. In **"The Crime of the Mathematics Professor,"** the role frequently taken by women in Lispector's stories is taken by a dog. In the final story of the collection, **"The Buffalo,"** the situation is reversed: the masculine role is played by the buffalo who destroys the protagonist of the story, a woman. In these two final stories, the conflicts between the male and female characters from previous stories are shown in their purest and most destructive forms.

The dog in **"The Crime of the Mathematics Professor"** has been the devoted companion of the male protagonist for some time. Dogs fulfill completely the terms of the description of "the other" given by Beauvoir when speaking of women. They have been bred for centuries for the sole purpose of being companion and friend to man. They are undeniably inferior beings, completely dependent on their masters for their continued existence.

The protagonist of the story has abandoned his dog. This act, which at first seems trivial, comes to haunt him, and the story records his effort both to understand the nature of his crime in abandoning his dog and to find some means of expiation. As he reflects on his relationship with the dog, he realizes that as time passed, the animal changed from a companion, who enhanced his sense of self, to a burden who seemed predatory and devouring. The only obligation the dog imposes on him is that he exist: "Of me, you demanded that I should be a man" (144). By being completely devoted to him, the dog demands from the professor a responsibility for his own existence that he is not willing to accept. The professor longs to relax into the unconsciousness of the inessential as the dog can; however, the dog's presence keeps him always aware of his autonomy as a man.

The professor tries to evade his consciousness of self by abandoning the dog. Unfortunately for him, the man's guilt prevents his action from having the desired effect. Although he successfully escapes the dog, he remains agonizingly aware of himself and his human responsibility. As expiation, he seeks once again to escape this awareness by performing the service of burial for a strange dog. When he buries this dog, he sees it as he had never seen his own dog, as a being apart from himself. This realization only heightens his sense of his responsibility as an individual; in abandoning his dog, he has not only rid himself of a parasite, but he has also deserted another being. By hiding the second dog under the earth, he now hopes to extinguish both his old consciousness of guilt and his new understanding of the first dog's separate existence.[7] However, he fails again. He finally leaves the dog unburied, "whole and unfamiliar," its eyes "open and crystallized" (146), an emblem of the inevitable separateness of existence.

By making the protagonist of her story a mathematics professor, Lispector emphasizes the logic and rationality often seen as masculine traits. The dog, a purely emotional creature, has apparently the easier role. It is sustained, materially and emotionally, by the man to whom it belongs and seems happy in adoring him. The burden ultimately is too much for the man to bear, however, and in ridding himself of it, he destroys the dog's reason for existence. The second dog is a symbolic projection of the fate of the first dog. It has gained the professor's recognition of its status as a separate being, a "strange, objective dog" (142), but it is also dead; the professor, in turn, is left still with the burden of his knowledge of "his weakness and his condition" as a human being (146). His crime, ultimately, is attempting to deny the terms of his existence as an autonomous being, but this denial is closely connected to his refusal to perceive his dog as anything but a projection of himself.[8]

In **"The Crime of the Mathematics Professor,"** Lispector presents the agony of a man who must, having rejected his "other," confront himself; in **"The Buffalo,"** we see the corresponding agony of a woman whose lover has abandoned her and who must attempt to construct an identity separate from his. As the story opens, the unnamed woman is strolling through zoological gardens. As a result of her lover's having abandoned her, just as the professor abandoned the dog, she has been brought suddenly and catastrophically to an awareness of the conditions of her normal existence, an existence based on the self-immolating love she feels for this man. In the garden, she searches for an alternate way to live, a way which would allow her to exist for herself only, and labels it, to distinguish it from the love which destroys her, as hate.

At first she finds no hate in the garden. Instead, each of the animals she sees there is tame, gentle, and loving, either actually female or the embodiment of typically feminine characteristics. The giraffe is virginal and innocent, while the hippopotamus is a motherly mass of soft round flesh. The elephant curbs its great power, allowing itself to be ruled by weaker beings, and the camel possesses a passive weary patience that sees it through its life. In all of these animals, the protagonist sees the message that she has no alternative to a life of selfless passivity.

She continues her search for some path to power, eventually coming to look for it in the essentially female capacity of giving birth. In her despair, however, she perceives this ability not as a means of creation but instead as a means of destruction:

> Rising from her womb, there came once more, imploring and in a slow wave, the urge to destroy. Her eyes moistened, grateful and black, in something near to happiness. It was not yet hatred: as yet it was only the tortured will to hate possessing her like some desire, the promise of a cruel flowering, a torment as of love, the craving for hatred, promising itself sacred blood and triumph, and the spurned female had spiritualized herself in great expectancy.
>
> (152)

She is trying to give birth to a new self whose existence will be based not on feminine love but on sustaining hatred. She has not achieved, however, the capacity of hating; to hate one must possess oneself, but her will to hate still owns her in much the same way her lover had owned her.

She still searches the garden for an animal on whom she can model her hatred and eventually finds such an animal, the buffalo.[9] While all the other animals have been characterized by images of female passivity and endurance, he presents an image of masculine power and self-sufficiency. In contrast to the other animals, he is completely self-possessed. The language that describes him emphasizes his separation and isolation: he is "compact," "narrow"; even his head seems "severed" from his body (154). The description ends with a simple assertion of his identity, without reference to anyone else: "In the distance, his body paraded slowly. He was a black buffalo" (154). He is definitely "the subject . . . the absolute," oblivious to the woman.[10] Having found this embodiment of her desire for self-possession, the woman attempts to assert her own being by killing him, thus allowing herself to take his place as subject, but she cannot. Instead, she must react to him as she has been taught to react to the masculine; she must love him to the exclusion of her own interests.

In doing so, she falls unwittingly back into the trap she has been trying to escape. She faints, literally losing her own consciousness in her love for the buffalo:

> The woman slowly shook her head, terrified by the hatred with which the buffalo, tranquil with hatred, watched her. . . . Caught, as she slipped, spellbound, along the railings—overcome by such giddiness, that before her body toppled gently to the ground, the woman saw the entire sky and a buffalo.
>
> (156)

While the buffalo can easily summon hatred sufficient to annihilate her, she is terrified by its power and can only react, once again, by relinquishing command of herself.[11] As she succumbs, she sees, juxtaposed, "the entire sky and a buffalo," freedom and the demanding masculinity which bars her from it.

Lispector offers no solutions for her characters nor does she show explicit concern for the social conditions that have shaped them. Instead, particularly through her use of animal imagery, she illuminates and magnifies the conditions of her characters' existence. In the early story **"The Chicken,"** she shows in simplified form the dilemma many of her women face: only in fulfilling their biological role can they find a measure of security, but this security will devour them in the end. In the two concluding stories of the collection, she uses animal imagery to show the destructiveness of both masculine and feminine roles. The mathematics professor comes to hate his dog because he cannot escape its self-denying devotion, but in destroying the animal, he finds that neither can he face an awareness of his own solitary existence. The woman in **"The Buffalo,"** who longs to feel herself solitary and separate, loses herself completely in contemplation of the buffalo's power. Neither subject nor object can exist without the other, nor can either truly become an independent being while defined as subject or object.

The only story in the collection that posits any sort of escape from the apparently endless parasitism between subject and object is the central story, **"The Smallest Woman in the World."** While the stories previously examined have contained animals with characteristics that could be seen as human, this story contains no animals, but rather a person, a woman who is viewed by other characters in the story as an animal. The smallest woman in the world is a pygmy who lives in equatorial Africa and who is found by a male explorer. The story is not constructed around her experiences but instead around the perception of her by the explorer and by the people who see the pictures he takes of her. In their minds, she is an alien thing, an object. She is several times referred to as an animal; the explorer says she is "black as a monkey" (89) and one of the women who sees her picture thinks "she looked just like a dog"

(90). However, in the climax of the story, the woman who has been portrayed as an object of contemplation suddenly becomes the subject of her own meditation and is seen as autonomous for the first time. She gains the status for which the chicken and the unnamed woman in **"The Buffalo"** strive, the condition that the dog in **"The Crime of the Mathematics Professor"** cannot survive.

However, in the early part of the story, as she is viewed by several groups of people, she becomes, as animals have been in other stories, an object on which the observers can project their own anxieties and views of life, just as the animals have been projections of human gender roles in other stories. The explorer ineptly names her "Little Flower," romanticizing her in the way in which females are often romanticized and objectified, but that delicate name is immediately contrasted with the woman's actual nature:

> At that moment, Little Flower scratched herself where one never scratches oneself. The explorer—as if he were receiving the highest prize of chastity to which man, always so full of ideals, dare aspire—the explorer who has so much experience of life, turned away his eyes.
>
> (90)

Little Flower is in some ways behaving here like an animal, unaware of the conventions of civilization.[12] She is also showing the essential artificiality and falseness of many of those conventions, however. She is not to be considered a "prize" nor alter her behavior to fit the abstract "ideals" of men; instead, she exists as herself, without consciousness of the expectations of others.

When the photographs taken of her appear in the Sunday supplement of the newspaper, many readers, themselves caught by false ideals, find in her picture an image of their own lives. A young girl on the verge of marriage finds a presentiment of her fate in the photograph, perceiving the pygmy woman as a "poor little thing" with "a sad expression" (91). In contrast, her mother refuses to identify herself with the pygmy; she replies to her daughter that "that is the sadness of an animal, not a human" (91). She, who has been married and who has found in her experience "defeat" cannot afford to see her own sadness in the face of the small woman. Instead, she must deny the suffering her daughter sees by objectifying the pygmy, seeing her as animal rather than human. The girl protests, but she protests with "despair," which perhaps foreshadows her future, in which she, like her mother, must find defeat in marriage. (91)

Another woman seeing the picture is reminded of a story told her in childhood by her cook, who had once lived in an orphanage. The girls in the orphanage, "not having any dolls to play with," had hidden the body of a dead companion and treated it as a doll: ". . . they played with the dead girl, bathing her and feeding her little tidbits, and they punished her only to be able to kiss and comfort her afterwards" (21). This story captures, in a particularly horrifying manner, the dilemma of love that is also illustrated in **"The Crime of the Mathematics Professor"** and **"The Buffalo."** When the loved one is viewed as an object, instead of as autonomous being, love becomes possession. The girls in the orphanage have no compassion for their dead comrade nor do they mourn those qualities of her being which are lost. Instead, they welcome the opportunity to "love" and cherish an object. Even more, they welcome their power over her: the power both to pamper and to punish. This memory, combined with the photograph of the pygmy, brings the woman to a sudden realization.

> . . . she considered the cruel necessity of loving. She considered the malignity of our desire to be happy. She considered the ferocity with which we want to play. And the number of times we murder for love. . . .
>
> (92)

She sees that love too often is comparable to the love of a child for a doll, becoming not a desire to cherish the loved one but a lust to own an attractive object. The woman attempts to distance herself from Little Flower, to see herself as "refined," "polished," "abstract," and civilized, just as other women in the story have needed to deny any camaraderie with this savage "raw" pygmy (92). However, this woman has reached an understanding which has eluded them. She has understood that love, often seen as the foundation of genteel society, is instead a savage force, driven by a "cruel" and "malign" desire for power through possession (92).

This vision is confirmed by the next vignette of readers of the Sunday supplement. An entire family, seeing the photograph of Little Flower, is possessed first by the desire to quantify her, to reduce her to centimeters measured on a wall, and then to possess her completely:

> And as they enjoyed themselves they made a startling discovery: she was even smaller than the most penetrating imagination could ever have invented. In the heart of each member of the family there arose the gnawing desire to possess that minute and indomitable thing for himself. . . . And indeed, who has not wanted to possess a human being just for himself?
>
> (92-93)

As the family continues to discuss the woman, the desire to own her, to dominate her "indomitable spirit," becomes clear in each of them. Indeed, her very uniqueness, both in her size and self-possession, causes them to desire even more to annex her to themselves, to make a pet of her. If the soul of the family is "roused to dedi-

cation" (93) by the sight of the woman, it is not roused out of any truly loving or charitable impulse but instead from the desire to devour and conquer this small woman who has so far escaped devouring and conquering. Her minuteness emphasizes their greater size: to rob her of her freedom would reinforce their belief in their own autonomy.

In the closing pages of the story, the thoughts of the "unique" thing herself are presented (94). She is happy because she remains to the explorer and everyone else an enigma:

> The unique thing itself was enjoying the ineffable sensation of not having been devoured yet. Not to have been devoured was something which at other times gave her the sudden impulse to leap from branch to branch. . . . And she went on enjoying her own gentle smile, she who was not being devoured. Not to be devoured is the most perfect sentiment. Not to be devoured is the secret objective of a whole existence.
>
> (94)

In many ways, these lines are central to understanding each of the stories in *Family Ties.* Being devoured is the fate of an animal whose individual existence has little intrinsic value and who is at the mercy of any predator, including humanity. The chicken is finally devoured by her family. The mathematics professor and his dog devour each other emotionally. The woman in **"The Buffalo"** searches throughout the zoological garden for the secret of not being devoured but fails to find it and is spiritually devoured by the buffalo. Little Flower, almost alone among Lispector's female characters in *Family Ties,* has escaped being devoured by refusing to see herself as an object for devouring. She, like the buffalo but without his malevolence, is completely self-possessed and autonomous.

In addition, Little Flower has learned to love without needing to possess or objectify what she loves. She loves the explorer, but she is content to leave him free and separate from herself. The narrator intrudes to explain:

> There is an old misunderstanding about the word "love," and if many children are born on account of that mistake, many others have lost the unique instant of birth simply on account of a susceptibility which exacts that it should be me, me that should be loved and not my money. But in the humidity of the jungle, there do not exist these cruel refinements; love is not to be devoured, love is to find boots pretty, love is to like the strange color of a man who is not black, love is to smile out of love at a ring that shines.
>
> (94-95)

Little Flower loves without self-absorption.[13] If in civilized countries love is too often confused with the desire to be possessed or to possess, it is also often experienced as a validation of the self. The central concern is not the relationship with the loved one, but a desire for the satisfaction of "me—me." Little Flower is deeply interested in herself, but nonetheless she is able to appreciate objects and people outside herself without needing to appropriate them to her own being. If she thinks to herself, "it is nice to possess, so nice to possess," that which she is glad to own is a "tree in which to live by herself" (95). She achieves the difficult feat of neither being devoured nor devouring.

The pygmy woman's successful retaining of her own autonomy is an achievement not replicated in *Family Ties.* If she is seen as an animal by others, she never loses her own consciousness of her unique being. She neither lets herself become an object nor makes herself a subject by defining someone else as inessential or subordinate. Instead, she cherishes each thing and person for itself. The animal imagery in *Family Ties* is primarily used to illustrate the consequences of failing in such cherishing, particularly in relationships between the sexes. The relationship of tamed animal and humanity is inevitably a relationship between master and possession, a relationship that may contain ties of affection, but that also imposes burdens on both parties. Little Flower illustrates both the individual being in those who are often seen as animal-like objects and the path to escape from the destructive tendency to so label and possess others.

### Notes

1. Much of the early criticism of Lispector focused on her use of existential themes: see, for example, Rita Herman, "Existence in *Lacos de Familia,*" *Luso-Brazilian Review* 4 (1967): 69-74; Massaud Moises, "Clarice Lispector: Fiction and Comic Vision," *Studies in Short Fiction* 8 (1972): 268-81; Giovanni Pontiero, "The Drama of Existence in *Lacos de Familia,*" *Studies in Short Fiction* 8 (1971): 256-67. However, as William Barrett points out in *Irrational Man: A Study is Existential Philosophy* (Garden City, New York: Doubleday and Company, 1958) the Sartrean brand of existentialism is almost "exclusively a masculine affair," leaving out the "totally ordinary woman, one of that great number whose being is the involvement with husband and children. . . ." (260-61). Such women are frequently at the center of Lispector's work and, in recent years, many commentators have written analyses of her work addressing those points which are excluded from a strictly Sartrean perspective. See, for instance, Helene Cixous, "L'approche de Clarice Lispector," *Poetique* 40 (1979): 408-17; Naomi Lindstrom," *Chasqui* 8 (1978): 43-52; Marta Peixoto, "*Family Ties*: Female Development in Clarice Lispector," *The Voyage in: Fictions of Female De-

velopment, ed. Elizabeth Abel, Marianne Hirsh, and Elizabeth Langland (Hanover, NH: UP of New England for Dartmouth College, 1983) 287-303.

2. Simone de Beauvoir, *The Second Sex,* trans. H. M. Pansley (New York: Vintage Books, 1952), xviii-xix.

3. For instance, see Dennis Seniff, "Self-Doubt in Clarice Lispector's *Lacos de Familia,*" *Luso-Brazilian Review* 14 (1977): 161-73. Seniff, in analyzing the significance of self-doubt in Lispector's work, most often considers that it serves a beneficent purpose when it leads a female character to return to her house and family, regardless of the circumstances of her life there.

4. The significance of animals in Lispector's fiction has been mentioned in several articles, although not linked to her portrayal of gender roles. Moises states that animals in Lispector's work serve as projections of the characters (274), an idea which has influenced my thought about her use of animals to reflect gender roles. I am also indebted to Herman who suggests that Lispector uses animals to simplify the dilemmas of human life to an instinctive level (71). In a somewhat similar vein, Pontiero, in the introduction to his translation of *Family Ties* (see below) notes that animal imagery in *Family Ties* serves to "define the vital links with primitive life" (20).

5. Clarice Lispector, "The Chicken," *Family Ties* trans. and introd. Giovanni Pontiero (Austin: Univ. Of Texas Press, 1972), p. 49. Further quotations from this and other stories in this collection will be from this translation and will be cited parenthetically in the text.

6. Peixoto, 300-01.

7. The following passage from *The Second Sex* is especially relevant to Lispector's characterization of the dog; "Shut up in the sphere of the relative, destined to the male from childhood, habituated to seeing in him a superb being who she cannot possibly equal, the woman who has not repressed her claim to humanity will dream of transcending her being toward one of these superior beings, of amalgamating herself with the sovereign subject. There is no other way out for her than to lose herself, body and soul, in him who is represented to her as the absolute, the essential." (721)

8. Several critics (see Herman 72 and Seniff 109) have noted that the mathematics professor commits a "crime" in attempting to escape his own human responsibility. They do not, however, address the significance of his sudden perception of the second dog as a being entirely apart from himself.

9. Rita Herman analyzes the interaction between the woman and the buffalo in the same terms as the interaction between the man and the dog in the previous story (70-71). She fails, however, to note the crucial difference in the gender of the protagonists.

10. Beauvoir, xix.

11. Peixoto, 296-97.

12. Peixoto, 302-03, examines in more detail the conflict between nature and civilization in this story.

13. Seniff, 168, notes that Little Flower "represents a new manner of love . . . and existence" but does not examine the significance of this new manner of love in detail.


**Judith Rosenberg (essay date winter 1989)**

SOURCE: Rosenberg, Judith. "Taking Her Measurements: Clarice Lispector and 'The Smallest Woman in the World.'" *Critique* 30, no. 2 (winter 1989): 71-6.

[*In the following essay, Rosenberg explores the sexual politics of competing power fantasies in "The Smallest Woman in the World."*]

Clarice Lispector's short story **"The Smallest Woman in the World"** begins "in the depths of equatorial Africa."[1] The French explorer and hunter, Marcel Pretre, comes "across a tribe of pygmies of surprising minuteness" (88). Among the smallest of these, he comes "face to face with a woman no more than forty-five centimeters tall, mature, black" (89), silent, and pregnant. He names her Little Flower and begins to observe her. He gathers data and sends his findings to newspapers that publish a life-sized color photograph of Little Flower. The narration shifts to the members of various urban families who, upon seeing the photograph of Little Flower, begin, like Pretre, to react, observe, and measure her. Back in Africa, Pretre has learned some of the tribe's few words, so he questions Little Flower. Throughout the narrative, Little Flower's only actions are to scratch herself or to smile; however, Lispector's omniscient narrator describes Little Flower's secret thoughts.

Lispector frames her work within myths familiar in Western literature. For **"The Smallest Woman in the World,"** she uses the myth of the great white hunter who penetrates the wilderness, slaughters or subdues the natives, and rapes their women. From the imperialist themes of Rudyard Kipling and Joseph Conrad to hunters like Bror Blixen and Denys Finch-Hatton, fictional and real-life narratives enact the same fantasy: to conquer and colonize. Lispector's hero, Marcel Pretre,

is the *explorador*, which, as Peixoto points out, means both *explorer* and *exploiter*. Furthermore, the French word *pretre* means *priest*. Pretre is awed by his discovery, is prepared to convert and control the heathen, but I would argue that Lispector's hero both exemplifies and parodies the myth. Instead of conquest, Pretre experiences embarrassment, shame, and loss of control that is intensified during the narrative in proportion to his diminishing comprehension. At midpoint, Lispector writes that Pretre, "instead of experiencing curiosity, enthusiasm, a sense of triumph, or the excitement of discovery—felt distinctly ill at ease" (93). By the end of the story

> The explorer tried to smile back at her without knowing exactly to which charm his smile was replying, and then became disturbed as only a full-grown man becomes disturbed.
>
> (95)

It is in the nature of authorship to experiment within a genre and create variations on a theme. The parodic element in Lispector's writing, however, cannot be explained by examining her work exclusively within the context of traditional genre.

The core of **"The Smallest Woman in the World"** is sexual politics. My reading of Lispector, which may provide a model for reading others of her work, examines the ways in which sexual fantasies compete. At the core of **"The Smallest Woman in the World"** is a female fantasy of autonomy. This fantasy, as it competes with the male fantasies of domination, charges **"The Smallest Woman in the World"** with power. Where other critics have stopped short of this core, I read Lispector from the dark center, which is Little Flower, and move my reading outward.

In every way, Little Flower seems to embody the object of male sexual desire. She is mature, black, silent, pregnant, and miniature. Her maturity signifies her sexual ripeness. As a female, she is denied authority and is made vulnerable. As a black female, she is further objectified in a system of racial politics that awards the black female as the prize the white man takes and believes he deserves. Little Flower's silence is a further sign of her desirability: it is woman's acquiescence to being seen and not heard.

Her pregnancy and her diminutive size enhance her desirability because both conditions are used as evidence in the biological argument for male superiority. A woman is limited by anatomy: by her menstrual cycle and by a nine-month confinement as part of her childbearing functions, and by her physique, which is smaller than the male's and reduces her to childlike status. Thus, women are characterized as chronically physically handicapped and biologically destined to subservience.

Lispector states, "Marcel Pretre came face to face with a woman no more than forty-five centimeters tall . . ." (89). Little Flower is about 18" in height. As "the smallest of the smallest" (88), she is the penultimate signifier of that male construct "the feminine." She would be prized in the way that Chinese men prized their women, already small when compared with other world cultures, after they were made even smaller through footbinding, a form of mutilation that further reduces the size of the female foot.[2] Using the language of commodity-exchange and of sexual fantasy, Lispector describes Pretre's thoughts as he gazes at his prize:

> This, then, was how the explorer discovered at his feet the smallest human creature that exists. His heart pounded, for surely no emerald is so rare. . . . There, before his eyes, stood a woman such as the delights of the most exquisite dream had never equaled.
>
> (90)

At this point in the narrative, Pretre names her "Little Flower," the name that fixes her into metaphor. As "Little Flower," she is the violet, daisy, lily, rose. She is both the bud and the full bloom, in either case, ripe for the plucking.

Why, then, doesn't Pretre "pluck" her? He tries to. In fact, his chief occupation—when he isn't gazing at her—is gathering her in the form of data, that is, recreating and appropriating her on paper. He can, thus, translate her body into print. He captures her image in a photograph, yet, when the photograph appears, it is not miniaturized but is a life-sized reproduction. Pretre cannot reduce her. Thus, while Pretre writes Little Flower, Clarice Lispector rewrites her. All the characteristics of the "feminine" that Little Flower embodies—maturity, blackness, silence, pregnancy, diminution—are recontextualized and, I argue, enlarged. How does this happen, and what are the effects?

In chemistry, distillation is a process that reduces a solution, making it less by eliminating other substances from its composition to yield a pure substance. Little Flower is the pure essence of femininity. Lispector presents the feminine not as weak and diluted but as an extract: refined, rare, valuable, and potent. She accomplishes this through the body of Little Flower. Little Flower uses her body to inscribe herself as autonomous, thereby resisting definition according to the male fantasy of the feminine. Little Flower scratches herself, smiles, and says *yes*. These three gestures revolutionize the female body and the text of the female body.

In fact, it is at the moment when Marcel Pretre names her that Little Flower—as a gesture of resistance—"scratched herself where one never scratches oneself" (90). Little Flower yields to the itch of her body, the desirous itch of her sexuality, and draws Pretre's gaze

to her dark vaginal space. This space should have been his to appropriate and penetrate in the same way that he has penetrated the dark space of the jungle. As she scratches the place that phallocentricity defines as no place, she points to the space contained within folds and discovers it. Her scratch makes her the text's "other" explorer, its only true discoverer: in effect, she puts the repressed space of the feminine on the map. Little Flower has just signified the unsignifiable. Her transgression is so enormous that Pretre can do nothing but avert his gaze. Pretre, "the explorer who has so much experience of life, turned away his eyes" (90).

Further into the narrative, Pretre resumes gazing, this time at Little Flower's pregnant belly, and he again feels uncomfortable. Lispector explains that Little Flower

> felt in [her] heart—perhaps also black . . . something still more rare, rather like the secret of its own secret: a minute child.
>
> (93)

At this point, Little Flower gestures with her smile. "She was smiling and warm, warm. Little Flower was enjoying herself. The unique thing was enjoying the ineffable sensation of not having been devoured yet. . . . Not to be devoured is the secret objective of a whole existence" (93-94). Instead of signaling a debilitating confinement, Little Flower's pregnancy is empowering. The child with which Little Flower is pregnant is the secret of Little Flower's existence. Little Flower is full of her self, and her self-fulfillment is proof that she has neither been devoured nor possessed: "And suddenly she was smiling. It was a smile that only someone who does not speak can smile. A smile that the uncomfortable explorer did not succeed in classifying" (94). Little Flower's smiling gesture is beyond language, a place that Pretre cannot/dare not enter. Little Flower defines her self, she possesses her self, that is, she is self-possessed, and, therefore, she cannot be possessed by another.

Her final revolutionary gesture is the answer "yes" to an undisclosed question of Pretre's. "If man could reduce woman to a single word, it would be 'yes.'"[3] It would be the "yes" Freud assigns to Dora in his case study of her when he asserts, "there is no such thing at all as an unconscious 'No.'"[4] Little Flower speaks only one word, "yes." In uttering the supreme signifier of consent, she fulfills the male fantasy that women never say "no," and that even when they say "no," they are signifying a "yes." Lispector rewrites the "yes" of concession into Little Flower's "yes" of affirmation. She

> answered 'yes.' That it was very nice to have a tree in which to live by herself, all by herself.

Lispector's novel, *The Hour of the Star,* begins with an invocation to the word *yes:*

Everything in the world began with a yes. One molecule said yes to another molecule and life was born.[5]

*Yes* is the signifier of sexual surrender. Does Little Flower's pregnancy signify *yes*? Who has fathered Little Flower's child? Perhaps no one. Though earlier, when Pretre is gathering data for the newspapers, we are told that Little Flower "lived at the top of a tree with her [*concubino*]"; at the end of the story, Little Flower tells us that she lives "all by herself." The strongest argument for women's dependency on man is her reproductive dependency. Little Flower embodies the male fear that man is reproductively irrelevant, that woman can reproduce without him.

**"The Smallest Woman in the World"** begins with a reference to containers: "And—like a box inside another box, inside yet another box—among the smallest pygmies in the world . . ." (88). In turn, the text of the story, **"The Smallest Woman in the World,"** is at the physical as well as thematic center of a larger text, the collection entitled ***Family Ties,*** in which it was published in Brazil in 1960. This publication date means that thirty years ago Clarice Lispector was already inventing language and discovering new ways to rewrite the feminine. Marta Peixoto and the French feminist Hélène Cixous are the only critics I have found who argue the feminist characteristics in Clarice Lispector's work. Peixoto points out,

In Lispector's eight novels, seven of the protagonists are female, as are most of the main characters in her five collections of short stories.[6]

Earl Fitz, one of Lispector's major critics, published in 1985 the first book in English to present "a general discussion of the most outstanding aspects of her work."[7] Though his survey identifies Lispector with feminism, Fitz does not develop an argument about gender. Most critics offer readings that locate Lispector within the tradition of Heidegger, Kierkegaard, Camus, and Sartre. Such readings confine Lispector within the context of male fantasies.

Lispector's writing is such a radical departure from literature that precedes it that there exists among readers, critics, and translators of her work an effort to normalize Lispector's texts. An example of this occurs in each of two translations of **"The Smallest Woman in the World"** from the original Portuguese to English, one by Giovanni Pontiero, the other by the American poet Elizabeth Bishop. In Bishop's case, it is particularly striking because, in a poem of hers entitled "Brazil, January 1, 1502," Bishop indicts the imperialist and sexual politics of colonialism. Yet her translation represses the sexual politics inherent in **"The Smallest Woman in the World"** in at least one instance: Lispector writes *concubino*, a word that, with its masculine *o* ending, does not exist in Portuguese. The existing term for concubine is *concubina,* engendered as a female form. Pontiero translates Lispector's term as *mate.* Bishop uses *spouse.* If Lispector had wanted to signify *mate* or *spouse,* she could have used their Portuguese equivalents such as *conjuge, consorte,* or *esposo.* Instead she chose to invent language. By their word choice, the translators perpetuate the structures of male fantasy.

Her text, **"The Smallest Woman in the World,"** is a map for a territory that, to date, remains unsettled. Current writers such as Hélène Cixous have inherited the journey into the dark continent. Cixous demonstrates her affinity for Lispector, as well as her stylistic departure, in the following passage:

. . . because you are Africa, you are black. Your continent is dark. Dark is dangerous. You can't see anything in the dark, you are afraid. . . . And we have internalized this fear of the dark. Women haven't had eyes for themselves. They haven't gone exploring in their house. Their sex still frightens them. Their bodies, which they haven't dared enjoy, have been colonized.[8]

My reading locates meaning inside **"The Smallest Woman in the World,"** and it travels outward as an attempt to open the text, to extend it, and to make it available for further and more varied explications.

*Notes*

1. This and all subsequent quotations, unless otherwise noted, are from Clarice Lispector, "The Smallest Woman in the World," *Family Ties,* trans. Giovanni Pontiero (Austin: UP Texas, 1984) 88.

2. Mary Daly, *Gyn/Ecology* (Boston: Beacon Press, 1978) 134 ff.

3. Denise Delorey, personal interview, November 11, 1987.

4. Sigmund Freud, *Dora: An Analysis of a Case of Hysteria,* ed. Philip Rieff (New York: Macmillan, 1963) 75.

5. Clarice Lispector, *The Hour of the Star,* trans. Giovanni Pontiero (New York: Carcanet Press, 1987) 11.

6. Marta Peixoto, "Family Ties: Female Development in Clarice Lispector," *The Voyage In,* eds. Elizabeth Abel, Marianne Hirsch, Elizabeth Langland (Hanover: UP of New England, 1983) 287.

7. Earl Fitz, *Clarice Lispector* (Boston: Twayne, 1985) Preface.

8. Hélène Cixous and Catherine Clement, *The Newly Born Woman,* trans. Betsy Wing (Minneapolis: UP Minnesota, 1986) 68.

**Ingrid R. Muller (essay date May 1991)**

SOURCE: Muller, Ingrid R. "The Problematics of the Body in Clarice Lispector's *Family Ties*." *Chasqui* 20, no. 1 (May 1991): 34-42.

[*In the following essay, Muller contends that the stories of* Family Ties *can best be read in the context of Western philosophical ideas about the "mind/body split."*]

Feminist readings of Clarice Lispector's collection of short stories, *Family Ties,* generally focus on the preponderance of women protagonists in the stories and their—mostly short-lived—attempts to assert themselves as autonomous human beings by escaping the narrowly defined roles imposed upon them by a male-dominated society. Thus A. M. Wheeler, in his article "Animal Imagery as Reflection of Gender Roles in Clarice Lispector's *Family Ties,*" states that the stories "primarily relate the struggle of women to realize themselves as subjects and to escape their role as objects" (125), and Magda Velloso Fernandes de Tolentino, in a comparative analysis of the story **"The Imitation of the Rose,"** asserts that Lispector "denounces the fact that women cannot indulge in their own search for self-fulfillment, but rather act as instruments of their men's comfort" (75). Marta Peixoto, in a similar vein, affirms that "through the plots of the stories and the inner conflicts of the heroines, Lispector challenges conventional roles, showing that the allegiances to others those roles demand lead to a loss of selfhood. The protagonists' efforts toward recuperating the self emerge as dissatisfaction, rage, or even madness" (288-89). Focusing on the women characters' difficulties in verbalizing their thoughts in the story **"The Daydreams of a Drunk Woman,"** Naomi Lindstrom concludes that "the total result is Lispector's fictional critique of woman's difficulties with verbal expression—a critique that parallels the concerns of feminism" ("Feminist Discourse Analysis" 9).

As Lindstrom's statement implies, Lispector's "feminism" does not express itself in an overt manner in the stories. In her analysis of Lispector's story **"Preciousness,"** Lindstrom recognizes that "many readers have perceived the Brazilian's writing to be essentially feminine, although this quality has been difficult to define critically" ("Discourse Analysis" 187), and Earl E. Fitz, in his study "Freedom and Self-Realization," concedes that "feminism is not present in her work as a clear-cut or easily defined feature" (58).

Although the presence of women characters who are trapped in their domestic roles—all of them, with one notable exception, middle-class women in an urban environment—is a dominant feature in the stories, narratives of feminist criticism founder because of the lack of a villain: the drama is played out largely in the minds of the women characters, while the men who occasionally appear on the scene generally take on the roles of puzzled bystanders witnessing their wives' eccentric behavior rather than representing agents of oppression. Nor does Lispector appear to point an accusing finger at the male establishment as a whole: her women characters generally live in comfortable circumstances and seem to have plenty of time for daydreaming and introspection; many of them cherish the security their social position as married women affords them, a fact which has led at least one critic to term the characters' return to domestic tranquility after a brief period of increased self-awareness as essentially positive in some of the stories (Seniff 163, 165-66, 169).

I suggest that the feelings of frustration and discontent Lispector's women characters experience are only indirectly related to their oppression by a patriarchic society. Instead, I propose that the stories be viewed in a broader perspective, namely, the problematic issue of the mind/body split, one of the fundamental principles of Western thought.

In the binary opposition mind/body, the mind is clearly privileged, inasmuch as it produces meaning and direction, and thus appears to provide a measure of control over one's existence, whereas the body is perceived as out in the world, one object among others, and as such highly vulnerable to outside forces which elude direct control: it is prey to injury, sickness, decay. In his study *Mind-Body: A Categorical Relation,* H. Tristram Engelhardt, Jr., observes that "thoughts and volitions are often set in opposition to the mute, cognitional and volitional opaqueness of the body. . . . With mind, one encounters a cognitional translucency opposed to the opacity and recalcitrance of the body. The experience of sickness and physical limitation present the body as an other which the mind is always endeavoring to make its own" (2).

If his fear of the contingencies of the body makes man's relationship to his body problematical, woman's relation to her body has become doubly problematic. "If the [male] intellectual, the cleric epitomizes the life of the mind," Jane Gallop states in *Thinking Through the Body,* "woman epitomizes the life of the body" (21). Man has projected the ambivalence he feels toward a body which largely escapes his control upon woman: she becomes the sorceress, the sphinx, the witch; she is, by nature, irrational, treacherous, *unheimlich,* often malevolent. By repudiating his body and the feeling of impotence it inspires in him, man becomes free to perceive himself as an autonomous being, while woman is made to carry the burden of the flesh. As the "representative of the body principle" she enables man to deal with "not only brute nature as it surrounds him, but also brute nature as it exists inside him, in his own mute unfathomable body. That body is in some intimate sense himself; yet it is not himself: it is in many ways the archenemy of his long-range, distinctively human, concerns" (Dinnerstein 125-26).

Colonizers have always felt the need to convince themselves of the inferior human status of the colonized: with woman incarnating all that is disturbing, uncanny and detrimental to the superior life of the mind, she can now, without further qualms, be harnessed to the yoke of a patriarchic system where she is largely reduced to the functions of wife and mother. Jane Gallop, rejecting man's attempt to define woman in terms of her usefulness to man, states that "the sons of a certain Western European tradition of subjugating the secondary body to a disembodied consciousness, are less and less able to maintain that domination, a domination which historically depended on other sexes, classes, and races to embody the body as well as care for the Master's body so he would not have to be concerned with it, so he could consider himself disembodied, autonomous, and free to will" (19-20).

It is not surprising then that, reduced to their physical functions by the narrow specifications of a male-dominated society, women have become profoundly alienated from their bodies. Adrienne Rich affirms in her autobiographical study of *Of Woman Born*: "I know of no woman—virgin, mother, lesbian, married, celibate—. . . for whom her body is not a fundamental problem" (290). Although Lispector's stories are not directly accessible to a feminist reading, the problematic relationship of women to their bodies forms one of the underlying principles in almost all of the stories in the collection *Family Ties,* most obviously in **"The Imitation of the Rose," "The Daydreams of a Drunk Woman," "The Buffalo"** and **"The Smallest Woman in the World."** With the significant exception of the pygmy woman in **"The Smallest Woman in the World,"** the women characters in these stories have recourse to a number of different strategies to deal with their bodies, of which their submission to the traditional female role is only one, albeit the one sought most often.

Woman's alienation from her body is most evident in Lispector's story **"The Imitation of the Rose,"** not only because Laura, the central character, uses a variety of different stratagems to rid herself of her body, but because she pursues her objective to its rigorous end: the total denial of the body. The tone of subtle irony which pervades the story reveals the contrast between Laura as she attempts to see herself, a meek, conventional, dull housewife, and her urge to assert herself: she observes the people around her with a critical eye, and she has no illusion about her inferior status as a housewife. After her release from the hospital, where she has undergone treatment during a psychotic episode, she sees herself as "finally returning to play an in-

significant role with gratitude" (34). What makes Laura's internal struggle so intense is that her stubborn determination to assert her individuality is matched by an equally strong internalization of the prescriptions of a male-dominated society: the daily glass of milk her doctor has prescribed for her becomes a symbol of the conditioning to which she has been subjected. Although, "in her humble opinion," Laura finds the doctor's orders contradictory, she blushes with pleasure when the doctor gives her a friendly pat on the back, and she scrupulously complies with his command to drink her milk, "that glass of milk which had finished up by gaining a secret power, which almost embodied with every sip the taste of a word and renewed that firm pat on the back . . ." (56).

Laura's problematic relationship to her body becomes apparent in her refusal to acknowledge her sexuality. She is unable to deal with the sexual aspect of her body except by using pseudoscientific terms. Embarrassed by her husband's repeatedly voiced admiration of her ample hips, she feels compelled to counter, each time he does so, with the explanation "that this resulted from ovarian insufficiency," while secretly labelling her husband's frank sexuality as "shameless" (60).

Laura's manner of dress is likewise calculated to defuse her sexuality: her brown dress—obviously a favorite—with the demure lace collar gives her "an almost child-like appearance, like some child from the past," and she perceives her "real life" as the time of her girlhood in Tijuca (59). In a similar vein, she takes refuge, in her relationship with her husband, in the sexually safe role of the child who tries to endear herself to the adult by her innocent charms; the sexual act becomes a kind of reward for good behavior: picturing her husband's reaction to her "impulsive" decision to have a bouquet of roses delivered to a friend, she anticipates with pleasure his look of surprise, certain that "Armando would look with kindness upon the impulses of his little wife and that night they would sleep together" (64).

One of the stratagems Laura employs to obliterate her body is camouflage. With her brown dress and brown hair and eyes she effectively blends into the environment. Reflecting upon her appearance, as she pictures herself walking down the street on her husband's arm, she congratulates herself on being "chestnut-haired as she obscurely felt a wife ought to be. To have black or blonde hair was an exaggeration, which, in her desire to make the right choice, she had never wanted. Then, as for green eyes, it seemed to her that if she had green eyes it would be as if she had not told her husband everything" (60-61).

Likewise, Laura appears to measure the excellence of a wife by the degree of her unobtrusiveness. In anticipation of a dinner party at the house of their friends Car-lota and João, she imagines with pleasure her husband being engaged in a conversation with João without paying attention to her; "a man at peace," she speculates, "was one who, oblivious of his wife's presence, could converse with another man about the latest news in the headlines" (53-54).

By the same token, Laura takes great care to efface all traces of her presence from her personal surroundings. "Laura," the narrator tells us, "experienced such pleasure in making something impersonal of her home; in a certain way perfect, because impersonal" (56).

In view of Laura's ultimate breakdown, the image she tries to create of herself as a busy little housewife "who had never had any ambitions except to be a wife to some man" (57), and her constant attempts to extol the importance of her domestic tasks must be seen in an ironic light. In fact, the bodily exhaustion she feels after doing her housework merely serves her as "a sort of compensation" (57) for the exhilarating feeling of superhuman power and independence she experienced during her illness: "In exhaustion she found a refuge, that discreet and obscure place from where, with so much constraint toward herself and others, she had once departed" (58).

In the end, Laura finds that she can no longer uphold her fiction of domestic bliss: contemplating the "luminous tranquility" of the roses she has bought at the market, she recalls, with mounting excitement, her former state of insanity in which she, like the roses, had become "superhuman and tranquil in her bright isolation" (57). Although she contrives to rid herself of the roses by having them delivered to a friend, she relapses once more into insanity; divesting herself of her body, she again becomes "luminous and remote" (72), a disembodied mind.

As Marta Peixoto observes, "an alert lack of fatigue, clarity of mind, a sense of independence, of possessing extraordinary powers, accompany her returning madness" (295). However, although Laura's escape into insanity effectively ends her internal struggle, it is difficult to maintain that madness, in this story, essentially "takes on a positive value" (Peixoto 299). The tragic loss of human identity Laura experiences after her relapse is conveyed to the reader by a shift of narrative focus to Laura's husband, Armando. As the narrator reports his reactions to his wife's alienation from reality, the reader, with Armando, watches helplessly and with a sense of doom as Laura withdraws to a remote, unearthly realm of existence: "From the open door he saw his wife sitting upright on the couch, once more alert and tranquil as if on a train. A train that had already departed" (72).

"The body," Adrienne Rich writes, "has been made so problematic for women that it has often seemed easier to shrug it off and travel as a disembodied spirit" (22). Laura's state of insanity in which, ironically, she perceives herself as "superhuman," prevents her from living a truly human existence as effectively as her previous reduced state of the dull little housewife. Magda Velloso Fernandes de Tolentino observes that "the irony lies in the fact that the only freedom allowed her is madness, which substitutes one status of marginality for another; closure just takes another form" (76). Moreover, the narrator makes it clear that Laura's escape into psychosis is not an easy cop-out: we are told that Armando watches his wife with "fear and respect," because he knows that "she had done everything possible not to become luminous and remote," before embarking, once more, on the road to insanity (72).

The Portuguese woman in Lispector's story **"The Daydreams of a Drunk Woman"** may, in some ways, be considered the reverse image of Laura in **"The Imitation of the Rose."** Whereas Laura negates and tries to obliterate her body, the Portuguese woman flaunts it: sensuous, healthy, conscious of her physicality, her laughter, the narrator tells us, comes "from the depths of that security of someone who has a body" (32). All is not well, though; as the story progresses, the reader becomes aware that her relationship to her body, for all that, is no less problematic. Although the woman's disgust at what she terms a "degrading and revolting existence" (32) frequently erupts in angry deprecations directed at herself and others, she is at a loss to account for the source of her dissatisfaction. Having internalized society's prescriptions which have reduced her to the functions of childbearer and sexual object, she seeks the causes of her discontent in herself: "Ah, what's wrong with me! she wondered desperately. Have I eaten too much? Heavens above! What *is* wrong with me?" (36). Only when she is drunk—her drunkenness serving as "a beacon that sweeps through the dawn while one is asleep" (32), does she become dimly aware of the problem, and even then she can express her feelings only metaphorically: "Her white flesh was as sweet as a lobster, the legs of a live lobster wriggling slowly in the air . . ." (32). Disgusted at the thought of being a lobster, a passive object of consumption, the urge to assert herself as an active and autonomous being subsequently produces a different image in her mind: "She was no longer a lobster, but a harsher sign—that of the scorpion. After all, she had been born in November" (32).

In the foreword to her study *Of Woman Born*, Adrienne Rich states that "woman's status as childbearer has been made into a major fact of her life. Terms like 'barren' or 'childless' have been used to negate any further identity" (xiii). In Lispector's story, the Portuguese woman tries to justify her existence and assert her personality by having recourse to society's glorification of motherhood: she is obsessed with the procreative potential of her body.

Imagery related to pregnancy and the proliferation of flesh abounds in the story. The triple mirror in the opening paragraph of the story becomes a symbol of the woman's physical multiplicity: the reader is introduced to her as she is standing in front of the dressing table, combing her hair, while "her open dressing gown revealed in the mirrors the intersected breasts of several women" (27-28). Later, at the restaurant, her drunkenness makes her feel "swollen and rotund like a large cow" (31). Reflecting upon her conversational skills, she speculates that "the words that a woman uttered when drunk were like being pregnant—mere words on her lips which had nothing to do with the secret core that seemed like pregnancy" (31). The woman despises the "barren" people in the restaurant, while she feels herself to be "plump and heavy and generous to the full" (33). Her contempt finds a welcome target in another female guest who has caught her eye because of her elegant attire; berating, in her mind, the woman's looks and refined manner, which she considers pure sham, her scorn is provoked in particular by the fact that the woman is "flat-chested" and erupts in a spiteful evaluation of the woman's procreative faculties: "And that pious ninny so pleased with herself in that hat and so modest about her slim waistline, and I'll bet she couldn't even bear her man a child" (33).

After returning home from the restaurant, the Portuguese woman undergoes a Kafkaesque metamorphosis, in which she herself and the objects around her suddenly take on the appearance of flesh: "Meanwhile she was becoming larger, more unsteady, swollen and gigantic. If only she could get closer to herself, she would find she was even larger. Each of her arms could be explored by someone who didn't even recognize that they were dealing with an arm, and someone could plunge into each eye and swim around without knowing that it was an eye. . . . Things of the flesh stricken by nervous twinges" (34).

Accustomed to think of herself in terms of the flesh, the woman, as her sense of self is being engulfed by her body, experiences a painful loss of control: "How sickening! How very annoying! When all is said and done, heaven help me—God knows best. What was one to do?" (35).

After the crisis has passed, the woman, in an ineffectual burst of energy, once more tries to prop up her sense of identity by having recourse to the image of herself as a childbearer: "Ah, she was feeling so well, so strong, as if she still had milk in those firm breasts" (36).

The Portuguese woman's efforts to enhance her self-esteem by thinking of herself as a desirable sexual object prove to be equally unsuccessful. Recalling the amorous advances her husband's business associate has made to her under the table at the restaurant, she falsely interprets them as a sign of respect: "When her husband's friend saw her so pretty and plump he immediately felt respect for her. And when she started to get embarrassed she did not know which way to look. Such misery! What was one to do?" (36). In the end, the woman's problem remains unresolved. The fact that she labels herself a "slut" signals her unquestioning acceptance of society's standards of female comportment and her lack of a sense of self as an autonomous human being.

The actions of the woman in the story **"The Buffalo,"** who has been spurned by her lover, must be seen as a last desperate effort to free herself from the bondage of her body and to salvage an identity which, at the beginning of the narrative, is already severely damaged. As Marta Peixoto observes, "the role of the woman in love limits severely the protagonist of '**The Buffalo.**' She only senses her deficiencies when her husband or lover abandons her and she is deprived of her source of identity" (296). Having allowed herself to be defined in terms of her usefulness to the male as a compassionate and nurturing female, she tries to recover her self-esteem by learning from the animals in the zoological gardens how to "find her own hatred" (147); instead, she finds that the bodies of the animals she encounters only mirror the sweetness and passivity of her own; the giraffe, perfectly attuned to its environment, is "more landscape than being" (148), the elephant and the camel exude patience and submission, and the hippopotamus is "a round mass of flesh, its round, mute flesh awaiting some other round, mute flesh" (148). The sight of the animals confirms her own status as a passive object, a mere body: "Then there was such a humble love in maintaining oneself only as flesh, there was such a sweet martyrdom in not knowing how to think" (148). The woman's attitude appears to bear out Adrienne Rich's argument in the final pages of her book *Of Woman Born,* in which she speaks out on the necessity of women to "repossess" their bodies. "We have tended either to *become* our bodies—blindly, slavishly, in obedience to male theories about us—," Rich declares, "or to try to exist in spite of them" (291-92).

Frustrated in her attempts to assert her individuality by hating the other, the woman turns her anger upon herself; her excursion becomes an orgy of self-destruction. By taking a ride on the roller coaster and surrendering her body to the play of exterior forces over which she has no control, she symbolically reenacts the humiliation she has suffered at the hands of her lover: "But suddenly there was that soaring of entrails, . . . the deep resentment with which she became mechanical, her body automatically buoyant . . . her humiliation, 'they were doing what they liked with her,' the terrible humiliation . . . the utter bewilderment of this spasmodic game as they did what they liked with her . . ." (150).

The woman's ultimate defeat takes place in her encounter with the buffalo, the only animal which appears to embody the hatred she has sought. However, instead of learning from him how to hate, she is overcome by the buffalo's hatred; in a staring down contest with the animal she falls, unconscious, to the ground. "Fainting," Peixoto observes, "signals, no doubt, her failure of nerve: a traditionally feminine strategy of withdrawal, it obliterates from consciousness her involvement and insights" (297).

The woman in this story employs strategies somewhat similar to those Laura uses in **"The Imitation of the Rose"** in her efforts to deal with the problematics of her body. She, too, attempts to obliterate her body by using camouflage; one of the markers Lispector employs is the brown coat—reminiscent of Laura's favorite brown dress—the woman is wearing, and, the narrator tells us, "she was not the sort of person others might notice" (152). However, whereas Laura seeks refuge in a disembodied mind, the woman in this story opts for a different solution: losing herself in the buffalo's gaze, "without wishing nor being able to escape" (156), she finds at last what she has come for, the annihilation, albeit temporary, of her self as a thinking and feeling body.

The figure of Little Flower, a pygmy living in the recesses of equatorial Africa, in the story **"The Smallest Woman in the World,"** forms a sharp contrast to the other women characters in *Family Ties*. "With the story of Little Flower," Marta Peixoto observes, "Lispector creates a comic parable of a native female power, sustained against all odds. The jungle inhabitant manages to retain the tranquil independence sought eagerly by city-bred women in their civilized world of enclosed spaces, prescribed behavior, and family ties" (302). Little Flower, as opposed to the other women characters, is the only woman whose self-image is fully intact, and who appears to be living in harmony with herself and her environment. "The pygmy woman's successful retaining of her own autonomy," A. M. Wheeler affirms, "is an achievement not replicated in *Family Ties*" (133). Far from denying her body, Little Flower lives through her body which she perceives as an integral part of her self.

The concept of control—the control of mind over body, the male over the female, the lover over the one he loves—is one of the main principles which underlie the structure of the story. The greater part of the story deals with the reaction of the civilized world to the discovery of the tiny woman who measures only forty-five centimeters in height; a full-size photograph of her minute body in the newspapers evokes feelings of profound unease in the readers. Trying to incorporate the pygmy woman in some way in their own societal system, they variously describe her as an animal or reify her as a sexual object, a plaything, a servant. The French explorer who discovers the pygmy is equally disturbed by the living, breathing presence of the little woman before him. The narrator ironically describes the explorer's attempts to regain control by inscribing her in the narrow categories of the mind: "Certainly it was only because he was sane that he managed to keep his head and not lose control. Sensing a sudden need to restore order, and to give a name to what exists, he called her Little Flower. And, in order to be able to classify her among the identifiable realities, he immediately began to gather data about her" (89).

The act of naming, another attempt at control, is described in a humorous manner. In this incident, too, the pygmy woman effectively eludes control: at the very moment the explorer, "with a delicacy of feeling of which even his wife would never have believed him capable," pronounces her name, "Little Flower scratched herself where one never scratches oneself" (90), causing the explorer to turn away his eyes in embarrassment. The incongruence of the explorer's official statement to the press, in which he describes the pygmy woman as "black as a monkey" (89), and the sentimental image evoked by her name denounces the idealization of the female body, and reveals the arbitrariness of conventional standards of female beauty. Commenting upon Little Flower's untimely itch, A. M. Wheeler remarks: "The explorer ineptly names her 'Little Flower,' romanticizing her in the way in which females are often romanticized and objectified, but that delicate name is immediately contrasted with the woman's actual nature" (130).

The Western concept of romantic love is alien to the little woman. Unlike the Portuguese woman in **"The Daydreams of a Drunk Woman,"** who vents her frustration at being locked into a dull marriage by dreaming about the Prince Charming who will be worthy of her love, Little Flower's idea of love, the narrator tells us, is untainted by the "cruel refinements" of Western culture (94), in which love is often sought as a means of control and self-enhancement. To the pygmy woman, love is a deeply joyous, sensuous feeling which embraces the person of the "yellow explorer" as well as his boots and the ring that shines on his finger. Wheeler points out that "in civilized countries love is too often confused with the desire to be possessed or to possess, it is also often experienced as a validation of the self. . . . Little Flower is deeply interested in herself, but nonetheless she is able to appreciate objects and people outside herself without needing to appropriate them to her own being" (132).

By the same token, pregnancy is experienced by the pygmy woman as a state of profound joy and sensuous pleasure: "If the unique thing itself was smiling it was because, inside her minute body, a great darkness had started to stir" (94). Other than her civilized sisters, Little Flower finds love and motherhood unproblematic; she conceives of her body as an intimate part of her self and as an immediate source of pleasure uncontaminated by the exigencies of the mind. For all that, the pygmy woman is not living in edenic bliss; her small tribe is surrounded by the savage tribe of the Bantus who are in the habit of netting the pygmies for food. Although doubly vulnerable because of her small size and her pregnancy, Little Flower accepts the fact that her existence is largely outside of her control, and is thus able to enjoy life to the fullest: "Little Flower was enjoying herself. The unique thing was enjoying the ineffable sensation of not having been devoured yet. . . . Not to be devoured is the most perfect sentiment. Not to be devoured is the secret objective of a whole existence" (93-94).

In many ways, **"The Smallest Woman in the World"** provides a key to the understanding of the other stories in the collection. It is significant that the central character in this story exhibits, in appearance and behavior, a number of animal characteristics; she is repeatedly referred to as an animal by the members of civilized society, and the narrator flatly informs us that "she looked just like a dog" (90). Yet, none of the other women characters in the stories possesses the kind of disinterestedness and integrity the pygmy woman exhibits: as A. M. Wheeler points out, Little Flower's love is completely nonpossessive (132), and her charms are not calculated to elicit approval and admiration from others to enhance her self-image. It is clear that Little Flower's animal nature is presented as a positive feature in the story; being an "animal," she is uncontaminated by the Western malady of the mind/body split, which makes the other women characters' relationships to their bodies so problematic.

In the article "Excerpts from the Chronicles of *The Foreign Legion*," which includes some of the rare commentaries Lispector has offered on her writing, Lispector states with reference to her story **"The Smallest Woman in the World"**: "I am convinced that this narrative too, stems from my affection for animals: I tend to regard them as the species closest to God, matter that did not invent itself . . ." (Pontiero 41). The tragedy of Western man, Lispector seems to imply in her stories, is that, in the course of "inventing himself," he has strayed from the living source of his existence and has become a victim of his own mental fabrications. Another of

Lispector's commentaries, in the same article, is more explicit. "In everything," she affirms, "your body will be your main asset. Our body is ever at our side. It is the one thing that never leaves us to the end" (41).

## Works Cited

Dinnerstein, Dorothy. *The Mermaid and the Minotaur: Sexual Arrangements and Human Malaise.* New York: Harper & Row, 1976.

Englehardt, Jr., H. Tristram. *Mind-Body: A Categorical Relation.* The Hague, Neth.: Martinus Nijhoff, 1973.

Fitz, Earl E. "Freedom and Self-Realization: Feminist Characterization in the Fiction of Clarice Lispector." *Modern Language Studies* 10.3 (1980): 51-61.

Gallop, Jane. *Thinking Through the Body.* New York: Columbia UP, 1988.

Lindstrom, Naomi. "A Discourse Analysis of 'Preciosidade' by Clarice Lispector." *Luso-Brazilian Review* 19 (1982): 187-94.

———. "A Feminist Discourse Analysis of Clarice Lispector's 'Daydreams of a Drunken Housewife.'" *Latin American Literary Review* 19 (1981): 7-16.

Lispector, Clarice. *Family Ties.* Trans. Giovanni Pontiero. Austin, TX: U of Texas P, 1960.

Peixoto, Marta. "Family Ties: Female Development in Clarice Lispector." *The Voyage in: Fictions of Female Development.* Hanover, NH: UP of New England for Dartmouth College, 1983: 287-303.

Pontiero, Giovanni. "Excerpts from the Chronicles of The Foreign Legion." By Clarice Lispector. *Review* 24 (1979): 37-43.

Rich, Adrienne. *Of Woman Born: Motherhood as Experience and Institution.* New York: Bantam, 1977.

Seniff, Dennis. "Self-Doubt in Clarice Lispector's Laços de família." *Luso-Brazilian Review* 14 (1977): 161-73.

Tolentino, Magda Velloso Fernandes de. "Family Bonds and Bondage within the Family: A Study of Family Ties in Clarice Lispector and James Joyce." *Modern Language Studies* 18.2 (1988): 73-78.

Wheeler, A. M. "Animal Imagery as Reflection of Gender Roles in Clarice Lispector's Family Ties." *Critique* 38.3 (1987): 125-34.

## Barbara Mathie (essay date 1991)

SOURCE: Mathie, Barbara. "Feminism, Language, or Existentialism: The Search for the Self in the Works of Clarice Lispector." In *Subjectivity and Literature from the Romantics to the Present Day,* edited by Philip Shaw and Peter Stockwell, pp. 121-34. London: Pinter Publishers, 1991.

[*In the following essay, Mathie discusses two Lispector short story collections in terms of whether the characters can achieve authentic experience, noting that only "Smallest Woman" is optimistic in his regard.*]

The title of this paper might seem to propose three alternative and mutually exclusive readings of the works of the Brazilian writer Clarice Lispector: that is to say, a feminist, a poststructuralist and an existentialist reading. However, I have no wish to propose one 'correct' reading; rather, I intend to show how all three readings can—I hesitate to say should—be simultaneously accepted.

Whereas existentialist and narratological readings of Clarice's work have already been widely discussed,[1] as has her poststructuralist stance regarding language and the construction of reality—a stance shared by many other Latin-American writers of the same period, for example Borges and Cortázar[2]—as Marta Peixoto points out in her article '*Family Ties*: Female Development in Clarice Lispector', the feminocentric nature of her writing is only now being recognized (1983: 287ff).

Obviously in this short paper I cannot hope to examine in detail the whole body that comprises the fiction of Clarice Lispector.[3] I shall, therefore, limit my analysis to two collections of short stories: *Laços de família* (*Family Ties*) (1970) first published in 1960, about halfway through Clarice's writing life, and a later collection, *A via crucis do corpo* (*The Via Crucis of the Flesh*) published in 1974.

My intention in choosing these two collections is to show that, despite her reluctance to be labelled as a *female* writer (a position echoed by her later champion Hélène Cixous, and by the theorist Julia Kristeva), and leaving aside the feminocentric surface structure—for example, a predominance of female characters—at the level of deep structure there lie firmly embedded in her work elements of recent (French) feminist theory, such as that introduced by both Cixous and Kristeva. Hélène Cixous herself considers the fiction of Clarice Lispector as a superlative example of *écriture féminine*.[4] Although Julia Kristeva does not, however, allow for the existence of an '*écriture féminine* or a *parler femme* that would be inherently feminine or female' she does allow for the concept of a marginal writing, bisexual rather than specifically feminine in nature; she does not allow for biological determinism however (in Moi 1985: 164).

Yet, between the two collections of stories cited here there is a fundamental difference. Fitz has already pointed out how *A via crucis do corpo* differs stylistically from Clarice's previous writing, and signals it as the text of 'a writer in transition' (Fitz 1988: 47). He sees the stories as considerably less lyrical in tone and as marking a change in the author's concerns; prior to *A via crucis do corpo* the concern is with the internal, isolated human, whereas those books that follow it are concerned with the external, and with the possibility of human communication.

However, it is my suggestion that while one can validly interpret the theme of *Laços de família* as being the (universal) isolation of the human condition, that is to stop short. What is common to almost all of the stories in this collection is the lack of space for discourses other than the patriarchal, a discourse which because of its adherence to a belief in an ultimate transcendental signifier, the phallus, necessarily renders the subject *être-en-soi* (being-in-itself).[5] This causes the protagonists to live inauthentic existences, as we shall see in the first part of this paper.

In the second collection of stories, however, Clarice adopts a new stance, positing a solution to this problem of lack of space. In the second part of this paper, I should like to examine how Clarice attempts to open up this new space and construct a discourse that is neither phallo- nor logocentric.

*Laços de família* (hereafter *LF*) is a collection of short stories of which three have male protagonists, although they are no less insignificant for being male.[6] All the other protagonists are female, although one of these females, in the story '**A galinha**' ('**The Chicken**'), is a chicken.

Each story centres around an epiphany, or *Gestalt;* that is to say a moment of supreme consciousness and self-awareness instigated by the protagonist's changed perception of an everyday object.[7] In '**Amor**' ('**Love**') for example, the protagonist, Ana, is precipitated into a state of crisis and self-awareness by the sight of a blind man chewing gum. I find it significant that the man is blind since it prevents Ana from being, in her relationship to him, an *être-pour-autrui,* an object in the eyes of others, which according to existentialist theory is an act of extreme *mauvaise foi* and one of the reasons underlying Sartre's proscription of love (Cranston 1962: 55-57).

Another element common to many of these stories is that the moment of awareness, the epiphany, although actually caused by the perception of an everyday object, occurs when the protagonist's social role remains temporarily undefined. For example, Ana's epiphany takes place when she is not limited and defined by her role of an urban, middle-class wife and mother. Ana herself speaks of 'na hora perigosa da tarde, quando a casa estave vazia sem precisar mais dela, o sol alto, cada membro da família distribuído nas suas funções' (during that dangerous hour in the afternoon when the house was empty, no longer needing her, the sun high in the sky, each member of the family elsewhere, busy with his own things) (*LF*: 19).[8]

The idea that women within patriarchal society are merely playing a role was first posited by Simone de Beauvoir, and explains her famous statement 'one is not born a woman, one becomes one'; in *Le Deuxième Sexe* (1956), de Beauvoir discusses the issue that within the confines of patriarchal society, the (biological) female *qua* female is always *other*, alienated without an individual identity and allocated the sole function of confirming male identity. This echoes Freud's concept of the gaze,'a phallic activity linked to anal desire for sadistic mastery of the object', for the female of patriarchy is rarely considered as more than (an) object; that is to say, as a male possession (Moi 1985: 134).

A theory of the gaze, Sartrean rather than Freudian, is the pivot around which the story **'Preciosidade'** (**'Preciousness'**) functions. In this story the young, female protagonist adopts a stance of *indifférence*. This is 'a kind of "blindness" towards others, or, more exactly, a deliberate refusal to accept that others are looking at me' (Cranston 1962: 57). And so she, the protagonist, intentionally avoids any interaction with those who surround her, except for in the classroom where, as we are told, she can be like a boy: 'Até que, enfim, a classe de aula . . . onde ela era tratada como um rapaz' (Until, at last, the classroom . . . where she was treated as if she were a boy) (*LF*: 98). For the girl to adopt this stance of *indifférence* is, as Naomi Lindstrom points out, an act of *mauvaise foi,* and also, in view of the protagonist's conscious efforts to be unkempt and unfeminine, indicative of her shirking her role as an adult woman within the confines of patriarchal society (Lindstrom 1982: 190).

The crisis in her (non-)existence occurs when she becomes aware that she is being followed by two young men (*LF*: 101). The sexual aspect of the fear of a young girl on her own is, of course, obvious but for her what is overriding is her fear that they might look at her; 'Êles vão olhar para mim, eu sei não, há mais niguém para êles olharem e êles vão olhar muito!' (They are going to look at me, I know it, there is no one else for them to look at, and they're going to look at me a lot!) (*LF*: 102). The climax of this episode occurs when they touch her and she is finally forced to recognize her existence *pour autrui*, as the alienated other, as the female sex object (*LF*: 102-3). The story ends, after her deliberating with herself, with her acceptance of her role as *être-pour-autrui:* '"Preciso cuidar mais de mim", pensou' ('I need to pay more attention to my appearance', she thought) (*LF*: 107). Thus she abandons her stance of *indifférence:* 'Até que, assim como

uma pessoa engorda, ela deixou, sem saber por que processo, de ser preciosa' (Until, in the same way as someone puts on weight, without realizing how, she stopped being 'affected') (*LF*: 108).

Yet, as the above quotation makes clear, this transformation was not so much a decisive action on her part, as ineluctable destiny.

What almost all the stories is this collection have in common, over and above their being structured around an epiphany, is the failure of the female protagonists to act upon what their 'experience' reveals to them. They do not initiate the quest for that eluding, indefinable grail which is an authentic existence as a semiotic *être-pour-soi,* as opposed to the inauthentic and symbolic state of *être-en-soi/pour-autrui.*

In these stories, as in Iberian Golden Age dramas, the modern detective story or the fairy story, any subversive action or event that threatens the monolithic order of the symbolic is *always* overcome, and harmony is restored.

In **'Amor'** (**'Love'**) Ana, while still in a state of crisis, finds herself drawn to the Botanic Gardens. The lyrical description of the gardens mentions their tropical lushness and abundance, but also present are death and putrification (*LF*: 23-25). This is a retreat to a pre-Lapsarian imaginary, or to Kristeva's semiotic *chora.*

Kristeva's theory of language acquisition substitutes the Lacanian terms of the 'imaginary' and the 'symbolic order' with the terms the 'semiotic' and the 'symbolic'. As with Lacan's concept of the imaginary (1977), the semiotic precedes the entry into language, and therefore, also the Oedipal crisis (the resolution of which results in the rupture of dyadic unity). This is reflected in the polysemy of the semiotic *chora,* 'which receives all things and in some mysterious way partakes of the intelligible and is most incomprehensible' (Moi 1985: 165): as there is no transcendental (phallic) signifier, there can be no fixed meaning. This means that love and hate, life and death and other such pairings—mutually exclusive within the confines of patriarchal binary thought—may co-exist; for, as Toril Moi points out, the pre-Oedipal mother is both masculine and feminine (1985: 165).

Yet, the semiotic cannot replace the symbolic (Moi 1985: 170). At the same time, however, 'there is no space for resistance within the terms of the symbolic order, and women who do not wish to repress their true femaleness can have no access to it' (Weedon 1987: 65). The use of the term 'femaleness' in the previous sentence does, however, require modification: for Kristeva, there is no such thing as a woman except in the most negative of senses. It is the phallocentric discourse of patriarchy which defines woman, and any such definition is in negative, marginalizing terms; as Kristeva says: 'I therefore understand by "woman" that which cannot be represented, that which is not spoken, that which remains outside naming and ideologies' (in Moi 1988: 163). What Kristeva advocates in place of 'femininity' is a theory of marginalization and subversion, not restricted in its application to the biological woman.

In this respect, Marta Peixoto points out the significance of the title of the collection of stories under discussion. The *family ties* of the title are what define and limit the female protagonists' existences (Peixoto 1983: 289). As we saw above, with reference to the story **'Amor'** (**'Love'**), Ana's crises (or epiphanies) occur *only* when she is not fully participating in the role of middle-class wife and mother. Patriarchal society is, of course, structured around the family, at the head of which is the father and his law, a law founded on the possession of the phallus: in Cixous' terms, it is the 'realm of the proper'.

Yet these defining bonds are not permanent as is illustrated in the story **'Feliz aniverário'** (**'Happy Birthday'**). As Peixoto points out in her article, the party in honour of the protagonist's eighty-ninth birthday is reduced to the level of empty ritual (1983: 287). The protagonist, the birthday girl, is described in passive terms, impotent now she holds only a puppet role:

> E, para adiantar o expediente, vestira a aniversariante logo depois do almoço. Pusera-lhe desde então a presilha em tôrno do pescoço e o broche, borrifara-lhe um pouco de água-de-colônia para disfarçar aquêle seu cheiro de guardado—sentara-a- à mesa. E desde duas horas a aniversariante estava sentada à cabeceira de longa mesa vazia, têsa na sala silenciosa.
>
> (*LF*: 61).

(And, to speed things up, she had dressed the birthday girl immediately after lunch. She had, at that point put the necklace around her neck and fastened it; she had sprinkled her with a little toilet water to hide that musty smell she had, and she had sat her at the table. And for last two hours the birthday girl had been sitting up straight at the head of the long, empty table in that silent room.)

The rest of the family are more concerned with themselves and with doing what is expected of them: her son José, the eldest of six sons, is especially worried about saying the correct thing (*LF*: 63ff).

The grandmother's moment of awareness occurs with the ritual cutting of the cake, symbolizing, for her, the final severing of the family ties. With a sudden show of rebellion, the grandmother spits vehemently, thereby upsetting everyone. Order is almost immediately re-established. However, the final words of the story re-

flect the pessimism of existentialism: of the grandmother we are told, 'A morte era o seu mistério' (Death was her mystery) (*LF*: 75), introducing the Sartrean belief that after death there is nothing, and that, consequently, a man or woman is the sum total of his or her acts. (Death is a favourite concern of Clarice, and in one of the stories of *A via crucis do corpo*—'Antes da ponte Rio-Niterói' ('Before the Bridge at River-Niterói')—she, as the intradiegetic narrator, considers the possible nature of death.)

In the title story of **'Laços de família'** maternal love is, again, the theme. By an act of chance (*le hasard*) the protagonist Catarina is thrown together with her mother in a taxi, and this results in Catarina's consciousness of her overwhelming love for her mother: 'Ninguém mais te pode amar senão eu . . . Não, não se podia dizer que amava sua mãe. Sue mãe lhe doía' (No one else can love you apart from me . . . No, she couldn't say that she loved her mother. Her mother made her ache) (*LF*: 112). This awareness of a primeval, semiotic love is all the more important as we have already been informed that Catarina's post-Oedipal tie was, as is the normal case, with her father (*LF*: 111-12). This awareness of love also occasions in Catarina a new awareness of the world surrounding her (*LF*: 114ff). It is also reflected in her relationship with her son who, since he has not yet fully mastered use of language nor acquired a sense of his own identity, is therefore pre-Oedipal:

> Em que momento é que a mão, apertando uma criança, dava-lhe esta prisão de amor que se abateria para ser sempre sôbre o futuro homen . . . Quem saberia jamais em que momento a mãe transferia ao filho a herança. E com que sombrio prazer. Agora mãe e filho comprendo-se dentro do mistério partilhado.
>
> (*LF*: 117-118).

(At what moment is it that a mother, hugging her child, gave him this prison of love that would descend forever upon the future man . . . Who could know at what moment a mother transferred to her son that inheritance. And with what sombre pleasure. Now mother and son understanding each other, together in the mystery they share.)

As Peixoto (1983: 293) points out, the father resents his exclusion from the dyadic unity between mother and infant, and uses his power to install the *feminine*: 'Mas tinha-se habituado a torná-la feminina dêste modo' (He had become used to making her feminine in this way) (*LF*: 118-19). It is, perhaps, superfluous to point out that the above quotation justifies the belief shared by de Beauvoir and Kristeva, amongst many, that a woman is created by patriarchy.

The third element that links these stories is the ineffable nature of the epiphanies. In **'Laços de família',** despite Catarina's burgeoning feelings for her mother, 'não tinham o que falar' (they had nothing to say) (*LF*: 112).

Likewise Ana, the protagonist of **'Amor'** (**'Love'**), attempts to communicate with her son, but cannot; she ends up frightening him instead with her momentary intensity (*LF*: 26).

This inability of the protagonists to vocalize, and therefore to lend reality to their new found consciousness, is, of course, because a return to the semiotic is a return to a state preceding language where the heterogeneous subject is, as yet, unsplit. Within the discourse of the symbolic, based on one transcendental signifier, the *logos* is fixed in meaning and the polysemic nature of the semiotic is, therefore, ineffable.

In her novel *A paixão segundo G.H.* (*The Passion according to G.H.*) (in Lucas 1976), Lispector examines fully the quest for authenticity and reality through language, and the ensuing muteness:

> Ah, mas para chegar à mudez, que grande esforço da voz. Minha voz é o modo como vou buscar a realidade; a realidade antes da minha linguagem, existia como um pensamento que não se pensa, mas por fatalidade fui e sou impelida a precisar saber o que o pensamento pensa . . . A realidade é a matéria prima, a linguagem é o modo como vou buscá-la . . . Mas—volto com o indizível.
>
> (Lucas 1976: 16-17)
>
> (Oh, but in order to become mute, what great efforts of the voice are required. My voice is the means by which I shall seek reality; reality even before my language existed as a thought, which is never thought, but by destiny I was and I am impelled to find out that which the thought thinks . . . Reality is the raw material, language is the means through which I can reach it . . . But—I always return with that which cannot be spoken.)

From an existentialist-poststructuralist point of view, if one accepts the fact that it is through language that any given reality is made manifest or created, if the *indizível* (that which cannot be spoken) were articulated in the (phal)logocentric discourse of patriarchal society, it would be fixed; that is to say, rendered *être-en-soi*.

The story entitled **'A menor mulher do mundo'** (**'The Smallest Woman in the World'**) is, perhaps, the only story in this collection that is in any way optimistic. Although, as Peixoto points out, this pygmy woman is representative of every possible minority—she is small, black, pregnant and female, in other words completely defenceless and marginalized—she has, nevertheless, succeeded in preserving her identity (1983: 301-02); she survives against all odds, including cannibalistic neighbours. Towards the end of the story she is described as being in possession of her own authentic identity:

> E então ela estava rindo. Era um riso como sòmente quem não fala ri. Êsse riso, o explorador constrangido não conseguiu classificar. E ela continuou fruindo o próprio riso macio, ela que não estava sendo devorada. Não ser devorado é o sentimento mais perfeito. Não ser devorado é o objectivo secreto de tôda uma vida.
>
> (*LF*: 84)
>
> (And then she was laughing. It could only be the laugh of someone who does not speak. This laugh the troubled explorer could not classify. She, who was not being devoured, continued enjoying her own smooth laugh. Not to be devoured is the most perfect sentiment. Not to be devoured is the secret objective of one's whole life.)

We are also told that in this community, a child is given his liberty 'quase que imediatamente' (almost immediately), thus freeing the mother from a subjugated existence as *autrui* (*LF*: 78). It is further related that this woman has a tree of her own, in which she lives; automatically, one thinks of the tree of life, although, it is also possible to interpret the tree as phallic, especially as it is spoken of as a *possession* (*LF*: 86). Yet it is my opinion that, although in possession of a tree and her own identity, Pequena Flor (Little Flower) who is named by (and perhaps therefore appropriated by) the explorer, is not situated within patriarchal discourse. This is because we are also told, more than once, that Pequena Flor cannot speak. Furthermore, her concept of love is of a love which does not devour the individuality of either party (*LF*: 84-85); that is to say a love in keeping with the tenets of existentialism (Cranston 1962: 57).

However, there are also three stories in the collection which have male protagonists. In the story **'Começos de uma fortuna'** (**'Beginnings of a Fortune'**) the adolescent Arturo is learning about life in the adult world. What is apparent throughout the story is Arturo's unease and tentativeness faced with the exploitative nature of capitalist (and patriarchal) society. Like the protagonist of **'Preciosidade'** (**'Preciousness'**) he is adolescent, but unlike her, for she attempts to resist entry into the adult world, he is both curiously tempted and repelled. Having recognized his parents as individuals (*LF*: 123), and acknowledging his growing separateness from them, he reflects upon the establishment of his own dynasty: 'Quando eu tiver minha mulher e meus filhos . . . tudo será diferente' (When I have my own wife and children . . . everything will be different). In this respect he obviously sees his own future as within the structures of patriarchy, with himself in the role of subject (*LF*: 124).

At the same time, he is unsure as to whether or not he wishes to take on this adult role, represented in the story by his indecision over whether or not to borrow money from his friend in order to take a girl to the cinema (*LF*: 125ff). In the end, after having been teased, he capitulates and borrows the money without being sure if the girl whom he took to the cinema was exploiting *him*, or if perhaps he should have taken advantage of *her* (*LF*: 128).

'O crime do professor de matemática' ('The Crime of the Mathematics Professor') features a protagonist whose career would point to him being the very embodiment of logic and rationality, as Di Antonio remarks (1985: 28); however, even he is unable to avoid certain feelings of Sartrean 'nausea'. His crisis is caused when he comes across a dead, unburied dog, which he determines to buy in an attempt to expiate his guilt over having earlier abandoned his own pet dog. This, however, he never manages to do. Di Antonio identifies the dog with the (instinctive) Jungian unconscious, which the professor is unable to buy under the tree of knowledge (1985: 29). It is not implausible to extend this interpretation, seeing the dog, an animal and therefore without language, as representing the semiotic and the act of burial as an attempt on the part of the symbolic, rational man to isolate himself from the subversive within himself. While Julia Kristeva maintains that it is impossible for the semiotic to take over the symbolic, she nevertheless posits a theory of the *sujet en procès,* or the disrupted subject. In the same way that Freud's repressed is never fully repressed, so too there are semiotic pulsions which can be released into the symbolic through expulsion or rejection. This allows for a subversive or revolutionary discourse, based on semiotic motility and the *sujet en procès* (a semiotic *être-pour-soi*). This is the theory in the philosophy of Julia Kristeva which is correlative and substitutive of Cixous' concept of *écriture féminine* (Moi 1985: 170).

It is, of course, entirely possible to interpret **'O crime do professor de matemática'** (**'The Crime of the Mathematics Professor'**) on a purely existentialist level. In Sartrean philosophy freedom is absolute: there is no absolute or transcendental moral code by which one can live one's life. Consequently, one has to make choices by which one can either be saved or be damned; one is responsible for these choices, and for one's acts. The concept of salvation and damnation might seem paradoxical when one is dealing with what, in the case of Sartre, is an atheist philosophy. This problem is examined in Sartre's *Huis clos,* where the three protagonists are in hell, but a hell of their own making: they are each other's hell ('L'enfer, ce sont les autres'). They are damned precisely because they are dead, and therefore can perform no new acts to wipe out their past deeds. Garcin asks: 'Can you judge a whole life by one act?', to which Inès responds 'It is deeds alone which show what a man has willed' (Cranston 1962: 35).

In Lispector's story there is no Sartrean hell; there are no other people; the crime is known only to the mathematics professor. His crime was not so much the abandoning of his pet as, rather, his attitude towards the dog: he tried to objectivize both himself and the dog in their mutual relationship, as in the Sartrean proscription of love. Love is seen as a process of 'infinite regress',

since in wanting to be loved, or in being loved, one's own transcendence is curtailed and one is objectivized, at least in relation to the person by whom one is loved. Correspondingly, in loving someone, one curtails the beloved's liberty (Cranston 1962: 56). This is complicated by the paradox that in desiring love, one merely seeks to be loved oneself; in desiring love/to be loved, one is an *être-pour-soi* seeking to be *en-soi,* and as such, one seeks to avoid ethical responsibility.

The professor's crime is, therefore, the former relationship with his dog, whom he even gave a human name: 'dei-te o nome de José para te dar um nome que te servisse ao mesmo tempo de alma' (I gave you the name José to give you a name that would, at the same time, serve as a soul) (*LF*: 143). Obviously, since the professor mis-recognizes his crime, he cannot expiate his crime.

The final story in *Laços de família* I want to consider is **'A imitação da rosa'** (**'The Imitation of the Rose'**). In this story, the protagonist, the childless Laura, has recently suffered a nervous breakdown. Although recognizing society's need to rationalize and to name everything, she attributes her illness to an 'insuficiência ovariana' (hormonal imbalance) (*LF*: 43). In an effort to compensate for her reduced social role—she has no children to furnish her with an identity as *autrui*—she takes an excessive interest in her home: 'em fazer da sua casa uma coisa impessoal; de certo modo perfeito por ser impessoal' (In making her house something impersonal; in a certain way perfect in its impersonal appearance) (*LF*: 39). It is the contemplation of some wild roses that causes Laura's delicate mental balancing act to fall apart. These roses represent the freedom and the integrity—they merely *are*—that are missing in Laura's life. Although she gives away the roses, it is too late, and when her husband returns home she was 'de nôvo alerta e tranqüila como num tren. Que já partira' (once more alert and serene, as if in a train. That had already left) (*LF*: 58).

In her attempts to exist *pour-soi*, she is considered as mad since society cannot accept her. In her outlining of the impossibility of an outright rejection of the symbolic, Toril Moi points out that a failure to engage in human relationships, that is to say discourse, would result in Lacanian psychosis (Moi 1985: 176).

Before discussing how in *A via crucis do corpo*, Clarice manages to resolve the problem of the lack of space for authentic existence as *être-pour-soi* within the discourse of patriarchy, I should like briefly to consider two novels which are situated chronologically between the two collections of short stories. These are *Uma aprendizagem ou o livro dos prazeres* (*An apprenticeship or the book of pleasures*) (1969) and *Água viva* (White Water) (1973).

*Uma aprendizagem ou o livro dos prazeres,* published in Brazil in 1969, is the novel that, in my opinion, marks Clarice's passage to a new phase of maturity, in which her characters are no longer quite so isolated in their human angst, managing instead to establish communication with their fellow humans. It is a text that differs considerably from those that precede it. First there are two central characters, and secondly, there is a much greater use of dialogue than previously common in Clarice's work. Like Clarice's other novels, the two characters embark upon a metaphysical journey. Here, however, Lóri and Ulisses are successful in attaining the grail, which is the fulfilment of love. In contrast to the constraining and limiting love of *Laços de família,* the love between the two protagonists of *Uma aprendizagem* is not based upon the infinite regressing of mutual objectivizing; it allows for individual freedom and self-fulfilment as an ever-growing *être-pour-soi.* As Fitz (1987: 431) points out, this psychological achievement is represented in the novel by the physical consummation of their love.

*Água viva,* published three years later in 1973, once again deals with the themes of love and freedom. Unlike *Uma aprendizagem* it is, however, more concerned with internal, psychological reality than with external relationships. As Fitz indicates, the novel is an unbroken stream of consciousness, centring around the female narrator's quest for rebirth as an individual. This will come about through the successful termination of a previous objectivizing relationship: "'Fui ao encontro de mim . . . Simplesmente eu sou eu. E você é você . . . Olha para mim e me ama, Não: tu olhas para ti e te amas'" (I went to an encounter with myself . . . I am simply me. And you are you . . . Look at me and love me, No: you look at yourself and love yourself) (Fitz 1985: 85).

Like *Laços de família, Água Viva* is once again highly lyrical in its language: it is, perhaps, a return to what preceded *Uma aprendizagem.* The novel ends with the female protagonist still in a state of flux, that is to say as *être-pour-soi,* yet, as Fitz points out, it is not quite a conclusion: we do not know whether the former lover will achieve that same degree of liberation—Fitz suggests that he will not (1985: 91). However, following on from the argument expressed in this analysis, for there to be any one, concrete 'conflict resolving conclusion' would involve a breach of existentialist and poststructuralist philosophy.

It is with the publication of *A via crucis do corpo* (hereafter *VC*) that the trend established in *Uma aprendizagem* continues to be expanded and developed. Like its forerunner, this collection of short stories affirms the possibility of successful human interaction, with non-hierarchical, non-exploitative relationships, although not in every story. Another similarity between *Via cru-* *cis* and *Uma aprendizagem* is the sexual element featured in both—often, though not always, as the means of communication, as in the story entitled **'Melhor do que arder'** (**'Better Than to Burn'**). As Fitz remarks, there is a link between sexuality and a sense of identity, for example in the story **'Miss Algrave'** (1988: 43).

The sexual element included in these stories is, of course, announced by the title of the collection: *A via crucis do corpo* (*The Via Crucis of the Flesh*). The translation of the title into English, however, ignores the dual meaning of the word in Portuguese, where *corpo* can also mean body. Although a valid interpretation of the title could be 'salvation through the flesh'— for the pain of the Way of the Cross (the Via Crucis) is superceded by the Resurrection—it is, perhaps better, to see this work as an example of the much heralded 'return of the body'. This return (or perhaps resurrection) of the body in literature is the replacing of the fixed, and allegedly transcendental, *logos*/phallus with the polysemic signifier that is the body; man's/woman's primal impulses (*triebe*) are corporal. Furthermore, for both Freud and Kristeva, 'the body forms the basis for the constitution of the subject' (Moi 1988: 166). For Kristeva, the disruption of the symbolic by the semiotic is through oral and anal expulsion or rejection; and since these impulses and desires, those of the pre-Oedipal child, are, contrary to patriarchal thinking never mastered, the subject is endlessly *en procès* (Moi 1988: 170). (Any total satisfaction of desire would, as Freud pointed out in 'Beyond the Pleasure Principle', result in death, although this mastery of desire (death drive) is what the phallocentric subject strives for.)

The return of the body is apparent in the story entitled **'Melhor do que arder'** (**'Better Than to Burn'**), the protagonist of which is a nun troubled by irrepressible sexual desire: 'Mas na hora em que o padre lhe tocava a boca para dar a hóstia tinha que se controlar para não morder a mão do padre' (But at the moment when the priest touched her mouth to give her the Sacrament she had to stop herself from biting his hand); 'Não podia mais ver o corpo quase nu do Cristo' (She could no longer look at the half-naked body of Christ) (*VC*: 92).

Although she attempts to annul and repress her desires by mortifying herself, she does so in vain, for as we have seen the primal impulses of the semiotic can never be fully repressed by the symbolic. In this story, however, the symbolic, as represented by the Church, is overthrown when the protagonist leaves the religious life and marries. Yet the use of the term 'overthrow' is misleading, for we have already seen how one cannot retreat into the semiotic; rather we should see this victory as a positing of the possibility of new parameters within which the subject is not redefined, but can be repositioned.

In one of the two title stories, **'O corpo'** (**'The Body'**), it is through female solidarity, however, that communication between the two protagonists is established, enabling once again an overthrow of the dominant phallogocentric symbolic. As well as meaning flesh and body the *corpo* also means corpse. The corpse in the story is that of Xavier, who is described as a *superhomem* (superman) and compared to that symbol of male sexuality, the bull (*VC*: 30-31). Not content with living bigamously with two women, he also frequents a prostitute, and it is this which leads the two women to rebel. First of all they go on strike in the kitchen and eventually go on to plan and carry through his murder (*VC*: 31-34). The solidarity between the two women in Xavier's life is built up gradually: we are told that Carmen would let Beatriz read her diary, and then that 'apesar de não serem homossexuais, se excitavam uma à outra e faziam amor. Amor triste' (although they were not homosexuals, they would caress each other and make love. Sad love) (*VC*: 30).

They murder Xavier, using one knife each, but yet they are not censured: in order to avoid excessive paper work, the police suggest that the two women flee to Montevideo and no more will be said of the matter. The phallus, Xavier, the *superhomem* who, as he admits, cannot be satisfied by the two women he lives with, is displaced. It is interesting that what replaces exclusive heterosexuality is not exclusive homosexuality, but bisexuality. Unlike some radical feminists who posit lesbianism as the only solution to the problem of patriarchy, Cixous, a passonate champion of Lispector, adheres to a solution of *other bisexuality,* which as Moi points out is 'multiple, variable and everchanging' (Moi 1985: 109). This postulation does not contradict Kristeva's aim of deconstructing the false and metaphysical gender identities defined by patriarchal discourse with its (would-be) transcendental signifier of the phallus.

The creation of (apparently) false gender identities is also the subject of the story **'Praça Mauá'.** The protagonists of the story are Luísa-Carla, a cabaret dancer, and the homosexual drag queen Celsinho-Moleirão. In their work at a nightclub they both assume false identities on a physical level: Luísa-Carla's make-up transforms her into 'uma boneca de louça' (a china doll) and Celsinho-Moleirão is, as mentioned, a transvestite who uses false eyelashes, and who, through taking hormones, has acquired a 'fac-simile de seios' (something akin to breasts) (*VC*: 79&81). The two protagonists fall out over a man whom they both desire, and Luísa-Carla accuses Celsinho-Moleirão of not being 'um homem de verdade' (a real man); he retorts that, since she does not even know how to crack an egg, she is not a real woman.

In this story, therefore, we see not only how the concept of 'womanhood' is defined, created and imposed by patriarchal discourse, but also an undoing of the traditional boundaries of 'masculine' and 'feminine'. In the first instance, Luísa-Carla is seen as not being a woman by Celsinho-Moleirão since she does not know how to cook, and, unlike him, she is also childless; yet at the same time, made-up and performing her erotic dances, she is the epitomy of male fantasy, though still not a real woman. Celsinho-Moleirão, like the character Molina in Manuel Puig's film *El beso de la mujer araña* (*The Kiss of the Spider Woman*), does not conform to patriarchal society's concept of the masculine, nor is he really a woman (he can have no idea of what it is like to be a (biological) woman from childhood in a patriarchal society) despite Luísa-Carla's admission at the end that Celsinho, who towards his adopted daughter was a 'verdedeira mãe' (a true mother) was 'mais mulher do que ela' (more of a woman than she) (*VC*: 80-81&84). In this story we are made to realize the arbitrariness of traditional gender divisions, and, as in the whole collection, there is not only a return of the body, but also a return of the marginalized subject; that is to say a repositioned subject who is *not* defined and written around the phallic signifier.

This repositioning of the subject is a theme explored again in **'Miss Algrave'.** Fitz maintains that 'the sexually-orientated scenes of *The Via Crucis of the Flesh* link a character's sexuality with the same character's sense of identity' (1988: 43). Yet, it must be pointed out that the sexuality expressed in these stories is, on the whole, a sexuality that within the context of patriarchal discourse is always marginalized. The non-phallocentric sexuality in this collection is the nucleus around which the stories are structured, and demonstrates the repositioning of the subject. It is a discovery of her sexual identity that liberates Miss Algrave, as Fitz remarks:

> the essential personality is established in terms of her being sexually repressed, isolated in her solitude, and painfully discontent with a superficial and inauthentic existence. Suddenly the unanticipated event happens and her sense of being is irrevocably altered.
>
> (1988: 47)

This 'unanticipated event' is the appearance of an extra-terrestrial being who initiates Miss Algrave sexually, giving her her sexual, and therefore, psychological freedom (*VC*: 20). When she asks who he is, she is given the answer 'Eu sou um eu' (I am an I): that is to say he is a being defined solely in relation to himself (*VC*: 20).

This process of liberation and self-discovery will and does continue, for we are told that Ixtlan will return (*VC*: 21). Yet this does not mean that Miss Algrave, now 'uma mulher realizada' (a whole woman) forms her life entirely around the extra-terrestrial; she has and will continue to have sexual relations with other men (*VC*: 22ff). Her social liberation is represented by her freeing herself from patriarchal domination in the form of the Church and her previous exploitative employer.

Although in this collection of short stories Clarice succeeds in establishing a non-phallogocentric discourse, there are nevertheless cases of exploitation. In **'Mas vai chover'** (**'But It's Going to Rain'**) the widow's sexual satisfaction in her relationship with the gigolo is short lived; it is not long before he begins to exploit her (*VC*: 98). He eventually demands a million *cruzeiros* as an inducement to continue his relationship with her, and leaves her when she cannot pay, despite her pitiful pleas. Although it may seem that in this story the evils of patriarchy are winning through, this is not entirely so. Once again, in this story, the primacy of the phallus is undermined for we are told that at the age of twenty-seven the gigolo, Alex, will become impotent.

Another distinctive feature of this collection that separates it from Clarice's previous fiction is that, unlike *A paixão segundo G.H.* and ***Laços de família,*** language plays a role, not as a lyrical mediator in the quest for authenticity, but as a means of communication. Fitz is correct in his assertion that these pieces are extremely unlyrical in tone, and there is little expressive dialogue between the characters; it is in the re-writing of a (his-)story that language becomes central, as well as the importance given to non-verbal language, in the form of sex (Fitz 1988: 41). It is this communication of the author to the reader that is essential.

Unlike ***Laços de famíla,*** some of these stories have an intradiegetic narrator. In **'Ruído de passos'** (**'The Sound of Footsteps'**) it is a third person narrator who directly addresses the protagonist: 'É a vida, senhora Raposo, é a vida. Até a benção da morte' (That's life, senhora Raposo, that's life. Until the blessing of death) (*VC*: 71). In this story the elderly female protagonist has to achieve sexual satisfaction on her own: once again Clarice posits an alternative, non-phallic form of sexual activity as valid.

In **'Antes da ponte Rio-Niterói'** (**'Before the Bridge over the River Niterói'**) the intradiegetic narrator is not only first person, but also admits to being unreliable. The narrator tells us:

> Mas estou me confundindo toda . . . As realidades dele são inventada. Peço desculpa porque além de contar os fatos também adivinho e o que adivinho aqui escrevo, escrivã que sou por fatalidade. Eu adivinho a realidade.
>
> (*VC*: 73)
>
> (But I'm getting all confused . . . All its realities are invented. Forgive me, for in addition to recounting the facts I also guess and what I guess I write down here, as the predestined writer that I am. I guess at reality.)

The story being told us is about a young girl whose leg is amputated, causing the girl's boyfriend to abandon her, even though she does not have long to live. In his relationship with her, the boyfriend has been cheating on the woman with whom he lives (*VC*: 74). This woman, however, decides to retaliate and pours boiling water into his ear leaving him 'surdo para sempre, logo ele que não perdoara defeito físico' (deaf for the rest of his life, he who would not forgive a physical imperfection) (*VC*: 75).

This obviously poststructuralist stance regarding the creation of fiction and reality, and the explicit blending of the boundaries between the two, is not unique to this story, occurring also in other stories such as **'A via crucis'.** However in **'Rio-Niterói'** it is constantly pointed out that the narrator (not necessarily the author) is inventing and imagining an event which took place in the distant past, if ever at all, and this could, in the light of the betrayed woman's revenge and the tone of the other stories in the collection, be seen as another example of subversive discourse in which the marginalized (woman) is able to depose the patriarchal.

Whereas in the stories of ***Laços de família*** Clarice's prose is highly lyrical and the stories themselves more drawn out, the style of *A via crucis* is more prosaic and the stories pared to the point of being almost schematic. This contrast in style between the two collections is a reflection of a shifting of what one might term the 'campo da batalha' (the battlefield). Prior to *A via crucis* the characters of her fiction tend to attempt to realize authenticity within the confines of patriarchal discourse and, naturally, fail. In *A via crucis* however, the struggle for realization of the self/subject is centred around the return of the pre-Oedipal body. It is only by substituting the polysemy of the pre-Oedipal body for the phallic signifier of the symbolic (with its concomitant desire for possession and mastery), that authenticity as *être-pour-soi* or *sujet en procès* can hope to be achieved by anyone (biologically) male or female, since the fixed phallogocentrism of patriarchal discourse must needs demand rigid, intransigent boundaries and definitions.

*Notes*

1. See, for example, Nunes (1973), de Sá (1979), and Fitz (1985).

2. See, for example, Fitz (1987).

3. For a detailed bibliography and biography, see Fitz (1985: 1-19).

4. See Cixous (1989).

5. In this study I am employing the Lacanian concept of the phallus, as defined by Weedon (1987: 53).

> meaning and the symbolic order as a whole, is fixed in relation to a primary transcendental signifier which Lacan calls the phallus, the signifier of

sexual difference, which guarantees the patriarchal structure of the symbolic order. The phallus signifies power and control in the symbolic order through control of the satisfaction of desire, the primary source of power within psychoanalytic theory.

6. These are: 'O Crime do Professor de Matemática', 'O Jantar', and 'Começos de uma Fortuna'.

7. For a more detailed discussion of the role of epiphany in Clarice Lispector, see Palls (1984).

8. All translations are my own.

### Bibliography

Anderson, R. (1985), 'Myth and Existentialism in Clarice Lispector's *O crime do professor de matemática*', *Luso-Brazilian Review,* Vol. XXII(1): 1-7.

de Beauvoir, S. (1956), *Le Deuxième Sexe,* Paris, Gallimard.

Cixous, H. (1987), 'Reaching the Point of Wheat, or a Portrait of the Artist as a Maturing Woman', *New Literary History,* Vol. 19(1): 1-21.

———. (1989), *L'Heure de Clarice Lispector,* Paris, des Femmes.

Cranston, M. (1962), *Sartre,* Edinburgh and London, Oliver and Boyd.

Di Antonio, R. (1985), 'Myth as a Unifying Force in *O crime do professor de matemática*', *Luso-Brazilian Review,* Vol. XXII(1): 27-35.

Fitz, E. E. (1980), 'Freedom and Self-realization: Feminist Characterization in the Fiction of Clarice Lispector', *Modern Language Studies,* Vol. 10(3): 51-61.

———. (1985), *Clarice Lispector,* Boston, Twayne.

———. (1987), 'A Discourse of Silence: The Post-Modernism of Clarice Lispector', *Contemporary Literature,* Vol. 28(4): 420-436.

———. (1988), 'A writer in Transition: Clarice Lispector and *A via crucis do corpo*', *Latin American Literary Review,* Vol. XVI(32) (July/August): 41-52.

Lacan, J. (1977), *Ecrits: A Selection,* London, Tavistock Publications.

Lindstrom, N. (1981), 'A Feminist Discourse Analysis of Clarice Lispector's "Daydreams of a Drunken Housewife"', *Latin American Literary Review,* Vol. 9 (Fall/Winter): 7-16.

———. (1982), 'A Discourse Analysis of "Preciosidade" by Clarice Lispector', *Luso-Brazilian Review,* Vol. IX(2): 187-195.

Lispector, C. (1969), *Uma aprendizagem ou o livro dos prazeres,* Rio de Janeiro, Editôra Sabiá.

———. (1970), *Laços de famíla* (5th edition), Rio de Janeiro, Editôra Sabiá.

———. (1973), *Agua Viva,* Rio de Janeiro, Editôra Sabiá.

———. (1974), *A via crucis do corpo* (1st edition), Rio de Janeiro, Editôra Artenova.

Lucas, F. (1976), *Poesia e Prosa no Brasil,* Belo Horizonte, Interlivros de Minas Gerais.

Moi, T. (1985), *Sexual/Textual Politics: Feminist Literary Theory,* London and New York, Routledge.

Nunes, B. (1973), *Clarice Lispector,* Bela Vista, São Paulo, Edições Quiron.

Palls, T. L. (1984), 'The Miracle of the Ordinary: Literary Epiphany in Virginia Woolf and Clarice Lispector', *Luso-Brazilian Review,* Vol. XXI(1): 63-78.

Piexoto, M. (1983), '*Family Ties*: Female Development in Clarice Lispector', in Abel, E., Hirsch, M. and Langland, E. (1983), *The Voyage In: Fictions of Female Development,* Hanover (N.H.) and London, University Press of New England for Dartmouth College, 287-303.

de Sá, O. (1979), *A Escritura de Clarice Lispector,* Rio de Janeiro, Editôra Vozez Ltda.

Senna, M. de (1986), '*A Imitação da Rosa* by Clarice Lispector: An Interpretation', *Portuguese Studies,* Vol. 2: 159-165.

Weedon, C. (1987), *Feminist Practice and Poststructuralist Theory,* Oxford, Basil Blackwell.

Wheeler, A. M. (1987), 'Animal Imagery as Reflection of Gender Role in Clarice Lispector's *Family Ties*', *Critique,* Vol. 23(3): 125-134.

### Kamala Platt (essay date 1992)

SOURCE: Platt, Kamala. "Race and Gender Representations in Clarice Lispector's 'A Menor Mulher do Mundo' and Carolina Maria de Jesus's *Quarto de Despejo.*" *Afro-Hispanic Review* 11, nos. 1-3 (1992): 51-7.

[*In the following essay, Platt compares de Jesus's* Quarto de Despejo *with "The Smallest Woman in the World," detailing the racist implications inherent in Lispector's depiction of Little Flower as a "subhuman" and "animal-like" representative of her race.*]

Brazil has, from the time of invasion by Portuguese colonizers, had a racial consciousness that differs from that which developed in the United States despite an at least superficially similar history of oppression of indigenous and African peoples by European colonizers. David T. Haberly in, *Three Sad Races,* compares racial constructs in U.S. and Brazilian literature thus:

> American literature, with pitifully few exceptions, has been written by whites, and about whites . . . [While] much of Brazil's literature has been preoccupied with an anguished search for a viable racial identity—a search that has been both personal and national in scope.
>
> (2)

Haberly finds these differences to be "the result of contrasting definitions of the nature of race and of the function of literature" (2) and points out that, unlike in the U.S., in Brazil a complex racial system based on genetic ancestry, actual physical characteristics, and cultural patterns—education, speech, dress, religion . . . is in operation. While he finds this system to be "equally founded upon prejudice toward nonwhite peoples" (3) he finds the racial identity of any given person to be mutable. Haberly identifies the position for literature within this system as

> almost exclusively the creature of the elite . . . [and] therefore an act of social self-affirmation, since that action and the abilities it presupposes are proof of membership in the elite. . . . And nonwhites who somehow manage to become consumers of literature thereby whiten themselves . . . .
>
> (5)

Haberly notes the extensive overlap of the producers and consumers of Brazilian literature and observes that while many literary figures in Brazil have been nonwhite, few have been "all black": "the achievements of those of mixed blood could always, in the final analysis, be explained away as the triumph of white genes over African or Indian genes." (6)

João da Cruz e Sousa, considered an outstanding Symbolist poet, demonstrates how this societal racism is internalized in the following passage:

> All the doors and passage-ways along the road of life are closed to me, a poor Aryan artist- yes, Aryan, because I acquired, by systematic study, all the qualities of that great race. To what end? A sad black man, detested by those with culture, beaten down by society, always humiliated, cast out of every bed, spat upon in every household like some evil leper! But how? To be an artist with this color?
>
> [in Magalhaes Junior, 1975: 130-1 (Haberly 106)]

Scholarly discussion has constructed Brazilian literature by focusing on Brazilian writers who have followed and/or manipulated European tradition in a Brazilian context. The concept of "whitening" has "paled" Brazilian literature just as its social intent was to whitewash Brazilian society. However, a more historically conscious survey of Brazilian writing uncovers multiple cultural self-identities. Among those who express an Afro-Brazilian racial identity is Carolina Maria de Jesus whose testimonio-like text *Quarto de Despejo* became world-famous[1]. She writes outside any "great works" genre, and that she has remained belief-system-wise as well, outside the whitening tradition, is illustrated in the following passage. "Se é que existe reincarnações, eu quero voltar sempre preta." (65) Likewise her self-identity as a woman reflects both pride in her gender and acknowledgement of the particular experiences of suffering endured and/or overcome.

Another woman who writes against the canonized Brazilian tradition, in that her writing expresses a woman's self-identity is Clarice Lispector.

However, unlike de Jesus's straightforward discussion of race—be it her own or the race of the people she meets—Clarice Lispector, when she presents race at all, presents it in stereotyping metaphors without historicization. Lispector's focus on female experience is central to the majority of her texts and much has been written about her descriptions of that experience. "Universal" female characters repeatedly appear as central characters in much of Lispector's work, however in reality these women are not at all universal but white upper middle class. The absence of diverse racial identities in most of her stories is conspicuous when looked at beside a text like *Quarto de Despejo* which describes experiences of being Black, female and poor on a daily basis. Lispector seems unfamiliar with, if not ignorant about Afro-Brazilian experiences. The mulattoes and Blacks that appear in her stories are cast as domestic servants and never play the major protagonist's role. **"A Menor Mulher do Mundo"** found in the collection *Laços de Família* is an exception. Thus I've chosen it as the focus of discussion. While I do not claim that this story represents Lispector's construction of nonwhite experience I find it useful as a singular example of fictional focus on African experience in her work. Appropriate analytical response to this story is complicated because, for example, Lispector uses animal and color symbolism in often grotesque and morbid ways throughout much of her writing. However the difference in this story is the depiction of the protagonist as representative of her race, prehuman emotionally, intellectually and socially, and animal-like. The conflation of these features clearly points to a racist portrayal of the African Pygmy woman. Her gender is used to magnify the "subhumanness" as I will demonstrate later. Having labeled the portrayal as racist I will discuss the specificity of this in the Brazilian context mentioned above, and in particular look at the differences in image between Lispector's character in *Pequena Flor* and De Jesus's self-image as Black. I contend in opposition to

Lispector, De Jesus's text reflects a respectful image of Blackness that corroborates with her positive identification as woman.

Clarice Lispector rarely acknowledges race as an element of human experience, and race is almost never discussed by the literary critics who discuss her but she consistently expresses a female consciousness and this has been written about profusely[2]. However in **"A Menor Mulher do Mundo"** the central figure is an African whose race is referred to constantly throughout the story. Lispector's portrayal of this African woman is very different from the familiar Lispector female character. Her skin color is most often described in animal metaphors and her size is used to infantilize and primitivize her personality. Given the universalist, existentialist character of Lispector's prose, one must ask how we are to read this description of race, as well as how one might interpret the absence of any multiracial focus in most of her other works. Using for comparison the Afra-Brazilian writer Carolina Maria de Jesus in her testimonio-like text *Quarto de Despejo* may help answer this question.

De Jesus presents her own life as an Afro-Brazilian woman and favela-dweller with acute and empowering political and personal insight developing a self-representation for Afro-Brazilian women that sharply contrasts with Lispector's portrayal of the African woman in **"A Menor Mulher do Mundo"**, the Afro-Brazilian women who appear as domestic servants in other Lispector texts, and middle class white women who are the universalized protaganists in most of Lispector's writing. De Jesus speaks from a position of powerlessness. As a victim of race, class and gender oppression, her voice defies and subverts her oppressors.

The political importance of Carolina's work is foregrounded by the form—"Testimonio represents an affirmation of the individual subject, even of individual growth and transformation, but in connection with a group or class situation marked by marginalization, oppression, and struggle" (Beverley 23) but also by the content. The clarity with which de Jesus portrays her feelings about herself as black and as woman (especially in terms of "in relationship to men") makes her self-image a powerful construction and her identity as group member 'idealized'. However I do not read that idealization to be self aggrandizing, but rather a sincere belief system from which she seems to act with conscientious consistence. This belief system sets her apart from most of the *faveladas,* from most women and from the "João da Cruz e Souzas" not to mention the 'nonblack' whitening mainsteam literary tradition in Brazil to which Lispector belongs.

In discussing the English translation of **Laços de Família, Family Ties,** Ana Sisnett identifies **"The Smallest Woman in the World"** as "racially charged" (6). She states, "Here, Lispector as author, is in an ambiguous position as critic/accomplice of racist ideology that holds Africa to be the land of cannibals and pygmies, the reserve of primitive freedom from the ills of Western society—"the end of the line" (989) (6). However Sisnett points out that "the story's fable tone ironically speaks more directly to the history of slavery and exploitation of Africa . . ." (8).

A close reading of the original Portuguese text reveals similar conclusions; I found nothing to suggest that Lispector is consciously "criticizing" the racist ideology expressed in her descriptive rhetoric though at points I find her descriptions to be sardonic if not ironic. Although, as Sisnett points out, *explorador* means either "explorer" or "exploiter" (7), that double meaning is hardly a precise choice by Lispector—were we to assume that Lispector is using the "informed" second meaning we would have to assume the same of colonial Portuguese travel narratives. The colonial relationship is set up in the second paragraph of the story when Marcel Pretre the *explorador* "descobriu realmente os menores pigmeus do mundo" and among them ("como uma caixa dentro de uma caixa, dentro de uma caixa") "o menor dos menores pigmeus do mundo," (77).

The following paragraph identifies "o menor dos menores pigmeus do mundo" as a woman who is "Escura como um macaco" (77). The choice of metaphor seems unlikely: one does not think of monkeys as particularly dark animals. Knowing Lispector's use of color and animalesque characteristics one can nonetheless only respond viscerally (as I think is intended) with the almost macabre disgust, "sweet nausea" the combination of horror and fascination at the portrayal of African woman as monkey. The artfullness of the image only exacerbates its awfulness. Additionally, the setting is painted as sublime and hellish—the quintessential 'orientalism' that Edward Said has identified—transported to African jungle. For instance: "Entre mosquitos e árvores mornas de umidade, entre as folhas ricas do verde mais preguiçoso . . ." (77) and in this setting of

> "no zumbido do calor, foi como se o francês tivesse inesperadamente chegado à conclusão última. Na certa, apenas por não ser louco, é que sua alma não desvairou nem perdeu os limites. Sentindo necessidade imediata de ordem, e de dar nome ao que existe, apelidou-a de Pequena Flor. E, para conseguir classificá-la entre as realidades reconhecíveis, logo passou a colher dados a seu respeito.

> (78)

I assume reading this passage selectively that Lispector is being ironic—the sarcasm against the anal-retentive Frenchman is far too strong—however, the next few sentences suggest that if this is a critique of the European it does not extend very deep. Next comes,

Sua raça de gente está aos poucos sendo exterminada. Poucos exemplares humanos restam dessa espécie que, não fosse o sonso perigo da África, seria povo alastrado. Fora doença, infectado hálito de águas, comida deficiente e feras rondantes, o grande risco para os escassos likoualas está nos selvafens bantos, ameaça que os rodeia em ar silencioso como em madrugada de batalha.

(78)

Are we to assume that genocide is a completely "natural" phenomenon according to Lispector? Disease, pollution and lack of resources are not, Lispector would have us believe, caused by humans but exist apart from them and the only human threat is other Africans who are of course *selvafens*. And in this African 'history lesson' the Pygmies are once again compared to monkeys, this time as prey. "Os bantos os caçam em rêdes, como fazem com os macacos" (78). One begins to wonder by the end of the paragraph whether the only thing "human" about these people is the "division of labor" (cynicism intended): "De onde as mulheres descem para cozinhar milho, moer mandioca e colher verduras; os homens, para caçar" (78). Not surprisingly we learn that their language consists of "gestos e sons animais" (79).

When the explorer discovers the smallest woman the reader again experiences the jolt from satire to decorative repulsion.

"Foi então que o explorador disse tìmidamente e com uma delicadeza de sentimentos de que sua esposa jamais o julgaria capaz:—Você é Pequena Flor. Nesse instante Pequena Flor coçou-se onde uma pessoa não se coça. O explorador—como se êstivesse recebendo o mais alto prêmio de castidade a que um homem ousa aspirar—sembre tão idealista, o explorador tão vivido, desviou os olhos.

(79)

The pattern repeats: Lispector follows a telling comment on European male-female relations—the comment on the lack of male intimacy with his wife played out on another woman—by a comment about the African woman that subverts her to animal or infant.

The next section of the story tells of the Brazilian response to the newspaper article where "A fotografia de Pequena Flor foi publicada no suplemento colorido dos jornais de domingo, onde coube em tamanho natural" (79). Here Lispector writes from a more familiar context and her writing is more layered with meaning and less cliche. Here also the African woman becomes almost completely objectified, in terms of both her race and gender. With the shift from jungle to urban Brazil Pequena Flor's animal image changes from monkey to dog. "O nariz chato, a cara preta, os olhos fundos, os pés espalmados. Parecia um cachorro" (80).

It is mainly women who respond to the newspaper's photojournalism and their responses vary from distress to a "perversa ternura" that could be read as a homophobic description of a perverse lesbian attraction/repulsion. Looking in a mirror with the picture one woman sees "a distância insuperavel de milênios" (insert again Sisnett's claim that Lispector makes the African "primitive"). Children also respond—a little girl is frightened and a little boy wants to use Pequena Flor to play a practical joke on his brother. A bride-to-be responds with compassion; one can read an empathy in the girl for Pequena Flor's expectancy, however the mother dispells it with her comment—"mas é tristeza de bicho, não a tristeza humana" (81). It is in very gender specific stereotypes that Lispector gets the strength of her images. For the Brazilians there is no racial differentialization discussed, and thus no stereotyping going on in this story, and most of the gender references seem either ironic or questionably harmless rather than violent or macabre[3]. In comparison the images used for the African woman seem less insightful and more ignorant. The exception to this and the strangest part of this section of the story is the cook's story of living in an orphanage.

lembrou-se do que uma cozinheira lhe contrara do tempo de orfanato. Não tendo boneca com que brincar, e a maternidade já pulsando terrível no coração das órfãs, as meninas sabidas haviam escondido da freira a morte de uma das garotas. Guardaram o cadáver num armário até a freira sair, e brincaram com a menina morta, deram-lhe banhos e comidinhas, puseramna de castigo somente para depois poder beijá-la, consolando-a.

(81)

That this story was told by the cook seems revealing—like the "savage" Africans the lower class are further down on a spectrum that extends to the smallest and the darkest, and the most female (i.e. pregnant) Pequena Flor.

The description of the child's corpse is comparable to de Jesus's description of a starving boy who dies from eating meat that is so old it is poison:

No outro dia encontraram o pretinho morto. Os dedos do seu pé abriram. O espaço era de vinte centimetros. Ele aumentou-se como se fosse de borracha. Os dedos do pé parecia leque. Não trazia documentos. Foi sepultado como um Zé qualquer. Ninguém procurou saber seu nome. Marginal não tem nome.

(41)

While both texts discuss disenfranchised Brazilian children de Jesus' description is filled with a rage charged by recognition of the injustice that causes the child's awful death, injustice that is as horrific as his death. The juxtaposition of de Jesus' following sentence emphasizes this and historicizes the situation: ". . . De quatro em quatro anos muda-se os políticos e não soluciona a fome, que tem a sua matriz nas favelas e as sucursaes nos lares dos operários" (41). Lispector presents the orphan's corpse for quite different effect—to draw an analogy with the African woman's body. In the parallel both groups are marginalized and presented as "subhuman" and no historicization occurs.

Lispector returns us to África for a last look at "a própria coisa rara" (83). She is experiencing simple emotions in her heart "quem sabe se negro também, pois numa Natureza que errou uma vez já não se pode mais confiar—". She is smiling at not having been eaten and of course her smile too is a "riso bestial". (84) Lispector then attributes love to the "própria coisa rara" as she is called through much of this section. However her love is one that cannot distinguish between the *explorador* and "o anel [e] . . . a bota do exporador" (85). Thus Pequena Flor's emotions too are infantalized.

The explorer meanwhile is asking questions and taking notes which is how he keeps himself in control—more commentary on the neurotic orderly European.

There is a consistent pattern in this story—the commentary on the Euro-Brazilians and the French explorer is informed by history and experience while the commentary on the Africans is based on ignorance and racist stereotyping. Though perhaps not consciously so, Lispector's vision is racist through a lack of history and her gender portrayals are informed by critical social/feminist commentary only when they focus on Euro-Brazilian middle class women. With de Jesus the patterns are very different but some episodes and discussions are comparable.

Carolina Maria de Jesus' self-representation as Black is consistant, emphasied by repetition, and straightforward. For instance the passage of 16 de junho:

> . . . Eu escrevia peças e apresentava aos diretores de circos. Eles respondiam-me:
>
> —É pena voce ser preta.
>
> Esquecendo êles que eu adoro a minha pele negra, e o meu cabelo rústico. Eu até acho o cabelo do negro mais educado do que o cabelo de branco. Porque o cabelo de preto onde põe, fica. É obediente. E o cabelo de branco, é só dar um movimento na cabeça êle já sai do lugar. É indisciplinado. Se é que existe reincarnações, eu quero voltar sempre preta.
>
> (65)

Carolina responds to a backhanded compliment, not by challenging its racist implications but by taking the stage with a challenge to the very basis of racism. She continues her monologue, carrying the argument back to humanity's origins.

> . . . Um dia, um branco disse-me:
>
> —Se os pretos tivessem chegado ao mundo depois dos brancos, aí os brancos podiam protestar com razão. Mas, nem o branco nem o preto conhece a sua origem.
>
> O branco é que diz que é superior. Mas que superioridade apresenta o branco? Se o negro bebe pinga, o branco bebe. A enfermidade que atinge o preto, atinge o branco. Se o branco sente fome, o negro também. A natureza não seleciona ninguém.
>
> (65)

Later in the text Carolina discusses race with global awareness and cross-cultural analysis.

> 20 de setembro . . . Fui no empório, levei 44 cruzeiros. Comprei um quilo de açúcar, um de feijão e dois ovos. Sobrou dois cruzeiros. Uma senhora que fez compra gastou 43 cruzeiros. E o senhor Eduardo disse:
>
> —Nos gastos quase que vocês empataram. Eu disse:
>
> —Ela é branca. Tem direito de gastar mais. Ela disse-me—A côr não influi.
>
> Então começamos a falar sobre o preconceito. Ela disse-me que nos Estados Unidos êles não querem negros nas escolas.
>
> Fico pensando: os norte-americanos são considerados os mais civilisados do mundo e ainda não conveceram que preterir o preto é o mesmo que preterir o sol. O homem não pode lutar com os produtos da Natureza. Deus criou todas as raças na mesma época. Se criasse os negros depois dos brancos, aí os brancos podia revoltarse.
>
> (119)

Carolina's discussion of her race at times reflects her wry humor as well as her self respect. For example: "Enfim, o mundo é como o branco quer. Eu não sou branca, não tenho nada com estas desorganizações" (70).

Carolina celebrates her identity as an Afro-Brazilian by observing important dates in Afro-Brazilian history:

> 13 de maio Hoje amanheceu chovendo. É um dia simpático para mim. É o dia da Abolição. Dia que comemoramos a libertação dos escravos.
>
> . . . Nas prisões os negros eram os bodes espiatórios. Mas os brancos agora são mais cultos. E não nos trata com desprêso. Que Deus ilumine os brancos para que os pretos sejam felizes.
>
> (32)

While she actively identifies with her race in her celebration of holidays such as the anniversary of the Brazilian abolition of slavery, her awareness of the power differentials between races, and her own affirmative self-perception as black, she also relates incidents in which she sees herself as different from most Blacks.

She parallels this distinction with her pride in being a woman and her disassociation with most other women, particularly those in the favela.

In discussing the role of Carolina's text as *testimonio,* I pointed out that through the form as well as the content the text is constructively politicized. Although I would not suggest that Lispector's short story form is inherently less politically constructed, I would suggest that the way Lispector uses the structure 'depoliticizes' it in a certain sense and 'repoliticizes' it in another sense. In other words, while she does not overtly express opinions about race or gender in the straightforward way that Carolina does, the ambiguity of her language allows for less controlled messages. Earl Fitz is, I believe, correct in his assessment of Lispector's texts as prime targets for the methodology of deconstruction. By deconstructing her cryptic codes and phrases, one can identify very consistent themes in her work. In **"A Menor Mulher do Mundo"** that theme represents the racism that is identified by many Afro-Brazilians.

While Carolina Maria de Jesus does not indicate that her reading includes writers such as Abdias de Nascimento, who focuses his writing, artwork and religious belief system on understanding and fighting against racism in Brazil, and while her writing may not be as deliberate as his, it reflects an Afro-Brazilian woman who is self-aware, and experientially aware of the conjuncts of suffering where Afro-Brazilian women are discriminated against in triple.

Wilfred Cartey describes the worlds of four Black writers in his article "I've Been Reading The Realities of Four Negro Writers": "Their outer realities, the face of the world on which they find themselves, are often painted by the heroes of these stories in hues that are dark indeed. The present is pain and the future is menacing" (34). He later observes that "From time to time Carolina's diary had entries on rainy days, and these are recurrent heavy choruses of despair . . ." (36). It is the experience of the emotions and events that informs Carolina's text and allows it to speak so consistently and convincingly. In **"A Menor Mulher do Mundo"** Clarice Lispector does not have the advantage of experience and it is most blatantly demonstrated in her depiction of African people. She all but ignores the fact that Brazil is a multiracial culture and focuses her description of "the other" in terms of race in a foreign land. Thus Afro-Brazilians like Carolina Maria de Jesus have no place in her texts[4].

De Jesus in her diary identified the world she also lived—a world where she suffered from racism, sexism and injustice. Clarice Lispector describes the world she saw infused with worlds she imagined—these too were heavy laden with oppression for women, but these women are not of the diversity the real world offers.

Clarice Lispector and Caroline Maria de Jesus not only offer different perspectives on race but through those differences they complicate our understandings of gender relations, class relations, and "politics". I end my comparisons with the last lines of their respective texts.

—Pois olhe—declarou de repente uma velha fechando o jornal com decisao—, pois olhe, eu só lhe digo uma coisa: Deus sabe o que faz.

(86)

1 de janeiro de 1960 Levantei as 5 horas e fui carregar água.

(182)

### Notes

1. Soon after publication *Quarto de Despejo* was printed in 22 different countries and Carolina got fan mail from such diverse sources as Fidel Castro in Cuba and impressed readers in Tibet. (Ebony 102) A record 10,000 copies were sold the first week in Brazil so two subsequent printings were planned immediately: this 80,000 copies equalled the number of copies of *Lolita* sold in the first month two years previously in the U.S. (*Time* 43) *Diciñario literario brasiliero* (1978) records over 100,000 copies following the initial three printings and translation into 29 languages. (337) *Nós Mulheres* cites 40 countries distributing it in 1977.

2. Even Earl Fitz in discussing Clarice Lispector in the "post modern" terminology of deconstruction does not examine race as a signifier in her work. One feminist critic reportedly mentions the disturbing nature of the racial portrayal in "A Menor Mulher Do Mundo" (Sisnett discussion) but the reference was not found.

3. I have chosen not to create a feminist bibliography on Lispector in the interest of balance in this paper and because I wish to foreground the issue of race, and record gender protrayal primarily as crosshatching of characterization/personality that complicates and compliments the race portrayal.

4. Lispector writes about Africans extensively in the travel accounts of a trip with her husband to África. These nonfiction accounts, published originally in *Journal do Brasil,* reflect the same kind of racial imperialism found in her fiction. (Sisnett) A subsequent comparative study of the portrayals of race in her fiction and nonfiction would be highly informative.

### Works Cited

Audalio. "A Favela Para O Mundo das Letras" *O Cruzeiro* 10 Sept. 1960: 149-50 152.

Bernd, Zila. *Introdução A Literatura Negra* São Paulo: editora brasiliense, 1988.

"Better to be Poor" *Ebony* Dec. 1966: 100-4.

Beverley, John. "The Margin at the Center: On Testi-monio (Testimonial Narrative)" *Modern Fiction Studies* 55, no. 1. Spring 1989.

Branco, Lúcia Catello and Ruth Silviano Brandão. *A Mulher Escrita* Rio de Janeiro: Casa-Maria Editorial—Milmam Edições Ltda., 1989.

Camargo, Oswaldo de. *O Negro Escrito: Apontamentos sobre a presença do negro na Literatura Brasileira.* Governo Quercia, 1987.

Cartey, Wiliam. "I've Been Reading The Realities of Four Negro Writers" *Columbia University Forum IX* iii summer 1966. 34-42.

Chaui, Marilena. "Nós, negros e mulatos" *Folha de São Paulo* 12/30/85.

Fontaine, Pierre-Michel. ed. *Race Class and Power in Brazil.* Los Angeles: Center for Afro-American Studies, 1985.

Freyre, Gilberto. *The Masters and the Slaves A Study in the Development of Brazilian Civilization.* Trans. Samuel Putnam. New York: Alfred A. Knopf, 1964.

Haberly, David T. *Three Sad Races Racial identity and national consciousness in Brazilian literature.* Cambridge: Cambridge University Press, 1983.

Jesus, Carolina Maria de. *La Favela.* La Habana: Casa de las Americas, 1965.

Jesus, Carolina Maria de. *Quarto de Despejo diario de uma favelada.* Sao Paulo: Livraria Francisco Alves, 1960.

"Life in a Garbage Room" *Time* Sept. 26, 1960: 43.

Lispector, Clarice. *Laços de Família* Brasil: Ficha Catalográfica, 1960.

"Memórias de Carolina de Jesus," *Nós Mulheres* No. 4 Mar/Apr., 1977.

Menezes, Raimundo. *Dicionário literário brasileiro.* 2nd ed. RJ: LTC Livros Técnicos e cientícos editora S.A.: 1978.

Monk, Abraham. *Black and White Race Relations in Brazil.* Buffalo N.Y.: Special Studies Council on International Studies State Univ. of New York at Buffalo, 1971.

Nascimento Abdias Do. *"Racial Democracy" in Brazil: Myth or Reality? (a dossier of Brazilian Racism).* Ibadan: Sketch Publ. Co. Ltd., 1977.

Sisnett, Ana. discussion April 26, 1991.

———. "Carolina Maria de Jesus" paper presented at the National Women's Studies Assoc. Conference, June 1987 Atlanta, Ga.

———. "Family Ties" unpublished review.

Spacks, Patricia Meyer. "Reflecting Women" *The Yale Review* Autumn 1973, 27-42.

## Marta Peixoto (essay date 1994)

SOURCE: Peixoto, Marta. "Female Power in *Family Ties.*" In *Passionate Fictions: Gender, Narrative, and Violence in Clarice Lispector,* pp. 24-38. Minneapolis: University of Minnesota Press, 1994.

[*In the following essay, Peixoto traces the nexus of gender and power in the story collection* Family Ties *and concludes that Little Flower's positive view of life in "Smallest Woman" is unique among the stories' protagonists.*]

In **"The Daydreams of a Drunk Woman,"** the opening story of *Laços de família* (1960; *Family Ties*) the young protagonist arrives home completely drunk after an evening out with her husband. She feels her body grow enormously as surrounding objects turn into her own flesh:

> And, as she half closed her eyes, everything became flesh, the foot of the bed flesh, the window flesh, the suit her husband had thrown on the chair flesh, and everything almost hurt. And she became bigger and bigger, hesitant, swollen, gigantic.
>
> (*FT* [**Family Ties**] 34)[1]

Many of the stories in the collection focus on such moments of physical or psychological aberration. The female protagonists are drawn into states of expanded perception in which they lose their "every-day soul, and how satisfying to lose it" (*FT* 31), and thus gain a power—exhilarating, threatening, and at times grotesque—normally inaccessible to them. But like the shrinking of swollen tissues, the power—or, more precisely, the illusion of power—recedes and dissipates, and the protagonists complacently take up again their normal, undistinguished lives.[2]

*Family Ties* contains Lispector's most celebrated, studied, and anthologized short stories, and yet the collection is rarely read in its entirety as a set of interacting texts. The more comprehensive perspective, although necessarily sacrificing the detailed reading that these stories invite and reward, allows us to discern patterns of interaction between gender and power in Lispector, an underlying theme of the collection and a persistent issue in all of her texts. These stories were written over a period of roughly a decade. Six of the thirteen stories had been published in another, little-noticed volume in 1952.[3] By 1955, at least four more of the *Family Ties* stories were completed, as were another four that

Lispector would include in a later collection, *The Foreign Legion* (1964).[4] *Family Ties* is not, then, a compilation of all the short narratives Lispector had written to date, but a selection of complementary texts. As one critic observes, "The threads of a very well woven net organize themselves in each story, threads that join with those of other stories, composing a web of meanings that never cease to refer to one another" (Santos 1990, 8). In this chapter I argue that gender and power form one such nexus, and I attempt to trace its variations in the interplay of texts within the collection.

Psychoanalysis tells us that the family assigns and enforces gender. Lispector's scrutiny of gender roles entails a critique of the family, where she places her characters and their intimate crises. Three of the thirteen stories have male protagonists: in these, gender and power are also at issue and always problematic. The men, observed in different stages of life, from adolescence to old age, uneasily measure their supposed prerogatives and assess the price of conforming to masculine roles. The female protagonists, mostly middle-class women in an urban setting, also range from youth to old age. The stories in which they appear can be read as versions of a single developmental tale that describes patterns of female possibilities, vulnerability, and power in Lispector's world; the smaller number of stories with male protagonists offer a counterpoint. Lispector assigns traditional female roles to her characters: adolescents confronting the fantasy or reality of sex, mature women relating to men and children, and a great-grandmother presiding over her birthday party. Through the plots and the descriptions of her heroines' inner conflicts, Lispector challenges conventional roles, showing that the allegiances to others demanded by those roles exact their toll from the women who occupy them. The protagonists' moments of access to forgotten ambitions and desires produce dissatisfaction, rage, or even madness. The stories present the dark side of family ties, where bonds of affection hurt and constrict; yet the institution of the family sustains the characters, who might rebel, but usually do not escape its grip.

All the stories in Lispector's collection turn on an epiphany, a moment of crucial revelation (Sant'Anna 1973, 198) when, in the midst of trivial events, or in response to a chance encounter, her characters suddenly become conscious of repressed desires or unsuspected dimensions of their psyches. Whereas the men come to terms with the implications of a socially defined masculinity, the women experience the reverse of their accepted roles as mother, daughter, wife, as gentle, pardoning, giving females. In their moments of changed awareness, they may realize not only their imprisonment, but also their function as jailers of women and men. The epiphanies, mysterious and transgressive, bring to consciousness repressed material with potentially subversive power. The negative terms that often describe these moments—"crisis," "nausea," "hell," "murder," "anger," "crime"—convey the guilt and fear that accompany the questioning of conventional roles for both men and women characters (Santa'Anna 1973, 199). Interior monologues shaped by antithesis, paradox, and hyperbole display a wealth of opposing moral and emotional forces that resist logical definition. The convulsions of language in Lispector function in a way similar to the melodramatic gestures and rhetoric Peter Brooks has found in the works of Balzac and Henry James, resembling what he terms "the violence and extremism of emotional reaction and moral implication" in their prose:

> The more elusive the tenor of the metaphor becomes, the more difficult it becomes to put one's finger on the nature of the spiritual reality alluded to—the more highly charged is the vehicle, the more strained with pressure to suggest a meaning beyond. . . . To the uncertainty of the tenor, corresponds the heightening of the vehicle.
>
> (Brooks 1985, 11)

In Lispector, the hyperactivity of language in moments of crisis dramatizes the force fields that move her characters' consciousness, without ever simplifying their dilemmas into unambiguously rational terms. After these crises, when the recognition of their restrictions gives the protagonists a glimpse of greater freedom, many pull back, returning to a confinement they cannot or will not change. The intensity of their conflicts may be enlightening for the reader, but the characters return to their previous situations, which they have questioned for only a moment.

Two of the three tales of adolescent initiation in *Family Ties* have women protagonists. In **"The Beginnings of a Fortune,"** a young boy suddenly fascinated with money grasps its connection with power and its usefulness in attracting girls. Yet he also sees that possession of "a fortune" would entail vulnerability to the greed of others. By the end of the story, he is, nevertheless, eager to continue acquiring money and financial information. The plots of the two stories with female protagonists, **"Preciousness"** and **"Mystery in São Cristóvão"** (see chapter 5 for further discussion), are parallel on a symbolic level: both hinge on the intrusion by several young men into a young woman's private domain. In **"Preciousness,"** an adolescent undergoes a violent sexual "initiation" when two young men, passing strangers, reach out and briefly touch her body. After the first shock, she accepts and turns to advantage this negative experience, darkly intuiting it as a lesson about her fragile individuality in a world of powerful men. **"Mystery in São Cristóvão"** reworks in parable form a similar version of female sexual initiation. Three young men trespass into "the forbidden ground of the garden" (*FT* 135) to steal hyacinths as a young girl watches from her window. The four participants share a mute epiphany; then, as the girl screams, the young men guiltily slip away, leaving behind a "hyacinth—still alive but with its stalk broken" (**FT** 138).

The male and female initiation tales offer, then, a number of contrasts: activity versus passivity; a young boy who seeks wealth and power versus young girls who are "precious" themselves, metaphorically identified with jewels and flowers; preoccupation with acquisition versus concern with self-protection; entrance into the world of economic and social exchange versus fearful retreat into oneself. Development, for the young girls, clearly will not proceed according to the male model.

It is in a context of attachment to and affiliation with others that the women characters develop. After being initiated into the vulnerability to which their female sexuality exposes them, they find protection and a measure of satisfaction in family ties. We see in other stories several of Lispector's women safely ensconced in a domestic life. The stories reflect the matrifocal organization of Brazilian society, where the extended family still prevails, so much so that the word *família usually refers not only to the small nuclear family, but also to a numerous network of relatives. The title story shows most clearly the ambivalent function of the family in the whole collection. In **Family Ties,** the power a woman wields within the family has a negative, constricting side: deprived of the chance to develop herself beyond the scope of the family, she attempts to control those close to her.*

**"Family Ties"** opens as Catherine says good-bye to her elderly mother at the train station, feeling an awkward tenderness and relief. With this scene between the two women, as well as with flashbacks and the narration of the emotional consequences of the mother's visit, the story touches on several types of family relationships: mother/daughter, mother-in-law/son-in-law, grandmother/grandson, husband/wife, and mother/son, all presented as subtle or not-so-subtle struggles for power. As Catherine looks at her mother through the train window, she becomes aware of the strong, but ambivalent, bonds they share:

> "No one else can love you except me," thought the woman, smiling with her eyes, and the weight of this responsibility put the taste of blood in her mouth. As if "mother and daughter" meant life and repugnance.
>
> (**FT** 117)

Relieved of her mother's company, the daughter recovered her "steady manner of walking—alone, it was much easier" (**FT** 119). However, that tie to her mother also facilitates an emotional availability: "She seemed ready to take advantage of the largesse of the whole

world—a path her mother had opened and that was burning in her breast" (**FT** 120). This very openness to others leads Catherine, it seems, to attempt to bind her son to her in the same way she was bound to her mother. The last third of the story is told from her husband's point of view. Excluded and jealous, he watches Catherine and their small son from a window, perceiving their intense interaction:

> At what moment is it that a mother, hugging her child, gives him this prison of love that would descend forever upon the future man. Later, her child, already a man, alone, would stand before this same window, drumming his fingers on the windowpane: imprisoned. . . . Who would ever know at what moment the mother transferred her inheritance to her child. And with what dark pleasure.
>
> (**FT** 122)

Here, the metaphorical prison entraps all members of the family: the father, who also speaks about his own predicament, sees the male as victim of the imprisoned and imprisoning female, the mother, who transmits this family tie to the next generation. The male power, deriving from his role in the world outside the home, does not prevail in the domestic world of intimate relationships, where his wife has a power at least equal to his own:

> He knew that if his wife took advantage of his situation as a young husband with a promising future, she also looked down on the situation, with those sly eyes, running off with her thin, nervous child. The man became uneasy. Because he could only go on giving her more success. And because he knew that she would help him to achieve it and would hate whatever they achieved.
>
> (**FT** 122)

Despite their dissatisfactions, it seems clear that at least the husband wishes to preserve the status quo. "'After dinner we'll go to the movies,' the man decided. Because after the movies it would be night at last, and this day would break up like the waves on the rocks of Arpoador" (**FT** 124). For the husband, the events of the day appear as minor, if recurrent, crises within the sustaining institution of the family.

The family as context for female development in Lispector's stories is, then, both positive and negative. Although it affords women the satisfaction of affirming ties to others, it also confines them to the subordinate role of ministering to others' needs and deprives them of an active agency in pursuing their private desires. The narrator of "Love" measures the rewards of a domestic life for the protagonist Anna, and hints at her sacrifices:

> Through indirect paths, she had happened upon a woman's destiny, with the surprise of fitting into it as if she had invented that destiny herself. The man whom she

had married was a real man, the children she mothered were real children. Her previous youth now seemed strange, like an illness of life. She had gradually emerged to discover that one could also live without happiness: by abolishing it she had found a legion of persons, previously invisible to her, who lived their lives as if they were working—with persistence, continuity, and cheerfulness.

(*FT* 38)

Several protagonists face their crises from a similar perspective. Women devoted to love, marriage, and children discover within themselves allegiances that subvert those roles. These stories follow the generic model that Susan J. Rosowski proposes in her article "The Novel of Awakening." Lispector's characters also attempt to find value "in a world that expects a woman to define herself by love, marriage, and motherhood" (Rosowski 1983, 68). For each protagonist, "an inner imaginative sense of personal value conflicts with her public role: an awakening occurs when she confronts the disparity between her two lives" (Rosowski 1983, 68). Lispector's protagonists also follow Rosowski's model in awakening to conflict and limitations. Their social world and their own conforming social selves cannot accommodate new allegiances. They discover that their loyalty to others has excluded possibilities for themselves. As Lispector puts it in a story from another collection, "To be loyal is not a clean thing. To be loyal is to be disloyal to everything else" (*FL* [*The Foreign Legion*], 53). Four stories from *Family Ties*—"Love," "The Imitation of the Rose," "The Buffalo," and "Happy Birthday"—are Lispector's versions of this kind of awakening.

In **"Love,"** Anna's everyday awareness of herself in her thriving domesticity is figured in images of prospering plants: "Like a farmer. She had planted the seeds she held in her hand, no others, but only those. And they were growing into trees" (*FT* 38). Although "at a certain hour of the afternoon the trees she had planted laughed at her" (*FT* 38), Anna feels steady in her chosen course until a casual encounter upsets her equilibrium. From a tram, she sees a blind man standing on the street, calmly chewing gum. His mechanical, indifferent acceptance of his fate perhaps mirrors for Anna her own blindness and restriction. The blind man is also a victim of the brutality of nature, which maims some of its creatures, a threat Anna usually forgets. When Anna continues her meditation in the botanical garden—a place that confines natural growth, forcing it to follow a prearranged plan—a nausea analogous to Sartre's *nausée* overtakes her: "a vague feeling of revulsion which the approach of truth provoked" (*FT* 44). The initial tranquility she perceives in this enclosed garden gives way to a disquieting vision of a secret activity taking place in the plants, as decay encroaches upon ripeness:

On the trees the fruits were black and sweet as honey. On the ground there lay dry fruit stones full of circumvolutions like small rotted cerebrums. The bench was stained purple with sap. . . . The rawness of the world was peaceful. The murder was deep. And death was not what one had imagined.

(*FT* 43)

The lesson she learns in the garden unsettles Anna's sureness about her immanent family world, about the seeds she planted that are growing into trees. At home, guilt-ridden for her transgressive thoughts, Anna feels both threatened and dangerous: "The slightest movement on her part and she would trample one of her children" (*FT* 47). In her final ruminations on the afternoon, Anna sees the blind man, "hanging among the fruits in the botanical garden" (*FT* 47). The blind man, as Anna's double, provides a frightening vision of her own destiny: death among the rotting fruit as a consequence of her stunted capacity for transcendence and lack of personal freedom in the life she has chosen. Yet, after a reassuringly ordinary evening at home, Anna seems content to forget her disturbing afternoon: "As if she were snuffing out a candle, she blew out the day's small flame" (*FT* 48), the light of her confused enlightenment, which could threaten her domestic life if it were allowed to burn.

**"The Imitation of the Rose"** contains a similar configuration of opposing forces: a familiar, domestic world threatened and undermined by the laws of another realm. For Laura, who has just returned from a mental hospital, images of light represent her powerful attraction to madness, suggesting that in madness she finds insights otherwise unavailable to her. Laura's dutiful relief at being "well" again, her drab descriptions of herself and her activities, contrast with her luminous, lively account of her mad self. Sleepiness, fatigue, obsession with method, cleanliness, and detail, a certain slowness of body and mind that bores others as well as herself— all these signal that Laura is "well." An alert wakefulness, clarity of mind, a sense of independence, of possessing extraordinary powers, accompany her returning madness.

In the encounter that sets off the struggle between sanity and madness, Laura admires the wild roses in her living room. The conflict between the impulse to send the roses to a friend and the desire to keep them for herself reflects Laura's lifelong struggle between accommodation to the wishes of others and assertion of her own subjectivity. She can only satisfy herself and what she perceives as society's demands by an exaggerated rendition of the role of a giving, submissive woman. The roses, in their beauty, exemplify a distinct, glorious self-sufficiency that Laura denies herself: "Something nice was either for giving or receiving, not only for possessing. And, above all, never for one to *be*. . . . A lovely thing lacked the gesture of giving" (*FT* 66). Yet as soon as Laura decides to give away the roses, her madness begins to return: "With parched lips she tried for an instant to imitate the roses inside herself. It was not even difficult" (*FT* 68-69). Tranquillity, self-sufficiency, and clarity signal Laura's changed state; she sits "with the serenity of the firefly that has its light" (*FT* 71). The story ends with the husband's view of Laura, whom he watches with a fear and respect that only her madness can elicit: "From the open door he saw his wife sitting upright on the couch, once more alert and tranquil as if on a train. A train that had already departed" (*FT* 72). This final image implies that only in madness can Laura assert her independence from the desires of others. She departs in the metaphorical train of madness, since other departures are beyond her capacity.

The role of woman in love limits severely the protagonist of "**The Buffalo,**" who only senses her deficiencies when her husband or lover abandons her, depriving her of support. Feeling mutilated and incomplete, she visits a zoo in a conscious search:

> But where, where could she find the animal that might teach her to have her own hatred? That hatred which belonged to her by right but which she could not attain in grief? . . . To imagine that perhaps she would never experience the hatred her forgiving had always been made of.
>
> (*FT* 152-53)

She senses that she is the one who is caged, "a female in captivity" (*FT* 153), while a free animal watches her from the other side. A visual confrontation with the buffalo—similar to Anna's with the blind man and Laura's with the roses, except that the buffalo returns her stare—allows her access to a wide and dangerous world, where she might free herself from her own compulsion to love and pardon. She looks to the buffalo, with its narrow haunches and hard muscles, as a masculine presence, the embodiment of her hatred and her strength "still imprisoned behind bars" (*FT* 155-56). She becomes terrified by the hatred that she projects onto the animal and that he in turn releases in her. As their encounter continues, it is couched in terms of a deadly struggle:

> Innocent, curious, entering deeper and deeper into those eyes that stared at her slowly, . . . without wanting or being able to escape, she was caught in a mutual murder. Caught as if her hand were stuck forever to the dagger she herself had thrust.
>
> (*FT* 156)

Perhaps not ready to allow herself to hate, the woman faints in the final scene: "Before her body thudded gently on the ground, the woman saw the whole sky and a buffalo" (*FT* 156). Fainting signals, no doubt, her failure of nerve: a traditionally feminine strategy of withdrawal, it obliterates from consciousness her involvement and insights. Yet the image of the open spaces of the sky, ambiguous as it is becomes in conjunction with the fainting, seems to offer, in a story cluttered with cages, the possibility of release.

The moments of insight mostly visited upon young and middle-aged protagonists are, in "**Happy Birthday,**" briefly available to an old woman celebrating her eighty-ninth birthday. She belatedly rejects her family, implicitly questioning her own role as a prototypical matriarch. Her power and the bonds of love have already been eroded, and her family gathers to mimic the appearance of closeness. The narrative method—a mosaic of interior monologues interspersed with dialogues and the narrator's remote, at times ironic, commentary—shows the resentment and hostility between members of the family and presents the protagonist as others see her as well as how she sees herself. In a Kafkaesque progression reminiscent of "The Judgment," the old woman at first appears decrepit and later demonstrates a surprising, malevolent vigor.

As the story opens, she is propped up, ready for the party: "There she was, stationed at the head of the table—an imposing old woman, large, gaunt, and dark. She looked hollow" (*FT* 75). She remains aloof and passive until urged to cut the cake: "And unexpectedly, the old lady grabbed the knife. And without hesitation, as if by hesitating for a second she might fall on her face, she dealt the first stroke with the grip of a murderess" (*FT* 78). Cutting the cake rouses the old woman from passivity; she goes on to shatter her image as dignified and respected mother. The metaphorical association of cutting/killing continues, linking the birthday gestures with those of a funeral: "The first cut having been made, as if the first shovel of earth had been thrown . . ." (*FT* 78). As the matriarch surveys her family "with her old woman's rage" (*FT* 80), Lispector resorts again to the recurring images of female imprisonment and powerlessness:

> She was the mother of them all. And, as her collar was choking her, she was the mother of them all, and powerless in her chair, she despised them. She looked at them, blinking. . . . How could she, who had been so strong, have given birth to those drab creatures with their limp arms and anxious faces? . . . The tree had been good. Yet it had rendered those bitter and unhappy fruits.
>
> (*FT* 79-80)

As her scorn and anger mount, the old woman curses, spits on the floor, and demands a glass of wine. The imagery and elements of the plot, with their origins in primitive and contemporary ritual—birthday party, funeral, spitting, cursing, wine—assimilate the old woman's revolt into the very institutions she challenges, suggesting that her anger and its ritualistic expression can be encompassed within their framework.

The old woman rails against her loss of power; in a sense she is a victim of old age. Her dominance stemmed from her personal capacity to play the most powerful role traditional Brazilian society allowed women: that of mother in a mother-dominated extended family. Her ability to command attention is eerily revived when she cuts the cake, spits, and curses. These actions serve as a crude demonstration of the willfulness that, in her prime, she would have manifested in more subtle and socially sanctioned ways. Yet this old woman, like Lispector's other protagonists, is also ultimately a victim of her social role. Her power issued from a control of others that is neither healthy nor enduring. One of her sons, observing that "she had not forgotten that same steady and direct gaze with which she had always looked at her . . . children, forcing them to look away," thinks that "a mother's love was difficult to bear" (*FT* 85). Because she cannot rule their lives she despises her children. By showing the lovelessness and will to power of this mother's love, Lispector suggests that the role of matriarch affords a false power that entraps women as well as their families.

After the old woman's outburst, the narrative method returns to external presentation. She relapses into an enigmatic passivity, clutching the ghost of her power: "Seated at the head of that messy table, with one hand clenched on the tablecloth as if holding a scepter, and with that silence which was her final word . . ." (*FT* 83). Like so many of Lispector's female protagonists, after a brief influx of power, she returns finally to her initial situation. As they move from youth to old age, the protagonists of *Family Ties* also trace a circular path, beginning and ending in passivity—from the withdrawal of a frightened young girl to the abstraction of an old woman whose power over her family, repressive in itself, is spent.

Through the plots and interior monologues of her characters, Lispector questions, as we have seen, the conventional roles she assigns to her protagonists. The tendency to subvert stereotypes in characters and plot recurs on the level of language. Lispector destroys and recreates the meanings of certain ordinary words, redefining them through paradoxical formulations. In **"Love,"** the title word acquires multiple and contradictory meanings as the protagonist attempts to align her confused yearnings with the *eros* and *caritas* she had always believed gave direction to her life. In **"The Imitation of the Rose,"** madness takes on a positive value, signifying the expansion of Laura's independence and

self-esteem—at the end of the story Laura is "serene and in full bloom" (*FT* 71)—without, of course, losing its acceptation of illness, the delusion of power. Anger in **"The Buffalo"** becomes the elusive object of a quest, whereas pardon is defined as covert hatred. A reversal of values also occurs in the imagery: the thriving plants, metaphorical analogues of Anna's domesticity, reappear on the literal level as the lush and rotting vegetation in the botanical garden; the birthday party is described in terms of a funeral; family ties appear as chains and cages. The tendency to redefine words and concepts, to reverse traditional metaphorical associations or to draw images from negative and antithetical realms supports and furthers Lispector's questioning of "a woman's destiny."

Lispector's protagonists, as they shift from one set of specific circumstances to another, repeatedly find themselves entrapped by their eager compliance with confining social roles. Their potential development—the ability to move toward the greater autonomy they desire in their moments of insight—again and again falters and stops short. For the youngest protagonists, the prison is their own fearful passivity in a society that accepts as normal the intrusions by men such as the ones they experience. Anna's attachment to domestic routines blocks her from participating in a wider social and moral world, which both frightens and exhilarates her, and whose outlines she only obscurely intuits. For Laura, living according to others' expectations and suppressing her own desires leads to madness, an illusory escape into another prison. The woman in **"The Buffalo"** is caged by her inability to recover emotions she had long repressed, and in **"Happy Birthday"** and **"Family Ties,"** mother-love itself imprisons. These women start out and remain in spiritual isolation. Locked in desired, yet limiting, relationships with husbands and children, they find no allies in other women—mothers, friends, or daughters—who if they appear at all are rivals and antagonists. Once the expansive insights of their epiphanic moments fade away, their only power lies in passing on an imprisoning motherly love to their children.

Two stories with adult male protagonists offer variants of the gender-linked crises of the women by probing the requirements of the masculine role. In **"The Crime of the Mathematics Teacher,"** the nameless protagonist, another of Lispector's *professores,* is defined by the clear thinking his profession demands: "There was no confusion in the man's mind. He understood himself with cold deliberation and without any loose threads" (*FT* 141). The narrator, however, makes much of his nearsightedness, of his putting on and removing his glasses, as if to imply that his lucidity is an obstacle to insight, just as the confusion of the female characters is a mode of understanding. The teacher attempts to expiate the crime of abandoning a dog whose love he was unable to reciprocate, and whose vulnerability tempted him to use it cruelly. "Each day you became a dog that could be abandoned," he thinks, addressing the absent dog. "One could choose. But you, trustfully, wagged your tail" (***FT*** 144). With questionable symmetry, the teacher atones for the abandonment by burying a substitute, a dead stray dog, in a private ritual. We now see, from the point of view of the perpetrator, the "crime" of betrayal, also committed by the man who abandoned the protagonist of **"The Buffalo"**: his "great unpunishable crime was not loving her" (***FT*** 156). The mathematics teacher reassures himself that "no one goes to hell for abandoning a dog that trusted in a man. For I knew that this crime was not punishable" (***FT*** 145).

In this story, the problem of being a man shades into the problem of being righteously human: because the teacher abuses his power he betrays his manhood. If, as one critic suggests, the dog symbolically represents a human partner in a love relationship (Santos 1986, 41), the teacher confronts from another perspective and with different results the issue that also troubles the women characters: how much caring does one owe to others and how much to oneself? The man discovers that his crime—"the debt that, disturbingly, no one required him to pay" (***FT*** 146)—is unpunishable, not only by society but also by himself. He compounds his initial betrayal with a further one. "And now, even more mathematical, he sought a way to eliminate that self-inflicted punishment" (***FT*** 146). He digs up the unknown dog, "[renewing] his crime forever. . . . And, as if that were still not enough, he began to descend the slopes, heading toward the intimacy of his family" (***FT*** 146). Being a man, in this story, necessarily entails not being enough of a man, with its requirements of living up to strict standards of virtue. Being man, however, also assures him of a power that not even his victim would question: "Powerful as I am, I need only choose to call you. Abandoned in the streets you would come leaping to lick my face with contentment and forgiveness" (***FT*** 146). The man's ritual, with its lucid but empty gestures that offer an illusion of symmetry and mathematical rigor, but in no way aid the victim of his crime, serves ultimately to reassert his right to infringe unchallenged the moral rules he himself would wish to uphold.

**"The Dinner,"** a story seldom discussed by critics,[5] also addresses the prerogatives and challenges of manhood. It is the only first-person narrative in ***Family Ties*** and, as such, presents a subject actually shaping a narrative, without a narrator's mediation. In a restaurant, a younger man watches with fascination and repulsion (emotions that converge readily in Lispector's fiction) a seemingly powerful old man who gulps down his red wine and red meat while fighting back tears. The plot consists exclusively of the young man's minute observations, supplemented by his own conjectures, of the grotesquely amplified movements of the old man, who eats his dinner and then leaves the restaurant.

Participating in a chain of voyeuristic acts, the reader witnesses the narrator's observation and private thoughts about the old man, who struggles with himself as he consumes his food, unaware of the sharp eyes that watch him. He resolutely takes nourishment, refusing to give way to a major grief, or so the narrator imagines, as he sees him falter and recover or wipe away tears. The young man sees him "as one of those elderly gentlemen who still command attention and power" (***FT*** 99), "still enormous and still capable of stabbing any one of us" (***FT*** 101), "the old child-eater." The strength of the patriarch derives from his single-minded use of others to increase his own power, a pursuit authorized by traditional gender roles and displayed in his greedy attack on the meat and wine. His command extends to his control of his emotions, in a spectacle that fascinates his observer. The narrator's reactions resemble those of the women characters in their epiphanic moments: "[The old man] expresses with gestures the most he can, but I, alas, fail to understand . . . I feel gripped by the heaving ecstasy of nausea. Everything seems to loom large and dangerous" (***FT*** 99-100). The narrator understands without understanding, as he witnesses a ruthless male power on the brink of collapse, the dark side of traditional masculinity, which in turn threatens his own sense of himself. "But I am still a man," he reassures himself in the final paragraph of the story, as he attempts to salvage his manhood from the spectacle he has just observed:

> When I have been betrayed or slaughtered, when someone has gone away forever, or I have lost the best of what I had left, or when I have learned that I am about to die—I do not eat. I have not yet attained this power, this edifice, this ruin. I push away my plate. I reject the meat and its blood.
>
> (***FT*** 101)

The power he has not yet attained, part and parcel of the role of "old patriarch," is a power he may not want, having witnessed—or imagined—the violence it requires.

Although in ***Family Ties*** Lispector focuses on the constraints of women caught in traditional roles, her dissection of gender does not result in simple feminist fables of powerless women preyed upon by ruthless men. The oppression is more subtle and far-reaching for both the men and the women who confront its impersonal injunctions. The Brazilian writer Rubem Braga comments, in a letter of March 4, 1957, in response to nine of Lispector's stories (judging by the date, several of the *Family Ties* stories would have been among them): "It's funny how you touch and enrich me at the same time that you hurt me a little, making me feel less solid and secure" (Clarice Lispector Archive). At least part of this discomfiture results, I would suggest, from Lispector's challenges to the fixities of gender roles.

In most of the stories, an unobtrusive narrator provides the gaze that frames the characters. Their struggles are observed with an ambivalent, ironic eye that alternately exalts and puts them down, oscillating between sympathy and disdain. These oscillations are particularly marked in the stories that transpose to a parodic register Lispector's scrutiny of female power. In **"A Chicken,"** a story that repeats the plot of failed escape from the confining roles of nurturing and submission, the limitations of the female role take on the sharpness of caricature. The protagonist, a chicken about to be killed for Sunday dinner, escapes her fate by setting off on a mad flight across the rooftops. Pursued and brought back by the man of the house, the flustered chicken lays an egg. The little girl who witnesses this surprising outcome persuades her mother to spare the chicken's life and adopts her as a pet. She seems to intuit a similarity between the chicken's predicament and the possibilities her own future may hold.

Another girl has the same understanding of chickens in a story from a different collection, which begins: "Once upon a time there was a little girl who observed chickens so closely that she knew their soul and their intimate desires" (Lispector 1971, 140). Gender determines the meaning of the chicken's adventure. During her escape the chicken is described as "stupid, timid, and free. Not victorious as a cock would be in flight" (*FT* 50). In her attempt to cast off the passivity expected of her and to assert her independence, the chicken echoes the central action of several other stories. Acquiring a "family tie" ends the chicken's adventure. It literally saves her life, but it does not provide her with enduring dignity or even safety. Her reprieve lasts many years, but not forever: "Until one day they killed her and ate her, and the years rolled on" (*FT* 52). Like the women she represents, the chicken's dilemma takes the form of an opposition between independence and nurturing: women may choose one role but not both, and Lispector's women end up settling for the nurturing role. Occasionally she recalls her "great escape":

> Once in a while, but ever more infrequently, she again remembered how she had stood out against the sky on the roof edge ready to cry out. At such moments, she filled her lungs with the stuffy air of the kitchen and, had females been given the power to crow, she would not have crowed but would have felt much happier.
>
> (*FT* 52)

Ellen Moers comments on women authors' use of birds "to stand in, metaphorically, for their own sex" (Moers 1976, 245). The chicken in this and later stories is Lispector's comically distorted image of the selfless, nurturing female incapable of sustained self-determination. The perspective implicit in this choice of metaphor, and in the abrupt shifts in tone from sentimentality to a blunt deflation, includes compassion, but also condescension, an attitude that carries over to Lispector's presentation of women in other stories of *Family Ties.* Most of the stories end with the female protagonists silent and described from an external vantage point, perhaps another sign of the author's desire to distance herself from her characters. In contrast to Lispector's first novel, where Joana boldly disdains the constrictions of feminine roles, in these short stories Lispector shows in excruciating detail protagonists bound in "women's destinies" and measures the extent of their disadvantage. It is tempting to suppose that these stories may have functioned for her as a kind of exorcism. Through this repeated exercise, Lispector could perhaps free herself—and her future women characters—for richer, more varied roles. Indeed, Lispector's imagination seems to require repeated incursions into the same themes. As one of her narrators states, "How many times will I have to live the same things in different situations?" (quoted in Hill 1976, 141). Lispector allows her later female protagonists greater independence and engages them in spiritual quests that are not invariably cut short by a return to confining domesticity.

The predominantly bleak view of female possibilities in *Family Ties* contains a curious exception, represented by the grotesque, almost fantastic protagonist of **"The Smallest Woman in the World."** This story elaborates on a supposedly documentary anecdote: a bewildered explorer meets the smallest member of the smallest tribe of African pygmies—a tiny pregnant woman, measuring a foot and a half—and names her Little Flower. Readers of the Sunday newspaper react to her story and see her life-size picture. With disconcerting shifts in tone, the little woman is alternately presented as subhuman ("as black as a monkey" [*FT* 89]; "she looked just like a dog" [*FT* 90]); and exquisitely suprahuman ("For surely no emerald is so rare. The teachings of the wise men of India are not so rare. The richest man in the world has never set eyes on such strange grace" [*FT* 90]).[6] Little Flower herself, oblivious both to her debasement and her exaltation, experiences an epiphany and also sparks moments of insight in other characters. Women of all ages seem fascinated by this hyperbolic representative of the fragility and powerlessness associated with their sex. One woman fights against an involuntary identification with Little Flower: "Looking into the bathroom mirror, the mother smiled, intentionally refined and polite, placing between her own face of abstract lines and the crude face of Little Flower, the insuperable distance of millennia" (*FT* 92).

Whereas people examine Little Flower's amazing smallness and supposed vulnerability with greedy interest, wanting to possess the miracle and even to use her as a servant or a pet, the small creature herself feels powerful and contented. Living constantly with the danger of being devoured by animals and members of other tribes, she experiences, as her epiphany, the triumph of having so far endured:

> She was laughing, warm, warm. . . . A laugh that the uncomfortable explorer did not succeed in classifying. And she went on enjoying her own gentle laugh, she who was not being devoured. Not to be devoured is the most perfect feeling.

> (*FT* 94)

Even her incipient motherhood will not lead her to confining bonds, for among the Likoualas a dubious practice prevails: "When a child is born, he is given his freedom almost at once" (*FT* 89). As her epiphany continues, Little Flower feels what "might be called love":

> She loved that sallow explorer. If she could have talked and told him that she loved him, he would have puffed up with vanity. A vanity that would have collapsed when she told him that she also loved the explorer's ring very much, and the explorer's boots.

> (*FT* 94)

Little Flower, unlike her urban counterparts, has no need to order and tame her chaotic desires; she merely enjoys them.

In answer to the explorer's question, Little Flower says it is "very nice to have a tree to live in that was hers, really hers. Because—and this she did not say but her eyes became so dark that they said it for her—because it is so nice to possess, so nice to possess" (*FT* 95). With the story of Little Flower, Lispector creates a comic parable of a native female power, sustained against all odds. The jungle inhabitant manages to retain the tranquil independence and unrepressed desires sought eagerly by city-bred women in their civilized world of enclosed spaces, prescribed behavior, and family ties. Lispector heaps on her protagonist multiple signs of powerlessness and oppression: membership in a black African tribe reminiscent of slavery and colonialism, the female sex, minute size, and the special dependence that pregnancy entails. She places her in opposition to a white male explorer (*explorador* in Portuguese means both "explorer" and "exploiter"). Yet the most vulnerable of women is not a victim. Unlike Laura, who cannot keep the roses, and unlike Lispector's other protagonists, who cannot hold on to and use their insights to change the forces that bind them, the

smallest woman in the world, alone in her tree house, possesses herself—Lispector's wry symbol of an effective female power, though not of the means to attain it.

### Notes

1. Quotations from *Family Ties* refer to Pontiero's translation (Lispector 1972), abbreviated *FT* and cited in the text.

2. This chapter is a revised and expanded version of "*Family Ties*: Female Development in Clarice Lispector," an essay that appeared in Abel, Hirsch, and Langland (1983, 287-303).

3. Clarice Lispector, *Alguns contos,* 1952. The collection contains, in this sequence: "Mystery in São Cristóvão," "Family Ties," "Beginnings of a Fortune," "Love," "A Chicken," and "The Dinner."

4. A letter from the Brazilian novelist Fernando Sabino dated March 30, 1955, gives his response to eight stories Lispector had sent him. Of these, four were included later in *Family Ties*: "The Imitation of the Rose," "The Daydreams of a Drunk Woman," "Happy Birthday," and "The Crime of the Mathematics Teacher." Sabino's response was fervently positive: "You have written eight stories as no one even remotely has been able to write in Brazil. You are writing like no one—saying what no one dared to say" (Clarice Lispector Archive).

5. Roberto Corrêa dos Santos's excellent analysis (1986, 45-57), the only discussion of this story I have seen, does not consider questions of gender.

6. Although page numbers in the text refer to the Pontiero translation, in my revision of it here I sometimes borrow from Elizabeth Bishop's excellent English version of "The Smallest Woman in the World" in Barbara Howes's anthology (1973, 320-28).

### Abbreviations

I use the following abbreviations for Lispector's works cited frequently throughout the book. The dates are those of the English translations.

*FL: The Foreign Legion* (Lispector 1986)

*FT: Family Ties* (Lispector 1972)

Page numbers follow the abbreviations and refer to the published English translations, although I often modify them for reasons of accuracy or to retain shades of meaning that are important to my interpretations.

Translations from Portuguese, French, and Spanish of quotations from interviews, letters, articles, and books, unless otherwise noted, are my own.

## Bibliography

Aleb, Elizabeth, Marianne Hirsch, and Elizabeth Langland, eds. 1983. *The Voyage In: Fictions of Female Development.* Hanover: University Press of New England.

Brooks, Peter. 1985. *The Melodramatic Imagination: Balzac, Henry James, Melodrama and the Mode of Excess.* 2d ed. New York: Columbia University Press.

Hill, Amariles G. 1976. A experiência de existir narrando. In *Seleta de Clarice Lispector,* eds. Renato C. Gomes and Amariles G. Hill. Rio de Janeiro: José Olympio.

Howes, Barbara, ed. 1973. *The Eye of the Heart: Short Stories from Latin America.* New York: Bobbs-Merrill.

Lispector, Clarice. 1952a. *Alguns contos.* Rio de Janeiro: Ministério de Educação e Saúde.

———. 1960. *Laços de família.* Rio de Janeiro: Francisco Alves.

———. 1971. *Felicidade clandestina.* Rio de Janeiro: Sabiá.

———. 1986a. *The Foreign Legion: Stories and Chronicles (A legião estrangeira).* Trans. Giovanni Pontiero. Manchester: Carcanet.

———. Clarice Lispector Archive. In the Arquivo-Museu de Literatura da Fundação Casa Rui Barbosa, Rio de Janeiro.

Moers, Ellen. 1976. *Literary Women: The Great Writers.* New York: Doubleday.

Rosowski, Susan J. 1983. The Novel of Awakening. In *The Voyage In: Fictions of Female Development,* eds. Elizabeth Abel, Marianne Hirsch, and Elizabeth Langland. Hanover: University Press of New England.

Sant'Anna, Affonso Romano. 1973. *Laços de família* e *Legião estrangeira.* In *Análise estrutural de romances brasileiros.* Petrópolis: Vozes.

Santos, Roberto Correa dos. 1986. *Clarice Lispector.* São Paulo: Atual.

———. 1990. Artes de fiandeira. Introduction to Clarice Lispector, *Laços de família,* 20th ed. Rio de Janeiro: Francisco Alves.

## M. Sheila McAvey (lecture date 1997)

SOURCE: McAvey, M. Sheila. "'The Smallest Woman in the World': Refractions of Identity in Elizabeth Bishop's Translation of Clarice Lispector's Tale." In *'In Worcester, Massachusetts': Essays on Elizabeth Bishop,* edited by Laura Jehn Menides and Angela G. Dorenkamp, pp. 279-86. New York: Peter Lang, 1999.

[*In the following essay, originally delivered as a lecture in 1997, McAvey suggests that working on her translation of "The Smallest Woman in the World" helped Elizabeth Bishop "to delve into her own powerful ambivalence about the need to enjoy being a physical body."*]

During the winter of 1962-63, Elizabeth Bishop took up Robert Lowell's suggestion that she include in her translations from Portuguese writers works by the Brazilian novelist Clarice Lispector. Bishop translated five of Lispector's stories. The three that are extant, **"The Smallest Woman in the World"** (**"SWW"**), **"A Hen,"** and **"Marmosets,"** appeared in 1964 in *Kenyon Review.*[1] Bishop's choice of Lispector, an acquaintance and writer whose feminism was an aspect, though a significant one, of her broader concern with the isolation of the human condition, was apt. A dominant theme in Lispector's writings, as in Bishop's works, is the question of how to define oneself as a woman and as an individual being in relation to others. **"The Smallest Woman in the World"** is typical Lispector, with its introspective style and the humorously sardonic outlook of its narrator. Its deeper appeals for Bishop, I would argue, are the emphasis on the theme of darkness that abides in maternal care and in love itself, as well as the tale's distinctive narrating voice that is, peculiarly, both amiable and cynical. The tale's satiric portrait of the earth-mother heroine and a rogues' gallery of urban maternal characters, who reel back from or obstinately ignore any consideration of their unmaternal selves, afforded Bishop a way to delve into her own powerful ambivalence about the need to enjoy being a physical body, a body that knows love, and the self-protective dread of those very needs.

Clarice Lispector could be categorized as a moralizing, feminist writer. She was indeed concerned with issues of individual conscience and societal norms, but her feminism was inextricable from her concern with the isolation of the human condition. Her feminism has been defined as "an uncompromising, assiduously held attitude . . . about the fact that . . . men and women are cursed because they must ponder their lonely fate even as they live it out to its inescapable end" (Fitz, "Freedom" 58). But that perspective leaves out Lispector's wily humor, particularly as it is manifested in her unflattering characterizations of women. Comparatively, we can see in Bishop's writings a similar tenor and subject matter: the same paradoxical dread of and desire for solitude, the uncertainty of identity, and the attraction-repulsion toward the female as mother figure, which underlies a profound ambivalence about what it means to be called "woman." In **"SWW,"** the title of which suggests much about her own self-image, Bishop found insistent echoes of harrowing memories and refractions of her own struggle to define herself. In addition, Bishop may well have encountered, in Lispector's stories, if not in Lispector's blunt philosophical realism, a way to describe her own conflicting views about women and mothering. Moreover, I would suggest that working with "SWW" provided Bishop an opportunity to take self-protective concealment behind the tapestry of another writer in order to delve into her own past.

Seeing, vision, what the "I/eye" defines as reality, is a recurrent theme in Lispector's story, "SWW," and not accidentally, in Bishop's writings, especially her post-1964 poems. One way of describing "SWW" is to say that it is a fantasy about seeing the world, and a detailed view of woman *as* the world and *in* the world. A mock fairy tale, the work concerns the discovery by a male French explorer of a 17¾-inch very pregnant Pygmy woman. The plot is structured by its narrating voice, which details both the explorer's response to this woman—whom "the greed of the most exquisite dream could never have imagined"—and the ambivalent reactions that a photograph of this marvel, published in a Sunday newspaper, arouses in readers, primarily female, who regard this woman-child from the safe remove of their urban world.

The tale opens with a mocking illustration of that favorite Romantic cliché, the maternal universe. The overworked vision of a lush world, animalistically alive and emphatically female, is the backdrop for the narrator's description of a delightfully humorous encounter between Marcel Pretre, "hunter and man of the world," and the story's eponymous heroine. The explorer's proud, manly bearing gets a jolt off-center when he confronts his prey, his holy grail: a child-size *woman,* not a male contender, who is obviously pregnant.

This male hunter, however rational he tries to be, is clearly flummoxed by the existence of a fecund female in a child-sized body. Reason is thrown into confusion; he is vulnerable. But, the narrator insists, M. Pretre doesn't die from shock. "Probably only because he was not insane, his soul neither wavered nor broke its bounds" (501). If the reader has not already smiled at M. Pretre's perplexed response in this confrontation with the sexual female, the narrator provides a description of the hilariously unselfconscious reaction of Little Flower to the explorer's masculine act of defining her with facts, a gesture that undermines his vaunted sense of himself:

> The explorer said timidly, and with a delicacy of feeling of which his wife would never have thought him capable: "You are Little Flower."
>
> At that moment, Little Flower scratched herself where no one scratches. The explorer—as if he were receiving the highest prize for chastity to which an idealistic man dares aspire—the explorer, experienced as he was, looked the other way.
>
> (502)

This ostensibly humorous image of the maternal, and thereby powerful, female is reconsidered more darkly at the end of this monumental encounter between *civilis* and nature. The explorer has calmed himself by methodically examining the miniature, sensual, woman standing at his feet; still, he finds himself "baffled" by the warm and bestial laughter of his prey. He assumes, as does the reader, that she is laughing at him, that, in her inarticulate awareness of the world, she has concluded that he is a prude. The narrator disabuses the reader of the idea that Little Flower has any such worldliness. The inquisitive, proud explorer cannot grasp that Little Flower, the jungle creature, is laughing delightedly because she has not been eaten by this much larger creature. The narrator reveals, to the reader, not to M. Pretre, that Little Flower's laughter arises from her animal pleasure in being still alive, in "not having been eaten yet" (505), a fate common to her tribe of Likoualas, who are customarily trapped and eaten by the carnivorous Bahundes tribe. Little Flower is feeling delighted with herself, and laughing for a very simple but self-centered reason: she is oblivious to the feelings, let alone the vanity, of the explorer.

M. Pretre remains baffled by Little Flower, but the narrator ensures that no such enchantment remains in the reader's mind. Ominously, the narrator reports, there is a darker motive for her laughter, one that provides an unexpected glimpse into the materialistic, greedily possessive soul of this maternal female. The reader is told of Little Flower's delight in the spectacle of the explorer's unusual skin color. It is sallow, white. However, the narrator warns, that delight, which might be called "profound love" in one who has no conception of love, is driven by another, less childlike motive. Little Flower, the "material girl" that the flamboyant entertainer Madonna extolled a decade ago, is in love with the novelties that she sees: M. Pretre's odd surface color, his ring, and his boots. This cynical portrait of maternity is rounded out with the narrator's bitter diatribe on the subject of love: "There is an old misunderstanding about the word love, and, if many children are born from this misunderstanding, many others have lost the unique chance of being born, only because of a susceptibility that demands that it be me! me! that is loved, and not my money" (506).

This cynical intrusion by the narrator forces the reader to confront significant, as well as sentimental, assumptions about the essence of love and of maternity embodied in the amoral Little Flower. The narrator intensifies uncertainty with a sardonic parting glimpse at the explorer and his wondrous "discovery." Little Flower, the fertile creature of nature, concludes her interview with M. Pretre by offering an unexpected "civilized" response to the explorer's mundane question about her habitat: "'Yes.' That it was very nice to have a tree of her own to live in. Because—she didn't say this but her eyes became so dark that they said it—because it is good to own, good to own, good to own" (506). Unsettled by this repeated phrase, the reader cannot avoid the disturbing truth beneath the Romantic, and sentimental, equation so dear to the heart of "civilized" minds, namely, that woman = maternal nature = pure love. So much for the narrator's initial portrait of Little Flower as Original Mother.[2]

The narrator's derisive, pessimistic evaluation of maternal care is unflinching. The description of M. Pretre's encounter with Little Flower frames a series of "portraits" of urban dwellers, primarily mothers, as they view the newspaper photograph of Little Flower that intrudes on their Sunday lives. These urban mothers, the narrator sneers, are corrupted and corrupting in their attention to their offspring, just like the jungle mother, who comes from a tribe of women incapable of protecting their young against disaster. The vignettes of urban domestic life that the narrator proceeds to describe compose a grim portrait of maternal love: self-deluded, ineffectual, and overwhelmingly self-centered.

To the narrator's eye, these civilized women enact a debilitating maternity and reveal a dreadful image of what it means to be a woman. In one vignette of domestic life, a young girl broods over the image of Little Flower, a yet-smaller female human being than herself, and comes to the distressing wisdom that no female can escape the tyrannical power of those who care for her. In another household, a young bride's untried maternal love for the "sad" Little Flower is exposed as ignorant condescension. Her mother delivers a contemptuous reprimand to her daughter regarding the great gulf that separates rational, "civilized" women from unreason of all sorts, especially emotions. This matron derides Little Flower as being, essentially, not female, not capable of human feelings such as sadness.

The narrator's mockery of sentimental definitions of maternal care is most severe in the centerpiece vignette of family love. This portrait, an exposé of the deliberate, self-centered willfulness masked under maternal love, echoes the unselfconscious but identically self-centered nature of Little Flower. The narrator details a mother's horrified reaction to her son's thoughtlessly cruel desire to acquire Little Flower as a toy. Pondering the "dangerous stranger" that her son has become, the mother considers "the cruel necessity of loving, . . . the malignity of our desire for happiness" (503). She senses the beast in her boy, and is even more horrified to sense the beast in her own soul, which, "more than her body, had engendered that being adept at life and happiness" (503-04). Willfully shutting out the thought of her own malign maternity, she determines—"obstinately," the narrator repeats—on a ludicrous solution:

she will buy her son a new suit. The narrator makes it clear that the absurdity of this maternal gesture to obliterate the Darwinian nature of her child's hunger for love is just as futile as the mother's subsequent gesture to mask her own inner nature. The narrator mocks her efforts to smooth her features with "a refined and social smile that should put millenia between herself and "the crude face of Little Flower." Her greed to protect against realities imprisons both mother and child in blindness to that essential aspect of the self.

Such corrosive maternal love is more the order in the civilized world than the exception, the narrator implies, offering yet another exemplum of greed calling itself love. A family groups together around the newspaper illustration of Little Flower and is consumed by an identical passion to own that small person. Such human desires should be acknowledged, the narrator snidely suggests: "To tell the truth, who hasn't wanted to own a human being just for himself?" (504) But, the narrator warns, concomitant with this grasping possession is the desire to avoid such responsibilities. Possessing another, the speaker jibes, "wouldn't always be convenient; there are times at which one doesn't want to have feelings" (504).

The tale's exhausting condemnation of maternal love concludes with the narrator's humorous portrait of an elderly newspaper reader's encounter with the photograph of Little Flower. This woman, long past the naive maternal whims of a bride and the strained exertions of actual maternal care, slams her newspaper shut against the implicit suggestion that a feral, female creature has the same reproductive capacity as herself. Maternal blindness to others' natures withers, in old age, to smug self-absorption.

Both the character of Little Flower and the distancing, sardonic voice of the narrator in this tale resonate with Elizabeth Bishop's own life and writings. Little Flower, the smallest woman in the world, embodies the conflicted feelings about mothers and mothering within Elizabeth Bishop: the sense of relief Bishop must have felt in "not having been eaten" by the loneliness of her isolated childhood, her delight in the fecundity of love, as well as in the pleasure of being a woman loved by another woman. However, Bishop's life had instilled into her a wariness towards women, towards love, and reinforced her guilt-ridden sense of herself as outsider. Little Flower, the mother *in potentis,* also represents Bishop's dark perception of maternal love from a child's point of view: the dread of her neediness, her greed for love, for companionship, which manifested itself in the series of sexual relationships that exposed a persistent emotional dissatisfaction that her lovers were incapable of countering. The "great darkness" growing in Little Flower is similar to the great darkness of Bishop's view of her childhood loss, and her probably inevitable loss of faith in the sustaining nourishment that was to be had through love.

Bishop's transplant to Brazil, however badly it ended in 1967, did alter her child's-eye vision of mothering. However, it is important to remember that Bishop never lost the *perspective* of being always the outsider, "the guest in other people's houses," as David Kalstone remarked (118). The fact that Bishop had been reworking childhood stories during this period of her life, particularly "In the Village" and the translation of a young Brazilian woman's diary, later entitled the *Diary of "Helena Morley,"* suggests a need to define herself.[3] Bishop's engagement with **"SWW,"** and specifically with the character Little Flower, enabled her to examine a female self, and the unusual narrating voice in **"SWW"** was another means of evoking and expressing Elizabeth Bishop's wariness about the self, women, and love. The narrator's sardonic humor and biting analyses of "civilized" maternal love suggests Bishop's own increasing pessimism regarding the human tendency to give and to withhold love. Possibly, in her eroding relationship with Lota de Macedo Soares, Bishop recognized the tale's disturbing dictum regarding "the cruel necessity of loving, . . . the malignity of our desire for happiness" (503).

In her close working with **"SWW,"** Bishop might have found a means to avoid direct memories of terrible personal experiences, and, through the voice of another writer, a way to examine the profoundly painful issues of identity, love, mothers. Clarice Lispector's story gave Bishop a safe way to contend with her own demons. In addition, ironically, Bishop's engagement with this writer, and with this story, might well have fostered her own development—or return—towards a pessimistic vision of human nature. **"The Smallest Woman in the World"** provided her with another "I/pair of eyes" with which she could puzzle over, yet again, what it means to be a woman, and how difficult it is to seek or trust in love after a childhood of traumatizing maternal loss.

## Notes

1. Lispector's first collection of short stories, *Some Stories [Algun Contos],* was published in 1952, during several years' residence in Washington, DC, with her husband and infants, and three years after publication of her third novel. In 1960, these six stories were included in a collection of thirteen tales entitled *Family Ties [Lacos de Familia].* This collection, which demonstrates Lispector's characteristic endeavor to capture the mind's stream of consciousness, is regarded as Lispector's most successful work, technically superior to her novels. Indeed, scholars and translators of her work such as Earl E. Fitz and Giovanni Pontiero note that the short-story format was Lispector's metier; in that form she best conveyed her characteristic technique: a sudden moment of epiphany, self-realization, when a character has a traumatic insight into her/his nature.

2. In naming her exotic heroine, Lispector played with the ironic connection between the creature "Little Flower" and the familiar appositive of the nineteenth-century French saint Therese Martin, the Little Flower. In largely Catholic Brazil, Lispector probably was aware of the saint's common name. Both the fictitious and the real woman are spunky in nature, but the behavioral gap between them is wide. Unlike the contentedly pregnant jungle flower, Therese Martin prided herself on her physical purity and her abstinence from daily human pleasures. Little Flower is a witty namesake to the virgin, Victorian saint. See Patricia O'Connor, *Therese of Lisieux: A Biography* (Huntington, Ind.: Our Sunday Visitor, 1983).

3. In the early years of her residence in Brazil, Bishop reworked a number of stories, that were scarcely veiled examinations of her childhood. For Bishop, prose represented a distinct way of looking back to her past, a period when her losses were multiple. The most anthologized of the stories "The Baptism" (1937), "The Farmer's Children" (begun in 1937 but published in 1947), "Gwendolyn" (1953), and "In the Village" (1953), all center on loss through death. It is clear that the dominant child's-eye view of lost maternal care in these stories held a powerful resonance for Bishop.

## Works Cited

Bishop, Elizabeth. *The Collected Prose.* Ed. Robert Giroux. New York: Farrar, Straus, Giroux, 1985.

———. *The Complete Poems, 1927-1979.* New York: Farrar, Straus, Giroux, 1983.

Fitz, Earl. *Clarice Lispector.* Boston: G. K. Hall, 1985.

———. "Freedom and Self-Realization: Feminist Characterization in the Fiction of Clarice Lispector." *Modern Language Studies* 10:3 (1980): 51-56.

Goldensohn, Lorrie. *Elizabeth Bishop: The Biography of a Poetry.* New York: Columbia UP, 1992.

Jozef, Bella. "Chronology: Clarice Lispector." Trans. Elizabeth Lowe. *Review* 24 (1979): 24-26.

Kalstone, David. *Becoming a Poet: Elizabeth Bishop with Marianne Moore and Robert Lowell.* Ed. Robert Hemenway. New York: Farrar, Straus, Giroux, 1989.

Lispector, Clarice. *Family Ties.* Trans. Giovanni Pontiero. New York: New Directions, 1992.

———. *The Foreign Legion.* Trans. Giovanni Pontiero. New York: New Directions, 1992.

———. "The Smallest Woman in the World," "A Hen," and "Marmosets." Trans. Elizabeth Bishop. *Kenyon Review* 26 (1964): 501-11.

Millier, Brett C. *Elizabeth Bishop: Life and the Memory of It.* Berkeley: U of California P, 1993.

Pontiero, Giovanni. "Excerpts from *The Chronicles of the Foreign Legion.*" *Review* 24 (1979): 37-43.

———. "The Drama of Existence in *Lacos de Familia.*" *Studies in Short Fiction* 8:1 (Winter 1977): 246-67.

# FURTHER READING

## Bibliography

Marting, Diane E., ed. *Clarice Lispector: A Bio-Bibliography.* Westport, Conn.: Greenwood Press, 1993. 327 p.

Bibliography of Lispector's major and minor works, including some critical assessments.

## Criticism

Fitz, Earl. *Clarice Lispector.* Boston: Twayne Publishers, 1985. 160 p.

Presents an overview of Lispector's life, work, and place in Brazilian literature.

Additional coverage of Lispector's life and career is contained in the following sources published by Thomson Gale: *Concise Dictionary of World Literary Biography,* **Vol. 3;** *Contemporary Authors,* **Vol. 139;** *Contemporary Authors New Revision Series,* **Vol. 71;** *Contemporary Authors—Obituary,* **Vol. 116;** *Contemporary Literary Criticism,* **Vol. 43;** *Dictionary of Literary Biography,* **Vols. 113, 307;** *Encyclopedia of World Literature in the 20th Century,* **Ed. 3;** *Feminist Writers;* *Hispanic Literature Criticism Supplement,* **Ed. 2;** *Hispanic Writers,* **Ed. 2;** *Latin American Writers;* *Literature of Developing Nations for Students,* **Vol. 1;** *Literature Resource Center;* *Reference Guide to Short Fiction,* **Ed. 2;** *Reference Guide to World Literature,* **Eds. 2, 3;** *Short Story Criticism,* **Vol. 34;** and *World Literature and Its Times,* **Ed. 1.**

# How to Use This Index

## The main references

> **Calvino, Italo**
> 1923-1985 ....... CLC 5, 8, 11, 22, 33, 39,
> 73; SSC 3, 48

**list all author entries in the following Gale Literary Criticism series:**

*AAL* = *Asian American Literature*
*BG* = *The Beat Generation: A Gale Critical Companion*
*BLC* = *Black Literature Criticism*
*BLCS* = *Black Literature Criticism Supplement*
*CLC* = *Contemporary Literary Criticism*
*CLR* = *Children's Literature Review*
*CMLC* = *Classical and Medieval Literature Criticism*
*DC* = *Drama Criticism*
*HLC* = *Hispanic Literature Criticism*
*HLCS* = *Hispanic Literature Criticism Supplement*
*HR* = *Harlem Renaissance: A Gale Critical Companion*
*LC* = *Literature Criticism from 1400 to 1800*
*NCLC* = *Nineteenth-Century Literature Criticism*
*NNAL* = *Native North American Literature*
*PC* = *Poetry Criticism*
*SSC* = *Short Story Criticism*
*TCLC* = *Twentieth-Century Literary Criticism*
*WLC* = *World Literature Criticism, 1500 to the Present*
*WLCS* = *World Literature Criticism Supplement*

## The cross-references

> See also CA 85-88, 116; CANR 23, 61;
> DAM NOV; DLB 196; EW 13; MTCW 1, 2;
> RGSF 2; RGWL 2; SFW 4; SSFS 12

**list all author entries in the following Gale biographical and literary sources:**

*AAYA* = *Authors & Artists for Young Adults*
*AFAW* = *African American Writers*
*AFW* = *African Writers*
*AITN* = *Authors in the News*
*AMW* = *American Writers*
*AMWR* = *American Writers Retrospective Supplement*
*AMWS* = *American Writers Supplement*
*ANW* = *American Nature Writers*
*AW* = *Ancient Writers*
*BEST* = *Bestsellers*
*BPFB* = *Beacham's Encyclopedia of Popular Fiction: Biography and Resources*
*BRW* = *British Writers*
*BRWS* = *British Writers Supplement*
*BW* = *Black Writers*
*BYA* = *Beacham's Guide to Literature for Young Adults*
*CA* = *Contemporary Authors*
*CAAS* = *Contemporary Authors Autobiography Series*
*CABS* = *Contemporary Authors Bibliographical Series*
*CAD* = *Contemporary American Dramatists*
*CANR* = *Contemporary Authors New Revision Series*
*CAP* = *Contemporary Authors Permanent Series*
*CBD* = *Contemporary British Dramatists*
*CCA* = *Contemporary Canadian Authors*
*CD* = *Contemporary Dramatists*
*CDALB* = *Concise Dictionary of American Literary Biography*
*CDALBS* = *Concise Dictionary of American Literary Biography Supplement*
*CDBLB* = *Concise Dictionary of British Literary Biography*

**CMW** = *St. James Guide to Crime & Mystery Writers*
**CN** = *Contemporary Novelists*
**CP** = *Contemporary Poets*
**CPW** = *Contemporary Popular Writers*
**CSW** = *Contemporary Southern Writers*
**CWD** = *Contemporary Women Dramatists*
**CWP** = *Contemporary Women Poets*
**CWRI** = *St. James Guide to Children's Writers*
**CWW** = *Contemporary World Writers*
**DA** = *DISCovering Authors*
**DA3** = *DISCovering Authors 3.0*
**DAB** = *DISCovering Authors: British Edition*
**DAC** = *DISCovering Authors: Canadian Edition*
**DAM** = *DISCovering Authors: Modules*
   **DRAM:** *Dramatists Module;* **MST:** *Most-studied Authors Module;*
   **MULT:** *Multicultural Authors Module;* **NOV:** *Novelists Module;*
   **POET:** *Poets Module;* **POP:** *Popular Fiction and Genre Authors Module*
**DFS** = *Drama for Students*
**DLB** = *Dictionary of Literary Biography*
**DLBD** = *Dictionary of Literary Biography Documentary Series*
**DLBY** = *Dictionary of Literary Biography Yearbook*
**DNFS** = *Literature of Developing Nations for Students*
**EFS** = *Epics for Students*
**EXPN** = *Exploring Novels*
**EXPP** = *Exploring Poetry*
**EXPS** = *Exploring Short Stories*
**EW** = *European Writers*
**FANT** = *St. James Guide to Fantasy Writers*
**FW** = *Feminist Writers*
**GFL** = *Guide to French Literature,* Beginnings to 1789, 1798 to the Present
**GLL** = *Gay and Lesbian Literature*
**HGG** = *St. James Guide to Horror, Ghost & Gothic Writers*
**HW** = *Hispanic Writers*
**IDFW** = *International Dictionary of Films and Filmmakers: Writers and Production Artists*
**IDTP** = *International Dictionary of Theatre: Playwrights*
**LAIT** = *Literature and Its Times*
**LAW** = *Latin American Writers*
**JRDA** = *Junior DISCovering Authors*
**MAICYA** = *Major Authors and Illustrators for Children and Young Adults*
**MAICYAS** = *Major Authors and Illustrators for Children and Young Adults Supplement*
**MAWW** = *Modern American Women Writers*
**MJW** = *Modern Japanese Writers*
**MTCW** = *Major 20th-Century Writers*
**NCFS** = *Nonfiction Classics for Students*
**NFS** = *Novels for Students*
**PAB** = *Poets: American and British*
**PFS** = *Poetry for Students*
**RGAL** = *Reference Guide to American Literature*
**RGEL** = *Reference Guide to English Literature*
**RGSF** = *Reference Guide to Short Fiction*
**RGWL** = *Reference Guide to World Literature*
**RHW** = *Twentieth-Century Romance and Historical Writers*
**SAAS** = *Something about the Author Autobiography Series*
**SATA** = *Something about the Author*
**SFW** = *St. James Guide to Science Fiction Writers*
**SSFS** = *Short Stories for Students*
**TCWW** = *Twentieth-Century Western Writers*
**WLIT** = *World Literature and Its Times*
**WP** = *World Poets*
**YABC** = *Yesterday's Authors of Books for Children*
**YAW** = *St. James Guide to Young Adult Writers*

# Literary Criticism Series
# Cumulative Author Index

**Alexeyev, Constantin Sergeivich**
  See Stanislavsky, Constantin
**Alexeyev, Konstantin Sergeyevich**
  See Stanislavsky, Constantin
**Alexie, Sherman** 1966- ........... **CLC 96, 154;**
  **NNAL; PC 53**
    See also AAYA 28; BYA 15; CA 138;
    CANR 65, 95, 133; CN 7; DA3; DAM
    MULT; DLB 175, 206, 278; LATS 1:2;
    MTCW 2; MTFW 2005; NFS 17; SSFS
    18
**al-Farabi** 870(?)-950 ............... **CMLC 58**
    See also DLB 115
**Alfau, Felipe** 1902-1999 ................. **CLC 66**
    See also CA 137
**Alfieri, Vittorio** 1749-1803 .......... **NCLC 101**
    See also EW 4; RGWL 2, 3; WLIT 7
**Alfonso X** 1221-1284 .................... **CMLC 78**
**Alfred, Jean Gaston**
    See Ponge, Francis
**Alger, Horatio, Jr.** 1832-1899 ... **NCLC 8, 83**
    See also CLR 87; DLB 42; LAIT 2; RGAL
    4; SATA 16; TUS
**Al-Ghazali, Muhammad ibn Muhammad**
    1058-1111 ............................ **CMLC 50**
    See also DLB 115
**Algren, Nelson** 1909-1981 .... **CLC 4, 10, 33;**
  **SSC 33**
    See also AMWS 9; BPFB 1; CA 13-16R;
    103; CANR 20, 61; CDALB 1941-1968;
    CN 1, 2; DLB 9; DLBY 1981, 1982,
    2000; EWL 3; MAL 5; MTCW 1, 2;
    MTFW 2005; RGAL 4; RGSF 2
**al-Hariri, al-Qasim ibn 'Ali Abu**
  **Muhammad al-Basri** 1054-1122
    ........................................ **CMLC 63**
    See also RGWL 3
**Ali, Ahmed** 1908-1998 ..................... **CLC 69**
    See also CA 25-28R; CANR 15, 34; CN 1,
    2, 3, 4, 5; DLB 323; EWL 3
**Ali, Tariq** 1943- ........................... **CLC 173**
    See also CA 25-28R; CANR 10, 99
**Alighieri, Dante**
    See Dante
    See also WLIT 7
**al-Kindi, Abu Yusuf Ya'qub ibn Ishaq** c.
    801-c. 873 ......................... **CMLC 80**
**Allan, John B.**
    See Westlake, Donald E.
**Allan, Sidney**
    See Hartmann, Sadakichi
**Allan, Sydney**
    See Hartmann, Sadakichi
**Allard, Janet** ...................................... **CLC 59**
**Allen, Edward** 1948- ........................ **CLC 59**
**Allen, Fred** 1894-1956 ................... **TCLC 87**
**Allen, Paula Gunn** 1939- ........ **CLC 84, 202;**
  **NNAL**
    See also AMWS 4; CA 112; 143; CANR
    63, 130; CWP; DA3; DAM MULT; DLB
    175; FW; MTCW 2; MTFW 2005; RGAL
    4; TCWW 2
**Allen, Roland**
    See Ayckbourn, Alan
**Allen, Sarah A.**
    See Hopkins, Pauline Elizabeth
**Allen, Sidney H.**
    See Hartmann, Sadakichi
**Allen, Woody** 1935- ........... **CLC 16, 52, 195**
    See also AAYA 10, 51; AMWS 15; CA 33-
    36R; CANR 27, 38, 63, 128; DAM POP;
    DLB 44; MTCW 1; SSFS 21
**Allende, Isabel** 1942- .. **CLC 39, 57, 97, 170;**
  **HLC 1; SSC 65; WLCS**
    See also AAYA 18, 70; CA 125; 130; CANR
    51, 74, 129; CDWLB 3; CLR 99; CWW
    2; DA3; DAM MULT; NOV; DLB 145;
    DNFS 1; EWL 3; FL 1:5; FW; HW 1, 2;
    INT CA-130; LAIT 5; LAWS 1; LMFS 2;

MTCW 1, 2; MTFW 2005; NCFS 1; NFS
    6, 18; RGSF 2; RGWL 3; SATA 163;
    SSFS 11, 16; WLIT 1
**Alleyn, Ellen**
    See Rossetti, Christina
**Alleyne, Carla D.** ............................ **CLC 65**
**Allingham, Margery (Louise)** 1904-1966
    ........................................... **CLC 19**
    See also CA 5-8R; 25-28R; CANR 4, 58;
    CMW 4; DLB 77; MSW; MTCW 1, 2
**Allingham, William** 1824-1889 ..... **NCLC 25**
    See also DLB 35; RGEL 2
**Allison, Dorothy E.** 1949- ........ **CLC 78, 153**
    See also AAYA 53; CA 140; CANR 66, 107;
    CN 7; CSW; DA3; FW; MTCW 2; MTFW
    2005; NFS 11; RGAL 4
**Alloula, Malek** ................................ **CLC 65**
**Allston, Washington** 1779-1843 ...... **NCLC 2**
    See also DLB 1, 235
**Almedingen, E. M.** .......................... **CLC 12**
    See Almedingen, Martha Edith von
    See also SATA 3
**Almedingen, Martha Edith von** 1898-1971
    See Almedingen, E. M.
    See also CA 1-4R; CANR 1
**Almodovar, Pedro** 1949(?)- .. **CLC 114, 229;**
  **HLCS 1**
    See also CA 133; CANR 72, 151; HW 2
**Almqvist, Carl Jonas Love** 1793-1866
    ........................................... **NCLC 42**
**al-Mutanabbi, Ahmad ibn al-Husayn Abu**
  **al-Tayyib al-Jufi al-Kindi** 915-965
    ........................................... **CMLC 66**
    See Mutanabbi, Al-
    See also RGWL 3
**Alonso, Damaso** 1898-1990 .............. **CLC 14**
    See also CA 110; 131; 130; CANR 72; DLB
    108; EWL 3; HW 1, 2
**Alov**
    See Gogol, Nikolai (Vasilyevich)
**al'Sadaawi, Nawal**
    See El Saadawi, Nawal
    See also FW
**al-Shaykh, Hanan** 1945- ................. **CLC 218**
    See Shaykh, al- Hanan
    See also CA 135; CANR 111; WLIT 6
**Al Siddik**
    See Rolfe, Frederick (William Serafino Aus-
    tin Lewis Mary)
    See also GLL 1; RGEL 2
**Alta** 1942- .................................... **CLC 19**
    See also CA 57-60
**Alter, Robert B(ernard)** 1935- ........ **CLC 34**
    See also CA 49-52; CANR 1, 47, 100
**Alther, Lisa** 1944- .......................... **CLC 7, 41**
    See also BPFB 1; CA 65-68; CAAS 30;
    CANR 12, 30, 51; CN 4, 5, 6, 7; CSW;
    GLL 2; MTCW 1
**Althusser, L.**
    See Althusser, Louis
**Althusser, Louis** 1918-1990 ........... **CLC 106**
    See also CA 131; 132; CANR 102; DLB
    242
**Altman, Robert** 1925-2006 ...... **CLC 16, 116**
    See also CA 73-76; CANR 43
**Alurista** ............................... **HLCS 1; PC 34**
    See Urista (Heredia), Alberto (Baltazar)
    See also CA 45-48R; DLB 82; LLW
**Alvarez, A.** 1929- ......................... **CLC 5, 13**
    See also CA 1-4R; CANR 3, 33, 63, 101,
    134; CN 3, 4, 5, 6; CP 1, 2, 3, 4, 5, 6, 7;
    DLB 14, 40; MTFW 2005
**Alvarez, Alejandro Rodriguez** 1903-1965
    See Casona, Alejandro
    See also CA 131; 93-96; HW 1

**Alvarez, Julia** 1950- ......... **CLC 93; HLCS 1**
    See also AAYA 25; AMWS 7; CA 147;
    CANR 69, 101, 133; DA3; DLB 282;
    LATS 1:2; LLW; MTCW 2; MTFW 2005;
    NFS 5, 9; SATA 129; WLIT 1
**Alvaro, Corrado** 1896-1956 .......... **TCLC 60**
    See also CA 163; DLB 264; EWL 3
**Amado, Jorge** 1912-2001 . **CLC 13, 40, 106;**
  **HLC 1**
    See also CA 77-80; 201; CANR 35, 74, 135;
    CWW 2; DAM MULT, NOV; DLB 113,
    307; EWL 3; HW 2; LAW; LAWS 1;
    MTCW 1, 2; MTFW 2005; RGWL 2, 3;
    TWA; WLIT 1
**Ambler, Eric** 1909-1998 ............. **CLC 4, 6, 9**
    See also BRWS 4; CA 9-12R; 171; CANR
    7, 38, 74; CMW 4; CN 1, 2, 3, 4, 5, 6;
    DLB 77; MSW; MTCW 1, 2; TEA
**Ambrose, Stephen E.** 1936-2002 ... **CLC 145**
    See also AAYA 44; CA 1-4R; 209; CANR
    3, 43, 57, 83, 105; MTFW 2005; NCFS 2;
    SATA 40, 138
**Amichai, Yehuda** 1924-2000 . **CLC 9, 22, 57,**
  **116; PC 38**
    See also CA 85-88; 189; CANR 46, 60, 99,
    132; CWW 2; EWL 3; MTCW 1, 2;
    MTFW 2005; PFS 24; RGHL; WLIT 6
**Amichai, Yehudah**
    See Amichai, Yehuda
**Amiel, Henri Frederic** 1821-1881 .. **NCLC 4**
    See also DLB 217
**Amis, Kingsley** 1922-1995 .... **CLC 1, 2, 3, 5,**
  **8, 13, 40, 44, 129**
    See also AITN 2; BPFB 1; BRWS 2; CA
    9-12R; 150; CANR 8, 28, 54; CDBLB
    1945-1960; CN 1, 2, 3, 4, 5, 6; CP 1, 2,
    3, 4; DA; DA3; DAB; DAC; DAM MST,
    NOV; DLB 15, 27, 100, 139, 326; DLBY
    1996; EWL 3; HGG; INT CANR-8;
    MTCW 1, 2; MTFW 2005; RGEL 2;
    RGSF 2; SFW 4
**Amis, Martin** 1949- .. **CLC 4, 9, 38, 62, 101,**
  **213**
    See also BEST 90:3; BRWS 4; CA 65-68;
    CANR 8, 27, 54, 73, 95, 132; CN 5, 6, 7;
    DA3; DLB 14, 194; EWL 3; INT CANR-
    27; MTCW 2; MTFW 2005
**Ammianus Marcellinus** c. 330-c. 395
    ........................................... **CMLC 60**
    See also AW 2; DLB 211
**Ammons, A.R.** 1926-2001 ..... **CLC 2, 3, 5, 8,**
  **9, 25, 57, 108; PC 16**
    See also AITN 1; AMWS 7; CA 9-12R;
    193; CANR 6, 36, 51, 73, 107, 156; CP 1,
    2, 3, 4, 5, 6, 7; CSW; DAM POET; DLB
    5, 165; EWL 3; MAL 5; MTCW 1, 2; PFS
    19; RGAL 4; TCLE 1:1
**Ammons, Archie Randolph**
    See Ammons, A.R.
**Amo, Tauraatua i**
    See Adams, Henry (Brooks)
**Amory, Thomas** 1691(?)-1788 ............ **LC 48**
    See also DLB 39
**Anand, Mulk Raj** 1905-2004 ..... **CLC 23, 93**
    See also CA 65-68; 231; CANR 32, 64; CN
    1, 2, 3, 4, 5, 6, 7; DAM NOV; DLB 323;
    EWL 3; MTCW 1, 2; MTFW 2005; RGSF
    2
**Anatol**
    See Schnitzler, Arthur
**Anaximander** c. 611B.C.-c. 546B.C.
    ........................................... **CMLC 22**
**Anaya, Rudolfo A.** 1937- ........ **CLC 23, 148;**
  **HLC 1**
    See also AAYA 20; BYA 13; CA 45-48;
    CAAS 4; CANR 1, 32, 51, 124; CN 4, 5,
    6, 7; DAM MULT, NOV; DLB 82, 206,
    278; HW 1; LAIT 5; LLW; MAL 5;
    MTCW 1, 2; MTFW 2005; NFS 12;
    RGAL 4; RGSF 2; TCWW 2; WLIT 1

**Andersen, Hans Christian** 1805-1875
.......... **NCLC 7, 79; SSC 6, 56; WLC 1**
See also AAYA 57; CLR 6, 113; DA; DA3;
DAB; DAC; DAM MST, POP; EW 6;
MAICYA 1, 2; RGSF 2; RGWL 2, 3;
SATA 100; TWA; WCH; YABC 1

**Anderson, C. Farley**
See Mencken, H(enry) L(ouis); Nathan,
George Jean

**Anderson, Jessica (Margaret) Queale** 1916-
.................. **CLC 37**
See also CA 9-12R; CANR 4, 62; CN 4, 5,
6, 7; DLB 325

**Anderson, Jon (Victor)** 1940- ........... **CLC 9**
See also CA 25-28R; CANR 20; CP 1, 3, 4,
5; DAM POET

**Anderson, Lindsay (Gordon)** 1923-1994
.................. **CLC 20**
See also CA 125; 128; 146; CANR 77

**Anderson, Maxwell** 1888-1959 ...... **TCLC 2,
144**
See also CA 105; 152; DAM DRAM; DFS
16, 20; DLB 7, 228; MAL 5; MTCW 2;
MTFW 2005; RGAL 4

**Anderson, Poul** 1926-2001 ............... **CLC 15**
See also AAYA 5, 34; BPFB 1; BYA 6, 8,
9; CA 1-4R, 181; 199; CAAE 181; CAAS
2; CANR 2, 15, 34, 64, 110; CLR 58;
DLB 8; FANT; INT CANR-15; MTCW 1,
2; MTFW 2005; SATA 90; SATA-Brief
39; SATA-Essay 106; SCFW 1, 2; SFW
4; SUFW 1, 2

**Anderson, Robert (Woodruff)** 1917-
.................. **CLC 23**
See also AITN 1; CA 21-24R; CANR 32;
CD 6; DAM DRAM; DLB 7; LAIT 5

**Anderson, Roberta Joan**
See Mitchell, Joni

**Anderson, Sherwood** 1876-1941 . **SSC 1, 46,
91; TCLC 1, 10, 24, 123; WLC 1**
See also AAYA 30; AMW; AMWC 2; BPFB
1; CA 104; 121; CANR 61; CDALB
1917-1929; DA; DA3; DAB; DAC; DAM
MST, NOV; DLB 4, 9, 86; DLBD 1; EWL
3; EXPS; GLL 2; MAL 5; MTCW 1, 2;
MTFW 2005; NFS 4; RGAL 4; RGSF 2;
SSFS 4, 10, 11; TUS

**Anderson, Wes** 1969- ..................... **CLC 227**
See also CA 214

**Andier, Pierre**
See Desnos, Robert

**Andouard**
See Giraudoux, Jean(-Hippolyte)

**Andrade, Carlos Drummond de** ..... **CLC 18**
See Drummond de Andrade, Carlos
See also EWL 3; RGWL 2, 3

**Andrade, Mario de** ...................... **TCLC 43**
See de Andrade, Mario
See also DLB 307; EWL 3; LAW; RGWL
2, 3; WLIT 1

**Andreae, Johann V(alentin)** 1586-1654
.................. **LC 32**
See also DLB 164

**Andreas Capellanus** fl. c. 1185- ... **CMLC 45**
See also DLB 208

**Andreas-Salome, Lou** 1861-1937 .. **TCLC 56**
See also CA 178; DLB 66

**Andreev, Leonid**
See Andreyev, Leonid (Nikolaevich)
See also DLB 295; EWL 3

**Andress, Lesley**
See Sanders, Lawrence

**Andrewes, Lancelot** 1555-1626 ........... **LC 5**
See also DLB 151, 172

**Andrews, Cicily Fairfield**
See West, Rebecca

**Andrews, Elton V.**
See Pohl, Frederik

**Andrews, Peter**
See Soderbergh, Steven

**Andreyev, Leonid (Nikolaevich)** 1871-1919
.................. **TCLC 3**
See Andreev, Leonid
See also CA 104; 185

**Andric, Ivo** 1892-1975 ....... **CLC 8; SSC 36;
TCLC 135**
See also CA 81-84; 57-60; CANR 43, 60;
CDWLB 4; DLB 147, 329; EW 11; EWL
3; MTCW 1; RGSF 2; RGWL 2, 3

**Androvar**
See Prado (Calvo), Pedro

**Angela of Foligno** 1248(?)-1309 ... **CMLC 76**

**Angelique, Pierre**
See Bataille, Georges

**Angell, Roger** 1920- ......................... **CLC 26**
See also CA 57-60; CANR 13, 44, 70, 144;
DLB 171, 185

**Angelou, Maya** 1928- .. **BLC 1; CLC 12, 35,
64, 77, 155; PC 32; WLCS**
See also AAYA 7, 20; AMWS 4; BPFB 1;
BW 2, 3; BYA 2; CA 65-68; CANR 19,
42, 65, 111, 133; CDALBS; CLR 53; CP
4, 5, 6, 7; CPW; CSW; CWP; DA; DA3;
DAB; DAC; DAM MST, MULT, POET,
POP; DLB 38; EWL 3; EXPN; EXPP; FL
1:5; LAIT 4; MAICYA 1; MAICYAS 1;
MAL 5; MBL; MTCW 1, 2; MTFW 2005;
NCFS 2; NFS 2; PFS 2, 3; RGAL 4;
SATA 49, 136; TCLE 1:1; WYA; YAW

**Angoulême, Marguerite d'**
See de Navarre, Marguerite

**Anna Comnena** 1083-1153 ........... **CMLC 25**

**Annensky, Innokentii Fedorovich**
See Annensky, Innokenty (Fyodorovich)
See also DLB 295

**Annensky, Innokenty (Fyodorovich)**
1856-1909 .............................. **TCLC 14**
See also CA 110; 155; EWL 3

**Annunzio, Gabriele d'**
See D'Annunzio, Gabriele

**Anodos**
See Coleridge, Mary E(lizabeth)

**Anon, Charles Robert**
See Pessoa, Fernando (Antonio Nogueira)

**Anouilh, Jean** 1910-1987 .... **CLC 1, 3, 8, 13,
40, 50; DC 8, 21**
See also AAYA 67; CA 17-20R; 123; CANR
32; DAM DRAM; DFS 9, 10, 19; DLB
321; EW 13; EWL 3; GFL 1789 to the
Present; MTCW 1, 2; MTFW 2005;
RGWL 2, 3; TWA

**Anselm of Canterbury** 1033(?)-1109
.................. **CMLC 67**
See also DLB 115

**Anthony, Florence**
See Ai

**Anthony, John**
See Ciardi, John (Anthony)

**Anthony, Peter**
See Shaffer, Anthony; Shaffer, Peter

**Anthony, Piers** 1934- ......................... **CLC 35**
See also AAYA 11, 48; BYA 7; CA 200;
CAAE 200; CANR 28, 56, 73, 102, 133;
CLR 118; CPW; DAM POP; DLB 8;
FANT; MAICYA 2; MAICYAS 1; MTCW
1, 2; MTFW 2005; SAAS 22; SATA 84,
129; SATA-Essay 129; SFW 4; SUFW 1,
2; YAW

**Anthony, Susan B(rownell)** 1820-1906
.................. **TCLC 84**
See also CA 211; FW

**Antiphon** c. 480B.C.-c. 411B.C. ... **CMLC 55**

**Antoine, Marc**
See Proust, (Valentin-Louis-George-Eugene)
Marcel

**Antoninus, Brother**
See Everson, William (Oliver)
See also CP 1

**Antonioni, Michelangelo** 1912- ...... **CLC 20,
144**
See also CA 73-76; CANR 45, 77

**Antschel, Paul** 1920-1970
See Celan, Paul
See also CA 85-88; CANR 33, 61; MTCW
1; PFS 21

**Anwar, Chairil** 1922-1949 ............. **TCLC 22**
See Chairil Anwar
See also CA 121; 219; RGWL 3

**Anzaldua, Gloria (Evanjelina)** 1942-2004
.................. **CLC 200; HLCS 1**
See also CA 175; 227; CSW; CWP; DLB
122; FW; LLW; RGAL 4; SATA-Obit 154

**Apess, William** 1798-1839(?) ....... **NCLC 73;
NNAL**
See also DAM MULT; DLB 175, 243

**Apollinaire, Guillaume** 1880-1918 ...... **PC 7;
TCLC 3, 8, 51**
See Kostrowitzki, Wilhelm Apollinaris de
See also CA 152; DAM POET; DLB 258,
321; EW 9; EWL 3; GFL 1789 to the
Present; MTCW 2; PFS 24; RGWL 2, 3;
TWA; WP

**Apollonius of Rhodes**
See Apollonius Rhodius
See also AW 1; RGWL 2, 3

**Apollonius Rhodius** c. 300B.C.-c. 220B.C.
.................. **CMLC 28**
See Apollonius of Rhodes
See also DLB 176

**Appelfeld, Aharon** 1932- .. **CLC 23, 47; SSC
42**
See also CA 112; 133; CANR 86; CWW 2;
DLB 299; EWL 3; RGHL; RGSF 2;
WLIT 6

**Apple, Max (Isaac)** 1941- .. **CLC 9, 33; SSC
50**
See also CA 81-84; CANR 19, 54; DLB
130

**Appleman, Philip (Dean)** 1926- ....... **CLC 51**
See also CA 13-16R; CAAS 18; CANR 6,
29, 56

**Appleton, Lawrence**
See Lovecraft, H. P.

**Apteryx**
See Eliot, T(homas) S(tearns)

**Apuleius, (Lucius Madaurensis)** c. 125-c.
164 .................. **CMLC 1, 84**
See also AW 2; CDWLB 1; DLB 211;
RGWL 2, 3; SUFW; WLIT 8

**Aquin, Hubert** 1929-1977 .............. **CLC 15**
See also CA 105; DLB 53; EWL 3

**Aquinas, Thomas** 1224(?)-1274 ... **CMLC 33**
See also DLB 115; EW 1; TWA

**Aragon, Louis** 1897-1982 .......... **CLC 3, 22;
TCLC 123**
See also CA 69-72; 108; CANR 28, 71;
DAM NOV, POET; DLB 72, 258; EW 11;
EWL 3; GFL 1789 to the Present; GLL 2;
LMFS 2; MTCW 1, 2; RGWL 2, 3

**Arany, Janos** 1817-1882 ............... **NCLC 34**

**Aranyos, Kakay** 1847-1910
See Mikszath, Kalman

**Aratus of Soli** c. 315B.C.-c. 240B.C.
.................. **CMLC 64**
See also DLB 176

**Arbuthnot, John** 1667-1735 ................. **LC 1**
See also DLB 101

**Archer, Herbert Winslow**
See Mencken, H(enry) L(ouis)

**Archer, Jeffrey** 1940- ....................... **CLC 28**
See also AAYA 16; BEST 89:3; BPFB 1;
CA 77-80; CANR 22, 52, 95, 136; CPW;
DA3; DAM POP; INT CANR-22; MTFW
2005

**Archer, Jeffrey Howard**
See Archer, Jeffrey

**Archer, Jules** 1915- .......................... **CLC 12**
See also CA 9-12R; CANR 6, 69; SAAS 5;
SATA 4, 85

**Archer, Lee**
See Ellison, Harlan

**Archilochus** c. 7th cent. B.C.- ...... **CMLC 44**
See also DLB 176

**Arden, John** 1930- ................. **CLC 6, 13, 15**
See also BRWS 2; CA 13-16R; CAAS 4;
CANR 31, 65, 67, 124; CBD; CD 5, 6;
DAM DRAM; DFS 9; DLB 13, 245;
EWL 3; MTCW 1

**Arenas, Reinaldo** 1943-1990 . **CLC 41; HLC 1**
See also CA 124; 128; 133; CANR 73, 106;
DAM MULT; DLB 145; EWL 3; GLL 2;
HW 1; LAW; LAWS 1; MTCW 2; MTFW
2005; RGSF 2; RGWL 3; WLIT 1

**Arendt, Hannah** 1906-1975 ....... **CLC 66, 98**
See also CA 17-20R; 61-64; CANR 26, 60;
DLB 242; MTCW 1, 2

**Aretino, Pietro** 1492-1556 .................. **LC 12**
See also RGWL 2, 3

**Arghezi, Tudor** ....................... **CLC 80**
See Theodorescu, Ion N.
See also CA 167; CDWLB 4; DLB 220;
EWL 3

**Arguedas, Jose Maria** 1911-1969 ... **CLC 10, 18; HLCS 1; TCLC 147**
See also CA 89-92; CANR 73; DLB 113;
EWL 3; HW 1; LAW; RGWL 2, 3; WLIT
1

**Argueta, Manlio** 1936- ..................... **CLC 31**
See also CA 131; CANR 73; CWW 2; DLB
145; EWL 3; HW 1; RGWL 3

**Arias, Ron** 1941- ............................... **HLC 1**
See also CA 131; CANR 81, 136; DAM
MULT; DLB 82; HW 1, 2; MTCW 2;
MTFW 2005

**Ariosto, Lodovico**
See Ariosto, Ludovico
See also WLIT 7

**Ariosto, Ludovico** 1474-1533 . **LC 6, 87; PC 42**
See Ariosto, Lodovico
See also EW 2; RGWL 2, 3

**Aristides**
See Epstein, Joseph

**Aristophanes** 450B.C.-385B.C. ...... **CMLC 4, 51; DC 2; WLCS**
See also AW 1; CDWLB 1; DA; DA3;
DAB; DAC; DAM DRAM, MST; DFS
10; DLB 176; LMFS 1; RGWL 2, 3;
TWA; WLIT 8

**Aristotle** 384B.C.-322B.C. ........... **CMLC 31; WLCS**
See also AW 1; CDWLB 1; DA; DA3;
DAB; DAC; DAM MST; DLB 176;
RGWL 2, 3; TWA; WLIT 8

**Arlt, Roberto (Godofredo Christophersen)**
1900-1942 ................. **HLC 1; TCLC 29**
See also CA 123; 131; CANR 67; DAM
MULT; DLB 305; EWL 3; HW 1, 2;
IDTP; LAW

**Armah, Ayi Kwei** 1939- ...... **BLC 1; CLC 5, 33, 136**
See also AFW; BRWS 10; BW 1; CA 61-
64; CANR 21, 64; CDWLB 3; CN 1, 2,
3, 4, 5, 6, 7; DAM MULT, POET; DLB
117; EWL 3; MTCW 1; WLIT 2

**Armatrading, Joan** 1950- ................. **CLC 17**
See also CA 114; 186

**Armin, Robert** 1568(?)-1615(?) ........ **LC 120**

**Armitage, Frank**
See Carpenter, John (Howard)

**Armstrong, Jeannette (C.)** 1948- ...... **NNAL**
See also CA 149; CCA 1; CN 6, 7; DAC;
SATA 102

**Arnette, Robert**
See Silverberg, Robert

**Arnim, Achim von (Ludwig Joachim von Arnim)** 1781-1831 . **NCLC 5, 159; SSC 29**
See also DLB 90

**Arnim, Bettina von** 1785-1859 .... **NCLC 38, 123**
See also DLB 90; RGWL 2, 3

**Arnold, Matthew** 1822-1888 .... **NCLC 6, 29, 89, 126; PC 5; WLC 1**
See also BRW 5; CDBLB 1832-1890; DA;
DAB; DAC; DAM MST, POET; DLB 32,
57; EXPP; PAB; PFS 2; TEA; WP

**Arnold, Thomas** 1795-1842 ........... **NCLC 18**
See also DLB 55

**Arnow, Harriette (Louisa) Simpson**
1908-1986 ......................... **CLC 2, 7, 18**
See also BPFB 1; CA 9-12R; 118; CANR
14; CN 2, 3, 4; DLB 6; FW; MTCW 1, 2;
RHW; SATA 42; SATA-Obit 47

**Arouet, Francois-Marie**
See Voltaire

**Arp, Hans**
See Arp, Jean

**Arp, Jean** 1887-1966 ...... **CLC 5; TCLC 115**
See also CA 81-84; 25-28R; CANR 42, 77;
EW 10

**Arrabal**
See Arrabal, Fernando

**Arrabal (Teran), Fernando**
See Arrabal, Fernando
See also CWW 2

**Arrabal, Fernando** 1932- .. **CLC 2, 9, 18, 58**
See Arrabal (Teran), Fernando
See also CA 9-12R; CANR 15; DLB 321;
EWL 3; LMFS 2

**Arreola, Juan Jose** 1918-2001 ...... **CLC 147; HLC 1; SSC 38**
See also CA 113; 131; 200; CANR 81;
CWW 2; DAM MULT; DLB 113; DNFS
2; EWL 3; HW 1, 2; LAW; RGSF 2

**Arrian** c. 89(?)-c. 155(?) ............... **CMLC 43**
See also DLB 176

**Arrick, Fran** ...................................... **CLC 30**
See Gaberman, Judie Angell
See also BYA 6

**Arrley, Richmond**
See Delany, Samuel R., Jr.

**Artaud, Antonin (Marie Joseph)** 1896-1948
...................... **DC 14; TCLC 3, 36**
See also CA 104; 149; DA3; DAM DRAM;
DFS 22; DLB 258, 321; EW 11; EWL 3;
GFL 1789 to the Present; MTCW 2;
MTFW 2005; RGWL 2, 3

**Arthur, Ruth M(abel)** 1905-1979 .... **CLC 12**
See also CA 9-12R; 85-88; CANR 4; CWRI
5; SATA 7, 26

**Artsybashev, Mikhail (Petrovich)** 1878-1927
...................................... **TCLC 31**
See also CA 170; DLB 295

**Arundel, Honor (Morfydd)** 1919-1973
...................................... **CLC 17**
See also CA 21-22; 41-44R; CAP 2; CLR
35; CWRI 5; SATA 4; SATA-Obit 24

**Arzner, Dorothy** 1900-1979 ............. **CLC 98**

**Asch, Sholem** 1880-1957 ................. **TCLC 3**
See also CA 105; EWL 3; GLL 2; RGHL

**Ascham, Roger** 1516(?)-1568 ............ **LC 101**
See also DLB 236

**Ash, Shalom**
See Asch, Sholem

**Ashbery, John** 1927- .. **CLC 2, 3, 4, 6, 9, 13, 15, 25, 41, 77, 125, 221; PC 26**
See Berry, Jonas
See also AMWS 3; CA 5-8R; CANR 9, 37,
66, 102, 132; CP 1, 2, 3, 4, 5, 6, 7; DA3;
DAM POET; DLB 5, 165; DLBY 1981;
EWL 3; INT CANR-9; MAL 5; MTCW
1, 2; MTFW 2005; PAB; PFS 11; RGAL
4; TCLE 1:1; WP

**Ashdown, Clifford**
See Freeman, R(ichard) Austin

**Ashe, Gordon**
See Creasey, John

**Ashton-Warner, Sylvia (Constance)**
1908-1984 ................................. **CLC 19**
See also CA 69-72; 112; CANR 29; CN 1,
2, 3; MTCW 1, 2

**Asimov, Isaac** 1920-1992 .... **CLC 1, 3, 9, 19, 26, 76, 92**
See also AAYA 13; BEST 90:2; BPFB 1;
BYA 4, 6, 7, 9; CA 1-4R; 137; CANR 2,
19, 36, 60, 125; CLR 12, 79; CMW 4;
CN 1, 2, 3, 4, 5; CPW; DA3; DAM POP;
DLB 8; DLBY 1992; INT CANR-19;
JRDA; LAIT 5; LMFS 2; MAICYA 1, 2;
MAL 5; MTCW 1, 2; MTFW 2005;
RGAL 4; SATA 1, 26, 74; SCFW 1, 2;
SFW 4; SSFS 17; TUS; YAW

**Askew, Anne** 1521(?)-1546 .................. **LC 81**
See also DLB 136

**Assis, Joaquim Maria Machado de**
See Machado de Assis, Joaquim Maria

**Astell, Mary** 1666-1731 ...................... **LC 68**
See also DLB 252; FW

**Astley, Thea (Beatrice May)** 1925-2004
...................................... **CLC 41**
See also CA 65-68; 229; CANR 11, 43, 78;
CN 1, 2, 3, 4, 5, 6, 7; DLB 289; EWL 3

**Astley, William** 1855-1911
See Warung, Price

**Aston, James**
See White, T(erence) H(anbury)

**Asturias, Miguel Angel** 1899-1974 ... **CLC 3, 8, 13; HLC 1; TCLC 184**
See also CA 25-28; 49-52; CANR 32; CAP
2; CDWLB 3; DA3; DAM MULT, NOV;
DLB 113, 290, 329; EWL 3; HW 1; LAW;
LMFS 2; MTCW 1, 2; RGWL 2, 3; WLIT
1

**Atares, Carlos Saura**
See Saura (Atares), Carlos

**Athanasius** c. 295-c. 373 ............... **CMLC 48**

**Atheling, William**
See Pound, Ezra (Weston Loomis)

**Atheling, William, Jr.**
See Blish, James (Benjamin)

**Atherton, Gertrude (Franklin Horn)**
1857-1948 ............................... **TCLC 2**
See also CA 104; 155; DLB 9, 78, 186;
HGG; RGAL 4; SUFW 1; TCWW 1, 2

**Atherton, Lucius**
See Masters, Edgar Lee

**Atkins, Jack**
See Harris, Mark

**Atkinson, Kate** 1951- ......................... **CLC 99**
See also CA 166; CANR 101, 153; DLB
267

**Attaway, William (Alexander)** 1911-1986
...................................... **BLC 1; CLC 92**
See also BW 2, 3; CA 143; CANR 82;
DAM MULT; DLB 76; MAL 5

**Atticus**
See Fleming, Ian; Wilson, (Thomas) Woodrow

**Atwood, Margaret** 1939- ...... **CLC 2, 3, 4, 8, 13, 15, 25, 44, 84, 135; PC 8; SSC 2, 46; WLC 1**
See also AAYA 12, 47; AMWS 13; BEST
89:2; BPFB 1; CA 49-52; CANR 3, 24,
33, 59, 95, 133; CN 2, 3, 4, 5, 6, 7; CP 1,

2, 3, 4, 5, 6, 7; CPW; CWP; DA; DA3; DAB; DAC; DAM MST, NOV, POET; DLB 53, 251, 326; EWL 3; EXPN; FL 1:5; FW; GL 2; INT CANR-24; LAIT 5; MTCW 1, 2; MTFW 2005; NFS 4, 12, 13, 14, 19; PFS 7; RGSF 2; SATA 50, 170; SSFS 3, 13; TCLE 1:1; TWA; WWE 1; YAW

**Atwood, Margaret Eleanor**
See Atwood, Margaret

**Aubigny, Pierre d'**
See Mencken, H(enry) L(ouis)

**Aubin, Penelope** 1685-1731(?) .............. **LC 9**
See also DLB 39

**Auchincloss, Louis** 1917- ... **CLC 4, 6, 9, 18, 45; SSC 22**
See also AMWS 4; CA 1-4R; CANR 6, 29, 55, 87, 130; CN 1, 2, 3, 4, 5, 6, 7; DAM NOV; DLB 2, 244; DLBY 1980; EWL 3; INT CANR-29; MAL 5; MTCW 1; RGAL 4

**Auchincloss, Louis Stanton**
See Auchincloss, Louis

**Auden, W(ystan) H(ugh)** 1907-1973
..... **CLC 1, 2, 3, 4, 6, 9, 11, 14, 43, 123; PC 1; WLC 1**
See also AAYA 18; AMWS 2; BRW 7; BRWR 1; CA 9-12R; 45-48; CANR 5, 61, 105; CDBLB 1914-1945; CP 1, 2; DA; DA3; DAB; DAC; DAM DRAM, MST, POET; DLB 10, 20; EWL 3; EXPP; MAL 5; MTCW 1, 2; MTFW 2005; PAB; PFS 1, 3, 4, 10; TUS; WP

**Audiberti, Jacques** 1899-1965 ......... **CLC 38**
See also CA 25-28R; DAM DRAM; DLB 321; EWL 3

**Audubon, John James** 1785-1851
..................................................... **NCLC 47**
See also AMWS 16; ANW; DLB 248

**Auel, Jean M(arie)** 1936- ......... **CLC 31, 107**
See also AAYA 7, 51; BEST 90:4; BPFB 1; CA 103; CANR 21, 64, 115; CPW; DA3; DAM POP; INT CANR-21; NFS 11; RHW; SATA 91

**Auerbach, Berthold** 1812-1882 ... **NCLC 171**
See also DLB 133

**Auerbach, Erich** 1892-1957 .......... **TCLC 43**
See also CA 118; 155; EWL 3

**Augier, Emile** 1820-1889 ............... **NCLC 31**
See also DLB 192; GFL 1789 to the Present

**August, John**
See De Voto, Bernard (Augustine)

**Augustine, St.** 354-430 ..... **CMLC 6; WLCS**
See also DA; DA3; DAB; DAC; DAM MST; DLB 115; EW 1; RGWL 2, 3; WLIT 8

**Aunt Belinda**
See Braddon, Mary Elizabeth

**Aunt Weedy**
See Alcott, Louisa May

**Aurelius**
See Bourne, Randolph S(illiman)

**Aurelius, Marcus** 121-180 ............ **CMLC 45**
See Marcus Aurelius
See also RGWL 2, 3

**Aurobindo, Sri**
See Ghose, Aurabinda

**Aurobindo Ghose**
See Ghose, Aurabinda

**Austen, Jane** 1775-1817 ..... **NCLC 1, 13, 19, 33, 51, 81, 95, 119, 150; WLC 1**
See also AAYA 19; BRW 4; BRWC 1; BRWR 2; BYA 3; CDBLB 1789-1832; DA; DA3; DAB; DAC; DAM MST, NOV; DLB 116; EXPN; FL 1:2; GL 2; LAIT 2; LATS 1:1; LMFS 1; NFS 1, 14, 18, 20, 21; TEA; WLIT 3; WYAS 1

**Auster, Paul** 1947- ............ **CLC 47, 131, 227**
See also AMWS 12; CA 69-72; CANR 23, 52, 75, 129; CMW 4; CN 5, 6, 7; DA3; DLB 227; MAL 5; MTCW 2; MTFW 2005; SUFW 2; TCLE 1:1

**Austin, Frank**
See Faust, Frederick (Schiller)

**Austin, Mary (Hunter)** 1868-1934
..................................................... **TCLC 25**
See also ANW; CA 109; 178; DLB 9, 78, 206, 221, 275; FW; TCWW 1, 2

**Averroes** 1126-1198 ......................... **CMLC 7**
See also DLB 115

**Avicenna** 980-1037 ......................... **CMLC 16**
See also DLB 115

**Avison, Margaret (Kirkland)** 1918- . **CLC 2, 4, 97**
See also CA 17-20R; CANR 134; CP 1, 2, 3, 4, 5, 6, 7; DAC; DAM POET; DLB 53; MTCW 1

**Axton, David**
See Koontz, Dean R.

**Ayckbourn, Alan** 1939- .... **CLC 5, 8, 18, 33, 74; DC 13**
See also BRWS 5; CA 21-24R; CANR 31, 59, 118; CBD; CD 5, 6; DAB; DAM DRAM; DFS 7; DLB 13, 245; EWL 3; MTCW 1, 2; MTFW 2005

**Aydy, Catherine**
See Tennant, Emma (Christina)

**Ayme, Marcel (Andre)** 1902-1967 .. **CLC 11; SSC 41**
See also CA 89-92; CANR 67, 137; CLR 25; DLB 72; EW 12; EWL 3; GFL 1789 to the Present; RGSF 2; RGWL 2, 3; SATA 91

**Ayrton, Michael** 1921-1975 ............... **CLC 7**
See also CA 5-8R; 61-64; CANR 9, 21

**Aytmatov, Chingiz**
See Aitmatov, Chingiz (Torekulovich)
See also EWL 3

**Azorin** ............................................... **CLC 11**
See Martinez Ruiz, Jose
See also DLB 322; EW 9; EWL 3

**Azuela, Mariano** 1873-1952 . **HLC 1; TCLC 3, 145**
See also CA 104; 131; CANR 81; DAM MULT; EWL 3; HW 1, 2; LAW; MTCW 1, 2; MTFW 2005

**Ba, Mariama** 1929-1981 ..................... **BLCS**
See also AFW; BW 2; CA 141; CANR 87; DNFS 2; WLIT 2

**Baastad, Babbis Friis**
See Friis-Baastad, Babbis Ellinor

**Bab**
See Gilbert, W(illiam) S(chwenck)

**Babbis, Eleanor**
See Friis-Baastad, Babbis Ellinor

**Babel, Isaac**
See Babel, Isaak (Emmanuilovich)
See also EW 11; SSFS 10

**Babel, Isaak (Emmanuilovich)** 1894-1941(?)
............... **SSC 16, 78; TCLC 2, 13, 171**
See Babel, Isaac
See also CA 104; 155; CANR 113; DLB 272; EWL 3; MTCW 2; MTFW 2005; RGSF 2; RGWL 2, 3; TWA

**Babits, Mihaly** 1883-1941 ............. **TCLC 14**
See also CA 114; CDWLB 4; DLB 215; EWL 3

**Babur** 1483-1530 ................................. **LC 18**

**Babylas** 1898-1962
See Ghelderode, Michel de

**Baca, Jimmy Santiago** 1952- ..... **HLC 1; PC 41**
See also CA 131; CANR 81, 90, 146; CP 6, 7; DAM MULT; DLB 122; HW 1, 2; LLW; MAL 5

**Baca, Jose Santiago**
See Baca, Jimmy Santiago

**Bacchelli, Riccardo** 1891-1985 ........ **CLC 19**
See also CA 29-32R; 117; DLB 264; EWL 3

**Bach, Richard** 1936- ......................... **CLC 14**
See also AITN 1; BEST 89:2; BPFB 1; BYA 5; CA 9-12R; CANR 18, 93, 151; CPW; DAM NOV, POP; FANT; MTCW 1; SATA 13

**Bach, Richard David**
See Bach, Richard

**Bache, Benjamin Franklin** 1769-1798
..................................................... **LC 74**
See also DLB 43

**Bachelard, Gaston** 1884-1962 ..... **TCLC 128**
See also CA 97-100; 89-92; DLB 296; GFL 1789 to the Present

**Bachman, Richard**
See King, Stephen

**Bachmann, Ingeborg** 1926-1973 ..... **CLC 69**
See also CA 93-96; 45-48; CANR 69; DLB 85; EWL 3; RGHL; RGWL 2, 3

**Bacon, Francis** 1561-1626 ... **LC 18, 32, 131**
See also BRW 1; CDBLB Before 1660; DLB 151, 236, 252; RGEL 2; TEA

**Bacon, Roger** 1214(?)-1294 .......... **CMLC 14**
See also DLB 115

**Bacovia, George** 1881-1957 ........... **TCLC 24**
See Vasiliu, Gheorghe
See also CDWLB 4; DLB 220; EWL 3

**Badanes, Jerome** 1937-1995 ........... **CLC 59**
See also CA 234

**Bagehot, Walter** 1826-1877 ............ **NCLC 10**
See also DLB 55

**Bagnold, Enid** 1889-1981 ............... **CLC 25**
See also BYA 2; CA 5-8R; 103; CANR 5, 40; CBD; CN 2; CWD; CWRI 5; DAM DRAM; DLB 13, 160, 191, 245; FW; MAICYA 1, 2; RGEL 2; SATA 1, 25

**Bagritsky, Eduard** ......................... **TCLC 60**
See Dzyubin, Eduard Georgievich

**Bagrjana, Elisaveta**
See Belcheva, Elisaveta Lyubomirova

**Bagryana, Elisaveta** ....................... **CLC 10**
See Belcheva, Elisaveta Lyubomirova
See also CA 178; CDWLB 4; DLB 147; EWL 3

**Bailey, Paul** 1937- ........................... **CLC 45**
See also CA 21-24R; CANR 16, 62, 124; CN 1, 2, 3, 4, 5, 6, 7; DLB 14, 271; GLL 2

**Baillie, Joanna** 1762-1851 ..... **NCLC 71, 151**
See also DLB 93; GL 2; RGEL 2

**Bainbridge, Beryl** 1934- ..... **CLC 4, 5, 8, 10, 14, 18, 22, 62, 130**
See also BRWS 6; CA 21-24R; CANR 24, 55, 75, 88, 128; CN 2, 3, 4, 5, 6, 7; DAM NOV; DLB 14, 231; EWL 3; MTCW 1, 2; MTFW 2005

**Baker, Carlos (Heard)** 1909-1987
..................................................... **TCLC 119**
See also CA 5-8R; 122; CANR 3, 63; DLB 103

**Baker, Elliott** 1922- ........................... **CLC 8**
See also CA 45-48; CANR 2, 63; CN 1, 2, 3, 4, 5, 6, 7

**Baker, Jean H.** ........................... **TCLC 3, 10**
See Russell, George William

**Baker, Nicholson** 1957- ........... **CLC 61, 165**
See also AMWS 13; CA 135; CANR 63, 120, 138; CN 6; CPW; DA3; DAM POP; DLB 227; MTFW 2005

**Baker, Ray Stannard** 1870-1946 .. **TCLC 47**
See also CA 118

**Baker, Russell** 1925- ....................... **CLC 31**
See also BEST 89:4; CA 57-60; CANR 11, 41, 59, 137; MTCW 1, 2; MTFW 2005

**Author Index**

**Beecher, Catharine Esther** 1800-1878
............................................ **NCLC 30**
See also DLB 1, 243

**Beecher, John** 1904-1980 .................... **CLC 6**
See also AITN 1; CA 5-8R; 105; CANR 8;
CP 1, 2, 3

**Beer, Johann** 1655-1700 ........................ **LC 5**
See also DLB 168

**Beer, Patricia** 1924- .......................... **CLC 58**
See also CA 61-64; 183; CANR 13, 46; CP
1, 2, 3, 4, 5, 6; CWP; DLB 40; FW

**Beerbohm, Max**
See Beerbohm, (Henry) Max(imilian)

**Beerbohm, (Henry) Max(imilian)** 1872-1956
............................................ **TCLC 1, 24**
See also BRWS 2; CA 104; 154; CANR 79;
DLB 34, 100; FANT; MTCW 2

**Beer-Hofmann, Richard** 1866-1945
............................................ **TCLC 60**
See also CA 160; DLB 81

**Beg, Shemus**
See Stephens, James

**Begiebing, Robert J(ohn)** 1946- ...... **CLC 70**
See also CA 122; CANR 40, 88

**Begley, Louis** 1933- .......................... **CLC 197**
See also CA 140; CANR 98; DLB 299;
RGHL; TCLE 1:1

**Behan, Brendan (Francis)** 1923-1964
............................ **CLC 1, 8, 11, 15, 79**
See also BRWS 2; CA 73-76; CANR 33,
121; CBD; CDBLB 1945-1960; DAM
DRAM; DFS 7; DLB 13, 233; EWL 3;
MTCW 1, 2

**Behn, Aphra** 1640(?)-1689 . **DC 4; LC 1, 30,
42; PC 13; WLC 1**
See also BRWS 3; DA; DA3; DAB; DAC;
DAM DRAM, MST, NOV, POET; DFS
16; DLB 39, 80, 131; FW; TEA; WLIT 3

**Behrman, S(amuel) N(athaniel)** 1893-1973
............................................ **CLC 40**
See also CA 13-16; 45-48; CAD; CAP 1;
DLB 7, 44; IDFW 3; MAL 5; RGAL 4

**Bekederemo, J. P. Clark**
See Clark Bekederemo, J.P.
See also CD 6

**Belasco, David** 1853-1931 ................ **TCLC 3**
See also CA 104; 168; DLB 7; MAL 5;
RGAL 4

**Belcheva, Elisaveta Lyubomirova** 1893-1991
............................................ **CLC 10**
See Bagryana, Elisaveta

**Beldone, Phil "Cheech"**
See Ellison, Harlan

**Beleno**
See Azuela, Mariano

**Belinski, Vissarion Grigoryevich** 1811-1848
............................................ **NCLC 5**
See also DLB 198

**Belitt, Ben** 1911- .............................. **CLC 22**
See also CA 13-16R; CAAS 4; CANR 7,
77; CP 1, 2, 3, 4, 5, 6; DLB 5

**Belknap, Jeremy** 1744-1798 ............. **LC 115**
See also DLB 30, 37

**Bell, Gertrude (Margaret Lowthian)**
1868-1926 .............................. **TCLC 67**
See also CA 167; CANR 110; DLB 174

**Bell, J. Freeman**
See Zangwill, Israel

**Bell, James Madison** 1826-1902 ....... **BLC 1;
TCLC 43**
See also BW 1; CA 122; 124; DAM MULT;
DLB 50

**Bell, Madison Smartt** 1957- ... **CLC 41, 102,
223**
See also AMWS 10; BPFB 1; CA 111; 183;
CAAE 183; CANR 28, 54, 73, 134; CN
5, 6, 7; CSW; DLB 218, 278; MTFW 2;
MTFW 2005

**Bell, Marvin (Hartley)** 1937- ...... **CLC 8, 31**
See also CA 21-24R; CAAS 14; CANR 59,
102; CP 1, 2, 3, 4, 5, 6, 7; DAM POET;
DLB 5; MAL 5; MTCW 1

**Bell, W. L. D.**
See Mencken, H(enry) L(ouis)

**Bellamy, Atwood C.**
See Mencken, H(enry) L(ouis)

**Bellamy, Edward** 1850-1898 .... **NCLC 4, 86,
147**
See also DLB 12; NFS 15; RGAL 4; SFW
4

**Belli, Gioconda** 1948- ...................... **HLCS 1**
See also CA 152; CANR 143; CWW 2;
DLB 290; EWL 3; RGWL 3

**Bellin, Edward J.**
See Kuttner, Henry

**Bello, Andres** 1781-1865 .............. **NCLC 131**
See also LAW

**Belloc, (Joseph) Hilaire (Pierre Sebastien
Rene Swanton)** 1870-1953 ........ **PC 24;
TCLC 7, 18**
See also CA 106; 152; CLR 102; CWRI 5;
DAM POET; DLB 19, 100, 141, 174;
EWL 3; MTCW 2; MTFW 2005; SATA
112; WCH; YABC 1

**Belloc, Joseph Peter Rene Hilaire**
See Belloc, (Joseph) Hilaire (Pierre Sebastien Rene Swanton)

**Belloc, Joseph Pierre Hilaire**
See Belloc, (Joseph) Hilaire (Pierre Sebastien Rene Swanton)

**Belloc, M. A.**
See Lowndes, Marie Adelaide (Belloc)

**Belloc-Lowndes, Mrs.**
See Lowndes, Marie Adelaide (Belloc)

**Bellow, Saul** 1915-2005 .... **CLC 1, 2, 3, 6, 8,
10, 13, 15, 25, 33, 34, 63, 79, 190, 200;
SSC 14; WLC 1**
See also AITN 2; AMW; AMWC 2; AMWR
2; BEST 89:3; BPFB 1; CA 5-8R; 238;
CABS 1; CANR 29, 53, 95, 132; CDALB
1941-1968; CN 1, 2, 3, 4, 5, 6, 7; DA;
DA3; DAB; DAC; DAM MST, NOV,
POP; DLB 2, 28, 299, 329; DLBD 3;
DLBY 1982; EWL 3; MAL 5; MTCW 1,
2; MTFW 2005; NFS 4, 14; RGAL 4;
RGHL; RGSF 2; SSFS 12, 22; TUS

**Belser, Reimond Karel Maria de** 1929-
See Ruyslinck, Ward
See also CA 152

**Bely, Andrey** ........................ **PC 11; TCLC 7**
See Bugayev, Boris Nikolayevich
See also DLB 295; EW 9; EWL 3

**Belyi, Andrei**
See Bugayev, Boris Nikolayevich
See also RGWL 2, 3

**Bembo, Pietro** 1470-1547 .................... **LC 79**
See also RGWL 2, 3

**Benary, Margot**
See Benary-Isbert, Margot

**Benary-Isbert, Margot** 1889-1979 ... **CLC 12**
See also CA 5-8R; 89-92; CANR 4, 72;
CLR 12; MAICYA 1, 2; SATA 2; SATA-
Obit 21

**Benavente (y Martinez), Jacinto** 1866-1954
.................... **DC 26; HLCS 1; TCLC 3**
See also CA 106; 131; CANR 81; DAM
DRAM, MULT; DLB 329; EWL 3; GLL
2; HW 1, 2; MTCW 1, 2

**Benchley, Peter** 1940-2006 ............. **CLC 4, 8**
See also AAYA 14; AITN 2; BPFB 1; CA
17-20R; 248; CANR 12, 35, 66, 115;
CPW; DAM NOV, POP; HGG; MTCW 1,
2; MTFW 2005; SATA 3, 89, 164

**Benchley, Peter Bradford**
See Benchley, Peter

**Benchley, Robert (Charles)** 1889-1945
............................................ **TCLC 1, 55**
See also CA 105; 153; DLB 11; MAL 5;
RGAL 4

**Benda, Julien** 1867-1956 .............. **TCLC 60**
See also CA 120; 154; GFL 1789 to the
Present

**Benedict, Ruth** 1887-1948 ............. **TCLC 60**
See also CA 158; CANR 146; DLB 246

**Benedict, Ruth Fulton**
See Benedict, Ruth

**Benedikt, Michael** 1935- .............. **CLC 4, 14**
See also CA 13-16R; CANR 7; CP 1, 2, 3,
4, 5, 6, 7; DLB 5

**Benet, Juan** 1927-1993 ...................... **CLC 28**
See also CA 143; EWL 3

**Benet, Stephen Vincent** 1898-1943 ... **PC 64;
SSC 10, 86; TCLC 7**
See also AMWS 11; CA 104; 152; DA3;
DAM POET; DLB 4, 48, 102, 249, 284;
DLBY 1997; EWL 3; HGG; MAL 5;
MTCW 2; MTFW 2005; RGAL 4; RGSF
2; SSFS 22; SUFW; WP; YABC 1

**Benet, William Rose** 1886-1950 .... **TCLC 28**
See also CA 118; 152; DAM POET; DLB
45; RGAL 4

**Benford, Gregory (Albert)** 1941- .... **CLC 52**
See also BPFB 1; CA 69-72, 175; CAAE
175; CAAS 27; CANR 12, 24, 49, 95,
134; CN 7; CSW; DLBY 1982; MTFW
2005; SCFW 2; SFW 4

**Bengtsson, Frans (Gunnar)** 1894-1954
............................................ **TCLC 48**
See also CA 170; EWL 3

**Benjamin, David**
See Slavitt, David R(ytman)

**Benjamin, Lois**
See Gould, Lois

**Benjamin, Walter** 1892-1940 ........ **TCLC 39**
See also CA 164; DLB 242; EW 11; EWL
3

**Ben Jelloun, Tahar** 1944-
See Jelloun, Tahar ben
See also CA 135; CWW 2; EWL 3; RGWL
3; WLIT 2

**Benn, Gottfried** 1886-1956 . **PC 35; TCLC 3**
See also CA 106; 153; DLB 56; EWL 3;
RGWL 2, 3

**Bennett, Alan** 1934- .................... **CLC 45, 77**
See also BRWS 8; CA 103; CANR 35, 55,
106, 157; CBD; CD 5, 6; DAB; DAM
MST; DLB 310; MTCW 1, 2; MTFW
2005

**Bennett, (Enoch) Arnold** 1867-1931
............................................ **TCLC 5, 20**
See also BRW 6; CA 106; 155; CDBLB
1890-1914; DLB 10, 34, 98, 135; EWL 3;
MTCW 2

**Bennett, Elizabeth**
See Mitchell, Margaret (Munnerlyn)

**Bennett, George Harold** 1930-
See Bennett, Hal
See also BW 1; CA 97-100; CANR 87

**Bennett, Gwendolyn B.** 1902-1981 ... **HR 1:2**
See also BW 1; CA 125; DLB 51; WP

**Bennett, Hal** ............................................ **CLC 5**
See Bennett, George Harold
See also CAAS 13; DLB 33

**Bennett, Jay** 1912- ............................ **CLC 35**
See also AAYA 10; CA 69-72; CANR 11,
42, 79; JRDA; SAAS 4; SATA 41, 87;
SATA-Brief 27; WYA; YAW

**Bennett, Louise** 1919-2006 . **BLC 1; CLC 28**
See also BW 2, 3; CA 151; CDWLB 3; CP
1, 2, 3, 4, 5, 6, 7; DAM MULT; DLB 117;
EWL 3

**Bennett-Coverley, Louise**
See Bennett, Louise

**Boyd, Nancy**
    See Millay, Edna St. Vincent
    See also GLL 1
**Boyd, Thomas (Alexander)** 1898-1935
    ................................ **TCLC 111**
    See also CA 111; 183; DLB 9; DLBD 16,
    316
**Boyd, William (Andrew Murray)** 1952-
    ................................ **CLC 28, 53, 70**
    See also CA 114; 120; CANR 51, 71, 131;
    CN 4, 5, 6, 7; DLB 231
**Boyesen, Hjalmar Hjorth** 1848-1895
    ................................ **NCLC 135**
    See also DLB 12, 71; DLBD 13; RGAL 4
**Boyle, Kay** 1902-1992 ....... **CLC 1, 5, 19, 58,**
    **121; SSC 5**
    See also CA 13-16R; 140; CAAS 1; CANR
    29, 61, 110; CN 1, 2, 3, 4, 5; CP 1, 2, 3,
    4, 5; DLB 4, 9, 48, 86; DLBY 1993; EWL
    3; MAL 5; MTCW 1, 2; MTFW 2005;
    RGAL 4; RGSF 2; SSFS 10, 13, 14
**Boyle, Mark**
    See Kienzle, William X.
**Boyle, Patrick** 1905-1982 ................ **CLC 19**
    See also CA 127
**Boyle, T. C.**
    See Boyle, T. Coraghessan
    See also AMWS 8
**Boyle, T. Coraghessan** 1948- .... **CLC 36, 55,**
    **90; SSC 16**
    See Boyle, T. C.
    See also AAYA 47; BEST 90:4; BPFB 1;
    CA 120; CANR 44, 76, 89, 132; CN 6, 7;
    CPW; DA3; DAM POP; DLB 218, 278;
    DLBY 1986; EWL 3; MAL 5; MTCW 2;
    MTFW 2005; SSFS 13, 19
**Boz**
    See Dickens, Charles (John Huffam)
**Brackenridge, Hugh Henry** 1748-1816
    ................................ **NCLC 7**
    See also DLB 11, 37; RGAL 4
**Bradbury, Edward P.**
    See Moorcock, Michael
    See also MTCW 2
**Bradbury, Malcolm (Stanley)** 1932-2000
    ................................ **CLC 32, 61**
    See also CA 1-4R; CANR 1, 33, 91, 98,
    137; CN 1, 2, 3, 4, 5, 6, 7; CP 1; DA3;
    DAM NOV; DLB 14, 207; EWL 3;
    MTCW 1, 2; MTFW 2005
**Bradbury, Ray** 1920- .. **CLC 1, 3, 10, 15, 42,**
    **98; SSC 29, 53; WLC 1**
    See also AAYA 15; AITN 1, 2; AMWS 4;
    BPFB 1; BYA 4, 5, 11; CA 1-4R; CANR
    2, 30, 75, 125; CDALB 1968-1988; CN
    1, 2, 3, 4, 5, 6, 7; CPW; DA; DA3; DAB;
    DAC; DAM MST, NOV, POP; DLB 2, 8;
    EXPN; EXPS; HGG; LAIT 3, 5; LATS
    1:2; LMFS 2; MAL 5; MTCW 1, 2;
    MTFW 2005; NFS 1, 22; RGAL 4; RGSF
    2; SATA 11, 64, 123; SCFW 1, 2; SFW 4;
    SSFS 1, 20; SUFW 1, 2; TUS; YAW
**Braddon, Mary Elizabeth** 1837-1915
    ................................ **TCLC 111**
    See also BRWS 8; CA 108; 179; CMW 4;
    DLB 18, 70, 156; HGG
**Bradfield, Scott** 1955- ...................... **SSC 65**
    See also CA 147; CANR 90; HGG; SUFW
    2
**Bradfield, Scott Michael**
    See Bradfield, Scott
**Bradford, Gamaliel** 1863-1932 ..... **TCLC 36**
    See also CA 160; DLB 17
**Bradford, William** 1590-1657 ............. **LC 64**
    See also DLB 24, 30; RGAL 4
**Bradley, David (Henry), Jr.** 1950- ... **BLC 1;**
    **CLC 23, 118**
    See also BW 1, 3; CA 104; CANR 26, 81;
    CN 4, 5, 6, 7; DAM MULT; DLB 33

**Bradley, John Ed** 1958- ................... **CLC 55**
    See also CA 139; CANR 99; CN 6, 7; CSW
**Bradley, John Edmund, Jr.**
    See Bradley, John Ed
**Bradley, Marion Zimmer** 1930-1999
    ................................ **CLC 30**
    See Chapman, Lee; Dexter, John; Gardner,
    Miriam; Ives, Morgan; Rivers, Elfrida
    See also AAYA 40; BPFB 1; CA 57-60; 185;
    CAAS 10; CANR 7, 31, 51, 75, 107;
    CPW; DA3; DAM POP; DLB 8; FANT;
    FW; MTCW 1, 2; MTFW 2005; SATA 90,
    139; SATA-Obit 116; SFW 4; SUFW 2;
    YAW
**Bradshaw, John** 1933- ................... **CLC 70**
    See also CA 138; CANR 61
**Bradstreet, Anne** 1612(?)-1672 ..... **LC 4, 30,**
    **130; PC 10**
    See also AMWS 1; CDALB 1640-1865;
    DA; DA3; DAC; DAM MST, POET; DLB
    24; EXPP; FW; PFS 6; RGAL 4; TUS;
    WP
**Brady, Joan** 1939- ........................... **CLC 86**
    See also CA 141
**Bragg, Melvyn** 1939- ...................... **CLC 10**
    See also BEST 89:3; CA 57-60; CANR 10,
    48, 89; CN 1, 2, 3, 4, 5, 6, 7; DLB 14,
    271; RHW
**Brahe, Tycho** 1546-1601 ...................... **LC 45**
    See also DLB 300
**Braine, John (Gerard)** 1922-1986 .... **CLC 1,**
    **3, 41**
    See also CA 1-4R; 120; CANR 1, 33; CD-
    BLB 1945-1960; CN 1, 2, 3, 4; DLB 15;
    DLBY 1986; EWL 3; MTCW 1
**Braithwaite, William Stanley (Beaumont)**
    1878-1962 ........ **BLC 1; HR 1:2; PC 52**
    See also BW 1; CA 125; DAM MULT; DLB
    50, 54; MAL 5
**Bramah, Ernest** 1868-1942 ........... **TCLC 72**
    See also CA 156; CMW 4; DLB 70; FANT
**Brammer, Billy Lee**
    See Brammer, William
**Brammer, William** 1929-1978 ......... **CLC 31**
    See also CA 235; 77-80
**Brancati, Vitaliano** 1907-1954 ...... **TCLC 12**
    See also CA 109; DLB 264; EWL 3
**Brancato, Robin F(idler)** 1936- ....... **CLC 35**
    See also AAYA 9, 68; BYA 6; CA 69-72;
    CANR 11, 45; CLR 32; JRDA; MAICYA
    2; MAICYAS 1; SAAS 9; SATA 97;
    WYA; YAW
**Brand, Dionne** 1953- ...................... **CLC 192**
    See also BW 2; CA 143; CANR 143; CWP
**Brand, Max**
    See Faust, Frederick (Schiller)
    See also BPFB 1; TCWW 1, 2
**Brand, Millen** 1906-1980 .................. **CLC 7**
    See also CA 21-24R; 97-100; CANR 72
**Branden, Barbara** ........................... **CLC 44**
    See also CA 148
**Brandes, Georg (Morris Cohen)** 1842-1927
    ................................ **TCLC 10**
    See also CA 105; 189; DLB 300
**Brandys, Kazimierz** 1916-2000 ....... **CLC 62**
    See also CA 239; EWL 3
**Branley, Franklyn M(ansfield)** 1915-2002
    ................................ **CLC 21**
    See also CA 33-36R; 207; CANR 14, 39;
    CLR 13; MAICYA 1, 2; SAAS 16; SATA
    4, 68, 136
**Brant, Beth (E.)** 1941- ...................... **NNAL**
    See also CA 144; FW
**Brant, Sebastian** 1457-1521 ............. **LC 112**
    See also DLB 179; RGWL 2, 3

**Brathwaite, Edward Kamau** 1930-
    ........................ **BLCS; CLC 11; PC 56**
    See also BRWS 12; BW 2, 3; CA 25-28R;
    CANR 11, 26, 47, 107; CDWLB 3; CP 1,
    2, 3, 4, 5, 6, 7; DAM POET; DLB 125;
    EWL 3
**Brathwaite, Kamau**
    See Brathwaite, Edward Kamau
**Brautigan, Richard (Gary)** 1935-1984
    .. **CLC 1, 3, 5, 9, 12, 34, 42; TCLC 133**
    See also BPFB 1; CA 53-56; 113; CANR
    34; CN 1, 2, 3; CP 1, 2, 3, 4; DA3; DAM
    NOV; DLB 2, 5, 206; DLBY 1980, 1984;
    FANT; MAL 5; MTCW 1; RGAL 4;
    SATA 56
**Brave Bird, Mary** ........................... **NNAL**
    See Crow Dog, Mary
**Braverman, Kate** 1950- .................. **CLC 67**
    See also CA 89-92; CANR 141
**Brecht, (Eugen) Bertolt (Friedrich)**
    1898-1956 .... **DC 3; TCLC 1, 6, 13, 35,**
    **169; WLC 1**
    See also CA 104; 133; CANR 62; CDWLB
    2; DA; DA3; DAB; DAC; DAM DRAM,
    MST; DFS 4, 5, 9; DLB 56, 124; EW 11;
    EWL 3; IDTP; MTCW 1, 2; MTFW 2005;
    RGHL; RGWL 2, 3; TWA
**Brecht, Eugen Berthold Friedrich**
    See Brecht, (Eugen) Bertolt (Friedrich)
**Bremer, Fredrika** 1801-1865 ......... **NCLC 11**
    See also DLB 254
**Brennan, Christopher John** 1870-1932
    ................................ **TCLC 17**
    See also CA 117; 188; DLB 230; EWL 3
**Brennan, Maeve** 1917-1993 .. **CLC 5; TCLC**
    **124**
    See also CA 81-84; CANR 72, 100
**Brenner, Jozef** 1887-1919
    See Csath, Geza
    See also CA 240
**Brent, Linda**
    See Jacobs, Harriet A(nn)
**Brentano, Clemens (Maria)** 1778-1842
    ................................ **NCLC 1**
    See also DLB 90; RGWL 2, 3
**Brent of Bin Bin**
    See Franklin, (Stella Maria Sarah) Miles
    (Lampe)
**Brenton, Howard** 1942- .................. **CLC 31**
    See also CA 69-72; CANR 33, 67; CBD;
    CD 5, 6; DLB 13; MTCW 1
**Breslin, James** 1930-
    See Breslin, Jimmy
    See also CA 73-76; CANR 31, 75, 139;
    DAM NOV; MTCW 1, 2; MTFW 2005
**Breslin, Jimmy** ........................... **CLC 4, 43**
    See Breslin, James
    See also AITN 1; DLB 185; MTCW 2
**Bresson, Robert** 1901(?)-1999 ......... **CLC 16**
    See also CA 110; 187; CANR 49
**Breton, Andre** 1896-1966 . **CLC 2, 9, 15, 54;**
    **PC 15**
    See also CA 19-20; 25-28R; CANR 40, 60;
    CAP 2; DLB 65, 258; EW 11; EWL 3;
    GFL 1789 to the Present; LMFS 2;
    MTCW 1, 2; MTFW 2005; RGWL 2, 3;
    TWA; WP
**Breton, Nicholas** c. 1554-c. 1626 ...... **LC 133**
    See also DLB 136
**Breytenbach, Breyten** 1939(?)- ....... **CLC 23,**
    **37, 126**
    See also CA 113; 129; CANR 61, 122;
    CWW 2; DAM POET; DLB 225; EWL 3
**Bridgers, Sue Ellen** 1942- ............... **CLC 26**
    See also AAYA 8, 49; BYA 7, 8; CA 65-68;
    CANR 11, 36; CLR 18; DLB 52; JRDA;
    MAICYA 1, 2; SAAS 1; SATA 22, 90;
    SATA-Essay 109; WYA; YAW

**Bridges, Robert (Seymour)** 1844-1930
.................................... **PC 28; TCLC 1**
See also BRW 6; CA 104; 152; CDBLB
1890-1914; DAM POET; DLB 19, 98
**Bridie, James** ..................................... **TCLC 3**
See Mavor, Osborne Henry
See also DLB 10; EWL 3
**Brin, David** 1950- ................................ **CLC 34**
See also AAYA 21; CA 102; CANR 24, 70,
125, 127; INT CANR-24; SATA 65;
SCFW 2; SFW 4
**Brink, Andre** 1935- ............ **CLC 18, 36, 106**
See also AFW; BRWS 6; CA 104; CANR
39, 62, 109, 133; CN 4, 5, 6, 7; DLB 225;
EWL 3; INT CA-103; LATS 1:2; MTCW
1, 2; MTFW 2005; WLIT 2
**Brinsmead, H. F.**
See Brinsmead, H(esba) F(ay)
**Brinsmead, H. F(ay)**
See Brinsmead, H(esba) F(ay)
**Brinsmead, H(esba) F(ay)** 1922- ..... **CLC 21**
See also CA 21-24R; CANR 10; CLR 47;
CWRI 5; MAICYA 1, 2; SAAS 5; SATA
18, 78
**Brittain, Vera (Mary)** 1893(?)-1970
.................................... **CLC 23**
See also BRWS 10; CA 13-16; 25-28R;
CANR 58; CAP 1; DLB 191; FW; MTCW
1, 2
**Broch, Hermann** 1886-1951 .......... **TCLC 20**
See also CA 117; 211; CDWLB 2; DLB 85,
124; EW 10; EWL 3; RGWL 2, 3
**Brock, Rose**
See Hansen, Joseph
See also GLL 1
**Brod, Max** 1884-1968 ................... **TCLC 115**
See also CA 5-8R; 25-28R; CANR 7; DLB
81; EWL 3
**Brodkey, Harold (Roy)** 1930-1996 . **CLC 56;**
**TCLC 123**
See also CA 111; 151; CANR 71; CN 4, 5,
6; DLB 130
**Brodsky, Iosif Alexandrovich** 1940-1996
See Brodsky, Joseph
See also AITN 1; CA 41-44R; 151; CANR
37, 106; DA3; DAM POET; MTCW 1, 2;
MTFW 2005; RGWL 2, 3
**Brodsky, Joseph** . **CLC 4, 6, 13, 36, 100; PC**
**9**
See Brodsky, Iosif Alexandrovich
See also AAYA 71; AMWS 8; CWW 2;
DLB 285, 329; EWL 3; MTCW 1
**Brodsky, Michael** 1948- ................... **CLC 19**
See also CA 102; CANR 18, 41, 58, 147;
DLB 244
**Brodsky, Michael Mark**
See Brodsky, Michael
**Brodzki, Bella** ............................... **CLC 65**
**Brome, Richard** 1590(?)-1652 ............ **LC 61**
See also BRWS 10; DLB 58
**Bromell, Henry** 1947- ......................... **CLC 5**
See also CA 53-56; CANR 9, 115, 116
**Bromfield, Louis (Brucker)** 1896-1956
.................................... **TCLC 11**
See also CA 107; 155; DLB 4, 9, 86; RGAL
4; RHW
**Broner, E(sther) M(asserman)** 1930-
.................................... **CLC 19**
See also CA 17-20R; CANR 8, 25, 72; CN
4, 5, 6; DLB 28
**Bronk, William (M.)** 1918-1999 ...... **CLC 10**
See also CA 89-92; 177; CANR 23; CP 3,
4, 5, 6, 7; DLB 165
**Bronstein, Lev Davidovich**
See Trotsky, Leon
**Bronte, Anne**
See Bronte, Anne

**Bronte, Anne** 1820-1849 ... **NCLC 4, 71, 102**
See also BRW 5; BRWR 1; DA3; DLB 21,
199; TEA
**Bronte, (Patrick) Branwell** 1817-1848
.................................... **NCLC 109**
**Bronte, Charlotte**
See Bronte, Charlotte
**Bronte, Charlotte** 1816-1855 ..... **NCLC 3, 8,**
**33, 58, 105, 155; WLC 1**
See also AAYA 17; BRW 5; BRWC 2;
BRWR 1; BYA 2; CDBLB 1832-1890;
DA; DA3; DAB; DAC; DAM MST, NOV;
DLB 21, 159, 199; EXPN; FL 1:2; GL 2;
LAIT 2; NFS 4; TEA; WLIT 4
**Bronte, Emily**
See Bronte, Emily (Jane)
**Bronte, Emily (Jane)** 1818-1848 .. **NCLC 16,**
**35, 165; PC 8; WLC 1**
See also AAYA 17; BPFB 1; BRW 5;
BRWC 1; BRWR 1; BYA 3; CDBLB
1832-1890; DA; DA3; DAB; DAC; DAM
MST, NOV, POET; DLB 21, 32, 199;
EXPN; FL 1:2; GL 2; LAIT 1; TEA;
WLIT 3
**Brontes**
See Bronte, Anne; Bronte, Charlotte; Bronte,
Emily (Jane)
**Brooke, Frances** 1724-1789 ........... **LC 6, 48**
See also DLB 39, 99
**Brooke, Henry** 1703(?)-1783 ................. **LC 1**
See also DLB 39
**Brooke, Rupert (Chawner)** 1887-1915
.................................... **PC 24; TCLC 2, 7; WLC 1**
See also BRWS 3; CA 104; 132; CANR 61;
CDBLB 1914-1945; DA; DAB; DAC;
DAM MST, POET; DLB 19, 216; EXPP;
GLL 2; MTCW 1, 2; MTFW 2005; PFS
7; TEA
**Brooke-Haven, P.**
See Wodehouse, P(elham) G(renville)
**Brooke-Rose, Christine** 1926(?)- .... **CLC 40,**
**184**
See also BRWS 4; CA 13-16R; CANR 58,
118; CN 1, 2, 3, 4, 5, 6, 7; DLB 14, 231;
EWL 3; SFW 4
**Brookner, Anita** 1928- . **CLC 32, 34, 51, 136**
See also BRWS 4; CA 114; 120; CANR 37,
56, 87, 130; CN 4, 5, 6, 7; CPW; DA3;
DAB; DAM POP; DLB 194, 326; DLBY
1987; EWL 3; MTCW 1, 2; MTFW 2005;
NFS 23; TEA
**Brooks, Cleanth** 1906-1994 ...... **CLC 24, 86,**
**110**
See also AMWS 14; CA 17-20R; 145;
CANR 33, 35; CSW; DLB 63; DLBY
1994; EWL 3; INT CANR-35; MAL 5;
MTCW 1, 2; MTFW 2005
**Brooks, George**
See Baum, L(yman) Frank
**Brooks, Gwendolyn** 1917-2000 ......... **BLC 1;**
**CLC 1, 2, 4, 5, 15, 49, 125; PC 7;**
**WLC 1**
See also AAYA 20; AFAW 1, 2; AITN 1;
AMWS 3; BW 2, 3; CA 1-4R; 190; CANR
1, 27, 52, 75, 132; CDALB 1941-1968;
CLR 27; CP 1, 2, 3, 4, 5, 6, 7; CWP; DA;
DA3; DAC; DAM MST, MULT, POET;
DLB 5, 76, 165; EWL 3; EXPP; FL 1:5;
MAL 5; MBL; MTCW 1, 2; MTFW 2005;
PFS 1, 2, 4, 6; RGAL 4; SATA 6; SATA-
Obit 123; TUS; WP
**Brooks, Mel** 1926-
See Kaminsky, Melvin
See also CA 65-68; CANR 16; DFS 21
**Brooks, Peter (Preston)** 1938- ........ **CLC 34**
See also CA 45-48; CANR 1, 107
**Brooks, Van Wyck** 1886-1963 ....... **CLC 29**
See also AMW; CA 1-4R; CANR 6; DLB
45, 63, 103; MAL 5; TUS

**Brophy, Brigid (Antonia)** 1929-1995
.................................... **CLC 6, 11, 29, 105**
See also CA 5-8R; 149; CAAS 4; CANR
25, 53; CBD; CN 1, 2, 3, 4, 5, 6; CWD;
DA3; DLB 14, 271; EWL 3; MTCW 1, 2
**Brosman, Catharine Savage** 1934- ... **CLC 9**
See also CA 61-64; CANR 21, 46, 149
**Brossard, Nicole** 1943- ........... **CLC 115, 169**
See also CA 122; CAAS 16; CANR 140;
CCA 1; CWP; CWW 2; DLB 53; EWL 3;
FW; GLL 2; RGWL 3
**Brother Antoninus**
See Everson, William (Oliver)
**Brothers Grimm**
See Grimm, Jacob Ludwig Karl; Grimm,
Wilhelm Karl
**The Brothers Quay**
See Quay, Stephen; Quay, Timothy
**Broughton, T(homas) Alan** 1936- ... **CLC 19**
See also CA 45-48; CANR 2, 23, 48, 111
**Broumas, Olga** 1949- ................ **CLC 10, 73**
See also CA 85-88; CANR 20, 69, 110; CP
5, 6, 7; CWP; GLL 2
**Broun, Heywood** 1888-1939 ........ **TCLC 104**
See also DLB 29, 171
**Brown, Alan** 1950- ........................... **CLC 99**
See also CA 156
**Brown, Charles Brockden** 1771-1810
.................................... **NCLC 22, 74, 122**
See also AMWS 1; CDALB 1640-1865;
DLB 37, 59, 73; FW; GL 2; HGG; LMFS
1; RGAL 4; TUS
**Brown, Christy** 1932-1981 ................. **CLC 63**
See also BYA 13; CA 105; 104; CANR 72;
DLB 14
**Brown, Claude** 1937-2002 . **BLC 1; CLC 30**
See also AAYA 7; BW 1, 3; CA 73-76; 205;
CANR 81; DAM MULT
**Brown, Dan** 1964- ........................... **CLC 209**
See also AAYA 55; CA 217; MTFW 2005
**Brown, Dee** 1908-2002 .............. **CLC 18, 47**
See also AAYA 30; CA 13-16R; 212; CAAS
6; CANR 11, 45, 60, 150; CPW; CSW;
DA3; DAM POP; DLBY 1980; LAIT 2;
MTCW 1, 2; MTFW 2005; NCFS 5;
SATA 5, 110; SATA-Obit 141; TCWW 1,
2
**Brown, Dee Alexander**
See Brown, Dee
**Brown, George**
See Wertmueller, Lina
**Brown, George Douglas** 1869-1902
.................................... **TCLC 28**
See Douglas, George
See also CA 162
**Brown, George Mackay** 1921-1996 . **CLC 5,**
**48, 100**
See also BRWS 6; CA 21-24R; 151; CAAS
6; CANR 12, 37, 67; CN 1, 2, 3, 4, 5, 6;
CP 1, 2, 3, 4, 5, 6; DLB 14, 27, 139, 271;
MTCW 1; RGSF 2; SATA 35
**Brown, (William) Larry** 1951-2004
.................................... **CLC 73**
See also CA 130; 134; 233; CANR 117,
145; CSW; DLB 234; INT CA-134
**Brown, Moses**
See Barrett, William (Christopher)
**Brown, Rita Mae** 1944- ....... **CLC 18, 43, 79**
See also BPFB 1; CA 45-48; CANR 2, 11,
35, 62, 95, 138; CN 5, 6, 7; CPW; CSW;
DA3; DAM NOV, POP; FW; INT CANR-
11; MAL 5; MTCW 1, 2; MTFW 2005;
NFS 9; RGAL 4; TUS
**Brown, Roderick (Langmere) Haig-**
See Haig-Brown, Roderick (Langmere)
**Brown, Rosellen** 1939- .............. **CLC 32, 170**
See also CA 77-80; CAAS 10; CANR 14,
44, 98; CN 6, 7

**Calvin, Jean**
See Calvin, John
See also DLB 327; GFL Beginnings to 1789
**Calvin, John** 1509-1564 ..................... **LC 37**
See Calvin, Jean
**Calvino, Italo** 1923-1985 .. **CLC 5, 8, 11, 22, 33, 39, 73; SSC 3, 48; TCLC 183**
See also AAYA 58; CA 85-88; 116; CANR 23, 61, 132; DAM NOV; DLB 196; EW 13; EWL 3; MTCW 1, 2; MTFW 2005; RGHL; RGSF 2; RGWL 2, 3; SFW 4; SSFS 12; WLIT 7
**Camara Laye**
See Laye, Camara
See also EWL 3
**Camden, William** 1551-1623 ............. **LC 77**
See also DLB 172
**Cameron, Carey** 1952- .................... **CLC 59**
See also CA 135
**Cameron, Peter** 1959- ..................... **CLC 44**
See also AMWS 12; CA 125; CANR 50, 117; DLB 234; GLL 2
**Camoens, Luis Vaz de** 1524(?)-1580
See Camoes, Luis de
See also EW 2
**Camoes, Luis de** 1524(?)-1580 ....... **HLCS 1; LC 62; PC 31**
See Camoens, Luis Vaz de
See also DLB 287; RGWL 2, 3
**Campana, Dino** 1885-1932 ............ **TCLC 20**
See also CA 117; 246; DLB 114; EWL 3
**Campanella, Tommaso** 1568-1639 ..... **LC 32**
See also RGWL 2, 3
**Campbell, John W(ood, Jr.)** 1910-1971
..................................................... **CLC 32**
See also CA 21-22; 29-32R; CANR 34; CAP 2; DLB 8; MTCW 1; SCFW 1, 2; SFW 4
**Campbell, Joseph** 1904-1987 ......... **CLC 69; TCLC 140**
See also AAYA 3, 66; BEST 89:2; CA 1-4R; 124; CANR 3, 28, 61, 107; DA3; MTCW 1, 2
**Campbell, Maria** 1940- ...... **CLC 85; NNAL**
See also CA 102; CANR 54; CCA 1; DAC
**Campbell, (John) Ramsey** 1946- ... **CLC 42; SSC 19**
See also AAYA 51; CA 57-60, 228; CAAE 228; CANR 7, 102; DLB 261; HGG; INT CANR-7; SUFW 1, 2
**Campbell, (Ignatius) Roy (Dunnachie)** 1901-1957 ................................. **TCLC 5**
See also AFW; CA 104; 155; DLB 20, 225; EWL 3; MTCW 2; RGEL 2
**Campbell, Thomas** 1777-1844 ...... **NCLC 19**
See also DLB 93, 144; RGEL 2
**Campbell, Wilfred** ........................... **TCLC 9**
See Campbell, William
**Campbell, William** 1858(?)-1918
See Campbell, Wilfred
See also CA 106; DLB 92
**Campbell, William Edward March** 1893-1954
See March, William
See also CA 108
**Campion, Jane** 1954- ............... **CLC 95, 229**
See also AAYA 33; CA 138; CANR 87
**Campion, Thomas** 1567-1620 ............ **LC 78**
See also CDBLB Before 1660; DAM POET; DLB 58, 172; RGEL 2
**Camus, Albert** 1913-1960 ..... **CLC 1, 2, 4, 9, 11, 14, 32, 63, 69, 124; DC 2; SSC 9, 76; WLC 1**
See also AAYA 36; AFW; BPFB 1; CA 89-92; CANR 131; DA; DA3; DAB; DAC; DAM DRAM, MST, NOV; DLB 72, 321, 329; EW 13; EWL 3; EXPN; EXPS; GFL

1789 to the Present; LATS 1:2; LMFS 2; MTCW 1, 2; MTFW 2005; NFS 6, 16; RGHL; RGSF 2; RGWL 2, 3; SSFS 4; TWA
**Canby, Vincent** 1924-2000 ............... **CLC 13**
See also CA 81-84; 191
**Cancale**
See Desnos, Robert
**Canetti, Elias** 1905-1994 ....... **CLC 3, 14, 25, 75, 86; TCLC 157**
See also CA 21-24R; 146; CANR 23, 61, 79; CDWLB 2; CWW 2; DA3; DLB 85, 124, 329; EW 12; EWL 3; MTCW 1, 2; MTFW 2005; RGWL 2, 3; TWA
**Canfield, Dorothea F.**
See Fisher, Dorothy (Frances) Canfield
**Canfield, Dorothea Frances**
See Fisher, Dorothy (Frances) Canfield
**Canfield, Dorothy**
See Fisher, Dorothy (Frances) Canfield
**Canin, Ethan** 1960- .......... **CLC 55; SSC 70**
See also CA 131; 135; MAL 5
**Cankar, Ivan** 1876-1918 .............. **TCLC 105**
See also CDWLB 4; DLB 147; EWL 3
**Cannon, Curt**
See Hunter, Evan
**Cao, Lan** 1961- ................................ **CLC 109**
See also CA 165
**Cape, Judith**
See Page, P(atricia) K(athleen)
See also CCA 1
**Capek, Karel** 1890-1938 ....... **DC 1; SSC 36; TCLC 6, 37; WLC 1**
See also CA 104; 140; CDWLB 4; DA; DA3; DAB; DAC; DAM DRAM, MST, NOV; DFS 7, 11; DLB 215; EW 10; EWL 3; MTCW 2; MTFW 2005; RGSF 2; RGWL 2, 3; SCFW 1, 2; SFW 4
**Capella, Martianus** fl. 4th cent. - .. **CMLC 84**
**Capote, Truman** 1924-1984 ...... **CLC 1, 3, 8, 13, 19, 34, 38, 58; SSC 2, 47, 93; TCLC 164; WLC 1**
See also AAYA 61; AMWS 3; BPFB 1; CA 5-8R; 113; CANR 18, 62; CDALB 1941-1968; CN 1, 2, 3; CPW; DA; DA3; DAB; DAC; DAM MST, NOV, POP; DLB 2, 185, 227; DLBY 1980, 1984; EWL 3; EXPS; GLL 1; LAIT 3; MAL 5; MTCW 1, 2; MTFW 2005; NCFS 2; RGAL 4; RGSF 2; SATA 91; SSFS 2; TUS
**Capra, Frank** 1897-1991 ................. **CLC 16**
See also AAYA 52; CA 61-64; 135
**Caputo, Philip** 1941- ....................... **CLC 32**
See also AAYA 60; CA 73-76; CANR 40, 135; YAW
**Caragiale, Ion Luca** 1852-1912 .... **TCLC 76**
See also CA 157
**Card, Orson Scott** 1951- ..... **CLC 44, 47, 50**
See also AAYA 11, 42; BPFB 1; BYA 5, 8; CA 102; CANR 27, 47, 73, 102, 106, 133; CLR 116; CPW; DA3; DAM POP; FANT; INT CANR-27; MTCW 1, 2; MTFW 2005; NFS 5; SATA 83, 127; SCFW 2; SFW 4; SUFW 2; YAW
**Cardenal, Ernesto** 1925- ........ **CLC 31, 161; HLC 1; PC 22**
See also CA 49-52; CANR 2, 32, 66, 138; CWW 2; DAM MULT, POET; DLB 290; EWL 3; HW 1, 2; LAWS 1; MTCW 1, 2; MTFW 2005; RGWL 2, 3
**Cardinal, Marie** 1929-2001 ............ **CLC 189**
See also CA 177; CWW 2; DLB 83; FW
**Cardozo, Benjamin N(athan)** 1870-1938
................................................. **TCLC 65**
See also CA 117; 164
**Carducci, Giosue (Alessandro Giuseppe)** 1835-1907 ................. **PC 46; TCLC 32**
See also CA 163; DLB 329; EW 7; RGWL 2, 3

**Carew, Thomas** 1595(?)-1640 ..... **LC 13; PC 29**
See also BRW 2; DLB 126; PAB; RGEL 2
**Carey, Ernestine Gilbreth** 1908-2006
................................................. **CLC 17**
See also CA 5-8R; CANR 71; SATA 2
**Carey, Peter** 1943- ....... **CLC 40, 55, 96, 183**
See also BRWS 12; CA 123; 127; CANR 53, 76, 117, 157; CN 4, 5, 6, 7; DLB 289, 326; EWL 3; INT CA-127; MTCW 1, 2; MTFW 2005; RGSF 2; SATA 94
**Carleton, William** 1794-1869 .......... **NCLC 3**
See also DLB 159; RGEL 2; RGSF 2
**Carlisle, Henry (Coffin)** 1926- ......... **CLC 33**
See also CA 13-16R; CANR 15, 85
**Carlsen, Chris**
See Holdstock, Robert P.
**Carlson, Ron** 1947- ........................... **CLC 54**
See also CA 105, 189; CAAE 189; CANR 27, 155; DLB 244
**Carlson, Ronald F.**
See Carlson, Ron
**Carlyle, Thomas** 1795-1881 .... **NCLC 22, 70**
See also BRW 4; CDBLB 1789-1832; DA; DAB; DAC; DAM MST; DLB 55, 144, 254; RGEL 2; TEA
**Carman, (William) Bliss** 1861-1929 . **PC 34; TCLC 7**
See also CA 104; 152; DAC; DLB 92; RGEL 2
**Carnegie, Dale** 1888-1955 ............ **TCLC 53**
See also CA 218
**Carossa, Hans** 1878-1956 ............. **TCLC 48**
See also CA 170; DLB 66; EWL 3
**Carpenter, Don(ald Richard)** 1931-1995
................................................. **CLC 41**
See also CA 45-48; 149; CANR 1, 71
**Carpenter, Edward** 1844-1929 ...... **TCLC 88**
See also CA 163; GLL 1
**Carpenter, John (Howard)** 1948- .. **CLC 161**
See also AAYA 2; CA 134; SATA 58
**Carpenter, Johnny**
See Carpenter, John (Howard)
**Carpentier (y Valmont), Alejo** 1904-1980
.... **CLC 8, 11, 38, 110; HLC 1; SSC 35**
See also CA 65-68; 97-100; CANR 11, 70; CDWLB 3; DAM MULT; DLB 113; EWL 3; HW 1, 2; LAW; LMFS 2; RGSF 2; RGWL 2, 3; WLIT 1
**Carr, Caleb** 1955- ............................. **CLC 86**
See also CA 147; CANR 73, 134; DA3
**Carr, Emily** 1871-1945 .................... **TCLC 32**
See also CA 159; DLB 68; FW; GLL 2
**Carr, John Dickson** 1906-1977 .......... **CLC 3**
See Fairbairn, Roger
See also CA 49-52; 69-72; CANR 3, 33, 60; CMW 4; DLB 306; MSW; MTCW 1, 2
**Carr, Philippa**
See Hibbert, Eleanor Alice Burford
**Carr, Virginia Spencer** 1929- .......... **CLC 34**
See also CA 61-64; DLB 111
**Carrere, Emmanuel** 1957- .............. **CLC 89**
See also CA 200
**Carrier, Roch** 1937- ................... **CLC 13, 78**
See also CA 130; CANR 61, 152; CCA 1; DAC; DAM MST; DLB 53; SATA 105, 166
**Carroll, James Dennis**
See Carroll, Jim
**Carroll, James P.** 1943(?)- .............. **CLC 38**
See also CA 81-84; CANR 73, 139; MTCW 2; MTFW 2005
**Carroll, Jim** 1951- ................... **CLC 35, 143**
See also AAYA 17; CA 45-48; CANR 42, 115; NCFS 5

**Cernuda (y Bidon), Luis** 1902-1963 ............................................ **CLC 54; PC 62**
See also CA 131; 89-92; DAM POET; DLB 134; EWL 3; GLL 1; HW 1; RGWL 2, 3

**Cervantes, Lorna Dee** 1954- ... **HLCS 1; PC 35**
See also CA 131; CANR 80; CP 7; CWP; DLB 82; EXPP; HW 1; LLW

**Cervantes (Saavedra), Miguel de** 1547-1616 . **HLCS; LC 6, 23, 93; SSC 12; WLC 1**
See also AAYA 56; BYA 1, 14; DA; DAB; DAC; DAM MST, NOV; EW 2; LAIT 1; LATS 1:1; LMFS 1; NFS 8; RGSF 2; RGWL 2, 3; TWA

**Cesaire, Aime** 1913- .... **BLC 1; CLC 19, 32, 112; DC 22; PC 25**
See also BW 2, 3; CA 65-68; CANR 24, 43, 81; CWW 2; DA3; DAM MULT, POET; DLB 321; EWL 3; GFL 1789 to the Present; MTCW 1, 2; MTFW 2005; WP

**Chabon, Michael** 1963- .. **CLC 55, 149; SSC 59**
See also AAYA 45; AMWS 11; CA 139; CANR 57, 96, 127, 138; DLB 278; MAL 5; MTFW 2005; SATA 145

**Chabrol, Claude** 1930- ..................... **CLC 16**
See also CA 110

**Chairil Anwar**
See Anwar, Chairil
See also EWL 3

**Challans, Mary** 1905-1983
See Renault, Mary
See also CA 81-84; 111; CANR 74; DA3; MTCW 2; MTFW 2005; SATA 23; SATA-Obit 36; TEA

**Challis, George**
See Faust, Frederick (Schiller)

**Chambers, Aidan** 1934- ................... **CLC 35**
See also AAYA 27; CA 25-28R; CANR 12, 31, 58, 116; JRDA; MAICYA 1, 2; SAAS 12; SATA 1, 69, 108, 171; WYA; YAW

**Chambers, James** 1948-
See Cliff, Jimmy
See also CA 124

**Chambers, Jessie**
See Lawrence, D(avid) H(erbert Richards)
See also GLL 1

**Chambers, Robert W(illiam)** 1865-1933 ............................................ **SSC 92; TCLC 41**
See also CA 165; DLB 202; HGG; SATA 107; SUFW 1

**Chambers, (David) Whittaker** 1901-1961 ............................................ **TCLC 129**
See also CA 89-92; DLB 303

**Chamisso, Adelbert von** 1781-1838 ............................................ **NCLC 82**
See also DLB 90; RGWL 2, 3; SUFW 1

**Chance, James T.**
See Carpenter, John (Howard)

**Chance, John T.**
See Carpenter, John (Howard)

**Chandler, Raymond (Thornton)** 1888-1959 ............................................ **SSC 23; TCLC 1, 7, 179**
See also AAYA 25; AMWC 2; AMWS 4; BPFB 1; CA 104; 129; CANR 60, 107; CDALB 1929-1941; CMW 4; DA3; DLB 226, 253; DLBD 6; EWL 3; MAL 5; MSW; MTCW 1, 2; MTFW 2005; NFS 17; RGAL 4; TUS

**Chang, Diana** 1934- ............................. **AAL**
See also CA 228; CWP; DLB 312; EXPP

**Chang, Eileen** 1920-1995 ...... **AAL; SSC 28; TCLC 184**
See Chang Ai-Ling; Zhang Ailing
See also CA 166

**Chang, Jung** 1952- ......................... **CLC 71**
See also CA 142

**Chang Ai-Ling**
See Chang, Eileen
See also EWL 3

**Channing, William Ellery** 1780-1842 ............................................ **NCLC 17**
See also DLB 1, 59, 235; RGAL 4

**Chao, Patricia** 1955- ....................... **CLC 119**
See also CA 163; CANR 155

**Chaplin, Charles Spencer** 1889-1977 ............................................ **CLC 16**
See Chaplin, Charlie
See also CA 81-84; 73-76

**Chaplin, Charlie**
See Chaplin, Charles Spencer
See also AAYA 61; DLB 44

**Chapman, George** 1559(?)-1634 ....... **DC 19; LC 22, 116**
See also BRW 1; DAM DRAM; DLB 62, 121; LMFS 1; RGEL 2

**Chapman, Graham** 1941-1989 ........ **CLC 21**
See Monty Python
See also CA 116; 129; CANR 35, 95

**Chapman, John Jay** 1862-1933 ...... **TCLC 7**
See also AMWS 14; CA 104; 191

**Chapman, Lee**
See Bradley, Marion Zimmer
See also GLL 1

**Chapman, Walker**
See Silverberg, Robert

**Chappell, Fred (Davis)** 1936- ... **CLC 40, 78, 162**
See also CA 5-8R; 198; CAAE 198; CAAS 4; CANR 8, 33, 67, 110; CN 6; CP 6, 7; CSW; DLB 6, 105; HGG

**Char, Rene(-Emile)** 1907-1988 ... **CLC 9, 11, 14, 55; PC 56**
See also CA 13-16R; 124; CANR 32; DAM POET; DLB 258; EWL 3; GFL 1789 to the Present; MTCW 1, 2; RGWL 2, 3

**Charby, Jay**
See Ellison, Harlan

**Chardin, Pierre Teilhard de**
See Teilhard de Chardin, (Marie Joseph) Pierre

**Chariton** fl. 1st cent. (?)- .............. **CMLC 49**

**Charlemagne** 742-814 ................... **CMLC 37**

**Charles I** 1600-1649 ...................... **LC 13**

**Charriere, Isabelle de** 1740-1805 . **NCLC 66**
See also DLB 313

**Chartier, Alain** c. 1392-1430 .............. **LC 94**
See also DLB 208

**Chartier, Emile-Auguste**
See Alain

**Charyn, Jerome** 1937- ............. **CLC 5, 8, 18**
See also CA 5-8R; CAAS 1; CANR 7, 61, 101; CMW 4; CN 1, 2, 3, 4, 5, 6, 7; DLBY 1983; MTCW 1

**Chase, Adam**
See Marlowe, Stephen

**Chase, Mary (Coyle)** 1907-1981 .......... **DC 1**
See also CA 77-80; 105; CAD; CWD; DFS 11; DLB 228; SATA 17; SATA-Obit 29

**Chase, Mary Ellen** 1887-1973 .......... **CLC 2; TCLC 124**
See also CA 13-16; 41-44R; CAP 1; SATA 10

**Chase, Nicholas**
See Hyde, Anthony
See also CCA 1

**Chateaubriand, Francois Rene de** 1768-1848 ............................................ **NCLC 3, 134**
See also DLB 119; EW 5; GFL 1789 to the Present; RGWL 2, 3; TWA

**Chatelet, Gabrielle-Emilie Du**
See du Chatelet, Emilie
See also DLB 313

**Chatterje, Sarat Chandra** 1876-1936(?)
See Chatterji, Saratchandra
See also CA 109

**Chatterji, Bankim Chandra** 1838-1894 ............................................ **NCLC 19**

**Chatterji, Saratchandra** .............. **TCLC 13**
See Chatterje, Sarat Chandra
See also CA 186; EWL 3

**Chatterton, Thomas** 1752-1770 ..... **LC 3, 54**
See also DAM POET; DLB 109; RGEL 2

**Chatwin, (Charles) Bruce** 1940-1989 ............................................ **CLC 28, 57, 59**
See also AAYA 4; BEST 90:1; BRWS 4; CA 85-88; 127; CPW; DAM POP; DLB 194, 204; EWL 3; MTFW 2005

**Chaucer, Daniel**
See Ford, Ford Madox
See also RHW

**Chaucer, Geoffrey** 1340(?)-1400 . **LC 17, 56; PC 19, 58; WLCS**
See also BRW 1; BRWC 1; BRWR 2; CD-BLB Before 1660; DA; DA3; DAB; DAC; DAM MST, POET; DLB 146; LAIT 1; PAB; PFS 14; RGEL 2; TEA; WLIT 3; WP

**Chavez, Denise** 1948- ...................... **HLC 1**
See also CA 131; CANR 56, 81, 137; DAM MULT; DLB 122; FW; HW 1, 2; LLW; MAL 5; MTCW 2; MTFW 2005

**Chaviaras, Strates** 1935-
See Haviaras, Stratis
See also CA 105

**Chayefsky, Paddy** ............................. **CLC 23**
See Chayefsky, Sidney
See also CAD; DLB 7, 44; DLBY 1981; RGAL 4

**Chayefsky, Sidney** 1923-1981
See Chayefsky, Paddy
See also CA 9-12R; 104; CANR 18; DAM DRAM

**Chedid, Andree** 1920- ...................... **CLC 47**
See also CA 145; CANR 95; EWL 3

**Cheever, John** 1912-1982 ... **CLC 3, 7, 8, 11, 15, 25, 64; SSC 1, 38, 57; WLC 2**
See also AAYA 65; AMWS 1; BPFB 1; CA 5-8R; 106; CABS 1; CANR 5, 27, 76; CDALB 1941-1968; CN 1, 2, 3; CPW; DA; DA3; DAB; DAC; DAM MST, NOV, POP; DLB 2, 102, 227; DLBY 1980, 1982; EWL 3; EXPS; INT CANR-5; MAL 5; MTCW 1, 2; MTFW 2005; RGAL 4; RGSF 2; SSFS 2, 14; TUS

**Cheever, Susan** 1943- ................. **CLC 18, 48**
See also CA 103; CANR 27, 51, 92, 157; DLBY 1982; INT CANR-27

**Chekhonte, Antosha**
See Chekhov, Anton (Pavlovich)

**Chekhov, Anton (Pavlovich)** 1860-1904 . **DC 9; SSC 2, 28, 41, 51, 85; TCLC 3, 10, 31, 55, 96, 163; WLC 2**
See also AAYA 68; BYA 14; CA 104; 124; DA; DA3; DAB; DAC; DAM DRAM, MST; DFS 1, 5, 10, 12; DLB 277; EW 7; EWL 3; EXPS; LAIT 3; LATS 1:1; RGSF 2; RGWL 2, 3; SATA 90; SSFS 5, 13, 14; TWA

**Cheney, Lynne V.** 1941- ................... **CLC 70**
See also CA 89-92; CANR 58, 117; SATA 152

**Chernyshevsky, Nikolai Gavrilovich**
See Chernyshevsky, Nikolay Gavrilovich
See also DLB 238

**Chernyshevsky, Nikolay Gavrilovich** 1828-1889 ................................. **NCLC 1**
See Chernyshevsky, Nikolai Gavrilovich

**Cherry, Carolyn Janice** 1942- ................... **CLC 35**
See Cherryh, C.J.
See also AAYA 24; BPFB 1; DLBY 1980; FANT; SATA 93; SCFW 2; SFW 4; YAW

**Cherryh, C.J.** 1942-
See Cherry, Carolyn Janice
See also CA 65-68; CANR 10, 147; SATA 172

**Clark, Walter Van Tilburg** 1909-1971
...................................................... **CLC 28**
See also CA 9-12R; 33-36R; CANR 63, 113; CN 1; DLB 9, 206; LAIT 2; MAL 5; RGAL 4; SATA 8; TCWW 1, 2

**Clark Bekederemo, J.P.** 1935- .......... **BLC 1; CLC 38; DC 5**
See Bekederemo, J. P. Clark; Clark, J. P.; Clark, John Pepper
See also BW 1; CA 65-68; CANR 16, 72; DAM DRAM, MULT; DFS 13; EWL 3; MTCW 2; MTFW 2005

**Clarke, Arthur C.** 1917- .. **CLC 1, 4, 13, 18, 35, 136; SSC 3**
See also AAYA 4, 33; BPFB 1; BYA 13; CA 1-4R; CANR 2, 28, 55, 74, 130; CLR 119; CN 1, 2, 3, 4, 5, 6; CPW; DA3; DAM POP; DLB 261; JRDA; LAIT 5; MAICYA 1, 2; MTCW 1, 2; MTFW 2005; SATA 13, 70, 115; SCFW 1, 2; SFW 4; SSFS 4, 18; TCLE 1:1; YAW

**Clarke, Austin** 1896-1974 .............. **CLC 6, 9**
See also CA 29-32; 49-52; CAP 2; CP 1, 2; DAM POET; DLB 10, 20; EWL 3; RGEL 2

**Clarke, Austin C.** 1934- ...... **BLC 1; CLC 8, 53; SSC 45**
See also BW 1; CA 25-28R; CAAS 16; CANR 14, 32, 68, 140; CN 1, 2, 3, 4, 5, 6, 7; DAC; DAM MULT; DLB 53, 125; DNFS 2; MTCW 2; MTFW 2005; RGSF 2

**Clarke, Gillian** 1937- ........................ **CLC 61**
See also CA 106; CP 3, 4, 5, 6, 7; CWP; DLB 40

**Clarke, Marcus (Andrew Hislop)** 1846-1881
.......................... **NCLC 19; SSC 94**
See also DLB 230; RGEL 2; RGSF 2

**Clarke, Shirley** 1925-1997 .............. **CLC 16**
See also CA 189

**Clash, The**
See Headon, (Nicky) Topper; Jones, Mick; Simonon, Paul; Strummer, Joe

**Claudel, Paul (Louis Charles Marie)** 1868-1955 .......................... **TCLC 2, 10**
See also CA 104; 165; DLB 192, 258, 321; EW 8; EWL 3; GFL 1789 to the Present; RGWL 2, 3; TWA

**Claudian** 370(?)-404(?) ................. **CMLC 46**
See also RGWL 2, 3

**Claudius, Matthias** 1740-1815 ...... **NCLC 75**
See also DLB 97

**Clavell, James** 1925-1994 ...... **CLC 6, 25, 87**
See also BPFB 1; CA 25-28R; 146; CANR 26, 48; CN 5; CPW; DA3; DAM NOV, POP; MTCW 1, 2; MTFW 2005; NFS 10; RHW

**Clayman, Gregory** ............................ **CLC 65**

**Cleaver, (Leroy) Eldridge** 1935-1998
.................................. **BLC 1; CLC 30, 119**
See also BW 1, 3; CA 21-24R; 167; CANR 16, 75; DA3; DAM MULT; MTCW 2; YAW

**Cleese, John (Marwood)** 1939- ....... **CLC 21**
See Monty Python
See also CA 112; 116; CANR 35; MTCW 1

**Cleishbotham, Jebediah**
See Scott, Sir Walter

**Cleland, John** 1710-1789 ................ **LC 2, 48**
See also DLB 39; RGEL 2

**Clemens, Samuel Langhorne** 1835-1910
See Twain, Mark
See also CA 104; 135; CDALB 1865-1917; DA; DA3; DAB; DAC; DAM MST, NOV; DLB 12, 23, 64, 74, 186, 189; JRDA; LMFS 1; MAICYA 1, 2; NCFS 4; NFS 20; SATA 100; YABC 2

**Clement of Alexandria** 150(?)-215(?)
...................................... **CMLC 41**

**Cleophil**
See Congreve, William

**Clerihew, E.**
See Bentley, E(dmund) C(lerihew)

**Clerk, N. W.**
See Lewis, C.S.

**Cleveland, John** 1613-1658 .............. **LC 106**
See also DLB 126; RGEL 2

**Cliff, Jimmy** ...................................... **CLC 21**
See Chambers, James
See also CA 193

**Cliff, Michelle** 1946- .......... **BLCS; CLC 120**
See also BW 2; CA 116; CANR 39, 72; CD-WLB 3; DLB 157; FW; GLL 2

**Clifford, Lady Anne** 1590-1676 ......... **LC 76**
See also DLB 151

**Clifton, Lucille** 1936- .. **BLC 1; CLC 19, 66, 162; PC 17**
See also AFAW 2; BW 2, 3; CA 49-52; CANR 2, 24, 42, 76, 97, 138; CLR 5; CP 2, 3, 4, 5, 6, 7; CSW; CWP; CWRI 5; DA3; DAM MULT, POET; DLB 5, 41; EXPP; MAICYA 1, 2; MTCW 1, 2; MTFW 2005; PFS 1, 14; SATA 20, 69, 128; WP

**Clinton, Dirk**
See Silverberg, Robert

**Clough, Arthur Hugh** 1819-1861
....................................... **NCLC 27, 163**
See also BRW 5; DLB 32; RGEL 2

**Clutha, Janet Paterson Frame** 1924-2004
See Frame, Janet
See also CA 1-4R; 224; CANR 2, 36, 76, 135; MTCW 1, 2; SATA 119

**Clyne, Terence**
See Blatty, William Peter

**Cobalt, Martin**
See Mayne, William (James Carter)

**Cobb, Irvin S(hrewsbury)** 1876-1944
.................................................. **TCLC 77**
See also CA 175; DLB 11, 25, 86

**Cobbett, William** 1763-1835 ......... **NCLC 49**
See also DLB 43, 107, 158; RGEL 2

**Coburn, D(onald) L(ee)** 1938- ......... **CLC 10**
See also CA 89-92; DFS 23

**Cocteau, Jean (Maurice Eugene Clement)** 1889-1963 .... **CLC 1, 8, 15, 16, 43; DC 17; TCLC 119; WLC 2**
See also CA 25-28; CANR 40; CAP 2; DA; DA3; DAB; DAC; DAM DRAM, MST, NOV; DLB 65, 258, 321; EW 10; EWL 3; GFL 1789 to the Present; MTCW 1, 2; RGWL 2, 3; TWA

**Codrescu, Andrei** 1946- .......... **CLC 46, 121**
See also CA 33-36R; CAAS 19; CANR 13, 34, 53, 76, 125; CN 7; DA3; DAM POET; MAL 5; MTCW 2; MTFW 2005

**Coe, Max**
See Bourne, Randolph S(illiman)

**Coe, Tucker**
See Westlake, Donald E.

**Coen, Ethan** 1958- .......................... **CLC 108**
See also AAYA 54; CA 126; CANR 85

**Coen, Joel** 1955- ............................. **CLC 108**
See also AAYA 54; CA 126; CANR 119

**The Coen Brothers**
See Coen, Ethan; Coen, Joel

**Coetzee, J.M.** 1940- ..... **CLC 23, 33, 66, 117, 161, 162**
See also AAYA 37; AFW; BRWS 6; CA 77-80; CANR 41, 54, 74, 114, 133; CN 4, 5, 6, 7; DA3; DAM NOV; DLB 225, 326, 329; EWL 3; LMFS 2; MTCW 1, 2; MTFW 2005; NFS 21; WLIT 2; WWE 1

**Coetzee, John Maxwell**
See Coetzee, J.M.

**Coffey, Brian**
See Koontz, Dean R.

**Coffin, Robert P(eter) Tristram** 1892-1955
...................................................... **TCLC 95**
See also CA 123; 169; DLB 45

**Cohan, George M.** 1878-1942 ....... **TCLC 60**
See also CA 157; DLB 249; RGAL 4

**Cohan, George Michael**
See Cohan, George M.

**Cohen, Arthur A(llen)** 1928-1986 .... **CLC 7, 31**
See also CA 1-4R; 120; CANR 1, 17, 42; DLB 28; RGHL

**Cohen, Leonard** 1934- ................. **CLC 3, 38**
See also CA 21-24R; CANR 14, 69; CN 1, 2, 3, 4, 5, 6; CP 1, 2, 3, 4, 5, 6, 7; DAC; DAM MST; DLB 53; EWL 3; MTCW 1

**Cohen, Leonard Norman**
See Cohen, Leonard

**Cohen, Matt(hew)** 1942-1999 .......... **CLC 19**
See also CA 61-64; 187; CAAS 18; CANR 40; CN 1, 2, 3, 4, 5, 6; DAC; DLB 53

**Cohen-Solal, Annie** 1948- ................ **CLC 50**
See also CA 239

**Colegate, Isabel** 1931- ..................... **CLC 36**
See also CA 17-20R; CANR 8, 22, 74; CN 4, 5, 6, 7; DLB 14, 231; INT CANR-22; MTCW 1

**Coleman, Emmett**
See Reed, Ishmael

**Coleridge, Hartley** 1796-1849 ....... **NCLC 90**
See also DLB 96

**Coleridge, M. E.**
See Coleridge, Mary E(lizabeth)

**Coleridge, Mary E(lizabeth)** 1861-1907
....................................................... **TCLC 73**
See also CA 116; 166; DLB 19, 98

**Coleridge, Samuel Taylor** 1772-1834
... **NCLC 9, 54, 99, 111, 177; PC 11, 39, 67; WLC 2**
See also AAYA 66; BRW 4; BRWR 2; BYA 4; CDBLB 1789-1832; DA; DA3; DAB; DAC; DAM MST, POET; DLB 93, 107; EXPP; LATS 1:1; LMFS 1; PAB; PFS 4, 5; RGEL 2; TEA; WLIT 3; WP

**Coleridge, Sara** 1802-1852 ........... **NCLC 31**
See also DLB 199

**Coles, Don** 1928- ........................... **CLC 46**
See also CA 115; CANR 38; CP 5, 6, 7

**Coles, Robert (Martin)** 1929- ........ **CLC 108**
See also CA 45-48; CANR 3, 32, 66, 70, 135; INT CANR-32; SATA 23

**Colette, (Sidonie-Gabrielle)** 1873-1954
.................... **SSC 10, 93; TCLC 1, 5, 16**
See Willy, Colette
See also CA 104; 131; DA3; DAM NOV; DLB 65; EW 9; EWL 3; GFL 1789 to the Present; MTCW 1, 2; MTFW 2005; RGWL 2, 3; TWA

**Collett, (Jacobine) Camilla (Wergeland)** 1813-1895 .............................. **NCLC 22**

**Collier, Christopher** 1930- .............. **CLC 30**
See also AAYA 13; BYA 2; CA 33-36R; CANR 13, 33, 102; JRDA; MAICYA 1, 2; SATA 16, 70; WYA; YAW 1

**Collier, James Lincoln** 1928- .......... **CLC 30**
See also AAYA 13; BYA 2; CA 9-12R; CANR 4, 33, 60, 102; CLR 3; DAM POP; JRDA; MAICYA 1, 2; SAAS 21; SATA 8, 70, 166; WYA; YAW 1

**Collier, Jeremy** 1650-1726 ................... **LC 6**

**Collier, John** 1901-1980 ....... **SSC 19; TCLC 127**
See also CA 65-68; 97-100; CANR 10; CN 1, 2; DLB 77, 255; FANT; SUFW 1

**Collier, Mary** 1690-1762 .................... **LC 86**
See also DLB 95

**Cormier, Robert** 1925-2000 ....... **CLC 12, 30**
See also AAYA 3, 19; BYA 1, 2, 6, 8, 9; CA 1-4R; CANR 5, 23, 76, 93; CDALB 1968-1988; CLR 12, 55; DA; DAB; DAC; DAM MST, NOV; DLB 52; EXPN; INT CANR-23; JRDA; LAIT 5; MAICYA 1, 2; MTCW 1, 2; MTFW 2005; NFS 2, 18; SATA 10, 45, 83; SATA-Obit 122; WYA; YAW

**Corn, Alfred (DeWitt III)** 1943- ..... **CLC 33**
See also CA 179; CAAE 179; CAAS 25; CANR 44; CP 3, 4, 5, 6, 7; CSW; DLB 120, 282; DLBY 1980

**Corneille, Pierre** 1606-1684 .. **DC 21; LC 28**
See also DAB; DAM MST; DFS 21; DLB 268; EW 3; GFL Beginnings to 1789; RGWL 2, 3; TWA

**Cornwell, David**
See le Carre, John

**Cornwell, Patricia** 1956- ................ **CLC 155**
See also AAYA 16, 56; BPFB 1; CA 134; CANR 53, 131; CMW 4; CPW; CSW; DAM POP; DLB 306; MSW; MTCW 2; MTFW 2005

**Cornwell, Patricia Daniels**
See Cornwell, Patricia

**Corso, Gregory** 1930-2001 ... **CLC 1, 11; PC 33**
See also AMWS 12; BG 1:2; CA 5-8R; 193; CANR 41, 76, 132; CP 1, 2, 3, 4, 5, 6, 7; DA3; DLB 5, 16, 237; MAL 5; MTCW 1, 2; MTFW 2005; WP

**Cortazar, Julio** 1914-1984 .. **CLC 2, 3, 5, 10, 13, 15, 33, 34, 92; HLC 1; SSC 7, 76**
See also BPFB 1; CA 21-24R; CANR 12, 32, 81; CDWLB 3; DA3; DAM MULT, NOV; DLB 113; EWL 3; EXPS; HW 1, 2; LAW; MTCW 1, 2; MTFW 2005; RGSF 2; RGWL 2, 3; SSFS 3, 20; TWA; WLIT 1

**Cortes, Hernan** 1485-1547 .................. **LC 31**

**Corvinus, Jakob**
See Raabe, Wilhelm (Karl)

**Corwin, Cecil**
See Kornbluth, C(yril) M.

**Cosic, Dobrica** 1921- ...................... **CLC 14**
See also CA 122; 138; CDWLB 4; CWW 2; DLB 181; EWL 3

**Costain, Thomas B(ertram)** 1885-1965
................................................ **CLC 30**
See also BYA 3; CA 5-8R; 25-28R; DLB 9; RHW

**Costantini, Humberto** 1924(?)-1987
................................................ **CLC 49**
See also CA 131; 122; EWL 3; HW 1

**Costello, Elvis** 1954- ...................... **CLC 21**
See also CA 204

**Costenoble, Philostene**
See Ghelderode, Michel de

**Cotes, Cecil V.**
See Duncan, Sara Jeannette

**Cotter, Joseph Seamon Sr.** 1861-1949
................................................ **BLC 1; TCLC 28**
See also BW 1; CA 124; DAM MULT; DLB 50

**Couch, Arthur Thomas Quiller**
See Quiller-Couch, Sir Arthur (Thomas)

**Coulton, James**
See Hansen, Joseph

**Couperus, Louis (Marie Anne)** 1863-1923
................................................ **TCLC 15**
See also CA 115; EWL 3; RGWL 2, 3

**Coupland, Douglas** 1961- ....... **CLC 85, 133**
See also AAYA 34; CA 142; CANR 57, 90, 130; CCA 1; CN 7; CPW; DAC; DAM POP

**Court, Wesli**
See Turco, Lewis (Putnam)

**Courtenay, Bryce** 1933- .................. **CLC 59**
See also CA 138; CPW

**Courtney, Robert**
See Ellison, Harlan

**Cousteau, Jacques-Yves** 1910-1997 . **CLC 30**
See also CA 65-68; 159; CANR 15, 67; MTCW 1; SATA 38, 98

**Coventry, Francis** 1725-1754 .............. **LC 46**

**Coverdale, Miles** c. 1487-1569 .......... **LC 77**
See also DLB 167

**Cowan, Peter (Walkinshaw)** 1914-2002
................................................ **SSC 28**
See also CA 21-24R; CANR 9, 25, 50, 83; CN 1, 2, 3, 4, 5, 6, 7; DLB 260; RGSF 2

**Coward, Noel (Peirce)** 1899-1973 .... **CLC 1, 9, 29, 51**
See also AITN 1; BRWS 2; CA 17-18; 41-44R; CANR 35, 132; CAP 2; CBD; CD-BLB 1914-1945; DA3; DAM DRAM; DFS 3, 6; DLB 10, 245; EWL 3; IDFW 3, 4; MTCW 1, 2; MTFW 2005; RGEL 2; TEA

**Cowley, Abraham** 1618-1667 .............. **LC 43**
See also BRW 2; DLB 131, 151; PAB; RGEL 2

**Cowley, Malcolm** 1898-1989 ............ **CLC 39**
See also AMWS 2; CA 5-8R; 128; CANR 3, 55; CP 1, 2, 3, 4; DLB 4, 48; DLBY 1981, 1989; EWL 3; MAL 5; MTCW 1, 2; MTFW 2005

**Cowper, William** 1731-1800 .... **NCLC 8, 94; PC 40**
See also BRW 3; DA3; DAM POET; DLB 104, 109; RGEL 2

**Cox, William Trevor** 1928-
See Trevor, William
See also CA 9-12R; CANR 4, 37, 55, 76, 102, 139; DAM NOV; INT CANR-37; MTCW 1, 2; MTFW 2005; TEA

**Coyne, P. J.**
See Masters, Hilary

**Cozzens, James Gould** 1903-1978 .... **CLC 1, 4, 11, 92**
See also AMW; BPFB 1; CA 9-12R; 81-84; CANR 19; CDALB 1941-1968; CN 1, 2; DLB 9, 294; DLBD 2; DLBY 1984, 1997; EWL 3; MAL 5; MTCW 1, 2; MTFW 2005; RGAL 4

**Crabbe, George** 1754-1832 ... **NCLC 26, 121**
See also BRW 3; DLB 93; RGEL 2

**Crace, Jim** 1946- ............. **CLC 157; SSC 61**
See also CA 128; 135; CANR 55, 70, 123; CN 5, 6, 7; DLB 231; INT CA-135

**Craddock, Charles Egbert**
See Murfree, Mary Noailles

**Craig, A. A.**
See Anderson, Poul

**Craik, Mrs.**
See Craik, Dinah Maria (Mulock)
See also RGEL 2

**Craik, Dinah Maria (Mulock)** 1826-1887
................................................ **NCLC 38**
See also Craik, Mrs.; Mulock, Dinah Maria
See also DLB 35, 163; MAICYA 1, 2; SATA 34

**Cram, Ralph Adams** 1863-1942 ... **TCLC 45**
See also CA 160

**Cranch, Christopher Pearse** 1813-1892
................................................ **NCLC 115**
See also DLB 1, 42, 243

**Crane, (Harold) Hart** 1899-1932 ........ **PC 3; TCLC 2, 5, 80; WLC 2**
See also AMW; AMWR 2; CA 104; 127; CDALB 1917-1929; DA; DA3; DAB; DAC; DAM MST, POET; DLB 4, 48; EWL 3; MAL 5; MTCW 1, 2; MTFW 2005; RGAL 4; TUS

**Crane, R(onald) S(almon)** 1886-1967
................................................ **CLC 27**
See also CA 85-88; DLB 63

**Crane, Stephen (Townley)** 1871-1900
.......... **SSC 7, 56, 70; TCLC 11, 17, 32; WLC 2**
See also AAYA 21; AMW; AMWC 1; BPFB 1; BYA 3; CA 109; 140; CANR 84; CDALB 1865-1917; DA; DA3; DAB; DAC; DAM MST, NOV, POET; DLB 12, 54, 78; EXPN; EXPS; LAIT 2; LMFS 2; MAL 5; NFS 4, 20; PFS 9; RGAL 4; RGSF 2; SSFS 4; TUS; WYA; YABC 2

**Cranmer, Thomas** 1489-1556 ............. **LC 95**
See also DLB 132, 213

**Cranshaw, Stanley**
See Fisher, Dorothy (Frances) Canfield

**Crase, Douglas** 1944- ...................... **CLC 58**
See also CA 106

**Crashaw, Richard** 1612(?)-1649 ......... **LC 24**
See also BRW 2; DLB 126; PAB; RGEL 2

**Cratinus** c. 519B.C.-c. 422B.C. .... **CMLC 54**
See also LMFS 1

**Craven, Margaret** 1901-1980 ............ **CLC 17**
See also BYA 2; CA 103; CCA 1; DAC; LAIT 5

**Crawford, F(rancis) Marion** 1854-1909
................................................ **TCLC 10**
See also CA 107; 168; DLB 71; HGG; RGAL 4; SUFW 1

**Crawford, Isabella Valancy** 1850-1887
................................................ **NCLC 12, 127**
See also DLB 92; RGEL 2

**Crayon, Geoffrey**
See Irving, Washington

**Creasey, John** 1908-1973 ................. **CLC 11**
See Marric, J. J.
See also CA 5-8R; 41-44R; CANR 8, 59; CMW 4; DLB 77; MTCW 1

**Crebillon, Claude Prosper Jolyot de (fils)** 1707-1777 ................................ **LC 1, 28**
See also DLB 313; GFL Beginnings to 1789

**Credo**
See Creasey, John

**Credo, Alvaro J. de**
See Prado (Calvo), Pedro

**Creeley, Robert** 1926-2005 ... **CLC 1, 2, 4, 8, 11, 15, 36, 78; PC 73**
See also AMWS 4; CA 1-4R; 237; CAAS 10; CANR 23, 43, 89, 137; CP 1, 2, 3, 4, 5, 6, 7; DA3; DAM POET; DLB 5, 16, 169; DLBD 17; EWL 3; MAL 5; MTCW 1, 2; MTFW 2005; PFS 21; RGAL 4; WP

**Creeley, Robert White**
See Creeley, Robert

**Crenne, Helisenne de** 1510-1560 ...... **LC 113**
See also DLB 327

**Crevecoeur, Hector St. John de**
See Crevecoeur, Michel Guillaume Jean de
See also ANW

**Crevecoeur, Michel Guillaume Jean de** 1735-1813 ............................. **NCLC 105**
See Crevecoeur, Hector St. John de
See also AMWS 1; DLB 37

**Crevel, Rene** 1900-1935 .............. **TCLC 112**
See also GLL 2

**Crews, Harry** 1935- .............. **CLC 6, 23, 49**
See also AITN 1; AMWS 11; BPFB 1; CA 25-28R; CANR 20, 57; CN 3, 4, 5, 6, 7; CSW; DA3; DLB 6, 143, 185; MTCW 1, 2; MTFW 2005; RGAL 4

**Crichton, Michael** 1942- .... **CLC 2, 6, 54, 90**
See also AAYA 10, 49; AITN 2; BPFB 1; CA 25-28R; CANR 13, 40, 54, 76, 127; CMW 4; CN 2, 3, 6, 7; CPW; DA3; DAM NOV, POP; DLB 292; DLBY 1981; INT CANR-13; JRDA; MTCW 1, 2; MTFW 2005; SATA 9, 88; SFW 4; YAW

**Drabble, Margaret** 1939- ..... **CLC 2, 3, 5, 8, 10, 22, 53, 129**
See also BRWS 4; CA 13-16R; CANR 18, 35, 63, 112, 131; CDBLB 1960 to Present; CN 1, 2, 3, 4, 5, 6, 7; CPW; DA3; DAB; DAC; DAM MST, NOV, POP; DLB 14, 155, 231; EWL 3; FW; MTCW 1, 2; MTFW 2005; RGEL 2; SATA 48; TEA

**Drakulic, Slavenka** 1949- ............... **CLC 173**
See also CA 144; CANR 92

**Drakulic-Ilic, Slavenka**
See Drakulic, Slavenka

**Drapier, M. B.**
See Swift, Jonathan

**Drayham, James**
See Mencken, H(enry) L(ouis)

**Drayton, Michael** 1563-1631 ................ **LC 8**
See also DAM POET; DLB 121; RGEL 2

**Dreadstone, Carl**
See Campbell, (John) Ramsey

**Dreiser, Theodore** 1871-1945 .......... **SSC 30; TCLC 10, 18, 35, 83; WLC 2**
See also AMW; AMWC 2; AMWR 2; BYA 15, 16; CA 106; 132; CDALB 1865-1917; DA; DA3; DAC; DAM MST, NOV; DLB 9, 12, 102, 137; DLBD 1; EWL 3; LAIT 2; LMFS 2; MAL 5; MTCW 1, 2; MTFW 2005; NFS 8, 17; RGAL 4; TUS

**Dreiser, Theodore Herman Albert**
See Dreiser, Theodore

**Drexler, Rosalyn** 1926- .................... **CLC 2, 6**
See also CA 81-84; CAD; CANR 68, 124; CD 5, 6; CWD; MAL 5

**Dreyer, Carl Theodor** 1889-1968 .... **CLC 16**
See also CA 116

**Drieu la Rochelle, Pierre** 1893-1945
............................................... **TCLC 21**
See also CA 117; 250; DLB 72; EWL 3; GFL 1789 to the Present

**Drieu la Rochelle, Pierre-Eugene** 1893-1945
See Drieu la Rochelle, Pierre

**Drinkwater, John** 1882-1937 ......... **TCLC 57**
See also CA 109; 149; DLB 10, 19, 149; RGEL 2

**Drop Shot**
See Cable, George Washington

**Droste-Hulshoff, Annette Freiin von**
1797-1848 ......................... **NCLC 3, 133**
See also CDWLB 2; DLB 133; RGSF 2; RGWL 2, 3

**Drummond, Walter**
See Silverberg, Robert

**Drummond, William Henry** 1854-1907
................................................... **TCLC 25**
See also CA 160; DLB 92

**Drummond de Andrade, Carlos** 1902-1987
............................. **CLC 18; TCLC 139**
See Andrade, Carlos Drummond de
See also CA 132; 123; DLB 307; LAW

**Drummond of Hawthornden, William**
1585-1649 ................................... **LC 83**
See also DLB 121, 213; RGEL 2

**Drury, Allen (Stuart)** 1918-1998 ..... **CLC 37**
See also CA 57-60; 170; CANR 18, 52; CN 1, 2, 3, 4, 5, 6; INT CANR-18

**Druse, Eleanor**
See King, Stephen

**Dryden, John** 1631-1700 .... **DC 3; LC 3, 21, 115; PC 25; WLC 2**
See also BRW 2; CDBLB 1660-1789; DA; DAB; DAC; DAM DRAM, MST, POET; DLB 80, 101, 131; EXPP; IDTP; LMFS 1; RGEL 2; TEA; WLIT 3

**du Bellay, Joachim** 1524-1560 ........... **LC 92**
See also DLB 327; GFL Beginnings to 1789; RGWL 2, 3

**Duberman, Martin (Bauml)** 1930- ... **CLC 8**
See also CA 1-4R; CAD; CANR 2, 63, 137; CD 5, 6

**Dubie, Norman (Evans)** 1945- ......... **CLC 36**
See also CA 69-72; CANR 12, 115; CP 3, 4, 5, 6, 7; DLB 120; PFS 12

**Du Bois, W(illiam) E(dward) B(urghardt)** 1868-1963 .... **BLC 1; CLC 1, 2, 13, 64, 96; HR 1:2; TCLC 169; WLC 2**
See also AAYA 40; AFAW 1, 2; AMWC 1; AMWS 2; BW 1, 3; CA 85-88; CANR 34, 82, 132; CDALB 1865-1917; DA; DA3; DAC; DAM MST, MULT, NOV; DLB 47, 50, 91, 246, 284; EWL 3; EXPP; LAIT 2; LMFS 2; MAL 5; MTCW 1, 2; MTFW 2005; NCFS 1; PFS 13; RGAL 4; SATA 42

**Dubus, Andre** 1936-1999 .... **CLC 13, 36, 97; SSC 15**
See also AMWS 7; CA 21-24R; 177; CANR 17; CN 5, 6; CSW; DLB 130; INT CANR-17; RGAL 4; SSFS 10; TCLE 1:1

**Duca Minimo**
See D'Annunzio, Gabriele

**Ducharme, Rejean** 1941- ................. **CLC 74**
See also CA 165; DLB 60

**du Chatelet, Emilie** 1706-1749 .......... **LC 96**
See Chatelet, Gabrielle-Emilie Du

**Duchen, Claire** ................................. **CLC 65**

**Duclos, Charles Pinot-** 1704-1772 ...... **LC 1**
See also GFL Beginnings to 1789

**Dudek, Louis** 1918-2001 ............ **CLC 11, 19**
See also CA 45-48; 215; CAAS 14; CANR 1; CP 1, 2, 3, 4, 5, 6, 7; DLB 88

**Duerrenmatt, Friedrich** 1921-1990 .. **CLC 1, 4, 8, 11, 15, 43, 102**
See Durrenmatt, Friedrich
See also CA 17-20R; CANR 33; CMW 4; DAM DRAM; DLB 69, 124; MTCW 1, 2

**Duffy, Bruce** 1953(?)- ....................... **CLC 50**
See also CA 172

**Duffy, Maureen (Patricia)** 1933- ..... **CLC 37**
See also CA 25-28R; CANR 33, 68; CBD; CN 1, 2, 3, 4, 5, 6, 7; CP 5, 6, 7; CWD; CWP; DFS 15; DLB 14, 310; FW; MTCW 1

**Du Fu**
See Tu Fu
See also RGWL 2, 3

**Dugan, Alan** 1923-2003 ................. **CLC 2, 6**
See also CA 81-84; 220; CANR 119; CP 1, 2, 3, 4, 5, 6, 7; DLB 5; MAL 5; PFS 10

**du Gard, Roger Martin**
See Martin du Gard, Roger

**Duhamel, Georges** 1884-1966 ........... **CLC 8**
See also CA 81-84; 25-28R; CANR 35; DLB 65; EWL 3; GFL 1789 to the Present; MTCW 1

**Dujardin, Edouard (Emile Louis)** 1861-1949
................................................... **TCLC 13**
See also CA 109; DLB 123

**Duke, Raoul**
See Thompson, Hunter S.

**Dulles, John Foster** 1888-1959 ..... **TCLC 72**
See also CA 115; 149

**Dumas, Alexandre (pere)** 1802-1870
............................. **NCLC 11, 71; WLC 2**
See also AAYA 22; BYA 3; DA; DA3; DAB; DAC; DAM MST, NOV; DLB 119, 192; EW 6; GFL 1789 to the Present; LAIT 1, 2; NFS 14, 19; RGWL 2, 3; SATA 18; TWA; WCH

**Dumas, Alexandre (fils)** 1824-1895 .... **DC 1; NCLC 9**
See also DLB 192; GFL 1789 to the Present; RGWL 2, 3

**Dumas, Claudine**
See Malzberg, Barry N(athaniel)

**Dumas, Henry L.** 1934-1968 ....... **CLC 6, 62**
See also BW 1; CA 85-88; DLB 41; RGAL 4

**du Maurier, Daphne** 1907-1989 . **CLC 6, 11, 59; SSC 18**
See also AAYA 37; BPFB 1; BRWS 3; CA 5-8R; 128; CANR 6, 55; CMW 4; CN 1, 2, 3, 4; CPW; DA3; DAB; DAC; DAM MST, POP; DLB 191; GL 2; HGG; LAIT 3; MSW; MTCW 1, 2; NFS 12; RGEL 2; RGSF 2; RHW; SATA 27; SATA-Obit 60; SSFS 14, 16; TEA

**Du Maurier, George** 1834-1896 .... **NCLC 86**
See also DLB 153, 178; RGEL 2

**Dunbar, Paul Laurence** 1872-1906 .. **BLC 1; PC 5; SSC 8; TCLC 2, 12; WLC 2**
See also AFAW 1, 2; AMWS 2; BW 1, 3; CA 104; 124; CANR 79; CDALB 1865-1917; DA; DA3; DAC; DAM MST, MULT, POET; DLB 50, 54, 78; EXPP; MAL 5; RGAL 4; SATA 34

**Dunbar, William** 1460(?)-1520(?) ..... **LC 20; PC 67**
See also BRWS 8; DLB 132, 146; RGEL 2

**Dunbar-Nelson, Alice** ........................ **HR 1:2**
See Nelson, Alice Ruth Moore Dunbar

**Duncan, Dora Angela**
See Duncan, Isadora

**Duncan, Isadora** 1877(?)-1927 ...... **TCLC 68**
See also CA 118; 149

**Duncan, Lois** 1934- ......................... **CLC 26**
See also AAYA 4, 34; BYA 6, 8; CA 1-4R; CANR 2, 23, 36, 111; CLR 29; JRDA; MAICYA 1, 2; MAICYAS 1; MTFW 2005; SAAS 2; SATA 1, 36, 75, 133, 141; SATA-Essay 141; WYA; YAW

**Duncan, Robert** 1919-1988 .. **CLC 1, 2, 4, 7, 15, 41, 55; PC 2, 75**
See also BG 1:2; CA 9-12R; 124; CANR 28, 62; CP 1, 2, 3, 4; DAM POET; DLB 5, 16, 193; EWL 3; MAL 5; MTCW 1, 2; MTFW 2005; PFS 13; RGAL 4; WP

**Duncan, Sara Jeannette** 1861-1922
................................................... **TCLC 60**
See also CA 157; DLB 92

**Dunlap, William** 1766-1839 ............ **NCLC 2**
See also DLB 30, 37, 59; RGAL 4

**Dunn, Douglas (Eaglesham)** 1942- .. **CLC 6, 40**
See also BRWS 10; CA 45-48; CANR 2, 33, 126; CP 1, 2, 3, 4, 5, 6, 7; DLB 40; MTCW 1

**Dunn, Katherine** 1945- .................... **CLC 71**
See also CA 33-36R; CANR 72; HGG; MTCW 2; MTFW 2005

**Dunn, Stephen** 1939- ............... **CLC 36, 206**
See also AMWS 11; CA 33-36R; CANR 12, 48, 53, 105; CP 3, 4, 5, 6, 7; DLB 105; PFS 21

**Dunn, Stephen Elliott**
See Dunn, Stephen

**Dunne, Finley Peter** 1867-1936 .... **TCLC 28**
See also CA 108; 178; DLB 11, 23; RGAL 4

**Dunne, John Gregory** 1932-2003 .... **CLC 28**
See also CA 25-28R; 222; CANR 14, 50; CN 5, 6, 7; DLBY 1980

**Dunsany, Lord** ......................... **TCLC 2, 59**
See Dunsany, Edward John Moreton Drax Plunkett
See also DLB 77, 153, 156, 255; FANT; IDTP; RGEL 2; SFW 4; SUFW 1

**Dunsany, Edward John Moreton Drax Plunkett** 1878-1957
See Dunsany, Lord
See also CA 104; 148; DLB 10; MTCW 2

**Duns Scotus, John** 1266(?)-1308 . **CMLC 59**
See also DLB 115

**du Perry, Jean**
See Simenon, Georges (Jacques Christian)

Eisenstein, Sergei (Mikhailovich) 1898-1948
............................................ **TCLC 57**
See also CA 114; 149

Eisner, Simon
See Kornbluth, C(yril) M.

Ekeloef, (Bengt) Gunnar 1907-1968
............................................ **CLC 27; PC 23**
See Ekelof, (Bengt) Gunnar
See also CA 123; 25-28R; DAM POET

Ekelof, (Bengt) Gunnar 1907-1968
See Ekeloef, (Bengt) Gunnar
See also DLB 259; EW 12; EWL 3

Ekelund, Vilhelm 1880-1949 ......... **TCLC 75**
See also CA 189; EWL 3

Ekwensi, C. O. D.
See Ekwensi, Cyprian (Odiatu Duaka)

Ekwensi, Cyprian (Odiatu Duaka) 1921-
............................................ **BLC 1; CLC 4**
See also AFW; BW 2, 3; CA 29-32R;
CANR 18, 42, 74, 125; CDWLB 3; CN 1,
2, 3, 4, 5, 6; CWRI 5; DAM MULT; DLB
117; EWL 3; MTCW 1, 2; RGEL 2; SATA
66; WLIT 2

Elaine ............................................ **TCLC 18**
See Leverson, Ada Esther

El Crummo
See Crumb, R.

Elder, Lonne III 1931-1996 .... **BLC 1; DC 8**
See also BW 1, 3; CA 81-84; 152; CAD;
CANR 25; DAM MULT; DLB 7, 38, 44;
MAL 5

Eleanor of Aquitaine 1122-1204 .. **CMLC 39**

Elia
See Lamb, Charles

Eliade, Mircea 1907-1986 ................ **CLC 19**
See also CA 65-68; 119; CANR 30, 62; CD-
WLB 4; DLB 220; EWL 3; MTCW 1;
RGWL 3; SFW 4

Eliot, A. D.
See Jewett, (Theodora) Sarah Orne

Eliot, Alice
See Jewett, (Theodora) Sarah Orne

Eliot, Dan
See Silverberg, Robert

Eliot, George 1819-1880 .... **NCLC 4, 13, 23,
41, 49, 89, 118; PC 20; SSC 72; WLC 2**
See Evans, Mary Ann
See also BRW 5; BRWC 1, 2; BRWR 2;
CDBLB 1832-1890; CN 7; CPW; DA;
DA3; DAB; DAC; DAM MST, NOV;
DLB 21, 35, 55; FL 1:3; LATS 1:1; LMFS
1; NFS 17, 20; RGEL 2; RGSF 2; SSFS
8; TEA; WLIT 3

Eliot, John 1604-1690 ........................... **LC 5**
See also DLB 24

Eliot, T(homas) S(tearns) 1888-1965
..... **CLC 1, 2, 3, 6, 9, 10, 13, 15, 24, 34,
41, 55, 57, 113; PC 5, 31; WLC 2**
See also AAYA 28; AMW; AMWC 1;
AMWR 1; BRW 7; BRWR 2; CA 5-8R;
25-28R; CANR 41; CBD; CDALB 1929-
1941; DA; DA3; DAB; DAC; DAM
DRAM, MST, POET; DFS 4, 13; DLB 7,
10, 45, 63, 245, 329; DLBY 1988; EWL
3; EXPP; LAIT 1:1; LMFS 2;
MAL 5; MTCW 1, 2; MTFW 2005; NCFS
5; PAB; PFS 1, 7, 20; RGAL 4; RGEL 2;
TUS; WLIT 4; WP

Elisabeth of Schonau c. 1129-1165
............................................ **CMLC 82**

Elizabeth 1866-1941 ...................... **TCLC 41**

Elizabeth I 1533-1603 ...................... **LC 118**
See also DLB 136

Elkin, Stanley L. 1930-1995 ..... **CLC 4, 6, 9,
14, 27, 51, 91; SSC 12**
See also AMWS 6; BPFB 1; CA 9-12R;
148; CANR 8, 46; CN 1, 2, 3, 4, 5, 6;
CPW; DAM NOV, POP; DLB 2, 28, 218,
278; DLBY 1980; EWL 3; INT CANR-8;
MAL 5; MTCW 1, 2; MTFW 2005;
RGAL 4; TCLE 1:1

Elledge, Scott ...................................... **CLC 34**

Eller, Scott
See Shepard, James R.

Elliott, Don
See Silverberg, Robert

Elliott, George P(aul) 1918-1980 ....... **CLC 2**
See also CA 1-4R; 97-100; CANR 2; CN 1,
2; CP 3; DLB 244; MAL 5

Elliott, Janice 1931-1995 .................. **CLC 47**
See also CA 13-16R; CANR 8, 29, 84; CN
5, 6, 7; DLB 14; SATA 119

Elliott, Sumner Locke 1917-1991 ... **CLC 38**
See also CA 5-8R; 134; CANR 2, 21; DLB
289

Elliott, William
See Bradbury, Ray

Ellis, A. E. .......................................... **CLC 7**

Ellis, Alice Thomas ........................... **CLC 40**
See Haycraft, Anna
See also CN 4, 5, 6; DLB 194

Ellis, Bret Easton 1964- .... **CLC 39, 71, 117,
229**
See also AAYA 2, 43; CA 118; 123; CANR
51, 74, 126; CN 6, 7; CPW; DA3; DAM
POP; DLB 292; HGG; INT CA-123;
MTCW 2; MTFW 2005; NFS 11

Ellis, (Henry) Havelock 1859-1939
............................................ **TCLC 14**
See also CA 109; 169; DLB 190

Ellis, Landon
See Ellison, Harlan

Ellis, Trey 1962- ............................... **CLC 55**
See also CA 146; CANR 92; CN 7

Ellison, Harlan 1934- ... **CLC 1, 13, 42, 139;
SSC 14**
See also AAYA 29; BPFB 1; BYA 14; CA
5-8R; CANR 5, 46, 115; CPW; DAM
POP; DLB 8; HGG; INT CANR-5;
MTCW 1, 2; MTFW 2005; SCFW 2;
SFW 4; SSFS 13, 14, 15, 21; SUFW 1, 2

Ellison, Ralph 1914-1994 .... **BLC 1; CLC 1,
3, 11, 54, 86, 114; SSC 26, 79; WLC 2**
See also AAYA 19; AFAW 1, 2; AMWC 2;
AMWR 2; AMWS 2; BPFB 1; BW 1, 3;
BYA 2; CA 9-12R; 145; CANR 24, 53;
CDALB 1941-1968; CN 1, 2, 3, 4, 5;
CSW; DA; DA3; DAB; DAC; DAM MST,
MULT, NOV; DLB 2, 76, 227; DLBY
1994; EWL 3; EXPN; EXPS; LAIT 4;
MAL 5; MTCW 1, 2; MTFW 2005; NCFS
3; NFS 2, 21; RGAL 4; RGSF 2; SSFS 1,
11; YAW

Ellmann, Lucy 1956- ........................ **CLC 61**
See also CA 128; CANR 154

Ellmann, Lucy Elizabeth
See Ellmann, Lucy

Ellmann, Richard (David) 1918-1987
............................................ **CLC 50**
See also BEST 89:2; CA 1-4R; 122; CANR
2, 28, 61; DLB 103; DLBY 1987; MTCW
1, 2; MTFW 2005

Elman, Richard (Martin) 1934-1997
............................................ **CLC 19**
See also CA 17-20R; 163; CAAS 3; CANR
47; TCLE 1:1

Elron
See Hubbard, L. Ron

El Saadawi, Nawal 1931- ............... **CLC 196**
See al'Sadaawi, Nawal; Sa'adawi, al-
Nawal; Saadawi, Nawal El; Sa'dawi,
Nawal al-
See also CA 118; CAAS 11; CANR 44, 92

Eluard, Paul ................. **PC 38; TCLC 7, 41**
See Grindel, Eugene
See also EWL 3; GFL 1789 to the Present;
RGWL 2, 3

Elyot, Thomas 1490(?)-1546 .............. **LC 11**
See also DLB 136; RGEL 2

Elledge, Scott ...................................... **CLC 34**

Elytis, Odysseus 1911-1996 ...... **CLC 15, 49,
100; PC 21**
See Alepoudelis, Odysseus
See also CA 102; 151; CANR 94; CWW 2;
DAM POET; DLB 329; EW 13; EWL 3;
MTCW 1, 2; RGWL 2, 3

Emecheta, Buchi 1944- ..... **BLC 2; CLC 14,
48, 128, 214**
See also AAYA 67; AFW; BW 2, 3; CA 81-
84; CANR 27, 81, 126; CDWLB 3; CN
4, 5, 6, 7; CWRI 5; DA3; DAM MULT;
DLB 117; EWL 3; FL 1:5; FW; MTCW
1, 2; MTFW 2005; NFS 12, 14; SATA 66;
WLIT 2

Emerson, Mary Moody 1774-1863
............................................ **NCLC 66**

Emerson, Ralph Waldo 1803-1882
.......... **NCLC 1, 38, 98; PC 18; WLC 2**
See also AAYA 60; AMW; ANW; CDALB
1640-1865; DA; DA3; DAB; DAC; DAM
MST, POET; DLB 1, 59, 73, 183, 223,
270; EXPP; LAIT 2; LMFS 1; NCFS 3;
PFS 4, 17; RGAL 4; TUS; WP

Eminem 1972- .................................. **CLC 226**
See also CA 245

Eminescu, Mihail 1850-1889 ........ **NCLC 33,
131**

Empedocles 5th cent. B.C.- ........... **CMLC 50**
See also DLB 176

Empson, William 1906-1984 .. **CLC 3, 8, 19,
33, 34**
See also BRWS 2; CA 17-20R; 112; CANR
31, 61; CP 1, 2, 3; DLB 20; EWL 3;
MTCW 1, 2; RGEL 2

Enchi, Fumiko (Ueda) 1905-1986 ... **CLC 31**
See Enchi Fumiko
See also CA 129; 121; FW; MJW

Enchi Fumiko
See Enchi, Fumiko (Ueda)
See also DLB 182; EWL 3

Ende, Michael (Andreas Helmuth)
1929-1995 ............................... **CLC 31**
See also BYA 5; CA 118; 124; 149; CANR
36, 110; CLR 14; DLB 75; MAICYA 1,
2; MAICYAS 1; SATA 61, 130; SATA-
Brief 42; SATA-Obit 86

Endo, Shusaku 1923-1996 .... **CLC 7, 14, 19,
54, 99; SSC 48; TCLC 152**
See Endo Shusaku
See also CA 29-32R; 153; CANR 21, 54,
131; DA3; DAM NOV; MTCW 1, 2;
MTFW 2005; RGSF 2; RGWL 2, 3

Endo Shusaku
See Endo, Shusaku
See also CWW 2; DLB 182; EWL 3

Engel, Marian 1933-1985 ... **CLC 36; TCLC
137**
See also CA 25-28R; CANR 12; CN 2, 3;
DLB 53; FW; INT CANR-12

Engelhardt, Frederick
See Hubbard, L. Ron

Engels, Friedrich 1820-1895 . **NCLC 85, 114**
See also DLB 129; LATS 1:1

Enright, D(ennis) J(oseph) 1920-2002
............................................ **CLC 4, 8, 31**
See also CA 1-4R; 211; CANR 1, 42, 83;
CN 1, 2; CP 1, 2, 3, 4, 5, 6, 7; DLB 27;
EWL 3; SATA 25; SATA-Obit 140

Ensler, Eve 1953- ............................ **CLC 212**
See also CA 172; CANR 126; DFS 23

Enzensberger, Hans Magnus 1929-
............................................ **CLC 43; PC 28**
See also CA 116; 119; CANR 103; CWW
2; EWL 3

Ephron, Nora 1941- ................... **CLC 17, 31**
See also AAYA 35; AITN 2; CA 65-68;
CANR 12, 39, 83; DFS 22

Epicurus 341B.C.-270B.C. .......... **CMLC 21**
See also DLB 176

**Epsilon**
See Betjeman, John

**Epstein, Daniel Mark** 1948- .............. **CLC 7**
See also CA 49-52; CANR 2, 53, 90

**Epstein, Jacob** 1956- ...................... **CLC 19**
See also CA 114

**Epstein, Jean** 1897-1953 ............... **TCLC 92**

**Epstein, Joseph** 1937- ............. **CLC 39, 204**
See also AMWS 14; CA 112; 119; CANR
50, 65, 117

**Epstein, Leslie** 1938- ........................ **CLC 27**
See also AMWS 12; CA 73-76, 215; CAAE
215; CAAS 12; CANR 23, 69; DLB 299;
RGHL

**Equiano, Olaudah** 1745(?)-1797 ....... **BLC 2;
LC 16**
See also AFAW 1, 2; CDWLB 3; DAM
MULT; DLB 37, 50; WLIT 2

**Erasmus, Desiderius** 1469(?)-1536 .... **LC 16,
93**
See also DLB 136; EW 2; LMFS 1; RGWL
2, 3; TWA

**Erdman, Paul E(mil)** 1932- ............. **CLC 25**
See also AITN 1; CA 61-64; CANR 13, 43,
84

**Erdrich, Karen Louise**
See Erdrich, Louise

**Erdrich, Louise** 1954- ....... **CLC 39, 54, 120,
176; NNAL; PC 52**
See also AAYA 10, 47; AMWS 4; BEST
89:1; BPFB 1; CA 114; CANR 41, 62,
118, 138; CDALBS; CN 5, 6, 7; CP 6, 7;
CPW; CWP; DA3; DAM MULT, NOV,
POP; DLB 152, 175, 206; EWL 3; EXPP;
FL 1:5; LAIT 5; LATS 1:2; MAL 5;
MTCW 1, 2; MTFW 2005; NFS 5; PFS
14; RGAL 4; SATA 94, 141; SSFS 14,
22; TCWW 2

**Erenburg, Ilya (Grigoryevich)**
See Ehrenburg, Ilya (Grigoryevich)

**Erickson, Stephen Michael** 1950-
See Erickson, Steve
See also CA 129; SFW 4

**Erickson, Steve** ................................. **CLC 64**
See Erickson, Stephen Michael
See also CANR 60, 68, 136; MTFW 2005;
SUFW 2

**Erickson, Walter**
See Fast, Howard

**Ericson, Walter**
See Fast, Howard

**Eriksson, Buntel**
See Bergman, (Ernst) Ingmar

**Eriugena, John Scottus** c. 810-877
................................................. **CMLC 65**
See also DLB 115

**Ernaux, Annie** 1940- ................. **CLC 88, 184**
See also CA 147; CANR 93; MTFW 2005;
NCFS 3, 5

**Erskine, John** 1879-1951 .............. **TCLC 84**
See also CA 112; 159; DLB 9, 102; FANT

**Eschenbach, Wolfram von**
See von Eschenbach, Wolfram
See also RGWL 3

**Eseki, Bruno**
See Mphahlele, Ezekiel

**Esenin, S.A.**
See Esenin, Sergei
See also EWL 3

**Esenin, Sergei** 1895-1925 ................ **TCLC 4**
See Esenin, S.A.
See also CA 104; RGWL 2, 3

**Esenin, Sergei Aleksandrovich**
See Esenin, Sergei

**Eshleman, Clayton** 1935- .................. **CLC 7**
See also CA 33-36R, 212; CAAE 212;
CAAS 6; CANR 93; CP 1, 2, 3, 4, 5, 6,
7; DLB 5

**Espada, Martin** 1957- ........................ **PC 74**
See also CA 159; CANR 80; CP 7; EXPP;
LLW; MAL 5; PFS 13, 16

**Espriella, Don Manuel Alvarez**
See Southey, Robert

**Espriu, Salvador** 1913-1985 ............... **CLC 9**
See also CA 154; 115; DLB 134; EWL 3

**Espronceda, Jose de** 1808-1842 .... **NCLC 39**

**Esquivel, Laura** 1951(?)- .. **CLC 141; HLCS
1**
See also AAYA 29; CA 143; CANR 68, 113;
DA3; DNFS 2; LAIT 3; LMFS 2; MTCW
2; MTFW 2005; NFS 5; WLIT 1

**Esse, James**
See Stephens, James

**Esterbrook, Tom**
See Hubbard, L. Ron

**Estleman, Loren D.** 1952- ................ **CLC 48**
See also AAYA 27; CA 85-88; CANR 27,
74, 139; CMW 4; CPW; DA3; DAM
NOV, POP; DLB 226; INT CANR-27;
MTCW 1, 2; MTFW 2005; TCWW 1, 2

**Etherege, Sir George** 1636-1692 ....... **DC 23;
LC 78**
See also BRW 2; DAM DRAM; DLB 80;
PAB; RGEL 2

**Euclid** 306B.C.-283B.C. ................ **CMLC 25**

**Eugenides, Jeffrey** 1960(?)- ..... **CLC 81, 212**
See also AAYA 51; CA 144; CANR 120;
MTFW 2005; NFS 24

**Euripides** c. 484B.C.-406B.C. ...... **CMLC 23,
51; DC 4; WLCS**
See also AW 1; CDWLB 1; DA; DA3;
DAB; DAC; DAM DRAM, MST; DFS 1,
4, 6; DLB 176; LAIT 1; LMFS 1; RGWL
2, 3; WLIT 8

**Evan, Evin**
See Faust, Frederick (Schiller)

**Evans, Caradoc** 1878-1945 .. **SSC 43; TCLC
85**
See also DLB 162

**Evans, Evan**
See Faust, Frederick (Schiller)

**Evans, Marian**
See Eliot, George

**Evans, Mary Ann**
See Eliot, George
See also NFS 20

**Evarts, Esther**
See Benson, Sally

**Everett, Percival**
See Everett, Percival L.
See also CSW

**Everett, Percival L.** 1956- ............... **CLC 57**
See Everett, Percival
See also BW 2; CA 129; CANR 94, 134;
CN 7; MTFW 2005

**Everson, R(onald) G(ilmour)** 1903-1992
................................................. **CLC 27**
See also CA 17-20R; CP 1, 2, 3, 4; DLB 88

**Everson, William (Oliver)** 1912-1994
.......................................... **CLC 1, 5, 14**
See Antoninus, Brother
See also BG 1:2; CA 9-12R; 145; CANR
20; CP 2, 3, 4, 5; DLB 5, 16, 212; MTCW
1

**Evtushenko, Evgenii Aleksandrovich**
See Yevtushenko, Yevgeny (Alexandrovich)
See also CWW 2; RGWL 2, 3

**Ewart, Gavin (Buchanan)** 1916-1995
................................................. **CLC 13, 46**
See also BRWS 7; CA 89-92; 150; CANR
17, 46; CP 1, 2, 3, 4, 5, 6; DLB 40;
MTCW 1

**Ewers, Hanns Heinz** 1871-1943 .... **TCLC 12**
See also CA 109; 149

**Ewing, Frederick R.**
See Sturgeon, Theodore (Hamilton)

**Exley, Frederick (Earl)** 1929-1992 ... **CLC 6,
11**
See also AITN 2; BPFB 1; CA 81-84; 138;
CANR 117; DLB 143; DLBY 1981

**Eynhardt, Guillermo**
See Quiroga, Horacio (Sylvestre)

**Ezekiel, Nissim (Moses)** 1924-2004 . **CLC 61**
See also CA 61-64; 223; CP 1, 2, 3, 4, 5, 6,
7; DLB 323; EWL 3

**Ezekiel, Tish O'Dowd** 1943- ............ **CLC 34**
See also CA 129

**Fadeev, Aleksandr Aleksandrovich**
See Bulgya, Alexander Alexandrovich
See also DLB 272

**Fadeev, Alexandr Alexandrovich**
See Bulgya, Alexander Alexandrovich
See also EWL 3

**Fadeyev, A.**
See Bulgya, Alexander Alexandrovich

**Fadeyev, Alexander** ...................... **TCLC 53**
See Bulgya, Alexander Alexandrovich

**Fagen, Donald** 1948- ........................ **CLC 26**

**Fainzilberg, Ilya Arnoldovich** 1897-1937
See Ilf, Ilya
See also CA 120; 165

**Fair, Ronald L.** 1932- ...................... **CLC 18**
See also BW 1; CA 69-72; CANR 25; DLB
33

**Fairbairn, Roger**
See Carr, John Dickson

**Fairbairns, Zoe (Ann)** 1948- ........... **CLC 32**
See also CA 103; CANR 21, 85; CN 4, 5,
6, 7

**Fairfield, Flora**
See Alcott, Louisa May

**Fairman, Paul W.** 1916-1977
See Queen, Ellery
See also CA 114; SFW 4

**Falco, Gian**
See Papini, Giovanni

**Falconer, James**
See Kirkup, James

**Falconer, Kenneth**
See Kornbluth, C(yril) M.

**Falkland, Samuel**
See Heijermans, Herman

**Fallaci, Oriana** 1930-2006 ........ **CLC 11, 110**
See also CA 77-80; CANR 15, 58, 134; FW;
MTCW 1

**Faludi, Susan** 1959- ........................ **CLC 140**
See also CA 138; CANR 126; FW; MTCW
2; MTFW 2005; NCFS 3

**Faludy, George** 1913- ...................... **CLC 42**
See also CA 21-24R

**Faludy, Gyoergy**
See Faludy, George

**Fanon, Frantz** 1925-1961 ... **BLC 2; CLC 74**
See also BW 1; CA 116; 89-92; DAM
MULT; DLB 296; LMFS 2; WLIT 2

**Fanshawe, Ann** 1625-1680 ................. **LC 11**

**Fante, John (Thomas)** 1911-1983 .. **CLC 60;
SSC 65**
See also AMWS 11; CA 69-72; 109; CANR
23, 104; DLB 130; DLBY 1983

**Far, Sui Sin** ...................................... **SSC 62**
See Eaton, Edith Maude
See also SSFS 4

**Farah, Nuruddin** 1945- ..... **BLC 2; CLC 53,
137**
See also AFW; BW 2, 3; CA 106; CANR
81, 148; CDWLB 3; CN 4, 5, 6, 7; DAM
MULT; DLB 125; EWL 3; WLIT 2

**Fargue, Leon-Paul** 1876(?)-1947 ... **TCLC 11**
See also CA 109; CANR 107; DLB 258;
EWL 3

**Farigoule, Louis**
See Romains, Jules

**Farina, Richard** 1936(?)-1966 .......... **CLC 9**
See also CA 81-84; 25-28R
**Farley, Walter (Lorimer)** 1915-1989
........................................ **CLC 17**
See also AAYA 58; BYA 14; CA 17-20R;
CANR 8, 29, 84; DLB 22; JRDA; MAI-
CYA 1, 2; SATA 2, 43, 132; YAW
**Farmer, Philip Jose** 1918- ...... **CLC 1, 19**
See also AAYA 28; BPFB 1; CA 1-4R;
CANR 4, 35, 111; DLB 8; MTCW 1;
SATA 93; SCFW 1, 2; SFW 4
**Farquhar, George** 1677-1707 ......... **LC 21**
See also BRW 2; DAM DRAM; DLB 84;
RGEL 2
**Farrell, J(ames) G(ordon)** 1935-1979
........................................ **CLC 6**
See also CA 73-76; 89-92; CANR 36; CN
1, 2; DLB 14, 271, 326; MTCW 1; RGEL
2; RHW; WLIT 4
**Farrell, James T(homas)** 1904-1979
............... **CLC 1, 4, 8, 11, 66; SSC 28**
See also AMW; BPFB 1; CA 5-8R; 89-92;
CANR 9, 61; CN 1, 2; DLB 4, 9, 86;
DLBD 2; EWL 3; MAL 5; MTCW 1, 2;
MTFW 2005; RGAL 4
**Farrell, Warren (Thomas)** 1943- ..... **CLC 70**
See also CA 146; CANR 120
**Farren, Richard J.**
See Betjeman, John
**Farren, Richard M.**
See Betjeman, John
**Fassbinder, Rainer Werner** 1946-1982
........................................ **CLC 20**
See also CA 93-96; 106; CANR 31
**Fast, Howard** 1914-2003 ...... **CLC 23, 131**
See also AAYA 16; BPFB 1; CA 1-4R, 181;
214; CAAE 181; CAAS 18; CANR 1, 33,
54, 75, 98, 140; CMW 4; CN 1, 2, 3, 4, 5,
6, 7; CPW; DAM NOV; DLB 9; INT
CANR-33; LATS 1:1; MAL 5; MTCW 2;
MTFW 2005; RHW; SATA 7; SATA-
Essay 107; TCWW 1, 2; YAW
**Faulcon, Robert**
See Holdstock, Robert P.
**Faulkner, William (Cuthbert)** 1897-1962
..... **CLC 1, 3, 6, 8, 9, 11, 14, 18, 28, 52,
68; SSC 1, 35, 42, 92; TCLC 141;
WLC 2**
See also AAYA 7; AMW; AMWR 1; BPFB
1; BYA 5, 15; CA 81-84; CANR 33;
CDALB 1929-1941; DA; DA3; DAB;
DAC; DAM MST, NOV; DLB 9, 11, 44,
102, 316, 330; DLBD 2; DLBY 1986,
1997; EWL 3; EXPN; EXPS; GL 2; LAIT
2; LATS 1:1; LMFS 2; MAL 5; MTCW
1, 2; MTFW 2005; NFS 4, 8, 13, 24;
RGAL 4; RGSF 2; SSFS 2, 5, 6, 12; TUS
**Fauset, Jessie Redmon** 1882(?)-1961
............... **BLC 2; CLC 19, 54; HR 1:2**
See also AFAW 2; BW 1; CA 109; CANR
83; DAM MULT; DLB 51; FW; LMFS 2;
MAL 5; MBL
**Faust, Frederick (Schiller)** 1892-1944
........................................ **TCLC 49**
See Brand, Max; Dawson, Peter; Frederick,
John
See also CA 108; 152; CANR 143; DAM
POP; DLB 256; TUS
**Faust, Irvin** 1924- ............................. **CLC 8**
See also CA 33-36R; CANR 28, 67; CN 1,
2, 3, 4, 5, 6, 7; DLB 2, 28, 218, 278;
DLBY 1980
**Fawkes, Guy**
See Benchley, Robert (Charles)
**Fearing, Kenneth (Flexner)** 1902-1961
........................................ **CLC 51**
See also CA 93-96; CANR 59; CMW 4;
DLB 9; MAL 5; RGAL 4
**Fecamps, Elise**
See Creasey, John

**Federman, Raymond** 1928- ......... **CLC 6, 47**
See also CA 17-20R, 208; CAAE 208;
CAAS 8; CANR 10, 43, 83, 108; CN 3,
4, 5, 6; DLBY 1980
**Federspiel, J(uerg) F.** 1931- ............. **CLC 42**
See also CA 146
**Feiffer, Jules (Ralph)** 1929- ..... **CLC 2, 8, 64**
See also AAYA 3, 62; CA 17-20R; CAD;
CANR 30, 59, 129; CD 5, 6; DAM
DRAM; DLB 7, 44; INT CANR-30;
MTCW 1; SATA 8, 61, 111, 157
**Feige, Hermann Albert Otto Maximilian**
See Traven, B.
**Feinberg, David B.** 1956-1994 ........ **CLC 59**
See also CA 135; 147
**Feinstein, Elaine** 1930- .................... **CLC 36**
See also CA 69-72; CAAS 1; CANR 31,
68, 121; CN 3, 4, 5, 6, 7; CP 2, 3, 4, 5, 6,
7; CWP; DLB 14, 40; MTCW 1
**Feke, Gilbert David** .......................... **CLC 65**
**Feldman, Irving (Mordecai)** 1928- ... **CLC 7**
See also CA 1-4R; CANR 1; CP 1, 2, 3, 4,
5, 6, 7; DLB 169; TCLE 1:1
**Felix-Tchicaya, Gerald**
See Tchicaya, Gerald Felix
**Fellini, Federico** 1920-1993 ....... **CLC 16, 85**
See also CA 65-68; 143; CANR 33
**Felltham, Owen** 1602(?)-1668 ............. **LC 92**
See also DLB 126, 151
**Felsen, Henry Gregor** 1916-1995 .... **CLC 17**
See also CA 1-4R; 180; CANR 1; SAAS 2;
SATA 1
**Felski, Rita** .................................... **CLC 65**
**Fenelon, Francois de Salignac de la Mothe-**
1651-1715 ................................. **LC 134**
See also DLB 268; EW 3; GFL Beginnings
to 1789
**Fenno, Jack**
See Calisher, Hortense
**Fenollosa, Ernest (Francisco)** 1853-1908
........................................ **TCLC 91**
**Fenton, James Martin** 1949- ... **CLC 32, 209**
See also CA 102; CANR 108; CP 2, 3, 4, 5,
6, 7; DLB 40; PFS 11
**Ferber, Edna** 1887-1968 ............. **CLC 18, 93**
See also AITN 1; CA 5-8R; 25-28R; CANR
68, 105; DLB 9, 28, 86, 266; MAL 5;
MTCW 1, 2; MTFW 2005; RGAL 4;
RHW; SATA 7; TCWW 1, 2
**Ferdowsi, Abu'l Qasem** 940-1020(?)
........................................ **CMLC 43**
See Firdawsi, Abu al-Qasim
See also RGWL 2, 3
**Ferguson, Helen**
See Kavan, Anna
**Ferguson, Niall** 1964- .................... **CLC 134**
See also CA 190; CANR 154
**Ferguson, Samuel** 1810-1886 ........ **NCLC 33**
See also DLB 32; RGEL 2
**Fergusson, Robert** 1750-1774 ............. **LC 29**
See also DLB 109; RGEL 2
**Ferling, Lawrence**
See Ferlinghetti, Lawrence
**Ferlinghetti, Lawrence** 1919(?)- ... **CLC 2, 6,
10, 27, 111; PC 1**
See also BG 1:2; CA 5-8R; CAD; CANR 3,
41, 73, 125; CDALB 1941-1968; CP 1, 2,
3, 4, 5, 6, 7; DA3; DAM POET; DLB 5,
16; MAL 5; MTCW 1, 2; MTFW 2005;
RGAL 4; WP
**Ferlinghetti, Lawrence Monsanto**
See Ferlinghetti, Lawrence
**Fern, Fanny**
See Parton, Sara Payson Willis
**Fernandez, Vicente Garcia Huidobro**
See Huidobro Fernandez, Vicente Garcia

**Fernandez-Armesto, Felipe** ............. **CLC 70**
See Fernandez-Armesto, Felipe Fermin
Ricardo
See also CANR 153
**Fernandez-Armesto, Felipe Fermin Ricardo**
1950-
See Fernandez-Armesto, Felipe
See also CA 142; CANR 93
**Fernandez de Lizardi, Jose Joaquin**
See Lizardi, Jose Joaquin Fernandez de
**Ferre, Rosario** 1938- .... **CLC 139; HLCS 1;
SSC 36**
See also CA 131; CANR 55, 81, 134; CWW
2; DLB 145; EWL 3; HW 1, 2; LAWS 1;
MTCW 2; MTFW 2005; WLIT 1
**Ferrer, Gabriel (Francisco Victor) Miro**
See Miro (Ferrer), Gabriel (Francisco
Victor)
**Ferrier, Susan (Edmonstone)** 1782-1854
........................................ **NCLC 8**
See also DLB 116; RGEL 2
**Ferrigno, Robert** 1948(?)- ............... **CLC 65**
See also CA 140; CANR 125
**Ferron, Jacques** 1921-1985 ............... **CLC 94**
See also CA 117; 129; CCA 1; DAC; DLB
60; EWL 3
**Feuchtwanger, Lion** 1884-1958 ....... **TCLC 3**
See also CA 104; 187; DLB 66; EWL 3;
RGHL
**Feuerbach, Ludwig** 1804-1872 ... **NCLC 139**
See also DLB 133
**Feuillet, Octave** 1821-1890 ........... **NCLC 45**
See also DLB 192
**Feydeau, Georges (Leon Jules Marie)**
1862-1921 ................................. **TCLC 22**
See also CA 113; 152; CANR 84; DAM
DRAM; DLB 192; EWL 3; GFL 1789 to
the Present; RGWL 2, 3
**Fichte, Johann Gottlieb** 1762-1814
........................................ **NCLC 62**
See also DLB 90
**Ficino, Marsilio** 1433-1499 ............... **LC 12**
See also LMFS 1
**Fiedeler, Hans**
See Doeblin, Alfred
**Fiedler, Leslie A(aron)** 1917-2003 .... **CLC 4,
13, 24**
See also AMWS 13; CA 9-12R; 212; CANR
7, 63; CN 1, 2, 3, 4, 5, 6; DLB 28, 67;
EWL 3; MAL 5; MTCW 1, 2; RGAL 4;
TUS
**Field, Andrew** 1938- ....................... **CLC 44**
See also CA 97-100; CANR 25
**Field, Eugene** 1850-1895 ................. **NCLC 3**
See also DLB 23, 42, 140; DLBD 13; MAI-
CYA 1, 2; RGAL 4; SATA 16
**Field, Gans T.**
See Wellman, Manly Wade
**Field, Michael** 1915-1971 ............. **TCLC 43**
See also CA 29-32R
**Fielding, Helen** 1958- ............. **CLC 146, 217**
See also AAYA 65; CA 172; CANR 127;
DLB 231; MTFW 2005
**Fielding, Henry** 1707-1754 ..... **LC 1, 46, 85;
WLC 2**
See also BRW 3; BRWR 1; CDBLB 1660-
1789; DA; DA3; DAB; DAC; DAM
DRAM, MST, NOV; DLB 39, 84, 101;
NFS 18; RGEL 2; TEA; WLIT 3
**Fielding, Sarah** 1710-1768 ............. **LC 1, 44**
See also DLB 39; RGEL 2; TEA
**Fields, W. C.** 1880-1946 ................. **TCLC 80**
See also DLB 44
**Fierstein, Harvey (Forbes)** 1954- ... **CLC 33**
See also CA 123; 129; CAD; CD 5, 6;
CPW; DA3; DAM DRAM, POP; DFS 6;
DLB 266; GLL; MAL 5

**Forester, C(ecil) S(cott)** 1899-1966
.......................... **CLC 35; TCLC 152**
See also CA 73-76; 25-28R; CANR 83;
DLB 191; RGEL 2; RHW; SATA 13

**Forez**
See Mauriac, Francois (Charles)

**Forman, James**
See Forman, James D(ouglas)

**Forman, James D(ouglas)** 1932- ..... **CLC 21**
See also AAYA 17; CA 9-12R; CANR 4,
19, 42; JRDA; MAICYA 1, 2; SATA 8,
70; YAW

**Forman, Milos** 1932- ...................... **CLC 164**
See also AAYA 63; CA 109

**Fornes, Maria Irene** 1930- ....... **CLC 39, 61,
187; DC 10; HLCS 1**
See also CA 25-28R; CAD; CANR 28, 81;
CD 5, 6; CWD; DLB 7; HW 1, 2; INT
CANR-28; LLW; MAL 5; MTCW 1;
RGAL 4

**Forrest, Leon (Richard)** 1937-1997
......................................... **BLCS; CLC 4**
See also AFAW 2; BW 2; CA 89-92; 162;
CAAS 7; CANR 25, 52, 87; CN 4, 5, 6;
DLB 33

**Forster, E(dward) M(organ)** 1879-1970
..... **CLC 1, 2, 3, 4, 9, 10, 13, 15, 22, 45,
77; SSC 27, 96; TCLC 125; WLC 2**
See also AAYA 2, 37; BRW 6; BRWR 2;
BYA 12; CA 13-14; 25-28R; CANR 45;
CAP 1; CDBLB 1914-1945; DA; DA3;
DAB; DAC; DAM MST, NOV; DLB 34,
98, 162, 178, 195; DLBD 10; EWL 3;
EXPN; LAIT 3; LMFS 1; MTCW 1, 2;
MTFW 2005; NCFS 1; NFS 3, 10, 11;
RGEL 2; RGSF 2; SATA 57; SUFW 1;
TEA; WLIT 4

**Forster, John** 1812-1876 ................ **NCLC 11**
See also DLB 144, 184

**Forster, Margaret** 1938- ................. **CLC 149**
See also CA 133; CANR 62, 115; CN 4, 5,
6, 7; DLB 155, 271

**Forsyth, Frederick** 1938- ......... **CLC 2, 5, 36**
See also BEST 89:4; CA 85-88; CANR 38,
62, 115, 137; CMW 4; CN 3, 4, 5, 6, 7;
CPW; DAM NOV, POP; DLB 87; MTCW
1, 2; MTFW 2005

**Forten, Charlotte L.** 1837-1914 ....... **BLC 2;
TCLC 16**
See Grimke, Charlotte L(ottie) Forten
See also DLB 50, 239

**Fortinbras**
See Grieg, (Johan) Nordahl (Brun)

**Foscolo, Ugo** 1778-1827 ............ **NCLC 8, 97**
See also EW 5; WLIT 7

**Fosse, Bob** 1927-1987
See Fosse, Robert L.
See also CA 110; 123

**Fosse, Robert L.** ............................ **CLC 20**
See Fosse, Bob

**Foster, Hannah Webster** 1758-1840
.................................................. **NCLC 99**
See also DLB 37, 200; RGAL 4

**Foster, Stephen Collins** 1826-1864
.................................................. **NCLC 26**
See also RGAL 4

**Foucault, Michel** 1926-1984 ..... **CLC 31, 34,
69**
See also CA 105; 113; CANR 34; DLB 242;
EW 13; EWL 3; GFL 1789 to the Present;
GLL 1; LMFS 2; MTCW 1, 2; TWA

**Fouque, Friedrich (Heinrich Karl) de la
Motte** 1777-1843 ...................... **NCLC 2**
See also DLB 90; RGWL 2, 3; SUFW 1

**Fourier, Charles** 1772-1837 ......... **NCLC 51**

**Fournier, Henri-Alban** 1886-1914
See Alain-Fournier
See also CA 104; 179

**Fournier, Pierre** 1916-1997 ............. **CLC 11**
See Gascar, Pierre
See also CA 89-92; CANR 16, 40

**Fowles, John** 1926-2005 ... **CLC 1, 2, 3, 4, 6,
9, 10, 15, 33, 87; SSC 33**
See also BPFB 1; BRWS 1; CA 5-8R; 245;
CANR 25, 71, 103; CDBLB 1960 to
Present; CN 1, 2, 3, 4, 5, 6, 7; DA3; DAB;
DAC; DAM MST; DLB 14, 139, 207;
EWL 3; HGG; MTCW 1, 2; MTFW 2005;
NFS 21; RGEL 2; RHW; SATA 22; SATA-
Obit 171; TEA; WLIT 4

**Fowles, John Robert**
See Fowles, John

**Fox, Paula** 1923- .................... **CLC 2, 8, 121**
See also AAYA 3, 37; BYA 3, 8; CA 73-76;
CANR 20, 36, 62, 105; CLR 1, 44, 96;
DLB 52; JRDA; MAICYA 1, 2; MTCW
1; NFS 12; SATA 17, 60, 120, 167; WYA;
YAW

**Fox, William Price (Jr.)** 1926- ......... **CLC 22**
See also CA 17-20R; CAAS 19; CANR 11,
142; CSW; DLB 2; DLBY 1981

**Foxe, John** 1517(?)-1587 ..................... **LC 14**
See also DLB 132

**Frame, Janet** .. **CLC 2, 3, 6, 22, 66, 96; SSC
29**
See Clutha, Janet Paterson Frame
See also CN 1, 2, 3, 4, 5, 6, 7; CP 2, 3, 4;
CWP; EWL 3; RGEL 2; RGSF 2; TWA

**France, Anatole** ............................... **TCLC 9**
See Thibault, Jacques Anatole Francois
See also DLB 123, 330; EWL 3; GFL 1789
to the Present; RGWL 2, 3; SUFW 1

**Francis, Claude** ................................. **CLC 50**
See also CA 192

**Francis, Dick**
See Francis, Richard Stanley
See also CN 2, 3, 4, 5, 6

**Francis, Richard Stanley** 1920- . **CLC 2, 22,
42, 102**
See Francis, Dick
See also AAYA 5, 21; BEST 89:3; BPFB 1;
CA 5-8R; CANR 9, 42, 68, 100, 141; CD-
BLB 1960 to Present; CMW 4; CN 7;
DA3; DAM POP; DLB 87; INT CANR-9;
MSW; MTCW 1, 2; MTFW 2005

**Francis, Robert (Churchill)** 1901-1987
....................................... **CLC 15; PC 34**
See also AMWS 9; CA 1-4R; 123; CANR
1; CP 1, 2, 3, 4; EXPP; PFS 12; TCLE
1:1

**Francis, Lord Jeffrey**
See Jeffrey, Francis
See also DLB 107

**Frank, Anne(lies Marie)** 1929-1945
..................................... **TCLC 17; WLC 2**
See also AAYA 12; BYA 1; CA 113; 133;
CANR 68; CLR 101; DA; DA3; DAB;
DAC; DAM MST; LAIT 4; MAICYA 2;
MAICYAS 1; MTCW 1, 2; MTFW 2005;
NCFS 2; RGHL; SATA 87; SATA-Brief
42; WYA; YAW

**Frank, Bruno** 1887-1945 ............... **TCLC 81**
See also CA 189; DLB 118; EWL 3

**Frank, Elizabeth** 1945- .................... **CLC 39**
See also CA 121; 126; CANR 78, 150; INT
CA-126

**Frankl, Viktor E(mil)** 1905-1997 .... **CLC 93**
See also CA 65-68; 161; RGHL

**Franklin, Benjamin**
See Hasek, Jaroslav (Matej Frantisek)

**Franklin, Benjamin** 1706-1790 . **LC 25, 134;
WLCS**
See also AMW; CDALB 1640-1865; DA;
DA3; DAB; DAC; DAM MST; DLB 24,
43, 73, 183; LAIT 1; RGAL 4; TUS

**Franklin, (Stella Maria Sarah) Miles
(Lampe)** 1879-1954 ................. **TCLC 7**
See also CA 104; 164; DLB 230; FW;
MTCW 2; RGEL 2; TWA

**Franzen, Jonathan** 1959- .............. **CLC 202**
See also AAYA 65; CA 129; CANR 105

**Fraser, Antonia** 1932- ............... **CLC 32, 107**
See also AAYA 57; CA 85-88; CANR 44,
65, 119; CMW; DLB 276; MTCW 1, 2;
MTFW 2005; SATA-Brief 32

**Fraser, George MacDonald** 1925- ..... **CLC 7**
See also AAYA 48; CA 45-48, 180; CAAE
180; CANR 2, 48, 74; MTCW 2; RHW

**Fraser, Sylvia** 1935- .......................... **CLC 64**
See also CA 45-48; CANR 1, 16, 60; CCA
1

**Frayn, Michael** 1933- ....... **CLC 3, 7, 31, 47,
176; DC 27**
See also AAYA 69; BRWC 2; BRWS 7; CA
5-8R; CANR 30, 69, 114, 133; CBD; CD
5, 6; CN 1, 2, 3, 4, 5, 6, 7; DAM DRAM,
NOV; DFS 22; DLB 13, 14, 194, 245;
FANT; MTCW 1, 2; MTFW 2005; SFW
4

**Fraze, Candida (Merrill)** 1945- ....... **CLC 50**
See also CA 126

**Frazer, Andrew**
See Marlowe, Stephen

**Frazer, J(ames) G(eorge)** 1854-1941
................................................. **TCLC 32**
See also BRWS 3; CA 118; NCFS 5

**Frazer, Robert Caine**
See Creasey, John

**Frazer, Sir James George**
See Frazer, J(ames) G(eorge)

**Frazier, Charles** 1950- ........... **CLC 109, 224**
See also AAYA 34; CA 161; CANR 126;
CSW; DLB 292; MTFW 2005

**Frazier, Ian** 1951- ............................. **CLC 46**
See also CA 130; CANR 54, 93

**Frederic, Harold** 1856-1898 . **NCLC 10, 175**
See also AMW; DLB 12, 23; DLBD 13;
MAL 5; NFS 22; RGAL 4

**Frederick, John**
See Faust, Frederick (Schiller)
See also TCWW 2

**Frederick the Great** 1712-1786 .......... **LC 14**

**Fredro, Aleksander** 1793-1876 ....... **NCLC 8**

**Freeling, Nicolas** 1927-2003 ........... **CLC 38**
See also CA 49-52; 218; CAAS 12; CANR
1, 17, 50, 84; CMW 4; CN 1, 2, 3, 4, 5,
6; DLB 87

**Freeman, Douglas Southall** 1886-1953
................................................. **TCLC 11**
See also CA 109; 195; DLB 17; DLBD 17

**Freeman, Judith** 1946- .................... **CLC 55**
See also CA 148; CANR 120; DLB 256

**Freeman, Mary E(leanor) Wilkins** 1852-1930
.......................... **SSC 1, 47; TCLC 9**
See also CA 106; 177; DLB 12, 78, 221;
EXPS; FW; HGG; MBL; RGAL 4; RGSF
2; SSFS 4, 8; SUFW 1; TUS

**Freeman, R(ichard) Austin** 1862-1943
................................................. **TCLC 21**
See also CA 113; CANR 84; CMW 4; DLB
70

**French, Albert** 1943- ........................ **CLC 86**
See also BW 3; CA 167

**French, Antonia**
See Kureishi, Hanif

**French, Marilyn** 1929- ........ **CLC 10, 18, 60,
177**
See also BPFB 1; CA 69-72; CANR 3, 31,
134; CN 5, 6, 7; CPW; DAM DRAM,
NOV, POP; FL 1:5; FW; INT CANR-31;
MTCW 1, 2; MTFW 2005

**French, Paul**
See Asimov, Isaac

**Genet, Jean** 1910-1986 . **CLC 1, 2, 5, 10, 14, 44, 46; DC 25; TCLC 128**
See also CA 13-16R; CANR 18; DA3; DAM DRAM; DFS 10; DLB 72, 321; DLBY 1986; EW 13; EWL 3; GFL 1789 to the Present; GLL 1; LMFS 2; MTCW 1, 2; MTFW 2005; RGWL 2, 3; TWA

**Genlis, Stephanie-Felicite Ducrest** 1746-1830 ................................................ **NCLC 166**
See also DLB 313

**Gent, Peter** 1942- ........................... **CLC 29**
See also AITN 1; CA 89-92; DLBY 1982

**Gentile, Giovanni** 1875-1944 ......... **TCLC 96**
See also CA 119

**Gentlewoman in New England, A**
See Bradstreet, Anne

**Gentlewoman in Those Parts, A**
See Bradstreet, Anne

**Geoffrey of Monmouth** c. 1100-1155 ................................................ **CMLC 44**
See also DLB 146; TEA

**George, Jean**
See George, Jean Craighead

**George, Jean Craighead** 1919- ........ **CLC 35**
See also AAYA 8, 69; BYA 2, 4; CA 5-8R; CANR 25; CLR 1; 80; DLB 52; JRDA; MAICYA 1, 2; SATA 2, 68, 124, 170; WYA; YAW

**George, Stefan (Anton)** 1868-1933 ................................................ **TCLC 2, 14**
See also CA 104; 193; EW 8; EWL 3

**Georges, Georges Martin**
See Simenon, Georges (Jacques Christian)

**Gerald of Wales** c. 1146-c. 1223 .. **CMLC 60**

**Gerhardi, William Alexander**
See Gerhardie, William Alexander

**Gerhardie, William Alexander** 1895-1977 ................................................ **CLC 5**
See also CA 25-28R; 73-76; CANR 18; CN 1, 2; DLB 36; RGEL 2

**Gerson, Jean** 1363-1429 .................... **LC 77**
See also DLB 208

**Gersonides** 1288-1344 .................. **CMLC 49**
See also DLB 115

**Gerstler, Amy** 1956- ........................ **CLC 70**
See also CA 146; CANR 99

**Gertler, T.** ............................................ **CLC 34**
See also CA 116; 121

**Gertsen, Aleksandr Ivanovich**
See Herzen, Aleksandr Ivanovich

**Ghalib** ................................... **NCLC 39, 78**
See Ghalib, Asadullah Khan

**Ghalib, Asadullah Khan** 1797-1869
See Ghalib
See also DAM POET; RGWL 2, 3

**Ghelderode, Michel de** 1898-1962 ... **CLC 6, 11; DC 15**
See also CA 85-88; CANR 40, 77; DAM DRAM; DLB 321; EW 11; EWL 3; TWA

**Ghiselin, Brewster** 1903-2001 ......... **CLC 23**
See also CA 13-16R; CAAS 10; CANR 13; CP 1, 2, 3, 4, 5, 6, 7

**Ghose, Aurabinda** 1872-1950 ........ **TCLC 63**
See Ghose, Aurobindo
See also CA 163

**Ghose, Aurobindo**
See Ghose, Aurabinda
See also EWL 3

**Ghose, Zulfikar** 1935- ............. **CLC 42, 200**
See also CA 65-68; CANR 67; CN 1, 2, 3, 4, 5, 6, 7; CP 1, 2, 3, 4, 5, 6, 7; DLB 323; EWL 3

**Ghosh, Amitav** 1956- ............... **CLC 44, 153**
See also CA 147; CANR 80; CN 6, 7; DLB 323; WWE 1

**Giacosa, Giuseppe** 1847-1906 ......... **TCLC 7**
See also CA 104

**Gibb, Lee**
See Waterhouse, Keith (Spencer)

**Gibbon, Edward** 1737-1794 ................ **LC 97**
See also BRW 3; DLB 104; RGEL 2

**Gibbon, Lewis Grassic** ..................... **TCLC 4**
See Mitchell, James Leslie
See also RGEL 2

**Gibbons, Kaye** 1960- ......... **CLC 50, 88, 145**
See also AAYA 34; AMWS 10; CA 151; CANR 75, 127; CN 7; CSW; DA3; DAM POP; DLB 292; MTCW 2; MTFW 2005; NFS 3; RGAL 4; SATA 117

**Gibran, Kahlil** 1883-1931 ... **PC 9; TCLC 1, 9**
See also CA 104; 150; DA3; DAM POET, POP; EWL 3; MTCW 2; WLIT 6

**Gibran, Khalil**
See Gibran, Kahlil

**Gibson, Mel** 1956- ........................... **CLC 215**

**Gibson, William** 1914- ..................... **CLC 23**
See also CA 9-12R; CAD; CANR 9, 42, 75, 125; CD 5, 6; DA; DAB; DAC; DAM DRAM, MST; DFS 2; DLB 7; LAIT 2; MAL 5; MTCW 2; MTFW 2005; SATA 66; YAW

**Gibson, William** 1948- ...... **CLC 39, 63, 186, 192; SSC 52**
See also AAYA 12, 59; AMWS 16; BPFB 2; CA 126; 133; CANR 52, 90, 106; CN 6, 7; CPW; DA3; DAM POP; DLB 251; MTCW 2; MTFW 2005; SCFW 2; SFW 4

**Gide, Andre (Paul Guillaume)** 1869-1951 .... **SSC 13; TCLC 5, 12, 36, 177; WLC 3**
See also CA 104; 124; DA; DA3; DAB; DAC; DAM MST, NOV; DLB 65, 321; 330; EW 8; EWL 3; GFL 1789 to the Present; MTCW 1, 2; MTFW 2005; NFS 21; RGSF 2; RGWL 2, 3; TWA

**Gifford, Barry (Colby)** 1946- .......... **CLC 34**
See also CA 65-68; CANR 9, 30, 40, 90

**Gilbert, Frank**
See De Voto, Bernard (Augustine)

**Gilbert, W(illiam) S(chwenck)** 1836-1911 ................................................ **TCLC 3**
See also CA 104; 173; DAM DRAM, POET; RGEL 2; SATA 36

**Gilbert of Poitiers** c. 1085-1154 .. **CMLC 85**

**Gilbreth, Frank B(unker), Jr.** 1911-2001 ................................................ **CLC 17**
See also CA 9-12R; SATA 2

**Gilchrist, Ellen (Louise)** 1935- . **CLC 34, 48, 143; SSC 14, 63**
See also BPFB 2; CA 113; 116; CANR 41, 61, 104; CN 4, 5, 6, 7; CPW; CSW; DAM POP; DLB 130; EWL 3; EXPS; MTCW 1, 2; MTFW 2005; RGAL 4; RGSF 2; SSFS 9

**Giles, Molly** 1942- .......................... **CLC 39**
See also CA 126; CANR 98

**Gill, Eric** ........................................... **TCLC 85**
See Gill, (Arthur) Eric (Rowton Peter Joseph)

**Gill, (Arthur) Eric (Rowton Peter Joseph)** 1882-1940
See Gill, Eric
See also CA 120; DLB 98

**Gill, Patrick**
See Creasey, John

**Gillette, Douglas** ............................. **CLC 70**

**Gilliam, Terry** 1940- ................. **CLC 21, 141**
See Monty Python
See also AAYA 19, 59; CA 108; 113; CANR 35; INT CA-113

**Gilliam, Terry Vance**
See Gilliam, Terry

**Gillian, Jerry**
See Gilliam, Terry

**Gilliatt, Penelope (Ann Douglass)** 1932-1993 ................................................ **CLC 2, 10, 13, 53**
See also AITN 2; CA 13-16R; 141; CANR 49; CN 1, 2, 3, 4, 5; DLB 14

**Gilligan, Carol** 1936- ...................... **CLC 208**
See also CA 142; CANR 121; FW

**Gilman, Charlotte (Anna) Perkins (Stetson)** 1860-1935 .... **SSC 13, 62; TCLC 9, 37, 117**
See also AMWS 11; BYA 11; CA 106; 150; DLB 221; EXPS; FL 1:5; FW; HGG; LAIT 2; MBL; MTCW 2; MTFW 2005; RGAL 4; RGSF 2; SFW 4; SSFS 1, 18

**Gilmour, David** 1946- ...................... **CLC 35**

**Gilpin, William** 1724-1804 ............ **NCLC 30**

**Gilray, J. D.**
See Mencken, H(enry) L(ouis)

**Gilroy, Frank D(aniel)** 1925- ............. **CLC 2**
See also CA 81-84; CAD; CANR 32, 64, 86; CD 5, 6; DFS 17; DLB 7

**Gilstrap, John** 1957(?)- .................... **CLC 99**
See also AAYA 67; CA 160; CANR 101

**Ginsberg, Allen** 1926-1997 ... **CLC 1, 2, 3, 4, 6, 13, 36, 69, 109; PC 4, 47; TCLC 120; WLC 3**
See also AAYA 33; AITN 1; AMWC 1; AMWS 2; BG 1:2; CA 1-4R; 157; CANR 2, 41, 63, 95; CDALB 1941-1968; CP 1, 2, 3, 4, 5, 6; DA; DA3; DAB; DAC; DAM MST, POET; DLB 5, 16, 169, 237; EWL 3; GLL 1; LMFS 2; MAL 5; MTCW 1, 2; MTFW 2005; PAB; PFS 5; RGAL 4; TUS; WP

**Ginzburg, Eugenia** ............................ **CLC 59**
See Ginzburg, Evgeniia

**Ginzburg, Evgeniia** 1904-1977
See Ginzburg, Eugenia
See also DLB 302

**Ginzburg, Natalia** 1916-1991 ..... **CLC 5, 11, 54, 70; SSC 65; TCLC 156**
See also CA 85-88; 135; CANR 33; DFS 14; DLB 177; EW 13; EWL 3; MTCW 1, 2; MTFW 2005; RGHL; RGWL 2, 3

**Giono, Jean** 1895-1970 ... **CLC 4, 11; TCLC 124**
See also CA 45-48; 29-32R; CANR 2, 35; DLB 72, 321; EWL 3; GFL 1789 to the Present; MTCW 1; RGWL 2, 3

**Giovanni, Nikki** 1943- ..... **BLC 2; CLC 2, 4, 19, 64, 117; PC 19; WLCS**
See also AAYA 22; AITN 1; BW 2, 3; CA 29-32R; CAAS 6; CANR 18, 41, 60, 91, 130; CDALBS; CLR 6, 73; CP 2, 3, 4, 5, 6, 7; CSW; CWP; CWRI 5; DA; DA3; DAB; DAC; DAM MST, MULT, POET; DLB 5, 41; EWL 3; EXPP; INT CANR-18; MAICYA 1, 2; MAL 5; MTCW 1, 2; MTFW 2005; PFS 17; RGAL 4; SATA 24, 107; TUS; YAW

**Giovene, Andrea** 1904-1998 .............. **CLC 7**
See also CA 85-88

**Gippius, Zinaida (Nikolaevna)** 1869-1945
See Hippius, Zinaida (Nikolaevna)
See also CA 106; 212

**Giraudoux, Jean(-Hippolyte)** 1882-1944 ................................................ **TCLC 2, 7**
See also CA 104; 196; DAM DRAM; DLB 65, 321; EW 9; EWL 3; GFL 1789 to the Present; RGWL 2, 3; TWA

**Gironella, Jose Maria (Pous)** 1917-2003 ................................................ **CLC 11**
See also CA 101; 212; EWL 3; RGWL 2, 3

**Gissing, George (Robert)** 1857-1903 ...................... **SSC 37; TCLC 3, 24, 47**
See also BRW 5; CA 105; 167; DLB 18, 135, 184; RGEL 2; TEA

**Gitlin, Todd** 1943- ........................... **CLC 201**
See also CA 29-32R; CANR 25, 50, 88

**Giurlani, Aldo**
See Palazzeschi, Aldo

Gordon, Charles William 1860-1937
See Connor, Ralph
See also CA 109

Gordon, Mary 1949- ......... **CLC 13, 22, 128, 216; SSC 59**
See also AMWS 4; BPFB 2; CA 102; CANR 44, 92, 154; CN 4, 5, 6, 7; DLB 6; DLBY 1981; FW; INT CA-102; MAL 5; MTCW 1

Gordon, Mary Catherine
See Gordon, Mary

Gordon, N. J.
See Bosman, Herman Charles

Gordon, Sol 1923- ............................ **CLC 26**
See also CA 53-56; CANR 4; SATA 11

Gordone, Charles 1925-1995 ....... **CLC 1, 4; DC 8**
See also BW 1, 3; CA 93-96, 180; 150; CAAE 180; CAD; CANR 55; DAM DRAM; DLB 7; INT CA-93-96; MTCW 1

Gore, Catherine 1800-1861 .......... **NCLC 65**
See also DLB 116; RGEL 2

Gorenko, Anna Andreevna
See Akhmatova, Anna

Gorky, Maxim .... **SSC 28; TCLC 8; WLC 3**
See Peshkov, Alexei Maximovich
See also DAB; DFS 9; DLB 295; EW 8; EWL 3; TWA

Goryan, Sirak
See Saroyan, William

Gosse, Edmund (William) 1849-1928
.......................... **TCLC 28**
See also CA 117; DLB 57, 144, 184; RGEL 2

Gotlieb, Phyllis (Fay Bloom) 1926-
.......................... **CLC 18**
See also CA 13-16R; CANR 7, 135; CN 7; CP 1, 2, 3, 4; DLB 88, 251; SFW 4

Gottesman, S. D.
See Kornbluth, C(yril) M.; Pohl, Frederik

Gottfried von Strassburg fl. c. 1170-1215
.......................... **CMLC 10**
See also CDWLB 2; DLB 138; EW 1; RGWL 2, 3

Gotthelf, Jeremias 1797-1854 ..... **NCLC 117**
See also DLB 133; RGWL 2, 3

Gottschalk, Laura Riding
See Jackson, Laura (Riding)

Gould, Lois 1932(?)-2002 ............. **CLC 4, 10**
See also CA 77-80; 208; CANR 29; MTCW 1

Gould, Stephen Jay 1941-2002 ...... **CLC 163**
See also AAYA 26; BEST 90:2; CA 77-80; 205; CANR 10, 27, 56, 75, 125; CPW; INT CANR-27; MTCW 1, 2; MTFW 2005

Gourmont, Remy(-Marie-Charles) de 1858-1915 .......................... **TCLC 17**
See also CA 109; 150; GFL 1789 to the Present; MTCW 2

Gournay, Marie le Jars de
See de Gournay, Marie le Jars

Govier, Katherine 1948- .................. **CLC 51**
See also CA 101; CANR 18, 40, 128; CCA 1

Gower, John c. 1330-1408 ..... **LC 76; PC 59**
See also BRW 1; DLB 146; RGEL 2

Goyen, (Charles) William 1915-1983
.......................... **CLC 5, 8, 14, 40**
See also AITN 2; CA 5-8R; 110; CANR 6, 71; CN 1, 2, 3; DLB 2, 218; DLBY 1983; EWL 3; INT CANR-6; MAL 5

Goytisolo, Juan 1931- .. **CLC 5, 10, 23, 133; HLC 1**
See also CA 85-88; CANR 32, 61, 131; CWW 2; DAM MULT; DLB 322; EWL 3; GLL 2; HW 1, 2; MTCW 1, 2; MTFW 2005

Gozzano, Guido 1883-1916 ................. **PC 10**
See also CA 154; DLB 114; EWL 3

Gozzi, (Conte) Carlo 1720-1806 ... **NCLC 23**

Grabbe, Christian Dietrich 1801-1836
.......................... **NCLC 2**
See also DLB 133; RGWL 2, 3

Grace, Patricia Frances 1937- ......... **CLC 56**
See also CA 176; CANR 118; CN 4, 5, 6, 7; EWL 3; RGSF 2

Gracian y Morales, Baltasar 1601-1658
.......................... **LC 15**

Gracq, Julien .............................. **CLC 11, 48**
See Poirier, Louis
See also CWW 2; DLB 83; GFL 1789 to the Present

Grade, Chaim 1910-1982 ................. **CLC 10**
See also CA 93-96; 107; EWL 3; RGHL

Graduate of Oxford, A
See Ruskin, John

Grafton, Garth
See Duncan, Sara Jeannette

Grafton, Sue 1940- ....................... **CLC 163**
See also AAYA 11, 49; BEST 90:3; CA 108; CANR 31, 55, 111, 134; CMW 4; CPW; CSW; DA3; DAM POP; DLB 226; FW; MSW; MTFW 2005

Graham, John
See Phillips, David Graham

Graham, Jorie 1950- ... **CLC 48, 118; PC 59**
See also AAYA 67; CA 111; CANR 63, 118; CP 4, 5, 6, 7; CWP; DLB 120; EWL 3; MTFW 2005; PFS 10, 17; TCLE 1:1

Graham, R(obert) B(ontine) Cunninghame
See Cunninghame Graham, Robert (Gallnigad) Bontine
See also DLB 98, 135, 174; RGEL 2; RGSF 2

Graham, Robert
See Haldeman, Joe

Graham, Tom
See Lewis, (Harry) Sinclair

Graham, W(illiam) S(idney) 1918-1986
.......................... **CLC 29**
See also BRWS 7; CA 73-76; 118; CP 1, 2, 3, 4; DLB 20; RGEL 2

Graham, Winston (Mawdsley) 1910-2003
.......................... **CLC 23**
See also CA 49-52; 218; CANR 2, 22, 45, 66; CMW 4; CN 1, 2, 3, 4, 5, 6, 7; DLB 77; RHW

Grahame, Kenneth 1859-1932 ..... **TCLC 64, 136**
See also BYA 5; CA 108; 136; CANR 80; CLR 5; CWRI 5; DA3; DAB; DLB 34, 141, 178; FANT; MAICYA 1, 2; MTCW 2; NFS 20; RGEL 2; SATA 100; TEA; WCH; YABC 1

Granger, Darius John
See Marlowe, Stephen

Granin, Daniil 1918- ....................... **CLC 59**
See also DLB 302

Granovsky, Timofei Nikolaevich 1813-1855
.......................... **NCLC 75**
See also DLB 198

Grant, Skeeter
See Spiegelman, Art

Granville-Barker, Harley 1877-1946
.......................... **TCLC 2**
See Barker, Harley Granville
See also CA 104; 204; DAM DRAM; RGEL 2

Granzotto, Gianni
See Granzotto, Giovanni Battista

Granzotto, Giovanni Battista 1914-1985
.......................... **CLC 70**
See also CA 166

Grass, Guenter
See Grass, Gunter
See also CWW 2; DLB 330; RGHL

Grass, Gunter 1927- . **CLC 1, 2, 4, 6, 11, 15, 22, 32, 49, 88, 207; WLC 3**
See Grass, Guenter
See also BPFB 2; CA 13-16R; CANR 20, 75, 93, 133; CDWLB 2; DA; DA3; DAB; DAC; DAM MST, NOV; DLB 75, 124; EW 13; EWL 3; MTCW 1, 2; MTFW 2005; RGWL 2, 3; TWA

Grass, Gunter Wilhelm
See Grass, Gunter

Gratton, Thomas
See Hulme, T(homas) E(rnest)

Grau, Shirley Ann 1929- ...... **CLC 4, 9, 146; SSC 15**
See also CA 89-92; CANR 22, 69; CN 1, 2, 3, 4, 5, 6, 7; CSW; DLB 2, 218; INT CA-89-92; CANR-22; MTCW 1

Gravel, Fern
See Hall, James Norman

Graver, Elizabeth 1964- ................. **CLC 70**
See also CA 135; CANR 71, 129

Graves, Richard Perceval 1895-1985
.......................... **CLC 44**
See also CA 65-68; CANR 9, 26, 51

Graves, Robert 1895-1985 . **CLC 1, 2, 6, 11, 39, 44, 45; PC 6**
See also BPFB 2; BRW 7; BYA 4; CA 5-8R; 117; CANR 5, 36; CDBLB 1914-1945; CN 1, 2, 3; CP 1, 2, 3, 4; DA3; DAB; DAC; DAM MST, POET; DLB 20, 100, 191; DLBD 18; DLBY 1985; EWL 3; LATS 1:1; MTCW 1, 2; MTFW 2005; NCFS 2; NFS 21; RGEL 2; RHW; SATA 45; TEA

Graves, Valerie
See Bradley, Marion Zimmer

Gray, Alasdair 1934- ....................... **CLC 41**
See also BRWS 9; CA 126; CANR 47, 69, 106, 140; CN 4, 5, 6, 7; DLB 194, 261, 319; HGG; INT CA-126; MTCW 1, 2; MTFW 2005; RGSF 2; SUFW 2

Gray, Amlin 1946- ........................... **CLC 29**
See also CA 138

Gray, Francine du Plessix 1930- .... **CLC 22, 153**
See also BEST 90:3; CA 61-64; CAAS 2; CANR 11, 33, 75, 81; DAM NOV; INT CANR-11; MTCW 1, 2; MTFW 2005

Gray, John (Henry) 1866-1934 ..... **TCLC 19**
See also CA 119; 162; RGEL 2

Gray, John Lee
See Jakes, John

Gray, Simon (James Holliday) 1936-
.......................... **CLC 9, 14, 36**
See also AITN 1; CA 21-24R; CAAS 3; CANR 32, 69; CBD; CD 5, 6; CN 1, 2, 3; DLB 13; EWL 3; MTCW 1; RGEL 2

Gray, Spalding 1941-2004 ...... **CLC 49, 112; DC 7**
See also AAYA 62; CA 128; 225; CAD; CANR 74, 138; CD 5, 6; CPW; DAM POP; MTCW 2; MTFW 2005

Gray, Thomas 1716-1771 ... **LC 4, 40; PC 2; WLC 3**
See also BRW 3; CDBLB 1660-1789; DA; DA3; DAB; DAC; DAM MST; DLB 109; EXPP; PAB; PFS 9; RGEL 2; TEA; WP

Grayson, David
See Baker, Ray Stannard

Grayson, Richard (A.) 1951- .......... **CLC 38**
See also CA 85-88; 210; CAAE 210; CANR 14, 31, 57; DLB 234

Greeley, Andrew M. 1928- ............. **CLC 28**
See also BPFB 2; CA 5-8R; CAAS 7; CANR 7, 43, 69, 104, 136; CMW 4; CPW; DA3; DAM POP; MTCW 1, 2; MTFW 2005

**Hobbs, Perry**
See Blackmur, R(ichard) P(almer)

**Hobson, Laura Z(ametkin)** 1900-1986
.................................... **CLC 7, 25**
See also BPFB 2; CA 17-20R; 118; CANR
55; CN 1, 2, 3, 4; DLB 28; SATA 52

**Hoccleve, Thomas** c. 1368-c. 1437 ..... **LC 75**
See also DLB 146; RGEL 2

**Hoch, Edward D(entinger)** 1930-
See Queen, Ellery
See also CA 29-32R; CANR 11, 27, 51, 97;
CMW 4; DLB 306; SFW 4

**Hochhuth, Rolf** 1931- ............. **CLC 4, 11, 18**
See also CA 5-8R; CANR 33, 75, 136;
CWW 2; DAM DRAM; DLB 124; EWL
3; MTCW 1, 2; MTFW 2005; RGHL

**Hochman, Sandra** 1936- ................ **CLC 3, 8**
See also CA 5-8R; CP 1, 2, 3, 4, 5; DLB 5

**Hochwaelder, Fritz** 1911-1986 ........ **CLC 36**
See Hochwalder, Fritz
See also CA 29-32R; 120; CANR 42; DAM
DRAM; MTCW 1; RGWL 3

**Hochwalder, Fritz**
See Hochwaelder, Fritz
See also EWL 3; RGWL 2

**Hocking, Mary (Eunice)** 1921- ........ **CLC 13**
See also CA 101; CANR 18, 40

**Hodgins, Jack** 1938- ......................... **CLC 23**
See also CA 93-96; CN 4, 5, 6, 7; DLB 60

**Hodgson, William Hope** 1877(?)-1918
.................................... **TCLC 13**
See also CA 111; 164; CMW 4; DLB 70,
153, 156, 178; HGG; MTCW 2; SFW 4;
SUFW 1

**Hoeg, Peter** 1957- .................... **CLC 95, 156**
See also CA 151; CANR 75; CMW 4; DA3;
DLB 214; EWL 3; MTCW 2; MTFW
2005; NFS 17; RGWL 3; SSFS 18

**Hoffman, Alice** 1952- ........................ **CLC 51**
See also AAYA 37; AMWS 10; CA 77-80;
CANR 34, 66, 100, 138; CN 4, 5, 6, 7;
CPW; DAM NOV; DLB 292; MAL 5;
MTCW 1, 2; MTFW 2005; TCLE 1:1

**Hoffman, Daniel (Gerard)** 1923- ...... **CLC 6,
13, 23**
See also CA 1-4R; CANR 4, 142; CP 1, 2,
3, 4, 5, 6, 7; DLB 5; TCLE 1:1

**Hoffman, Eva** 1945- ........................ **CLC 182**
See also AMWS 16; CA 132; CANR 146

**Hoffman, Stanley** 1944- ..................... **CLC 5**
See also CA 77-80

**Hoffman, William** 1925- ................. **CLC 141**
See also CA 21-24R; CANR 9, 103; CSW;
DLB 234; TCLE 1:1

**Hoffman, William M.**
See Hoffman, William M(oses)
See also CAD; CD 5, 6

**Hoffman, William M(oses)** 1939- .... **CLC 40**
See Hoffman, William M.
See also CA 57-60; CANR 11, 71

**Hoffmann, E(rnst) T(heodor) A(madeus)**
1776-1822 ............ **NCLC 2; SSC 13, 92**
See also CDWLB 2; DLB 90; EW 5; GL 2;
RGSF 2; RGWL 2, 3; SATA 27; SUFW
1; WCH

**Hofmann, Gert** 1931-1993 ............... **CLC 54**
See also CA 128; CANR 145; EWL 3;
RGHL

**Hofmannsthal, Hugo von** 1874-1929 . **DC 4;
TCLC 11**
See also CA 106; 153; CDWLB 2; DAM
DRAM; DFS 17; DLB 81, 118; EW 9;
EWL 3; RGWL 2, 3

**Hogan, Linda** 1947- .... **CLC 73; NNAL; PC
35**
See also AMWS 4; ANW; BYA 12; CA 120,
226; CAAE 226; CANR 45, 73, 129;
CWP; DAM MULT; DLB 175; SATA
132; TCWW 2

**Hogarth, Charles**
See Creasey, John

**Hogarth, Emmett**
See Polonsky, Abraham (Lincoln)

**Hogarth, William** 1697-1764 ............ **LC 112**
See also AAYA 56

**Hogg, James** 1770-1835 ......... **NCLC 4, 109**
See also BRWS 10; DLB 93, 116, 159; GL
2; HGG; RGEL 2; SUFW 1

**Holbach, Paul-Henri Thiry** 1723-1789
.................................... **LC 14**
See also DLB 313

**Holberg, Ludvig** 1684-1754 ................. **LC 6**
See also DLB 300; RGWL 2, 3

**Holcroft, Thomas** 1745-1809 ........ **NCLC 85**
See also DLB 39, 89, 158; RGEL 2

**Holden, Ursula** 1921- ........................ **CLC 18**
See also CA 101; CAAS 8; CANR 22

**Holderlin, (Johann Christian) Friedrich**
1770-1843 .................... **NCLC 16; PC 4**
See also CDWLB 2; DLB 90; EW 5; RGWL
2, 3

**Holdstock, Robert**
See Holdstock, Robert P.

**Holdstock, Robert P.** 1948- ............. **CLC 39**
See also CA 131; CANR 81; DLB 261;
FANT; HGG; SFW 4; SUFW 2

**Holinshed, Raphael** fl. 1580- ............. **LC 69**
See also DLB 167; RGEL 2

**Holland, Isabelle (Christian)** 1920-2002
.................................... **CLC 21**
See also AAYA 11, 64; CA 21-24R; 205;
CAAE 181; CANR 10, 25, 47; CLR 57;
CWRI 5; JRDA; LAIT 4; MAICYA 1, 2;
SATA 8, 70; SATA-Essay 103; SATA-Obit
132; WYA

**Holland, Marcus**
See Caldwell, (Janet Miriam) Taylor
(Holland)

**Hollander, John** 1929- ........ **CLC 2, 5, 8, 14**
See also CA 1-4R; CANR 1, 52, 136; CP 1,
2, 3, 4, 5, 6, 7; DLB 5; MAL 5; SATA 13

**Hollander, Paul**
See Silverberg, Robert

**Holleran, Andrew** ............................ **CLC 38**
See Garber, Eric
See also CA 144; GLL 1

**Holley, Marietta** 1836(?)-1926 ...... **TCLC 99**
See also CA 118; DLB 11; FL 1:3

**Hollinghurst, Alan** 1954- ........... **CLC 55, 91**
See also BRWS 10; CA 114; CN 5, 6, 7;
DLB 207, 326; GLL 1

**Hollis, Jim**
See Summers, Hollis (Spurgeon, Jr.)

**Holly, Buddy** 1936-1959 ................ **TCLC 65**
See also CA 213

**Holmes, Gordon**
See Shiel, M(atthew) P(hipps)

**Holmes, John**
See Souster, (Holmes) Raymond

**Holmes, John Clellon** 1926-1988 ..... **CLC 56**
See also BG 1:2; CA 9-12R; 125; CANR 4;
CN 1, 2, 3, 4; DLB 16, 237

**Holmes, Oliver Wendell, Jr.** 1841-1935
.................................... **TCLC 77**
See also CA 114; 186

**Holmes, Oliver Wendell** 1809-1894
.................................... **NCLC 14, 81; PC 71**
See also AMWS 1; CDALB 1640-1865;
DLB 1, 189, 235; EXPP; PFS 24; RGAL
4; SATA 34

**Holmes, Raymond**
See Souster, (Holmes) Raymond

**Holt, Victoria**
See Hibbert, Eleanor Alice Burford
See also BPFB 2

**Holub, Miroslav** 1923-1998 .............. **CLC 4**
See also CA 21-24R; 169; CANR 10; CD-
WLB 4; CWW 2; DLB 232; EWL 3;
RGWL 3

**Holz, Detlev**
See Benjamin, Walter

**Homer** c. 8th cent. B.C.- ... **CMLC 1, 16, 61;
PC 23; WLCS**
See also AW 1; CDWLB 1; DA; DA3;
DAB; DAC; DAM MST, POET; DLB
176; EFS 1; LAIT 1; LMFS 1; RGWL 2,
3; TWA; WLIT 8; WP

**Hongo, Garrett Kaoru** 1951- .............. **PC 23**
See also CA 133; CAAS 22; CP 5, 6, 7;
DLB 120, 312; EWL 3; EXPP; RGAL 4

**Honig, Edwin** 1919- .......................... **CLC 33**
See also CA 5-8R; CAAS 8; CANR 4, 45,
144; CP 1, 2, 3, 4, 5, 6, 7; DLB 5

**Hood, Hugh (John Blagdon)** 1928-
.................................... **CLC 15, 28; SSC 42**
See also CA 49-52; CAAS 17; CANR 1,
33, 87; CN 1, 2, 3, 4, 5, 6, 7; DLB 53;
RGSF 2

**Hood, Thomas** 1799-1845 ............. **NCLC 16**
See also BRW 4; DLB 96; RGEL 2

**Hooker, (Peter) Jeremy** 1941- ......... **CLC 43**
See also CA 77-80; CANR 22; CP 2, 3, 4,
5, 6, 7; DLB 40

**Hooker, Richard** 1554-1600 ............... **LC 95**
See also BRW 1; DLB 132; RGEL 2

**hooks, bell** 1952(?)- .......................... **CLC 94**
See also BW 2; CA 143; CANR 87, 126;
DLB 246; MTCW 2; MTFW 2005; SATA
115, 170

**Hooper, Johnson Jones** 1815-1862
.................................... **NCLC 177**
See also DLB 3, 11, 248; RGAL 4

**Hope, A(lec) D(erwent)** 1907-2000 ... **CLC 3,
51; PC 56**
See also BRWS 7; CA 21-24R; 188; CANR
33, 74; CP 1, 2, 3, 4, 5; DLB 289; EWL
3; MTCW 1, 2; MTFW 2005; PFS 8;
RGEL 2

**Hope, Anthony** 1863-1933 ............. **TCLC 83**
See also CA 157; DLB 153, 156; RGEL 2;
RHW

**Hope, Brian**
See Creasey, John

**Hope, Christopher (David Tully)** 1944-
.................................... **CLC 52**
See also AFW; CA 106; CANR 47, 101;
CN 4, 5, 6, 7; DLB 225; SATA 62

**Hopkins, Gerard Manley** 1844-1889
.................................... **NCLC 17; PC 15; WLC 3**
See also BRW 5; BRWR 2; CDBLB 1890-
1914; DA; DA3; DAB; DAC; DAM MST,
POET; DLB 35, 57; EXPP; PAB; RGEL
2; TEA; WP

**Hopkins, John (Richard)** 1931-1998 . **CLC 4**
See also CA 85-88; 169; CBD; CD 5, 6

**Hopkins, Pauline Elizabeth** 1859-1930
.................................... **BLC 2; TCLC 28**
See also AFAW 2; BW 2, 3; CA 141; CANR
82; DAM MULT; DLB 50

**Hopkinson, Francis** 1737-1791 .......... **LC 25**
See also DLB 31; RGAL 4

**Hopley-Woolrich, Cornell George** 1903-1968
See Woolrich, Cornell
See also CA 13-14; CANR 58, 156; CAP 1;
CMW 4; DLB 226; MTCW 2

**Horace** 65B.C.-8B.C. ........ **CMLC 39; PC 46**
See also AW 2; CDWLB 1; DLB 211;
RGWL 2, 3; WLIT 8

**Horatio**
See Proust, (Valentin-Louis-George-Eugene)
Marcel

**Jawien, Andrzej**
  See John Paul II, Pope
**Jaynes, Roderick**
  See Coen, Ethan
**Jeake, Samuel, Jr.**
  See Aiken, Conrad (Potter)
**Jean Paul** 1763-1825 ........................ **NCLC 7**
**Jefferies, (John) Richard** 1848-1887
  .................................... **NCLC 47**
  See also DLB 98, 141; RGEL 2; SATA 16;
  SFW 4
**Jeffers, (John) Robinson** 1887-1962
  ... **CLC 2, 3, 11, 15, 54; PC 17; WLC 3**
  See also AMWS 2; CA 85-88; CANR 35;
  CDALB 1917-1929; DA; DAC; DAM
  MST, POET; DLB 45, 212; EWL 3; MAL
  5; MTCW 1, 2; MTFW 2005; PAB; PFS
  3, 4; RGAL 4
**Jefferson, Janet**
  See Mencken, H(enry) L(ouis)
**Jefferson, Thomas** 1743-1826 ....... **NCLC 11,
103**
  See also AAYA 54; ANW; CDALB 1640-
  1865; DA3; DLB 31, 183; LAIT 1; RGAL
  4
**Jeffrey, Francis** 1773-1850 ............ **NCLC 33**
  See Francis, Lord Jeffrey
**Jelakowitch, Ivan**
  See Heijermans, Herman
**Jelinek, Elfriede** 1946- ................... **CLC 169**
  See also AAYA 68; CA 154; DLB 85, 330;
  FW
**Jellicoe, (Patricia) Ann** 1927- .......... **CLC 27**
  See also CA 85-88; CBD; CD 5, 6; CWD;
  CWRI 5; DLB 13, 233; FW
**Jelloun, Tahar ben** 1944- .............. **CLC 180**
  See Ben Jelloun, Tahar
  See also CA 162; CANR 100
**Jemyma**
  See Holley, Marietta
**Jen, Gish** ................... **AAL; CLC 70, 198**
  See Jen, Lillian
  See also AMWC 2; CN 7; DLB 312
**Jen, Lillian** 1955-
  See Jen, Gish
  See also CA 135; CANR 89, 130
**Jenkins, (John) Robin** 1912- ........... **CLC 52**
  See also CA 1-4R; CANR 1, 135; CN 1, 2,
  3, 4, 5, 6, 7; DLB 14, 271
**Jennings, Elizabeth (Joan)** 1926-2001
  ....................... **CLC 5, 14, 131**
  See also BRWS 5; CA 61-64; 200; CAAS
  5; CANR 8, 39, 66, 127; CP 1, 2, 3, 4, 5,
  6, 7; CWP; DLB 27; EWL 3; MTCW 1;
  SATA 66
**Jennings, Waylon** 1937-2002 ........... **CLC 21**
**Jensen, Johannes V(ilhelm)** 1873-1950
  .................................... **TCLC 41**
  See also CA 170; DLB 214, 330; EWL 3;
  RGWL 3
**Jensen, Laura (Linnea)** 1948- ........ **CLC 37**
  See also CA 103
**Jerome, Saint** 345-420 ................. **CMLC 30**
  See also RGWL 3
**Jerome, Jerome K(lapka)** 1859-1927
  .................................... **TCLC 23**
  See also CA 119; 177; DLB 10, 34, 135;
  RGEL 2
**Jerrold, Douglas William** 1803-1857
  .................................... **NCLC 2**
  See also DLB 158, 159; RGEL 2
**Jewett, (Theodora) Sarah Orne** 1849-1909
  ...................... **SSC 6, 44; TCLC 1, 22**
  See also AMW; AMWC 2; AMWR 2; CA
  108; 127; CANR 71; DLB 12, 74, 221;
  EXPS; FL 1:3; FW; MAL 5; MBL; NFS
  15; RGAL 4; RGSF 2; SATA 15; SSFS 4

**Jewsbury, Geraldine (Endsor)** 1812-1880
  .................................... **NCLC 22**
  See also DLB 21
**Jhabvala, Ruth Prawer** 1927- ...... **CLC 4, 8,
29, 94, 138; SSC 91**
  See also BRWS 5; CA 1-4R; CANR 2, 29,
  51, 74, 91, 128; CN 1, 2, 3, 4, 5, 6, 7;
  DAB; DAM NOV; DLB 139, 194, 323,
  326; EWL 3; IDFW 3, 4; INT CANR-29;
  MTCW 1, 2; MTFW 2005; RGSF 2;
  RGWL 2; RHW; TEA
**Jibran, Kahlil**
  See Gibran, Kahlil
**Jibran, Khalil**
  See Gibran, Kahlil
**Jiles, Paulette** 1943- ................... **CLC 13, 58**
  See also CA 101; CANR 70, 124; CP 5;
  CWP
**Jimenez (Mantecon), Juan Ramon**
  1881-1958 ...... **HLC 1; PC 7; TCLC 4,
183**
  See also CA 104; 131; CANR 74; DAM
  MULT, POET; DLB 134, 330; EW 9;
  EWL 3; HW 1; MTCW 1, 2; MTFW
  2005; RGWL 2, 3
**Jimenez, Ramon**
  See Jimenez (Mantecon), Juan Ramon
**Jimenez Mantecon, Juan**
  See Jimenez (Mantecon), Juan Ramon
**Jin, Ba** 1904-2005
  See Pa Chin
  See also CA 244; CWW 2; DLB 328
**Jin, Xuefei**
  See Ha Jin
**Jodelle, Etienne** 1532-1573 .............. **LC 119**
  See also DLB 327; GFL Beginnings to 1789
**Joel, Billy** ............................... **CLC 26**
  See Joel, William Martin
**Joel, William Martin** 1949-
  See Joel, Billy
  See also CA 108
**John, Saint** 10(?)-100 ............. **CMLC 27, 63**
**John of Salisbury** c. 1115-1180 .... **CMLC 63**
**John of the Cross, St.** 1542-1591 ....... **LC 18**
  See also RGWL 2, 3
**John Paul II, Pope** 1920-2005 ....... **CLC 128**
  See also CA 106; 133; 238
**Johnson, B(ryan) S(tanley William)**
  1933-1973 ............................ **CLC 6, 9**
  See also CA 9-12R; 53-56; CANR 9; CN 1;
  CP 1, 2; DLB 14, 40; EWL 3; RGEL 2
**Johnson, Benjamin F., of Boone**
  See Riley, James Whitcomb
**Johnson, Charles (Richard)** 1948- ... **BLC 2;
CLC 7, 51, 65, 163**
  See also AFAW 2; AMWS 6; BW 2, 3; CA
  116; CAAS 18; CANR 42, 66, 82, 129;
  CN 5, 6, 7; DAM MULT; DLB 33, 278;
  MAL 5; MTCW 2; MTFW 2005; RGAL
  4; SSFS 16
**Johnson, Charles S(purgeon)** 1893-1956
  .................................... **HR 1:3**
  See also BW 1, 3; CA 125; CANR 82; DLB
  51, 91
**Johnson, Denis** 1949- ..... **CLC 52, 160; SSC
56**
  See also CA 117; 121; CANR 71, 99; CN
  4, 5, 6, 7; DLB 120
**Johnson, Diane** 1934- ............. **CLC 5, 13, 48**
  See also BPFB 2; CA 41-44R; CANR 17,
  40, 62, 95, 155; CN 4, 5, 6, 7; DLBY
  1980; INT CANR-17; MTCW 1
**Johnson, E(mily) Pauline** 1861-1913
  .................................... **NNAL**
  See also CA 150; CCA 1; DAC; DAM
  MULT; DLB 92, 175; TCWW 2

**Johnson, Eyvind (Olof Verner)** 1900-1976
  .................................... **CLC 14**
  See also CA 73-76; 69-72; CANR 34, 101;
  DLB 259, 330; EW 12; EWL 3
**Johnson, Fenton** 1888-1958 .............. **BLC 2**
  See also BW 1; CA 118; 124; DAM MULT;
  DLB 45, 50
**Johnson, Georgia Douglas (Camp)**
  1880-1966 .................................. **HR 1:3**
  See also BW 1; CA 125; DLB 51, 249; WP
**Johnson, Helene** 1907-1995 ............... **HR 1:3**
  See also CA 181; DLB 51; WP
**Johnson, J. R.**
  See James, C(yril) L(ionel) R(obert)
**Johnson, James Weldon** 1871-1938 . **BLC 2;
HR 1:3; PC 24; TCLC 3, 19, 175**
  See also AFAW 1, 2; BW 1, 3; CA 104;
  125; CANR 82; CDALB 1917-1929; CLR
  32; DA3; DAM MULT, POET; DLB 51;
  EWL 3; EXPP; LMFS 2; MAL 5; MTCW
  1, 2; MTFW 2005; NFS 22; PFS 1; RGAL
  4; SATA 31; TUS
**Johnson, Joyce** 1935- ...................... **CLC 58**
  See also BG 1:3; CA 125; 129; CANR 102
**Johnson, Judith (Emlyn)** 1936- .. **CLC 7, 15**
  See Sherwin, Judith Johnson
  See also CA 25-28R; 153; CANR 34; CP 6,
  7
**Johnson, Lionel (Pigot)** 1867-1902
  .................................... **TCLC 19**
  See also CA 117; 209; DLB 19; RGEL 2
**Johnson, Marguerite Annie**
  See Angelou, Maya
**Johnson, Mel**
  See Malzberg, Barry N(athaniel)
**Johnson, Pamela Hansford** 1912-1981
  ........................... **CLC 1, 7, 27**
  See also CA 1-4R; 104; CANR 2, 28; CN
  1, 2, 3; DLB 15; MTCW 1, 2; MTFW
  2005; RGEL 2
**Johnson, Paul** 1928- ...................... **CLC 147**
  See also BEST 89:4; CA 17-20R; CANR
  34, 62, 100, 155
**Johnson, Paul Bede**
  See Johnson, Paul
**Johnson, Robert** ............................ **CLC 70**
**Johnson, Robert** 1911(?)-1938 ...... **TCLC 69**
  See also BW 3; CA 174
**Johnson, Samuel** 1709-1784 ........ **LC 15, 52,
128; WLC 3**
  See also BRW 3; BRWR 1; CDBLB 1660-
  1789; DA; DAB; DAC; DAM MST; DLB
  39, 95, 104, 142, 213; LMFS 1; RGEL 2;
  TEA
**Johnson, Uwe** 1934-1984 . **CLC 5, 10, 15, 40**
  See also CA 1-4R; 112; CANR 1, 39; CD-
  WLB 2; DLB 75; EWL 3; MTCW 1;
  RGWL 2, 3
**Johnston, Basil H.** 1929- ................. **NNAL**
  See also CA 69-72; CANR 11, 28, 66;
  DAC; DAM MULT; DLB 60
**Johnston, George (Benson)** 1913- ... **CLC 51**
  See also CA 1-4R; CANR 5, 20; CP 1, 2, 3,
  4, 5, 6, 7; DLB 88
**Johnston, Jennifer (Prudence)** 1930-
  ....................... **CLC 7, 150, 228**
  See also CA 85-88; CANR 92; CN 4, 5, 6,
  7; DLB 14
**Joinville, Jean de** 1224(?)-1317 ... **CMLC 38**
**Jolley, (Monica) Elizabeth** 1923- ... **CLC 46;
SSC 19**
  See also CA 127; CAAS 13; CANR 59; CN
  4, 5, 6, 7; DLB 325; EWL 3; RGSF 2
**Jones, Arthur Llewellyn** 1863-1947
  See Machen, Arthur
  See also CA 104; 179; HGG
**Jones, D(ouglas) G(ordon)** 1929- .... **CLC 10**
  See also CA 29-32R; CANR 13, 90; CP 1,
  2, 3, 4, 5, 6, 7; DLB 53

Author Index

1890-1914; CLR 39, 65; CWRI 5; DA; DA3; DAB; DAC; DAM MST, POET; DLB 19, 34, 141, 156, 330; EWL 3; EXPS; FANT; LAIT 3; LMFS 1; MAICYA 1, 2; MTCW 1, 2; MTFW 2005; NFS 21; PFS 22; RGEL 2; RGSF 2; SATA 100; SFW 4; SSFS 8, 21, 22; SUFW 1; TEA; WCH; WLIT 4; YABC 2

**Kircher, Athanasius** 1602-1680 ........ **LC 121**
See also DLB 164

**Kirk, Russell (Amos)** 1918-1994 . **TCLC 119**
See also AITN 1; CA 1-4R; 145; CAAS 9; CANR 1, 20, 60; HGG; INT CANR-20; MTCW 1, 2

**Kirkham, Dinah**
See Card, Orson Scott

**Kirkland, Caroline M.** 1801-1864
................................................. **NCLC 85**
See also DLB 3, 73, 74, 250, 254; DLBD 13

**Kirkup, James** 1918- .......................... **CLC 1**
See also CA 1-4R; CAAS 4; CANR 2; CP 1, 2, 3, 4, 5, 6, 7; DLB 27; SATA 12

**Kirkwood, James** 1930(?)-1989 ........ **CLC 9**
See also AITN 2; CA 1-4R; 128; CANR 6, 40; GLL 2

**Kirsch, Sarah** 1935- ....................... **CLC 176**
See also CA 178; CWW 2; DLB 75; EWL 3

**Kirshner, Sidney**
See Kingsley, Sidney

**Kis, Danilo** 1935-1989 ...................... **CLC 57**
See also CA 109; 118; 129; CANR 61; CDWLB 4; DLB 181; EWL 3; MTCW 1; RGSF 2; RGWL 2, 3

**Kissinger, Henry A(lfred)** 1923- .... **CLC 137**
See also CA 1-4R; CANR 2, 33, 66, 109; MTCW 1

**Kittel, Frederick August**
See Wilson, August

**Kivi, Aleksis** 1834-1872 ................. **NCLC 30**

**Kizer, Carolyn** 1925- .... **CLC 15, 39, 80; PC 66**
See also CA 65-68; CAAS 5; CANR 24, 70, 134; CP 1, 2, 3, 4, 5, 6, 7; CWP; DAM POET; DLB 5, 169; EWL 3; MAL 5; MTCW 2; MTFW 2005; PFS 18; TCLE 1:1

**Klabund** 1890-1928 ....................... **TCLC 44**
See also CA 162; DLB 66

**Klappert, Peter** 1942- ...................... **CLC 57**
See also CA 33-36R; CSW; DLB 5

**Klein, A(braham) M(oses)** 1909-1972
.................................................... **CLC 19**
See also CA 101; 37-40R; CP 1; DAB; DAC; DAM MST; DLB 68; EWL 3; RGEL 2; RGHL

**Klein, Joe**
See Klein, Joseph

**Klein, Joseph** 1946- ....................... **CLC 154**
See also CA 85-88; CANR 55

**Klein, Norma** 1938-1989 ................. **CLC 30**
See also AAYA 2, 35; BPFB 2; BYA 6, 7, 8; CA 41-44R; 128; CANR 15, 37; CLR 2, 19; INT CANR-15; JRDA; MAICYA 1, 2; SAAS 1; SATA 7, 57; WYA; YAW

**Klein, T(heodore) E(ibon) D(onald)** 1947-
.................................................... **CLC 34**
See also CA 119; CANR 44, 75; HGG

**Kleist, Heinrich von** 1777-1811 ..... **NCLC 2, 37; SSC 22**
See also CDWLB 2; DAM DRAM; DLB 90; EW 5; RGSF 2; RGWL 2, 3

**Klima, Ivan** 1931- .................... **CLC 56, 172**
See also CA 25-28R; CANR 17, 50, 91; CDWLB 4; CWW 2; DAM NOV; DLB 232; EWL 3; RGWL 3

**Klimentev, Andrei Platonovich**
See Klimentov, Andrei Platonovich

**Klimentov, Andrei Platonovich** 1899-1951
.................................... **SSC 42; TCLC 14**
See Platonov, Andrei Platonovich; Platonov, Andrey Platonovich
See also CA 108; 232

**Klinger, Friedrich Maximilian von** 1752-1831 ................... **NCLC 1**
See also DLB 94

**Klingsor the Magician**
See Hartmann, Sadakichi

**Klopstock, Friedrich Gottlieb** 1724-1803
.................................................... **NCLC 11**
See also DLB 97; EW 4; RGWL 2, 3

**Kluge, Alexander** 1932- .................... **SSC 61**
See also CA 81-84; DLB 75

**Knapp, Caroline** 1959-2002 ............. **CLC 99**
See also CA 154; 207

**Knebel, Fletcher** 1911-1993 ............. **CLC 14**
See also AITN 1; CA 1-4R; 140; CAAS 3; CANR 1, 36; CN 1, 2, 3, 4, 5; SATA 36; SATA-Obit 75

**Knickerbocker, Diedrich**
See Irving, Washington

**Knight, Etheridge** 1931-1991 .. **BLC 2; CLC 40; PC 14**
See also BW 1, 3; CA 21-24R; 133; CANR 23, 82; CP 1, 2, 3, 4, 5; DAM POET; DLB 41; MTCW 2; MTFW 2005; RGAL 4; TCLE 1:1

**Knight, Sarah Kemble** 1666-1727 ....... **LC 7**
See also DLB 24, 200

**Knister, Raymond** 1899-1932 ........ **TCLC 56**
See also CA 186; DLB 68; RGEL 2

**Knowles, John** 1926-2001 . **CLC 1, 4, 10, 26**
See also AAYA 10; AMWS 12; BPFB 2; BYA 3; CA 17-20R; 203; CANR 40, 74, 76, 132; CDALB 1968-1988; CLR 98; CN 1, 2, 3, 4, 5, 6, 7; DA; DAC; DAM MST, NOV; DLB 6; EXPN; MTCW 1, 2; MTFW 2005; NFS 2; RGAL 4; SATA 8, 89; SATA-Obit 134; YAW

**Knox, Calvin M.**
See Silverberg, Robert

**Knox, John** c. 1505-1572 ................... **LC 37**
See also DLB 132

**Knye, Cassandra**
See Disch, Thomas M.

**Koch, C(hristopher) J(ohn)** 1932- .. **CLC 42**
See also CA 127; CANR 84; CN 3, 4, 5, 6, 7; DLB 289

**Koch, Christopher**
See Koch, C(hristopher) J(ohn)

**Koch, Kenneth** 1925-2002 ....... **CLC 5, 8, 44**
See also AMWS 15; CA 1-4R; 207; CAD; CANR 6, 36, 57, 97, 131; CD 5, 6; CP 1, 2, 3, 4, 5, 6, 7; DAM POET; DLB 5; INT CANR-36; MAL 5; MTCW 2; MTFW 2005; PFS 20; SATA 65; WP

**Kochanowski, Jan** 1530-1584 ............. **LC 10**
See also RGWL 2, 3

**Kock, Charles Paul de** 1794-1871
.................................................... **NCLC 16**

**Koda Rohan**
See Koda Shigeyuki

**Koda Rohan**
See Koda Shigeyuki
See also DLB 180

**Koda Shigeyuki** 1867-1947 ........... **TCLC 22**
See Koda Rohan
See also CA 121; 183

**Koestler, Arthur** 1905-1983 . **CLC 1, 3, 6, 8, 15, 33**
See also BRWS 1; CA 1-4R; 109; CANR 1, 33; CDBLB 1945-1960; CN 1, 2, 3; DLBY 1983; EWL 3; MTCW 1, 2; MTFW 2005; NFS 19; RGEL 2

**Kogawa, Joy Nozomi** 1935- ..... **CLC 78, 129**
See also AAYA 47; CA 101; CANR 19, 62, 126; CN 6, 7; CP 1; CWP; DAC; DAM MST, MULT; FW; MTCW 2; MTFW 2005; NFS 3; SATA 99

**Kohout, Pavel** 1928- ......................... **CLC 13**
See also CA 45-48; CANR 3

**Koizumi, Yakumo**
See Hearn, (Patricio) Lafcadio (Tessima Carlos)

**Kolmar, Gertrud** 1894-1943 .......... **TCLC 40**
See also CA 167; EWL 3; RGHL

**Komunyakaa, Yusef** 1947- . **BLCS; CLC 86, 94, 207; PC 51**
See also AFAW 2; AMWS 13; CA 147; CANR 83; CP 6, 7; CSW; DLB 120; EWL 3; PFS 5, 20; RGAL 4

**Konrad, George**
See Konrad, Gyorgy

**Konrad, Gyorgy** 1933- ........... **CLC 4, 10, 73**
See also CA 85-88; CANR 97; CDWLB 4; CWW 2; DLB 232; EWL 3

**Konwicki, Tadeusz** 1926- ...... **CLC 8, 28, 54, 117**
See also CA 101; CAAS 9; CANR 39, 59; CWW 2; DLB 232; EWL 3; IDFW 3; MTCW 1

**Koontz, Dean R.** 1945- ............. **CLC 78, 206**
See also AAYA 9, 31; BEST 89:3, 90:2; CA 108; CANR 19, 36, 52, 95, 138; CMW 4; CPW; DA3; DAM NOV, POP; DLB 292; HGG; MTCW 1; MTFW 2005; SATA 92, 165; SFW 4; SUFW 2; YAW

**Koontz, Dean Ray**
See Koontz, Dean R.

**Kopernik, Mikolaj**
See Copernicus, Nicolaus

**Kopit, Arthur (Lee)** 1937- ..... **CLC 1, 18, 33**
See also AITN 1; CA 81-84; CABS 3; CAD; CD 5, 6; DAM DRAM; DFS 7, 14; DLB 7; MAL 5; MTCW 1; RGAL 4

**Kopitar, Jernej (Bartholomaus)** 1780-1844
.................................................... **NCLC 117**

**Kops, Bernard** 1926- ......................... **CLC 4**
See also CA 5-8R; CANR 84; CBD; CN 1, 2, 3, 4, 5, 6, 7; CP 1, 2, 3, 4, 5, 6, 7; DLB 13; RGHL

**Kornbluth, C(yril) M.** 1923-1958 ... **TCLC 8**
See also CA 105; 160; DLB 8; SCFW 1, 2; SFW 4

**Korolenko, V.G.**
See Korolenko, Vladimir G.

**Korolenko, Vladimir**
See Korolenko, Vladimir G.

**Korolenko, Vladimir G.** 1853-1921
.................................................... **TCLC 22**
See also CA 121; DLB 277

**Korolenko, Vladimir Galaktionovich**
See Korolenko, Vladimir G.

**Korzybski, Alfred (Habdank Skarbek)** 1879-1950 .................................... **TCLC 61**
See also CA 123; 160

**Kosinski, Jerzy** 1933-1991 ... **CLC 1, 2, 3, 6, 10, 15, 53, 70**
See also AMWS 7; BPFB 2; CA 17-20R; 134; CANR 9, 46; CN 1, 2, 3, 4; DA3; DAM NOV; DLB 2, 299; DLBY 1982; EWL 3; HGG; MAL 5; MTCW 1, 2; MTFW 2005; NFS 12; RGAL 4; RGHL; TUS

**Kostelanetz, Richard (Cory)** 1940- . **CLC 28**
See also CA 13-16R; CAAS 8; CANR 38, 77; CN 4, 5, 6; CP 2, 3, 4, 5, 6, 7

**Kostrowitzki, Wilhelm Apollinaris de** 1880-1918
See Apollinaire, Guillaume
See also CA 104

**Kotlowitz, Robert** 1924- .................... **CLC 4**
See also CA 33-36R; CANR 36

**Lagerloef, Selma (Ottiliana Lovisa)**
.................................... **TCLC 4, 36**
See Lagerlof, Selma (Ottiliana Lovisa)
See also CA 108; MTCW 2

**Lagerlof, Selma (Ottiliana Lovisa)**
1858-1940
See Lagerloef, Selma (Ottiliana Lovisa)
See also CA 188; CLR 7; DLB 259; RGWL
2, 3; SATA 15; SSFS 18

**La Guma, Alex** 1925-1985 . **BLCS; CLC 19;
TCLC 140**
See also AFW; BW 1, 3; CA 49-52; 118;
CANR 25, 81; CDWLB 3; CN 1, 2, 3;
CP 1; DAM NOV; DLB 117, 225; EWL
3; MTCW 1, 2; MTFW 2005; WLIT 2;
WWE 1

**Lahiri, Jhumpa** 1967- ........................ **SSC 96**
See also DLB 323

**Laidlaw, A. K.**
See Grieve, C(hristopher) M(urray)

**Lainez, Manuel Mujica**
See Mujica Lainez, Manuel
See also HW 1

**Laing, R(onald) D(avid)** 1927-1989
................................................. **CLC 95**
See also CA 107; 129; CANR 34; MTCW 1

**Laishley, Alex**
See Booth, Martin

**Lamartine, Alphonse (Marie Louis Prat) de**
1790-1869 .................. **NCLC 11; PC 16**
See also DAM POET; DLB 217; GFL 1789
to the Present; RGWL 2, 3

**Lamb, Charles** 1775-1834 .... **NCLC 10, 113;
WLC 3**
See also BRW 4; CDBLB 1789-1832; DA;
DAB; DAC; DAM MST; DLB 93, 107,
163; RGEL 2; SATA 17; TEA

**Lamb, Lady Caroline** 1785-1828 . **NCLC 38**
See also DLB 116

**Lamb, Mary Ann** 1764-1847 ...... **NCLC 125**
See also DLB 163; SATA 17

**Lame Deer** 1903(?)-1976 ................... **NNAL**
See also CA 69-72

**Lamming, George (William)** 1927- . **BLC 2;
CLC 2, 4, 66, 144**
See also BW 2, 3; CA 85-88; CANR 26,
76; CDWLB 3; CN 1, 2, 3, 4, 5, 6, 7; CP
1; DAM MULT; DLB 125; EWL 3;
MTCW 1, 2; MTFW 2005; NFS 15;
RGEL 2

**L'Amour, Louis** 1908-1988 ........ **CLC 25, 55**
See also AAYA 16; AITN 2; BEST 89:2;
BPFB 2; CA 1-4R; 125; CANR 3, 25, 40;
CPW; DA3; DAM NOV, POP; DLB 206;
DLBY 1980; MTCW 1, 2; MTFW 2005;
RGAL 4; TCWW 1, 2

**Lampedusa, Giuseppe (Tomasi) di**
................................................. **TCLC 13**
See Tomasi di Lampedusa, Giuseppe
See also CA 164; EW 11; MTCW 2; MTFW
2005; RGWL 2, 3

**Lampman, Archibald** 1861-1899 .. **NCLC 25**
See also DLB 92; RGEL 2; TWA

**Lancaster, Bruce** 1896-1963 ............ **CLC 36**
See also CA 9-10; CANR 70; CAP 1; SATA
9

**Lanchester, John** 1962- .................... **CLC 99**
See also CA 194; DLB 267

**Landau, Mark Alexandrovich**
See Aldanov, Mark (Alexandrovich)

**Landau-Aldanov, Mark Alexandrovich**
See Aldanov, Mark (Alexandrovich)

**Landis, Jerry**
See Simon, Paul

**Landis, John** 1950- .......................... **CLC 26**
See also CA 112; 122; CANR 128

**Landolfi, Tommaso** 1908-1979 .. **CLC 11, 49**
See also CA 127; 117; DLB 177; EWL 3

**Landon, Letitia Elizabeth** 1802-1838
................................................. **NCLC 15**
See also DLB 96

**Landor, Walter Savage** 1775-1864
................................................. **NCLC 14**
See also BRW 4; DLB 93, 107; RGEL 2

**Landwirth, Heinz** 1927-
See Lind, Jakov
See also CA 9-12R; CANR 7

**Lane, Patrick** 1939- ........................ **CLC 25**
See also CA 97-100; CANR 54; CP 3, 4, 5,
6, 7; DAM POET; DLB 53; INT CA-97-
100

**Lane, Rose Wilder** 1887-1968 ..... **TCLC 177**
See also CA 102; CANR 63; SATA 29;
SATA-Brief 28; TCWW 2

**Lang, Andrew** 1844-1912 ............. **TCLC 16**
See also CA 114; 137; CANR 85; CLR 101;
DLB 98, 141, 184; FANT; MAICYA 1, 2;
RGEL 2; SATA 16; WCH

**Lang, Fritz** 1890-1976 ............. **CLC 20, 103**
See also AAYA 65; CA 77-80; 69-72;
CANR 30

**Lange, John**
See Crichton, Michael

**Langer, Elinor** 1939- ........................ **CLC 34**
See also CA 121

**Langland, William** 1332(?)-1400(?) .. **LC 19,
120**
See also BRW 1; DA; DAB; DAC; DAM
MST, POET; DLB 146; RGEL 2; TEA;
WLIT 3

**Langstaff, Launcelot**
See Irving, Washington

**Lanier, Sidney** 1842-1881 ...... **NCLC 6, 118;
PC 50**
See also AMWS 1; DAM POET; DLB 64;
DLBD 13; EXPP; MAICYA 1; PFS 14;
RGAL 4; SATA 18

**Lanyer, Aemilia** 1569-1645 ... **LC 10, 30, 83;
PC 60**
See also DLB 121

**Lao Tzu** c. 6th cent. B.C.-3rd cent. B.C.
................................................. **CMLC 7**

**Lao-Tzu**
See Lao Tzu

**Lapine, James (Elliot)** 1949- ........... **CLC 39**
See also CA 123; 130; CANR 54, 128; INT
CA-130

**Larbaud, Valery (Nicolas)** 1881-1957
................................................. **TCLC 9**
See also CA 106; 152; EWL 3; GFL 1789
to the Present

**Lardner, Ring**
See Lardner, Ring(gold) W(ilmer)
See also BPFB 2; CDALB 1917-1929; DLB
11, 25, 86, 171; DLBD 16; MAL 5;
RGAL 4; RGSF 2

**Lardner, Ring W., Jr.**
See Lardner, Ring(gold) W(ilmer)

**Lardner, Ring(gold) W(ilmer)** 1885-1933
................................. **SSC 32; TCLC 2, 14**
See Lardner, Ring
See also AMW; CA 104; 131; MTCW 1, 2;
MTFW 2005; TUS

**Laredo, Betty**
See Codrescu, Andrei

**Larkin, Maia**
See Wojciechowska, Maia (Teresa)

**Larkin, Philip (Arthur)** 1922-1985 .. **CLC 3,
5, 8, 9, 13, 18, 33, 39, 64; PC 21**
See also BRWS 1; CA 5-8R; 117; CANR
24, 62; CDBLB 1960 to Present; CP 1, 2,
3, 4; DA3; DAB; DAM MST, POET;
DLB 27; EWL 3; MTCW 1, 2; MTFW
2005; PFS 3, 4, 12; RGEL 2

**La Roche, Sophie von** 1730-1807
................................................. **NCLC 121**
See also DLB 94

**La Rochefoucauld, Francois** 1613-1680
................................................. **LC 108**

**Larra (y Sanchez de Castro), Mariano Jose
de** 1809-1837 .................. **NCLC 17, 130**

**Larsen, Eric** 1941- ........................... **CLC 55**
See also CA 132

**Larsen, Nella** 1893(?)-1963 ..... **BLC 2; CLC
37; HR 1:3**
See also AFAW 1, 2; BW 1; CA 125; CANR
83; DAM MULT; DLB 51; FW; LATS
1:1; LMFS 2

**Larson, Charles R(aymond)** 1938- . **CLC 31**
See also CA 53-56; CANR 4, 121

**Larson, Jonathan** 1960-1996 ........... **CLC 99**
See also AAYA 28; CA 156; DFS 23;
MTFW 2005

**La Sale, Antoine de** c. 1386-1460(?)
................................................. **LC 104**
See also DLB 208

**Las Casas, Bartolome de** 1474-1566
................................................. **HLCS; LC 31**
See Casas, Bartolome de las
See also DLB 318; LAW

**Lasch, Christopher** 1932-1994 ...... **CLC 102**
See also CA 73-76; 144; CANR 25, 118;
DLB 246; MTCW 1, 2; MTFW 2005

**Lasker-Schueler, Else** 1869-1945 .. **TCLC 57**
See Lasker-Schuler, Else
See also CA 183; DLB 66, 124

**Lasker-Schuler, Else**
See Lasker-Schueler, Else
See also EWL 3

**Laski, Harold J(oseph)** 1893-1950
................................................. **TCLC 79**
See also CA 188

**Latham, Jean Lee** 1902-1995 .......... **CLC 12**
See also AITN 1; BYA 1; CA 5-8R; CANR
7, 84; CLR 50; MAICYA 1, 2; SATA 2,
68; YAW

**Latham, Mavis**
See Clark, Mavis Thorpe

**Lathen, Emma** ................................ **CLC 2**
See Hennissart, Martha; Latsis, Mary J(ane)
See also BPFB 2; CMW 4; DLB 306

**Lathrop, Francis**
See Leiber, Fritz (Reuter, Jr.)

**Latsis, Mary J(ane)** 1927-1997
See Lathen, Emma
See also CA 85-88; 162; CMW 4

**Lattany, Kristin**
See Lattany, Kristin (Elaine Eggleston)
Hunter

**Lattany, Kristin (Elaine Eggleston) Hunter**
1931- .......................................... **CLC 35**
See Hunter, Kristin
See also AITN 1; BW 1; BYA 3; CA 13-
16R; CANR 13, 108; CLR 3; CN 7; DLB
33; INT CANR-13; MAICYA 1, 2; SAAS
10; SATA 12, 132; YAW

**Lattimore, Richmond (Alexander)** 1906-1984
................................................. **CLC 3**
See also CA 1-4R; 112; CANR 1; CP 1, 2,
3; MAL 5

**Laughlin, James** 1914-1997 ............. **CLC 49**
See also CA 21-24R; 162; CAAS 22; CANR
9, 47; CP 1, 2, 3, 4, 5, 6; DLB 48; DLBY
1996, 1997

**Laurence, Margaret** 1926-1987 .... **CLC 3, 6,
13, 50, 62; SSC 7**
See also BYA 13; CA 5-8R; 121; CANR
33; CN 1, 2, 3, 4; DAC; DAM MST; DLB
53; EWL 3; FW; MTCW 1, 2; MTFW
2005; NFS 11; RGEL 2; RGSF 2; SATA-
Obit 50; TCWW 2

**Laurent, Antoine** 1952- .................. **CLC 50**

**Lauscher, Hermann**
See Hesse, Hermann

**Lautreamont** 1846-1870 . **NCLC 12; SSC 14**
See Lautreamont, Isidore Lucien Ducasse
See also GFL 1789 to the Present; RGWL
2, 3

**Lautreamont, Isidore Lucien Ducasse**
See Lautreamont
See also DLB 217

**Lavater, Johann Kaspar** 1741-1801
.................................................. **NCLC 142**
See also DLB 97

**Laverty, Donald**
See Blish, James (Benjamin)

**Lavin, Mary** 1912-1996 ........ **CLC 4, 18, 99;**
**SSC 4, 67**
See also CA 9-12R; 151; CANR 33; CN 1,
2, 3, 4, 5, 6; DLB 15, 319; FW; MTCW
1; RGEL 2; RGSF 2; SSFS 23

**Lavond, Paul Dennis**
See Kornbluth, C(yril) M.; Pohl, Frederik

**Lawes, Henry** 1596-1662 .................... **LC 113**
See also DLB 126

**Lawler, Ray**
See Lawler, Raymond Evenor
See also DLB 289

**Lawler, Raymond Evenor** 1922- ..... **CLC 58**
See Lawler, Ray
See also CA 103; CD 5, 6; RGEL 2

**Lawrence, D(avid) H(erbert Richards)**
1885-1930 .......... **PC 54; SSC 4, 19, 73;**
**TCLC 2, 9, 16, 33, 48, 61, 93; WLC 3**
See Chambers, Jessie
See also BPFB 2; BRW 7; BRWR 2; CA
104; 121; CANR 131; CDBLB 1914-
1945; DA; DA3; DAB; DAC; DAM MST,
NOV, POET; DLB 10, 19, 36, 98, 162,
195; EWL 3; EXPP; EXPS; LAIT 2, 3;
MTCW 1, 2; MTFW 2005; NFS 18; PFS
6; RGEL 2; RGSF 2; SSFS 2, 6; TEA;
WLIT 4; WP

**Lawrence, T(homas) E(dward)** 1888-1935
.......................................................... **TCLC 18**
See Dale, Colin
See also BRWS 2; CA 115; 167; DLB 195

**Lawrence of Arabia**
See Lawrence, T(homas) E(dward)

**Lawson, Henry (Archibald Hertzberg)**
1867-1922 ................ **SSC 18; TCLC 27**
See also CA 120; 181; DLB 230; RGEL 2;
RGSF 2

**Lawton, Dennis**
See Faust, Frederick (Schiller)

**Layamon** fl. c. 1200- ..................... **CMLC 10**
See Laȝamon
See also DLB 146; RGEL 2

**Laye, Camara** 1928-1980 .... **BLC 2; CLC 4,**
**38**
See Camara Laye
See also AFW; BW 1; CA 85-88; 97-100;
CANR 25; DAM MULT; MTCW 1, 2;
WLIT 2

**Layton, Irving** 1912-2006 .... **CLC 2, 15, 164**
See also CA 1-4R; 247; CANR 2, 33, 43,
66, 129; CP 1, 2, 3, 4, 5, 6, 7; DAC; DAM
MST, POET; DLB 88; EWL 3; MTCW 1,
2; PFS 12; RGEL 2

**Layton, Irving Peter**
See Layton, Irving

**Lazarus, Emma** 1849-1887 ..... **NCLC 8, 109**

**Lazarus, Felix**
See Cable, George Washington

**Lazarus, Henry**
See Slavitt, David R(ytman)

**Lea, Joan**
See Neufeld, John (Arthur)

**Leacock, Stephen (Butler)** 1869-1944
..................................... **SSC 39; TCLC 2**
See also CA 104; 141; CANR 80; DAC;
DAM MST; DLB 92; EWL 3; MTCW 2;
MTFW 2005; RGEL 2; RGSF 2

**Lead, Jane Ward** 1623-1704 .............. **LC 72**
See also DLB 131

**Leapor, Mary** 1722-1746 .................... **LC 80**
See also DLB 109

**Lear, Edward** 1812-1888 .... **NCLC 3; PC 65**
See also AAYA 48; BRW 5; CLR 1, 75;
DLB 32, 163, 166; MAICYA 1, 2; RGEL
2; SATA 18, 100; WCH; WP

**Lear, Norman (Milton)** 1922- ......... **CLC 12**
See also CA 73-76

**Leautaud, Paul** 1872-1956 ............. **TCLC 83**
See also CA 203; DLB 65; GFL 1789 to the
Present

**Leavis, F(rank) R(aymond)** 1895-1978
.......................................................... **CLC 24**
See also BRW 7; CA 21-24R; 77-80; CANR
44; DLB 242; EWL 3; MTCW 1, 2;
RGEL 2

**Leavitt, David** 1961- ........................ **CLC 34**
See also CA 116; 122; CANR 50, 62, 101,
134; CPW; DA3; DAM POP; DLB 130;
GLL 1; INT CA-122; MAL 5; MTCW 2;
MTFW 2005

**Leblanc, Maurice (Marie Emile)** 1864-1941
.......................................................... **TCLC 49**
See also CA 110; CMW 4

**Lebowitz, Fran(ces Ann)** 1951(?)- .. **CLC 11,**
**36**
See also CA 81-84; CANR 14, 60, 70; INT
CANR-14; MTCW 1

**Lebrecht, Peter**
See Tieck, (Johann) Ludwig

**le Carre, John** 1931- .................... **CLC 9, 15**
See also AAYA 42; BEST 89:4; BPFB 2;
BRWS 2; CA 5-8R; CANR 13, 33, 59,
107, 132; CDBLB 1960 to Present; CMW
4; CN 1, 2, 3, 4, 5, 6, 7; CPW; DA3;
DAM POP; DLB 87; EWL 3; MSW;
MTCW 1, 2; MTFW 2005; RGEL 2; TEA

**Le Clezio, J. M.G.** 1940- ......... **CLC 31, 155**
See also CA 116; 128; CANR 147; CWW
2; DLB 83; EWL 3; GFL 1789 to the
Present; RGSF 2

**Le Clezio, Jean Marie Gustave**
See Le Clezio, J. M.G.

**Leconte de Lisle, Charles-Marie-Rene**
1818-1894 ............................... **NCLC 29**
See also DLB 217; EW 6; GFL 1789 to the
Present

**Le Coq, Monsieur**
See Simenon, Georges (Jacques Christian)

**Leduc, Violette** 1907-1972 ............. **CLC 22**
See also CA 13-14; 33-36R; CANR 69;
CAP 1; EWL 3; GFL 1789 to the Present;
GLL 1

**Ledwidge, Francis** 1887(?)-1917 ... **TCLC 23**
See also CA 123; 203; DLB 20

**Lee, Andrea** 1953- ............. **BLC 2; CLC 36**
See also BW 1, 3; CA 125; CANR 82;
DAM MULT

**Lee, Andrew**
See Auchincloss, Louis

**Lee, Chang-rae** 1965- ...................... **CLC 91**
See also CA 148; CANR 89; CN 7; DLB
312; LATS 1:2

**Lee, Don L.** ........................................ **CLC 2**
See Madhubuti, Haki R.
See also CP 2, 3, 4, 5

**Lee, George W(ashington)** 1894-1976
....................................... **BLC 2; CLC 52**
See also BW 1; CA 125; CANR 83; DAM
MULT; DLB 51

**Lee, Harper** 1926- .. **CLC 12, 60, 194; WLC**
**4**
See also AAYA 13; AMWS 8; BPFB 2;
BYA 3; CA 13-16R; CANR 51, 128;
CDALB 1941-1968; CSW; DA; DA3;

DAB; DAC; DAM MST, NOV; DLB 6;
EXPN; LAIT 3; MAL 5; MTCW 1, 2;
MTFW 2005; NFS 2; SATA 11; WYA;
YAW

**Lee, Helen Elaine** 1959(?)- .............. **CLC 86**
See also CA 148

**Lee, John** ......................................... **CLC 70**

**Lee, Julian**
See Latham, Jean Lee

**Lee, Larry**
See Lee, Lawrence

**Lee, Laurie** 1914-1997 ..................... **CLC 90**
See also CA 77-80; 158; CANR 33, 73; CP
1, 2, 3, 4, 5, 6; CPW; DAB; DAM POP;
DLB 27; MTCW 1; RGEL 2

**Lee, Lawrence** 1941-1990 ............... **CLC 34**
See also CA 131; CANR 43

**Lee, Li-Young** 1957- .......... **CLC 164; PC 24**
See also AMWS 15; CA 153; CANR 118;
CP 6, 7; DLB 165, 312; LMFS 2; PFS 11,
15, 17

**Lee, Manfred B.** 1905-1971 ............. **CLC 11**
See Queen, Ellery
See also CA 1-4R; 29-32R; CANR 2, 150;
CMW 4; DLB 137

**Lee, Manfred Bennington**
See Lee, Manfred B.

**Lee, Nathaniel** 1645(?)-1692 ............. **LC 103**
See also DLB 80; RGEL 2

**Lee, Shelton Jackson**
See Lee, Spike
See also AAYA 4, 29

**Lee, Spike** 1957(?)- ............ **BLCS; CLC 105**
See Lee, Shelton Jackson
See also BW 2, 3; CA 125; CANR 42;
DAM MULT

**Lee, Stan** 1922- ................................ **CLC 17**
See also AAYA 5, 49; CA 108; 111; CANR
129; INT CA-111; MTFW 2005

**Lee, Tanith** 1947- ............................. **CLC 46**
See also AAYA 15; CA 37-40R; CANR 53,
102, 145; DLB 261; FANT; SATA 8, 88,
134; SFW 4; SUFW 1, 2; YAW

**Lee, Vernon** ...................... **SSC 33; TCLC 5**
See Paget, Violet
See also DLB 57, 153, 156, 174, 178; GLL
1; SUFW 1

**Lee, William**
See Burroughs, William S.
See also GLL 1

**Lee, Willy**
See Burroughs, William S.
See also GLL 1

**Lee-Hamilton, Eugene (Jacob)** 1845-1907
.......................................................... **TCLC 22**
See also CA 117; 234

**Leet, Judith** 1935- ........................... **CLC 11**
See also CA 187

**Le Fanu, Joseph Sheridan** 1814-1873
......................... **NCLC 9, 58; SSC 14, 84**
See also CMW 4; DA3; DAM POP; DLB
21, 70, 159, 178; GL 3; HGG; RGEL 2;
RGSF 2; SUFW 1

**Leffland, Ella** 1931- ......................... **CLC 19**
See also CA 29-32R; CANR 35, 78, 82;
DLBY 1984; INT CANR-35; SATA 65;
SSFS 24

**Leger, Alexis**
See Leger, (Marie-Rene Auguste) Alexis
Saint-Leger

**Leger, (Marie-Rene Auguste) Alexis**
**Saint-Leger** 1887-1975 . **CLC 4, 11, 46;**
**PC 23**
See Perse, Saint-John; Saint-John Perse
See also CA 13-16R; 61-64; CANR 43;
DAM POET; MTCW 1

**Leger, Saintleger**
See Leger, (Marie-Rene Auguste) Alexis
Saint-Leger

**Maclean, Norman (Fitzroy)** 1902-1990
........................................ **CLC 78; SSC 13**
See also AMWS 14; CA 102; 132; CANR
49; CPW; DAM POP; DLB 206; TCWW
2

**MacLeish, Archibald** 1892-1982 .. **CLC 3, 8,
14, 68; PC 47**
See also AMW; CA 9-12R; 106; CAD;
CANR 33, 63; CDALBS; CP 1, 2; DAM
POET; DFS 15; DLB 4, 7, 45; DLBY
1982; EWL 3; EXPP; MAL 5; MTCW 1,
2; MTFW 2005; PAB; PFS 5; RGAL 4;
TUS

**MacLennan, (John) Hugh** 1907-1990
........................................ **CLC 2, 14, 92**
See also CA 5-8R; 142; CANR 33; CN 1,
2, 3, 4; DAC; DAM MST; DLB 68; EWL
3; MTCW 1, 2; MTFW 2005; RGEL 2;
TWA

**MacLeod, Alistair** 1936- ......... **CLC 56, 165;
SSC 90**
See also CA 123; CCA 1; DAC; DAM
MST; DLB 60; MTCW 2; MTFW 2005;
RGSF 2; TCLE 1:2

**Macleod, Fiona**
See Sharp, William
See also RGEL 2; SUFW

**MacNeice, (Frederick) Louis** 1907-1963
........................................ **CLC 1, 4, 10, 53; PC 61**
See also BRW 7; CA 85-88; CANR 61;
DAB; DAM POET; DLB 10, 20; EWL 3;
MTCW 1, 2; MTFW 2005; RGEL 2

**MacNeill, Dand**
See Fraser, George MacDonald

**Macpherson, James** 1736-1796 ......... **LC 29**
See Ossian
See also BRWS 8; DLB 109; RGEL 2

**Macpherson, (Jean) Jay** 1931- ........ **CLC 14**
See also CA 5-8R; CANR 90; CP 1, 2, 3, 4,
6, 7; CWP; DLB 53

**Macrobius** fl. 430- ......................... **CMLC 48**

**MacShane, Frank** 1927-1999 .......... **CLC 39**
See also CA 9-12R; 186; CANR 3, 33; DLB
111

**Macumber, Mari**
See Sandoz, Mari(e Susette)

**Madach, Imre** 1823-1864 .............. **NCLC 19**

**Madden, (Jerry) David** 1933- ..... **CLC 5, 15**
See also CA 1-4R; CAAS 3; CANR 4, 45;
CN 3, 4, 5, 6, 7; CSW; DLB 6; MTCW 1

**Maddern, Al(an)**
See Ellison, Harlan

**Madhubuti, Haki R.** 1942- . **BLC 2; CLC 6,
73; PC 5**
See Lee, Don L.
See also BW 2, 3; CA 73-76; CANR 24,
51, 73, 139; CP 6, 7; CSW; DAM MULT,
POET; DLB 5, 41; DLBD 8; EWL 3;
MAL 5; MTCW 2; MTFW 2005; RGAL
4

**Madison, James** 1751-1836 ......... **NCLC 126**
See also DLB 37

**Maepenn, Hugh**
See Kuttner, Henry

**Maepenn, K. H.**
See Kuttner, Henry

**Maeterlinck, Maurice** 1862-1949 ... **TCLC 3**
See also CA 104; 136; CANR 80; DAM
DRAM; DLB 192; EW 8; EWL 3; GFL
1789 to the Present; LMFS 2; RGWL 2,
3; SATA 66; TWA

**Maginn, William** 1794-1842 ........... **NCLC 8**
See also DLB 110, 159

**Mahapatra, Jayanta** 1928- .............. **CLC 33**
See also CA 73-76; CAAS 9; CANR 15,
33, 66, 87; CP 4, 5, 6, 7; DAM MULT;
DLB 323

**Mahfouz, Naguib** 1911(?)-2006 .... **CLC 153;
SSC 66**
See Mahfuz, Najib
See also AAYA 49; BEST 89:2; CA 128;
CANR 55, 101; DA3; DAM NOV;
MTCW 1, 2; MTFW 2005; RGWL 2, 3;
SSFS 9

**Mahfouz, Naguib Abdel Aziz Al-Sabilgi**
See Mahfouz, Naguib

**Mahfuz, Najib** ........................... **CLC 52, 55**
See Mahfouz, Naguib
See also AFW; CWW 2; DLBY 1988; EWL
3; RGSF 2; WLIT 6

**Mahon, Derek** 1941- .......... **CLC 27; PC 60**
See also BRWS 6; CA 113; 128; CANR 88;
CP 1, 2, 3, 4, 5, 6, 7; DLB 40; EWL 3

**Maiakovskii, Vladimir**
See Mayakovski, Vladimir (Vladimirovich)
See also IDTP; RGWL 2, 3

**Mailer, Norman** 1923- . **CLC 1, 2, 3, 4, 5, 8,
11, 14, 28, 39, 74, 111**
See also AAYA 31; AITN 2; AMW; AMWC
2; AMWR 2; BPFB 2; CA 9-12R; CABS
1; CANR 28, 74, 77, 130; CDALB 1968-
1988; CN 1, 2, 3, 4, 5, 6, 7; CPW; DA;
DA3; DAB; DAC; DAM MST, NOV,
POP; DLB 2, 16, 28, 185, 278; DLBD 3;
DLBY 1980, 1983; EWL 3; MAL 5;
MTCW 1, 2; MTFW 2005; NFS 10;
RGAL 4; TUS

**Mailer, Norman Kingsley**
See Mailer, Norman

**Maillet, Antonine** 1929- ........... **CLC 54, 118**
See also CA 115; 120; CANR 46, 74, 77,
134; CCA 1; CWW 2; DAC; DLB 60;
INT CA-120; MTCW 2; MTFW 2005

**Maimonides, Moses** 1135-1204 .... **CMLC 76**
See also DLB 115

**Mais, Roger** 1905-1955 ................... **TCLC 8**
See also BW 1, 3; CA 105; 124; CANR 82;
CDWLB 3; DLB 125; EWL 3; MTCW 1;
RGEL 2

**Maistre, Joseph** 1753-1821 ........... **NCLC 37**
See also GFL 1789 to the Present

**Maitland, Frederic William** 1850-1906
........................................ **TCLC 65**

**Maitland, Sara (Louise)** 1950- ........ **CLC 49**
See also BRWS 11; CA 69-72; CANR 13,
59; DLB 271; FW

**Major, Clarence** 1936- .. **BLC 2; CLC 3, 19,
48**
See also AFAW 2; BW 2, 3; CA 21-24R;
CAAS 6; CANR 13, 25, 53, 82; CN 3, 4,
5, 6, 7; CP 2, 3, 4, 5, 6, 7; CSW; DAM
MULT; DLB 33; EWL 3; MAL 5; MSW

**Major, Kevin (Gerald)** 1949- .......... **CLC 26**
See also AAYA 16; CA 97-100; CANR 21,
38, 112; CLR 11; DAC; DLB 60; INT
CANR-21; JRDA; MAICYA 1, 2; MAIC-
YAS 1; SATA 32, 82, 134; WYA; YAW

**Maki, James**
See Ozu, Yasujiro

**Makine, Andrei** 1957- .................... **CLC 198**
See also CA 176; CANR 103; MTFW 2005

**Malabaila, Damiano**
See Levi, Primo

**Malamud, Bernard** 1914-1986 . **CLC 1, 2, 3,
5, 8, 9, 11, 18, 27, 44, 78, 85; SSC 15;
TCLC 129, 184; WLC 4**
See also AAYA 16; AMWS 1; BPFB 2;
BYA 15; CA 5-8R; 118; CABS 1; CANR
28, 62, 114; CDALB 1941-1968; CN 1, 2,
3, 4; CPW; DA; DA3; DAB; DAC; DAM
MST, NOV, POP; DLB 2, 28, 152; DLBY
1980, 1986; EWL 3; EXPS; LAIT 4;
LATS 1:1; MAL 5; MTCW 1, 2; MTFW
2005; NFS 4, 9; RGAL 4; RGHL; RGSF
2; SSFS 8, 13, 16; TUS

**Malan, Herman**
See Bosman, Herman Charles; Bosman,
Herman Charles

**Malaparte, Curzio** 1898-1957 ....... **TCLC 52**
See also DLB 264

**Malcolm, Dan**
See Silverberg, Robert

**Malcolm, Janet** 1934- .................... **CLC 201**
See also CA 123; CANR 89; NCFS 1

**Malcolm X** .... **BLC 2; CLC 82, 117; WLCS**
See Little, Malcolm
See also LAIT 5; NCFS 3

**Malebranche, Nicolas** 1638-1715 ..... **LC 133**
See also GFL Beginnings to 1789

**Malherbe, Francois de** 1555-1628 ....... **LC 5**
See also DLB 327; GFL Beginnings to 1789

**Mallarme, Stephane** 1842-1898 ..... **NCLC 4,
41; PC 4**
See also DAM POET; DLB 217; EW 7;
GFL 1789 to the Present; LMFS 2; RGWL
2, 3; TWA

**Mallet-Joris, Francoise** 1930- .......... **CLC 11**
See also CA 65-68; CANR 17; CWW 2;
DLB 83; EWL 3; GFL 1789 to the Present

**Malley, Ern**
See McAuley, James Phillip

**Mallon, Thomas** 1951- .................. **CLC 172**
See also CA 110; CANR 29, 57, 92

**Mallowan, Agatha Christie**
See Christie, Agatha (Mary Clarissa)

**Maloff, Saul** 1922- ............................. **CLC 5**
See also CA 33-36R

**Malone, Louis**
See MacNeice, (Frederick) Louis

**Malone, Michael (Christopher)** 1942-
........................................ **CLC 43**
See also CA 77-80; CANR 14, 32, 57, 114

**Malory, Sir Thomas** 1410(?)-1471(?)
........................................ **LC 11, 88; WLCS**
See also BRW 1; BRWR 2; CDBLB Before
1660; DA; DAB; DAC; DAM MST; DLB
146; EFS 2; RGEL 2; SATA 59; SATA-
Brief 33; TEA; WLIT 3

**Malouf, David** 1934- ................... **CLC 28, 86**
See also BRWS 12; CA 124; CANR 50, 76;
CN 3, 4, 5, 6, 7; CP 1, 3, 4, 5, 6, 7; DLB
289; EWL 3; MTCW 2; MTFW 2005;
SSFS 24

**Malraux, (Georges-)Andre** 1901-1976
........................................ **CLC 1, 4, 9, 13, 15, 57**
See also BPFB 2; CA 21-22; 69-72; CANR
34, 58; CAP 2; DA3; DAM NOV; DLB
72; EW 12; EWL 3; GFL 1789 to the
Present; MTCW 1, 2; MTFW 2005;
RGWL 2, 3; TWA

**Malthus, Thomas Robert** 1766-1834
........................................ **NCLC 145**
See also DLB 107, 158; RGEL 2

**Malzberg, Barry N(athaniel)** 1939- .. **CLC 7**
See also CA 61-64; CAAS 4; CANR 16;
CMW 4; DLB 8; SFW 4

**Mamet, David** 1947- . **CLC 9, 15, 34, 46, 91,
166; DC 4, 24**
See also AAYA 3, 60; AMWS 14; CA 81-
84; CABS 3; CAD; CANR 15, 41, 67, 72,
129; CD 5, 6; DA3; DAM DRAM; DFS
2, 3, 6, 12, 15; DLB 7; EWL 3; IDFW 4;
MAL 5; MTCW 1, 2; MTFW 2005;
RGAL 4

**Mamet, David Alan**
See Mamet, David

**Mamoulian, Rouben (Zachary)** 1897-1987
........................................ **CLC 16**
See also CA 25-28R; 124; CANR 85

**Mandelshtam, Osip**
See Mandelstam, Osip (Emilievich)
See also EW 10; EWL 3; RGWL 2, 3

**Mandelstam, Osip (Emilievich)**
1891(?)-1943(?) ....... **PC 14; TCLC 2, 6**
See Mandelshtam, Osip
See also CA 104; 150; MTCW 2; TWA

**Mander, (Mary) Jane** 1877-1949 .. **TCLC 31**
See also CA 162; RGEL 2

**Mandeville, Bernard** 1670-1733 ......... **LC 82**
See also DLB 101

**Mandeville, Sir John** fl. 1350- ..... **CMLC 19**
See also DLB 146

**Mandiargues, Andre Pieyre de** ....... **CLC 41**
See Pieyre de Mandiargues, Andre
See also DLB 83

**Mandrake, Ethel Belle**
See Thurman, Wallace (Henry)

**Mangan, James Clarence** 1803-1849
.................................................... **NCLC 27**
See also RGEL 2

**Maniere, J.-E.**
See Giraudoux, Jean(-Hippolyte)

**Mankiewicz, Herman (Jacob)** 1897-1953
.................................................... **TCLC 85**
See also CA 120; 169; DLB 26; IDFW 3, 4

**Manley, (Mary) Delariviere** 1672(?)-1724
.................................................. **LC 1, 42**
See also DLB 39, 80; RGEL 2

**Mann, Abel**
See Creasey, John

**Mann, Emily** 1952- ........................... **DC 7**
See also CA 130; CAD; CANR 55; CD 5,
6; CWD; DLB 266

**Mann, (Luiz) Heinrich** 1871-1950 .. **TCLC 9**
See also CA 106; 164, 181; DLB 66, 118;
EW 8; EWL 3; RGWL 2, 3

**Mann, (Paul) Thomas** 1875-1955 ...... **SSC 5,
80, 82; TCLC 2, 8, 14, 21, 35, 44, 60,
168; WLC 4**
See also BPFB 2; CA 104; 128; CANR 133;
CDWLB 2; DA; DA3; DAB; DAC; DAM
MST, NOV; DLB 66; EW 9; EWL 3; GLL
1; LATS 1:1; LMFS 1; MTCW 1, 2;
MTFW 2005; NFS 17; RGSF 2; RGWL
2, 3; SSFS 4, 9; TWA

**Mannheim, Karl** 1893-1947 .......... **TCLC 65**
See also CA 204

**Manning, David**
See Faust, Frederick (Schiller)

**Manning, Frederic** 1882-1935 ....... **TCLC 25**
See also CA 124; 216; DLB 260

**Manning, Olivia** 1915-1980 ......... **CLC 5, 19**
See also CA 5-8R; 101; CANR 29; CN 1,
2; EWL 3; FW; MTCW 1; RGEL 2

**Mannyng, Robert** c. 1264-c. 1340
.................................................. **CMLC 83**
See also DLB 146

**Mano, D. Keith** 1942- ................. **CLC 2, 10**
See also CA 25-28R; CAAS 6; CANR 26,
57; DLB 6

**Mansfield, Katherine** ....... **SSC 9, 23, 38, 81;
TCLC 2, 8, 39, 164; WLC 4**
See Beauchamp, Kathleen Mansfield
See also BPFB 2; BRW 7; DAB; DLB 162;
EWL 3; EXPS; FW; GLL 1; RGEL 2;
RGSF 2; SSFS 2, 8, 10, 11; WWE 1

**Manso, Peter** 1940- ......................... **CLC 39**
See also CA 29-32R; CANR 44, 156

**Mantecon, Juan Jimenez**
See Jimenez (Mantecon), Juan Ramon

**Mantel, Hilary (Mary)** 1952- ......... **CLC 144**
See also CA 125; CANR 54, 101; CN 5, 6,
7; DLB 271; RHW

**Manton, Peter**
See Creasey, John

**Man Without a Spleen, A**
See Chekhov, Anton (Pavlovich)

**Manzano, Juan Franciso** 1797(?)-1854
.................................................... **NCLC 155**

**Manzoni, Alessandro** 1785-1873 .. **NCLC 29,
98**
See also EW 5; RGWL 2, 3; TWA; WLIT 7

**Map, Walter** 1140-1209 ............... **CMLC 32**

**Mapu, Abraham (ben Jekutiel)** 1808-1867
.................................................... **NCLC 18**

**Mara, Sally**
See Queneau, Raymond

**Maracle, Lee** 1950- ........................... **NNAL**
See also CA 149

**Marat, Jean Paul** 1743-1793 ............. **LC 10**

**Marcel, Gabriel Honore** 1889-1973
.................................................... **CLC 15**
See also CA 102; 45-48; EWL 3; MTCW 1,
2

**March, William** ............................ **TCLC 96**
See Campbell, William Edward March
See also CA 216; DLB 9, 86, 316; MAL 5

**Marchbanks, Samuel**
See Davies, Robertson
See also CCA 1

**Marchi, Giacomo**
See Bassani, Giorgio

**Marcus Aurelius**
See Aurelius, Marcus
See also AW 2

**Marguerite**
See de Navarre, Marguerite

**Marguerite d'Angouleme**
See de Navarre, Marguerite
See also GFL Beginnings to 1789

**Marguerite de Navarre**
See de Navarre, Marguerite
See also RGWL 2, 3

**Margulies, Donald** 1954- ................. **CLC 76**
See also AAYA 57; CA 200; CD 6; DFS 13;
DLB 228

**Marie de France** c. 12th cent. - .... **CMLC 8;
PC 22**
See also DLB 208; FW; RGWL 2, 3

**Marie de l'Incarnation** 1599-1672 ..... **LC 10**

**Marier, Captain Victor**
See Griffith, D(avid Lewelyn) W(ark)

**Mariner, Scott**
See Pohl, Frederik

**Marinetti, Filippo Tommaso** 1876-1944
.................................................... **TCLC 10**
See also CA 107; DLB 114, 264; EW 9;
EWL 3; WLIT 7

**Marivaux, Pierre Carlet de Chamblain de**
1688-1763 ................... **DC 7; LC 4, 123**
See also DLB 314; GFL Beginnings to
1789; RGWL 2, 3; TWA

**Markandaya, Kamala** ................. **CLC 8, 38**
See Taylor, Kamala
See also BYA 13; CN 1, 2, 3, 4, 5, 6, 7;
DLB 323; EWL 3

**Markfield, Wallace (Arthur)** 1926-2002
.................................................... **CLC 8**
See also CA 69-72; 208; CAAS 3; CN 1, 2,
3, 4, 5, 6, 7; DLB 2, 28; DLBY 2002

**Markham, Edwin** 1852-1940 ........ **TCLC 47**
See also CA 160; DLB 54, 186; MAL 5;
RGAL 4

**Markham, Robert**
See Amis, Kingsley

**Marks, J.**
See Highwater, Jamake (Mamake)

**Marks-Highwater, J.**
See Highwater, Jamake (Mamake)

**Markson, David M(errill)** 1927- ..... **CLC 67**
See also CA 49-52; CANR 1, 91; CN 5, 6

**Marlatt, Daphne (Buckle)** 1942- ... **CLC 168**
See also CA 25-28R; CANR 17, 39; CN 6,
7; CP 4, 5, 6, 7; CWP; DLB 60; FW

**Marley, Bob** ....................................... **CLC 17**
See Marley, Robert Nesta

**Marley, Robert Nesta** 1945-1981
See Marley, Bob
See also CA 107; 103

**Marlowe, Christopher** 1564-1593 ....... **DC 1;
LC 22, 47, 117; PC 57; WLC 4**
See also BRW 1; BRWR 1; CDBLB Before
1660; DA; DA3; DAB; DAC; DAM
DRAM, MST; DFS 1, 5, 13, 21; DLB 62;
EXPP; LMFS 1; PFS 22; RGEL 2; TEA;
WLIT 3

**Marlowe, Stephen** 1928- ................. **CLC 70**
See Queen, Ellery
See also CA 13-16R; CANR 6, 55; CMW
4; SFW 4

**Marmion, Shakerley** 1603-1639 ........ **LC 89**
See also DLB 58; RGEL 2

**Marmontel, Jean-Francois** 1723-1799 . **LC 2**
See also DLB 314

**Maron, Monika** 1941- ................... **CLC 165**
See also CA 201

**Marot, Clement** c. 1496-1544 .......... **LC 133**
See also GFL Beginnings to 1789

**Marquand, John P(hillips)** 1893-1960
.................................................... **CLC 2, 10**
See also AMW; BPFB 2; CA 85-88; CANR
73; CMW 4; DLB 9, 102; EWL 3; MAL
5; MTCW 2; RGAL 4

**Marques, Rene** 1919-1979 . **CLC 96; HLC 2**
See also CA 97-100; 85-88; CANR 78;
DAM MULT; DLB 305; EWL 3; HW 1,
2; LAW; RGSF 2

**Marquez, Gabriel Garcia**
See Garcia Marquez, Gabriel

**Marquis, Don(ald Robert Perry)** 1878-1937
.................................................... **TCLC 7**
See also CA 104; 166; DLB 11, 25; MAL
5; RGAL 4

**Marquis de Sade**
See Sade, Donatien Alphonse Francois

**Marric, J. J.**
See Creasey, John
See also MSW

**Marryat, Frederick** 1792-1848 ....... **NCLC 3**
See also DLB 21, 163; RGEL 2; WCH

**Marsden, James**
See Creasey, John

**Marsh, Edward** 1872-1953 ............ **TCLC 99**

**Marsh, (Edith) Ngaio** 1895-1982 ...... **CLC 7,
53**
See also CA 9-12R; CANR 6, 58; CMW 4;
CN 1, 2, 3; CPW; DAM POP; DLB 77;
MSW; MTCW 1, 2; RGEL 2; TEA

**Marshall, Allen**
See Westlake, Donald E.

**Marshall, Garry** 1934- ..................... **CLC 17**
See also AAYA 3; CA 111; SATA 60

**Marshall, Paule** 1929- ....... **BLC 3; CLC 27,
72; SSC 3**
See also AFAW 1, 2; AMWS 11; BPFB 2;
BW 2, 3; CA 77-80; CANR 25, 73, 129;
CN 1, 2, 3, 4, 5, 6, 7; DA3; DAM MULT;
DLB 33, 157, 227; EWL 3; LATS 1:2;
MAL 5; MTCW 1, 2; MTFW 2005;
RGAL 4; SSFS 15

**Marshallik**
See Zangwill, Israel

**Marsten, Richard**
See Hunter, Evan

**Marston, John** 1576-1634 ................... **LC 33**
See also BRW 2; DAM DRAM; DLB 58,
172; RGEL 2

**Martel, Yann** 1963- ....................... **CLC 192**
See also AAYA 67; CA 146; CANR 114;
DLB 326; MTFW 2005

**Martens, Adolphe-Adhemar**
See Ghelderode, Michel de

**McKay, Festus Claudius** 1889-1948
See McKay, Claude
See also BW 1, 3; CA 104; 124; CANR 73;
DA; DAC; DAM MST, MULT, NOV,
POET; MTCW 1, 2; MTFW 2005; TUS

**McKuen, Rod** 1933- ............ **CLC 1, 3**
See also AITN 1; CA 41-44R; CANR 40;
CP 1

**McLoughlin, R. B.**
See Mencken, H(enry) L(ouis)

**McLuhan, (Herbert) Marshall** 1911-1980
.................................................. **CLC 37, 83**
See also CA 9-12R; 102; CANR 12, 34, 61;
DLB 88; INT CANR-12; MTCW 1, 2;
MTFW 2005

**McManus, Declan Patrick Aloysius**
See Costello, Elvis

**McMillan, Terry** 1951- . **BLCS; CLC 50, 61,
112**
See also AAYA 21; AMWS 13; BPFB 2;
BW 2, 3; CA 140; CANR 60, 104, 131;
CN 7; CPW; DA3; DAM MULT, NOV,
POP; MAL 5; MTCW 2; MTFW 2005;
RGAL 4; YAW

**McMurtry, Larry** 1936- ..... **CLC 2, 3, 7, 11,
27, 44, 127**
See also AAYA 15; AITN 2; AMWS 5;
BEST 89:2; BPFB 2; CA 5-8R; CANR
19, 43, 64, 103; CDALB 1968-1988; CN
2, 3, 4, 5, 6, 7; CPW; CSW; DA3; DAM
NOV, POP; DLB 2, 143, 256; DLBY
1980, 1987; EWL 3; MAL 5; MTCW 1,
2; MTFW 2005; RGAL 4; TCWW 1, 2

**McMurtry, Larry Jeff**
See McMurtry, Larry

**McNally, Terrence** 1939- .. **CLC 4, 7, 41, 91;
DC 27**
See also AAYA 62; AMWS 13; CA 45-48;
CAD; CANR 2, 56, 116; CD 5, 6; DA3;
DAM DRAM; DFS 16, 19; DLB 7, 249;
EWL 3; GLL 1; MTCW 2; MTFW 2005

**McNally, Thomas Michael**
See McNally, T.M.

**McNally, T.M.** 1961- .................. **CLC 82**
See also CA 246

**McNamer, Deirdre** 1950- .......... **CLC 70**

**McNeal, Tom** ........................... **CLC 119**

**McNeile, Herman Cyril** 1888-1937
See Sapper
See also CA 184; CMW 4; DLB 77

**McNickle, (William) D'Arcy** 1904-1977
.................................................. **CLC 89; NNAL**
See also CA 9-12R; 85-88; CANR 5, 45;
DAM MULT; DLB 175, 212; RGAL 4;
SATA-Obit 22; TCWW 1, 2

**McPhee, John** 1931- .................. **CLC 36**
See also AAYA 61; AMWS 3; ANW; BEST
90:1; CA 65-68; CANR 20, 46, 64, 69,
121; CPW; DLB 185, 275; MTCW 1, 2;
MTFW 2005; TUS

**McPherson, James Alan** 1943-
................. **BLCS; CLC 19, 77; SSC 95**
See also BW 1, 3; CA 25-28R; CAAS 17;
CANR 24, 74, 140; CN 3, 4, 5, 6; CSW;
DLB 38, 244; EWL 3; MTCW 1, 2;
MTFW 2005; RGAL 4; RGSF 2; SSFS
23

**McPherson, William (Alexander)** 1933-
.................................................. **CLC 34**
See also CA 69-72; CANR 28; INT
CANR-28

**McTaggart, J. McT. Ellis**
See McTaggart, John McTaggart Ellis

**McTaggart, John McTaggart Ellis** 1866-1925
.................................................. **TCLC 105**
See also CA 120; DLB 262

**Mead, George Herbert** 1863-1931
.................................................. **TCLC 89**
See also CA 212; DLB 270

**Mead, Margaret** 1901-1978 ............. **CLC 37**
See also AITN 1; CA 1-4R; 81-84; CANR
4; DA3; FW; MTCW 1, 2; SATA-Obit 20

**Meaker, Marijane** 1927-
See Kerr, M. E.
See also CA 107; CANR 37, 63, 145; INT
CA-107; JRDA; MAICYA 1, 2; MAIC-
YAS 1; MTCW 1; SATA 20, 61, 99, 160;
SATA-Essay 111; YAW

**Medoff, Mark (Howard)** 1940- ... **CLC 6, 23**
See also AITN 1; CA 53-56; CAD; CANR
5; CD 5, 6; DAM DRAM; DFS 4; DLB
7; INT CANR-5

**Medvedev, P. N.**
See Bakhtin, Mikhail Mikhailovich

**Meged, Aharon**
See Megged, Aharon

**Meged, Aron**
See Megged, Aharon

**Megged, Aharon** 1920- ................... **CLC 9**
See also CA 49-52; CAAS 13; CANR 1,
140; EWL 3; RGHL

**Mehta, Deepa** 1950- ................... **CLC 208**

**Mehta, Gita** 1943- ..................... **CLC 179**
See also CA 225; CN 7; DNFS 2

**Mehta, Ved** 1934- ....................... **CLC 37**
See also CA 1-4R, 212; CAAE 212; CANR
2, 23, 69; DLB 323; MTCW 1; MTFW
2005

**Melanchthon, Philipp** 1497-1560 ....... **LC 90**
See also DLB 179

**Melanter**
See Blackmore, R(ichard) D(oddridge)

**Meleager** c. 140B.C.-c. 70B.C. ..... **CMLC 53**

**Melies, Georges** 1861-1938 ........... **TCLC 81**

**Melikow, Loris**
See Hofmannsthal, Hugo von

**Melmoth, Sebastian**
See Wilde, Oscar (Fingal O'Flahertie Wills)

**Melo Neto, Joao Cabral de**
See Cabral de Melo Neto, Joao
See also CWW 2; EWL 3

**Meltzer, Milton** 1915- ................... **CLC 26**
See also AAYA 8, 45; BYA 2, 6; CA 13-
16R; CANR 38, 92, 107; CLR 13; DLB
61; JRDA; MAICYA 1, 2; SAAS 1; SATA
1, 50, 80, 128; SATA-Essay 124; WYA;
YAW

**Melville, Herman** 1819-1891 ... **NCLC 3, 12,
29, 45, 49, 91, 93, 123, 157; SSC 1, 17,
46, 95; WLC 4**
See also AAYA 25; AMW; AMWR 1;
CDALB 1640-1865; DA; DA3; DAB;
DAC; DAM MST, NOV; DLB 3, 74, 250,
254; EXPN; EXPS; GL 3; LAIT 1, 2; NFS
7, 9; RGAL 4; RGSF 2; SATA 59; SSFS
3; TUS

**Members, Mark**
See Powell, Anthony

**Membreno, Alejandro** .................... **CLC 59**

**Menand, Louis** 1952- ..................... **CLC 208**
See also CA 200

**Menander** c. 342B.C.-c. 293B.C. .. **CMLC 9,
51; DC 3**
See also AW 1; CDWLB 1; DAM DRAM;
DLB 176; LMFS 1; RGWL 2, 3

**Menchu, Rigoberta** 1959- . **CLC 160; HLCS
2**
See also CA 175; CANR 135; DNFS 1;
WLIT 1

**Mencken, H(enry) L(ouis)** 1880-1956
.................................................. **TCLC 13**
See also AMW; CA 105; 125; CDALB
1917-1929; DLB 11, 29, 63, 137, 222;
EWL 3; MAL 5; MTCW 1, 2; MTFW
2005; NCFS 4; RGAL 4; TUS

**Mendelsohn, Jane** 1965- .................. **CLC 99**
See also CA 154; CANR 94

**Mendoza, Inigo Lopez de**
See Santillana, Inigo Lopez de Mendoza,
Marques de

**Menton, Francisco de**
See Chin, Frank (Chew, Jr.)

**Mercer, David** 1928-1980 .................. **CLC 5**
See also CA 9-12R; 102; CANR 23; CBD;
DAM DRAM; DLB 13, 310; MTCW 1;
RGEL 2

**Merchant, Paul**
See Ellison, Harlan

**Meredith, George** 1828-1909 ............. **PC 60;
TCLC 17, 43**
See also CA 117; 153; CANR 80; CDBLB
1832-1890; DAM POET; DLB 18, 35, 57,
159; RGEL 2; TEA

**Meredith, William (Morris)** 1919- ... **CLC 4,
13, 22, 55; PC 28**
See also CA 9-12R; CAAS 14; CANR 6,
40, 129; CP 1, 2, 3, 4, 5, 6, 7; DAM
POET; DLB 5; MAL 5

**Merezhkovsky, Dmitrii Sergeevich**
See Merezhkovsky, Dmitry Sergeyevich
See also DLB 295

**Merezhkovsky, Dmitry Sergeevich**
See Merezhkovsky, Dmitry Sergeyevich
See also EWL 3

**Merezhkovsky, Dmitry Sergeyevich**
1865-1941 ............................... **TCLC 29**
See Merezhkovsky, Dmitrii Sergeevich;
Merezhkovsky, Dmitry Sergeevich
See also CA 169

**Merimee, Prosper** 1803-1870 .. **NCLC 6, 65;
SSC 7, 77**
See also DLB 119, 192; EW 6; EXPS; GFL
1789 to the Present; RGSF 2; RGWL 2,
3; SSFS 8; SUFW

**Merkin, Daphne** 1954- .................... **CLC 44**
See also CA 123

**Merleau-Ponty, Maurice** 1908-1961
.................................................. **TCLC 156**
See also CA 114; 89-92; DLB 296; GFL
1789 to the Present

**Merlin, Arthur**
See Blish, James (Benjamin)

**Mernissi, Fatima** 1940- ................. **CLC 171**
See also CA 152; FW

**Merrill, James** 1926-1995 .... **CLC 2, 3, 6, 8,
13, 18, 34, 91; PC 28; TCLC 173**
See also AMWS 3; CA 13-16R; 147; CANR
10, 49, 63, 108; CP 1, 2, 3, 4; DA3; DAM
POET; DLB 5, 165; DLBY 1985; EWL 3;
INT CANR-10; MAL 5; MTCW 1, 2;
MTFW 2005; PAB; PFS 23; RGAL 4

**Merriman, Alex**
See Silverberg, Robert

**Merriman, Brian** 1747-1805 ......... **NCLC 70**

**Merritt, E. B.**
See Waddington, Miriam

**Merton, Thomas (James)** 1915-1968
................. **CLC 1, 3, 11, 34, 83; PC 10**
See also AAYA 61; AMWS 8; CA 5-8R;
25-28R; CANR 22, 53, 111, 131; DA3;
DLB 48; DLBY 1981; MAL 5; MTCW 1,
2; MTFW 2005

**Merwin, W.S.** 1927- ... **CLC 1, 2, 3, 5, 8, 13,
18, 45, 88; PC 45**
See also AMWS 3; CA 13-16R; CANR 15,
51, 112, 140; CP 1, 2, 3, 4, 5, 6, 7; DA3;
DAM POET; DLB 5, 169; EWL 3; INT
CANR-15; MAL 5; MTCW 1, 2; MTFW
2005; PAB; PFS 5, 15; RGAL 4

**Metastasio, Pietro** 1698-1782 ........... **LC 115**
See also RGWL 2, 3

**Metcalf, John** 1938- ......... **CLC 37; SSC 43**
See also CA 113; CN 4, 5, 6, 7; DLB 60;
RGSF 2; TWA

**Metcalf, Suzanne**
See Baum, L(yman) Frank

**Mew, Charlotte (Mary)** 1870-1928 . **TCLC 8**
See also CA 105; 189; DLB 19, 135; RGEL
2

**Mewshaw, Michael** 1943- .................. **CLC 9**
See also CA 53-56; CANR 7, 47, 147;
DLBY 1980

**Meyer, Conrad Ferdinand** 1825-1898
........................................ **NCLC 81; SSC 30**
See also DLB 129; EW; RGWL 2, 3

**Meyer, Gustav** 1868-1932
See Meyrink, Gustav
See also CA 117; 190

**Meyer, June**
See Jordan, June

**Meyer, Lynn**
See Slavitt, David R(ytman)

**Meyers, Jeffrey** 1939- ................... **CLC 39**
See also CA 73-76; 186; CAAE 186; CANR
54, 102; DLB 111

**Meynell, Alice (Christina Gertrude
Thompson)** 1847-1922 ............ **TCLC 6**
See also CA 104; 177; DLB 19, 98; RGEL
2

**Meyrink, Gustav** ........................... **TCLC 21**
See Meyer, Gustav
See also DLB 81; EWL 3

**Michaels, Leonard** 1933-2003 .... **CLC 6, 25;
SSC 16**
See also AMWS 16; CA 61-64; 216; CANR
21, 62, 119; CN 3, 45, 6, 7; DLB 130;
MTCW 1; TCLE 1:2

**Michaux, Henri** 1899-1984 .......... **CLC 8, 19**
See also CA 85-88; 114; DLB 258; EWL 3;
GFL 1789 to the Present; RGWL 2, 3

**Micheaux, Oscar (Devereaux)** 1884-1951
.................................................... **TCLC 76**
See also BW 3; CA 174; DLB 50; TCWW
2

**Michelangelo** 1475-1564 ..................... **LC 12**
See also AAYA 43

**Michelet, Jules** 1798-1874 ............. **NCLC 31**
See also EW 5; GFL 1789 to the Present

**Michels, Robert** 1876-1936 ........... **TCLC 88**
See also CA 212

**Michener, James A.** 1907(?)-1997 .... **CLC 1,
5, 11, 29, 60, 109**
See also AAYA 27; AITN 1; BEST 90:1;
BPFB 2; CA 5-8R; 161; CANR 21, 45,
68; CN 1, 2, 3, 4, 5, 6; CPW; DA3; DAM
NOV, POP; DLB 6; MAL 5; MTCW 1, 2;
MTFW 2005; RHW; TCWW 1, 2

**Mickiewicz, Adam** 1798-1855 ........ **NCLC 3,
101; PC 38**
See also EW 5; RGWL 2, 3

**Middleton, (John) Christopher** 1926-
.................................................... **CLC 13**
See also CA 13-16R; CANR 29, 54, 117;
CP 1, 2, 3, 4, 5, 6, 7; DLB 40

**Middleton, Richard (Barham)** 1882-1911
.................................................... **TCLC 56**
See also CA 187; DLB 156; HGG

**Middleton, Stanley** 1919- ........ **CLC 7, 38**
See also CA 25-28R; CAAS 23; CANR 21,
46, 81, 157; CN 1, 2, 3, 4, 5, 6, 7; DLB
14, 326

**Middleton, Thomas** 1580-1627 .... **DC 5; LC
33, 123**
See also BRW 2; DAM DRAM, MST; DFS
18, 22; DLB 58; RGEL 2

**Migueis, Jose Rodrigues** 1901-1980
.................................................... **CLC 10**
See also DLB 287

**Mikszath, Kalman** 1847-1910 ....... **TCLC 31**
See also CA 170

**Miles, Jack** ................................. **CLC 100**
See also CA 200

**Miles, John Russiano**
See Miles, Jack

**Miles, Josephine (Louise)** 1911-1985
................................ **CLC 1, 2, 14, 34, 39**
See also CA 1-4R; 116; CANR 2, 55; CP 1,
2, 3, 4; DAM POET; DLB 48; MAL 5;
TCLE 1:2

**Militant**
See Sandburg, Carl (August)

**Mill, Harriet (Hardy) Taylor** 1807-1858
.................................................. **NCLC 102**
See also FW

**Mill, John Stuart** 1806-1873 ... **NCLC 11, 58**
See also CDBLB 1832-1890; DLB 55, 190,
262; FW 1; RGEL 2; TEA

**Millar, Kenneth** 1915-1983 ............. **CLC 14**
See Macdonald, Ross
See also CA 9-12R; 110; CANR 16, 63,
107; CMW 4; CPW; DA3; DAM POP;
DLB 2, 226; DLBD 6; DLBY 1983;
MTCW 1, 2; MTFW 2005

**Millay, E. Vincent**
See Millay, Edna St. Vincent

**Millay, Edna St. Vincent** 1892-1950 ... **PC 6,
61; TCLC 4, 49, 169; WLCS**
See Boyd, Nancy
See also AMW; CA 104; 130; CDALB
1917-1929; DA; DA3; DAB; DAC; DAM
MST, POET; DLB 45, 249; EWL 3;
EXPP; FL 1:6; MAL 5; MBL; MTCW 1,
2; MTFW 2005; PAB; PFS 3, 17; RGAL
4; TUS; WP

**Miller, Arthur** 1915-2005 ... **CLC 1, 2, 6, 10,
15, 26, 47, 78, 179; DC 1; WLC 4**
See also AAYA 15; AITN 1; AMW; AMWC
1; CA 1-4R; 236; CABS 3; CAD; CANR
2, 30, 54, 76, 132; CD 5, 6; CDALB
1941-1968; DA; DA3; DAB; DAC; DAM
DRAM, MST; DFS 1, 3, 8; DLB 7, 266;
EWL 3; LAIT 1, 4; LATS 1:2; MAL 5;
MTCW 1, 2; MTFW 2005; RGAL 4;
RGHL; TUS; WYAS 1

**Miller, Henry (Valentine)** 1891-1980
...... **CLC 1, 2, 4, 9, 14, 43, 84; WLC 4**
See also AMW; BPFB 2; CA 9-12R; 97-
100; CANR 33, 64; CDALB 1929-1941;
CN 1, 2; DA; DA3; DAB; DAC; DAM
MST, NOV; DLB 4, 9; DLBY 1980; EWL
3; MAL 5; MTCW 1, 2; MTFW 2005;
RGAL 4; TUS

**Miller, Hugh** 1802-1856 ............... **NCLC 143**
See also DLB 190

**Miller, Jason** 1939(?)-2001 ................. **CLC 2**
See also AITN 1; CA 73-76; 197; CAD;
CANR 130; DFS 12; DLB 7

**Miller, Sue** 1943- ............................. **CLC 44**
See also AMWS 12; BEST 90:3; CA 139;
CANR 59, 91, 128; DA3; DAM POP;
DLB 143

**Miller, Walter M(ichael, Jr.)** 1923-1996
.................................................. **CLC 4, 30**
See also BPFB 2; CA 85-88; CANR 108;
DLB 8; SCFW 1, 2; SFW 4

**Millett, Kate** 1934- ......................... **CLC 67**
See also AITN 1; CA 73-76; CANR 32, 53,
76, 110; DA3; DLB 246; FW; GLL 1;
MTCW 1, 2; MTFW 2005

**Millhauser, Steven** 1943- .... **CLC 21, 54, 109;
SSC 57**
See also CA 110; 111; CANR 63, 114, 133;
CN 6, 7; DA3; DLB 2; FANT; INT CA-
111; MAL 5; MTCW 2; MTFW 2005

**Millhauser, Steven Lewis**
See Millhauser, Steven

**Millin, Sarah Gertrude** 1889-1968 . **CLC 49**
See also CA 102; 93-96; DLB 225; EWL 3

**Milne, A. A.** 1882-1956 ............. **TCLC 6, 88**
See also BRWS 5; CA 104; 133; CLR 1,
26, 108; CMW 4; CWRI 5; DA3; DAB;
DAC; DAM MST; DLB 10, 77, 100, 160;
FANT; MAICYA 1, 2; MTCW 1, 2;
MTFW 2005; RGEL 2; SATA 100; WCH;
YABC 1

**Milne, Alan Alexander**
See Milne, A. A.

**Milner, Ron(ald)** 1938-2004 .... **BLC 3; CLC
56**
See also AITN 1; BW 1; CA 73-76; 230;
CAD; CANR 24, 81; CD 5, 6; DAM
MULT; DLB 38; MAL 5; MTCW 1

**Milnes, Richard Monckton** 1809-1885
.................................................... **NCLC 61**
See also DLB 32, 184

**Milosz, Czeslaw** 1911-2004 ... **CLC 5, 11, 22,
31, 56, 82; PC 8; WLCS**
See also AAYA 62; CA 81-84; 230; CANR
23, 51, 91, 126; CDWLB 4; CWW 2;
DA3; DAM MST, POET; DLB 215; EW
13; EWL 3; MTCW 1, 2; MTFW 2005;
PFS 16; RGHL; RGWL 2, 3

**Milton, John** 1608-1674 .... **LC 9, 43, 92; PC
19, 29; WLC 4**
See also AAYA 65; BRW 2; BRWR 2; CD-
BLB 1660-1789; DA; DA3; DAB; DAC;
DAM MST, POET; DLB 131, 151, 281;
EFS 1; EXPP; LAIT 1; PAB; PFS 3, 17;
RGEL 2; TEA; WLIT 3; WP

**Min, Anchee** 1957- ........................... **CLC 86**
See also CA 146; CANR 94, 137; MTFW
2005

**Minehaha, Cornelius**
See Wedekind, Frank

**Miner, Valerie** 1947- ....................... **CLC 40**
See also CA 97-100; CANR 59; FW; GLL
2

**Minimo, Duca**
See D'Annunzio, Gabriele

**Minot, Susan (Anderson)** 1956- ..... **CLC 44,
159**
See also AMWS 6; CA 134; CANR 118;
CN 6, 7

**Minus, Ed** 1938- ............................. **CLC 39**
See also CA 185

**Mirabai** 1498(?)-1550(?) ..................... **PC 48**
See also PFS 24

**Miranda, Javier**
See Bioy Casares, Adolfo
See also CWW 2

**Mirbeau, Octave** 1848-1917 .......... **TCLC 55**
See also CA 216; DLB 123, 192; GFL 1789
to the Present

**Mirikitani, Janice** 1942- ..................... **AAL**
See also CA 211; DLB 312; RGAL 4

**Mirk, John** (?)-c. 1414 ..................... **LC 105**
See also DLB 146

**Miro (Ferrer), Gabriel (Francisco Victor)**
1879-1930 ................................ **TCLC 5**
See also CA 104; 185; DLB 322; EWL 3

**Misharin, Alexandr** ........................... **CLC 59**

**Mishima, Yukio** ... **CLC 2, 4, 6, 9, 27; DC 1;
SSC 4; TCLC 161; WLC 4**
See Hiraoka, Kimitake
See also AAYA 50; BPFB 2; GLL 1; MJW;
RGSF 2; RGWL 2, 3; SSFS 5, 12

**Mistral, Frederic** 1830-1914 ......... **TCLC 51**
See also CA 122; 213; GFL 1789 to the
Present

**Mistral, Gabriela**
See Godoy Alcayaga, Lucila
See also DLB 283; DNFS 1; EWL 3; LAW;
RGWL 2, 3; WP

**Mistry, Rohinton** 1952- .. **CLC 71, 196; SSC
73**
See also BRWS 10; CA 141; CANR 86,
114; CCA 1; CN 6, 7; DAC; SSFS 6

**Mitchell, Clyde**
See Ellison, Harlan

**Mitchell, Emerson Blackhorse Barney** 1945-
.................................................... **NNAL**
See also CA 45-48

**Muir, Edwin** 1887-1959 ..... **PC 49; TCLC 2, 87**
See Moore, Edward
See also BRWS 6; CA 104; 193; DLB 20, 100, 191; EWL 3; RGEL 2

**Muir, John** 1838-1914 .................... **TCLC 28**
See also AMWS 9; ANW; CA 165; DLB 186, 275

**Mujica Lainez, Manuel** 1910-1984 . **CLC 31**
See Lainez, Manuel Mujica
See also CA 81-84; 112; CANR 32; EWL 3; HW 1

**Mukherjee, Bharati** 1940- ... **AAL; CLC 53, 115; SSC 38**
See also AAYA 46; BEST 89:2; CA 107, 232; CAAE 232; CANR 45, 72, 128; CN 5, 6, 7; DAM NOV; DLB 60, 218, 323; DNFS 1, 2; EWL 3; FW; MAL 5; MTCW 1, 2; MTFW 2005; RGAL 4; RGSF 2; SSFS 7, 24; TUS; WWE 1

**Muldoon, Paul** 1951- ......... **CLC 32, 72, 166**
See also BRWS 4; CA 113; 129; CANR 52, 91; CP 2, 3, 4, 5, 6, 7; DAM POET; DLB 40; INT CA-129; PFS 7, 22; TCLE 1:2

**Mulisch, Harry (Kurt Victor)** 1927-
................................................. **CLC 42**
See also CA 9-12R; CANR 6, 26, 56, 110; CWW 2; DLB 299; EWL 3

**Mull, Martin** 1943- ......................... **CLC 17**
See also CA 105

**Muller, Wilhelm** ............................ **NCLC 73**

**Mulock, Dinah Maria**
See Craik, Dinah Maria (Mulock)
See also RGEL 2

**Multatuli** 1820-1881 ..................... **NCLC 165**
See also RGWL 2, 3

**Munday, Anthony** 1560-1633 ............. **LC 87**
See also DLB 62, 172; RGEL 2

**Munford, Robert** 1737(?)-1783 ........... **LC 5**
See also DLB 31

**Mungo, Raymond** 1946- ................... **CLC 72**
See also CA 49-52; CANR 2

**Munro, Alice** 1931- ... **CLC 6, 10, 19, 50, 95, 222; SSC 3, 95; WLCS**
See also AITN 2; BPFB 2; CA 33-36R; CANR 33, 53, 75, 114; CCA 1; CN 1, 2, 3, 4, 5, 6, 7; DA3; DAC; DAM MST, NOV; DLB 53; EWL 3; MTCW 1, 2; MTFW 2005; RGEL 2; RGSF 2; SATA 29; SSFS 5, 13, 19; TCLE 1:2; WWE 1

**Munro, H(ector) H(ugh)** 1870-1916
See Saki
See also AAYA 56; CA 104; 130; CANR 104; CDBLB 1890-1914; DA; DA3; DAB; DAC; DAM MST, NOV; DLB 34, 162; EXPS; MTCW 1, 2; MTFW 2005; RGEL 2; SSFS 15

**Murakami, Haruki** 1949- ............... **CLC 150**
See Murakami Haruki
See also CA 165; CANR 102, 146; MJW; RGWL 3; SFW 4; SSFS 23

**Murakami Haruki**
See Murakami, Haruki
See also CWW 2; DLB 182; EWL 3

**Murasaki, Lady**
See Murasaki Shikibu

**Murasaki Shikibu** 978(?)-1026(?) . **CMLC 1, 79**
See also EFS 2; LATS 1:1; RGWL 2, 3

**Murdoch, Iris** 1919-1999 . **CLC 1, 2, 3, 4, 6, 8, 11, 15, 22, 31, 51; TCLC 171**
See also BRWS 1; CA 13-16R; 179; CANR 8, 43, 68, 103, 142; CBD; CDBLB 1960 to Present; CN 1, 2, 3, 4, 5, 6; CWD; DA3; DAB; DAC; DAM MST, NOV; DLB 14, 194, 233, 326; EWL 3; INT CANR-8; MTCW 1, 2; MTFW 2005; NFS 18; RGEL 2; TCLE 1:2; TEA; WLIT 4

**Murfree, Mary Noailles** 1850-1922
................................. **SSC 22; TCLC 135**
See also CA 122; 176; DLB 12, 74; RGAL 4

**Murglie**
See Murnau, F.W.

**Murnau, Friedrich Wilhelm**
See Murnau, F.W.

**Murnau, F.W.** 1888-1931 ............... **TCLC 53**
See also CA 112

**Murphy, Richard** 1927- .................. **CLC 41**
See also BRWS 5; CA 29-32R; CP 1, 2, 3, 4, 5, 6, 7; DLB 40; EWL 3

**Murphy, Sylvia** 1937- ...................... **CLC 34**
See also CA 121

**Murphy, Thomas (Bernard)** 1935- . **CLC 51**
See Murphy, Tom
See also CA 101

**Murphy, Tom**
See Murphy, Thomas (Bernard)
See also DLB 310

**Murray, Albert L.** 1916- .................. **CLC 73**
See also BW 2; CA 49-52; CANR 26, 52, 78; CN 7; CSW; DLB 38; MTFW 2005

**Murray, James Augustus Henry** 1837-1915
................................................. **TCLC 117**

**Murray, Judith Sargent** 1751-1820
................................................. **NCLC 63**
See also DLB 37, 200

**Murray, Les(lie Allan)** 1938- ........... **CLC 40**
See also BRWS 7; CA 21-24R; CANR 11, 27, 56, 103; CP 1, 2, 3, 4, 5, 6, 7; DAM POET; DLB 289; DLBY 2001; EWL 3; RGEL 2

**Murry, J. Middleton**
See Murry, John Middleton

**Murry, John Middleton** 1889-1957
................................................. **TCLC 16**
See also CA 118; 217; DLB 149

**Musgrave, Susan** 1951- .............. **CLC 13, 54**
See also CA 69-72; CANR 45, 84; CCA 1; CP 2, 3, 4, 5, 6, 7; CWP

**Musil, Robert (Edler von)** 1880-1942
................................. **SSC 18; TCLC 12, 68**
See also CA 109; CANR 55, 84; CDWLB 2; DLB 81, 124; EW 9; EWL 3; MTCW 2; RGSF 2; RGWL 2, 3

**Muske, Carol** ................................. **CLC 90**
See Muske-Dukes, Carol (Anne)

**Muske-Dukes, Carol (Anne)** 1945-
See Muske, Carol
See also CA 65-68, 203; CAAE 203; CANR 32, 70; CWP; PFS 24

**Musset, Alfred de** 1810-1857 ........... **DC 27; NCLC 7, 150**
See also DLB 192, 217; EW 6; GFL 1789 to the Present; RGWL 2, 3; TWA

**Musset, Louis Charles Alfred de**
See Musset, Alfred de

**Mussolini, Benito (Amilcare Andrea)** 1883-1945 .............................. **TCLC 96**
See also CA 116

**Mutanabbi, Al-**
See al-Mutanabbi, Ahmad ibn al-Husayn Abu al-Tayyib al-Jufi al-Kindi
See also WLIT 6

**My Brother's Brother**
See Chekhov, Anton (Pavlovich)

**Myers, L(eopold) H(amilton)** 1881-1944
................................................. **TCLC 59**
See also CA 157; DLB 15; EWL 3; RGEL 2

**Myers, Walter Dean** 1937- ...... **BLC 3; CLC 35**
See Myers, Walter M.
See also AAYA 4, 23; BW 2; BYA 6, 8, 11; CA 33-36R; CANR 20, 42, 67, 108; CLR 4, 16, 35, 110; DAM MULT, NOV; DLB 33; INT CANR-20; JRDA; LAIT 5; MAI-

CYA 1, 2; MAICYAS 1; MTCW 2; MTFW 2005; SAAS 2; SATA 41, 71, 109, 157; SATA-Brief 27; WYA; YAW

**Myers, Walter M.**
See Myers, Walter Dean

**Myles, Symon**
See Follett, Ken

**Nabokov, Vladimir (Vladimirovich)** 1899-1977 ..... **CLC 1, 2, 3, 6, 8, 11, 15, 23, 44, 46, 64; SSC 11, 86; TCLC 108; WLC 4**
See also AAYA 45; AMW; AMWC 1; AMWR 1; BPFB 2; CA 5-8R; 69-72; CANR 20, 102; CDALB 1941-1968; CN 1, 2; CP 2; DA; DA3; DAB; DAC; DAM MST, NOV; DLB 2, 244, 278, 317; DLBD 3; DLBY 1980, 1991; EWL 3; EXPS; LATS 1:2; MAL 5; MTCW 1, 2; MTFW 2005; NCFS 4; NFS 9; RGAL 4; RGSF 2; SSFS 6, 15; TUS

**Naevius** c. 265B.C.-201B.C. .......... **CMLC 37**
See also DLB 211

**Nagai, Kafu** ............................... **TCLC 51**
See Nagai, Sokichi
See also DLB 180

**Nagai, Sokichi** 1879-1959
See Nagai, Kafu
See also CA 117

**Nagy, Laszlo** 1925-1978 ...................... **CLC 7**
See also CA 129; 112

**Naidu, Sarojini** 1879-1949 ............. **TCLC 80**
See also EWL 3; RGEL 2

**Naipaul, Shiva** 1945-1985 ......... **CLC 32, 39; TCLC 153**
See also CA 110; 112; 116; CANR 33; CN 2, 3; DA3; DAM NOV; DLB 157; DLBY 1985; EWL 3; MTCW 1, 2; MTFW 2005

**Naipaul, V.S.** 1932- . **CLC 4, 7, 9, 13, 18, 37, 105, 199; SSC 38**
See also BPFB 2; BRWS 1; CA 1-4R; CANR 1, 33, 51, 91, 126; CDBLB 1960 to Present; CDWLB 3; CN 1, 2, 3, 4, 5, 6, 7; DA3; DAB; DAC; DAM MST, NOV; DLB 125, 204, 207, 326; DLBY 1985, 2001; EWL 3; LATS 1:2; MTCW 1, 2; MTFW 2005; RGEL 2; RGSF 2; TWA; WLIT 4; WWE 1

**Nakos, Lilika** 1903(?)-1989 ............. **CLC 29**

**Napoleon**
See Yamamoto, Hisaye

**Narayan, R.K.** 1906-2001 ..... **CLC 7, 28, 47, 121, 211; SSC 25**
See also BPFB 2; CA 81-84; 196; CANR 33, 61, 112; CN 1, 2, 3, 4, 5, 6, 7; DA3; DAM NOV; DLB 323; DNFS 1; EWL 3; MTCW 1, 2; MTFW 2005; RGEL 2; RGSF 2; SATA 62; SSFS 5; WWE 1

**Nash, (Frediric) Ogden** 1902-1971
................. **CLC 23; PC 21; TCLC 109**
See also CA 13-14; 29-32R; CANR 34, 61; CAP 1; CP 1; DAM POET; DLB 11; MAICYA 1, 2; MAL 5; MTCW 1, 2; RGAL 4; SATA 2, 46; WP

**Nashe, Thomas** 1567-1601(?) ....... **LC 41, 89**
See also DLB 167; RGEL 2

**Nathan, Daniel**
See Dannay, Frederic

**Nathan, George Jean** 1882-1958 .. **TCLC 18**
See Hatteras, Owen
See also CA 114; 169; DLB 137; MAL 5

**Natsume, Kinnosuke**
See Natsume, Soseki

**Natsume, Soseki** 1867-1916 ...... **TCLC 2, 10**
See Natsume Soseki; Soseki
See also CA 104; 195; RGWL 2, 3; TWA

**Natsume Soseki**
See Natsume, Soseki
See also DLB 180; EWL 3

**Ostrovsky, Alexander** 1823-1886 . **NCLC 30, 57**
  See Ostrovsky, Aleksandr Nikolaevich
**Otero, Blas de** 1916-1979 ................ **CLC 11**
  See also CA 89-92; DLB 134; EWL 3
**O'Trigger, Sir Lucius**
  See Horne, Richard Henry Hengist
**Otto, Rudolf** 1869-1937 ................ **TCLC 85**
**Otto, Whitney** 1955- ........................ **CLC 70**
  See also CA 140; CANR 120
**Otway, Thomas** 1652-1685 .. **DC 24; LC 106**
  See also DAM DRAM; DLB 80; RGEL 2
**Ouida** .............................................. **TCLC 43**
  See De la Ramee, Marie Louise (Ouida)
  See also DLB 18, 156; RGEL 2
**Ouologuem, Yambo** 1940- ............. **CLC 146**
  See also CA 111; 176
**Ousmane, Sembene** 1923- .. **BLC 3; CLC 66**
  See Sembene, Ousmane
  See also BW 1, 3; CA 117; 125; CANR 81;
  CWW 2; MTCW 1
**Ovid** 43B.C.-17 ................... **CMLC 7; PC 2**
  See also AW 2; CDWLB 1; DA3; DAM
  POET; DLB 211; PFS 22; RGWL 2, 3;
  WLIT 8; WP
**Owen, Hugh**
  See Faust, Frederick (Schiller)
**Owen, Wilfred (Edward Salter)** 1893-1918
  ................ **PC 19; TCLC 5, 27; WLC 4**
  See also BRW 6; CA 104; 141; CDBLB
  1914-1945; DA; DAB; DAC; DAM MST,
  POET; DLB 20; EWL 3; EXPP; MTCW
  2; MTFW 2005; PFS 10; RGEL 2; WLIT
  4
**Owens, Louis (Dean)** 1948-2002 ....... **NNAL**
  See also CA 137, 179; 207; CAAE 179;
  CAAS 24; CANR 71
**Owens, Rochelle** 1936- ...................... **CLC 8**
  See also CA 17-20R; CAAS 2; CAD;
  CANR 39; CD 5, 6; CP 1, 2, 3, 4, 5, 6, 7;
  CWD; CWP
**Oz, Amos** 1939- .... **CLC 5, 8, 11, 27, 33, 54; SSC 66**
  See also CA 53-56; CANR 27, 47, 65, 113,
  138; CWW 2; DAM NOV; EWL 3;
  MTCW 1, 2; MTFW 2005; RGHL; RGSF
  2; RGWL 3; WLIT 6
**Ozick, Cynthia** 1928- ........ **CLC 3, 7, 28, 62, 155; SSC 15, 60**
  See also AMWS 5; BEST 90:1; CA 17-20R;
  CANR 23, 58, 116; CN 3, 4, 5, 6, 7;
  CPW; DA3; DAM NOV, POP; DLB 28,
  152, 299; DLBY 1982; EWL 3; EXPS;
  INT CANR-23; MAL 5; MTCW 1, 2;
  MTFW 2005; RGAL 4; RGHL; RGSF 2;
  SSFS 3, 12, 22
**Ozu, Yasujiro** 1903-1963 ................ **CLC 16**
  See also CA 112
**Pabst, G. W.** 1885-1967 .............. **TCLC 127**
**Pacheco, C.**
  See Pessoa, Fernando (Antonio Nogueira)
**Pacheco, Jose Emilio** 1939- .............. **HLC 2**
  See also CA 111; 131; CANR 65; CWW 2;
  DAM MULT; DLB 290; EWL 3; HW 1,
  2; RGSF 2
**Pa Chin** ........................................ **CLC 18**
  See Jin, Ba
  See also EWL 3
**Pack, Robert** 1929- ........................ **CLC 13**
  See also CA 1-4R; CANR 3, 44, 82; CP 1,
  2, 3, 4, 5, 6, 7; DLB 5; SATA 118
**Padgett, Lewis**
  See Kuttner, Henry
**Padilla (Lorenzo), Heberto** 1932-2000
  .............................................. **CLC 38**
  See also AITN 1; CA 123; 131; 189; CWW
  2; EWL 3; HW 1

**Page, James Patrick** 1944-
  See Page, Jimmy
  See also CA 204
**Page, Jimmy** 1944- .......................... **CLC 12**
  See Page, James Patrick
**Page, Louise** 1955- .......................... **CLC 40**
  See also CA 140; CANR 76; CBD; CD 5,
  6; CWD; DLB 233
**Page, P(atricia) K(athleen)** 1916- .... **CLC 7, 18; PC 12**
  See Cape, Judith
  See also CA 53-56; CANR 4, 22, 65; CP 1,
  2, 3, 4, 5, 6, 7; DAC; DAM MST; DLB
  68; MTCW 1; RGEL 2
**Page, Stanton**
  See Fuller, Henry Blake
**Page, Stanton**
  See Fuller, Henry Blake
**Page, Thomas Nelson** 1853-1922 ...... **SSC 23**
  See also CA 118; 177; DLB 12, 78; DLBD
  13; RGAL 4
**Pagels, Elaine**
  See Pagels, Elaine Hiesey
**Pagels, Elaine Hiesey** 1943- ........... **CLC 104**
  See also CA 45-48; CANR 2, 24, 51, 151;
  FW; NCFS 4
**Paget, Violet** 1856-1935
  See Lee, Vernon
  See also CA 104; 166; GLL 1; HGG
**Paget-Lowe, Henry**
  See Lovecraft, H. P.
**Paglia, Camille** 1947- ...................... **CLC 68**
  See also CA 140; CANR 72, 139; CPW;
  FW; GLL 2; MTCW 2; MTFW 2005
**Paige, Richard**
  See Koontz, Dean R.
**Paine, Thomas** 1737-1809 ............. **NCLC 62**
  See also AMWS 1; CDALB 1640-1865;
  DLB 31, 43, 73, 158; LAIT 1; RGAL 4;
  RGEL 2; TUS
**Pakenham, Antonia**
  See Fraser, Antonia
**Palamas, Costis**
  See Palamas, Kostes
**Palamas, Kostes** 1859-1943 ............. **TCLC 5**
  See Palamas, Kostis
  See also CA 105; 190; RGWL 2, 3
**Palamas, Kostis**
  See Palamas, Kostes
  See also EWL 3
**Palazzeschi, Aldo** 1885-1974 ........... **CLC 11**
  See also CA 89-92; 53-56; DLB 114, 264;
  EWL 3
**Pales Matos, Luis** 1898-1959 .......... **HLCS 2**
  See Pales Matos, Luis
  See also DLB 290; HW 1; LAW
**Paley, Grace** 1922- . **CLC 4, 6, 37, 140; SSC 8**
  See also AMWS 6; CA 25-28R; CANR 13,
  46, 74, 118; CN 2, 3, 4, 5, 6, 7; CPW;
  DA3; DAM POP; DLB 28, 218; EWL 3;
  EXPS; FW; INT CANR-13; MAL 5;
  MBL; MTCW 1, 2; MTFW 2005; RGAL
  4; RGSF 2; SSFS 3, 20
**Palin, Michael (Edward)** 1943- ....... **CLC 21**
  See Monty Python
  See also CA 107; CANR 35, 109; SATA 67
**Palliser, Charles** 1947- ...................... **CLC 65**
  See also CA 136; CANR 76; CN 5, 6, 7
**Palma, Ricardo** 1833-1919 ........... **TCLC 29**
  See also CA 168; LAW
**Pamuk, Orhan** 1952- ...................... **CLC 185**
  See also CA 142; CANR 75, 127; CWW 2;
  WLIT 6
**Pancake, Breece Dexter** 1952-1979
  See Pancake, Breece D'J
  See also CA 123; 109

**Pancake, Breece D'J** ......... **CLC 29; SSC 61**
  See Pancake, Breece Dexter
  See also DLB 130
**Panchenko, Nikolai** .......................... **CLC 59**
**Pankhurst, Emmeline (Goulden)** 1858-1928
  .............................................. **TCLC 100**
  See also CA 116; FW
**Panko, Rudy**
  See Gogol, Nikolai (Vasilyevich)
**Papadiamantis, Alexandros** 1851-1911
  .............................................. **TCLC 29**
  See also CA 168; EWL 3
**Papadiamantopoulos, Johannes** 1856-1910
  See Moreas, Jean
  See also CA 117; 242
**Papini, Giovanni** 1881-1956 .......... **TCLC 22**
  See also CA 121; 180; DLB 264
**Paracelsus** 1493-1541 ........................ **LC 14**
  See also DLB 179
**Parasol, Peter**
  See Stevens, Wallace
**Pardo Bazan, Emilia** 1851-1921 ....... **SSC 30**
  See also EWL 3; FW; RGSF 2; RGWL 2, 3
**Pareto, Vilfredo** 1848-1923 ........... **TCLC 69**
  See also CA 175
**Paretsky, Sara** 1947- ...................... **CLC 135**
  See also AAYA 30; BEST 90:3; CA 125;
  129; CANR 59, 95; CMW 4; CPW; DA3;
  DAM POP; DLB 306; INT CA-129;
  MSW; RGAL 4
**Parfenie, Maria**
  See Codrescu, Andrei
**Parini, Jay (Lee)** 1948- ........... **CLC 54, 133**
  See also CA 97-100, 229; CAAE 229;
  CAAS 16; CANR 32, 87
**Park, Jordan**
  See Kornbluth, C(yril) M.; Pohl, Frederik
**Park, Robert E(zra)** 1864-1944 .... **TCLC 73**
  See also CA 122; 165
**Parker, Bert**
  See Ellison, Harlan
**Parker, Dorothy (Rothschild)** 1893-1967
  ...... **CLC 15, 68; PC 28; SSC 2; TCLC 143**
  See also AMWS 9; CA 19-20; 25-28R; CAP
  2; DA3; DAM POET; DLB 11, 45, 86;
  EXPP; FW; MAL 5; MBL; MTCW 1, 2;
  MTFW 2005; PFS 18; RGAL 4; RGSF 2;
  TUS
**Parker, Robert B.** 1932- ................... **CLC 27**
  See also AAYA 28; BEST 89:4; BPFB 3;
  CA 49-52; CANR 1, 26, 52, 89, 128;
  CMW 4; CPW; DAM NOV, POP; DLB
  306; INT CANR-26; MSW; MTCW 1;
  MTFW 2005
**Parker, Robert Brown**
  See Parker, Robert B.
**Parkin, Frank** 1940- ........................ **CLC 43**
  See also CA 147
**Parkman, Francis, Jr.** 1823-1893 . **NCLC 12**
  See also AMWS 2; DLB 1, 30, 183, 186,
  235; RGAL 4
**Parks, Gordon** 1912-2006 ... **BLC 3; CLC 1, 16**
  See also AAYA 36; AITN 2; BW 2, 3; CA
  41-44R; 249; CANR 26, 66, 145; DA3;
  DAM MULT; DLB 33; MTCW 2; MTFW
  2005; SATA 8, 108
**Parks, Gordon Alexander Buchanan**
  See Parks, Gordon
**Parks, Suzan-Lori** 1964(?)- ............... **DC 23**
  See also AAYA 55; CA 201; CAD; CD 5,
  6; CWD; DFS 22; RGAL 4
**Parks, Tim(othy Harold)** 1954- ..... **CLC 147**
  See also CA 126; 131; CANR 77, 144; CN
  7; DLB 231; INT CA-131
**Parmenides** c. 515B.C.-c. 450B.C.
  .............................................. **CMLC 22**
  See also DLB 176

**Porter, Katherine Anne** 1890-1980 .. **CLC 1, 3, 7, 10, 13, 15, 27, 101; SSC 4, 31, 43**
See also AAYA 42; AITN 2; AMW; BPFB 3; CA 1-4R; 101; CANR 1, 65; CDALBS; CN 1, 2; DA; DA3; DAB; DAC; DAM MST, NOV; DLB 4, 9, 102; DLBD 12; DLBY 1980; EWL 3; EXPS; LAIT 3; MAL 5; MBL; MTCW 1, 2; MTFW 2005; NFS 14; RGAL 4; RGSF 2; SATA 39; SATA-Obit 23; SSFS 1, 8, 11, 16, 23; TCWW 2; TUS

**Porter, Peter (Neville Frederick)** 1929-
.................................... **CLC 5, 13, 33**
See also CA 85-88; CP 1, 2, 3, 4, 5, 6, 7; DLB 40, 289; WWE 1

**Porter, William Sydney** 1862-1910
See Henry, O.
See also CA 104; 131; CDALB 1865-1917; DA; DA3; DAB; DAC; DAM MST; DLB 12, 78, 79; MTCW 1, 2; MTFW 2005; TUS; YABC 2

**Portillo (y Pacheco), Jose Lopez**
See Lopez Portillo (y Pacheco), Jose

**Portillo Trambley, Estela** 1927-1998
.................................................... **HLC 2**
See Trambley, Estela Portillo
See also CANR 32; DAM MULT; DLB 209; HW 1

**Posey, Alexander (Lawrence)** 1873-1908
.................................................... **NNAL**
See also CA 144; CANR 80; DAM MULT; DLB 175

**Posse, Abel** ........................................ **CLC 70**

**Post, Melville Davisson** 1869-1930
.................................................... **TCLC 39**
See also CA 110; 202; CMW 4

**Potok, Chaim** 1929-2002 .. **CLC 2, 7, 14, 26, 112**
See also AAYA 15, 50; AITN 1, 2; BPFB 3; BYA 1; CA 17-20R; 208; CANR 19, 35, 64, 98; CLR 92; CN 4, 5, 6; DA3; DAM NOV; DLB 28, 152; EXPN; INT CANR-19; LAIT 4; MTCW 1, 2; MTFW 2005; NFS 4; RGHL; SATA 33, 106; SATA-Obit 134; TUS; YAW

**Potok, Herbert Harold** -2002
See Potok, Chaim

**Potok, Herman Harold**
See Potok, Chaim

**Potter, Dennis (Christopher George)**
1935-1994 .................... **CLC 58, 86, 123**
See also BRWS 10; CA 107; 145; CANR 33, 61; CBD; DLB 233; MTCW 1

**Pound, Ezra (Weston Loomis)** 1885-1972
........ **CLC 1, 2, 3, 4, 5, 7, 10, 13, 18, 34, 48, 50, 112; PC 4; WLC 5**
See also AAYA 47; AMW; AMWR 1; CA 5-8R; 37-40R; CANR 40; CDALB 1917-1929; CP 1; DA; DA3; DAB; DAC; DAM MST, POET; DLB 4, 45, 63; DLBD 15; EFS 2; EWL 3; EXPP; LMFS 2; MAL 5; MTCW 1, 2; MTFW 2005; PAB; PFS 2, 8, 16; RGAL 4; TUS; WP

**Povod, Reinaldo** 1959-1994 ............. **CLC 44**
See also CA 136; 146; CANR 83

**Powell, Adam Clayton, Jr.** 1908-1972
.................................... **BLC 3; CLC 89**
See also BW 1, 3; CA 102; 33-36R; CANR 86; DAM MULT

**Powell, Anthony** 1905-2000 . **CLC 1, 3, 7, 9, 10, 31**
See also BRW 7; CA 1-4R; 189; CANR 1, 32, 62, 107; CDBLB 1945-1960; CN 1, 2, 3, 4, 5, 6; DLB 15; EWL 3; MTCW 1, 2; MTFW 2005; RGEL 2; TEA

**Powell, Dawn** 1896(?)-1965 ............. **CLC 66**
See also CA 5-8R; CANR 121; DLBY 1997

**Powell, Padgett** 1952- ...................... **CLC 34**
See also CA 126; CANR 63, 101; CSW; DLB 234; DLBY 01

**Powell, (Oval) Talmage** 1920-2000
See Queen, Ellery
See also CA 5-8R; CANR 2, 80

**Power, Susan** 1961- ........................... **CLC 91**
See also BYA 14; CA 160; CANR 135; NFS 11

**Powers, J(ames) F(arl)** 1917-1999 ... **CLC 1, 4, 8, 57; SSC 4**
See also CA 1-4R; 181; CANR 2, 61; CN 1, 2, 3, 4, 5, 6; DLB 130; MTCW 1; RGAL 4; RGSF 2

**Powers, John J(ames)** 1945-
See Powers, John R.
See also CA 69-72

**Powers, John R.** ............................... **CLC 66**
See Powers, John J(ames)

**Powers, Richard** 1957- ...................... **CLC 93**
See also AMWS 9; BPFB 3; CA 148; CANR 80; CN 6, 7; MTFW 2005; TCLE 1:2

**Pownall, David** 1938- ........................ **CLC 10**
See also CA 89-92, 180; CAAS 18; CANR 49, 101; CBD; CD 5, 6; CN 4, 5, 6, 7; DLB 14

**Powys, John Cowper** 1872-1963 .. **CLC 7, 9, 15, 46, 125**
See also CA 85-88; CANR 106; DLB 15, 255; EWL 3; FANT; MTCW 1, 2; MTFW 2005; RGEL 2; SUFW

**Powys, T(heodore) F(rancis)** 1875-1953
.................................................... **TCLC 9**
See also BRWS 8; CA 106; 189; DLB 36, 162; EWL 3; FANT; RGEL 2; SUFW

**Pozzo, Modesta**
See Fonte, Moderata

**Prado (Calvo), Pedro** 1886-1952 .. **TCLC 75**
See also CA 131; DLB 283; HW 1; LAW

**Prager, Emily** 1952- ......................... **CLC 56**
See also CA 204

**Pratchett, Terry** 1948- ...................... **CLC 197**
See also AAYA 19, 54; BPFB 3; CA 143; CANR 87, 126; CLR 64; CN 6, 7; CPW; CWRI 5; FANT; MTFW 2005; SATA 82, 139; SFW 4; SUFW 2

**Pratolini, Vasco** 1913-1991 .......... **TCLC 124**
See also CA 211; DLB 177; EWL 3; RGWL 2, 3

**Pratt, E(dwin) J(ohn)** 1883(?)-1964
.................................................... **CLC 19**
See also CA 141; 93-96; CANR 77; DAC; DAM POET; DLB 92; EWL 3; RGEL 2; TWA

**Premchand** .................................... **TCLC 21**
See Srivastava, Dhanpat Rai
See also EWL 3

**Prescott, William Hickling** 1796-1859
.................................................... **NCLC 163**
See also DLB 1, 30, 59, 235

**Preseren, France** 1800-1849 ........ **NCLC 127**
See also CDWLB 4; DLB 147

**Preussler, Otfried** 1923- .................. **CLC 17**
See also CA 77-80; SATA 24

**Prevert, Jacques (Henri Marie)** 1900-1977
.................................................... **CLC 15**
See also CA 77-80; 69-72; CANR 29, 61; DLB 258; EWL 3; GFL 1789 to the Present; IDFW 3, 4; MTCW 1; RGWL 2, 3; SATA-Obit 30

**Prevost, (Antoine Francois)** 1697-1763
.................................................... **LC 1**
See also DLB 314; EW 4; GFL Beginnings to 1789; RGWL 2, 3

**Price, Reynolds** 1933- ....... **CLC 3, 6, 13, 43, 50, 63, 212; SSC 22**
See also AMWS 6; CA 1-4R; CANR 1, 37, 57, 87, 128; CN 1, 2, 3, 4, 5, 6, 7; CSW; DAM NOV; DLB 2, 218, 278; EWL 3; INT CANR-37; MAL 5; MTFW 2005; NFS 18

**Price, Richard** 1949- ................... **CLC 6, 12**
See also CA 49-52; CANR 3, 147; CN 7; DLBY 1981

**Prichard, Katharine Susannah** 1883-1969
.................................................... **CLC 46**
See also CA 11-12; CANR 33; CAP 1; DLB 260; MTCW 1; RGEL 2; RGSF 2; SATA 66

**Priestley, J(ohn) B(oynton)** 1894-1984
.................................................... **CLC 2, 5, 9, 34**
See also BRW 7; CA 9-12R; 113; CANR 33; CDBLB 1914-1945; CN 1, 2, 3; DA3; DAM DRAM, NOV; DLB 10, 34, 77, 100, 139; DLBY 1984; EWL 3; MTCW 1, 2; MTFW 2005; RGEL 2; SFW 4

**Prince** 1958- .................................... **CLC 35**
See also CA 213

**Prince, F(rank) T(empleton)** 1912-2003
.................................................... **CLC 22**
See also CA 101; 219; CANR 43, 79; CP 1, 2, 3, 4, 5, 6, 7; DLB 20

**Prince Kropotkin**
See Kropotkin, Peter (Aleksieevich)

**Prior, Matthew** 1664-1721 ................. **LC 4**
See also DLB 95; RGEL 2

**Prishvin, Mikhail** 1873-1954 ......... **TCLC 75**
See Prishvin, Mikhail Mikhailovich

**Prishvin, Mikhail Mikhailovich**
See Prishvin, Mikhail
See also DLB 272; EWL 3

**Pritchard, William H(arrison)** 1932-
.................................................... **CLC 34**
See also CA 65-68; CANR 23, 95; DLB 111

**Pritchett, V(ictor) S(awdon)** 1900-1997
.................. **CLC 5, 13, 15, 41; SSC 14**
See also BPFB 3; BRWS 3; CA 61-64; 157; CANR 31, 63; CN 1, 2, 3, 4, 5, 6; DA3; DAM NOV; DLB 15, 139; EWL 3; MTCW 1, 2; MTFW 2005; RGEL 2; RGSF 2; TEA

**Private 19022**
See Manning, Frederic

**Probst, Mark** 1925- ......................... **CLC 59**
See also CA 130

**Procaccino, Michael**
See Cristofer, Michael

**Proclus** c. 412-c. 485 ..................... **CMLC 81**

**Prokosch, Frederic** 1908-1989 ..... **CLC 4, 48**
See also CA 73-76; 128; CANR 82; CN 1, 2, 3, 4; CP 1, 2, 3, 4; DLB 48; MTCW 2

**Propertius, Sextus** c. 50B.C.-c. 16B.C.
.................................................... **CMLC 32**
See also AW 2; CDWLB 1; DLB 211; RGWL 2, 3; WLIT 8

**Prophet, The**
See Dreiser, Theodore

**Prose, Francine** 1947- ............... **CLC 45, 231**
See also AMWS 16; CA 109; 112; CANR 46, 95, 132; DLB 234; MTFW 2005; SATA 101, 149

**Protagoras** c. 490B.C.-420B.C. .... **CMLC 85**
See also DLB 176

**Proudhon**
See Cunha, Euclides (Rodrigues Pimenta) da

**Proulx, Annie**
See Proulx, E. Annie

**Proulx, E. Annie** 1935- ............. **CLC 81, 158**
See also AMWS 7; BPFB 3; CA 145; CANR 65, 110; CN 6, 7; CPW 1; DA3; DAM POP; MAL 5; MTCW 2; MTFW 2005; SSFS 18, 23

**Proulx, Edna Annie**
See Proulx, E. Annie

**Ragni, Gerome** 1942-1991 .............. **CLC 17**
See also CA 105; 134

**Rahv, Philip** ............................ **CLC 24**
See Greenberg, Ivan
See also DLB 137; MAL 5

**Raimund, Ferdinand Jakob** 1790-1836
............................................. **NCLC 69**
See also DLB 90

**Raine, Craig (Anthony)** 1944- ........ **CLC 32, 103**
See also CA 108; CANR 29, 51, 103; CP 3, 4, 5, 6, 7; DLB 40; PFS 7

**Raine, Kathleen (Jessie)** 1908-2003 . **CLC 7, 45**
See also CA 85-88; 218; CANR 46, 109; CP 1, 2, 3, 4, 5, 6, 7; DLB 20; EWL 3; MTCW 1; RGEL 2

**Rainis, Janis** 1865-1929 ................ **TCLC 29**
See also CA 170; CDWLB 4; DLB 220; EWL 3

**Rakosi, Carl** ............................... **CLC 47**
See Rawley, Callman
See also CA 228; CAAS 5; CP 1, 2, 3, 4, 5, 6, 7; DLB 193

**Ralegh, Sir Walter**
See Raleigh, Sir Walter
See also BRW 1; RGEL 2; WP

**Raleigh, Richard**
See Lovecraft, H. P.

**Raleigh, Sir Walter** 1554(?)-1618 ...... **LC 31, 39; PC 31**
See Ralegh, Sir Walter
See also CDBLB Before 1660; DLB 172; EXPP; PFS 14; TEA

**Rallentando, H. P.**
See Sayers, Dorothy L(eigh)

**Ramal, Walter**
See de la Mare, Walter (John)

**Ramana Maharshi** 1879-1950 ....... **TCLC 84**

**Ramoacn y Cajal, Santiago** 1852-1934
............................................. **TCLC 93**

**Ramon, Juan**
See Jimenez (Mantecon), Juan Ramon

**Ramos, Graciliano** 1892-1953 ....... **TCLC 32**
See also CA 167; DLB 307; EWL 3; HW 2; LAW; WLIT 1

**Rampersad, Arnold** 1941- .............. **CLC 44**
See also BW 2, 3; CA 127; 133; CANR 81; DLB 111; INT CA-133

**Rampling, Anne**
See Rice, Anne
See also GLL 2

**Ramsay, Allan** 1686(?)-1758 .............. **LC 29**
See also DLB 95; RGEL 2

**Ramsay, Jay**
See Campbell, (John) Ramsey

**Ramuz, Charles-Ferdinand** 1878-1947
............................................. **TCLC 33**
See also CA 165; EWL 3

**Rand, Ayn** 1905-1982 ..... **CLC 3, 30, 44, 79; WLC 5**
See also AAYA 10; AMWS 4; BPFB 3; BYA 12; CA 13-16R; 105; CANR 27, 73; CDALBS; CN 1, 2, 3; CPW; DA; DA3; DAC; DAM MST, NOV, POP; DLB 227, 279; MTCW 1, 2; MTFW 2005; NFS 10, 16; RGAL 4; SFW 4; TUS; YAW

**Randall, Dudley (Felker)** 1914-2000
......................................... **BLC 3; CLC 1, 135**
See also BW 1, 3; CA 25-28R; 189; CANR 23, 82; CP 1, 2, 3, 4, 5; DAM MULT; DLB 41; PFS 5

**Randall, Robert**
See Silverberg, Robert

**Ranger, Ken**
See Creasey, John

**Rank, Otto** 1884-1939 ................ **TCLC 115**

**Ransom, John Crowe** 1888-1974 . **CLC 2, 4, 5, 11, 24; PC 61**
See also AMW; CA 5-8R; 49-52; CANR 6, 34; CDALBS; CP 1, 2; DA3; DAM POET; DLB 45, 63; EWL 3; EXPP; MAL 5; MTCW 1, 2; MTFW 2005; RGAL 4; TUS

**Rao, Raja** 1908-2006 ................. **CLC 25, 56**
See also CA 73-76; CANR 51; CN 1, 2, 3, 4, 5, 6; DAM NOV; DLB 323; EWL 3; MTCW 1, 2; MTFW 2005; RGEL 2; RGSF 2

**Raphael, Frederic (Michael)** 1931- .. **CLC 2, 14**
See also CA 1-4R; CANR 1, 86; CN 1, 2, 3, 4, 5, 6, 7; DLB 14, 319; TCLE 1:2

**Ratcliffe, James P.**
See Mencken, H(enry) L(ouis)

**Rathbone, Julian** 1935- ................. **CLC 41**
See also CA 101; CANR 34, 73, 152

**Rattigan, Terence (Mervyn)** 1911-1977
........................................ **CLC 7; DC 18**
See also BRWS 7; CA 85-88; 73-76; CBD; CDBLB 1945-1960; DAM DRAM; DFS 8; DLB 13; IDFW 3, 4; MTCW 1, 2; MTFW 2005; RGEL 2

**Ratushinskaya, Irina** 1954- ............ **CLC 54**
See also CA 129; CANR 68; CWW 2

**Raven, Simon (Arthur Noel)** 1927-2001
............................................. **CLC 14**
See also CA 81-84; 197; CANR 86; CN 1, 2, 3, 4, 5, 6; DLB 271

**Ravenna, Michael**
See Welty, Eudora

**Rawley, Callman** 1903-2004
See Rakosi, Carl
See also CA 21-24R; 228; CANR 12, 32, 91

**Rawlings, Marjorie Kinnan** 1896-1953
............................................. **TCLC 4**
See also AAYA 20; AMWS 10; ANW; BPFB 3; BYA 3; CA 104; 137; CANR 74; CLR 63; DLB 9, 22, 102; DLBD 17; JRDA; MAICYA 1, 2; MAL 5; MTCW 2; MTFW 2005; RGAL 4; SATA 100; WCH; YABC 1; YAW

**Ray, Satyajit** 1921-1992 ............ **CLC 16, 76**
See also CA 114; 137; DAM MULT

**Read, Herbert Edward** 1893-1968 .... **CLC 4**
See also BRW 6; CA 85-88; 25-28R; DLB 20, 149; EWL 3; PAB; RGEL 2

**Read, Piers Paul** 1941- .......... **CLC 4, 10, 25**
See also CA 21-24R; CANR 38, 86, 150; CN 2, 3, 4, 5, 6, 7; DLB 14; SATA 21

**Reade, Charles** 1814-1884 ........ **NCLC 2, 74**
See also DLB 21; RGEL 2

**Reade, Hamish**
See Gray, Simon (James Holliday)

**Reading, Peter** 1946- ...................... **CLC 47**
See also BRWS 8; CA 103; CANR 46, 96; CP 5, 6, 7; DLB 40

**Reaney, James** 1926- ...................... **CLC 13**
See also CA 41-44R; CAAS 15; CANR 42; CD 5, 6; CP 1, 2, 3, 4, 5, 6, 7; DAC; DAM MST; DLB 68; RGEL 2; SATA 43

**Rebreanu, Liviu** 1885-1944 .......... **TCLC 28**
See also CA 165; DLB 220; EWL 3

**Rechy, John** 1934- .... **CLC 1, 7, 14, 18, 107; HLC 2**
See also CA 5-8R, 195; CAAE 195; CAAS 4; CANR 6, 32, 64, 152; CN 1, 2, 3, 4, 5, 6, 7; DAM MULT; DLB 122, 278; DLBY 1982; HW 1, 2; INT CANR-6; LLW; MAL 5; RGAL 4

**Rechy, John Francisco**
See Rechy, John

**Redcam, Tom** 1870-1933 .............. **TCLC 25**

**Reddin, Keith** 1956- ...................... **CLC 67**
See also CAD; CD 6

**Redgrove, Peter (William)** 1932-2003
............................................. **CLC 6, 41**
See also BRWS 6; CA 1-4R; 217; CANR 3, 39, 77; CP 1, 2, 3, 4, 5, 6, 7; DLB 40; TCLE 1:2

**Redmon, Anne** ............................... **CLC 22**
See Nightingale, Anne Redmon
See also DLBY 1986

**Reed, Eliot**
See Ambler, Eric

**Reed, Ishmael** 1938- ... **BLC 3; CLC 2, 3, 5, 6, 13, 32, 60, 174; PC 68**
See also AFAW 1, 2; AMWS 10; BPFB 3; BW 2, 3; CA 21-24R; CANR 25, 48, 74, 128; CN 1, 2, 3, 4, 5, 6, 7; CP 1, 2, 3, 4, 5, 6, 7; CSW; DA3; DAM MULT; DLB 2, 5, 33, 169, 227; DLBD 8; EWL 3; LMFS 2; MAL 5; MSW; MTCW 2; MTFW 2005; PFS 6; RGAL 4; TCWW 2

**Reed, John (Silas)** 1887-1920 .......... **TCLC 9**
See also CA 106; 195; MAL 5; TUS

**Reed, Lou** ........................................ **CLC 21**
See Firbank, Louis

**Reese, Lizette Woodworth** 1856-1935
......................................... **PC 29; TCLC 181**
See also CA 180; DLB 54

**Reeve, Clara** 1729-1807 ................ **NCLC 19**
See also DLB 39; RGEL 2

**Reich, Wilhelm** 1897-1957 ........... **TCLC 57**
See also CA 199

**Reid, Christopher (John)** 1949- ...... **CLC 33**
See also CA 140; CANR 89; CP 4, 5, 6, 7; DLB 40; EWL 3

**Reid, Desmond**
See Moorcock, Michael

**Reid Banks, Lynne** 1929-
See Banks, Lynne Reid
See also AAYA 49; CA 1-4R; CANR 6, 22, 38, 87; CLR 24; CN 1, 2, 3, 7; JRDA; MAICYA 1, 2; SATA 22, 75, 111, 165; YAW

**Reilly, William K.**
See Creasey, John

**Reiner, Max**
See Caldwell, (Janet Miriam) Taylor (Holland)

**Reis, Ricardo**
See Pessoa, Fernando (Antonio Nogueira)

**Reizenstein, Elmer Leopold**
See Rice, Elmer (Leopold)
See also EWL 3

**Remarque, Erich Maria** 1898-1970
............................................. **CLC 21**
See also AAYA 27; BPFB 3; CA 77-80; 29-32R; CDWLB 2; DA; DA3; DAB; DAC; DAM MST, NOV; DLB 56; EWL 3; EXPN; LAIT 3; MTCW 1, 2; MTFW 2005; NFS 4; RGHL; RGWL 2, 3

**Remington, Frederic S(ackrider)** 1861-1909
............................................. **TCLC 89**
See also CA 108; 169; DLB 12, 186, 188; SATA 41; TCWW 2

**Remizov, A.**
See Remizov, Aleksei (Mikhailovich)

**Remizov, A. M.**
See Remizov, Aleksei (Mikhailovich)

**Remizov, Aleksei (Mikhailovich)** 1877-1957
............................................. **TCLC 27**
See Remizov, Alexey Mikhaylovich
See also CA 125; 133; DLB 295

**Remizov, Alexey Mikhaylovich**
See Remizov, Aleksei (Mikhailovich)
See also EWL 3

**Renan, Joseph Ernest** 1823-1892
......................................... **NCLC 26, 145**
See also GFL 1789 to the Present

**Renard, Jules(-Pierre)** 1864-1910 . **TCLC 17**
See also CA 117; 202; GFL 1789 to the Present

**Rivera, Tomas** 1935-1984 ................. **HLCS 2**
See also CA 49-52; CANR 32; DLB 82;
HW 1; LLW; RGAL 4; SSFS 15; TCWW
2; WLIT 1
**Rivers, Conrad Kent** 1933-1968 ....... **CLC 1**
See also BW 1; CA 85-88; DLB 41
**Rivers, Elfrida**
See Bradley, Marion Zimmer
See also GLL 1
**Riverside, John**
See Heinlein, Robert A.
**Rizal, Jose** 1861-1896 ................... **NCLC 27**
**Roa Bastos, Augusto** 1917-2005 ..... **CLC 45;**
**HLC 2**
See also CA 131; 238; CWW 2; DAM
MULT; DLB 113; EWL 3; HW 1; LAW;
RGSF 2; WLIT 1
**Roa Bastos, Augusto Jose Antonio**
See Roa Bastos, Augusto
**Robbe-Grillet, Alain** 1922- ... **CLC 1, 2, 4, 6,**
**8, 10, 14, 43, 128**
See also BPFB 3; CA 9-12R; CANR 33,
65, 115; CWW 2; DLB 83; EW 13; EWL
3; GFL 1789 to the Present; IDFW 3, 4;
MTCW 1, 2; MTFW 2005; RGWL 2, 3;
SSFS 15
**Robbins, Harold** 1916-1997 ............... **CLC 5**
See also BPFB 3; CA 73-76; 162; CANR
26, 54, 112, 156; DA3; DAM NOV;
MTCW 1, 2
**Robbins, Thomas Eugene** 1936-
See Robbins, Tom
See also CA 81-84; CANR 29, 59, 95, 139;
CN 7; CPW; CSW; DA3; DAM NOV,
POP; MTCW 1, 2; MTFW 2005
**Robbins, Tom** ......................... **CLC 9, 32, 64**
See Robbins, Thomas Eugene
See also AAYA 32; AMWS 10; BEST 90:3;
BPFB 3; CN 3, 4, 5, 6, 7; DLBY 1980
**Robbins, Trina** 1938- ...................... **CLC 21**
See also AAYA 61; CA 128; CANR 152
**Roberts, Charles G(eorge) D(ouglas)**
1860-1943 ................. **SSC 91; TCLC 8**
See also CA 105; 188; CLR 33; CWRI 5;
DLB 92; RGEL 2; RGSF 2; SATA 88;
SATA-Brief 29
**Roberts, Elizabeth Madox** 1886-1941
................................ **TCLC 68**
See also CA 111; 166; CLR 100; CWRI 5;
DLB 9, 54, 102; RGAL 4; RHW; SATA
33; SATA-Brief 27; TCWW 2; WCH
**Roberts, Kate** 1891-1985 ................. **CLC 15**
See also CA 107; 116; DLB 319
**Roberts, Keith (John Kingston)** 1935-2000
................................ **CLC 14**
See also BRWS 10; CA 25-28R; CANR 46;
DLB 261; SFW 4
**Roberts, Kenneth (Lewis)** 1885-1957
................................ **TCLC 23**
See also CA 109; 199; DLB 9; MAL 5;
RGAL 4; RHW
**Roberts, Michele (Brigitte)** 1949- .. **CLC 48,**
**178**
See also CA 115; CANR 58, 120; CN 6, 7;
DLB 231; FW
**Robertson, Ellis**
See Ellison, Harlan; Silverberg, Robert
**Robertson, Thomas William** 1829-1871
................................ **NCLC 35**
See Robertson, Tom
See also DAM DRAM
**Robertson, Tom**
See Robertson, Thomas William
See also RGEL 2
**Robeson, Kenneth**
See Dent, Lester

**Robinson, Edwin Arlington** 1869-1935
........................ **PC 1, 35; TCLC 5, 101**
See also AMW; CA 104; 133; CDALB
1865-1917; DA; DAC; DAM MST,
POET; DLB 54; EWL 3; EXPP; MAL 5;
MTCW 1, 2; MTFW 2005; PAB; PFS 4;
RGAL 4; WP
**Robinson, Henry Crabb** 1775-1867
................................ **NCLC 15**
See also DLB 107
**Robinson, Jill** 1936- ........................ **CLC 10**
See also CA 102; CANR 120; INT CA-102
**Robinson, Kim Stanley** 1952- .......... **CLC 34**
See also AAYA 26; CA 126; CANR 113,
139; CN 6, 7; MTFW 2005; SATA 109;
SCFW 2; SFW 4
**Robinson, Lloyd**
See Silverberg, Robert
**Robinson, Marilynne** 1944- ..... **CLC 25, 180**
See also AAYA 69; CA 116; CANR 80, 140;
CN 4, 5, 6, 7; DLB 206; MTFW 2005;
NFS 24
**Robinson, Mary** 1758-1800 ......... **NCLC 142**
See also DLB 158; FW
**Robinson, Smokey** ...................... **CLC 21**
See Robinson, William, Jr.
**Robinson, William, Jr.** 1940-
See Robinson, Smokey
See also CA 116
**Robison, Mary** 1949- ................. **CLC 42, 98**
See also CA 113; 116; CANR 87; CN 4, 5,
6, 7; DLB 130; INT CA-116; RGSF 2
**Roches, Catherine des** 1542-1587 .... **LC 117**
See also DLB 327
**Rochester**
See Wilmot, John
See also RGEL 2
**Rod, Edouard** 1857-1910 ............... **TCLC 52**
**Roddenberry, Eugene Wesley** 1921-1991
See Roddenberry, Gene
See also CA 110; 135; CANR 37; SATA 45;
SATA-Obit 69
**Roddenberry, Gene** ...................... **CLC 17**
See Roddenberry, Eugene Wesley
See also AAYA 5; SATA-Obit 69
**Rodgers, Mary** 1931- ........................ **CLC 12**
See also BYA 5; CA 49-52; CANR 8, 55,
90; CLR 20; CWRI 5; INT CANR-8;
JRDA; MAICYA 1, 2; SATA 8, 130
**Rodgers, W(illiam) R(obert)** 1909-1969
................................ **CLC 7**
See also CA 85-88; DLB 20; RGEL 2
**Rodman, Eric**
See Silverberg, Robert
**Rodman, Howard** 1920(?)-1985 ...... **CLC 65**
See also CA 118
**Rodman, Maia**
See Wojciechowska, Maia (Teresa)
**Rodo, Jose Enrique** 1871(?)-1917 ... **HLCS 2**
See also CA 178; EWL 3; HW 2; LAW
**Rodolph, Utto**
See Ouologuem, Yambo
**Rodriguez, Claudio** 1934-1999 ........ **CLC 10**
See also CA 188; DLB 134
**Rodriguez, Richard** 1944- .. **CLC 155; HLC**
**2**
See also AMWS 14; CA 110; CANR 66,
116; DAM MULT; DLB 82, 256; HW 1,
2; LAIT 5; LLW; MTFW 2005; NCFS 3;
WLIT 1
**Roelvaag, O(le) E(dvart)** 1876-1931
See Rolvaag, O(le) E(dvart)
See also CA 117; 171
**Roethke, Theodore (Huebner)** 1908-1963
...... **CLC 1, 3, 8, 11, 19, 46, 101; PC 15**
See also AMW; CA 81-84; CABS 2;
CDALB 1941-1968; DA3; DAM POET;
DLB 5, 206; EWL 3; EXPP; MAL 5;
MTCW 1, 2; PAB; PFS 3; RGAL 4; WP

**Rogers, Carl R(ansom)** 1902-1987
................................ **TCLC 125**
See also CA 1-4R; 121; CANR 1, 18;
MTCW 1
**Rogers, Samuel** 1763-1855 ............ **NCLC 69**
See also DLB 93; RGEL 2
**Rogers, Thomas Hunton** 1927- ....... **CLC 57**
See also CA 89-92; INT CA-89-92
**Rogers, Will(iam Penn Adair)** 1879-1935
................. **NNAL; TCLC 8, 71**
See also CA 105; 144; DA3; DAM MULT;
DLB 11; MTCW 2
**Rogin, Gilbert** 1929- ........................ **CLC 18**
See also CA 65-68; CANR 15
**Rohan, Koda**
See Koda Shigeyuki
**Rohlfs, Anna Katharine Green**
See Green, Anna Katharine
**Rohmer, Eric** .............................. **CLC 16**
See Scherer, Jean-Marie Maurice
**Rohmer, Sax** ............................... **TCLC 28**
See Ward, Arthur Henry Sarsfield
See also DLB 70; MSW; SUFW
**Roiphe, Anne** 1935- ..................... **CLC 3, 9**
See also CA 89-92; CANR 45, 73, 138;
DLBY 1980; INT CA-89-92
**Roiphe, Anne Richardson**
See Roiphe, Anne
**Rojas, Fernando de** 1475-1541 .. **HLCS 1, 2;**
**LC 23**
See also DLB 286; RGWL 2, 3
**Rojas, Gonzalo** 1917- ...................... **HLCS 2**
See also CA 178; HW 2; LAWS 1
**Roland (de la Platiere), Marie-Jeanne**
1754-1793 ................................ **LC 98**
See also DLB 314
**Rolfe, Frederick (William Serafino Austin**
**Lewis Mary)** 1860-1913 ........ **TCLC 12**
See Al Siddik
See also CA 107; 210; DLB 34, 156; RGEL
2
**Rolland, Romain** 1866-1944 .......... **TCLC 23**
See also CA 118; 197; DLB 65, 284; EWL
3; GFL 1789 to the Present; RGWL 2, 3
**Rolle, Richard** c. 1300-c. 1349 ..... **CMLC 21**
See also DLB 146; LMFS 1; RGEL 2
**Rolvaag, O(le) E(dvart)** ................. **TCLC 17**
See Roelvaag, O(le) E(dvart)
See also DLB 9, 212; MAL 5; NFS 5;
RGAL 4
**Romain Arnaud, Saint**
See Aragon, Louis
**Romains, Jules** 1885-1972 ................. **CLC 7**
See also CA 85-88; CANR 34; DLB 65,
321; EWL 3; GFL 1789 to the Present;
MTCW 1
**Romero, Jose Ruben** 1890-1952 ... **TCLC 14**
See also CA 114; 131; EWL 3; HW 1; LAW
**Ronsard, Pierre de** 1524-1585 ...... **LC 6, 54;**
**PC 11**
See also DLB 327; EW 2; GFL Beginnings
to 1789; RGWL 2, 3; TWA
**Rooke, Leon** 1934- .................... **CLC 25, 34**
See also CA 25-28R; CANR 23, 53; CCA
1; CPW; DAM POP
**Roosevelt, Franklin Delano** 1882-1945
................................ **TCLC 93**
See also CA 116; 173; LAIT 3
**Roosevelt, Theodore** 1858-1919 .... **TCLC 69**
See also CA 115; 170; DLB 47, 186, 275
**Roper, William** 1498-1578 ................. **LC 10**
**Roquelaure, A. N.**
See Rice, Anne
**Rosa, Joao Guimaraes** 1908-1967 . **CLC 23;**
**HLCS 1**
See Guimaraes Rosa, Joao
See also CA 89-92; DLB 113, 307; EWL 3;
WLIT 1

**Schelling, Friedrich Wilhelm Joseph von** 1775-1854 ............... **NCLC 30**
See also DLB 90

**Scherer, Jean-Marie Maurice** 1920-
See Rohmer, Eric
See also CA 110

**Schevill, James (Erwin)** 1920- .......... **CLC 7**
See also CA 5-8R; CAAS 12; CAD; CD 5, 6; CP 1, 2, 3, 4, 5

**Schiller, Friedrich von** 1759-1805 .... **DC 12; NCLC 39, 69, 166**
See also CDWLB 2; DAM DRAM; DLB 94; EW 5; RGWL 2, 3; TWA

**Schisgal, Murray (Joseph)** 1926- ...... **CLC 6**
See also CA 21-24R; CAD; CANR 48, 86; CD 5, 6; MAL 5

**Schlee, Ann** 1934- ........................... **CLC 35**
See also CA 101; CANR 29, 88; SATA 44; SATA-Brief 36

**Schlegel, August Wilhelm von** 1767-1845
........................................ **NCLC 15, 142**
See also DLB 94; RGWL 2, 3

**Schlegel, Friedrich** 1772-1829 ....... **NCLC 45**
See also DLB 90; EW 5; RGWL 2, 3; TWA

**Schlegel, Johann Elias (von)** 1719(?)-1749
........................................................ **LC 5**

**Schleiermacher, Friedrich** 1768-1834
........................................ **NCLC 107**
See also DLB 90

**Schlesinger, Arthur M(eier), Jr.** 1917-
........................................................ **CLC 84**
See also AITN 1; CA 1-4R; CANR 1, 28, 58, 105; DLB 17; INT CANR-28; MTCW 1, 2; SATA 61

**Schlink, Bernhard** 1944- ................. **CLC 174**
See also CA 163; CANR 116; RGHL

**Schmidt, Arno (Otto)** 1914-1979 ..... **CLC 56**
See also CA 128; 109; DLB 69; EWL 3

**Schmitz, Aron Hector** 1861-1928
See Svevo, Italo
See also CA 104; 122; MTCW 1

**Schnackenberg, Gjertrud** 1953- .... **CLC 40; PC 45**
See also AMWS 15; CA 116; CANR 100; CP 5, 6, 7; CWP; DLB 120, 282; PFS 13

**Schnackenberg, Gjertrud Cecelia**
See Schnackenberg, Gjertrud

**Schneider, Leonard Alfred** 1925-1966
See Bruce, Lenny
See also CA 89-92

**Schnitzler, Arthur** 1862-1931 ... **DC 17; SSC 15, 61; TCLC 4**
See also CA 104; CDWLB 2; DLB 81, 118; EW 8; EWL 3; RGSF 2; RGWL 2, 3

**Schoenberg, Arnold Franz Walter** 1874-1951
........................................................ **TCLC 75**
See also CA 109; 188

**Schonberg, Arnold**
See Schoenberg, Arnold Franz Walter

**Schopenhauer, Arthur** 1788-1860
........................................ **NCLC 51, 157**
See also DLB 90; EW 5

**Schor, Sandra (M.)** 1932(?)-1990 .... **CLC 65**
See also CA 132

**Schorer, Mark** 1908-1977 ................. **CLC 9**
See also CA 5-8R; 73-76; CANR 7; CN 1, 2; DLB 103

**Schrader, Paul (Joseph)** 1946- ....... **CLC 26, 212**
See also CA 37-40R; CANR 41; DLB 44

**Schreber, Daniel** 1842-1911 ........ **TCLC 123**

**Schreiner, Olive (Emilie Albertina)** 1855-1920 ............................... **TCLC 9**
See also AFW; BRWS 2; CA 105; 154; DLB 18, 156, 190, 225; EWL 3; FW; RGEL 2; TWA; WLIT 2; WWE 1

**Schulberg, Budd (Wilson)** 1914- ...... **CLC 7, 48**
See also BPFB 3; CA 25-28R; CANR 19, 87; CN 1, 2, 3, 4, 5, 6, 7; DLB 6, 26, 28; DLBY 1981, 2001; MAL 5

**Schulman, Arnold**
See Trumbo, Dalton

**Schulz, Bruno** 1892-1942 ..... **SSC 13; TCLC 5, 51**
See also CA 115; 123; CANR 86; CDWLB 4; DLB 215; EWL 3; MTCW 2; MTFW 2005; RGSF 2; RGWL 2, 3

**Schulz, Charles M.** 1922-2000 ......... **CLC 12**
See also AAYA 39; CA 9-12R; 187; CANR 6, 132; INT CANR-6; MTFW 2005; SATA 10; SATA-Obit 118

**Schulz, Charles Monroe**
See Schulz, Charles M.

**Schumacher, E(rnst) F(riedrich)** 1911-1977
........................................................ **CLC 80**
See also CA 81-84; 73-76; CANR 34, 85

**Schumann, Robert** 1810-1856 .... **NCLC 143**

**Schuyler, George Samuel** 1895-1977
........................................................ **HR 1:3**
See also BW 2; CA 81-84; 73-76; CANR 42; DLB 29, 51

**Schuyler, James Marcus** 1923-1991 . **CLC 5, 23**
See also CA 101; 134; CP 1, 2, 3, 4, 5; DAM POET; DLB 5, 169; EWL 3; INT CA-101; MAL 5; WP

**Schwartz, Delmore (David)** 1913-1966
.................... **CLC 2, 4, 10, 45, 87; PC 8**
See also AMWS 2; CA 17-18; 25-28R; CANR 35; CAP 2; DLB 28, 48; EWL 3; MAL 5; MTCW 1, 2; MTFW 2005; PAB; RGAL 4; TUS

**Schwartz, Ernst**
See Ozu, Yasujiro

**Schwartz, John Burnham** 1965- ..... **CLC 59**
See also CA 132; CANR 116

**Schwartz, Lynne Sharon** 1939- ....... **CLC 31**
See also CA 103; CANR 44, 89; DLB 218; MTCW 2; MTFW 2005

**Schwartz, Muriel A.**
See Eliot, T(homas) S(tearns)

**Schwarz-Bart, Andre** 1928-2006 ... **CLC 2, 4**
See also CA 89-92; CANR 109; DLB 299; RGHL

**Schwarz-Bart, Simone** 1938- ... **BLCS; CLC 7**
See also BW 2; CA 97-100; CANR 117; EWL 3

**Schwerner, Armand** 1927-1999 .......... **PC 42**
See also CA 9-12R; 179; CANR 50, 85; CP 2, 3, 4, 5, 6; DLB 165

**Schwitters, Kurt (Hermann Edward Karl Julius)** 1887-1948 .................. **TCLC 95**
See also CA 158

**Schwob, Marcel (Mayer Andre)** 1867-1905
........................................................ **TCLC 20**
See also CA 117; 168; DLB 123; GFL 1789 to the Present

**Sciascia, Leonardo** 1921-1989 . **CLC 8, 9, 41**
See also CA 85-88; 130; CANR 35; DLB 177; EWL 3; MTCW 1; RGWL 2, 3

**Scoppettone, Sandra** 1936- ............. **CLC 26**
See Early, Jack
See also AAYA 11, 65; BYA 8; CA 5-8R; CANR 41, 73, 157; GLL 1; MAICYA 2; MAICYAS 1; SATA 9, 92; WYA; YAW

**Scorsese, Martin** 1942- ...... **CLC 20, 89, 207**
See also AAYA 38; CA 110; 114; CANR 46, 85

**Scotland, Jay**
See Jakes, John

**Scott, Duncan Campbell** 1862-1947
........................................................ **TCLC 6**
See also CA 104; 153; DAC; DLB 92; RGEL 2

**Scott, Evelyn** 1893-1963 ................... **CLC 43**
See also CA 104; 112; CANR 64; DLB 9, 48; RHW

**Scott, F(rancis) R(eginald)** 1899-1985
........................................................ **CLC 22**
See also CA 101; 114; CANR 87; CP 1, 2, 3, 4; DLB 88; INT CA-101; RGEL 2

**Scott, Frank**
See Scott, F(rancis) R(eginald)

**Scott, Joan** ......................................... **CLC 65**

**Scott, Joanna** 1960- ......................... **CLC 50**
See also CA 126; CANR 53, 92

**Scott, Paul (Mark)** 1920-1978 ..... **CLC 9, 60**
See also BRWS 1; CA 81-84; 77-80; CANR 33; CN 1, 2; DLB 14, 207, 326; EWL 3; MTCW 1; RGEL 2; RHW; WWE 1

**Scott, Ridley** 1937- ......................... **CLC 183**
See also AAYA 13, 43

**Scott, Sarah** 1723-1795 ..................... **LC 44**
See also DLB 39

**Scott, Sir Walter** 1771-1832 ... **NCLC 15, 69, 110; PC 13; SSC 32; WLC 5**
See also AAYA 22; BRW 4; BYA 2; CD-BLB 1789-1832; DA; DAB; DAC; DAM MST, NOV, POET; DLB 93, 107, 116, 144, 159; GL 3; HGG; LAIT 1; RGEL 2; RGSF 2; SSFS 10; SUFW 1; TEA; WLIT 3; YABC 2

**Scribe, (Augustin) Eugene** 1791-1861
........................................ **DC 5; NCLC 16**
See also DAM DRAM; DLB 192; GFL 1789 to the Present; RGWL 2, 3

**Scrum, R.**
See Crumb, R.

**Scudery, Georges de** 1601-1667 ......... **LC 75**
See also GFL Beginnings to 1789

**Scudery, Madeleine de** 1607-1701 . **LC 2, 58**
See also DLB 268; GFL Beginnings to 1789

**Scum**
See Crumb, R.

**Scumbag, Little Bobby**
See Crumb, R.

**Seabrook, John**
See Hubbard, L. Ron

**Seacole, Mary Jane Grant** 1805-1881
........................................ **NCLC 147**
See also DLB 166

**Sealy, I(rwin) Allan** 1951- .............. **CLC 55**
See also CA 136; CN 6, 7

**Search, Alexander**
See Pessoa, Fernando (Antonio Nogueira)

**Sebald, W(infried) G(eorg)** 1944-2001
........................................................ **CLC 194**
See also BRWS 8; CA 159; 202; CANR 98; MTFW 2005; RGHL

**Sebastian, Lee**
See Silverberg, Robert

**Sebastian Owl**
See Thompson, Hunter S.

**Sebestyen, Igen**
See Sebestyen, Ouida

**Sebestyen, Ouida** 1924- .................. **CLC 30**
See also AAYA 8; BYA 7; CA 107; CANR 40, 114; CLR 17; JRDA; MAICYA 1, 2; SAAS 10; SATA 39, 140; WYA; YAW

**Sebold, Alice** 1963(?)- .................... **CLC 193**
See also AAYA 56; CA 203; MTFW 2005

**Second Duke of Buckingham**
See Villiers, George

**Secundus, H. Scriblerus**
See Fielding, Henry

**Sedges, John**
See Buck, Pearl S(ydenstricker)

**Skelton, John** 1460(?)-1529 ... **LC 71; PC 25**
See also BRW 1; DLB 136; RGEL 2

**Skelton, Robin** 1925-1997 .............. **CLC 13**
See Zuk, Georges
See also AITN 2; CA 5-8R; 160; CAAS 5;
CANR 28, 89; CCA 1; CP 1, 2, 3, 4, 5, 6;
DLB 27, 53

**Skolimowski, Jerzy** 1938- .............. **CLC 20**
See also CA 128

**Skram, Amalie (Bertha)** 1847-1905
................................................... **TCLC 25**
See also CA 165

**Skvorecky, Josef** 1924- ....... **CLC 15, 39, 69,
152**
See also CA 61-64; CAAS 1; CANR 10,
34, 63, 108; CDWLB 4; CWW 2; DA3;
DAC; DAM NOV; DLB 232; EWL 3;
MTCW 1, 2; MTFW 2005

**Slade, Bernard** 1930- ................. **CLC 11, 46**
See Newbound, Bernard Slade
See also CAAS 9; CCA 1; CD 6; DLB 53

**Slaughter, Carolyn** 1946- ................ **CLC 56**
See also CA 85-88; CANR 85; CN 5, 6, 7

**Slaughter, Frank G(ill)** 1908-2001 .. **CLC 29**
See also AITN 2; CA 5-8R; 197; CANR 5,
85; INT CANR-5; RHW

**Slavitt, David R(ytman)** 1935- .... **CLC 5, 14**
See also CA 21-24R; CAAS 3; CANR 41,
83; CN 1, 2; CP 1, 2, 3, 4, 5, 6, 7; DLB
5, 6

**Slesinger, Tess** 1905-1945 .............. **TCLC 10**
See also CA 107; 199; DLB 102

**Slessor, Kenneth** 1901-1971 ............ **CLC 14**
See also CA 102; 89-92; DLB 260; RGEL
2

**Slowacki, Juliusz** 1809-1849 ........ **NCLC 15**
See also RGWL 3

**Smart, Christopher** 1722-1771 ... **LC 3, 134;
PC 13**
See also DAM POET; DLB 109; RGEL 2

**Smart, Elizabeth** 1913-1986 ............ **CLC 54**
See also CA 81-84; 118; CN 4; DLB 88

**Smiley, Jane (Graves)** 1949- ..... **CLC 53, 76,
144**
See also AAYA 66; AMWS 6; BPFB 3; CA
104; CANR 30, 50, 74, 96; CN 6, 7; CPW
1; DA3; DAM POP; DLB 227, 234; EWL
3; INT CANR-30; MAL 5; MTFW 2005;
SSFS 19

**Smith, A(rthur) J(ames) M(arshall)**
1902-1980 ................................. **CLC 15**
See also CA 1-4R; 102; CANR 4; CP 1, 2,
3; DAC; DLB 88; RGEL 2

**Smith, Adam** 1723(?)-1790 ............... **LC 36**
See also DLB 104, 252; RGEL 2

**Smith, Alexander** 1829-1867 ........ **NCLC 59**
See also DLB 32, 55

**Smith, Anna Deavere** 1950- ............ **CLC 86**
See also CA 133; CANR 103; CD 5, 6; DFS
2, 22

**Smith, Betty (Wehner)** 1904-1972 ... **CLC 19**
See also BPFB 3; BYA 3; CA 5-8R; 33-
36R; DLBY 1982; LAIT 3; RGAL 4;
SATA 6

**Smith, Charlotte (Turner)** 1749-1806
........................................ **NCLC 23, 115**
See also DLB 39, 109; RGEL 2; TEA

**Smith, Clark Ashton** 1893-1961 ....... **CLC 43**
See also CA 143; CANR 81; FANT; HGG;
MTCW 2; SCFW 1, 2; SFW 4; SUFW

**Smith, Dave** ................................. **CLC 22, 42**
See Smith, David (Jeddie)
See also CAAS 7; CP 3, 4, 5, 6, 7; DLB 5

**Smith, David (Jeddie)** 1942-
See Smith, Dave
See also CA 49-52; CANR 1, 59, 120;
CSW; DAM POET

**Smith, Iain Crichton** 1928-1998 ...... **CLC 64**
See also BRWS 9; CA 21-24R; 171; CN 1,
2, 3, 4, 5, 6; CP 1, 2, 3, 4, 5, 6; DLB 40,
139, 319; RGSF 2

**Smith, John** 1580(?)-1631 ..................... **LC 9**
See also DLB 24, 30; TUS

**Smith, Johnston**
See Crane, Stephen (Townley)

**Smith, Joseph, Jr.** 1805-1844 ........ **NCLC 53**

**Smith, Kevin** 1970- ......................... **CLC 223**
See also AAYA 37; CA 166; CANR 131

**Smith, Lee** 1944- ......................... **CLC 25, 73**
See also CA 114; 119; CANR 46, 118; CN
7; CSW; DLB 143; DLBY 1983; EWL 3;
INT CA-119; RGAL 4

**Smith, Martin**
See Smith, Martin Cruz

**Smith, Martin Cruz** 1942- . **CLC 25; NNAL**
See also BEST 89:4; BPFB 3; CA 85-88;
CANR 6, 23, 43, 65, 119; CMW 4; CPW;
DAM MULT, POP; HGG; INT CANR-
23; MTCW 2; MTFW 2005; RGAL 4

**Smith, Patti** 1946- .......................... **CLC 12**
See also CA 93-96; CANR 63

**Smith, Pauline (Urmson)** 1882-1959
................................................... **TCLC 25**
See also DLB 225; EWL 3

**Smith, Rosamond**
See Oates, Joyce Carol

**Smith, Sheila Kaye**
See Kaye-Smith, Sheila

**Smith, Stevie** 1902-1971 ... **CLC 3, 8, 25, 44;
PC 12**
See also BRWS 2; CA 17-18; 29-32R;
CANR 35; CAP 2; CP 1; DAM POET;
DLB 20; EWL 3; MTCW 1, 2; PAB; PFS
3; RGEL 2; TEA

**Smith, Wilbur** 1933- ........................ **CLC 33**
See also CA 13-16R; CANR 7, 46, 66, 134;
CPW; MTCW 1, 2; MTFW 2005

**Smith, William Jay** 1918- .................. **CLC 6**
See also AMWS 13; CA 5-8R; CANR 44,
106; CP 1, 2, 3, 4, 5, 6, 7; CSW; CWRI
5; DLB 5; MAICYA 1, 2; SAAS 22;
SATA 2, 68, 154; SATA-Essay 154; TCLE
1:2

**Smith, Woodrow Wilson**
See Kuttner, Henry

**Smith, Zadie** 1975- ......................... **CLC 158**
See also AAYA 50; CA 193; MTFW 2005

**Smolenskin, Peretz** 1842-1885 ...... **NCLC 30**

**Smollett, Tobias (George)** 1721-1771 .. **LC 2,
46**
See also BRW 3; CDBLB 1660-1789; DLB
39, 104; RGEL 2; TEA

**Snodgrass, W.D.** 1926- ..... **CLC 2, 6, 10, 18,
68; PC 74**
See also AMWS 6; CA 1-4R; CANR 6, 36,
65, 85; CP 1, 2, 3, 4, 5, 6, 7; DAM POET;
DLB 5; MAL 5; MTCW 1, 2; MTFW
2005; RGAL 4; TCLE 1:2

**Snorri Sturluson** 1179-1241 ........ **CMLC 56**
See also RGWL 2, 3

**Snow, C(harles) P(ercy)** 1905-1980 .. **CLC 1,
4, 6, 9, 13, 19**
See also BRW 7; CA 5-8R; 101; CANR 28;
CDBLB 1945-1960; CN 1, 2; DAM NOV;
DLB 15, 77; DLBD 17; EWL 3; MTCW
1, 2; MTFW 2005; RGEL 2; TEA

**Snow, Frances Compton**
See Adams, Henry (Brooks)

**Snyder, Gary** 1930- ........ **CLC 1, 2, 5, 9, 32,
120; PC 21**
See also AMWS 8; ANW; BG 1:3; CA 17-
20R; CANR 30, 60, 125; CP 1, 2, 3, 4, 5,
6, 7; DA3; DAM POET; DLB 5, 16, 165,
212, 237, 275; EWL 3; MAL 5; MTCW
2; MTFW 2005; PFS 9, 19; RGAL 4; WP

**Snyder, Zilpha Keatley** 1927- .......... **CLC 17**
See also AAYA 15; BYA 1; CA 9-12R;
CANR 38; CLR 31; JRDA; MAICYA 1,
2; SAAS 2; SATA 1, 28, 75, 110, 163;
SATA-Essay 112, 163; YAW

**Soares, Bernardo**
See Pessoa, Fernando (Antonio Nogueira)

**Sobh, A.**
See Shamlu, Ahmad

**Sobh, Alef**
See Shamlu, Ahmad

**Sobol, Joshua** 1939- ......................... **CLC 60**
See Sobol, Yehoshua
See also CA 200; RGHL

**Sobol, Yehoshua** 1939-
See Sobol, Joshua
See also CWW 2

**Socrates** 470B.C.-399B.C. ............. **CMLC 27**

**Soderberg, Hjalmar** 1869-1941 .... **TCLC 39**
See also DLB 259; EWL 3; RGSF 2

**Soderbergh, Steven** 1963- .............. **CLC 154**
See also AAYA 43; CA 243

**Soderbergh, Steven Andrew**
See Soderbergh, Steven

**Sodergran, Edith (Irene)** 1892-1923
See Soedergran, Edith (Irene)
See also CA 202; DLB 259; EW 11; EWL
3; RGWL 2, 3

**Soedergran, Edith (Irene)** 1892-1923
................................................... **TCLC 31**
See Sodergran, Edith (Irene)

**Softly, Edgar**
See Lovecraft, H. P.

**Softly, Edward**
See Lovecraft, H. P.

**Sokolov, Alexander V(sevolodovich)** 1943-
See Sokolov, Sasha
See also CA 73-76

**Sokolov, Raymond** 1941- .................. **CLC 7**
See also CA 85-88

**Sokolov, Sasha** ................................. **CLC 59**
See Sokolov, Alexander V(sevolodovich)
See also CWW 2; DLB 285; EWL 3; RGWL
2, 3

**Solo, Jay**
See Ellison, Harlan

**Sologub, Fyodor** ............................... **TCLC 9**
See Teternikov, Fyodor Kuzmich
See also EWL 3

**Solomons, Ikey Esquir**
See Thackeray, William Makepeace

**Solomos, Dionysios** 1798-1857 ....... **NCLC 15**

**Solwoska, Mara**
See French, Marilyn

**Solzhenitsyn, Aleksandr I.** 1918- . **CLC 1, 2,
4, 7, 9, 10, 18, 26, 34, 78, 134; SSC 32;
WLC 5**
See Solzhenitsyn, Aleksandr Isayevich
See also AAYA 49; AITN 1; BPFB 3; CA
69-72; CANR 40, 65, 116; DA; DA3;
DAB; DAC; DAM MST, NOV; DLB 302;
EW 13; EXPS; LAIT 4; MTCW 1, 2;
MTFW 2005; NFS 6; RGSF 2; RGWL 2,
3; SSFS 9; TWA

**Solzhenitsyn, Aleksandr Isayevich**
See Solzhenitsyn, Aleksandr I.
See also CWW 2; EWL 3

**Somers, Jane**
See Lessing, Doris

**Somerville, Edith Oenone** 1858-1949
................................................ **SSC 56; TCLC 51**
See also CA 196; DLB 135; RGEL 2; RGSF
2

**Somerville & Ross**
See Martin, Violet Florence; Somerville,
Edith Oenone

**Sommer, Scott** 1951- ....................... **CLC 25**
See also CA 106

**Susann, Jacqueline** 1921-1974 .......... **CLC 3**
 See also AITN 1; BPFB 3; CA 65-68; 53-
 56; MTCW 1, 2
**Su Shi**
 See Su Shih
 See also RGWL 2, 3
**Su Shih** 1036-1101 ........................ **CMLC 15**
 See Su Shi
**Suskind, Patrick** ............................. **CLC 182**
 See Sueskind, Patrick
 See also BPFB 3; CA 145; CWW 2
**Suso, Heinrich** c. 1295-1366 ........ **CMLC 87**
 See also DLB 179; LMFS 1
**Sutcliff, Rosemary** 1920-1992 .......... **CLC 26**
 See also AAYA 10; BYA 1, 4; CA 5-8R;
 139; CANR 37; CLR 1, 37; CPW; DAB;
 DAC; DAM MST, POP; JRDA; LATS
 1:1; MAICYA 1, 2; MAICYAS 1; RHW;
 SATA 6, 44, 78; SATA-Obit 73; WYA;
 YAW
**Sutro, Alfred** 1863-1933 ................. **TCLC 6**
 See also CA 105; 185; DLB 10; RGEL 2
**Sutton, Henry**
 See Slavitt, David R(ytman)
**Suzuki, D. T.**
 See Suzuki, Daisetz Teitaro
**Suzuki, Daisetz T.**
 See Suzuki, Daisetz Teitaro
**Suzuki, Daisetz Teitaro** 1870-1966
 ........................................ **TCLC 109**
 See also CA 121; 111; MTCW 1, 2; MTFW
 2005
**Suzuki, Teitaro**
 See Suzuki, Daisetz Teitaro
**Svevo, Italo** .................. **SSC 25; TCLC 2, 35**
 See Schmitz, Aron Hector
 See also DLB 264; EW 8; EWL 3; RGWL
 2, 3; WLIT 7
**Swados, Elizabeth (A.)** 1951- .......... **CLC 12**
 See also CA 97-100; CANR 49; INT CA-
 97-100
**Swados, Harvey** 1920-1972 ................ **CLC 5**
 See also CA 5-8R; 37-40R; CANR 6; CN
 1; DLB 2; MAL 5
**Swan, Gladys** 1934- ........................... **CLC 69**
 See also CA 101; CANR 17, 39; TCLE 1:2
**Swanson, Logan**
 See Matheson, Richard (Burton)
**Swarthout, Glendon (Fred)** 1918-1992
 ........................................ **CLC 35**
 See also AAYA 55; CA 1-4R; 139; CANR
 1, 47; CN 1, 2, 3, 4, 5; LAIT 5; SATA 26;
 TCWW 1, 2; YAW
**Swedenborg, Emanuel** 1688-1772 .... **LC 105**
**Sweet, Sarah C.**
 See Jewett, (Theodora) Sarah Orne
**Swenson, May** 1919-1989 ..... **CLC 4, 14, 61,**
 **106; PC 14**
 See also AMWS 4; CA 5-8R; 130; CANR
 36, 61, 131; CP 1, 2, 3, 4; DA; DAB;
 DAC; DAM MST, POET; DLB 5; EXPP;
 GLL 1; MAL 5; MTCW 1, 2; MTFW
 2005; PFS 16; SATA 15; WP
**Swift, Augustus**
 See Lovecraft, H. P.
**Swift, Graham** 1949- ................. **CLC 41, 88**
 See also BRWC 2; BRWS 5; CA 117; 122;
 CANR 46, 71, 128; CN 4, 5, 6, 7; DLB
 194, 326; MTCW 2; MTFW 2005; NFS
 18; RGSF 2
**Swift, Jonathan** 1667-1745 ... **LC 1, 42, 101;**
 **PC 9; WLC 6**
 See also AAYA 41; BRW 3; BRWC 1;
 BRWR 1; BYA 5, 14; CDBLB 1660-1789;
 CLR 53; DA; DA3; DAB; DAC; DAM
 MST, NOV, POET; DLB 39, 95, 101;
 EXPN; LAIT 1; NFS 6; RGEL 2; SATA
 19; TEA; WCH; WLIT 3

**Swinburne, Algernon Charles** 1837-1909
 ................. **PC 24; TCLC 8, 36; WLC 6**
 See also BRW 5; CA 105; 140; CDBLB
 1832-1890; DA; DA3; DAB; DAC; DAM
 MST, POET; DLB 35, 57; PAB; RGEL 2;
 TEA
**Swinfen, Ann** ...................................... **CLC 34**
 See also CA 202
**Swinnerton, Frank (Arthur)** 1884-1982
 ........................................ **CLC 31**
 See also CA 202; 108; CN 1, 2, 3; DLB 34
**Swinnerton, Frank Arthur** 1884-1982
 ........................................ **CLC 31**
 See also CA 108; DLB 34
**Swithen, John**
 See King, Stephen
**Sylvia**
 See Ashton-Warner, Sylvia (Constance)
**Symmes, Robert Edward**
 See Duncan, Robert
**Symonds, John Addington** 1840-1893
 ........................................ **NCLC 34**
 See also DLB 57, 144
**Symons, Arthur** 1865-1945 ............ **TCLC 11**
 See also CA 107; 189; DLB 19, 57, 149;
 RGEL 2
**Symons, Julian (Gustave)** 1912-1994
 ........................................ **CLC 2, 14, 32**
 See also CA 49-52; 147; CAAS 3; CANR
 3, 33, 59; CMW 4; CN 1, 2, 3, 4, 5; CP 1,
 3, 4; DLB 87, 155; DLBY 1992; MSW;
 MTCW 1
**Synge, (Edmund) J(ohn) M(illington)**
 1871-1909 .............. **DC 2; TCLC 6, 37**
 See also BRW 6; BRWR 1; CA 104; 141;
 CDBLB 1890-1914; DAM DRAM; DFS
 18; DLB 10, 19; EWL 3; RGEL 2; TEA;
 WLIT 4
**Syruc, J.**
 See Milosz, Czeslaw
**Szirtes, George** 1948- .......... **CLC 46; PC 51**
 See also CA 109; CANR 27, 61, 117; CP 4,
 5, 6, 7
**Szymborska, Wislawa** 1923- .. **CLC 99, 190;**
 **PC 44**
 See also CA 154; CANR 91, 133; CDWLB
 4; CWP; CWW 2; DA3; DLB 232; DLBY
 1996; EWL 3; MTCW 2; MTFW 2005;
 PFS 15; RGHL; RGWL 3
**T. O., Nik**
 See Annensky, Innokenty (Fyodorovich)
**Tabori, George** 1914- ......................... **CLC 19**
 See also CA 49-52; CANR 4, 69; CBD; CD
 5, 6; DLB 245; RGHL
**Tacitus** c. 55-c. 117 ............................. **CMLC 56**
 See also AW 2; CDWLB 1; DLB 211;
 RGWL 2, 3; WLIT 8
**Tagore, Rabindranath** 1861-1941 ....... **PC 8;**
 **SSC 48; TCLC 3, 53**
 See also CA 104; 120; DA3; DAM DRAM,
 POET; DLB 323; EWL 3; MTCW 1, 2;
 MTFW 2005; PFS 18; RGEL 2; RGSF 2;
 RGWL 2, 3; TWA
**Taine, Hippolyte Adolphe** 1828-1893
 ........................................ **NCLC 15**
 See also EW 7; GFL 1789 to the Present
**Talayesva, Don C.** 1890-(?) .............. **NNAL**
**Talese, Gay** 1932- ............................... **CLC 37**
 See also AITN 1; CA 1-4R; CANR 9, 58,
 137; DLB 185; INT CANR-9; MTCW 1,
 2; MTFW 2005
**Tallent, Elizabeth** 1954- .................... **CLC 45**
 See also CA 117; CANR 72; DLB 130
**Tallmountain, Mary** 1918-1997 ........ **NNAL**
 See also CA 146; 161; DLB 193
**Tally, Ted** 1952- ................................. **CLC 42**
 See also CA 120; 124; CAD; CANR 125;
 CD 5, 6; INT CA-124

**Talvik, Heiti** 1904-1947 ................. **TCLC 87**
 See also EWL 3
**Tamayo y Baus, Manuel** 1829-1898
 ........................................ **NCLC 1**
**Tammsaare, A(nton) H(ansen)** 1878-1940
 ........................................ **TCLC 27**
 See also CA 164; CDWLB 4; DLB 220;
 EWL 3
**Tam'si, Tchicaya U**
 See Tchicaya, Gerald Felix
**Tan, Amy** 1952- ..... **AAL; CLC 59, 120, 151**
 See also AAYA 9, 48; AMWS 10; BEST
 89:3; BPFB 3; CA 136; CANR 54, 105,
 132; CDALBS; CN 6, 7; CPW 1; DA3;
 DAM MULT, NOV, POP; DLB 173, 312;
 EXPN; FL 1:6; FW; LAIT 3, 5; MAL 5;
 MTCW 2; MTFW 2005; NFS 1, 13, 16;
 RGAL 4; SATA 75; SSFS 9; YAW
**Tandem, Carl Felix**
 See Spitteler, Carl
**Tandem, Felix**
 See Spitteler, Carl
**Tanizaki, Jun'ichiro** 1886-1965 .. **CLC 8, 14,**
 **28; SSC 21**
 See Tanizaki Jun'ichiro
 See also CA 93-96; 25-28R; MJW; MTCW
 2; MTFW 2005; RGSF 2; RGWL 2
**Tanizaki Jun'ichiro**
 See Tanizaki, Jun'ichiro
 See also DLB 180; EWL 3
**Tannen, Deborah** 1945- .................. **CLC 206**
 See also CA 118; CANR 95
**Tannen, Deborah Frances**
 See Tannen, Deborah
**Tanner, William**
 See Amis, Kingsley
**Tante, Dilly**
 See Kunitz, Stanley
**Tao Lao**
 See Storni, Alfonsina
**Tapahonso, Luci** 1953- .......... **NNAL; PC 65**
 See also CA 145; CANR 72, 127; DLB 175
**Tarantino, Quentin (Jerome)** 1963-
 ........................................ **CLC 125, 230**
 See also AAYA 58; CA 171; CANR 125
**Tarassoff, Lev**
 See Troyat, Henri
**Tarbell, Ida M(inerva)** 1857-1944
 ........................................ **TCLC 40**
 See also CA 122; 181; DLB 47
**Tarkington, (Newton) Booth** 1869-1946
 ........................................ **TCLC 9**
 See also BPFB 3; BYA 3; CA 110; 143;
 CWRI 5; DLB 9, 102; MAL 5; MTCW 2;
 RGAL 4; SATA 17
**Tarkovskii, Andrei Arsen'evich**
 See Tarkovsky, Andrei (Arsenyevich)
**Tarkovsky, Andrei (Arsenyevich)** 1932-1986
 ........................................ **CLC 75**
 See also CA 127
**Tartt, Donna** 1964(?)- ....................... **CLC 76**
 See also AAYA 56; CA 142; CANR 135;
 MTFW 2005
**Tasso, Torquato** 1544-1595 ............. **LC 5, 94**
 See also EFS 2; EW 2; RGWL 2, 3; WLIT
 7
**Tate, (John Orley) Allen** 1899-1979 . **CLC 2,**
 **4, 6, 9, 11, 14, 24; PC 50**
 See also AMW; CA 5-8R; 85-88; CANR
 32, 108; CN 1, 2; CP 1, 2; DLB 4, 45, 63;
 DLBD 17; EWL 3; MAL 5; MTCW 1, 2;
 MTFW 2005; RGAL 4; RHW
**Tate, Ellalice**
 See Hibbert, Eleanor Alice Burford
**Tate, James (Vincent)** 1943- .... **CLC 2, 6, 25**
 See also CA 21-24R; CANR 29, 57, 114;
 CP 1, 2, 3, 4, 5, 6, 7; DLB 5, 169; EWL
 3; PFS 10, 15; RGAL 4; WP

**Thomas, Ross (Elmore)** 1926-1995 . **CLC 39**
See also CA 33-36R; 150; CANR 22, 63; CMW 4

**Thompson, Francis (Joseph)** 1859-1907
.................................................. **TCLC 4**
See also BRW 5; CA 104; 189; CDBLB 1890-1914; DLB 19; RGEL 2; TEA

**Thompson, Francis Clegg**
See Mencken, H(enry) L(ouis)

**Thompson, Hunter S.** 1937(?)-2005 . **CLC 9, 17, 40, 104, 229**
See also AAYA 45; BEST 89:1; BPFB 3; CA 17-20R; 236; CANR 23, 46, 74, 77, 111, 133; CPW; CSW; DA3; DAM POP; DLB 185; MTCW 1, 2; MTFW 2005; TUS

**Thompson, James Myers**
See Thompson, Jim (Myers)

**Thompson, Jim (Myers)** 1906-1977(?)
.................................................. **CLC 69**
See also BPFB 3; CA 140; CMW 4; CPW; DLB 226; MSW

**Thompson, Judith (Clare Francesca)** 1954-
.................................................. **CLC 39**
See also CA 143; CD 5, 6; CWD; DFS 22

**Thomson, James** 1700-1748 ... **LC 16, 29, 40**
See also BRWS 3; DAM POET; DLB 95; RGEL 2

**Thomson, James** 1834-1882 .......... **NCLC 18**
See also DAM POET; DLB 35; RGEL 2

**Thoreau, Henry David** 1817-1862
.. **NCLC 7, 21, 61, 138; PC 30; WLC 6**
See also AAYA 42; AMW; ANW; BYA 3; CDALB 1640-1865; DA; DA3; DAB; DAC; DAM MST; DLB 1, 183, 223, 270, 298; LAIT 2; LMFS 1; NCFS 3; RGAL 4; TUS

**Thorndike, E. L.**
See Thorndike, Edward L(ee)

**Thorndike, Edward L(ee)** 1874-1949
.................................................. **TCLC 107**
See also CA 121

**Thornton, Hall**
See Silverberg, Robert

**Thorpe, Adam** 1956- ...................... **CLC 176**
See also CA 129; CANR 92; DLB 231

**Thubron, Colin (Gerald Dryden)** 1939-
.................................................. **CLC 163**
See also CA 25-28R; CANR 12, 29, 59, 95; CN 5, 6, 7; DLB 204, 231

**Thucydides** c. 455B.C.-c. 395B.C.
.................................................. **CMLC 17**
See also AW 1; DLB 176; RGWL 2, 3; WLIT 8

**Thumboo, Edwin Nadason** 1933- ....... **PC 30**
See also CA 194; CP 1

**Thurber, James (Grover)** 1894-1961
.............. **CLC 5, 11, 25, 125; SSC 1, 47**
See also AAYA 56; AMWS 1; BPFB 3; BYA 5; CA 73-76; CANR 17, 39; CDALB 1929-1941; CWRI 5; DA; DA3; DAB; DAC; DAM DRAM, MST, NOV; DLB 4, 11, 22, 102; EWL 3; EXPS; FANT; LAIT 3; MAICYA 1, 2; MAL 5; MTCW 1, 2; MTFW 2005; RGAL 4; RGSF 2; SATA 13; SSFS 1, 10, 19; SUFW; TUS

**Thurman, Wallace (Henry)** 1902-1934
...................... **BLC 3; HR 1:3; TCLC 6**
See also BW 1, 3; CA 104; 124; CANR 81; DAM MULT; DLB 51

**Tibullus** c. 54B.C.-c. 18B.C. ......... **CMLC 36**
See also AW 2; DLB 211; RGWL 2, 3; WLIT 8

**Ticheburn, Cheviot**
See Ainsworth, William Harrison

**Tieck, (Johann) Ludwig** 1773-1853
.............................. **NCLC 5, 46; SSC 31**
See also CDWLB 2; DLB 90; EW 5; IDTP; RGSF 2; RGWL 2, 3; SUFW

**Tiger, Derry**
See Ellison, Harlan

**Tilghman, Christopher** 1946- .......... **CLC 65**
See also CA 159; CANR 135, 151; CSW; DLB 244

**Tillich, Paul (Johannes)** 1886-1965
.................................................. **CLC 131**
See also CA 5-8R; 25-28R; CANR 33; MTCW 1, 2

**Tillinghast, Richard (Williford)** 1940-
.................................................. **CLC 29**
See also CA 29-32R; CAAS 23; CANR 26, 51, 96; CP 2, 3, 4, 5, 6, 7; CSW

**Tillman, Lynne** ? ........................... **CLC 231**
See also CA 173; CANR 144

**Timrod, Henry** 1828-1867 ............. **NCLC 25**
See also DLB 3, 248; RGAL 4

**Tindall, Gillian (Elizabeth)** 1938- ..... **CLC 7**
See also CA 21-24R; CANR 11, 65, 107; CN 1, 2, 3, 4, 5, 6, 7

**Tiptree, James, Jr.** ................. **CLC 48, 50**
See Sheldon, Alice Hastings Bradley
See also DLB 8; SCFW 1, 2; SFW 4

**Tirone Smith, Mary-Ann** 1944- ...... **CLC 39**
See also CA 118; 136; CANR 113; SATA 143

**Tirso de Molina** 1580(?)-1648 ........... **DC 13; HLCS 2; LC 73**
See also RGWL 2, 3

**Titmarsh, Michael Angelo**
See Thackeray, William Makepeace

**Tocqueville, Alexis (Charles Henri Maurice Clerel Comte) de** 1805-1859 . **NCLC 7, 63**
See also EW 6; GFL 1789 to the Present; TWA

**Toer, Pramoedya Ananta** 1925-2006
.................................................. **CLC 186**
See also CA 197; 251; RGWL 3

**Toffler, Alvin** 1928- ...................... **CLC 168**
See also CA 13-16R; CANR 15, 46, 67; CPW; DAM POP; MTCW 1, 2

**Toibin, Colm** 1955- ...................... **CLC 162**
See also CA 142; CANR 81, 149; CN 7; DLB 271

**Tolkien, J(ohn) R(onald) R(euel)** 1892-1973
....... **CLC 1, 2, 3, 8, 12, 38; TCLC 137; WLC 6**
See also AAYA 10; AITN 1; BPFB 3; BRWC 2; BRWS 2; CA 17-18; 45-48; CANR 36, 134; CAP 2; CDBLB 1914-1945; CLR 56; CN 1; CPW 1; CWRI 5; DA; DA3; DAB; DAC; DAM MST, NOV, POP; DLB 15, 160, 255; EFS 2; EWL 3; FANT; JRDA; LAIT 1; LATS 1:2; LMFS 2; MAICYA 1, 2; MTCW 1, 2; MTFW 2005; NFS 8; RGEL 2; SATA 2, 32, 100; SATA-Obit 24; SFW 4; SUFW; TEA; WCH; WYA; YAW

**Toller, Ernst** 1893-1939 ................. **TCLC 10**
See also CA 107; 186; DLB 124; EWL 3; RGWL 2, 3

**Tolson, M. B.**
See Tolson, Melvin B(eaunorus)

**Tolson, Melvin B(eaunorus)** 1898(?)-1966
.............................. **BLC 3; CLC 36, 105**
See also AFAW 1, 2; BW 1, 3; CA 124; 89-92; CANR 80; DAM MULT, POET; DLB 48, 76; MAL 5; RGAL 4

**Tolstoi, Aleksei Nikolaevich**
See Tolstoy, Alexey Nikolaevich

**Tolstoi, Lev**
See Tolstoy, Leo (Nikolaevich)
See also RGSF 2; RGWL 2, 3

**Tolstoy, Aleksei Nikolaevich**
See Tolstoy, Alexey Nikolaevich
See also DLB 272

**Tolstoy, Alexey Nikolaevich** 1882-1945
.................................................. **TCLC 18**
See Tolstoy, Aleksei Nikolaevich
See also CA 107; 158; EWL 3; SFW 4

**Tolstoy, Leo (Nikolaevich)** 1828-1910
...... **SSC 9, 30, 45, 54; TCLC 4, 11, 17, 28, 44, 79, 173; WLC 6**
See Tolstoi, Lev
See also AAYA 56; CA 104; 123; DA; DA3; DAB; DAC; DAM MST, NOV; DLB 238; EFS 2; EW 7; EXPS; IDTP; LAIT 2; LATS 1:1; LMFS 1; NFS 10; SATA 26; SSFS 5; TWA

**Tolstoy, Count Leo**
See Tolstoy, Leo (Nikolaevich)

**Tomalin, Claire** 1933- ................... **CLC 166**
See also CA 89-92; CANR 52, 88; DLB 155

**Tomasi di Lampedusa, Giuseppe** 1896-1957
See Lampedusa, Giuseppe (Tomasi) di
See also CA 111; DLB 177; EWL 3; WLIT 7

**Tomlin, Lily** 1939(?)-
See Tomlin, Mary Jean
See also CA 117

**Tomlin, Mary Jean** .......................... **CLC 17**
See Tomlin, Lily

**Tomline, F. Latour**
See Gilbert, W(illiam) S(chwenck)

**Tomlinson, (Alfred) Charles** 1927- .. **CLC 2, 4, 6, 13, 45; PC 17**
See also CA 5-8R; CANR 33; CP 1, 2, 3, 4, 5, 6, 7; DAM POET; DLB 40; TCLE 1:2

**Tomlinson, H(enry) M(ajor)** 1873-1958
.................................................. **TCLC 71**
See also CA 118; 161; DLB 36, 100, 195

**Tonna, Charlotte Elizabeth** 1790-1846
.................................................. **NCLC 135**
See also DLB 163

**Tonson, Jacob** fl. 1655(?)-1736 .......... **LC 86**
See also DLB 170

**Toole, John Kennedy** 1937-1969 .... **CLC 19, 64**
See also BPFB 3; CA 104; DLBY 1981; MTCW 2; MTFW 2005

**Toomer, Eugene**
See Toomer, Jean

**Toomer, Eugene Pinchback**
See Toomer, Jean

**Toomer, Jean** 1894-1967 . **BLC 3; CLC 1, 4, 13, 22; HR 1:3; PC 7; SSC 1, 45; TCLC 172; WLCS**
See also AFAW 1, 2; AMWS 3, 9; BW 1; CA 85-88; CDALB 1917-1929; DA3; DAM MULT; DLB 45, 51; EWL 3; EXPP; EXPS; LMFS 2; MAL 5; MTCW 1, 2; MTFW 2005; NFS 11; RGAL 4; RGSF 2; SSFS 5

**Toomer, Nathan Jean**
See Toomer, Jean

**Toomer, Nathan Pinchback**
See Toomer, Jean

**Torley, Luke**
See Blish, James (Benjamin)

**Tornimparte, Alessandra**
See Ginzburg, Natalia

**Torre, Raoul della**
See Mencken, H(enry) L(ouis)

**Torrence, Ridgely** 1874-1950 ........ **TCLC 97**
See also DLB 54, 249; MAL 5

**Torrey, E(dwin) Fuller** 1937- .......... **CLC 34**
See also CA 119; CANR 71

**Torsvan, Ben Traven**
See Traven, B.

**Torsvan, Benno Traven**
See Traven, B.

**Torsvan, Berick Traven**
See Traven, B.

**Twain, Mark** .... **SSC 6, 26, 34, 87; TCLC 6, 12, 19, 36, 48, 59, 161, 185; WLC 6**
See Clemens, Samuel Langhorne
See also AAYA 20; AMW; AMWC 1; BPFB 3; BYA 2, 3, 11, 14; CLR 58, 60, 66; DLB 11; EXPN; EXPS; FANT; LAIT 2; MAL 5; NCFS 4; NFS 1, 6; RGAL 4; RGSF 2; SFW 4; SSFS 1, 7, 16, 21; SUFW; TUS; WCH; WYA; YAW

**Tyler, Anne** 1941- ...... **CLC 7, 11, 18, 28, 44, 59, 103, 205**
See also AAYA 18, 60; AMWS 4; BEST 89:1; BPFB 3; BYA 12; CA 9-12R; CANR 11, 33, 53, 109, 132; CDALBS; CN 1, 2, 3, 4, 5, 6, 7; CPW; CSW; DAM NOV, POP; DLB 6, 143; DLBY 1982; EWL 3; EXPN; LATS 1:2; MAL 5; MBL; MTCW 1, 2; MTFW 2005; NFS 2, 7, 10; RGAL 4; SATA 7, 90, 173; SSFS 17; TCLE 1:2; TUS; YAW

**Tyler, Royall** 1757-1826 ................. **NCLC 3**
See also DLB 37; RGAL 4

**Tynan, Katharine** 1861-1931 ......... **TCLC 3**
See also CA 104; 167; DLB 153, 240; FW

**Tyndale, William** c. 1484-1536 ......... **LC 103**
See also DLB 132

**Tyutchev, Fyodor** 1803-1873 ......... **NCLC 34**

**Tzara, Tristan** 1896-1963 .. **CLC 47; PC 27; TCLC 168**
See also CA 153; 89-92; DAM POET; EWL 3; MTCW 2

**Uchida, Yoshiko** 1921-1992 ................. **AAL**
See also AAYA 16; BYA 2, 3; CA 13-16R; 139; CANR 6, 22, 47, 61; CDALBS; CLR 6, 56; CWRI 5; DLB 312; JRDA; MAICYA 1, 2; MTCW 1, 2; MTFW 2005; SAAS 1; SATA 1, 53; SATA-Obit 72

**Udall, Nicholas** 1504-1556 ................. **LC 84**
See also DLB 62; RGEL 2

**Ueda Akinari** 1734-1809 ............. **NCLC 131**

**Uhry, Alfred** 1936- ......................... **CLC 55**
See also CA 127; 133; CAD; CANR 112; CD 5, 6; CSW; DA3; DAM DRAM, POP; DFS 11, 15; INT CA-133; MTFW 2005

**Ulf, Haerved**
See Strindberg, (Johan) August

**Ulf, Harved**
See Strindberg, (Johan) August

**Ulibarri, Sabine R(eyes)** 1919-2003
................. **CLC 83; HLCS 2**
See also CA 131; 214; CANR 81; DAM MULT; DLB 82; HW 1, 2; RGSF 2

**Unamuno (y Jugo), Miguel de** 1864-1936
... **HLC 2; SSC 11, 69; TCLC 2, 9, 148**
See also CA 104; 131; CANR 81; DAM MULT, NOV; DLB 108, 322; EW 8; EWL 3; HW 1, 2; MTCW 1, 2; MTFW 2005; RGSF 2; RGWL 2, 3; SSFS 20; TWA

**Uncle Shelby**
See Silverstein, Shel

**Undercliffe, Errol**
See Campbell, (John) Ramsey

**Underwood, Miles**
See Glassco, John

**Undset, Sigrid** 1882-1949 . **TCLC 3; WLC 6**
See also CA 104; 129; DA; DA3; DAB; DAC; DAM MST, NOV; DLB 293; EW 9; EWL 3; FW; MTCW 1, 2; MTFW 2005; RGWL 2, 3

**Ungaretti, Giuseppe** 1888-1970 .. **CLC 7, 11, 15; PC 57**
See also CA 19-20; 25-28R; CAP 2; DLB 114; EW 10; EWL 3; PFS 20; RGWL 2, 3; WLIT 7

**Unger, Douglas** 1952- ................. **CLC 34**
See also CA 130; CANR 94, 155

**Unsworth, Barry (Forster)** 1930- ... **CLC 76, 127**
See also BRWS 7; CA 25-28R; CANR 30, 54, 125; CN 6, 7; DLB 194, 326

**Updike, John** 1932- ...... **CLC 1, 2, 3, 5, 7, 9, 13, 15, 23, 34, 43, 70, 139, 214; SSC 13, 27; WLC 6**
See also AAYA 36; AMW; AMWC 1; AMWR 1; BPFB 3; BYA 12; CA 1-4R; CABS 1; CANR 4, 33, 51, 94, 133; CDALB 1968-1988; CN 1, 2, 3, 4, 5, 6, 7; CP 1, 2, 3, 4, 5, 6, 7; CPW 1; DA; DA3; DAB; DAC; DAM MST, NOV, POET, POP; DLB 2, 5, 143, 218, 227; DLBD 3; DLBY 1980, 1982, 1997; EWL 3; EXPP; HGG; MAL 5; MTCW 1, 2; MTFW 2005; NFS 12, 24; RGAL 4; RGSF 2; SSFS 3, 19; TUS

**Updike, John Hoyer**
See Updike, John

**Upshaw, Margaret Mitchell**
See Mitchell, Margaret (Munnerlyn)

**Upton, Mark**
See Sanders, Lawrence

**Upward, Allen** 1863-1926 ............. **TCLC 85**
See also CA 117; 187; DLB 36

**Urdang, Constance (Henriette)** 1922-1996
................. **CLC 47**
See also CA 21-24R; CANR 9, 24; CP 1, 2, 3, 4, 5, 6; CWP

**Urfe, Honore d'** 1567(?)-1625 .......... **LC 132**
See also DLB 268; GFL Beginnings to 1789; RGWL 2, 3

**Uriel, Henry**
See Faust, Frederick (Schiller)

**Uris, Leon** 1924-2003 ................. **CLC 7, 32**
See also AITN 1, 2; BEST 89:2; BPFB 3; CA 1-4R; 217; CANR 1, 40, 65, 123; CN 1, 2, 3, 4, 5, 6; CPW 1; DA3; DAM NOV, POP; MTCW 1, 2; MTFW 2005; RGHL; SATA 49; SATA-Obit 146

**Urista (Heredia), Alberto (Baltazar)** 1947-
................. **HLCS 1**
See Alurista
See also CA 182; CANR 2, 32; HW 1

**Urmuz**
See Codrescu, Andrei

**Urquhart, Guy**
See McAlmon, Robert (Menzies)

**Urquhart, Jane** 1949- ................. **CLC 90**
See also CA 113; CANR 32, 68, 116, 157; CCA 1; DAC

**Usigli, Rodolfo** 1905-1979 ............... **HLCS 1**
See also CA 131; DLB 305; EWL 3; HW 1; LAW

**Usk, Thomas** (?)-1388 ................. **CMLC 76**
See also DLB 146

**Ustinov, Peter (Alexander)** 1921-2004
................. **CLC 1**
See also AITN 1; CA 13-16R; 225; CANR 25, 51; CBD; CD 5, 6; DLB 13; MTCW 2

**U Tam'si, Gerald Felix Tchicaya**
See Tchicaya, Gerald Felix

**U Tam'si, Tchicaya**
See Tchicaya, Gerald Felix

**Vachss, Andrew** 1942- ................. **CLC 106**
See also CA 118, 214; CAAE 214; CANR 44, 95, 153; CMW 4

**Vachss, Andrew H.**
See Vachss, Andrew

**Vachss, Andrew Henry**
See Vachss, Andrew

**Vaculik, Ludvik** 1926- ................. **CLC 7**
See also CA 53-56; CANR 72; CWW 2; DLB 232; EWL 3

**Vaihinger, Hans** 1852-1933 ......... **TCLC 71**
See also CA 116; 166

**Valdez, Luis (Miguel)** 1940- .... **CLC 84; DC 10; HLC 2**
See also CA 101; CAD; CANR 32, 81; CD 5, 6; DAM MULT; DFS 5; DLB 122; EWL 3; HW 1; LAIT 4; LLW

**Valenzuela, Luisa** 1938- ......... **CLC 31, 104; HLCS 2; SSC 14, 82**
See also CA 101; CANR 32, 65, 123; CDWLB 3; CWW 2; DAM MULT; DLB 113; EWL 3; FW; HW 1, 2; LAW; RGSF 2; RGWL 3

**Valera y Alcala-Galiano, Juan** 1824-1905
................. **TCLC 10**
See also CA 106

**Valerius Maximus** fl. 20- ............. **CMLC 64**
See also DLB 211

**Valery, (Ambroise) Paul (Toussaint Jules)** 1871-1945 ............... **PC 9; TCLC 4, 15**
See also CA 104; 122; DA3; DAM POET; DLB 258; EW 8; EWL 3; GFL 1789 to the Present; MTCW 1, 2; MTFW 2005; RGWL 2, 3; TWA

**Valle-Inclan, Ramon (Maria) del** 1866-1936
................. **HLC 2; TCLC 5**
See del Valle-Inclan, Ramon (Maria)
See also CA 106; 153; CANR 80; DAM MULT; DLB 134; EW 8; EWL 3; HW 2; RGSF 2; RGWL 2, 3

**Vallejo, Antonio Buero**
See Buero Vallejo, Antonio

**Vallejo, Cesar (Abraham)** 1892-1938
................. **HLC 2; TCLC 3, 56**
See also CA 105; 153; DAM MULT; DLB 290; EWL 3; HW 1; LAW; RGWL 2, 3

**Valles, Jules** 1832-1885 ................. **NCLC 71**
See also DLB 123; GFL 1789 to the Present

**Vallette, Marguerite Eymery** 1860-1953
................. **TCLC 67**
See Rachilde
See also CA 182; DLB 123, 192

**Valle Y Pena, Ramon del**
See Valle-Inclan, Ramon (Maria) del

**Van Ash, Cay** 1918-1994 ................. **CLC 34**
See also CA 220

**Vanbrugh, Sir John** 1664-1726 .......... **LC 21**
See also BRW 2; DAM DRAM; DLB 80; IDTP; RGEL 2

**Van Campen, Karl**
See Campbell, John W(ood, Jr.)

**Vance, Gerald**
See Silverberg, Robert

**Vance, Jack** 1916-
See Queen, Ellery; Vance, John Holbrook
See also CA 29-32R; CANR 17, 65, 154; CMW 4; MTCW 1

**Vance, John Holbrook** ................. **CLC 35**
See Vance, Jack
See also DLB 8; FANT; SCFW 1, 2; SFW 4; SUFW 1, 2

**Van Den Bogarde, Derek Jules Gaspard Ulric Niven** 1921-1999 ............. **CLC 14**
See Bogarde, Dirk
See also CA 77-80; 179

**Vandenburgh, Jane** ............. **CLC 59**
See also CA 168

**Vanderhaeghe, Guy** 1951- ............... **CLC 41**
See also BPFB 3; CA 113; CANR 72, 145; CN 7

**van der Post, Laurens (Jan)** 1906-1996
................. **CLC 5**
See also AFW; CA 5-8R; 155; CANR 35; CN 1, 2, 3, 4, 5, 6; DLB 204; RGEL 2

**van de Wetering, Janwillem** 1931- . **CLC 47**
See also CA 49-52; CANR 4, 62, 90; CMW 4

**Van Dine, S. S.** ............. **TCLC 23**
See Wright, Willard Huntington
See also DLB 306; MSW

Vivekananda, Swami 1863-1902 ... **TCLC 88**

Vizenor, Gerald Robert 1934- ...... **CLC 103; NNAL**
See also CA 13-16R, 205; CAAE 205; CAAS 22; CANR 5, 21, 44, 67; DAM MULT; DLB 175, 227; MTCW 2; MTFW 2005; TCWW 2

Vizinczey, Stephen 1933- ................. **CLC 40**
See also CA 128; CCA 1; INT CA-128

Vliet, R(ussell) G(ordon) 1929-1984
............................................................. **CLC 22**
See also CA 37-40R; 112; CANR 18; CP 2, 3

Vogau, Boris Andreyevich 1894-1938
See Pilnyak, Boris
See also CA 123; 218

Vogel, Paula A. 1951- ......... **CLC 76; DC 19**
See also CA 108; CAD; CANR 119, 140; CD 5, 6; CWD; DFS 14; MTFW 2005; RGAL 4

Voigt, Cynthia 1942- ......................... **CLC 30**
See also AAYA 3, 30; BYA 1, 3, 6, 7, 8; CA 106; CANR 18, 37, 40, 94, 145; CLR 13, 48; INT CANR-18; JRDA; LAIT 5; MAICYA 1; MAICYAS 1; MTFW 2005; SATA 48, 79, 116, 160; SATA-Brief 33; WYA; YAW

Voigt, Ellen Bryant 1943- ............... **CLC 54**
See also CA 69-72; CANR 11, 29, 55, 115; CP 5, 6, 7; CSW; CWP; DLB 120; PFS 23

Voinovich, Vladimir 1932- ........ **CLC 10, 49, 147**
See also CA 81-84; CAAS 12; CANR 33, 67, 150; CWW 2; DLB 302; MTCW 1

Voinovich, Vladimir Nikolaevich
See Voinovich, Vladimir

Vollmann, William T. 1959- .... **CLC 89, 227**
See also CA 134; CANR 67, 116; CN 7; CPW; DA3; DAM NOV, POP; MTCW 2; MTFW 2005

Voloshinov, V. N.
See Bakhtin, Mikhail Mikhailovich

Voltaire 1694-1778 ....... **LC 14, 79, 110; SSC 12; WLC 6**
See also BYA 13; DA; DA3; DAB; DAC; DAM DRAM, MST; DLB 314; EW 4; GFL Beginnings to 1789; LATS 1:1; LMFS 1; NFS 7; RGWL 2, 3; TWA

von Aschendrof, Baron Ignatz
See Ford, Ford Madox

von Chamisso, Adelbert
See Chamisso, Adelbert von

von Daeniken, Erich 1935- .............. **CLC 30**
See also AITN 1; CA 37-40R; CANR 17, 44

von Daniken, Erich
See von Daeniken, Erich

von Eschenbach, Wolfram c. 1170-c. 1220
............................................................. **CMLC 5**
See Eschenbach, Wolfram von
See also CDWLB 2; DLB 138; EW 1; RGWL 2

von Hartmann, Eduard 1842-1906
............................................................. **TCLC 96**

von Hayek, Friedrich August
See Hayek, F(riedrich) A(ugust von)

von Heidenstam, (Carl Gustaf) Verner
See Heidenstam, (Carl Gustaf) Verner von

von Heyse, Paul (Johann Ludwig)
See Heyse, Paul (Johann Ludwig von)

von Hofmannsthal, Hugo
See Hofmannsthal, Hugo von

von Horvath, Odon
See von Horvath, Odon

von Horvath, Odon
See von Horvath, Odon

von Horvath, Odon 1901-1938 ..... **TCLC 45**
See von Horvath, Oedoen
See also CA 118; 194; DLB 85, 124; RGWL 2, 3

von Horvath, Oedoen
See von Horvath, Odon
See also CA 184

von Kleist, Heinrich
See Kleist, Heinrich von

Vonnegut, Kurt, Jr.
See Vonnegut, Kurt

Vonnegut, Kurt 1922- .. **CLC 1, 2, 3, 4, 5, 8, 12, 22, 40, 60, 111, 212; SSC 8; WLC 6**
See also AAYA 6, 44; AITN 1; AMWS 2; BEST 90:4; BPFB 3; BYA 3, 14; CA 1-4R; CANR 1, 25, 49, 75, 92; CDALB 1968-1988; CN 1, 2, 3, 4, 5, 6, 7; CPW 1; DA; DA3; DAB; DAC; DAM MST, NOV, POP; DLB 2, 8, 152; DLBD 3; DLBY 1980; EWL 3; EXPN; EXPS; LAIT 4; LMFS 2; MAL 5; MTCW 1, 2; MTFW 2005; NFS 3; RGAL 4; SCFW; SFW 4; SSFS 5; TUS; YAW

Von Rachen, Kurt
See Hubbard, L. Ron

von Sternberg, Josef
See Sternberg, Josef von

Vorster, Gordon 1924- ..................... **CLC 34**
See also CA 133

Vosce, Trudie
See Ozick, Cynthia

Voznesensky, Andrei (Andreievich) 1933-
............................................................. **CLC 1, 15, 57**
See Voznesensky, Andrey
See also CA 89-92; CANR 37; CWW 2; DAM POET; MTCW 1

Voznesensky, Andrey
See Voznesensky, Andrei (Andreievich)
See also EWL 3

Wace, Robert c. 1100-c. 1175 ...... **CMLC 55**
See also DLB 146

Waddington, Miriam 1917-2004 ..... **CLC 28**
See also CA 21-24R; 225; CANR 12, 30; CCA 1; CP 1, 2, 3, 4, 5, 6, 7; DLB 68

Wagman, Fredrica 1937- ................... **CLC 7**
See also CA 97-100; INT CA-97-100

Wagner, Linda W.
See Wagner-Martin, Linda (C.)

Wagner, Linda Welshimer
See Wagner-Martin, Linda (C.)

Wagner, Richard 1813-1883 ... **NCLC 9, 119**
See also DLB 129; EW 6

Wagner-Martin, Linda (C.) 1936- .. **CLC 50**
See also CA 159; CANR 135

Wagoner, David (Russell) 1926- .. **CLC 3, 5, 15; PC 33**
See also AMWS 9; CA 1-4R; CAAS 3; CANR 2, 71; CN 1, 2, 3, 4, 5, 6, 7; CP 1, 2, 3, 4, 5, 6, 7; DLB 5, 256; SATA 14; TCWW 1, 2

Wah, Fred(erick James) 1939- ........ **CLC 44**
See also CA 107; 141; CP 1, 6, 7; DLB 60

Wahloo, Per 1926-1975 ..................... **CLC 7**
See also BPFB 3; CA 61-64; CANR 73; CMW 4; MSW

Wahloo, Peter
See Wahloo, Per

Wain, John (Barrington) 1925-1994
.................................. **CLC 2, 11, 15, 46**
See also CA 5-8R; 145; CAAS 4; CANR 23, 54; CDBLB 1960 to Present; CN 1, 2, 3, 4, 5; CP 1, 2, 3, 4, 5; DLB 15, 27, 139, 155; EWL 3; MTCW 1, 2; MTFW 2005

Wajda, Andrzej 1926- ............. **CLC 16, 219**
See also CA 102

Wakefield, Dan 1932- ........................ **CLC 7**
See also CA 21-24R, 211; CAAE 211; CAAS 7; CN 4, 5, 6, 7

Wakefield, Herbert Russell 1888-1965
............................................................. **TCLC 120**
See also CA 5-8R; CANR 77; HGG; SUFW

Wakoski, Diane 1937- .... **CLC 2, 4, 7, 9, 11, 40; PC 15**
See also CA 13-16R, 216; CAAE 216; CAAS 1; CANR 9, 60, 106; CP 1, 2, 3, 4, 5, 6, 7; CWP; DAM POET; DLB 5; INT CANR-9; MAL 5; MTCW 2; MTFW 2005

Wakoski-Sherbell, Diane
See Wakoski, Diane

Walcott, Derek 1930- .. **BLC 3; CLC 2, 4, 9, 14, 25, 42, 67, 76, 160; DC 7; PC 46**
See also BW 2; CA 89-92; CANR 26, 47, 75, 80, 130; CBD; CD 5, 6; CDWLB 3; CP 1, 2, 3, 4, 5, 6, 7; DA3; DAB; DAC; DAM MST, MULT, POET; DLB 117; DLBY 1981; DNFS 1; EFS 1; EWL 3; LMFS 2; MTCW 1, 2; MTFW 2005; PFS 6; RGEL 2; TWA; WWE 1

Waldman, Anne (Lesley) 1945- ......... **CLC 7**
See also BG 1:3; CA 37-40R; CAAS 17; CANR 34, 69, 116; CP 1, 2, 3, 4, 5, 6, 7; CWP; DLB 16

Waldo, E. Hunter
See Sturgeon, Theodore (Hamilton)

Waldo, Edward Hamilton
See Sturgeon, Theodore (Hamilton)

Walker, Alice 1944- ..... **BLC 3; CLC 5, 6, 9, 19, 27, 46, 58, 103, 167; PC 30; SSC 5; WLCS**
See also AAYA 3, 33; AFAW 1, 2; AMWS 3; BEST 89:4; BPFB 3; BW 2, 3; CA 37-40R; CANR 9, 27, 49, 66, 82, 131; CDALB 1968-1988; CN 4, 5, 6, 7; CPW; CSW; DA; DA3; DAB; DAC; DAM MST, MULT, NOV, POET, POP; DLB 6, 33, 143; EWL 3; EXPN; EXPS; FL 1:6; FW; INT CANR-27; LAIT 3; MAL 5; MBL; MTCW 1, 2; MTFW 2005; NFS 5; RGAL 4; RGSF 2; SATA 31; SSFS 2, 11; TUS; YAW

Walker, Alice Malsenior
See Walker, Alice

Walker, David Harry 1911-1992 ..... **CLC 14**
See also CA 1-4R; 137; CANR 1; CN 1, 2; CWRI 5; SATA 8; SATA-Obit 71

Walker, Edward Joseph 1934-2004
See Walker, Ted
See also CA 21-24R; 226; CANR 12, 28, 53

Walker, George F(rederick) 1947- . **CLC 44, 61**
See also CA 103; CANR 21, 43, 59; CD 5, 6; DAB; DAC; DAM MST; DLB 60

Walker, Joseph A. 1935-2003 .......... **CLC 19**
See also BW 1, 3; CA 89-92; CAD; CANR 26, 143; CD 5, 6; DAM DRAM, MST; DFS 12; DLB 38

Walker, Margaret 1915-1998 . **BLC; CLC 1, 6; PC 20; TCLC 129**
See also AFAW 1, 2; BW 2, 3; CA 73-76; 172; CANR 26, 54, 76, 136; CN 1, 2, 3, 4, 5, 6; CP 1, 2, 3, 4, 5, 6; CSW; DAM MULT; DLB 76, 152; EXPP; FW; MAL 5; MTCW 1, 2; MTFW 2005; RGAL 4; RHW

Walker, Ted ...................................... **CLC 13**
See Walker, Edward Joseph
See also CP 1, 2, 3, 4, 5, 6, 7; DLB 40

Wallace, David Foster 1962- .. **CLC 50, 114; SSC 68**
See also AAYA 50; AMWS 10; CA 132; CANR 59, 133; CN 7; DA3; MTCW 2; MTFW 2005

Wallace, Dexter
See Masters, Edgar Lee

**Wallace, (Richard Horatio) Edgar** 1875-1932 .................................................. **TCLC 57**
See also CA 115; 218; CMW 4; DLB 70; MSW; RGEL 2

**Wallace, Irving** 1916-1990 .......... **CLC 7, 13**
See also AITN 1; BPFB 3; CA 1-4R; 132; CAAS 1; CANR 1, 27; CPW; DAM NOV, POP; INT CANR-27; MTCW 1, 2

**Wallant, Edward Lewis** 1926-1962 .. **CLC 5, 10**
See also CA 1-4R; CANR 22; DLB 2, 28, 143, 299; EWL 3; MAL 5; MTCW 1, 2; RGAL 4; RGHL

**Wallas, Graham** 1858-1932 .......... **TCLC 91**

**Waller, Edmund** 1606-1687 ... **LC 86; PC 72**
See also BRW 2; DAM POET; DLB 126; PAB; RGEL 2

**Walley, Byron**
See Card, Orson Scott

**Walpole, Horace** 1717-1797 ........... **LC 2, 49**
See also BRW 3; DLB 39, 104, 213; GL 3; HGG; LMFS 1; RGEL 2; SUFW 1; TEA

**Walpole, Hugh (Seymour)** 1884-1941 .................................................. **TCLC 5**
See also CA 104; 165; DLB 34; HGG; MTCW 2; RGEL 2; RHW

**Walrond, Eric (Derwent)** 1898-1966 .................................................. **HR 1:3**
See also BW 1; CA 125; DLB 51

**Walser, Martin** 1927- ............... **CLC 27, 183**
See also CA 57-60; CANR 8, 46, 145; CWW 2; DLB 75, 124; EWL 3

**Walser, Robert** 1878-1956 ... **SSC 20; TCLC 18**
See also CA 118; 165; CANR 100; DLB 66; EWL 3

**Walsh, Gillian Paton**
See Paton Walsh, Gillian

**Walsh, Jill Paton** .............................. **CLC 35**
See Paton Walsh, Gillian
See also CLR 2, 65; WYA

**Walter, Villiam Christian**
See Andersen, Hans Christian

**Walters, Anna L(ee)** 1946- ................ **NNAL**
See also CA 73-76

**Walther von der Vogelweide** c. 1170-1228 .................................................. **CMLC 56**

**Walton, Izaak** 1593-1683 ................ **LC 72**
See also BRW 2; CDBLB Before 1660; DLB 151, 213; RGEL 2

**Wambaugh, Joseph (Aloysius), Jr.** 1937- .................................................. **CLC 3, 18**
See also AITN 1; BEST 89:3; BPFB 3; CA 33-36R; CANR 42, 65, 115; CMW 4; CPW 1; DA3; DAM NOV, POP; DLB 6; DLBY 1983; MSW; MTCW 1, 2

**Wang Wei** 699(?)-761(?) ..................... **PC 18**
See also TWA

**Warburton, William** 1698-1779 ........ **LC 97**
See also DLB 104

**Ward, Arthur Henry Sarsfield** 1883-1959
See Rohmer, Sax
See also CA 108; 173; CMW 4; HGG

**Ward, Douglas Turner** 1930- .......... **CLC 19**
See also BW 1; CA 81-84; CAD; CANR 27; CD 5, 6; DLB 7, 38

**Ward, E. D.**
See Lucas, E(dward) V(errall)

**Ward, Mrs. Humphry** 1851-1920
See Ward, Mary Augusta
See also RGEL 2

**Ward, Mary Augusta** 1851-1920 .. **TCLC 55**
See Ward, Mrs. Humphry
See also DLB 18

**Ward, Nathaniel** 1578(?)-1652 .......... **LC 114**
See also DLB 24

**Ward, Peter**
See Faust, Frederick (Schiller)

**Warhol, Andy** 1928(?)-1987 ............. **CLC 20**
See also AAYA 12; BEST 89:4; CA 89-92; 121; CANR 34

**Warner, Francis (Robert le Plastrier)** 1937- .................................................. **CLC 14**
See also CA 53-56; CANR 11; CP 1, 2, 3, 4

**Warner, Marina** 1946- ............. **CLC 59, 231**
See also CA 65-68; CANR 21, 55, 118; CN 5, 6, 7; DLB 194; MTFW 2005

**Warner, Rex (Ernest)** 1905-1986 .... **CLC 45**
See also CA 89-92; 119; CN 1, 2, 3, 4; CP 1, 2, 3, 4; DLB 15; RGEL 2; RHW

**Warner, Susan (Bogert)** 1819-1885 .................................................. **NCLC 31, 146**
See also DLB 3, 42, 239, 250, 254

**Warner, Sylvia (Constance) Ashton**
See Ashton-Warner, Sylvia (Constance)

**Warner, Sylvia Townsend** 1893-1978 ............ **CLC 7, 19; SSC 23; TCLC 131**
See also BRWS 7; CA 61-64; 77-80; CANR 16, 60, 104; CN 1, 2; DLB 34, 139; EWL 3; FANT; FW; MTCW 1, 2; RGEL 2; RGSF 2; RHW

**Warren, Mercy Otis** 1728-1814 .... **NCLC 13**
See also DLB 31, 200; RGAL 4; TUS

**Warren, Robert Penn** 1905-1989 . **CLC 1, 4, 6, 8, 10, 13, 18, 39, 53, 59; PC 37; SSC 4, 58; WLC 6**
See also AITN 1; AMW; AMWC 2; BPFB 3; BYA 1; CA 13-16R; 129; CANR 10, 47; CDALB 1968-1988; CN 1, 2, 3, 4; CP 1, 2, 3, 4; DA; DA3; DAB; DAC; DAM MST, NOV, POET; DLB 2, 48, 152, 320; DLBY 1980, 1989; EWL 3; INT CANR-10; MAL 5; MTCW 1, 2; MTFW 2005; NFS 13; RGAL 4; RGSF 2; RHW; SATA 46; SATA-Obit 63; SSFS 8; TUS

**Warrigal, Jack**
See Furphy, Joseph

**Warshofsky, Isaac**
See Singer, Isaac Bashevis

**Warton, Joseph** 1722-1800 . **LC 128; NCLC 118**
See also DLB 104, 109; RGEL 2

**Warton, Thomas** 1728-1790 ........ **LC 15, 82**
See also DAM POET; DLB 104, 109; RGEL 2

**Waruk, Kona**
See Harris, (Theodore) Wilson

**Warung, Price** ............................... **TCLC 45**
See Astley, William
See also DLB 230; RGEL 2

**Warwick, Jarvis**
See Garner, Hugh
See also CCA 1

**Washington, Alex**
See Harris, Mark

**Washington, Booker T(aliaferro)** 1856-1915 .................................................. **BLC 3; TCLC 10**
See also BW 1; CA 114; 125; DA3; DAM MULT; LAIT 2; RGAL 4; SATA 28

**Washington, George** 1732-1799 ........ **LC 25**
See also DLB 31

**Wassermann, (Karl) Jakob** 1873-1934 .................................................. **TCLC 6**
See also CA 104; 163; DLB 66; EWL 3

**Wasserstein, Wendy** 1950-2006 ...... **CLC 32, 59, 90, 183; DC 4**
See also AMWS 15; CA 121; 129; 247; CABS 3; CAD; CANR 53, 75, 128; CD 5, 6; CWD; DA3; DAM DRAM; DFS 5, 17; DLB 228; EWL 3; FW; INT CA-129; MAL 5; MTCW 2; MTFW 2005; SATA 94; SATA-Obit 174

**Waterhouse, Keith (Spencer)** 1929- .................................................. **CLC 47**
See also CA 5-8R; CANR 38, 67, 109; CBD; CD 6; CN 1, 2, 3, 4, 5, 6, 7; DLB 13, 15; MTCW 1, 2; MTFW 2005

**Waters, Frank (Joseph)** 1902-1995 . **CLC 88**
See also CA 5-8R; 149; CAAS 13; CANR 3, 18, 63, 121; DLB 212; DLBY 1986; RGAL 4; TCWW 1, 2

**Waters, Mary C.** ............................. **CLC 70**

**Waters, Roger** 1944- ......................... **CLC 35**

**Watkins, Frances Ellen**
See Harper, Frances Ellen Watkins

**Watkins, Gerrold**
See Malzberg, Barry N(athaniel)

**Watkins, Gloria Jean**
See hooks, bell

**Watkins, Paul** 1964- ......................... **CLC 55**
See also CA 132; CANR 62, 98

**Watkins, Vernon Phillips** 1906-1967 .................................................. **CLC 43**
See also CA 9-10; 25-28R; CAP 1; DLB 20; EWL 3; RGEL 2

**Watson, Irving S.**
See Mencken, H(enry) L(ouis)

**Watson, John H.**
See Farmer, Philip Jose

**Watson, Richard F.**
See Silverberg, Robert

**Watts, Ephraim**
See Horne, Richard Henry Hengist

**Watts, Isaac** 1674-1748 ...................... **LC 98**
See also DLB 95; RGEL 2; SATA 52

**Waugh, Auberon (Alexander)** 1939-2001 .................................................. **CLC 7**
See also CA 45-48; 192; CANR 6, 22, 92; CN 1, 2, 3; DLB 14, 194

**Waugh, Evelyn (Arthur St. John)** 1903-1966 .. **CLC 1, 3, 8, 13, 19, 27, 44, 107; SSC 41; WLC 6**
See also BPFB 3; BRW 7; CA 85-88; 25-28R; CANR 22; CDBLB 1914-1945; DA; DA3; DAB; DAC; DAM MST, NOV, POP; DLB 15, 162, 195; EWL 3; MTCW 1, 2; MTFW 2005; NFS 13, 17; RGEL 2; RGSF 2; TEA; WLIT 4

**Waugh, Harriet** 1944- ....................... **CLC 6**
See also CA 85-88; CANR 22

**Ways, C. R.**
See Blount, Roy (Alton), Jr.

**Waystaff, Simon**
See Swift, Jonathan

**Webb, Beatrice (Martha Potter)** 1858-1943 .................................................. **TCLC 22**
See also CA 117; 162; DLB 190; FW

**Webb, Charles (Richard)** 1939- ........ **CLC 7**
See also CA 25-28R; CANR 114

**Webb, Frank J.** ........................... **NCLC 143**
See also DLB 50

**Webb, James, Jr.**
See Webb, James

**Webb, James** 1946- ......................... **CLC 22**
See also CA 81-84; CANR 156

**Webb, James H.**
See Webb, James

**Webb, James Henry**
See Webb, James

**Webb, Mary Gladys (Meredith)** 1881-1927 .................................................. **TCLC 24**
See also CA 182; 123; DLB 34; FW; RGEL 2

**Webb, Mrs. Sidney**
See Webb, Beatrice (Martha Potter)

**Webb, Phyllis** 1927- ......................... **CLC 18**
See also CA 104; CANR 23; CCA 1; CP 1, 2, 3, 4, 5, 6, 7; CWP; DLB 53

**Webb, Sidney (James)** 1859-1947 . **TCLC 22**
See also CA 117; 163; DLB 190

**Webber, Andrew Lloyd** .................... **CLC 21**
See Lloyd Webber, Andrew
See also DFS 7

# Literary Criticism Series
# Cumulative Topic Index

This index lists all topic entries in Thompson Gale's *Children's Literature Review* (CLR), *Classical and Medieval Literature Criticism* (CMLC), *Contemporary Literary Criticism* (CLC), *Drama Criticism* (DC), *Literature Criticism from 1400 to 1800* (LC), *Nineteenth-Century Literature Criticism* (NCLC), *Short Story Criticism* (SSC), and *Twentieth-Century Literary Criticism* (TCLC). The index also lists topic entries in the Gale Critical Companion Collection, which includes the following publications: *The Beat Generation* (BG), *Feminism in Literature* (FL), *Gothic Literature* (GL), and *Harlem Renaissance* (HR).

Topic Index

# *SSC* Cumulative Nationality Index

## ALGERIAN

Camus, Albert **9**

## AMERICAN

Abish, Walter **44**
Adams, Alice (Boyd) **24**
Aiken, Conrad (Potter) **9**
Alcott, Louisa May **27**
Algren, Nelson **33**
Anderson, Sherwood **1, 46, 91**
Apple, Max (Isaac) **50**
Auchincloss, Louis (Stanton) **22**
Baldwin, James (Arthur) **10, 33**
Bambara, Toni Cade **35**
Banks, Russell **42**
Barnes, Djuna **3**
Barth, John (Simmons) **10, 89**
Barthelme, Donald **2, 55**
Bass, Rick **60**
Beattie, Ann **11**
Bellow, Saul **14**
Benét, Stephen Vincent **10, 86**
Berriault, Gina **30**
Betts, Doris (Waugh) **45**
Bierce, Ambrose (Gwinett) **9, 72**
Bowles, Paul (Frederick) **3**
Boyle, Kay **5**
Boyle, T(homas) Coraghessan **16**
Bradbury, Ray (Douglas) **29, 53**
Bradfield, Scott **65**
Bukowski, Charles **45**
Cable, George Washington **4**
Caldwell, Erskine (Preston) **19**
Calisher, Hortense **15**
Canin, Ethan **70**
Capote, Truman **2, 47, 93**
Carver, Raymond **8, 51**
Cather, Willa (Sibert) **2, 50**
Chabon, Michael **59**
Chambers, Robert W. **92**
Chandler, Raymond (Thornton) **23**
Cheever, John **1, 38, 57**
Chesnutt, Charles W(addell) **7, 54**
Chopin, Kate **8, 68**
Cisneros, Sandra **32, 72**
Coover, Robert (Lowell) **15**
Cowan, Peter (Walkinshaw) **28**
Crane, Stephen (Townley) **7, 56, 70**
Davenport, Guy (Mattison Jr.) **16**
Davis, Rebecca (Blaine) Harding **38**
Dick, Philip K. **57**
Dixon, Stephen **16**
Dreiser, Theodore (Herman Albert) **30**
Dubus, André **15**
Dunbar, Paul Laurence **8**
Dybek, Stuart **55**
Elkin, Stanley L(awrence) **12**
Ellison, Harlan (Jay) **14**
Ellison, Ralph (Waldo) **26, 79**
Fante, John **65**
Farrell, James T(homas) **28**
Faulkner, William (Cuthbert) **1, 35, 42, 92**

Fisher, Rudolph **25**
Fitzgerald, F(rancis) Scott (Key) **6, 31, 75**
Ford, Richard **56**
Freeman, Mary E(leanor) Wilkins **1, 47**
Gaines, Ernest J. **68**
Gardner, John (Champlin) Jr. **7**
Garland, (Hannibal) Hamlin **18**
Garrett, George (Palmer) **30**
Gass, William H(oward) **12**
Gibson, William (Ford) **52**
Gilchrist, Ellen (Louise) **14, 63**
Gilman, Charlotte (Anna) Perkins (Stetson) **13, 62**
Glasgow, Ellen (Anderson Gholson) **34**
Glaspell, Susan **41**
Gordon, Caroline **15**
Gordon, Mary **59**
Grau, Shirley Ann **15**
Hammett, (Samuel) Dashiell **17**
Hannah, Barry **94**
Harris, Joel Chandler **19**
Harrison, James (Thomas) **19**
Harte, (Francis) Bret(t) **8, 59**
Hawthorne, Nathaniel **3, 29, 39, 89**
Heinlein, Robert A(nson) **55**
Hemingway, Ernest (Miller) **1, 25, 36, 40, 63**
Henderson, Zenna (Chlarson) **29**
Henry, O. **5, 49**
Howells, William Dean **36**
Hughes, (James) Langston **6, 90**
Hurston, Zora Neale **4, 80**
Huxley, Aldous (Leonard) **39**
Irving, Washington **2, 37**
Jackson, Shirley **9, 39**
James, Henry **8, 32, 47**
Jewett, (Theodora) Sarah Orne **6, 44**
Johnson, Denis **56**
Jones, Thom (Douglas) **56**
Kelly, Robert **50**
Kincaid, Jamaica **72**
King, Stephen (Edwin) **17, 55**
Lahiri, Jhumpa **96**
Lardner, Ring(gold) W(ilmer) **32**
Le Guin, Ursula K(roeber) **12, 69**
Ligotti, Thomas (Robert) **16**
Lish, Gordon (Jay) **18**
London, Jack **4, 49**
Lovecraft, H(oward) P(hillips) **3, 52**
Maclean, Norman (Fitzroy) **13**
Malamud, Bernard **15**
Marshall, Paule **3**
Mason, Bobbie Ann **4**
McCarthy, Mary (Therese) **24**
McCullers, (Lula) Carson (Smith) **9, 24**
McPherson, James Alan **95**
Melville, Herman **1, 17, 46, 95**
Michaels, Leonard **16**
Millhauser, Steven **57**
Mori, Toshio **83**
Murfree, Mary Noailles **22**
Nabokov, Vladimir (Vladimirovich) **11, 86**
Nin, Anaïs **10**
Norris, (Benjamin) Frank(lin Jr.) **28**

Oates, Joyce Carol **6, 70**
O'Brien, Tim **74**
O'Connor, Frank **5**
O'Connor, (Mary) Flannery **1, 23, 61, 82**
O'Hara, John (Henry) **15**
Olsen, Tillie **11**
Ozick, Cynthia **15, 60**
Page, Thomas Nelson **23**
Paley, Grace **8**
Pancake, Breece D'J **61**
Parker, Dorothy (Rothschild) **2**
Perelman, S(idney) J(oseph) **32**
Phillips, Jayne Anne **16**
Poe, Edgar Allan **1, 22, 34, 35, 54, 88**
Pohl, Frederik **25**
Porter, Katherine Anne **4, 31, 43**
Powers, J(ames) F(arl) **4**
Price, (Edward) Reynolds **22**
Pynchon, Thomas (Ruggles Jr.) **14, 84**
Roth, Philip (Milton) **26**
Salinger, J(erome) D(avid) **2, 28, 65**
Salter, James **58**
Saroyan, William **21**
Selby, Hubert Jr. **20**
Silko, Leslie (Marmon) **37, 66**
Singer, Isaac Bashevis **3, 53**
Spencer, Elizabeth **57**
Spofford, Harriet Prescott **87**
Stafford, Jean **26, 86**
Stegner, Wallace (Earle) **27**
Stein, Gertrude **42**
Steinbeck, John (Ernst) **11, 37, 77**
Stuart, Jesse (Hilton) **31**
Styron, William **25**
Suckow, Ruth **18**
Taylor, Peter (Hillsman) **10, 84**
Thomas, Audrey (Callahan) **20**
Thurber, James (Grover) **1, 47**
Toomer, Jean **1, 45**
Trilling, Lionel **75**
Twain, Mark (Clemens, Samuel) **6, 26, 34, 87**
Updike, John (Hoyer) **13, 27**
Vinge, Joan (Carol) D(ennison) **24**
Vonnegut, Kurt Jr. **8**
Walker, Alice (Malsenior) **5**
Wallace, David Foster **68**
Warren, Robert Penn **4, 58**
Welty, Eudora **1, 27, 51**
Wescott, Glenway **35**
West, Nathanael **16**
Wharton, Edith (Newbold Jones) **6, 84**
Wideman, John Edgar **62**
Williams, William Carlos **31**
Williams, Tennessee **81**
Wodehouse, P(elham) G(renville) **2**
Wolfe, Thomas (Clayton) **33**
Wolff, Tobias **63**
Woolson, Constance Fenimore **90**
Wright, Richard (Nathaniel) **2**
Yamamoto, Hisaye **34**

**ITALIAN**

Boccaccio, Giovanni **10, 87**
Calvino, Italo **3, 48**
Ginzburg, Natalia **65**
Levi, Primo **12**
Moravia, Alberto **26**
Pavese, Cesare **19**
Pirandello, Luigi **22**
Svevo, Italo (Schmitz, Aron Hector) **25**
Verga, Giovanni (Carmelo) **21, 87**

**JAMAICAN**

Senior, Olive (Marjorie) **78**

**JAPANESE**

Abe, Kobo **61**
Akutagawa, Ryunosuke **44**
Dazai Osamu **41**
Endo, Shūsaku **48**
Kawabata, Yasunari **17**
Oe, Kenzaburo **20**
Shiga, Naoya **23**
Tanizaki, Junichirō **21**

**MEXICAN**

Arreola, Juan José **38**
Castellanos, Rosario **39, 68**
Fuentes, Carlos **24**
Rulfo, Juan **25**

**NEW ZEALANDER**

Frame, Janet **29**
Mansfield, Katherine **9, 23, 38, 81**

**POLISH**

Agnon, S(hmuel) Y(osef Halevi) **30**
Borowski, Tadeusz **48**
Conrad, Joseph **9, 71**
Peretz, Isaac Loeb **26**

Schulz, Bruno **13**
Singer, Isaac Bashevis **3, 53, 80**

**PUERTO RICAN**

Ferré, Rosario **36**

**RUSSIAN**

Babel, Isaak (Emmanuilovich) **16, 78**
Bulgakov, Mikhail (Afanas'evich) **18**
Bunin, Ivan Alexeyevich **5**
Chekhov, Anton (Pavlovich) **2, 28, 41, 51, 85**
Dostoevsky, Fedor Mikhailovich **2, 33, 44**
Gogol, Nikolai (Vasilyevich) **4, 29, 52**
Gorky, Maxim **28**
Kazakov, Yuri Pavlovich **43**
Leskov, Nikolai (Semyonovich) **34, 96**
Nabokov, Vladimir (Vladimirovich) **11, 86**
Olesha, Yuri **69**
Pasternak, Boris (Leonidovich) **31**
Pilnyak, Boris **48**
Platonov, Andrei (Klimentov, Andrei
 Platonovich) **42**
Pushkin, Alexander (Sergeyevich) **27, 55**
Solzhenitsyn, Aleksandr I(sayevich) **32**
Tolstoy, Leo (Nikolaevich) **9, 30, 45, 54**
Turgenev, Ivan (Sergeevich) **7, 57**
Zamyatin, Yevgeny **89**
Zoshchenko, Mikhail (Mikhailovich) **15**

**SCOTTISH**

Davie, Elspeth **52**
Doyle, Arthur Conan **12**
Oliphant, Margaret (Oliphant Wilson) **25**
Scott, Walter **32**
Spark, Muriel (Sarah) **10**
Stevenson, Robert Louis (Balfour) **11, 51**

**SOUTH AFRICAN**

Gordimer, Nadine **17, 80**
Head, Bessie **52**

**SPANISH**

Alarcón, Pedro Antonio de **64**
Cela, Camilo José **71**
Cervantes (Saavedra), Miguel de **12**
Pardo Bazán, Emilia **30**
Unamuno (y Jugo), Miguel de **11, 69**
de Zayas y Sotomayor, María **94**

**SWEDISH**

Lagervist, Par **12**

**SWISS**

Hesse, Hermann **9, 49**
Meyer, Conrad Ferdinand **30**
Keller, Gottfried **26**
Walser, Robert **20**

**TRINIDADIAN**

Naipaul, V(idiadhar) S(urajprasad) **38**

**UKRAINIAN**

Aleichem, Sholom **33**

**URUGUAYAN**

Onetti, Juan Carlos **23**
Quiroga, Horacio **89**

**WELSH**

Evans, Caradoc **43**
Lewis, Alun **40**
Machen, Arthur **20**
Thomas, Dylan (Marlais) **3, 44**

**YUGOSLAVIAN**

Andrić, Ivo **36**

# *SSC*-96 Title Index